Y0-AFX-642

ANNUAL REVIEW OF
SOCIOLOGY

ANNUAL REVIEW OF SOCIOLOGY

VOLUME 25, 1999

KAREN S. COOK, *Co-Editor*
Duke University

JOHN HAGAN, *Co-Editor*
University of Toronto

www.AnnualReviews.org   science@annurev.org   650-493-4400
ANNUAL REVIEWS   4139 EL CAMINO WAY   P.O. BOX 10139   PALO ALTO, CALIFORNIA 94303-0139

ANNUAL REVIEWS
Palo Alto, California, USA

International Standard Serial Number: 0360-0572
International Standard Book Number: 0-8243-2225-8
Library of Congress Catalog Card Number: 75-648500

Annual Review and publication titles are registered trademarks of Annual Reviews

The paper used in this publication meets the minimum requirements of American National Standards for Information Sciences—Permanence of Paper for Printed Library Materials, ANSI Z39.48-1992

Annual Reviews and the Editors of its publications assume no responsibility for the statements expressed by the contributors to this *Annual Review.*

TYPESETTING BY RUTH M. SAAVEDRA AND THE ANNUAL REVIEWS EDITORIAL STAFF
PRINTED AND BOUND IN THE UNITED STATES OF AMERICA

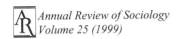
Annual Review of Sociology
Volume 25 (1999)

CONTENTS

(continued)

RELATED ARTICLES IN OTHER *ANNUAL REVIEWS*

From the *Annual Review of Anthropology*, Volume 28, 1999:

Evolutionary Psychology, DM Jones
Life History Theory and Applications, K Hill

From the *Annual Review of Political Science*, Volume 2, 1999:

Historical Institutionalism in Comparative Politics, K Thelen
Ending Revolutions and Building New Governments, A Stinchcombe
Behavioral Approaches to Decision Theory, B Joones
Coping with Tragedies of the Commons, E Ostrum
Instititonalism and the European Union: Beyond International Relations and Comparative Politics, JA Caporaso and J Jupille
Political Parties and Democracy, SC Stokes
What Do We Know About Democratization After Twenty Years, B Geddes

From the *Annual Review of Psychology*, Volume 50, 1999:

Emotion, JT Cacioppo and WL Gardner
Interpersonal Processes: the Interplay of Cognitive, Motivational, and Behavioral Activities in Social Interaction, M Snyder and AA Stukas, Jr
Organizational Change and Development, KE Weick and RE Quinn
The Psychological Underpinnings of Democracy: A Selective Review of Research on Political Tolerance, Interpersonal Trust, and Social Capital, JL Sullivan and JE Transue

From the *Annual Review of Public Health*, Volume 20, 1999:

What We Have Learned About Public Health in the Twentieth Century: An Overview, E Free and JE Fielding

For the convenience of readers, a detachable order form/envelope is bound into the back of this volume.

Annu. Rev. Sociol. 1999. 25:1–18

LOOKING BACK AT 25 YEARS OF SOCIOLOGY AND THE *ANNUAL REVIEW OF SOCIOLOGY*

Neil J. Smelser

Center for Advanced Study in the Behavioral Sciences, Stanford, California 94305;
e-mail: neil@casbs.stanford.edu

ABSTRACT

This essay engages the daunting task of encapsulating and reflecting on the 25 year history of the *Annual Review of Sociology*. After giving a short account of my own involvement in *ARS*, I give a brief rendition of what sociology as a field has been during the past quarter century—that is, what was "out there" to be reflected in the pages of *ARS*. I lay out some statistics on trends in the size, countries, and universities represented, coauthorship patterns, and gender ratios in *ARS*. These statistics are very informative but contain few surprises. Next I trace and analyze an issue that has commmanded the attention of editors of *ARS* throughout its history—unity or diversity of sociology as a discipline. Finally I conclude that the *ARS* does indeed reflect the field in ways that can be documented, but that this process of reflection is subject to many imprecisions generated by the editorial process itself.

INTRODUCTION

In accepting the assignment for this essay, I did not realize how complex it would turn out to be. If I had been given two or three times the space allotted, it would not have sufficed. Accordingly, I have had to be schematic in preparing my remarks. I will limit my comments to six topics:

- An autobiographical note, as it relates to the *Annual Review of Sociology* (hereafter *ARS*)

- A brief overview of trends in sociological theory and research in the past quarter-century

- Some descriptive data about the *ARS*

1

0360-0572/99/0001-0001$08.00

- The theme of unity and diversity of sociology
- The dynamics of "reflecting" the discipline in the *ARS*
- Some concrete examples of "reflecting"

A Biographical and Parental Note

There is a role in academia—partly created by oneself, partly assigned by others—that might be called "representing the discipline." It takes several forms: (*a*) writing about the status of the field, including its trends and problems; (*b*) acting in a "canonical" capacity, such as editor of a publication of one's professional association; and (*c*) serving in an organization whose work affects the world of knowledge and research. Although one does not always directly represent one's discipline in this role—in fact, there is a taboo on being too partisan—it is not possible to avoid being identified as speaking for one's field to some degree. This representative role has both symbolic and political dimensions, both stemming from the fact that it is oneself and not someone else doing the representing.

By a variety of circumstances I have found myself in representative roles to an unusual degree. I became Editor of the *American Sociological Review* at a young age in 1962. Over a 30-year period I have written or edited four texts representing general sociology (Smelser 1967a, 1973; Smelser 1981, 1984, 1988, 1991, 1995; Smelser 1988; Smelser 1994). On several "official" occasions—special sessions at the annual meetings of the American Sociological Association and a special conference of the American Academy of Political and Social Science—I have been asked to comment on the nature and scope of sociology and its relations to the other social sciences (Smelser 1967b, 1969). I compiled and edited a volume on citation patterns in the behavioral and social sciences (Smelser 1987). I served as chair of the Sociology Panel for the Behavioral and Social Sciences Survey (BASSS), sponsored by the Social Science Research Council and the National Academy of Sciences in the 1960s (Smelser & Davis 1969), and as member and chair of a special committee of the Commission on the Behavioral and Social Sciences and Education (National Research Council) on the past, present, and future of the social sciences in the 1980s (Adams et al 1982, Smelser & Gerstein 1986, Gerstein et al 1988, Luce et al 1989). Over the years I have served on the governing boards of the Social Science Research Council, the Center for Advanced Study in the Behavioral Sciences, and the Russell Sage Foundation. And now I am the co-editor (with Paul Baltes, Max Planck Institute on Human Development, Berlin) of the *International Encyclopedia of the Social and Behavioral Sciences*, a 27-volume compilation to be published by Elsevier Science in 2001.

This penchant for representing also appeared in the genesis and early history of the *ARS*. It was the Sociology Panel of the BASS Survey, which I chaired, that called for the creation of an annual review of sociology, explaining that "the objective of this publication would be to review findings and trends from the various fields of sociology on an annual basis" (Smelser & Davis 1969, p. 168). The recommendation was not controversial. The ASA Council echoed it in 1972, at a time when I was serving on the council as vice-president elect. The ASA approached Annual Reviews, Inc., of Palo Alto, California, publisher of most other such reviews, and after a feasibility study the first editorial committee was appointed to plan for the first volume, to appear in 1975. I was named one of the first two associate editors (along with James Coleman), with Alex Inkeles as the first editor. I served in that capacity for Volumes 1–3 and 6 and as a member of the planning committee for Volumes 1–5 and 8.

The conclusion of this biographical excursus is that, with this special personal history, it is appropriate that I comment on the first quarter century of the *ARS*. I am honored to do so, because this publication has had a very successful career, and itself is now fully established as a major "representative" of sociology.

Some Threads in Sociological Theory and Research, 1975 to the Present

The last quarter of the twentieth century is an engaging time in the history of the discipline. This period began after one of the most tumultuous decades of the century—from the early 1960s to the early 1970s. From the standpoint of sociology's societal environment, it was the decade of civil rights, student protest, urban racial disturbances, the war on poverty, the crystallization of a new feminist movement, a souring of American society over the Vietnam war, and the assassinations of several of the decade's charismatic figures. Mirroring these conflictful events, sociologists squared off against one another in college and university faculties, in relations between faculties and students, and in the professional association. The divisions concerned those issues in the larger society, plus a number peculiar to the discipline—the "relevance" of sociological knowledge for social reform and revolution, scientific vs humanistic sociology, the proper training of graduate students, the role of students in the governance of academic departments, the political role of the American Sociological Association, and not least, the deification and vilification of particular sociologists, dead and living.

Much of the turbulence in sociology during the 1960s was shaped by the rejection of a memory about the foregoing decade—the 1950s, which were portrayed by many as the affluent, complacent, and politically conservative Eisenhower years. Those years were also remembered as a period of hegemony—within sociology—of an uncritical sociological positivism and a functionalism insensitive to, if not apologetic for, problems and contradictions in

American society. Similarly, many of the theoretical and ideological developments since the 1960s have been a matter of coming to terms with—embracing, rejecting, modifying, elaborating—the memory of that memorable decade. In both cases the imaging of the past has included a motivated stereotyping by all parties involved that seems to be an unavoidable feature of generational dynamics.

It is easy to overdramatize these generational shifts and conflicts and to mistake them for the whole story. To avoid that effect, let me make explicit my impression that the continuity of the sociological enterprise outweighs the dramatic theoretical and ideological debates. Most sociologists engaged in research and teaching continue to perceive and believe that the world consists of empirical social facts and social problems, and they continue to describe, analyze, and explain these phenomena from a variety of sociological perspectives. They employ largely eclectic, not monolithic, frameworks, even though most sociologists have theoretical preferences. The discipline's theoretical and ideological movements do condition their selection of research issues, their teaching, and their choice of sociological friends, but the big picture is one of laboring in the vineyards, not fighting mighty wars. We must keep this observation before us as we ask how a medium such as an annual review "reflects" the discipline.

With this point in mind, we may remind ourselves that the 1970s were marked by the continuing vitalization of neo-Marxian, neo-Weberian, critical-theory, and radical-sociology perspectives. All of them took as polemic targets the functionalism, quietism, and conservatism of the 1950s as well as the sociologists thought to represent them. Similarly, modernization theory was criticized as too Western centered and too focused on internal dynamics of and obstacles to development. As alternatives, we witnessed the rise of dependency theory and world-system theory, both more internationalist and both to the political left of modernization theory.

These macro-perspectives, although they changed the focus of the sociological positivism of the foregoing decade, did little to challenge that position philosophically (neo-Marxist thinkers did reject "functionalist" positivism as subordinated to the capitalist class and state system, but they did not forsake their own brand of positivism). That task was taken up by the so-called "microscopic revolution," which also crystallized in the late 1960s and 1970s. This revolution involved the vitalization of social behaviorism, symbolic interactionism, ethnomethodology, hermeneutics, and phenomenology generally. These perspectives differed from one another, but they shared an assault on sociological realism, treating roles, social structures, and culture as produced by and reproduced in—or derived from—a crucible of micro-interactions among persons. Except for social behaviorism, these perspectives also raised epistemological objections to a sociological science based on objective social facts.

These theoretical developments ramified into subfields of sociology, creating differences of emphases and conflicts in them. We witnessed the appearance of labeling theory and radical criminology as alternatives to traditional views of deviance as rule-breaking. Feminist sociology developed liberal, critical, radical, and Marxist subdivisions, as did family sociology. Stratification research developed a split between status attainment and structural approaches to mobility, reflecting a liberal-radical split as well. Similar subdivisions appeared in the study of political sociology and community power relations, collective behavior and social movements, race and ethnic relations, and others.

Research methods did not escape the turmoil. The 1970s witnessed not only advances in statistical methods, mathematical modeling, and computation, but also a consolidation of and campaigns for comparative/historical/archival and ethnographic/field methods and semiotics as contenders for legitimate methodological status.

The most significant theoretical development in the 1980s and 1990s was the precipitous collapse of the Marxist and related approaches, first in political and academic circles in Eastern and Western Europe, then in the collapse of communism and the Soviet empire, and then more generally. The Marxist impulse survived in diluted form in revisionist critical theory (associated with Habermas), focusing more on the state apparatus than on market capitalism, and on cultural capital (associated with Bourdieu).

Notable but less dramatic developments included the following:

- A continuing stagnation of interest in general theory—Parsonian "grand theory," systems theory, theories of society, and other variants that enjoyed currency in mid-century and into the 1960s. Interest in general issues focuses more on phenomena that reach across disciplinary lines (for example, risk, rationality) and interdisciplinary research.

- A vitalization of the sociology of culture, reflecting not so much culture as force for social integration (the functionalist stress), but rather culture as medium for hegemonic domination, as individual and group "project," and as "industry," producing and being reproduced.

- The consolidation of the sociology of gender, race, and poverty as dominant foci of inequality, with a corresponding eclipse of class.

- The critical discussion of agency theory, associated with the work of Giddens and others.

- A growing salience of rational-choice theory, stemming from writings by some economists, game theorists, and political scientists, as well as the sociological work of Coleman and others.

- The spread of the intellectual movement referred to variously and imprecisely as postmodernism (including poststructuralism and aspects of multiculturalism). This movement combined an alienation from "rational" aspects of modem society, an antiscience impulse, an identification with the oppressed, and a fascination with "difference" and the uniqueness of "the other," which rejects general principles and grand narratives. Postmodernism has had modest impact in sociology, compared with anthropology and several subjects in the humanities, but it has affected feminist sociology, the sociology of culture, and the sociology of science.

In addition to all these developments, sociology has, throughout the quarter-century, continued to play "catch-up" with larger societal changes. By this term I mean that when some dramatic change, trend, problem, or event rises to social and political visibility, it generates a flurry of theoretical discussion, debate, and empirical research in sociology, sometimes resulting in a new subtradition if not subfield of the discipline, particularly if the item resonates with ongoing sociological preoccupations. Illustrations of this phenomenon in the last quarter-century include the bursts of research on student activism, the impact of the computer on the work place, drugs, satanism, esoteric cults, single-parent families, family violence, step-parenting, adult children living with parents, homelessness, immigration, identity politics, and globalism.

All these developments—solidification of competing sociological perspectives, infusion of these perspectives into subfields, development of conflicts based on these perspectives, growth of new subfields, "chasing social problems," crystallization of different research methods—in large part lie behind the continuing trend toward specialization of the field. This specialization has been the subject of much agonizing among sociologists. Some acknowledge its inevitability and positive contribution to the accumulation of knowledge; others proclaim fragmentation, disarray, loss of identity, and crisis; others seek themes of unity and coherence; and still others heed but go on with their labors.

At the same time, I sense a certain routinization of differences, with the shrill partisanship of the 1960s and 1970s giving way to greater mutual tolerance—a kind of peaceful pluralism—in the 1980s and 1990s, even though inherited differences persist. As the century ends, I sense a deep ambivalence: a sure knowledge that sociology is a solidly institutionalized and enduring enterprise, but also a sense of profound unease and loss of mission. The unease is fed by gnawing doubts about the coherence of the enterprise of sociology, by internal political conflicts, by periodic efforts and threats to phase out the field in a few private colleges and universities, and by the unsteady funding situation for the behavioral and social sciences in governmental and foundation circles. These few remarks on the status of sociology in the past several decades should serve as a background as we look at how the *Annual Review of Sociology* has reflected the discipline during its existence.

A Few Descriptive Data

The *ARS* has kept its "annual" promise by appearing every year since Volume 1 was published in 1975. Its average size has been fairly stable. In what might be called the "thin period"—1975–1982—the number of articles averaged exactly 16, with a low of 13 (1982) and a high of 21 (1978). In 1983, however, the number jumped to 26, the all-time high, and between that year and 1997 the average was 20.6 articles, with a high of 26 in 1983 and a low of 17 in 1994. These data are not remarkable, but the steadiness of the past 15 years reflects the fact that the *ARS* has become a going concern in the world of academic sociology.

What kinds of institutions are reflected in the *Annual Review*? I recorded the institutions of all authors from 1975 through 1997, using the categories of US Public, US Private, Canadian, Non-North American, and Other (non-academic institutions such as government agencies). Table 1 reveals the breakdown.

This display reveals an overwhelming dominance of American colleges and universities; no identifiable secular trends in the balance between American private and public institutions; and very low numbers of Canadian, Non-North American, and Other.

The low level of non-North American institutions shows that *ARS* is not a perfect reflection of sociology if we make the reasonable assumption that the field has become steadily more internationalized in the last quarter of the twentieth century. International representation "bulges" slightly in the publication's middle years. I believe this blip traces to the fact that in 1982 the editorial committee added three non-US sociologists—John Goldthorpe (United Kingdom), Natalie Rogoff Ramsoy (Norway), and Erwin Scheuch (West Germany)—as a "Corresponding Committee." This arrangement continued, with changing membership, until 1993, when it was apparently discontinued. The existence of the Corresponding Committee coincides almost exactly with the small bulge of international authors.

Table 1   Types of institution represented by author, *Annual Review of Sociology*, 1975–1997

	1975-79 No.	%	1980–84 No.	%	1985–89 No.	%	1990–94 No.	%	1995–97 No.	%
US Public	61	51.2	66	54.5	79	53.7	86	56.6	43	49.4
US Private	46	37.7	49	33.7	44	29.9	50	32.2	43	39.1
Canadian	2	1.7	2	1.7	2	1.4	2	1.3	6	6.9
Non-North American	5	4.2	7	5.8	16	10.9	11	7.2	1	4.6
Other	5	4.2	6	4.9	6	4.1	3	2.0	1	2.3

Table 2 Universities most represented in *Annual Review of Sociology*, 1975–1997

University	No. of authors
Wisconsin-Madison	31
Michigan	27
Stanford	23
North Carolina-Chapel Hill	21
California-Los Angeles	18
Harvard	15
Chicago	14
Duke	14
California-Berkeley	14
Washington State	13
Cornell	12
Indiana	11
Washington-Seattle	11

Which American institutions of higher education had highest representation? The cumulative count for institutions most represented (by author) is found in Table 2. That table, too, reveals no surprises. The major research universities have dominated, and the "great Midwest empirical tradition" (including North Carolina) insofar as that is anything real, has a commanding presence. Some might regard Stanford's position (third) as worthy of comment. I hesitate to make much of this, but geographical proximity (Annual Reviews' central office is in Palo Alto) and familiarity with local talent might be mentioned as factors contributing to its high ranking. Institutions producing fewer than 10 articles are numerous, diverse, and widespread, and they provide little information that would merit explanation or speculation.

I also ran an "author/article" count to determine if there might be any trends toward increasing or decreasing multiple authorship. No real trend in either direction is discernible. The ratios were 1.44 for 1975–79, 1.32 for 1980–84, 1.41 for 1985–89, 1.52 for 1990–94, and 1.64 for 1995–97.

Finally, I calculated the percentage of women authors in the *ARS* from 1975 to 1997. Those percentages, represented in five-year intervals, are found in Table 3. What is found is an expected trend, moving more or less steadily upward and certainly reflecting broader changes in the sociological profession and the society at large. One might ask why the numbers did not "take off" earlier, because the feminist movement was by 1975 already firmly in the minds of sociologists. The great jump came between the first half and the second half of the 1980s. One factor in accounting for this change, I believe, was the appointment of Alice Rossi as member of the editorial committee. Her term ran from 1983 to 1988, and she actively pressed for the inclusion of women authors.

Table 3   Percentage of women authors, *Annual Review of Sociology*, 1975–1997

	1975–79	1980–84	1985–89	1990–94	1995–97
No. men	102	105	106	106	61
No. women	19	16	41	46	35
% women	18.6	13.1	27.9	30.7	36.4

On the Unity and Diversity of Sociology

I vividly remember discussions by the first editorial committee on two related topics: how to represent sociology and how to organize the volumes of *ARS*. The vividness of my recollection stems in part from the fact that I myself had been struggling with issues of scope, subdivisions, and unity of sociology for several years preceding the convening of the first editorial committee. A brief account of my struggle might set the scene for the committee's discussions and resolutions.

In the mid-1960s I wrote an essay (Smelser 1967b) in which I defined and set apart from one another the fields of anthropology, economics, history, political science, psychology, and sociology, and I attempted to specify some relations among them. In retrospect I regard that as a rash effort, even though I had already studied in all of them at various points in my young academic career. I did not acknowledge it at the time, but this exercise presupposed that each of the fields was an identifiable entity, capable of specification of its relations with those other entities—disciplines—that surrounded it. I now regard that supposition as both naive and inadequate.

About four years later, I was asked to give a normative presentation on "the optimum scope of sociology"—mentioned above—before an august gathering of twenty sociologists that included Herbert Blumer, Philip Hauser, George Homans, Paul Lazarsfeld, Robert Merton, Wilbert Moore, Talcott Parsons, and Robin Williams. At the same meeting James Coleman was asked to speak on "methods" of sociology and Peter Blau on the "objectives" of sociology.

As I recall that event, it also seems rash that I presumed to tell this score of established and rising people what our discipline was about, but I accepted the assignment. By that time I was slightly less naive, and I gave a more complex account of sociology. At the outset, I sought to disarm my variegated audience with a permissive statement, uttered under the heading of "one field, many frameworks":

> . . . sociology, by comparison with some other sciences, lacks a single, accepted conceptual framework. The field is difficult to distinguish from others because it contains a diversity of frameworks, some of which it shares with other fields such as psychology and social anthropology. If anything, then, sociology is too comprehensive, diffuse, soft in the center, and fuzzy around the edges. (Smelser 1969, p. 5).

Not content with this indeterminacy, I next ventured the view that sociology was in fact distinguished by five distinctive and core perspectives or levels of analysis:

- The demographic and ecological

- The person in social context (social psychological)

- The group (including organizations)

- The social structural (including roles and institutions)

- The cultural

I suggested further that, in order for an investigation to be considered sociological, it had to choose some dependent variable falling within one of these perspectives, and to explain variations in this variable by reference to some independent variable, also within the perspectives. In that way I addressed the issue of "optimum scope," or the issue of diversity within the framework of unity.

Robert Nisbet, one of the commentators on my subject, picked up the tension in my remarks and observed that they combined two versions of me: first, a Free Sociological Momentum (FSM—apt enough for its day) version, which permitted an almost unlimited range of activities under the heading of sociological investigation; and second, a more authoritarian streak that demanded that analysis, in order to be considered properly sociological, had to be related to and to draw from the core perspectives. Nisbet was worried that the latter would inhibit scholarly imagination and creativity. I could not fully answer his challenge to draw a firm line between permissiveness and constraint, but neither could he. He clearly preferred the FSM version, but admitted, "granted that for a discipline to exist worth the naming, there must be something distinctive in its naming" (Nisbet 1969, p. 33). This was the way that the tension between diversity and unity worked out at that moment in 1967; it was basically unresolved.

The editorial committee planning the *Annual Review of Sociology* was also constrained to make some decisions about the unity and the diversity of sociology. This was a different task from the one I faced in my two previous efforts. My efforts were aimed at neatening the field conceptually, making sense of a vast array of research and writing. The editorial committee had a more directed task. It had to say how it was going to represent the field, in the form of research articles, to a diverse reading audience, by developing a common framework within which its peculiarities fit.

We attacked our presentation of the field as follows: On the one hand, the complexity, dynamism, and evident disorderliness of much ongoing sociological work did not permit the portrayal of a field advancing each year in a systematic and orderly way as a field. On the other hand, none of us on the editorial committee was prepared to throw our hands up and confess that sociology is whatever sociologists do, and that we would present some interesting but unrelated things each year. What line between these two extremes might be drawn?

The committee had an advantage in answering this question, because we shared a common commitment to sociology as a scientific enterprise. But there were differences as well. Renee Fox and I, with our Parsons training, leaned toward a more inclusive, integrative scheme for organizing the volumes; Alex Inkeles, Peter Rossi, and James Coleman, most influenced by Robert Merton and Paul Lazarsfeld, also preferred a systematic approach, but one less elaborate and inclusive. John Clausen, Ralph Turner, and Carl Taueber came from the more problem-oriented Chicago tradition, and they were less enamored of general organizing schemes than the rest of us.

After long discussion and negotiation, we fashioned a solution of the unity-diversity issue that all could accept with varying degrees of enthusiasm. We laid out some ten foci of sociological analysis and decided that these foci would be headings to which all review articles, however specialized, could be assigned. Not every heading would necessarily appear in every issue, but we believed that the framework would be useful "for the next few years" (Editorial Committee 1975, p. v). The headings were the following:

- Differentiation and Stratification
- Political Sociology
- Social Processes
- Institutions
- Individual and Society
- Formal Organization
- Urban Sociology
- Demography
- Policy
- Theory and Methods

Looking back at this list, it strikes me that it was "macro" in emphasis, with "Individual and Society" as the only repository for social psychology, that urban sociology perhaps did not merit a full heading, and that "culture" was a conspicuous omission. The most obvious characteristic of our strategy of general headings for specialized articles, however, is that we were fashioning a compromise solution to the "unity vs. diversity" issue. We were announcing to readers that we were commissioning highly specialized articles on recognizable "strands of research." At the same time, we supplied a coherent framework into which ongoing work could fit. But again, in making each issue selective rather than comprehensive, we acknowledged the unreality of the proposition that an annual review could track the movement of an entire discipline every year.

As it turned out, the organizing framework enjoyed much more staying power than we might have predicted. In 1976 there was a never to-be repeated addition of a "Bicentennial Article" heading, under which we put two entries. In 1977 we added a heading of "Sociology of World Regions," which became a permanent heading but has always contained few entries. In 1978 another category—"Historical Sociology"—was added. It again became permanent, but also with limited numbers of entries. In 1979 the editorial committee permitted itself a moment of self-congratulation on its formula:

> We annually rededicate ourselves to a sociology defined around basic issues, sharing coherent paradigms and methods, which produces important findings and generates cumulative knowledge. Without denying that sociology is a house of many mansions we see no reason not to give full play to the lasting accomplishments of our profession. And we see every reason to help all who are serious enough to desire an intellectual currency in subfields other than those in which they specialize. (Editorial Committee 1979, p. v).

This statement called attention to the "unity" side of the tension. Two years later, however, the committee acknowledged that "in recent years specialized lines of research have proliferated, as have journals that focus on different topics." It has become "more difficult," it added, for every social scientist to maintain "a broad perspective and [keep] informed about developments over a wide range of activities" (Editorial Committee 1981, p. v). All the more reason, it argued, to have periodic stocktakings in the *ARS*. The committee also softened its "unity" emphasis a bit more by explaining that "we view the categories as a heuristic device rather than a rigid structure" and acknowledged that "any classification of subfields cannot be universally acceptable" (Editorial Committee 1981, p. v). By 1993 the committee seemed almost ready to throw in the towel, announcing that "Volume 19 is one of our most diverse" and adding "these articles have little in common but they provide an unusually broad sweep of contemporary sociology" (Editorial Committee 1993, p. viii).

A few other changes in categories were made over the years. In 1979 "Political Sociology" became "Political and Economic Sociology." In the same year, "Culture" appeared. It disappeared the following year, but then reappeared in an "Institutions and Culture" category in 1984. Also in 1984 "Urban" became "Urban and Rural Community Sociology." In 1986 a category called "Prefatory Chapter" appeared, as the editorial committee decided to dedicate one chapter per volume to a reflective statement by a distinguished senior sociologist (George Homans was the first selection). Beyond those modifications—all of which expanded categories while keeping the total number around a dozen—the *ARS* has revealed a remarkable continuity of intellectual organization, at the same time reminding readers of the complexity, specialization, and breadth of the discipline. How change was built into this representative continuity is the next topic for inquiry.

The Process of "Reflecting" a Discipline

In one sense the issue of reflecting is almost trivial, perhaps uninteresting. Of course, in undertaking to publish a review of a discipline, the publishers and editors have already decided, as a matter of self–conscious mission, to reflect it. Certainly that role was in the minds of the BASS Panel of Sociology that recommended the establishment of a review for sociology. It was also in the minds of the ASA Council that endorsed that recommendation. Moreover, that role was made explicit in the editorial statement of mission found in the first volume:

> The publication of this annual review provides the sociological community with a special opportunity for taking stock of progress in its various subfields at intervals. It is our hope that the articles in the *Annual Review of Sociology* will identify critical issues, sort out research evidence bearing on them, and then facilitate the systematic assessment of what we know. (Editorial Committee 1975, p. v)

Several years later, in 1983, the editors commented that that year's issue was the largest and most diverse yet, and that it "reflect[ed] the state of the discipline" and "the continuing ferment in sociology." The editors elaborated by calling attention to the fact that many traditional approaches were being "challenged"—sociology of science, family sociology, and the traditional writing of the history of sociology, for example—and noted the importation of perspectives from "outside the sociological mainstream" (Editorial Committee 1983, v–vi).

Such assertions of a self–conscious mission to reflect, however, leave unanswered a number of additional questions that surface when one acknowledges that the editorial committee and the contributing authors are not completely passive agents in the reflecting process but are actually choosing ways to carry it out. More particularly, we should ask at least three questions:

- By what criteria are different topics, aspects, or facets of ongoing work judged to be relevant for selection?
- How does the choice process work? Does it involve systematic gaps in information or systematic biases on the part of those who organize and execute the review?
- Does the actual process of selecting, writing, delivering, and editing affect the reflecting process?

I cannot answer these questions precisely in this retrospective essay and could do so only if I had been a permanent fly on the wall throughout all the deliberations, decisions, and writing and editorial activities that have produced the *ARS* volumes. I can, however, call on impressions from the pages of the review, on my own several years as one of the planners and editors of the *ARS*, and on a range of other editorial experiences.

WHAT MAKES FOR RELEVANCE?   Several factors might draw editors' attention to the desirability of commissioning a review article:

- The perceived importance or centrality of a line of research activity to "core" areas of sociology. Such perceptions are not neutral; there is disagreement and controversy among sociologists about the core. Several years ago, Joan Huber suggested that quantitative work in demography, stratification, and formal organizations constitutes the "core" of sociology (Huber 1995). That essay set off a mini-storm of voices who criticized her assessments and argued for a different set of priorities. It seems best to regard the "core" of the field as a matter of continuous examination, conflict, and negotiation.

- The perceived quality and quantity of research conducted in a given line of work. As the editorial committee commented in Volume 18: "There must be a literature for us to review. Not infrequently, our desire to do an important Annual Review essay founders on the lack of research on the topic" (Editorial Committee 1992, p. v).

- The perceived novelty or importance of a research technique.

- The perceived novelty or importance of a statement by an individual or group of scholars that initiates, revives, or revitalizes a line of theory and empirical research.

- The perceived relevance of a line of research that works toward the solution of—or at least is relevant to—a sociological problem.

- A perceived tension, controversy, or debate in the field.

- The perceived importance in the larger society of (*a*) an important trend—for example, regressive movements in income, (*b*) a dramatic event or set of events—the OPEC crisis, the Jonestown massacre, the Watergate crisis, (*c*) a social movement—the civil rights or the feminist movement, the moral majority—plus the development of research in the literature. Not all phenomena under these headings are chosen. They are more likely to be chosen if they resonate with some enduring sociological preoccupation (e.g. inequality, family stability). Earlier I referred to this tendency as sociology's tendency to "chase social problems."

In the process of editorial selection some combination of all these criteria are at least implicitly in mind as decisions are made.

SOME IMPRECISIONS IN THE REFLECTING PROCESS   When an editorial board convenes to plan future issues, we may safely assume that it attempts, collectively and in good faith, to reflect the discipline and be true to the mission of the publication. Yet in these undertakings, the "true" process of reflecting immediately becomes imprecise. First, different committee members invariably give different weight to the different criteria of relevance listed above, and for that reason they will differ among themselves in assessing how interesting or important a line of research is and in arguing for or against its inclusion. Second, editorial committee members, individually and collectively, are limited in their knowledge of the discipline because they specialize in certain parts of it and not others, because they do not read everything, and because they are involved in some collegial networks and not others. Third, editorial committees are not willing to pay the transaction costs of surveying and gathering information about parts of the discipline they do not know about. And finally, individual committee members, being human, will unconsciously or consciously push for inclusion of topics and research traditions they know and love best or that "grab" them and for exclusion of others.

The imprecision of reflecting is made greater in selecting authors and preparing manuscripts. Some authors decline invitations. The figures vary and are no doubt not available for the history of the *ARS*, but every commissioning editor experiences a mix of successes and failures. This factor affects the process of reflecting in unknown ways. Furthermore, acceptance of an assignment does not mean delivery of the product. The editorial committee for Volume 1 (of which I was a member) acknowledged candidly that it had experienced a default and delinquency rate of 25%, and it apologized to its readers for resulting gaps in coverage. No other editorial committee has commented on that issue. We thought that rate was atypically high, but apparently delinquency and default remain significant issues. In any event, default and delinquency are two additional sources of the imperfection that accumulates in the journey from the ideal of truly reflecting the discipline to its actual representation in the published volumes.

Some Illustrations in Reflecting

The name of the reflecting game, then, is imprecision, both in the *ARS* and in all other enterprises that try to reflect. It is subject to ignorance, unrepresentativeness, biases, lags, aborted efforts, and other sources of error. With that in mind, I have deliberately refrained from carrying out elaborate (to say nothing of quantitative) analyses of the contents of the *ARS* over the years. Nevertheless, in going over the two dozen volumes, I wrote down a heading I called "timeliness" and entered what I noticed in that category. Given all the imprecision I have emphasized, that seemed the most appropriate method. In the final section of this essay, I record, illustratively, some of these notes.

A FEW OBVIOUS ILLUSTRATIONS OF REFLECTING   The pages of the ARS give evidence that the editors took cognizance of noteworthy publications of socio-logical relevance, novel "traditions" of sociological work, visible situations in society, and dramatic social events. A few obvious examples will suffice: arti-cles on biology and sociobiology (Barchas 1976, Boorman & Levitt 1980); countermovements in society (Lo 1982); resource mobilization theory (Jenkins 1983); homosexuality (Risman & Schwartz 1988); sociology of sport (Frey & Eitzen 1991); religious cults since Jonestown (Barker 1986); and homelessness (Schlay & Rossi 1992). There were no doubt some "misses" as well. For example, the early volumes show no entries on youth movements or students, with only two articles on generations (Kertzer 1983, Braungart & Braungart 1986), touching on the burst of sociological literature on students in the 1960s and early 1970s.

THEORY AND METHODS   Theory and methods has been one of the major cate-gorical headings of the *ARS* throughout its publication history. The treatment of the two topics, however, has been very different. Only two articles on gen-eral sociological theory appeared. The first was in Volume 1, in which Botto-more announced that there was no general theory but rather a competition—"functionalism no longer occupies such a prominent place as a sociological paradigm" (Bottomore 1975:192). The second (Sciulli & Gerstein 1985) noted the numerous cumulated assaults on Parsons from the 1960s through the 1980s but remarked on a certain amount of continued general interest in Parsons in German and American theoretical circles. Other observers have noticed the diminution of interest in general theory (e.g. Turk 1988), and the pages of *ARS* certainly show that. Theoretical articles continued to appear, but they focused on specialized subareas of sociology. A few illustrations are theoretical arti-cles on formal (i.e. mathematical and logical) theorizing (Freese 1980), justice (Pepinsky 1986), social problems (Schneider 1985), industrialization (Walton 1987), and collective action (Oliver 1993). This development yields further evidence of continuing specialization in sociology.

With respect to methods, the editors' choice of articles records increasing catholicity of research methods, noted earlier. An ample number of "main-stream" articles discuss statistics, surveys, and formal modeling (e.g. Sudman 1976, Hannan & Tuma 1979, Blalock 1984, Winship & Mare 1992). At the same time, "alternative" methods receive more than equal attention. Illustra-tions are urban ethnography (Suttles 1976), observational field research (McCall 1984), evaluation research (Gordon & Morse 1975, Rossi & Wright 1984), and the life story approach (Bertaux & Kohli 1984).

GENDER   Changes in both number and contents of articles on gender offer perhaps the clearest instance of reflection in the *ARS*. In the very first issue, one article on "Sex Roles in Transition" (Lipman-Blumen & Tickamyer 1975) appeared, covering the literature available and devoting one and one-half pages to the feminist writings of Betty Friedan. A period of silence followed, but 1982 produced another article on sex roles (Miller & Garrison 1982), this one having a more evident feminist emphasis. Three more appeared in the late 1980s—one on women's labor force participation and the distribution of income (Treas 1987), one on comparable worth (England & Dunn 1988), and one on sex difference in earnings (Marini 1989)—all reflecting a focus on economic and structural aspects of women's experience. In fact, Volume 15 (1989) aptly symbolized the "cultural turn" in gender studies, with both the article on women's earnings and a second on "gender and social reproduction" (Laslett & Brenner 1989). By the mid-1990s articles on gender were a regular feature of the *ARS*, with nine of the 39 articles in the 1996 and 1997 issues devoted to theoretical, institutional, and cultural aspects of feminist sociology and gender studies.

I have similar reflective stories to tell about the representation of the microsociological revolution, race, and immigration in the history of *ARS*, but they are roughly similar to the gender story and would add a lot of citations but few additional insights. Suffice it to say, in conclusion, that the editors, working through all the imprecisions created by their own selective perceptions of sociology, their lack of information and their biases, and the failures experienced in persuading authors to write and to deliver manuscripts, nevertheless achieved an interesting and instructive reflection of sociology in the annals of the *Annual Review of Sociology*.

Visit the *Annual Reviews* home page at http://www.AnnualReviews.org.

Literature Cited

Adams RM, Smelser NJ, Treiman DJ, eds. 1982. *Behavioral and Social Science Research: A National Resource.* Washington, DC: Natl. Acad.

Barchas PR. 1976. Interface of sociological and biological processes. *Annu. Rev. Sociol.* 2:299–333

Barker E. 1986. Cult and anticult since Jonestown. *Annu. Rev. Sociol.* 12:329–46

Bertaux D, Kohli M. 1984. The life-story approach: a continental view. *Annu. Rev. Sociol.* 10:257–37

Blalock HM. 1984. Contextual effects: theoretical and methodological issues. *Annu. Rev. Sociol.* 10:353–72

Boorman S, Levitt PR. 1980. The comparative evolutionary biology of social behavior. *Annu. Rev. Sociol.* 6:213–33

Bottomore T. 1975. Competing paradigms in macrosociology. *Annu. Rev. Sociol.* 1: 191–202

Braungart RG, Braungart MM. 1986. Lifecourse and generational politics. *Annu. Rev. Sociol.* 12:205–31

Editorial Committee. 1975. Preface. *Annu. Rev. Sociol.* 1:v–vi

Editorial Committee 1979. Preface. *Annu. Rev. Sociol.* 5:v

Editorial Committee 1981. Preface. *Annu. Rev. Sociol.* 7:v–vii

Editorial Committee 1983. Preface. *Annu. Rev. Sociol.* 9:v–vi

Editorial Committee 1992. Preface. *Annu. Rev. Sociol.* 18:v–vi

Editorial Committee 1993. Preface. *Annu. Rev. Sociol.* 19:vii

England P, Dunn D. 1988. Evaluating work and comparable worth. *Annu. Rev. Sociol.* 14:227–48

Freese L. 1980. Formal theorizing. *Annu Rev. Sociol.* 6:1878–212

Frey JH, Eitzen DS. 1991. Sport and Society. *Annu. Rev. Sociol.* 17:503–22

Gerstein DR, Luce, RD, Smelser NJ, Sperlich, S, eds. 1988. *The Behavioral and Social Sciences: Achievements and Opportunities.* Washington, DC: Natl. Acad.

Gordon G, Morse EV. 1975. Evaluation research. *Annu. Rev. Sociol.* 1:339–61

Hannan MT, Tuma N. 1979. Methods for temporal analysis. *Annu. Rev. Sociol.* 5:303–28

Huber J. 1995. Centennial essay: institutional perspectives on sociology. *Am. J. Sociol.* 100:196–216

Kertzer DI. 1983. Generation as a social problem. *Annu. Rev. Sociol.* 9:125–49

Jenkins JC. 1983. Resource mobilization theory and the study of social movements. *Annu. Rev. Sociol.* 9:527–53

Laslett B, Brenner J. 1989. Gender and social reproduction: historical perspectives. *Annu. Rev. Sociol.* 15:381–404

Lipman-Blumen J, Tickamyer AR. 1975. Sex roles in transition. *Annu. Rev. Sociol.* 1:297–337

Lo CYH. 1982. Countermovements and conservative movements in the contemporary U.S. Annu. Rev. Sociol. 8:107–34

Luce RD, Smelser NJ, Gerstein DR, eds. 1989. *Leading Edges in Social and Behavioral Science.* New York: Russell Sage Found.

Marini MM. 1989. Sex differences in earnings in the United States. *Annu. Rev. Sociol.* 15:343–80

McCall GJ. 1984. Systematic field observation. *Annu Rev. Sociol.* 10:263–82

Miller J, Garrison HH. 1982. The division of labor at home and in the workplace. *Annu. Rev. Sociol.* 8:237–62

Nisbet RA. 1969. Comment on Smelse's paper, in *A Design for Sociology: Scope, Objectives, and Methods,* Monograph 9 in a series sponsored by the Am. Acad. Polit. Soc. Sci. Philadelphia: Am. Acad. Polit. Soc. Sci., p. 30–35

Oliver PE. 1993. Formal models of collective action. *Annu. Rev. Sociol.* 19:271–300

Pepinsky HE. 1986. A sociology of justice. *Annu. Rev. Sociol.* 12:93–108

Risman B, Schwartz P. 1988. Sociological re-search on male and female homosexuality. *Annu. Rev. Sociol.* 14:125–47

Rossi PH, Wright J. 1984. Evaluation research: an assessment. *Annu. Rev. Sociol.* 10:331–52

Schlay AB, Rossi PH. 1992. Social science research and contemporary studies of homelessness. *Annu. Rev. Sociol.* 18:129–60

Schneider JW. 1985. Social problems theory: the constructionist view. *Annu. Rev. Sociol.* 11: 209–29

Sciulli D, Gerstein D. 1985. Social theory and Talcott Parsons in the 1980s. *Annu. Rev. Sociol.* 11:369–87

Smelser NJ, ed. 1967a. *Sociology: An Introduction.* New York: Wiley. 2nd ed. 1973

Smelser NJ. 1967b. Sociology and the other social sciences. In *The Uses of Sociology,* ed. PF Lazarsfeld, WH Sewell, HL Wilensky, pp. 3–44. New York: Basic Books

Smelser NJ. 1969. The optimum scope of sociology. In *A Design for for Sociology: Scope, Objectives And Methods,* Monograph 9 in a series sponsored by the Am. Acad. Polit. Soc. Sci. Philadelphia, PA: Am. Acad. Polit. Soc. Sci., pp. 1–22

Smelser NJ. 1981 *Sociology.* Englewood Cliffs, NJ: Prentice–Hall. 2nd ed. 1984, 3rd ed. 1988, 4th ed. 1991, 5th ed. 1995

Smelser, NJ, ed. 1987. *Contemporary Classics in the Social and Behavioral Sciences.* Philadelphia, PA: ISI Press

Smelser NJ, ed. 1988. *Handbook of Sociology.* Newbury Park, CA: Sage

Smelser NJ. 1994. *Sociology.* Oxford: Blackwell and UNESCO

Smelser NJ, Davis JA, eds. 1969. *Sociology.* Englewood Cliffs, NJ: Prentice-Hall

Smelser NJ, Gerstein DR, eds. 1986. *Behavioral and Social Science: Fifty Years of Discovery.* Washington, DC: Natl. Acad.

Sudman S. 1976. Sample surveys. *Annu. Rev. Sociol.* 2:107–20

Suttles GD. 1976. Urban ethnography: situational and normative accounts. *Annu. Rev. Sociol.* 2:1–18

Treas J. 1987. The effect of women's labor force participation on the distribution of income in the United States. *Annu. Rev. Sociol.* 13:259–88

Turk H. 1988. Sociological theory. In *The Future of Sociology,* ed. EF Borgatta, K Cook, pp. 18–41. Newbury Park, CA: Sage

Walton J. 1987. Theory and research on industrialization. *Annu. Rev. Sociol.* 13:89–108

Winship C, Mare RD. 1992. Models for sample selection bias. *Annu. Rev. Sociol.* 18: 327–50

Annu. Rev. Sociol. 1999. 25:19–46

THE SOCIOLOGY OF ENTREPRENEURSHIP

Patricia H. Thornton

Department of Sociology, Duke University, Durham, North Carolina 27708;
e-mail: thornton@soc.duke.edu

KEY WORDS: entrepreneurs, new ventures, organizational founding, demand side perspective, intrapreneurship, venture capital, initial public offerings,

ABSTRACT

Recent research on entrepreneurship by sociologists has focused on subsectors of the discipline rather than on entrepreneurship as a class. This review draws insights from diverse literatures to develop a sociological perspective on entrepreneurship as a whole. Until recently, the supply-side perspective, which focuses on the individual traits of entrepreneurs, has been the dominant school of research. Newer work from the demand-side perspective has focused on rates, or the context in which entrepreneurship occurs. This review emphasizes this less developed demand-side perspective—in particular, the influence of firms and markets on how, where, and why new enterprises are founded. I take stock of the differences and separation in the two perspectives and argue that sociological frameworks, an embeddedness perspective, institutional and ecological theory, and multilevel models can be used to integrate the two schools and extend their research implications.

INTRODUCTION

Entrepreneurship occurs at significantly higher rates than at any time in the last 100 years (Gartner & Shane 1995). Recent survey evidence suggests that entrepreneurship is a meaningful lifestyle and career identity for many, with 4% of all adults, 1 in 25, trying to start a new firm at any given time (Reynolds & White 1997:7).

Along with the increase in entrepreneurship has come growth in the number of endowed chairs in business schools; positions in research institutions, foundations, professional organizations; and journals in the field of entrepreneurship (Katz 1991, Robinson & Haynes 1991, Sandberg & Gatewood 1991). Yet in spite of these developments, entrepreneurship researchers complain that the field lacks a distinct professional identity, one defined by a unified body of knowledge based on generally accepted social science theories (Bull & Willard 1993). Surveys describe the field as organized by camps, where the lack of cross-level and cross-disciplinary interaction tends to obscure the overall picture of what gives rise to entrepreneurship (Wortman 1987, Herron et al 1992, Gartner & Shane 1995). Many commentaries on the field have called for an increase in the quality, interdisciplinary nature, and development of unifying schemes to integrate diverse pieces of research on entrepreneurship (e.g., Bygrave & Hofer 1991). The purpose of this review is to examine sociological research on entrepreneurship and draw selectively from other specialized literatures to create an agenda for further development of a sociological perspective on entrepreneurship.

I define entrepreneurship as the creation of new organizations (Gartner 1988), which occurs as a context-dependent, social and economic process (Reynolds 1991, Low & Abrahamson 1997). I draw from diverse literatures to take stock of what we know about how, where, and why new enterprise is founded. A central problem with answering this question is that despite the large and eclectic literature on entrepreneurship, relatively little is known about the specific contexts of organizational founding (Reynolds & White 1997). For example, ecologists have systematically studied founding rates, but they have focused on the development of universal concepts rather than on the particular context (Amburgey & Rao 1996). As Baum & Haveman (1997:304) note: "research has treated foundings as identical additions to homogeneous populations.... Organizational attributes cannot be used as explanatory variables in analyses of founding because they cannot be observed for organizations that do not yet exist."

The entrepreneurship literature can be classified into two schools: one taking the supply-side perspective and the other, the demand-side perspective. The supply-side school focuses on the availability of suitable individuals to occupy entrepreneurial roles; the demand-side, on the number and nature of the entrepreneurial roles that need to be filled. The demand-side perspective suggests a number of ways to examine the context of organizational founding, such as the generation of new ventures by organizational hierarchies (Freeman 1986), the activity of the professions (Wholey et al 1993), the policy of nation-states (Dobbin & Doud 1997), the development of markets (White 1981, King & Levine 1993), and the advent of technological change (Shane 1996). This review focuses on the following contexts for the development of entrepreneurship: the influences of two types of firms-organizational hierarchies and venture capital firms—and the influences of two types of markets—initial public offerings (IPOs) and corporate acquisitions. I suggest that integrative frameworks from sociology, a social embeddedness perspective, ecological and institution theories, and multilevel models be used to link supply and demand perspectives. Last, I discuss sources of heterogeneity according to four different levels of analysis: individual, organizational, market, and environmental.

I have chosen to examine the contextual analysis of organizational founding in terms of firms and markets because they are both highly organized institutions in the United States and are also relatively underexamined as engines of entrepreneurship. Preliminary results from the Entrepreneurship Research Consortium indicate that a significant proportion of new start-ups are sponsored by existing organizations. Over one quarter of the people who say they were involved in trying to start new ventures were doing it for their current employer, rather than starting out on their own (Reynolds & Rong 1997). Second, a focus on firms and markets is appropriate given the maturity of many US industries. Third, the sociological aspects of how venture capital firms and initial public offering (IPO) and acquisition markets affect the founding of critical high-growth and high-technology organizations are underexamined (Florida & Kenney 1988b:35). Finally, data from the last five years shows that start-ups backed by venture capital are increasing as a percentage of all new business incorporations (VentureOne Corporation 1997, Statistical Abstract of the United States 1997).

The supply-side school examines entrepreneurship by focusing on the individual characteristics of entrepreneurs, specifying potential mechanisms for agency and change, whereas the demand-side emphasizes the push and pull of context. Clearly, the founding of a firm may be dependent on the individual entrepreneur, as supply-side analysts suggest, but it is also clear that an individual cannot mobilize without an infrastructure. I suggest that multilevel models be used to examine the influence of both these forces (DiPrete & Forristal 1994).

The idea that individuals and organizations affect and are affected by their social context is a seminal argument in both classic and contemporary sociology and has been applied to the study of entrepreneurship at different levels of analysis. For example, Weber's (1904) research illustrated how religious doctrine provided the cultural legitimation needed to shape the economic behavior of individuals in ways that, in the aggregate, led to the rise of capitalism. Weber's metatheory catalyzed the supply-side perspective and led psychologists to develop research programs on culture and personality as the ushers of entrepreneurship (McClelland 1961). Similarly, Burt (1992) has shown how entrepreneurs' chances of success are determined by the structure of their networks. Individual entrepreneurs with deep "structural holes" in their networks—that is, an absence of contact redundancy and substitution increase their chances of successfully identifying and optimizing entrepreneurial opportunities because they are central to and well positioned to manipulate a structure that is more likely to produce higher levels of information.

DEFINING SUPPLY AND DEMAND PERSPECTIVES

The categorization of the supply and demand perspectives stems both from Weber and from the economic concept that there is a supply and demand for entrepreneurship (Casson 1995). The supply perspective has been criticized for its single-cause logic and its lack of rigorous and appropriate research methods; the demand perspective has been attacked for its lack of a theory of action. Moreover, these two perspectives represent different methatheoretical assumptions and levels of analysis-micro and macro, respectively. I consider the two perspectives together here, however, because both advance causal theories. It has been argued that individual traits tend to be enduring, whereas social structures tend to be context- and time-dependent (Scott 1995). For example, the findings on individuals' "need for achievement" (McClelland 1975) change very little within society over short periods of time, but Gartner & Shane (1995) have shown that the measure changes considerably at the societal level over time periods greater than ten years. Considering both supply and demand perspectives promises to advance thorny questions about which explanatory factors are universal across time and contexts and which factors are particular to time and context.

Supply-Side Perspective

The central argument of the supply-side perspective and its traits-oriented approach is that special types of individuals create entrepreneurship. To advance economically, societies need an adequate supply of these special individuals. In this perspective, differences in the rate, form, and location of entrepreneurs and entrepreneurship are attributed to differences in psychological, social, cultural, and ethnic characteristics of individuals. Thus, supply-side psychologists have asked whether entrepreneurs have psychological traits and backgrounds that differentiate them from other populations such as managers. Such research has examined individuals' need for achievement, locus of control, risk-taking propensity, problem-solving style and innovativeness, leadership style, values, and socialization experience. This line of inquiry has yielded mixed results (Brockhaus & Horwitz 1986). While individuals are a key ingredient in how and why new organizations are founded, the idea that psychological traits alone account for entrepreneurship has been largely abandoned. See Shaver and Scott (1991) for a review of the substantial research based on the psychological perspective.

Sociological supply-side approaches have examined how attributes of culture (Weber 1904, Shane 1993), social class, and ethnic group (Aldrich &

Waldinger 1990, Light & Rosenstein 1995) produce entrepreneurial behavior. Following the supply-side logic, such research holds that differences in entrepreneurship can be predicted by differences in individuals—that is, that if one can accurately describe the personality or social group of an individual entrepreneur, one can then infer how, why, and where new businesses are founded.

While the majority of entrepreneurship research has been conducted from the supply-side perspective, considerable evidence underscores the causal logic critique of the supply-side perspective. For example, Baumol (1986) has illustrated that differences in the rates of development across diverse cultures are declining, and Gereffi & Hempel (1996) have shown that entrepreneurial institutions are spreading globally. IPO markets are developing in countries previously thought to have nonentrepreneurial cultures (Edmundson et al 1996), and policy documents in Third World countries are beginning to use the concept of entrepreneur in describing the role of women in economic development (Chin & Brauchi 1995). These examples imply that in addition to individual and cultural differences, entrepreneurs and entrepreneurship are determined by forces operating within other, larger contexts.

Both sociologists and psychologists have criticized supply-side studies for their lack of rigorous and appropriate research methods (Frey 1984, Brockhaus & Horwitz 1986, Aldrich 1990). A common research design flaw is sampling on the dependent variable—that is, successful entrepreneurs and firms. Such studies leave unanswered the question of whether an entrepreneurial person created a successful business or a successful business created an entrepreneurial person. Other criticisms focus on the lack of controls for important variables such as age, education, gender, and work experience, which makes the generalizability of findings problematic. Another criticism of supply-side research centers on the use of cross-sectional methods, which disregard important temporal and contextual events and processes. This is problematic because recent empirical studies illustrate that entrepreneurship is a dynamic phenomenon that exists across time and space (Gartner & Shane 1995), with the definition of an entrepreneur and what is defined as entrepreneurship changing over the life course of individuals and industrial contexts (Brockhaus & Horwitz 1986, Vesper 1990). In sum, supply-side perspectives by themselves are too simple, making economic activity too much a function of individuals and underplaying the role of external structural influences (Martinelli 1994).

While much has been learned about the personal attributes, behaviors, and other characteristics associated with entrepreneurs, there has been little progress in relating types of entrepreneurs to the formation of new ventures. Because the challenges of founding new organizations vary by context, different types of enterprises are likely to require different types of entrepreneurs. Unless context is taken into account, the links between the actions of individuals in founding new organizations and the founding rate are likely to remain elusive (Low & Abrahamson 1997).

Demand-Side Perspective

The demand-side perspective was first developed by Marxists, economists, and geographers (Light & Rosenstein 1995). Glade (1967:251) defined the demand perspective as an "opportunity structure, an 'objective' structure of economic opportunity and a structure of differential advantage in the capacity of the system's participants to perceive and act upon such opportunities." In contrast to the supply-side emphasis on stasis and individuals, the demand-side perspective advances the study of entrepreneurship by asking what entrepreneurs actually do—the decisions they make within social settings that are changing over time. However, Glade's contextual approach misses the micro-macro link; as Martinelli (1994:486) notes, "he cannot go from behavior of the individual to the higher-social phenomena, other than by claiming that growth stems from the capability of the actor to take advantage of the situation."

Newer work from a demand-side perspective, which is gaining popularity in business schools and among economic sociologists, draws from ecological and institutional theories in organizational sociology (Gartner 1989, Aldrich 1990, Aldrich & Wiedenmayer 1993, Bull & Willard 1993). Romanelli (1989) characterizes this approach with her idea that the availability of resources encourages founders to emerge. Similarly, in case studies Freeman (1986) found that semiconductor organizations create entrepreneurs that spin off new organizations because they give knowledge and resources to employees and identify models of organization, market niches, and entrepreneurial opportunities. High employee turnover may be coupled with cultures that support and revere those who leave to found new ventures. The ecological perspective, while methodologically rigorous, has been criticized by entrepreneurship scholars as lacking a theory of agency and context because it aggregates events at the population level of analysis. Institutional theory has also been criticized for having an underdeveloped theory of agency (DiMaggio 1988). However, both perspectives are developing in directions that promise to address both the issue of agency and the micro-macro link.

INFLUENCES OF FIRMS   There is debate on whether it is the internal core or the periphery of organizations—that is, the hierarchy or the market—that provides the greatest source of new ventures for the economy. Aldrich & Zimmer (1986) argue for the peripheral view, noting that the majority of new small businesses are funded informally by the owner's personal savings, family, and network of friends. Similarly, Birch's analyses (1987) support the peripheral view that small new firms are the primary source of new ventures. Reynolds & White (1997) present an overview of both sides of this debate. Harrison (1994) argues that the aggregate importance of new independent ventures has been exaggerated and that entrepreneurship by new ventures is largely under the control of large corporations. Arrow (1983) states that because of the increasing cost of innovation, large firms play a greater role in innovation and economic growth than do small firms. However, because there is a market for research outcomes, small firms have become less inhibited about research for which large development expenditures are necessary.

Organization theorists in sociology and economics have done considerable research on the rise of the large corporation as a central mechanism for resource allocation and market control in the United States during the later half of the twentieth century (Chandler 1962, 1977, Rumelt 1974, Armour & Teece 1978, Williamson 1985, Fligstein 1985, 1990, Palmer et al 1987, 1993, Roy 1997). Fligstein (1985) found that by 1979 the multidivisional firm (M-form) had become the dominant form of industrial enterprise. Ingram & Baum (1997:70) have documented the increasing prevalence of multiunit establishments in the service sector, accounting for 25% of all service revenue in 1955 and 40% in 1987, with this trend continuing upward. Chandler (1980:11) makes clear the distinction between M-form and unitary-form firms:

> The traditional firm was a single-unit enterprise, with an individual or a small number of owners operating a shop, store, factory, and a bank or transportation line out of a single office. Normally, this type of firm undertook to fulfill only a single economic function, produce or sell a single line of products, and operated in one geographic region. Before the rise of the modern firm, the activities of these small, personally owned and managed enterprises were coordinated and monitored primarily by market and price mechanisms. The modern multiunit enterprise, in contrast, has come to operate in different locations, often carrying out a number of economic activities and producing or selling several lines of goods and services. The operation of its units and the transactions among them have been internalized within the firm. The activities of these units have come to be monitored and coordinated by the decisions of salaried managers rather than by market mechanisms.

While we know a considerable amount about the conditions that give rise to organizational hierarchies, we know very little about their effects on innovation—that is, on the creation of entrepreneurs and the founding of new ventures.

To gain insights, I turn to the interdisciplinary literatures on organization theory and more specifically on corporate venturing for guiding propositions on the role of large organizations in founding new ventures. Some of these views state that large organizations suppress entrepreneurship, while others argue that they promote it. There is evidence to support both arguments; however, no systematic studies exist that compare these two competing perspectives (Rumelt 1987).

According to one variant of the institutional perspective, organizations have remarkable inertia that reflects the historical conditions at the time of their founding. However, new forms arise and surviving organizations reinvent themselves by an entrepreneurial response to the institutional changes in their environments. Classic case histories support these arguments (Selznick 1949, Kimberly 1975, Zald & Denton 1963). This pattern of adaptational organizational change is driven by the distribution of resources in the environment such as increasing urbanization and literacy, changes in state policies, political revolution, and the development of a market economy (Stinchcombe 1965). The institutional perspective points to potential independent variables concerning how the environment may influence entrepreneurial activity in existing organizations.

The structural inertia thesis (Hannan & Freeman 1984) emphasizes that selection processes favor organizations that have stable structures because they are more reliable and accountable than organizations that experiment with change. The inertia thesis is a useful concept to draw upon in understanding which organizations are likely contexts for innovation and the founding of new ventures. However, Freeman's (1986) case studies of the semiconductor industry indicate a positive relationship between inertia and the organizational production of entrepreneurs. The effect of slowness in transferring technology and reallocating funding among divisions creates frustration that actually pushes potential entrepreneurs out the door faster. Freeman's findings are consistent with psychological studies on the push effect of previous work experience (Brockhaus & Horwitz 1986).

Agency theory argues that governance forms in which the principal and agent are integrated provide greater incentive for entrepreneurship (Jensen & Meckling 1976). In this view, individuals are less likely to create new ventures if they are employees in professionally managed corporations than if they are independent entrepreneurs. This is because employees have divergent goals from principals and because managers act to promote the security of their own position rather than risk strategies of new venturing. Shane (1995) found support for this agency argument by performing time-series regression analysis of rates of entrepreneurship versus real rates of economic growth. These findings suggest that ownership form is an important context variable.

The key idea of transaction cost theory that is central to entrepreneurship is that exchange is not costless and that sometimes it is less costly to use the market to govern exchanges and at other times it is less costly to use the firm (Swedberg 1994). Rumelt (1987) argues that firms are centers of sustained resources and that they engage in explicit strategies to spawn new enterprises because functions once attributed to capital markets have been transferred to the hierarchy. However, transaction cost theory does not focus per se on the means or processes that an entrepreneur employs in a large organization but instead focuses on what determines the payoff for entrepreneurial activity. Payoff incentives can be blunted by an owner who exerts strong control over residual returns. For example, the manipulation of transfer pricing and cost accounting rules can obfuscate the rise of and results of innovation; hence, causal ambiguity and general office intrusion blunt payoff incentives for entrepreneurship in large organizations (Williamson 1985). While seldom applied to the study of entrepreneurship, the transaction cost theory can be useful in framing intraorganizational differences concerning employee incentives, which in turn can form the basis for hypotheses about which firms are more likely to engage in corporate venturing.

In the corporate venturing literature, Burgelman (1983:1349) defines corporate entrepreneurship as "the process whereby firms engage in diversification through internal development, which requires new resource combinations to extend the firm's activities in areas unrelated or marginally related to its current domain of competence." Hornsby et al (1993) argue that corporate entrepreneurship is a means by which firms enhance the entrepreneurial abilities of their employees. Trends such as the increasing prevalence of M-form firms, the maturation of industries, and increasing competition have given rise to corporate venturing as a means for firms to remain competitive (Merrifield 1993). In Galunic's 1996 inductive case study of ten divisions within a large high-technology corporation, he observed that the creation of new divisions and the recreation of existing ones occurred in response to industry and divisional life cycles.

Zahra (1993) found that a company's good financial performance is associated positively with corporate entrepreneurship. However, it is not clear whether it is corporate entrepreneurship that induces positive financial performance. In a review of Du Pont's 85 "new-direction" businesses, several determinants for success were identified: the possession of proprietary technology, heavy investment, conservative financial management, patient development, and outstanding people. Other lessons learned from venturing activities were the importance of the following: tolerance of failure, separation of venture and established businesses, corporate sponsorship, flexible planning to manage uncertainty, training of entrepreneurial leaders, and recognition and rewards for intrapreneurial individuals. For further reviews of corporate venturing, see Block & MacMillan (1993).

The central findings of those investigating corporate venturing indicate that the types of entrepreneurship best suited to large organizations may be (*a*) ventures based on the redeployment of the firm's resources and the extension of its competitive positions and (*b*) ventures that require large project administration and longer term resources. Ventures more attractive to individuals and small firms may be ones based on opportunities created by new and emerging markets (Rumelt 1987). Other variables that strongly influence whether organizations start new ventures are the characteristics of the organizational culture in which corporate employees operate and the reaction of organizational participants to changes in social and economic environments.

In general, the research on corporate venturing is atheoretical and poorly designed, and definitions of success are inadequately described. However, this work does illustrate that there is considerable intraorganizational heterogeneity. Here, advances can be gained by borrowing ethnographic and interpretive approaches (Smircich 1983) and organization theory and quantitative methods in sociology to guide studies of entrepreneurship. With respect to the latter, Krackhardt's (1995) application of Burt's structural hole theory to explain differences in entrepreneurial opportunity within corporations is a step in that direction.

Venture Capital Firms   Venture capital firms control a type of financing that addresses a variety of barriers to innovation: the inertia of large corporations, the risk aversion of traditional financial markets, and the liability of newness inherent in business start-ups (Florida & Kenney 1988a). Because there has been little sociological study of venture capital firms and financial markets (Adler & Adler 1984), I first describe these organizations and institutions and then suggest avenues for using a sociological perspective in future research.

Venture capital firms provide seed, start-up, mezzanine, and bridge-stage funding for new ventures. The economic logic underpinning the business of professionally managed risk capital is the assumption that investment in entrepreneurial companies, while carrying higher risk, can provide higher returns than conventional investments. New ventures that are well suited to venture capital financing include high-technology and high-growth businesses with a fast "burn-rate" of capital in a variety of industries, including communications, electronics, health care, and retailing and consumer products, among others.

Venture capitalists form partnerships and syndications to share expertise, spread risk, and raise pools of money from sources such as university endowments, pension funds, and previously successful entrepreneurs, known as "angels." Institutional investors that participate in venture capital have tended to spread their risk by participating as limited partners in a varied portfolio of venture capital investment pools (Brophy & Guthner 1988). The organization of venture capital firms more closely resembles network than hierarchical forms of organization (Powell 1990). While the first venture capital firm began in the 1930s, venture capital did not become a highly organized form of financing until a change in federal legislation in the late 1970s, which for the first time allowed typically risk-averse pension funds to invest in venture capital funds.

Venture capital differs from debt capital because venture capitalists are actively involved in helping set up, manage, and oversee the founding and development of new firms. Florida & Kenney (1988b:43) provide data showing that venture capital is "spatially fixed" around high concentrations of financial institutions and technology-intensive enterprises. They note that a growing body of literature recognizes a dynamic complementarity existing between large companies, universities, and small companies. Venture capitalists enhance such environments by acting as both catalyst and capitalist, providing the resources and the contacts to facilitate new business start-ups, spinoffs, and expansions. Because they sit at the center of extended networks linking financiers, entrepreneurs, corporate executives, headhunters and consultants, venture capitalists have a propulsive effect on the rates of business formations.

The use of venture capital has been on the rise. From 1992 to 1997, available venture capital funds increased by 158% , from $4.1 billion to $10.4 billion. These funds supported 952 ventures in 1992 and 2429 ventures in 1997, an increase of 155%. The median age of companies financed by venture capital in 1996 was two years and ten months. Early-stage venture capital is the most expensive to raise, and its abundance varies with market cycles. The number of firms receiving initial venture capital rose from 327 in 1992 to 628 in 1996. In 1996, 39% of all venture capital funded early-stage start-up companies (VentureOne Corporation 1996, 1997).

INFLUENCES OF MARKETS   Markets for initial public offerings (IPOs) are linked to venture capital firms because an IPO is a sequentially planned exit strategy for founding entrepreneurs and venture capitalists. Venture capital firms "harvest" their successful investment in firms that have shown solid results and high growth potential through their relationships with stock underwriters, who can take the fledgling firms public. An IPO allows a company to access public capital markets to reduce its debt, provide greater liquidity for investors, commit to expansion, and therefore be more attractive to lenders. An IPO provides a publicly traded share price, which gives both management and shareholders outside information about the company's value. The share price at which the owners of the company agree to trade their ownership for cash depends on the overall market conditions, the characteristics of the company, and the policies of investment bankers. In 1996, 275 companies went public, raising a total of $11.2 billion, compared with approximately 140 companies that raised $5.8 billion in 1992. The average age of companies going public in the decade of the 1990s is approximately 7.9 years, and the average pre-offering valuation in 1996 was over $125 million (VentureOne Corporation 1997).

Acquisition markets   An alternative to an IPO, an acquisition is another form of second-stage financing that also provides an exit strategy for founding entrepreneurs and venture capitalists. The lateral entry of the large corporation via acquisition provides the acquired firm with immediate access to sources of capital and other resources, thus increasing the rapidity with which the newer firm becomes established. Arguing that the market for corporate control is an important context in which to examine innovation and entrepreneurship, Hitt et al (1996) found that firms that grow by acquisition tend to invest less in internal venturing. Because there is a market for research outcomes, there is a symbiotic relationship between large firms that seek to externalize the risk of research and development by acquiring new firms and new firms that seek acquisition in order to gain access to the distribution and financial muscle of large organizations (Arrow 1983). This empirically underexamined form of entrepreneurship is prevalent in industries such as biotechnology and pharmaceuticals. In 1996, 155 venture-backed companies were acquired. This tally does not include acquisitions of companies that had already gone public, because an IPO is also considered a liquidity event. The market for acquisitions has been growing steadily and in 1996 accounted for $21.3 billion in assets.

SOCIOLOGICAL EMBEDDEDNESS PERSPECTIVE   An important perspective for understanding social and economic environments is the embeddedness approach (Granovetter 1985, Lie 1997). In his seminal 1985 essay, Granovetter argues that economic environments are embedded in social and structural relationships that modify neoclassical predictions of atomistic economic behavior. Contrasting his argument to Williamson's (1975) classic dichotomy of "markets and hierarchies," Granovetter illustrates how economic processes, whether governed by market or hierarchy, are affected by their embeddedness in social and structural relations. The character of venture capital firms and IPO and acquisition markets exemplifies both relational and spatial embeddedness.

   With respect to relational embeddedness, Eisenhardt & Forbes (1984) describe how in venture-backed Silicon Valley companies, one cohort of successful companies seeds successive generations. This phenomenon makes the market for venture capital "regenerative" in relation to successful ventures, because such ventures create "angels" and "serial entrepreneurs" who provide the financial, human, and social capital to start new ventures. Working this same vein, Florida & Kenney (1988a,b) develop a formal model of the types of firms in the network that are catalysts, and they document the regional clustering of venture capital resource flows.

   Both IPO and acquisition markets are also relationally embedded with venture capital firms because they are tied to their "harvest cycle," being the main liquidation mechanisms of successful founding entrepreneurs and venture capital investors. Venture-backed firms seeking placement on the IPO or acquisition market are also subject to status-ordering processes controlled by opinion leaders such as industry analysts and leading bankers (Podolny 1993, Haunschild 1994). As Podolny's work with established firms indicates, choosing the most prestigious investment bank as an underwriter sends a favorable signal to the market. The case of IPOs is interesting since most venture-backed firms have yet to turn a profit, and their status is shaky and dependent on inside knowledge and networks within a particular industrial context. These characteristics raise a new line of questioning about what we know about the status ordering and embeddedness of markets. For example, does the salience of status ordering still hold in a context in which there are young markets and firms that have had little opportunity to establish a reputation? Also, how do status relations affect IPO markets and the rate of foundings with respect to the liability of adolescence?

Spatial factors such as the density and proximity of venture capital firms have an effect on the founding of new ventures. While Florida & Kenney identified the spatial clustering of venture capital resources, Schoonhoven & Eisenhardt (1992) used the concept of clustering, or what they termed incubator regions, to predict the comparative birth rate of new organizations in a cross-regional analysis. Also taking a spatial approach, Reynolds et al (1995) used two types of independent variables to predict regional differences in the birth of new firms in the United States between 1976 and 1988: regional features such as economic diversity, volatile industries, employment policy flexibility; and features that reflected the population itself, such as career opportunity and personal wealth.

In sum, the work on incubator regions provides solid evidence that geographic areas that have higher concentrations of resources, such as a large number of venture capital firms and relevant specialized service companies, have higher birth rates of new ventures. First introduced in work on geographic areas (Pennings 1982), the gist of this explanation is that density and proximity are determinants of the entrepreneurial behavior, organizing capacity, and competitive advantages of regions. This argument is pervasive, used initially in classic organizational sociology (Stinchcombe 1965) and later in the business strategy literature (Porter 1990).

 · While the regional-factors work predicts the context in which certain forms of new enterprise are likely to be founded, it is not regions that start new businesses. To predict how and why new ventures are founded, we must ask other questions. At the individual level, are the entrepreneurs who are making use of resources in incubator regions—the ones whom supply-side psychologists claim have a high need for achievement (McClelland 1961) and a high internal locus of control (Rotter 1966)? How do the entrepreneurs' backgrounds—their prior start-up experience and social ties (Eisenhardt & Schoonhoven 1990)— affect the new businesses they found? At the organizational level, what type of organizational structures and cultures produce which forms of genealogical progeny—those that are "integrated" and have flat hierarchies or those that are "fragmented" with deep hierarchies (Martin 1992, Saxenian 1994)? At the environmental level, do such start-ups happen during periods of resource competition, resource munificence, or technological discontinuity (Tushman & Anderson 1986)?

Additional research should link the work on regional variation with the role of individuals and firms in starting new ventures. This integrated approach can also address a number of important theoretical questions of interest to sociologists who study the origin and change of institutions, because it provides a setting for observing both interest and agency effects and universal versus particular effects. Future studies should also advance beyond the level of anecdote and descriptive analysis.

The work on regional variation heralds the need to reconcile the anomalous findings of research on incubator regions and research on density dependence based on population ecology theory. The findings of Schoonhoven & Eisenhardt imply that the effects of competition, the backbone of ecology, are less important than the effects of cooperation and spatial proximity, features that facilitate organizational learning (Ingram & Baum 1997)—that is, the easy transmission of technical and managerial know-how from one generation of entrepreneurs and firms to the next.

In response to these anomalies, the ecological literature has shifted toward an emphasis on contextual analysis. (See Baum & Oliver 1996 for a review of the ecological perspective and level of analysis.) The spatial effects of legitimation and competition are beginning to be examined according to political boundaries such as cities, states, regions, and nation-states; such studies have been made in the context of US and German breweries (Carroll & Wade 1991), Italian cooperative banks (Freeman & Lomi 1994), and automobile manufacturers (Hannan et al 1995). While too early to be definitive, preliminary evidence indicates that organizations compete locally but organizational populations evolve globally. This evidence, however, further confuses how different levels of action might be linked (Lomi & Larsen 1996).

The commodity-chains perspective offers an alternative explanation for where new enterprise is likely to locate. In shifting global markets, resource dependencies and transaction-cost exchange relations among leading and subservient firms drive the processes and location of new venture formation. Contrary to ecological work, this perspective suggests that cultural and political (nation-state) boundaries—as distinct from firm, market, and industry boundaries—are increasingly inconsequential in enterprise formation (Gereffi 1994).

Aldrich (1990) offers another explanation for where enterprise is likely to be founded by focusing on the relationship between spatial proximity and information transmission. Because venture capitalists fund "ideas," an asset that bankers cannot easily value, they assure control of these abstract assets by requiring board seats and boilerplate management agreements. Suchman (1995) found that venture capital financing agreements in Silicon Valley became more routinized over time and that routinization declined with geographical distance. These findings provide systematic evidence of the mechanisms that venture capitalists use in spreading knowledge that leads to founding new organizations.

The limited sociological literature on acquisition activity presents several research implications. While both economists and sociologists have observed that the market for acquisitions occurs in waves (Golbe & White 1988, Thornton 1995, Stearns & Allan 1996), sociologists have empirically examined the collective properties of acquisition activity. On the basis of an industry case study, Thornton (1995) has argued that the market for acquisitions is contingent on the competitive and cooperative structure of the particular industry as well as on universal models in the larger business environment. In an organizational field of the largest US firms, Stearns & Allan (1996) found that mimicry of new innovations in corporate financing led to the 1980s merger wave. Using a sample of large industrial firms, Amburgey & Miner (1992) showed how acquisition activity has momentum effects. Also sampling large industrial firms, Haunschild (1993) was able to predict the pattern of acquisition activity on the basis of corporate board networks. Based on a sample of the 100 largest firms in the United States, Fligstein (1990) illustrated that the state influences the market for acquisitions because antitrust policies tend to give rise to new innovations in integration. For example, the prohibition against horizontal and vertical integration gave rise to diversified integration as a new form of enterprise.

All these sociological attributes—local industry and global cross-industry pressures, networks, mimicry, momentum, and the activities of the state—are likely to affect the market for acquisitions and therefore, second-stage funding for fledgling new ventures. Because acquisitions occur in waves, one would expect this pattern to affect opportunity structures for entrepreneurs and the liabilities of the adolescence of organizations. Moreover, the advent of investor capitalism (Useem 1996), coupled with the rise of the market for acquisitions, has made an acquisition an established option for entrepreneurs. Historically, such changes in business practices are likely to accompany a shift in logic—in this case, a shift from thinking of a business as a relatively permanent lifestyle to considering it a time-limited, successive endeavor. Such a shift implies a change in an entrepreneur's identity and career path (i.e., to that of serial entrepreneur) and, concomitantly, an increased chance of new ventures (Gartner & Shane 1995). These conjectures await formal testing.

INTEGRATING FRAMEWORKS

The knowledge base of entrepreneurship research has been generated by three founding disciplines: psychology (McClelland 1961), economics (Schumpeter

1934), and sociology (Weber 1904). Each of these disciplines asks different questions, employs different metatheories, and focuses at different levels of analysis (Martinelli 1994). While the social embeddedness of firms and markets is a useful concept to suggest ways to contextualize organizational founding, other approaches relevant to a sociological perspective are ecological and institutional theories and multilevel models (DiPrete & Forristal 1994).

Ecological and Institutional Perspectives

Greenfield & Strickon (1981) were the first to suggest a population perspective as a new paradigm for entrepreneurship. However, it is Aldrich's (1990) work on population ecology that has migrated from sociology to propel demand-side research on entrepreneurship. Aldrich argues for a refocus on "rates," because studying individual traits of entrepreneurs fails to provide information on the environmental context within which entrepreneurs interpret and make sense of their actions (Aldrich & Wiedenmayer 1993). Reynolds (1992) suggests that population and organizational ecology is a productive paradigm in which to develop research on the societal context of entrepreneurship.

The strength of population ecology's formal theory and methods lends clarity to generating falsifiable hypotheses and to advancing understanding of organizational founding at the population level. As Aldrich (1999) notes, one sign of population ecology theory's sophistication is the developing use of computer simulations for hypothesis testing. Population ecology has developed useful concepts such as the liabilities of newness and adolescence that are applicable to framing organizational and environmental effects on new ventures. However, the current theory does not provide any explanation for the role of individual action in influencing founding conditions (Hannan & Carroll 1992, Hofer & Bygrave 1992). Ecological data sets do not contain information on such microprocesses. Population ecology theory has emphasized the importance of outside forces or unconscious action as causal forces, rather than individuals' goals and intents. It has generally adhered to the important goal of developing and testing general theory on the patterns of founding and disbanding of organizational populations.

However, ecological research is beginning to advance a contextual focus. In studying the founding rate of baseball teams and leagues, Land et al (1994) demonstrate that, in addition to the conventional density-dependent effects, spatial and relational embeddedness also affect founding rates. Using the concept of structural mutualism, they show that league foundings have a positive impact on team foundings. Linking entrepreneurs' choices to a founding rate analysis of the structure of the Manhattan hotel industry, Baum & Haveman (1997) show that entrepreneurs located new hotels geographically close to established hotels that were similar in price but different in size. Barnett & Carroll (1995), pacesetters in use of the ecological paradigm, suggested a focus on content and adaptation, and this invitation is encouraging the participation of new scholars and perspectives (Amburgey & Rao 1996).

The strength of the institutional perspective is that it does not have restrictive scope conditions with respect to the rationality of actors, historical time, and level of analysis. It has breadth in the sense that the socially constructed nature of "actors" can be rational individuals or seemingly irrational organizations and their environments (Scott 1995, Scott 1997). This theoretical flexibility provides the ability to link the micro supply-side and macro demand-side perspectives. For example, Van de Ven & Garud (1989), using a case study of the cochlear implants industry, made the first theoretical statement encompassing both micro and macro levels. Using a recursive, emergent social systems model (Romanelli 1991), Van de Ven & Garud argue that the odds of a firm successfully developing an innovation are largely a function of the extant infrastructure at the industrial level. This community infrastructure facilitates and constrains entrepreneurs, but it is entrepreneurs who construct and change the infrastructure. This infrastructure emerges and changes through the accretion of numerous institutional, resource, and proprietary events that co-produce each other through the actions of many public- and private-sector actors over an extended period (Ventresca & Lacey, forthcoming, Whitley 1996).

While such institutionally oriented research reflects "thick descriptions" of the context of human networks that enact the emergence of new ventures, it needs to advance beyond the case-study stage to include large-sample studies and formal models. Ingram & Inman's (1996) study of hotel foundings in the Niagara Falls market is one example that integrates historical description with quantitative modeling of how institutional structure increased the founding rate (in this case, how the development of parks influenced the development of nearby hotels). Further advances hinge on the use of longitudinal quantitative methods and attention to historical detail to capture important time-dependent relationships, such as the life cycles of individuals and organizations in relation to population life cycles. The study by Van de Ven & Grazman (1994) on a genealogy of the Twin Cities' health care organizations is a step in that direction.

Multilevel Models

If we build on ecological and institutional approaches, future entrepreneurship research should address the effects of individual-level traits, organizational and market-level variables, and population-level characteristics in models of the founding of new ventures. However, as Aldrich (1992) states, to generalize about entrepreneurs, individuals need to be studied; to generalize about new ventures, organizations need to be studied. While an integrative approach promises to advance our understanding of who becomes an entrepreneur and how, why, and where organizations are founded, it is not an easy task. One potential solution is to use multilevel models.

DiPrete & Forristal (1994) provide a useful review of recent advances in the application of multilevel models to substantive problems in sociology. They take as their starting point Blalock's (1984) definition: "The essential feature of all contextual-effects models is an allowance for macro processes that are presumed to have an impact on the individual actor over and above the effects of any individual-level variables that may be operating" (quoted in DiPrete & Forristal 1994:354). They then note, "If we generalize his use of the term 'individual' to apply to any unit that is micro relative to some other macro level in the analysis, his definition is still quite serviceable" (333). In other words, if we extrapolate, the idea of context can include individual contexts (e.g., psychological traits, background characteristics, cognitive schemas), spatial contexts, (countries, states, regions, communities), temporal contexts (history), organizational contexts (U-form, M-form, network form), and social/cultural/economic contexts (ethnic groups, social classes, economic sectors, cultural logics). We can also identify precedents, such as Fligstein's 1987 work using the functional backgrounds of CEOs to predict shifts in conceptions of control prevailing in an organizational field of Fortune 500 firms.

While DiPrete & Forristal (1994) review the assumptions of various multilevel models, they also caution that there is no general theory of multilevel relationships. They point out that many researchers theorize at multiple levels of analysis but use data at only one level, or use data at multiple levels but theorize at one level, both of which can raise issues of the ecological fallacy (see Blalock 1984 for a summary). Because of such obstacles, it is important to identify sources of heterogeneity at different levels of analysis.

Sources of Heterogeneity

INDIVIDUALS   Due to space limitations, I have not elaborated on literature reviewed elsewhere that examines the psychological traits, individual backgrounds, and behavioral characteristics of entrepreneurs. However, I do want to emphasize that new insights can be gleaned by building on the classic variables highlighted in psychology (the need for achievement, risk-taking propensity, and locus of control) and by integrating advances from the literatures in cognitive psychology and decision biases (March 1988). For example, Dosi & Lovallo (1997:42) use an eclectic mix of experimental evidence and literature review to argue that decision-making biases have important ramifications for the nature of entrepreneurship and for how and why entrepreneurs found new ventures. Such integration introduces to the study of entrepreneurship concepts such as organizational learning, allocation of attention, decision-making under uncertainty, unrealistic optimism, competitive blind spots, and competitive groups (March 1991, Lant & Baum 1995). These concepts provide a theoretical bridge from the rational models that underlie the psychological work on entrepreneurs to sociological interest in individual irrationalities and collectivism. Moreover, melding the insights from cognitive psychology and decision bias work with those from institutional theory affords a focus on both the signal the environment delivers and the way internal representations of the world are constructed. It provides one way of perceiving how individuals' actions scale up to organizational outcomes, how new ventures and industries are spawned, and a way to treat sticky metatheorical issues of individualism versus structuralism (Mayhew 1980).

ORGANIZATIONS   We understand more about how interorganizational differences affect organizational founding than we do about how intraorganizational differences matter. Hannan & Freeman (1987) showed that the relationships among different types of organizational forms in a population affect the emergence and the diversity of new ventures—for example, that the growth of industrial unions restrained the founding rate of craft unions. Studies on resource partitioning and organizational size and mutualism also illustrate that diversity among types and forms of organizations has important consequences for founding rates (Carroll 1985, Barnett & Carroll 1987). Similarly, Baum & Oliver (1996) showed that nonprofit forms proliferated over for-profit forms of organizations.

However, an important and unexplored form of heterogeneity is the influence of large, diversified, M-form organizations. The multidivisional (M-form) represents a now-established sea change in organizational populations, and we have no studies of its effects on founding rates. The M-form organization presents a problematic context to study because M-forms span industries and different resource pools, thereby violating theoretical assumptions of homogeneous population boundaries (Thornton & Tuma 1995). Van de Ven & Grazman (1994) have approached this problem using event histories to study how existing organizations may be recombined or new organizations developed from the resources and ancestral forms in a population of organizations.

According to resource partitioning theory, interorganizational heterogeneity evolves endogenously as industries mature over time because a few generalist firms that exploit mass markets come to dominate the industry. This in turn should increase the founding rate of new businesses because entrepreneurs take advantage of the opportunity to found specialist organizations as demand rises in areas that have been neglected by generalists, creating new niche markets. However, it may be unrealistic to assume that generalists (M-forms) will not attempt to exploit these new niche markets and compete with the entrepreneurs starting new ventures. There are numerous examples of large firms that have relatively autonomous divisions organized to stratify the marketplace. For example, retailing firms like the Gap use a divisionalized parent-firm structure as a strategy to avoid diluting the status of its low- and high-prestige brands (Podolny 1993). These observations warrant research to further develop resource partitioning theory.

The M-form also is an appreciable source of intraorganizational heterogeneity, which has psychological, sociological, and economic dimensions for entrepreneurship (Arrow 1983:16). Reviewing the literature on corporate hierarchies and venturing reveals that intraorganizational differences—that is, differences in internal structure within similar organizational forms—do affect the founding of new ventures. Studies of differences in organizational culture, identities, and managerial ideologies and styles within corporate hierarchies align well with attempts by economic sociologists to understand the autonomy of cultural effects in economic environments (Zukin & DiMaggio 1990). Direct measures of internal organizational structure also promise to advance ecological research on foundings, which so far has relied on gross measures of industrial concentration and organization size to understand how internal differentiation of organizational forms influences founding rates.

The description of venture capital firms suggests that their social organization has important effects on organizational founding. Advancing our understanding of this influence hinges on finding ways of quantifying the social embeddedness of relationships among entrepreneurs, angels, law firms, venture capital firms, and other financial institutions. Venture capital presents an interesting sociological topic because its social organization defies the neoclassical economic principles of financial markets, in which, under conditions of perfect information, investments flow freely across organizational and spatial boundaries to enterprises that offer the highest rate of return. With respect to venture capital—backed firms, however, the free flow of investments is controlled instead by the organizational and spatial networks characteristic of the venture capital industry.

MARKETS   Using case studies, Freeman (1986) illustrated that foundings occur in waves that correspond with market cycles. Also, the reciprocal effects of markets and firms (Fligstein 1996) are one way to examine what determines the timing of when new ventures are founded. Because of the coupling of markets and firms, the timing of market cycles in relation to organizational founding raises several lines of inquiry. How does a shock in one market affect another—for example, in the relationship between IPO and acquisition markets? When IPO and acquisition markets are in a down cycle, they decrease liquidation options for venture capital firms. How do venture capital firms influence the patterns of IPO markets, and vice versa, with respect to organizational founding? In what context do acquisition waves produce waves of organizational founding or disbanding? How does the collective nature of the market for acquisitions, in terms of momentum and mimicry, affect liabilities of new-ness and adolescence of firms? How do status-ordering processes mediate how venture capital firms and the IPO market affect the founding of new ventures (White 1987)?

ENVIRONMENTS   Because the potential for founding new ventures depends on entrepreneurs' finding and utilizing opportunities in the environment, examining sources of environmental heterogeneity is one way to understand how and where new ventures are founded. Here, there are several issues to advance that hinge on the level of analysis employed and on endogenous and exogenous effects. Reconciling the effects of density dependence with the findings on incubator regions is one way to advance the research on organizational founding. Does the increasing density in maturing industries make the plight of entrepreneurs more difficult, as ecological theory would imply? Or, does it translate into increasing resource munificence, thereby increasing the ability of entrepreneurs in a particular space to garner resources for founding new ventures? So far the work on incubator regions would lead us to believe that environments with higher density—because they offer greater opportunities for mutualism and resource exchanges among firms—are more prone to learning, imitation, and collective action, all elements necessary to building infra-structure. However, not all organizations in a population benefit equally from any set of available resources. Baum & Singh (1994) have shown that founding rates were depressed when organizations had niche overlap—that is, when organizations competed for the same resources.

The contradictions in the predictions generated by studies of incubator regions vs. those of population ecology theory may be related to differences in the level of analysis. That is, the way organizations are selected for inclusion in empirical research may determine whether or not an analysis captures most of the competition effects (Singh 1993, Thornton & Tuma 1995). In population ecology theory, populations refer to entire industries, regardless of geographical dispersion. In contrast, studies of incubator regions focus on the geographical distribution of firms and largely ignore the variables of industry size, maturity, and concentration—all variables related to the distribution of resources and, most likely, to the founding rate.

Another potential explanation for these discrepant findings involves technological innovations that introduce competence-destroying discontinuities into an environment (Tushman & Anderson 1986). Entrepreneurial ventures that take advantage of competence-destroying technologies would no longer be in direct competition with established firms. Nevertheless, it might still be in the best interests of a start-up firm to locate in the region of established firms, due to the proximity of other firms in the industry, suppliers, and an existing skilled workforce. A further explanation for the discrepancies in the findings is that the populations of organizations of ecological studies are largely located in low techology or diminishing returns sectors. However, the work on incubator regions focuses on high technology of increasing return sectors (Arthur 1990, Bygrave 1995).

Conceptual frameworks are needed both to move research beyond the descriptive level, as in the case of incubator regional analysis, and to contextualize ecological effects. In trying to determine the best environmental context for successful foundings, Low & Abrahamson (1997) have developed a model that groups different organizational and competitive challenges into three stages of industry evolution: emerging, growth, and mature. This typology has two axes: one details transmission mechanisms, movements, bandwagons, and clones; the other axis contains context characteristics, entrepreneur networks, behaviors, stakeholders, and strategy/structure. In sum, answering the question of how and where new enterprises are founded requires conducting more research aimed at discovering which resources, in which industries, at which stage of industry evolution are more significant than others.

Modeling Contextual Heterogeneity

Sociological methodology is progressing rapidly in its use of multilevel models (DiPrete & Forristal 1994). Strang & Tuma (1993), for example, have developed a heterogeneous diffusion model that incorporates individual- and contextual-level variables into an event-history framework to represent the social structural relationships that are thought to channel diffusion. Such models can combine individual-, organizational-, and environmental-level variables to understand how individual behavior is influenced by individual factors and by the social structure of inter-actor influences (Davis & Greve 1997). Extending the application of these models to explore the issues highlighted in this review—for example, to create a model of the influences of corporate hierarchies or venture capital firm networks on organizational foundings—would represent a significant advance in entrepreneurship research.

This new class of models addresses the methodological problem of how to incorporate population heterogeneity, time nonstationarity, and varying degrees of interdependence among members of the population in the same modeling framework. These models decompose noncontagious and contagious influences, separating the contagious influence in terms of the susceptibility of the focal individual or organization to influence by other individuals and organizations, the infectiousness of previous individuals and organizations, and the social proximity of the focal individual and organization to previous individuals and organizations. This review has highlighted sociological perspectives in the founding of new ventures, such as embeddedness, imitation, and momentum effects, in which the previous occurrence of one event or practice by one actor affects the rate for the population. These methods can advance what we know about the conditions under which individual entrepreneurs are networked, and the genealogy of the firms and the characteristics of the resource environments from which they diffuse, in predicting the founding of new ventures. These models are not a simple solution because there is caution about their use with incomplete populations, making the data collection requirements appear daunting. However, ongoing research is examining the consequences of less complete data and the implications of less costly sampling for obtaining valid results (Greve et al 1993).

CONCLUSION

Over the last thirty years, Weber's theory on the origin of the entrepreneurial spirit as a cultural account of individualism has been the metatheory underlying the dominant supply-side perspectives in entrepreneurship research. Theory development and empirical research from a demand-side perspective are currently underdeveloped but on the rise. This review boosts the demand perspective by focusing on the influences exerted by firms and markets. It suggests that sociological frameworks, an embeddedness perspective, ecological and institutional theories, and multilevel models could be used to integrate analyses of individual, organizational, market, and environmental characteristics in explaining how, where, and why new ventures are founded. In sociology, there have been recurrent reminders of the importance of the totality of interpretation, as evidenced by periodic essays to "bring back" men (Homans 1964), firms (Baron & Bielby 1980), states (Skocpol 1985), society (Friedland & Alford 1991), and work (Barley 1996). Rapid advances in theoretical and empirical work in sociology are now providing avenues for "bringing back" the study of entrepreneurship into sociological research.

ACKNOWLEDGMENTS

I acknowledge the research assistance of Emily Faville and the helpful comments of Howard Aldrich, Kenneth Spenner, Nancy Tuma, and Intersouth Partners.

Visit the *Annual Reviews home page* at
http://www.AnnualReviews.org.

Literature Cited

Adler P, Adler PA. 1984. *The Social Dynamics of Financial Markets*. Greenwich, CT: JAI

Aldrich H. 1990. Using an ecological approach to study organizational founding rates. *Entrepreneurship Theory Pract.* 14(3):7–24

Aldrich H. 1992. Methods in our madness? Trends in entrepreneurship research. In *The State of the Art of Entrepreneurship*, ed. DL Sexton, JD Kasarda, pp. 191–213. Boston: PWS-Kent

Aldrich H. 1999. *Organizations Evolving*. London: Sage

Aldrich H, Waldinger R. 1990. Ethnicity and entrepreneurship. *Annu. Rev. Sociol.* 16: 111–35

Aldrich H, Wiedenmayer G. 1993. From traits to rates: an ecological perspective on organizational foundings. *Adv. in Entrepreneurship, Firm Emergence, Growth* 1: 145–95

Aldrich H, Zimmer C. 1986. Entrepreneurship through social networks. In *The Art and Science of Entrepreneurship*, ed. D Sexton, R Smilor, pp. 3–23. Cambridge, MA: Ballinger

Amburgey TL, Miner AS. 1992. Strategic momentum: the effects of repetitive, positional and contextual momentum on merger activity. *Strategic Manage. J.* 13: 335–48

Amburgey TL, Rao H. 1996. Organizational ecology: past, present, and future directions. *Acad. Manage. J.* 39(5):1265–86

Armour HO, Teece DJ. 1978. Organizational structure and economic performance: a test of the multidivisional hypothesis. *Bell J. Econ.* 9(1):106–22

Arrow KJ. 1983. Innovation in large and small firms. In *Entrepreneurship: Price Institute for Entrepreneurial Studies*, ed. J Ronen, pp. 15–27. Lexington, MA: Lexington

Arthur WB. 1990. Positive feedbacks in the economy. *Sci. Am.* February, 1990:92–99

Barley SR. 1996. Technicians in the workplace: ethnographic evidence for bringing work into organization studies. *Admin. Sci. Q.* 41:404–41

Barnett WP, Carroll GR. 1987. Competition and commensalism among early telephone companies. *Admin. Sci. Q.* 30:400–21

Barnett WP, Carroll GR. 1995. Modeling internal organizational change. *Annu. Rev. Sociol.* 12:217–36

Baron JN, Bielby WT. 1980. Bringing the firms back in: stratification, segmentation, and the organization of work. *Am. Sociol. Rev.* 45:737–65

Baum AC, Haveman HA. 1997. Love thy neighbor? Differentiation and agglomeration in the Manhattan hotel industry, 1898–1990. *Admin. Sci. Q.* 42(2):304–338

Baum JAC, Oliver C. 1996. Toward an institutional ecology of organizational founding. *Acad. Manage. J.* 39(5):1378–1427

Baum JAC, Singh JV. 1994. Organizational niche overlap and the dynamics of organizational founding. *Organ. Sci.* 5:483–502

Baumol WJ. 1986. Entrepreneurship and a century of growth. *J. Bus. Venturing* 1: 141–45

Birch D. 1987. *Job Creation in America: How Our Smallest Companies Put the Most People to Work*. New York: Free

Blalock HM. 1984. Contextual-effects models: theoretical and methodological issues. *Annu. Rev. Sociol.* 10:353–72

Block Z, MacMillan IC. 1993. *Corporate Venturing: Creating New Business Within the Firm*. Boston, MA: Harvard Bus. School Press

Brockhaus RH Sr, Horwitz PS. 1986. The psychology of the entrepreneur. In *The Art and Science of Entrepreneurship*, ed. DL Sexton, RW Smilor, pp. 25–48. Cambridge, MA: Ballinger

Brophy DJ, Guthner MW. 1988. Publicly traded venture capital funds: implications for institutional fund of funds investors. *J. Bus. Venturing* 3:187–206

Bull I, Willard GE. 1993. Towards a theory of entrepreneurship. *J. Bus. Venturing* 8: 183–95

Burgelman RA. 1983. A process model of internal corporate venturing in the diversified major firm. *Admin. Sci. Q.* 28:223–44

Burt RS. 1992. *Structural Holes: The Social Structure of Competition*. Cambridge, MA: Harvard Univ. Press

Bygrave WD. 1995. Theory building in the entrepreneurship paradigm. In *Entrepreneurship Perspectives on Theory Building*, ed. I Bull, H Thomas, G Willard, pp. 129–158. Oxford, UK: Elsevier

Bygrave WD, Hofer CW. 1991. Theorizing about entrepreneurship. *Entrepreneurship Theory Practice* 16(2):13–22

Carroll GR. 1985. Concentration and specialization: dynamics of niche width in populations of organizations. *Am. J. Sociol.* 90: 1262–83

Carroll GR, Wade JB. 1991. Density dependence in the evolution of the American brewing industry across different levels of analysis. *Soc. Sci. Res.* 20:271–302

Casson M. 1995. *Entrepreneurship and Busi-*

ness Culture. Aldershot, UK: Edward El-gar

Chandler AD. 1962. *Strategy and Structure: Chapters in the History of the American Industrial Enterprise.* Cambridge, MA: MIT Press

Chandler AD. 1977. *The Visible Hand: The Managerial Revolution in American Business.* Cambridge, MA: Harvard Univ. Press

Chandler AD. 1980. The United States: seedbed of managerial capitalism. In *Managerial Hierarchies,* ed. AD Chandler, H Daems, pp. 9–40. Cambridge, MA: Harvard Univ. Press

Chin K, Brauchi MW. 1995. Tens of thousands of women sitting around talking. *Wall Street J.,* September 8

Davis GF, Greve HR. 1997. Corporate elite networks and governance changes in the 1980s. *Am. J. Sociol.* 103:1–37

DiMaggio PJ. 1988. Interest and agency in institutional theory. In *Institutional Patterns and Organizations: Culture and Environment,* ed. L Zucker, pp.3–21. Cambridge, MA: Ballinger

DiPrete TA, Forristal JD. 1994. Multilevel models: methods and substance. *Annu. Rev. Sociol.* 20:331–57

Dobbin F, Dowd TJ. 1997. How policy shapes competition: early railroad foundings in Massachusetts. *Admin. Sci. Q.* 42: 501–29

Dosi G, Lovallo D. 1997. Rational entrepreneurs or optimistic martyrs? Some considerations on technological regimes, corporate entries, and the evolutionary role of decision biases. In *Technological Innovation: Oversights and Foresights,* ed. R Garzed, PR Nayyar, B Shapira, pp. 41–68. Cambridge: Cambridge Univ. Press

Edmundson G, Flynn J, Glasgall J. 1996. Come home little startups: Europe wants its own NASDAQ to capture more IPOs. *Bus. Wk.,* February 26

Eisenhardt KM, Forbes N. 1984. Technical entrepreneurship: an international perspective. *Columbia J. World Bus.* 19:31–38

Eisenhardt KM, Schoonhoven K. 1990. Organizational growth: linking founding teams, strategy, environment and growth among U.S. semi–conductor ventures. *Admin. Sci. Q.* 28:274–91

Fligstein N. 1985. The spread of the multidivisional form among large firms, 1919–1979. *Am. Sociol. Rev.* 50:377–91

Fligstein N. 1987. The intraorganizational power struggle: the rise of finance presidents in large corporations. *Am. Sociol. Rev.* 52:44–58

Fligstein N. 1990. *The Transformation of Corporate Control.* Cambridge, MA: Harvard Univ. Press

Fligstein N. 1996. Markets as politics: a political-cultural approach to market institutions. *Am. J. Sociol.* 61(4):656–73

Florida RL, Kenney M. 1998a. Venture capital–financed innovation and technological change in the USA. *Res. Policy* 17: 119–37

Florida RL, Kenney M. 1998b. Venture capital, high technology and regional development. *Regional Stud.* 22:33–48

Freeman J. 1986. Entrepreneurs as organizational products: semiconductor firms and venture capital firms. *Adv. Stud. Entrepreneurship, Innovation, and Econ. Growth* 1:33–52

Freeman J, Lomi A. 1994. Resource partitioning and the founding of banking cooperatives in Italy. In *Evolutionary Dynamics of Organizations,* ed. J Baum, J. Singh, pp 269–93. New York: Oxford Univ. Press

Frey RS. 1984. Need for achievement, entrepreneurship, and economic growth: a critique of the McClelland thesis. *Soc. Sci. J.* 21:125–34

Friedland R, Alford RR. 1991. Bringing society back in: symbols, practices, and institutional contradictions. In *The New Institutionalism in Organizational Analysis,* ed. WW Powell, PJ DiMaggio, pp. 232–66. Chicago: Univ. Chicago Press

Galunic C. 1996. Recreating divisional domains: coevolution and the multibusiness firm. *Best Proc., Acad. Manage., 56th,* Cincinnati, ed. DP Moore, pp. 219–23. Statesboro: Georgia Southern Univ. Off. Publ.

Gartner WB. 1988. Who is an entrepreneur? is the wrong question. *Entrepreneurship Theory Practice* 13(4):47–68

Gartner WB, Shane SA. 1995. Measuring entrepreneurship over time. *J. Bus. Venturing* 10:283–301

Gereffi G. 1994. The international economy and economic development. In *The Handbook of Economic Sociology,* ed. NJ Smelser, R Swedberg, pp. 206–33. Princeton, NJ: Princeton Univ. Press

Gereffi G, Hempel L. 1996. Latin America in the global economy: Running faster to stay in place. *NACLA Report on the Americas* 29(4):18–27

Glade WP. 1967. Approaches to a theory of entrepreneurial formation. *Explorations in Entrepreneurial History,* 2nd ser., 4(3): 245–59

Golbe DL, White LJ. 1988. A time-series analysis of mergers and acquisitions in the U.S. economy. In *Corporate Takeovers: Causes and Consequences,* ed. A Auerback, pp. 265–303. Chicago: Univ. Chicago Press

Granovetter M. 1985. Economic action and social structure: the problem of embeddedness. *Am. J. Sociol.* 91(3):481–510

Greenfield SM, Strickon A. 1981. A new paradigm for the study of entrepreneurship and social change. *Am. J. Sociol.* 87: 467–99

Greve HR, Tuma NB, Strang D. 1993. *Estimation of diffusion processes from incomplete data.* Presented in part at the Annu. Meet. of the Am. Sociol. Assoc., 88th, Miami Beach, FL

Hannan MT, Carroll GR. 1992. *Dynamics of Organizational Populations.* New York: Oxford Univ. Press; Revised version, Dept. Sociol. Stanford Univ., unpublished

Hannan MT, Carroll GR. 1992. *Dynamics of Organizational Populations.* New York: Oxford Univ. Press

Hannan MT, Carroll GR, Dundon EA, Torres JC. 1995. Organizational evolution in multinational context: entries of automobile manufacturers in Belgium, Britain, France, Germany, and Italy. *Am. Sociol. Rev.* 60:509–28

Hannan MT, Freeman J. 1984. Structural inertia and organizational change. *Am. Sociol. Rev.* 49:149–64

Hannan MT, Freeman J. 1987. The ecology of organizational founding: American labor unions, 1836–1985. *Am. J. Sociol.* 92: 910–43

Harrison B. 1994. *Lean and Mean: The Changing Landscape of Corporate Power in the Age of Flexibility.* New York: Basic

Haunschild PR. 1993. Interorganizational imitation: the impact of interlocks on corporate acquisition activity. *Admin. Sci. Q.* 38(4):564–92

Haunschild PR. 1994. How much is that company worth?: Interorganizational relationships, uncertainty, and acquisition premiums. *Admin. Sci. Q.* 39(3):391–411

Herron L, Sapienza HJ, Smith-Cook D. 1992. Entrepreneurship theory from an interdisciplinary perspective. *Entrepreneurship Theory Pract.* 16(3):5–11

Hitt M, Hoskinson RE, Johnson RA, Moesel DD. 1996. The market for corporate control and financial innovation. *Am. Manage. J.* 39(5):1084–1119

Hofer CW, Bygrave WD. 1992. Researching entrepreneurship. *Entrepreneurship Theory Pract.* 16(3):91–100

Homans GC. 1964. Bringing men back in. *Am. Sociol. Rev.* 29:809–18

Hornsby JS, Naffziger DW, Kuratko DF, Montagno RV. 1993. An interactive model of the corporate entrepreneurship process.

Entrepreneurship. *Theory Pract.* 17(2): 29–37

Ingram P, Baum JAC. 1997. Chain affiliation and the failure of Manhattan hotels, 1889–1980. *Admin. Sci. Q.* 42:68–102

Ingram P, Inman C. 1996. Institutions, intergroup competition, and the evolution of hotel populations around Niagara Falls. *Admin. Sci. Q.* 41:629–58

Jensen MC, Meckling WH. 1976. Theory of the firm: managerial behavior, agency costs and ownership structure. *J. Finan. Econ.* 3:305–60

Katz JA. 1991. The institution and infrastructure of entrepreneurship. *Entrepreneurship Theory Pract.* 15(3): 85–102

Kimberly JR. 1975. Environmental constraints and organizational structure: a comparative analysis of rehabilitation organizations. *Admin. Sci. Q.* 20:1–9

King RG, Levine R. 1993. Finance, entrepreneurship, and growth. *J. Monetary Econ.* 32:513–42

Krackhardt D. 1995. Entrepreneurial opportunities in an entrepreneurial firm: a structural approach. *Entrepreneurship Theory Pract.* 19(3):53–69

Land K, Davis WR, Blau J. 1994. Organizing the boys of summer: the evolution of U.S. minor-league baseball, 1883–1990. *Am. J. Sociol.* 100(3):781–813

Lant TK, Baum JAC. 1995. Cognitive sources of socially constructed competitive groups. In *The Institutional Construction of Organizations,* ed. WR Scott, S Christensen, pp. 15–38. Thousand Oaks, CA: Sage

Lie J. 1997. Sociology of markets. *Annu. Rev. Sociol.* 23:341–60

Light I, Rosenstein C. 1995. *Race, Ethnicity, and Entrepreneurship in Urban America.* New York: Aldine De Gruyter

Lomi A, Larsen ER. 1996. Interacting locally and evolving globally: a computational approach to the dynamics of organizational populations. *Acad. Manage. J.* 39(4): 1287–1321

Low MR, Abrahamson E. 1997. Movements, bandwagons, and clones: industry evolution and the entrepreneurial process. *J. Bus. Ventures* 12:435–57

March JG. 1988. *Decisions and Organizations.* Oxford, UK: Basil Blackwell

March JG. 1991. Exploration and exploitation in organizational learning. *Organ. Sci.* 2(1):71–87

Martin J. 1992. *Cultures in Organizations: Three Perspectives.* New York: Oxford Univ. Press

Martinelli A. 1994. Entrepreneurship and management. In *The Handbook of Eco-*

nomic Sociology, ed. NJ Smelser, R Swedberg, pp. 476–503. Princeton, NJ: Princeton Univ. Press

Mayhew, B. 1980. Structuralism versus individualism: Part 1, shadowboxing in the dark. *Soc. Forces* 59 (2): 535–375

McClelland DC. 1961. *The Achieving Society*. New York: D. Van Nostrand

McClelland DC. 1975. *Power: The Inner Experience*. New York: Irvington/Halstead

Merrifield DB. 1993. Intrapreneurial corporate renewal. *J. Bus. Venturing* 8:383–89

Palmer DA, Friedland R, Jennings PD, Powers M. 1987. The economics and politics of structure: the multidivisional form and the large U.S. corporation. *Admin. Sci. Q.* 32: 25–48

Palmer DA, Jennings PD, Zhou X. 1993. Late adoption of the multidivisional form by large U.S. corporations. *Admin. Sci. Q.* 38:100–31

Pennings JM. 1982. The urban quality of life and entrepreneurship. *Acad. Manage. J.* 25(1):63–79

Podolny JM. 1993. A status–based model of market competition. *Am. J. Sociol.* 98(4): 829–72

Porter ME. 1990. *The Competitive Advantage of Nations*. New York: Free

Powell W. 1990. Neither markets nor hierarchies: network forms of organization. In *Research in Organizational Behavior*, ed. BM Staw, LL Cummings, 12:295–336. Greenwich, CT: JAI

Reynolds PD. 1991. Sociology and entrepreneurship: concepts and contributions. *Entrepreneurship Theory Pract.* 16(2): 47–70

Reynolds PD, Miller B, Maki WR. 1995. Explaining regional variation in business births and deaths: U.S. 1976–88. *Small Bus. Econ.* 7:389–407

Reynolds PD, Rong J. 1997. Summary Report. *First Pilot Study, National Panel Study of U.S. Business Startups*, February 25

Reynolds PD, White S. 1997. *The Entrepreneurial Process: Economic Growth, Men, Women, and Minorities*. Westport, CT: Quorum

Robinson P, Haynes M. 1991. Entrepreneurship education in America's major universities. *Entrepreneurship Theory Pract.* 15(3):41–52

Romanelli E. 1989. Organization birth and population variety: a community perspective on origins. In *Research in Organizational Behavior*, ed. LL Cummings, BM Staw, 11:211–46. Greenwich, CT: JAI

Romanelli E. 1991. The evolution of new organizational forms. *Annu. Rev. Sociol.* 17: 79–103

Rotter JB. 1966. Generalized expectations for internal versus external control of reinforcement. *Psychol. Monogr.* 80(1):1–28

Roy WG. 1997. *Socializing Capital: The Rise of the Large Industrial Corporation in America*. Princeton, NJ: Princeton Univ. Press

Rumelt RP. 1974. *Strategy, Structure and Economic Performance*. Cambridge, MA: Harvard Univ. Press

Rumelt RP. 1987. Theory, strategy, and entrepreneurship. In *The Competitive Challenge: Strategies for Industrial Innovation*, ed. DJ Teece, pp. 137–58. Cambridge, MA: Ballinger

Sandberg WR, Gatewood EJ. 1991. A profile of entrepreneurship research centers: orientations, interests, activities, and resources. *Entrepreneurship Theory Pract.* Spring, pp. 11–24

Saxenian A. 1994. *Regional Advantage: Culture and Competition in Silicon Valley and Route 128*. Cambridge, MA: Harvard Univ. Press

Schoonhoven CB, Eisenhardt KM. 1992. Entrepreneurial environments: incubator region effects on the birth of new technology–based firms. In *High Technology Venturing*, ed. L Gomez-Mejia, M Lawless, III, pp. 210–252. Greenwich, CT: JAI

Schumpeter JA. 1934. *The Theory of Economic Development*. Cambridge, MA: Harvard Univ. Press

Scott WR. 1995. *Institutions and Organizations*. Newbury Park, CA: Sage

Scott WR. 1997. *Organizations: Rational, Natural, and Open Systems*. Englewood Cliffs, NJ: Prentice Hall

Selznick P. 1949. *TVA and the Grass Roots*. Berkeley, CA: Univ. California Press

Shane S. 1993. Cultural influences on national rates of innovation. *J. Bus. Venturing* 8: 59–73

Shane S. 1995. Is the independent entrepreneurial firm a valuable organizational form? In *Best Proc., Acad. Manage., 55th*, Vancouver, ed. DP Moore, pp. 110–13. Statesboro: Ga. Southern Univ. Off. Publ.

Shane S. 1996. Explaining variation in rates of entrepreneurship in the United States: 1899–1988. *J. Manage.* 22(5):747–81

Shaver KG, Scott LR. 1991. Person, process, choice: the psychology of new venture creation. *Entrepreneurship Theory Pract.* 16(2):16:2

Singh JV. 1993. Review essay: density dependence theory–current issues, future promise. *Am. J. Sociol.* 99:464–73

Skocpol T. 1985. Bringing the state back in: strategies of analysis in current research. In *Bringing the State Back In*, ed. P Evans et al, pp. 3–43. New York: Cambridge Univ. Press

Smircich L. 1983. Concepts of culture and organizational analysis. *Admin. Sci. Q.* 28(3):339–58

Statistical Abstract of the United States. 1997. *The National Data Book.* Washington, DC: US Dep. Commerce

Stearns L, Allan K. 1996. Economic behavior in an institutional setting: the merger wave of the 1980s. *Am. Sociol. Rev.* 61:699–718

Stinchcombe A. 1965. Social structure and social organization. In *The Handbook of Organizations*, ed. JG March, pp. 142–93. Chicago: Rand McNally

Strang D, Tuma NB. 1993. Spatial and temporal heterogeneity in diffusion. *Am. J. Sociol.* 99(3):614–39

Suchman M. 1995. Localism and globalism in institutional analysis: the emergence of contractual norms in venture finance. In *The Institutional Construction of Organizations: International and Longitudinal Studies*, ed. WR Scott, S Christensen, pp. 39–66. Thousand Oaks, CA: Sage

Swedberg R. 1994. Markets as social structures. In *The Handbook of Economic Sociology*, ed. N Smelser, R Swedberg, pp. 255–82. Princeton, NJ: Princeton Univ. Press.

Thornton PH. 1995. Accounting for acquisition waves: evidence from the U.S. college publishing industry. In *The Institutional Construction of Organizations: International and Longitudinal Studies*, ed. WR Scott, S Christensen, pp. 199–225. Thousand Oaks, CA: Sage

Thornton PH, Tuma NB. 1995. The problem of boundaries in contemporary research on organizations. In *Best Proc., Acad. Manage., 55th*, Vancouver, ed. DP Moore, pp 276–80

Tushman ML, Anderson P. 1986. Technological discontinuities and organizational environments. *Admin. Sci. Q.* 31:439–65

Useem M. 1996. *Investor Capitalism: How Money Managers are Changing the Face of Corporate America.* New York: Basic

Van de Ven AH. 1993. The development of an infrastructure for entrepreneurship. *J. Bus. Venturing* 8:211–30

Van de Ven AH, Garud R. 1989. A framework for understanding the emergence of new industries. *Res. Technol. Innovation Manage. Policy* 4:295–325

Van de Ven AH, Grazman DN. 1994. *From generation to generation: a genealogy of Twin Cities health care organizations, 1853–1993.* Presented at the Annu. Meet. Acad. Manage., Dallas

Ventresca M, Lacey R. 1999. Origins and activities of industry entrepreneurs in the formation of the US online database industry, 1969–1982. In *The Entrepreneurial Dynamic: The Origins of Entrepreneurship and its Role in Industry Evolution*, ed. CB Schoonhoven, E Romanelli. Forthcoming

VentureOne Corporation. 1996, 1997. *National Venture Capital Association Annual Report.* Newark, NJ: Venture Econ. Info. Serv.

Vesper KH. 1990. *New Venture Strategies.* Englewood Cliffs, NJ: Prentice Hall

Weber M. 1904. *The Protestant Ethic and the Spirit of Capitalism.* New York: Routledge

White H. 1981. Production markets as induced role structures. In *Sociological Methodology*, ed. S Leinhardt, pp. 1–57. San Francisco: Jossey–Bass

White HC. 1981. Where do markets come from? *Am. J. Sociol.* 87:517–47

Whitley R. 1996. Business systems and global commodity chains: competing or complementary forms of economic organization. *Competition & Change* 1: 411–25

Wholey DR, Christianson JB, Sanchez SM. 1993. The effect of physician and corporate interests on the formation of health maintenance organizations. *Am. J. Sociol.* 99(1):164–200

Williamson OE. 1975. *Markets and Hierarchies: Analysis and Antitrust Implications.* New York: Free/MacMillan

Williamson OE. 1985. *The Economic Institutions of Capitalism: Firms, Markets, Relational Contracting.* New York: Free

Wortman MS. 1987. Entrepreneurship: an integrating topology and evaluation of the empirical research in the field. *J. Manage.* 13:259–79

Zahra SA. 1993. A conceptual model of entrepreneurship as firm behavior: a critique and extension. *Entrepreneurship Theory Pract.* 17(4): 5–21

Zald MN, Denton P. 1963. From evangelism to general service: the transformation of the YMCA. *Admin. Sci. Q.* 8:214–34

Zukin S, DiMaggio P, eds. 1990. *Structures of Capital: The Social Organization of the Economy.* Cambridge, MA: Cambridge Univ. Press

Annu. Rev. Sociol. 1999. 25:47–71

WOMEN'S MOVEMENTS IN THE THIRD WORLD: Identity, Mobilization, and Autonomy

R. Ray and A. C. Korteweg

Department of Sociology, 410 Barrows Hall, University of California, Berkeley, California 94720; e-mail: rakaray@uclink4.berkeley.edu, korteweg@socrates.berkeley.edu

KEY WORDS: women's interests, state, democratization, nationalism, political opportunities

ABSTRACT

Sociology has paid insufficient attention to third world women's movements. In this review, for which we draw upon a variety of interdisciplinary sources, we focus on three questions: the issue of women's interests; the conditions under which women mobilize—particularly the effects of democratization, nationalist, religious, and socialist movements; and the issue of state and organizational autonomy. We argue that the concept of a political opportunity structure inadequately captures the role that states in the third world play in determining the possibilities of third world women's movements. We call for more comparative work with a focus on the local rather than on the macro level. This will help us to better understand both the ways in which women's collective identities and interests are constructed and the ideological and material conditions under which mobilizations actually take place.

INTRODUCTION

In a much reviewed and cited article on the relationship between first and third world feminisms, Chandra Mohanty (1991) argued that for too long, women in the third world have been considered not agents of their own destiny, but victims (1991:56). A potent image has been constructed, even in feminist scholarship, of an "average third world woman" who "leads an essentially truncated life based on her feminine gender (read: sexually constrained) and her being 'third world' (read: ignorant, poor, uneducated, tradition-bound, domestic, family-oriented, victimized, etc.)" (p. 56).

47

Our review of the literature on third world women's movements finds that sociologists are no less guilty of ignoring women's activism in the third world. Mainstream sociology journals have but a handful of articles on the topic, and thus we have included, for purposes of our review, a variety of inter-disciplinary sources to give readers a fuller appreciation of the available lit-erature.

We have found that while there is a trend toward the increased visibility of women's activism and the circumstances under which women in third world countries organize, there is a central dilemma in the literature, which we shall call the dilemma of particularism versus universalism. In other words, there are still too many individual case studies that heighten the perception of uniqueness and nonreplicability on the one hand, and too many studies that tend to assume that all women want the same thing, on the other, without enough dialogue between the two.

To bridge the gap between universalism and particularism, we need sys-tematic comparative work. While several excellent comparative studies of women's movements in Western Europe and the United States have appeared (Jenson 1987, Ferree 1995, Gelb 1989), there are few for the many countries that comprise the third world (for exceptions, see Jayawardena 1986, Mogha-dam 1992, Baffoun 1994, Thayer 1997). In this review we bring together the various writings on women's movements in the third world in order to facili-tate the comparative study of such movements. By "women's movements" we mean the range of activities in which women engage to better the circum-stances of their lives. We do not ourselves use the term feminist unless the authors or activists under discussion self-identify as such.

The theme of this essay is our call for less universalistic claims about women's mobilization and for more attention to the theorizing of the local and particular. Thus, we focus on books and articles that discuss and compare his-torically specific movements, rather than on those that emphasize large-scale structural forces or economic transformations as the explanation for women's movements. Our attention to specific, local political forces leads us to call for the expansion of a concept central to the comparative study of social move-ments—political opportunity structure.

The essay is organized around three broad questions. First, the question of women's interests; second, the question of conditions under which women mobilize; and third, the question of the relationship of women's movements to the state and also to other movements.

WOMEN'S INTERESTS

Literature on women's activism has shown that women are mobilized not only as women but also as mothers, workers, peasants, and citizens. Initially, scholars focused on interests, specifically whether such a thing as "women's interests" could be identified. More recently the focus has been on identities, specifically how identities mobilize women.

Perhaps the most influential writer on the question of interests was Maxine Molyneux (1985), who dismissed the concept of "women's interests," claiming that women as a group have many interests. She did, however, specify that women have "gender interests," which can be practical or strategic. Practical gender interests arise from women's position in the sexual division of labor and tend to involve struggles not for liberation but for the ability to fulfill their roles as wives and mothers. These interests, which stem from women's lived experiences, are inductively derived. Strategic gender interests, on the other hand, are derived deductively, seek to change the rules under which women live, and can be arrived at only after practical interests have been taken into account.

This formulation of gender interests has framed much of the discussion on women's movements. Thus, in her analysis of women's movements in the transition to democracy in Brazil, Sonia Alvarez (1990) uses Molyneux's definition, but prefers the adjectives "feminine" and "feminist" to "practical" and "strategic gender interests." Sternbach et al (1992) articulate the frustrations of self-defined feminists (*feministas*) with women activists (*mujeres*) who use the language of practical, not strategic, interests. Indeed, Chinchilla (1992) argues that the central task of feminist practice is to link the two. As the history of the *encuentros* (Latin American bi-annual continent-wide feminist meetings or exchanges) shows, the distinction articulated by Molyneux did indeed resonate with Latin American feminists, who initially broke away from movements that did not explicitly pursue strategic gender interests, but who found themselves returning to and building alliances with the more "feminine" mujeres (Sternbach et al 1992). The contrast between practical and strategic interests does seem to be self-consciously deployed, at least in Latin American feminist movements, pointing to the thriving links between analysis and activism.

Despite the popularity of these concepts, the distinction between strategic and practical interests remains troubling because it tends to echo assumptions about the divide between middle class and non–middle class women (Barrig 1989, Alvarez 1990), as well as between women of the first and the third worlds. Practical gender interests, not strategic ones, are seen to be driving many third world women's movements. So, for example, the editor of *Gender & Society* writes in her introduction to a special issue on women and development, that third world "grassroots women's politics is practical," whereas middle class women's politics is feminist (Lorber 1990:294).

Several scholars have explicitly critiqued Molyneux's model. Saskia Wieringa's (1992) investigation of two women's organizations in Indonesia undermines Molyneux's framework by showing that what matters is not meeting practical interests per se, but the manner in which the interests are met. The pursuit of practical interests by the right wing PKK (Pembinaan Kesejahteraan Keluarga or Family Welfare Guidance), she argues, simply entrenched women's subordination further, while the pursuit of the same interests by the socialistic Gerwani (Gerakan Wanita Indonesia or Indonesian Women's Movement) radicalized women. Critiquing Molyneux's inductive/deductive dichotomy in her analysis of the Chipko movement in India (a grassroots environmental movement in which both women and men participated), Bina Agarwal (1992) says that the shift from practical to strategic interests is internally generated through the experience of participation in Chipko, not externally identified through analysis. Lilia Rodriguez's (1994) analysis of barrio women in Ecuador indicates similar possibilities for a transition from practical to strategic interests. Finally, writing about Sudan, Sondra Hale claims that there is such a thing as women's interests "when women's issues seem at variance with the interests of men" (Hale 1993:150).

Ray (1999) and Lind (1992) question the creation of interests in Molyneux's framework. Starting from the perspective that multiple and shifting identities inform interests, Ray argues that interests themselves, are, for Molyneux, predetermined, even if they are prioritized differently at different moments. Further, Molyneux's formulation of the temporal order between strategic and practical gender interests, where strategic interests can only be formulated after practical interests are met, is a distinction that cannot be sustained. Basing her conclusions on popular women's protests in Ecuador, Amy Lind complicates the relationship between interest formation and class, arguing that "[b]asic needs are not tied solely to survival but rather to constructions of identity and relations of power"(1992:147).

While the concept of women's interests lies at the heart of much scholarship done in this field, Ray and Lind's questioning of Molyneux's frame reflects an increasing interest in the concept of women's collective identity. Thus, the question has moved from the objective criteria through which women's oppression is judged— their interests—to more subjective criteria—their identities. In other words, rather than imputing identity from articulated interests, and asking whether meeting these interests would change subjectively held identity, scholars now center identity, asking what subjectively held sense of self motivates women to act collectively. These identities are not always self-evident and do not "emerge automatically" from a structural position but rather are created in the process of struggle (Berger 1992).

The literature considers several sets of competing identities, some of which are in tension with each other. Kumar (1993) argues that the Indian women's movement switched from mobilizing around women's identity as mothers to women's identity as daughters, thus shifting the focus from suffering and sacrifice to strength and rights. Kim (1996) highlights the different identities of married and unmarried women in her work on militancy in Korean factories, while Cooper (1995) discusses the way different identities of married and unmarried women in Niger are constructed as they participate in separate organizations. The literature from the Middle East makes clear that in many parts of the world where Islamic movements are on the rise, women find themselves torn between their identities as women and their cultural identity as Muslims, a plight that Leila Ahmed calls "excruciating" (quoted in Kandiyoti 1991:7). Some women resolve this dilemma by adopting the veil, where the veil can suggest both conformist and feminist meanings (MacLeod 1992).

Several authors have focused on motherhood as the motivating identity for women's social action. Kevin Neuhouser argues that women participate in collective action in defense of their roles as mothers, in conditions under which they can no longer fulfill their "gender-specific responsibilities" (Neuhouser 1995:40; see also Sarti 1989). Stamp argues that Kenyan women deploy a "'combative motherhood' to counter assaults against their rights *and* against egalitarian gender relations" (1995:384, emphasis added).

At contention in these articles is the extent to which collective action undertaken in defense of traditional identities spills over into feminist consciousness or consciousness of gender subordination. The case of the Madres de la Plaza de Mayo (Schirmer 1989, Femenía 1987, Navarro 1989) makes clear that while mothers began their organizing to address the conditions that made them unable to be mothers, they came also to address broader human rights issues. Indeed, Safa (1990), Schirmer (1989), and Rodriguez (1994) argue that even traditional mobilizations can result in transformed identities, as do Haj (1992) for women's activism as wives and mothers in the cause of Palestinian liberation, and Agarwal (1992) for women's activism in defense of their environment. These transformations occur, despite the fact that, for example, the women involved in Latin-American human rights movements refuse the label "feminist" (Schirmer 1989).

Analysis of the various identities through which women are mobilized cannot be complete without the recognition of the increased visibility of women in right wing movements in many parts of the world. The realization that many of these women are mobilized as mothers has been the focus of considerable discussion, particularly in India (Sarkar & Butalia 1995, Kumar 1993) and South Africa (Hassim 1993). Here too, the authors examine the extent to which the concept of motherhood is reworked into a political identity, as well as the extent to which mobilization by right wing movements undermines feminist interests. Until the rise of right wing mobilization, scholars had simply assumed that mobilization on behalf of gender interests was good. Successful right wing mobilization forces a rethinking and redefinition of the concept, for if gender interests are partial and are attained at the cost of other women, can they still be considered gender interests?

The literature shows that rigid distinctions such as feminine versus feminist or strategic versus practical interests limit our understanding of gender. The perspective that partial, but no less real, identities inform interests enables a richer and more complex analysis. However, these identities are not themselves formed in a vacuum and are mobilized at certain times and not at others. Given this, we need to focus on the conditions under which particular identities are mobilized.

PRECONDITIONS TO WOMEN'S MOBILIZATION

We have argued for a perspective that sees women's identities as shaping their interests, where these interests in turn inform mobilization. However, interests and identities themselves are formed within structural, political, and cultural contexts, and their mobilization occurs in reaction to and is facilitated by these (pre)conditions. In the literature, there currently exist two conceptualizations of conditions under which women mobilize. These conditions are either structural and universal or historically and locationally specific, with local variations obstructing or facilitating the specific forms of women's movements.

The representatives of the first position argue that a rise in the levels of urbanization, industrialization, and education leads to an increase in women's mobilization (Chafetz & Dworkin 1986, Margolis 1993; for a critique see Basu 1995, Papanek 1993). Kandiyoti (1988) makes a more nuanced structural argument, identifying factors such as women's rights to land as a key variable in understanding the range of women's resistance. Structural arguments tend to emphasize the forces of capitalism (Gordon 1995, Robertson 1996), or long-term processes of modernization, which are slow to change (Margolis 1993, Chafetz & Dworkin 1986), at the expense of more immediate political, local, and cultural practices.

It has become increasingly evident that this focus on the spread of capitalism, or on general processes of urbanization, industrialization, and education obscures rather than illuminates the processes that shape women's movements. The structure of the economy and demographic factors such as a surplus of women or an increase in the age of marriage do not in themselves determine the interests and identities that mobilize women, nor do they occur in similar sequences everywhere. The analyses of the specificities of oppression are vital if we are to understand the nature of the rebellion to which it gives rise. For example, Samira Haj (1992) argues that the assumption of women's oppression particular to nuclear families fails to explain the situation of women who are not in such families, and thus fails to explain the situation of the majority of third world women.

In the second approach to the preconditions of mobilization, women's abilities to form collective identities and articulate their interests are shaped by political, local, and historically contingent processes (Neuhouser 1995, Basu 1992, Seidman 1993, 1999, Lazreg 1990). This approach is exemplified by the editors of a recent volume about feminist organizations who note that "feminist organizations are outcomes of situationally and historically specific processes. In each time and place, feminism reflects its history and prior developments, as well as present opportunities and constraints" (Ferree & Martin 1995:2). Kandiyoti's later work reminds us that women's struggles ought to be treated as "both intensely local, grappling with their own histories and specificities, and international, in that they have been in dialogue, both collaborative and adversarial, with broader currents of thought and activism" (quoted in Sharoni 1995:28).

In general, the second approach then can better explain women's mobilization against repressive military regimes, participation in colonial struggles or struggles for socialism, and their support of fundamentalist politics. We suggest that this approach enables us to identify specific constellations of factors, sometimes called "political opportunity structures" in the dominant literature on social movements, that enable or thwart mobilizing even as we pay close attention to the specificities of time and space. The concept of political opportunity structure usually refers to changes in access to power or shifts in the ruling alignments that enable those outside the polity to gain access to it. The most well-known works that use this concept have focused on the realignments of political parties, or on shifting alliances and coalitions between parties (see McAdam 1982, Tarrow 1994, Klandermans 1990). If we wish to apply this concept to the third world, however, we must be prepared to expand it to include more fundamental changes in the nature of the state, such as the transition from colonialism to independence or from dictatorship to democracy. In other words, the assumption of a relatively stable state, made by the literature on political opportunity structures, must be challenged.

In order to show how this expanded conceptualization of political opportunity structures enables theorizing based on the locally and historically specific, we have identified the relationship of women's movements to four historically contingent processes that involve shifts in regime type—democratization, anticolonial and nationalist struggles, socialist, and religious/fundamentalist movements. These studies show that (*a*) women's movements are fundamentally shaped by political processes, particularly crises of the state, and (*b*) there is considerable variation in the outcomes even within each of these processes. Comparative work illuminates how international and national processes interact with local and regional variations to transform women's identities and interests and to create particular forms of mobilization (Chinchilla 1992, Jaquette 1989, Jelin 1990, Thayer 1997, Basu 1992, Schirmer 1989).

Democratization

The Latin American debate about democratization takes the region-wide phenomenon of repressive military governments and the process of democratization and shows how variations in the nature of the ruling classes and the military regimes enabled the mobilization of different aspects of women's identity.
The literature looks at mobilization based on motherhood, on the one hand,
and on "feminism," on the other. One important issue the literature addresses
is the conditions under which women have been able to translate mobilization
against authoritarian regimes into institutional political power as their countries made the transition to democracy.

According to the literature, women's mobilization around human rights issues in bureaucratic authoritarian regimes was explicitly grounded in their
identities as mothers. Schirmer (1989), Femenía (1987), and Noonan (1995)
discuss groups such as the Madres de la Plaza de Mayo in Argentina, the Mutual Support Group (GAM) in Guatemala, and the Group of Relatives of the
Detained-Disappeared (Agrupacíon) in Chile, which mobilized around the issue of forced disappearances. These authors argue that while the state valorized traditional notions of motherhood and family, women inverted this image
by using their motherhood status to agitate for the return of the disappeared
(dead or alive), and the punishment of their torturers and murderers. Schirmer
shows that in these three countries women mobilized as mothers despite differences in their class status, previous experiences, and political ideologies.

The idea that repressive regimes' attitudes toward gender unintentionally
created the space for women to organize also reverberates in analyses of the
rise of self-identified feminist movements in Latin America (Alvarez 1989,
1990, Chuchryk 1989, Jaquette 1989, Sternbach et al 1992). In the case of
Brazil the regime was unable to perceive women as political actors in their
own right. Alvarez argues that the political space this created, in conjunction
with women's experience with the sexist practices of left wing oppositional
organizations, sparked the articulation of a feminist consciousness. Many of
the feminist movements in Latin-America shared a similar trajectory. Thus,
Sternbach et al argue, "the realities of both state repression and class warfare
were instrumental in shaping a Latin American feminist praxis distinct from
that of feminist movements elsewhere" (1992:397).

In sum, during periods of flux generated by transitions to democracy, all
classes of women may find the "political opportunities" to push for change
(Alvarez 1990, Chuchryk 1989, Jaquette 1989, Waylen 1994). However, once
the process of democratization starts, some women's demands continue to be
addressed while others are increasingly discredited. Schirmer's analysis of
women's human rights movements offers one example of how newly legitimated churches and political parties marginalize radical women as they at-

tempt to form a new state. While women's human rights groups played a crucial role in undermining the legitimacy of repressive regimes, Schirmer argues
that "once these groups are successful in helping to change the repressive
terrain by claiming important political space, they may be eclipsed by the
dominant political forces...[which grant them] little institutional hearing"
(1989:27).

However, the retrenchment of gender relations is not uniform across nations. As a comparison of Brazil and Peru shows, movement strategies and
success are shaped by differences in the nature of the repressive regime and in
the processes of democratization. During Brazil's first wave of democratic
elections, political parties actively courted feminist and women's organizations and women responded by supporting specific political parties, hoping to
usher in "a new, democratic regime... more supportive of gender-specific demands for equality and justice" (Alvarez 1990:11). Brazilian women thus won
some institutional political representation, but throughout the 1980s they continued to organize autonomously as well. In Peru, on the other hand, the military government was established in 1968 against the dominant classes and was
initially supported by sections of the left. Women's popular mobilization,
which started only after the introduction of structural adjustment policies in
the late 1970s, took the form of communal kitchens and other local organizations—but they did not take the form of demands for more democracy. In contrast to Brazil, Peruvian feminist mobilization remained separate from both
popular mobilization and state institutions and gained little institutional power
(Barrig 1989).

Comparing democratization processes in Argentina, Chile, and Brazil,
Waylen shows that the longer the transition period, the greater women's involvement in transition policies. However, even this involvement has not
translated into continued institutional power for women (Waylen 1994:343).
One reason for women's elision from the newly democratic political sphere,
researchers conclude, is that the party system, revived during the transition to
democracy, has historically been male terrain (Barrig 1989, Waylen 1994,
also Neuhouser 1995).

Anticolonial and Nationalist Struggles

Many of the women's movements in the third world have been tied to nationalist and anticolonial projects. This historical fact alerts us to the need to examine the complex relationships between women's movements in the first and
third worlds, on the one hand, and between women's movements in the third
world and the nationalist movements with which they are linked, on the other.
Judith Tucker (1993) writes that the very existence of European feminism has
been a problem for women working within nationalist and anticolonialist
movements, both because of the image of third world women created in the

West (as Mohanty 1991 argues) and because demands from third world women are more easily suspect if they are seen as connected to a movement in an imperial power (see also Stamp 1995).

Accounts of anticolonial struggles in Algeria and Palestine show that notions of gender are actively deployed by both sides in anticolonial struggles. In Algeria, the French promised to liberate women from the confinement imposed by Islam, while participation in the anticolonial struggle offered women a way to challenge the boundaries historically placed on their activities (Lazreg 1990). Haj (1992) shows how the Israeli occupying forces sexually abuse women to undermine their participation in Palestinian liberation movements, using the idea that sexual abuse defiles women to turn them into collaborators. However, she argues, this use of the culture of gender by the Israelis has ceased to be effective, as the younger generation has started to redefine proper sexual/gendered behavior.

Given that gender is so deeply implicated in both sides of the nationalist struggle, how do we understand the relationship between women's liberation and national liberation? Many scholars argue that, in the past, women who made their specific interests subsidiary to national ones found that they were left out in the cold once the struggle was won. The idea that "women's interests" have been subordinated to national interests has been often repeated, contested, and modified. In a provocative essay Partha Chatterjee (1989) declared that the woman question was decided with the nationalist question because the former was less central to the struggle for Indian independence than the explicitly gendered nationalist project. Thapar (1994) and Sarkar (1992) argue that, while participation in the anticolonial struggle did indeed expand the sphere of movement for middle class women, ultimately, because women's interests were secondary, the liberation they achieved remained a by-product of national liberation. Bharati Ray (1988), on the other hand, maintains that women's consciousness did indeed expand in unexpected ways, and thus women's emancipation was directly served by the struggle for Indian independence.

Marnia Lazreg (1994) argues that we must keep the question of women's participation in anticolonial struggles separate from the question of unequal shares that fall to women once independence is achieved. Resisting the view that Algerian women, like women in other nationalist movements, were "duped" by "unscrupulous men" into joining the Algerian movement, Lazreg argues forcefully that given the context of colonial rule in Algeria, women's active participation in the movement was a "rational response to an otherwise irrational historical situation" (1994:118–119). In the war against the French, women, no less than men, chose to engage in a struggle that "transcended their everyday lives," not simply for a better living, but for the idea of a free nation. The new Algerian state, like many others, only partially implemented policies beneficial to women. This failure of the nationalist project with regard to them prompted women to create an independent women's movement in both India and Algeria (Lazreg 1994, Kumar 1993, Jayawardena 1986).

While discussions of the relationship between women's movements and national liberation occurred after the fact in Algeria and India, more recent liberation movements have been acutely aware of the possible tensions between the two movements. Looking at South Africa, Beall et al (1989) argue that separating the women's movement from the nationalist movement generates a false dichotomy between these two struggles. They articulate a position, based in socialist-feminism, that national liberation is a form of class struggle and should take precedence over gender and race struggles. However, they argue, participants in class (and national liberation) struggles should understand that these struggles are themselves deeply gendered. Souad Dajani (1993) too claims an inseparability between women's issues and political concerns in the case of Palestine. Palestinian women have been displaced and oppressed largely as a result of Israeli occupation, she argues, and thus for them "the struggle for women's rights and the struggle for socio-economic and national self-determination become one and the same" (Dajani 1993:107).

In contrast, Mervat Hatem (1993) argues that nationalist discourses used in Arab countries have limited the possibilities of women's movements, and thus women's movements must seek an independent voice. According to Hatem, feminists worked within three dominant nationalist discourses: modernist-Islamist, Marxist, and dependency. Ultimately all three discourses subordinated women to the nation's needs. Taking an intermediary position between Hatem and Dajani, Sharoni (1995) suggests that while the Palestinian nationalist struggle, like others before it, has not adequately dealt with issues of gender, the Intifada itself has created a distinctive Palestinian women's peace movement on the one hand and an Israeli women's peace movement on the other. As Seidman (1993), Berger (1992), and Sharoni (1995) indicate, the participation of women in women-only organizations for national liberation gives them the capacity to develop gender consciousness and make gender specific demands. And further, Haj (1992) points out, we must make a distinction between armed liberation struggles, which tend to include mainly young men (as in Algeria), and unarmed liberation struggles based on the mobilization of many segments the populace—men and women, young and old. These civilian mobilizations, she argues, create conditions more conducive for women's active participation.

Not only are the links between women's liberation and national liberation extremely complicated, national movements are themselves internally differentiated, and the political ideologies of their component parts affect the women's movements they inspire, as the South African case shows. Women's participation in Inkatha, the Zulu nationalist party in South Africa, was based on a (revised) version of traditional culture in which women were the politically passive keepers of the home while men were the politically active warriors (Hassim 1993). In contrast, women's involvement with the African National Congress and other organizations was based on their awareness of the need for progressive changes in political and economic structures. Ultimately, however, the articles on South Africa do offer some hope. Gay Seidman (1993), for example, argues that women in South Africa have learned the lessons from these previous liberation struggles and that their commitment, as well as the commitment of their male comrades and the international community, will help create a more positive outcome.

Religious and Fundamentalist Movements

The rise of religious nationalisms in the Middle East and South Asia is closely related to the outcome of nationalist struggles. In the literature, a general consensus exists that both Islamist and Hindu fundamentalist movements arose as a populist reaction to western domination on the one hand and the failure of the nationalist project for the poor and lower middle classes on the other (Shukrallah 1994, Baffoun 1994). Both Kandiyoti and Chatterjee argue that in a colonial context, the family came to be seen by the colonized as the only untouched space, and thus control over women and the family became the most significant symbolic markers of nationalist resistance. "Westernized" women in Iran, for example, were considered "gharbzadeh"or "Western-struck" in Iran, and the most "dangerous bearers of moral decay" (Kandiyoti 1991:8; see also Moghadam 1994). How have these movements that specifically target women affected women's activism? Scholars of the Middle East warn us that despite an overall logic that is similar across several countries, the outcomes for women and for the possibilities of feminism are not the same. There is considerable variation in the extent to which Islamists have been able to win victories, as well as the spheres in which these have been won.

For Egypt, Margot Badran (1994) argues, the rise of Islamism has generated a new brand of "gender activism." Both secular feminists and Islamic feminists practice this brand of pragmatic politics, which advocates a public role for women in society, whereas secular feminists feel compelled to reject the explicit label of "feminism" in the newly conservative atmosphere. Azza Karam (1997) identifies three coexisting feminisms in Egypt—secular feminists who do not believe liberation is possible within the tenets of established religion; Islamist feminists who value the complementarity of the sexes and believe that western ideas of equality (sameness) oppress women further; and Muslim feminists who try to make Islam compatible with United Nations' positions on women's rights. Of the three, Muslim feminists are the pragmatic feminists who believe that it is self-defeating to try to create feminism incompatible with Islam for it is sure to be rejected by the rest of society. Whether they recognize two or three feminisms, these authors agree that Islamic movements have tempered secular feminism, while the presence of secular feminism has given rise to a certain sort of Islamic feminism as well. The clearest separation between secular and religion-based feminisms, argues Moghadam, centers on the issues of the *hijab* (the veil) and the *Sharia* (Islamic law) (1993).

The effect of Islam on women's movements is mediated by both the policies and the ideologies of the state. In Tunisia and Algeria, for example, an authoritarian one-party state derives its legitimacy from the anticolonial liberation movements. Both states are faced with Islamist movements, but because of state policies, the movements have not had the same effects on women. Women's groups have been able to make headway in Tunisia partly because, argues Baffoun, a "feminist legislature" passed several laws beneficial to women, overriding customary social practice (Baffoun 1994:176). Women were also allowed to form voluntary associations. Further, declaring that Islam was a religion that belonged to all, the Tunisian state denied Islamist parties legal status. In Algeria, on the other hand, women were "expelled" from social, economic, and political spheres after independence, despite the "socialism" of the Algerian state, and Islamic precepts were imbricated in state ideology. While Islamists have been able to make far more headway in Algeria than in Tunisia, the passage of the deeply misogynistic family law in 1984 revitalized the women's movement in Algeria (Moghadam 1993).

The cases of Algeria and Tunisia support Haj (1992), Kandiyoti (1997), and Lazreg's (1990) argument that we cannot understand the struggles in the Middle East solely through the lens of Islam. Looking at Algeria, Lazreg argues that Islam needs to be understood as a multifaceted cultural paradigm whose influence waxes and wanes as economic and political circumstances change. After all, she argues, when women left their homes to actively participate in the struggle against France, Islam did not challenge them (1994). Kandiyoti argues further that the emphasis on proper Islamic conduct for women is not about Islam at all, but rather about social control (Kandiyoti 1997).

In India, right wing Hindu mobilization has occurred for many of the same reasons as Islamic mobilization in the Middle East. The essays in a 1995 volume edited by Tanika Sarkar and Urvashi Butalia (1995) attempt to understand how and why these women came to be attracted to the Hindu right and not to the women's movement. Historian Tanika Sarkar situates the recruiting ground for the Hindu right in the upwardly mobile trading or middle-ranking service sectors and argues that the Hindu right, with its emphasis on purity, *shakti* (women's strength), and physical fitness has bestowed, "among women of a specific conservative milieu... a limited but real empowerment" (Sarkar 1995:210).

The increasing attraction of non-elite women to religious nationalist movements has led several scholars to question the failure of the secular feminist movement to make feminism relevant. Elite feminism's assumption of "unproblematic access to authority" (Shaheed 1998); the sometimes easy refusal to be involved in partisan politics (Jalal 1991); the physical and social separation of elite feminists from poorer women (Banerjee 1995); or, in the case of Bangladesh, the failure to address the mass rape of rural women by Pakistani soldiers during the Bangladesh independence movement in 1971–1972 (Feldman 1998) have all served to further divide elite feminists from other women.

Socialism

Women's participation in the transition to socialism and the extent to which women subsequently benefited was written about often in the 1970s and 1980s, initially with hope, and then with a sense of betrayal or resignation. While the decline of socialist regimes may make these writings seem outdated, we include them here both because they spurred women's movements and because they form a crucial reference point for other writings on third world women's movements. Scholars such as Omvedt argue further that while inspired by Marxist movements, for example, Indian women's movements mounted a powerful theoretical challenge to Marxism (Omvedt 1993).

Socialism, the editors of a 1989 anthology claimed, has always held out a "promissory note" to women (Kruks et al 1989), and women in socialist countries from China to Nicaragua had high expectations and hopes of their revolutionary governments. What might affect the extent to which women did get involved, and what might affect the degree to which their concerns were taken into account? Three sorts of reasons are given for the constraints that Socialism puts on the mobilization of women: the rigidity of ideology, the organization and structure of socialist/communist parties, and the exigencies of the transition.

Ideologically, socialist regimes and parties are blamed for their productionist bias, and their acceptance of Engels' solution that women's emancipation comes from fuller participation in the public, economic sphere (Kruks et al 1989). One effect of the productionist bias on socialist parties and regimes is their conservatism with regard to the cultural aspects of gender. Socialist regimes are accused of being too similar to nonsocialist regimes and parties culturally, and thus they are unable to push forward any liberation of women that challenges the tenets of received culture. While the Chinese experiment, particularly with the cultural revolution, was radical from this point of view, it tended to erase difference in rhetoric but not in reality (Young 1989).

Amrita Basu points out in her examination of the Communist Party of India—Marxist in the Indian state of West Bengals that the party accepted middle-class and upper-caste norms of gender at the cost of radical challenges that did arise among lower-caste women (Basu 1992). Sondra Hale (1993) criticizes revolutionary parties in Sudan for attempting to erase indigenous cultures and suggests that gender can be revolutionized by building onto indigenous structures and cultures. The relative success of women's liberation in Nicaragua, by contrast, can be attributed to the Sandinista Front's emphasis on ideological and political struggle over economic orthodoxy (Chinchilla 1990). Indeed it is the fostering of political empowerment, Chinchilla argues, that enables an increase in material benefits for women. In other words, the logic of emancipation in the Nicaraguan revolution reversed Marxist orthodoxy.

Various authors have pointed to the organizational principle of democratic centralism, which, in practice, is more centralist than democratic, is intolerant of autonomy, and therefore unable to hear or accede to women's voices (Basu 1992, Jayawardena 1988). Others point to a lack of political will among some party leaders (Chinchilla 1990). Thus, many advocate that women's groups should at the same time work both from within the party and from without. We take up this strand in the following section on autonomy.

Sometimes the constraints imposed on women's mobilization appear to be strategic. In the case of revolutionary China, both Judith Stacey (1983) and Christina Gilmartin (1989) suggest that the Chinese Communist Party (CCP) did indeed include a programmatic concern with women's emancipation on their agenda, yet dropped these concerns when they [the CCP] were threatened. Gilmartin (1989) shows that the CCP started out with the position that women's issues had to be addressed in the course of the revolution, not after. Only when threatened by the Guomindang, who labeled Communist women as promiscuous, did the CCP begin to revise their women's programs drastically. Stacey (1983) argues that the CCP had to back away from moves toward collectivization when "peasant patriarchs" resisted it as threatening their patriarchal authority. In other examples, Muriel Nazzari (1989) sees Cuba's embattled economy as the main constraint to women's emancipation; writing about Vietnam and Nicaragua, Christine Pelzer White (1989) and Maxine Molyneux (1989) show how women's dreams of gender equality slip away in a society permanently mobilized for war. Though the Sandinista women's organization had been ready to deal with issues such as the legalization of abortion or the value of women's labor, it was compelled to put them aside and devote its energies to the war effort. However, the extent to which these potential constraints, could, with political will, have been overcome, is a question several authors raise.

STATE AND ORGANIZATIONAL AUTONOMY

The review of the literature on the preconditions to, and the nature of, women's mobilization highlights two recurring themes which we draw out in the following section: the nature of the state, and the issue of organizational autonomy.

The Nature of the State

The four processes and their variations outlined above draw our attention to the preeminent role of the state—in both its local and regional forms—for women's mobilization. How activists understand the nature of the state profoundly shapes the form and content of their activism. While it is true, as Afshar (1987) warns, that third world countries have inconsistent policies regarding women, both internally and compared to each other, it is also true, as Alexander & Mohanty (1996) argue, that in the third world especially feminism cannot escape state intervention. As postcolonial states attempt to build their power base and increase legitimacy, often constrained by their dependency on foreign capital, they control, survey, and discipline women's lives. Thus, special attention has to be paid to state interests and state capacities in any analysis of the political opportunities within which third world women must organize.

There are various ways in which the policies of third world states shape women's lives and thus create the possibilities of women's activism. Economically, as many feminist scholars have argued, the policies of developing countries either make women invisible or actively exploit them (Boserup 1970, Kannabiran & Kannabiran 1996, Kabeer 1994). In Thailand and the Philippines, whose economies benefit substantially from the sex-trade, the state is an "active agent" in structuring exploitation (Heng 1996:32). Looking at the political sphere, Moran argues that the Liberian colonial state introduced, and the postcolonial state continued, a policy of imposing a single hierarchy of sex (in which men dominate women) where, preceding colonialism, women and men each represented their own interests (Moran 1989). States also directly legislate sexuality and family. Alexander (1991) has shown that in Trinidad and Tobago the state attempts to maintain social control by regulating morality in a manner informed by the legacy of colonial rule. Looking at the Islamic world, Kandiyoti (1991) has argued that secular states attempt to consolidate their power by undermining traditional community structures. In this context the family and particularly women's role in it becomes one of the primary sites of state-building struggles. Finally, states directly intervene in women's organizing. Fearful of challenges against them, many newly independent regimes have forbidden any form of autonomous political organizing, including women's organizations, leaving only inadequate party-sponsored women's groups as avenues for change (Kandiyoti 1991).

Given the nature of the state, both activists and scholars debate whether women should pursue legal reforms within the state or stay outside of it (Stamp 1995). Some groups believe that effective reform can only come through the state (see for example Barrig 1989 and Alvarez 1990). Bush, on the other hand, argues that the state is invested in patriarchy and at best can only partially serve women's needs (Bush 1992). Indeed, Gandhi & Shah (1991) argue that the state co-opts women's issues, and they point to the ways in which each new piece of legislation that seemingly favors women has afforded the state—not women—more power. Analogously, Sarti (1989) argues that the political institutionalization of the women's movement is inversely related to its existence as a social movement in civil society. Taking both sides of the argument into account, some scholars and activists are more pragmatic, advising organizations to work selectively with the state while maintaining awareness of its limitations (Alvarez 1990, Jaquette 1989, Wieringa 1992).

Much of the social movement literature on the first world is informed by the image of a stable state. However, as we have seen, many third world women organize in order to effect regime change. To grasp the relationship between third world women's movements and state structures, we have to pay attention not only to variation among third world states but also to historical change within each individual state. As regimes shift from authoritarian to post-authoritarian, colonial to post-colonial, secular to post-secular, the conditions under which women mobilize and the identities that become salient are transformed.

Organizational Autonomy

The question of autonomy arises not only in the context of the state but also when activist women collaborate with other movements for social change. This is an issue of particular importance for women's movements precisely because so many of them have emerged out of other progressive movements. In this section we discuss connections between women's movements and other organizations and movements.

Most scholars who write about women's movements believe that the autonomy of women's movements is an unqualified good. This is partly because experience has taught that the left seems to be incapable of overcoming the "natural" division of labor between men and women (Molyneux 1981). Proponents of autonomy see left parties as hierarchical and nondemocratic. The predominantly male leadership of the left, critics claim, is threatened by feminist demands and makes only half-hearted attempts to bring women into the fold, avoiding issues not considered to be in men's interest (Sen 1989). Looking at the Indian Left, Katzenstein argues that it was the autonomy of the Indian women's movement that enabled them to focus on the issue of violence against women (Katzenstein 1989). Further, women's issues are used strategically and may be dropped when expedient, as Stacey (1983) and Gilmartin (1989) have made evident in their studies of Chinese Communists, and Islah Jad (1995) has argued for the Palestinian movement.

Those who argue against the autonomy of women's movements claim that affiliation to a larger organization enhances the efficacy of the women's movements (Wieringa 1985). From this perspective, it is preferable to compromise on one's principles to some extent and to be effective, rather than retain them and be marginalized. In the context of South Africa, as we have seen, Beall et al (1989) argue that the concept of autonomy is irrelevant, as does Dajani (1993) in the context of Palestine. Barrig (1989) argues that in Peru the emphasis on autonomy grew out of a narrow definition of gender interests, which in turn led to feminists' isolation from other women's and progressive movements. Writing about Pakistan, Jalal argues that in the absence of ties to broad-based progressive groups, gender issues will not be put on the political agenda (Jalal 1991). Challenging the division between feminist and nonfeminist struggles, Amrita Basu argues that we should not equate feminism with autonomous organizing because that would ignore the many "democracy, nationalist, and human rights struggles" of which women are a vital part and in which they have come to challenge the dominant relations of gender (Basu 1995:19).

In the end, perhaps it is difficult to argue conclusively whether autonomy is inherently better or worse for a women's organization. As Hellman cautions, the concept of autonomy should not be fetishized, for the dialectical relationship between movements and parties is more important than autonomy per se (1992). One strategic solution to the problem of the relationship between political parties and autonomous women's organizations is the idea of double militancy, suggested by Latin American feminists (Sternbach et al 1992). In this way, women can be involved both in democratic struggles and in feminist struggles, with one, ideally, influencing the other. Theoretically, the concept of political field allows for a more tempered approach to the question of autonomy (Ray 1998, 1999). Political fields structure the actions, rhetoric, and effectiveness of organizations in them. From this perspective, autonomy is more or less effective depending upon the political field within which women's organizations are embedded. Thus, for example, autonomous organizations in a political field dominated by one political party are less effective than those in a more fragmented political field.

INTERNATIONAL CONNECTIONS   The question of autonomy can also be posed in the context of international connections. There is no doubt that efforts such as the International Women's Decade declared by the United Nations provided the impetus for and legitimacy of organizing around women's issues in many countries (Sarti 1989, Omvedt 1993). Yet, that decade, and the intervening international conferences, including the most recent one at Beijing, foreground the relationships and uneven dependencies between the women's movements of the first and third world, even as they highlight the possibilities for international solidarity (Charlesworth 1996, Howard & Allen 1996; see also special issues of *Signs* 1996 and of *Feminist Studies* 1996).

The underlying theme of the 1995 Beijing conference, women's rights as human rights, was part of a general push for the consideration of a universal standard of human rights (Howard & Allen 1996, Peters & Wolper 1995). Framing women's rights as human rights uses the human rights platform as developed by the United Nations to better women's lives in terms of their physical, cultural, social, political, and economic well-being. Charlotte Bunch, among others, argues that this is one way to get gender-based violence on the mainstream agenda of organizations such as the United Nations and Amnesty International (Bunch 1995, Friedman 1995, Stamatopoulou 1995). The adoption of this perspective on women's rights implies that these organizations should add violations of human rights in the private sphere to their present focus on violations in the public sphere.

However, the women's-rights-as-human-rights frame implies a universalizing stance for which western feminism has been rightly critiqued. Addressing this problem directly, many who argue for framing women's rights as human rights claim that it does not have to imply homogenization (Howard & Allen 1996; see also Bunch 1995, Rao 1995, Friedman 1995). Rao (1995) argues that national leaders have often deployed reified notions of culture to resist addressing the question of women's status. Defining culture as "a series of constantly contested and negotiated social practices whose meanings are influenced by the power and status of their interpreters and participants," she argues that treating women's rights as human rights can and should become part of local and national cultural practices everywhere (1995:173).

Those who argue for women's rights as human rights assume that there is a global solution to what they perceive as the ultimately universal, if locally varying, problems of women; they turn to supranational institutions to put pressure on individual states to address the issues they feel are important. In the end, however, what human rights mean and how they can be applied depend on the factors we have highlighted throughout this paper—the formation of identities, interests, and the impact of locally and nationally specific processes on women's mobilizations.

CONCLUSION

This exploration of the rich and varied literatures on women's movements in the third world has highlighted women's own conceptualizations of their lives, needs, and desires, which affect not only identity and interest formation but also mobilization based on them. These identities and interests are shaped by structural preconditions that (*a*) impact locally specific women's movements and their potential for success and (*b*) affect the ability of women's movements to influence nation building and regime change. Furthermore, the review of the literature shows that the relationships between women's movements and the state, between women's movements and other movements, and between women's movements themselves are extremely complex. Universal discourses such as the increasingly popular human rights framework used by some feminists seem promising in their ability to mobilize potentially powerful international institutions on behalf of women, yet simultaneously threaten to overlook the very embeddedness in locally and nationally specific structures that make women's movements so powerful.

In this review we have problematized the tendency of theory to focus on the universals at the expense of the local, yet have pointed to the possibilities of using larger concepts of identity, autonomy, and political opportunities within which to situate the local. As these concepts are relevant to social movements in general, this observation leads us to ask what is unique about women's movements in the third world? On the one hand, this review has shown such a wide variety of women's movements as to question the existence of the entity "third world women's movement." On the other hand, the commonalties in the preconditions that inform women's mobilizing derive from those very experiences that mark the first world as separate from the third world (such as colonialism and political/economic dependency). It is not the forces of modernization per se, but rather the specific historical trajectories that are shared by parts of the third world, that enable us to claim that while there is not a third world woman's movement, there are indeed third world women's movements.

We end this review with two recommendations. First, considering the depth of work presented here, the lack of attention paid to it by sociologists is, to say the least, surprising. Our review has shown that concepts such as political opportunity structures would be expanded and deepened if understandings of regime change and conditions of postcolonialism were to be incorporated. Second, we call for a shift in focus in comparative work, from the macro level to the local where larger political, cultural, and economic processes are played out. This shift would enable us to better understand the ways in which women's collective identities and interests are constructed and the ideological and material conditions under which mobilizations actually take place.

ACKNOWLEDGMENTS

We would like to thank Kim Boss, Michael Burawoy, and members of the Bryn Mawr College Gender Colloquium for their invaluable suggestions.

> **Visit the *Annual Reviews home page* at http://www.AnnualReviews.org.**

Literature Cited

Afshar H. 1987. Introduction. In *Women State and Ideology: Studies from Africa and Asia*, ed. H Afshar, pp. 1–9. Albany: State Univ. New York Press

Agarwal B. 1992. The gender and environment debate: lessons from India. *Fem. Stud.* 18(1):119–58

Alexander MJ. 1991. Redrafting morality: the post–colonial state and the Sexual Offenses Bill in Trinidad and Tobago. In *Third World Women and the Politics of Feminism*, ed. C Mohanty, A Russo, L Torres, pp. 133–52. Bloomington/Indianapolis: Ind. Univ. Press

Alexander MJ, Mohanty CT. 1996. Introduction: genealogies, legacies, movements. In *Feminist Genealogies, Colonial Legacies, Democratic Futures*, ed. MJ Alexander, CT Mohanty, pp. xiii–xlii. New York/London: Routledge

Alvarez SE. 1990. *Engendering Democracy in Brazil*. Princeton, NJ: Princeton Univ. Press

Alvarez SE. 1989. Women's movements and gender politics in the Brazilian transition. In *The Women's Movement in Latin America: Feminism and the Transition to Democracy*, ed. JS Jaquette, pp. 18–71. Boston, MA: Unwin Hyman

Badran M. 1994. Gender activism: feminists and Islamists in Egypt. In *Identity Politics and Women*, ed. VM Moghadam, pp. 202–27. Boulder, CO: Westview

Baffoun A. 1994. Feminism and Muslim fundamentalism: the Tunisian and Algerian cases. In *Identity Politics and Women*, ed. VM Moghadam, pp. 167–82. Boulder, CO: Westview

Banerjee S. 1995. Hindu nationalism and the construction of woman: the Shiv Sena organises women in Bombay. In *Women and Right Wing Movements: Indian Experi-*ences, ed. T Sarkar, U Butalia, pp. 216–32. London/New Jersey: Zed Books

Barrig M. 1989. The difficult equilibrium between bread and roses: women's organizations and the transition from dictatorship to democracy in Peru. In *The Women's Movement in Latin America: Feminism and the Transition to Democracy*, ed. JS Jaquette, pp. 114–48. Boston, MA: Unwin Hyman

Basu A. 1992. *Two Faces of Protest: Contrasting Modes of Women's Activism in India*. Berkeley: Univ. Calif. Press

Basu A. 1995. Introduction. In *The Challenge of Local Feminisms: Women's Movements in Global Perspective*, ed. A Basu, pp. 1–21. Boulder, CO: Westview

Beall J, Hassim S, Todes A. 1989. 'A Bit on the Side'?: Gender struggles in the politics of transformation in South Africa. *Fem. Rev.* 33:30–56

Berger I. 1992. Categories and contexts: reflections on the politics of identity in South Africa. *Fem. Stud.* 18(2):284–94

Boserup E. 1970. *Women's Role in Economic Development*. New York: St. Martin's

Bunch C. 1995. Transforming human rights from a femininst perspective. In *Women's Rights, Human Rights: International Feminist Perspectives*, ed. J Peters, A Wolper, pp. 11–17. New York: Routledge

Bush DM. 1992. Women's movements and state policy reform aimed at domestic violence against women: a comparison of the consequences of movement mobilization in the U.S. and India. *Gender Soc.* 6(4): 587–608

Chafetz JS, Dworkin AG. 1986. *Female Revolt: Women's Movements in World and Historical Perspective*. Totowa, NJ: Rowman & Allenheld

Charlesworth H. 1996. Women as Sherpas: Are global summits useful for women? *Fem. Stud.* 22(3):537–47

Chatterjee P. 1989. The nationalist resolution of the women's question. In *Recasting Women: Essays in Colonial History*, ed. K Sanghar, S Vaid. New Delhi: Kali for Women

Chinchilla NS. 1990. Revolutionary popular feminism in Nicaragua: articulating class, gender, and national sovereignty. *Gender Soc.* 4(3):370–97

Chinchilla NS. 1992. Marxism, feminism and the struggle for democracy in Latin America. In *The Making of Contemporary Social Movements in Latin America*, ed. A Escobar, S Alvarez. Boulder, CO: Westview

Chuchryk PM. 1989. Feminist anti–authoritarian politics: the role of women's organizations in the Chilean transition to democracy. In *The Women's Movement in Latin America: Feminism and the Transition to Democracy*, ed. JS Jaquette, pp. 149–84. Boston, MA: Unwin Hyman

Cooper BM. 1995. The politics of difference and women's associations in Niger: of 'prostitutes,' the public, and politics. *Signs* 20(4):851–82

Dajani S. 1993. Palestinian women under Israeli occupation. In *Arab Women*, ed. JE Tucker. Bloomington/Indianapolis: Ind. Univ. Press

Feldman S. 1998. (Re)presenting Islam: manipulating gender, shifting state practices, and class frustrations in Bangladesh. In *Appropriating Gender: Women's Activism and Politicized Religion in South Asia*, ed. P Jeffery, A Basu, pp. 33–52. New York/London: Routledge

Femenia NA. 1987. Argentinian's Mothers of Plaza de Mayo: the mourning process from junta to democracy. *Fem. Stud.* 13(1):9–18

Feminist Studies. 1996. Special Issue. 22(3)

Ferree MM. 1995. Patriarchies and feminisms: the two women's movements of post–unification Germany. *Soc. Polit.* 2(1):10–24

Ferree MM, Martin PY. 1995. *Feminist Organizations: Harvest of the New Women's Movement*. Philadelphia, PA: Temple Univ. Press

Friedman E. 1995. Women's human rights: the emergence of a movement. In *Women's Rights, Human Rights: International Feminist Perspectives*, ed. J Peters, A Wolper, pp. 18–35. New York: Routledge

Gandhi N, Shah N. 1991. *The Issues at Stake: Theory and Practice in the Contemporary Women's Movement in India*. New Delhi: Kali for Women

Gelb J. 1989. *Feminism and Politics: A Comparative Perspective*. Berkeley: Univ. Calif. Press

Gilmartin C. 1989. Gender, politics, and patriarchy in China: the experiences of early women communists, 1920–27. In *Promissory Notes: Women in the Transition to Socialism*, ed. S Kruks, R Rapp, MB Young, pp. 82–105. New York: Monthly Rev.

Gordon A. 1995. Gender, ethnicity, and class in Kenya: 'Burying Otieno' revisited. *Signs* 20(4):883–912

Haj S. 1992. Palestinian women and patriarchal relations. *Signs* 17(4):761–78

Hale S. 1993. Transforming culture or fostering second–hand consciousness? Women's Front organizations and revolutionary parties–the Sudan case. In *Arab Women*, ed. JE Tucker, pp. 149–74. Bloomington/Indianapolis: Ind. Univ. Press

Hassim S. 1993. Family, motherhood and Zulu nationalism: the politics of the Inkatha Women's Brigade. *Fem. Rev.* 43:1–25

Hatem M. 1993. Toward the development of post–Islamist and post–nationalist feminist discourses in the Middle East. In *Arab Women*, ed. JE Tucker, pp. 29–48. Bloomington/Indianapolis: Ind. Univ. Press

Hellman JA. 1992. The study of new social movements in Latin America and the question of autonomy. In *The Making of Social Movements in Latin America*, ed. A Escobar, SE Alvarez, pp. 52–61. Boulder, CO: Westview

Heng G. 1996. A great way to fly: nationalism, the state and varieties of third world feminism. In *Feminist Genealogies, Colonial Legacies, Democratic Futures*, ed. MJ Alexander, CT Mohanty. New York/London: Routledge

Howard JA, Allen C. 1996. Reflections on the Fourth World Conference on Women and NGO Forum '95 – Introduction. *Signs* 22(1):181–85

Jad I. 1995. Claiming feminism, claiming nationalism: women's activism in the occupied territories. In *The Challenge of Local Feminisms: Women's Movements in Global Perspective*, ed. A Basu, pp. 226–48. Boulder, CO: Westview

Jalal A. 1991. The convenience of subservience: women and the state of Pakistan. In *Women, Islam and the State*, ed. D Kandiyoti, pp. 77–114. Philadelphia, PA: Temple Univ. Press

Jaquette JS, ed. 1989. *The Women's Movement in Latin America: Feminism and the Transition to Democracy*. Boston: Unwin Hyman

Jayawardena K. 1986. *Feminism and Nationalism in the Third World*. London: Zed Books

Jayawardena K. 1988. Some comments on feminism and the left in South Asia. *South Asia Bull.* 8:88–91

Jelin E, ed. 1990. *Women and Social Change in Latin America.* London: Zed Books

Jenson J. 1987. Changing discourse, changing ideas. In *Women's Movements of the United States and Western Europe*, ed. MF Katzenstein, CM Mueller, pp. 64–88. Philadelphia, PA: Temple Univ. Press

Kabeer N. 1994. *Reversed Realities: Gender Hierarchies in Development Thought.* London/New York: Verso

Kandiyoti D. 1988. Bargaining with patriarchy. *Gender Soc.* 2(3):274–90

Kandiyoti D. 1991. *Women, Islam and the State.* Philadelphia, PA: Temple Univ. Press

Kandiyoti D. 1997. Beyond Beijing: obstacles and prospects for the Middle East. In *Muslim Women and the Politics of Participation: Implementing the Beijing Platform*, ed. M Afkhami, E Friedl, pp. 3–10. Syracuse, NY: Syracuse Univ. Press

Kannabiran V, Kannabiran K. 1996. Looking at ourselves: the women's movement in Hyderabad. In *Feminist Genealogies, Colonial Legacies, Democratic Futures*, ed. MJ Alexander, CT Mohanty. New York/London: Routledge

Karam AM. 1997. Women, Islamisms, and the state: dynamics of power and contemporary feminisms in Egypt. In *Muslim Women and the Politics of Participation: Implementing the Beijing Platform*, ed. M Afkhami, E Friedl, pp. 18–28. Syracuse, NY: Syracuse Univ. Press

Katzenstein MF. 1989. Organizing against violence: strategies of the Indian women's movement. *Pac. Aff.* 62(1):53–71

Kim S-k. 1996. Big companies don't hire us, married women: exploitation and empowerment among women workers in South Korea. *Fem. Stud.* 22(3):555–71

Klandermans PB. 1990. Linking the "old" and "new": movement networks in the Netherlands. In *Challenging the Political Order: New Social and Political Movements in Western Democracies*, ed. R Dalton, M Kuechler, pp. 122–36. New York: Oxford Univ. Press

Kruks S, Rapp R, Young MB. 1989. Introduction. In *Promissory Notes: Women in the Transition to Socialism*, ed. S Kruks, R Rapp, MB Young, pp. 7–12. New York: Monthly Rev.

Kumar R. 1993. *A History of Doing: An Illustrated Account of Movements for Women's Rights and Feminism in India, 1800–1990.* New Delhi: Kali for Women

Lazreg M. 1994. *The Eloquence Of Silence: Algerian Women In Question.* New York: Routledge

Lazreg M. 1990. Gender and politics in Algeria: unraveling the religious paradigm. *Signs* 15(4):755–80

Lind AC. 1992. Power, gender and development: popular women's organization and the politics of needs in Ecuador. In *The Making of Social Movements in Latin America*, ed. A Escobar, SE Alvarez, pp. 134–49. Boulder, CO: Westview

Lorber J. 1990. From the Editor. In *Special Issue on Women and Development in the Third World. Gender Soc.* 4(3):293–95

MacLeod AE. 1992. Hegemonic relations and gender resistance: the new veiling as accommodating protest in Cairo. *Signs* 17(3):533–57

Margolis DR. 1993. Women's movements around the world: cross-cultural comparisons. *Gender Soc.* 7(3):379–99

McAdam D. 1982. *Political Process and the Development of Black Insurgency, 1930–1970.* Chicago: Univ. Chicago Press

Moghadam VM. 1992. Revolution, Islam and women: sexual politics in Iran and Afghanistan. In *Nationalisms and Sexualities*, ed. A Parker, M Russo, D Sommer, P Yaeger, pp. 424–46. New York/London: Routledge

Moghadam VM. 1993. *Modernizing Women: Gender and Social Change in the Middle East.* Boulder, CO/London: Lynne Reinner

Moghadam VM. 1994. *Identity Politics and Women.* Boulder, CO: Westview

Mohanty CT. 1991. Under western eyes: feminist scholarship and colonial discourses. In *Third World Women and the Politics of Feminism*, ed. CT Mohanty, A Russo, L Torres, pp. 51–80. Bloomington/Indianapolis: Ind. Univ. Press

Molyneux M. 1989. Women's role in the Nicaraguan revolutionary process: the early years. In *Promissory Notes: Women in the Transition to Socialism*, ed. S Kruks, R Rapp, MB Young, pp. 127–47. New York: Monthly Rev.

Molyneux M. 1981. Women in socialist societies: problems of theory and practice. In *Of Marriage and the Market*, ed. K Young, C Wolkowitz, R McCullagh, pp. 55–90. London: LSE Books

Molyneux M. 1985. Mobilization without emancipation? Women's interests, state and revolution in Nicaragua. *Fem. Stud.* 11(2):227–53

Moran MH. 1989. Collective action and the 'representation' of African women: a Liberian case study. *Fem. Stud.* 15(3):443–60

Navarro M. 1989. The Mothers of the Plaza de Mayo in Argentina. In *Power and Popular Protest: Latin American Social Movements*, ed. S Eckstein. Berkeley: Univ. Calif. Press

Nazarri M. 1989. The "Woman Question" in Cuba: an analysis of material constraints on its resolution. In *Promissory Notes: Women in the Transition to Socialism*, ed. S Kruks, R Rapp, MB Young, pp. 109–26. New York: Monthly Rev.

Neuhouser K. 1995. 'Worse than Men:' Gendered mobilizations in an urban Brazilian squatter settlement, 1971–91. *Gender Soc.* 9(1):38–59

Noonan RK. 1995. Women against the State: political opportunities and collective action frames in Chile's transition to democracy. *Sociol. Forum* 10(1):81–111

Omvedt G. 1993. *Reinventing Revolution: New Social Movements and the Socialist Tradition in India*. Armonk/New York/London: M.E. Sharpe

Papanek H. 1993. Theorizing about women's movements globally: comment on Diane Margolis. *Gender Soc.* 7(3):379–99

Peters J, Wolper A. 1995. *Women's Rights, Human Rights: International Feminist Perspectives.* New York: Routledge

Rao A. 1995. The politics of gender and culture in international human rights discourse. In *Women's Rights, Human Rights: International Feminist Perspectives*, ed. J Peters, A Wolper, pp. 167–75. New York: Routledge

Ray B. 1988. Freedom movement and women's awakening in Bengal, 1911–1929. *Indian Hist. Rev.* XVII(1–2):130–63

Ray R. 1998. Women's movements and political fields: a comparison of two Indian cities. *Soc. Probl.* 45(1): 21–36

Ray R. 1999. *Fields of Protest: Women's Movements in India.* Minneapolis: Univ. Minn. Press

Robertson C. 1996. Grassroots in Kenya: women genital mutilation, and collective action, 1920–1990. *Signs* 21(3):615–42

Rodriguez L. 1994. Barrio women: Between the urban and the feminist movement. *Lat. Am. Perspect.* 21(3):32–48

Safa HI. 1990. Women's social movements in Latin America. *Gender Soc.* 4(3):354–69

Sarkar T. 1992. The Hindu wife and the Hindu nation: domesticity and nationalism in 19th century Bengal. *Stud. Hist.* 8(2): 213–35

Sarkar T, Butalia U, eds. 1995. *Women and Right Wing Movements: Indian Experiences.* London/New Jersey: Zed Books

Sarti C. 1989. The panorama of feminism in Brazil. *New Left Rev.* 173:75–90

Schirmer JG. 1989. 'Those Who Die for Life Cannot Be Called Dead:' Women in human rights Protest in Latin America. *Fem. Rev.* 32:3–29

Seidman GW. 1993. No freedom without the women: mobilization and gender in South-Africa, 1970-1992. *Signs* 18(2):291–320

Seidman G. 1999. Gendered citizenship: South Africa's democratic transition and the construction of a gendered state. *Gender Soc.* Forthcoming

Sen I. 1989. Feminists, women's movement and the working class. *Econ. Polit. Wkly.* 24(29):1639–41

Shaheed F. 1998. The other side of the discourse: women's experiences of identity, religion, and activism in Pakistan. In *Appropriating Gender: Women's Activism and Politicized Religion in South Asia*, ed. P Jeffery, A Basu, pp. 143–64. New York/London: Routledge

Sharoni S. 1995. *Gender and the Israeli–Palestinian Conflict: the Politics of Women's Resistance*. Syracuse, NY: Syracuse Univ. Press

Shukrallah H. 1994. The impact of the Islamic movement in Egypt. *Fem. Rev.* 47:15–32

Signs. 1996. Special Issue. 22(1)

Stacey J. 1983. *Patriarchy and Socialist Revolution in China.* Berkeley: Univ. Calif. Press

Stamatopoulou E. 1995. Women's rights and the United Nations. In *Women's Rights, Human Rights: International Feminist Perspectives*, ed. J Peters, A Wolper, pp. 36–48. New York: Routledge

Stamp P. 1995. Burying Otieno: the politics of gender and ethnicity in Kenya. In *Rethinking the Political: Gender, Resistance, and the State*, ed. J Brenner, B Laslett, Y Arat, pp. 351–88. Chicago/London: Univ. Chicago Press

Sternbach NS, Navarro-Aranguren M, Chuchryk P, Alvararez SE. 1992. Feminisms in Latin America: from Bogotá to San Bernardo. *Signs* 17(2):393–434

Tarrow S. 1994. *Power in Movement: Social Movements, Collective Action and Politics.* Cambridge, UK: Cambridge Univ. Press

Thapar S. 1994. Women as activists; women as symbols: a study of the Indian nationalist movement. *Fem. Rev.* 44:81–96

Thayer M. 1997. Identity, revolution, and democracy: lesbian movements in Central America. *Soc. Probl.* 44(3):386–407

Tucker JE. 1998. *Arab Women.* Bloomington/Indianapolis: Ind. Univ. Press

Waylen G. 1994. Women and democratization: conceptualizing gender relations in transition politics. *World Polit.* 46:327–54

White CP. 1989. Vietnam: war, socialism, and the politics of gender relations. In *Promissory Notes: Women in the Transition to Socialism,* ed. S Kruks, R Rapp, MB Young, pp. 172–92. New York: Monthly Rev.

Wieringa S. 1985. *The Perfumed Nightmare: Some Notes on the Indonesian Women's Movement.* The Hague: Inst. Soc. Stud.

Wieringa S. 1992. Ibu or the beast: gender interests in two Indonesian women's organizations. *Fem. Rev.* 41:98–113

Young MB. 1989. Chicken Little in China: Women after the Cultural Revolution. In *Promissory Notes: Women in the Transition to Socialism*, ed. S Kruks, R Rapp, MB Young, pp. 233–47. New York: Monthly Rev.

Annu. Rev. Sociol. 1999. 25:73–93

SEXUALITY IN THE WORKPLACE:
Organizational Control, Sexual Harassment, and the Pursuit of Pleasure

Christine L. Williams[1], Patti A. Giuffre[2], and Kirsten Dellinger[3]

[1]Department of Sociology, University of Texas, Austin, Texas 78712, e-mail: clw@la.utexas.edu; [2]Department of Sociology, Southwest Texas State University, San Marcos, Texas 78666, e-mail: pg07@swt.edu; [3]Department of Sociology and Anthropology, University of Mississippi, University, Mississippi 38677, e-mail: kdelling@olemiss.edu

KEY WORDS   consensual sexuality, office romance, intimate relationships

ABSTRACT

Flirting, bantering, and other sexual interactions are commonplace in work organizations. Not all of these interactions constitute harassment or assault; consensual sexual relationships, defined as those reflecting positive and autonomous expressions of workers' sexual desire, are also prevalent in the workplace and are the focus of this paper. We begin by reviewing research on the distinction between sexual harassment and sexual consent. Next we examine popular and business literatures on office romance. Finally we discuss sociological research on consensual sexual relationships, including research on mate selection, organizational policy, and workplace culture. We argue that sexual behaviors must be understood in context, as an interplay between organizational control and individual agency.

INTRODUCTION

Sexual bantering, flirting, and dating are commonplace at work, but with few exceptions, sociologists have not paid much attention to these behaviors. The Weberian assumption that organizations progressively shed particularistic and irrational elements as they bureaucratize has deflected attention from love, sex, and relationships at work. The myth of the self-made professional also

73

contributes to this lacuna. Although Jessie Bernard noted over thirty years ago that men's top-level careers typically rely on the unpaid support of a wife at home, the conviction persists that individuals achieve success based on their own hard work and merit. To suggest that sexual relationships routinely shape (and are shaped by) our employment experiences violates values and beliefs that are fundamental to our capitalist culture. The research emphasis on sexual harassment may also contribute to downplaying the ubiquity of consensual sex in the workplace. Some sexual harassment researchers have suggested that women who do not label their sexual experiences as sexual harassment are suffering from false consciousness, implying that all sexual behavior is harmful to women (whether they think it is or not) and therefore ought to be eliminated from workplaces.

Despite sociologists' relative lack of attention to consensual sex in the workplace, public attention has been riveted on the issue thanks to several highly publicized sex scandals. Among the most notorious are the 1991 congressional hearings on the alleged sexual harassment of Anita Hill by Clarence Thomas, nominee to the Supreme Court; the sexual assault on female officers at a party during the 1991 annual convention of Navy fighter pilots; the dismissal of Air Force pilot Kelly Flinn for adultery in 1997; the 1998 trial and acquittal of the top ranking Army enlisted man on charges of sexual harassment; and the independent counsel investigations of President Clinton's sexual affairs with subordinates. These cases and others received saturation media coverage, prompting one commentator to label "sex and its place in American life" as the dominant theme of the 1990s (Stan 1995).

All too frequently, the public debates sparked by these cases have been polarized between those who argue that sex doesn't belong in the workplace, and those who argue that virtually "anything goes" as far as consenting adults are concerned (Stan 1995). Feminists are as split as any other group on this issue. Lynn Chancer identifies a schism between "sex" and "sexism" among feminist concerns: "One feminist goal ... is that women be able to enjoy sexual freedom. Another, just as necessary, is that women be able to attain freedom from sexism" (Chancer 1998:2). Those who focus their energy on the former goal, often referred to as "pro-sex" feminists, are pitted in debates against those committed to fighting discrimination and eradicating sexual harassment from the workplace, a position associated with the works of Catharine MacKinnon and Andrea Dworkin and often labeled "radical feminist." "Pro-sex" feminists argue that women are oppressed by restrictions on sexual expression. They point out that such restrictions are frequently supported by social and political conservatives devoted to preserving an image of pure and virtuous womanhood. From this perspective, women's sexual desire should be expressed, even in workplaces, because it is a potentially subversive force for undermining this patronizing and patriarchal image of women. Those associated with "radical feminism," on the other hand, maintain that heterosexuality is oppressive to women, particularly in workplaces that are dominated and controlled by men. In this view, sexual consent is possible only between equals; therefore heterosexual relationships that take place at work are inherently involuntary and unequal since men (in general) have more power, income, and status than women. (See also Hallinan 1993, LeMoncheck 1997.)

Both positions, in their extreme forms, are untenable. Sexual relationships at work are not always liberating and mutually fulfilling, nor are they always sexually harassing and harmful. Individuals can and do make distinctions between sexual harassment and assault on the one hand, and pleasurable, mutually desired sexual interactions and relationships on the other. Sexual interactions include a wide range of behaviors, including flirting with coworkers or clients (in person or via email); consuming pornography; sexual joking, bantering and touching; and coworker dating, sexual affairs, cohabitation and marriage. Fully understanding how behaviors such as these come to be labeled consensual or coercive raises fundamental questions that call out for systematic study by sociologists: How pervasive is consensual sexual activity in the workplace? How do workers distinguish between wanted and unwanted sexual advances? What are the consequences of consensual sexual behavior for men's and women's careers? How do organizations distinguish between wanted and unwanted sexual activity? And why do some organizations accommodate consensual sexual relationships, and others resist or prohibit them?

This chapter reviews the literature on these topics, focusing on research conducted in the United States. We begin with a discussion of research examining the difference between consensual and harassing sexuality in the workplace. By clarifying the meaning of sexual harassment, we believe we will be in a better position to understand consensual sexual activity.

SEXUAL HARASSMENT AND SEXUAL CONSENT

Some might question our starting premise on the grounds that consensual sexual relationships have nothing whatever to do with sexual harassment (e.g. Gallop 1997, Schultz 1998). This argument contends that sexual harassment is objectionable not because it is sexual per se, but rather because its effects are damaging to women's careers and employment or educational opportunities. These writers acknowledge that workplace discrimination against women often takes a sexual form—e.g., sexual put-downs, staring, come-ons, touching—but these behaviors should only be prohibited if they result in loss of opportunities.

Certainly, from a purely legal perspective, this argument is correct: Sexual harassment is technically against the law only insofar as it is a form of gender discrimination. According to Mane Hajdin:

> From the viewpoint of the law, even the fact that a victim of sexual harass-
> ment has suffered harm is not in itself a ground for providing a legal remedy,
> no matter how grave the harm might be....The ultimate question that a court
> dealing with [a sexual harassment] case needs to resolve is not "Has the
> plaintiff suffered harm?" but rather, "Has the plaintiff, in suffering the harm,
> been discriminated against on the basis of sex?" The evidence of the harm
> suffered by the victim is legally relevant only insofar as it can contribute to
> answering the latter question. (Hajdin 1997:123)

In a court of law, the victim of sexual harassment must show that she (or he) was treated differently than were the men (or the women) who were similarly situated, and consequently suffered a loss of opportunities or benefits. In 1998, the US Supreme Court affirmed the principle that all litigated sexual harassment cases must involve gender discrimination. The Court allowed a case of sexual harassment involving a heterosexual man suing his heterosexual male coworkers to go to trial, but Justice Scalia wrote that the male plaintiff must still prove that his coworkers' behavior toward him was "not merely tinged with offensive sexual connotation, but actually constituted discrimination because of sex" (*New York Times*, March 5, 1998, p. A17). The issue of consent is immaterial according to this legal perspective: The only pertinent question should be whether or not the particular sexual behaviors resulted in gender discrimination.

Nevertheless, in actual court proceedings, the issue of sexual consent is often paramount in proving or disproving a charge of sexual harassment. Evidence of a prior intimate relationship may undermine the credibility of a sexual harassment plaintiff (Schultz 1998, Summers & Myklebust 1992). In a study of a disciplinary tribunal hearing on sexual harassment in a Canadian university, Ehrlich & King (1996) found that consent was the central issue: Complainants were questioned repeatedly about why they didn't resist the defendant's sexual advances by yelling out or locking their doors. The authors argue that the presumption of the defendant as well as the tribunal members was that behavior that is not resisted to the "utmost" implies consent, which can undermine charges of sexual harassment.

Workers themselves often conceive of sexual behaviors at work along a continuum, ranging from pleasurable, to tolerable, to harassing. Some studies have attempted to ascertain how workers "draw the line" between sexual harassment and consensual sexual behaviors. In a study of restaurants, Giuffre & Williams (1994) found that waiters and waitresses eagerly engaged in a great deal of flirtatious, sexual bantering with coworkers of their same race/ethnicity, class, and sexual orientation, but they defined identical behaviors by coworkers of different backgrounds as sexual harassment. The widespread use of double standards in assessing sexual harassment suggests that it is not the sexual behavior per se that some workers find objectionable, but rather, characteristics of the individual who engages in the behavior. This study raises concerns that already-marginalized groups (racial/ethnic minority members; gays and lesbians; working class men) may be singled out and targeted for enforcement of the sexual harassment policies that exist today in many workplaces.

Workers also may be more likely to tolerate objectionable sexual behaviors if they consider them a requirement of their jobs. Service workers subjected to constant sexual comments, leering, and touching from customers may be reluctant to complain about these behaviors to managers. For example, Adkins (1995) found that women hired for several different jobs in the British tourism industry were required to engage in sexualized interactions with customers and coworkers. A catering manager describes the work of her female assistants:

> She "expected" women workers to be able to cope with sexual behaviour and attention from men customers as "part of the job." She said that if "the women catering assistants complain, or say things like they can't cope, I tell them it happens all the time and not to worry about it...it's part of the job...if they can't handle it then they're not up to working here." (Adkins 1995:130)

While some women may enjoy and even profit from sexualized interactions at work, resisting these behaviors may be impossible. In this particular case, reporting sexually offensive behavior to the catering manager would not result in a complaint of sexual harassment; more likely, it would result in the loss of a job. Those who stay in these jobs therefore must develop their own personal strategies to cope with the constant sexual harassment.

In the service jobs they studied, Folgero & Fjeldstad (1995) found that those who did actively complain of sexual harassment were admonished by their coworkers to either "take it or leave it." Many workers believe that any reasonable person should tolerate the sexual demands of the job. As Folgero & Fjeldstad point out (1995:311), "in a cultural setting where sexual harassment is generally accepted as part of the job, feelings of harassment may be suppressed to a degree where the victim actively denies that the problem exists." In these instances, workers may label as sexual harassment only those experiences that transcend the work role, involve violence, or take place after work hours, as in the case of stalking. (See also Giuffre & Williams 1994, Williams 1998, cf Haavio-Mannila et al 1988.)

These studies all suggest that sexual harassment and sexual consent are not polar opposites, in contrast to the assumption of much legal theory. Instead, they are interrelated and overlapping moments in a complex and context-specific process. Thus, in work contexts where subjection to sexual harassment is part of the job, the concept of "consent" is problematic, yet many workers tolerate and even endorse these features of their jobs. In these cases, the boundary between sexual harassment and sexual consent is often blurred, from the vantage points both of employees and of researchers interested in documenting and ultimately eradicating sexual harassment.

But what about jobs that give workers more autonomy in defining their own sexual desires and practices? Do workers ever seek out jobs for sexual excitement and adventure? Do men and women ever enjoy their sexual experiences in the workplace? These questions tend to be ignored in the studies of sexual harassment we have reviewed, in part because they have been designed to document the unacceptable range of sexual behavior.

In this paper, we shift the focus to consensual relationships, which we define as those reflecting positive and autonomous expressions of workers' sexual desire. Our goal is to preserve a place for workers' agency in our understanding of workplace sexuality, without denying the organizational constraints on their behavior. But very little sociological research has explored the pleasurable and consensual end of the sexual spectrum. As editor Beth Schneider lamented in a special issue of *Gender & Society* devoted to sexuality research, "There is still a severe shortage of research on the narratives and experiences of the joys of sexuality" (1994:296). We now turn to a brief overview of the few sources of existing data on this topic.

OFFICE ROMANCE LITERATURE

Nonacademic sources of information about consensual sex in the workplace abound. Magazines and news organizations frequently commission surveys on workplace flirting, dating, and marriage, but this kind of study has more to do with titillating readers and expanding sales than generating reliable information about work organizations. An Associated Press story released on Valentine's Day 1998, reported on one such survey commissioned by *Details* magazine. It polled the magazine's subscribers' opinions about a range of intimate and personal behaviors in the workplace, from smiling and socializing after work, to wearing tight, provocative clothing and telling sexual jokes. Perhaps not surprisingly, the survey found that a large percentage of respondents engaged in these behaviors, leading the AP writer to conclude that "like red roses and Valentine's Day, office romances are now part of many a love life."

There is also a vast literature on "office romance" that has been generated by business researchers and consultants. This literature can be grouped into three categories: empirical studies, policy analyses, and how-to advice for managers. The empirical studies focus on assessing the impact of intimate, sexual relationships on productivity, and on generating policy guidelines to control and monitor employee behavior. A number of studies survey managers about whether their companies have policies regulating office romance and solicit their opinions on the motives of the participants, and the effects of such relationships on workers' productivity. A comprehensive review of this literature (Pierce et al 1996) reports mixed and inconclusive results from these studies: Some find that office romances increase job productivity and worker morale; others find the opposite. On the benefits side, studies find that workplace romance can inject excitement into the work group; enhance communication and cooperation; stimulate creativity; and create a happier work environment (Mainiero 1986, Crary 1987, Anderson & Hunsaker 1985, Dillard & Broetzmann 1989). On the negative side, studies find that romances can take time and energy away from work (late arrivals, early departures, long lunches); increase gossip; arouse jealousy and suspicion due to favoritism; and increase vulnerability to charges of sexual harassment (Anderson & Hunsaker 1985, Mainiero 1986, Powell 1993, Pierce & Aguinis 1997).

Numerous shortcomings detract from the value of most of these studies for sociologists. Most are based on anecdotal evidence or on convenience samples, such as MBA students or people waiting in airports (Dillard's work is an exception). Many are third party studies, soliciting opinions about office romance from individuals who may or may not have any personal experience with such relationships. Almost all of the studies use closed-ended surveys and pay little to no attention to organizational context. Finally, these studies are of limited value because they tend to focus exclusively on heterosexual relationships among white collar employees, ignoring those of gays and lesbians, and any relationships that may develop among blue collar workers and those employed in service industries and the professions.

The management literature also includes articles addressing policy concerns. Many of these urge managers to institute policies to stop office affairs if they suspect that productivity is adversely affected by them (e.g. Anderson & Hunsaker 1985, Dillard & Broetzmann 1989, Lobel et al 1994). For instance, one study of intimate heterosexual relationships concludes with the following advice:

> Because this type of relationship can have both positive and negative consequences, managers have a vital role to play: fostering positive outcomes while intervening to minimize any negative repercussions (Lobel et al 1994:15).

The means that managers have at their disposal to "minimize any negative repercussions" of office romance include transferring and even firing the employees. There are virtually no legal limits on employers' ability to impose and enforce prohibitions against fraternization between employees, even away from the workplace (Massengill & Peterson 1995). The constitutionally guaranteed right to privacy does not protect individuals involved in intimate relationships at work (Hallinan 1993). In fact, employers can require employees to disclose information about intimate relationships that involve actual or perceived conflicts of interest. Failure to disclose can be legal grounds for discharge (Segal 1993).

Almost half of all states have laws prohibiting discrimination against workers on the basis of marital status. Some people who marry coworkers have attempted to use these laws to protect them from job loss or transfer, but in most instances, these efforts have not been successful in challenging rules prohibiting corporate romance and relationships (Wolkenbreit 1997).

The practice of firing or transferring individuals involved in consensual sexual relationships may be especially detrimental for women workers. In cases involving heterosexual couples, the woman may bear the brunt of such management decisions, because she is likely to occupy a lower- level position in the organization compared to the man (Quinn 1977, Anderson & Hunsacker 1985, Wolkenbreit 1997). Laws prohibiting employment discrimination against women may not apply in these cases if the two partners do not occupy similar positions in the organizational hierarchy. Courts have found that it is legal to fire the subordinate member of the couple and not the superordinate—even if that negatively impacts more women than men—as long as the rule is enforced equally on all subordinates, regardless of gender (Massengill & Peterson 1995, cf Young 1995). Gender discrimination resulting from such policies is difficult to prove for two additional reasons. Because only a small number of women are typically affected by the policy in any given organization, the statistical evidence needed to prove disparate impact is usually lacking or unconvincing in the courtroom (Wolkenbreit 1997). And finally, because some companies allow the couple to decide which member must leave their job, a variety of factors might enter into their choice, such as income, seniority, and opportunities. Although all of these considerations are clearly linked to gender, courts may view them as independent causal factors, making gender discrimination arguments difficult to prove (Wolkenbreit 1997; see also Hallinan 1993).

In sum, there are few legal protections available for employees who lose their jobs because they date, cohabitate with, or marry a coworker. The management literature generally supports companies' power to regulate these relationships. Thus, most of the management policy literature and several of the law journal articles we reviewed (e.g. Hallinan 1993, Herbst 1996) recommend instituting a clear, written policy prohibiting fraternization (especially between supervisors and subordinates) and uniformly enforcing it.

Finally, in addition to research and policy studies, the management literature also contains a genre of "how to" books and essays, providing "hands-on" advice to businessmen and women regarding sexual relationships. These works are typically based on informal, journalistic interviews with corporate executives (e.g. Westoff 1985, Neville 1990, Baridon & Eyler 1994). Business workers usually are advised to avoid sexual relationships, in part to protect themselves against charges of sexual harassment and in part to enhance their productivity and economic success. Some writers provide check-lists to aid individuals in deciding whether or not to pursue a sexual relationship on the job, as in the following example (cited in Powell 1993:144–45):

1. Be aware of office norms about romance before acting.
2. Evaluate the potential risks to career advancement.
3. Don't mess around with a boss—or mentor.
4. Maintain strict boundaries between personal and professional roles.
5. Clarify at the start exactly what you want from the relationship.
6. Identify the possible areas in which partners may become competitive.
7. Anticipate possible conflict-of-interest situations.
8. Be sensitive to the reactions of colleagues and management.
9. Remember that the romance will not remain a secret for long.
10. Discuss "contingency plans" at the start of the romance.

Overall, the value of this literature to sociologists is mixed. It offers very little reliable information about what is actually taking place in organizations and why. But it does provide interesting insights into how management experts understand sexuality and its place in organizations. Most of these writers rely on a very reified image of sexuality, as an irrational, biological force that must be controlled and channeled for organizations to profit and for individuals to succeed. Almost every book and article in the genre follows the same format: They begin with a variant of the statement, "In the last decade, women have been entering the labor force in record numbers" (Dillard & Witteman 1985:99). Office romance is considered the inevitable result: "Today's organizational woman works, interacts, travels, socializes, and relaxes with her male colleagues more than ever before. Such intense involvement is a potential breeding ground for both sexual attraction and romantic relationships" (Warfield 1987:22). These romances are threatening to organizations: "The introduction of gender into workplace groupings opens up issues such as jealousy, triangles, favoritism, territoriality, mismatched attraction, exploitation, and awkward breakups" (Baridon & Eyler 1994:149). But expert help is available: "Whether [corporations] like it or not, whether it is good for business or bad, corporate romance is as inevitable as earthquakes in California, and it must be explored and understood so that this often unpredictable social force can be properly channeled" (Westoff 1985:21).

The view of sexuality contained in these writings is very similar to the conventional Freudian perspective that sexuality must be repressed for civilization to function productively. Sexuality (id) is counterposed to rationality (ego) and is considered disruptive, antisocial, dangerous, and in need of control. Many sociologists today reject this perspective, arguing instead that society actively promotes some specific expressions of sexuality while it discourages others. The discourse of experts (in contemporary society, anyone from talk-show hosts to psychologists to business consultants) is particularly influential in defining and enforcing the boundaries between "normal" and "abnormal" sexuality. Jeffrey Weeks sums up this position:

> Sexuality is something that society produces in complex ways. It is a result of diverse social practices that give meaning to social activities, of social definitions and self-definitions, of struggles between those who have the power to define and regulate, and those who resist. Sexuality is not given, it is a product of negotiation, struggle and human agency. (Weeks 1986:25)

This broader definition of sexuality emphasizes that social institutions, including the workplace, define and shape sexual desire, and also that social groups often negotiate and resist pressures toward conformity with social norms (see also Williams & Britton 1995).

From this perspective, managers can be seen, through their expert advice literature, as actively shaping workers' sexual desire. This opens up interesting questions for sociological investigation. For instance, by providing check lists like the one cited above, are consultants privileging certain sexual practices and marginalizing others? Do any groups benefit more than others from anti-dating policies (e.g. married vs single, men vs women)? And what are the social and psychological consequences of implementing this advice? It is possible that these policies may make prohibited liaisons riskier and hence sexier to workers. Furthermore, because they typically police only heterosexual relationships, they may contribute to the invisibility of gays and lesbians in many workplaces, but by prohibiting all sexual relationships, such policies may force heterosexuals into the closet as well. Unfortunately, we know virtually nothing about workers' reactions to such policies, how pervasive they are, how consistently they are enforced, and their impact on different groups of workers. Thus the "office romance" literature is suggestive of fruitful avenues for sociological research, but it begs as many questions as it answers.

SOCIOLOGICAL STUDIES OF WORKPLACE SEXUALITY

As noted, few sociologists have ever examined consensual sexual behavior in the workplace. However, pockets of information are scattered in diverse literatures. Some insight into the topic can be gleaned from research on sexual partnering or mate selection. For instance, we can gain an overall impression of the prevalence of consensual sexuality from the nation-wide survey on American sexual behavior by Laumann et al (1994). This survey asked respondents where they met their current sexual partners, and a substantial proportion—about 15%—said that they met at work.

Research on marriage patterns in particular occupations is also a potential source of information on the scope of consensual sexual behavior. Studies of workers in specific occupations often include information about their family members. Thus, we know that women physicians often marry men physicians (Myers 1988); many women research scientists are married to scientists (Pycior et al 1996); and faculty members frequently marry other faculty members (Astin & Milem 1997). Of course this research on marriage partners is limited to legally sanctioned heterosexual relationships; less is known about workplace relationship patterns among gays, lesbians, and unmarried heterosexuals. Furthermore, this admittedly partial information is available only for a narrow range of occupations. We have relatively more information about the prevalence of marriage-at-work among professionals and small business owners (e.g. Kranendonk 1997), and less information about workers in blue collar and service occupations. Presumably, certain occupations would lend themselves more to consensual sexual unions than others. The mix of workers (age, gender, sexual orientation, race/ethnicity), their relative isolation or proximity, hours requirements, and opportunities for social interaction during the day are all important aspects of jobs that may have an impact on the prevalence of consensual sexual behavior (Mainiero 1986, Haavio-Mannila et al 1988, Powell 1993). But no one has yet undertaken a systematic study of the prevalence of consensual sexual relationships, including marriage patterns, over the gamut of occupations.

Ascertaining the prevalence of sexual relationships among workers in different jobs would not inform larger questions of organizational structure and culture, however. Specific hospitals, universities, factories, and stores may be more or less amenable to the formation of sexual relationships among employees, but there have been no studies to date that have explored general patterns among organizations.

Some information about the structural constraints imposed on workers' intimate relationships is available from the employee manuals of specific organizations and from publicized court cases that contest specific personnel policies. Our brief examination of these sources suggests that there is a wide range of corporate policy and expectations regarding consensual relationships in the workplace. (References for this section are included under "Newspapers and Magazines Consulted" in the Literature Cited.)

At one extreme are organizations that prohibit and closely monitor all intimate involvements among employees. This category includes religious organizations, which typically scrutinize the sexual behavior of their clergy, and the military, which has strict antifraternization policies and bars the employment of gays and lesbians. Some business organizations also fit in this category. Prior to 1994 (when they lost a court battle over this issue), Walmart fired any employee who acknowledged committing adultery. In 1997, Staples Inc. fired the president of the company and a secretary whom he had been dating for violating the company's no fraternization policy. Some businesses, such as the Cracker Barrel restaurant chain, bar the employment of gays and lesbians. Dual-career married partners are often accommodated by these organizations (such is the case in the US military), but some have antinepotism policies, such as UPS (United Parcel Service), although this is increasingly rare (Reed & Bruce 1993, Werbel & Hames 1996).

At the other extreme are organizations that facilitate if not encourage the formation of sexual relationships. Family businesses, including direct sales organizations such as Amway, explicitly seek out and invite the employment of family members (Biggart 1989). Historically black colleges have welcomed the employment of dual-career married couples (Perkins 1997), as do some colleges and universities in remote rural areas (Ferber & Loeb 1997). In the corporate world, there is apparently more acceptance of dating and fraternization in specific industries, such as natural foods (e.g. Ben & Jerry's and Odwalla), and high tech (e.g. Apple, Microsoft, Xerox, Oracle, and Borland Computers). In these organizations, workers are encouraged to socialize at company-sponsored events, and to work-out at the company gymnasium. Ben & Jerry's hosts winter solstice parties for its employees where it subsidizes hotel rooms to discourage drinking and driving. A personnel manager at the company is quoted as saying, "We expect that our employees will date, fall in love, and become partners." They make no effort to limit personal relationships among employees. Some companies in this category, such as AT&T and Johnson's Wax, previously had more restrictive policies that were changed in response to employee litigation.

Most work organizations probably fall somewhere in the middle, promoting some types of sexual relationships and prohibiting others. Several universities now prohibit dating between faculty members and their students as part of their sexual harassment or "amorous relationship" policies, but they permit other types of sexual relationships, such as marriage between faculty members. (Some universities now have "partner programs" that set aside salary lines to hire faculty spouses. See Ferber & Loeb 1997.) Similarly, many corporations (IBM, General Motors, General Electric) enforce an antidating policy only on supervisors and their subordinates. IBM, for example, requires employees to inform management if they are dating a subordinate and to submit to a job transfer. Interestingly, the policy stipulates that it is the supervisor who is required to transfer to a new job.

It would be a fruitful exercise to systematically map out this range for a large number of work organizations in order to ascertain what if any characteristics are shared in common by organizations with similar policies. It may be the case that organizations with steeper hierarchies are more restrictive than "flatter" organizations. Sociologists could also assess the links between specific policy approaches and employment opportunities for various groupings of workers (e.g. men and women; heterosexuals, gays, and lesbians; factory workers, service workers, professionals, etc.) It would be interesting to know, for example, if liberal policies are associated with enhanced or restricted job opportunities for women workers.

Perhaps the best sources of sociological information about consensual sexuality are workplace ethnographies. Several ethnographers are currently interested in the overlap between the public and private lives of employees. A number of recent studies provide rich insights into how organizations monitor and control intimate relationships at work, and also how workers resist that control and pursue sexual pleasure on the job. We briefly review findings from a variety of workplace settings that point the way to fruitful avenues for further study.

In her ethnography of "Amerco," Hochschild (1997) explores why executives, managers, and factory workers in a company with family-friendly policies do not seem to make use of them in order to alleviate "the time bind" surrounding the balancing of work and family needs. While there are structural reasons why workers don't utilize these policies (fear of losing hours, not being seen as a "serious" player, failure of executives to wholeheartedly endorse a family-friendly work culture, etc), Hochschild argues that there has been a cultural shift in the valuation of home and work. She found that many workers, despite their complaints of a time crunch, preferred to spend time at work because they were emotionally supported, appreciated, and rewarded there.

Modern participatory management techniques invite workers to feel relaxed at work by blurring the distinction between work and play (dress down days, free cokes), and by taking on "the role of a helpful relative" in solving employees' personal problems. Hochschild also claims that work may become more interesting than home because the workplace offers a " natural theater" in which workers can "follow the progress of jealousies, sexual attractions, simmering angers" that may be less dramatic at home (1997:201). She argues that several social trends have caused courtship and mate selection to move into the sphere of work:

> The later age for marriage, the higher proportion of unmarried people, and the high divorce rate all create an ever-replenishing courtship pool at work. The gender desegregation of the workplace, and the lengthened working day also provide opportunity for people to meet and develop romantic or quasi-romantic ties. At the factory, romance may develop in the lunchroom, pub, or parking lot; and for upper management levels, at conferences, in "fantasy settings" in hotels and dimly lit restaurants (1996:27).

For example, in Hochschild's interviews with factory workers at Amerco, one man described the joking and "meaningless" flirting relationships that he and his male coworkers have with single women on the shop floor. These women, who have the reputation of "coming on" to married men, are labeled "marriage busters." Hochschild also reports that older women come to work early "to gossip about the cut of a young women's jersey or her new hair coloring—or like the men, they would consider the latest bulletins from the 'marriage busting' front" (1997:188). Although this is merely one example,

Hochschild's ethnographic approach to studying the workplace, and her attention to personal and emotional relationships at work, illustrate the ubiquitous interest in consensual sexuality in a variety of occupations in one work organization.

The term "professional" usually connotes an attitude toward work that is knowledgeable, trustworthy, and asexual. It is a term that is often reserved for very high status occupations, such as doctors, lawyers, and engineers. But a study of doctors and nurses (Giuffre 1995, 1997) found that many health care professionals experience a highly sexualized work culture, which includes a great deal of bantering, touching, and flirting with coworkers. According to a male anesthesiologist:

> You can go into a typical heart operation. We joke all the time about sex. It's a coping mechanism for people in an operating room for stressful situations. People come up to me and hug me, or massage my back, and that's all it's meant to be. Outsiders might think, "Gee, is she coming on to him?" But they don't know that you might have been doing that for six years. Everybody does it. (Giuffre 1997:8)

Of course, in many cases, these sexual interactions do mean more, and they lead to long term intimate relationships.

But several men and women interviewed considered the frequent sexual bantering and touching an important part of their job because it helps them to cope with the stressful nature of their work. The pleasure that many derive from sexual interactions leads some to be wary of efforts to rid their workplaces of sexual harassment. According to a woman urologist:

> Sexual banter happens partly because of the high stress situations. In the operating room, it's even more stressful. You all go in and put on these scrubs. It removes social and sexual boundaries....[There's] teasing and joking and pinching and elbowing. It's fun. That's one reason people like being in that arena. That's part of the camaraderie....I think it's been limited somewhat by all of the sexual harassment cases. It's sad that if someone who I'm working with nudges up to me and elbows me, and I say, "I'm glad I wore my metal bra today to protect myself from your elbow," it's sad that you can't say that in peace anymore. It's a way that men and women interact. It's a form of flirtation. (Giuffre 1997:6)

The sexualized work culture in the operating room is consensual and fun in her view, and it should be beyond the scope of sexual harassment policy. This finding suggests that at least some workers, including highly placed professional women, would likely resent and resist organizations' efforts to monitor and regulate their sexual behaviors and relationships with coworkers, even for the purpose of eradicating sexual harassment.

On the other hand, doctors and nurses in Giuffre's study were very circumspect about engaging in sexual interactions with their patients. Sexual relationships with patients are strictly prohibited and can result in job loss and legal problems for health care professionals (Friedman & Boumil 1995). Physicians and nurses must therefore learn to "desexualize" their interactions with patients, by repressing their personal sexual feelings and denying the sexual desires of their patients (Henslin & Biggs 1998). Thus, even in this highly sexualized work culture, health care professionals recognize as legitimate certain organizational restrictions on their sexual behavior.

What happens when workers violate such restrictions? In Britton's (1995, 1997) ethnographic study of guards in a men's and a women's prison, the topic of sexual relationships between guards and inmates surfaced frequently. At the men's prison, women officers are seen by supervisors and male officers as "willing or unwilling victims of seduction by male inmates" (1995:96), and consequently they are viewed as "weak." There were stories of women who lost their jobs because they developed relationships with inmates. Many women officers attempt to rid their interactions with inmates of any possible sexual interpretation by closely following institutional procedures. Although this lessened the chance that they would be labeled "weak"and sexually vulnerable, it also made it more difficult for them to get along with male officers who expected a degree of flexibility when implementing institutional rules during work with the inmates. Thus, women officers in the men's prison face a double bind: They are disadvantaged by the perception that they will have consensual sexual relationships with male inmates, as well as by their efforts to avoid this perception by sticking closely to institutional procedures.

In the case of the women's prison, lesbian relationships between guards and inmates were a frequent topic of discussion and gossip. Like women who work in many nontraditional occupations, women prison guards are frequently stereotyped as lesbian. This makes them especially susceptible to rumors about relationships with female inmates. In fact, women officers were seen as equally if not more likely to enter into relationships with inmates as were male officers (the converse was not the case at the men's prison), and women were as likely as men to be fired for having sex with inmates. Several officers claimed that there was a high number of inmate/guard relationships as a result of the structural set-up of the women's prison facility barracks, where 34 inmates are guarded by one officer for eight hour shifts. This arrangement of the prison, so unlike the "panopticon" design of the men's prison, promotes rumors about prohibited sexual liaisons and may even facilitate the formation of such relationships.

In the prison and the hospital, as in other "total" institutions, employees are typically forbidden from entering into sexual relationships with "clients." However, as mentioned previously in this article, sexual interactions with clients are part of many jobs in the service sector. Maika Loe (1996), who was employed for six months by the euphemistically renamed "Bazooms" national restaurant chain, discusses how sexual behavior can be built into job descriptions, and also how workers attempt to reshape and negotiate with these demands. At Bazooms, young women workers are hired to wait on mostly male customers. They are required to wear skimpy uniforms, and their figures, make-up, and hair are strictly monitored. In addition to serving food, the "Bazooms Girls," as they are officially called, are required to play with hula hoops, to dance with customers on their birthdays and special occasions (while giving instructions on how to shake salt-and-pepper containers like maracas), and to place orders by reaching up to a line into the kitchen (which exposes their midriffs) while singing.

The culture of the Bazooms workplace is completely sexualized. New workers are required to sign consent forms that certify they are aware of this sexualized environment and they are comfortable with it. Calendars featuring "Bazooms Girls" wearing bikinis are prominently displayed, as are jokes that characterize the waitresses as stupid and gullible ("Caution: Blondes Thinking").

Remarkably, there is a great deal of competition for these jobs: Loe writes that she was one of sixty "lucky" women hired out of an applicant pool of 800! Why do women want to work there? Loe claims that they have a variety of motives: Some are motivated by economic need and limited prospects, but many come to Bazooms to affirm their femininity:

> Working at Bazooms can be "a huge self-esteem boost" (Lori), because Bazooms girls are getting what some consider to be positive attention in the form of flirting, flattery, and daily affirmation that they are indeed sexy, desirable women. Not only do Bazooms girls get attention and affirmations, but they are making commission as well....My fellow waitresses who were single moms tended to be more interested in the tips; others may have been more concerned with affirmation and self-esteem. (Loe 1996:418)

The boost to self-esteem is short-lived and tenuous, however. The women at Bazooms constantly struggle with managers (all men) and customers to protect their autonomy and agency. They also incessantly monitor themselves (and their coworkers) about their appearance and self-worth. Not surprisingly, a high turnover among waitresses is the result.

Organizations sometimes appropriate workers' sexuality and sexual pleasure in more informal ways. Yelvington (1996) conducted an ethnographic study of flirting in a Trinidadian factory. According to Yelvington, all non-kin male-female relationships in Trinidad are sexualized. Through flirting, men and women express their sexuality and sexual desire, but they also use it to exercise power in specifically gendered, ethnic, and class-specific ways.

Yelvington, an anthropologist, studied sexual interactions in a factory stratified by race/ethnicity and gender: All the supervisors were white and East Indian men, and all the line workers were Black and East Indian, and most were women. He found that the white supervisors often flirt with the young Black and East Indian women factory workers, who usually play along with it:

> What the women told me was that they had taken stock of their relative posi-
> tions of influence and power within the factory hierarchy (they were at the
> bottom) and that they need to play along with the supervisor's advances, to
> insinuate the possibility of a future sexual relationship, so that they could en-
> sure smooth workplace relations, and ultimately, keep their jobs. (Yelving-
> ton 1996:323)

Yelvington argues that this flirting between white supervisors and female line workers reproduces the history of white men's access to Black and East Indian women under slavery and indenture. He notes that supervisors who are East Indian do not flirt with the Black women, because doing so would cause them to lose symbolic capital, but they do flirt with the East Indian women line workers.

Yelvington also found a great deal of flirting between men and women line workers. Both men and women sexually objectify each other. Men typically flirt with women in a confrontational verbal style, while women's flirting usu-ally is done with sexy looks and suggestive body language. Yelvington ex-plains that women flirt to "engage [men's] attentions for instrumental pur-poses," such as getting men to collect boxes of parts for them. Occasionally, women do aggressively "heckle" (verbally bait or harass) men; for example, when three women looked out the factory window and caught a man urinating outside, they teased him about his penis. Yelvington sees women's initiation of flirting as a way for women to mitigate and resist men's control. He con-cludes that "Flirting plays with sexual attraction while being a conduit for power relations, and these multiple meanings are fraught with contradiction and value conflict. The culturally 'acceptable' and valorized practice of flirting shades into threat and coercion, which are less acceptable and more able to be resisted legitimately" (Yelvington 1996:328).

Each of the studies that we have reviewed so far describes workplaces that are infused with a heterosexual culture that privileges heterosexual workers. Are there any organizations that value other expressions of sexuality and workers with alternative sexual identities? Dellinger's (1998) study of two organizations in the magazine publishing industry suggests that the official ideology of an organization can greatly impact the organization's willingness to tolerate and, in some cases, to value the contributions of gay, lesbian, and bi-sexual workers. One of the organizations she studied publishes a heterosexual men's pornographic magazine, and the other, a feminist magazine. At the feminist magazine, lesbian perspectives are valued for providing alternative and critical insights into the editorial content of the magazine and for adding an interesting, "exotic" element to workplace interactions and discussions. At the pornographic magazine, the perspectives of gays and lesbians are not valued per se, but in some jobs gays and lesbians may be the preferred workers. The men entrusted with escorting the models to company functions and nude photo shoots, for example, are both gay. Dellinger noted that gay men, and to a lesser extent lesbians, may be sought after for certain jobs because they are seen as better able than heterosexuals to distance themselves and their own sexual desires from the material at hand. In other words, they are perceived to view the pornographic material as simply a "product" to be dealt with objectively. Although in both organizations, gays and lesbians face barriers to achieving the top positions, Dellinger's study suggests that not all occupations within organizations presume and privilege heterosexual workers.

These ethnographies illustrate a range of organizational responses to sexuality. They each provide rich, detailed information about particular workplace contexts. But how generalizable are their findings? More information from a wider array of organizations is needed before we can reach any reliable conclusions, but a few preliminary observations are possible.

Perhaps most importantly, these ethnographies demonstrate that in the study of sexuality in the workplace, context is paramount. The same behavior in different organizational contexts can have different meanings and consequences. Thus, while many service workers are paid to be sexy and to engage in sexual innuendo with customers, in other jobs, mere rumors of sexual behavior or desire can destroy a career, as is the case in the prison or hospital.

The consequences of organizational sexuality for women's careers seem especially significant. Because young women are defined as (hetero)sexually attractive, they are the preferred workers in certain serving jobs. Many women find pleasure in this recognition of their sexual attractiveness, and some profit from it. Yet defining women's value as workers in terms of their sexuality is always short-lived, and may discriminate against older, "less attractive" women. Equating women workers with sexuality may also make women especially vulnerable to dismissal or transfer in organizations that forbid sexual relationships between employees and clients, as is the case in total organizations.

We also see from these studies that different expressions of sexuality are hegemonic in different contexts. Usually heterosexual married individuals are privileged, but occasionally singles, and more rarely, gays and lesbians may be the preferred workers. We need to have more information about the work contexts that are welcoming to nonheterosexuals. Finally, these studies indicate that sexual practices vary considerably among countries. Behavior that is expected and normative in Trinidad may be highly unusual and deviant in another country. A country's laws and norms regarding sexual harassment are likely to have an important impact on the workplace culture of organizations.

CONCLUSION

Sexuality takes many forms in the workplace, and it has multiple and contradictory meanings and consequences. The various literatures we have reviewed show that organizations attempt to control and to monitor sexual behavior among workers, but also that workers resist and negotiate these constraints. Many men and women enjoy the sexualized elements of their work lives, but they nevertheless draw boundary lines between enjoyable, tolerable, and unacceptable sexual behavior. These boundary lines are context-specific, and they can vary for different categories of workers (professional, service, blue collar, etc). Sexual behavior that would scandalize and result in sexual harassment lawsuits in one context could be part of the job description in another.

However, the fact that men and women workers enjoy sexualized interactions in a particular context does not preclude the possibility of dangerous or damaging outcomes. Individuals may use double standards to decide who can and who cannot participate in the sexualized culture of the workplace. Marginalized groups may be overrepresented among those who are excluded, making members of these groups more likely than dominant group members to be charged with sexual harassment for engaging in sexual behaviors. Some organizations also use double standards in deciding who can and cannot engage in sexual relationships, and which relationships are valued and privileged. Furthermore, enjoyable and consensual sexual behavior can be coopted for organizations' purposes, producing ambivalent reactions in the workforce. The waitresses at "Bazooms," for example, are flattered by the public acknowledgment of their sexual attractiveness, yet they lament that they are exploited in ways that deny their sexual agency and self-esteem. Sex at work is rarely either pleasurable or harmful; apparently, it is usually both.

Sociologists still have a great deal to learn about sexuality in the workplace. Our review of the literature has suggested some of the ways that the social organization of sexuality at work may be linked to workplace inequality, stratification, and discrimination—and also to job satisfaction, self-esteem, and happiness. But many unanswered questions remain. Human beings are sexual and consequently so are the places where they work. Organizations will never be able to rid themselves of sexuality (an undesirable goal at any rate), but they should do a better job of shielding workers from harassment and discrimination. Achieving a better understanding of the pleasures and the perils of sexuality at work is an important step in this quest for more humane workplaces.

Literature Cited

Adkins L. 1995. *Gendered Work: Sexuality, Family, and the Labour Market*. Bristol: Open Univ. Press

Anderson CI, Hunsaker PL. 1985. Why there's romancing at the office and why it's everybody's problem. *Personnel* 62:57–63

Astin HS, Milem JF. 1997. The status of academic couples in U.S. institutions. See Ferber & Loeb 1997, pp. 128–55

Baridon AP, Eyler DR. 1994. *Working Together: The New Rules and Realities for Managing Men and Women at Work*. New York: McGraw Hill

Biggart NW. 1989. *Charismatic Capitalism: Direct Selling Organizations in America*. Berkeley: Univ. Calif. Press

Britton DM. 1995. *Sex, violence and supervision: a study of the prison as a gendered organization*. PhD thesis. Univ. Texas, Austin

Britton DM 1997. Gendered organizational logic: policy and practice in men's and women's prisons. *Gender Soc.* 11:796–818

Chancer LS. 1998. *Reconcilable Differences: Confronting Beauty, Pornography, and the Future of Feminism*. Berkeley: Univ. of Calif. Press

Crary M. 1987. Managing attraction and intimacy at work. *Organ. Dynamics* 15:27–41

Dellinger KA. 1998. *Contextualizing workplace opportunities: a comparative case study of gender and sexuality at a feminist and a men's pornographic magazine*. PhD thesis. Univ. Texas, Austin

Dillard JP, Broetzmann SM. 1989. Romantic relationships at work: perceived changes in job-related behaviors as a function of participant's motive, partner's motive, and gender. *J Appl. Soc. Psychol.* 19:93–110

Dillard JP, Witteman H. 1985. Romantic relationships at work: organizational and personal influences. *Hum. Commun. Res.* 12:99–116

Ehrlich S, King R. 1996. Consensual sex or sexual harassment: negotiating meaning. In *Rethinking Language and Gender Research: Theory and Practice*, ed. VL Bergvall, JM Bing, AF Freed, pp. 153–72. London: Longman

Ferber MA, Loeb JW. 1997. *Academic Couples: Problems and Promises*. Urbana: Univ. Ill. Press

Folgero IS, Fjeldstad IH. 1995. On duty—off guard: cultural norms and sexual harassment in service organizations. *Organ. Stud.* 16(2):299–313

Friedman J, Boumil MM. 1995. *Betrayal of*

Trust: Sex and Power in Professional Relationships*. Westport, CT: Praeger

Gallop J. 1997. *Feminist Accused of Sexual Harassment*. Durham: Duke Univ. Press

Giuffre PA. 1997. *Labeling sexual harassment in hospitals: a case study of doctors and nurses*. Presented at the Sociologists Against Sexual Harassment meeting, Toronto

Giuffre PA. 1995. *The management of sexuality: a case study of doctors and nurses*. Presented at the Am. Sociol. Assoc. annual meeting, Washington, DC

Giuffre PA, Williams CL. 1994. Boundary lines: labeling sexual harassment in restaurants. *Gender Soc.* 8:378–401

Hajdin M. 1997. Why the fight against sexual harassment is misguided. In *Sexual Harassment: A Debate*, ed. L LeMoncheck, M Hajdin, pp. 97–163. Lanham, MD: Rowman & Littlefield

Hallinan KM. 1993. Invasion of privacy or protection against sexual harassment: co-employee dating and employer liability. *Columbia J. Law Soc. Problems* 26:435–64

Henslin JM, Biggs MA. 1998. Behavior in public places: the sociology of the vaginal examination. In *Down to Earth Sociology: Introductory Readings*, ed. JM Henslin. New York: Free Press

Herbst MS. 1996. Employers may regulate some workplace romances. *Natl. Law J.* (February 26): C19-20

Haavio-Mannila E, Kauppinen-Toropainen K, Kandolin I. 1988. The effect of sex composition of the workplace on friendship, romance, and sex at work. In *Women and Work: An Annual Review*, Vol. 3, ed. BA Gutek, AH Stromberg, L Larwood. Newbury Park: Sage

Hochschild AR. 1997. *The Time Bind: When Work becomes Home and Home becomes Work*. New York: Metropolitan Books

Hochschild AR. 1996. The emotional geography of work and family life. In *Gender Relations in Public and Private*, ed. L Morris, ES Lyon. New York: St. Martin's Press

Kranendonk B. 1997. *Married and Making a Living: Couples Who Own Small Franchise Businesses*. New York: Garland

Laumann EO, Gagnon JH, Michael RT, Michaels S. 1994. *The Social Organization of Sexuality: Sexual Practices in the United States*. Chicago: Univ. Chicago Press

LeMoncheck L. 1997. *Loose Women, Lecherous Men: A Feminist Philosophy of Sex*. New York: Oxford Univ. Press

Lobel SA, Quinn RE, St. Clair L, Warfield A. 1994. Love without sex: the impact of psychological intimacy between men and women at work. *Organ. Dynamics* 23:4–17

Loe M. 1996. Working for men–at the intersection of power, gender, and sexuality. *Sociol. Inquiry* 66:399–421

Mainiero LA. 1986. A review and analysis of power dynamics in organizational romances. *Acad. Manage. Rev.* 11:750–62

Massengill D, Peterson DJ. 1995. Legal challenges to no fraternization rules. *Labor Law J.* 46:429–35

Myers MF. 1988. *Doctors' Marriages: A Look at the Problems and Solutions.* New York: Plenum Medical Book

Neville K. 1990. *Corporate Attractions: An Inside Account of Sexual Harassment with the New Sexual Rules for Men and Women on the Job.* Washington, DC: Acropolis Books

Perkins LM. 1997. For the good of the race: married African-American academics—a historical perspective. See Ferber & Loeb 1997, pp. 80-105

Pierce CA, Aguinis H. 1997. Bridging the gap between romantic relationships and sexual harassment in organizations. *J. Organ. Behav.* 18:197–200

Pierce CA, Byrne D, Aguinis H. 1996. Attraction in organizations: a model of workplace romance. *J. Organ. Behav.* 15:5–32

Powell GN. 1993. *Women and Men in Management.* Newbury Park: Sage

Pycior HM, Slack NG, Abir-Am PG. 1996. *Creative Couples in the Sciences.* New Brunswick, NJ: Rutgers Univ. Press

Quinn RE. 1977. Coping with Cupid: the formation, impact and management of romantic relationships in organizations. *Admin. Sci. Q.* 22:30–45

Reed CM, Bruce WM. 1993. Dual-career couples in the public sector: a survey of personnel policies and practices. *Public Personnel Manage.* 22:187–99

Schneider B. 1994. [Editor's introduction] *Gender Soc.* 8:293–96

Schultz V. 1998. Reconceptualizing sexual harassment. *Yale Law J.* 107:1683–1805

Segal JA. 1993. Love: what's work got to do with it? *HR Magazine* 38:37–41

Stan AM. 1995. *Debating Sexual Correctness: Pornography, Sexual Harassment, Date Rape, and the Politics of Sexual Equality.* New York: Delta

Summers RJ, Myklebust K. 1992. The influence of a history of romance on judgements and responses to a complaint of sexual harassment. *Sex Roles* 27:345–57

Warfield A. 1987. Co-worker romances: impact on the work group and on career-oriented women. *Personnel* May: 22–35

Weeks J. 1986. *Sexuality.* London: Tavistock.

Werbel JD, Hames DS. 1996. Anti-nepotism reconsidered: the case of husband and wife employment. *Group Organ. Manage.* 21: 365–79

Westoff LA. 1985. *Corporate Romance: How to Avoid It, Live Through It, or Make It Work for You.* New York: Times Books

Williams CL. 1998. Sexual harassment in organizations: a critique of current research and policy. *Sexuality Culture* 1:19-43

Williams CL, Britton DM. 1995. Sexuality and work. In *Introduction to Social Problems,* ed. C Calhoun, G Ritzer. New York: McGraw-Hill Primis

Wolkenbreit R. 1997. In order to form a more perfect union: applying no-spouse rules to employees who meet at work. *Columbia J. Law Soc. Problems* 31:119–65

Yelvington, KA. 1996. Flirting in the factory. *J. Royal Anthropol. Inst.* 2:313–333

Young BS. 1995. Family matters. *HR Magazine* 40:30–31

Newspapers and Magazines Consulted

Austin-American Statesman, 2-14-98
Details Magazine, February 1998
Fortune Magazine, 10-3-94
New York Times, 4-24-96, 10-26-97, 2-16-98
Newsweek, 6-16-97
Psychology Today, March-April, 1995.
USA Today Magazine, November, 1995
Wall Street Journal, 2-14-95, 2-4-98
Washington Post, 11-2-97, 1-29-98

Annu. Rev. Sociol. 1999. 25:95–119

WHAT HAS HAPPENED TO THE US LABOR MOVEMENT? Union Decline and Renewal

Dan Clawson[1] and Mary Ann Clawson[2]

[1]Department of Sociology, University of Massachusetts at Amherst, Amherst, Massachusetts 01003; e-mail: clawson@sadri.umass.edu, and [2]Department of Sociology, Wesleyan University, Middletown, Connecticut 06459; e-mail: mclawson@wesleyan.edu

KEY WORDS: trade unions, labor organizing, AFL-CIO, employer anti-union offensive, labor movement future

---

ABSTRACT

For many years, US trade unions declined in union density, organizing capacity, level of strike activity, and political effectiveness. Labor's decline is variously attributed to demographic factors, inaction by unions themselves, the state and legal system, globalization, neoliberalism, and the employer offensive that ended a labor-capital accord. The AFL-CIO New Voice leadership elected in 1995, headed by John Sweeney, seeks to reverse these trends and transform the labor movement. Innovative organizing, emphasizing the use of rank-and-file intensive tactics, substantially increases union success; variants include union building, immigrant organizing, feminist approaches, and industry-wide non–National Labor Relations Board (or nonboard) organizing. The labor movement must also deal with participatory management or employee involvement programs, while experimenting with new forms, including occupational unionism, community organizing, and strengthened alliances with other social movements.

INTRODUCTION

In 1995, the American Federation of Labor—Congress of Industrial Organizations (AFL-CIO), the body that unites most United States unions into a feder-

0360-0572/99/0815-0095$08.00

ated organization, experienced its first contested election, in which the insurgent slate won, and the victors, led by John Sweeney as president, announced their intent to transform the labor movement (Sweeney 1996, Welsh 1997). Only rarely does a massive institution directly and publicly confront the spectre of its own demise; even more rarely does a bureaucratic organization, albeit one with social movement origins, attempt rejuvenation through a return to its activist roots. This moment of critique and attempted reconstruction prompts a similar response from social scientists, including sociologists, who have devoted surprisingly little attention to the labor movement.

As a discipline centrally concerned with processes of institutional functioning, social movement activism, and class differentiation and domination, this relative neglect is striking. Even scholars who study class or the labor process tend to neglect the importance of group processes of struggle, "focusing on atomized individual workers as the unit of analysis" (Lembcke et al 1994:117). This emphasis has both impoverished sociology and led labor studies "to recede from the intellectual scene, principally becoming a professional area for training union officials and negotiators" (Lembcke et al 1994:114). But outstanding work of the past ten to fifteen years exemplifies the rewards of a renewed focus on the labor movement; four recent collections are especially notable as introductions, each including the work of both academic and labor scholars (Bronfenbrenner et al 1998, Fraser & Freeman 1997, Friedman et al 1994, Mantsios 1998; for a review of earlier work, see Freeman & Medoff 1984 and Cornfield 1991).

Unions provide a laboratory for the analysis of a variety of social phenomena. Thirteen million members are in AFL-CIO unions, including over five million women, two million African Americans, and one million Latino/as, with many additional members in nonfederated organizations like the National Education Association. Even at the present time, strikes involve some 300,000 members per year, and unions successfully organize more than 250,000 workers yearly, with perhaps an equivalent number involved in unsuccessful organizing campaigns. These actions offer social movement scholars an underused resource: the opportunity for systematic study of widely practiced, and often highly risky, forms of collective action. At the same time, labor studies and the labor movement can only profit from contact with sociology's broader contextualization and more explicit theorizing.

The overriding reality that frames the recent history of the labor movement and the social science literature we examine is a dramatic change in the relations between business and unions. Until recently, the dominant scholarly perspective assumed the existence of a postwar "accord" between management and labor, an arrangement whereby business accepted unions and unions became the de facto allies of management, helping to regulate and coopt worker discontent (Aronowitz 1973, Burawoy 1979, Fantasia 1988, Piven &

Cloward 1977). For many critics on the left, the accord meant that unions had lost their oppositional character, while capital valued the benefits conferred by a unionized workforce.

This understanding has been shaken by events of the late 1970s and early 1980s, when corporate forces assumed a far more confrontational stance, and unions found themselves under relentless attack. The vehemence of the employer mobilization suggests that the accord may never have been as fully accepted by capital as many had supposed, that instead capital may simply have recognized the strength of labor and concluded that certain kinds of opposition were not (then) feasible.

The labor movement has responded to this assault in a variety of ways. Some approaches call for a new militancy, supported by innovative and aggressive organizing to confront employer opposition, while others seek ways to recreate the accord and reestablish unions as valued partners. This essay considers directions for the future of the movement by examining explanations for union decline and initiatives for labor's revitalization.

UNION DECLINE

The fact of union decline is beyond dispute. Private sector union density (the percentage of the labor force in unions) declined from 39% in 1954 to 10% today. Decline in membership strength has been accompanied during the past two decades by a larger loss of efficacy. From 1969 to 1979, strikes involved more than 950,000 workers in every year; from 1987 to 1996, by contrast, despite a larger labor force, strikes never involved even half a million workers. Many more strikes were broken, with employees losing their jobs. From 1945 to 1980, union wage settlements almost always involved wage increases; thereafter, unions frequently made concessions on both wages and benefits (Griffin et al 1990, Moody 1988:165-91, Wrenn 1985). Politically as well, unions had diminishing clout, in part because of increasing Republican dominance, but even more so because unions exercised less and less leverage within the Democratic party.

Five major perspectives, found both within the labor movement and among scholars, attempt to explain such changes. These focus respectively on (*a*) demographic changes, (*b*) the role of the union itself as an institution, (*c*) the state, especially the legal system, (*d*) globalization and neoliberalism, and (*e*) the employer anti-union offensive.

Demographic Factors

Even with no change in unions or the legal climate, union strength would decline if unions were strong in population groups and sectors of the economy that were shrinking. Depending on the time period studied, the methodology used, and the comprehensiveness of the factors taken into account, analysts believe that structural and compositional factors account for 20% to 60% of the decrease in union density (Dickens & Leonard 1985, Farber 1990, Freeman 1985, Goldfield 1987, Western 1997). Many of the significant factors are widely discussed and easily understood: geographic shifts from the Rustbelt to the Sunbelt, occupational shifts from blue collar to white collar, and changes in the gender distribution of the work force. Other factors are less obvious: Western's (1997:120) analyses indicate that the tremendous growth in the US labor force explains nearly 9 percentage points of the 15% postwar American union decline, because a rapidly growing labor force diminishes union density unless unions make huge efforts to organize new workers. Although Western provides probably the best examination of these factors, he himself prefers institutional explanations, criticizing the assumption of the econometric approach that "the key agents are workers and employers, rather than unions." This leads, he says, to an institutionally "thin view of labor movements," which fails to recognize the central role of "organizing effort and the active construction of shared interests" (1997:103).

The Union Itself

If, as Western suggests, unionization results from active effort, then the labor movement must bear a significant share of the blame for its own decline. Goldfield (1987:208) defines the problem as a lack of will: "Unions can put out the necessary effort to win when they have to" but "most of the time... do not put out this sufficient effort." An AFL-CIO report similarly argues, "instead of organizing, unions hunkered down" and "collectively chose the shortsighted strategy of trying to protect current contracts of members instead of organizing new members" (AFL-CIO 1996:5). In consequence, the most dynamic sectors of the economy, including service occupations "employing large numbers of women and people of color," as well as "the growing ranks of professional, technical, and white collar employees, except for those in the public sector," were "left nearly untouched by union activity" during the postwar decades of labor's greatest strength (Bronfenbrenner et al 1998:5–6).

The flawed record of unions vis á vis women and racial minorities is reflected not only in failures of organizing, but by an internal reluctance or inability to address issues raised by the feminist and civil rights movements. Women's presence as union members, for example, falls short of their presence in the labor force as a whole, while gains in leadership have been "quite modest" in relation to gains in membership (Milkman 1985:302, Melcher et al 1992, Cornfield 1993, Roby 1995). More fundamentally, Milkman argues, women have been organized not as women, but "as members of occupational groups which happened to be largely female in composition," with the result that women were "now squarely *in*, but generally still not *of* the labor move-ment" (Milkman 1985:302). To the extent that men and women differ in pre-ferred cultural styles and forms of leadership, unions have tended to reflect and to value male (often macho) approaches (Cobble 1993, Feldberg 1987, Sacks 1988).

While the late 1960s saw the emergence of the League of Revolutionary Black Workers as a rank-and-file protest movement (Geschwender 1977), more recent responses such as the Coalition of Labor Union Women and the Coalition of Black Trade Unionists have been largely concentrated among elected officials and staff, focusing, in the case of CLUW, on placing more women in leadership positions "without challenging the basic structure or character of the labor movement" (Milkman 1985:305).

Labor became increasingly distant from other social movements, and un-ions were not seen—either by unions themselves or by social movement activ-ists—as a primary means of addressing the issues raised by the civil rights, feminist, and environmental movements. Instead these concerns were primar-ily addressed through new legal rights, governmental regulation, new social movement organizations, and class action lawsuits. Unions participated in these processes but were not generally regarded as crucial actors.

The decline of organizing in the postwar era coincides with an increased fo-cus on contract negotiation and the enforcement of work rules through the grievance system, both of which led to an increase in union staff. Within this framework, the union's shop-floor presence was expressed primarily through its negotiation of work rules and their enforcement through the grievance pro-cedure. Grievances were virtually the only way for workers to address working conditions and conflicts with supervisors within a Taylorist organization of production; the grievance procedure accomplishes this through a multi-step, quasi-judicial process that strengthens the role of staff and attenuates workers' involvement (Spencer 1977). Burawoy (1979:110) notes the individualizing effect of the grievance process: "Each time a *collective* grievance or an issue of principle outside the contract, affecting the entire membership... is raised" the union representative responded "Have you got a grievance? ... If you haven't, give the floor to someone else."

The limitations of the staff-driven union were also evident in politics. Form's (1995) detailed study of Ohio demonstrates that "most union officials think they have a political education program, but most members are not aware of it" (p. 255). Four-fifths were not aware of their union's political action program (p. 251), and very few members were involved in electoral and party activities. Croteau (1995) argues workers hold many progressive political views, but—for a variety of reasons, with the weakness of unions one of the most important—workers doubt their ability to have a political impact and hence see little point in getting involved.

Proponents of an institutional explanation of union decline emphasize that internal factors rendered unions less likely to devote energy and resources to the task of organizing, and less likely to present to potential members a vision of a dynamic, compelling movement organization. This is, however, an interactive process; unions did not devote more energy and resources to organizing in part because of the powerful barriers to effective organizing that originate outside of the union itself, barriers rooted in labor law and in the vigor and resourcefulness of employer opposition to unionization.

The State and Legal System

The United States has not had a social democratic or labor party, and the legal frame creates more difficult conditions for unions here than in virtually any other democracy. The stated purpose of the New Deal industrial relations system was to institutionalize relations between employers and workers and thus provide them with a mechanism, collective bargaining, for resolving differences with minimal disruption (McCammon 1990, 1993, 1994). Unions are part of a legal regime that shapes and channels worker organization and activism through specification of legally permissible and impermissible modes of collective action and through the law's very definition of workplace representation.

Schizophrenia is the dominant characteristic of US labor law. For union recognition, American labor law grants/guarantees workers the right to "self-organize" via the formation of unions, a right realized through the federally mandated and supervised representation election that establishes a particular union as the sole legally recognized bargaining agent for that workplace (or bargaining unit). At the same time, the law protects the right of employers to influence and intervene in this process: "Unique among industrial democracies, US labor law allows employers actively to oppose their employees' decision to unionize" (Comstock & Fox 1994:90, Tomlins 1985), and a series of court and administrative decisions have further narrowed employee-union rights while expanding employer rights (Brody 1997, Gross 1995). A similar split operates in regard to strikes: Workers are guaranteed the right to strike and may not be penalized for doing so, but employers are guaranteed the right to maintain production during a strike and may hire permanent replacement workers. Thus, workers may not be fired for engaging in a strike, but they may be permanently replaced—an academic distinction at best (Fantasia 1993).

Globalization and Neoliberalism

The US legal system creates uniquely unfavorable conditions for organizing or striking, but this framework takes on greater significance in the context of two 1970s changes—a capitalist offensive that involved both political mobilization and relentless hostility to unions (Clawson &Clawson 1987), and a complex of economic changes generally referred to as globalization, but which also includes a hegemonic neoliberal discourse and the ideological triumph of the market over all alternative forms of structuring activity.

Western (1997) finds that, in advanced industrial societies, through the 1970s, the trajectory of union strength varied from one country to another. In 13 of the 18 countries studied, for example, union density increased during the 1970s—with the United States the most notable exception. As globalization, the market, and neoliberalism took hold in the 1980s, however, union power weakened in almost all advanced industrial societies. An important contributing factor was the fragmentation of labor markets, as bargaining moved from an industry to a company level, or from a company to a plant level, with workers increasingly competing against one another (Moody 1988). Silver (1995) confirms a sharp drop in labor unrest in core countries in the 1980s but shows that this is paired with a slight rise in labor unrest in the semiperiphery and a sharp rise in the periphery; she argues labor movements are weakened in areas of capital emigration and strengthened in areas of capital in-migration.

Globalization hurts unions in at least two ways. First, "a growing proportion of core workers are now in direct competition with semiperipheral labor"; second, "as the state's ability to manage its share of the world economy declines, movements that rely on state power suffer as well" (Boswell & Stevis 1997:291, 289). Capital's operations are vastly more globalized than those of unions, whose efforts at international solidarity have been fragmentary and, so far at least, largely ineffective (Boswell & Stevis 1997, Borgers 1996).

Floating exchange rates, the increased power of the International Monetary Fund, and de-regulation were politically instituted, as was the current culturally dominant understanding that these are technologically mandated, beyond human control, exogenous to politics, and in effect the only rational way to organize almost any activity. Once instituted, however, these forms exercise a substantial independent effect, constantly reinforced by a pervasive effort to maintain and extend neoliberal interpretations (Tilly 1995, Moody 1997). Under floating exchange rates, state policy is driven primarily by financial flows, not job markets. The world system is considerably more polycentric than it was forty years ago; neither production nor labor markets are confined to national borders. Although the United States is one of the economies least vulnerable to world markets, it is perhaps the most thoroughly dominated by neoliberalism. Out-sourcing, privatization, and the growth of part-time and contingent employment are often as significant as "globalization" per se. Together these processes pose enormous problems for labor unions, whose very existence *necessitates* the restriction and regulation of labor markets. In order to succeed, unions *must* raise the price of labor above what would exist if conditions were left entirely to capital and the market.

Employer Offensive

Although these changes are world-wide, the level of employer hostility to labor is unique to the United States. This hostility is found in many areas—decertifications, concession bargaining, and strikes, for example—but is most marked in organizing campaigns. The 1970s saw the emergence of systematic attempts by employers to maintain "union free" workplaces through delays, "information campaigns," and outright intimidation (Friedman et al 1994). One early indicator of increasing employer resistance to organizing was a decline in the proportion of elections where employers simply agreed to hold the election, without contesting the process through the National Labor Relations Board. "In 1962, 46.1 percent of all NLRB elections were conducted as consent elections," contrasted with only 8.6% in 1977 (Prosten 1979:39). Delay typically represents both a tactic and an indicator of a larger management strategy, most often associated with the use of consulting firms for systematic anti-union campaigns.

Studies conducted by Bronfenbrenner (1993, 1997) and by Bronfenbrenner & Juravich (1998) give the most comprehensive picture of such campaigns. Looking at NLRB elections in both 1986–1987 and 1994, Bronfenbrenner & Juravich (1998:22–23) find that 87% of employers used outside consultants, while 64% held five or more captive audience meetings, in which the company requires all employees to listen to anti-union presentations during work hours—a level of access, within a coercive atmosphere, that cannot be equaled by union organizers, who are are barred from company property and can talk to workers only away from the job. Bronfenbrenner & Juravich found, moreover, that 76% used one-on-one meetings with supervisors, who were trained by the outside consultants to query the worker about his or her views, make the anti-union case, and demand a response.

Finally, in what is surely the most devastating action an employer can take, 28% discharged one or more workers for union activity. Similarly, Weiler's analysis of NLRB data show that in 1980 the odds were one in twenty that a union supporter would be fired for supporting an organizing drive (Weiler 1983:1781), and even in cases where employers are ruled to have illegally fired a worker, they can, using the appeals process, delay reinstatement for up to three years (Weiler 1983:1795). Moreover, "of employees who did go back, nearly 80% were gone within a year or two, and most blamed their departure on vindictive treatment by the employer" (Weiler 1983:1792). Levitt's (1993) memoir, *Confessions of a Union Buster*, a detailed narrative of years of systematic anti-union activity by a leading (and now repentant) management consultant, gives a sense of these tactics in operation, tactics which lead Geoghegan (1991:255) to conclude: "an employer who didn't break the law would have to be what economists call an 'irrational firm.'"

The chilling impact that such coercive tactics exert on workers' right to organize may be seen in their effects on representation elections. Bronfenbrenner & Juravich (1998) find that union win rates were much lower when the employer used more than five aggressive tactics (32%) than when the employer used five or less (48%); a logit analysis shows that "the probability of the union winning the election declined by 7 percent for each aggressive antiunion tactic the employer used" (p. 32). As Seeber & Cooke (1983) concluded, on the basis of an earlier state-by-state analysis of NLRB data, using the proportion of consent elections as a proxy for employer resistance, this resistance is "the salient factor in the recent decline in union organizing success" (p. 43; see also Farber 1990, Fantasia 1993, Freeman & Kleiner 1990). One study argued that employer resistance did not matter (Getman et al 1976), but this study has been subjected to devastating criticism (Dickens 1983). Increasingly, employers continue the same tactics *after* the union wins an election, so that even if the union "wins," 20 to 25% of the time no contract is ever negotiated (Cooke 1985, Prosten 1979, Weiler 1984).

Employer hostility is most visible during organizing drives (or strikes), but Kochan et al (1986) compellingly argue that this is only a fraction of the problem (p. 79). Citing Dickens & Leonard's (1985) finding that "union coverage would still have fallen if unions had won 100% of the elections held since 1950," Kochan et al locate the causes of union decline in a more fundamental and far-reaching management strategy: operating within the collective bargaining framework at unionized worksites while simultaneously using expansion over time to create a nonunion sector supported by new modes of personnel management. Guided by an informal rule of thumb that "no plant which is unionized will be expanded onsite" (quoted in Kochan et al 1986:263), employers have channeled investment into nonunion production sites, which offer a technological edge as well as a wage and benefit differential over the increasingly obsolescent unionized units. In this account, corporate power lies principally in its control over investment decisions and personnel innovation, rather than the ability to engage in short-term, case-by-case manipulation of labor law.

THE FUTURE OF LABOR

On the most obvious level, labor's challenge is clear: Simply to maintain their current proportion of the workforce, unions must organize 300,000 workers a year; to gain significant ground unions would need to organize a million a year (Rothstein 1996a). The enormity of the task suggests it will not be accomplished incrementally through a superior replication of present practice (but see Shostak 1991).

Each stage of capitalism—whether we call it a social structure of accumulation or a regulatory regime—has been associated with a characteristic form of union. The craft system of the late nineteenth century spawned the American Federation of Labor and a set of craft-based unions; the mass production (Taylorism, Fordism) of the mid twentieth century is associated with the Congress of Industrial Organizations and industrial unionism. Social movement theorists argue that such large-scale transformations are contingent on major shifts in the structure of political opportunities, the incentives for collective action, and the ability of economic and social institutions to inhibit resistance (Tarrow 1994, Piven & Cloward 1979). Probably only two things are certain. First, although labor history is a rich and necessary source of insight, *if* there is a new surge of unionism, it will take a different form (or forms) from the past. Second, institutional transformation does not appear de novo, but rather emerges as a synthesis of previously existing initiatives and experiments, successful practices and apparent failures. In this section we attempt to identify contemporary sites of innovation and proposals for change, examining the strikes of the 1980s, emerging models of organizing, attempts to revitalize unions as activist organizations, and the conceptualization and development of new forms of organization, both inside and outside unions as they are presently constituted.

Strikes in the Eighties

The strike is part of an established repertoire of collective action; its success requires solidarity by a large fraction of the workforce, at a considerable economic cost, by people usually operating close to the margin, for an open-ended period of time. Roughly from 1948 to 1975, the available form in the United States was a strike officially declared by the union and acceded to by management, involving workers withholding services and picketing, with the picketing usually symbolic but widely honored (in an indication of the cultural legitimacy and counter-hegemonic recognition accorded unions), and the resolution a compromise depending on which side could (economically) outlast the other.

That form was challenged in the late 1970s by an employer offensive built around hiring scabs, restoring production, and systematically working to break the union (Clawson et al 1982). Union busting responses to strikes were well under way by the time President Reagan fired PATCO workers, but that action, and labor's failure to respond effectively, legitimated what had been a minority tendency.

Unions responded in a variety of ways, none completely effective. As noted earlier, the sheer volume of strikes dropped dramatically, and unions developed creative alternatives to the strike using brief in-plant actions to build worker solidarity and pressure the company to settle (Moody 1988:238).

But some unions chose militant confrontation. Two strikes in particular—the Arizona miners' strike against the Phelps Dodge Company and the strike of packing house workers against Hormel (the P-9 strike)—were the focus of extensive media coverage and produced a voluminous literature, both journalistic and scholarly, including two books on the Phelps Dodge strike (Kingsolver 1989, Rosenblum 1995) and four (plus a feature length documentary film) on P-9 (Hage & Klauda 1989, Green 1990, Rachleff 1993, Schleuning 1994).

Taken as social movement events, these strikes displayed innovative mobilization strategies that often galvanized their locals to creative displays of militancy. The P-9 strike is the exemplar, with its use of community mass meetings, demonstrations, and outreach to other trade unionists, both regionally and nationally. Two practices are especially noteworthy. The corporate campaign sought to broaden the struggle by pressuring the financial institutions that supported the company, involving members more actively in the strike and building public support by taking the workers' case to the community and the media. Equally noteworthy in these strikes was the emergence of forms of women's activism that went beyond the traditional auxiliary function to include study groups, direct action campaigns, and community leadership (Schleuning 1994, Kingsolver 1989).

These strikes were also important because of the way in which they were made to represent the labor movement. For many observers, the P-9 local appeared as a model of inventive working-class activism that demonstrated the potential of union action. But the best known strikes of this type, including P-9, were defeated, so that union struggles were increasingly identified as acts of isolated resistance, dead-end actions, doomed to failure no matter how energetic their struggles. When a union won such a strike, as at Ravenswood (Juravich & Bronfenbrenner 1999), the margin of success appeared to depend on the national and local union both fully supporting a militant struggle (both P-9 and Phelps Dodge involved major conflicts between the local and national), combined with a somewhat more vulnerable ownership structure. Nonetheless the victory was limited in character and came at a high price. Finally, these strikes raised the issue of how best to respond to demands for concessions: When is it more effective to resist all demands for lowered wages and loss of benefits and work rules, and when is it advisable to make a strategic retreat in order to save the union as an institution and the collective bargaining framework itself.

Another union response involved a new strategy: espousing a nontraditional issue that mobilizes new constituencies and combining that with a classic strike to increase pressure on the employer. Probably the most notable examples of this in the 1980s were strikes (at Yale University, San Jose, and Contra Costa County, California) focused on the issue of comparable worth and women's pay. In each case, the strike was preceded by a long period of agitation, education, and explicit attempts to build community and political support (Blum 1991, Johnston 1994, Ladd-Taylor 1985), and the pressure to settle came as much from a successful public relations campaign as from economic disruption. The 1997 UPS strike, focused on part-time and contingent work, was another noteworthy incident; we do not as yet have a scholarly study.

Models of Organizing

Because of the unremitting and aggressive hostility of so many employers to unionization, and because the law permits employers to actively intervene in the election process, the fact that a majority of workers at a given site want representation is no longer sufficient to achieve certification, despite the intent of federal labor law. Bronfenbrenner (1994) found, for example, that 73% of the time unions did not file for an election until a majority of the unit was signed up —and nonetheless only 43% of the campaigns were won.

What is the likelihood that that will change, and where would change come from? Piven & Cloward (1977:36–37) argue that "Protest wells up in response to momentous changes in the institutional order. It is not created by organizers and leaders ... Protest movements are shaped by institutional conditions, and not by the purposive efforts of leaders and organizers." (See also Tarrow 1994, McAdam 1982.) In contrast, Voss & Sherman (1997), focusing not on periods of mass insurgency but rather on union organizing today, argue that the key to both the level of organizing activity and the use of innovative tactics is pressure from above, typically from the national union, not an upsurge from below—workers get mobilized because an organizer activates and channels them, and local unions undertake organizing because the national union pressures and rewards them for doing so. We would argue both analyses are correct: To use the Kuhnian analogy, Piven & Cloward identify what is crucial to the key periods of activity that bring paradigm shifts; Voss & Sherman show what happens in between, in periods of what might be called normal science. The current period, we would argue, is one of normal science, but the normal science of today's unions is in active search of a new paradigm and is experimenting with innovative forms.

One early step by the AFL-CIO was the creation of the Organizing Institute (OI) to train organizers, many of them recent college graduates (Foerster 1996). OI training heavily emphasized housecalls—organizers and union activists visiting workers in their homes (away from employer interference)— and focused on professional organizers willing to travel anywhere for a campaign and then move long distances for the next campaign. In opposition to this, Early (1998) has argued for reliance on local organizers, many of them rank-and-file workers, rooted in their communities.

Bronfenbrenner & Juravich's (1998) random sample of organizing campaigns in 1986–1987 and 1994, examining both employer and union tactics, stresses that "it takes more than housecalls." Employers' antiunion tactics reduce the union win rate; a change in labor law, or enforcement of existing law, would obviously benefit unions. But even in the absence of such changes, which do not appear imminent, union tactics matter, and success depends on using a wide range of different forms of worker involvement: "The probability of the union winning the election increases by as much as 9 percent for each rank-and-file intensive tactic the union uses" (p. 32). As contrasted with the house call model, this approach emphasizes the fostering of social networks throughout the worksite and looks beyond the certification vote toward the building of an activist union through its emphasis on leadership development and worker involvement.

This research has been widely discussed in union circles and influenced leading organizers and locals but has not been widely incorporated into practice: "In 1994 only 15 percent of the lead organizers surveyed ran comprehensive campaigns that used more than five rank-and-file-intensive tactics" (Bronfenbrenner & Juravich 1998:29). This may be explained by Voss & Sherman's (1997) finding that "fully innovative" locals shared three characteristics: a perception of the seriousness of union decline, pressure for organizing from the national union, and the presence in the local of organizers with social movement experience gained outside the labor movement.

Rank-and-file intensive tactics, however, may take many different forms. We examine four case studies, each of them among the 15% that use more than five rank-and-file tactics, to indicate some of those possible forms. First, Fantasia's (1988) study of a hospital workers' organizing drive explicitly focuses on the use of a "union building," or rank and file intensive approach, and shows the process by which the organizer facilitates the active mobilization of workers into the organizing process. Markowitz (1998) supplements and extends this by contrasting two campaigns that sharply differed in the extent to which they involved the workers in the organizing process, and the consequences of this for workers' relation to the union, and the meaning of union, after the organizing drive ended. Both find that rank-and-file intensive organizing campaigns create a new culture among workers, developing their abilities and transforming their political understanding.

Second, Delgado (1993) examines what is often seen as an overwhelming barrier to organizing: a workforce composed primarily of undocumented workers. Contrary to expectation, he found that, at least for Los Angeles area Latino workers in light manufacturing in the mid 1980s, fear of discharge was a more significant obstacle than fear of deportation. The campaign's success depended not only on the normal strengths of union building approaches, but also on the mobilization of ethnic solidarities between the workers and the Latino organizers, and the creation of community, especially through drinking and (company sponsored) soccer games. Studies of California show that even in the more hostile climate of the 1990s, immigration status, although it is one additional factor to be considered, by no means prevents organizing and continues to offer sources of strength as well as vulnerability (Milkman 1999). Kwong (1997) reports a very different experience for Chinese undocumented workers in New York; although they too can be organized when unions make the effort, their fear of deportation is much higher.

The campaigns to organize Harvard clerical workers provide a third example of innovative organizing, this one self-consciously based on the fact that most of the workers organized, and most of the organizers, were women (Hoerr 1997). Much union organizing raises the level of confrontation; at Harvard the aim was to reduce the level of fear. Thus, the union's central slogan was that "it's not anti-Harvard to be pro-union," and on the day of the voting, union supporters surprised Harvard by decorating the campus with thousands of colored balloons, to create a festive, implicitly "feminine," atmosphere—a tactic that Harvard protested as an unfair labor practice. These gendered differences in style may help explain Milkman's (1992) finding that if a workplace is predominantly male, union organizing is likely to succeed; as the proportion of women increases and the workforce becomes more mixed, the likelihood of organizing success drops significantly; as the proportion of women increases still further, the highest levels of success are attained when the workforce is predominantly women.

A fourth instructive case is Los Angeles Justice for Janitors (Waldinger et al 1998, Fisk et al 1999), probably the most widely discussed campaign of the past twenty years. Successful and creative in at least two major ways, its first innovation was the insistence that it is not enough to organize 1 or 2 or 10 worksites; unless the union can organize a substantial proportion of the total industry, it cannot significantly affect wages and working conditions.

Second, the campaign used the strategy of organizing outside the NLRB framework, in response to employers' ability to frustrate labor law. This meant that the union ignored the formal employers, the cleaning contractors who technically hired the workers, and instead targeted the building owners who in fact determined wage rates. Cleaning contractors typically had short-term contracts with building owners; success in organizing one or another of them would simply have meant dismissal by the building owner and replacement by a competitor. Moreover, running a "nonboard" campaign meant that the union did not need to win 50.1 percent of the votes in an election, and the campaign did not attempt to do so. It was instead based on a high level of commitment by a militant minority of workers, many of them mobilized in their ethnic communities as well as their workplaces, combining massive civil disobedience with an aggressive corporate campaign. The lead organizer for the campaign has explicitly developed this as a theory of a new way to organize; his suggestions have stimulated active debate (Lerner 1998).

Union, at Work and as Institution

The terms "union" and "labor movement" capture a contradiction. The "union" is an institution, a legally constituted collective bargaining agent that represents workers in complex economic and juridical relations with employers and government. The "labor movement" is a more fluid formation whose very existence depends on high-risk activism, mass solidarity, and collective experiences with transformational possibilities. Given a capitalist economy, the union's long-term survival depends on an ability to deliver wages, benefits, and a systematized defense of workers' everyday workplace rights. But, as the last two decades have demonstrated, the sustained opposition of employers means that the presumed legitimacy of the union, its taken-for-granted character, ultimately depends on the existence of a labor movement, an ability by unions to constitute and reconstitute themselves as social movements.

Many contemporary workers have no experience of labor militance; they understand the union primarily as a servicing institution rather than a vehicle for collective action. In response, labor movement reformers have called for a rejection of the "servicing model" in favor of an "internal organizing" or "union-building" approach to revitalize dormant locals.

This approach envisions a greater involvement of workers in the basic operation of the union with a decreasing reliance on staff (Banks & Metzgar 1989, Conrow 1991). Within a literature that is still largely prescriptive, Fletcher & Hurd's (1998) study stands out as a critical analysis of current best practice. The locals studied involved workers in new roles as grievance handlers, organizers, and political activitists, but successful implementation required intensive efforts at education and consensus-building, thus challenging the initial expectation that the move away from servicing would produce a more economic use of time and resources and a reduction in staff burnout. As one of the people they interviewed reported, "It is a myth that the organizing model will free staff; you constantly have to train members to do things you could do faster yourself" (p. 43). Finally, by differentiating locals that emphasized internal activities such as grievance representation from more externally oriented locals that prioritized organizing of nonunion sites, Fletcher & Hurd argue that evaluation of participatory models must include consideration of the ends to which participation is directed. Thus conceived, internal organizing raises "larger questions about the strategic direction of the entire labor movement" (53).

Strategic questions for labor are also raised by the emergence of participatory management systems. Such programs range from quality circles, voluntary or involuntary, to sites where the work process itself is organized around a team system of production. As management's major initiative to transform workplace relations, employee involvement programs in both organized and unorganized sites represent a challenge to labor that may rival the more flagrant attempts to combat unionization described earlier.

Such programs are characterized by their emphasis on group process, cultivation of nonadversarial relationships, and solicitation of workers' input, all grounded in the assertion of a unity of interest between management and workers (Parker 1985, Parker & Slaughter 1988). Workers often welcome the promise of a greater voice in the production process, as well as opportunities for skill enhancement, a more humane workplace atmosphere, and a heightened respect for their contributions (Smith 1996, Milkman 1997, Graham 1995). But while some employee involvement programs have provided workers with a voice, however modest, such expectations are more often disappointed. Milkman finds a polarization of skills rather than an overall upgrading, with many workers experiencing greater deskilling. In many cases, employee involvement at unionized worksites has resulted in speedups and increased workplace stress (Juravich 1998), leading once hopeful workers to conclude that "management simply could not be trusted" (Milkman 1997:174).

Because they involve discussion of mandatory subjects of bargaining (work-load, hours, grievances) in a management-controlled setting, these programs become a form of company union and thus violate current labor law. In 1994, President Clinton's Commission on the Future of Worker-Management Relations (Dunlop Commission) recommended relaxing prohibitions against company unions, a goal long sought by the business community in order to legitimate and expand employer-dominated participation programs (Kochan 1995:353, Juravich 1998). Possible implementation of such a proposal is an especially serious threat to organizing efforts, given the widespread use of participatory schemes to preempt or resist unionization, a point made by Grenier's (1987) ethnography of a total quality management program and by Rundle's (1998) survey of NLRB election campaigns, which found that employee involvement (EI) programs are often established during and in response to union organizing drives and are highly effective in helping to defeat them.

How then should organized labor respond to employee involvement systems? In practice, most unions have accepted workplace participation with varying degrees of enthusiasm. In Tom Juravich's (1998:85) informed estimate, "In many unions the employee involvement staff is larger, with more resources and institutional power, than the organizing staff." Advocates of total rejection emphasize the programs' character as a "conscious attempt to undermine existing union organization" (Graham 1995:195, Parker 1985, Parker & Slaughter 1988) and to shift "the balance of power in industrial social relations" (Fantasia et al 1988:469). Research indicates that unionized settings are actually more efficient than nonunion workplaces with employee involvement (Kelley & Harrison 1992), but companies fiercely resist unionization and actively promote EI. Programs offer a management-controlled means to connect to workers as a collectivity and to supplant informal work groups, a traditional source of solidarity, with a management-dominated team structure that uses peer pressure to maintain work discipline rather than to promote resistance (Shaiken et al 1997, Graham 1995). The image of a unified team works to deny the possibility that workers' interests differ from management's; as Parker has noted, QWL training manuals portray a world in which "solutions... are never disadvantageous to workers" and "poor lighting is usually the answer" (1985: 16). Thus, employee involvement programs appear as efforts to move toward what Burawoy (1985) terms hegemonic management systems and away from "despotic" systems more likely to incite workers' resistance.

Against this, some academics who maintain associations with both labor and management advocate the institutionalization of certain types of extraunion labor-management representation systems. Heckscher argues that "*some* independent structure of employee voice remains essential," that "the present system, as codified under the National Labor Relations Act of 1935, is inadequate" and that "existing unions probably cannot drive the change" (Heckscher 1996, pp. xiii–xiv). Rogers & Streeck (1994, 1995) argue for a system of works councils, to supplement unions with "a 'second channel' of industrial relations" whose purpose is "to give workers a voice in the governance of the shop floor and the firm, and to facilitate communication and cooperation between management and labor on production-related matters, more or less free of direct distributive conflict over wages" (Rogers & Streeck 1994:97).

These scholars see their proposals as related to, but distinct from, current management schemes. Although these scholars support the continued presence of already-existing unions as collective bargaining agents, they emphasize the need to provide other workers a "voice"—even if that voice is less than a union. Their own accounts suggest that such more autonomous arrangements historically emerge as a product, rather than a cause, of workers' empowerment and are unlikely to develop at a time of labor weakness. Such proposals were indeed considered by the Dunlop Commission, but Kochan (1995:355) reports "the problem was that, aside from some academics, there was no constituency in favor of this!", with business representatives opposed and "lack of strong endorsement by labor" (p. 363). One indication of the extent to which unions have lost control of the framing of public debate on labor issues is that discussion of labor reform has focused on such proposals and even more so on management's wish to remove restrictions on company unions (the Team Act), rather than on the labor law reforms advocated by unions.

Some forces within the labor movement support at least a critical engagement with existing management-initiated participation schemes, arguing for their potential to heighten workers' control and consciousness. In Banks & Metzgar's (1989) influential formulation, employee involvement should be treated as a form of "union organizing on a new terrain," used as an opportunity "to enhance worker and union power" (p. 12). Best-case studies suggest that unions can have significant influence over the unilateral character of these programs and can even use them to advance workers' interests. But Juravich (1998) warns that, in most programs, management's strategic goals "become paramount" and go unchallenged by an alternate union agenda. Thus, he calls for "systematic evaluation of these programs and their impact on workers and their unions" (p. 87), placed within the context of broader labor movement strategies and concerns.

New Forms

Any discussion of the future of the labor movement is necessarily speculative. Twin starting points help frame the discussion—who is (and is not) covered by labor law, and recent changes in the character of work, especially in the most dynamic sectors of the economy. Current labor law is designed to protect long-term, full-time, nonsupervisory, rule-bound, workers with a single employer; that is, "the rights of a worker who is fast disappearing" (Carre et al 1994). Employment is increasingly likely to be part-time and contingent; even professionals frequently work as consultants. White collar and service work frequently, though by no means always, involves less differentiation and more familiar interaction across employment boundaries, and service workers often operate in a triangular relationship with managers on the one hand and clients, customers, students, or patients on the other. It is increasingly unclear who is a "worker" as more and more people are reclassified as some form of "manager" and often identify as such, even when their duties are little changed. These trends especially affect women workers; Cobble (1994:291) estimates that "the current legal and institutional framework of the NLRA disenfranchised more than half of the current female workforce... Women are less organized than men in large part because they have less opportunity to participate in choosing a union."

Appropriate to the form of production that produced it, industrial unionism is unsuited to many post-industrial workplaces; they demand new forms of employee organization and representation. We conclude by briefly indicating some of these possibilities—occupational organizing, community-based actions, and connections to other social movements.

Cobble (1991) and Kimeldorf (1999) describe the multi-employer bargaining strategies of early twentieth century unions—waitstaff and dockworkers—trades in which rights and benefits were linked to the occupation, rather than to a specific employer. During periods of strength, the union regulated wages and conditions in the industry, operating on a larger field than any employer; workers set performance standards, and the union at least attempted to control the labor supply. Building trades unions continue to operate with such an industry- or occupation-wide framework; efforts by the International Brotherhood of Electrical Workers exemplify the use of industry-wide approaches to restore union influence in construction work (Lewis & Mirand 1998, Condit et al 1998). Some approximation of Cobble's "occupational" or Wial's (1994) "network-based" unionism was also a foundation of the Los Angeles Justice for Janitors campaign.

Such cases shift the focus of bargaining from the individual employer to an industry-wide structure, but presume that involved workers are unequivocally union members. Other models go farther, seeking to provide some form of union-like involvement for workers who may be unwilling or, given present realities, unable to participate in collective bargaining relationships (Bonacich 1999). The Garment Workers Justice Centers operated by UNITE are one attempt to create such a form (Ness 1998); these centers are open to all garment workers and their families, whether or not any of them are union members, and provide classes (say, in English as a second language), a social space, and legal help (with citizenship, employer violations of minimum wage and overtime regulations, etc). A variant of this could also be used by professional and technical workers in what Heckscher (1996) terms associational unionism, "an open professional association with a willingness to pressure employers" (xx) that occupies the space somewhere between a current union and professional association. Such organizations could serve as a bridge to full unionization, as in the case of the National Education Association; alternatively they could continue as associations offering services and advocacy.

The primary US union form is organized around an employer and a work site, but community-based unions also have a long history and active present (Lynd 1996, Brecher & Costello 1990), institutionalized in the Central Labor Council (CLC), which includes representatives of each of the unions in a city or other geographic area. Although most CLCs were weak or moribund, the New Voice AFL-CIO leadership made it a priority to revive them, for example by—for the first time—bringing together representatives of CLCs from around the country (Gapasin & Wial 1998). CLCs are an obvious organizational vehicle for the occupational unionism discussed above, for political mobilization, and for a variety of innovative new forms of organizing, from multi-union campaigns to community card check recognition, whereby a Central Labor Council, Jobs with Justice chapter, or other group creates a Workers' Rights Justice Board composed of ministers, elected officials, and respected community leaders. Employers are then pressured to agree to forego normal NLRB procedures and to recognize the union if the Workers Rights Justice Board certifies that a majority of the workforce have signed union authorization cards. [Several Canadian provinces permit card check recognition; it appears inconceivable that Congress would authorize such a labor law reform in the United States—(Weiler 1984.)]

The third and final form of alternative labor movement structure is one that breaks down the boundaries between labor and other movements, one that in many ways transcends "the union" as a form. To some degree this has always been the case—many of the key union victories depended on community-wide mobilizations and support. Consider boycotts. Because union members cannot legally picket stores or restaurants that carry the products of a struck employer, existing labor law coerces labor to work with coalitions that transcend the union.

Community organizations are not subject to the nation's labor laws, and recently the Supreme Court ruled that the First Amendment staunchly protects the boycotting activities of such organizations. "Thus, Ochoa Perez of LA-MAP (Los Angeles Manufacturing Action Project) may find new reasons for appreciating the strategic value of East LA's soccer associations and country-of-origin clubs" (Forbath 1997:140). More generally, many kinds of boycotts and pressure campaigns achieve their impact not because of the strictly labor dimension, but through association with some other cause (the environment, women's rights); even labor issues are often understood outside of a union framework (as in anti-sweatshop campaigns [Rothstein 1996b]). Thus, both legal requirements and the need to reach a broader public are pushing unions to build broad coalitions with other groups and movements.

New forms of union, and a new labor movement, will not be created easily. LA-MAP is a case in point. In the early 1990s, several exciting organizing campaigns triumphed in the Los Angeles area—Justice for Janitors, a militant strike and self-organizing campaign by largely Mexican-American drywall workers (with many of the key leaders coming from a single small Mexican town), and others (Milkman 1999). In response to these successes, nine unions each pledged seed money to initiate LA-MAP, which incorporated in one project many of the progressive innovations widely discussed in the labor movement as the basis for renewal and transformation. The intent was strategic: a multi-union effort to organize entire industrial sectors, rather than simply isolated "hot shops," so that it would be possible to bargain wages and working conditions for the industry as a whole. It was community based, targeting the key manufacturing corridor in Los Angeles, which positioned it to tap into family, neighborhood, church, and ethnic networks and establish connections with social movement and community groups. But this bold effort to create a next generation labor movement foundered as (with the exception of the Teamsters) the unions that had pledged initial seed money withdrew their support when the time came to commit the much larger sums needed to make the project viable (Delgado 1999).

A successful LA-MAP might have served as the catalyst for a dramatically transformed regional labor movement, given its use of innovations widely regarded as vital to the future of labor. It is not surprising that this hugely ambitious effort did not succeed and that it was a source of internal union conflict. Unions are understandably reluctant to embark on bold and untested initiatives given that most successful social movements are preceded by a long string of failed attempts (Weinbaum 1997). Even perceptive analysts conclude that the failure of these attempts demonstrates that change—at least major change, a new paradigm—is impossible. When and if the movement takes off, analysts look back to its precursors and show how previous efforts had laid the groundwork and shown the possibilities.

At this point, no one can know the future of the labor movement. We have reviewed many of the issues and activities likely to be significant, but the future will hold numerous surprises. Labor activity, for example, has concentrated on manufacturing and low-wage service work, but much of the employment growth has been in highly educated and white collar employment. The new forms within the labor movement often emphasize the community, ethnic group, occupation or profession, moving away from workplace relations as the source of worker solidarity and the strike as labor's major strategic weapon. A new surge of labor activity, should it develop, might return to an emphasis on workplaces and strikes, might move to community and occupational forms, or might develop an as-yet-unanticipated form incorporating and transcending both. Labor's future is contested not only between labor and capital; struggles within unions will determine the character of union leadership and the strategies taken in future activity, just as happened in the 1930s (Stepan-Norris & Zeitlin 1989). Both labor activists and scholarly analysts are self-consciously seeking new directions; the field is vibrant and innovative, both practically and intellectually.

> **Visit the *Annual Reviews* home page at**
> **http://www.AnnualReviews.org.**

Literature Cited

AFL–CIO. 1996. Elected Leadership Task Force on Organizing. *Organizing for Change, Changing to Organize!*

Aronowitz S. 1973. *False Promises*. New York: McGraw-Hill

Banks A, Metzgar J. 1989. Participating in management: union organizing on a new terrain. *Labor Res. Rev.* 8 (2):1–58

Blum LM. 1991. *Between Feminism and Labor: The Significance of the Comparable Worth Movement.* Berkeley: Univ. Calif. Press

Bonacich E. 1999. Intense challenges, tentative possibilities: organizing immigrant garment workers in Los Angeles. See Milkman 1999. In press

Borgers F. 1996. The challenges of economic globalization for U.S. labor. *Crit. Soc.* 22: 67–88

Boswell T, Stevis D. 1997. Globalization and

international labor organizing. *Work Occup.* 24:288–308

Brecher J, Costello T, eds. 1990. *Building Bridges:The Emerging Grassroots Coalition of Labor and Community*. New York: Mon. Rev.

Brody D. 1997. Labor elections: Good for workers? *Dissent* Summer:71–77

Bronfenbrenner K. 1993. *Seeds of resurgence: successful union strategies for winning certification elections and first contracts in the 1980s and beyond*. PhD thesis. Cornell Univ., Ithaca, NY

Bronfenbrenner K. 1997. The role of union strategies in NLRB certification elections. *Indust. Labor Relat. Rev.* 50:195–212

Bronfenbrenner K, Friedman S, Hurd RW, Oswald RA, Seeber RL, eds. 1998. *Organizing to Win: New Research on Union Strategies*. Ithaca, NY: ILR/Cornell Univ. Press

Bronfenbrenner K, Juravich T. 1998. It takes more than house calls: organizing to win with a comprehensive union–building strategy. See Bronfenbrenner et al 1998, pp. 19–36

Bronfenbrenner KL. 1994. Employer behavior in certification elections and first-contract campaigns: implications for labor law reform. See Friedman et al 1994, pp. 75–89

Burawoy M. 1979. *Manufacturing Consent: Changes in the Labor Process Under Monopoly Capitalism*. Chicago: Univ. Chicago Press

Burawoy M. 1985. *The Politics of Production*. New York: Verso

Carre FJ, duRivage V, Tilly C. 1994. Representing the part-time and contingent workforce: challenges for unions and public policy. See Friedman et al 1994, pp. 314–23

Clawson D, Clawson MA. 1987. Reagan or business? Foundations of the new conservatism. In *The Structure of Power in America: The Corporate Elite as a Ruling Class*, ed. M Schwartz, pp. 201–17. New York: Holmes & Meier

Clawson D, Johnson K, Schall J. 1982. Fighting union busting in the 80's. *Radic. Am.* 16 (4–5):45–62

Cobble DS. 1991. *Dishing It Out: Waitresses and Their Unions in the Twentieth Century*. New York: Cambridge Univ. Press.

Cobble DS, ed. 1993. *Women and Unions: Forging a Partnership*. Ithaca, NY: ILR Press

Cobble DS. 1994. Making postindustrial unionism possible. See Friedman et al 1994, pp. 285–302

Comstock P, Fox MB. 1994. Employer tactics

and labor law reform. See Friedman et al 1994, pp. 90–109

Condit B, Davis T, Grabelsky J, Kotler F. 1998. Construction organizing: a case study of success. See Bronfenbrenner et al 1998, pp. 309–19

Conrow T. 1991. Contract servicing from an organizing model. *Labor Res. Rev.* 17 (Spring):45–59

Cooke WN. 1985. The failure to negotiate first contracts: determinants and policy implications. *Indust. Labor Relat. Rev.* 38: 163–78

Cornfield D. 1991. The US labor movement: its development and impact on social inequality and politics. *Annu. Rev. Sociol.* 17: 27–49

Cornfield D. 1993. Integrating U.S. labor leadership: union democracy and the ascent of ethnic and racial minorities and women into national union offices. *Res. Sociol. Organ.* 2:51–74

Croteau D. 1995. *Politics and the Class Divide: Working People and the Middle Class Left*. Philadelphia: Temple Univ. Press

Delgado H. 1993. *New Immigrants, Old Unions: Organizing Undocumented Workers in Los Angeles*. Philadelphia, PA: Temple Univ. Press

Delgado H. 1999. The Los Angeles Manufacturing Action Project: lessons learned, an opportunity squandered? See Milkman 1999. In press

Dickens WT. 1983. The effect of company campaigns on certification elections. *Indust. Labor Relat. Rev.* 36:560–75

Dickens WT, Leonard J. 1985. Accounting for the decline in union membership, 1950–1980. *Indust. Labor Relat. Rev.* 38: 323–34

Early S. 1998. Membership–based organizing. See Mantsios 1998, pp. 82–103

Fantasia R. 1988. *Cultures of Solidarity: Consciousness, Action, and Contemporary American Workers*. Berkeley: Univ. Calif. Press

Fantasia R. 1993. The assault on American labor. In *Social Problems*, ed. C Calhoun, G Ritzer, pp. 673–79. New York: McGraw-Hill

Fantasia R, Clawson D, Graham G. 1988. A critical view of worker participation in American industry. *Work Occup.* 15: 468–88

Farber HS. 1990. The decline of unionization in the United States: What can be learned from recent experience. *J. Labor Econ.* 8: S75–105

Feldberg RL. 1987. Women and trade unions: Are we asking the right questions? In *Hid-*

den Aspects of Women's Work, ed. C Bose, R Feldberg, N Sokoloff, pp. 299–322. New York: Praeger

Fisk CL, Mitchell DJB, Erickson CL. 1999. Union representation of immigrant janitors in Southern California: economic and legal challenges. See Milkman 1999. In press

Fletcher B Jr, Hurd RW. 1998. Beyond the organizing model: the transformation process in local unions. See Bronfenbrenner et al 1998, pp. 37–53

Foerster A. 1996. *"Don't whine, organize!" The AFL–CIO Organizing Institute: a rejuvenation of U.S. labor?* Presented at Annu. Meet. Am. Soc. Assoc., New York

Forbath WE. 1997. Down by law? History and prophecy about organizing in hard times and a hostile legal order. See Fraser & Freeman 1997, pp. 132–51

Form W. 1995. *Segmented Labor, Fractured Politics: Labor Politics in American Life*. New York: Plenum

Fraser S, Freeman JB, eds. 1997. *Audacious Democracy: Labor, Intellectuals, and the Social Reconstruction of America*. New York: Houghton Mifflin

Freeman RB. 1985. Why are unions faring poorly in NLRB representation elections? In *Challenges and Choices Facing American Labor*, ed. TA Kochan, pp. 45–64. Cambridge: MIT Press

Freeman RB, Kleiner MM. 1990. Employer behavior in the face of union organizing drives. *Indust. Labor Rel. Rev.* 43:351–65

Freeman RB, Medoff JL. 1984. *What Do Unions Do?* New York: Basic Books

Friedman S, Hurd RW, Oswald RA, Seeber RL, eds. 1994. *Restoring the Promise of American Labor Law*. Ithaca, NY: ILR Press

Gapasin F, Wial H. 1998. The role of Central Labor Councils in union organizing in the 1990s. See Bronfenbrenner et al 1998, pp. 54–67

Geoghegan T. 1991. *Which Side Are You On? Trying to be for Labor When It's Flat on Its Back*. New York: Farrar, Strauss, & Giroux

Geschwender JA. 1977. *Class, Race, and Worker Insurgency: The League of Revolutionary Black Workers*. New York: Cambridge Univ. Press

Getman JG, Goldberg SB, Herman JB. 1976. *Union Representation Elections: Law and Reality*. New York: Russell Sage Found.

Goldfield M. 1987. *The Decline of Organized Labor in the United States*. Chicago: Univ. Chicago Press

Graham L. 1995. *On the Line at Subaru–Isuzu: The Japanese Model and the American Worker*. Ithaca NY: ILR Press

Green H. 1990. *On Strike at Hormel: The Struggle for a Democractic Labor Movement*. Philadelphia: Temple Univ. Press

Grenier G. 1987. *Inhuman Relations: Quality Circles and Anti Unionism in American Industry*. Philadelphia: Temple Univ. Press

Griffin LJ, McCammon HJ, Botsko C. 1990. The "unmaking" of a movement? The crisis of U.S. trade unions in comparative perspective. In *Change in Societal Institutions*, ed. M Hallinan, D Klein, A Glass, pp. 169–94. New York: Plenum

Gross JA. 1995. *Broken Promise: The Subversion of U.S. Labor Relations Policy, 1947–1994*. Philadelphia: Temple Univ. Press

Hage D, Klauda P. 1989. *No Retreat, No Surrender: Labor's War at Hormel*. New York: Morrow

Heckscher CC. 1988/1996. *The New Unionism: Employee Involvement in the Changing Corporation*. Ithaca, NY: ILR/Cornell Univ. Press

Hoerr J. 1997. *We Can't Eat Prestige: The Women Who Organized Harvard*. Philadelphia: Temple Univ. Press

Johnston P. 1994. *Success While Others Fail: Social Movement Unionism and the Public Workplace*. Ithaca, NY: ILR Press

Juravich T. 1998. Employee involvement, work reorganization, and the new labor movement: toward a radical integration. *New Labor Forum* 2:84–91

Juravich T, Bronfenbrenner K. 1999. *Ravenswood*. Ithaca, NY: Cornell/ILR Press

Kelley MR, Harrison B. 1992. Unions, technology, and labor–management cooperation. In *Unions and Economic Competitiveness*, ed. L Mishel, PB Voos, pp. 247–77. Armonk, NY: Sharpe

Kimeldorf H. 1999. *Syndicalism, Pure and Simple: Wobblies, Craft Unionists, and the Battle for American Labor*. Berkeley: Univ. Calif. Press

Kingsolver B. 1989. *Holding the Line: Women in the Great Arizona Mine Strike of 1983*. Ithaca, NY: ILR/Cornell Univ. Press

Kochan TA. 1995. Using the Dunlop Report to achieve mutual gains. *Indust. Relat.* 34: 350–65

Kochan TA, Katz HC, McKersie RB. 1986. *The Transformation of American Industrial Relations*. New York: Basic Books

Kwong P. 1997. *Forbidden Workers: Illegal Chinese Immigrants and American Labor*. New York: The New Press

Ladd–Taylor M. 1985. Women workers and the Yale strike. *Fem. Stud.* 11:465–90

Lembcke J, Jipson A, McGuire P. 1994. Labor's crisis and the crisis of labor studies: toward a retheorized sociology of labor. In

From the Left Bank to the Mainstream, ed. P McQuire, D McQuarie, pp. 108–27. Dix Hills, NY: General Hall Inc.

Lerner S. 1998. Taking the offensive, turning the tide. See Mantsios 1998, pp. 69–81

Levitt MJ. 1993. *Confessions of a Union Buster*. New York: Crown

Lewis J, Mirand B. 1998. Creating an organizing culture in today's building and construction trades: a case study of IBEW Local 46. See Bronfenbrenner et al 1998, pp. 320–38

Lynd S, ed. 1996. *"We are All Leaders": The Alternative Unionism of the Early 1930s*. Urbana, IL: Univ. Ill. Press

Mantsios G, ed. 1998. *A New Labor Movement for the New Century*. New York: Mon. Rev.

Markowitz L. 1998. After the organizing ends: workers' self–efficacy, activism, and union frameworks. *Soc. Probl.* 45:356–82

McAdam D. 1982. *Political Process and the Development of Black Insurgency, 1930–1970*. Chicago, IL: Univ. Chicago Press

McCammon H. 1990. Legal limits on labor militancy: U.S. Labor law and the right to strike since the New Deal. *Soc. Probl.* 37: 206–29

McCammon H. 1993. From repressive intervention to integrative prevention: the U.S. state's legal management of labor militancy 1881–1978. *Soc. Forces* 71:569–601

McCammon H. 1994. Disorganizing and reorganizing conflict: outcomes of the state's legal regulation of the strike since the Wagner Act. *Soc. Forces* 72:1011–49

Melcher D, Eichstedt JL, Eriksen S, Clawson D. 1992. Women's participation in local union leadership: the Massachusetts experience. *Indust. Labor Relat. Rev.* 45: 267–80

Milkman R. 1985. Women workers, feminism and the labor movement since the 1960s. In *Women, Work and Protest: A Century of U.S. Women's Labor History*, ed. R Milkman, pp. 300–22. Boston: Routledge & Kegan Paul

Milkman R. 1997. *Farewell to the Factory: Auto Workers in the Late Twentieth Century*. Berkeley: Univ. Calif. Press

Milkman R. 1999. *Immigrants and Union Organizing in California*. Ithaca, NY: Cornell Univ. Press. In press

Moody K. 1988. *An Injury to All: The Decline of American Unionism*. London: Verso

Moody K. 1997. *Workers in a Lean World: Unions in the International Economy*. New York: Verso

Ness I. 1998. Organizing immigrant commu-

nites: UNITE's workers center strategy. See Bronfenbrenner et al 1998, pp. 87–101

Parker M. 1985. *Inside the Circle: A Union Guide to QWL*. Boston: South End Press

Parker M, Slaughter J. 1988. *Choosing Sides: Unions and the Team Concept*. Boston: South End Press

Piven FF, Cloward R. 1977. *Poor People's Movements: Why They Succeed, How They Fail*. New York: Vintage

Prosten R. 1979. The rise in NLRB election delays: measuring business' new resistance. *Mon. Labor Rev.* 102(2):38–40

Rachleff P. 1993. *Hard Pressed in the Heartland: The Hormel Strike and the Future of the Labor Movement*. Boston: South End Press

Roby P. 1995. Becoming shop stewards: perspectives on gender and race in ten trade unions. *Labor Stud. J.* 20:65–82

Rogers J, Streeck W. 1994. Workplace representation overseas: the works council story. In *Working Under Different Rules*, ed. RB Freeman, pp. 97–156. New York: Russell Sage

Rogers J, Streeck W, eds. 1995. *Works Councils: Consultation, Representation, and Cooperation in Industrial Relations*. Chicago: Univ. Chicago Press

Rosenblum JD. 1995. *Copper Crucible: How the Arizona Miners' Strike of 1983 Recast Labor–Management Relations in America*. Ithaca, NY: Cornell/ILR Press

Rothstein R. 1996a. Toward a more perfect union: new labor's hard road. *The Am. Prospect* 26 (May–June):47–53

Rothstein R. 1996b. The Starbucks solution: can voluntary codes raise global living standards? *The Am. Prospect* 27 (July–Aug.):36–42

Rundle J. 1998. Winning hearts and minds in the era of employee–involvement programs. See Bronfenbrenner et al 1998, pp. 213–31

Sacks KB. 1988. Gender and grassroots leadership. In *Women and the Politics of Empowerment*, ed. A Bookman, S Morgen, pp. 77–94. Philadelphia: Temple Univ. Press

Schleuning NJ. 1994. *Women, Community, and the Hormel Strike of 1985–86*. Westport, CT: Greenwood

Seeber RL, Cooke WN. 1983. The decline in union success in NLRB representation elections. *Indust. Relat.* 22:34–44

Shaiken H, Lopez S, Mankita I. 1997. Two routes to team production: Saturn and Chrysler compared. *Indust. Relat.* 36:17–45

Shostak AB. 1991. *Robust Unionism: Innovations in the Labor Movement*. Ithaca, NY: ILR Press

Silver B. 1995. World–scale patterns of labor–capital conflict: labor unrest, long waves, and cycles of world hegemony. *Review* 18:155–94

Smith V. 1996. Employee involvement, involved employees: participative work arrangements in a white–collar service occupation. *Soc. Probl.* 43:166–79

Stepan–Norris J, Zeitlin M. 1989. "Who gets the bird?" or, how the Communists won power and trust in America's unions: the relative autonomy of intraclass political struggles. *Am. Sociol. Rev.* 54:503–23

Sweeney JJ. 1996. *America Needs a Raise: Fighting for Economic Security and Social Justice.* Boston: Houghton Mifflin

Tarrow S. 1994. *Power in Movement: Social Movements, Collective Action and Politics.* Cambridge, Engl: Cambridge Univ. Press

Tilly C. 1995. Globalization threatens labor's rights. *Int. Labor Work.–Class Hist.* 47: 1–23

Tomlins C. 1985. *The state and the unions: labor relations, law, and the organized labor movement in America, 1880–1960.* New York: Cambridge Univ. Press

Voss K, Sherman R. 1997. *Putting the "move" back in labor movement: tactical innovation and contemporary American unions.* Presented at Annu. Meet. Am. Soc. Assoc., Toronto

Waldinger R, Erickson C, Milkman R, Mitchell DJB, Valenzuela A, et al. 1998. Helots no more: A case study of the Justice for Janitors campaign in Los Angeles. See Bronfenbrenner et al 1998, pp. 102–19

Weiler P. 1983. Promises to keep: securing workers' rights to self–organization under the NLRA. *Harv. Law Rev.* 98:351–420

Weiler P. 1984. Striking a new balance: freedom of contract and the prospects for union representation. *Harv. Law Rev.* 96: 1769–827

Weinbaum E. 1997. *Failure paves the road to success: plant closing struggles.* Presented at Annu. Meet. Am. Soc. Assoc., Toronto

Welsh RW. 1997. Building and changing: a new beginning at the AFL–CIO. See Fraser & Freeman 1997, pp. 73–84

Western B. 1997. *Between Class and Market: Postwar Unionization in the Capitalist Democracies.* Princeton, NJ: Princeton Univ. Press

Wrenn R. 1985. The decline of American labor. *Social. Rev.* 15:89–117

Annu. Rev. Sociol. 1999. 25:121–44

OWNERSHIP ORGANIZATION AND FIRM PERFORMANCE

David L. Kang[1] and Aage B. Sørensen[2]

[1]Graduate School of Business Administration, Harvard University, Boston, Massachusetts 02163; e-mail: dkang@hbs.edu; [2]Department of Sociology, Harvard University, Cambridge, Massachusetts 02138

KEY WORDS: firm performance, corporate governance, property rights, agency theory

ABSTRACT

This essay reviews research on the type and degree of fragmentation of firm ownership with an emphasis on the consequences of ownership organization for firm performance. We use a property rights approach to synthesize sociological, organizational, legal, and economic research that has examined the effect of ownership organization on firm performance. Agency theorists generally assume that shareholders are homogenous and that their influence on firm performance is directly proportional to the percentage of equity they hold. However, empirical research following this approach has failed to produce definitive evidence. Class analysis perspectives interpret these inconclusive results as demonstrating that, regardless of ownership organization, firms are run to serve the capitalist class. An alternative interpretation is that shareholders are not homogeneous but that certain types of shareholders use their formal authority, social influence, and expertise to "capture" property rights and strongly influence firm performance. The influence of different types of owners may depend on industry characteristics, and we review literature pointing to a contingency theory of ownership organization.

INTRODUCTION

Recent work in organizational sociology has made considerable progress toward understanding how certain features of the governance systems found in modern public corporations affect a range of important firm outcomes. The functional backgrounds of corporate officers, the proportion of outsider directors, the separation of the Chairman and CEO positions, and the social net-

0360-0572/99/0815-0121$08.00

works found across firms have been used to predict outcomes such as poison pill adoption, corporate diversification policies, and the use of the multidivisional organizational form. This research has generally downplayed the role of ownership in corporate governance and assumed that ownership and control are effectively separated. By contrast, financial economic research continues to question the role of ownership in understanding control of the firm, although this research tradition has produced highly mixed results on the relationship between ownership organization and performance.

The study of ownership organization and its effect on performance should not be left completely to financial economic research. The study of who controls the use of capital and how this control affects the creation and distribution of wealth in society has long been an important line of intellectual inquiry, originating with Marx. Studying the relationships of individuals and firms to property with a broader and more flexible approach may provide important insights into the efficiency and distributive consequences of modern capitalist firms, or so we hope to show. The actual and potential contributions of sociology to this line of inquiry seem particularly important at the present time, and it is therefore timely to assess what is known, and not known, about the effects of ownership organization on firm performance. We propose an approach based on "ownership type" that views ownership as a key organizational variable in determining firm outcomes.

In the sociological and economic literature on organizations, the modern firm is usually seen as a large organization with four main groups of actors: shareholders, boards of directors, top executives and other managers, and workers. Shareholders are thought of as "owners"; they provide financial capital and in return receive a contractual promise of economic returns from the operations of the firm. Directors act as fiduciaries of the corporation who may approve certain strategy and investment decisions but whose main responsibility is to hire and fire top managers. Managers operate the firms; they make most business decisions and employ and supervise workers. Workers carry out the activities that create the firm's output.

This image of the modern firm accurately reflects the organization of many large public corporations that dominate the US economy. However, many other firms are organized in ways that merge two or more of these tasks: Owners may be both investing and managing, workers may be owners, managers may acquire large shares of ownership, and so forth. In entrepreneurial firms, one person fuses all four tasks: investing, monitoring, managing, and working. In fact, owner-managed firms were the origin of capitalist production and dominated the US economy until the twentieth century. However, as firms in industries such as steel, railroads, and oil expanded their operations, individual and family owners found that they did not have enough wealth to finance large-scale industrial operations (Chandler 1977). Firms began the practice of issuing shares to raise the large amounts of capital necessary for growth and geographic expansion. As a result, many firms, particularly large firms, are no longer owner-managed firms but corporations, sometimes with thousands of shareholders each of whom owns only a small fraction of the shares.

The fragmentation of the owner-managed firm and its consequences have interested sociologists, legal scholars, and economists for a very long time. Karl Marx discussed the fragmentation in Volume III of *Capital*, characterizing the resulting separation as "the abolition of capital as private property within the framework of capitalist production itself " (1867). The consequence of this fragmentation for the class structure has generated a debate among sociologists, to which we return below. However, the main impetus to studying the consequences of the fragmentation of the owner-managed firm in organizational sociology and economics was Berle & Means' *The Modern Corporation and Private Property* (1932). Berle & Means document the "separation of ownership and control" and depict the corporation as a largely autonomous entity, where executives and managers successfully pursue their own objectives of growth and stability rather than maximizing the returns to the shareholders. A large literature in organizational sociology and economics adopts this "managerialist" perspective which assumes autonomous managers control firms.

OWNERSHIP ORGANIZATION AND FIRM PERFORMANCE: AN OVERVIEW

In this essay, we review research and scholarship on the organization of ownership resulting from the fragmentation of the original owner-managed firm and the consequences of these ownership patterns, especially for firm performance. Our perspective differs from the conventional separation of ownership and control conception. The contrast between the large autonomous and management-controlled corporation and the owner-managed firm is an oversimplification. There are more than two types of ownership organization. Modern firms have a variety of ownership patterns, and exploring ownership type recognizes that large-block shareholders are not homogenous and that certain types of owners have a disproportionately large impact on corporate governance. Some very large firms are dominated by large-block shareholders who have a seat on the board of directors, some by shareholders who sustain their ownership blocks over time, and some by families owning large bocks of shares. Recent research has shown, using accounting and stock price-based measures, that each of these ownership types is associated with enhanced performance (Kang 1998a).

Additional ownership types include top executives, employee stock ownership plans, buyers, suppliers, different types of institutional investors, leveraged buyouts, and venture capital. Top executive stock ownership has recently received considerable attention, as there is currently a trend toward compensating executives with stock options. However, little compelling evidence exists of the effects of these developments on firm performance (Loderer & Martin 1997, Bhagat & Black 1998). Employee stock ownership has been found to have some positive effects on profitability, productivity, and compensation (Blasi et al 1996). Although buyers and suppliers have been identified as having potentially important relationships through cross-holdings of equity, only anecdotal evidence suggests that these owners affect performance (Porter 1992).

Another important ownership type is institutional investors, such as public pension funds and private mutual funds, which now hold approximately 60% of all outstanding US equities. A small number of these investors, usually public pension funds such as CalPERs, have recently become more active in corporate governance, largely through the use of media condemnation or "jawboning" to influence managers. Research on the effect of this shareholder activism or "relational investing" on firm performance has produced mixed results (Bethel et al 1998, Bhagat et al 1997). These investors typically do not conduct proxy fights and do not try to elect members to the board of directors. Research has failed to produce strong evidence on a correlation between the percentage of shares owned by institutions and firm performance (Chaganti & Damanpour 1991, Black 1998). Finally, anecdotal evidence suggests that specialized investment funds run by skilled managers who purchase large blocks of shares may in some cases improve the firm performance (Pound 1992).

Firms may fundamentally change their ownership patterns over time. A particularly interesting and controversial example of changing ownership patterns can be found in the recent wave of buyouts, called leveraged buy-outs (LBOs), of large public corporations by investment groups, which use enormous amounts of debt to transform public corporations into private, owner-dominated firms. The value of LBOs and their resulting changes in ownership patterns have been widely debated, as some researchers have presented evidence that the reorganization of ownership patterns improved the efficiency of the firm, while others argue these gains occurred at the expense of workers and communities (Jensen 1989, Kaplan 1991, Shleifer & Summers 1988). Another interesting example of changing ownership forms are the many entrepreneurial firms that begin as private firms that rely on venture capitalists at founding, but then within a few years use initial public offerings to place a significant portion of equity in the hands of public shareholders. Research on venture capital suggests that this form of concentrated ownership may lead to increased performance, although there is now evidence that firms may continue to perform well even after venture capitalists have sold their equity stakes (Sahlman 1990, Black & Gilson 1998, Mikkelson et al 1997).

Our review integrates sociological literature on ownership with approaches from managerial economics that use a principal-agent perspective on the relationship between the various groups of actors in the modern corporation. We first survey ideas about property rights that present a framework for analysis of ownership organization and its consequences. We then present the principal-agent conception of the firm that has inspired much of the research on the consequences of ownership fragmentation, and we examine the empirical evidence on the relationship between ownership concentration and performance. A review of the debate on the consequences of ownership fragmentation for the class structure follows. We then review organizational approaches to the analysis of the relationship between ownership organization and firm governance and suggest a synthesis of theory in understanding ownership and performance that sees the "fit" between certain ownership types and the industry context as shaping firm performance.

PROPERTY AND THE LEGAL RIGHTS OF SHAREHOLDERS

Our basic thesis is that the organization of ownership matters for firm performance because the organization of ownership allocates property rights, or control of assets, to various actors involved in a firm—in the owner-managed firm to a single actor, in the typical corporation to many actors. These property rights present opportunities for actors to realize their interests and affect firm performance. For example, family owners of large blocks of shares may force firms to remain in less profitable geographical locations. Or, managers may use their control of operational decisions to divert firms into unprofitable endeavors that may benefit managers' careers but decrease the return to shareholders.

Property rights here are conceived of broadly as the rights to the benefits, use of, and disposal of goods and assets. The metaphor of property as a "bundle of rights" is useful in conceptualizing how organizational actors are able to influence organizational outcomes (Hohfeld 1913). As noted by Corbin, "Our concept of property has shifted, incorporeal rights have become property. And, finally, 'property' has ceased to describe any *res*, or object of sense, at all, and has become merely a bundle of legal relations—rights, powers, privileges, immunities" (1922:429). In the classic "atom of property" (Berle & Means 1932), the benefit, use, and disposal rights are fused. In the conception of the classic owner-managed firm, the same individual receives the benefits from the asset she controls, decides completely about its uses, and can dispose of the property fully. The separation of ownership and control in the modern corporation described by Berle & Means is a particular fragmentation of these rights, where benefit rights and use rights have been separated.

The fusion of all rights in the "atom of property" is the exception rather than the rule. Even in ordinary market transactions, rights are often not completely fused. With goods sold with warranties, the seller retains some of the use rights by making the warranty dependent on meeting certain obligations—regular oil changes for cars, for example. Prospective buyers can gain some of the benefit rights, as when customers pick and choose the best cherries in a batch without the owner being easily able to prevent it (Barzel 1997).

Rights become fragmented in two main ways. First, they may be simply assumed or captured because the original holder of the right cannot protect the right because the costs are too high. It may be too costly to ascertain the properties of the good or asset, such as in the cherry-picking example. Or, free-rider problems may make it too costly for an individual to monitor the asset, such as when executives use cash flow to acquire corporate jets. Second, rights become fragmented because they are delegated by contracts. Contracts are sometimes explicit or complete contracts, as in the warranty example. However, contracts are often incomplete because of the high transaction costs of negotiating every possible future contingency, and they are therefore subject to further fragmentation due to capture. For example, employment contracts are usually incomplete contracts, where the delegation of use rights to employees is done by the original owners, who retain control over benefit rights. These benefit rights are subject to capture as employees use bargaining powers derived from firm specific skills or collective actions to capture rents (Sørensen 1996).

Rights and contracts transferring or delegating rights may be enforced by the state, making them legal rights. However many rights are captured or transferred without legal support as when managers control cash flows to live more glamorously. Legal rights may be seen as one of several possible means to obtain what Barzel (1997) calls economic property rights, which are what people ultimately seek. Economic rights can be defined, following Barzel (1997:3), as the ability to consume some good, or the services of an asset, directly, or to consume it indirectly through exchange. These rights are not constant; they are dependent on the efforts of protection, the capture attempts by others, and governmental protection through police and the courts.

Legal rights are important because they protect economic rights and define the basic context for the exercise and transfer of rights. In particular, legal rules are the foundation of modern corporate governance, as the property rights of shareholders are created and defined by federal securities regulations and case law. Shareholders may be viewed as parties that have explicitly contracted for a relatively well-defined subset of rights as prescribed under the corporate charter. A close examination of the formal legal rights assigned shareholders reveals three key rights:

> 1. The right to share pro rata (that is, the same amount for each share) in dividend payments, if and when the directors exercise their discretion to declare dividends, and to share pro rata in distributions in liquidation of the enter-

prise. 2. The right to vote, on a one share—one vote basis, upon the election of directors and certain major corporate changes such as mergers with other companies and liquidations. 3. A restricted but not negligible right to information in the form of a shareholder's right to inspect corporate books and records. (Clark 1986:13)

Shareholders in public corporations have very limited rights compared to the "owners" found in other legal forms of organizing such as partnerships. Under the legal doctrine of limited liability, shareholders of public corporations do not bear the risk of facing legal claims against their personal assets. By contrast, partners not only risk their initial investment, but they also are personally liable for legal claims brought against the partnership. Therefore, shareholders' legal powers within the corporation should be viewed as highly limited in scope and very different from the broad legal powers given to "owners" of other organizational forms or other types of assets.

The legal limits in shareholder power are important in understanding control of the corporation because shareholders seldom have physical control over the complex assets of the corporation. Property law initially defined ownership in terms of the physical possession of assets (Berle & Means 1932). As Oliver Wendall Holmes discusses in *The Common Law*, "But what are the rights of ownership? They are substantially the same as those incident to possession. Within the limits prescribed by policy, the owner is allowed to exercise his natural powers over the subject-matter uninterfered with, and is more or less protected in excluding other people from such interference. The owner is allowed to exclude all, and is accountable to no one but him" (1881:246). However, in the modern corporation it is not the shareholders, but rather the managers and workers, who come closest to physically "possessing" the firm's assets. These assets are often complex, such as in the case of large-scale production facilities and research laboratories. Most shareholders cannot determine whether these assets are being used correctly, lacking both the information and expertise needed to monitor the activities that take place.

Most shareholders only own a small fraction of the total number of shares and face considerable costs in conducting effective monitoring. Although shareholders have legal rights to benefits from corporate assets, these benefit rights may routinely be captured by other organizational participants, including board members, managers, workers, or other shareholders. The central issue that occupies our review is the inability of shareholders with their limited use rights to capture many of these benefit rights.

The existence of rights and the potential for obtaining or capturing benefit rights provide incentives that are opportunities for actors to increase their wealth. They act on these opportunities according to the formal authority, social influence, and expertise that govern their behavior. Therefore, this broad conception of property rights allows for the integration of economic ideas that feature a narrow conception of contracts and exchanges with sociological ideas about the social processes and structures that shape people's responses to incentives and the opportunities they present. Ownership is a complex economic and sociological phenomenon occurring in a legal context that creates incentives and opportunities to capture property rights and take actions that shape firm performance.

AGENCY THEORY AND THE THEORY OF THE FIRM

The property rights perspective directly informs the rich literatures on the firm found in legal theory and organizational economics, where the distinction between the market and the firm for organizing transactions has been a major concern. The idea that property rights rarely are absolute and that benefit, use, and disposal rights often are fragmented explains why firms often incur agency costs (Jensen & Meckling 1976) and transaction costs (Williamson 1985). These are the costs associated with transfer, capture, and protection of rights (Barzel 1997:4). In particular, the view that principals delegate rights to agents and are therefore faced with the problem of alignment of the agents' interests in order to maximize firm performance has generated an important literature in managerial economics.

An agency relation is one where a "principal" delegates authority to an "agent" to perform some service for the principal. These relations may occur in a variety of social contexts involving the delegation of authority, including clients and service providers such as lawyers, citizens and politicians, political party members and party leaders, rulers and state officials, employers and employees, and stockholders and managers of corporations (Kiser 1998). Sociologists have recently used ideas regarding principal-agent relations to explore a wide range of social phenomena (Kiser 1998). Sociological research using agency theory approaches includes Adams' (1996) discussion of agency problems involved in colonial control, Kiser's (Kiser & Tong 1992, Kiser & Schneider 1994, Kiser 1994) work on the organizational structure of early modern tax administration, Gorski's (1993) analysis of the "disciplinary revolution" in Holland and Prussia, and Hamilton & Biggart's (1980, 1984, 1985) arguments about control in state government bureaucracies. Similarly, current work in political science has also used agency theory approaches to explore state policy implementation (Weingast & Moran 1983, Bendor & Moe 1985, Wood 1988, Kiewiet & McCubbins 1991).

Applied in the corporate governance context, agency theory recognizes how fragmented property rights may significantly affect firm performance. Agency theorists conceptualize the firm as a "nexus of contracts" where rights are delegated to the various groups of actors (Jensen & Meckling 1976). This contractual view provides an elegant formal conception of the firm, where all contracts can be treated as formally alike. Firms perform well when the system of contracts offers an efficient alternative to other organizational forms and to markets. Firms that survive minimize agency costs and provide the quality of the product or service demanded at the lowest price, while covering the full costs of production. Maximizing claims for shareholders is thought to be consistent with these efficiency criteria (Fama & Jensen 1983). The aspect of the organization of ownership emphasized in this literature is the alignment of the parties' interests through the use of contracts, in particular using contracts to align the interests of managers with the interests of shareholders.

Agency theorists suggest that the separation of ownership and control is often the best available organizational design, as the benefits of increased access to capital and professional management typically outweigh the costs associated with delegating control of business decisions to managers (Fama & Jensen 1983). However, in the absence of strong corporate governance systems, public corporations may suffer in performance when self-interested managers pursue their own interests rather than the interests of shareholders (Jensen 1989). Managers have opportunities for pursuing their own interests—in prestige, luxurious accommodations and modes of transportation, and high salaries—because they have been delegated rights through their contracts to control cash flows and information in their firms. Modern public corporations often are faced with considerable agency costs. It is expensive to gather information and assess managerial actions, and particular shareholders only gain a fraction of any pecuniary benefits produced, proportional to the percentage of total equity they own (Shleifer & Vishny 1989). This creates collective action problems. Gains are available to all shareholders regardless of whether they have incurred the costs of monitoring, a problem that contributes to the separation of ownership and control (Berle & Means 1932). Because the costs of participating in corporate governance typically exceed the benefits, and because of the problem of free riding, dispersed shareholders are generally unlikely to participate in corporate governance.

Large-block shareholders potentially have an important role in reducing agency costs in public corporations. Because large-block owners must obtain sufficient returns to make their participation in corporate governance cost-effective, public corporations with concentrated owners are thought to enjoy lower agency costs, resulting in superior performance relative to corporations with fragmented ownership (Fama & Jensen 1983, Jensen 1989, 1993). One way to align the interests of shareholders and managers is for firms to raise a large portion of the capital they require by issuing debt rather than equity. Debt covenants require periodic debt repayments, forcing managers to generate cash and pay it out rather than use it to invest in new projects or perquisites. The heavy use of debt financing also enables individual shareholders to own a larger proportion of the firm's total equity for a given amount of capital invested, as the total value of the equity outstanding is considerably smaller in highly leveraged firms. As a result, the large-block shareholders found in LBOs have substantial voting rights in corporate governance and the financial incentive to monitor closely the activities of the firm. Agency theorists argue that these changes in ownership, combined with changes in top management teams, improve the efficiency of firms (Jensen 1989). Agency theory provides an elegant argument for how ownership organization affects firm perform-ance. We consider next the empirical evidence on the link between organiza-tion and performance that bears on this argument.

CONCENTRATED OWNERSHIP, CONTROL, AND FIRM PERFORMANCE

Considerable empirical research explores the link between concentration of ownership and performance from both economic and sociological perspec-tives. Large-sample financial economic studies measuring the effect of con-centrated ownership on performance in public corporations find mixed results when examining the overall concentration of ownership and the percentage of shares held by insiders or institutional investors (Demsetz & Lehn 1985, Holderness & Sheehan 1988, Zeckhauser & Pound 1990, Cho 1998, Black 1998). For example, in their study of 511 large US public corporations, Dem-setz & Lehn (1985) suggest that concentrated ownership rises to its appropri-ate level for each industrial context such that it has no measurable effect on performance, a conclusion we shall return to later.

Many studies have simply dichotomized ownership concentration by char-acterizing firms as manager-controlled or owner-controlled. Managerial control is inferred when the concentration of ownership is low so that the largest shareholder holds between four or five percent (Salancik & Pfeffer 1980, Berle & Means 1932) to as high as 20% (Burch 1972). A study that dis-tinguished among owner-controlled, manager-controlled, and owner-managed firms found that owner-controlled and owner-managed firms pro-duced significantly higher rates of return on investment than did manager-controlled firms (McEachern 1975). However, most studies using ownership thresholds indicate little or no difference, either in profit margin rate or rate of return to stockholders, or between owner-controlled and manager-controlled firms (Kamerschen 1968, Monsen et al 1968, Lewellen 1969, Larner 1970, Hindley 1970, J Palmer 1973). This large literature using ownership thresholds has been reviewed by Scherer (1988).

The mixed results on the relationship between ownership concentration and performance can be given one of three possible interpretations. One interpreta-tion is that the Berle & Means thesis about the separation of ownership and control is an empirical "pseudofact," where existing empirical measures of "control" do not sufficiently account for the complex social context in which ownership occurs. Zeitlin argues that modern public corporations, whether appearing outwardly to be run by managers, owner-managers, or large shareholders, are ultimately governed in the interest of the capitalist class in the manner conceived of by Marxist scholarship (1974). We address this perspective in greater detail below.

A second interpretation is that surviving firms enjoy the level of ownership concentration that is most efficient for their industrial and institutional environment. This is the interpretation suggested by Demsetz & Lehn (1985), Kole (1994) and Cho (1998). Ownership organization is considered endogenous and not an independent influence on performance. However, this approach assumes that ownership structures are in equilibrium and does not address the possibility that longitudinal evidence on ownership and performance may reveal that certain ownership structures are generally associated with increased firm performance. Other evidence also suggests that the matter is more complicated. For example, research that distinguishes among different types of large-block institutional investors finds that large mutual funds, foundations, and pension funds are more likely to affect organizational decision-making than other large-block shareholders (Brickley et al 1988). We review below other research that suggests that the characteristics of large-block owners matter for performance.

A third interpretation of the mixed empirical evidence found regarding the effects of ownership concentration on firm performance is that examining formal ownership rights does not adequately capture important social dimensions of ownership. Agency theory's view of the firm as a nexus of contracts where property rights are precisely meted out by contracts may not sufficiently explain firm outcomes (Demsetz & Lehn 1985, Morck et al 1988). Focusing on the delegation of the formal rights of shareholders is conceptually appealing because it helps avoid the problem of reification, where the corporation is thought of as a single entity and the legal rights arising from corporate assets are thought of as indivisible. However, simply defining property rights in corporate assets in terms of principal-agent relationships or formal, contractual rights may overlook interesting and important questions regarding who "captures" these property rights and how this affects firm performance. The theory and evidence for this interpretation is considered below, after we consider the class analysis perspective.

CLASS ANALYSIS, OWNERSHIP, AND PROFIT

Marx proposed a model for capitalist production that saw capitalists forced by competition to act to maximize profits and the rate of exploitation, resulting in maximum firm performance. In general, this analysis pays little attention to the particular characteristics of capitalists and the manner in which ownership is organized. However, as previously noted, Marx did present a brief discussion of joint stock companies and saw them as the "abolition of capital as private property." This statement has been given two very different interpretations. One interpretation, first proposed by Dahrendorf (1959), is consistent with the Berle & Means' (1932) fragmentation of ownership tradition and agency theory. The second interpretation, suggested by Zeitlin (1974), argues that the "abolition of capital" should be understood as a transformation of capital rather than an elimination of capital.

Dahrendorf argues that Marx understood the "socialization of ownership" as weakening capitalism by reducing the incentives of capitalists to maximize performance, thus resulting in a fundamental change in capitalist society and the transformation of capitalism from within into "industrial society" (Dahrendorf 1959). In particular, managers will be less likely than owners to maximize the efforts of workers. As a result, firm performance is likely to decline, with the distributive consequence that wealth is transferred from shareholders to workers. Dahrendorf suggested that professional managers are not simply the capitalist oppressors of workers, but rather that "Capital—and therefore capitalism—has dissolved and given way in the economic sphere" to independent conflict fronts, where the subjected classes of industry and of political society are no longer identical, as opposed to the politically and economically oppressed worker class described by Marx (Dahrendorf 1959:47).

Similarly, work by Wright suggests that modern capitalism has resulted in a situation where managers occupy "contradictory" locations because "they share class interests with two different classes but have interests identical to neither" (1980:331). If the firm performs well, the managers' value on the market for managerial talent will increase somewhat. However, because they often work closely with workers, managers may feel closer social ties with workers, and they may be willing to transfer the shareholders' money to workers rather than to extract the maximum amount of labor possible from them (Shleifer & Summers 1988).

Zeitlin interprets Marx as seeing a transformation into a new, but still capitalist, capitalism. Corporations may appear outwardly to be controlled by managers, but capitalists such as large-block family owners and their "kinship" groups may actually control these firms, causing managers to work in the interests of the "proprietary interests" of the capitalist class (Zeitlin 1974). Zeitlin argues that as an empirical matter, the separation of ownership and control has been greatly exaggerated and suggests large-block owners actually controlled many of the public corporations originally studied by Berle & Means. These large-block owners were often families, where founders had passed down "control" of the corporation through the transfer of significant, though not majority, ownership stakes to their heirs (Zeitlin et al 1975). In any event, it does not much matter for performance who controls the firms, as all the main actors are believed to work in the interest of the capitalist class. Zeitlin criticizes empirical work on ownership and performance and suggests that the concept of "control" requires a more context-specific understanding.

Other research in this tradition suggests that managers are a group of networked elites that use interlocked boards of directors to pursue their own interests as well as promoting the general interests of large business (Useem 1980). Domhoff suggests that "The growth and interconnections of corporations... have meant the rise of a more sophisticated executive elite which now possesses a certain autonomy from any specific property interest. It's the power of property, but that property is not always or even usually of one coherent and narrow type. It is, in operating fact, class-wide property" (1967:40).

The argument that firms are run in the interest of the capitalist class, regardless of ownership organization, raises the question of how the capitalist class exercises its influence. This question has produced a large literature in sociology and political science, reviewed, for example, by Glasberg & Schwartz (1983), on who controls the large corporations: large-block shareholders including families, banks, or the managers themselves. Control has been defined in terms of the power to determine the broad policies guiding the corporation, including decisions regarding capital structure, product diversification, corporate structure, and mergers (Herman 1981, Fligstein & Brantley 1992). However, much of the organizational literature on interlocks pays considerable attention to identifying patterns of interlocking directorships and much less attention to what control means for the performance of firms (Useem 1980, Palmer 1983).

The class analysis perspective suggests either that Marx had foreseen the Berle & Means thesis and a fundamental transformation of capitalist society, or that he had envisioned the continuation of capitalism with new key actors such as elite managers and banks acting in the interests of the capitalist class. Research using the latter perspective suggests that although managers may not always have their interests aligned with the particular shareholders that are their principals, their interests may be aligned with the capitalist class as a whole. Neither interpretation has produced evidence on variation in firm performance by ownership organization.

Class approaches to the topic of ownership organization and performance have raised important questions regarding the distributive consequences of the ownership patterns found in modern corporations. As Dahrendorf notes, "class is always a category for purposes of the analysis of the dynamics of social conflict and its structural roots, and as such it has to be separated strictly from stratum as a category for describing hierarchical systems at a given point in time" (1959:76). Zeitlin argues that understanding families as "kinship units" that perpetuate class relations is one useful approach (1974). Yet, surprisingly little sociological research has attempted to understand how the evolution of ownership organization has affected modern class relations. Recent economic research on ownership distribution in US society has found that increasing institutional ownership has increased the disparity in income distribution in the US population (Poterba & Samwick 1995). The question of who gains from superior performance in corporations—who enjoys the benefit rights to corporate profit—appears worthy of more extensive sociological inquiry, as the efficiency and distributive consequences of economic activity are highly intertwined and have together shaped the legal rules surrounding corporate governance (Bromley 1989, Roe 1991, 1994).

ORGANIZATIONAL STUDIES AND OWNERSHIP TYPE

Most research in the sociology of organizations fundamentally assumes that managers control the modern public corporation. This approach, known as "managerialism," assumes that most of the use rights and benefit rights that arise from corporate property have already been captured by managers, and that the most important areas for inquiry are those that investigate social influences on managers. Because managerialism is assumed, most organizational research on "corporate governance" has focused on variables other than ownership. At the same time, this organizational research has deemphasized the question of organizational performance, instead focussing primarily on other organizational outcomes. For example, managers have been characterized as having "conceptions of control" where their actions regarding strategic decisions are seen as being greatly shaped by institutional factors that affect a very broad range of dependent variables, primarily focused on firm strategy (Fligstein 1990, Fligstein & Brantley 1992). Other organizational research has explored how networks of intercorporate relations affect the adoption of organizational practices such as poison pills and golden parachutes (Davis 1991, Davis & Greve 1997), the payment of acquisition premiums (Haunschild 1993), financing, and capital structure (Mizruchi & Stearns 1994), and intercorporate coordination (Palmer et al 1986). Additional organizational research on corporate governance has focused on board characteristics and how they affect the payment of greenmail (Kosnik 1987), CEO turnover (Ocasio 1994), and diversification strategy (Westphal & Zajac 1997). Research that has surveyed the effects of board composition has found an uncertain relationship between board composition and firm performance (Bhagat & Black 1998). Organizational research on corporate governance finds that managers engage in "symbolic action" by announcing, but not actually implementing, actions that engender positive stock market reactions (Westphal & Zajac 1998). Although organizational research has explored many important aspects of corporate governance, this research typically uses concentration of ownership simply as a control variable, having very little to say on how ownership patterns affect organizational performance.

Taking "managerialism" for granted and concentrating on how resource dependency and institutional forces affect managers does not sufficiently recognize informal and formal empirical evidence that certain types of large-block shareholders exercise influence in corporate governance using formal authority and informal power. Agency theory's emphasis on the importance of ownership concentration offers an important starting point in understanding ownership organization. As argued above, the mixed evidence for the link between ownership concentration and performance may reflect that in agency theory, ownership is seen as a purely economic variable, where owners are homogenous and the influence of ownership is a function of ownership concentration. Owners with comparably sized ownership stakes may vary considerably in their capacity to influence managers and the firm because concentrated ownership limits managers' potential alternative sources of support for their decisions (Salancik & Pfeffer 1980). Different types of shareholders have different sets of benefit rights and use rights, and their willingness and ability to monitor managers may vary according to the amount of contractual and non-contractual benefit rights and use rights they possess. Although shareholders may sometimes have complex goals, increasing their benefits by increasing the economic value of their large-block ownership stake is very likely to be their primary goal. At the same time, some benefits outside of stock price appreciation may be important. This may be critical for some ownership types, such as family large-block owners. Not only may shareholders differ in their objectives, they may also differ in how likely it is that they can realize their objectives. In particular, large-block owners have three potential bases of power that they may leverage to influence firm outcomes: formal authority, social influence, and expertise.

Three Bases of Shareholder Power

All shareholders have some power based on their legal rights, or formal authority (Weber 1968). These powers include the right to vote on ratification of nominations to the board of directors and the right to approve some major business decisions such as mergers and acquisitions (Clark 1986). If shareholders are of sufficient size to overcome free rider problems, they may obtain active roles in the governance structure of the firm, such as a seat on the board of directors, which provide them with additional formal authority and direct involvement in key strategic decisions. When ownership is coupled to a "strategic position" such as a high executive office or a directorship, it enables their possessors to participate in making key decisions (Herman 1981). Although directors are frequently criticized for being passive "pawns" of management, outside-director shareholders are more likely to be "potentates" (Lorsch & MacIver 1989) who overcome the problems of passive, dysfunctional boards. Several financial economic studies have found a nonmonotonic relationship between the magnitude of insider stock ownership and firm performance (Morck et al 1988, McConnell & Servaes 1990, Cho 1998). For example, Morck et al find that insider ownership between 0 and 5% increases firm performance, insider ownership between 5% and 25% decreases performance, but that insider ownership above 25% again increases performance (1988).

Second, shareholders also have power based on social influence that they develop through interactions that occur in the context of formal organizational roles, through repeated interactions between owners and managers over time, and through rich histories of relationships that may develop between owners and workers over several generations. Consistent with this view, large-block shareholders who maintain their ownership stakes increase their social influence over time. Social influence is an important base of power, as interpersonal relations significantly shape important resource allocation decisions in organizations (Pfeffer 1992). Social influence is important in corporate governance as suggested by the finding that CEOs able to appoint more outsiders to their board are more likely to have golden parachutes (Wade et al 1990). General evidence on the importance of social influence is provided by research that has focused on demographic backgrounds of participants as a source of political power (Zajac & Westphal 1995, 1996).

Third, certain types of large-block shareholders may have power based on their expertise. Expertise is a superior understanding of the firm and its industry and general business skills that can be used in managing critical environmental dependencies (French & Raven 1968, Pfeffer & Salancik 1978, Finkelstein 1992). This expertise is often acquired through participation in the firm's governance structure, such as serving on the board of directors, observing and participating in important strategic decisions over time, and in managing the firm. Owners with expertise are likely to have well-informed discussions with managers regarding the strategic direction of the firm. Managers are very likely to respond to large-block owners whom they regard as sophisticated, as expertise allows owner power to become legitimated—expected and desired rather than contested in the social context of corporate governance (Pfeffer 1981, Ocasio 1994).

Exploring Ownership Type

As we have outlined, there are many different "ownership types" of large-block investors: shareholders who have a seat on the board of directors, shareholders who sustain their ownership blocks over time, families, top executives, institutional investors such as public pension funds and mutual funds, LBO and MBO associations, and venture capital funds (Kang 1996). They differ in the length of their involvement with firms, and their effect on performance depends on the industrial and competitive context in which the firm operates. We briefly illustrate how length of involvement and context may condition the influence of ownership types on performance.

We have already argued that length of involvement should be important for social influence and expertise of large-block shareholders, and long involvement should also make large owners more likely to assume positions of formal authority on boards of directors. For example, owner types such as family owners often have very long associations with the firms they originally founded. They should therefore gain considerable social influence and expertise as noted above. Family owners often "control" public corporations, where the extent of stock ownership by the controlling family affected managerial tenure (Allen & Panian 1982), family owners affect the susceptibility to takeover (Davis & Stout 1992), and family ownership suppressed adoption of the multidivisional form during the 1960s, but not during the 1980s (Palmer et al 1987, 1993).

Although many anecdotal accounts describe both high-performing and poorly performing family-controlled firms, there is a lack of theory and evidence on how family owners might affect performance in large publicly held US corporations. Research on the effect of large-block family ownership on performance in modern corporations has produced mixed results (Demsetz & Lehn 1985, Fligstein & Brantley 1992, Johansson 1993). One possible explanation for these mixed results is that the power that large-block family shareholders have may diminished over time as their formal authority, social influence, and expertise may decline in later generations. This "Buddenbrooks effect" occurs where early-generation family owners enjoy superior performance and make superior strategic decisions, while later-generation family owners do not enjoy superior performance and make less effective strategic decisions (Kang 1998b).

By contrast, other owner types are unlikely to develop a long history of social influence in the firm. This is the case for many institutional investors and LBO associations. The increased importance of institutional investors in particular has led some to suggest that US corporations may suffer from a "time horizon" problem, where managers are unable to make necessary strategic investments because of capital market pressures for immediate shareholder returns (Porter 1992). However, the price of publicly traded shares is thought to reflect the present value of all future streams of cash flows from the corporation, and empirical studies provide only anecdotal evidence on the "time horizon" problem.

The literature on corporate governance may further suggest that the effect of ownership type on performance is likely to be contingent on industry and competitive context, as the formal authority, social influence, and expertise of each ownership type will vary contingent on characteristics of the industry and competitive environment in which the firm operates. Financial economic research suggests some industries are "transparent" where firms are relatively simple to monitor, whereas others are "opaque" where firms are difficult to monitor, based on whether or not capital and investments are highly firm specific (Zeckhauser & Pound 1990). Transparent industries, such as textiles and steel, are characterized by less firm-specific capital and investments, where most shareholders are more easily able to monitor managers. By contrast, opaque industries, such as microprocessors and pharmaceuticals, are those with highly specific capital investments, where most shareholders are unlikely to have the expertise and information necessary to monitor managers.

Certain types of large-block owners may be more able to increase firm performance under "transparent" industry conditions, whereas other types of large-block shareholders may be more appropriate for "opaque" conditions. For example, in the US textile industry, a "transparent" industry, large-block outside director owners, large-block owners who sustain their ownership over time, and large-block family owners each were found to be associated with increased firm performance (Kang 1996). By contrast, large-block owner-managers may be most effective in "opaque" industries, where their high levels of expertise and continual access to information allow them to participate effectively in corporate governance.

In addition, the social characteristics of industries may influence the effects of large-block owners on performance. In industries with a strong history of owner involvement, active participation of owners in corporate governance may be expected and accepted by managers, as political institutions and shared understandings of interdependencies, or "conceptions of control," occur within each industry (DiMaggio & Powell 1983, Fligstein & Brantley 1992).

Firms also compete in industries that are emerging, growing, mature, or declining. The stage of the industry in this "corporate lifecycle" may influence how ownership structures affect firm performance. Research on venture capital firms indicates how these firms actively nurture and monitor startup companies through a series of stages (Sahlman 1990). Research on LBO associations have indicated how in declining industries with overcapacity, the discipline imposed by debt obligations combined with changes in management can lead to the creation of value (Jensen 1989).

Finally, the overall stability of the industry is likely to influence the effects of large-block owners on performance. Certain periods may be characterized by "environmental turbulence" (Haleblian & Finkelstein 1993) where industry shifts require strategic decisions that may reveal whether or not large-block shareholders "control" the corporation. Contingent on industry conditions, shareholders may have "active" or "latent" power (Herman 1981).

These important aspects of industry conditions may be developed into a "contingency theory of corporate governance" (Kang 1996), which suggests different types of owners are more or less effective at capturing property rights and increasing corporate performance, contingent on the specific industry context. Such a theory of corporate governance suggests that, one, there is no one best firm ownership structure, two, not all ownership structures are equally effective, and three, the best way to structure ownership depends on industry characteristics. This approach parallels Lawrence & Lorsch's work on organizational structure in *Organizations and Environments*, where they argue that, one, there is no one best way to organize, two, not all ways of organizing are equally effective, and three, the best way to organize depends on the nature of the environment to which the organization relates (Lawrence & Lorsch 1967).

Therefore, the "fit" between different types of owners and particular industry and competitive conditions then should determine the relationship between ownership organization and performance. A contingency approach to corporate governance offers an alternative to proposed solutions that assert certain investors, such as public pension funds, are ideal "active" investors across all industries (Pound 1992). The fit between different types of shareholders and firms may depend on the stage of the firm in the corporate lifecycle. Start-up firms often feature large-block ownership by founders, growth firms are often owned by venture capitalists, mature firms often feature family owners, and declining industries are often owned by LBO associations.

CONCLUSION

We have reviewed theory and evidence about ownership as an important sociological and organizational variable that affects firm performance. Nearly twenty-five years have passed since the "astonishing consensus" that managers, rather than owners, control modern corporations was found to be a social scientific "pseudofact" (Zeitlin 1974). However, the assumption of "managerialism" is again prevalent, as recent organizational research downplays the importance of ownership and instead focuses on other varieties of social structures, social relationships, and institutions that may constrain managers. Owners are now routinely depicted as fungible, where there is assumed to be virtually no social component in owner-manager relations. Although agency theory has brought important insights on the incentives of participants in corporations, its depiction of the corporation as being composed of principal and agent relationships has focused attention away from the interesting and important question of how power relationships develop among organizational participants. In particular, certain types of large-block shareholders may have sufficient formal authority, social influence, and expertise to capture property rights to gain control of the firm, giving them disproportionately large amounts of benefit and use rights. Ownership types offer an alternative approach to measuring ownership structure purely in terms of ownership concentration, or simply classifying firms as owner-controlled or manager-controlled. The relationships between owners and managers have an important social dimension that cannot be expressed simply in contractual terms.

Our review suggests a contingency theory of corporate governance where the effect of ownership on firm performance is contingent on the "fit" between owner types and the industry context. Certain types of large-block owners may lead to increased firm performance, contrary to the "managerialist" assumption that ownership structure does not matter. We do not suggest managers are unimportant in determining firm performance. Historical accounts suggest a key failure of "personal capitalism" was that British enterprises controlled by owner-managers failed to employ the full staffs of professional managers necessary to govern the increasingly complex organizations, distribution channels, and production processes that characterized the Second Industrial Revolution (Chandler 1990). Corporations must employ highly skilled professional managers, but certain types of large-block shareholders may increase the effectiveness of these managers by shaping strategic decisions in ways that are associated with increased corporate performance.

The importance of studying ownership is likely to increase as the nature and structure of ownership continues to evolve in the US economy and in the world. Capital markets are possibly becoming increasingly efficient, with information on firm strategy and investment decisions more readily accessible to investors. At the same time, modern corporations have become less reliant on physical assets and are more dependent on intangible assets such as intellectual property and highly skilled employees who are often given ownership stakes as a form of compensation. Recent changes in ownership patterns are also likely to increase the importance of understanding the distributive consequences of the effect of ownership structure on performance, as the efficiency and distributive consequences of ownership are highly intertwined. Finally, although there may be a significant degree of "separation of ownership and control" in the United States, this is certainly not the case in most of the other wealthy economies in the world, where much of the theory developed on the Berle & Means corporation may only have limited relevance (La Porta et al 1998). Therefore, we conclude that ownership is an important but neglected sociological and organizational variable that deserves continued academic inquiry.

Literature Cited

Adams J. 1996. Principals and agents, colonialists and company men:the decay of colonial control in the Dutch East Indies. *Am. Sociol. Rev.* 61(1):12–28

Allen MP, Panian SK. 1982. Power, performance, and succession in the large corporation. *Admin. Sci. Q.* 27(4):538–47

Barzel Y. 1997. *Economic Analysis of Property Rights.* Cambridge, UK: Cambridge Univ. Press. 2nd ed.

Bendor J, Moe TM. 1985. An adaptive model of bureaucratic politics. *Am. Polit. Sci. Rev.* 79:755–74

Berle AA, Means GC. 1932. *The Modern Corporation and Private Property.* New York: Harcourt, Brace & World

Bethel JE, Liebskind JP, Opler T. 1998. Block share purchases and corporate performance. *J. Financ.* 53(2):605–34

Bhagat S, Black B. 1998. The uncertain relationship between board composition and firm performance. In *Corporate Governance: The State of the Art and Emerging Research,* ed. L Hopt, M Roe, E Wymeersch, S. Prigge. Oxford, UK: Oxford Univ. Press

Bhagat S, Black BS, Blair M. 1997. *Relational investing and firm performance. Work. Pap.* Columbia Law Sch., Cent. Law Econ. Stud.

Black BS. 1998. Shareholder activism and corporate governance in the United States. In *The New Palgrave Dictionary of Economics and the Law,* ed. P Newman. New York: Groves Dictionaries

Black BS, Gilson R. 1998. Venture capital and the structure of capital markets:Banks versus stock markets. *J. Financ. Econ.* 47(3): 243–77

Blasi J, Conte M, Kruse D. 1996. Employee stock ownership and corporate performance among public companies. *Ind. Labor Relat. Rev.* 50(1):60–79

Brickley JA, Lease RC, Smith CW. 1988. Ownership structure and voting on antitakeover amendments. *J. Financ. Econ.* 20(1–2):267–91

Bromley DW. 1989. *Economic Interests and Institutions: The Conceptual Foundations of Public Policy.* New York: Basil Blackwell

Burch PH. 1972. *The Managerial Revolution Reassessed.* Lexington, MA: Heath

Chaganti R, Damanpour F. 1991. Institutional ownership, capital structure and firm performance. *Strat. Manage. J.* 12:479–91

Chandler AD. 1977. *The Visible Hand:The Managerial Revolution in American Business.* Cambridge, MA: Harvard Univ. Press

Chandler AD. 1990. *Scale and Scope:The Dynamics of Industrial Capitalism.* Cambridge, MA: Harvard Univ. Press

Cho M. 1998. Ownership structure, investment, and the corporate value: an empirical analysis. *J. Financ. Econ.* 47(1): 103–21

Clark RC. 1986. *Corporate Law.* Boston, MA: Little, Brown

Corbin A. 1922. Taxation of seats on the stock exchange. *Yale Law J.* 31:429

Dahrendorf R. 1959. *Class and Class Conflict In Industrial Society.* Stanford, CA: Stanford Univ. Press

Davis GF. 1991. Agents without principles? The spread of the poison pill through the intercorporate network. *Admin. Sci. Q.* 36(4):583–613

Davis GF, Greve H. 1997. Corporate elite networks and governance changes in the 1980s. *Am. J. Sociol.* 103(1):1–37

Davis GF, Stout SK. 1992. Organization theory and the market for corporate control: dynamic analysis of the characteristics of large takeover targets, 1980–1990. *Admin. Sci. Q.* 37(4):605–33

Demsetz H, Lehn K. 1985. The structure of corporate ownership: causes and consequences. *J. Polit. Econ.* 93(6):1155–77

DiMaggio P, Powell WW. 1983. The iron cage revisited: institutional isomorphism and collective rationality in organizational fields. *Am. Sociol. Rev.* 48(2):147–60

Domhoff GW. 1967. *Who Rules America?* Englewood Cliffs, NY: Prentice Hall

Fama EF, Jensen MC. 1983. Separation of ownership and control. *J. Law Econ.* 26(2):301–25

Finkelstein S. 1992. Power in top management teams: dimensions, measurement and validation. *Acad. Manage. J.* 35(3):505–38

Fligstein N. 1990. *The Transformation of Corporate Control.* Cambridge, MA: Harvard Univ. Press

Fligstein N, Brantley P. 1992. Bank control, owner control, or organizational dynamic: Who controls the large modern corporation? *Am. J. Sociol.* 98(2):280–307

French JRP, Raven B. 1968. The bases of social power. In *Group Dynamics,* ed. D Cartwright, A Zander, pp. 259–69. New York: Harper & Row. 3rd ed.

Glasberg D, Schwartz M. 1983. Ownership and control of corporations. *Annu. Rev. Sociol.* 9:311–32

Gorski P. 1993. The protestant ethic revisited:

disciplinary revolution and state formation in Holland and Prussia. *Am. J. Sociol.* 99(2):265–316

Haleblian J, Finkelstein S. 1993. Top management team size, CEO dominance, and firm performance: the moderating roles of environmental turbulence and discretion. *Acad. Manage. J.* 36(4):844–63

Hamilton G, Biggart NW. 1980. Making the dilettante and expert: personal staffs in public bureaucracies. *J. Appl. Behav. Sci.* 16(2):192–210

Hamilton G, Biggart NW. 1984. *Governor Reagan, Governor Brown.* New York: Columbia Univ. Press

Hamilton G, Biggart NW. 1985. Why people obey: theoretical observations on power and obedience in complex organizations. *Sociol. Perspect.* 28(1):3–28

Haunschild PR. 1993. Interorganizational imitation: the impact of interlocks on corporate acquisition activity. *Admin. Sci. Q.* 38(4):564–92

Herman ES. 1981. *Corporate Control, Corporate Power.* Cambridge, MA: Cambridge Univ. Press

Hindley BV. 1970. Separation of ownership and control in the modern corporations. *J. Law Econ.* 13(1):185–221

Hohfeld WN. 1913. Some fundamental legal conceptions as applied in jural reasoning. *Yale Law J.* 23(16):30

Holderness CG, Sheehan DP. 1988. The role of majority shareholders in publicly held corporations. *J. Financ. Econ.* 20:317–46

Holmes OW. 1881. *The Common Law.* Boston, MA: Little, Brown. 1946. Reprint

Jensen MC. 1989. Eclipse of the public corporation. *Harv. Bus. Rev.* 67(5):61–74

Jensen MC. 1993. The modern industrial revolution, exit, and the failure of internal control systems. *J. Financ.* 48(3):831–80

Jensen MC, Meckling WH. 1976. Theory of the firm: managerial behavior, agency costs and ownership structure. *J. Financ. Econ.* 3(4):305–60

Johansson A. 1993. Structures, managers and owners: the case of the post–war Swedish paint industry. *Bus. Hist.* 35(2):87–98

Kamerschen DR. 1968. The influence of ownership and control on profit rates. *Am. Econ. Rev.* 58(3):42–44

Kang DL. 1996. *The impact of ownership type on organizational performance.* PhD thesis. Harvard Univ. Unpublished

Kang DL. 1998a. *The impact of ownership type on organizational performance: a study of the U.S. textile industry 1983–1992. Harvard Bus. Sch. Work. Pap. 98–109*

Kang DL. 1998b. *The "Buddenbrooks Effect": The generational effects of family ownership on resource allocation decisions and performance in public corporations. Harvard Bus. Sch. Work. Pap. 99–029*

Kaplan S. 1991. The staying power of leveraged buyouts. *J. Financ. Econ.* 29(2):287–313

Kiewiet DR, McCubbins M. 1991. *The Logic of Delegation.* Chicago: Univ. Chicago

Kiser E. 1994. Markets and hierarchies in early modern fiscal systems: a principal-agent analysis. *Polit. Soc.* 22(3):284–315

Kiser E. 1998. *Comparing varieties of agency theory in economics, political science, and sociology: an illustration from state policy implementation. Work. Pap. Univ. Wash.*

Kiser E, Schneider J. 1994. Bureaucracy and efficiency: an analysis of taxation in early modern Prussia. *Am. Sociol. Rev.* 59(2):187–204

Kiser E, Tong X. 1992. Determinants of the amount and type of corruption in state fiscal bureacracies: an analysis of late imperial China. *Comp. Polit. Stud.* 25(3):300–31

Kole S. 1994. *Managerial ownership and firm performance: Incentives or rewards? Work. Pap. 93-10.* Univ. Rochester, Rochester, NY

Kosnik R. 1987. Greenmail: a study of board performance in corporate governance. *Admin. Sci. Q.* 32(2):163–85

La Porta R, Lopez-de-Silanes F, Shleifer A. 1998. *Corporate ownership around the world. Work. Pap.* Nat. Bur. Econ. Res.

Larner RJ. 1970. *Management Control and the Large Corporation.* New York: Dunellen

Lawrence PR, Lorsch JW. 1967. *Organization and Environment.* Boston, MA: Harvard Bus. Sch. Press

Lewellen WG. 1969. Management and ownership in the large firms. *J. Financ.* 24:299–322

Loderer C, Martin K. 1997. Executive stock ownership and performance: tracking faint traces. *J. Financ. Econ.* 45(2):223–55

Lorsch JW, MacIver E. 1989. *Pawns or Potentates: The Reality of America's Corporate Boards.* Boston, MA: Harvard Bus. Sch. Press

Marx K. 1867. *Capital.* New York: The Modern Library

McConnell JJ, Servaes H. 1990. Additional evidence on equity ownership and corporate value. *J. Financ. Econ.* 27(2):595–612

McEachern WA. 1975. *Managerial Control and Performance.* Lexington, MA: Lexington Books

Mikkelson W, Partch M, Shah K. 1997. Ownership and operating performance of companies that go public. *J. Financ. Econ.* 44: 279–307

Mizruchi MS, Stearns LB. 1994. A longitudinal study of borrowing by large American corporations. *Admin. Sci. Q.* 39(1):118–40

Monsen RJ, Chiu JS, Cooley DE. 1968. The effect of separation of ownership and control on the performance of the large firm. *Q. J. Econ.* 82:435–51

Morck R, Shleifer A, Vishny RW. 1988. Management ownership and market valuation. *J. Financ. Econ.* 20:293–315

Ocasio W. 1994. Political dynamics and the circulation of power: CEO succession in U.S. industrial corporations, 1960–1990. *Admin. Sci. Q.* 39:285–312

Palmer D. 1983. Broken ties: interlocking directorates and intercorporate coordination. *Admin. Sci. Q.* 28(1):40–55

Palmer D, Friedland R, Jennings RD, Powers ME. 1987. The economics and politics of structure: the multidivisional form and the large U.S. corporation. *Admin. Sci. Q.* 32(1):25–48

Palmer D, Friedland R, Singh J. 1986. The ties that bind: organizational and class bases of stability in a corporate interlock network. *Am. Sociol. Rev.* 51(6):781–96

Palmer D, Jennings PD, Zhou X. 1993. Late adoption of the multidivisional form by large U.S. corporations: institutional, political, and economic accounts. *Admin. Sci. Q.* 38:100–31

Palmer J. 1973. The profit–performance effects of the separation of ownership and control in large U.S. industrial corporations. *Bell J. Econ. Manage. Sci.* 4(1): 293–303

Pfeffer J. 1981. *Power in Organizations.* New York: Harper Bus.

Pfeffer J. 1992. *Managing With Power: Politics and Influence in Organizations.* Boston, MA: Harvard Bus. Sch. Press

Pfeffer J, Salancik GR. 1978. *The External Control of Organizations.* New York: Harper & Row

Porter ME. 1992. *Capital Choices: Changing the Way America Invests in Industry.* Washington, DC: Council on Competitiveness

Poterba JM, Samwick AA. 1995. Stock ownership patterns, stock market fluctuations, and consumption. *Brook. Pap. Econ. Activity* 2:295–372

Pound J. 1992. *The rise of the political model of corporate governance and corporate control.* Cambridge, MA: John F. Kennedy Sch. Gov., Harvard Univ.

Roe M. 1991. A political theory of American corporate finance. *Columbia Law. Rev.* 91: 10–67

Roe M. 1994. *Strong Managers, Weak Owners.* Princeton, NJ: Princeton Univ. Press

Sahlman WA. 1990. The structure and governance of venture-capital organizations. *J. Financ. Econ.* 27(2):473–524

Salancik GR, Pfeffer J. 1980. Effects of ownership and performance on executive tenure in U.S. corporations. *Acad. Manage. J.* 23(4):653–64

Scherer FM. 1988. Corporate ownership and control. In *The U.S. Business Corporation: An Institution in Transition,* ed. JR Meyer, JM Gustafson, pp. 43–66. Cambridge, MA: Ballinger

Shleifer A, Summers L. 1988. Breach of trust in hostile takeovers. In *Corporate Takeovers: Causes and Consequence,* ed. AJ Auerbach, pp. 65–88. Chicago: Univ. Chicago Press

Shleifer A, Vishny RW. 1989. Management entrenchment: the case of manager-specific investments. *J. Financ. Econ.* 25(1):123–39

Sørensen AB. 1996. The structural basis of social inequality. *Am. J. Sociol.* 101(5): 1333–65

Useem M. 1980. Corporations and the corporate elite. *Annu. Rev. Sociol* 6:41–77

Wade J, O'Reilly C, Chandratat I. 1990. Golden parachutes: CEOs and the exercise of social influence. *Admin. Sci. Q.* 35(4): 587–603

Weber M. 1968. *Economy and Society: An Interpretive Sociology,* Vols. 1–3, ed. G Roth, C Wittich. New York: Bedminister

Weingast B, Moran M. 1983. Bureaucratic discretion or congressional control?: regulatory policy making by the federal trade commission. *J. Polit. Econ.* 91(5): 765–800

Westphal JD, Zajac EJ. 1997. Defections from the inner circle: social exchange, reciprocity, and the diffusion of board independence in U.S. corporations. *Admin. Sci. Q.* 42(1):161–83

Westphal JD, Zajac EJ. 1998. The symbolic management of stockholders: corporate governance reforms and shareholder reactions. *Admin. Sci. Q.* 43(1):127–53

Williamson O. 1985. *The Economic Institutions of Capitalism.* New York: Free Press

Wood BD. 1988. Principals, bureaucrats, and responsiveness in clean air enforcements. *Am. Polit. Sci. Rev.* 82(1):214-34

Wright EO. 1980. Varieties of Marxist conceptions of class structure. *Polit. Soc.* 9: 223–70

Zajac EJ, Westphal JD. 1995. Who shall govern? CEO/board power, demographic similarity, and new director selection. *Admin. Sci. Q.* 40(1):60–83

Zajac EJ, Westphal JD. 1996. Director reputation, CEO–board power, and the dynamics of board interlocks. *Admin. Sci. Q.* 41(3): 507–29

Zeckhauser R, Pound J. 1990. Are large shareholders effective monitors? An investigation of share ownership and corporate performance. In *Asymmetric Information, Corporate Finance, and Investment,* ed. R

Hubbard, pp. 149–80. Boston, MA: Harvard Bus. Sch. Press

Zeitlin M. 1974. Corporate control and ownership: the large corporation and the class. *Am. J. Sociol.* 79(5):1073–119

Zeitlin M, Ewen LA, Ratcliff RE. 1975. New princes for old? The large corporation and the capitalist class in Chile. *Am. J. Sociol.* 80(1):87–123

Annu. Rev. Sociol. 1999. 25:145–68

DECLINING VIOLENT CRIME RATES IN THE 1990S: Predicting Crime Booms and Busts

Gary LaFree

Department of Sociology, University of New Mexico, Albuquerque, New Mexico
87131; e-mail: lafree@unm.edu.

KEY WORDS: crime trends, crime waves, crime theories, longitudinal analysis, ahistoricism

---

ABSTRACT

The United States in the 1990s has experienced the greatest sustained decline
in violent crime rates since World War II—even though rates thus far have
not fallen as rapidly as they increased during the crime boom of the 1960s
and early 1970s. I review a set of exogenous and policy-related explanations
for the earlier crime boom and for the crime bust of the 1990s. I argue that our
understanding of crime trends is hampered by a lack of longitudinal analysis
and by ahistorical approaches. I identify a set of questions, concepts, and
research opportunities raised by taking a more comprehensive look at crime
waves.

INTRODUCTION

Recent declines in rates of violent crime in the United States caught many
policymakers and researchers off guard. These declines were perhaps more
surprising in that they came on the heels of dire predictions about the rise of a
generation of "superpredators" who would soon unleash the full force of their
destructive capacities on an already crime-weary nation (Bennett et al 1996,
Fox & Pierce 1994).

I argue in this paper that changes such as those involving the recent downturn in violent crime rates usually surprise researchers because we rely mostly

145

on cross-sectional analysis and rarely study social phenomenon like crime trends in a longitudinal context. I begin this article by looking more closely at the recent downturn in violent crime rates, comparing it to trends since World War II. I then summarize and evaluate several common explanations for changing violent crime rates. Finally, I identify a set of concepts that might be useful for moving our thinking about social phenomenon such as crime toward a more longitudinal framework.

Studying Crime Trends in Postwar America

I concentrate here on violent crime trends for the United States. While violent crime generally includes murder, rape, robbery, and aggravated assault, researchers agree that data are probably most accurate for murder and robbery (Gove et al 1985, O'Brien 1996). A focus on the United States is strategic in that it accounts for the greatest volume of research, although such a focus simultaneously underscores the strategic importance of developing more cross-national comparisons.

Researchers interested in studying violent crime trends in the United States are limited to two main data sources: the Uniform Crime Reports (UCR), collected annually since 1930 by the Federal Bureau of Investigation; and the National Crime Victimization Survey (NCVS), collected every six months since 1973 by the Bureau of Justice Statistics (Rand et al 1997). Space limitations prevent a detailed assessment of the strengths and weaknesses of these data sets (Biderman & Lynch 1991, LaFree 1998a:Ch. 2). I concentrate here on the UCR because it provides the longest uninterrupted crime series data for the United States.

Figure 1 shows UCR trends for murder and robbery, 1946 to 1997. I begin the series in 1946 because of serious validity problems with pre-World War II UCR data. I use "longitudinal" throughout this paper to refer to studies based on annual time-series analysis.

My first concern is to identify the major trends in violent crime rates during the post-World War II period. In fact, considering this issue provides insight because it illustrates how little emphasis we have placed on longitudinal changes in crime rates. We lack even a basic shared vocabulary to describe crime changes in precise language. I use the term crime "boom" to refer to a rapid increase in crime rates and crime "bust" to a rapid decline.

Converting the annual rates depicted in Figure 1 to annual percentage changes shows that the longest sustained increases in murder and robbery rates occurred from the early 1960s to the mid-1970s. Taken together, murder rates increased by 113.04% from 1963 to 1974 and robbery rates increased by 222.47% from 1961 to 1971. While rape and aggravated assault rates are generally less reliable, they also increased dramatically during this period; both

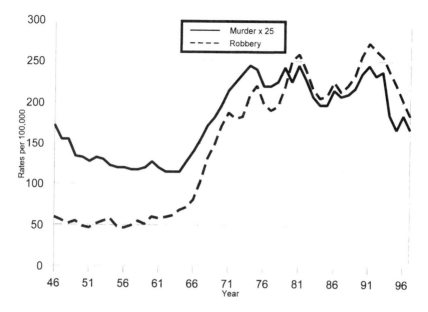

Figure 1 Murder and robbery rates, 1946–1997; data supplied by the U.S. Federal Bureau of Investigation, "Crime in the United States," *Uniform Crime Reports* annual, 1946 to 1997 (Washington, DC: Government Printing Office).

nearly tripled from the 1960s to the early 1970s. Hence, the most persuasive evidence for a postwar violent crime boom comes from the years about 1961 to 1974. While there were other periods of increase (especially the late 1970s and the late 1980s), none was as steep or as sustained.

Evidence for a single crime bust is less clear. Thus far at least, none of the four violent crimes rates have shown declines that were as long or as steep as the increases of the 1960s and early 1970s. Still, Figure 1 shows that, from 1991 to 1997, murder rates declined in five of six years and robbery rates declined in all six years. In fact, for both murder and robbery, the largest sustained declines of the postwar period have occurred in the 1990s. Murder rates dropped by 30.6% and robbery rates by 31.8% from 1991 to 1997. Rape and aggravated assault rates have also registered declines in the 1990s: rape rates fell by 15.1% and aggravated assault rates by 11.8%.

EXPLAINING POSTWAR VIOLENT CRIME TRENDS

One of the most important justifications for taking a longitudinal approach to crime trends is that it provides insights that are unavailable in cross-sectional

designs. With regard to the trends shown in Figure 1, two insights are especially important. First, postwar US violent crime trends sometimes changed
very rapidly. In the space of just over ten years in the 1960s and early 1970s,
murder rates more than doubled and robbery rates more than tripled. Likewise,
in the space of only six years in the 1990s, murder and robbery rates fell by
about a third. The simple rapidity of these changes calls into question explanations of crime based on fixed biological characteristics, deep-seated psychological characteristics, or slow-moving social characteristics.

Second, a longitudinal perspective underscores the obvious but often neglected fact that events like the crime boom of the 1960s and the crime bust of
the 1990s are situated in distinct historical periods. This fact reminds us of the
importance of considering not only what causes crime to increase or decline in
general, but more specifically, what particular historical events were directly
associated with these changes.

In the sections that follow, I divide common explanations for postwar crime
trends into exogenous and public policy effects. I specifically consider how
well each explanation fits the timing of the 1960s crime boom and the 1990s
crime bust.

Exogenous Effects

I define exogenous effects as those that are largely independent of crime policy. The three exogenous effects that have probably been most frequently
linked to violent crime by researchers are economic stress, political legitimacy, and family disorganization. Other exogenous effects with special relevance for crime trends are the proportion of young people, drug markets, and
changes in the public's routine activities.

ECONOMIC STRESS   The proposition that increased levels of economic stress
raise crime rates cuts across otherwise competing models, including theories
of social disorganization (Shaw & McKay 1942, Kornhauser 1978), social
strain (Merton 1938, Cloward & Ohlin 1960), violent subcultures (Wolfgang
1967, Blau & Blau 1982:118), conflict (Taylor et al 1973, Chambliss 1988),
criminal motivation (Cohen et al 1980, Cantor & Land 1985), and macroeconomics (Becker 1968, Brenner 1976). While specific arguments vary enor-
mously, most theorists assume that economic stress undermines legitimacy
and weakens social bonds.

Economic stress models of US crime rates work well for the early postwar
period when a strong economy was paired with low, stable crime rates. The
war jolted the US economy out of a devastating depression, matched the un-
damaged industrial plants of the United States against the war-torn factories of
Europe and Japan, and established America as a supermarket to the world
(Levy 1987, Wallerstein 1995). However, connections between economic

stress variables and crime trends are less certain for the middle postwar period (from about 1961 to 1973), when rapidly accelerating crime rates were paired with what appeared to be a fairly robust economy. This problem is well expressed by Wilson's (1975:3) influential challenge to researchers to explain "the paradox" of "crime amidst plenty." One possible explanation for this seeming paradox is that crime trends are dependent on specific economic stress measures.

Measures of economic stress can usefully be divided into absolute measures (which refer to how individuals or groups of individuals are doing in comparison to some fixed level of economic well-being) and relative measures (which emphasize how one individual or group of individuals is doing compared to other individuals or groups; LaFree 1998a:119–20). Common absolute measures of economic stress are poverty, median income, and unemployment; common relative measures are income inequality and inflation. Of the two types, relative measures have thus far been more successful at explaining longitudinal crime trends in the postwar United States (Devine et al 1988, LaFree & Drass 1996). While absolute measures of economic stress like unemployment and median income were generally favorable during the middle postwar years, relative measures like income inequality and inflation were far less favorable.

Although it is still too early to tell, economic stress perspectives may also help explain the crime bust of the 1990s. In 1996, the federal spending deficit reached its lowest level since 1979 (*US Economic Report to the President* 1997). In 1994, the poverty rate began to fall for the first time in five years and income inequality began a modest decline (*US Economic Report to the President* 1997). In 1997, unemployment reached its lowest level since 1973 (*US Economic Report to the President* 1997). After reaching double digits in the 1970s and early 1980s, inflation cooled off during the 1990s, remaining under 3% from 1990 to 1996 (*US Economic Report to the President* 1997).

POLITICAL LEGITIMACY   Weber (1947:324) defines legitimate power (or "authority") as "the probability that certain commands (or all commands) from a given source will be obeyed by a given group of persons" and adds that a basic criterion of legitimate power is a "minimum of voluntary submission" (p. 329). All societies face the ongoing problem of legitimizing their rules and laws and transmitting this legitimacy to succeeding generations. Legitimation is the process of explaining and justifying the social rules to new societal members (Berger & Luckmann 1967:93). This reasoning suggests that crime and deviance rates may be related to trends in the legitimacy of political institutions.

Before the mid-1960s, most researchers assumed that challenges to political legitimacy such as protests and riots were directly related to crime rates

(Useem 1998). Social disorganization (Davies 1962, Smelser 1962), breakdown (Tilly et al 1975, Useem 1985), tension (Lodhi & Tilly 1973), anomie (Merton 1938), and strain (Cloward & Ohlin 1960) theories all share the assumption that crime and collective political action are positively related because both flow from social breakdown. When there is a breakdown in social organization, informal sources of social control—family, work, school, voluntary organizations—lose their ability to channel individuals into conventional behavior. The resulting disorganization frees social actors to engage in a wide variety of antisocial behavior, including crime and collective action (Durkheim 1951, Smelser 1962).

But after the mid-1960s, this view of the association between collective political action and crime was increasingly discredited. The most articulate of these challenges came from resource mobilization theorists (McCarthy & Zald 1977, Oberschall 1978, Snyder & Tilly 1972), who argued that unlike crime and other forms of social pathology, collective action requires both access to resources and the development of a well-defined organizational structure. Because collective action and crime have different requirements, resource mobilization theorists reasoned that perspectives that assume that they spring from similar social forces are incorrect.

Probably owing in large part to the complexities of measuring political legitimacy, there are few longitudinal studies examining its relationship to crime. Using a content analysis of news stories recorded in the *New York Times Annual Index*, LaFree & Drass (1997) compare total event counts for collective political action associated with the civil rights movement to total rates of robbery, murder, and burglary for the United States, 1955 to 1991. They find a strong positive relationship between civil rights–related collective action and crime rates from 1955 to the early 1970s, but an increasingly negative relationship between the two thereafter. They interpret this as partial support for both social disorganization and resource mobilization perspectives: Social disorganization theory is supported in that street crime increased along with political unrest in the early postwar period; but resource mobilization theory is supported in that, compared to crime, collective political action declined more rapidly in the middle and late postwar years.

Arguments about the relationship between political legitimacy and crime seem better suited to explaining the crime boom of the 1960s than the crime bust of the 1990s. Still, there is evidence that the free fall in levels of political trust recorded in the 1960s has ended. This interpretation is consistent with many of the measures tapped since 1958 by the biennial national election survey on American attitudes toward government (Miller 1996). For example, for the past 40 years, this survey has asked respondents, "How much of the time can you trust the US government to do what is right?" The proportion of Americans answering "most of the time or just about always" declined rapidly during the 1960s and 1970s, scoring just over 25% in 1980 (LaFree 1998a: 102). But since 1980, the percentage who express trust in the federal government has held steady (just under 30%) and even begun to rise a bit. In fact, levels of trust tapped by this measure were higher in 1996 than in 1980 (LaFree 1998a:102). Other measures of public confidence in government tracked by the national election survey data provide similar evidence (LaFree 1998a: 104).

More generally, in the 1990s, there was no organized collective political action that remotely resembled the scope of the civil rights movement or the antiwar protests of the 1960s and 1970s.

FAMILY DISORGANIZATION   Measures of family disorganization have been among the most popular postwar explanations of crime trends in the United States. Again, while individual theories vary greatly, most emphasize one or more of three connections between family organization and crime. First, throughout human history, families have helped to regulate crime rates by serving as the primary institution for passing social rules and values from one generation to the next (Davis 1948). With few exceptions, children have more frequent and longer contacts with family members than with others, and family contacts are generally earlier and more emotionally intense than other contacts.

Second, families control crime by directly regulating the behavior of their members. Families may limit the delinquent behavior of their children by restricting their activities, by maintaining actual physical surveillance over them, and by knowing their whereabouts when they are out of sight (Hirschi 1995:128). Relatedly, families control the behavior of children simply by commanding their love and respect. A good deal of research confirms that children who care about their families will be more likely to avoid behavior that they know may result in shame, embarrassment, or inconvenience for family members (Hirschi 1995:128, Braithwaite 1989:48).

And finally, families reduce crime by protecting their members. Thus, families reduce the criminal victimization of family members by shielding them from property crimes such as burglary and theft, and also by guarding them from potential physical harm from unwanted suitors, molesters, muggers, and rapists (Hirschi 1995).

Despite the interest in connections between family organization and crime, there have been few longitudinal studies. Cohen & Felson (1979:600), however, created a longitudinal measure they call a "household activity ratio" by adding the number of married households with women in the paid labor force to the total number of non–husband-wife households. They use this measure to estimate changes in the amount of activity engaged in away from households. But it can also be interpreted as a measure of the amount of time individuals spend outside of traditional nuclear families. In their analysis of homicide, rape, aggravated assault, robbery, and burglary from 1947 to 1974, Cohen and Felson confirm that increases in the proportion of time individuals spend away from traditional families is consistently associated with increases in all of these street crimes; a finding largely confirmed in a later longitudinal study of murder, robbery, and burglary in the United States from 1948 to 1985 (Devine et al 1988).

The idea that rapid changes in the family are associated with the 1960s crime boom has obvious appeal. Although it is important not to overstate the homogeneity of the American family directly following World War II (Coontz 1992), the aggregate changes were nevertheless substantial. In the 1950s, divorce rates were lower than they would be for the next fifty years, and the proportion of American households containing individuals with no family connections hovered around 10% (US Bureau of the Census 1975:64). After the 1960s, rates of divorce, children born to unmarried parents, and single-parent families rapidly increased, and the total number of Americans living entirely outside of families skyrocketed (Goldscheider & Waite 1991).

Revolutionary changes in the economy no doubt contributed to these changes. The steady movement of men away from agricultural labor at home to positions in the paid labor force, which had already begun in earnest during the industrial revolution, continued to gain momentum during the postwar period (Coleman 1993:4). Women joined the paid labor force in record numbers during the postwar years (Burggraf 1997:18). And the amount of time children and young adults spent away from families and in schools rapidly accelerated (LaFree 1998a:159–61). These changes totally restructured the American family.

Connections between family organization and crime seem less certain for the crime bust of the 1990s. Still, there is some evidence of growing family stability. Divorce rates per 1000 married women peaked in 1979 and declined slightly into the 1990s (US Bureau of the Census 1996a:104). The proportion of births to unwed mothers was still increasing in the 1990s, but more slowly than it was in earlier decades (US Bureau of the Census 1995). Several economic indicators of family change also held steady or even reversed direction at the end of the twentieth century. For example, trends in female labor force participation and the formation of nonfamily households were flat in the 1990s (US Bureau of the Census 1996a:6, 394).

And importantly, the end of the twentieth century comes more than three decades after the most rapid changes in family organization began. Blended, dual-career, male-household manager, single-parent, and even gay family forms are becoming increasingly institutionalized. As these alternatives to the traditional family become more routinized, their ability to prevent deviance and crime should increase. In fact, there is evidence that some specific types of violent crime—notably, intimate partner homicides—have actually declined along with falling marriage rates (Rosenfeld 1997) and the increasing availability of domestic violence services (Dugan et al 1999).

Other Exogenous Effects

AGE STRUCTURE   The idea that changes in violent crime rates are due to the simple availability of young people over time has been one of the most common explanations of crime in postwar America. Of 24 longitudinal studies on the effects of age structure on homicide reviewed by Marvell & Moody (1991), 19 reported a significant positive relationship with the proportion of young people (measured variously as between 14 and 34 years of age). Moreover, 16 of these 19 studies found "strong" or "moderate" relationships between age and murder rates whereas only one of the negative relationship studies did. Among six time series studies of robbery, all six found a significant positive relationship with age.

In fact, the presumed strength of the relationship between age structure and crime rates lead Hirschi & Gottfredson (1983:124) to pronounce it "invariant" across cultures, historical periods, and types of crime. Indeed, like violent crime trends, the proportion of youth was relatively low following World War II, began to escalate in the 1960s, reached a peak in the early 1970s, and then declined somewhat into the 1980s and 1990s (LaFree 1998a:44). However, the importance of the age-crime relationship is easily exaggerated. Blumstein & Rosenfeld (1999:11) point out that the crime bust of the 1990s has been accompanied by a period in which age cohorts in the late teens and early 20s have been growing rather than declining in size. More generally, the authors note (1999:11) that age-composition changes are relatively small, with cohort sizes growing at a rate of about 1% per year. By contrast, age-specific crime rates have at times increased or decreased by as much as 20%.

DRUG MARKETS   The expansion and contraction of drug markets have also been suggested as an explanation for postwar American violent crime trends. Thus, Wilson (1975:ch. 8) draws connections between the crime boom of the 1960s and dramatic increases in heroin use. Many commentators have argued that the increases in rates of serious violent crime among juveniles in the middle and late 1980s were directly linked to the rapid rise of crack cocaine use (Blumstein 1995, Baumer et al 1998). Moreover, Blumstein & Rosenfeld (1999) argue that the crime bust of the 1990s may be explained in part by the declining number of new crack users and the increasing stability of drug markets.

As with several of the other explanations reviewed here, it is difficult to tell to what extent evolving drug markets have caused violent crime trends or are simply correlated with them. Blumstein's (1995) careful analysis of connections between the crack cocaine epidemic and the rise in youthful firearm violence provides evidence for a causal connection. However, some have argued that the nearly simultaneous, rapid increases in drug use that accompanied the violent crime boom of the 1960s may well be a spurious correlation (Goode 1989).

CHANGES IN ROUTINE ACTIVITIES   "Routine activity" explanations for changes in violent crimes have been most systematically advanced by Cohen and Felson and their associates (Cohen & Felson 1979, Cohen et al 1980). They argue that economic and social development in the United States has brought about changes in routine activities, increasing the dispersion of activities away from the home and consequently heightening opportunities for crime. They note that for a crime to occur the necessary elements ("motivated offenders," "suitable targets," and the absence of "capable guardians") must converge, and they argue that these elements were increasingly likely to co-occur in the United States during the high crime growth decades of the 1960s and 1970s. In particular, Cohen & Felson (1979:598–600) argue that the increasing dispersion of activities away from households coincided with dramatic increases in the proportion of violent crimes committed by strangers.

Felson (1998:ch. 9) also offers a routine activities explanation for the crime bust of the 1990s, emphasizing especially recent changes in property targets and access to cash. Felson argues that as valuable, easy-to-steal items like electronic equipment have become more widespread, their prices and thus the value of stealing them have dropped commensurately. Likewise, the explosive growth in credit card use, point of sale transactions, and money machines have greatly reduced the number and value of property crime targets.

Routine activity theories have contributed to our understanding of crime trends by focusing attention on the impact of situational variables. However, thus far researchers have not been able to demonstrate conclusively how situational variables are linked to violent crime trends or the extent to which any linkages are unique to situational as opposed to other variables (Birkbeck & LaFree 1993:126–9).

Public Policy Effects

I define public policy effects as the effects of those policies aimed directly or indirectly at reducing crime rates. The most obvious connection here is the effects of the criminal justice system. However, policymakers have also supported education and welfare programs at least partly in terms of crime reduction (*President's Commission 1967*:66).

CRIMINAL JUSTICE SYSTEM EFFECTS   The two parts of the criminal justice system that have probably been most frequently associated with violent crime trends in the postwar United States are police and prisons.

Police initiatives   Poor relations between the police and communities were a common explanation for the crime boom of the 1960s (Wilson 1975:109). However, much greater research attention has been focused on the role of police in the crime bust of the 1990s. The last decade of the twentieth century has witnessed a nationwide adoption—or revival—of policing styles variously called "community policing" or "community oriented policing" (Roth & Moore 1995). The best publicized example of the impact of this reorientation on violent crime trends has occurred in New York City (Kelling & Coles 1996). In the early 1990s, New York City police began a citywide campaign against "quality of life" offenses—drinking in public, urinating in the streets, making excessive noise, and other forms of incivility (Anderson 1997:52). Police especially targeted aggressive young toughs who were especially threatening to neighborhoods.

The results have been widely heralded. Only 985 homicides occurred in New York City in 1996—a 57% decline from the peak of 2262 in 1990 (Anderson 1997:53). Similar results are being attributed to changed policing strategies in other cities (Kennedy et al 1996). However, the exact connections between changes in policing and declining rates of violent crime are difficult to gauge because crime rates have decreased both in cities that have changed policing styles and cities that have not. Moreover, no one has been able to establish the extent to which policing strategies interact with other variables thought to be related to crime rates.

Incarceration rates   The argument that increased incarceration reduces crime, especially through its effects on deterrence and/or incapacitation, has also been frequently advanced to explain postwar crime trends (Devine et al 1988, Blumstein et al 1978). Several researchers using annual time-series data for the United States report consistent positive effects of imprisonment on violent crime rates (Cantor & Land 1987, Bowker 1981). Devine et al (1988) found a strong connection between annual changes in homicide, robbery, and burglary rates and changes in prison population, controlling for a variety of economic and social variables, 1948 to 1985; a finding updated and replicated for homicides, robberies, and assaults by Marvell & Moody (1997).

From the end of World War II until the mid-1970s, imprisonment rates in the United States hovered around 100 prisoners per 100,000 US residents (*US Bureau of Justice Statistics 1997a*:518). In fact, imprisonment rates in 1973 were about the same as they had been in 1946. But from 1974 to 1996, US imprisonment rates more than quadrupled, reaching a century high of 427 per 100,000 residents (*US Bureau of Justice Statistics 1997b*:1). From 1990 to 1996 alone, imprisonment rates increased by 43.8% (*US Bureau of Justice Statistics 1997b*:1). Freeman (1995:172) provides the startling conclusion that by 1995, the number of American men under the supervision of corrections had surpassed the total number of unemployed men. While much research confirms that informal social controls are generally more effective than formal controls such as imprisonment in reducing crime (Braithwaite 1989, Tyler 1990), nevertheless, increases in formal sanctions of this magnitude have undoubtedly dampened US crime rates in the 1990s.

EDUCATION AND WELFARE EFFECTS   Schools, like families, can discourage crime by reducing criminal motivation, by increasing the effectiveness of social control, and in principal at least, by protecting students from the criminal behavior of others. There is a well-known tendency for offenders to be drawn from those with low levels of educational attainment (Elliott & Voss 1974). There is also evidence that juveniles who accept the legitimacy of education and who have high educational aspirations and long-term educational goals are less likely to engage in delinquency (Liska 1971:12, Figueira-McDonough 1984:325). Schools can reduce crime by effectively monitoring and supervising the behavior of children under their custody (Toby 1995:152–58). More generally, research shows that juveniles are less likely to commit crime when they are strongly attached to school (Braithwaite 1989:28–29) and when they are more successful in school (Agnew 1985:151).

Despite the great interest in the potential impact of expanding educational attainment on crime, there have been few longitudinal studies (Long & Witte 1981). The crime bust of the 1990s does coincide with continued expansion of educational attainment. During the 1990s, the proportion of 14 to 17 year olds enrolled in school topped 96%, the proportion of 18 and 19 year olds in school reached 59.4%, and the total proportion of young adults 20 to 24 years old in school reached 31.5% (US Department of Education 1997:15).

But educational attainment also expanded rapidly in the 1960s and 1970s— at the same time as the crime boom. In fact, any connection between educational attainment and crime is likely complex. For example, Carnoy (1972) argues that the effects of educational attainment are complicated by its relativity: expanding educational attainment may improve prospects for graduates but may also lower prospects for nongraduates. LaFree & Drass (1996:618) point out that the capacity of educational attainment to create more egalitarian social conditions ultimately depends on the strength of the economy. Their time-series analysis of murder, robbery, and burglary arrest rates for United States 1957 to 1990 showed that whether increasing levels of educational attainment reduced arrest rates for whites and African Americans depended on levels of income inequality.

The most obvious connection between welfare spending and crime is welfare's presumed ability to ameliorate economic stress and thereby reduce the motivation of potential offenders to commit crime and to improve the effectiveness of informal social control mechanisms. These connections would presumably apply most directly to those violent crimes with immediate economic benefits like robbery and some types of homicide. In an annual time-series analysis, Devine et al (1988) found that total spending on Aid to Families with Dependent Children and other public relief was consistently associated with declining burglary rates and marginally associated with declining robbery rates, 1948 to 1985. However, spending on welfare had no effect on homicide rates. In addition, cross-national studies generally support the conclusion that countries that spend more on public assistance have lower rates of child homicide victimization (Fiala & LaFree 1988; Gartner 1990).

In 1948, total US welfare spending amounted to $83 *per capita* (in 1995 dollars; *US Bureau of the Census 1985*:26–28). Spending rates increased only slightly during the early postwar period, reaching $116 *per capita* in 1960 (pp. 26–28). But from the mid-1960s to the late 1970s, increases in welfare spending were rapid. From 1964 to 1978 alone, total *per capita* welfare spending (again, in 1995 dollars) more than quadrupled—from $121 per year to $551 dollars per year (*US Bureau of the Census* 1996b:1).

Connecting levels of welfare spending to the crime bust of the 1990s seems more problematic. In 1996, Congress replaced Aid to Families with Dependent Children (AFDC) and several other long-established programs with the Temporary Assistance for Needy Families (TANF) program (Watts 1997). The new law sets up a system of block grants to the states, mandates that federal funding for TANF programs be capped at $16.4 billion annually through the year 2002, and stipulates that recipients can only receive TANF benefits for a maximum of five years. However, because of the way these changes are being phased in, it is too early to tell what impact if any they will have on violent crime rates. Moreover, recent changes in the welfare system have been implemented during a period when the economy has been relatively strong.

IMPEDIMENTS TO THE STUDY OF CRIME WAVES

Undoubtedly, a simple lack of usable time-series data has been a major impediment to the longitudinal analysis of crime and related phenomena. Even in those relatively rare circumstances in which a given variable has been collected reliably over time, it is seldom possible to gather more than 50 years worth of annual data. This means that time-series analysis must confront many of the same limitations that face comparative research in general: small sample sizes, limited variables, and data based on convenience rather than theory (Lieberson 1991, Ragin 1987). Although longitudinal analysis of crime rates has grown more sophisticated over time, methodological and analytical problems have made it difficult to test competing explanations (LaFree 1998b: 135–7). But there are at least two more fundamental impediments to longitudinal studies of crime waves; one springs from sociology in general and the other is more specific to the study of crime waves.

Ahistoricism and Crime

The general impediment is the ahistoricism that has characterized much quantitative time-series research in sociology. Isaac & Griffin (1989) claim that this ahistoricism is in turn rooted in three common and rarely examined assumptions: theory and history should be separated; time may be treated ahistorically; and quantitative methods should take primacy over historical considerations.

SEPARATING THEORY AND HISTORY   Isaac & Griffin (1989) argue that most quantitative time-series analyses handle theories and their derivative hypotheses as independent of history, which "becomes something 'out there,' needing no explicit theorization" (p. 875). This separation treats social processes as if they were independent of history so that determinants of social phenomena are expected to be similar, for example, in the contemporary United States, England in the eighteenth century, or ancient Greece.

An example of this ahistoricism in criminology can be found in the now voluminous quantitative literature on connections between criminal processing and offender's race (Kleck 1981, Blumstein et al 1983). As cross-sectional research accumulates over time, it is easy to interpret each new study as if it were testing relationships between criminal justice outcomes and race for all time. Thus, research which concludes that there is little evidence of discrimination against African Americans in criminal processing at a given point in time (e.g. Kleck 1981) is sometimes incorrectly used to draw conclusions about the viability of race discrimination theories of criminal processing in other periods. Similarly, research that demonstrates discrimination against African Americans in a particular period (e.g. Russell 1998) is sometimes incorrectly used to support theories of discrimination across all periods.

AHISTORICAL TIME   Isaac & Griffin's second point is that much longitudinal sociology research treats time as a "linear organizing device" marking incremental, equal units (1989: 875). This ahistorical time is conceptualized as undifferentiated and external to events and relationships and assumes that relationships between independent and dependent variables are consistent over given measures of time.

But whether relationships between measures of crime and other variables are consistent over time is an empirical question. For example, comparing annual event counts for the total number of collective actions taken in support of the civil rights movement (e.g. sit-ins, demonstrations, riots) to total annual arrest rates for robbery, homicide, and burglary, LaFree & Drass (1997) found that the relationship between crime arrest rates and rates of collective political action was historically contingent: positive and statistically significant for a period from 1955 to 1972, but unrelated or negatively related thereafter.

PRIMACY OF METHODOLOGY OVER HISTORY   Isaac & Griffin's third point is that quantitative longitudinal studies in sociology are usually governed more by statistical than historical criteria. Because of the emphasis on statistical significance, researchers frequently push to expand the length of their time series analysis even when this expansion is unrelated or antithetical to theoretically critical historical events. Because of the difficulties of obtaining sufficient data to permit a quantitative analysis, this consideration is especially germane to the developing area of longitudinal analysis of crime trends.

Crime Waves in Criminology

The more specific impediment to the development of an empirical study of crime waves is a longstanding tendency by researchers to treat crime waves as socially constructed epiphenomena, rather than as empirical facts with important theoretical and policy implications. This view is exemplified by Erikson's (1966) influential study of deviance in the Puritan colonies of Massachusetts in the seventeenth century. Erikson identifies three "crime waves" during the first sixty years of settlement: the Antinomian controversy (a challenge to the community's religious establishment), the arrival of the Quakers from Pennsylvania, and the Salem witch hysteria. But he then argues that all three waves were not fueled by increases in crime rates—which remained relatively stable over the six decades—but were instead efforts to shift public attention away from other problems and create social unity.

Like Erikson, the few researchers who have studied crime waves in contemporary America (Fishman 1978, Graber 1980) have most often interpreted them as social constructs, often emphasizing the generally weak connections between concern about crime and actual crime rates. For example, Fishman (1978) argues that crime waves are constructed when the news media devotes considerable attention to a small number of crimes, encouraging law enforcement agents to bring evidence only of these crimes forward. Relatedly, Beckett (1997) compares increases in rates of street crime in the 1960s and 1970s to levels of public concern about crime and to levels of punishment. While she does not conclude that the increases in crime were imaginary, she nevertheless concentrates on the weak relationship between actual crime levels and public fear of crime to argue against the rise in public support for more punitive crime policies.

PROMISING DIRECTIONS

The study of crime waves might be advanced by examining research in other fields where the behavior of waves has been studied more intensively: including mathematics and engineering (Chui 1992, 1995, Bailey 1975); economics, history and political science (Fischer 1996, Goldstein 1988, Gurr 1977); and epidemiology (Potterat et al 1985, Wallace & Wallace 1990). By treating crime waves as an important research issue, we immediately raise several largely unexplored questions about their nature and their relationship to individual behavior.

Waves and Individual Decision-Making

Perhaps the most fundamental issue advanced by taking crime waves more seriously is the implications raised for the individual decision to commit crime. Just as individual investors would be profoundly affected by whether they happened to enter the stock market in 1928 or 1998, so too, apart from any psychological make-up or deep-seated biological characteristics, individual decisions to commit crimes are going to be profoundly affected by their chance location in history. This is because individual decisions are in part a product of how many other individuals are engaging in crime at a given point in time. Schelling (1978:14) states this interrelationship between individual action and broader social trends in general terms: "People are responding to an environment that consists of other people responding to their environment, which consists of people responding to an environment of people's responses."

This way of conceptualizing criminal decision-making is compatible with Matza's (1964) influential work on delinquency and drift. Matza argues (p. 28) that delinquents are not locked into crime in any absolute way, but rather exist in a "limbo between convention and crime, responding in turn to the demands of each, flirting now with one, now the other...." Such reasoning suggests that it may well be easier for juveniles to "drift" into crime when they occupy a point in time that is characterized by high levels of criminal activity. Thus, holding constant biological drives, psychological predispositions, fear of punishment, morality and other factors, a given individual will be more likely to commit crime during a crime boom than a crime bust. Crime booms may thus lower thresholds for committing crime and contribute to "bandwagon" effects (Granovetter 1978:1425). Crime busts may raise thresholds for committing crime and contribute to "snob" effects.

Wave Length

The length of waves and whether these lengths are similar across cultures and historical periods are also largely unexplored. Reviews of economic cycles by Goldstein (1988:7) and Fischer (1996:273–77) distinguish between hegemony cycles (about 150 years), long waves or Kondratieff cycles (about 50 years), Kuznet cycles or long swings (about 20 years), Labrousse intercycles (about 10 years) and business, trade, or Julgar cycles (about 5 years). However, few criminologists have made similar attempts to specify the length of crime waves.

Gurr et al's (1977:623–24) study of crime trends in London, Stockholm, New South Wales, and Calcutta, 1820 to 1970, suggests that there may be considerable variation in crime wave lengths for different countries and time periods. For example, starting in the 1840s, London's murder and manslaughter rates declined steadily until the 1920s—a period of about 80 years. New South Wales also showed similar long-term declines. By contrast, declines in murder and manslaughter rates for Stockholm that began in the 1840s were interrupted twenty years later by a rapid resurgence in rates. Calcutta's rates changed even more rapidly. Figure 1 presented earlier shows that violent crime rates in the post-World War II United States increased most rapidly for a period of about 15 years—from the early 1960s to the mid-1970s.

Wave Shape

The shape of crime waves has also received little attention. Goldstein (1988:7) notes that waves can be divided into an expansion phase or upswing and a stagnation phase or downswing. The transition point from upswing to downswing is called a "peak," and the transition point from stagnation to expansion is called a "trough." Application of these distinctions to Gurr et al's (1977) data suggests that from 1873 to 1971, the city of Calcutta experienced murder and manslaughter peaks in about 1880, 1910, and at the end of the data collection period in 1971; and murder and manslaughter troughs in about 1890 and 1950. For the postwar United States, LaFree (1998a:22) shows that murder rates reached peaks in 1974, 1980, and 1991 and troughs in 1957, 1976, and 1984.

An important related issue is whether crime waves exhibit symmetric or asymmetric connections with other variables. Lieberson (1985:174) points out that because most research and theory in the behavioral sciences is based on cross-sectional data, researchers most often simply assume symmetry between independent and dependent variables: "the question of whether an increase in (some variable) X yields an increase (or a decline) in Y is not distinguished from the question of whether a decline in X yields a decline (or an increase) in Y." This assumption rules out the possibility that some longitudinal relations are fully or partially irreversible. For example, perhaps a severe economic depression raises crime rates permanently, even when the economy returns to its post-depression levels. Or relatedly, perhaps an economy that is first depressed and then returns to its former level results in crime rates either higher or lower than they were initially.

In a rare test for symmetry in the criminology literature, Cohen & Land (1987) examine the longitudinal relationship between age structure (population aged 15 to 24) and crime (murder and motor vehicle theft rates) in the United States, 1947 to 1984. They conclude that there is evidence for symmetry between crime and age structure for this period. By contrast, LaFree & Drass's (1997) study of the relationship between crime rates (homicide, robbery, and burglary) and collective political action cited earlier finds an asymmetrical relationship: crime rates and collective action were positively associated from 1955 to the early 1970s, but unrelated or negatively related thereafter.

Waves and Linearity

Longitudinal analysis also raises the possibility of nonlinear relationships over time between crime and its determinants. At present the literature in this area is largely unsystematic and scattered. However, from diverse sources, we can offer several useful sensitizing concepts: including, tipping points (Schelling 1978, Granovetter 1978), threshold models (Granovetter 1978, Wallace 1991), contagion effects (Crane 1991, Loftin 1986, Wallace &Wallace 1990), epidemic theories (Crane 1991), diffusion models (Burt 1987, Granovetter & Soong 1983, Pitcher et al 1978), and bandwagon effects (Granovetter 1978). While the exact application of these concepts varies greatly, all of them are grounded in the assumption that under the right circumstances, trends in social problems like crime may be nonlinear. Berry (1991:9) notes that the two general forms this nonlinearity can take are "accelerating acceleration" and "decelerating deceleration."

These concepts all suggest that rates of specific types of behavior may accelerate (or decelerate) rapidly once the occurrence of this behavior in a particular community reaches a critical level. For example, Schelling (1971) shows that "white flight" behaves as a "tipping point" phenomena such that when a given neighborhood reaches a particular concentration of African Americans, white flight increases inevitably and precipitously. Similarly, Rowe & Rodger's (1991) research on the average age at which teenagers lose their virginity in a given community can be interpreted in terms of a community-based tipping point: when levels of nonvirginity reach a certain level, they begin to accelerate dramatically.

Granovetter and his colleagues (1978, Granovetter & Soong 1983) develop a more formal approach to related issues through the concept of "thresholds." Granovetter (1978:1422) defines individual thresholds as that point where the perceived individual benefits of doing a particular thing exceed the perceived costs. Granovetter uses the decision to participate in a riot as an example. The cost to a given individual of joining a riot declines as riot size increases because the probability of being apprehended is smaller when more people are involved. Granovetter points out that different individuals will bring with them different thresholds for joining a riot. For example, political radicals may have low thresholds for joining riots: the benefits of rioting are high to them, the cost of arrest low. But at the same time, apart from individual predispositions, thresholds for everyone are lowered when a particular type of behavior becomes more common.

Crane (1991:1227) builds a "contagion model" of thresholds by assuming that social problems spread mostly through peer influence; an assumption he grounds in the criminology literature demonstrating the importance of peer influence on juvenile delinquency and other deviant behavior (Kandel 1980). This assumption raises the possibility that there may be identifiable levels of the incidence of social problems within given populations such that when the incidence reaches this critical point, the process changes explosively. Crane finds support for this possibility with data showing that when neighborhood levels of dropping out of school and teenage pregnancy reach certain levels, they jump dramatically, rather than showing continuing linear increases. Crane (1991) argues that the effect of neighborhood organization on social problems (including violent crime) in urban ghettos may also take this contagious form.

Key issues raised by sensitizing concepts such as these include the possibility that: (*a*) violent crime rates might increase explosively in response to key variables reaching a particular threshold or tipping point; (*b*) violent crime rates within communities or nations sometimes behave like epidemics, changing rapidly in a short time; (*c*) individual predispositions to violent behavior are affected by the context in which such behavior is already occurring in a given community or nation; and (*d*) violent crime rates do not always respond in a direct, linear way to predictive variables such as economic stress or age structure.

Synchronous and Asynchronous Waves

Another issue opened by considering the longitudinal properties of crime trends is the extent to which trends are synchronous across various geographical units and time periods. In a review of economic "long cycles," Goldstein (1988:4) argues that the long-term ups and downs of national economies are synchronous among core nations. Moreover, as the number of nations at the economic core has expanded in the modern period, economic synchrony has spread to larger regions of the world. Similar explorations could be applied to violent crime trends. Gurr et al (1977:619) conclude that historical crime trends for London, Stockholm, and New South Wales appear to be largely synchronous: "one might almost conclude that some common social and political dynamics created public order over the course of a century...then went crazily unsprung." By contrast, Gurr et al conclude that crime rates for Calcutta appear to be asynchronous with the other three cities.

CONCLUSIONS

Based on violent crime trends for the postwar United States, the best case for existence of a crime boom is the period from the early 1960s to the mid-1970s.

The 1990s have thus far represented the best case for a crime bust—although rates have thus far not fallen as fast in the 1990s as they increased in the 1960s.

The greatest impediment to longitudinal analysis is simple data availability. Annual crime data for the United States from the National Crime Victimization Survey extend only to 1973; UCR data extend back to 1930 but are less complete before 1960 and are extremely incomplete before World War II. Still, imagine how our interpretation of crime trends will change by 2045, when researchers should have a reasonably accurate, 100-year crime series. We can perhaps appreciate the implications of having an expanded longitudinal data set by projecting backward: How would our conclusions about crime trends differ if we had a usable crime series that extended back 100 years?

An approximation is provided by Eckberg (1995), who uses state-level death registration data and econometric modeling techniques to create an estimate of annual US murder rates from 1900 to 1989. Eckberg's estimates show that murder rates in the first three decades of the twentieth century were about the same as they were in the 1970s and 1980s. Judged from this perspective, the low murder rates of the 1940s and 1950s, rather than the high rates of the 1970s and 1980s, are the aberration. Eckberg's data also allow us to conclude that the decline in murder rates from 1931 (9.7 per 100,000) to 1957 (4.7 per 100,000) was steeper than the murder rate decline logged thus far in the 1990s (9.8 per 100,000 in 1991 compared to 6.7 per 100,000 in 1997).

More generally, imagine the kinds of analyses that could be done if a valid set of longitudinal data on violent crimes and other variables existed for the past century. For example, we could compare the effects of alcohol prohibition in the 1920s to the war on drugs of the 1980s; the crime boom of the early 1900s to the boom of the 1960s; and the impact of police reform and reorganization in the early 1900s compared to the community policing reforms of the 1990s.

Among the roles of social science, prediction is the most precarious. If crime rates continue to drop during the last few years of the twentieth century, then history will likely interpret the 1990s as a period of major crime declines in the United States. If, on the other hand, crime rates again begin to increase over the next few years, the first half of the 1990s will more closely resemble the early 1980s—a period when most street crime rates faltered before heading upward again.

Campbell (1994:2) predicts that the continuing accumulation of machine readable longitudinal data will soon create "a revolution" in social science forecasting. Clearly, the feasibility of doing longitudinal analysis and forecasting in areas such as violent crime rates improves every year. We can speed up these developments by devoting more time and energy to longitudinal approaches.

ACKNOWLEDGMENTS

The author would like to thank Bert Useem and Richard Wood for helpful comments on an earlier draft and the Harry Frank Guggenheim Foundation for research support.

> **Visit the *Annual Reviews home page* at**
> **http://www.AnnualReviews.org.**

Literature Cited

Agnew R. 1985. A revised strain theory of delinquency. *Soc. Forc.* 64:151–67

Anderson DC. 1997. The mystery of the falling crime rate. *Am. Prospect.* (May–June):49–55

Bailey NTJ. 1975. *The Mathematical Theory of Infectious Diseases and its Application.* New York: Hafner

Baumer E, Lauritsen JL, Rosenfeld R, Wright R. 1998. The influence of crack cocaine on robbery, burglary and homicide rates: a cross–city, longitudinal analysis. *J. Res. Crime Delinq.* 35:316–40

Becker G. 1968. Crime and punishment: an economic approach. *J. Polit. Econ.* 75:167–217

Beckett K. 1997. *Making Crime Pay: Law and Order in Contemporary American Politics.* New York: Oxford Univ. Press

Bennett W, DiIulio J, Walters J. 1996. *Body Count.* New York: Simon & Schuster

Berger PL, Luckmann T. 1967. *The Social Construction of Reality: A Treatise in the Sociology of Knowledge.* Garden City, NY: Anchor Books

Berry BJL. 1991. *Long-Wave Rhythms in Economic Development and Political Behavior.* Baltimore, MD: Johns Hopkins Univ. Press

Biderman AD, Lynch J. 1991. *Understanding Crime Incidence Statistics.* New York: Springer-Verlag

Birkbeck C, LaFree G. 1993. The situational analysis of crime and deviance. *Annu. Rev. Sociol.* 19:113–37

Blau JR, Blau PM. 1982. The cost of inequality: metropolitan structure and violent crime. *Am. Sociol. Rev.* 47:114–29

Blumstein A. 1995. Youth violence, guns and the illicit-drug industry. *J. Crim. Law Criminol.* 86:10–36

Blumstein A, Cohen J, Martin SE, Tonry MH.
1983. *Research on Sentencing: the Search for Reform.* Vol. 1. Washington, DC: Natl. Acad. Press

Blumsetin A, Cohen J, Nagel D, eds. 1978. *Deterrence and Incapacitation: Estimating the Effects of Criminal Sanctions on Crime Rates.* Washington, DC: Natl. Acad. Sci.

Blumstein A, Rosenfeld R. 1999. Explaining recent trends in US homicide rates. *J. Crim. Law Criminol.* In press

Bowker LH. 1981. Crime and the use of prisons in the United States: a time–series analysis. *Criminology* 27:206–12

Braithwaite J. 1989. *Crime, Shame and Reintegration.* Cambridge, UK: Cambridge Univ. Press

Brenner HM. 1976. *Estimating the social costs of national economic policy: implications for mental and physical health and criminal aggression. Paper No. 5,* Joint Econ. Com., Congress of the United States. Washington, DC: US Gov. Print. Off.

Burggraf SP. 1997. *The Feminine Economy and Economic Man: Reviving the Role of the Family in the Post Industrial Age.* Reading, MA: Addison–Wesley

Burt RS. 1987. Social contagion and innovation: cohesion versus structural equivalence. *Am. J. Sociol.* 92:1287–1335

Campbell RT. 1994. A data-based revolution in the social sciences. *ICPSR Bull.* 14:1–4

Cantor DI, Land KC. 1985. Unemployment and crime rates in the post-world war II United States: a theoretical and empirical analysis. *Am. Sociol. Rev.* 50:317–32

Carnoy M, ed. 1972. *Schooling in a Corporate Society.* New York: McKay

Chambliss WJ. 1988. *Exploring Criminology.* New York: Macmillan

Chui CK. 1992. *An Introduction to Wavelets.* Boston: Academic Press

Chui CK. 1995. *Wavelets: Theory, Algorithms and Applications.* Boston: Academic Press

Cloward RA, Ohlin LE. 1960. *Delinquency and Opportunity: A Theory of Delinquent Gangs.* New York: Free Press

Cohen LE, Felson M. 1979. Social change and crime rate trends: a routine activity approach. *Am. Sociol. Rev.* 44:588–608

Cohen LE, Felson M, Land KC. 1980. Property crime rates in the United States: a macrodynamic analysis, 1947–1977 with *ex ante* forecasts for the mid-1980s. *Am. J. Sociol.* 86:90–118

Cohen LE, Land KC. 1987. Age structure and crime: symmetry versus asymmetry and the projection of crime rates through the 1990s. *Am. Sociol. Rev.* 52:170–83

Coleman JS. 1993. The rational reconstruction of society. *Am. Sociol. Rev.* 58:1–15

Coontz S. 1992. *The Way We Never Were: American Families and the Nostalgia Trap.* New York: Basic

Crane J. 1991. The epidemic theory of ghettos and neighborhood effects on dropping out and teenage childbearing. *Am. J. Sociol.* 96:1226–59

Davies JC. 1962. Toward a theory of revolution. *Am. Sociol. Rev.* 27:5–19

Davis K. 1948. *Human Society.* New York: Macmillan

Devine JA, Sheley JF, Smith MD. 1988. Macroeconomics and social–control policy influences on crime rate changes, 1948–1985. *Am. Sociol. Rev.* 53:407–20

Dugan L, Nagin D, Rosenfeld R. 1999. Explaining the decline in intimate partner homicide: the effects of changing domesticity, women's status, and domestic violence resources. *Homicide Stud.* In press

Durkheim E. 1951. *Suicide.* Tr. by George Simpson. New York: Free Press

Eckberg DL. 1995. Estimates of early twentieth–century U.S. homicide rates: an econometric forecasting approach. *Demography* 32:1–16

Elliott DS, Voss H. 1974. *Delinquency and Dropout.* Lexington, MA: DC Heath

Erikson K. 1966. *Wayward Puritans.* New York: Wiley

Felson M. 1998. *Crime and Everyday Life.* 2nd ed. Thousand Oaks, CA: Sage

Fiala R, LaFree G. 1988. Cross-national determinants of child homicide. *Am. Sociol. Rev.* 53:432–45

Figueira–McDonough J. 1984. Feminism and delinquency. *Br. J. Criminol.* 24:325–42

Fischer DH. 1996. *The Great Wave: Price Revolutions and the Rhythm of History.* New York: Oxford Univ. Press

Fishman M. 1978. Crime waves as ideology. *Soc. Prob.* 25:531–43

Fox JA, Pierce G. 1994. American killers are getting younger. *USA Today* January: 24–6

Freeman RB. 1995. The labor market. In *Crime,* ed. JQ Wilson, J Petersilia, pp. 171–91. San Francisco, CA: Inst. Contemp. Stud.

Gartner R. 1990. The victims of homicide: a temporal and cross–national comparison. *Am. Sociol. Rev.* 55:92–106

Goldscheider FK, Waite LJ. 1991. *New Families, No Families? The Transformation of the American Home.* Berkeley: Univ. Calif. Press

Goldstein JS. 1988. *Long Cycles: Prosperity and War in the Modern Age.* New Haven: Yale

Goode E. 1989. *Drugs in American Society,* 3rd ed. New York: McGraw Hill

Gove WR, Hughes M, Geerken M. 1985. Are Uniform Crime Reports a valid indicator of the index crimes? An affirmative answer with minor qualifications. *Criminology* 23:451–501

Graber DA. 1980. *Crime, News and the Public.* New York: Praeger

Granovetter M. 1978. Threshold models of collective behavior. *Am. J. Sociol.* 83: 1420–43

Granovetter M, Soong R. 1983. Threshold models of diffusion and collective behavior. *J. Math. Sociol.* 9:165–79

Gurr TR. 1977. Crime trends in modern democracies since 1947. *Int. Annals Criminol.* 16:41–85

Gurr TR, Grabosky PN, Hula RC. 1977. *The Politics of Crime and Conflict: A Comparative History of Four Cities.* Beverly Hills: Sage

Hirschi T. 1995. The family. In *Crime,* ed. JQ Wilson, J Petersilia, pp. 121–40. San Francisco, CA: Inst. Contemp. Stud.

Hirschi T, Gottfredson M. 1983. Age and the explanation of crime. *Am. J. Sociol.* 89: 552–84

Isaac LW, Griffin LJ. 1989. Ahistoricism in time–series analyses of historical process: critique, redirection, and illustrations from U.S. labor history. *Am. Sociol. Rev.* 54: 873–90

Kandel DB. 1980. Drug and drinking behavior among youth. *Annu. Rev. Sociol.* 6: 235–85

Kelling G, Coles CM. 1996. *Fixing Broken Windows: Restoring Order and Reducing Crime in Our Communities.* New York: Free Press

Kennedy DM, Piehl AM, Braga AA. 1996. Youth violence in Boston: gun markets, serious youth offenders, and a use–reduction strategy. *Law Contemp. Probl.* 59: 147–83

Kleck G. 1981. Racial discrimination in criminal sentencing. *Am. Sociol. Rev.* 46: 783–804

Kornhauser R. 1978. *Social Sources of Delinquency.* Chicago: Univ. Chicago Press

LaFree G. 1998a. *Losing Legitimacy: Street Crime and the Decline of Social Institutions in America.* Boulder, CO: Westview

LaFree G. 1998b. A summary and review of cross–national comparative studies of homicide. In *Homicide Studies: A Sourcebook of Social Research,* ed. D Smith, MA Zahn, pp. 125–45. Thousand Oaks, CA: Sage

LaFree G, Drass KA. 1996. The effect of changes in intraracial income inequality and educational attainment on changes in arrest rates for African Americans and whites, 1957 to 1990. *Am. Sociol. Rev.* 61:614–34

LaFree G, Drass KA. 1997. African–American collective action and crime, 1955–91. *Soc. Forc.* 75:835–53

Levy F. 1987. *Dollars and Dreams.* New York: Russell Sage

Lieberson S. 1985. *Making it Count: The Improvement of Social Research and Theory.* Berkeley: Univ. Calif. Press

Lieberson S. 1991. Small N's and big conclusions: an examination of the reasoning in comparative studies based on a small number of cases. *Soc. Forc.* 70:307–20

Liska A. 1971. Aspirations, expectations, and delinquency: stress and additive models. *Soc. Q.* 12:99–107

Lodhi AQ, Tilly C. 1973. Urbanization, crime and collective violence in nineteenth century France. *Am. J. Sociol.* 79:296–318

Loftin C. 1986. Assaultive violence as a contagious social process. *Bull. NY Acad. Med.* 62:550–55

Long SK, Witte AD. 1981. Current economic trends: implications for crime and criminal justice. In *Crime and Criminal Justice in a Declining Economy,* ed. K Wright, pp. 69–143. Cambridge, MA: Oelgeschlager, Gunn & Hain

Marvell TB, Moody CE. 1991. Age structure and crime rates: the conflicting evidence. *J. Quant. Criminol.* 7: 237–73

Marvell TB, Moody CE. 1997. The impact of prison growth on homicide. *Homicide Stud.* 1:205–33

Matza D. 1964. *Delinquency and Drift.* New York: Wiley

McCarthy JD, Zald MN. 1977. Resource mobilization and social movements. *Am. J. Sociol.* 82:1212–41

Merton RK. 1938. Social structure and anomie. *Am. Sociol. Rev.* 3:672–82

Miller WE. 1996. *American National Election Studies Cumulative Data File, 1952–1996.* Ann Arbor, MI: Ctr. Polit. Stud.

Oberschall A. 1978. Theories of social conflict. *Annu. Rev. Sociol.* 4:291–315

O'Brien R. 1996. Police productivity and crime rates: 1973–1992. *Criminology* 34: 183–208

Pitcher BL, Hamblin RL, Miller JLL. 1978. The diffusion of collective violence. *Am. Sociol. Rev.* 43:23–35

Potterat J, Rothenberg R, Woodhorse D, Muth J, Pratts C, Fogle J. 1985. Gonorrhea as a social disease. *Sex. Transm. Dis.* 12: 25–32

President's Commission on Law Enforcement and the Administration of Justice. 1967. *The Challenge of Crime in a Free Society.* Washington, DC: US Gov. Print. Off.

Ragin C. 1987. *The Comparative Method: Moving Beyond Qualitative and Quantitative Strategies.* Berkeley: Univ. Calif. Press

Rand MR, Lynch JP, Cantor D. 1997. *Criminal Victimization, 1973–95.* Washington, DC: Dep. Justice

Rosenfeld R. 1997. Changing relationships between men and women: a note on the decline in intimate partner homicide. *Homicide Stud.* 1:72–83

Roth JA, Moore, MH. 1995. Reducing violent crimes and intentional injuries. *Res. in Action,* October:1–10. Washington, DC: Natl. Inst. Justice

Rowe DC, Rodgers JL. 1991. An "epidemic" model of adolescent sexual intercourse: applications to national survey data. *J. Biosoc. Sci.* 23:211–19

Russell KK. 1998. *The Color of Crime: Racial Hoaxes, White Fear, Black Protectionism, Police Harassment, and other Macroaggressions.* New York Univ. Press

Schelling TC. 1971. Dynamic models of segregation. *J. Math. Sociol.* 1:143–86

Schelling TC. 1978. *Micromotives and Macrobehavior.* New York: Norton

Shaw CR, McKay H. 1942. *Juvenile Delinquency and Urban Areas.* Chicago: Univ. Chicago Press

Smelser N. 1962. *Theory of Collective Behavior.* New York: Free Press

Snyder D, Tilly C. 1972. Hardship and collective violence in France, 1830–1960. *Am. Sociol. Rev.* 37:520–32

Taylor I, Walton P, Young J. 1973. *The New Criminology: For a Social Theory of Deviance.* Boston: Routledge & Kegan Paul

Tilly C, Tilly L, Tilly R. 1975. *The Rebellious Century, 1830–1930.* Cambridge: Harvard Univ. Press

Toby J. 1995. The schools. In *Crime,* ed. JQ Wilson, J Petersilia, pp. 141–70. San Francisco, CA: Inst. Contemp. Stud.

Tyler TR. 1990. *Why People Obey the Law.* New Haven: Yale Univ. Press

US Bureau of the Census. 1975. *Historical Statistics of the United States: Colonial Times to 1970.* Washington, DC: US Gov. Print. Off.

US Bureau of the Census. 1985. *Historical Statistics on Governmental Finance and Employment 1985.* Washington, DC: US Gov. Print. Off.

US Bureau of the Census. 1995. *Statistical Abstract of the United States, 1995.* Washington, DC: US Gov. Print. Off.

US Bureau of the Census. 1996a. *Statistical Abstract of the United States, 1996.* Washington, DC: US Gov. Print. Off.

US Bureau of the Census. 1996b. *Governmental Finances: 1984–1992, Series GF/92–5.* Washington, DC: US Gov. Print. Off.

US Bureau of Justice Statistics. 1997a. *Sourcebook of Criminal Justice Statistics 1996.* Washington, DC: Dep. Justice

US Bureau of Justice Statistics. 1997b. *Prisoners in 1996.* Washington, DC: Dep. Justice

US Department of Education. 1997. *Digest of Education Statistics 1996.* Washington, DC: Natl. Ctr. for Educ. Statist.

Useem B. 1985. Disorganization and the New Mexico prison riot of 1980. *Am. Sociol. Rev.* 50:677–88

Useem B. 1998. Breakdown theories of collective action. *Annu. Rev. Sociol.* 24:215–38

Wallace R. 1991. Social disintegration and the spread of AIDs: threshold for propagation along "sociogeographic" networks. *Soc. Sci. M.* 33:1155–62

Wallace R, Wallace D. 1990. Origins of public health collapse in New York City: the dynamics of planned shrinkage, contagious urban decay and social disintegration. *Bull. NY Acad. Med.* 66:391–434

Wallerstein I. 1995. *After Liberalism.* New York: New Press

Watts J. 1997. The end of work and the end of welfare. *Contemp. Sociol.* 26:409–12

Weber M. 1947. *The Theory of Social and Economic Organizations.* New York: Oxford Univ. Press

Wilson JQ. 1975. *Thinking About Crime.* New York: Basic

Wolfgang ME. 1967. *The Subculture of Violence.* Newbury Park, CA: Sage

Annu. Rev. Sociol. 1999. 25:169–90

GENDER AND SEXUAL HARASSMENT

Sandy Welsh

Department of Sociology, University of Toronto, 203 College Street, Toronto, Ontario, Canada, M5T 1P9; e-mail: welsh@chass.utoronto.ca

KEY WORDS: measurement, organizational context, consequences of harassment

ABSTRACT

Research on sexual harassment is still in its infancy. Over the past 20 years, research has moved from prevalence studies to more sophisticated empirical and theoretical analyses of the causes and consequences of sexual harassment. This review provides an overview of the prevalence and measurement of harassment along with some suggestions for developing standard measures of sexual harassment. Researchers are encouraged to include organizational forms of harassment in their measures, along with commonly understood individual forms. The most prominent and promising explanations of harassment are discussed including societal, organizational, and individual level approaches. Of particular promise are approaches incorporating the gendered nature of organizational structures and processes. Research on the responses to and consequences of sexual harassment are also presented. The review ends with a discussion of overlooked areas and directions for future research, including the need for more advanced survey data collection techniques and qualitative research.

Even social scientists didn't study it,and they study everything that moves.
Catherine MacKinnon (1987:106; commenting on the lack of information about sexual harassment)

Twenty years ago, the study of sexual harassment focussed on whether or not sexual harassment was a social problem worthy of study and on descriptive analyses of its prevalence. In recent years, research has shifted to more sophisticated empirical and theoretical analyses of the causes and consequences of this phenomenon. Research now exists that attempts to answer many of the fundamental questions surrounding sexual harassment: What is sexual harass-

0360-0572/99/0815-0169$08.00

ment? How prevalent is sexual harassment? What are the predictors of sexual harassment? And what are the responses to and consequences of sexual harassment? This review outlines the major accomplishments in this field, some of its pitfalls, and research directions for the future.

WHAT IS SEXUAL HARASSMENT?

From a legal standpoint, sexual harassment is a form of sex discrimination composed of two forms of behavior: quid pro quo harassment and hostile environment harassment. Quid pro quo harassment involves sexual threats or bribery that are made a condition of employment or used as the basis for employment decisions. Hostile environment harassment captures those behaviors, such as sexual jokes, comments, and touching, that interfere with an individual's ability to do her/his job or that create an "intimidating, hostile or offensive working environment" (US EEOC 1980). This includes forms of gender harassment such as gender-based hazing and put-downs. After examining US legal decisions in sexual harassment cases, Schultz (1998b) comes to the following conclusion:

> Of course making a woman the object of sexual attention can also work to undermine her image and self-confidence as a capable worker. Yet, much of the time, harassment assumes a form that has little or nothing to do with sexuality but everything to do with gender. (p. 1687)

At its core, sexual harassment is often about letting women know they are not welcome in certain workplaces and that they are not respected members of the work group (Reskin & Padavic 1994). Sexual harassment continues to hamper employment opportunities for many women and men.

THE PREVALENCE AND MEASUREMENT OF SEXUAL HARASSMENT

How Prevalent Is Sexual Harassment?

Considerable variation exists in the estimated proportions of women reporting experiences with sexual harassment. [1] Depending on the sample used, 16% to 90% of working women experience sexual harassment in their lifetime (e.g. Brooks & Perot 1991, Gutek 1985, Terpstra & Baker 1989, US MSPB 1981). The recent US National Women's Study conducted by the Crime Victims and Treatment Center found 12% of women experienced harassment in their life-

---

[1]Most studies focus on the sexual harassment of women. Men's experiences are an understudied aspect of sexual harassment and are discussed later in this review. This discussion focuses on workplace sexual harassment. Researchers interested in the phenomenon of public harassment are referred to research by Gardner (1995).

time (Dansky & Kilpatrick 1997:164). Researchers agree that this study under-estimates nonverbal forms of hostile environment harassment (e.g. posting of pornography in the workplace and graffiti) and harassment perpetrated by co-workers. In Canada, studies using random samples of the general population, estimate that lifetime sexual harassment rates for women vary from 23% (Welsh & Nierobisz 1997) to 51% (Gruber 1997). Gruber's (1990) content analysis of 18 sexual harassment surveys found the median prevalence rate to be 44%. When coworker behavior is included, the prevalence rate ranges from 40% to 50% (Fitzgerald et al 1995c). The brief overview of prevalence rates highlights one of the major problems confronting the empirical study of sexual harassment, as these differences are attributed, in part, to survey measurement issues.

Measuring Sexual Harassment

Some measurement issues identified as problematic in research on sexual har-assment include differences in sampled populations, response rates, number of sexual harassment items, and context and time frame of questions (see Gruber 1990, 1992, Fitzgerald & Shullman 1993, Arvey & Cavanaugh 1995, Welsh & Nierobisz 1997). For example, studies with higher survey response rates that use random samples tend to report lower prevalence rates than do other stud-ies. As well, in early sexual harassment surveys there was little consensus as to how sexual harassment was defined. Most surveys provided a list of sexual be-haviors derived in part from the EEOC definition. Often these lists of behav-iors were neither mutually exclusive nor exhaustive (Fitzgerald & Shullman 1993, Gruber 1992). Survey items also tended to be nonspecific such as asking about "pressure for relationships" or experiencing "sexual remarks and teas-ing" (e.g. CHRC 1983). Extremely brief items are problematic for they may be interpreted differently by survey respondents. To overcome this, Fitzgerald & Shullman (1993) advocate the use of detailed and behaviorally based items to ensure that respondents interpret survey items in a similar manner. These types of items also improve respondents' recall of their experiences (Sudman & Bradburn 1982). As well, items should ask respondents about "unwanted" sex-ual experiences and should not use the term "sexual harassment" (Fitzgerald & Shullman 1993). In response to these early measurement problems, two com-prehensive and fairly consistent schemes for measuring sexual harassment have emerged in the literature: the Sexual Experiences Questionnaire (Fitzger-ald et al 1988) and the Inventory of Sexual Harassment (Gruber 1992).

The Sexual Experiences Questionnaire (SEQ) presents sexual harassment as a three-dimensional construct consisting of gender harassment, unwanted sexual attention, and sexual coercion (e.g., Fitzgerald et al 1988, 1995b, Gel-fand et al 1995). Each dimension of harassment utilizes multiple indicators. Gender harassment represents sexist and derogatory comments and jokes about women in general. Unwanted sexual attention consists of unsolicited sexual remarks, questions and/or sexual touching. Finally, sexual coercion captures all forms of sexual solicitations. The three harassment dimensions of the SEQ parallel legal constructs, with gender harassment and unwanted sexual attention linked to hostile environment harassment and sexual coercion linked to quid pro quo harassment (Fitzgerald et al 1997b:11). Overall, the founders of the SEQ define sexual harassment as a "psychological construct" consisting of "unwanted sex-related behavior at work that is appraised by the recipient as offensive, exceeding her resources, or threatening her well-being" (Fitzgerald et al 1997b:15).

To increase the reliability of responses, survey items of the SEQ are "behaviorally-based," including references to specific sexual behaviors (Fitzgerald & Shullman 1993, Welsh & Nierobisz 1997). Responses are classified on either a three-point or five-point Likert scale, measuring how often the harassment occurred (Gefland et al 1995, Fitzgerald et al 1995a). In one study of a public utility company, Fitzgerald et al (1995a) report alpha reliability coefficients of .82 for gender harassment, .85 for unwanted sexual attention, and .42 for sexual coercion (p. 435). The low value for sexual coercion reflects the lower base rate of this type of harassment compared to others. Since the SEQ builds on the empirically based categories of Till (1980), Fitzgerald et al (1997b) believe content validity is built into their measure. As well, most items are highly correlated with the criterion item "I have been sexually harassed" (Fitzgerald et al 1997b:13). Based on these types of analyses, the SEQ creators believe their instrument is designed to meet existing reliability and validity standards (Fitzgerald et al 1997b, 1995a) with initial reviews concurring (Arvey & Cavanaugh 1995).

The second measure, the Inventory of Sexual Harassment (ISH), was developed through the content analysis of previously published sexual harassment studies and court cases (Gruber 1992). The ISH consists of three categories of harassment: verbal comments, verbal requests, and nonverbal displays. This scheme captures severity of the harassment because sexual behaviors within each category fall on a continuum of less-to-more severe (see Gruber 1992, 1997, Gruber et al 1996 for details). Using the ISH, Gruber and colleagues (Gruber et al 1996, Gruber 1997) present evidence of the "universality" of women's sexual harassment experiences in the United States, Canada, and Europe. Although the ISH is critiqued for conflating legal distinctions between quid pro quo and hostile environment harassment, it can be used to add a level of specificity to the general SEQ categories (Fitzgerald et al 1997b:12; see Welsh et al 1998, for example).

More work on measurement is needed. First, separate indicators or subscales of frequency, duration, directness, and offensiveness for specific types of harassment should be developed further. Because both the causes and impact of harassment are not consistent across all types of harassment, these more refined measures are necessary (Fitzgerald & Shullman 1993, Gruber et al 1996, Gruber 1998). Second, cumulative or multidimensional measures of sexual harassment should be developed, as most harassment behaviors do not occur in isolation (Gruber et al 1996, Fitzgerald et al 1995b; for examples, see Schneider et al 1997, Macmillan et al 1996). Third, researchers other than the creators of the SEQ and the ISH need to perform reliability and validity tests on these measures (e.g. Stockdale & Hope 1997). These two measurement schemes represent the first step in developing standard harassment measures. Yet other researchers are slow to incorporate either the SEQ or the ISH and to test their relative reliability and validity. For example, the US National Women's Study conducted in the early 1990s used its own method of classification. Although the costs of incorporating multiple measures of sexual harassment into surveys is high, analyses are needed as to the relative strengths and weaknesses of available measures of sexual harassment. And finally, as is discussed in the next section, more attention is needed to the range of harassing behaviors included in sexual harassment measures. For the past 20 years, sociological research on sexual harassment has been limited by the ways surveys have been constructed.[2] This has resulted in sexual harassment being viewed primarily as an unambiguous individual phenomenon of men harassing women (Williams 1997). Yet, what constitutes sexual harassment may be subjective, based on an individual's perceptions or the organizational context in which she works. In the following section, I discuss some of the implications of the subjective nature of sexual harassment for using survey data.

Is It Sexual Harassment? Labeling Sexual Behaviors

Although survey respondents often report being the targets of unwanted sexual behaviors, many respondents do not define these behaviors as sexual harassment (e.g. Fitzgerald et al 1997b). Yet, when using survey responses, it is common for researchers to define all unwanted sexual behaviors as sexual harassment, whether the respondent defines them as such (see Gruber 1998 for notable exception). This phenomenon has led some to focus on the gap between objective and subjective perceptions of harassment or the likelihood respondents will label their experiences as sexual harassment (e.g. Vaux 1993, Folgero & Fjeldstad 1995, Williams 1997).

Some explanations are offered as to why respondents may be unwilling to label, or be more sensitive to, certain types of unwanted sexual behavior. First, social psychologists find women and men both with more traditional sex-role attitudes label fewer behaviors as sexual harassment (e.g. Johnson et al 1991, Tangri & Hayes 1997). In terms of experiencing harassment though, this find-

---

[2]In psychology, research also relied on analogue studies of college students.

ing is not consistent across all work contexts. Rosenberg and colleagues (1993) found female attorneys with feminist orientations were less likely than their more traditional counterparts to report experiences with sexual harassment. Second, individual differences such as sexual orientation, race, and the organizational position of the harasser influence the self-labeling of harassment experiences (Giuffre & Williams 1994). Giuffre & Williams (1994) offer a compelling explanation for the process behind self-labeling. Heterosexual norms in workplaces make sexual interaction between coworkers of the same race and sexual orientation seem less problematic. It is when sexual interaction crosses racial, sexual orientation, or organizational power lines that targets of the behavior are more likely to label their experiences as sexual harassment. Third, the characteristics of the harassment matter as targets of harassment are more likely to label severe, pervasive, or frequent sexual behaviors as sexual harassment (Stockdale et al 1995). [3]

Recent qualitative studies highlight how organizational culture contributes to employees' willingness and ability to label sexual behaviors as sexual harassment (e.g. Folgero & Fjeldstad 1995). In some masculine work cultures, women, in order to be seen as competent and as teamplayers, may not define their experiences as sexual harassment (Collinson & Collinson 1996). As well, in other workplaces, sexual behaviors commonly understood as sexual harassment may in fact be requirements of the job (Williams 1997:4). That is, organizations may sanction or mandate the sexualized treatment of workers. For example, management may require waitresses to wear tight skirts (Loe 1996), customers in bars may be encouraged to "talk dirty" to waitresses by ordering drinks with sexually-loaded names like "Screaming Orgasm" (Williams 1997:22; Giuffre & Williams 1994:387), or for new female coal miners sexualized hazing rituals may be considered part of their initiation into workgroups (e.g. Yount 1991). [4]

In these sexually charged or permissive work cultures, degrading and sexual behaviors become an "institutionalized" component of work and, thus,

---

[3]Much debate exists over whether or not men and women hold different perceptions of sexual harassment. Gender differences in perceptions of harassment tend to disappear when the context of the harassment (frequencey, severity, and pervasiveness) are considered (Gutek & O'Connor 1995). Gutek (1995) provides a good overview of this issue and concludes that what women and men perceive as harassment, or as more or less severe harassment, is similar.

[4]Beyond the scope of this review is the enjoyment and power some women gain through sexual interactions at work (e.g. Pringle 1988). See Williams (1997) for a recent discussion of this issue and how it links to sexual harassment. Also related to the issue of power is that of consent, especially as typified by professor-student consensual relations (e.g. Refinetti 1997). Discussions of sexual consent are intertwined with issues of "political correctness," with what are appropriate policies for harassment and freedom of speech (Holloway & Jefferson 1996). This review does not have space to do justice to these arguments. Interested readers are referred to the volume on "Sexual harassment and sexual consent" in the journal *Sexuality and Culture* (1997).

may not be considered sexual harassment (Williams 1997). This process of institutionalization involves the normalization of sexual harassment, whereby "individual workers may not define their experiences as sexual harassment, even if they feel sexually degraded by them" (Williams 1997:26, Loe 1996).

To what extent do we need to worry about the gap between experiencing unwanted sexual behaviors and labeling these behaviors sexual harassment? Some believe we have little to worry about in terms of the validity of harassment measures because the perception of the target is incorporated into measures by default (Tangri & Hayes 1997:122). For Fitzgerald et al (1997b), the main implication of self-labeling is that experiences respondents do not label as harassment are less likely to enter the legal system. This does not mean these experiences have no effect. Respondents who were the objects of unwanted sexual behaviors, regardless of whether they labeled their experiences as sexual harassment, experienced more negative psychological and work-related outcomes than respondents who did not experience any unwanted sexual behaviors (Fitzgerald et al 1997b:23). In terms of survey measurement, the inclusion of an item which asks "did you consider this sexual harassment?" can be used to determine how differences in outcomes may be affected by self-labeling. This is not the answer for all research issues though. In some instances, unambiguous measures that parallel legal definitions of harassment are useful, such as when examining the effect of sexual harassment policies on the occurrence of sexual harassment (e.g. Gruber 1998).

Yet, some aspects of the problems regarding self-labeling of harassment are not resolved by asking the respondent whether or not their experience constituted sexual harassment. Williams (1997) believes this problem will continue to complicate the validity of harassment measures due to the limited range of behaviors incorporated into social science conceptualizations. For example, the experience of institutionalized forms of harassment, where workers consent to sexual behaviors as part of their job, are not likely to be captured by survey items that specify respondents should report "unwanted" sexual behaviors (Williams 1997:23). To overcome this, some researchers suggest turning to ethnographic methods to uncover ambiguous forms of sexual harassment and to bridge the gap between objective and subjective measures (Williams 1997, Avery & Cavanaugh 1995).

This highlights an underlying tension between survey research and qualitative methods when studying sexual harassment. Williams (1997) criticizes survey research for emphasizing the harassment of women by men and for overlooking how heterosexual norms in organizations exploit workers' sexuality and may lead to same-sex harassment. Yet, it is not survey methods per se that are the problem. Just as the courts are slow to take up forms of harassment that do not fit "our top-down, male-female sexual come-on image of harassment" (Schultz 1998a, 1998b), so are social science researchers. We know that workers tolerated hostile work environments long before these environments were recognized as such legally (Fitzgerald et al 1997b:7). And, as qualitative research illustrates, workers continue to tolerate same-sex harassment and organizationally sanctioned harassment not captured in current measurement schemes. As we gain a better understanding of the range and context of unwanted sexual behaviors, sexual harassment's effective empirical measurement becomes not only more critical but more complicated.

THEORIES AND EXPLANATIONS OF SEXUAL HARASSMENT

If there is a weakness in studies of sexual harassment, it is the lack of systematic theoretical explanations for why sexual harassment occurs. As Tangri & Hayes (1997:113) point out, most sexual harassment studies offer descriptive models that primarily describe covariates and do not offer explanations as to why sexual harassment occurs. Grounded in feminist, social psychological, and psychological frameworks, several models exist that break explanations of harassment into the primary correlates of sexual harassment (e.g. target characteristics, occupational/organizational characteristics, and offender characteristics) and theoretical explanations of sexual harassment (e.g. sex-role spillover and power-dominance models, e.g. Stockdale 1996, Fitzgerald & Shullman 1993, Hulin et al 1996). In the following section, I first outline the most prominent explanations and theories of sexual harassment found in sociological analyses of sexual harassment. This builds on Tangri et al's (1982) influential discussion of the "Sociocultural" model and the "Organizational" model. Tangri and colleagues (1982) also discuss the "natural/biological model" which proposes sexual harassment is the natural outcome of men's stronger sex drive and men's role as the sexual aggressor (e.g. Studd & Gattiker 1991). For an update and critique of this model, researchers may consult Tangri &47 Hayes (1997).

Societal Level Explanations and the Sociocultural Model

The sociocultural model posits that sexual harassment is a product of culturally legitimated power and status differences between men and women (Farley 1978, MacKinnon 1979). Sociocultural explanations fit with the "feminist" or "dominance" model that emphasizes sexual harassment's origins in patriarchal society (e.g. MacKinnon 1979, Cockburn 1991, Stanko 1985, Rospenda et al 1998, Padavic & Orcutt 1997). Sexual harassment is perceived to be an outgrowth of the gender socialization process and is a mechanism by which men assert power and dominance over women both at work and in society (Tangri et al 1982). Proponents of this approach emphasize gender as a key predictor of who is at risk of harassment, in light of empirical evidence that women experience more harassment than men (Tangri et al 1982, Gutek 1985, USMPSB 1981).

The sociocultural model also emphasizes how individual-level correlates, such as age and marital status, mediate women's low status and lack of sociocultural power (e.g. Kauppinen-Toropainen & Gruber 1993, Padavic & Orcutt 1997). For example, single women and young women may be viewed as more available for sexual interaction than do other women, and hence, they may experience higher levels of sexual harassment than other women (e.g., Gruber & Bjorn 1982, Lafontaine & Tredeau 1986, US MSPB 1981). Some argue that age not only captures the "impact of youth per se" but is also a proxy for low seniority or poor job status (Gruber 1998:312). Individual-level correlates of age and marital status are mediated by occupational context (Kauppinen-Toropainen & Gruber 1993). For example, among older women in the United States, those who are professionals experience less harassment than do nonprofessional women (Kauppinen-Toropainen & Gruber 1993).

Organizational-Level Explanations

A diverse set of explanations for sexual harassment focus on the role of organizations, ranging from theoretical explanations of power to descriptions of organizational characteristics that are correlated with the likelihood of sexual harassment. Underlying many of these explanations are the ways power differences in organizations promote sexual harassment and perpetuate inequality (Rospenda et al 1998:42).

FORMAL AND INFORMAL ORGANIZATIONAL POWER   Some organizational models emphasize how inequities in structural or formal power in organizations lead to harassment. Individuals with formal organizational power, such as managers, may use their position to harass subordinates (e.g., Benson & Thomson 1982, MacKinnon 1979). An underlying assumption is that it is men holding managerial positions who are harassing women subordinates. However, research showing that harassers are more likely to be co-workers (e.g. Gutek 1985) and that harassers may sometimes be subordinates (Grauerholz 1989, McKinney 1994, Rospenda et al 1998) highlights the limitations of such explanations.

Most researchers agree that conceptualizations of organizational power must be broadened to include interpersonal modes of power (see Cleveland & Kerst 1993 for extensive review; Grauerholz 1996). For example, co-workers with individual or informal sources of power, such as personality, expertise, and access to critical information, may be more likely to engage in harassment than others (Cleveland & Kerst 1993). In terms of contrapower harassment, whereby a subordinate harasses someone with formal organizational power, sociocultural power may compensate for the lack of organizational power (e.g. McKinney 1990, 1992). Rospenda and associates illustrate how sociocultural and interpersonal forms of power are used by perpetrators to subordinate the victim's organizational power, as seen in the case of a white female senior faculty member harassed by a black administrator (1998:55). While formal organizational power still has contextualized effects in terms of who is harassed and how targets react to their harassment, it is clear that harassment studies need to incorporate the multiple hierarchies of power which "can make people simultaneously powerful and powerless in relation to others" (Miller 1997:50). By doing so, we move away from always conceptualizing the harasser as male and powerful and the target as female and powerless.

NUMERICAL AND NORMATIVE DOMINANCE   Numerically skewed sex ratios in work situations, such as female-dominated and male-dominated work groups, play a prominent role in explanations of sexual harassment. Some approaches focus on the gender roles associated with female and male-dominated work situations (e.g. sex role spillover), while others discuss the issue in terms of numerical dominance of males over females in certain workplaces (contact hypothesis). Those interested in whether these approaches are considered theories, hypotheses, or descriptions of correlates are referred to previous reviews of sexual harassment research (e.g. Tangri & Hayes 1997, Stockdale 1996). In this review, I focus on the process by which numerically skewed work situations are linked to sexual harassment. In the following two sections, I discuss the primary ways normative dominance (gender roles) and numerical dominance (workgroup gender ratios) in work situations are used to explain the occurrence of sexual harassment (e.g. Gruber 1998).

Sex role spillover   Sex role spillover theory is considered one of the primary theories of sexual harassment (Tangri & Hayes 1997, Stockdale 1996). According to Gutek, when women's gender roles take precedence over their work roles, sex role "spillover" occurs (Gutek & Morach 1982, Gutek 1985). This happens most often when the gender ratio is heavily skewed toward either men or women because skewed situations render "femaleness" more salient and visible (Kanter 1977, Stockdale 1996a:10). Under these circumstances, sexual harassment is more likely. For example, in female-dominated work situations, feminine roles become equated with the job, such as expectations that nurses are "nurturing" or waitresses are "sexy" (Gutek 1985, Nieva & Gutek 1981). In male-dominated workplaces, where women are competing with men for jobs, men attempt to emphasize women coworkers' status as women over their status as workers (DiTomaso 1989:88). Doing this allows men to put women in their "proper" subordinate position. Overall, sex-role spillover theory highlights how gender-based normative expectations prevail in numerically skewed work situations.

  Support for this approach has been mixed. Women in male-typed jobs are more likely to experience sexual harassment than women in female-typed and integrated occupations (Gutek & Morasch 1982, Gutek & Cohen 1987), but

they are not necessarily more likely to label their experiences as sexual harassment (Konrad & Gutek 1986, Ragins & Scandura 1995). Studies of sex-role
spillover are limited by their use of occupational sex ratios as proxies for sex
roles. Social constructionists provide a more fundamental critique of sex-role
spillover theory. Based on critiques of sex-role theory in general, sex-role spillover theory conceptualizes gender and sexuality as elements that are "smug-
gled" into gender-neutral, asexual organizations by gendered workers (Rogers
& Henson 1997:216). Measures of occupational sex ratios do not capture the
gendered organizational processes that foster sex role spillover.

The contact hypothesis and numerical dominance   The contact hypothesis
(Gutek et al 1990, Gruber 1998) views harassment as a function of the contact
between men and women in the workplace, rather than emphasizing the gender
role expectations associated with certain jobs. Here, numerical dominance is
seen as distinct from, though interrelated to, normative dominance (Gruber
1998). For example, a female secretary who works in an environment numerically dominated by males and who has more contact with men, will experience
more severe harassment than her counterparts in integrated workplaces or
those numerically dominated by females (e.g. Gutek et al 1990, Gruber 1997).
Direct support for the contact hypothesis is found when measures of contact
are based on respondents' reports of daily contact with men as opposed to occupational sex ratios (e.g. Kauppinen-Toropainen & Gruber 1993, Gutek et
al 1990, Gruber 1998).

Complicating numerical dominance are male-dominated or "doubly-male"
workgroups where both numerical and normative dominance are present. In
these "male preserves" (see Gruber 1997 for overview; Gruber 1998, Martin
1980, DiTomaso 1989) or "masculine job gender contexts" (Hulin et al 1996),
"the traditionality of an *occupation* creates a work culture that is an extension
of male culture, and numerical dominance of the *workplace* by men heightens
the visibility of, and hostility toward, women workers who are perceived as
violating men's territory" (Gruber 1998:303). Ultimately this leads to extensive and aggressive forms of sexual harassment not usually found in other
workgroups (e.g. Stanko 1985, Martin & Jurik 1996).

Gruber's (1998) analysis represents one of the few empirical attempts to
tease out the relative effects of numerical (gender ratio of workgroup) and normative dominance (occupational sex ratio) on sexual harassment experiences.
He finds that the amount of contact with men, or the gender ratio of workgroups, is helpful for understanding both the likelihood of experiencing
harassment and the occurrence of specific types of harassment. The effect of
normative dominance, or occupational sex ratios, provides less explanatory
power than does numerical dominance. It also is not significantly related to
physical threats and sexual materials, forms of sexual harassment common to

male-dominated workplaces. Gender predominance, an interaction term of the gender ratio of workgroups and occupational sex ratios used to capture the combination of normative and numerical dominance found in male preserves, was an important predictor of exposure to sexual materials and physical threats. Gruber concludes that studies that rely solely on occupational sex ratios as their measure of gender dominance probably overestimate the effect of gendered occupational roles and underestimate the effect of the numerical gendered context. Overall, most survey-based studies attempting to capture normative and numerical dominance are hindered by the use of occupational and workgroup gender ratios as proxies for underlying gendered processes and organizational structures. These processes are not easily captured by survey measures. Qualitative studies can complement quantitative studies by demonstrating how numerical and normative dominance are interrelated and where they diverge (e.g. Rogers & Henson 1997, Collinson & Collinson 1996).

ORGANIZATIONAL CULTURE   Because organizational culture represents the norms of appropriate behavior and values held by organizational members (Hall 1994), it is not surprising researchers are turning to culture to explain why sexual harassment occurs in some organizations and not in others (e.g. Kauppinen-Toropainen & Gruber 1993, Hulin et al 1996, Pryor et al 1993). Early on, Gutek (1985) proposed that "unprofessional" or disorganized ambiances, such as antagonistic relationships between coworkers or drinking on the job, would increase the likelihood of sexual harassment of women. More recently, Ragins & Scandura (1995) discuss how the physical nature of blue-collar work promotes a "physical culture" resulting in more aggressive forms of sexual harassment (p. 449).

Organizational cultures that tolerate sexual harassment are linked to increased incidents of sexual harassment (e.g. Hulin et al 1996, Pryor et al 1993). Pryor and associates' (1993) person/situation framework illustrates how men who are highly likely to sexually harass are encouraged to do so by "local" norms of sexual and aggressive behaviors supported by supervisors and peers. In contrast, proactive sexual harassment policies, or attempts to modify the workplace culture through training sessions and official complaint procedures, are particularly effective for reducing hostile environment harassment (Gruber 1998).

THE ORGANIZATION OF WORK   Relatively few studies incorporate how the technical organization of work, such as task characteristics, interacts with the social organization of work (e.g. DiTomaso 1989, Kauppinen-Toropainen & Gruber 1993, Lach & Gwartney-Gibbs 1993). In part, this gap is due to the influence of psychologists on the area and their predominant interest in individuals and their interactions (e.g. Stockdale 1996, Hulin et al 1996). Looking

at the organization of work, alienating work conditions, such as physically demanding or repetitive jobs, may be partly responsible for women's experiences of sexual harassment in male-typed jobs. Some researchers see men's
harassment of women and sexual horseplay in the workplace as an attempt to
forge human contact and to overcome boring work (e.g. Hearn & Parkin
1987:85; Hearn 1985). On the other hand, engaging in sexually aggressive
behavior and harassment may be an act of resistance that demonstrates opposition to women's presence in traditionally male jobs (e.g. Miller 1997, Hearn &
Parkin 1987). As Cockburn reminds us, "men's morale and solidarity in their
struggle against the boss is sometimes achieved directly at the expense of
women" (1991:148).

GENDERED ORGANIZATIONS AND DOING GENDER   Recent attention by sexual
harassment researchers to the gendered processes of organizations (e.g. Acker
1990) and to "doing gender" (e.g. West & Zimmerman 1987, West & Fenstermaker 1995) has begun to clarify how the organization of work is connected to
sexual harassment. As stated by Rogers & Henson (1997:234), "sexual harassment is about particular constructions of gender, especially organizational
imperatives to 'do gender' in a particular manner" (Lorber 1994, West & Zimmerman 1987). For example, the deferential behavior of temporary workers,
stemming from the feminized and powerless status of their job, increases
workers' vulnerability and potential for experiencing sexual harassment (Rogers
& Henson 1997:224; see also Folgero & Fjeldstad 1995). Not surprising, studies that focus on the socially constructed nature of sexual harassment are qualitative. This research represents an important advance in the field by moving
beyond variables of sex-ratios and organizational culture to explain sexual harassment, drawing our attention to how organizational norms of heterosexuality
and power construct gender and facilitate sexual harassment (e.g. Schneider
1982, Collinson & Collinson 1989, Williams 1997, Rospenda et al 1998).

Individual-Level Explanations

A variety of approaches focus on individual-level characteristics of harassment targets to explain whether sexual harassment is likely to occur. Some of
these were discussed above, such as sociocultural characteristics and sources
of individual power (e.g. Gruber & Bjorn 1986). The link between offender
characteristics and sexual harassment has been examined by psychologists.
Using insights from research on the proclivities of rapists, Pryor (1987, Pryor
et al 1993) finds men who score high on his Likelihood-to-Sexually-Harass
scale are more likely than other men to harass women in circumstances that
tolerate sexual contact between men and women. For an overview of individual-level psychological approaches to sexual harassment, such as the role
of sexual arousal, readers may find Stockdale (1996) informative.

REACTIONS TO SEXUAL HARASSMENT

Research suggests that women's responses to sexual harassment fall along a continuum of avoidance, diffusion, negotiation, and confrontation (Gruber 1989). Most women do not report their experiences of sexual harassment. Instead they are more likely to ignore the harassment (Benson & Thomson 1982, Cochran et al 1997, Gruber & Bjorn 1982, Loy & Stewart 1984), to deflect the harassment by joking or going along with it (Gutek 1985, USMSPB 1981 1987), or to avoid the harasser (Cochran et al 1997, Culbertson et al 1992, Gutek 1985, Schneider 1991; see Yoder & Aniakudo 1995 for exception). In Culbertson et al's (1992) study of the US Navy, only 12% of the enlisted women and 5% of the women officers who experienced harassment filed formal complaints. Women do not report harassment for a variety of reasons ranging from a fear of retaliation or disbelief to a fear of losing ones' job or making the situation worse (Loy & Stewart 1984, Cochran et al 1997, Schneider 1991, Fitzgerald et al 1995c). Assertive or direct responses tend to occur in a variety of contexts, such as when the harassment is severe (Brooks & Perot 1991, Cochran et al 1997, Gutek & Koss 1993, Livingston 1982, USMSPB 1981); when the harasser is not a supervisor (Gruber & Smith 1995); when policies and procedures are in place to combat sexual harassment (Gruber & Smith 1995); when the percentage of women in an occupation is either at parity with men or a threatening minority (Gruber & Bjorn 1986, Gruber & Smith 1995); and, finally, when the harassment target holds feminist attitudes (Gruber & Smith 1995, Brooks & Perot 1991). Respondents who are more tolerant of sexual harassment are less likely to see their experiences as severe and hence respond less assertively (Cochran et al 1997). Moving beyond assertive versus nonassertive responses to harassment, Fitzgerald et al (1995c) offer a framework of externally and internally focused strategies. This framework includes behavioral strategies such as avoidance and seeking social support as well as cognitive or emotion-management strategies such as denial and detachment. Fitzgerald and colleagues argue for the incorporation of cognitive strategies in order to shift the question from why victims do not respond assertively to the multiple ways women respond to sexual harassment.

Qualitative studies suggest that responses to sexual harassment are grounded in the organization of power relations at work. Women and men temporary workers, with little control over employment assignments, have little recourse but to tolerate or ignore the harassment if they wish to continue receiving work assignments (Rogers & Henson 1997:230). On the other hand, African-American women firefighters, already considered outsiders and marginalized due to their race and gender, believe they have nothing to lose from fighting back against sexual harassment and confronting their harassers (Yoder & Aniakudo 1996). These studies support Williams' (1997) argument for contextualizing our understanding of sexual harassment. Although both temporary workers and African-American women firefighters are marginalized or vulnerable workers, they respond to sexual harassment in dramatically different ways.

CONSEQUENCES OF SEXUAL HARASSMENT

Numerous studies outline the job-related, psychological, and somatic health consequences of sexual harassment. In terms of job consequences, sexual harassment is found to result in lowered morale, absenteeism (USMSPB 1981, 1987), decreased job satisfaction (Gruber 1992), decreased perception of equal opportunity (Newell et al 1995), and damaged interpersonal work-relationships (Culbertson et al 1992, DiTomaso 1989, Gutek 1985). Some victims are forced to quit or they lose their jobs (Coles 1986, Crull 1982, Gutek 1985, USMSPB 1981 1987). Organizations also pay a price for harassment in terms of lost productivity, job turnover, and medical claims (USMBPB 1987). The psychological and physical health consequences of sexual harassment are also well-documented. Sexual harassment is linked to anxiety, depression, sleep disturbances, nausea, stress, and headaches (Crull 1982, Fitzgerald 1993, Gutek & Koss 1993).

Research on the consequences of harasssment is limited. Most studies tend to list possible outcomes, with little regard to the prevalence of outcomes or the complex processes underlying them (Gutek & Koss 1993:42). Recent research by psychologists attempts to respond to this critique. Early results from the National Women's Study (Dansky & Kilpatrick 1997) provide evidence of a long-term link among depression, lifetime post-traumatic stress disorder, and sexual harassment. However, this study is limited by a reliance on retrospective accounts. Schneider et al's (1997) job-stress model provides evidence that sexual harassment has a distinct negative effect on psychological and job-related outcomes, even after controlling for respondents' general level of job stress or negative disposition (see also Fitzgerald et al 1997a). Fitzgerald et al (1995c) also recommend including measures of victim vulnerability, such as victimization history, personal resources, attitudes, and control, to explain the impact of sexual harassment on targets. Results from a two-wave longitudinal study on the effects of workplace harassment on coping, self-medication, and health over time will be available in the near future (Richman et al 1997).

Psychologists are responsible for much of the research on the psychological consequences of sexual harassment. For their part, sociologists should be asking questions about the life course effects of sexual harassment on women's lives. That is, sexual harassment represents a turning point in the lives of some targets, altering their progression through life-course sequences and hindering their chances for positive work and family outcomes. To utilize the life-course perspective, sexual harassment researchers need to gather longitudinal data.

The need for different types of data as well as substantive areas in need of more research are discussed next.

STUDYING SEXUAL HARASSMENT: AN AGENDA FOR THE FUTURE

Longitudinal Research and Multiplicity Sampling

Sexual harassment research in the past 10 years has moved away from a focus on prevalence rates to more sophisticated multivariate analyses of the antecedents and consequences of sexual harassment (e.g. Padavic & Orcutt 1997). Restricting many of the empirical analyses of harassment is a reliance on cross-sectional survey data. One positive trend away from this is the movement toward longitudinal data collection (e.g. Richman et al 1997) because an understanding of the organizational context of harassment requires longitudinal data. For example, current analyses of the effect of organizational culture generally rely on respondents' perceptions of culture *after* they were sexually harassed. Without longitudinal data, the meaning behind the correlation between organizational tolerance and incidences of sexual harassment is unclear (Pryor et al 1993).

Organizational researchers are also turning to multiplicity or "bottom-up" sampling techniques to create samples linked across macro and micro levels (e.g. Parcel et al 1991:74, Kalleberg et al 1996). Future surveys of sexual harassment should incorporate this kind of sampling. By linking interviews with individuals, supervisors, and human resource managers, multiplicity sampling could provide data on the relationship between sexual harassment, organizational policies and context, and job-related outcomes. It is time for the use of more sophisticated data collection techniques if we are to continue to build our theoretical and empirical understandings.

Uncovering Gendered Processes: The Need for Qualitative Research

To counter the reliance on survey methods, a growing number of researchers are calling for the use of qualitative methods to study sexual harassment (Avery & Cavanaugh 1995, Williams 1997). This is partly due to a belief that important concepts and processes are not adequately captured by survey items. For example, much is written about the connection between sexual harassment and the gendered nature of organizations in terms of how "organizational forms structure and are themselves structured by gender" (Savage & Witz 1992:8, Acker 1990, Adkins 1992). Yet, as discussed earlier, these gendered processes are difficult to capture using discrete survey items. As a result, researchers often use measures of gender roles and management's tolerance for sexual harassment as proxies for gendered processes existing in organizations. These measures do not tap the depth or identify the subtle ways in which organizational processes may "institutionalize" sexual harassment as part of the job. Good examples of this research include recent studies of the restaurant industry (Giuffre & Williams 1994) and temporary work (Rogers & Henson 1997). As well, qualitative research is capable of uncovering the ambiguity that surrounds sexuality and sexual harassment in organizations (Williams 1997).

Race and Sexual Harassment

Several overviews comment on the paucity of research concerning sexual harassment, race and ethnicity (e.g. Murrell 1996, Fitzgerald & Shullman 1993, Barak 1997). Much of this discussion is conceptual with an emphasis on the distinction between sexism and "sexual racism" (e.g. Murrell 1996:56, Collins 1990) and on how racialized norms of sexual attractiveness limit job opportunities for women of color (e.g. Williams 1997:29). A few early empirical studies found no overall difference in harassment rates for women of color and white women (e.g. Gutek 1985, USMSPB 1981). On the other hand, some evidence exists that women of color experience more severe forms of sexual harassment (e.g. Gruber & Bjorn 1982). Rospenda et al's (1998) analysis moves beyond the issue of prevalence to show how race intersects with class and gender in instances of contrapower harassment. For example, they theorize how norms of black masculinity may be a factor in the reluctance of a black male faculty member to report the harassment by a white male secretary (Rospenda et al 1998:50). In many ways, MacKinnon's quote cited at the beginning of the article still characterizes the state of research on race and sexual harassment.

Sexual Harassment of Men and Same-Sex Harassment

The sexual harassment of men, as well as same-sex harassment, are understudied phenomena (Vaux 1993, Williams 1997, Fitzgerald et al 1997). In terms of the sexual harassment of men, Gutek's (1985) study found that men were more likely to interpret "social-sexual" behavior as nonthreatening, whereas women interpreted the same behavior as threatening. Men also identify some behaviors as harassing that are not identified by women (Berdahl et al 1996). These behaviors include those perpetrated by women, such as verbal comments that negatively stereotype men (e.g. "Men are pigs"). Men also report being labelled as unmasculine (e.g. being called "fag" or "pussy") when they do not participate with their male colleagues in jokes about women (Fitzgerald et al 1997b:24). In order to understand the harassment of men, research on masculinity provides a useful starting point (e.g. Connell 1995).

Related to the sexual harassment of men are issues of same-sex harassment. Not only does the harassment of gays and lesbians need to be considered (e.g. Woods & Lucas 1993, Hall 1989), but the harassment of heterosexual men by heterosexual men should be examined. As discussed elsewhere in this review, studies illustrate how sexuality and "hyper-masculinity" are part of many organizational cultures (e.g. Williams 1997). Heterosexual norms exclude or sexualize women, but they also constrain the behavior of men. As others have mentioned, researchers need to incorporate the complexity of sexual exploitation and harassment found in organizations (e.g. Vaux 1993). As Williams point out, focusing on the harassment of women by men ignores "other sexualized power dynamics in the workplace" (1997:33).

CONCLUSION

This review only touches the surface of many issues with which researchers are currently struggling. Beyond the specific scope of this review, but in need of further study, is the relationship of complaints of sexual harassment to legal and institutional environments. Studies of the outcomes of sexual harassment cases focus on victim, perpetrator, and sexual harassment characteristics without utilizing theoretical insights from the sociology of law (e.g. Terptrsa & Baker 1992, 1988). Black's (1993) work provides an avenue for conceptualizing how organizational status may predict the outcome of third party intervention into sexual harassment. And, similar to research on the "legalization of the workplace" (e.g. Sutton et al 1994, Edelman 1992), the organizational adoption of sexual harassment policies and the potential increased regulation of workers' sexual interaction could be examined using insights from institutional approaches. Issues in the study of sexual harassment at work can draw from and inform a variety of sociological perspectives not previously considered.

What we know about sexual harassment is that its definition and occurrence is contextualized by organizational and individual factors. Gender will continue to remain central to the study of harassment, whether conceptualized as quantitative measures of gender ratios or more qualitative understandings of gender roles and gendered organizational processes. At this point, though, no unified theoretical framework has developed for explaining the occurrence of sexual harassment. Recent insights from social constructionists and other analyses of gendered organizations are among the most promising. As researchers move beyond cross-sectional surveys to more advanced survey techniques and more encompassing ethnographic studies, the task of sorting out the effects of gender, individual perceptions and organizational context on sexual harassment will be assisted. As well, criminological theories are underutilized in the study of sexual harassment. One possible avenue is to incorporate routine activity theory that can provide insight into the interaction between organizational context and the presence of guardians and motivated offenders. The study of sexual harassment is in beginning stages, which means researchers are still struggling with issues related to measurement, data collection, and theoretical development. Yet it is these challenges that make this area one worth pursuing.

ACKNOWLEDGMENTS

Special thanks to Annette Nierobisz for helpful discussions, research assistance, and editorial comments. I also thank Bill Magee, Myrna Dawson, and Michael Schreiner for comments and suggestions on an earlier draft of this article.

Visit the *Annual Reviews home page* at
http://www.AnnualReviews.org.

Literature Cited

Acker J. 1990. Hierarchies, jobs, bodies: a theory of gendered organizations. *Gender & Society* 4(2):139–58

Adkins L. 1992. Sexual work and the employment of women in the service industries. In *Gender and Bureaucracy*, ed. M Savage, A Witz, pp. 207–28. Oxford: Blackwell

Arvey RD, Cavanaugh MA. 1995. Using surveys to assess the prevalence of sexual harassment: some methodological problems. *J. Soc. Issues* 51(1):39–52

Barak A. 1997. Cross-cultural perspectives on sexual harassment. See O'Donohue 1997, pp. 263–300

Benson DJ, Thomson GE. 1982. Sexual harassment on a university campus: the confluence of authority relations, sexual interest and gender stratification. *Soc. Probl.* 29:236–51

Berdahl JL, Magley VJ, Waldo CR. 1996. The sexual harassment of men? Exploring the concept with theory and data. *Psychol. Women Q.* 20(4): 527–47

Black D. 1993. *The Social Structure of Right and Wrong.* San Diego, CA: Academic

Brooks L, Perot AR. 1991. Reporting sexual harassment: exploring a predictive model. *Psychol. Women Q.* 15(1):31–47

Cleveland JN, Kerst ME. 1993. Sexual harassment and perceptions of power: an under-articulated relationship. *J. Voc. Behav.* 42: 49–67

Cochran CC, Frazier PA, Olson AM. 1997. Predictors of responses to unwanted sexual harassment. *Psychol. Women Q.* 21(2): 207–26

Cockburn C. 1991. *In the Way of Women: Men's Resistance to Sex Equality in Organizations.* Ithaca, NY: ILR

Coles FS. 1986. Forced to quit: sexual harassment complaints and agency response. *Sex Roles* 14:81–95

Collins PH. 1990. *Black Feminist Thought: Knowledge, Consciousness, and the Politics of Empowerment.* Boston: Irwin Hyman

Collinson D, Collinson M. 1989. Sexuality in the workplace: the domination of men's sexuality. See Hearn et al 1989, pp. 91–109

Collinson M, Collinson D. 1996. 'It's only Dick': the sexual harassment of women managers in insurance sales. *Work, Employment & Society* 10(1):29–56

Connell RW. 1995. *Masculinities.* Berkeley: Univ. Calif. Press

Crull P. 1982. Stress effects of sexual harassment on the job: implications for counseling. *Am. J. Orthopsychiatry* 52:539–44

Culbertson AL, Rosenfeld P, Booth–Kewley S, Magnusson P. 1992. *Assessment of Sexual Harassment in the Navy: Results of the 1989 Navy-wide Survey.* San Diego, CA: Navy Personnel Res. Dev. Ctr.

Dansky BS, Kilpatrick DG. 1997. Effects of sexual harassment. See O'Donohue 1997, pp. 152–74

DiTomaso N. 1989. Sexuality in the workplace: discrimination and harassment. See J Hearn et al 1989, pp. 71–90

Edelman LB. 1992. Legal ambiguity and symbolic structures: organizational mediation of civil rights law. *Am. J. Sociol.* 97(6): 1531–76

Farley L. 1978. *Sexual Shakedown: The Sexual Harassment of Women On the Job.* New York: McGraw–Hill

Fitzgerald LF 1993. Sexual harassment: violence against women in the workplace. *Am. Psychol.* 48:1070–76

Fitzgerald LF, Drasgow F, Hulin C, Gelfand M, Magley V. 1997a. The antecedents and consequences of sexual harassment in organizations. *J. Appl. Psychol.* 82(2):578–89

Fitzgerald LF, Hulin C, Drasgow F. 1995a. The antecedents and consequences of sexual harassment in organizations: An integrated model. In *Job Stress in a Changing*

Workforce, ed. Keita G, Hurrell J Jr, pp. 55–73. Washington, D.C.: American Psychological Association

Fitzgerald LF, Gefland M, Drasgow R. 1995b. Measuring sexual harassment: Theoretical and psychometric advances. *Basic and Appl. Soc. Psychol.* 17(4):425–45

Fitzgerald LF, Shullman S. 1993. Sexual harassment: A research agenda for the 1990s. *J. Voc. Behav.* 42:5–27

Fitzgerald LF, Shullman S, Bailey N, Richards M, Sweeker J, et al. 1988. The incidence and dimensions of sexual harassment in academia and the workplace. *J. Voc. Behav.* 32:152–75

Fitzgerald, LF, Swan S, Fischer K. 1995c. Why didn't she just report him? The psychological and legal implications of women's responses to sexual harassment. *J. Soc. Issues* 51(1):117–38

Fitzgerald LF, Swan S, Magley V. 1997b. But was it really sexual harassment? Legal behavioral and psychological definitions of the workplace victimization of women. See W O'Donohue 1997, pp. 5–28

Folgero IS, Fjeldstad IH. 1995. On duty-off guard: cultural norms and sexual harassment in service organizations. *Org. Stud.* 16(2):299–313

Gardner CB. 1995. *Passing By: Gender and Public Harassment.* Berkeley: Univ. Calif. Press

Gelfand M, Fitzgerald LF, Drasgow F. 1995. The structure of sexual harassment: a confirmatory analysis across culture and settings. *J. Voc. Behav.* 47:164–77

Giuffre PA, Williams CL. 1994. Boundary lines: labeling sexual harassment in restaurants. *Gender & Soc.* 8:378–401

Grauerholz E. 1989. Sexual harassment of women professors by students: exploring the dynamics of power, authority and gender in a university setting. *Sex Roles.* 21(11/12):789–801

Grauerholz E. 1996. Sexual harassment in the academy: the case of women professors. See Stockdale 1996, 5:29–50

Gruber JE. 1989. How women handle sexual harassment: a literature review. *Sociol. Soc. Res.* 74:3–9

Gruber JE. 1990. Methodological problems and policy implications in sexual harassment research. *Pop. Res. Policy Rev.* 9: 235–54

Gruber JE. 1992. A typology of personal and environmental sexual harassment: research and policy implications from the 1990s. *Sex Roles* 22:447–64

Gruber JE. 1997. An epidemiology of sexual harassment: evidence from North America and Europe. See O'Donohue 1997, pp. 84–98

Gruber JE. 1998. The impact of male work environments and organizational policies on women's experiences of sexual harassment. *Gender & Soc.* 12(3):301–20

Gruber JE, Bjorn L. 1982. Blue-collar blues: the sexual harassment of women autoworkers. *Work Occup.* 9(Aug.):271–98

Gruber JE, Bjorn L. 1986. Women's responses to sexual harassment: an analysis of sociocultural, organzational, and personal resource models. *Soc. Sci. Q.* 67: 814–26

Gruber JE, Kauppinen-Toropainen K, Smith M. 1996. Sexual harassment types and severity: linking research and policy. See Stockdale1996, pp. 151–73

Gruber JE, Smith M. 1995. Women's responses to sexual harassment: a multivariate analysis. *Basic Appl. Soc. Psychol.* 17: 543–62

Gutek BA. 1985. *Sex and the Workplace: The Impact of Sexual Behavior and Harassment on Women, Men, and Organizations.* San Francisco: Jossey–Bass

Gutek BA. 1995. How subjective is sexual harassment? An examination of rater effects. *Basic Appl. Soc. Psychol.* 17(4): 447–67

Gutek BA, Cohen AG. 1987. Sex ratios, sex role spillover and sex at work: a comparison of men's and women's experiences. *Hum. Relat.* 40(2):97–115

Gutek BA, Cohen AG, Konrad AM. 1990. Predicting social–sexual behavior at work: a contact hypothesis. *Acad. Mgmt. J.* 33: 560–77

Gutek BA, Koss M. 1993. Changed women and changed organizations: consequences and coping with sexual harassment. *J. Voc. Behav.* 42:28–48

Gutek BA, Morasch B. 1982. Sex ratios, sexrole spillover, and sexual harassment of women at work. *J. Soc. Issues* 38:55–74

Gutek BA, O'Connor M. 1995. The empirical basis for the reasonable woman standard. *J. Soc. Issues* 51:151–66

Hall M. 1989. Private experiences in the public domain: Lesbians in organizations. See J Hearn et al 1989, pp. 125–38

Hall RH. 1994. *Sociology of Work: Perspectives, Analyses, and Issues.* Thousand Oaks: Pine Forge

Hearn J. 1985. Men's sexuality at work. In *The Sexuality of Men*, ed. A Metcalf, M Humphries, pp. 110–28. London: Pluto

Hearn J, Sheppard DL, Tancred-Sheriff P, Burrell G. 1989. *The Sexuality of Organization.* London: Sage

Hearn J, Parkin W. 1987. *'Sex' at 'Work': The Power and Paradox of Organisation Sexuality.* Brighton: Wheatsheaf

Holloway W, Jefferson T. 1996. PC or not PC: sexual harassment and the question of ambivalence. *Hum. Relat.* 49(3): 373–93

Hulin, C, Fitzgerald LF, Drasgow F. 1996. Organizational influences on sexual harassment. See Stockdale 1996, pp. 127–51

Johnson CB, Stockdale MS, Saal FE. 1991. Persistence of men's misperceptions of friendly cues across a variety of interpersonal encounters. *Psychol. Women Q.* 15: 463–75

Kalleberg AD, Knocke PV, Marsden PV, Spaeth, JL. 1996. *Organizations in America: Analyzing Their Structures and Human Resource Practices.* Thousand Oaks, CA: Sage

Kanter RM. 1977. *Men and Women of the Corporation.* New York: Basic Books

Kauppinen–Toropainen K, Gruber JE. 1993. Antecedents and outcomes of woman- unfriendly experiences. *Psychol. Women Q.* 17:421–56

Konrad AM, Gutek BA. 1986. Impact of work experience on attitudes toward sexual harassment. *Admin. Sci. Q.* 31:422–38

Lach DH, Gwartney–Gibbs PA. 1993. Sociological perspectives on sexual harassment and workplace dispute resolution. *J. Voc. Behav.* 42:102–15

Lafontaine E, Tredeau L. 1986. The frequency, sources and correlates of sexual harassment among women in traditional male occupations. *Sex Roles* 15(Oct.): 433–42

Livingston J. 1982. Responses to sexual harassment on the job: legal, organizational, and individual actions. *J. Soc. Issues* 38: 5–22

Loe M. 1996. Working for men—at the intersection of power, gender, and sexuality. *Sociol. Inquiry* 66(4):399–421

Lorber, J. 1994. *Paradoxes of Gender.* New Haven, CT: Yale Univ. Press

Loy P, Stewart L. 1984. The extent and effects of the sexual harassment of working women. *Sociol. Focus* 17:31–43

MacKinnon C. 1979. *Sexual Harassment of Working Women.* New Haven: Yale Univ. Press

MacKinnon C. 1987. *Feminism Unmodified: Discourses on Life and Law.* Cambridge, MA: Harvard Univ. Press

Macmillan R, Nierobisz A, Welsh S. 1996. *Gender in public: harassment and fear of crime among women.* Pres. Am. Sociol. Assoc. Meet., New York

Martin S. 1980. *Breaking and Entering: Policewomen on Patrol.* Berkeley: Univ. Calif. Press

Martin S, Jurik N. 1996. *Doing Justice, Doing Gender.* Thousand Oaks, CA: Sage

McKinney K. 1990. Sexual harassment of university faculty by colleagues and students. *Sex Roles* 23:421–38

McKinney K. 1992. Contrapower sexual harassment: the effects of student sex and type of behavior on faculty perceptions. *Sex Roles* 27(11–12):627–43

McKinney K. 1994. Sexual harassment and college faculty members. *Deviant Behav.* 15(2):171–91

Miller LL. 1997. Not just weapons of the weak: gender harassment as a form of protest for Army men. *Soc. Psychol. Q.* 60(1): 32–51

Murrell AJ. 1996. Sexual harassment and women of color: issues, challenges, and future directions. See Stockdale 1996, pp. 51–66

Newell CE, Rosenfeld P, Culbertson AL. 1995. Sexual harassment experiences and equal opportunity perceptions of Navy women. *Sex Roles* 32(3–4):159–68

Nieva VF, Gutek BA. 1981. *Women and Work: A Psychological Perspective.* New York: Praeger

O'Donohue W. 1997. *Sexual Harassment: Theory, Research and Treatment.* New York: Allyn & Bacon

Orcutt JD. 1997. Perceptions of sexual harassment in the Florida legal system: a comparison of dominance and spillover explanations. *Gender & Soc.* 11(5):682–98

Padavid I, Orcutt JD. 1997. Perceptions of sexual harassment in the Florida legal system: a comparison of dominance and spillover explanations. *Gender Soc.* 11(5): 682–98

Parcel TL, Kaufman RL, Jolly L. 1991. Going up the ladder: multiplicity sampling to create linked macro-to-micro organizational samples. *Sociol. Methodol.* 21:43–79

Pringle R. 1988. *Secretaries Talk: Sexuality, Power and Work.* London: Verso

Pryor J. 1987. Sexual harassment proclivities in men. *Sex Roles* 17:269–90

Pryor J, Lavite C, Stoller L. 1993. A social psychological analysis of sexual harassment: the person/situation interaction. *J. Voc. Behav.* 42:68–83

Ragins BR, Scandura TA. 1995. Antecedents and work–related correlates of reported sexual harassment: an empirical investigation of competing hypotheses. *Sex Roles* 32(7– 8):429–55

Refinetti R. 1997. Sexual harassment, sexual consent, and beyond. *Sexuality & Culture* 1:5–17

Reskin B, Padavic I. 1994. *Women and Men at Work.* Thousand Oaks, CA: Pine Forge

Richman JA, Rospenda KM, Nawyn SJ, Flaherty JA. 1997. Workplace harassment and the self–medicalization of distress: a conceptual model and case illustrations. *Cont. Drug Probl.* 24:179–200

Rogers J, Henson K. 1997. "Hey, why don't you wear a shorter skirt?" Structural vulnerability and the organization of sexual harassment in temporary clerical employment. *Gender & Soc.* 11(2):215–37

Rosenberg J, Perlstadt H, Phillips WRF. 1993. Now that we are here: discrimination, disparagement, and harassment at work and the experience of women lawyers. *Gender & Soc.* 7:415–33

Rospenda KM, Richman JA, Nawyn SJ. 1998. Doing power: the confluence of gender, race, and class in contrapower sexual harassment. *Gender & Soc.* 12(1):40–60

Savage M, Witz A. 1992. *Gender and Bureaucracy.* Oxford: Blackwell

Schneider BE. 1982. Consciousness about sexual harassment among heterosexual and lesbian women workers. *J. Soc. Issues* 38(4):75–98

Schneider BE. 1991. Put up or shut up: workplace sexual assaults. *Gender & Soc.* 5: 533–48

Schneider K, Swan S, Fitzgerald LF. 1997. Job-related and psychological effects of sexual harassment in the workplace: empirical evidence from two organizations. *J. Appl. Psychol.* 82:401–15

Schultz V. 1998a. Sex is the least of it: Let's focus harassment law on work, not sex. *The Nation* May 25

Schultz V. 1998b. Reconceptualizing sexual harassment. *Yale Law Rev.* 107:1683–805

Stanko EA. 1985. *Intimate Intrusions: Women's Experience of Male Violence.* Boston: Routledge & Kegan Paul

Stockdale MS. 1996a. *Sexual Harassment in the Workplace: Perspectives, Frontiers and Response Strategies,* Vol. 5, Women and Work Series. Thousand Oaks, CA: Sage

Stockdale MS. 1996. What we know and what we need to learn about sexual harassment. See Stockdale 1996, pp. 3–25

Stockdale MS, Hope KG. 1997. Confirmatory factor analysis of the U.S. Merit System's Protection Board's survey of sexual harassment: the fit of a three-factor model. *J. Voc. Behav.* 51:338–57

Stockdale MS, Vaux A, Cashin J. 1995. Acknowledging sexual harassment: a test of alternative models. *Basic Appl. Soc. Psychol.* 17:469–96

Studd M, Gattiker U. 1991. The evolutionary psychology of sexual harassment in organizations. *Ethiol. Soc. Biol.* 12:249–90

Sudman S, Bradburn NM. 1982. *Asking Questions: A Practical Guide to Questionnaire Design.* San Francisco: Jossey-Bass

Sutton JR, Dobbin F, Meyer JW, Scott WR. 1994. The legalization of the workplace. *Am. J. Sociol.* 99:944–71

Tangri S, Burt M, Johnson L. 1982. Sexual harassment at work: three explanatory models. *J. Soc. Issues* 38(Winter):33–54

Tangri S, Hayes SM. 1997. Theories of sexual harassment. See W O'Donohue, pp. 99–111

Terpstra DE, Baker DD. 1988. Outcomes of sexual harassment charges. *Acad. Mgmt. J.* 31: 185–94

Terpstra DE, Baker DD. 1989. The identification and classification of reactions to sexual harassment. *J Org. Behav.* 10:1–14

Terpstra DE, Baker DD. 1992. Outcomes of federal court decisions on sexual harassment. *Acad. Mgmt. J.* 35:181–90

Till FJ. 1980. *Sexual Harassment: A Report on the Sexual Harassment of Students.* Washington, DC: National Advisory Council on Women's Educational Program

US Equal Employment Opportunity Commission (EEOC). 1980. Guidelines on discrimination because of sex. *Fed. Reg.* 43: 74676–7

US Merit System Protection Board. 1981. *Sexual Harassment in the Workplace: Is It a Problem?* Washington, DC: US Gen. Post Off.

US Merit Systems Protection Board. 1987. *Sexual Harassment of Federal Workers: An Update.* Washington, DC: US GPO

Vaux A. 1993. Paradigmatic assumptions in sexual harassment research: being guided without being misled. *J. Voc. Behav.* 42: 116–35

Welsh S, Nierobisz A. 1997. How prevalent is sexual harassment? A research note on measuring sexual harassment in Canada. *Can. J. Sociol.* 22(4):505–22

Welsh, S, Nierobisz A, Berman E. 1998. *Remedies for harassment: sexual harassment complaints and the Canadian Human Rights Commission.* Pres. North Central Sociol. Assoc. Meet., Cleveland, OH

West C, Fenstermaker S. 1995. Doing difference. *Gender & Soc.* 9:8–37

West C, Zimmerman DH. 1987. Doing gender. *Gender & Soc.* 1:125–51

Williams C. 1997. Sexual harassment in organizations: a critique of current research and policy. *Sexuality Culture* 1:19–43

Woods JD, Lucas JH. 1993. *The Corporate Closet: The Professional Lives of Gay Men in America.* New York: Free Press

Yoder J, Aniakudo P. 1995. The response of African-American women firefighters to gender harassment at work. *Sex Roles* 32(3–4):125–37

Yount K. 1991. Ladies, flirts, and tomboys: strategies for managing sexual harassment in an underground coal mine. *J. Cont. Ethnogr.* 19:396–422

Annu. Rev. Sociol. 1999. 25:191–216

THE GENDER SYSTEM AND INTERACTION

Cecilia L. Ridgeway

Department of Sociology, Stanford University, Stanford, California 94305-2047;
e-mail: ridgeway@leland.stanford.edu

Lynn Smith-Lovin

Department of Sociology, University of Arizona, Tucson, Arizona 85721;
e-mail: smithlov@u.arizona.edu

KEY WORDS: sex differences, social behavior, social status, identity, social networks

ABSTRACT

The gender system includes processes that both define males and females as different in socially significant ways and justify inequality on the basis of that difference. Gender is different from other forms of social inequality in that men and women interact extensively within families and households and in other role relations. This high rate of contact between men and women raises important questions about how interaction creates experiences that confirm, or potentially could undermine, the beliefs about gender difference and inequality that underlie the gender system. Any theory of gender difference and inequality must accommodate three basic findings from research on interaction. (*a*). People perceive gender differences to be pervasive in interaction. (*b*). Studies of interaction among peers with equal power and status show few gender differences in behavior. (*c*). Most interactions between men and women occur in the structural context of roles or status relationships that are unequal. These status and power differences create very real interaction effects, which are often confounded with gender. Beliefs about gender difference combine with structurally unequal relationships to perpetuate status beliefs, leading men and women to recreate the gender system in everyday interaction. Only peer interactions that are not driven by cultural beliefs about the general competence of men and women or interactions in which women are status- or power-advantaged over men are likely to undermine the gender system.

0360-0572/99/0815-0191$08.00

INTRODUCTION

Gender is a system of social practices within society that constitutes people as different in socially significant ways and organizes relations of inequality on the basis of the difference (Ridgeway & Smith-Lovin 1999). The continued, everyday acceptance of the gender system requires that both people's experiences and widely shared cultural beliefs confirm for them that men and women are sufficiently different in ways that justify men's greater power and privilege. In this, gender is similar to other systems of difference and inequality such as race and class. Gender is distinctive, however, in that its constitutive cultural beliefs and confirmatory experiences must be sustained in the context of constant interaction, often on familiar terms, between those advantaged and disadvantaged by the system. As a consequence, events at the interactional level have a special potency for the gender system. As interactional events enact gender relations over diverse contexts, they confirm or undermine gender beliefs. Thus, interaction plays an important role in sustaining or modifying the gender system as a whole in the face of continually changing material and social structural conditions (Ridgeway 1997).

There are several reasons why men and women interact frequently compared to people on opposite sides of class and race divides. Because whom you interact with is partly determined by who is available, the fact that gender divides people into two equal-sized groups creates the maximum structural likelihood of cross-gender contact for both sexes (Blau & Schwartz 1984). Sexual behavior and reproduction also increase the rate of contact between men and women. In addition, gender crosscuts kin. Most people interact with other-sex family members such as parents, siblings, or children.

The frequent rate of contact between men and women not only makes interaction a powerful arena in the gender system; it also affects the basic rules that people use to frame interaction itself (West & Zimmerman 1987, Ridgeway 1997). Interacting with another requires at least a minimal cultural definition of who self and other are. Perhaps because it is a simple, fast, habitually used cultural dichotomy, research shows that people automatically sex categorize (i.e. label as female or male) any concrete other with whom they interact, even when other definitions, such as teacher-student, are available (Brewer & Lui 1989). This may seem "natural," but ethnomethodologists have shown that sex categorization in everyday interaction is a thoroughly social process. It relies on cues of appearance and behavior that are culturally presumed to stand for physical sex differences (Kessler & McKenna 1978, West & Zimmerman 1987). Sex category is one of only two or three "primary" social categories constituted in our culture as essential to make another sufficiently sensible in relation to self so that interaction can proceed (Brewer & Lui 1989).

Although gender is deeply involved in the fundamental organization of interaction, people are many things in interaction in addition to their sex. Dichotomous sex categories make simple orienting frames, but by the same token they are too diffuse to define behavior adequately in most contexts. People also classify self and other in additional and more situationally specific ways, including age, ethnicity, and institutional role. As additional categorizations occur, research shows that they are cognitively nested within the fundamental understanding of the person as male or female (Brewer & Lui 1989, Stangor et al 1992). As a result, the interactional conduct of gender is always enmeshed in other identities and activities. It cannot be observed in a pure, unentangled form. Gender is a background identity that modifies other identities that are often more salient in the setting than it is.

If gender is a background identity that is interactionally present but enmeshed with other identities, how are culturally shared beliefs about the typical natures, differences, and inequality of men and women produced and reproduced in peoples' experiences? The answer is likely to lie in repeating patterns of associations across interactional contexts between the background identity of male or female and a diversity of situationally specific positions of equality or inequality. To the extent that such repeating patterns of association occur between sex category and interactional power and prestige, they are likely to facilitate shared understandings of men and women as different and unequal. They also reinforce gender as a fundamental personal identity for individuals and structure its meaning for them.

Two factors are likely to shape the patterns of association that occur in interaction between sex category and situational power and prestige. The structural contexts in which cross-sex and same-sex contact occur may interactionally advantage one sex more often than the other. In addition, cultural gender beliefs and identities, themselves a product of interactional patterns, are likely to shape the way actors organize their interactions within the constraints of their structural context.

As this suggests, we see cultural beliefs about gender difference and inequality and corresponding gender identities as both products and producers of the gender organization of interaction. We see a similarly reciprocal relation between the structural contexts in which men and women come together and their gender beliefs and identities: Beliefs and identities affect the network contacts that men and women seek and, thus, the structural contexts in which they meet.

These assumptions guide the organization of our review. First, we examine network studies because they offer us a picture of the typical patterns of interaction between men and women. They also offer a description of the structural contexts in which interaction creates stable network ties and the role relationships in which these interactions are embedded. Then we turn to the gender organization of interaction itself, focusing on the impact of formal positional differences, of cultural beliefs about gender status, and of gender identity processes. We shift then to examine how unequal interaction mediates cultural beliefs about gender and how interaction processes affect network contacts and structures.

NETWORKS OF MALE-FEMALE INTERACTION

Although men and women interact frequently, only a minority of these interactions occur between men and women who, except for gender, are otherwise peers in the power and status associated with their social roles and positions. Researchers find that gender homophily, the tendency for network connections to be same-sex rather than cross-sex, begins virtually as soon as children are able to choose their playmates (Block 1979, Lever 1978, Eder & Hallinan 1978). Since this homophily occurs at about the same time that children develop the knowledge that sex is a permanent personal characteristic, it is probably shaped by identity processes (Kohlberg 1974, Block 1979). The implications of this childhood division may be profound. Networks and knowledge co-evolve, with network connections creating shared knowledge which, in turn, increases the propensity to interact (Carley 1986, 1991). The common activities that occur in childhood play groups create gendered knowledge, which strengthens the perception of gender differences and erodes the common ground upon which intimate, status-equal friendship relationships between males and females must be based. Researchers have argued that these gendered subcultures increase the potential for misunderstanding between men and women (Maltz & Borker 1982, Tannen 1990).

Although peer friendship relations remain gender homophilous into adulthood, there are many similarities in men's and women's networks. Adult women and men have discussion networks of about the same size (Fischer 1982, Marsden 1987); young, unmarried men and women, in particular, have very similar patterns of interaction. Marriage and childbearing introduce subtle changes in networks, however, because of the gendered nature of family life. Wellman (1985) found that childbearing significantly reduced cross-sex contacts for women, drawing them into a female world of play groups and school activities. Women typically have a higher proportion of contacts with kin and neighbors than men (Fischer & Oliker 1983, Marsden 1987); although men get drawn into a more family-oriented female kinship network with the birth of a new child, this family embeddedness fades as the child ages (Munch et al 1997).

Women are much more likely to know friends through their husband's work ties than men are to know their wives' work friends (Fischer & Oliker 1983). Aldrich (1989) suggests that women are more supportive of their husbands' networks than husbands are of their wives'. Structural factors also may be at work. Women are more likely to move with their husbands' work opportunities than men are to move with their wives' job changes. In a study of recent job changers in four white-collar occupations, Campbell (1988) found that children and geographic mobility had a much bigger impact on women's networks than on men's. Women's network ties to co-workers shrank in response to having young children and to moving because of their spouse's job. When the women in Campbell's study moved because of their husband's career opportunities, the diversity of their networks also decreased.

Voluntary group activities help create and reinforce the gender segregation of interaction. Voluntary activities create a highly sex-segregated environment for social interaction: Half of all groups are exclusively female and one fifth are all male (McPherson & Smith-Lovin 1986). Women are more likely to belong to small groups organized around social and religious activities, whereas men belong to more large, work-oriented groups (McPherson & Smith-Lovin 1982). Far from providing a venue where men and women meet as informal peers, interactions within the voluntary sector tend to reinforce gender segregation in society overall (Marsden 1988, 1990). The typical female voluntary association membership generates face-to-face contacts with 29 other members, fewer than 4 of whom are men. The typical men's membership produces contacts with 37 other members, 8 of whom are women (because men's organizations are larger and more likely to be gender integrated) (McPherson & Smith-Lovin 1986).

The picture that emerges from the research about social networks is one in which women seldom meet men in status-equal, role-similar interactions (Smith-Lovin & McPherson 1993). Beginning in childhood, much interaction is gender homophilous. Boys and girls develop in gendered subcultures surrounding play activities and, after a brief period of greater interaction as young, unmarried adults, move into highly differentiated adult worlds. Women interact with other women in child-centered or neighborhood settings, keep religious and kinship contacts alive through regular maintenance, and share intimate friendships with other women. Men interact with a wider range of people, including some women, in the context of larger, more heterogeneous groups. The men are drawn temporarily into kinship ties with the birth of a child, but those contacts fade in importance as the child ages and the nuclear family reasserts itself as the primary basis of men's intimacy and social support.

Men and women meet each other in contexts where institutional roles heavily structure their interaction. Kinship, work, and couple-oriented social events are the primary settings for these interactions. When a woman talks with a man, she is most likely to do so as a mother, a wife, a daughter, an employee, a purchaser of services, or perhaps as the wife of his male friend. Contacts between men and women are most likely to occur in large political or business-related associations (McPherson & Smith-Lovin 1986), where men are more likely to hold higher status positions.

Women's networks are more likely than men's to be densely interconnected because of the kinship structures and small groups in which they are generated; the people with whom women interact are more likely to know one another well while the people to whom men are tied are more likely to be disconnected from one another. Therefore, women are less likely to experience the autonomy that comes from conflicting or disconnected affiliations. In a sense, women's social worlds are more like a small town, where everyone knows everyone else, while men's are based in a wider variety of disconnected institutional spheres. Men get diverse information from their larger numbers of weak ties (Granovetter 1973, Lin 1999) and have more opportunities to generate power through exclusivity of exchange relations (Molm & Cook 1995) or through brokerage opportunities (Burt 1992).

One special case where we have a great deal of information about the patterns and character of contacts between men and women is the workplace. There are a wealth of studies exploring the social capital that white-collar, managerial-level workers accumulate and its effects on their career advancement. The sex-segregated nature of work creates a biased opportunity structure for work interaction between men and women. Women are found in different, often less attractive, jobs than men (Reskin 1993); this segregation is especially strong at the firm level where workers actually interact (Bielby & Baron 1986). This means that although men and women may interact in the workplace, most of their interactions will be cross-occupation (e.g. nurses with doctors, secretaries with managers), with men occupying the higher paying, higher authority position (South et al 1982).

In the relatively rare instances where men and women are in similar occupations, jobs, and hierarchical levels, they have surprisingly similar networks. In particular, they are equally likely to hold central positions in informal organizational networks (Brass 1985, Miller 1986, Ibarra 1992) and to have similar personal networks (Aldrich et al 1989, Moore 1990, Burt 1992). But since women are much rarer at the higher ranks in most occupations and organizations, organizational demography constrains the pool of potential network contacts that are both gender homophilous and high status for most women workers (Ibarra 1992). High-status women can have supportive contacts with highly placed people (mostly male) or with other women (mostly lower status than themselves), but not both simultaneously (Ibarra 1997).

These subtle network pressures on women in high status positions lead to some interesting differences in the ability of women to translate network characteristics into career advancement. Men are more able to translate educational attainment and external professional contacts into central positions in informal organizational networks (Ibarra 1992, Miller 1986). Furthermore, men are better able to use some network structures to their advantage. Burt (1992) found that men's mobility was enhanced by ties to people who were not directly connected to one another (i.e. bridging ties that crossed structural holes in the network). Women, on the other hand, needed strong ties to strategic partners in the organization to advance quickly. Ibarra (1997) also found that fast-track men advanced most quickly when their networks bridged structural holes, while fast-track women built networks that were higher in both tie strength and range of contacts within and outside the organization. These organizational network findings confirm Granovetter's (1983, 1985) conclusion that weak ties are less advantageous for people in insecure positions, whether economically or socially. Women's lower status and legitimacy in the managerial world means that they need strong ties to sponsors and mentors that allow them to "borrow" social capital (to use Burt's economic language). Men can use the information and structural power that comes from weak, bridging ties, because they do not have the legitimacy problems that women face.

In sum, the literature on work networks tells us two important things. First, managerial women (or women in blue-collar jobs traditionally dominated by men) are less likely than similar men to have ties with same-sex others who are in their same position or who are just above them in the hierarchy. Therefore, they will find it more difficult to find role models or sources of information about how to handle the special problems that they may experience either because of work-family conflicts or because of their less legitimated token status (Ibarra 1996). To have gender-homophilous ties, women must have networks that range further outside their own organization (Ibarra 1992, 1997) or outside their own hierarchical level within the organization. Second, the legitimacy problems that women face lead networks to work differently for them. Close ties to a superior who can sponsor them are more important for women; these ties are often with a man, given the organizational demography of managerial positions. Although these male mentors may not provide solutions to the special problems that women face, they do offer connections that confer status and opportunity.

THE OVERDETERMINED NATURE OF INEQUALITY IN MALE-FEMALE INTERACTION

Gender and Positions of Authority

Network studies show that cross-sex interaction is usually embedded in unequal, institutionalized role relationships. Women are most frequently in the low status position (e.g., mentor and protégé, boss and secretary). Even when women and men appear to occupy the same status position, differences in their legitimacy and the ways in which informal networks work for them may produce interactional effects that have far-reaching implications.

Since cognitive sex categorization makes gender a background identity for actors in these encounters, they experience men in more powerful roles, behaving assertively and agentically, while women act in a more supportive manner in their less powerful roles. Eagly's (1987, Eagly & Steffen 1984, Eagly & Wood 1991) role theory of gender differences argues that stereotypic beliefs about the agentic versus communal traits of men and women derive from this gendered division of labor. Powerful, high-status roles are disproportionately played by men in society and homemaker roles are played almost entirely by women. The gendered division of labor in society also gives men and women different experiences from which they may acquire different skills and interests.

Role theory argues that interactional behavior is shaped by the most salient role in a setting. In most contexts this is an institutional role such as a job. Thus, role theory predicts that men and women will act similarly in similar formal roles. Gender roles are a primary determinant of behavior only when they are salient in the situation or other roles are ambiguous. When gender roles are salient, stereotypic expectations for agency and communion create gender differences in behavior.

Are the structural constraints of position the primary source of men and women's behavior in unequal formal roles, as role theory predicts, or is behavior strongly shaped by individuals' gendered skills and traits? If gendered traits play a large role, they would affect the selection of men and women into powerful versus subordinate roles as well as the way that they act in those roles.

The evidence clearly supports the importance of structural constraints independent of gendered traits. In positions of similar formal authority, few differences appear between men and women in the way they interact with either same- or other-sex subordinates. Johnson (1994) randomly assigned men and women to positions of authority in same- and mixed-sex contexts. She found no gender differences in their managerial behavior. In an extensive meta-analysis of leadership studies, Eagly & Johnson (1990) similarly found no differences in how task directed male and female leaders acted and only very slight differences (effect size $d = 0.04$) in how interpersonally oriented they were.

In a familial context, positions of power or role also shape men and women's behavior in similar ways. In a study of heterosexual and homosexual couples, Kollock et al (1985) showed that the member a couple rated as more powerful in shared decisions generally talked more and interrupted the partner more than the less powerful member did, regardless of sex or sex of partner. Risman (1998) reports that men cast in the position of primary caretaker for a child adapt to behave similarly to women who mother.

On the other hand, gender-atypical occupants of power positions are sometimes perceived by others as less legitimate in such roles. Problems of legitimacy can make it more difficult for women in positions of power to exercise directive power or dominance compared to men in equivalent positions (Butler & Geis 1990, Kanter 1977, Ridgeway & Berger 1986). Eagly et al (1992) found only a slight overall tendency for male leaders to be evaluated more favorably than female leaders in a meta-analytic study. But when leaders behaved in a directive, autocratic style, there was a moderate-sized tendency ($d = 0.30$) for women to be evaluated more negatively than men. Perhaps in reaction to such legitimacy pressures, meta-analysis indicates a small tendency ($d = 0.22$) for women leaders to be more democratic and participatory than men. Such legitimacy problems suggest that there is a prescriptive edge to expectations created by gender beliefs (Fiske & Stevens 1993). Perhaps this is not surprising given the pressures of maintaining beliefs about difference and inequality in the context of frequent interaction.

The frequency of such power stratified encounters between men and women encourages cultural beliefs about gender differences (Eagly & Steffen 1984). Yet formally stratified roles are not the only factor that produces gender difference and inequality in interaction. Men and women do encounter one another as formal role peers in important contexts, such as educational institutions, some jobs, and romantic contexts. People also have considerable contact with same-sex peers. Widely shared evaluative or status beliefs about gender and people's gendered identities have their strongest impact on behavior in these less formally stratified interactional contexts. These factors, too, play a critical role in the enactment of difference and inequality.

Differences in legitimacy in work positions mean that even men and women who hold structurally equivalent formal positions are actually operating in different social contexts. Ibarra (1997) has noted that women's lack of legitimacy in managerial roles (especially in dealing with clients outside the firm) can limit the usefulness of role-modeling from men who act as their mentors.

Gender Status and Behavior in Interaction

One of the major accounts of gender inequality among formal peers derives from expectation states theory (Berger et al 1977, Carli 1991, Ridgeway 1993, Wagner & Berger 1997). Eagly's (1987) role theory makes predictions about such settings that are similar to, although less detailed than, those of expectation states theory. Space limitations prevent us from describing them as well (for a comparison of the theories, see Aries 1996, Ridgeway & Diekema 1992).

Expectation states theory argues that actors use cultural beliefs about the status implications of their distinguishing characteristics to organize their interaction in goal-oriented settings (Berger et al 1977). Gender is a status characteristic in many countries in that beliefs that associate higher status and competence with men than with women are widely held (Broverman et al 1972, Williams & Best 1990). As Foschi and colleagues (1994) argue, recent social changes may be weakening gender status beliefs in the United States, especially among college students. Most current research, however, continues to find evidence of gender status effects.

Expectation states theory claims that gender becomes salient in a setting when it either differentiates the actors (a mixed-sex context) or is culturally linked to the task at hand. When gender is salient, gender status beliefs shape the expectations actors form for the competence of men and women in the setting. These often unconscious performance expectations shape behavior in a self-fulfilling way. They affect the likelihood that a man, compared to a woman, will speak up and make suggestions to the group and that others will respond positively to those suggestions, ask for the person's opinions, and accept influence from the person. In this way, performance expectations, shaped by gender status beliefs, create a power and prestige order among men and women in the setting (Lockheed 1985, Wagner & Berger 1997, Wood & Karten 1986).

In mixed sex groups, then, the theory predicts that men will be more influential, participate more, be more assertive, and be less inclined to agree than similar women. When the task or setting is stereotypically masculine (e.g., car repair), gender's direct relevance to the setting will exaggerate these behavioral differences, increasing men's power and prestige advantage over women. When the task is stereotypically feminine (e. g., child care), the theory predicts that women will have a slight power and prestige advantage over men. In same-sex groups, on the other hand, gender status will not be salient unless the task is gender typed. As a result, men's and women's participation and assertive, task-oriented behavior should be similar in same-sex groups with a gender-neutral task.

These predictions hold for men and women who are otherwise equals. When other status characteristics (e.g., education, valued skills, occupation, ethnicity) are salient in the situation as well as gender, the theory argues that actors combine the implications of each, weighted by its relevance to the situational goal, to form aggregated performance expectations for each actor compared to another. In some situations, more relevant status characteristics may outweigh the effect of gender status. According to expectation states, then, although sex categorization may occur in all interactions, the impact of gender status on behavior varies greatly. It depends on the salience of gender status beliefs in the situation and their relevance to the task at hand, compared to other status information that is also salient.

Expectation states theory provides a good account of the gender organization of behaviors that are task directed or enact a power and prestige hierarchy. These include participation, influence, emergent leadership, assertive gestures and gaze, and tentative speech. With the exception of agreement, which is part of the influence process, the theory does not address the supportive, socioemotional aspects of interaction. We review research and associated explanations of socioemotional behavior after a consideration of power and prestige behaviors.

PARTICIPATION, INFLUENCE, AND LEADERSHIP   Several studies show that, other things being equal, men in mixed sex groups talk more (James & Drakich 1993, Dovidio et al 1988), make more task suggestions (Wood & Karten 1986), are more influential (Pugh & Wahrman 1983, Lockheed 1985, Wagner et al 1986; but see Stewart 1988), and are more likely to be selected leader than are women (Eagly & Karau 1991, Fleischer & Chertoff 1986, Nyquist & Spence 1986, Wentworth & Anderson 1984). Yet in same-sex groups no differences appear between men and women in participation, task suggestions (Carli 1991, Johnson et al 1996, Wagner & Berger 1997), or willingness to accept influence from others (Pugh & Wahrman 1983). Wood & Karten (1986) demonstrated that men's tendency to speak more and engage in more active task behaviors in mixed sex discussions was mediated by status-based assumptions that the men were more competent. When performance expectations for men and women in the situation were equalized, gender differences in behavior disappeared.

In a meta-analytic study of emergent leadership in mixed sex contexts, Eagly & Karau (1991) found that the overall tendency for men to become leaders rather than women varied with the gender typing of the leadership and task. As expectation states theory predicts, the likelihood that men became leaders was especially high when the task was culturally masculine, moderate when the task was gender neutral, and low or negative when the task was culturally feminine or leadership was social in nature. Several studies have shown that gender differences in leadership disappear or favor women in mixed sex groups when the task turns to one favoring the interests and expected competence of women (Dovidio et al 1988, Wentworth & Anderson 1984, Yamada et al 1983).

The gender organization of assertive versus deferential gestures and speech shows a similar pattern. There are gender differences that favor men in mixed sex interaction but these interact with the gender typing of the task or setting, giving men a stronger advantage in masculine tasks and a weak disadvantage in feminine tasks. In same-sex groups there are few differences between men's and women's assertive gestures and speech.

GAZE AND GESTURES   A large body of research on gaze, reviewed by Ellyson et al (1992), indicates that, other factors being equal, men show more visual dominance in mixed sex interaction than do women. Visual dominance is a pattern of looking at the other more while speaking than while listening. It is associated with perceived competence and influence. In same-sex groups men and women differ little in visual dominance. They both show similarly greater visual dominance when in high-status rather than low-status positions in the interaction (Ellyson et al 1992).

The relevance of gender to the setting affects gaze and gestures as well. Dovidio et al (1998) found that when mixed sex dyads turned from a gender neutral task to a masculine task, men's greater visual dominance and rate of gesturing became exaggerated, but when the dyad shifted to discuss a feminine task, women displayed more visual dominance and gestured more than men. These shifts in gaze and gesture patterns accompanied corresponding changes in participation rates and speech initiations, indicating changes in the behavioral power and prestige orders of the dyads.

TENTATIVE SPEECH   Lakoff (1975) has suggested that women, due to their lower status, use more tentative, deferential speech forms, especially with men, and that these forms make the speaker appear less convincing. Studies do show that women are more likely to use tag questions (Brouwer et al 1979, Crosby & Nyquist 1977, Eakins & Eakins 1978, McMillan et al 1977), hedges, and disclaimers (Bradley 1981, Crosby & Nyquist 1977, Eakins & Eakins 1978), and hypercorrect, "superpolite" grammatical constructions (Crosby & Nyquist 1977, Lakoff 1975, McMillan et al 1977). Although tag questions may convey uncertainty in task-oriented contexts, subsequent studies show that they may also be used to support the speech of another (see Aries 1996 for a review).

Maltz & Borker (1982) and Tannen (1990) have argued that women learn more supportive, less dominance oriented speech styles in childhood peer groups that are sex segregated. In mixed sex contexts, according to this view, women's more supportive speech style is misinterpreted as tentative and deferential. This "gendered subcultures" argument, in contrast to that of Lakoff (1975) and expectation states theory, predicts greater gender differences in tentative speech forms between men and women in same-sex groups than in mixed sex groups. In task directed settings, however, research does not support this prediction. In a well designed study, Carli (1990) has shown that women use more hedges, disclaimers, and tag questions than similar men in mixed sex task discussion, but there are no gender differences in these speech forms in same-sex discussions.

INTERRUPTIONS   In an influential early study, Zimmerman & West (1975) reported that whereas interruptions are rare in same-sex contexts, men interrupt women in mixed-sex interaction as an assertion of power over the conversation. More powerful actors do tend to interrupt more (Drass 1986, Kollock et al

1985, Roger & Nesshoever 1987, Roger & Schumaker 1983). As subsequent evidence has accumulated, however, it is less clear that there are gender differences in overall interruption rates (James & Clarke 1993). The matter is complicated by the fact that some interruptions express active listenership rather than disrupt the other's speech. The evidence suggests that men more often disruptively interrupt women than other men, whereas women do not discriminate in whom they interrupt (Smith-Lovin & Brody 1989).

CREDIT FOR PERFORMANCE   In addition to shaping patterns of participation, influence, gaze, and tentative versus assertive speech, scholars have shown that the activation of gender status beliefs in mixed sex interaction can affect the credit women receive for their performances compared to similar men. Gender status beliefs evoke double standards for judging competence, so that a performance of the same quality is seen as less indicative of ability in a woman than a man (Biernat & Kobrynowicz 1997, Foschi 1996). Similarly, LaFrance et al (1997) show that women's actions in mixed-sex pairs are depicted in less causal language than men's actions are.

COUNTERVEILING EVIDENCE   There is one set of evidence that contradicts the broad pattern of support for gender status as the primary cause of gender differences in assertive, task directed behaviors and influence among formal peers. These are studies that use Bales' (1970) Interaction Process Analysis (IPA) to code the percentages of each person's behavior in an encounter that are task-oriented and instrumental versus supportive and socioemotional. Such studies generally find that men in task groups have higher percentages of task behavior and women have somewhat higher percentages of socioemotional behavior. In conflict with the expectation states account, these differences are marginally larger between men and women in same-sex groups than in mixed sex groups (Anderson & Blanchard 1982, Carli 1989, Piliavin & Martin 1978, Strodtbeck & Mann 1956).

As several scholars point out, however, the contradiction is an artifact of the IPA coding scheme (Aries 1996, Carli 1991, Wheelan & Verdi 1992). IPA records relative percentages rather than absolute numbers of task-directed behaviors and classifies as socioemotional all acts that contain any socioemotional element. Thus, a task suggestion accompanied by a smile or laugh is coded as a socioemotional behavior. In fact, studies show no differences in the total number of task behaviors that men and women produce in same-sex groups (Johnson et al 1996, Wagner & Berger 1997).

SOCIOEMOTIONAL BEHAVIOR   The likely explanation for the IPA results is that women display more socioemotional behaviors than men, especially in same-sex groups. Research shows that women use verbal forms that support the speech of others more than men and engage in more backchanneling (i.e., simultaneous speech that supports the other's speech) (Eakins & Eakins 1978, Johnson et al 1996, McLaughlin et al 1981). Women also use more expressive intensifiers than men (Carli 1990) and are nonverbally warmer (Hall 1984, Wood & Rhodes 1992). These gender differences are often strongest in same-sex groups (Carli 1990).

Women's higher rate of socioemotional behaviors in interaction is attributed to several sources. When gender status is salient (in mixed-sex or gender-relevant settings), women face legitimacy problems when they seek to be highly influential. Accompanying their assertive efforts with socioemotional "softeners" assuages resistance and increases their influence in the group, as research shows (Carli 1990, Carli et al 1995, Ridgeway 1982, Shackleford et al 1996). Also, simply being in a lower status position casts a person, regardless of sex, in a supportive, agreeing role (Gerber 1996).

Status factors alone, however, do not explain women's increased socioemotional behaviors in female groups. In a modification of the gendered subcultures argument, Carli (1990) suggests that people have gendered schemas for socioemotional behavior in same-sex interaction. Whether or not this is the case, it appears that people signal or mark gender identity and, thus, gender difference across interaction contexts primarily through behaviors in the socioemotional realm. It is interesting that the identity marked by socioemotional behavior is female or not: Adding socioemotional behaviors is distinctively female, but a socioemotionally neutral style is not definitively male. As linguists note, it is the exception to the dominant form that is marked in language (e.g., woman doctor).

In sum, gender status beliefs become salient in mixed sex or gender relevant situations and create unequal competence expectations for similar men and women. These expectations organize a broad array of assertive, goal-oriented behaviors, both verbal and nonverbal, creating a gender hierarchy of influence and esteem among the actors. Men's advantage in this behavioral hierarchy is moderate in gender-neutral settings but becomes stronger when the task is masculine typed. When the task is culturally feminine, women have a slight advantage over men in the behavioral hierarchy. Because gender status combines with other salient status distinctions to affect behavior, gender status effects can be overwhelmed by other, counteracting status characteristics (e.g., woman computer whiz) that are more relevant in the situation than gender is.

The evidence shows that gender inequality in male-female interaction is created primarily by situational factors. These include unequal formal roles and salient gender status beliefs. As a result, behavioral difference and inequality are quite sensitive to changes in the structure of situations and vary across contexts. A general pattern of inequality in male-female interaction only occurs because it is overdetermined by situational factors. Gender status beliefs support the assignment and enactment of unequal formal roles between men and women. Unequal roles, in turn, create interactional experiences that sustain status beliefs. Status beliefs themselves import inequality into interactions between men and women who are formal peers.

Cultural gender beliefs imply difference as well as inequality. Across mixed- and same-sex contexts, gender difference and identity, rather than status in the situation, seem to be marked most consistently by socioemotional behaviors rather than task-directed behaviors.

Gender Identities in Interaction

In the sections above, we reviewed how status and power structures associated with gender create inequality in interaction. Another central theme in the literature involves the meanings associated with gender identities and how they are expressed in interaction. Two traditions share this emphasis on meaning: the "doing gender" perspective (West & Fenstermaker 1995, West & Zimmerman 1987) and the structural symbolic interactionist perspectives (Stryker 1980, Burke & Tully 1977). The two perspectives differ dramatically in their typical methods and language, but they share some important insights about the ubiquitous character of gender in interaction.

In particular, both perspectives focus on how gender and its cultural meanings are expressed in a large variety of institutional contexts, across different situations, embedded in different role relationships. They suggest how gender can flavor the expression of power- and status-unequal relationships, as well as shaping the character of peer, status-equal interactions.

"Doing gender" is an ethnomethodological approach that argues gender is an interactional accomplishment, something that must be continually enacted in local situations to persist as a social phenomenon. Cultural norms dictate that there are two and only two sexes, each with inherent natures that justify male dominance. However, these norms cannot be maintained unless people present themselves in ways that allow others to categorize them as male or female. Gender, in this perspective, is the local management of conduct in relation to normative conceptions of appropriate behavior and attitudes for one's sex category (West & Zimmerman 1987). Thus, gender is an adverb rather than a noun—something that modifies the ways that role behaviors are enacted, rather than a personal characteristic. Gender qualifies how a person carries out any behavior in any situation, so that the behavior can be recognized as a culturally competent gender performance by others. The concept of gender as something that one "does" has been very influential as a theoretical point, but researchers have been slow to operationalize this insight to orient empirical work on interaction (see Brines 1994 for a notable exception). The structural symbolic interactionists have been much more explicit about how cultural meanings associated with gender get transformed into behaviors specific to institutional situations.

Modern structural symbolic interactionists see identities as a set of cultural meanings that are learned through a variety of mechanisms, including interaction behaviors, people's emotional reactions, material culture, and other institutional arrangements (Heise 1979). These meanings then act as a reference point for interpreting events that occur and for guiding behavior (Heise 1979, Smith-Lovin & Heise 1988, Burke & Reitzes 1981, Burke 1991). In other words, structural symbolic interactionists now view identity and behavior as a control system, such that identity meanings disturbed by interpersonal interaction are restored by new behaviors and cognitions that are produced in response to the disturbance.

Gender is often viewed as a "master identity" because it is evoked across a large variety of contexts, rather than being associated with specific institutional roles (Stets & Burke 1996). It serves as a background personal identity, based on one's sex category, even while more specific roles are being enacted. Feminine identities like female, woman, lady, wife, and mother are more positively evaluated, less powerful, and a bit more expressive than their male counterparts (male, man, gentleman, husband, and father) (Kroska 1997). Institutional roles that require or strongly suggest a particular gender (e.g., family roles like son and daughter, or gender-segregated occupational roles like secretary and welder) will incorporate these gender meanings as part of the role-identity's connotation. When someone is a gender-atypical occupant of a role-identity, the gender marks and modifies the meaning of the identity in systematic ways (Averett & Heise 1988). While a "female judge" is a very powerful, grave person, the addition of the modifier "female" will make her seem a little more positive, less powerful, and more expressive than her male counterparts who occupy the unmarked identity ("judge," because we assume "male") (Averett & Heise 1988).

The gendered meanings of identities shape behavior. In general, we expect women to behave in a more positive, less powerful, more expressive way. In this sense, the structural symbolic interactionists' view is closely related to traditional socialization approaches to gender: People learn meanings about what it is to be masculine or feminine and then enact those meanings across a variety of situations. The control system introduces a crucial difference, however, because it explains how situational factors can have such an important impact on the way in which gender meanings are played out. For example, we see how situational role-identities can powerfully shape or even overwhelm gender. A woman acting as a mother may show strongly feminine behavior (because gendered meanings are so central to the meaning of "mother"), but when she goes to a business meeting to enact the role-identity of boss, the fact that she is a "female boss" may only slightly modify the manner in which she carries out that role. Most importantly, the control perspective illustrates how recent events can shape what behaviors are needed to maintain meanings. If an interaction is making one seem more feminine than one's fundamentally held gender identity, then more assertive behavior might result, even if the identity standard were quite feminine. On the other hand, a woman who has had to engage in a nasty fight with a service person to carry out some household task may respond by being unusually unassertive and emotional to her husband a few moments later; the traditional femininity in the latter encounter helps to restore meanings that were upset in the former confrontation. In this way, the control system view of the structural symbolic interactionist mirrors the basic insight of the "doing gender" perspective. Different actions will serve to express and maintain gender identities within different situational contexts.

Researchers have applied the new control theories to the dynamics of conversation. Robinson & Smith-Lovin (1992) looked at how gender identities shaped discussions among male and female students in six-person task groups. Since common conversational behaviors like "interrupt" and "talk to" have meanings that shape impressions of the speaker and the recipient, men and women respond somewhat differently in such discussions. Stets & Burke (1996) used the same logic to study how married couples discussed disagreements. They found that spouses with a more masculine identity used more negative behavior in the marital interactions, while those with a feminine identity used more positive behavior. This finding echoes an earlier result from Drass (1986), who showed that self-meanings of masculinity and femininity could shape conversational dynamics even in same-sex discussions. Burke et al (1988) applied the perspective to more powerful behaviors: physical and sexual abuse during dating relationships.

The fact that identity meanings are controlled in interaction does not mean that they cannot change. Persistent disconfirmations of our self-relevant meanings can lead us to adjust so that our identities better fit the impressions being produced in actual experiences. Burke & Cast (1997) explored how the gender identities of newly married couples shifted over a three-year period that included the birth of their first child. The interactions surrounding the birth led to an increase in gender identity differences, as the new mother and father played out their parental roles. However, role-taking processes in which a spouse takes his or her partner's perspective on the interactions served to create convergence in gender identities. Verta Taylor (1999) showed how social movements purposefully create new identity meanings. In an ethnographic study of a post-partum self-help group, Taylor followed how new mothers' identities were transformed to create a more positive, assertive emotional state.

Although they arise from very different intellectual traditions, both the doing-gender perspective and the structural symbolic interaction theories stress similar changes to the traditional gender role socialization perspective. They both emphasize that gender is accomplished in a situational context.

Which behaviors support gender conceptions vary from one interaction to another, depending on the institutional background, the recent history of the interaction, and the roles occupied by the participants. Both perspectives stress the meanings associated with behaviors as well as identities. Behaviors in interaction provide social confirmation or disconfirmation of gendered identities because they have cultural meanings that interactants share.

The primary difference between the two perspectives is the degree of specificity about these cultural meanings and how they are assessed in empirical work. The original proponents of the doing gender perspective, West & Zimmerman (1987:127), defined gender as "the activity of managing situated conduct in light of normative conceptions of attitudes and activities appropriate for one's sex category," placing the emphasis squarely on the behavioral accomplishment of gendered meanings. But, as Kroska (1998:307) pointed out, advocates of the doing gender perspective rarely measure these normative conceptions, but rather infer them from differences in behavior by sex category. Kroska showed how combining the basic insight of the doing gender perspective with the greater formalism of the identity control theories can produce theoretical progress. She examined how the meanings associated with common household tasks (e.g. cleaning a kitchen, feeding a baby) might produce the extraordinarily stable division of labor in the home. Viewing gender ideology as an identity to which people are committed in varying degrees helped to explain the sometimes weak correlations that have been observed between these attitudes and actual household behavior. Blending the doing gender and identity control ideas helps us introduce a dynamic, situational aspect to the basic insight of traditional socialization theory, that people learn cultural meanings about what it is to be a man or woman that shape their behavior in a wide variety of situations. It refocuses our attention on the meanings of social actions as well as identities. It also helps us cope with the empirical fact that gender behavior looks very different in different institutional contexts (and sometimes appears to disappear altogether, when institutional roles are dominant and gender is not salient).

THE ROLE OF UNEQUAL INTERACTION IN MEDIATING BELIEFS ABOUT GENDER

Gendered identity meanings develop in response to widely shared cultural beliefs about men and women. Several scholars have noted the striking correspondence between such beliefs about men and women and stereotypes of high- and low-status people more generally (i.e., respected, competent, leaderlike versus supportive, less competent, and followerlike) (Conway et al 1996, Geis et al 1984, Gerber 1996). Given sex categorization in interaction and male-female interaction that is most often status ordered, men and women commonly experience one another as acting in high- and low-status ways. It is reasonable to expect that these repeated experiences would affect widely shared beliefs about men's and women's attributes.

Research suggests that interactional experiences can induce people to take on status beliefs about their distinguishing characteristics. After repeated encounters between people who differed in resources that led to influence, such as pay, as well as a distinguishing characteristic, actors believed that most people see those in the advantaged category of the characteristic as more respected and competent than, but not as nice as, those in the disadvantaged category (Ridgeway et al 1998). Once created, actors can spread status beliefs to others by treating them according to the beliefs (Ridgeway & Glasgow 1996).

Since men and women interact frequently, but usually under conditions where men have more resources (e. g., pay, formal position, contacts, information) that advantage them in the influence hierarchies that develop, mixed-sex interaction continually refreshes gender status beliefs (Ridgeway 1991). It reinforces them as social facts for individuals and maintains their effective consensuality. Because widespread status beliefs change more slowly than material conditions (Ridgeway 1997), men and women, implicitly acting on gender status beliefs, rewrite gender inequality into new conditions and organizational forms. Thus, interaction can conserve gender inequality, in modified form, over changes in the social structure of society (Ridgeway 1997).

Besides fostering gender status beliefs, constant sex categorization and frequent cross-sex interaction raise the salience of gender as a personal identity both for individuals and in cultural beliefs. A person's multiple identities can be thought of as hierarchically arranged in terms of commitment or embeddedness within social networks (Ibarra & Smith-Lovin 1997, Stryker & Serpe 1982). Enactments of gender as a background, modifying identity across a wide variety of social contexts, embed it within a broad range of personal networks, heightening its salience and affective importance for the individual. At the same time, such extensive expressions of gender identity reinforce the importance of cultural beliefs associated with gender and imbue them with diffuse relevance to diverse activities. Thus, interaction helps produce gender identity and gender status beliefs as well as being shaped by them.

INTERACTION PROCESSES AFFECT NETWORK STRUCTURES

In the section above, we reviewed how ubiquitous sex categorization and the structural inequality of men and women lead to unequal interaction and the formation of beliefs about essential differences between men and women. Now we turn to the reciprocal effect: how interactional processes, sex categorization, and gender beliefs shape the degree to which men and women interact. Since most network research has focused on the outcomes of networks rather than their sources, this topic reveals fewer empirical studies.

Homophily on gender operates both through the opportunities that are presented for men and women to interact (induced homophily) and through the choice to interact with others who view the world in the same way (choice homophily) (McPherson & Smith-Lovin 1987). People select to interact with those who confirm their own view of the world, especially their self-views (Swann et al 1987, Robinson & Smith-Lovin 1992a). To the extent that men and women occupy "different worlds" because of their structural positions, they will be more likely to form gender-homophilious friendships and other peer relations (Carley 1986, 1991). To the extent that people enjoy interacting with those who accord them status or power (Kemper 1978, Heise 1999), we would expect men to seek out women for intimate friendships more often than women seek out men. Women, on the other hand, can operate in the absence of some constraints by interacting in all-female groups. Robinson & Smith-Lovin (1992b) find, for example, that men have higher success than women in getting a laugh for a joke when they are in mixed sex groups but that women make more jokes than men in same-sex groups.

Individuals vary, of course, in how central gender identity is in their self structure. A social identity perspective may help to explain the considerable variability in the extent to which people in the same structural position construct ego networks that are gender homophilous (Ibarra 1995, Chatman & Brown 1996, Ely 1994, Wharton 1992). The salience of gender identity is likely to vary depending on factors such as personal history, organizational context, exposure to social movement activities, parents' ideologies, and other factors. The extent to which people select for gender-homophilous networks also is determined by the legitimacy of men and women within a particular position. Ibarra (1996) showed how the legitimacy problems that women faced as they were promoted into a role requiring interaction with clients led them to seek out female mentors who had faced similar problems.

In sum, interaction processes affect with whom one interacts in several interrelated ways. First, since men and women often occupy different structural positions, they come to know different things, view the world in different ways, and prefer gender-homophilous friendships. Second, since women are often structurally disadvantaged in interactions with men, sex category is likely to remain socially constructed as a salient difference. Third, gender identity salience will vary across individuals in predictable ways, based on personal biography and structural context, producing concomitant variations in the gender homophily of ego networks. Finally, the special legitimacy and interactional problems that women face may lead them to seek out other women as appropriate role models, mentors, and friends. As we note above, most of these observations apply equally to any other social category that is ordered by status, power, and prestige. The unique features of gender are that it involves two roughly equal-sized populations, increasing the potential role of choice homophily, and that it is spread more evenly across many other structural and geographic divides, decreasing its strong correlation with other salient factors that might reinforce interactional differences.

CONCLUSION

Any theory of gender difference and inequality must accommodate three basic findings from research on interaction. 1. People perceive gender differences to be pervasive in interaction. 2. Actual studies of interaction among equal-status, equal-power peers indicate relatively few gender differences in behavior. Those that occur are concentrated in the socio-emotional, nonverbal domains that are commonly considered to be less central to instrumental outcomes. Equal status/power contacts between men and women may be the most problematic for the gender system, since they undermine both difference and inequality (Reskin 1988). 3. Most interactions between men and women occur within the structural context of role or status relationships that are unequal. Unequal role/status relationships between men and women produce many differences in interactional behavior that are commonly associated with gender.

Together, these findings point to a process by which cultural conceptions of gender that justify inequality are constructed from the way gender is enmeshed in the conduct of other roles/identities across diverse structural contexts. Additional research is needed on several aspects of this process. 1. We need a better understanding of the way gender combines with other identities/roles/statuses and shapes the way they are played. This research could focus on how statuses combine to create expectations in a group, on how less legitimate authority figures play out their roles, on how multiple identities combine in situated action, or on how people "do" gender in different institutional domains. 2. We need further investigation of the structural sources of interactional differences between men and women and the processes by which these differences are incorporated into our cultural meanings of what it is to be a man or woman. 3. We have reasonably effective theories and evidence on how status, power, and identity shape interaction and on how interaction affects beliefs about identity and status. We are especially lacking, however, in investigations of how these cultural beliefs and interactional patterns help form and perpetuate network structures that provide the contexts of cross-sex and same-sex interaction. Such research is needed to close the circle of causality between structure and interaction out of which gender appears to emerge.

Visit the *Annual Reviews home page* at
http://www.AnnualReviews.org.

Literature Cited

Anderson LR, Blanchard PN. 1982. Sex differences in task and social-emotional behavior. *Basic Appl. Soc. Psychol.* 3:109–39

Aldrich H. 1989. Networking among women entrepreneurs. In *Women-Owned Businesses*, ed. O Hagan, C Rivchun, D Sexton, pp. 103–32. New York: Praeger

Aldrich H, Reese PR, Dubini P. 1989. Women on the verge of a breakthrough? Networking among entrepreneurs in the United States and Italy. *Entrepreneurship Reg. Dev.* 1:339–56

Aries E. 1996. *Men and Women in Interaction: Reconsidering the Differences.* New York: Oxford Univ. Press

Averett CP, Heise DR. 1988. Modified social identities: amalgamations, attributions and emotions. In *Analyzing Social Interaction: Research Advances in Affect Control Theory,* ed. L Smith-Lovin, DR Heise, pp. 103–32. New York: Gordon & Breach

Bales RF. 1970. *Personality and Interpersonal Behavior.* New York: Holt, Rinehart & Winston

Berger J, Fisek H, Norman R, Zelditch M. 1977. *Status Characteristics and Social Interaction.* New York: Elsevier

Bielby WT, Baron JN. 1986. Men and women at work: sex segregation and statistical discrimination. *Am. J. Sociol.* 91:759–99

Biernat M, Kobrynowicz D. 1997. Gender- and race-based standards of competence: lower minimum standards but higher ability standards for devalued groups. *J. Pers. Soc. Psychol.* 72:544–57

Blau P, Schwartz J. 1984. *Crosscutting Social Circles: Testing a Macrostructural Theory of Intergroup Relations.* New York: Academic

Blier MJ, Blier-Wilson LA. 1989. Gender differences in self-rated emotional expressiveness. *Sex Roles* 21:287–96

Block JH. 1979. Socialization influences on personality development in males and females. In *APA Master Lecture Series on Issues of Sex and Gender in Psychology,* ed. MM Parks. Washington, DC: Am. Psychol. Assoc.

Bradley PH. 1981. The folk-linguistics of women's speech: an empirical examination. *Commun. Monogr.* 48:73–90

Brass DJ. 1985. Men's and women's networks: a study of interaction patterns and influence in an organization. *Acad. Manag. J.* 28:2:327–43

Brewer M, Lui L. 1989. The primacy of age and sex in the structure of person categories. *Soc. Cognit.* 7:262–74

Brines J. 1994. Economic dependency, gender, and the division of labor at home. *Am. J. Sociol.* 100:652–88

Brouwer D, Gerritsern MM, De Haan D. 1979. Speech differences between men and women: on the wrong track? *Lang. Soc.* 8:33–50

Broverman I, Vogel S, Broverman D, Clarkson F, Rosenkrantz P. 1972. Sex-role stereotypes: a reappraisal. *J. Soc. Issues* 28:59–78

Burke PJ. 1991. Identities processes and social stress. *Am. Sociol. Rev.* 56:836–49

Burke PJ, Cast AD. 1997. Stability and change in the gender identities of newly married couples. *Soc. Psychol. Q.* 60:277–90

Burke PJ, Reitzes DC. 1981. The link between identity and role performance. *Soc. Psychol. Q.* 44:83–92

Burke PJ, Stets JE, Pirog-Good MA. 1988. Gender identity, self-esteem, and physical and sexual abuse in dating relationships. *Soc. Psychol. Q.* 51:272–85

Burke PJ, Tully JC. 1977. The measurement of role identity. *Soc. Forc.* 55:881–97

Burt RS. 1992. *Structural Holes.* Cambridge, MA: Harvard Univ. Press

Butler D, Geis FL. 1990. Nonverbal affect responses to male and female leaders: implications for leadership evaluations. *J. Pers. Soc. Psychol.* 58:48–59

Campbell KE. 1988. Gender differences in job-related networks. *Work Occup.* 15:179–200

Carley KM. 1986. An approach for relating social structure to cognitive structure. *J. Math. Sociol.* 12:137–89

Carley KM. 1991. A theory of group stability. *Am. Sociol. Rev.* 56:331–54

Carli LL. 1989. Gender differences in interaction style and influence. *J. Pers. Soc. Psychol.* 56:565–76

Carli LL. 1990. Gender, language and influence. *J. Pers. Soc. Psychol.* 59:941–51

Carli LL. 1991. Gender, status, and influence. In *Advances in Group Processes,* ed. EJ Lawler, B Markovsky, CL Ridgeway, H Walker. 8:89–113. Greenwich, CT: JAI

Carli LL, LaFleur SJ, Loeber CC. 1995. Nonverbal behavior, gender, and influence. *J. Pers. Soc. Psychol.* 68:1030–41

Chatman JA, Brown RA. 1996. *It takes two to tango: demographic similarity, social identity and friendship.* Presented at Stanford Conf. on Power, Politics and Influence, Stanford, CA

Conway M, Pizzamiglio MT, Mount M. 1996. Status, communality, and agency: implications for stereotypes of gender and other groups. *J. Pers. Soc. Psychol.* 71:25–38

Crosby F, Nyquist L. 1977. The female register: an empirical study of Lakoff's hypotheses. *Lang. Soc.* 6:313–22

Dovidio JF, Brown CE, Heltman K, Ellyson SL, Keating CF. 1988. Power displays between women and men in discussions of gender linked tasks: a multichannel study. *J. Pers. Soc. Psychol.* 55:580–87

Drass KA. 1986. The effect of gender identity on conversation. *Soc. Psychol. Q.* 49: 294–301

Eagly AH. 1987. *Sex Differences in Social Behavior: A Social-Role Interpretation.* Hillsdale, NJ: Earlbaum

Eagly AH, Johnson BT. 1990. Gender and the emergence of leaders: a meta-analysis. *Psychol. Bull.* 108:233–56

Eagly AH, Karau SJ. 1991. Gender and leadership style: a meta-analysis. *J. Pers. Soc. Psychol.* 60:685–710

Eagly AH, Wood W. 1991. Explaining sex differences in social behavior: a meta-analytic perspective. *Pers. Soc. Psychol. Bull.* 17:306–15

Eagly AH, Makhijani MG, Klonsky BG. 1992. Gender and the evaluation of leaders: a meta-analysis. *Psychol. Bull.* 111:543–88

Eagly AH, Steffen VJ. 1984. Gender stereotypes stem from the distribution of women and men into social roles. *J. Pers. Soc. Psychol.* 46:735–54

Eakins B, Eakins RG. 1978. Verbal turn-taking and exchanges in faculty dialogue. In *Proc. Conf. Sociol. of Languages of Am. Women,* ed. BL Dubois, I Crouch, pp. 53–62. San Antonio, TX: Trinity Univ. Press

Eder D, Hallinan MA. 1978. Sex differences in children's friendships. *Am. Sociol. Rev.* 43:237–50

Ellyson SL, Dovidio JF, Brown CE. 1992. The look of power: gender differences and similarities. In *Gender, Interaction, and Inequality,* ed. C Ridgeway, pp. 50–80. New York: Springer–Verlag

Ely RJ. 1994. The effects of organizational demographics and social identity on relationships among professional women. *Admin. Sci. Q.* 39:203–38

Fischer C. 1982. *To Dwell Among Friends.* Chicago: Univ. Chicago

Fischer C, Oliker S. 1983. A research note on friendship, gender and the life cycle. *Soc. Forc.* 62:124–32

Fiske ST, Stevens LE. 1993. What's so special about sex? Gender stereotyping and discrimination. In *Gender Issues in Contemporary Society,* ed. S Oskamp, M Costanzo, pp. 173–96. Newbury Park, CA: Sage

Fleischer RA, Chertkoff JM. 1986. Effects of dominance and sex on leader selection in dyadic work groups. *J. Pers. Soc. Psychol.* 50:94–99

Foschi M. 1996. Double standards in the evaluation of men and women. *Social Psychol. Q.* 59:237–54

Foschi M, Lai L, Sigerson K. 1994. Gender and double standards in the assessment of job applicants. *Soc. Psychol. Q.* 57:326–39

Geis FL, Brown V, Jennings J, Corrado-Taylor D. 1984. Sex vs. status in sex-associated stereotypes. *Sex Roles* 11:771–85

Gerber GL. 1996. Status in same-gender and mixed-gender police dyads: effects on personality attributions. *Soc. Psychol. Q.* 59: 350–63

Granovetter MS. 1973. *Getting a Job: A Study of Contacts and Careers.* Cambridge, MA: Harvard Univ. Press

Granovetter MS. 1983. The strength of weak ties: a network theory revisited. In *Sociological Theory,* ed. R Collins, pp. 201–33. San Francisco: Jossey-Bass

Granovetter MS. 1985. Economic action and social structure: the problem of embeddedness. *Am. J. Sociol.* 91:481–510

Hall J. 1984. *Nonverbal Sex Differences: Communication Accuracy and Expressive Style.* Baltimore: Johns Hopkins Univ. Press

Heise DR. 1979. *Understanding Events: Affect and the Construction of Social Action.* New York: Cambridge Univ. Press

Heise DR 1999. Controlling affective experience interpersonally. *Soc. Psyc. Q.* 62: 5–15

Ibarra H. 1992. Homophily and differential returns: sex differences in network structure and access in an advertising firm. *Admin. Sci. Q.* 37:422–47

Ibarra H. 1995. Race, opportunity and diversity of social circles in managerial networks. *Acad. Manag. J.* 38:673–703

Ibarra H. 1996. *Inauthentic selves: image, identity and social network in professional adaptation.* Paper presented at Annu. Meet. Acad. Manag., Cincinnati

Ibarra H. 1997. Paving an alternative route: gender differences in managerial networks. *Soc. Psychol. Q.* 60:91–102

Ibarra H, Smith-Lovin L. 1997. New directions in social network research in gender and organizational careers. In *Handbook of Organizational Behavior,* ed. S Jackson, C Cooper, pp. 359–84. New York: Wiley

James D, Clarke S. 1993. Women, men and interruptions: a critical review. In *Gender and Conversational Interaction,* ed. D Tannen, pp. 231–80. New York: Oxford Univ. Press

James D, Drakich J. 1993. Understanding gender differences in amount of talk: a critical review of research. In *Gender and Conversational Interaction,* ed. D Tannen, pp. 281–312. New York: Oxford Univ. Press

Johnson C. 1994. Gender, legitimate authority, and leader-subordinate conversations. *Am. Sociol. Rev.* 59:122–35

Johnson C, Clay-Warner J, Funk SJ. 1996. Effects of authority structures and gender on interaction in same-sex task groups. *Soc. Psychol. Q.* 59:221–36

Kanter RM. 1977. *Men and Women of the Corporation.* New York: Basic Books

Kemper TD. 1978. *A Social Interactional Theory of Emotions.* New York: Wiley

Kessler S, McKenna W. 1978. *Gender: An Ethnomethodological Approach.* New York: Wiley

Kohlberg K. 1974. A cognitive-developmental analysis of children's sex role concepts and attitudes. In *The Psychology of Sex Differences,* ed. E Maccoby, C Jacklin. Stanford, CA: Stanford Univ. Press

Kollock P, Blumstein P, Schwartz P. 1985. Sex and power in interaction: conversational privileges and duties. *Am. Sociol. Rev.* 50:34–46

Kroska A. 1997. The division of labor in the home: a review and reconceptualization. *Soc. Psychol. Q.* 60:304–22

LaFrance M, Brownell H, Hahn E. 1997. Interpersonal verbs, gender, and implicit causality. *Soc. Psychol. Q.* 60:138–52

Lakoff R. 1975. Language and women's place. *Lang. Soc.* 2:45–79

Lever J. 1978. Sex differences in the complexity of children's play and games. *Am. Sociol. Rev.* 43:4:471–83

Lin N. 1999. Social networks and status attainment. *Annu. Rev. Sociol.* 25: In press

Lockheed ME. 1985. Sex and social influence: a meta-analysis guided by theory. In *Status, Rewards, and Influence,* ed. J Berger, M Zeldtich, pp. 406–29. San Francisco: Jossey-Bass

Maltz DN, Borker RA. 1982. A cultural approach to male-female miscommunication. In *Language and Social Identity,* ed. JJ Gumperz, pp. 196–216. Cambridge, UK: Cambridge Univ. Press

Marsden PV. 1987. Core discussion networks of Americans. *Am. Sociol. Rev.* 52:122–31

Marsden PV. 1988. Homogeneity in confiding relations. *Soc. Networks* 10:57–76

Marsden PV. 1990. Network diversity, substructures and opportunities for contact. In *Structures of Power and Constraint: Papers in Honor of Peter M. Blau,* ed. C Calhoun, M Meyer, WR Scott, pp. 397–410. New York: Cambridge Univ. Press

McLaughlin ML, Cody MJ, Kane ML, Robey CS. 1981. Sex differences in story receipt and story sequencing behaviors in dyadic conversations. *Hum. Commun. Res.* 7: 99–116

McMillan JR, Clifton AK, McGrath D, Gale WS. 1977. Women's language: uncertainty or interpersonal sensitivity and emotionality? *Sex Roles* 3:545–59

McPherson JM, Smith-Lovin L. 1982. Women and weak ties: differences by sex in the size of voluntary organizations. *Am. J. Sociol.* 87:883–904

McPherson JM, Smith-Lovin L. 1986. Sex segregation in voluntary associations. *Am. Sociol. Rev.* 51:61–79

McPherson JM, Smith-Lovin L. 1987. Homophily in voluntary organizations: status distance and the composition of face-to-face groups. *Am. Sociol. Rev.* 52:370–79

Miller J. 1986. *Pathways in the Workplace.* Cambridge, UK: Cambridge Univ. Press

Molm LD, Cook, KS. 1995. Social exchange theory. In *Sociological Perspectives on Social Psychology,* ed. KS Cook, GA Fine, JS House, pp. 209–35. New York: Allyn & Bacon

Moore G. 1990. Structural determinants of men's and women's personal networks. *Am. Sociol. Rev.* 55:726–35

Munch A, McPherson JM, Smith-Lovin L. 1997. Gender, children and social contact: the effects of childrearing for men and women. *Am. Sociol. Rev.* 62:509–20

Nyquist L, Spence JT. 1986. Effects of dispositional dominance and sex role expectations on leadership behaviors. *J. Pers. Soc. Psychol.* 50:87–93

Piliavin JA, Martin RR. 1978. The effects of the sex composition of groups on style of social interaction. *Sex Roles* 4:281–96

Pugh M, Wahrman R. 1983. Neutralizing sexism in mixed-sex groups: Do women have to be better than men? *Am. J. Sociol.* 88: 746–62

Reskin BF, ed. 1984. *Sex Segregation in the Workplace: Trends, Explanations and Remedies.* Washington, DC: Natl. Acad.

Reskin BF. 1988. Bringing the men back in: sex differentiation and the devaluation of women's work. *Gender Soc.* 2:58–81

Reskin BF. 1993. Sex segregation in the workplace. *Annu. Rev. Sociol.* 19:241–70

Ridgeway CL. 1982. Status in groups: the importance of motivation. *Am. Sociol. Rev.* 47:76–88

Ridgeway CL. 1991. The social construction of status value: gender and other nominal characteristics. *Soc. Forc.* 70:367–86

Ridgeway CL. 1993. Gender, status, and the social psychology of expectations. In *The-*

ory on Gender/Feminism on Theory, ed. P England, pp. 175–98. New York: Aldine

Ridgeway CL. 1997. Interaction and the conservation of gender inequality: considering employment. Am. Sociol. Rev. 62: 218–35

Ridgeway CL, Berger J. 1986. Expectations, legitimation, and dominance behavior in task groups. Am. Sociol. Rev. 51:603–17

Ridgeway CL, Boyle EH, Kuipers KJ, Robinson DT. 1998. How do status beliefs develop? The role of resources and interactional experience. Am. Sociol. Rev. 63: 331–50

Ridgeway CL, Diekema D. 1992. Are gender differences status differences? In Gender, Interaction, and Inequality, ed. CL Ridgeway, pp. 157–80. New York: Springer-Verlag

Ridgeway CL, Glasgow K. 1996. Acquiring status beliefs from behavior in interaction. Presented at Annu. Meet. Am. Sociol. Assoc., New York

Ridgeway CL, Smith-Lovin L. 1999. Gender and interaction. In Handbook of Gender Sociology, ed. J Chafetz. In press

Risman B. 1998. Gender Vertigo: American Families in Transition. New Haven, CT: Yale Univ. Press

Robinson DT, Smith-Lovin L. 1992a. Selective interaction as a strategy for identity maintenance: an affect control model. Soc. Psychol. Q. 55:1:12–28

Robinson DT, Smith-Lovin L. 1992b. Who gets the laugh: humor and status in task groups. Presented at Annu. Mtg. Southern Sociol. Society, New Orleans

Roger D, Nesshoever W. 1987. Individual differences in dyadic conversational strategies: a further study. Br. J. Soc. Psychol. 26:247–55

Roger D, Schumaker A. 1983. Effects of individual differences on dyadic conversational strategies. J. Pers. Soc. Psychol. 45:700–5

Shackelford S, Wood W, Worchel S. 1996. Behavioral styles and the influence of women in mixed-sex groups. Soc. Psychol. Q. 59:284–93

Smith-Lovin L, Brody C. 1989. Interruptions in group discussion: the effects of gender and group composition. Am. Sociol. Rev. 54:424–35

Smith-Lovin L, Heise DR. 1988. Analyzing Social Interaction: Research Advances in Affect Control Theory. New York: Gordon & Breach

Smith-Lovin L, McPherson JM. 1991. You are who you know: a network perspective on gender. In Theory on Gender/Feminism on Theory, ed P. England, pp. 223–51. New York: Aldine

South SJ, Bonjean CM, Corder J, Markham JT. 1982. Sex and power in the federal bureaucracy: a comparative analysis of male and female supervisors. Work Occup. 9:233–54

Stangor C, Lynch L, Duan C, Glass B. 1992. Categorization of individuals on the basis of multiple social features. J. Pers. Soc. Psychol. 62:207–18

Stets JE, Burke PJ. 1996. Gender, control and interaction. Soc. Psychol. Q. 59:193–220

Stewart P. 1988. Women and men in groups: a status characteristics approach to interaction. In Status Generalization: New Theory and Research, ed. M Webster, M Foschi, pp. 69–85. Stanford, CA: Stanford Univ. Press

Strodtbeck FL, Mann RD. 1956. Sex role differentiation in jury deliberations. Sociometry 19:468–73

Stryker S. 1980. Symbolic Interactionism: A Social Structural Version. Menlo Park, CA: Benjamin/Cummings

Stryker S, Serpe RT. 1982. Commitment, identity salience, and role behavior. In Personality, Roles and Social Behavior, ed.W Ickes, E Knowles, pp. 199–218. New York: Springer-Verlag

Swann WB Jr, Griffin JJ Jr, Predmore SC, Gaines B. 1987. The cognitive-affective crossfire: when self-consistency confronts self-enhancement. J. Pers. Soc. Psychol. 52:881–89

Tannen D. 1990. You Just Don't Understand: Women and Men in Conversation. New York: William Morrow

Taylor V. 1999. Emotions and identity in women's self-help movements. In Self, Identity and Social Movements, ed. S Stryker, T Owens, R White. Minneapolis: Univ. Minn. Press. In press

Wagner DG, Berger J. 1997. Gender and interpersonal task behaviors: status expectation accounts. Sociol. Perspect. 40:1–32

Wagner DG, Ford RS, Ford TW. 1986. Can gender inequalities be reduced? Am. Sociol. Rev. 51:47–61

Wellman B. 1985. Domestic work, paid work and net work. In Understanding Personal Relationships, ed S Duck, D Perlman, pp. 159–91. London: Sage

Wentworth DK, Anderson LR. 1984. Emergent leadership as a function of sex and task type. Sex Roles 11:513–24

West C, Fenstermaker S. 1995. Doing difference. Gender Soc. 9:8–37

West C, Zimmerman D. 1987. Doing gender. Gender Soc. 1:125–51

Wharton AS. 1992. The social construction of gender and race in organizations: a social identity and group mobilization perspective. In *Res. Sociol. Org.*, ed. P Tolbert, S Bacharach, 10:55–84

Wheelan SA, Verdi AF. 1992. Differences in male and female patterns of communication in groups: a methodological artifact? *Sex Roles* 27:1–15

Williams JE, Best DL. 1990. *Measuring Sex Stereotypes: A Multinational Study.* Newbury Park, CA: Sage

Wood W, Karten SJ. 1986. Sex differences in interaction style as a product of perceived sex differences in competence. *J. Pers. Soc. Psychol.* 50:341–47

Wood W, Rhodes N. 1992. Sex differences in interaction style in task groups. In *Gender, Interaction, and Inequality,* ed. CL Ridgeway, pp. 97–121. New York: Springer-Verlag

Yamada EM, Tjosvold D, Draguns JG. 1983. Effects of sex-linked situations and sex composition on cooperation and style of interaction. *Sex Roles* 9:541–53

Zimmerman DH, West C. 1975. Sex roles, interruptions and silences in conversation. In *Language and Sex: Difference and Dominance,* ed. B Thorne, N Henley, pp. 105–29. Rowley, MA: Newbury

Annu. Rev. Sociol. 1999. 25:217–44

BRINGING EMOTIONS INTO SOCIAL EXCHANGE THEORY

Edward J. Lawler

School of Industrial and Labor Relations, and Department of Sociology, Cornell University, Ithaca, New York 14853; e-mail: ejl3@cornell.edu

Shane R. Thye

Department of Sociology, University of South Carolina, Columbia, South Carolina 29208; e-mail: srthye00@garnet.cla.sc.edu

KEY WORDS: social exchange, emotion, social formation, bargaining, negotiation power

ABSTRACT

We analyze and review how research on emotion and emotional phenomena can elaborate and improve contemporary social exchange theory. After identifying six approaches from the psychology and sociology of emotion, we illustrate how these ideas bear on the context, process, and outcome of exchange in networks and groups. The paper reviews the current state of the field, develops testable hypotheses for empirical study, and provides specific suggestions for developing links between theories of emotion and theories of exchange.

INTRODUCTION

Social exchange theory assumes self-interested actors who transact with other self-interested actors to accomplish individual goals that they cannot achieve alone. *Self-interest* and *interdependence* are central properties of social exchange. Whether it is two lovers who share a warm and mutual affection, or two corporations who pool resources to generate a new product, the basic form of interaction remains the same. Two or more actors, each of whom has something of value to the other, decide whether to exchange and in what amounts.

Such actors are normally viewed as unemotional beings who have information, cognitively process it, and make decisions concerning the pattern and nature of exchange with others. In this paper we explore how emotions can be brought into social exchange theory.

Within the exchange tradition, emotions are a relatively vacuous "catchall" category for phenomena that cannot be subsumed by behavioral or rational choice principles. The classic works on exchange contain references to emotion of various sorts (Thibaut & Kelley 1959, Homans 1961, Blau 1964) and even sustained concern with some emotionally tinged phenomena, such as "sentiment" in Homans (1961). In the related literature on justice and equity, emotional reactions are assumed to be more important, but even there, they are not theorized to any great extent (Molm & Cook 1995, Hegtvedt & Markovsky 1995). This is true of most sociological theories and traditions; in fact, it is only in the last 10 to 15 years that emotions became a prominent research area in the discipline (Kemper 1990a,b, Gordon 1981, Scheff 1983, Thoits 1989).

A close examination of many common exchange relations suggests that emotions both enter and pervade social exchange processes. Friendship relations are often propelled by strong affection or feelings of joy; corporate mergers may result from fear or anger; economic partnerships may thrive because they produce positive feelings such as confidence or pleasure. The context of exchange may have a discernible emotional tone, invoke particular emotion rules, and generate corrective measures when emotions surface or are expressed (Hochschild 1979). The processes of exchange may cause individuals to feel good, satisfied, relieved, excited, and so forth (Lawler & Yoon 1996). The outcome of social exchange may generate pride or shame directed at one's self (Scheff 1990a) or anger or gratitude directed toward the other (Weiner 1986). We believe that emotional dynamics have a more central role in social exchange than typically assumed. This is the motivation for writing this paper.

Emotion is neglected primarily because of metatheoretical conceptions at the core of exchange theory, in particular, behavioral and rational choice assumptions about actors. From a behavioral (reinforcement) perspective, emotions are essentially epiphenomenal, that is, inseparable from reinforcements and punishments (Homans 1961, Emerson 1972a,b). As rational-choice principles were introduced into exchange theorizing, it became increasingly clear that actors who engage in "cognitive work" may not strictly conform to either rational choice or reinforcement principles. One reason is judgmental biases (see Molm 1994, Plous 1993). Exchange theorists have been willing to incorporate the idea of an information-processing, cognizing actor but slow to introduce the idea of an emoting actor. There are, however, exceptions. Several recent papers examine the role of emotion in exchange (see Lovaglia 1995, Molm & Cook 1995, Willer et al 1997), and interest among rational choice theorists is revealed by a 1993 special issue of *Rationality and Society* on emotion and choice.

To fill the void, we offer a selective review and analysis of the juxtaposition between emotion theories and exchange theories. The purpose is to identify avenues by which emotions and emotional processes can enrich or improve exchange theorizing and research. We pose questions that warrant attention, provide answers using work from both emotion and exchange traditions, and apply select theories of emotion to social exchange phenomena. In general terms we are concerned with restricted exchange, broadly defined as a direct exchange involving contingencies between actors' behaviors (Ekeh 1974). Emerson (1981) identified two kinds of restricted exchange—reciprocal and negotiated. Reciprocal exchange entails sequential giving with unspecified terms and obligations; negotiated exchange entails an agreement with speci-fied terms and obligations. In each case, exchange is a joint task and actors have an incentive to accomplish or consummate it in some fashion.

The organization of this paper is based on three main points of entry for emotion phenomena into social exchange—exchange context, exchange pro-cess, and exchange outcomes. Emotions are part of and can alter the context of exchange as well as be caused and produced by the exchange process and/or the results of negotiated exchanges. Before turning to our primary task, how-ever, it is important to review recent efforts in sociology and psychology to develop the concept and measurement of emotion.

CONCEPTUALIZING EMOTIONS

Broadly, we define an emotion as a relatively short-lived positive or negative evaluative state that has neurological and cognitive elements (Schachter & Singer 1962, Izard 1991). Emotions are internal states that are not under the complete control of actors. We agree that the question is, what people do with them? There are many unanswered questions about the nature and definition of emotions. How many emotions are there (Kemper 1987)? Are some emotions more fundamental and others more derivative (Watson & Tellegen 1985, Izard 1991, Kemper 1987, Scheff 1990b)? Are emotions culturally specific or uni-versal (Lutz 1988, Izard 1971, Scherer 1984, 1988)? Our purpose is not to ad-dress all or even many of these issues directly, but to help social-exchange re-searchers cut a path through such sticky conceptual issues.

Over the last ten or so years, psychologists have attempted to develop con-cepts and measures of emotion based on the words people use to describe their own feelings and those of others. This approach, which might be termed psy-chometric, has addressed two conceptual issues: first, whether there are a small number of dimensions (two or three) that can concisely capture funda-mental emotions beneath the apparent diversity of feeling-words used by people themselves; second, whether some emotions are categorically different than others.[1]

These questions have inspired two competing models. One indicates that emotions lie on continua, that is, they vary as a matter of degree over a few fundamental dimensions (Guttman 1954, Russell 1980, Watson & Tellegen 1985, Russell et al 1989, Mano 1991). Perhaps the best-known solution here is Russell's (1980) circumplex model of affect, which maps the universe of emotion as points on a circle in two-dimensional bipolar space. One dimension of the circumplex captures emotional valence (pleasure-displeasure); the other dimension is oriented perpendicular to the first and reflects the level of arousal (high-low). Although some debate has arisen over how the dimensions should be named (Larsen & Diener 1992), and how many dimensions are optimal (Osgood 1966, Russell & Mehrabian 1977), there is considerable evidence that many people do organize their emotions in this way (Russell 1980, 1983, 1991, Watson & Tellegen 1985, Watson et al 1984, Russell & Ridgeway 1983, Haslam 1995).

The second model stipulates that the experience of emotion is not as continuous or seamless as the circumplex might suggest (Clore et al 1987, Oatley & Johnson-Laird 1987, Ekman 1980, 1992, Izard 1977, Batra & Holbrook 1990, Osgood 1966, Storm & Storm 1987, Wierzbicka 1992). These researchers argue that emotions are discrete events, and that the circumplex model can be decomposed into a small number of distinct regions that represent fundamental emotions, each qualitatively different from the others. The usual suspects for a list of fundamental or basic emotions include anger, fear, joy or pleasure, frustration, and sadness; such emotions ostensibly differ along an important dimension that the circumplex does not capture. For example, Larsen & Diener (1992) point out that anger and fear are very close to one another on the circumplex (i.e., both emotions are negative and active) and yet these emotions tend to result in very different behaviors. Whereas anger may lead a person to fight, fear might cause a person to retreat. Frijda and associates (Frijda 1986, Frijda et al 1989) provide evidence that different emotions do in fact activate different levels of action readiness.

The above suggests that all emotions vary along a few abstract dimensions, but also that each emotion may have a few concrete properties that make it unique from others. We see an inherent tradeoff between continuous models that focus on the abstract or general properties of emotion, and discrete models

---

[1]There are many debates in this literature, most of which are beyond the scope of our discussion. For example, emotions have been construed as (a) continuously graded or sharp categories (Russell 1980, Clore et al 1987), (b) infused with cognition or separate systems (Lazarus 1982, 1984, 1995, Zajonc 1980, 1984), (c) culturally specific or mostly pancultural (Lutz 1988, Izard 1971, Shaver et al 1992), (d) accompanied by diffuse or specific physiological arousal (Schachter & Singer 1962, Levenson et al 1992), and the list goes on.

that emphasize the more concrete or specific aspects. Neither model is necessarily better than the other; the question becomes, what is the theoretical payoff for a general versus specific concept of emotion? In the social exchange literature, which is still relatively young, we suggest that the circumplex model provides researchers with a good abstract account of the emotional universe overall, and it also has the advantage of pointing to dimensions that intuitively seem important to social exchange (e.g. pleasure and arousal). The processes and outcomes of exchange can and do generate variable degrees of pleasure and arousal in the form of excitement (Lawler & Yoon 1996).

APPROACHES TO EMOTION AND SOCIAL EXCHANGE

What emotion theories or frameworks have implications for exchange contexts, processes, or outcomes? There are innumerable frameworks for classifying or grouping the types of emotion or emotional processes; in fact, there has been an outpouring of such efforts in the last 10 to 15 years. Kemper has contributed a number of important works, including his contrast of fundamental emotions that are neurologically wired versus other emotions that are socially constructed (Kemper 1978, 1987). Averill (1992:2) developed a comprehensive, multilevel, 15-category classification of variables that cause emotional behaviors. Izard (1991) revised his differentiated-emotions theory, which bears some resemblance to Kemper's notion of fundamental emotions. Ortony and associates (1988) developed a framework that argues for three classes of emotion based on the cognitive object involved: events, actions, or objects. Sociological researchers such as Hochschild (1979, 1983), Clark (1990), Heise (1979), and Collins (1981, 1989) developed conceptual distinctions directed at a particular theoretical problem or domain.

Based on our analysis of these frameworks we identify six approaches to the study of emotion, two for each facet of exchange: context, process, and outcome. In the case of exchange context, a cultural-normative approach (Hochschild 1990) treats emotions as part of the normative context, while a structural-relational approach (Collins 1975, Kemper 1978) treats actors' social positions as fundamental causes of emotions and feelings. In the case of exchange process, a social-cognitive perspective (Isen 1987, Bower 1991) views emotions as shaping actors' perceptions and interpretations of the other and situation, and sensory-informational theories (Heise 1979, Frank 1988) view emotions as important signals (or bits of information) that are displayed to actors and others. Finally, for exchange outcomes, a social-attribution approach (Weiner 1985, 1986) analyzes the emotions produced by actors' attributions of credit/blame for good/bad outcomes, and the social-formations approach (Collins 1981, Lawler & Yoon 1996) indicates how emotional reactions to exchange outcomes impact relations over time. Each approach poses a unique set of theoretical questions. We briefly introduce these below and explore them more deeply in the sections that follow.

To analyze the exchange context, the cultural-normative approach starts from the premise that any social context invokes expectations about what sort of emotions are appropriate to experience and, in particular, to express in a visible or public manner (Hochschild 1990, Clark 1990, Thoits 1990). For example, the norms for displaying emotions at a funeral, wedding, or job interview are socially defined and circumscribed. Behavior that is consistent with the prevailing emotional norms both affirms and reestablishes those norms while fostering an emotional tone, i.e., a prevailing emotional environment, that is salient to new entrants. Thus, exchange contexts should have norms for displaying emotions in addition to an emotional tone tied to the particular exchange context.

Taking a different slice of the exchange context, structural/relational approaches begin from the premise that social positions impact the emotions people are likely to feel. The core idea is captured by Collins' (1975) theory of social stratification, which essentially claims that giving orders makes people feel good while taking orders makes people feel bad. This may be due to different capabilities to generate rewards and avoid costs, the degree of respect and social esteem they receive from others, and/or the overall sense of control they have in the particular social context. Such explanations have stimulated exchange theorists to address a variety of questions linking power, status, and emotion (Kemper 1978, 1987, Kemper & Collins 1990, Ridgeway & Johnson 1990, Lovaglia & Houser 1996).

To analyze the process of exchange, sensory-informational approaches begin with the notion that emotions are signals to self (Heise 1966, 1987) and/or to others (Frank 1988, 1993). For example, feeling bad as a result of violating an emotion norm is an internal signal that will likely produce restitutive action such as an apology. Issues for exchange theories include the role of emotions in signaling information to the actor and determining when such emotions are displayed to others.

From a social cognitive approach, emotions modify or adjust cognitions central to the exchange processes. A general question is how do emotional states influence actors' perceptions of each other, their predictions for future encounters, and the way they deal with uncertainty? For example, given that exchange contexts inherently involve uncertainty, emotions that promote more optimistic rather than more pessimistic information processing can have important consequences for the exchange process and outcomes.

To analyze exchange outcomes, a social-attribution approach starts from the notion that attributions of credit or blame to self, the other, or the situation are likely to have emotional effects on actors. Specific emotions (gratitude, pity, shame, anger, pride, etc) should vary with the nature of the consequences (positive-negative) and attribution target (self, other, situation). For example, credit to self yields pride while blame to other yields anger (Weiner 1985). It is also possible that attributions are directed at social relationships or larger social units as a specific component of the situation (Hewstone 1989). This means that as a joint task, social exchange may generate social attributions, which have effects on the order, cohesion, and solidarity of relations and groups.

The social-formations approach treats emotions as integral to the process through which relationships and groups form and remain salient (Collins 1975, Lawler & Yoon 1993, 1996). This idea can be traced to Durkheim's classic notion, abstracted as follows: When people engage in joint activity with others, they tend to experience an uplift (elation) which heightens their sense of collective or group membership. Joint activity reaffirms and strengthens social solidarity because of the shared emotions and feelings it produces. From this perspective it is important to understand how and when social exchange produces shared positive feelings and whether those feelings result in stronger affective attachments to an exchange relation or network.

These six approaches capture key elements of the exchange context, exchange process, and exchange outcomes. These elements hang together in a systematic way as shown in Figure 1. Within the exchange context, structural-relational conditions are fundamental causes of emotions actually felt and emotion norms shape their expression or display. Within the exchange process, emotions have signaling functions for self and for others, and they may bias how members perceive one another in present and future interaction. Exchange outcomes—such as the frequency and nature of exchange—generate another layer of emotions that can increase/decrease social cohesion when the emotions are attributed to exchange relations, networks, or groups. Each of these six theoretical themes is elaborated in the next three sections.

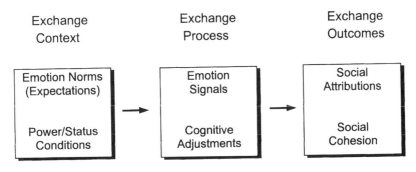

Figure 1   Where emotions enter the exchange process.

EXCHANGE CONTEXT AND EMOTIONS

Cultural/Normative Approaches

From this perspective, emotions are socially constructed, displayed, and managed in the context of the various social roles, memberships, identities, or categories that individuals occupy (Clark 1990, Gordon 1990). This idea can be traced to the symbolic interactionism of Goffman (1959), who theorized that social situations entail scripts for acceptable behavior. A script is a recipe or norm for appropriate behavior in a given situation. Emotional reactions often follow scripts, but more importantly, emotion norms can be construed as scripts. For example, it is both acceptable and expected to experience and display emotion when a musical piece is concluded at an orchestra concert. The same expression and display in the middle of the first movement, however, is a stern violation in this context. A good deal of the theoretical and empirical work in this tradition has focused on situations that elicit a particular emotion but prohibit it from being displayed. In this sense, the cultural/normative approach maintains a focus on the interplay between social context (e.g., roles and identities) and outcomes (e.g., emotional displays). When there is a discrepancy between the emotions we experience and those we may appropriately display, individuals experience what Thoits (1985, 1990) calls "emotional deviance" and may attempt to regulate their expression through what Hochschild (1983) terms "emotion management."

Hochschild (1975, 1979, 1983) observed that emotions and their rules for display occur in the context of norms that are implicitly or explicitly attached to a given job. In her book, *The Managed Heart,* Hochschild (1983) documents that flight attendants (*a*) often experience strong emotions as a result of rude travelers, and (*b*) are trained to inhibit their true feelings. The result is that individuals want to express emotions but cannot, and thus they manage their emotions to alleviate the tension. She proposes two basic strategies through which this occurs. *Surface acting* involves changing one's outward behavior with the hope of altering inner feelings. For example, flight attendants who force themselves to smile after being insulted report feeling better. *Deep acting* occurs when individuals attempt to regulate their physiological activity (e.g., "just calm down and breathe slowly") or shift their focus of attention (e.g., "just ignore it and you will feel better").

Social exchange contexts may also have emotion norms that vary with the nature of the relationship. Business relationships—such as explicit contracting between representatives of different corporations—will likely have a norm of emotional neutrality; in fact, being "professional" in such contexts is being in control of one's emotions. Bargainers suppress the urge to display their excitement in order not to "tip their hand" to the opposing party and raise suspicion.

By the same token, anger or contempt for the other party is held in check. There is much surface acting in these exchanges.

The opposite also may occur. At times actors intentionally reveal a false emotion for strategic purposes. Professional gamblers feign nervousness, joy, or confidence to create impressions that give them an advantage. "Bluffing" is a strategic act and inherent feature of many economic exchange contexts. Ironically, in contexts where bluffing is normatively expected—such as the poker table or used-car lot— it may actually lose effectiveness. In contrast, in very close relations, it is partially the emotional displays that are themselves the objects of exchange. The true expression of emotion becomes a valuable commodity above and beyond any material goods.

The cultural-normative perspective implies that the generalizability of social exchange principles is limited or conditioned by the emotional environment, e.g., emotion norms, emotion management, etc. Most contemporary exchange theories assume (and most empirical tests explicitly create) a relatively sterile and dispassionate environment with a neutral emotional tone. This inhibits the development and expression of emotion, enhances surface acting, and fosters an overall emotional context that makes the formation and maintenance of strong relations problematic. One can imagine that the typical exchange context is similar in some respects to that described by Hochschild's flight attendants. In any case, the management and regulation of emotion norms across various exchange contexts are important avenues for future research.

Structural/Relational Approaches

The orienting idea of the structural-relational approach is that positional differences create differences in felt emotion, and these have important effects on exchange relations and networks. Structural-relational theories predict emotion from specific relational attributes, such as one's position in a power or status hierarchy. By way of comparison, cultural normative theories focus on symbolic or emergent social definitions and norms in groups with common identities (gangs, flight attendants, etc). In general, structural-relational theories tend to have a more deterministic flavor, making causal predictions for which emotions emerge given a set of structural conditions; whereas cultural-normative approaches are more conceptual and interpretive.

Kemper's (1978, 1987, 1990c) theory of emotion falls squarely in the structural tradition, given its focus on two relational attributes: power and status. His basic assumption is that an increase in power or status will result in positive emotions, while a decrease in power or status will lead to negative emotions. More specifically, Kemper (1978, 1990c) predicts that an increase in relative power results in feelings of security, while a decrease in relative power leads to fear or anxiety. The term "relative" in the preceding sentence is important. The theory predicts an individual feels secure when her or his own power is directly increased over another, or when their power is indirectly increased due to a reduction in the power of the opposing party. The theory focuses on emotions caused by power or status dynamics that actually transpire, but it also suggests that anticipatory emotions occur when one expects a change in power or status whether or not it actually occurs.

Turning to status, changes again stimulate emotional responses (Kemper 1990c). An increase in status produces satisfaction or happiness, while a decrease in status produces shame, anger, or depression. The case of status loss is more complex than that for status gain. Consider an x—y relationship in which person x suffers a loss in relative status. If x attributes the status loss to person y and believes it is not justified or legitimate, then the theory predicts x should be angry. But when x assumes responsibility for the status loss, then the emotion is likely to be shame. Finally, if an uncontrollable external agent is responsible for status loss, then depression is the predicted result.

Kemper offers a rigorous theory that connects power and status dynamics to emotional phenomena. He distinguishes the emotional consequences of power and status conditions, and recent research affirms that power and status dimensions produce somewhat different emotions or emotional processes. Let us consider some of this research by exchange theorists.

EMOTIONS PRODUCED BY POWER   In exchange theory, power is defined as a structural potential based in the pattern and quality of exchange opportunities (Emerson 1972b, 1981, Willer & Anderson 1981). The classical example of structural power is a three-actor dating network, A—B—C, where the centrally located B has the option of dating two people each of whom has no dating alternatives. Assuming that interactions between one dyad preclude interactions in the other, then A or C must always be excluded on any given night of dating. By the same token, position B will always be guaranteed to have a partner, and so we say that B occupies a high power position.

There is considerable evidence that actors who bargain from high power positions, like actor B in the three line shown above, tend to experience positive emotions. Willer and associates (1997) tested this proposition directly. They measured the emotions of all three actors after a series of bilateral negotiations in the three-actor line. The results show that B tended to report strong positive emotions following exchanges, while A and C reported negative emotional reactions. The finding that power differences yield corresponding emotional reactions has also been reported by Lawler & Yoon (1993, 1996).

Molm (1991) provides further evidence on the relationship between power and emotion. She reports an interesting asymmetry between the base of power (reward versus punishment) and satisfaction with the exchange relation. Data from a series of experiments indicate that a single unit of punishment decreases satisfaction more than a single unit of reward increases satisfaction. That is, punishment power has a stronger effect than reward power on emotional reactions. The finding that individuals respond more strongly to negative outcomes is consistent with research on collective action (Hardin 1991) and exchange networks (Skvoretz & Zhang 1997, Thye et al 1997). In sum, the evidence reviewed above indicates that actors who occupy low power positions of various types experience negative emotions, while actors in high power positions experience positive emotions.

EMOTIONS PRODUCED BY STATUS   Those who study status processes in face-to-face discussion groups have arrived at similar conclusions. Bales (1950, 1953) argued that positive emotional behaviors, such as acting friendly or expressing agreement, are functional to the group because such behaviors promote positive task outcomes. Bales reasoned that in collective and task-oriented groups, negative emotions emerge when individual group members disagree, and these have deleterious effects by diverting attention and time from the task. Positive socioemotional behaviors help members maintain a task focus and deal with disputes along the way (Bales & Slater 1955, Bales & Hare 1965). Shelly (1993) suggests further that positive sentiments can shape interaction and influence, as does status in expectation states theory.

Ridgeway & Johnson (1990) develop an expectation states theory of status and socioemotional behavior, explaining why high- and low-status persons experience different emotions. They argue that group members with positive status characteristics are targets of higher performance expectations, and as a result, they receive positive feedback from group interactions and encounter very few disagreements from lower status group members. In the event a high status member is challenged by a status subordinate, the former will typically attribute the disagreement externally (e.g., "You clearly do not know what you're talking about!"). In comparison, lower performance expectations are associated with members who possess the low states of status characteristics; they receive more criticism for expressing their ideas and tend to attribute criticisms internally (e.g., "You're right, that is a silly idea."). The combined result of differential performance expectations, selective feedback, and attributional biases is that high status members experience positive emotion and are more free to display these feelings. By the same token, low status group members experience negative emotions and are more apt to conceal them from the group.

Lovaglia & Houser (1996) propose the notion of "status compatible emotions" to explain how emotions combine with status to produce influence in groups. They suggest that positive emotion is compatible with high status, while negative emotion is compatible with low status. They conducted a series of experiments, and the results indicated that for both high- and low-status subjects, positive emotional reactions tended to decrease resistance to social influence, while negative emotion tended to increase resistance to influence attempts. These findings suggest that high status group members experience positive emotions and, as a consequence, become more open to the task suggestions made by lower status others. At the same time low status members experience negative emotions and consequently become more steadfast in their conviction. This research details how emotional reactions combine with status characteristics to determine patterns of social influence in groups.

EXCHANGE PROCESS AND EMOTIONS

Sensory/Informational Approaches

These theories emphasize that emotions convey information within or between individuals. This can happen in multiple ways. First, individuals can sense their own emotional reactions and use this information to make inferences about themselves and the environment. A person who overreacts to a friend's mild criticism may, ex post facto, infer their friendship is drifting apart. Second, the display or visibility of an emotion to others may inform those others of one's own internal reactions or disposition. In this example, the friend who was the target of the emotional outburst may make the same inference. This section discusses theories that detail how emotions signal information to the self and others. We use Heise's (1979) affect control theory[2] to illustrate signaling to self and Frank's (1988) theory of moral sentiments to illustrate signaling to the other.

In affect control theory, emotions signal the self. Briefly, the theory assumes that individuals carry with them a set of "fundamental" meanings regarding themselves, other persons, objects or behaviors (Smith-Lovin & Heise 1988). Fundamental meanings refer to the evaluation of a person, object or action out of context. For example, most individuals probably believe that doctors, birthday cakes, and volunteer work are somewhat positive. Meaning is thought to vary along three primary dimensions: good-bad (evaluation), powerful-powerless (potency), and lively-quiet (activity). The evidence suggests that people from varying cultures and social strata organize fundamental meanings along these dimensions (Heise 1966). Transient meanings occur when objects, behaviors, and situations are strung together in more complex scenarios (e.g., the doctor abused her child). As a single unit of analysis, transient meanings can also be measured. Affect control theory assumes that individuals seek consistency between fundamental meanings (i.e., that which they believe to be true), and transient meanings (i.e., that which they experience at a given moment). Emotional reactions reflect whether or not this consistency is maintained.

---

[2]The affect control theory home page is at http://www.indiana.edu/~socpsy/ACT/Index.html.

In affect control theory, emotion is the result of a cognitive appraisal. The theory asserts that individuals occupy identities that provide baselines from which transient impressions (or events) are interpreted. An emotional reaction occurs when one experiences an event and then assesses how well it fits her or his fundamental understanding of the people, identities, and actions involved. When the fit between one's fundamental understanding and transient impressions is good, emotions felt are consistent with the identity. An example is a person with a positive self identity (e.g., community volunteer) who experiences a positive, confirming event (e.g., an award recognizing service). Here the fundamental meaning associated with the identity is consistent with the positive transient meaning, and the theory predicts that positive emotions will ensue. When a person holds a negative identity (e.g., criminal) and experiences a consistent confirming event (e.g., an indictment), then negative emotions will be the result. The overarching assumption is consistency; events that confirm identities result in emotions with the same valence.

Applied to exchange theory, affect control theory suggests that the emotions experienced in exchange are contingent on the actors' identities. As noted earlier, certain identities—such as corporate representative, professional arbitrator, or merchandise buyer—involve contextual norms that demand control of one's emotional displays. Other identities such as colleague, friend, or husband are more forgiving in this respect, in that they normatively allow or generate richer emotional experiences. One implication is that as the exchange context changes from purely instrumental to partially expressive, the salience of certain identities will shift, resulting in a wider range and greater depth of emotions.

It's worth noting that emotions in affect control theory are both social and relational. Heise (1987) suggests that when another person is a salient part of the environment, our transient experiences can move in the direction of that person's identity. For example, when talking with a powerful senator, a person may have transient impressions such as awe or gratitude. When these emotions are displayed for others to see, we essentially broadcast our private appraisals outward. Thus, while emotions signal the self in affect control theory, they also may be communicated to others.

Such communication of emotion is the focus of Frank's (1988, 1993) theory of moral sentiments. Frank begins with a rational-choice model of human action that assumes behavior is driven by immediate self-interest. He notes that the unbridled pursuit of self-interest, however, results in an interesting paradox: Actors who are always attempting to maximize their local self-interest blindly stumble into social dilemmas. The dilemma is that such actors can never reap the benefits of collaboration, even when it promises greater rewards in the long run. A purely self-interested actor would always steal if she or he could safely do so without cost or detection; in a population of egoists, marriages could never survive external temptations, business partners would cheat one another, etc. These are instances of what Frank calls "the problem of commitment."

Frank (1988, 1993) argues that emotions help individuals resolve the problem of commitment by fostering prosocial tendencies that are reciprocated over time. He claims that emotional reactions such as love, sorrow, and sympathy are powerful incentives that curb self-interest. A spouse who is considering an affair, for example, may refrain out of love or respect for her partner. Workers who receive cash payments may nevertheless report all income to the IRS out of fear, guilt, or a sense of national identity. In this way emotional/affective processes short-circuit and regulate the desire for immediate self gratification.

Notice that although emotions help promote long-term behavioral commitment for any given person, the unilateral experience of emotion is not enough to fully solve the commitment problem. Long-term committed relationships can only emerge when each party (*a*) experiences commitment-inducing emotions and (*b*) can detect (and be detected by) others with the same capacity. The first trait gives one the ability to control passing temptations; the second ensures that individuals with high "moral fiber" are likely to locate similar others. Frank suggests that individuals communicate their emotional makeup through subtle behavioral gestures and cues that have evolved through biological mechanisms.

To summarize, the theory of moral sentiments postulates that emotions allow commitment to emerge, but long-term committed relationships prosper only when emotional reactions are coordinated at the dyadic level. Frank provides a convincing argument for the importance of emotional expressions to the development of trust and commitment. The broad implication for exchange theory is that communicated emotions are an inherent part of social interaction, and these are particularly important to the development of cohesive or solidary relations.

Cognitive Approaches

A rather large body of psychological research examines how emotions influence cognition. Mood, affect, and feelings all have been shown to impact how people process information and the degree to which they reveal a concern for others. It is now well established that individuals in a positive mood perceive, encode, interpret, and remember events in a more positive light than do individuals in a negative mood (Bower 1981, 1991, Isen 1987). For example, Isen and colleagues (1978) have shown that subjects in a positive mood tend to have better recall for positive trait adjectives such as "kind" or "friendly" learned at an earlier point in time. Others find a tendency for individuals in a given mood state to have greater recall for material learned while in that same mood state, a phenomenon known as state-dependent learning (Bartlett et al 1982, Bower et al 1981). Overall there is little doubt that emotions (both positive and negative) affect how information is encoded and retrieved from memory.

Emotional states also have been shown to bias social judgments (Bower 1991). Wright & Bower (1992) found that, compared to subjects in a neutral mood, those in a good mood tended to overestimate the probability of positive events and underestimate the probability of negative events. Subjects in a bad mood did just the opposite—they overestimated the probability of negative events and saw positive events as less likely. Johnson & Tversky (1983) report comparable biases with respect to subjective frequencies. In a series of experiments, they found that subjects in a bad mood tended to overestimate the frequency of other bad events. Others found that positive emotions correlate with the tendency to make risky decisions, but only when the potential for loss is small or inconsequential (Isen & Patrick 1983, Isen & Geva 1987). All of this research indicates that moods do in fact shape social judgments.

What is not so well understood is exactly *why* moods alter social judgments. We identified four distinct models of judgment in the psychological literature. According to the priming model advanced by Bower (1981, 1991), the common thread that weds these research findings together is that positive or negative emotional states activate and make salient cognitive structures of the same valence. A distinct, but related, model suggests that mood-congruent social judgments result from efforts to maintain one's current mood state (Isen 1987, Wegener et al 1995). These ideas are particularly relevant to exchange theories, as they suggest that pleasant/unpleasant social exchanges trigger cognitions of the same tone that build on one another over time and ultimately bias information processing. This is one basis for "bounded rationality."

A third model assumes that individuals make decisions, in part, by sensing their current emotional reactions and using this data as input (Schwarz & Clore 1983, Schwarz 1990, Clore & Parrott 1994). From this perspective, emotional reactions operate as stimuli that sometimes can be confused with more objective information. We have all made decisions that just don't feel right, and when this happens, it is tempting to cast aside more reasoned thought and judgment. This raises an interesting possibility for exchange theory. If emotional states function as information, then it is at least possible that emotions originating from earlier exchanges with other people might carry-over into the current exchange context. The emotional consequence of a morning speeding ticket might still be felt in that afternoon's business meeting. Research on sympathetic activation and excitation transfer provide conceptual and empirical support for this possibility (Zillman 1983).

Perhaps the most provocative ideas for exchange theory come from the reduced capacity model, which holds that emotions disrupt attention or diminish cognitive capacity (Eysenck 1977, Isen 1987, Mackie & Worth 1989, 1991). Considerable research documents that emotional experiences tend to result in superficial information processing. For example, Mackie & Worth (1989, 1991) report that subjects in a positive mood are less attentive to messages and have poorer recall of their content compared to subjects in a neutral mood. Presumably, emotional reactions consume cognitive resources that might be directed elsewhere. Mackie & Worth provide further evidence in support of this idea, reporting that subjects who feel positive simply take longer to read and interpret a message, which again suggests lowered cognitive ability.

Turning to negative emotion, studies show that high-fear subjects tend to rely more on group stereotypes and process messages less carefully (Wilder & Shapiro 1989, Baron, Inman, Kao & Logan 1992). For example, Wessel & Merckelbach (1997) found that spider phobics exposed to a large live spider (i.e., the high-fear group) had less recall for minor details than did non–spider phobics (i.e., the low-fear group). However, at least one recent experiment questions these ideas. Baron and colleagues (1994) report that high fear patients about to receive a dental filling actually process cavity-related information more carefully than patients in a low fear condition. They argue that lazy information processing may actually result from attentional shifts toward the stressor, rather than an overall diminution of cognitive ability.

Applied to exchange theory, lazy information processing may enhance the cohesion and solidarity of exchange relations and groups by promoting relaxed accounting. Individuals who adopt a relaxed or "loose" accounting system do not keep precise records of the benefits or costs to actors, whereas restrictive accounting systems are characterized by continuous and precise tallying of such information. Kollock (1993) used computer simulation to demonstrate that relaxed accounting systems produce more mutual cooperation in prisoner's dilemma games. The immediate implication is that if positive emotions promote lazy information processing and relaxed accounting systems, this may in turn promote mutual cooperation, commitment, trust, and solidarity in those relations. Overall, there are good reasons to believe emotions bias how individuals perceive and interpret their exchanges with others. In the following section we illustrate one such bias with an application to elementary theory.

AN APPLICATION   There is an interesting theoretical link between social cognition research and the elementary theory of power in social relations (Willer 1981, Willer & Markovsky 1993). Willer and associates put forth a resistance theory that suggests power is partially determined by what actors hope (or aspire) to receive in exchange with others. From cognitive theories we hypothesize that if individuals in exchange relations experience positive and negative emotions, these systematically bias what they hope to receive as they negotiate exchange. Resistance theory asserts that actors possess a certain level of "resistance" to exchange depending on their best expected payoff (Pmax) and the payoff at confrontation when no exchange occurs (Pcon). According to the theory, A's resistance (R_A) to a given offer (P_A) is given by the following equation,

$$R_A = \frac{P_A \text{ max} - P_A}{P_A - P_A \text{con}}.$$

This suggests that actors resist exchange when they expect to receive more than they are offered (Pmax $- P_A$ is large) or when the profit they are offered barely outweighs the profit from no exchange at all (P_A $-$ Pcon is small). The theory asserts that exchanges between A and B occur when the resistance of A is equal to the resistance of B such that

$$R_A = \frac{P_A \text{ max} - P_A}{P_A - P_A \text{con}} = \frac{P_B \text{ max} - P_B}{P_B - P_B \text{con}} = R_B.$$

To briefly illustrate, assume actors A and B must agree on how to divide 20 units of profit or each will earn nothing. Assuming each unit of profit is indivisible, each actor can reasonably hope to take no more than 19 of the possible 20 units. If either actor requests all 20 units then the incentive to exchange dissipates. Thus we have $P_A$max = $P_B$max = 19. If A and B fail to reach agreement then they each earn nothing making $P_A$con = $P_B$con = 0. It follows that

$$R_A = \frac{19 - P_A}{P_A - 0} = \frac{19 - P_B}{P_B - 0} = R_B.$$

Since any agreement between A and B must sum to 20 units, we set $P_B = (20 - P_A)$ and solve to find $P_A = 10$ and therefore $P_B = 10$. In dyadic exchange where each party has no alternative, the resistance model predicts an equal division of the profit pool.

The relevant point for our purposes is that resistance to exchange entails the weighing of best hopes (P_{max}) against worst fears (P_{con}). Recall from our earlier discussion that actors in a positive mood tend to overestimate the probability of positive outcomes, while actors in a negative mood state tend to be less optimistic and view negative events as more likely (Wright & Bower 1992). When incorporated into resistance theory, this finding implies that emotions bias P_{max} in the direction of one's emotional state during the negotiations.

Consider the following example. Again let actors A and B negotiate how to divide a 20-point profit pool under the conditions specified above. Further, assume that A is in a positive mood while B is in a somewhat negative mood. For ease of calculation, let's assume the emotions of A and B are reliably measured, then standardized on a scale (E^*) ranging from 0 to 1 such that larger values reflect more positive emotion. Let $E_A{}^* = 1.0$ and $E_B^* = .70$. Use this bias to calculate $P_A$max = (1.0)19 = 19 and $P_B$max = .70(19) = 13.3. Plugging these new values into the resistance equation and solving for P_A yields a slight profit advantage for A such that $P_A = 11.76$ and $P_B = 8.23$. This example demonstrates how emotional reactions, because they act on the judgments of exchange-related information, might affect social exchange outcomes.

Thus, actors in a positive mood should perceive P_{max} to be approximately its full value, or at least higher than the P_{max} for those in a negative mood state. Similarly, actors in a relatively negative mood should have reduced profit aspirations and perceive their P_{max} to be lower. The combined effect of these emotions is a slight profit advantage for actors with positive feelings and higher profit aspirations. This is, of course, a testable prediction.

EXCHANGE OUTCOMES AND EMOTIONS

Attributional Approaches

Weiner (1985, 1986) puts forth an attribution theory of emotion that addresses how actors interpret the often vague and global feelings they experience in interaction or exchange with others. He argues that when an actor experiences a successful or blocked goal opportunity, the result is a generalized emotional reaction that is global and diffuse. Weiner terms these "primitive" emotions. They are dependent on the outcome of the interaction but not associated with anything in particular. Importantly, such emotions generate an attribution process through which actors attempt to understand and interpret the sources (causes) of the interaction outcomes. Thus, the global (i.e., primitive) emotions are "outcome dependent" and "attribution independent."

In Weiner's (1985) theory, positive emotions (pleasure, happiness) follow a positive event and negative emotions (sadness) follow a negative event, an idea quite compatible with exchange theorizing. He holds that the attribution process reshapes these emotional reactions, further differentiating the generalized emotions into more specific affective reactions. The sense of sadness following a spoiled job interview may be transformed into shame (if attributed to self) or anger (if attributed to the other). These specific emotions are "attribution dependent" because they result directly from the causal attributions associated with the event. Through this attribution process, more specific emotions evolve and become attached to particular objects (i.e., self, other, situation).

The object targeted by the attribution process actually determines the specific emotion that emerges. As noted, guilt or shame result from negative outcomes attributed to one's self, and anger results from negative events attributed to arbitrary or illegitimate acts of others. Pride results from attributions of positive events to self, and gratitude results from attributions of positive events to the other. Weiner's theory posits a series of feedback loops through which attribution-specific emotions are formed and guide an individual's future behavior. As with other attribution theories, however, the emphasis is on attributions to individuals based on their behavior. In social exchange such individualized attributions are more difficult because exchange outcomes are joint products of two or more actors' behaviors.

Weiner's approach nevertheless represents an important contribution to the study of emotion. He recognizes that some emotions result from events that require very little cognitive processing, while others emerge after more careful thought or reflection. In this sense, he finds a viable middle ground in the classic debate regarding the primacy of affect versus cognition (Lazarus 1984, Zajonc 1984). By differentiating global from specific emotions and elucidating the specific types of attributions that lead from one to another, his theory suggests a dynamic picture of the way emotions unfold in exchange relations.

To develop an explicit link to exchange theory, two shifts are needed in Weiner's framework. First, the primitive, global emotions should be viewed as internal reinforcements/punishments that people consciously feel and attempt to explain or understand. Involuntary, global emotional reactions then are motivating states in exchange relations because, once they are part of conscious awareness, actors strive to reproduce positive feelings and avoid negative feelings. This theoretical shift narrows the emotions of concern to those that are global and detected (perceived) by the actors themselves. For exchange theorizing, it seems quite reasonable to suppose that people involved in exchange relations sometimes feel good or bad as a result of the exchange; they are motivated to reproduce the positive and eliminate the negative emotions; and therefore they try to understand and interpret their own emotional reactions.

The second shift needed is that the objects of attributions should include "social units" in addition to self, other, and situation. This is implied by the jointness and "social embeddedness" of exchange. If social units—such as exchange relations, networks, groups, or larger organizations and communities—become targets or perceived causes of global feelings, then emotion attributions have important implications for solidarity-related phenomena such as compliance (Hechter 1987), solidarity (Markovsky & Lawler 1994), affective attachments (Kanter 1968, Lawler 1992), and relational cohesion (Lawler and Yoon 1996). Social units perceived as the cause of positive feelings in exchange should generate stronger individual-to-collective attachments than those perceived as a source of negative feelings from exchange. The social-formations perspective examined next elaborates these implications.

Social-Formation Approaches

Two basic ideas are the foundation of the social-formations approach. The first is directly from social exchange theory: that mutual dependencies are the underlying structural conditions for cohesion and solidarity in social units (Emerson 1972a,b, Hechter 1987, Molm & Cook 1995, Lawler & Yoon 1996). Mutual dependence is the degree to which two or more actors in a relation, network, or group are dependent on each other for valued rewards. Emerson

(1972b) explicitly indicated that cohesion was a function of the sum or average of each actor's dependence on the other.[3]

The second idea originates in Durkheim (1915) and has been developed more recently by Collins (1975, 1981, 1989, 1993). This is that joint activities generate uplift, elation, confidence, or other emotions that affirm and make salient social ties and group memberships. This is the centerpiece of Collins' (1981, 1989) theory of interaction ritual chains. Theories in the social-formations tradition explain how the emotions and feelings that social exchange generates, in turn, foster cohesion or solidarity.

How can we theorize the degree and consequence of jointness in social exchange contexts? Kelley & Thibaut (1978) distinguished three types of dependencies: reflexive control, fate control, and behavioral control. These refer respectively to the degree that actors' outcomes are determined by their own behavior (independence), the behavior of the other (dependence), or a combination of their own and others' behavior (interdependence). Mutual fate control establishes the foundation for trading resources or behaviors that do not produce new value to be divided but still involve contingencies. In contrast, mutual behavioral control promotes the negotiation of coordinated behaviors that have multiplicative effects on resources or exchange outcomes (Molm 1994). These forms of dependence are interwoven, and it is reasonable to hypothesize that the greater the degree of mutual behavioral control (interdependence) and the lower the degree of mutual reflexive control (independence), the more actors take account of each other and the more they see the results of their exchange—positive or negative—as produced jointly.

In discussing Weiner's (1985, 1986) theory, we already proposed that interdependence makes the relevant social units (dyads, groups, organizations, etc) causal objects in actors' attributions. How and when might such attributions occur? Lawler & Yoon (1993, 1995, 1996, 1998) addressed this question in their theory of relational cohesion. They argued that structural conditions of dependence—relative and total (mutual) dependencies—make exchanges between some pairs of actors more likely than others. Specifically, when mutual dependence is high, then actors should find one another more attractive relative to other potential exchange partners. When relative dependence is equal as opposed to unequal, then they should find it easier to reach agreement because neither has an a priori bargaining advantage that raises fairness issues. The theory indicates that exchange frequencies across pairs of actors in a network or group will vary depending on these conditions of dependence (Lawler & Yoon 1996).

---

[3]The same point is also built into Molm's (1987) idea of "average power" and Bacharach & Lawler's (1981) notion of "total power."

The theory of relational cohesion goes on to argue that structural dependence relations do not have a direct impact on the formation of cohesive exchange relations; the effects are indirect and mediated by exchange frequencies and the emotions produced. Successful exchange generates global feelings of pleasure/satisfaction and interest/excitement, emotions that are "primitive" in Weiner's terms. Actors are motivated to interpret and understand the causes of these feelings, and in the process, their exchange relations become more salient. In this way, globalized positive emotions lead actors to view the exchange relation or group as a cohesive object, and they then are willing to take risks or make sacrifices on its behalf. Several studies by Lawler & Yoon (1993, 1995, 1996, 1998) demonstrate that the endogenous process—from exchange frequency, to positive emotions, to perceived cohesion—produces commitment to exchange relations. Through this process, the exchange relation becomes an expressive object of attachment for actors.

The emotional aspects of social formation processes can be elaborated by Collins' theory of interaction ritual chains. Interaction ritual is infused with emotion and expressiveness. Collins argues that interactions require and produce emotional energy, a global, undirected reserve of positive feelings (e.g., confidence, uplift). Emotional energy is a "common denominator" across situations and relations, and it is fundamentally what binds group members together. Emotions are synchronized, microlevel events that spread across interactions and have macrolevel effects on the group structure and stability.

To Collins (1981, 1989, 1993), an interaction ritual entails (*a*) at least two people, who (*b*) have a mutual focus on some object or action. A church prayer, faculty meeting, or long-distance telephone conversation are potential contexts for interaction ritual. The conditions for enhanced social solidarity include not only a mutual focus but also (*c*) the experience of a common mood or emotion and, by implication, the sharing of that emotion, as well as (*d*) the strengthening of feelings over time. All of these conditions, with the possible exception of the last, seem to fit the conditions usually found in social exchange—a mutual focus and common mood. When these conditions are satisfied, Collins (1989:18) asserts that a social boundary begins to emerge within which "participants feel like members of a little group, with moral obligations to one another." In this way, socially based emotions set the stage for or reaffirm symbolic group membership and social solidarity. Collins' theory specifies an emotional foundation for group formation in contrast to the predominantly cognitive one found in social identity theorizing (Kramer & Brewer 1984, Kramer 1991). There are strong affinities between Collins' work and recent theory and research on emotion in social exchange.

To conclude, the core ideas of the social-formations approach to emotion in exchange can be stated as follows: *Mutual dependencies (or interdependencies) produce joint activities which, in turn, generate positive/negative emo-*

tions or feelings; to the extent that these emotions are attributed to the relevant social unit, they produce stronger/weaker individual-collective ties, and those groups memberships command more/less cooperation and compliance. When emotions produce stronger individual-collective ties, relational or group memberships appear more distinctive than before and stand out more vis-à-vis alternative memberships. Feedback effects also occur such that mutual dependencies are enhanced by the consequences they produce. The growth and decline of exchange-based relations and groups might be understood in these terms.

CONCLUSION

The sociology of emotions and the sociology of exchange are highly distinct, incommensurable traditions with very different assumptions about actors and human behavior (e.g., Emerson 1972a, Kemper 1990a, Collins 1981, Scheff 1990b, Hochschild 1983, Molm & Cook 1995). The actors of exchange theories are individualistic, instrumental, and emotionally vacuous, whereas those of emotion theories are socially oriented, expressive, and emotionally deep and complex. The former are driven by reason, the latter by passion. Yet research from a variety of domains shows that passion and reason are intertwined, and this poses an important question: What role do emotions play in social exchange?

We illustrate the potential fruitfulness of building emotion and emotional processes into exchange theorizing by surveying a range of sociological and psychological work on emotions. Emotion theories raise many questions of relevance to social exchange (e.g., Hochschild 1983, Heise 1987, Frank 1988); they suggest new testable propositions that refine existing exchange predictions (e.g., Bower 1991), expand the range of phenomena treated by exchange theorizing (e.g., Lovaglia & Houser 1996, Lawler & Yoon 1996) and point toward a richer exchange-theory explanation for social cohesion and solidarity than is possible with extant cognitive or rational-choice principles (see Hechter 1987). Our coverage has been necessarily selective, yet we have identified six traditions in the emotions literature that contain implicit or explicit claims about emotional aspects of social exchange—its context, process, or outcomes.

Together, the six approaches reveal a multitude of theoretical junctures at which emotional phenomena can complement, deepen, or broaden exchange theorizing and research. A *cultural-normative* perspective (e.g., Hochschild 1979, 1983) sensitizes us to the fact that exchange contexts necessarily entail emotion norms that limit the public expression of emotions, and result in actors managing their emotions to fit their roles or positions. *Structural-relational* approaches posit different emotions for actors with high power–status versus actors with low power–status, and analyze when these emotions maintain or undermine interpersonal relations (e.g., Ridgeway & Johnson 1990, Lovaglia & Houser 1996). *Sensory-information* approaches cast emotions as signals within the exchange process, revealing the intentions and trustworthiness of exchange partners (e.g., Frank 1988), or indicating whether an actor's felt emotions are consistent with his or her identity in that context (e.g., Heise 1987). *Cognitive* theory and research indicate that positive (or negative) emotions enhance, correspondingly, an actor's perceived probability of positive (or negative) behaviors by an exchange partner. *Attribution theory* helps us understand why and how actors explain and interpret global feelings generated by exchange outcomes (e.g., Weiner 1986). The *social-formations* approach elucidates the conditions under which these global feelings strengthen or weaken the cohesion of exchange relations or person-to-group ties (e.g., Collins 1981, Lawler & Yoon 1996).

The six approaches also imply distinct emotional underpinnings for different forms of social exchange (see Emerson 1972b, Ekeh 1974, Molm & Cook 1995 for a classification of forms of exchange). Of particular relevance is the contrast between negotiated and reciprocal exchange—respectively, a context where actors repeatedly negotiate the terms of a trade versus a context involving the sequential provision of unilateral benefits (e.g., favors, gifts, etc) with unspecified timing and obligations (Blau 1964, Emerson 1981, Molm & Cook 1995). Negotiated-exchange contexts usually promote and reward dispassionate, unemotional images or presentations of self in the actual process of negotiating, i.e., a "professional demeanor" or "affective neutrality" in Parsons' (1951) terms. Reciprocal exchange allows a wider array of emotional expressions and a greater variety of emotion norms to emerge.

We hypothesize that the cohesion and solidarity of relations based on reciprocal exchange should be quite sensitive to emotional expressions in the exchange process. For example, experiencing and expressing gratitude, in response to a favor, help assure the giver that the recipient will likely reciprocate sometime in the future; expressing anger in response to a denial of a favor is an implied threat not to provide benefits in the future; expressing sadness may invoke shame or guilt in the other and engender backtracking or restitutive behavior. In reciprocal exchange, emotions expressed are also behaviors exchanged, and these affective exchanges should have important effects on trust and commitment; these are critical because the sequential character of reciprocal exchange entails more or different types of risk than the binding agreements of negotiated exchange (Molm 1994). Thus, emotion expressions are integral parts of the exchange process in reciprocal (nonnegotiated) social exchange.

In negotiated exchange, emotion expressions that reveal intentions may give the partner information to use as leverage, so the risk is revealing too much, not too little. The emotional consequences of the joint outcomes (i.e. frequency of and profit from agreements made) should be more important than emotional expressions in the exchange process. First, jointness is more salient and the sense of common activity therefore stronger. Second, actors in negotiated exchange are more likely to perceive a shared responsibility for the outcomes and target the relation, network, or group. The upshot is that (ceterus paribus) the cohesion effects of successful exchange (i.e. outcomes) should be stronger for negotiated exchange than reciprocal exchange, whereas the cohesion effects for emotional expressions in the exchange process (i.e. displays) should be stronger for reciprocal exchange than for negotiated exchange.

In conclusion, we propose, based on our analysis here, that exchange relations, groups, and networks are more likely to endure if emotions (a) felt and expressed correspond with contextual norms and actors' identities, (b) are openly shared so as to promote mutual trust, and (c) are attributed to the relevant social units. Relations and groups that regularly satisfy these criteria should yield greater compliance, obligation, sacrifice, and collective action than can be explained by extant social exchange theorizing (e.g. Ekeh 1974, Hechter 1987). In this sense, bringing emotion into exchange theory has the potential to generalize and deepen social exchange explanations of social order and solidarity. We believe general questions about social exchange and social order are important avenues for future theorizing and research because exchange serves as a bridging phenomenon forging ties across differentiated parts of social systems (Ekeh 1974). Emotions and emotional processes warrant a central role in such theorizing.

ACKNOWLEDGMENTS

We thank Karen Hegtvedt, Murray Webster, and Jeongkoo Yoon for helpful comments on an earlier version of this chapter.

> **Visit the *Annual Reviews home page* at**
> **http://www.AnnualReviews.org.**

Literature Cited

Averill JR. 1992. The structural bases of emotional behavior: a metatheoretical analysis. See Clark 1992, pp. 1–24

Bacharach SB, Lawler EJ. 1981. *Bargaining: Power, Tactics, and Outcomes.* San Francisco: Jossey-Bass

Bales RF. 1950. *Interaction Process Analysis: A Method for the Study of Small Groups.* Cambridge, MA: Addison-Wesley

Bales RF. 1953. The equilibrium problem in small groups. In *Working Papers in the Theory of Action,* ed. T Parsons, RF Bales, EA Shils, pp. 111–61. Glencoe, IL: Free Press

Bales RF, Hare P. 1965. Diagnostic use of the interaction profile. *J. Soc. Psychol.* 67: 239–58

Bales RF, Slater PE. 1955. Role differentiation in small decision making groups. In *The Family, Socialization and Interaction*

Processes, ed. T Parsons, PE Slater, pp. 259–306. Glencoe, IL: Free Press

Baron RS, Inman ML, Kao CF, Logan H. 1992. Negative emotion and superficial social processing. *Motivation Emotion* 16(4):323–46

Baron R, Logan H, Lilly J, Inman M, Brennan M. 1994. Negative emotion and message processing. *J. Exp. Soc. Psychol.* 30: 181–210

Bartlett JC, Burleson G, Santrock JW. 1982. Emotional mood and memory in young children. *J. Exp. Child Psychol.* 34(1): 59–76

Batra R, Holbrook MB. 1990. Developing a typology of affective responses to advertising. *Psychol. Market.* 7(1):11–25

Berger J, Zelditch M Jr, Anderson B, eds. 1972. *Sociological Theories in Progress,* Vol. 2. Boston: Houghton Mifflin

Blau PM. 1964. *Exchange and Power in Social Life.* New York: Wiley

Bower GH. 1981. Mood and memory. *Am. Psychol.* 36(2):129–48

Bower GH. 1991. Mood congruity of social judgments. See Forgas 1991, pp. 31–53

Bower GH, Gilligan SG, Monteiro KP. 1981. Selectivity of learning caused by affective states. *J. Exp. Soc. Psychol.* 110(4): 451–73

Clark C. 1990. Emotions and micropolitics in everyday life: some patterns and paradoxes of place. See Kemper 1990a, pp. 305–33

Clark MS, ed. 1992. *Emotion.* Newbury Park, CA: Sage

Clore GL, Ortony A, Foss MA. 1987. The psychological foundations of the affective lexicon. *J. Pers. Soc. Psychol.* 53(4): 751–66

Clore GL, Parrott GW. 1994. Cognitive feelings and metacognitive judgments. *Eur. J. Soc. Psychol.* 24:101–15

Collins R. 1975. *Conflict Sociology.* New York: Academic

Collins R. 1981. On the microfoundations of macrosociology. *Am. J. Sociol.* 86(5):984–1014

Collins R. 1989. Toward a neo-median sociology of mind. *Symb. Inter.* 12(1):1–32

Collins R. 1993. Emotional energy as the common denominator of rational action. *Ration. Soc.* 5(2):203–30

Cook KS, Fine GA, House JS, eds. 1995. *Sociological Perspectives on Social Psychology.* Boston: Allyn & Bacon

Durkheim E. 1915. *The Elementary Forms of Religious Life.* New York: Free Press

Ekeh PP. 1974. *Social Exchange Theory: The Two Traditions.* Cambridge, MA: Harvard Univ. Press

Ekman P. 1980. *The Face of Man: Expressions of Universal Emotions in a New Guinea Village.* New York: Garland STMP Press

Ekman P. 1992. An argument for basic emotion. *Cognition Emotion* 6:169–200

Emerson RM. 1972a. Exchange theory. Part I: A psychological basis for social exchange. See Berger et al 1972, pp. 38–57

Emerson RM. 1972b. Exchange theory. Part II: Exchange rules and networks. See Berger et al 1972, pp. 58–87

Emerson RM. 1981. Social exchange theory. See Rosenberg & Turner 1981, pp. 30–65

Eysenck MW. 1977. *Human Memory: Theory, Research and Individual Differences.* Elmsford, NY: Pergamon

Forgas JP, ed. 1991. *Emotion and Social Judgments.* Oxford: Pergamon

Frank RH. 1988. *Passions within Reason: the Strategic Role of Emotions.* New York: Norton

Frank RH. 1993. The strategic role of emotions: reconciling over- and undersocialized accounts of behavior. *Ration. Soc.* 5(2): 160–84

Frijda NH. 1986. *The Emotions.* Cambridge, MA: Cambridge Univ. Press

Frijda NH, Kuipers P, Schure E. 1989. Relations among emotion, appraisal, and emotional action readiness. *J. Pers. Soc. Psychol.* 57:212–29

Gordon SL. 1981. The sociology of sentiments and emotion. See Rosenberg & Turner 1981, pp. 562–92

Gordon SL. 1990. Social structure effects on emotions. See Kemper 1990a, pp. 145–79

Goffman E. 1959. *The Presentation of Self in Everyday Life.* New York: Doubleday

Guttman L. 1954. An outline of some new methodology in social research. *Pub. Opin. Q.* 18:395–404

Hardin R. 1991. *Collective Action.* Baltimore, MD: Johns Hopkins Univ. Press

Haslam N. 1995. The discreteness of emotion concepts: categorical structure in the affective circumplex. *Pers. Soc. Psychol. Bull.* 21(10):1012–19

Hechter M. 1987. *Principles of Group Solidarity.* Berkeley: Univ. Calif. Press

Heise DR. 1966. Social status, attitudes and word connotations. *Sociol. Inquiry* 36(2): 227–39

Heise DR. 1987. Affect control theory: concepts and model. *J. Math. Sociol.* 13:1–33

Heise DR. 1979. *Understanding Events.* New York: Cambridge Univ. Press

Hegtvedt KA, Markovsky B. 1995. Justice and injustice. See Cook et al 1995, pp. 257–80

Hewstone M. 1989. *Causal Attribution: From Cognitive Processes to Collective Beliefs.* Oxford, UK: Blackwell

Hochschild AR. 1975. The sociology of feeling and emotion: selected possibilities. In *Another Voice,* ed. M Millman, R Kanter, pp. 280–307. New York: Anchor

Hochschild AR. 1979. Emotion work, feeling rules, and social structure. *Am. J. Sociol.* 85(3):551–75

Hochschild AR. 1983. *The Managed Heart: The Commercialization of Human Feeling.* Berkeley: Univ. Calif. Press

Hochschild AR. 1990. Ideology and emotion management: a perspective path. See Kemper 1990a, pp. 117–42

Homans GC. 1961. *Social Behavior: Its Elementary Forms.* New York: Harcourt Brace

Isen AM. 1987. Positive affect, cognitive processes, and social behavior. In *Adv. in Exp. Soc. Psychol,* ed. L Berkowitz, 20:203–53. New York: Academic

Isen AM, Geva N. 1987. The influence of positive affect on acceptable level of risk: the person with a large canoe has a large worry. *Org. Behav. Hum. Decision Proc.* 39(2):145–54

Isen AM, Patrick R. 1983. The effects of positive feelings on risk-taking: when the chips are down. *Org. Behav. Hum. Decision Proc.* 31(2):194–202

Isen AM, Shalker TE, Clark M, Karp L. 1978. Affect, accessibility of material in memory and behavior: a cognitive loop? *J. Pers. Soc. Psychol.* 36(1):1–12

Izard CE. 1971. *The Face of Emotion.* New York: Appleton–Century–Crofts

Izard CE. 1977. *Human Emotions.* New York: Plenum

Izard CE. 1991. *The Psychology of Emotions.* New York: Plenum

Johnson EJ, Tversky A. 1983. Affect, generalization, and the perception of risk. *J. Pers. Soc. Psychol.* 45(1):20–31

Kanter RM. 1968. Commitment and social organization: a study of commitment mechanisms in utopian communities. *Am. Sociol. Rev.* 33:499–517

Kelley HH, Thibaut JW. 1978. *Interpersonal Relations: A Theory of Interdependence.* New York: Wiley

Kemper TD. 1978. *A Social Interactional Theory of Emotions.* New York: Wiley

Kemper TD. 1987. How many emotions are there? Wedding the social and the autonomic components. *Am. J. Sociol.* 93: 263–89

Kemper TD, ed. 1990a. *Research Agendas in the Sociology of Emotions.* New York: SUNY Press

Kemper TD.1990b. Themes and variations in the sociology of emotions. See Kemper 1990a, pp. 3–23

Kemper TD.1990c. Social relations and emotions: a structural approach. See Kemper 1990a, pp. 207–37

Kemper TD, Collins R. 1990. Dimensions of microinteraction. *Am. J. Sociol.* 96(1): 32–68

Kollock P. 1993. An eye for an eye leaves everyone blind: cooperation and accounting systems. *Am. Sociol. Rev.* 58:768–86

Kramer RM. 1991. Intergroup relations and organizational dilemmas: the role of categorization processes. In *Research in Organizational Behavior,* ed. B Staw, L Cummins, 13:191–228. Greenwich, CT: JAI

Kramer RM, Brewer MB. 1984. Effects of group identity on resource use in a simulated commons dilemma. *J. Pers. Soc. Psychol.* 46:1044–57

Larsen RJ, Diener E. 1992. Promises and problems with the circumplex model of emotion. See Clark 1992, pp. 25–59

Lawler EJ. 1992. Affective attachments to nested groups: a choice-process theory. *Am. Sociol. Rev.* 57:327–39

Lawler EJ, Yoon J. 1993. Power and the emergence of commitment behavior in negotiated exchange. *Am. Sociol. Rev.* 58: 465–81

Lawler EJ, Yoon J. 1995. Structural power and emotional processes in negotiations: a social exchange approach. In *Negotiation as a Social Process,* ed. R Kramer, D Messick, pp. 143–65. Newbury Park, CA: Sage

Lawler EJ, Yoon J. 1996. Commitment in exchange relations: test of a theory of relational cohesion. *Am. Sociol. Rev.* 61: 89–108

Lawler EJ, Yoon J. 1998. Network structure and emotion in exchange relations. *Am. Sociol. Rev.* 63:871–94

Lazarus RS. 1982. Thoughts on the relation between emotion and cognition. *Am. Psychol.* 37(9):1019–24

Lazarus RS. 1984. On the primacy of cognition. *Am. Psychol.* 39(2):124–29

Lazarus RS. 1995. Cognition and emotion from the RET viewpoint. *J. Ration. Emotive Cogn. Behav. Ther.* 13(1):29–54

Levenson RW, Ekman P, Heider K, Friesen WV. 1992. Emotion and autonomic nervous system activity in the Minangkabau of West Sumatra. *J. Pers. Soc. Psychol.* 62(6):972–88

Lovaglia MJ. 1995. Power and status: exchange, attribution, and expectation states. *Small Group Res.* 26(3):400–26

Lovaglia MJ, Houser J. 1996. Emotional reactions and status in groups. *Am. Sociol. Rev.* 61:867–83

Lutz C. 1988. *Unnatural Emotions: Everyday*

Sentiments on a Micronesian Atoll and their Challenge to Western Theory. Chicago: Univ. Chicago Press

Mackie DM, Worth LT. 1989. Processing deficits and the mediation of positive affect in persuasion. *J. Pers. Soc. Psychol.* 57:27–40

Mackie DM, Worth LT. 1991. Feeling good, but not thinking straight: the impact of positive mood on persuasion. See Forgas 1991, pp. 201–19

Mano H. 1991. The structure and intensity of emotional experiences: method and context convergence. *Multivariate Behav. Res.* 26(3):389–411

Markovsky B, Lawler EJ. 1994. A new theory of group solidarity. In *Advances in Group Processes,* ed. B Markovsky, K Heimer, J O'Brien, EJ Lawler, 11:113–37. Greenwich, CT: JAI

Molm LD. 1987. Extending power dependence theory: power processes and negative outcomes. In *Advances in Group Processes,* 4178–98: ed. DJ Lawler, E Markovsky. Greenwich, CT: JAI

Molm LD. 1991. Affect and social exchange: satisfaction in power-dependence relations. *Am. Sociol. Rev.* 56:475–93

Molm LD. 1994. Dependence and risk: transforming the structure of social exchange. *Soc. Psychol. Q.* 57(3):163–76

Molm LD, Cook KS. 1995. Social exchange and exchange networks. In *Sociological Perspectives on Social Psychology,* ed. FA Fine, JS House, pp. 209–35. Boston: Allyn & Bacon

Oatley K, Johnson-Laird PN. 1987. Toward a cognitive theory of emotion. *Cogn. Emotion* 1:29–50

Ortony A, Clore GL, Collins A. 1988. *The Cognitive Structures of Emotions.* Cambridge, MA: Cambridge Univ. Press

Osgood CE. 1966. Dimensionality of the semantic space for communication via facial expressions. *Scand. J. Psychol.* 7:1–30

Parsons T. 1951. *The Social System.* New York: Free Press

Plous S. 1993. *The Psychology of Judgment and Decision Making.* New York: McGraw-Hill

Ridgeway C, Johnson C. 1990. What is the relationship between socioemotional behavior and status in task groups. *Am. J. Sociol.* 95(5):1189–212

Rosenberg M, Turner RH, eds. 1981. *Social Psychology: Sociological Perspectives.* New York: Basic

Russell JA. 1980. A circumplex model of affect. *J. Pers. Soc. Psychol.* 39(6):1161–78

Russell JA. 1983. Pancultural aspects of the human conceptual organization of emotions. *J. Pers. Soc. Psychol.* 45(6):1281–88

Russell JA. 1991. Culture and the categorization of emotions. *Psychol. Bull.* 110(3):426–50

Russell JA, Mehrabian A. 1977. Evidence for a three factor theory of emotions. *J. Res. Pers.* 11(3):273–94

Russell JA, Ridgeway D. 1983. Dimensions underlying children's emotion concepts. *Dev. Psychol.* 19(6):795–804

Russell JA, Weiss A, Mendelsohn GA. 1989. Affect grid: a single-item scale of pleasure and arousal. *J. Pers. Soc. Psychol.* 57(3):493–502

Schachter S, Singer JE. 1962. Cognitive, social and physiological determinants of emotional state. *Psychol. Rev.* 69:379–99

Scheff TJ. 1983. Toward integration in the social psychology of emotions. *Annu. Rev. Sociol.* 18:500–5

Scheff TJ. 1990a. Socialization of emotions: pride and shame as causal agents. See Kemper 1990a, pp. 281–304

Scheff TJ. 1990b. *Microsociology: Discourse, Emotion and Social Structure.* Chicago: Univ. Chicago Press

Scherer KR. 1984. Emotion as a multicomponent process: a model and some cross-cultural data. *Rev. Pers. Soc. Psychol.* 5: 37–63

Scherer KR. 1988. *Facets of Emotion: Recent Research.* Hillsdale, NJ: Lawrence Earlbaum

Schwarz N. 1990. Feelings as information: informational and motivational functions of affective states. In *Handbook of Motivation and Cognition: Foundations of Social Behavior,* ed. RM Sorrentino, ET Higgins, pp. 265–96. New York: Guilford

Schwarz N, Clore GL. 1983. Mood, misattribution, and judgments of well-being: informative and directive functions of affective states. *J. Pers. Soc. Psychol.* 45(3):513–23

Shaver PR, Wu S, Schwartz JC. 1992. Cross-cultural similarities and differences in emotion and its representation. See Clark 1992, pp. 175–212

Shelly RK. 1993. How sentiments organize interaction. In *Advances in Group Processes,* ed. EJ Lawler, B Markovsky, K Heimer, J O'Brien, 10:113–32. Greenwich, CT: JAI

Skvoretz J, Zhang P. 1997. Actors' responses to outcomes in exchange networks: the process of power development. *Sociol. Perspect.* 40:183–97

Smith-Lovin L, Heise DR, eds. 1988. *Analyzing Social Interaction: Advances in Affect*

Control Theory. New York: Gordon & Breach

Storm C, Storm T. 1987. A taxonomic study of the vocabulary of emotions. *J. Pers. Soc. Psychol.* 53(4):1063–70

Thoits PA. 1985. Self-labeling processes in mental illness: the role of emotional deviance. *Am. J. Sociol.* 92:221–49

Thoits PA. 1989. The sociology of emotions. *Annu. Rev. Sociol.* 15:317–42

Thoits PA. 1990. Emotional deviance: research agendas. See Kemper 1990a, pp. 180–203

Thibaut JW, Kelly HH. 1959. *The Social Psychology of Groups.* New York: Wiley

Thye SR, Lovaglia MJ, Markovsky B. 1997. Responses to social exchange and social exclusion in networks. *Soc. Forc.* 75(3): 1031–47

Watson D, Clark LA, Tellegen A. 1984. Cross-cultural convergence in the structure of mood: a Japanese replication and a comparison with U.S. findings. *J. Pers. Soc. Psychol.* 47(1):127–44

Watson D, Tellegen A. 1985. Toward a consensual structure of mood. *Psychol. Bull.* 98(2):219–35

Wegener DT, Petty RE, Smith SM. 1995. Positive mood can increase or decrease message scrutiny: the hedonic contingency view of mood and message processing. *J. Pers. Soc. Psychol.* 69(1):5–15

Weiner B. 1985. An attributional theory of achievement motivation and emotion. *Psychol. Rev.* 92:548–73

Weiner B. 1986. *An Attributional Theory of Motivation and Emotion.* New York: Springer-Verlag

Wessel I, Merckelbach H. 1997. The impact of anxiety on memory for details in spider phobics. *Appl. Cog. Psychol.* 11(3):223–31

Wierzbicka A. 1992. Defining emotion concepts. *Cogn. Sci.* 16:539–81

Wilder DA, Shapiro P. 1989. The effects of anxiety on impression formation in a group context: an anxiety-assimilation hypothesis. *J. Exp. Soc. Psychol.* 25(6):481–99

Willer D. 1981. The basic concepts of elementary theory. See Willer & Anderson 1981, pp. 25–53

Willer D, Anderson B. 1981. *Networks Exchange and Coercion: The Elementary Theory and Its Applications.* New York: Elsevier

Willer D, Lovaglia MJ, Markovsky B. 1997. Power and influence: a theoretical bridge. *Soc. Forc.* 76(2):571–603

Willer D, Markovsky B. 1993. Elementary theory: its development and research program. In *Theoretical Research Programs: Studies in Theory Growth*, ed. J Berger, M Zelditch, pp. 323–63. Stanford, CA: Stanford Univ. Press

Wright WF, Bower GH. 1992. Mood effects on subjective probability assessment. *Org. Behav. Hum. Decision Proc.* 52:276–91

Zajonc RB. 1980. Thinking and feeling: preferences need no inferences. *Am. Psychol.* 35(2):151–75

Zajonc RB. 1984. On the primacy of affect. *Am. Psychol.* 39(2):117–23

Zillman D. 1983. Transfer of excitation in emotional behavior. In *Social Psychophysiology: A Sourcebook*, ed. JT Cacioppo, RE Petty, pp. 215–40. New York: Guilford

Annu. Rev. Sociol. 1999. 25:245–69

APHORISMS AND CLICHÉS: The Generation and Dissipation of Conceptual Charisma

Murray S. Davis

900 Contra Costa Avenue, Berkeley, California 94707; msdavis@value.net

KEY WORDS: sociology, rhetoric, cognition, knowledge, interesting

ABSTRACT

The motivating engines of intellectual life are not true ideas but interesting ones. This article investigates the aphorism, the purest form of an interesting idea that draws the mind onward. It begins by examining the linguistic style of aphorisms, their reconceptions of experience from deceptive surfaces to more fundamental truths, their psychological and social effects on the vanity and status of their creators and conveyers, and the decline of their conceptual charisma into cliché until a surprising modification restarts the aphorism-cliché cycle. The investigation of aphorisms broadens to their intellectual and cultural contexts by examining their expansion into articles and collection into books, the different aspects of a topic revealed by aphoristic perspectives and scientific sequences, and the similarities (and differences) between aphoristic and postmodern ways of knowing. This article ends with a series of aphorisms on the cognitive substance of alluring knowledge, which distinguish some of the components of interesting ideas.

INTRODUCTION

We chase the interesting, which continually eludes us; we are chased by boredom, which continually catches us.

The first criterion by which people judge anything they encounter, even before deciding whether it is true or false, is whether it is interesting or boring.

The truth of a theory is not even the main criterion of its acceptance, for an interesting falsehood will attract more followers than a boring truth.

0360-0572/99/0815-0245$08.00

What makes a theory interesting is its implications, the set of further instances to which it can be applied. By evoking the desire to complete this set, to close its gestalt, the charisma of a theory draws the mind onward.

The interesting is the motivating engine of the mental life: Unlike theories that are merely true, theories that are interesting configure incomplete gestalts in the mind, which—as they accelerate toward potential closure—produce pleasurable endorphins in the brain.

The interesting is more interesting than the true because Truth, as the final goal of knowledge, is static, whereas the Interesting, as the revelation of a potential understanding that propels the mind toward Truth, is dynamic.

The interesting determines the true—not the other way around. Rather than ascertaining the truth of a theory before applying it to additional topics, we become more convinced of a theory's core concepts the more provocative we find its peripheral implications.

THE APHORISM: THE LINGUISTIC STYLE OF ALLURING KNOWLEDGE

Lexicology

Def.: APHORISM *n.* The finest thoughts in the fewest words.

Defining "aphorism" with an aphorism unites definition and illustration—a union especially appropriate for this term because morphologically an aphorism is succinct, and etymologically it means definition (from the Greek: *aphorizein* [*apo*: from; *horizein* horizon, boundary] to delimit, mark off, divide, define).

In form, aphorisms are always terse and trenchant, demonstrating maximum comprehension in minimum expression. Like the above aphorism, their parts are often parallel and opposed. Unlike the above aphorism, their whole is sometimes paradoxical when their parts are antithetical:

> The great misfortune for intellectual merit is that it has to wait until the good is praised by those who produce only the bad...(Schopenhauer 1970: 224).

In content, aphorisms are deep and wide. The observations they report range vertically from perceptive to profound, and horizontally from all members of one class to all members of all classes. The *Oxford English Dictionary* defines an aphorism as "a short, pithy sentence containing a truth of general import."

Some critics (Smith 1943, Auden & Kronenberger 1966) contrast the aphorism's universal application to humanity with the epigram's particular application to a person. (Epigrams, these critics claim, are also more concise, witty, and caustic than aphorisms.) Although this distinction ignores the many short observations on intermediate social groupings—specific genders, classes, nationalities, occupations, institutions, etc—it does point out the important dimension of the aphorism's generality.

Roget's International Thesaurus, under the heading "Wise Sayings," lists several synonyms of "aphorism," which indicate its other dimensions. A "maxim" or a "motto" is a guide to conduct rather than thought. A "slogan" has a purpose other than insight, reenforcing a product perception or political prejudice rather than reorienting a perspective. An "adage" or a "proverb" is a traditional rather than novel saying. A "commonplace," "truism," "platitude," "cliché," "chestnut," "bromide," or "saw" stresses a saying's loss of vitality, which sedates rather than awakens its audience. Many new aphorisms revitalize old ones by negating or reversing familiar quotations, turning comforting platitudes into unsettling paradoxes, such as Oscar Wilde's "Only the shallow know themselves" and "Work is the curse of the drinking classes."

The *OED* points out that "aphorism" was first used in a scientific context as the title of Hippocrates's book of medical observations (which began with the famous "Life is short, art is long, opportunity fleeting, experimenting dangerous, reasoning difficult..."). Renaissance philosophers maintained its scientific derivation, defining "aphorism" as the "concise statement of a principle of a science," eventually expanded to include principles of morality and philosophy. Later philosophers disconnected it from its scientific origins, increasingly distinguishing "aphorism," a plausible truth, from "axiom," a self-evident truth, "theorem," a theoretically demonstrable truth, and "hypothesis," an empirically provable truth.

In short, an "aphorism" is located at the intersection of five distinctive dimensions, from which its partial synonyms move away: (*a*) intellectuality (from insight to conduct), (*b*) plausibility (from the possible to the undeniable, demonstrable, or provable), (*c*) generality (from universal to individual), (*d*) novelty (from new perspective to customary perspective), and (*e*) vitality (from stimulating to soporific).

Phenomenology[1] and Cognition

The principal process of intellectual life is not the discovery of new truths but the dulling of old ones. Because our experience of cognition continually fades, it must be continually refreshed:

---

[1] I will use "phenomenology" (and its derivatives) in several senses, depending on its context: (*a*) experience, (*b*) the cognition of experience, (*c*) the scientific investigation of experience, (*d*) the experience of cognition, and (*e*) the cognition of the experience of cognition. I also use it in Hegel's sense as the development of thinking, but not in Husserl's strict sense as the philosophical investigation of experience.

> In philosophy equally as in poetry it is the highest and most useful preroga-
> tive of genius to produce the strongest impressions of novelty, while it res-
> cues admitted truths from the neglect caused by the very circumstance of
> their universal admission. Extremes meet. Truths, of all others the most aw-
> ful and interesting, are too often considered *so* true that they lose all the
> power of truth, and lie bedridden in the dormitory of the soul, side by side
> with the most despised and exploded errors.
>
> Coleridge, *Aids to Reflection*: Aphorism 1.

Unlike the comic wit that revitalizes cognitive experience by recategorizing its exterior characteristics (Davis 1993), aphoristic insight revitalizes it by peeling its conceptually calloused outer layer to reveal fresh features beneath.

Aphorisms, derived from the experience of those most perceptive about experience, point out that common conceptions of experience create illusions that conceal the real. Aphorists reinterpret the world to bring out the contradictions between surface conceptions and fundamental realities: What seems to be unified is basically separate, and vice versa; what seems to be social is basically individual, and vice versa; what seems to be high status is basically low status, and vice versa; what seems to be determined is basically voluntary, and vice versa; what seem to be causes are actually effects, and vice versa—and in general exteriors are the opposite of interiors. By reversing the polarity of our ideas about the world, aphorisms regenerate intellectual excitement.

Aphoristic observations do not describe the whole world because no true aphorism reports its boring parts where surface conceptions coincide with fundamental realities, where things are what they seem. Instead aphorisms plow through the world to turn over its soil, reinvigorating experience by turning conceptions of it inside out.

Psychology and Sociology

Perhaps the most important discovery of psychology and sociology is that every activity affects its actor's status, in his/her or others' eyes. Activities are subtly distorted, however, if this secondary effect becomes their primary purpose. The aphoristic tradition has both contributed to and been influenced by this discovery. The content of aphoristic observation has shifted from the natural to the social world. Since the Renaissance, most aphorists have excavated the human psyche, uncovering the base motivations that underlie its noble activities. "Our virtues are merely vices in disguise," goes La Rochefoucauld's summary epigraph to his *Maxims*. And Nietzsche summarizes his scattered observations in "a theory of the derivation of all good impulses from wicked ones" (*Beyond Good and Evil*: #23). Because the relative status of activities and motivations depends on social standards, many aphorists try to derive the altruistic activities Western society has regarded as high status from the egocentric motivations it has regarded as low status:

> In most people, gratitude is only a secret longing for greater benefits.
>
> La Rochefoucauld, *Maxims*: #298.

> By doing good...one exercises one's power upon others...who are in some way already dependent upon us...
>
> Nietzsche, *The Gay Science*: #13.

Thus the classical aphorists view human nature like modern "rational choice" economists (who find maximizing self-interest behind seemingly selfless activities) and sociobiologists (who find passing on one's own genes behind aid to others).

Those who deny common assumptions must go on to point out what deludes those who mistakenly hold them. For the aphoristic tradition considered here, the cause of self-delusion is self-esteem (variously termed vanity, pride, conceit, self-love, *amore-propre*), which many people can maintain only by repressing the recognition that their intentions are less reputable than they would like to believe.

> "I have done that." says my memory. "I cannot have done that." says my pride, and remains adamant. Eventually, memory yields.
>
> Nietzsche, *Beyond Good and Evil*: #68.

Aphorists remove the veil of avowed intentions to reveal actual intentions.

Aphorists have some of the most pessimistic perspectives on human nature—cynical about intentions, skeptical about justifications—because they continually discover motivations deemed to be base behind actions claimed to be noble (according to the standards of their society).

But aphorists themselves can be infected by the same pernicious psychological and social processes as those about whom they aphorize. All aphorists imply that they are wiser than others, for only they have peered beneath the surface of the psyche to discover its fundamental motivations. Exposing the vanity of others, however, can increase the vanity of the exposer, for it is difficult to avoid patronizing those who not only act for reprehensible reasons but do not know it. (Even aphorists who disparage themselves, their own groups, or their common humanity can still take pride in their perceptiveness.) Every aphorism that degrades its object's status upgrades its subject's (even if subject and object are the same). It is not accidental that many of the prototypal sixteenth and seventeenth century aphorists were aristocrats.[2]

---

[2]See Auden & Kronenberger 1966: vii-viii; La Rochefoucauld 1959: 15-16. Among the renowned early aphorists, Bacon, La Rochefoucauld, Chamfort, Halifax, and Chesterfield were social aristocrats. Many later aphorists were cultural aristocrats: well-known on the public stage as speakers like Emerson; as popular writers and journalists like Voltaire, Johnson, Twain, Mencken, and Bierce; as politicians like Churchill; or as dramatists like Goethe, Wilde, and Shaw. A third group—Pascal, Blake, Schopenhauer, Nietzsche, Wittgenstein, and Cicoran—were spiritual aristocrats, psychologically intense though socially reclusive.

Aphorisms might not have lasted as a literary form had they enhanced the self-esteem only of their authors. Their amplifications of self-esteem ripple outward from aphorist to audience, who also feel they belong to an elite group, superior to those unaware that the front of human existence differs from its backside. Being succinct in form and general in content,[3] aphorisms are modular enough for their audience to slip easily into their own speech or writing. Like proverbs (which frequently recommend opposite actions: e.g., "Look before you leap" and "Cross that bridge when you come to it"), aphorisms are a resource that can provide their audience with social support for almost any opinion or advice. Unlike proverbs, their social support comes not from tradition and community but from influential individuals. Although people quote the aphorisms of others ostensibly to articulate their own ideas, like those who want to embellish their physical image with stylish ornaments, they may also want to embellish their social image by transferring some status from the quoted to the quoter—not always succeeding:

> I quote others only to speak my own mind better.... [But] the injudicious writers of our century, who scatter about their valueless works whole passages from old authors to increase their own reputations, do just the reverse. For the infinitely greater brilliance of the ancients makes their own writing look so pale, dull, and ugly that they lose much more than they gain.
>
> Montaigne, Essays: Chap. 26.

In their pas de deux of dominance, aphorists try to stay one step ahead of their audience by undermining the arrogance of those who use (or overuse) their aphorisms:

> Maxims or axioms are, like abridgements, the work of men of genius who have, or seem to have, labored on behalf of the lazy or the mediocre. The lazy swallow a maxim whole, dispensing with the observations that have led the author to his conclusion. They give a generality to the maxim that the author, unless mediocre himself, has not claimed for it.
>
> Chamford, Maxims and Thoughts: #1.

---

[3]Their content makes writing aphorisms more difficult for sociologists than psychologists. Psychologists can make concise generalizations about presumably universal human nature whereas sociologists must both generalize and qualify, noting group and individual deviance from their generalizations—which requires more words. Their form, however, makes writing aphorisms easier for sociologists. A literary mode that is parallel and paradoxical can felicitously express the many social processes that are dual and dialectical. For example:

> The same equality that makes him independent from every other citizen makes him isolated when confronting the majority.
>
> Tocqueville, *Democracy in America*: Vol. 2, Part 1, Chap. 2.

And a much quoted public speaker disparaged his epigone with a statement only the shameless can cite:

> I hate quotations. Tell me what you know.
> Emerson, *Journals*, 1849.

Finally, the aphorist can expose the vanity that can contaminate everyone connected with the exposé:

> ...Those who write against vanity want the prestige of having written well, their readers the prestige of having read them, as do I who write this, and perhaps too you who read this.
> Pascal, *Pensées*: #150.

The intellectual diffusion of aphorisms from aphorist to audience initiates the dynamics of the aphorism-cliché cycle. Phenomenologically and cognitively, an aphorism whose entire set of implications has been worked out no longer stimulates those who hear or read it. Psychologically and sociologically, an aphorism whose repeaters stand on ever lower rungs of the intellectual stratification ladder no longer elevates those who say or write it. The nadir of this cycle motivates every connoisseur of aphorisms to stab every Polonius they know. Only by killing the cliché, if not the cliché-monger, can the idea's vitality and reputability be restored—restarting the cycle.

Bartlett's Familiar Quotations

One cannot discuss the phenomenological-cognitive and psychological-social functions of aphorisms without mentioning *Bartlett's*, their premier font of inspiration and hall of fame. *Bartlett's* itself has been ambivalent about which function to emphasize.

The "commonplace books," which compiled anonymous adages and attributed aphorisms since the Renaissance, culminated in John Bartlett's *Familiar Quotations* (1980, 1995) in 1855. This literary genre, which began as religious meditation manuals, evolved into intellectual fashion manuals cataloging the cultural references that everyone who wanted to appear an educated person should know. Bartlett codified many of the well-known quotations of his time "to show...the obligations our language owes to various authors for numerous phrases and familiar quotations which have become 'household words'." Bartlett's list perfected his partially educated readers' familiarity with these quotations and provided a crib sheet for uneducated readers who wanted to appear educated. Later editors shifted their criteria of inclusion from descriptive—quotations that are familiar—to prescriptive—quotations that *ought* to be familiar, those that have "literary power, intellectual and historical significance, originality, and timeliness." Inclusion in *Bartlett's*, however, may confer enough status by itself to transform unfamiliar quotations into familiar ones, and little known aphorists into well-known ones.

The latest editors have reverted from the novel to the banal by choosing more quotations from those whose celebrity (in popular culture, sports, or politics) made them seem insightful than from those whose insights made them—or should have made them—celebrities.

Successive editions of *Bartlett's* have vacillated between emphasizing the aphorism's psychological-social and phenomenological-cognitive functions, between serving those searching for a famous quotation and those browsing for general inspiration. Only a "personal selection" of aphorisms (e.g., Auden & Kronenberger 1966) focuses on the latter exclusively.

THE EXPANSION OF APHORISMS INTO ARTICLES

The standard literary form published in academic journals is the article. An article is an aphorism exploded. Writers for journals must inflate an aphorism's compressed solidity into an article's bloated superfluity, puffing up the kernel of an idea into the popcorn of a treatise. No one has better contrasted these two ways to deliver knowledge than Sir Francis Bacon in 1605:

> Another diversity of method, whereof the consequence is great, is the delivery of knowledge in aphorisms, or in [the methodical exposition of the modern academic article]; wherein we may observe that it has been too much taken into custom, out of a few axioms or observations upon any subject to make a solemn and formal art, filling it with some discourses, and illustrating it with examples, and digesting it into a sensible method. But writing in aphorisms has many excellent virtues, whereto writing in [methodical expositions] does not approach.
>
> For first, it [tests] the writer, whether he be superficial or solid: for aphorisms, except they should be ridiculous, cannot be made but of the pith and heart of sciences; for discourse of illustration is cut off; recitals of examples are cut off; discourse of connection and order is cut off; descriptions of practice are cut off. So there remains nothing to fill the aphorisms but some good quantity of observation: and therefore no man [is competent], nor in reason will attempt, to write aphorisms, but he that is sound and grounded. But in [methodical expositions], "such is the power of order and connection, such the beauty that may crown the commonplace," [Horace, *Ars Poetica*] that a man shall make a great show of an art, which, if it were disjointed, would come to little. Secondly, [methodical expositions] are more fit to win consent or belief, but less fit to point to action; for [their circular arguments], one part illuminating another, [are superficially convincing]. But particulars being dispersed do best agree with [ordinary actions'] dispersed directions. And lastly, aphorisms, representing a knowledge broken [i.e., incomplete], do invite men to inquire further; whereas [methodical expositions], carrying the show of a total, do secure men, as if they were at furthest [i.e., give the false sense of security of fully understanding the subject]
>
> (1996: 234-235) [spelling and idioms modernized].

Unfortunately, Bacon's prolixity contradicts his preference. Had he described the relative inferiority of articles in aphoristic form, he might have said: "Only those who need spelled out for them all the connections, exemplifications, verifications, qualifications, and implications of a thesis prefer the fluff of an article to the substance of an aphorism."

Unlike the aristocratic aphorists, who never argue or explain but only assert, the democratic writers of academic articles are supposed never to assert but only to argue or explain. The aphorist's goal is to stimulate the few, the article writer's to convince the many. Since aphorisms belong to the logic of discovery rather than the logic of verification, their truth is irrelevant to their contribution to understanding, which is the reorientation of thinking itself. Aphorisms are "prescientific" in the sense that their novel insights may eventually produce more interesting hypotheses for science to prove or disprove. Unverified aphoristic observations were useful in prescientific fields like medicine and agriculture, and they are useful in nonscientific fields like law, art, and politics. Only a "social science" pretentious enough to claim today that it is not prescientific or nonscientific would exclude them from precisely the areas of investigation that most need their insights.

Even most readers of articles, however, prefer to comprehend and remember only their core ideas. By underlining or highlighting the article to remove its superfluous words, the reader reduces what the author elaborated. Rather than forcing the reader to recompress what the article writer decompressed, the aphorist simply gives the reader the basic idea, efficiently saving the reader the bother of recreating it. The thoughtful aphorist has already taken the reader's notes.

The abstract, which prefaces many journal articles today, resembles the aphorism. Most abstracts, however, are merely carelessly written afterthoughts rather than carefully conceived forethoughts. Since abstracts are widely read in this era of computer searches, an elegant aphoristic abstract could become more influential than the article it abstracts.

Writing at the beginning of modern science, Bacon had the prescience to describe the distortion produced if the article ever displaced the aphorism totally as the literary vehicle that delivers knowledge: the intellectual excitement dissipated by articles, which elaborate relatively few new ideas, will no longer be regenerated by aphorisms, which disseminate relatively many fresh ideas for potential elaboration.

THE COLLECTION OF APHORISMS INTO BOOKS

The Individual Aphorism and the Collection of Aphorisms

Aphorisms are not easily collected because each aphorism is autonomous, complete in itself, and essentially separate from all other aphorisms. An aphorism is both detached (from a notebook or a larger literary work) and unattached (to other thoughts or an extended exposition). Samuel Johnson defined an aphorism as an "unconnected proposition."

An aphorism collection is the intellectual equivalent of the twelve-tone or serial system in music. Being a closed thought, definitively expressed, one aphorism provides no problematic tone for another to resolve. Consisting only of stressed notes, an aphorism collection provides no absolute ground against which a figure can be emphasized. (Readers who would mark any aphorism that appeared in another context are forced to mark only the *relatively* "best" ones in a collection of aphorisms, creating a background out of the ones they find *relatively* less provocative.) A collection of aphorisms, unlike an ordinary book or article, is not skimmable.

Aphorism collections try to connect what wants to stand alone, try to link what has no hooks. Each aphorism wants to go its own way, unconstrained by other aphorisms or by their collective whole. A collection of aphorisms (probably Nietzsche's) reminded Wagner of "performing fleas." By bringing out discrepancies that would otherwise remain unnoticed, and relativizing assertions that would otherwise seem unconditioned, collecting aphorisms can weaken their power. A whole can be less than the sum of its parts as well as more. In another way, though, collecting aphorisms can strengthen their power. An organization can realign the diverse orientations of several aphorisms, compelling their diffuse insights to converge on a common topic, even aligning them sequentially to elucidate it progressively.

Since each aphorism and each systematic organization of aphorisms tends toward self-completion, each level tries to organize the other around itself. An aphorism's sudden revelation momentarily blinds the reader to all other truths, temporarily transforming a component of a collection into the whole. But the systematic organization's classification scheme confines each aphorism to its place relative to all the other components of the collection. The opposing tendencies of both these totalizing entities—aphorism and collection—produce the peculiar tension of the aphorism collection.

Aphoristic Perspectives and Scientific Sequences

Collections of humanistic aphorisms may resemble collections of scientific or pseudoscientific propositions—e.g., Euclid's *Elements*, Wittgenstein and Russell's *Tractatus Logico-Philosophicus*, Newton's *Principia*, Spinoza's *Ethics*, or some more recent pretentious sociologies—in their similar categorical and numerical organization. But they differ not only in the certainty of *what* is connected (plausible aphorisms vs. self-evident axioms, demonstrable theorems, provable laws, or their corollaries) but also in the methodicalness of *how*.

Collections of scientific propositions are typically interconnected systematically. Their collectors line up each proposition individually along a common topic, rigorously following a hierarchical and sequential logic. Each proposition in the line, more specific than the last, clarifies their common topic gradually from its grosser to its finer aspects.

In contrast, collections of humanistic aphorisms are typically interconnected associatively. Their collectors assemble each aphorism concerned with a common topic into a category, loosely arranged according to a democratic and perspectival logic. Each aphorism in the category, equal to the others, spotlights a different aspect of their common topic; all of them floodlight the entire topic from multiple perspectives.

This intellectual method—which I will call *logical pointillism* or, when applied to social life, as it usually is, *sociological pointillism*—generates a scintillating image of a topic from the many points of insight that galvanize its particular aspects. In the same way that standardizing diffuse waves of radiant energy into a laser beam amplifies light, categorizing aphorisms to focus their diverse orientations amplifies their insights—enough to make their common topic cognitively fluoresce. Just as Seurat's perceptual pointillism captured the dynamics of visual experience more realistically than traditional painting, logical pointillism comprehends a topic more resonantly than a sequence of scientific propositions about it. Rather than image a topic linearly, as a sequence of scientific propositions does, a category of humanistic aphorisms images a topic multidimensionally through the conceptual "dots" or cognitive pixels of many pointed and vibrant insights, which oscillate consciousness between its surface and its substance. Pointillistic logics activate the mind more than do other intellectual methods: Each aphorism swings the mind from outside to inside a topic, whereas a category of aphorisms swings it from side to side across their common topic—stimulating the mind to fill in the empty conceptual space between points of clarity.

More generally, logical, or sociological, pointillism can make the entire world, especially the social world, sparkle like a cut diamond: each aphorism illuminates one of its facets; a coherent collection of aphorisms intensifies the brilliance of all of them.[4]

---

[4]Sociological pointillism, which contrasts with the more continuous and ordered semi-scientific approaches of Marx, Durkheim, Weber, and Freud, derives from the perspectival and fragmented approach of the *fin de siecle* German sociologist Georg Simmel. Simmel has been accused of "impressionism," both philosophical and sociological, for being concerned merely with discontinuous appearances. Though post-impressionistic, pointillism is vulnerable to the same accusation, for it is part of the same aesthetic tradition. But sociological pointillists are not concerned *merely* with discontinuous appearances. They articulate them only to contrast them more precisely with the unified underlying processes that produce them. Indeed they are concerned less with either fragmented surfaces or unified foundations than with the observer's cognitive oscillation between them, for their opposition activates the synthesizing potential of his or her mind.

APHORISM: SELF AND SOCIETY

Objective and Subjective Aspects

Aphorisms refer not only forward and outward to the world they ostensibly concern but also backward and inward to their creator. The humanities have increasingly diverged from the sciences over the question of whether to focus on what text asserts about the objective *world* or suggests about the subjective *world viewer*.

In these newer humanistic perspectives, though to various extents, the subjective mind creates the objective world. Consequently, those who comment on their environment reveal their own nature as much as their environment's. The more an observer organizes and articulates the world, the more he or she organizes and articulates the world viewer, for world-creation reflects self-creation.

What distinguishes the great aphorists is that all their aphorisms can be traced back to a common attitude toward the world. Behind their many aphorisms stands a single principle applied to a variety of topics: Pascal's "self-fragility," La Rochefoucauld's "self-interest," Schopenhauer's "self-denial," Nietzsche's "self-empowerment." Cioran's (1992) attitude of "self-despair," for instance, permeates all his aphorisms, as illustrated by these few:

> Apparently matter, jealous of life, seeks to discover its weak points and to punish its initiatives, its betrayals. For life is life only by infidelity to matter (5).

> ...Whoever does not die young will regret it sooner or later (15).

> To have accomplished nothing and to die overworked (85).

Aphorisms about the outer world disclose the inner self, but in different degrees. Aphorisms cannot be completely classified as either objective observations or subjective opinions; rather, each aphorism is located on a continuum of objectivity and subjectivity, for aphorists express their thoughts with different levels of commitment. Cioran (1992) points out the fluctuating psychological *distance* between aphorists and their aphorisms:

> In any book governed by the Fragment, truths and whims keep company throughout. How to sift them, to decide which conviction, which caprice? One proposition, a momentary impulse, precedes or follows another, a life's companion raised to the dignity of an obsession.... It is the reader who must assign the roles, since in more than one instance, the author himself hesitates to take sides...(Epigraph).

That writing about the world can expose the writer as much as the world has been well known, for scientists have always taken great pains to conceal the distinctive selves who wrote their works (except, significantly, for their name). Montaigne, however, was the first writer to revel in self-revelation, the first to write *solely* for the purpose of discovering what kind of self his writing about the world implied: "...finding myself entirely unprovided with and empty of other material, I proposed myself to myself for theme and subject" (Book 2, Chapter 8). But he did not distinguish the writer revealed *indirectly* by one's writing about the world from the writer revealed *directly* by one's writing about oneself.

Modern and Postmodern Aspects

Aphorisms ceased to be a major mode of publication two centuries ago. Since about 1800, few social observers have used them as the main vehicle through which to introduce their new ideas (Nietzsche being the most notable exception). Only the value of aphorisms as a resource for their audience has prevented this literary tradition from fading further, for the speakers and writers who retransmit aphorisms have come to rely on their preservation in *Bartlett's* and other reference works.

Aphorisms declined because they have less affinity with modern society (whose intellectual arbiters require all new ideas be elaborated systematically, connected theoretically, and verified empirically) than they had with premodern society (whose seventeenth and eighteenth century classical aphorists created their paradigmatic form). Aphorisms may again become popular because they have an affinity with postmodern society (whose communicative characteristics could increase audience receptivity to them).[5]

The aphoristic form is well suited to the discontinuities of postmodern society. Its shortness can help postmodern audiences fill their many small splinters of empty time. Its conciseness can make aphorisms appropriate for the "sound bites" that fill postmodern media's brief time slots for news. Its modularity can adapt aphorisms to postmodern culture's *collage*, in which items originally invented for one purpose are frequently used for another, for "a truth of general import" can be easily transported between contexts.

The aphoristic content also mirrors postmodern epistemology, which reduces the breadth, but increases the depth, of human understanding. Like the postmodernist, the aphorist believes it is better to explain a thing in itself than to locate it in a rigorously organized whole. Only local understandings are possible. But only local understandings are necessary because every component is

---

[5]Although "postmodern" is a fashionable term devoid of definite content, it has the heuristic value of allowing prognosticators to contrast what they believe are avant-garde and passé social phenomena. Pointing out the ways the aphorism is compatible with postmodernism helps manifest the distinctive characteristics that give this form of communication a progressive aura. But I also point out their incompatibilities.

a synecdoche of its whole. To understand a component is to understand its whole. For a postmodern sociologist, to understand an ethnic or gender identity group is to understand a whole society. For an aphorist:

> I summed up all systems in a phrase, and all existence in an epigram.
> Oscar Wilde, *Letter to Lord Alfred Douglas*.

Aphoristic closure can produce a momentarily satisfying intellectual fulfillment rarely found elsewhere by the postmodern psyche. But if the form and content of aphorisms are postmodern, their density and effect are not. An aphorism is a compacted thought, whose complete decompression requires contemplation. Unfolding its implications may be too tedious for those used to the hollow concepts and "lite ideas" that dominate the popular media. Even though aphorisms seem well suited to the *internet*, they are not. Those who search the internet for information must search elsewhere for insight. Easy to read but hard to comprehend, an aphorism would strike those who try to surf through it like a rock.

Moreover, an aphorism's perspective shift on one topic has repercussions on all topics, requiring more cognitive readjustments than most people today care to make. True aphorisms are not the ideal sound bites they appear, for they shift perspectives too much for a mass media that wants to divert its audience but not disconcert them.

Finally, aphorists, like postmodernists, distinguish between appearance and reality. But postmodernists, who maintain an ironic distance from reality, are content to live in the world of appearances, whereas aphorists, who maintain an ironic distance from appearance, are never content so long as appearance continues to separate from reality. Consequently, aphorists undermine the meaning of postmodern life as much as the meanings of modern and premodern life. It seems appropriate to end an article on the aphoristic style of interesting ideas by illustrating its themes with a series of aphorisms on their cognitive substance (see also Davis 1971).

THE INTERESTING: THE COGNITIVE SUBSTANCE OF ALLURING KNOWLEDGE

Invention

The world can be interesting only because it seems—is?—bilevel, only because its front and rear, surface and structure, appearance and reality differ—which allows the mind to move from one level of understanding to another.

The Pediatrics of Intellectual Life: Those who believe that a phenomenon *is* what it seems begin to consider whether it might be *more* than it seems.

The phenomenology of cognition can reveal the appeal of paradigm formation and transformation: It is exciting to discover a truth because the unattached elements the truth connects seem to "speed up" as they gravitate toward their appropriate place in its gestalt. But it is even more exciting to convert them from an old truth to a new one, for the conceptual force needed to pry attached elements out of their original gestalt before reattaching them to a new gestalt seems to accelerate them even more.

Whoever wishes to live on through his/her ideas should start by examining well-known ideas to discover what characteristics account for their enduring renown.

Interesting ideas, an examination discloses, are (*a*) *novel*—for they externally contradict a conventional baseline; (*b*) *extendible*—for they are easily elaborated to apply to new topics; (*c*) *reorganizational*—for they separate what seemed coupled or couple what seemed separate; (*d*) *reflexive*—for they provide their own justification by applying their thesis to themselves; (*e*) *ambiguous*—for they contain internal contradictions that allow multiple interpretations; (*f*) *sociable*—for they create the social group that carries them; and (*g*) *transient*—for they alter the conceptual background against which they first appeared interesting.

Novelty

Is there a transformation formula for innovative ideas? Some common logical process that determines how a new idea develops from an old one? Even a rote application of this transformation formula to any field today could make the uncreative sound avant-garde.

One must know what is obvious before one can know what is interesting, for the interesting refutes the accepted assumptions of the common sense world.

The interesting characteristic easiest to find is the dimension on which something's difference from the norm is extreme: most, least, highest, lowest, heaviest, lightest, etc.

Unlike ordinary thinking that regards change between positive and negative extremes as progressive and incremental, dialectical thinking regards these extremes as more similar to each other than either is to their midpoint.

Brilliant chess sacrifices deny the common sense expectation that relative power increases or decreases linearly by showing that it may change curvilinearly: the sacrifice produces a short-term loss (of material) that brings about a long-term gain (of position). (Likewise the best chess problems are solved by the "worst" moves: those that at first appear only to weaken position.)

Inspired musical performances first set up a basic pattern, then modify it increasingly but without breaking it melodically or harmonically—until the performer's ability to sustain the resultant strain seems to surpass the very limits of ordinary human endurance.

Many endeavors attempt to make some relationship more efficient or effective. When everyone else is working toward this objective by trying to modify one side of the relationship, the clever suggest modifying the other. If the objective is to make an engine burn gasoline more efficiently, unlike those trying to improve the gas, the clever suggest improving the engine. If the objective is an effective foreign policy, unlike those trying to find the best means to accomplish it, the clever suggest lowering the foreign policy goal to make it more attainable.

Rather than regard people as moving through a stationary environment, the insightful regard the environment as moving through stationary people (at least mentally).

A provocative perception shifts focus on a phenomenon from its central to its peripheral aspects. The prosaic see someone waving a hand. The perceptive see "armpit display."

Ingenious: The ability to articulate one of the antitheses to a traditional thesis. Often attributed to the social theorists who shifted their audience's conception of the principal agency of social life from human to nonhuman: to the economy (Marx), to the society (Durkheim), to the culture (Simmel).

The Dialectic of Intellectual History: An idea becomes interesting only in relation to the baseline of another, opposite, idea. Freudianism, for instance, became interesting only against the background of rationalism. If rationalism were not the dominant ideology in the first half of the twentieth century, most people would have found Freudianism irrelevant or obvious. Today Freudianism is less interesting because rationalism is less dominant (thanks, in part, to Freudianism).

Assumed ideas form the ground from which avant-garde ideas stand out. Profundities appear only against a background of platitudes.

The assumed ideas in every society not only reflect what its majority believe, but also determine the reaction against them of its avant-garde intellectuals. Imagine a society whose language encourages field rather than atomistic thinking (unlike our own but like those in Jorge Luis Borges' short story "*Tlon, Uqbar, Orbis Tertius*"). Most members of such a society would regard individuals as interconnected, whereas its avant-garde intellectuals would theorize that individuals are actually isolated from each other and from their environment—reversing the views of equivalent groups in our society.

Extendability

An idea applied to what is beyond the edge of awareness elicits the response: "So what?" An idea applied to what is too close to the center of attention elicits the response: "Of course!" But an idea that shifts what is at the edge of awareness to the center of attention elicits the response: "That's interesting!" Regardless of the content, the formal shift itself generates the intellectual excitement of recognition.

An interesting idea spreads out in waves. Its cognitive power is its ability to connect the discrete phenomena it encounters into a single theoretical system.

Mind surfing: catching hold of an idea and riding it through various elaborations until its potential to sustain interest is exhausted, dumping the surfer into an insipid commonplace.

An idea is born not clear and distinct but surrounded by a penumbra of spreading implications of fading clarity. Like this one.

To elaborate an idea means to specify its implications, to apply it to other members of the same set to which it was originally applied (e.g., black power—gay power—gray power). (Thus, idea shifts in logic resemble vowel shifts in linguistics.)

In *The Image of the City* Kevin Lynch produced a phenomenology of urban life that distinguished "path," node," "edge," "district," and "landmark." These concepts produce an equally insightful phenomenology of institutions by organizing members' experience of their daily rounds in, say, hospitals or universities.

An idea's implications are interesting when its applications are not obvious, when its further instances are not nearby members of the same set as its original instances.

The most important criterion for evaluating any social (and other) theory is its *fluff/substance ratio*. Fluff = its application to obvious instances. Substance = its application to nonobvious instances (in the relevant set).

The fundamental secret behind intellectual and practical life, the cognitive process that creates the most insightful thoughts and effective actions, is *analogy*.

Those who currently regard the world as chaotic will be more interested in discovering analogies between its many features that seem unrelated than in discriminating differences between its fewer features that seem similar.

The similarity of their body parts (e.g. arms, legs) originally motivated human beings to look for the analog aspects of the world, which has led them to develop language and the humanities. But the symmetry of their body parts (e.g. left, right) also motivated them to look for its binary aspects, which has led them to develop mathematics and the sciences. Different ways of relating the parts of the body, then, have produced divergent ways of thinking about the world.

As binary or digital thinking becomes more prevalent, analog thinking will become more valued—at least among the intelligentsia who will realize how digital thinking impoverishes the human psyche by extending consciousness in only one of its potential directions.

Reorganization

As researchers continue to subdivide the world, theorists can no longer comprehend the world directly by interrelating its components, but only indirectly by first grouping them into categories and then interrelating these categories: the cognitive equivalent of representative government.

Pluralists would not bother to point out the complexity of the world unless they assumed that most people oversimplify it. Monists would not bother to reduce the world to one basic factor unless they assumed that most people's view of the world is overly complex.

Pluralists reinforce the distinction between their categories that monists undermine. Pluralists argue that each category is irreducible to the other(s) because it operates according to different rules (e.g. Descartes: mind-body; Newton: metaphysics-science; Kant: faith-reason). Monists argue that all the other categories are merely epiphenomena of one prime category whose rules override theirs (e.g. Marx: economics; Nietzsche: power; Freud: sex).

Pluralism is defensive; monism offensive. Pluralists help their followers wall off established areas of research, allowing them to elaborate one intellectual category without worrying about attacks on it from adherents of another. Thus, Newton fortified science against religious refutations and Kant fortified theology against rational refutations. Monists, like Marx and Freud, help their followers to extend their approach aggressively into new areas of research, allowing them to reconceptualize in terms of their novel thesis topics that had seemed unsuitable for it.

Between two seemingly unrelated phenomena, a *pun* reveals a linguistic relation that is obvious and trivial whereas a *profundity* reveals an empirical relation that is subtle and important. Is this a pun or a profundity?

If an "explanation" is a description of the less familiar in terms of the more familiar, and if the "interesting" is the contradiction between the apparent and the real, then an *interesting explanation*—which describes a less familiar phenomenon in terms of a more familiar model when the connotations (secondary characteristics) of phenomenon and model are contradictory—is simultaneously synthetic and analytic, integrating and differentiating. It is interesting to explain intimate relationships in terms of an automobile model because it implies that their seemingly human processes are "really" mechanical.

Hegel's dialectic from the point of view of the Synthesis: *The Synthesis itself*, looking backwards, *creates the Thesis and Antithesis from which it was born.* Although any Thesis has many Antitheses, in retrospect, only one can be the parent of a particular Synthesis.

Vertically synthetic social science theories are especially provocative. Based on the Gnostic thought model, they connect the most spiritual and the most earthly, the greatest good and the worst evil.

Ideal Synthesis: Simmel looked for the spiritual in the earthly, finding metaphysical principles in seemingly trivial pot handles, whereas Goffman looked for the earthly in the spiritual, finding the fabrication behind the sincere. It is this dialectic between highest and lowest, and not that between mere opposites, that also accounts for the power and appeal of Freud's work (which connects the highest cultural achievements with the lowest, most disparaged biological urge) and Marx's work (which connects the highest hope for a utopian social organization with the lowest, most disdained social class).

Moral Synthesis: Simmel connected values in the upward "appreciative" direction, finding good in the seeming evil (e.g. discovering the positive functions of social conflict). Goffman connected them in the downward "critical" direction, finding evil in the seeming good (e.g.

discovering concentration camps in mental hospitals). Along with Marx and Freud, Nietzsche connected them in both directions, degrading what their society regarded as good (e.g. Christianity is motivated by "ressentiment"), elevating what their society regarded as evil (e.g. "the will to power is the will to life").

There is a fine line between the interesting, which contradicts a widely held cognitive assumption, and the outrageous, which contravenes a strongly held moral conviction. Any social thinker who crosses this line should do so deliberately.

Reflexivity

Erving Goffman begins his book *Frame Analysis* by discussing Prefaces, comments on Prefaces, comments on comments on Prefaces, etc. An infinitely reflexive algorithm like this one can make a theory compelling, for its momentum entices readers to follow it out while its complexity retards their actually doing so.

Marijuana users believe their thoughts are "profound" because each thought seems to have more implications than they can work out. For instance, marijuana can tempt its users to reiterate the reflexivity of metaphysical meditations, motivating the search for ever more inclusive answers:
  Why am I saying this?
  Why am I saying "Why am I saying this?"?
  Why am I saying "Why am I saying 'Why am I saying this?'?"? etc.

Reflexivity elaborates a theory up logical levels.

Reflexivity is the last elaboration of a thought system, designed to make it seem self-contained and therefore "complete." Hegel tried to distinguish his thought system from others by applying its thesis to itself. By describing the historical path of humanity's increasing self-consciousness, Hegel's own thought system becomes its final stage, for—at last!— consciousness has become aware of itself.

Theorists, like Hegel, who apply reflexivity to their own theories make them appear more profound, absolutized through self-affirmation. But theorists, like Mannheim, who apply reflexivity to the theories of other theorists make them appear less profound, relativized through self-denial. "So's yourself!" is the most effective way to parry a theory that tries to undermine others by relativizing them.

If the general principle of sociology is true (if all phenomena, including knowledge, are socially determined), then it does not matter which of sociology's competing intellectual paradigms is theoretically correct, for each would be accepted or rejected for nonlogical (i.e. sociological) reasons.

Ethnomethodology suffers the same reflexivity problem as the sociology of knowledge. Ethnomethodologists, who contend that "'what really is' is only what people attend to" must themselves attend to aspects of the world that are there only because ethnomethodologists attend to them. Ethnomethodology should include an ethnomethodology of ethnomethodology.

Those who lose interest in reflexivity, whose insoluble cycles rapidly become tiresome, can renew their interest with *meta*reflexivity, an infinite regression of reflections on reflexivity itself, etc.

Ambiguity

An ambiguous thought system consists of several contradictory gestalts.

An unequivocal thought system does not give its explicators enough to do. They can add value to their interpretations only by pointing out ambiguities in seemingly clear thought systems or clarifying seemingly ambiguous ones. Consequently, theorists who develop new thought systems have a duty to their disciples to contradict themselves occasionally.

The internal contradictions of a thought system affect its intellectual reception. Its audience will regard the idea system as profound if synthesizing its contradictions seems possible but not obvious, as absurd if synthesizing them seems impossible.

Ambiguity, which blurs differences, is midway between congruity, which denies them, and incongruity, which affirms them. If supporters try to show the coherence of a thought system by minimizing its ambiguities, critics try to show its incoherence by emphasizing them.

Interpreters can enhance the reputation of their favorite theorist by increasing his or her ambiguities as well as decreasing them: Those who presume that Theorist A believed X have criticized him for not considering Not-X; but in fact Theorist A also believed Not-X, although he did not emphasize it. Critics have presumed that Hegel believed the Spirit developed only in ideas, but he actually believed it developed in both ideas and reality, although he wrote about the latter less.

An ambiguous theory is more likely to catch on than an unambiguous theory. Ambiguity not only gives a theory's adherents the psychological "joy" of clarifying it for themselves, but as each interpreter argues for his or her interpretation of what the theorist must have really meant, their conflict also creates the social "buzz" that attracts the attention of a wider audience.

Sociability

Sociologists of knowledge should reorient their field from studying groups that possess the end products of intellect to studying the processes—ideological and sociological—by which these groups acquire them.

Successful intellectual movements establish a social base that conveys refinements of their original ideas to current and potential members. One person's novel ideas about a topic remain idiosyncratic and capricious until picked up by a group. The group expands their limited appeal internally by generalizing and systematizing them from the combined viewpoints of its members, and externally by simplifying and segmenting them for translation to different audiences.

Truth alone is not enough to make a theory influential. Theories that flourish must have a *reproductive advantage*, not only intellectually but socially. They must be interesting enough for continued cognitive appeal (providing adherents with intellectual resources for reconceptualizing ever new topics), and practical enough for sustained status advancement (providing adherents with social resources for publications, jobs, and students).

Is the cognitive power of an idea system stronger than the social competence of those who believe in it? Are potential adherents to the idea system more attracted by its intellectual ability to explain phenomena or by the charm of its believers? The relative power of cognitive and social factors on the viability of ideas becomes apparent only when they get out of phase, when the ideas of low status groups are appealing and the ideas of high status groups are appalling.

The internal contradictions of an idea system affect its social reception. An idea system (like that of Marx, Durkheim, Weber, Simmel, Freud, or Parsons in the social sciences) will become "classic" if it appeals to different groups, each latching onto an interpretation derived from one of its contradictory gestalts.

Thought systems become popular by speaking to multiple audiences: Shakespeare and Freud spoke to different age groups by dealing with problems of the young and the old. The Bible and Marx spoke to different educational strata by communicating on several levels: (*a*) slogans for the uneducated; (*b*) ideas for undergraduates; (*c*) complexities for scholars (whose raison d'être is disentangling intermixed thought models).

All great writers (e.g. Plato, Shakespeare, Marx, Nietzsche, Freud) share a common characteristic: their ideas can be corrupted. A world view can be corrupted only if it is dynamically ambiguous, consisting of several partially overlapping models. Each generation focuses on the model that resonates with its social conditions, which the next generation, responding to new social conditions, interprets as a corruption of the author's original intent.

Transiency

Intellectual Curse: "May you waste your life elaborating a dying paradigm!"

It is important to study not only the creation of theories but also their decline and death. "The Last Years of Talcott Parsons' Sociology" would be a particularly interesting case study of late twentieth century intellectual history.

The Geriatrics of Intellectual Life: Interpretations of a phenomenon increasingly take on lives of their own—if it is more than it seems, the "more" increasingly separates from the "seems"—until some maverick recalls the original experience of the phenomenon by skimming off its interpretive overlay.

It is poignant to watch an interesting idea die before its time, before its set of implications has been filled in. Although only a subset of its implications, the analogies that clarify and enliven a well-loved thesis can lose their meaning for students as the grounds of their metaphors and similes historically recede. (Comparisons to commodities and technologies become unintelligible rapidly, comparisons to nature more slowly.) No matter how fresh and insightful the analogy seems at first, those who compare a psychological or social process to DOS or a VCR will discover that, in the not-too-distant future, few still understand what they were talking about.

The fruitfulness of a theory, its potential for many surprisingly appropriate applications, declines the farther or more frequently its concepts are extended from their paradigm, for its application to new topics will eventually become either nebulous or obvious—which even poisons the fruit of its original application retrospectively. The theories of Marx, Freud, and Parsons provide "paradigmatic" examples of *this* theory.

The same recentering that allows a fresh point of view to solve a problem not only can create new ones but can reopen old ones that the previous perspective had solved. The solution to the immediate problem may be dazzling enough to obscure these other problems, but not forever.

In the history of intellectual schools, the vital strengths of the first generation innovators become the mechanical weaknesses of the second generation imitators.

When a school's second generation elaborates its founder's theories too greatly, its third generation is more likely to adopt a new theory than to master all the baroque elaborations of the old one. Thus, the decline of Parsonianism in the 1960's and 1970's, and Positivism in the 1980's and 1990's. But if enough time has elapsed to forget the second generation's elaborations, the theory may again become attractive. Thus the resurrection of Marxism, seemingly dead of hypertrophy in the 1930's, in the 1960's and 1970's.

Cellular aging provides a model for ideological decline: (*a*) a great theorist enunciates a theory, (*b*) the theorist's direct disciples misunderstand a small percentage of the theory, (*c*) as the theory is transmitted over several generations, misunderstandings accumulate, (*d*) the increasingly misunderstood theory finally reaches a point where it appears—or can easily be made to look—ridiculous, inducing the last receiving generation to break away from it.

The cognitive power of an idea can be undermined by the social incompetence of those who disseminate it. Reason may still be more interesting than Unreason but it now has less charismatic advocates.

Relativism is the AIDS of ideology, weakening the ability of an idea system to protect itself from infection by other ideologies. Relativism lowers the self-confidence of those who believe in an ideology by enticing them to take counter ideologies seriously.

The delegitimizing power of Relativism is overrated, for it is self-denying. Ideas seem relative only from one point of view, which by definition has no more claim to truth than any other point of view.

It is better for a theory to be no longer interesting than never to have been interesting at all; for having once possessed interesting characteristics, a theory retains the potential to be revitalized.

Someone should start a flea market of ideas: where people with esoteric and nostalgic tastes could browse among quaint, old, worn, but still serviceable thoughts to find those that could be made interesting again with just a little tinkering and polishing.

> Visit the *Annual Reviews home page* at
> http://www.AnnualReviews.org.

Literature Cited

Auden WH, Kronenberger L, eds. 1996. *The Viking Book of Quotations: A Personal Selection.* New York: Viking

Bartlett J, ed. 1980. *Familiar Quotations.* New York: Little Brown. 15th ed.

Bartlett J, ed. 1995. *Familiar Quotations.* New York: Time Warner Electronic Publ. 16th ed.

Bacon F. 1996. *The Advancement of Learning.* In *Francis Bacon: A Critical Edition,* ed. B Vickers. London: Oxford Univ. Press

Cioran E. 1992. *Anathemas and Admirations.* Trans. R Howard. London: Quartet Books

Davis MS. 1971. That's Interesting! Towards a phenomenology of sociology and a sociology of phenomenology. *Philos. Soc. Sci.* 1(4):309–44

Davis MS. 1993. *What's So Funny? The Comic Conception of Culture and Society.* Chicago: Univ. Chicago Press

Ehrlich E, DeBruehl M, eds. 1996. *International Thesaurus of Quotations.* New York: HarperCollins

Gross J, ed. 1962. *The Oxford Book of Aphorisms.* New York: Oxford Univ.

Hyman R, ed. 1962. *The Quotation Dictionary.* New York: Collier Books

La Rochefoucauld F. 1959 (1665). *Maxims.* Trans. L Kronenberger. New York: Vintage

La Rochefoucauld F. 1959. *Maxims.* Trans L. Tancock. New York: Penguin

Nietzsche F. 1977 (1879). *Assorted Opinions and Maxims.* Trans. R Hollingdale. In *The Nietzsche Reader,* ed. R Hollingdale. New York: Penguin

Oxford 1981. *The Concise Oxford Dictionary of Quotations.* New York: Oxford Univ. Press

Pascal B. 1966 (1670). *Pensées.* Trans. A Krailsheimer. New York: Penguin

Pascal B. 1958. *Pensées.* Trans. W Trotter. New York: Dutton

Schopenhauer A. 1970 (1851). *Essays and Aphorisms.* Trans. R Hollingdale. New York: Penguin

Annu. Rev. Sociol. 1999. 25:271–305

THE DARK SIDE OF ORGANIZATIONS: Mistake, Misconduct, and Disaster

Diane Vaughan

Department of Sociology, Boston College, Chestnut Hill, Massachusetts 02167;
e-mail: vaughand@bc.edu

KEY WORDS: analogical theorizing, cognition, culture, deviance, rational choice

ABSTRACT

In keeping with traditional sociological concerns about order and disorder, this essay addresses the dark side of organizations. To build a theoretical basis for the dark side as an integrated field of study, I review four literatures in order to make core ideas of each available to specialists in the others. Using a Simmelian-based case comparison method of analogical theorizing, I first consider sociological constructs that identify both the generic social form and the generic origin of routine nonconformity: how things go wrong in socially organized settings. Then I examine three types of routine nonconformity with adverse outcomes that harm the public: mistake, misconduct, and disaster produced in and by organizations. Searching for analogies and differences, I find that in common, routine nonconformity, mistake, misconduct, and disaster are systematically produced by the interconnection between environment, organizations, cognition, and choice. These patterns amplify what is known about social structure and have implications for theory, research, and policy.

INTRODUCTION

Weber warned that a society dominated by organizations imbued with legal-rational authority would suffer negative consequences. Tracing that historic transformation, Coleman (1974) affirmed Weberian pessimism. He observed

271

0360-0572/99/0815-0271$08.00

that this change altered social relations: Individuals not only interacted with individuals as before, they also interacted with organizations, and organizations interacted with other organizations. Coleman's primary insight was that this structural transformation produced both perceived and real loss of power for individuals. But the rise of formal organizations also wrought new possibilities for adverse societal consequences as a result of mistake, misconduct, and disaster. Surprisingly, these harmful actions and the extensive social costs to the public—the dark side of organizations—are not claimed as central to the domain of sociologists who define their specialization as organizations, occupations, and work, although prima facie, they would appear to fall within it. Organizational sociologists have affirmed that formal organizations can deviate from the rationalist expectations of the Weberian model; also, the pathologies that harm members are part of mainstream organization theory. But only recently have textbooks included harmful outcomes and organizational pathologies that adversely affect the public (Perrow 1986, Hall 1996, Scott 1998), and collections addressed failure, crime, and deviance in and by organizations (Anheier 1998, Bamberger & Sonnenstuhl 1998, Hodson & Jensen 1999).

Ironically, many organizational sociologists have been working on the dark side for a long time, as this essay shows. Moreover, scholars in medical sociology, deviance and social control, and the sociology of science, technology, and risk have studied mistake, misconduct, and disaster produced in and by organizations, as have scholars in other disciplines. The irony here is that we learn much about how things go wrong, but absent the tools of organization theory, the full set of socially organized circumstances that produce these harmful outcomes remains obscure. Specialization within and between disciplines segregates knowledge, with four consequences. First, the tensions and affinities in relevant work are not visible, theoretical matters for debate have not been identified, and the dialogue essential to intellectual development is absent. Second, both the social origins and cumulative significance of harmful organizational outcomes are masked. Third, the sociological basis for policy implications—for organizations, the public, and agents of social control—remains underdeveloped. Finally, a broader theoretical issue is at stake. This topic moves us away from rational choice assumptions about means-ends oriented social action toward explanations of socially patterned variations from that model.

A substantial body of scholarship exists, but the dark side of organizations is not an integrated field. The purpose of this essay is to legitimate it as a field of study, bridging disciplinary boundaries by reviewing four literatures in order to make core ideas of each available to specialists in the others. Much has been written about improving and/or regulating organizations to reduce the possibility of harmful outcomes, but unmasking causal structures and processes is the focus here. I begin by searching the sociological literature for general principles—theories and concepts—that help explain both the social form and generic origin of routine nonconformity: how things go wrong in socially organized settings. Then I review the literatures on mistake, misconduct, and disaster, three types of routine nonconformity with adverse outcomes that harm the public. Using a Simmelian-based case comparison method of analogical theorizing that legitimates theory building from comparing similar phenomena occurring in different social settings (Simmel 1950; Vaughan 1992, 1999a), I identify analogies and differences across these three types to show where progress has been made, assess the adequacy of this work, and speculate about future directions.

ROUTINE NONCONFORMITY: THE SYSTEMATIC PRODUCTION OF ORGANIZATIONAL DEVIANCE

Merton's (1936, 1940, 1968) thinking is the foundation of any consideration of the dark side of organizations. He observed that any system of action inevitably generates secondary consequences that run counter to its objectives. Unanticipated consequences of purposive social action can be differentiated into consequences to the actor(s) and consequences to others that are mediated through social structure, culture, and civilization (1936:895). Actors can be individuals or organizations. His point is that outcomes can be unexpected; the consequences may be either optimal or suboptimal. Our primary concern is unanticipated suboptimal outcomes.

A conceptual language that helps organize the literature does not exist, so the first step is to invent a conceptual definition (tentative and subject to later revision) that helps us consider the form and origin of unanticipated suboptimal outcomes. Formal organizations are designed to produce means-ends oriented social action by formal structures and processes intended to assure certainty, conformity, and goal attainment. Therefore, I will define *an event, activity, or circumstance, occurring in and/or produced by a formal organization, that deviates from both formal design goals and normative standards or expectations, either in the fact of its occurrence or in its consequences, and produces a suboptimal outcome* as organizational deviance. This conceptual definition is sufficiently broad to include conforming behavior by individual members as well as deviant behavior by individual members. Therefore, it encompasses mistake, misconduct, and disaster, one differing from the other not in its general fit with this definition but in its particulars: the normative standards or expectations violated (internal rules; legal mandates; social expectations), the categories of the public harmed, the extent of harmful social consequences, the social group whose expectations are violated, and/or the response of some public to the incident.

To define organizational deviance is not to explain it, however, and we are concerned with both form and origin. To the sociologically uninitiated, the language and personal experience of mistake might suggest that some types of organizational deviance result from coincidence, synchronicity, or chance. Sociologists have written about chance (Sumner [1906] 1940, Aubert 1965, Zelizer 1979, Meltzer & Mannis 1992, Paget 1993, Becker 1994, Mannis & Meltzer 1994, Tilly 1996), but we don't know how or to what extent chance explains social life. Alternatively, a breakdown in some normally well-functioning organizational system may occur, leading to unanticipated suboptimal outcomes. However, my search of the sociological literature for theories and concepts with explanatory power shows that whatever the role of chance or system breakdown, much organizational deviance is a routine by-product of the characteristics of the system itself. Organizational deviance, in its generic form, can be understood as routine nonconformity: a predictable and recurring product of all socially organized systems. In this essay, I use routine nonconformity and the systematic production of organizational deviance as interchangeable constructs, both denoting the causal origins of unanticipated negative outcomes.

This finding is consistent with Durkheim's thesis that the pathological is an inextricable part of every social system because the conditions of the normal are the preconditions of the pathological ([1895]1966:47–75). It follows that the same characteristics of a system that produce the bright side will regularly provoke the dark side from time to time. For example, the simple system that enables the owner to walk the dog (dog, owner, and the leash that joins them) ordinarily functions in an acceptable way, but this system produces an unanticipated suboptimal outcome when the dog is startled or surprised by some aspect of the environment, so backs up, gives chase, runs a zigzag, or circles so that the leash entangles the owner, causing an embarrassing stumble or fall. Only apparently simple, the dog-owner-leash system also encompasses the external environment and the interpretive capacities of dog and owner.

Analogically, the sociological theories and concepts assembled below assert that the system responsible for the production of routine nonconformity includes (*a*) the environment of organizations, (*b*) organization characteristics (structure, processes, tasks), and (*c*) the cognitive practices of individuals within them. Although these three levels of analysis are topically separated for this discussion, the literature shows that the social origin of routine nonconformity is in the connections between them. Carrying the analogy further, this review affirms that aspects of social organization typically associated with the bright side also are implicated in the dark side. Finally, it shows not nly that unanticipated suboptimal outcomes are a routine aspect of social life, but also that a conceptual apparatus already exists for studying them as socially organized phenomena. Not in all cases did the originators make the link between their theoretical constructs and routine nonconformity; I have drawn out the implications when doing so seemed theoretically appropriate.

Environment and Routine Nonconformity

Less is known about how the environment contributes to routine nonconformity than is known about the role of organization characteristics or cognition and choice. Traditionally in organization theory, the environment includes both the organization set (networks and other kinds of interorganizational relations), and the general conditions of the social context (political, technological, economic, legal, demographic, ecological, and cultural). It has been described as complex, aggressive and changing, turbulent, and as conveying jolts to unsuspecting organizations (Hall 1996). Environmental uncertainty is a concept frequently associated with routine nonconformity. Because organizations have difficulty accurately predicting circumstances that might affect their future activities, unexpected negative outcomes are possible even when initial conditions are diagnosed as optimal (see, e.g., Pressman & Wildavsky 1973, Wilson et al 1996, cf. Perrow & Guillen). Poorly understood social conditions even can lead to the failure of the organization to survive. Stinchcombe's "liabilities of newness" (1965:148) explain comparative death rates of new and old organizations: A higher proportion of new organizations are likely to fail than old. The liabilities of newness include the necessity of generating and learning new roles; costs in time, worry, conflict, and inefficiency; the absence of standard routines; the necessity of relying on social relations among strangers; the absence of stable ties with consumers. Although Stinchcombe used liabilities of newness to explain the development of populations of organizational forms, his concept also may apply to analogical circumstances at other levels of analysis, explaining why new programs, products, or services by individual organizations get into trouble, or even the problems of neophytes in organizations.

When power is used as the central explanatory concept, the focus shifts from organizations adapting to an uncertain environment to organizations actively defining, creating, and shaping it to suit their needs (Perrow 1986, 1991). Power struggles may result in cooptation and goal displacement, two classic concepts relevant to routine nonconformity (Selznick 1949). In order to survive, all organizations must compete for resources that help them meet goals. Often, these resources are scarce because their nature limits supply, because the activities of regulators, competitors, and suppliers make them scarce, or because of pre-existing commitments that keep organizations from getting the resources they want. In this competition, power is both a means and an end. Cooptation, the process of mediating threats to stability from the environment by absorbing new elements into the leadership or policy-determining structure of an organization, can result in compromise that deflects an organization from its original goals, so that outcomes deviate from normative standards or expectations.

To these concepts may be added two recent theories that locate causes of routine nonconformity in the environment: the new institutionalism (Powell & DiMaggio 1991) and the economic embeddedness perspective (Granovetter 1985). The new institutionalism explains that organizational forms and behaviors reflect prevailing values and beliefs that have become institutionalized. Cultural rules constitute actors (states, organizations, professions, and individuals), thus defining legitimate goals for them to pursue and affecting action and meaning at the local level. Legitimacy in the institutional realm can be not only a means to some end, but an end in itself. Because the generalized rules of the institutionalized environment are often inappropriate to specific situations, outcomes may be suboptimal and, to some extent, unpredictable. For Granovetter, attempts at purposive action are embedded in concrete, ongoing systems of social relations that affect them (1985:487). In contrast to the new institutionalism, agency is central to the embeddedness perspective. Both contingency and constraint explain economic action; thus, the embeddedness perspective is another tool for explaining the systematic production of organizational deviance. Granovetter points out the ironic link between the bright side and the dark side: The very concrete social relations and structures (or networks) in the environment that play a role in generating trust and discouraging wrongdoing in economic exchange also increase opportunities for deceit and deviance (1985:491–93).

Organization Characteristics and Routine Nonconformity

STRUCTURE Meyer & Rowan (1977) debunk the Weberian notion of efficient structure with their "myth and ceremony" argument. They show that organizations sometimes incorporate structures and practices that conform to institutionalized cultural beliefs in order to gain legitimacy, but these structures and practices may be inefficient or inappropriate to their tasks, so unexpected adverse outcomes result. Interestingly, the embeddedness perspective also applies intra-organizationally: The relational ties within organizations that generate trust and control malfeasance provide members with opportunities for deceit and misconduct (Granovetter 1985:499–502). In addition to these theories, concepts relating structure to routine nonconformity are plentiful. Complexity can make an organization unwieldy so that the upper levels cannot control the subunits. But centralization and formalization, instituted to keep things from going wrong, also have their dark side. High levels of centralization provide greater coordination but less flexibility; consistent policy that is inappropriate for specific situations; rapid decision-making in a crisis but cumbersome procedures that stall routine decisions (Staw et al 1981). Formalization can never cover all conditions; moreover, the number of written rules and procedures, their recency, perceived relevance, complexity, vagueness, and/or acceptability have known association with the systematic production of organizational deviance (Blau 1955, Vaughan 1982a, Oliver 1991, Elsbach & Sutton 1992).

"Structural secrecy" refers to the way division of labor, hierarchy, and specialization segregate knowledge about tasks and goals (Vaughan 1996). Structural secrecy implies that (*a*) information and knowledge will always be partial and incomplete, (*b*) the potential for things to go wrong increases when tasks or information cross internal boundaries, and (*c*) segregated knowledge minimizes the ability to detect and stave off activities that deviate from normative standards and expectations. Structural secrecy is reinforced as messages are transformed as they pass through the system, either by the deletion of information or by distortion (Guetzkow 1965). "Uncertainty absorption" occurs as an organization's technical language and classification schemes prevent some kinds of information from being communicated (March & Simon 1958:165). More information typically is viewed by people in organizations as the solution. Unfortunately, information can contribute to routine nonconformity both when there is too little and when there is too much (Feldman 1989). Confronted by these obstacles, decision-makers employ the "micropolitics of knowledge" (Lazega 1992). They sort through knowledge claims, determining the relevance of information by its social appropriateness as well as its technical accuracy. The result is an informal network that excludes certain knowledge claims, perpetuating partial understanding and the possibility of unexpected negative outcomes.

PROCESSES   Case studies hold memorable lessons about how organizational processes systematically produce unanticipated outcomes that deviate from formal design goals and normative standards. Either explicitly or implicitly, power as process, rather than structure, is a central concept in these cases. Classics show how informal organization contributes to routine nonconformity at both the top of the hierarchy (Dalton 1959) and the bottom (Roethlisberger & Dickson 1947, Burawoy 1979). A substantial literature connects routine decision making by organizational elites with unanticipated adverse outcomes for disadvantaged others. In his portrayal of how working class kids get working class jobs, Willis (1977) showed how education policy designed to enable students to do better after high school in fact promotes rebellion that perpetuates their working class condition. Most recently, Diamond (1992) revealed how the demands of corporate balance sheets and regulations distort the daily rituals of nursing homes for the elderly, eroding quality care, and Chambliss (1996) showed how the bureaucratic machinery of health care converts ethical decisions about hospital patient care to conflicts between occupational groups, with adverse consequences for patients.

Power struggles about subunit goals can produce unanticipated suboptimal outcomes when the most powerful subunit or coalition consistently triumphs, so some valuable policies are never enacted and some socially harmful policies may be (Fligstein 1990). Parallel processes that make sense in terms of different subunits pursuing their own goals may produce a joint outcome not intended by anyone and directly counter to the interests motivating individual actions (Giddens 1984:9–14). Finally, Mechanic (1962) located a cause of routine nonconformity in the power of lower participants to subvert the formal goals of organizations. But he, too, made a connection between the bright side and the dark side of organizations. The power of lower participants, surely a deviation from design expectations in most hierarchical organizations, may produce conformity and positive outcomes when that power is used to prevent organizational acts with harmful social consequences.

Learning, in the organizational behavior literature, is a process normally associated with the bright side. How organizations learn the wrong thing is understudied (March et al 1991), although not ignored. Crozier (1964) found that a bureaucratic system of organization cannot correct its errors because the feedback process does not function well. The response to error increases the rigidity of the organization, perpetuating the production of routine nonconformity. Verifying this ironic consequence, other scholars offer concepts that explain why attempts to put out a fire may inadvertently fan the flame. "Deviance amplification" (Weick 1979) is the result of causal loops typified by interdependence and feedback that makes any small deviation grow, with major unanticipated consequences. Schulman (1989) found that decisions to correct errors can spiral into "error-amplifying decision traps." A simple error is transformed into organizational pathology by resonate changes in organization structure: Efforts to correct and cover up involve more participants and more actions that increase both the amount of deviation and the possibility of discovery. These responses to error are systematic in origin and defeat the goals they are intended to achieve.

TASKS   Hughes (1951) was the first sociologist to look for theoretical principles associated with task-related errors in the workplace. For Hughes, occupation is the key concept. Arguing that unexpected negative outcomes are indigenous to the work process, he theorized about variations in their frequency and probability due to variation in amount of occupational skill, frequency of performance of the skill, and role in the workplace as a social system. Risk is also a central concept for Hughes: the distribution of risk among occupational roles and how systems delegate, spread, or concentrate both the risk of mistakes at work and the losses that result from them. His prescience about the theoretical importance of risk is borne out in the discussions of mistake, misconduct, and disaster that follow.

Tasks involve technologies. Understanding the link between tasks, technology, and routine nonconformity as a generic social form requires treating technology both as an object with a determinate physical essence that has consequences that are real and as an artifact embedded in social context within which it has meaning (Knorr Cetina 1997). Taking the former perspective, several richly detailed analyses of work-related technology have laid bare its vast unanticipated consequences (Turkle 1995, Tenner 1996, Rochlin 1997). Following Perrow (1984), a large body of work shows how the characteristics of the technology contribute to negative outcomes (see section on disaster.) Taking the latter perspective, scholars have examined scientific and technical practice using ethnomethodological and other interactionist perspectives to focus on the social construction/production of knowledge and meaning (Knorr Cetina 1981). For example, in her research on human/computer interaction in the design of intelligent machines, Suchman (1987) examined the discrepancy between "plans" as models for action and "situated actions" as actions taken in the context of particular, concrete circumstances.

Because of scientific and technical uncertainty, all judgments are made under conditions of imperfect knowledge, so that routine nonconformity is a normal by-product of techno-scientific work. Many concepts lend themselves to the study of the relationship between uncertainty, imperfect knowledge, and unanticipated adverse outcomes. "Interpretive flexibility" is the capacity for scientific or technological facts to be given different meanings by different actors (Pinch & Bijker 1984). "Tacit knowledge" refers to intuitive understandings about practice that cannot be articulated; it is acquired by the "core set"— those who carry out the task (Collins 1974, 1981). By definition, the core set cannot express essential understandings to others. Thus, decision-makers outside the core set will always have imperfect knowledge, which in turn may lead to unanticipated suboptimal outcomes. In conditions of uncertainty, actors convert disorder to order (Collins 1992). Despite these efforts, fundamental ambiguities remain, so that adverse outcomes are always a possibility. Wynne (1988) notes that normal technology is "unruly": Engineering typically occurs under conditions of ambiguity in unclear circumstances, with rules emerging from practice and experience rather than preceding it. "Representational technologies" are models, diagrams, records, and other artifacts that are means of making decisions in all kinds of technical work (Lynch & Woolgar 1988). These technologies stand in for and represent some incident, process, or object but are true only in the sense that they shape understanding of it, converting uncertainty to certainty. But the more general the formal representation, the more elements unique to a work situation are lost: the ad hoc strategies, workarounds, and local knowledge that keep organizations going (Star 1995).

Cognition, Choice, and Routine Nonconformity

Psychologists provide many insights that point to cognitive origins of unanticipated suboptimal outcomes (see Heimer 1988, Reason 1990, DiMaggio 1997). However, this discussion focuses on sociological constructs that demonstrate the influence of social context on decision processes, choice, and action. This work is abundant, theoretically rich, and at three levels of analysis. It begins to clarify the relationship between environment, organization, cognition, and routine nonconformity.

At the institutional level, structuration theory and cultural theory are explanatory tools that emphasize how aspects of the environment can shape cognitive limits to rationality. Giddens' structuration theory locates the origins of routine nonconformity in the gap between the known and understanding about its significance (1984:xxiii). He argues that this discrepancy will always have the potential to produce unanticipated consequences, which will feed back to promote social reproduction of institutionalized practices because of routinization: "Repetitive activities, located in one context of time and space, have regularized consequences, unintended by those who engage in those activities, in more or less 'distant' time-space contexts" (1984:14). Giddens leaves the details of this process to the imagination, but Tilly (1996) supplies an answer. Asserting that error is incessant in social interaction, Tilly explains that responses to error produce stable social structure and processes because they are drawn from historically accumulated cultural understandings and embedded social relations that modify, rather than contradict, what came before.

Other scholars have considered how institutionalized cultural understandings mediate between the environment and the cognitive practices of individuals. Cultural knowledge is instrumental in complexity reduction (Sackmann 1991), thereby shaping and narrowing understanding so that unexpected adverse outcomes are one possibility. How culture travels from the institutional level to "manifest in people's heads" remains a central theoretical and empirical dilemma (DiMaggio 1997:272). New institutionalists posit culture as a mediating link: Institutionalized cultural beliefs have a complexity reduction effect that determines what individuals will consider rational at a given moment (DiMaggio & Powell 1983, Zucker 1977). Another strand of theory takes for granted institutionalized cultural knowledge, instead trying to track the problem of culture and cognition. It shows how cultural knowledge contributes to unanticipated negative outcomes by enabling individuals to violate normative standards. Cultural understandings affect interpretive work, so that people may see their own conduct as conforming, even when the behavior in question is objectively deviant. One line of thought is that by drawing on largely unconscious cultural knowledge, individuals make the problematic nonproblematic by formulating a definition of the situation that makes sense of it in cultural terms, so that in their view their action is acceptable and non-deviant prior to an act (Stokes & Hewitt 1976, Zucker 1977, Morrill et al 1997, Vaughan 1996). Alternatively, individuals may justify organizational deviance in retrospect by constructing accounts that bring their actions into harmony with social expectations. The effect is to legitimate deviant actions. By drawing on cultural scripts, individual engagement in routine nonconformity can encompass violation of normative standards and expectations that are either internal or external to the organization.

At the organizational level of analysis, many classics have exposed cognitive limits to rationality. Barnard (1938) argued that organization elites set the premises of decision-making by setting up routines, so that internal activity is often the result of habit and routine-following rather than consideration of multiple options. Veblen's "trained incapacity," Merton's "bureaucratic personality," and Thompson's "bureaupathology" identified how bureaucratic systems can create extreme rule-mindedness that deflects individuals from actions that are most beneficial to the organization. March & Simon (1958) emphasized that the norm of rationality itself cannot be viewed as a set standard but must be seen rather as a guideline from which deviation is expected. They located systematic limits to rationality in the inability of organizations to provide adequate information for decisions and individual cognitive constraints that limit the ability to adequately assess the information at hand. Decision-making is typified by "bounded rationality" and "satisficing." Bounded rationality modifies rational choice theory; the "garbage can model" rejects it in favor of organizational anarchy (Cohen et al 1972). The metaphor of the garbage can reveals a decision-making process in which problems and solutions are loosely coupled, so that one problem may get transformed into a different one or may disappear due to inattention; solutions may arise that no one envisioned, or no solutions may appear at all. This perspective suggests that unexpected interactions and outcomes can occur in systems of varying complexity.

At the micro-level, theory in social psychology has relentlessly pursued the ambiguous bases of decision-making and its outcomes. Symbolic interactionism, in all its variations, contests the assumption of an objective reality in which "truth" and "error" can be reliably ascertained by individuals. It gives primacy to agency, interpretative work, spontaneous nonrational action, situated and emergent meanings, and the symbolic foundations of thought. The constraining qualities of the social world are influential, yet the emphasis on agency and meaning construction underscores the potential for unanticipated consequences as a normal product of the ongoing creation, negotiation, interpretation, and ordering of the social. Goffman, for example, specialized in exposing the micro-origins of routine nonconformity. He demonstrated that in

social interaction things are never as they seem because impression management and deception, intentional and unintentional, are integral aspects of social interaction. The role of social context as interpretive device and constraint
is exemplified by his concept of framing (1974), in which an observation, experience, or idea is selected for attention and linked to a more general form in
order to make sense of it, forming a condition for future action. Errors in
framing (1974:308–21) may result in what he calls "ordinary troubles," among
them actions that have unanticipated suboptimal outcomes (cf. Emerson &
Messinger 1977).

   Two theories combine aspects of symbolic interactionism to explain cognitive processes associated with routine nonconformity. Weick (1995) makes
sensemaking, loose coupling, organizing, and enactment central concepts. Because the actor's subjective understanding and the loose coupling between
information and action dominate interpretive processes, unanticipated suboptimal consequences are constant possibilities. For Weick, environment and
organization are enacted moment to moment as people perceive and select the
objects and activities on which sensemaking will be based. Misperception is a
function of the normal selectivity of the process; rationality is a definition of
the situation bestowed only in retrospect. Manning (1992) combines loose
coupling, dramaturgy, and semiotics to examine organizational communication. Because meanings cannot be separated from social structure and social
relations, communication consists of signs symbolically marking authority,
power, and differences. Communication is comprised of multiple realities
emanating from multiple organization roles, so paradoxes and contradictions
are common. Misunderstandings and incomplete knowledge are typical (Putnam 1986, Martin et al 1983, Boden 1994).

Summary   To legitimate the dark side of organizations as an integrated field
of study, we have searched the sociological literature for theories and concepts
that help explain, generically, how things go wrong in socially organized settings. This search is by no means complete, limited by the agenda to consider
mistake, misconduct, and disaster in these same pages. Also, because the goal
is to identify relevant causal mechanisms for the first time, the important
question of the variable relationship between the principles identified and the
frequency and probability of unexpected adverse outcomes is assumed but not
discussed. Nonetheless, three things are clear. First, numerous theories and
concepts exist that explain routine nonconformity as a generic phenomenon.
These can be used in research on mistake, misconduct, and disaster so that
similarities and differences can be identified and the development of general
theory about the dark side of organizations can begin across types. Second,
identifying patterns from an inductive analysis of this literature shows that
the social form of routine nonconformity includes aspects of environment, or-

ganization characteristics (structure, processes, tasks), and cognition/choice. Third, the theories and concepts found implicate the macro-micro connection in the systematic production of organizational deviance: Its origin is in the nested and dynamic interrelationship between environment, organization characteristics, cognition, and choice. Now we turn to the three types of routine nonconformity that have unanticipated consequences that harm the public. I use the levels of analysis and subcategories inductively derived from the search for general sociological principles to organize this discussion, looking for analogies and differences across the three types (Simmel 1950, Vaughan 1992, 1999a). As before, I concentrate on both social form and origin, presenting central themes in order to facilitate discourse across disciplinary boundaries.

MISTAKE, MISCONDUCT, AND DISASTER

Recall that organizational deviance was defined as an event, activity, or circumstance, occurring in and/or produced by a formal organization, that deviates from both formal organizational design goals and normative standards or expectations, either in the fact of its occurrence or in its consequences, and that produces an unanticipated suboptimal outcome. Because this definition could include conforming behavior by individual members as well as deviant behavior by individual members, it provides an heuristic device for considering mistake, misconduct, and disaster. However, shifting from routine nonconformity as a generic social form to these three types creates a new definitional difficulty. Mistake, misconduct, and disaster are socially defined in relation to the norms of some particular group. Whether an incident or activity producing an unexpected negative outcome is viewed as conforming or deviant, whether it is defined as mistake, misconduct, or disaster will vary by group. Also, it will vary by level of analysis: Intentional fudging at the individual level could be viewed as conformity at the group level, transformed into mistake at the organizational level and misconduct at the institutional level (S Zerilli 1998, personal communication). Further, mistake, misconduct, and disaster are defined only in retrospect when outcomes are known, and these understandings are historically contingent.

Emerson observed that instead of using criteria from outside the setting to examine mistake and error, sociologists should investigate the local notions of competent performance honored and used in particular social settings: how actors judge each others' decisions and formulate them as "mistakes" (RM Emerson, unpublished observations). Equally important is determining who has the right to say what a failure is (Hughes 1951), and how those understandings are produced and transformed into misconduct or disaster (Star & Gerson 1987). But indicative of a nascent field of study, this research has only begun.

Therefore, to preserve openness of meaning, I create broad conceptual definitions of mistake, misconduct, and disaster below, dividing the research into these types based on how scholars refer to their own work and a few common characteristics of the phenomena that are evident in the literature.

MISTAKE

The sociology of mistake is in its infancy. The few sociologists who have studied it have investigated mistake in nonroutine work in organizations when it has direct, tangible social harm: loss of life, injury, psychological consequences, property damage, and mistreatment by an agent of social control. For many, mistake was a small part of a multifaceted project. A point on which all agree is that mistake is systematically produced as a part of the social organization of work. However, organizations usually are a barely visible backdrop, their environments, structures, and processes often unnamed. Theory and the theoretical debates found in developed areas of study are absent. One common pursuit is grounded typologies that often go beyond description to explanation (Singer 1978, Bosk 1979, Belli & Schuman 1996). With the exception of Roth's (1991) helpful compendium of research and anecdote, no attempt has been made to integrate this work to build a sociology of mistake. Nonetheless, a solid basis is there.

For a definition of mistake sufficiently broad to organize this discussion, we use the definition of organizational deviance above, which stresses the violation of formal design goals and normative standards and expectations. Then, to distinguish mistake from misconduct and disaster, we further specify that definition to include acts of omission or commission by individuals or groups of individuals, acting in their organization roles, that produce unexpected adverse outcomes with a contained social cost: e.g., mistake in a hospital may harm an individual actor or small number of actors, with varying direct social cost to them. The definitional problem noted above immediately appears, for if mistakes are aggregated across all hospitals, their organizational-technical system origins and extensive harmful social consequences might well qualify as disasters.

Environment and Mistake

The most complex treatment of environment and mistake analyzes wrongful conviction in the criminal justice system. Huff et al (1996) first show the relation between institutionalized cultural beliefs and mistake, then how mistake is produced by structural conditions of the system. The other complex treatment is Freidson's (1970, 1975) analysis of how the various fragmented bodies that regulate medicine create differential performance standards. Thus, the regulatory environment, by its failure, becomes a structural origin of mistake. However, most research reduces environment to a single dimension: competition for scarce resources (income, profits, and funding). The workings of interorganizational power, politics, and conflicts of interest, associated with routine nonconformity in the last section, have not been studied.

Competitive pressures have been explored two ways. One is by analyzing some aspect of the competitive environment without showing how it affects mistake at the micro-level: e.g., Landau & Chisholm (1995) argue that norms of efficiency drive industries and organizations, not norms of effectiveness; Singer (1978) shows that errors are quasi-institutionalized because they are literally profitable for organizations to commit; Guillemin (1994) notes the rapid diffusion of untested hospital-based technologies in the medical market place during periods of institutional expansion. The second is to identify competition for scarce resources but instead analyze the micro-processes through which it materializes in the workplace: e.g., McKee & Black (1992) found economic concerns of hospitals caused cutbacks in staff, so that junior doctors made mistakes because of inadequate supervision; in building construction, deadlines and demands for productivity produce mistake (Reimer 1976); Guillemin & Holmstrom (1986) found the institutional goal of keeping beds filled was one factor in latent experiments in newborn intensive care units that went on without scientific protocol.

Organization Characteristics and Mistake

STRUCTURE   Little is known about the relationship between structure and mistake. Dwyer (1991) found that work site control by the dominant group (managers, individuals, unions) and the methods of control are related to the incidence of workplace mistakes, injuries, and death. The only other aspect of structure specifically linked to mistake is complexity (Roth 1991). In building construction, Reimer (1976) found that division of labor among subcontractors creates irreversible errors, so that buildings are constructed by an accumulation of blunders.

PROCESSES   Research shows more about the processes of power and hierarchy than its structure. Zerilli (1998) analyzed ceremonial confession as a form of institutionalized interaction, whereby professionals in organizations (priests, police, therapists, terrorists) have the official responsibility of bringing about the act of individual confession. The ritualistic tactics of confessional-making are such that they may elicit mistaken accounts from individuals, with misdiagnosis and harmful outcome the institutional response. Not so surprisingly, since mistakes-in-progress are elusive, more is known about how the powerful respond to mistake than to the patterns of interaction that produce it. Light (1972) showed that the explicit therapeutic failure and possible error inherent in patient suicide threatened psychiatrists, who institutionalized a review process that preserved the professional project and protected the practitioner from blame. Repeatedly, research shows how organizational hierarchies suppress mistakes and deny responsibility, protecting the status of profession, organization, and individuals (Millman 1977, Bosk 1979, Jackall 1988, Leibel 1991, Edmondson 1996, Rosenthal et al 1999). This research reveals formal and informal patterns that are institutionalized, throwing workplace culture into broad relief, yet its richness is still to be mined, for culture is not named nor are the theoretical implications drawn out.

TASKS   The greatest concentration of research on mistake is fine-grained ethnographic analysis of tasks. History matters: Tasks that are structurally and temporally separate can generate mistake through accumulation. Contemplating the string of medical misdiagnoses that later took her life, Paget (1993) noted how action unfolds in time, so that one mistake is compounded by others, until harm is irreversible. Hughes' (1951) prescience about mistake and risk as indigenous to the task are verified in this empirical work. Uncertainty, risk, and task complexity were first noted by Fox (1959); Paget (1988:58) called medical work "error-ridden activity" because it is inexact, uncertain, and practiced on the human body; Huff et al (1996) locate risk and uncertainty in the complexity of offense and offender; Reimer (1976) links uncertainty to the transitional nature of the building construction work site. How uncertainty, risk, and task complexity vary and how they intersect with cognition and mistake remain to be studied.

Cognition, Choice, and Mistake

Traditionally, cognition and mistake are the turf of cognitive psychologists (see Rasmussen 1986, Reason 1990), but sociologists have begun a cognitive sociology of mistake. Three lines of inquiry have developed. The first explores processes that "neutralize" and "normalize" certain kinds of mistake, so that people in the workplace see them as routine and nonremarkable (Freidson 1975, Millman 1977, Bosk 1979). The second examines the construction of accounts by professionals when confronted with possible evidence of their own error (Stelling & Bucher 1973, Mulkay & Gilbert 1982, Mizrahi 1984). The third illuminates how social and cultural conditions affect cognition and choice, resulting in professional misdiagnosis. For example, social worker error in diagnosing abused children was explained by high observation costs, gradual accumulation of information, and lack of time to review and revise as more information became available (Munro 1996). Research using ethnomethodology and labeling theory exposes how institutionalized professional cultural beliefs affect cognition and mistake: Rosenhan's (1973) research admitting sane pseudo-patients into mental hospitals undetected; Pfohl's (1978) analysis of official reviews of inmates in institutions for the criminally insane by teams of mental health professionals; Sudnow's (1965) "normal crimes," a study of basic conceptual equipment with which judges, lawyers, police, and probation workers organize their daily work.

Summary   The strength of this work lies in its indication of common patterns within each level of analysis, regardless of size, complexity, task, or kind of organization. These patterns begin to suggest the social origin and form of mistake. The most valuable contribution to the dark side of organizations is the field research that shows responses to mistakes as they are occurring in the work setting: These insights into ethnocognition and organizational deviance have not been possible in research on misconduct and disaster. The possibilities for future research and theorizing are unlimited. Environment, organization characteristics, and cognition and choice all need study. Of the sociological theories and concepts described in the previous section that explain routine nonconformity, only a few have been tapped and none systematically. We need to know more about the human/technology interface and mistake, and about how the individual experience of mistake and emotion affects the propensity for subsequent mistakes. Also, research has been imbalanced. Sociologists have focused on mistakes that directly harm individuals or property, omitting mistakes that are just as relentless but more mundane: mistakes in reports, the lead news story, hiring, the pornographic novel stitched into the binding of an academic monograph, products that cannot be assembled or fail and have to be recalled. Employees and organizations devote enormous resources to prevent incidents of routine nonconformity from being publicly defined as mistake. This, too, is worthy of research: The social organization of clean-up work also has social costs that eventually are paid by the public.

MISCONDUCT

In contrast to mistake, the sociology of misconduct in and by organizations is a mature, thriving enterprise. But deeper inquiry has produced harder questions. Key conceptual debates remain unsettled: Is it "white-collar crime," "occupational crime," "corporate crime," "abuse of power," "organizational deviance," or "abuse of trust"? The result is research in many conceptual traditions. But a mechanism for coherence has emerged. Despite differences, many offenses originate in formal and complex organizations. Beginning in the mid-1960s, scholars trained in the sociology of organizations and of deviance and social control began combining the two, creating theories that pointedly gave explanatory primacy to the organizational locus of wrongdoing. This development is institutionalized, evident in (*a*) the systematic inclusion of organizations in causal theories, (b) the shifting premises of theoretical debate (initially, the relationship between individual actors and organizational actors; most recently, the relative explanatory power of rational choice theory and organization theory), (c) regular discussion of organizations in textbooks, articles, and chapters, and (d) research using ever more sophisticated organizational analysis and theory.

For a definition of organizational misconduct sufficiently broad to organize this review, we use the definition of organizational deviance above. To distinguish misconduct from mistake and disaster, we further specify that definition to include acts of omission or commission by individuals or groups of individuals acting in their organizational roles who violate internal rules, laws, or administrative regulations on behalf of organization goals. The extent of adverse consequences and harm to the public will vary with the act, so social cost may be contained or diffused. As with mistake, when incidents are aggregated, harm is extensive and social cost is high. Because deviation from both formal design goals and normative standards or expectations is a requisite of routine nonconformity, organized crime is excluded from this discussion.

Environment and Misconduct

The competitive and regulatory environments have received extensive research scrutiny. The role of the regulatory environment in the social origin of misconduct is uncontested: Although effective in specific cases, sources of regulatory failure are socially organized and systematic across cases, thereby undermining the efficacy of deterrence. Power enters into this equation in the ability of regulated organizations to affect both the structure of the regulatory environment and specific regulatory outcomes. Further, powerful offenders can resist grass roots efforts at social control because they construct public accounts that legitimate their actions and because individuals and organizations are dependent upon them for goods and services (see Edelman & Suchman 1997). The relationship between the competitive environment and organizational misconduct is equally well established but still puzzling. The most frequent hypothesis, derived from Mertonian strain theory ([1938]1968), is that organizations with blocked access to opportunities for economic success will violate: Thus, marginal and failing firms will be more likely to offend, a prediction consistent with Merton's about the working class and street crime but inconsistent with research on crimes of the powerful and the influence of power on the regulatory enterprise. Quantitative research on corporate violations separates environment into complex industry variables, market structure, and fluctuating economic conditions. The results are contradictory and weak (see Jamieson 1994, Geis & Salinger 1998).

However, qualitative research suggests this use of the Mertonian hypothesis is overly restrictive. Power—powerful organization offenders, contests of power—is as essential to understanding the competitive environment as it is to comprehending regulatory failure (Snider & Pearce 1995, Michalowski & Kramer 1987). Analysis of misconduct by nonprofits, governments, and business shows (a) competition not just for profits and economic success but for many kinds of scarce resources essential to survival, suggesting that quantitative studies wrongly narrow competitive pressures to economic success and profits; and (b) misconduct not limited to marginal and failing organizations (e.g., Grabowsky 1989, Fleischer et al 1992, LaFollette 1992, Simon 1994, Zuckerman 1977). These findings call into question the data sources for quantitative research: typically, agency enforcement actions on corporations. Lacking power, marginal or failing business firms simply may be more likely to get caught. This possibility is reinforced by Delaney (1992), who debunks firm financial figures as the product of strategies and power relations, not indicators of firm health. Qualitative research suggests revising the Mertonian hypothesis as follows: Given the universality of competitive pressures, all organizations may be structurally induced to violation, regardless of ranking in the organizational stratification system. The powerful may compete for scarce resources to sustain rank, others may compete for upward mobility, and still others to keep from losing ground or dropping out of the competition altogether.

Culture is an aspect of the environment scholars hold important. Often referred to as normative environment, its role in the social origin of organizational misconduct has been located in many places: in normative ambiguity for white-collar offenses (Aubert 1952), culturally approved success goals and anomie (Merton [1938]1968), a tiered system of meaning in an industry (Denzin 1977), cultures of risk taking (Black et al 1995), the culture of capitalism (Finney & Lesieur 1982), occupational cultures (Green 1997), and industry cultures (Leonard & Weber 1970). However, the cultural environment typically is noted as important without precision in conceptual definition, its empirical referent, or its connection to the actions of organizations and their members. A new interest is network analysis linking organizations and actors in networks of collusion that subvert the legitimate economy (Barlow 1993, Baker & Faulkner 1993, Calavita et al 1997). This research builds upon theories of interorganizational relations, paving the way for future studies of power struggles and the political environment.

Organization Characteristics and Misconduct

Theorists uniformly hold that structures, processes, and tasks are opportunity structures for misconduct because they provide (a) normative support for misconduct, (b) the means for carrying out violations, and (c) concealment that minimizes detection and sanctioning.

STRUCTURE   Scholars have studied the role of formal structure in "crime co-ercive systems" and "crime facilitative systems" (Needleman & Needleman 1979); the diffusion of knowledge, misconduct, and responsibility (Stone 1975, Wheeler & Rothman 1982, Clinard 1983, Kram et al 1989); and varia-tion in subunit vulnerability (Frey 1994, Simpson & Koper 1997). Unexamined is complexity: centralization, decentralization, geographic dispersion, number of component parts, and layers of hierarchy and how they vary in relation to misconduct. Also, much scholarship affirms that an individual offender's posi-tion in a structure explicates the social organization of misconduct (e.g., Quinney 1963, Vaughan 1983, Daly 1989, Shapiro 1990, Shover & Bryant 1993). This latter research agenda, if pursued, promises insights that transcend types of organizations and types of violations.

PROCESSES   A central contribution has been scholarship establishing how the competitive, regulatory, and cultural environments translate into organiza-tional processes, leading individuals to engage in misconduct on behalf of or-ganization goals. Research shows how environmental strain materializes in performance pressures that affect individual actions and the development of internal culture that supports achieving the organization's goals illegitimately. Top administrators are responsible for performance pressures indirectly (by establishing out-of-reach goals or not providing sufficient resources necessary to attain goals) and directly (by actively conceiving and enacting violative behavior). Now, scholars are studying the impact of administrative decisions on misconduct in more detail: managerial succession, CEO background, de-centralized management, and product dominant strategies (Simpson & Koper 1997); downsizing (Friedrichs 1997); and escalating commitment (Ermann & Rabe 1995).

Traditionally, organization culture is treated unidimensionally: It provides normative support for wrongdoing. This view is sustained by Sutherland's (1949) learning theory, which explains that employees are socialized into membership in a group where the norms favor violation of internal rules, laws, or administrative regulations; ethnographies that show socialization and on-the-job training for techniques of rule violating behavior used to execute rou-tine tasks (e.g., Bensman & Gerver 1963, Vaz 1979, Punch 1985, Shulman 1997); and research showing that willingness to use illegitimate means on the organization's behalf is sealed by a reinforcing system of rewards and punish-ments. However, this unidimensional view of culture is challenged by theory that emphasizes cultural complexity and variation (Vaughan 1983, Coleman & Ramos 1998), and more dramatically, by ethnographies that show conflicting cultures due to differences in professions, rank, and informal cliques (Jackall 1988, Chambliss 1996, Morrill 1995).

TASKS   Cressey (1953) argued that the skills necessary to misconduct are simply the skills necessary to do the job in the first place, but only recently has the relationship between tasks and misconduct been studied. Friedrichs (1996) notes the conspicuous rise of "finance crime"—large-scale illegality that occurs in finance and financial institutions—and "technocrime"—use of new technologies such as computers, facsimile machines, electronic surveillance, and accounting technologies. The transformation of routine tasks by these technologies contributes to misconduct because they are employed in new, complex transaction systems that are difficult to monitor and control (Vaughan 1982b). Sociologists have investigated accounting tactics (Passas 1996), manipulation of markets and financial capitalism (Levi 1981, Abolafia 1996, Zey 1993), and espionage (Hagan 1997). Some are studying the diffusion of these innovations (Calavita et al 1997, Baker & Faulkner 1997).

Cognition, Choice, and Misconduct

Traditionally, decisions to violate have been explained by the amoral calculator hypothesis, a form of rational choice theory: Confronted with blocked access to legitimate means to organization goals, decision-makers will calculate the costs and benefits of using illegitimate means; if benefits outweigh the costs, actors will violate (Kagan & Scholtz 1984). Whereas in the sociology of mistake, the concepts of risk and uncertainty were associated with tasks, in organizational misconduct, they are located in cognition, decisions to violate, and the probable reaction of regulators. However, these concepts usually are not directly studied, disappearing into costs, benefits, and the probability of punishment. In what is possibly the most important new development, the rational choice assumptions behind the amoral calculator hypothesis are being examined within the context of social psychological and organization theory (Coleman 1987, Reed & Yeager 1996, Ermann & Rabe 1997, Lofquist 1997, Simpson 1998, Simpson et al 1998, Vaughan 1998). This research promises advances connecting institutions, organizations, and culture with interpretation, meaning, and individual action.

Summary   Research and theory suggest that, like mistake, the social form of organizational misconduct includes aspects of environment, organization characteristics (structure, processes, and tasks), and cognition and is systematically produced by these three in combination. Most significant for understanding the dark side of organizations is recent research integrating these three levels of analysis. This direction has potential. Behind the unsettled debates about the appropriate conceptual definition (occupational crime, organizational deviance, etc) is an unrecognized, covert debate about what the appropriate level of analysis is (Vaughan 1999b). The reason the definitional issue remains provocative and lively is that, as this review shows, all levels of analysis apply. The existence of this covert debate accentuates the legitimacy of each level of analysis, thus substantiating the importance of merging them. Moreover, the benefit of the disagreement is that each conceptual tradition has produced knowledge at all levels, ready to be integrated. Often, scholars have identified aspects of environment and organizations as "criminogenic," showing how aspects of environment, organization characteristics, and cognitive practice normally associated with the bright side of organizations are systematically related to the dark side. Although recent research has begun to inquire into variation, the central question still is: When do they produce conduct and when do they produce misconduct?

DISASTER

The study of disasters has deeper roots than its topicality suggests. Historically, interest lay in the impact of disaster and the organizational response; inquiry into the social origin examined human factors in accidents. Unnoticed in that array was prescient work locating the cause of accidents in power and the structural and cognitive limits embedded in organizations and technologies. Landau (1969) located the social origin in large, complex, and tightly ordered systems in which parts are interdependent such that the failure of a part can result in the failure of the system. Erikson (1976) showed the corporate power and cost/safety trade-offs behind the Buffalo Creek dam collapse. Turner (1976, 1978) analyzed 84 accidents and disasters across industries, finding that social, technical, and administrative arrangements systematically produced disasters. Then in 1984, Perrow's *Normal Accidents* and Short's "The Social Fabric at Risk" charged the intellectual community and changed the research agenda. The result is a body of work showing how institutions, organizations, technologies, and cognitive practices contribute to accidents and disasters.

This review encompasses disaster studies: research its authors identify as investigations into the origin of accidents and disasters. Disaster is a type of routine nonconformity that significantly departs from normative experience for a particular time and place. It is a physical, cultural, and emotional event incurring social loss, often possessing a dramatic quality that damages the fabric of social life. For an accident to be defined as a disaster, the accident would need to be large-scale, unusually costly, unusually public, unusually unexpected, or some combination (Turner & Pidgeon 1997:19). Mistake and misconduct often occur in the prehistory of accidents and disasters, the latter two distinguished from mistake and misconduct by the social cost and quality of surprise. To be sufficiently broad to encompass both accidents and disasters, we start with the previous definition of organizational deviance, further specifying it as organizational-technical systems failures that include acts of omission or commission by individuals or groups of individuals acting in their organization roles, with outcomes that either in the fact of their occurrence or consequences are unexpected, adverse, and of high social impact and cost regardless of number of lives and amount of property lost.

Environment and Disaster

Research firmly links the social origin to political, competitive, regulatory, and cultural environments. Sagan (1993, 1994) presents convincing evidence that power and politics contribute to accidents. Indeed, the history of technology is a history of conflicts of interest that resulted in suboptimal decisions about technology and technological products (Cowan 1983, Hughes 1983, MacKenzie 1990). Equally interesting is how the political environment permeates competitive, regulatory, and cultural environments. Competition and scarcity set the stage for accidents when they lead to cost/safety trade-offs, so safety tends to be the goal displaced. Quantitative research now is looking at producers' ability to afford safety, costs of regulation, and the safety record (Marcus et al 1993, Verma & Marcus 1995). The regulatory environment gets more attention from sociolegal scholars than disaster specialists, but both demonstrate that it contributes to accidents when subject to power-dependence relations that undermine (*a*) effective monitoring, investigating, and sanctioning of producers and users and (*b*) effective response to incidents, so they develop into accidents and disasters. Organizations producing and using risky technologies are both victims of political shifts in regulatory policy (Tompkins 1990) and powerful actors that shape it (Kroll-Smith & Couch 1990, Cable et al 1998).

In mistake and misconduct, cultural environment appears as an independent variable; in disaster studies, it is usually a dependent variable. Producers and users of science and technology have the power to affect what is culturally defined as an acceptable risk so that debates about hazards go on in an environment that is compatible with their interests. Cultural legitimacy also is gained by displacing blame from organizations and institutions to operator error (Perrow 1984) and by the creation of "fantasy documents," official plans to respond to accidents that are culturally reassuring but lack appropriate resources, strategies, and knowledge for an effective response to crisis (Clarke 1999). Historic environmental change has multiplied the potential for accidents and disasters, most notably as large technical systems developed with the capacity for normal accidents (Mayntz & Hughes 1988). But turbulence may also matter. Eisenhardt (1993) argues that accidents are associated with "high velocity environments" marked by rapid and discontinuous change in demand, competitors, technology, and/or regulation, such that information is often inaccurate, unavailable, or obsolete. How a high velocity environment can be identified and its effects on accidents and disasters defined both remain to be worked out, but one known result is the failure of formal agents of social control to effectively monitor rapid changes in scientific and technical knowledge (Jasanoff 1986).

Organization Characteristics and Disaster

STRUCTURE   Perrow (1984) established complexity as a core concept in disaster studies: Accidents are normal in complex systems, an outcome of types of interaction of system parts (complex or linear) and types of coupling (tight or loose). Also salient are the effects of organization complexity on information flows, undermining knowledge about potential hazards (LaPorte 1982, Bella 1987, Freudenberg 1992, Gusterson 1996, Turner & Pidgeon 1997). Hierarchy and power are profoundly implicated in accidents. Executive goals and resource allocations can trickle down, impeding the efforts of people doing the risky work (Perrow 1984, Shrivastava 1987, Bogard 1989, Vaughan 1997, Clarke 1999, Marcus & Nichols 1999). Turner (1978:179) found that errors at the top have greater accident potential because errors compound as they move down through the hierarchy. Perrow (1983) explains why military and top industrial management are indifferent to good human-factors design, favoring technologies that reinforce the power structure and result in unwarranted claims of operator error. In addition, group and subunit conflicts can displace goals, resulting in less-than-optimal technology (Thomas 1994).

PROCESSES   Two patterns repeat in disaster research. First, analogous to organizational misconduct, environmental strain translates into internal processes that are associated with accidents: conflicting goals, performance pressures, deadlines, escalating commitment, reward systems that reinforce productivity and undermine safety, and decline of resource slack. Second, analogous to mistake, history matters: Turner (1978) found that man-made disasters had long incubation periods, typified by rule violations, discrepant events that accumulated unnoticed, and cultural beliefs about hazards that together prevented intervention that might have staved off harmful outcomes.

Striking and new are the discoveries about rules. The conjunction of competition, history, and rule violations suggests that only poorly run organizations have violations and accidents, but well-run organizations also exhibit this pattern. Routine nonconformity has multiple logics: Rule violations occur because of mistake, misconduct, institutional arrangements, informal organization, and cultural understandings (Perrow 1984, Braithwaite 1985, Shrivastava 1987, Osborn & Jackson 1988, Clarke 1989, Sagan 1993, Vaughan 1996, Perin 1998). For example, Snook (1996) identified "practical drift": an incremental uncoupling of practice from written procedures designed to handle the worst-case condition when subunits are tightly coupled. This gap between written rules and action impairs effective response in a crisis, when tight coupling is called for. Ironically, conforming to rules also can contribute to accidents and disasters. Weick (1993), in a stunning analysis of why firefighters died in the 1949 Mann Gulch disaster, revealed that the few who survived dropped their heavy tools and ran, while those who perished conformed to the organization mandate always to carry their tools.

TASKS One strand of task-oriented research locates risk and uncertainty in the technology because it is complex, uncertain, and therefore inherently risky: The technology makes tasks difficult and accidents likely. As the technical system varies, so does the ability of operators, managers, organizations, and institutions to control it (Perrow 1984). Recent research has opened up the unexplored world of the people who do the risky work. This new work discloses "the operational realities of risk handling" (Carroll & Perin 1995:22), showing how the technology mystifies and how organizational and institutional factors affect the work process, contributing to failures. Both intelligent technology and intelligent humans have limited ability to cope with inconceivable occurrences, promoting "the reasonable choice of disaster" (Lanir 1989); people are taught modes of success, not modes of failure (Schulman 1993); training is for single failures, not complex interactive ones (Meshkati 1991); risk-handling resources are inadequate (Perin 1995); minor flaws and errors are accepted due to deadlines (Pate-Cornell 1990); schedules, resources, and commitments to hardware produce questionable fixes rather than change (Starbuck & Milliken 1988a).

Cognition, Choice, and Disaster

Scholarship on cognition, choice, and the social origin of accidents and disasters locates risk and uncertainty in interpretation and sensemaking about technologies. The guiding assumption is that all technologies have interpretive flexibility, resulting in disputed knowledge claims about the technical world (Pinch 1991). How individuals construct risk and uncertainty and how they produce technical knowledge are the central problematics. Social context is all-important: Risk and uncertainty of a situation or object vary with the social location of the actor; experts disagree about facts both before accidents and after. Many aspects of social context are salient for cognition (Short & Clarke 1992, Roberts 1993, Weick & Roberts 1993, Cushing 1994, Weick et al 1999). Unfortunately but understandably, studies of ethnocognition as incidents, accidents, and disasters unfold are rare. The productive alternative has been participant observation of people doing risky work safely, which has yielded concepts related to cognition and effective teamwork, such as "heedful interrelating" and "collective mind" (Weick & Roberts 1993, Weick et al 1999). These studies of process show how better organizations catch mistakes by employing advanced collective cognition before things snowball into disasters.

However, knowledge about the effect of culture on choice in the preconditions of accidents and disasters is accumulating (see Turner & Pidgeon 1997: Ch.11). Turner (1976) found cultural beliefs contributed to "failures of foresight:" a history of discrepant events that were ignored or misinterpreted. Prior to accidents, decision-makers saw "ill-structured" problems that afterwards became "well-structured" to decision-makers and investigators alike when the adverse outcome altered their world view. Two studies show how institutional and organizational cultural beliefs promote failures of foresight by affecting the interpretation of information: A "disqualification heuristic" leads decision-makers to neglect information that contradicts their conviction that a technical system is safe (Clarke 1993), and the "normalization of deviance" can neutralize signals of danger, enabling people to conform to institutional and organizational mandates even when personally objecting to a line of action (Vaughan 1996). Not only do "fantasy documents" affect societal cultural beliefs about risky technologies, they also persuade employees of the safety of their own enterprise (Clarke & Perrow 1996). After accidents, government, industry, and professional cultural beliefs frame facts, limiting what investigations can learn from failures (Gephart 1984, Starbuck & Milliken 1988b, Carroll 1995, 1998).

Summary　The achievements of disaster studies are several. First, like mistake and misconduct, research into causes affirms that environment, organizations, and cognition are all implicated. Second, in contrast to mistake and misconduct, most scholarship uses organization theory, showing the socially organized origins of accidents and disasters in comprehensive complexity. Third, research has new insights about how power, rules, and culture create failures. Finally, many scholars have responded to the high demand for sociological insights from organizations that produce and use risky technologies. They consult and lecture, fomenting an incipient revolution. Miraculously, many practitioners are beginning to look beyond operator error, directing preventive strategies toward the institutions, organizations, and systems that contribute to accidents.

When assessing disaster studies, it is typical to worry about "The Great Divide": Normal Accident Theory (NAT) studies failures, emphasizes structure, and argues that complex systems will inevitably fail; High Reliability Theory (HRT) studies safe systems, emphasizes process, and argues for effective prevention. These different orientations show in detail how the same aspects of organizations that contribute to the bright side also contribute to the dark side. Hotly debated between NAT and HRT are the effects of centralization, decentralization, tight and loose coupling, and redundancy, but research has not sorted out under what conditions they will produce safety or increase the probability of accidents. However, much current scholarship mediates these polarities, perhaps indicating the growing maturity of the field: Debates illuminate similarities as well as differences (LaPorte 1994); scholars studying failure link structure to process and cognition (Clarke 1992, 1993; Vaughan 1996); scholars studying high reliability organizations compare failures and safe organizations (Weick 1990, 1993; Roberts & Libuser 1993); scholars studying a risky industry, rather than successes or failures (Carroll & Perin 1995), and integrative efforts compare variations in structure, process, performance, and accidents (Schulman 1993, Marcus 1995).

Weick (1987) has skillfully shown how the same processes that produce the bright side (safety) can produce the dark side (accidents and disasters): Training, often used to prevent errors, can create them; information richness introduces inefficiency, too little produces inaccuracy; teams have multiple points of view that enhance safety, but as they become a cohesive group they share assumptions, so the "requisite variety" important to safety is lost. Additional progress is possible if future research, regardless of orientation, more carefully specifies social context: the unit of analysis (system, organization, subunit, work group), its complexity, the complexity and coupling of the technology, relevant aspects of competitive and regulatory environments, presence or absence of resource slack, and especially the characteristics of the task. Neither "side" is doing this, so the generalizability of all findings is unclear. The division of labor, which has HRT mainly exploring process and NAT focusing more on structure, has been most problematic for developing broad causal principles upon which to base strategies for control. For both theoretical and practical reasons, we need to know, e.g., how variation in structure affects the possibility of collective cognition and its success or failure as a preventive. The debate about whether redundancy contributes to accidents (NAT) or prevents them (HRT) may be a function of different disciplinary training and research styles that result in two different definitions of redundancy: structural redundancy versus process redundancy. The greatest advances may come when individual projects strive to merge levels of analysis, examining the link between environmental factors, organization characteristics, and ethnocognition in tasks of people doing risky work.

THEORIZING THE DARK SIDE

This essay is a Simmelian examination of the dark side of organizations, first exploring the social form and origin of routine nonconformity, then of mistake, misconduct, and disaster as three types. Studying the dark side of organizations exposes the operational inadequacy of society's institutional bases. It increases our understanding of social structure, showing that routine nonconformity, mistake, misconduct, and disaster are not anomalous events, but systematic products of complex structures and processes. Consequently, it challenges not only Weberian notions of rationality, but also the decontextualized, means-ends orientation of rational choice theory, showing that behavior is rational within situational contexts and that social context can decouple rational choice from outcomes, so organizations produce unanticipated negative consequences that deviate from formal design goals and normative standards and expectations. Debunking myths of operator error and individual wrongdoing, this review affirms that policy for preventive strategies must go beyond individuals to institutional and organizational factors that shape individual cognition and action.

To lay a foundation for the dark side of organizations as an integrated field of study, I have analyzed four literatures in order to make key ideas of each available to specialists in the others. Using an inductive case comparison method that identifies social form and origin by attending to both analogies and differences, two central analogies stand out: first, routine nonconformity and the three types have a common form that includes aspects of environment, organizations, and socio-cognition; and second, common origin is located in connections between these levels of analysis that systematically produce organizational deviance. Analogous structures and processes are easy to identify because patterns clearly repeat across routine nonconformity and its types. But drawing conclusions about differences within these categories is more tentative because the absence of some characteristic may reflect substantive topic differences in research maturity (e.g., mistake is "young") and research access and interest rather than differences of form. But some differences can be singled out as directions for future research.

Only a few sociological constructs linked to the social origin of routine nonconformity have been used in research on mistake, misconduct, and disaster. Theories and concepts (e.g., the embeddedness perspective, environmental uncertainty, liabilities of newness, goal displacement, error-amplifying decision traps, trained incapacity, core set) could be extended to study the three types. Reciprocally, theories and concepts associated with mistake, misconduct, and disaster could guide the study of routine nonconformity or be swapped between types (e.g., anomie, the trickle-down effect, practical drift, the disqualification heuristic, system complexity, requisite variety). Also, advances in one area can provide theoretical insight and research direction for another. For example, the regulatory environment has been extensively studied in organizational misconduct but virtually ignored in mistake and disaster; tasks have priority in research on mistake and disaster but are neglected in misconduct; science and technology are central in disaster studies but unexplored in mistake and misconduct; power and politics are emphasized in misconduct and disaster but minimally addressed in mistake. Risk and uncertainty are fundamental but are conceptually underdeveloped in all three types.

Building the dark side of organizations as an integrated field also would include some topics that are challenging methodologically because the subject matter is, after all, organizational deviance. First, studies of ethnocognition are necessary. Second, we might hypothesize that in virtually all socially organized settings, routine nonconformity is met with efforts to keep it from becoming publicly identified as mistake, misconduct, or disaster. What is the social organization of this clean-up work, and what is the effect on social structure? Third, how do understandings develop about what is an incident of routine nonconformity, who gets to decide what is and what is not, and how is routine nonconformity converted to mistake, misconduct, or disaster? Finally, there is the unresolved question of when conditions combine to produce the bright side and when they culminate in the dark side of organizations.

This discussion has been cast as a dark side/bright side dichotomy to emphasize variation from the usual treatment of organizational behavior. However, the variable relationship between structures and processes identified and the frequency and probability of unexpected suboptimal outcomes is an important question. Answers are likely to be forthcoming when scholars examine how the conjunction of environmental, organizational, and socio-cognitive elements combine to produce variation in individual choice and action. Necessarily, this agenda would add to and draw from historical sociology, investigating changes in law, science, technology, and knowledge that affect the incidence of unanticipated adverse outcomes, understandings about what is culpable and what is tolerable, and social definitions of what is normative and deviant at a particular historic moment; economic sociology, for research on markets, competition, institutionalized inequality, and social costs; rational choice sociology, examining the disjunction between rational choice and outcomes; and cultural sociology, for analyzing how culture mediates environment, organization characteristics, cognition, and choice. Much can also be learned from the strong theoretical interdisciplinary work on the dark side of organizations (e.g., Jervis 1970, 1976, 1997, Lerner 1986, Gaba et al 1987, Moe 1991, Sagan 1994, Reason 1997, Klein 1998, Allison & Zelikow 1999).

ACKNOWLEDGMENTS

My thanks to Sal Zerilli for conversations fundamental to my thinking and for help assembling the literature on which this essay is based; to Robert Gibbons and the participants in his MIT Organizational Behavior seminar for their response to an early outline of these ideas; and John Carroll, Lee Clarke, Karl Weick, and an anonymous reviewer for thoughtful comments on the penultimate draft. Special thanks to the many kind colleagues who responded to requests by sending bundles of their most recent work.

Visit the *Annual Reviews home page* at
http://www.AnnualReviews.org.

Literature Cited

Abolafia M. 1996. *Making Markets.* Cambridge, MA: Harvard Univ. Press
Allison G, Zelikow P. 1999. *Essence of Decision.* New York: Longman. 2nd ed.
Anheier H, ed. 1998. *When Things Go Wrong.* Thousand Oaks, CA: Sage
Aubert V. 1952. White-collar crime and social structure. *Am. J. Sociol.* 58:263–71
Aubert V. 1965. *The Hidden Society.* Totowa, NJ: Bedminster
Baker W, Faulkner R. 1993. The social organization of conspiracy. *Am. Sociol. Rev.* 58: 837–60
Baker W, Faulkner R. 1997. *Diffusion of fraud.* Presented at Int. Soc. Networks Conf., San Diego
Bamberger PA, Sonnenstuhl WJ, eds. 1998. *Research in the Sociology of Organizations,* Vol. 15. Stamford, CT: JAI
Barlow HD. 1993. From fiddle factors to networks of collusion. *Criminol. Law Soc. Change* 20:319–37
Barnard C. 1938. *The Functions of the Executive.* Cambridge, MA: Harvard Univ. Press
Becker HS. 1994. 'Foi por acaso': conceptualizing coincidence. *Sociol. Q.* 35:183–94
Bella D. 1987. Organizations and systematic distortion of information. *Prof. Issues Eng.* 113:360–70
Belli RE, Schuman H. 1996. The complexity of ignorance. *Qual. Sociol.* 19:423–30
Bensman J, Gerver I. 1963. Crime and punishment in the factory. *Am. Sociol. Rev.* 28: 588–98
Blau P. 1955. *The Dynamics of Bureaucracy.* Chicago: Univ. Chicago Press. 2nd ed.
Boden D. 1994. *The Business of Talk.* Bristol, UK: Polity
Bogard W. 1989. *The Bhopal Tragedy.* Boulder, CO: Westview
Bosk C. 1979. *Forgive and Remember.* Chicago: Univ. Chicago Press
Braithwaite J. 1985. *To Punish or Persuade.* Albany: State Univ. NY Press
Burawoy M. 1979. *Manufacturing Consent.* Chicago: Univ. Chicago Press
Cable S, Shriver T, Hastings D. 1998. The silenced majority. In *Research in Social Problems and Public Policy,* ed. W Freudenberg, T Youn. Greenwich, CT: JAI
Calavita K, Pontell H, Tillman R. 1997. *Big Money Crime.* Berkeley: Univ. Calif. Press

Carroll J. 1995. Incident reviews in high-hazard industries. *Ind. Environ. Crisis Q.* 9:175–97
Carroll J. 1998. Organizational learning activities in high-hazard industries. *J. Manage. Stud.* 35:699–717
Carroll J, Perin C. 1995. *Organizing and Managing for Safe Production. Rep. NSP95-005,* MIT Cent. Energy Environ. Policy Res.
Chambliss D. 1996. *Beyond Caring.* Chicago: Univ. Chicago Press
Clarke L. 1989. *Acceptable Risk?* Berkeley: Univ. Calif. Press
Clarke L. 1992. Context dependency and risk decision making. In *Organizations, Uncertainties, and Risk,* ed. L Clarke, JF Short, pp. 27–38. Boulder, CO: Westview
Clarke L. 1993. The disqualification heuristic. In *Research in Social Problems and Public Policy,* Vol. 5, ed. W Freudenberg, T Youn. Greenwich, CT: JAI
Clarke L. 1999. *Mission Improbable.* Chicago: Univ. Chicago Press
Clarke L, Perrow C. 1996. Prosaic organizational failures. *Am. Behav. Sci.* 39: 1040–56
Clinard M. 1983. *Corporate Ethics and Crime.* Beverly Hills, CA: Sage
Cohen MA, Lofquist WS, Rabe GA, eds. 1997. *Debating Corporate Crime.* Cincinnati, OH: Anderson
Cohen MD, March JG, Olsen JP. 1972. Garbage can model of organizational choice. *Admin. Sci. Q.* 17:1–25
Coleman JS. 1974. *Power and the Structure of Society.* Philadelphia: Univ. Phila. Press
Coleman JW. 1987. Toward an integrated theory of white-collar crime. *Am. J. Sociol.* 93:406–39
Coleman JW, Ramos LL. 1998. Subcultures and deviant behavior in the organizational context. See Bamberger & Sonnenstuhl 1998, pp. 3–34
Collins HM. 1974. The TEA set. *Sci. Stud.* 4:165–86
Collins HM. 1981. The place of the 'core-set' in modern science. *Hist. Sci.* 19:6–19
Collins HM. 1992. *Changing Order.* Chicago: Univ. Chicago Press
Cowan RS. 1983. *More Work for Mother.* New York: Basic Books

Cressey D. 1953. *Other People's Money.* Glencoe, IL: Free Press

Crozier M. 1964. *The Bureaucratic Phenomenon.* Chicago: Univ. Chicago Press

Cushing S. 1994. *Fatal Words.* Chicago: Univ. Chicago Press

Dalton M. 1959. *Men Who Manage.* New York: Wiley

Daly K. 1989. Gender and varieties of white-collar crime. *Criminology* 27:769–94

Delaney KJ. 1992. *Strategic Bankruptcy.* Berkeley: Univ. Calif. Press

Denzin N. 1977. Notes on the criminogenic hypothesis. *Am. Sociol. Rev.* 42:905–20

Diamond T. 1992. *Making Gray Gold.* Chicago: Univ. Chicago Press

DiMaggio P. 1997. Culture and cognition. *Annu. Rev. Sociol.* 23:263–87

DiMaggio P, Powell WW. 1983. Introduction. In *The New Institutionalism in Organizational Analysis,* ed. WW Powell, P DiMaggio. Chicago: Univ. Chicago Press

Durkheim E. [1895]1966. *The Rules of Sociological Method.* New York: Free Press

Dwyer T. 1991. *Life and Death at Work.* New York: Plenum

Edelman LB, Suchman MC. 1997. The legal environments of organizations. *Annu. Rev. Sociol.* 23:479–515

Edmondson AC. 1996. Learning from mistakes is easier said than done. *J. Appl. Behav. Sci.* 32:5–28

Eisenhardt K. 1993. High reliability organizations meet high velocity environment. See Roberts 1993

Elsbach K, Sutton RI. 1992. Acquiring organizational legitimacy through illegitimate actions. *Acad. Manage. J.* 35:699–738

Emerson RM, Messinger S. 1977. The micropolitics of trouble. *Soc. Probl.* 25: 121–34

Erikson K. 1976. *Everything in Its Path.* New York: Simon & Schuster

Ermann DM, Rabe GA. 1995. Corporate concealment of tobacco hazards. *Dev. Behav.* 16:223–44

Ermann DM, Rabe GA. 1997. Organizational processes (not rational choices) produce most corporate crimes. See Cohen et al 1997, pp. 53–68

Feldman M. 1989. *Order Without Design.* Stanford, CA: Stanford Univ. Press

Finney H, Lesieur H. 1982. A contingency theory of organizational crime. In *Research in the Sociology of Organizations,* ed. SB Bacharach, pp. 255–99. Greenwich, CT: JAI

Fleischer A, Goff B, Tollison RD. 1992. *The National Collegiate Athletic Association: A Study in Cartel Behavior.* Chicago: Univ. Chicago Press

Fligstein N. 1990. *The Transformation of Corporate Control.* Cambridge, MA: Harvard Univ. Press

Fox R. 1959. *Experiment Perilous.* Glencoe, IL: Free Press

Freidson E. 1970. *Profession of Medicine.* New York: Dodd, Mead & Co.

Freidson E. 1975. *Doctoring Together.* Chicago: Univ. Chicago Press

Freudenberg W. 1992. Risk analysis and the organizational amplification of risks. *Risk* 3:1–35

Frey JH. 1994. Deviance of organizational subunits. *Sociol. Focus* 18:110–22

Friedrichs D. 1996. *Trusted Criminals.* Belmont, MA: Wadsworth

Friedrichs D. 1997. The downsizing of America and white collar crime. *Criminol. Law Soc. Change* 26:351–66

Gaba DM, Maxwell MS, DeAnda A. 1987. Anesthetic mishaps. *Anesthesiology* 66: 670–76

Geis G, Salinger L. 1998. Antitrust and organizational deviance. See Bamberger & Sonnenstuhl 1998, pp. 71–110

Gephart RP. 1984. Making sense of organizationally based environmental disasters. *J. Manage.* 10:205–25

Giddens A. 1984. *The Constitution of Society.* Berkeley: Univ. Calif. Press

Goffman E. 1974. *Frame Analysis.* New York: Harper & Row

Grabowsky PN. 1989. *Wayward Governance.* Canberra: Aust. Inst. Criminol.

Granovetter M. 1985. Economic action and social structure. *Am. J. Sociol.* 91:481–510

Green GS. 1997. *Occupational Crime.* Chicago: Nelson/Hall

Guetzkow H. 1965. Communications in organizations. See March 1965, pp. 534–73

Guillemin, J. 1994. Experiment and illusion in reproductive medicine. *Hum. Nat.* 5: 1–21

Guillemin J, Holmstrom LL. 1986. *Mixed Blessings.* New York: Oxford Univ. Press

Gusterson H. 1996. *Nuclear Rites.* Berkeley: Univ. Calif. Press

Hagan FE. 1997. *Political Crime.* Boston: Allyn & Bacon

Hall R. 1996. *Organizations.* Englewood Cliffs, NJ: Prentice Hall. 6th ed.

Heimer C. 1988. Social structure, psychology, and the estimation of risk. *Annu. Rev. Sociol.* 14:491–519

Hodson R, Jensen G, eds. 1999. Crime at work. *Work Occup.* In press

Huff CR, Rattner A, Sagarin E. 1996. *Convicted But Innocent.* Thousand Oaks, CA: Sage

Hughes EC. 1951. Mistakes at work. *Can. J. Econ. Polit. Sci.* 17:320–27

Hughes TP. 1983. *Networks of Power*. Baltimore, MD: Johns Hopkins Univ. Press

Jackall R. 1988. *Moral Mazes*. New York: Oxford Univ. Press

Jamieson K. 1994. *The Organization of Corporate Crime*. Thousand Oaks, CA: Sage

Jasanoff S. 1986. *Risk Management and Political Culture*. New York: Sage

Jervis R. 1970. *The Logic of Images in International Relations*. New York: Columbia Univ. Press

Jervis R. 1976. *Perceptions and Misperceptions in International Politics*. Princeton, NJ: Princeton Univ. Press

Jervis R. 1997. *System Effects*. Princeton, NJ: Princeton Univ. Press

Kagan R, Scholz JT. 1984. The criminology of the corporation and regulatory enforcement strategies. In *Enforcing Regulation*, ed. K Hawkins, J Thomas. Boston: Kluwer-Nijhoff

Klein G. 1998. *Sources of Power*. Cambridge, MA: MIT Press

Knorr Cetina K. 1981. *The Manufacture of Knowledge*. Oxford, UK: Pergamon

Knorr Cetina K. 1997. Sociality with objects. *Theory Cult. Soc.* 14:1–30

Kroll-Smith JS, Couch SR. 1990. *The Real Disaster is Above Ground*. Lexington, KY: Univ. Ky. Press

Kram KE, Yeager PC, Reed GE. 1989. Decisions and dilemmas. In *Research in Corporate Social Performance and Policy*. ed. JE Post, pp. 21–54. Greenwich, CT: JAI

LaFollette M. 1992. *Stealing into Print*. Berkeley: Univ. Calif. Press

Landau M. 1969. Redundancy, rationality, and the problem of duplication and overlap. *Public Admin. Rev.* July/Aug:346–57

Landau M, Chisholm D. 1995. The arrogance of optimism. *J. Cont. Crisis Manage.* 3: 67–78

Lanir Z. 1989. The reasonable choice of disaster. *J. Strateg. Stud.* 12:479–93

LaPorte TR. 1982. On the design and management of nearly error-free organizational control systems. In *Accident at Three Mile Island*, ed. D Sills, VB Shelanski, CP Wolf. Boulder, CO: Westview

LaPorte TR. 1994. A strawman speaks up. *J. Cont. Crisis Manage.* 2:207–11

Lazega E. 1992. *The Micropolitics of Knowledge*. New York: Aldine de Gruyter

Leibel W. 1991. When scientists are wrong. *J. Bus. Ethn.* 10:601–4

Leonard WN, Weber M. 1970. Automakers and dealers: a study of criminogenic market forces. *Law Soc. Rev.* 4:407–24

Lerner AW. 1986. There is more than one way to be redundant. *Admin. Soc.* 18:334–59

Levi M. 1981. *The Phantom Capitalists*. Aldershot, UK: Gower

Light D. 1972. Psychiatry and suicide: the management of a mistake. *Am. J. Sociol.* 77:821–38

Lofquist WS. 1997. Agency, structure, and corporate crime. See Cohen et al 1997, pp. 1–30

Lynch M, Woolgar S, eds. 1988. *Representation in Scientific Practice*. Cambridge, MA: MIT Press

MacKenzie D. 1990. *Inventing Accuracy*. Cambridge, MA: MIT Press

Manning PK. 1992. *Organizational Communication*. New York: Aldine

Mannis JG, Meltzer BN. 1994. Chance in human affairs. *Sociol. Theory* 12:1

March JG, ed. 1965. *Handbook of Organizations*. Chicago: Rand McNally

March JG, Simon HA. 1958. *Organizations*. New York: Wiley

March JG, Sproull LS, Tamuz M. 1991. Learning from samples of one or fewer. *Organ. Sci.* 2:1–13

Marcus A. 1995. Managing with danger. *Ind. Environ. Crisis Q.* 9:139–51

Marcus A, McAvoy E, Nichols M. 1993. Economic and behavioral perspectives on safety. In *Research in Organizational Behavior*, Vol. 15, ed. S Bacharach, pp. 323–55. Greenwich, CT: JAI

Marcus A, Nichols M. 1999. Warnings heeded. *Organ. Sci.* In press

Martin J, Feldman MS, Hatch MJ, Sitkin S. 1983. The uniqueness paradox in organization. *Admin. Sci. Q.* 28:438–53

Mayntz R, Hughes TP, eds. 1988. *The Development of Large Technical Systems*. Boulder, CO: Westview

McKee M, Black N. 1992. Does the current use of junior doctors in the United Kingdom affect the quality of medical care? *Soc. Sci. Med.* 34:549–58

Mechanic D. 1962. Sources of power of lower participants in complex organizations. *Admin. Sci. Q.* 7:349–64

Meltzer BN, Mannis JG. 1992. Emergence and human contact. *J. Psychol.* 126: 333–42

Merton RK. 1936. The unanticipated consequences of purposive social action. *Am. Sociol. Rev.* 1:894–904

Merton RK. 1938. Social structure and anomie. *Am. Sociol. Rev.* 3:672–82

Merton RK. 1940. Bureaucratic structure and personality. *Soc. Forces* 17:560–68

Merton RK. 1968. *Social Structure and Social Theory*. New York: Free Press

Meshkati N. 1991. Human factors in large-scale technological systems' accidents. *Ind. Crisis Q.* 5:133–54

Meyer JW, Rowan B. 1977. Institutional-ized organizations. *Am. J. Sociol.* 83: 340–63

Michalowski RJ, Kramer RC. 1987. The space between laws. *Soc. Probl.* 34:34–53

Millman M. 1977. *The Unkindest Cut.* New York: Morrow

Mizrahi T. 1984. Managing medical mistakes. *Soc. Sci. Med.* 19:135–46

Moe T. 1991. Politics and the theory of organi-zation. *J. Law Econ. Org.* 7:106–29

Morrill C. 1995. *The Executive Way.* Chicago: Univ. Chicago Press

Morrill C, Snyderman E, Dawson EJ. 1997. It's not what you do, but who you are. *Sociol. Forum* 12:519–43

Mulkay M, Gilbert GN. 1982. Accounting for error. *Sociology.* 16:165–83

Munro E. 1996. Avoidable and unavoidable mistakes in child protection work. *Br. J. Soc. Wkly.* 26:793–808

Needleman ML, Needleman C. 1979. Organi-zational crime. *Sociol. Q.* 20:517–28

Oliver C. 1991. Strategic responses to institu-tional processes. *Acad. Manage. Rev.* 16: 145–79

Osborn R, Jackson D. 1988. Leaders, riverboat gamblers, or purposeful unintended conse-quences in the management of complex, dangerous technologies. *Acad. Manage. J.* 31:924–47

Paget MA. 1988. *The Unity of Mistakes.* Phila-delphia: Temple Univ. Press

Paget MA. 1993. *A Complex Sorrow.* Philadel-phia: Temple Univ. Press

Passas N. 1996. Accounting for fraud. In *The Ethics of Accounting and Finance,* ed. WM Hoffman, JB Kamm, RE Frederick, ES Petry. Westport, CT: Quorum

Pate-Cornell ME. 1990. Organizational as-pects of engineering safety systems. *Sci-ence* 250:1210–16

Perin C. 1995. Organizations as contexts. *Ind. Environ. Crisis Q.* 9:152–74

Perin C. 1998. Operating as experimenting. *Sci. Tech. Hum. Values* 23:36–57

Perrow C. 1983. The organizational context of human factors engineering. *Admin. Sci. Q.* 28:521–41

Perrow C. 1984. *Normal Accidents.* New York: Basic Books

Perrow C. 1986. *Complex Organizations.* New York: Random House. 3rd. ed.

Perrow C. 1991. A society of organizations. *Theory Soc.* 20:763–94

Perrow C, Guillen M. 1990. *The AIDS Disas-ter.* New Haven, CT: Yale Univ. Press

Pfohl SJ. 1978. *Predicting Dangerousness.* Lexington, MA: Lexington Books

Pinch T. 1991. How do we treat technical un-certainty in systems failure? In *Social Re-sponses to Large Technical Systems,* ed. TR LaPorte. Amsterdam: Klewer

Pinch TJ, Bijker WE. 1984. The social con-struction of facts and artefacts. *Soc. Stud. Sci.* 14:399–441

Powell W, DiMaggio P. 1991. *The New Insti-tutionalism in Organizational Analysis.* Chicago: Univ. Chicago Press

Pressman JL, Wildavsky A. 1973. *Implemen-tation.* Berkeley: Univ. Calif. Press

Punch M. 1985. *Conduct Unbecoming.* Lon-don: Tavistock

Putnam L. 1986. Contradictions and para-doxes in organizations. In *Organization Communication: Emerging Perspectives,* Vol. 1, ed. I Thayer. Norwood, MA: Ablex

Quinney ER. 1963. Occupations structure and criminal behavior. *Soc. Probl.* 11: 179–85

Rasmussen J. 1986. *Information Processing and Human-Machine Interaction.* Amster-dam: North-Holland

Reason J. 1990. *Human Error.* Cambridge: Cambridge Univ. Press

Reason J. 1997. *Managing the Risks to Organizational Accidents.* Aldershot, UK: Ashgate

Reed G, Yeager PC. 1996. Organizational of-fending and neoclassical criminology. *Criminology* 34:357–82

Reimer JW. 1976. Mistakes at work. *Soc. Probl.* 23:255–67

Roberts K, ed. 1993. *New Challenges to Un-derstanding Organizations.* New York: Macmillan

Roberts KH, Libuser C. 1993. From Bhopal to banking. *Organ. Dyn.* 21:15–26

Rochlin GI. 1997. *Trapped in the Net.* Prince-ton: Princeton Univ. Press

Roethlisberger FJ, Dickson WJ. 1947. *Man-agement and the Worker.* Cambridge, MA: Harvard Univ. Press

Rosenhan DL. 1973. On being sane in insane places. *Science* 179:1–9

Rosenthal M, Mulcahy L, Lloyd-Bostock S. 1999. *Medical Mistakes.* London: Open Univ. Press

Roth JA. 1991. *Mistakes at Work.* Dep. So-ciol., Univ. Calif., Davis

Sackmann SA. 1991. *Cultural Knowledge in Organizations.* Newbury Park, CA: Sage

Sagan S. 1993. *The Limits of Safety.* Princeton: Princeton Univ. Press

Sagan S. 1994. The perils of proliferation. *Int. Secur.* 18:66–107

Sagan S. 1994. Toward a political theory of or-ganizational reliability. *J. Cont. Crisis Manage.* 2:228–40

Schulman PR. 1989. The 'logic' of organiza-tional irrationality. *Admin. Soc.* 21: 31–33

Schulman PR. 1993. The analysis of high reliability organizations. See Roberts 1993

Scott WR. 1998. *Organizations.* Upper Saddle River, NJ: Prentice Hall. 4th ed.

Selznick P. 1949. *TVA and the Grass Roots.* Berkeley: Univ. Calif. Press

Shapiro S. 1990. Collaring the crime, not the criminal. *Am. Soc. Rev.* 55:346–65

Short JF. 1984. The social fabric at risk. *Am. Soc. Rev.* 49:711–25

Short JF, Clarke L, eds. 1992. *Organizations, Uncertainties, and Risk.* Boulder, CO: Westview

Shover N, Bryant K. 1993. Theoretical explanations of corporate crime. In *Understanding Corporate Criminality*, ed. M Blankensmith, pp. 141–76. New York: Garland

Shrivastava P. 1987. *Bhopal.* Cambridge: Ballinger

Shulman D. 1997. *The social organization of workplace deception.* PhD thesis. Northwest. Univ.

Simmel G. 1950. *The Sociology of Georg Simmel.* Transl. ed. K Wolff. New York: Free Press

Simon D. 1994. *Crimes of the Criminal Justice System.* Cincinnati, OH: Anderson

Simpson S. 1998. *Why Corporations Obey the Law.* New York: Cambridge Univ. Press

Simpson S, Koper C. 1997. Top management characteristics, organizational strain, and antitrust offending. *J. Quant. Criminol.* 13:373–404

Simpson S, Paternoster R, Piquero N. 1998. Exploring the micro-macro link in corporate crime research. See Bamberger & Sonnenstuhl 1998, pp. 35–70

Singer B. 1978. Assessing social error. *Soc. Policy* 9:27–34

Snook SA. 1996. *Practical drift.* PhD thesis. Harvard Univ., Cambridge, MA

Snider L, Pearce F. 1995. *Corporate Crime.* Toronto: Univ. Toronto Press

Star SL, ed. 1995. *Ecologies of Knowledge.* Albany: State Univ. NY Press

Star SL, Gerson E. 1987. The management and dynamics of anomalies in scientific work. *Sociol. Q.* 28: 147–69

Starbuck W, Milliken FJ. 1988a. Challenger: fine-tuning the odds until something breaks. *J. Manage. Stud.* 25:319–40

Starbuck W, Milliken FJ. 1988b. Executives' perceptual filters. In *The Executive Effect,* ed. DC Hambrick. Greenwich, CT: JAI

Staw BM, Sandelands LE, Dutton JE. 1981. Threat-rigidity effects in organizational behavior. *Admin. Sci. Q.* 26:501–24

Stelling J, Bucher R. 1973. Vocabularies of realism in professional socialization. *Soc. Sci. Med.* 76:661–75

Stinchcombe AL. 1965. Social structure and organizations. See March 1965, pp. 142–93

Stokes R, Hewitt JP. 1976. Aligning actions. *Am. Sociol. Rev.* 41:838–49

Stone CD. 1975. *Where the Law Ends.* New York: Harper

Suchman LA. 1987. *Plans and Situated Actions.* Cambridge, UK: Cambridge Univ. Press

Sudnow D. 1965. Normal crimes. *Soc. Probl.* 12:255–76

Sumner WG. [1906]1940. *Folkways.* New York: New Am. Library

Sutherland EH. 1949. *White-Collar Crime.* New York: Dryden

Tenner E. 1996. *Why Things Bite Back.* New York: Knopf

Thomas R. 1994. *What Machines Can't Do.* Berkeley: Univ. Calif. Press

Tilly C. 1996. The invisible elbow. *Sociol. Forum* 2:589–601

Tompkins PK. 1990. On risk communication as interorganizational control. In *Nothing to Fear*, ed. A Kirby, pp. 203–39. Tucson: Univ. Ariz. Press

Turkle S. 1995. *Life On The Screen.* New York: Simon & Schuster

Turner B. 1976. The organizational and interorganizational development of disasters. *Admin. Sci. Q.* 21:378–97

Turner B. 1978. *Man-Made Disasters.* London: Wykeham

Turner B, Pidgeon N. 1997. *Man-made Disasters.* London: Butterworth-Heinemann. 2nd ed.

Vaughan D. 1982a. Toward understanding unlawful organizational behavior. *Mich. Law Rev.* 80:1377–1402

Vaughan D. 1982b. Transaction systems and unlawful organizational behavior. *Soc. Probl.* 29:373–79

Vaughan D. 1983. *Controlling Unlawful Organizational Behavior.* Chicago: Univ. Chicago Press

Vaughan D. 1992. Theory elaboration. In *What is a Case?* ed. C Ragin H Becker, pp. 173–202. New York: Cambridge Univ. Press

Vaughan D. 1996. *The Challenger Launch Decision.* Chicago: Univ. Chicago Press

Vaughan D. 1997. The trickle-down effect. *Calif. Manage. Rev.* 39:80–102

Vaughan D. 1998. Rational choice, situated action, and the social control of organizations. *Law Soc. Rev.* 32:23–61

Vaughan D. 1999a. *Theorizing: Analogy, Cases, and Comparative Social Organization.* Chicago: Univ. Chicago Press. In press

Vaughan D. 1999b. Boundary work: levels of analysis, the macro-micro link, and the social control of organizations. In *Social Science, Social Policy, and the Law,* ed. P Ewick, R Kagan, A Sarat. New York: Russell Sage

Vaz E. 1979. Institutionalized rule violation in professional hockey. In *Sport Sociology,* ed. A Yiannakis. Dubuque, IA: Kendall-Hunt

Verma K, Marcus A. 1995. Causes and effects of rising production costs in US nuclear power industry. *Ind. Environ. Crisis Q.* 9:242–58

Weick KE. 1979. *The Social Psychology of Organizing.* Reading, MA: Addison-Wesley

Weick KE. 1987. Organization culture as a source of high reliability. *Calif. Manage. Rev.* 28:112–27

Weick KE. 1990. The vulnerable system. *J. Manage.* 16:571–93

Weick KE. 1993. The collapse of sensemaking in organizations. *Admin. Sci. Q.* 38:628–52

Weick KE. 1995. *Sensemaking in Organizations.* Thousand Oaks, CA: Sage

Weick KE, Roberts KH. 1993. Collective mind in organizations. *Admin. Sci. Q.* 38:357–81

Weick KE, Sutcliffe KM, Obstfeld D. 1999.

Organizing for high reliability. In *Research in Organizational Behavior*, ed. B Staw, R Sutton. Greenwich CT: JAI. In press

Wheeler S, Rothman ML. 1982. The organization as weapon in white-collar crime. *Mich. Law Rev.* 80:1403–26

Willis P. 1977. *Learning to Labor.* New York: Columbia Univ. Press

Wilson DC, Hickson DJ, Miller S. 1996. How organizations can overbalance. *Am. Behav. Sci.* 39:995–1010

Wynne B. 1988. Unruly technology. *Soc. Stud. Sci.* 18:147–67

Zelizer V. 1979. *Morals and Markets.* New York: Columbia Univ. Press

Zerilli S. 1998. *Four common tactics of confession-makers.* MA thesis. Boston College, Chestnut Hill, MA

Zey M. 1993. *Banking on Fraud.* New York: Aldine

Zucker L. 1977. The role of institutionalization in cultural persistence. *Am. Sociol. Rev.* 42:726–43

Zuckerman H. 1977. Deviant behavior and social control in science. In *Deviance and Social Change,* ed. E Sagarin, pp. 87–138. Beverly Hills: Sage

Annu. Rev. Sociol. 1999. 25:307–33

FEMINIZATION AND JUVENILIZATION OF POVERTY: Trends, Relative Risks, Causes, and Consequences

Suzanne M. Bianchi

Department of Sociology, University of Maryland, College Park, Maryland 20742-1315; e-mail: bianchi@bss1.umd.edu

KEY WORDS: poverty, gender, children, inequality, family

ABSTRACT

This paper reviews trends in "feminization" and "juvenilization" of poverty showing that the relative risks of poverty increased for women in the 1970s but decreased for working-age women in the early 1980s. Relative risks of poverty increased for children between the 1970s and 1990s particularly in comparison with the elderly. Four factors affect these trends: First, the increase in women's employment and decline in the gender wage gap enhanced the likelihood that women remained above the poverty level. Second, the decline in manufacturing employment and "family wage" jobs for men increased the likelihood that less-educated men (and their families) fell into poverty in the early 1980s. These two factors combined to halt the feminization of poverty among the working-age population. At the same time, a third trend, the increase in "nonmarriage," elevated the proportion of single parents who were young, never-married mothers and complicated the collection of child support from nonresident fathers. This tended to concentrate poverty in mother-child families. Finally, public transfers of income, especially Social Security, were far more effective in alleviating poverty among the elderly than among children, a factor dramatically increasing the "juvenilization" of poverty after 1970.

0360-0572/99/0815-0307$08.00

Poverty in the United States is a serious problem for women and children particularly those in single-parent families. However, assessing trends in the "feminization" and "juvenilization" of poverty turns out to be a trickier business than it might at first seem. First, are "feminization" and "juvenilization" best assessed by trends in the percentage of the poverty population that is female (or juvenile), by the absolute poverty rates of women and children, or by the relative risks of poverty for different groups (i.e., men versus women, adults versus children)? Second, what factors are implicated in the heightened poverty levels of women and children, and what factors seem to be correlated with changes over time in their relative risks of poverty? Finally, and perhaps most importantly, what are the effects of poverty, particularly for those who grow up poor? This chapter reviews the empirical evidence and research literature in an attempt to shed light on each of these questions.

TRENDS

The Feminization of Poverty: The Case of Adult Women

The term "feminization of poverty" was coined by Diana Pearce in a 1978 article in *Urban and Social Change Review* in which she argued that poverty was "rapidly becoming a female problem" and that women accounted "for an increasingly large proportion of the economically disadvantaged" (Pearce 1978:28). Pearce lamented an irony—during the same period that women's employment increased dramatically and affirmative action legislation enhanced opportunities for women in educational institutions and the labor force, their likelihood of living in poverty was increasing relative to men.

What was the evidence for the "feminization of poverty"? Pearce noted that in 1976, two of three poor adults were women; that female-headed families were increasing rapidly, and that the number of poor female-headed families doubled between 1950 and 1974.[1] She also suggested that female-headed

---

[1]"Female-headed families" was the common parlance at the time Pearce described the feminization of poverty. With the 1980 Census, and after lobbying by feminist scholars (see Presser 1999), the Census Bureau discontinued use of the term "head" in describing household and family relationships. However, the term female-headed families continues to be used by researchers outside the Census Bureau when describing households that include a mother living with her dependent children, with no adult male present. I share the feminist dissatisfaction with the "headship" terminology in the case of two-parent families and am pleased that the Census Bureau moved to the householder concept in 1980. Yet, I think in the case of mothers living with their children, the concept of "head" may still be appropriate. Mothers are presumably in charge of these households and their financial difficulties in "managing" or "heading" these households is what generated the interest in the "feminization of poverty" in the first place. Hence, in this chapter, I use the terms "female-headed families" "mother-child families" and the Census Bureau's current terminology, "female-maintained families" or "families with a female householder" interchangeably to describe families (or households) that include a mother, her children, and no spouse present.

families were losing ground vis-à-vis families with an adult male present in the household, noting that the ratio of income in female-headed families to other families had declined between 1950 and 1974. In a later piece, Pearce suggested that if trends continued, nearly all the poor would be living in female-headed families by the year 2000 (Pearce 1988:514).

Usage of the term "feminization of poverty" quickly became widespread. The picture of impoverished women and children captured public attention—especially the paradox that while women attempted to improve their lot vis-à-vis men, they were losing ground. Some blamed women's own choices, particularly their eschewing of marriage, for their plight (Murray 1984), whereas others saw women as merely victims of a cruel hoax, equality without the means of self-sufficiency (Pearce 1978, 1988). All sides seemed to accept the fact that poverty was increasingly becoming a woman's problem and that something detrimental was happening to single mothers and their children.

From the beginning, what the term "feminization" meant and to whom it referred were not always clear. Did "feminization" merely mean that the number of poor females exceeded the number of poor males, or did it imply that women's poverty rates were higher than men's? With respect to poverty rates, did feminization imply that the absolute likelihood of living in poverty was higher for women than men or was the concept about the relative poverty risks (i.e., the ratio of women's to men's poverty rates)? Finally, was the "feminization of poverty" about the chances of living in poverty among adult women, or was it about the heightened likelihood of poverty among those who lived in mother-child families—particularly children, male as well as female children?

Statistics cited to support the feminization of poverty tended to blur these distinctions. Oft quoted figures, such as the percentage of the poor who were female or the proportion of poor families that were female headed (e.g., Shortridge 1984: Figure 1), gave little evidence of how big a problem poverty was for women (as opposed to men) or how much the problem was intensifying. One of the statistics cited by Pearce (1978:128), that 70% of the aged poor were women, seemed shocking. Yet, given women's longer life expectancy, without information on how many of the aged were women,[2] or the percentages of men and women elderly who lived in poverty, it was difficult to know how concentrated poverty was among older women or whether things were getting worse for them relative to older men (McLanahan et al 1989).

In an attempt to more systematically assess trends in poverty for women and men, McLanahan, Sorenson, & Watson (1989) argued that "feminization of poverty" conveyed the notion that the risks of poverty were rising for women relative to men—that rather than examining how many poor women there were for every poor man, one needed to examine poverty rates for

---

[2]About 58% of the over–age 65 population in both 1970 and 1996 were women.

women and men and assess feminization by the trend in the ratio of women's to men's poverty rates. From their analysis of female/male poverty ratios, McLanahan, Sorenson & Watson (1989) concluded that poverty was indeed feminizing between 1950 and 1980: Among adult whites and blacks, at all ages, the ratio of women's to men's poverty rates increased during the period. Among whites, women's poverty rates were 10% higher than men's in 1950, but almost 50% higher by 1980. The rise was especially dramatic for those over age 65: Elderly women's poverty rates were 13% higher than men's in 1950 but climbed to 76% higher by 1980. Trends were similar for blacks, though increases in relative risks were not quite as extreme and changes tended to lag those for whites.

Although Pearce had not been systematic in measuring poverty, McLanahan et al's analysis (1989) confirmed Pearce's assessment of the trend: Women's risks of poverty relative to men's had increased during the 1950s, 1960s, and, to a lesser extent, during the 1970s. Ironically, or so it seemed, this increase in relative risks was taking place as women surged into the labor force, the women's movement took hold, and affirmative action legislation was enacted.

A different paradox was not much noted in the "feminization of poverty" literature, however. At the same time women's relative risks of poverty were increasing, their absolute risks of poverty were declining fairly substantially. This was particularly true for elderly women: As white elderly women's relative risks of poverty climbed from 1.13 to 1.76 those of men, their absolute poverty levels declined from 62% poor in 1950 to 15% poor in 1980 (McLanahan et al 1989: Table 2). Yet because poverty rates were lower for elderly men in 1950—and declined at an even faster pace—elderly women's relative position deteriorated.[3]

The "feminization of poverty" was noted in the 1970s, studied in the decade that followed, and then largely assumed to persist and given little empirical attention after the mid-1980s. Attention turned increasingly to the plight of children in poverty and the relative poverty risks for children who lived with one versus two parents. Only recently have two studies, one by England (1997) and another by McLanahan & Kelly (1997), carried forward the analysis of trends in the relative poverty of women and men. The results are somewhat surprising.

Figure 1 uses annual Current Population Survey (CPS) data to plot three-year moving averages of the ratio of women's to men's poverty rates. Data are for all women, age 18 and older, and for three age groups (18–29, 30–64, and 65 years and over). There are year-to-year fluctuations in the overall ratio, but

---

[3]The divergence in absolute and relative measures of elderly women's poverty points up a potential weakness in relying solely on relative measures to assess feminization of poverty. With ratio variables, it is sometimes easy to overlook the fact that changes in the denominator of a relative measure can be as important as changes in the numerator in understanding trends.

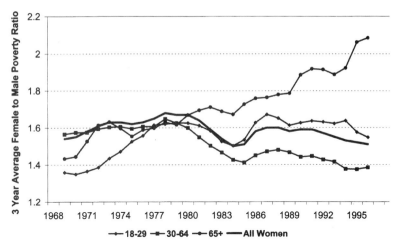

Figure 1   Women's relative poverty risks by age 1968–1997

the trend between 1968 and the late 1970s is upward: Women's poverty rates were 55% higher than men's in 1968 and climbed until they peaked at 72% higher than men's in 1978. Poverty was clearly feminizing.

During the early 1980s, the ratio dropped substantially. In the recessionary years of the early 1980s, women's poverty rates remained higher than men's but dropped from 72% to 47% higher.[4]

After the mid-1980s, the poverty ratio was above the level of the early 1980s but lower than during the 1970s. Women's poverty rates tended to fluctuate between 50% and 60% higher than men's (rising with the economic recovery of the late 1980s but falling again in the 1990s.)

The rates for all women, shown in Figure 1, mask differing trends by age, however. England (1997) and McLanahan & Kelly (1997) present figures that suggest that poverty has continued to feminize among very young women (those under age 25) and among elderly women (over age 65). However, among those in the prime working ages, the ratio of women's to men's poverty rates has declined (McLanahan & Kelly 1997: Table 1; England 1997: Table 4). The CPS data plotted in Figure 1 suggest that poverty ratios of working age women to men (age 30 to 64) were relatively stable in the 1970s and then declined from 1.60 in 1980 to 1.39 in 1996.

On the other hand, the ratio of female poverty rates to male rates for those over age 65 rose from 1.43 to 2.09 between 1968 and 1996. That is, the only group of women to record continued improvement in terms of declining abso-

_____

[4]Both women's and men's poverty rates rose with the recession of the early 1980s, but men's rates rose relatively more than women's rates.

lute poverty rates in the 1980s and 1990s—the elderly—was also the group to witness continued and substantial "feminization" of poverty. The divergence between the trend in the absolute poverty levels of women and the trend in their poverty rates relative to men requires some circumspection about measures as well as the interpretations we attach to the notion of the "feminization of poverty."

The Feminization of Poverty: The Case of Mother-Child Families

Perhaps it was hyperbole, but Pearce (1988) suggested a decade ago that the United States was headed in the direction of having all its poor living in female-headed families by the end to the century. That has not happened. In 1994, of the 38.1 million persons officially in poverty, about 14.4 million, or 38%, lived in families with a female householder, no husband present. An additional 5.0 million poor individuals were women who lived alone or with nonrelatives. About 57% of the total number in poverty were females (US Bureau of the Census, 1996).

Nonetheless, there are grounds for asserting that poverty is increasingly concentrated in mother-child families. As the number of persons living in mother-only families has grown, so also has the proportion of the poor who are in these families. In 1966, only about one fourth of the members of poor families lived in mother-child families, compared with more than 50% by the latter 1990s. But as noted in the previous section, knowing how many poor are in female-maintained families provides only partial information. We must also examine the absolute poverty levels in these families. And, if poverty in families has "feminized," it may be either because the risks of residing in poverty have increased relatively more in mother-child families than in other types of families or because the composition of the group of mother-child families has shifted toward those most vulnerable to poverty (i.e., young, never-married mothers with children).

Poverty rates declined in mother-child families—from 60% to 40% poor—as their numbers grew rapidly between 1959 and 1979 (Garfinkel & McLanahan 1986). After 1980, the growth in mother-child families slowed, but the likelihood of poverty increased somewhat for women and children in these families and tended to fluctuate between 44% and 47%. After 1980, the growth in mother-child families was dominated by the increase in young, never-married mothers and their children, whereas in the 1960s and 1970s, growth had been primarily an increase in divorced or separated mothers (Bianchi 1995).

In terms of the relative risks of poverty in female-maintained compared with other types of families, poverty was feminizing in the 1960s, particularly in the latter half of the 1960s as poverty rates came down for all families with children but came down precipitously for those with an adult male present in the household. (See Table 1.) The reverse happened in the early 1980s: Poverty rose among two-parent families, after years of decline. Poverty also rose in mother-child families but not as dramatically. Hence, between the mid-1970s and the mid-1980s, the risks of poverty in mother-child families declined relative to other families. Whereas poverty rates in mother-child families were seven times those for two-parent families in 1974, they declined to five times those in two-parent families by 1984. Poverty rates rose relatively more in two-parent families than in single-parent families during this period (Bane & Ellwood 1989, Fuchs & Reklis 1992). Since the mid-1980s, the percentage of mother-child families in poverty has fluctuated, and the ratio of their poverty rate to that of married-couple families has been higher than in 1984.

To summarize, low income is a major problem for many women, especially those trying to rear children alone. Yet an assessment of the "feminization of poverty" is complicated by the lack of precision in the concept and the array of statistics used to support a claim of "feminized" poverty. Trends differ depending upon whether the focus is on relative risks or absolute levels of poverty. In absolute terms, women are at greater risk of poverty than men and mother-child families experience much higher poverty levels than two-parent families. But with respect to relative risks and trends in the "feminization of poverty," there are significant and important nonlinearities and peculiarities. These include the "de-feminization" of poverty after 1980 among adult, working-age women, the fluctuation in relative risks of mother-child families compared with two-parent families, and the dramatic rise in relative poverty risks for elderly women vis-à-vis elderly men even as their absolute poverty levels dropped precipitously.

The Juvenilization of Poverty

Over the course of the 1980s, social scientists became increasingly concerned about the rising poverty rates among children. After reaching a low point in the

Table 1   Trends in poverty rates and ratios for mother-child and two-parent families: 1959–1994

	1959	1969	1974	1979	1984	1989	1994
Percent in poverty							
Mother-child families	59.9	44.9	43.7	39.6	45.7	42.8	44.0
All families	20.3	10.8	12.1	12.6	17.2	15.5	17.2
Married couple families	na	na	6.0	6.1	9.4	7.3	8.3
Ratio of percent in poverty							
Mother-child/all families	2.95	4.16	3.61	3.14	2.66	2.76	2.53
Mother-child/married couple families	na	na	7.28	6.49	4.86	5.86	5.30

Source: U.S. Bureau of the Census, Current Population Survey

1970s, poverty rates increased among children in the 1980s. The elevation in poverty rates in the early 1980s captured public attention for two reasons. First, increased poverty among children was not confined to children in mother-child families. In a widely cited article that appeared in *Science* in 1989, Mary Jo Bane and David Ellwood (1989) pointed out that poverty was rising among children in two-parent families and researchers increasingly turned their attention to declining male wages in explanations of poverty trends (Bianchi 1993, Blank 1991). Second, increased child poverty in the 1980s was at odds with trends for the other "dependent" segment of the population, the elderly. Poverty rates among the elderly continued to decline in the 1980s while rates rose among children.

Attention to the plight of children was heightened for the demographic community by Samuel Preston (1984), who, in his Presidential Address to the Population Association of America in 1984, noted a seeming demographic anomaly: During the 1970s, the number of children shrank as a result of the "Baby Bust", the decline in fertility after the mid-1960s. On the other hand, the number of elderly grew rapidly due in part to medical improvements that led to an unprecedented increase in life expectancy. Based on sheer population size, one might have predicted both declining well-being for the elderly, as population pressure created more competition for resources, and improved well-being for children, as fewer of them vied for public dollars. But, according to Preston, just the opposite had occurred—things had gotten better for the elderly and worse for children. Prominent in his argument was a focus on trends in poverty for the two population groups.

As shown in Figure 2, over the past three decades, poverty has "juvenilized." Children's poverty rates rose relative to adult rates during the 1970s and 1980s. Relative to the elderly, children's rates of poverty rose dramatically between the late 1960s, when children's odds of poverty were only about 60% those for the elderly, and the early 1990s, when children's poverty rates climbed to almost twice those of the elderly.

For children, as for adult women, the distinction between absolute poverty levels and relative poverty rates is important. Rates of child poverty came down dramatically between the Great Depression of the 1930s and the mid-1970s (Hernandez 1993, Bianchi 1990, 1993, Lichter 1997). In 1959, when the official poverty figures were established, 27% of children were counted as poor, and this declined to 14–15% by the 1970s. During the same period, the poverty decline for the elderly was even sharper—36% of the elderly were poor in 1959; by the mid-1970s their rate of poverty dropped to 14–15%, a rate roughly equal to that of children's. After the mid-1970s, trends diverged for the two groups. The elderly continued to experience declines in poverty, with their poverty rate decreasing to 10–11% by the mid-1990s. Children's poverty rates, on the other hand, rose after the mid-1970s. During the 1980s and 1990s,

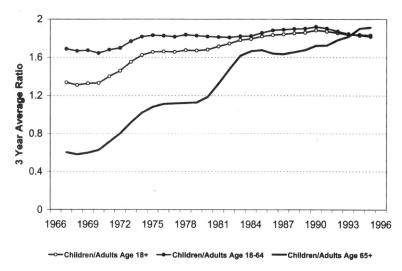

Figure 2 Children's relative poverty risks, 1966–1996

children's rates fluctuated between 20% and 23%, never dropping below about 20% poor after 1981. Hence, children's relative risks of poverty skyrocketed vis-à-vis the elderly.[5]

A Note on Children's Material Hardship

While there is little question, using official rates, that poverty has juvenilized (Lichter 1997), Mayer & Jencks (1994) question what this means for children.[6]

They argue that measures of serious hardship suggest continued improvement in the living standards that children enjoy—especially in the most

[5]Children as a percentage of all persons who are poor has not strayed much from the 40% mark. In the late 1960s, about 42–43% of the poor were children and in the mid-1990s, about 40% of the poor were children. But, this stability does not take into account that in 1966, children accounted for 36% of the population whereas in 1994 they made up only 27% of the population. If their relative risks of poverty were similar to adults, they should have accounted for a much smaller share of the poor than 40% in the 1990s.

[6]Mayer & Jencks (1994) note that using different adjustments for inflation gives a sizable range of poverty estimates for children. Secondly, the official poverty definition, which excludes income from nonrelatives such as cohabiting partners of the a child's mother, may underestimate income available to children. Third, Consumer Expenditure Survey data indicate that consumption by households with children may not have declined. This raises the possibility that more income may go unreported now than in the past, something that is also suggested by ethnographic evidence (e.g., Edin & Lein 1997). Finally, the official measure of poverty does not include the value of non-cash assistance, such as food stamps or Medicaid, both of which have been important for poor households in the past three decades.

income-deprived of households (Mayer & Jenks 1994). Mayer (1997b) paints a picture of poor children who are increasingly better housed over time. For example, the percentage of children in the lowest income quintile living in homes without a complete bathroom, with leaky roofs, holes in the floor, no central heat, no electric outlets, or no sewer or septic system has declined substantially. Children have become less likely to live in crowded housing conditions, though home ownership has declined and crime in children's neighborhoods has increased. Mayer & Jencks (1994) argue that a relatively high-quality housing stock in central cities has been vacated by the middle class, increasing the ability of the poor to live in uncrowded housing with amenities like indoor plumbing, electric lights, even air conditioning. However, the safety of the neighborhoods surrounding this housing stock may have deteriorated over time.

Mayer (1997b) also finds poor children today to be more likely to receive medical attention than in the past. In terms of health, the percentage of poor children who had not visited a doctor in the previous year declined, especially in the 1970s. Poor children are more likely to be immunized than in the past. In terms of consumer durables, children at the bottom of the income distribution became more likely to live in families that owned an air conditioner and had telephone service. In sum, Mayer (1997) argues, these indicators at least raise the possibility that trends in the official poverty measure based on money income do not adequately capture trends in material hardship of children. On indicators of housing, health, and certain consumption items, children's material conditions seem to have improved over time, even among the poorest income quintile. On these indicators, the most dramatic improvement took place during the 1970s, but conditions have not deteriorated since then, and some indicators (e.g., access to air conditioning) suggest continued improvement.

CAUSES OF THE "FEMINIZATION" AND "JUVENILIZATION" OF POVERTY

Having surveyed the trends in poverty—both trends in absolute poverty levels and relative poverty risks of women and men, mother-child versus two-parent families, and children compared with the elderly—we must ask what factors illuminate the trends? In the1970s, Pearce (1978) argued that the feminization of poverty was occurring for three reasons: 1. Women couldn't earn enough to be self-sufficient because of occupational segregation and low wages. 2. The private transfer system for supporting children was seriously flawed—men failed to pay child support. 3. The public transfer system/safety net was too meager to help. Aid to Families with Dependent Children (AFDC), the major public transfer program for women raising children alone, had multiple problems, and women didn't have access to better alternatives.

Each of these potential "causes" of "feminized" poverty—women's low earnings, lack of private transfers especially child support, and meager public assistance—remain worthy of investigation in the 1990s. But in addition, given the decline in the poverty risks of working-age women and the rise in child poverty in two-parent families in the early 1980s, trends in labor force attachment and earnings of men, especially less-educated men in unskilled or semiskilled jobs, also require examination.

Finally, the trend toward "juvenilization" of poverty, and the seemingly divergent path of children and the elderly, require attention to the public and private transfer systems that benefit children and the elderly. Children rely heavily on the transfer of earned income from their parents, and many poor children also rely on support, such as welfare, that derives from taxes paid by workers. The elderly rely on income generated from their own prior labor force participation (e.g. pension income) and savings, from social insurance programs that are financed by taxing the earnings of the working-age population (e.g., Social Security and Medicare), and, in some cases, their own continued (part-time) labor force participation. The question to be answered is: Why has the income flowing to one group, the poor or near-poor elderly, apparently been more adequate than to the other group, poor or near-poor children?

Women's Increased Employment and Earnings

The gains women were making in the labor force in the 1980s and 1990s were not readily apparent in the 1970s, when the "feminization of poverty" was noted by Pearce (1978). Women earned less than men, and the average earnings of women who were full-time, year-round workers had remained unchanged (fluctuating around 55% to 59% of men's earnings) since the mid-1950s (Spain & Bianchi 1996). During the 1950s, the gender segregation of occupations had actually increased and then declined only slightly in the 1960s (Blau & Hendrichs 1979, Jacobs 1989). At the beginning of the 1970s, it seemed as if women's progress toward equality in areas where it really mattered—better jobs and higher wages—was permanently stalled.

Now, two decades later, it is much easier to see that women made substantial progress in narrowing the gap in both occupational attainment and average wages after 1970 (Blau 1998). Although in 1990 over half of the female labor force would have to change occupations to be distributed across categories as were men, the decline in occupational segregation after 1970 was dramatic, especially when compared to the 1950s and 1960s (Bianchi & Rytina 1986, Bianchi 1995, Cotter et al 1995). Between 1980 and 1995, the ratio of women's to men's earnings among full-time, year-round workers, the most commonly used barometer of gender wage inequality, rose from 60% to 71% (Bianchi & Spain 1996: Figure 5 and Table 8). Women's hourly wages increased from 64% to 79% of men's. The decline in occupational gender segregation and narrowing of the gender wage gap coincided with an important alteration in female labor force patterns.

Women's employment increased substantially throughout the post-World War II period, but in the 1950s and 1960s the increase was greatest among women in their forties and fifties, women past the most intense years of child-rearing (Bianchi 1995, Goldin 1990, Smith & Ward 1989). In these decades, women worked before marriage and children, dropped out of the labor force to rear their children, and returned to the labor force after their children had grown, after a long absence from the labor force. Their pattern of lifetime attachment to the labor force was discontinuous.

During the 1970s and 1980s, the lifetime pattern of female labor participation shifted dramatically. The largest increases in rates of women's employment occurred among younger women, women in their twenties and thirties. Participation rates increased for those who in the past had been the least likely to be employed—married mothers with pre-school-age children. The result was a shift in the lifetime pattern of labor force participation of women. Recent cohorts of women are much more likely to be attached to the labor force throughout adulthood, and hence their patterns of employment have become much more similar to those of men.

The end result of this shift was that after 1970, the average work experience of women workers increased dramatically, an increase that paralleled the decline in the gender wage gap (Bianchi & Spain 1996, O'Neill & Polacheck 1993, Wellington 1993). It became increasingly difficult to predict whether a woman would engage in market work based on her marital and motherhood status. With the increase in work experience, it probably also become increasingly difficult—both unprofitable and illegal—for employers to discriminate based on gender as well.

The narrowing of the gender wage gap has led to considerable debate between those who attribute the narrowing primarily to gains made by women in education, work experience, and resulting real wage gains (Cotter et al 1997, O'Neill & Polacheck 1993) and those who argue that the narrowing is much more a result of stagnation or decline in male wages than it is improvement in female wages (Bernhardt et al 1995). Ample evidence indicates that income inequality has increased among both male and female workers (Levy 1995) and that less educated workers have been disadvantaged in the labor market during the past two decades (Levy & Murnane 1992). The question here is: To what extent do declining male wages (rather than rising female wages) explain the halt in the "feminization of poverty" in the 1980s?

Decline in Wages of Low-Skill Male Workers

One of the major explanations of the rise and then stability of high poverty rates for children in the 1980s, despite macroeconomic growth, has been the failure of growth to "trickle down" to poor children (Blank 1991), even poor children living with a male breadwinner (Bane & Ellwood 1989). Due to the decline in wages of less-educated workers relative to more-educated, more experienced workers (Bound & Johnson 1992, Katz & Murphy 1992, Juhn et al 1993, Levy & Murnane 1992, Blackburn et al 1991), children who resided with a parent who had a high school education or less were at increased risk of poverty relative to children living with a college-educated parent.

Levy (1995) has argued that the economic restructuring to improve productivity in manufacturing, delayed for a time after the oil price shocks of 1973 but inevitably set in motion by the tight monetary policy instituted in 1979 to control inflation, ultimately resulted in a substantially decreased demand for semiskilled workers in the United States. Manufacturing productivity was revived in the 1980s, but the losers were semi-skilled workers, those who had not gone beyond high school. During the 1980s, total durable goods employment declined by 1 million workers (Levy 1995:11).

Those facing import competition were the first to make changes. Due to large deficits and the globalization of trade and the availability of cheaper labor pools outside the United States, demand for low-skill labor declined as production jobs were either automated or moved overseas (Borjas et al 1992, Murphy & Welch 1992). At first, low-skill workers (with less than a high school education) were most affected—perhaps women even more than men as textile manufacturing moved outside US borders. Juhn (1992) shows that the declining employment of low-skill male workers between 1967 and 1987, though not initially due to wage changes, can be explained almost fully (for whites; partially, for blacks) by declining wages after 1973. Duration of spells of non-employment also lengthened.

By the 1980s, the demand for semi-skilled labor also declined, and men were especially vulnerable because it was men who were in the unionized, manufacturing jobs paying "family wages" that were undergoing transition. As Wetzel (1995:76) notes "before 1975, spending on domestically produced goods stimulated rapid job growth in goods-producing industries and provided "middle class" jobs with comparatively low educational requirements for millions of Americans." In reality, it was American men who held these jobs— women had never gained access and, hence, benefited primarily by being married to a worker who had one of these semiskilled jobs. After 1980, construction employment grew, but otherwise "employment in manufacturing and mining, where men outnumber women three to one and wages are high relative to the schooling levels of workers," declined considerably. (Wetzel 1995:76 and Table 2.2.).

Blau & Kahn (1997) ask the interesting question: "How has the dramatic decline in the gender gap in wages been achieved in the face of changes in the overall wage structure that were increasingly unfavorable to low-wage workers?" The answer is particularly informative for understanding how, at least in relative terms, poverty was becoming more concentrated among women until sometime in the 1970s, and then the trend halted when economic conditions deteriorated for both men and women at the bottom of the income distribution.

Blau & Kahn (1997) argue that, relative to men, it was high-wage rather than low-wage women workers who had more of a struggle to achieve equality in the 1980s. The supply of college-educated women workers increased faster than that of less-educated women workers. The gap between the wages of highly educated women and of men widened because of the high returns to skill in the 1980s and the lesser work experience of highly skilled women relative to men. At lower skill levels, occupational and industry trends and deunionization (e.g., the decline in durable manufacturing, discussed by Wetzel and Levy) resulted in more job loss for men than women while women increased their work experience vis-à-vis men. Also, the "unexplained" portion of the pay gap (capturing either discrimination or unexplained differences such as "motivation") diminished.

Blau & Kahn suggest that shifts in demand for labor benefitted women relative to men at lower skill levels but men relative to women at high skill levels. Hence, among workers close to the poverty level or below it, men lost out more than women, and this helps explain the end of the feminization of poverty in the early 1980s. The effect of the rising supply of women workers increased competition for jobs and was unfavorable to women as a group, but these negative supply effects were stronger for more highly educated women.

One of the ironies noted in the original formulation of the "feminization of poverty" thesis was that increased poverty for women occurred while affirmative action supposedly opened doors for women. There is some evidence to suggest that any affirmative action benefits for women ended in the 1980s (Leonard 1989)—that is, ended at the very time poverty stopped "feminizing." However, Blau & Kahn (1997) note that feedback effects of earlier affirmative action efforts of the 1960s and 1970s may have encouraged women to invest in their education and made employers less likely to stereotype and discriminate statistically—in effect, setting in motion actions that continued even after retrenchment in affirmative action efforts.[7]

Women's increasing ability to support themselves financially and men's decreased access to "family wage" jobs in the 1980s coincides reasonably well with the halt in the "feminization" of poverty among working-age adults after

---

[7]Goldin's (1990) historical analysis of women's employment and earnings over the last two centuries illustrates the complexity of sorting out trends in the gender wage gap and increases/decreases in discriminatory treatment of women. Her analysis suggests that narrowing wage gaps do not always signal declining discrimination and, reciprocally, increasing wage gaps can accompany more equal opportunities for women, at least in the short-run.

1980. But to understand poverty trends in single-parent families and child poverty, trends in family structure, child support, and welfare are also implicated. Changes in these factors are interrelated with trends in the earnings of women and men. For example, Wilson (1987) argues that a major factor in the declining rates of marriage among blacks is the disappearance of "family wage" jobs for men. McLanahan & Kelly (1997) estimate that the continued (albeit slower) increase in female-headed families in the 1980s would have kept feminizing poverty except that changes in labor force participation and earnings favored women and lowered the relative poverty ratios of women compared to men.

Increase in Never-Married Single Mothers and the Transfer of Child Support

By far the most common path to single parenting in the 1960s and 1970s was for a woman to marry, have one or more children within marriage, experience a marital disruption, and then raise dependent children on her own. Another path to single parenting became increasingly common in the 1980s and 1990s, especially among blacks. This was for an unmarried women to have a child and raise that child on her own. Between 1960 and the early 1990s, the proportion of female family householders who had never married and who had children increased from 4% to 31% (Bianchi 1995). Between 1983 and 1992, the proportion of children in single-parent homes with a never married parent rose 10 percentage points to 34% (Saluter 1991, Saluter 1993:29).

An economic profile of never-married mothers shows them to be very distinct from divorced mothers. Never-married mothers are much younger and less well-educated than divorced mothers. Consequently, only 39% of children with a never-married mother live with a parent who is employed, compared with 69% of those with a divorced mother. The median income of children with a never-married mother is only about one half that of children with a divorced mother. Almost two thirds of children with a never-married mother live in poverty compared with 38% of those with divorced mothers. Perhaps most important, whereas about one half of divorced mothers with children under age 21 report receiving some child support from the nonresident father of her children, that percentage drops to 17% among never-married mothers (Bianchi & Spain 1996: Table 10).

After low wages for women, the second reason Pearce (1978) noted for the "feminization of poverty" in the 1960s and 1970s was the failure of the private transfer system. When marriages dissolved or were never formed, mothers ended up caring for the children and fathers failed to financially support those children. Some argued that, ironically, the reform of divorce proceedings in the wake of the women's movement, making it easier to divorce and making it more difficult for women to be granted alimony awards, left women more vulnerable and unprotected than before reform (Weitzman 1985). Most importantly, enforcement of child support awards was minimal: Fathers failed to pay child support with relative impunity.

If court orders of support were difficult to obtain and enforce for divorced mothers, they were even more problematic for mothers who did not marry the father of their children. Hence, as the source of growth in the number of single parents shifted away from divorced mothers and to never-married mothers, particularly in the 1980s, the hurdles to the private transfer of funds from absent parents to their children grew. Now, paternity had to be established before a court order could be pursued. If welfare mothers pursued court action and were successful, only $50 of the support actually reached a mother and her children. The remainder went to the state to defray the cost of AFDC payments. Edin & Lein (1997), in their ethnographic work with low-income mothers, found widespread complicity of welfare mothers and fathers in avoiding the official child support system: Many mothers realized more gain from informal or occasional in-kind payments from the fathers of their children then they did by complying with the requirements to help identify the fathers of their children to the legal and administrative system. Fathers also reported little incentive to comply—and few sanctions—since so little of the income they provided would be directly passed through to their children.

Increased attention was given to the failures of the private transfer system in the 1980s and 1990s, in part because it was one strategy for better securing the well-being of poor women and children that had gained widespread political support. For liberals, it was difficult to argue with measures that would better secure the support for poor children. Particularly for feminists, measures that would enhance gender equality in the support of children seemed desirable. And conservatives, who argued that the problem with welfare was that it eroded recipients' sense of responsibility for their own lives, saw stricter child support enforcement as a way of enhancing male responsibility for their children and potentially lessening the state's role in supporting poor children.

At the end of the 1970s, the Census Bureau began collecting systematic national data on the receipt of child support by custodial mothers. The first collection, in 1979, showed that only about one third of women with children under age 21 received any support for those children. Estimates using data collected in the early 1980s suggested that the potential for increased child support collection from reform efforts was substantial: Instead of the $7 billion that was actually being collected in child support obligations, the potential for collection was near $30 billion (Garfinkel & Oellerich 1989). Data showed that the problem was both establishment of awards and collection of awards.

That is, only about 60% of mothers had an informal agreement or court-ordered child support award. Among those who had awards, a large fraction either did not receive any payments (about one quarter) or did not receive the full amount owed (an additional one quarter) (Lester 1991, Scoon-Rogers & Lester 1995).

Garfinkel & McLanahan (1995:213) note that in 1975, child support legislation and enforcement was almost entirely left up to the states, but since then there have been a series of federal laws enacted aimed at setting up a national child support enforcement bureaucracy or infrastructure, eliminating judicial discretion in setting award amounts, moving toward standard guidelines for setting amounts, increasing paternity establishment, and otherwise increasing compliance (for example, via mandatory withholding of child support obligations from wages). They argue that there has been considerable progress made in shoring up the private transfer system but that the changes are taking place very gradually requiring assessment of progress over relatively long intervals, 10 to 15 years.

Hanson et al (1996) assess trends in child support for the 1979 to 1990 period. On the surface, trends do not seem to support an assessment of progress. The rate of establishing awards dropped between 1978 and 1989, from 57% to 50% among custodial families recently eligible for child support (Hanson et al 1996: Table 1). Award amounts declined by 21% and there was a parallel decline in the proportion of an award amount that was actually received by the custodial parent over the 1978-89 period.[8]

Why has the decline in awards and payments occurred when child support enforcement has been strengthening? Hanson et al (1996) estimate that the decline in award rates was due primarily to a demographic shift—the increase in the proportion of new child support cases due to a nonmarital birth rather than a divorce. Secondly, award rates declined due to the decrease in earnings of nonresident fathers. These two changes went hand in hand: Nonmarital births tended to occur to mothers and fathers who were younger and had lower earnings than parents who divorce. If shifts in the marital status of parents and earnings of absent fathers had not occurred, Hanson et al (1996:Table 3) suggest that award rates would actually have increased a percentage point (rather than declining 7 percentage points). With regard to declining award amounts in the 1980s, nonresident fathers' lower average earnings, fewer children per award, and the failure of award amounts to be adjusted upward for inflation ex-

[8]Among all custodial mothers, not just those recently eligible for child support, there is stability but little decline: 59.1% had an award in 1978, 57.7% in 1989. Also, between 1978 and 1989, the average award payment declined by 12.5% among all custodial mothers with awards (Lester 1991:Table B and Table E). Hanson et al (1996: Appendix Table A1) estimate a 22.4% decline in payments for their sample of those who became eligible to receive child support in the immediate three years.

plain the decline.[9] The major factors explaining the decline in child support despite improvements in enforcement—less marriage and declining wages of fathers—may well be linked (Wilson 1987). Oppenheimer et al (1997) report that young men's increased difficulty in becoming established in the labor market in a secure job over the 1979–1990 period resulted in considerable delay in marriage. The delay in marriage among young men and women, particularly blacks—much more so than any change in nonmarital fertility rates—was the major factor increasing the proportion of births outside marriage in the 1980s (Smith et al 1996).

What can we conclude about the role of private transfers and trends in the feminization and juvenilization of poverty? There is little question that in terms of the likelihood of mother-child families residing in poverty, the failure of fathers to pay child support heightens the risk of poverty (Garfinkel et al 1994). However, examination of "income packaging" in female-headed families shows that child support is only one source—and rarely the major source—of income in these families (Knox & Bane 1994).

The declines in awards and amounts seem to coincide with increasing relative risks of income poverty for children over the period. However, they do not provide much explanatory power for the relative risks of poverty for adult women and men, as they suggest that absent parents, usually men, transferred relatively less income to custodial parents, usually women, at the end of the 1980s than at the beginning. Also, income transfers were worsening during a time (the early 1980s) when the position of female-maintained families may have improved relative to two-parent families.

Meager Government Support For Women and Children

Why have children lost ground vis-à-vis the elderly? Sources of public transfers differ greatly for the two groups, with those going to children less generous and declining over time and those going to the elderly more generous and much less susceptible, at least politically, to erosion over the past two decades. Ozawa (1995) shows that cash, non–means tested income keeps the elderly out of poverty while children most often rely on means-tested, non-cash income. Jensen et al (1993) analyze trends in the 1970s and 1980s and find that there has been an increase since 1970 in the percentage of children receiving public assistance, a sharp rise in children's reliance on public assistance rather than

---

[9]Interestingly, although the coefficient of mother's income on award rates and amounts is negative—suggesting mother's increased earnings works against child support—these effects are small and nonsignificant. Although others have reported that women's increased earnings may have hurt them in child support dispositions (Robbins 1992), these findings have been disputed on methodological grounds (Hanson et al 1996). Consistent with past findings (Bellar & Graham 1993), Hanson et al (1996) report that women's increased labor force participation and earnings do not seem to be a major factor in the decline in child support awards and amounts.

parental earnings, but a stagnation in the ameliorative effects of public assistance on child poverty during the 1980s. A number of studies that compare the United States with other European countries show the United States to be far less generous in its public support of children (e.g., Bergmann 1996, Rainwater 1995, Smeeding et al 1997). Forster (1994) compares the poverty experience of female-head families and children in various OECD countries before and after taxes/transfers and shows that the US tax and public transfer system does the least of any of the countries to alleviate child poverty.

Burtless (1994) has tracked trends in spending on the poor between 1960 and 1990, showing that overall, spending on the poor increased greatly when the economy was doing well in the 1960s, but that public willingness to support programs for the poor declined dramatically after the economic downturn that began in 1974. Burtless also documents a trend away from cash assistance and toward in-kind assistance.

A distinction is usually made between "means-tested" or welfare programs and social insurance programs such as Social Security, Medicare, and unemployment compensation (Sawhill 1988). The former are highly targeted as low income is a requirement for receipt. The latter offer protections to (potentially) everyone against certain causes of poverty such as short-term job loss, disability, or old age. The elderly have been covered under social insurance programs, primarily Social Security and Medicare, and their benefits have been indexed to the Consumer Price Index (CPI) so that they have kept up with inflation.[10]

Children, on the other hand, have more often been covered by means tested programs such as AFDC (until 1996, now TANF—Temporary Assistance to Needy Families), Medicaid, or food stamps. AFDC benefit levels have eroded over time as they were never indexed to the CPI. The introduction of Medicaid and Food Stamp assistance prevented a decline in benefits in the 1970s, but after 1980 welfare benefits to families with children declined in real terms (Moffitt 1992). Public transfers reach poor children but they do not lift them from

---

[10]Burtless (1994) points out that the universality of the social insurance programs benefiting the elderly are both its strength and weakness. Because receipt is widespread, programs such as Social Security and Medicare have considerable public support. However, because Social Security and Medicare are not targeted on the poor, equity issues are raised when low-income wage workers are taxed to provide benefits to non-poor elderly. Whether programs such as Social Security will be substantially curtailed in the future is currently being debated as the impending retirement of the large Baby Boom generation looms on the horizon. But to date, poverty among the elderly has been reduced appreciably by Social Security, much more appreciably than has been the case for any program benefitting low income children. Burtless (1994:64) notes that Social Security has a dramatic effect on the poverty rates of the elderly. For example, he claims that in the mid-1980s, whereas 56% of the elderly would have been poor before receiving Social Security, poverty rates were reduced to 14% after including Social Security transfers.

poverty to nearly the extent that social insurance transfers eliminate poverty among the elderly (Danziger & Weinberg 1994).

Effects of Poverty on Children

One of the reasons the increase in child poverty in the 1980s—both absolutely and relative to the elderly and working age adult population—has been of such great concern is because of the presumed negative impact of low income on children's development. Duncan & Brooks-Gunn (1997a,b) propose multiple pathways through which poverty affects child outcomes. The most direct is perhaps through a child's health and nutrition: Lack of money directly exposes children to greater risks of hunger, of environmental hazards such as lead ex- posure, and of poor birth outcomes. Indeed, one of the major governmental programs for the poor, WIC, is specifically targeted at improving birth and early childhood outcomes. Poor children are 1.7 times more likely to weigh un- der 2500 grams at birth, 3.5 times more likely to have dangerously high blood- lead levels, twice as likely to experience stunting (being in the lowest 5% of height for age), and twice as likely to have short-stay hospital periods during the preceding year. Poor children are 10 times more likely to have experienced hunger (food insufficiency) at least once in the past year. Mortality rates in infancy and childhood are also much higher among the poor.

Poor children's cognitive ability and school achievement are also lower than among non-poor children. Goldstein (1990), in a review of cognitive test scores at age 4, reports that children from low socioeconomic status families have IQ test scores 10–15 points lower than children from higher socioeco- nomic families. Four health conditions—low birth weight, lead absorption, anemia, and ear infections—more prevalent among low income children, may account for 2 points. Poor children are 30% to 40% more likely to experience developmental delays and learning disabilities and are twice as likely to repeat a grade in school, be expelled, or drop out before graduating from high school (Duncan & Brooks-Gunn 1997a:Table 1.)

Behavioral outcomes differ between poor and non-poor children, especially among adolescent and older children. Parents of poor children are more likely to report that their child has had an emotional or behavioral problem (though less likely to report that a child has been treated for such a problem). Nonmari- tal birth rates are three times as high for poor as for non-poor teenage girls. Poor teens and young adults are twice as likely to be "idle," that is, neither working nor in school. Reported cases of neglect and child abuse are almost seven times higher among poor than non-poor children, and poor children are twice as likely to be in families victimized by violent crimes (Duncan & Brooks-Gunn 1997a).

Poor parents provide less stimulating home environments (fewer toys and materials to foster child development) and have styles of disciplining their children that may be less conducive to good child outcomes (McLoyd 1990, Duncan et al 1998). The implication is that these inadequacies flow from the limited financial resources of poor children's families (e.g., lack of money to purchase books). Studies that measure these aspects of children's families, according to Duncan & Books-Gunn (1997b), account for a substantial portion of the effect of income on cognition and achievement in the early years. (Studies cited in support are Duncan et al 1994, Korenman et al 1995, Brooks-Gunn et al 1993.) Goldstein's (1990) review of studies of four-year-old children suggests that differential home environments may account for 7 points of the 10–15 point difference in IQ scores between children from families of low and high socioeconomic status.

It is hypothesized that parental interactions with their children may differ in poor families and that these differences result in poorer outcomes. For example, middle-class mothers may talk to their young children more, engage their children in more verbal interaction, than do lower-class mothers. Poverty may be associated with harsher discipline, e.g. spanking, and this may result in poor child outcomes (McLeod & Shanahan 1993) or more conflict in adolescence (Conger et al 1994, 1997, Simons et al 1996). However, others find that the linkages between poverty, poorer parenting practices, and poor child outcomes are not all that strong. Mayer (1997a,b), based on analyses of longitudinal data (e.g., the NLSY and the PSID), finds that parent-child interactions are important for child outcomes, but that the data do not suggest that parents' income is highly predictive of parenting practices. Hanson et al (1997) also report very weak linages between income and parenting practices.

Studies of adolescents also point to poor parental mental health, perhaps caused in part by worries about money, as a factor in adult-adolescent conflict and poor behavior outcomes for teens (Conger et al 1997, McLoyd et al 1994). However, problems of causal ordering arise, as poor mental or emotional health on the part of parents may be a cause of poverty rather than a result (Mayer 1997a).

Finally, poverty often constrains parents' choice of residence: Poor parents live in less safe neighborhoods and send their children to lower-quality schools. These neighborhood effects, a result of income constraints, may add to aspects of families that create poor child outcomes (Wilson 1987). Living in less affluent neighborhoods is associated with lower test scores, poorer parenting practices, and less advantageous learning environments in the home (Brooks-Gunn et al 1993, Brooks-Gunn et al 1997, Klebanov et al 1994). Also, poor parents change residences more often, and the sheer disruption caused by frequent moves has been shown to be detrimental to children's educational functioning (Astone & McLanahan 1994, Tucker et al 1998).

Despite all the research, there continues to be debate about how much money matters to outcomes for children. Duncan et al (1998) argue that in certain circumstances money matters a lot. When they examine the complete history of poverty for children, following them from birth to age 18, they conclude that poverty, early in a child's life (during the pre-school years) more so than later (during middle childhood and adolescence), is most detrimental to "good" young adult outcomes. Deep, long-term poverty is extremely problematic for children,and effects are strongest on academic achievement (high school graduation, college attendance, years of school completed) and less strong on behavioral outcomes (teen births).

Mayer (1997a) argues that income matters but its effect on any one outcome is not all that large. She does not find a large effect of money on outcomes such as test scores, school completion, educational attainment, teen childbearing, single motherhood, idleness, and earnings in young adulthood, and Mayer believes this is because "government policies have done a lot to ensure that poor children get basic necessities most of the time" (Mayer 1997a:143).

Mayer (1997a) notes that in most social science research, there have been one of two types of theories that have been used to understand how parental income might affect children's life chances.One view, which she labels an "investment theory" approach, suggests that poor families are less well able to purchase those things that would enhance their children's life chances and this is why poor children are less successful, on average. On the other hand, the "good-parent" theory suggests that it is not income and the lack of investment by parents, per se, that results in poorer child outcomes but rather that low income reduces the effectiveness and quality of parenting. Parents' stress is high in poor families, and this leads to less effective parenting (Huston 1994). Reminiscent of the "culture of poverty" argument, this theory suggests that poor parents, as a result of their low income, develop values and behaviors that, while adaptive, may mean that they do not become role models of success for their children. Proponents of the different perspectives all see money as important to the explanation of child outcomes, but those subscribing to the poor role model theory would not expect that merely increasing income will improve child outcomes. The problem, as Mayer sees it, is that poor families differ from non-poor families in more than just access to income.[11]

[11]One of the problems in assessing the impact of poverty on child outcomes is that often data sets with good indicators of child well-being have rather poor measures of income. This leads to considerable error in the estimation of the effects of income on child outcomes. Separating effects of family structure, parental education, and family income is difficult because these factors are intertwined in complex ways, but a number of studies have attempted to do this with large, nationally representative data sets. These studies, reported in Duncan & Brooks-Gunn (1997a) and summarized by McLanahan (1997), suggest that, to the extent that "causal" factors can be isolated, the effects of income are stronger than the effects of family structure on cognition and achievement, but that family structure matters more than income for behavioral outcomes.

SUMMARY AND CONCLUSION

To summarize the trends in the "feminization and juvenilization" of poverty:

Adult Women   Between 1950 and the mid- to late-1970s, poverty feminized, but it did so as absolute poverty levels declined for women. In the early 1980s, this reversed: Poverty was no longer feminizing, except among the elderly (and perhaps young adults). At the same time, absolute poverty levels rose somewhat for working age women but continued to decline for the elderly.

Families   Poverty became more concentrated in mother-child families in the 1960s and early 1970s, less concentrated in these families in the late 1970s and early 1980s, and again more concentrated in single-parent families after the mid-1980s. However, if the official poverty measure were altered—to better capture in-kind transfer income such as food stamps, adjust for taxes and tax credits for childcare or the Earned Income Tax Credit (EITC), and move to a household-based accounting scheme where income of cohabiting partners and other nonrelatives were included in assessing poverty—all changes that have been recommended by a National Academy of Sciences Panel for improving the measurement of poverty and that are currently being implemented at least on an experimental basis by the Census Bureau (Citro & Michael 1995)—the relative poverty rates of married couples and single-parent families might be altered. According to Betson & Michael (1997), these changes would increase the proportion of poor children living in two-parent families and reduce the share in single-parent families.

Children   Using the official measure of poverty, poverty has "juvenilized" since 1960. Especially relative to the elderly, children's risks of poverty have increased over time. Children's absolute levels of poverty rose in the 1980s in both two-parent and one-parent families and remained high (over 20%) throughout the 1990s as poverty levels for the elderly continued to decline. However, researchers have raised questions about how well the official measure captures children's material hardship. As poverty rates increased and remained high for children, children's access to better quality housing, medical care, and other amenities such as air conditioning and telephones, appears to have improved (Mayer 1997b, Jencks & Mayer 1989).

Important to understanding these trends are several factors: 1. the increase in women's employment and earnings in the 1980s and 1990s; 2. the decline in manufacturing employment and "family wage" jobs that negatively affected less-educated workers but probably had a greater impact on men then women in the 1980s; 3. the increase in "non-marriage" and resulting shift in single-parent families from those with a divorced parent, usually a mother, to those with a never-married mother in the 1980s; 4. the likely interaction between trends in men's earnings and the movement away from marriage among the poor and the negative effect this had on private transfers of fathers' income to children even as child support enforcement was improved in the 1980s and 1990s; and 5. the divergent trends in the effectiveness of public transfers to alleviate poverty among children and the elderly.

Finally, it is the interpretation of these trends in "feminization" or "juvenilization" of poverty and the assessment of the consequences for women (and men) and their children that is most important. Do the trends suggest increasing "fairness" or "unfairness" in the life circumstances of women and men? How detrimental are the developmental consequences of a childhood spent in poverty? Is it money or "something else" that is needed to improve the life chances of poor children? It is these "equity" and "life chances" questions that are the most difficult to answer but that also warrant the most attention, both in terms of social science research and public debate.

ACKNOWLEDGMENTS

I would like to thank Jane Dye and Lekha Subaiya for research assistance and Sara McLanahan, Stanley Presser, Daphne Spain, and especially, Reeve Vanneman, for helpful comments. I am also indebted to the support provided by the William and Flora Hewlett Foundation to the Center on Population, Gender, and Social Inequality at the University of Maryland.

> **Visit the *Annual Reviews home page* at**
> **http://www.AnnualReviews.org.**

Literature Cited

Astone NM, McLanahan SS. 1994. Family structure, residential mobility, and school dropout: a research note. *Demography* 31: 575–84

Bane MJ, Ellwood DT. 1989. One fifth of the nations' children: Why are they poor? *Science* 245:1047–53

Beller AH, Graham J. 1993. *Small Change: The Economics of Child Support*. New Haven, CT: Yale Univ. Press

Bergmann BR. 1996. *Saving Our Children from Poverty: What the United States Can Learn From France*. New York: Russell Sage

Bernhardt A, Morris M, Handcock MS. 1995. Women's gains or men's losses? A closer look at the shrinking gender gap in earnings. *Am. J. Sociol.* 101:302–28

Betson DM, Michael RT. 1997. Why so many children are poor. *Future Child.* 7:25–39

Bianchi SM. 1990. America's children: mixed prospects. *Popul. Bull.* 45:1–43

Bianchi SM. 1993. Children of poverty: Why are they poor? In *Child Poverty and Public Policy*, ed. JA Chafel. Washington, DC: Urban Inst. Press

Bianchi SM. 1995. Changing economic roles of women and men. In *State of the Union. Vol. 1. Economic Trends,* ed. R Farley, pp. 107–54. New York: Russell Sage

Bianchi, SM, Rytina N. 1986. The decline in occupational sex segregation during the 1970s: Census and CPS comparisons. *Demography* 23:79–86

Bianchi SM, Spain D. 1996. Women, work, and family in America. *Popul. Bull.* 51: 1–48

Blackburn ML, Bloom DE, Freeman RB. 1991. *Changes in earnings differentials in the 1980s: concordance, convergence, causes, and consequences. NBER Work. Pap. No. 3901*

Blank R. 1991. *Why were poverty rates so high in the 1980s? NBER Work. Pap. 3878*

Blau FD. 1998. Trends in the well-being of American women, 1970–1995. *J. Econ. Lit.* 35:112–65

Blau FD, Hendricks WE. 1979. Occupational segregation by sex: trends and prospects. *J. Hum. Resourc.* 14:197–210

Blau FD, Kahn LM. 1997. Swimming upstream: trends in the gender wage differential in the 1980s. *J. Labor Econ.* 15:1–42

Borjas G Jr, Froman RB, Katz LF. 1992. On the labor market effects of immigration and trade. In *The Economic Effects of Immigration in Source and Receiving Countries*, ed. G Borjas, R Freedman. Chicago: Univ. Chicago Press

Bound J, Johnson G. 1992. Changes in the structure of wages during the 1980s: an evaluation of alternative explanations. *Am. Econ. Rev.* 82:371–92

Brooks-Gunn J, Duncan GJ, Aber JL. 1997. *Neighborhood Poverty: Context and Consequences for Children.* Vol. 1. New York: Russell Sage

Brooks-Gunn J, Duncan GJ, Klebanov PK, Sealand N. 1993. Do neighborhoods influence child and adolescent behavior? *Am. J. Sociol.* 99:335–95

Burtless G. 1994. Public spending on the poor: historical trends and economic limits. See Danziger et al 1994, pp. 51–84

Chase-Lansdale PL, Brooks-Gunn J, eds. 1995. *Escaping from Poverty: What Makes a Difference for Children?* New York: Cambridge Univ. Press

Citro C, Michael RT. 1995. *Measuring Poverty: A New Approach.* Washington, DC: Natl. Acad.

Conger RD, Conger KJ, Elder GH Jr. 1997. Family economic hardship and adolescent adjustment: mediating and moderating processes. See Duncan & Brooks-Gunn 1997b, pp. 288–310

Conger RD, Ge X, Elder GH Jr, Lorenz FO, Simons RL. 1994. Economic stress, coercive family process and developmental problems of adolescents. *Child Dev.* 65: 541–61

Cotter DA, DeFiore JM, Hermsen JM, Kowalewski BM, Vanneman R. 1995. Occupational gender desegregation in the 1980s. *Work Occup.* 22:3–21

Cotter DA, DeFiore JM, Hermsen JM, Kowalewski BM, Vanneman R. 1997. Same data, different conclusions: comment on Bernhardt et al. *Am. J. Sociol.* 102: 1143–62

Danziger SH, Sandefur GD, Weinberg DH, eds. 1994. *Confronting Poverty: Prescriptions for Change.* New York: Russell Sage

Danziger SH, Weinberg DH. 1994. The historical record: trends in family income, inequality, and poverty. See Danziger et al 1994, pp. 51–84

Duncan GJ, Brooks-Gunn J. 1997a. The effects of poverty on children. *Future Child.* 7:55–71

Duncan GJ, Brooks-Gunn J. 1997b. *Consequences of Growing Up Poor.* New York: Russell Sage

Duncan GJ, Brooks–Gunn J, Klebanov PK. 1994. Economic deprivation and early childhood development. *Child Dev.* 65: 296–318

Duncan GJ, Yeung WJ, Brooks-Gunn J, Smith JR. 1998. How much does childhood poverty affect on the life chances of children? *Am. Sociol. Rev.* 63:406–24

Edin K, Lein L. 1997. *Making Ends Meet: How Single Mothers Survive Welfare and Low-Wage Work.* New York: Russell Sage

England P. 1997. *Gender and access to money: What do trends in earnings and household poverty tell us? Pap. Conf. Reconfigurations of Class Gender*, Canberra, Aust., Aug.

Faber HS. 1995. *Are lifetime jobs disappearing? Job duration in the United States: 1973–93. Work. Pap. No. 5014.* Cambridge, MA: Natl. Bur. Econ. Res.

Farley R, ed. 1995. *State of the Union.* Vol. 1. *Economic Trends.* New York: Russell Sage

Forster MF. 1994. *The effects on net transfers on low income families among non-elderly families. OECD Econ. Stud. No. 22*

Freeman J, ed. 1988. *Women: A Feminist Perspective.* Mountain View, CA: Mayfield. 3rd ed.

Fuchs VR, Reklis DM. 1992. America's children: economic perspectives and policy options. *Science* 255:41–46

Furstenberg FF Jr. 1995. Dealing with dads: the changing roles of fathers. See Chase-Lansdale & Brooks-Gunn 1995, pp. 189–210

Furstenberg FF Jr. 1988. Good dads–bad dads: the two faces of fatherhood. In *The Changing American Family and Public Policy*, ed. AJ Cherlin, pp. 193–218. Washington, DC: Urban Inst. Press

Garfinkel I. 1992. *Assuring Child Support: An Extension of Social Security.* New York: Russell Sage

Garfinkel I, McLanahan S. 1986. *Single Mothers and Their Children: A New American Dilemma.* Washington, DC: Urban Inst. Press

Garfinkel I, McLanahan S. 1995. The effects of child support reform on child well-being. See Chase-Lansdale & Brooks-Gunn 1995, pp. 211–38

Garfinkel I, McLanahan S, Robins PK, eds. 1994. *Child Support and Child Well-Being*. Washington, DC: Urban Inst. Press

Garfinkel I, Oellerich D. 1989. Noncustodial father's ability of pay child support. *Demography* 26:219–34

Goldin C. 1990. *Understanding the Gender Gap*. New York: Oxford Univ. Press

Goldstein N. 1990. *Explaining socioeconomic differences in children's test scores. Work. Pap. H–90–1.* Harvard Univ. Malcolm Wiener Cent. Soc. Policy, John F. Kennedy Sch. Gov.

Hanson TL, Garfinkel I, McLanahan SS, Miller CK. 1996. Trends in child support outcomes. *Demography* 33:483–96

Hanson TL, McLanahan S, Thomson E. 1997. Economic resources, parental practices, and children's well-being. See Duncan & Brooks-Gunn 1977b, pp. 190–238

Hernandez DJ. 1993. *America's Children: Resources from Family, Government, and the Economy*. New York: Russell Sage

Huston AC 1994. Children in poverty: designing research to affect policy. *Soc. Policy Rep.* 8:1–12

Jacobs J. 1989. Long-term trends in occupational segregation by sex. *Am. J. Sociol.* 95:160–73

Jensen L, Eggebeen D, Lichter D. 1993. Child poverty and the ameliorative effects of public assistance. *Soc. Sci. Q.* 74:542–59

Juhn C. 1992. Decline of male labor market participation: the role of declining market opportunities. *Q. J. Econ.* 107:79–121

Juhn C, Murphy KM, Pierce B. 1993. Wage inequality and the rise in returns to skill. *J. Polit. Econ.* 101:410–42

Katz LF, Murphy KM. 1992. Changes in relative wages, 1963–87: supply and demand factors. *Q. J. Econ.* 107:35–78

Leonard JS. 1989. Women and affirmative action. *J. Econ. Perspect.* 3:61–75

Klebanor PK, Brooks-Gunn J, Duncan GH. 1994. Does neighborhood and family affect parenting, mental health, and social suport? *J. Marriage Fam.* 56:441–55

Knox VW, Bane MJ. 1994. Child support and schooling. See Garfinkel et al 1994, pp. 285–316

Korenman S, Miller JE, Sjaastad JE. 1995. Long-term poverty and child development in the United States: results from the NLSY. *Child. Youth Serv. Rev.* 17:127–55

Lester G. 1991. Child support and alimony: 1989. *U.S. Bureau of the Census, Curr. Popul. Rep. Ser. P60–173.* Washington, DC: US Gov. Print. Off.

Levy F. 1987. *Dollars and Dreams:The Changing American Income Distribution*. New York: Russell Sage

Levy F. 1995. Incomes and income inequality. See Farley 1995, pp. 1–58

Levy F, Murnane RJ. 1992. U.S. earnings levels and earnings inequality: a review of recent trends and proposed explanations. *J. Econ. Lit.* 30:1333–81

Lichter DT. 1997. Poverty and inequality among children. *Annu. Rev. Sociol.* 23: 121–45

Mayer SE. 1997a. *What Money Can't Buy: Family Income and Children's Life Chances*. Cambridge, MA: Harvard Univ. Press

Mayer SE. 1997b. Trends in the economic well-being and life chances of America's children. See Duncan & Brooks-Gunn 1997b, pp. 49–69

Mayer SE, Jencks C. 1994. *Has poverty really increased among children since 1970? Work. Pap. 94–14.* Evanston, IL: Northwest. Univ. Cent. Urban Aff. Policy Res.

Mayer SE, Jencks C. 1989. Poverty and the distribution of material hardship. *J. Hum. Resourc.* 24:88–111

McLanahan SS. 1997. Parent absence or poverty: Which matters more? See Duncan & Brooks-Gunn 1997b, pp. 35–48

McLanahan SS, Kelly EL. 1997. *The feminization of poverty: past and future.* Unpublished pap.

McLanahan SS, Sorenson A, Watson D. 1989. Sex differences in poverty, 1950–80. *Signs* 15:102–22

McLeod JD, Shanahan MJ. 1993. Poverty, parenting, and children's mental health. *Am. Sociol. Rev.* 58:351–66

McLoyd VC. 1990. The impact of economic hardship on black families and children: psychological distress, parenting, and socioemotional development. *Child Dev.* 61: 311–46

McLoyd VC, Jayaratne TB, Ceballo R, Borquez J. 1994. Unemployment and work interruption among African American single mothers: effects on parenting and adolescent socioemotional functioning. *Child Dev.* 65:562–89

Moffitt R. 1992. Incentive effects of the U.S. welfare system: a review. *J. Econ. Lit.* 30: 1–61

Murphy KM, Welch F. 1992. Wage differentials in the 1980s: the role of international trade. In *Workers and Their Wages: Changing Patterns in the United States,* ed. M. Kosters. Washington, DC: Am. Enterprise Inst.

Murray C. 1984. *Losing Ground: American Social Policy, 1950–1980.* New York: Basic Books

O'Neill J, Polachek S. 1993. Why the gender

gap in wages narrowed in the 1980s. *J. Labor Econ.* 11:205–28

Oppenheimer VK, Kalmijn M, Lim N. 1997. Men's career development and marriage timing during a period of rising inequality. *Demography* 34:311–30

Ozawa MN. 1995. Anti-poverty effects of public income transfers on children. *Child. Youth Serv. Rev.* 17:43–59

Pearce D. 1978. The feminization of poverty: women, work, and welfare. *Urban Soc. Change Rev.* 11:128–36

Pearce D. 1988. Farewell to alms: women's fare under welfare. See Freeman 1988, pp. 502–15

Presser HB. 1999. Decapitating the U.S. Census Bureau's head of household: feminist mobilization in the 1970s. *Fem. Econ.* In press

Preston S. 1984. Children and the elderly: divergent paths for America's dependents. *Demography* 21:435–57

Rainwater L. 1995. Poverty and the income package of working parents: the United States in comparative perspective. *Child. Youth Serv. Rev.* 17:11–41

Robins PK 1992. Why did child support award levels decline from 1978 to 1985? *J. Hum. Resour.* 27:362–79

Saluter AF. 1991. Marital status and living arrangements: March 1990. U.S. Bureau of the Census. *Curr. Popul. Rep. Ser. P20-450.* Washington, DC: US Gov. Print. Off.

Saluter AF. 1993. Marital status and living arrangements: March 1992. U.S. Bureau of the Census. *Curr. Popul. Rep. Ser. P20-468.* Washington, DC: US Gov. Print. Off.

Sawhill IV. 1988. Poverty in the U.S.: Why is it so persistent? *J. Econ. Lit.* 26:1073–119

Scoon-Rogers L, Lester G. 1995. Child support for custodial mothers and fathers: 1991. U.S. Bureau of the Census. *Curr. Popul. Rep. Ser. P60-187.* Washington, DC: US Gov. Print. Off.

Shortridge K. 1984. Poverty is a woman's problem. In *Women: A Feminist Perspective*, ed. J Freeman, p. 492–501. Mountain View, CA: Mayfield

Simons RL, et al. 1996. *Understanding Differences Between Divorced and Intact Families.* Thousand Oaks, CA: Sage

Smeeding TM, Rainwater L, Danziger S. 1997. *Child poverty in advanced economies: the economy, the family, and the state.* Presented. at Annu. Meet. Am. Sociol. Assoc., Toronto, Can.

Smith HL, Morgan SP, Koropeckyj-Cox T. 1996. A decomposition of trends in the nonmarital fertility ratios of blacks and whites in the United States, 1960–92. *Demography* 33:141–51

Smith JP, Ward M. 1989. Women in the labor market and the family. *J. Econ. Perspect.* 3:9–23

Spain D, Bianchi SM. 1996. *Balancing Act: Motherhood, Marriage, and Employment Among American Women.* New York: Russell Sage

Tucker CJ, Marx J, Long L. 1998. 'Moving On': residential mobility and children's school lives. *Sociol. Educ.* 71:111–29

US Bur. Census. 1996. Income, poverty, and valuation of noncash benefits: 1994. *Curr. Pop. Rep. Ser. P60-189.* Washington, DC: US Gov. Print. Off.

Weitzman LJ. 1985. *The Divorce Revolution.* New York: Free Press

Wellington A. 1993. Changes in the male/female wage gap, 1976–85. *J. Hum. Resourc.* 28:383–411

Wetzel, JR. 1995. Labor force, unemployment, and earnings. See Farley 1995, pp. 59–106

Wilson WJ. 1987. *The Truly Disadvantaged: The Inner City, the Underclass, and Public Policy.* Chicago: Univ. Chicago

Annu. Rev. Sociol. 1999. 25:335–61

THE DETERMINANTS AND CONSEQUENCES OF WORKPLACE SEX AND RACE COMPOSITION

Barbara F. Reskin,[1] *Debra B. McBrier,*[2] *and Julie A. Kmec*[3]

[1]Department of Sociology, Harvard University, Cambridge, Massachusetts 02138; e-mail: reskin@wjh.harvard.edu; [2]Department of Sociology, University of Miami, Coral Gables, Florida 33124-2208; [3]Department of Sociology, University of Pennsylvania, Philadelphia, Pennsylvania 19104; e-mail: jkmec@sas.upenn.edu

KEY WORDS: sex composition, organizational demography, organizational sex ratios, organizational race ratios

ABSTRACT

This chapter reviews research on the determinants and consequences of race and sex composition of organizations. Determinants include the composition of the qualified labor supply; employers' preferences, including the qualifications they require; the response of majority groups; and an establishment's attractiveness, size, and recruiting methods. The race and sex composition of an establishment affects workers' cross-group contact; stress, satisfaction, and turnover; cohesion; stereotyping; and evaluation. Composition also affects organizations themselves, including their performance, hiring and promotion practices, levels of job segregation, and wages and benefits. Theory-driven research is needed (*a*) on the causal mechanisms that underlie the relationships between organizational composition and its determinants and consequences and (*b*) on the form of the relationships between organizational composition and workers outcomes (e.g., cross-group contact, cohesion, turnover, etc.). Research is needed on race and ethnic composition, with a special focus on the joint effects of race and sex.

INTRODUCTION

Almost 20 years ago, Baron & Bielby (1980) appealed to researchers studying stratification in labor markets to "bring the firm back in." "Firms," they argued,

0360-0572/99/0815-0335$08.00

"link the 'macro' and 'micro' dimensions of work organization and inequality" (p. 738). They practiced what they preached, publishing pathbreaking studies of the impact of organizational characteristics on the level of sex segregation in California firms (see, e.g., Bielby & Baron 1986, Baron & Bielby 1986) and California state agencies (see, e.g., Baron et al 1991, Baron & Newman 1989). Researchers have since begun to collect survey data on work organizations (see, e.g., Kalleberg et al 1996, Osterman 1994). These data, along with studies of work group dynamics, support a growing body of scholarship on the determinants of the sex and race composition of organizations and on the consequences of that composition for workers and for the organizations themselves. Many of these analyses have been guided by the renewed attention to the importance of organizational demography for workers and establishments (Pfeffer 1983, Martin 1985, Baron & Newman 1989, Davis-Blake 1992, Mittman 1992, Shenhav & Haberfeld 1992, Tsui et al 1992), often built on the insights of Kanter (1977) and P Blau (1977).

The sex and race composition of an organization is an important expression of its social structure. In the aggregate, compositions of organizations are indicative of the extent to which sex and race serve as bases of workers' differentiation across the economy. Thus, organizations' composition allows the study of the determinants of sex- and race-based ascription in employment in general. Establishments' race and sex compositions shape the demographic mix in which Americans work and their likelihood of contact with persons from their own and other races and sexes. Establishments provide a context in which researchers can test competing theories about how composition affects workers from numerical minority and majority groups. Thus, scholars can use establishment data to address a question of considerable moment in contemporary political dialogue: the consequences of diversity within organizations.

Researchers have addressed some of the above questions with data on occupations or industries. But occupations and industries do not employ workers or constitute the settings in which people work. Establishments are both actors in employment decisions and the settings in which workers perform. Hence, understanding the factors that affect the race and sex composition of establishments, and the effects of those compositions on workers and organizations, illuminates not only what establishments do, but when and why their decisions matter for workers and work groups.

Composition refers to the prevalence of some attribute or the distribution of some variable within a unit. To describe an organization's composition with respect to some demographic characteristic, we need to know the distribution of some demographic trait within the organization (e.g., the number of females and males). When data are available on the share a sex or race has of the pool from which establishments recruit (e.g., similar organizations, the industry, the local labor force), researchers can assess whether sex-race groups are under-, over-, or proportionally represented in organizations.

Researchers have drawn attention to the sex or race segregation of workers across occupations, and some have examined sex and race segregation by industry (Jacobs 1989, Reskin 1993, Cotter et al 1998). In the context of employment, segregation refers to the degree to which two or more groups are differently distributed across work settings. Thus, an organization in which sexes or races are employed proportionally to their share of the labor pool may nonetheless be highly segregated if job assignments are based on sex or race, and a one-sex–dominated establishment could nevertheless be perfectly integrated across jobs if the minority sex was represented in the same proportion in every job.

After briefly describing the race and sex composition of US establishments, we review research on the causes of sex and race composition of organizations. We then review studies of the consequences of composition for workers and their employers.

SEX AND RACE COMPOSITION OF ORGANIZATIONS

Organizations can be described in terms of their degree of differentiation on various dimensions. This chapter shows that a consequential and highly variable dimension of organizational differentiation is sex and race composition. According to the National Organizations Study (NOS), a 1991 nationally representative survey of organizations (Kalleberg et al 1996), one fifth of the employees in an average establishment are minorities, in keeping with minorities' share of the US labor force (US Bur. Census 1998:Table 621). However, almost one in four establishments employed no minorities, and in slightly more than one quarter of organizations, minority employees numbered less than one in ten (BF Reskin, unpublished data). Thus, in over half of US establishments studied, minorities are substantially underrepresented.

Women are distributed more evenly across establishments than are minorities. On average, almost half of an establishment's full-time employees are female. However, in one establishment in nine, less than 10% of full-time employees are female, whereas in one in 14, more than 90% are female [computed from NOS data (Kalleberg et al 1996)]. In sum, US work organizations are far from homogeneous with respect to sex and race composition. We turn to factors that give rise to the variations.

FACTORS AFFECTING SEX AND RACE COMPOSITIONS OF ORGANIZATIONS

There is a large body of research literature on the effects of sex and race on employment. Scholars emphasize both sex and race differences in the characteristics of the labor supply and race- and sex-linked considerations that affect an employer's hiring practices. Although we drew on this scholarship—especially research on the determinants of occupational or job segregation—to identify important causal factors, our review is limited to research on establishments.

Composition of the Labor Pools

The sex and race composition of establishments that are indifferent to a worker's race and sex and that use sex- and race-neutral recruitment methods should be roughly proportional to that of the supply of qualified workers in the labor pool. All else being equal, the larger a group's share of the qualified labor supply, the more of its members firms will employ. The larger the establishment relative to the size of the labor pool, the more its composition will depend on the composition of the labor supply (Szafran 1982:182, Cohn 1985:196).

The labor pools from which establishments hire may be the local or regional labor market, the establishment's industry, or the labor markets for the occupations that the establishment draws on, so the sex and race composition of these entities will influence an establishment's composition.[1] For example, an establishment's proximity to African American populations affects the likelihood of blacks applying for employment in that firm and the firm's likelihood of employing them (Holzer 1996:91). Among small- to medium-sized establishments, the more female-intensive the industry, the greater women's share of the jobs (Carrington & Troske 1994:521–23). In a national probability sample of establishments, women's share of full-time jobs in establishments was positively related to their share of jobs in the establishment's industry ($r = 0.71$; BF Reskin, unpublished data).

To the extent that the skills and credentials of prospective workers vary by sex or race within the pools from which establishments hire or employers mistakenly believe that they do, variation in employers' demand for skills will distribute the sexes and races unevenly across establishments. Skills are not identically distributed by sex and race (Farkas & Vicknair 1996). School segregation and tracking by race and sex have produced race and sex differences in educational attainment and majors, and hiring discrimination and occupational segregation have generated differences in experience and skills. Differences in the jobs that establishments comprise mean that establishments may differ in the skill levels they seek in workers, so it stands to reason that sex and race differences in skill or experience will affect an establishment's race and

---

[1]Geographic location affects an establishment's employment practices by limiting its labor market and serving as a proxy for local customs that affect an employer's hiring practices (Baron 1984:49). However, regional differences in residential segregation, industrial mix, unionism, employment norms, and cultural attitudes in the institutional community may obscure regional effects of demographic composition (Jones & Rosenfeld 1989:687).

sex composition. Little research exists on how the skills establishments require affect its composition. Surveys of employers indicate that retail and service-sector firms are more likely than manufacturing and public-service establishments to exclude black men (by making personality and appearance job qualifications) (Moss & Tilly 1996:260; P Moss & C Tilly, unpublished data). In addition, firms in four urban labor markets that required general experience were less likely to employ black females than those that did not require general experience, and requiring the use of arithmetic or computers reduced the likelihood of employing black males (Holzer 1996:100–1).[2] We know almost nothing about what factors lead firms to require skills that are distributed unequally across the sexes or races.

Statistical Discrimination

The more establishments use race or sex as proxy for an individual's skills, potential productivity, or employment costs—in other words, the more establishments practice statistical discrimination on the basis of race or sex—the more the representation of women and minorities will depart from that of the qualified labor supply (Mittman 1992:16). A tendency to discriminate statistically will exacerbate the effect of sex or race differences in skills or credentials in a labor pool on an establishment's composition. Small, nonbureaucratized establishments are hypothetically more likely than are large bureaucracies to practice statistical discrimination, because they are less likely to have regular procedures for assessing a worker's qualifications. However, there is no research on what kinds of firms are more likely to practice statistical discrimination or how statistical discrimination affects the sex and race composition of an establishment.

Hiring Discrimination

Some employers are openly reluctant to hire nonwhites or women (Neckerman & Kirschenman 1991, Kennelly 1998; P Moss & C Tilly, unpublished data) because they are hostile toward or uncomfortable with persons from certain race-sex groups or because social dissimilarity hinders trust (Tolbert & Oberfield 1991:306).[3] Others, however, pursue equal-employment or affirmative action hiring (Konrad & Linnehan 1995, Holzer & Neumark 1999). Variation among employers in hiring discrimination contributes to their varying compositions. The associations between the sex or race of employers and the compo-

---

[2]Although suburban firms require fewer skills for entry-level workers than do urban firms, the latter are more likely than the former to employ blacks (Holzer 1996:95).

[3]This propensity for "homosocial reproduction" (Kanter 1977:48, 63) may be especially apparent in establishments that have created organizational cultures into which they want employees to fit (Baron 1984:50–57).

sition of their employees are consistent with discrimination. Firms whose owners and supervisors are black disproportionately employ black workers (Carrington & Troske 1998b:251), and female-owned establishments are more likely than male-owned establishments to employ women, net of other firm characteristics, such as size (Carrington & Troske 1994:521–22).

Relative Numbers, Group Power, and Threat

The demographic makeup of the labor supply influences an organization's composition through its potential to affect the balance of power between groups. Some sociologists have argued that the greater the representation of minorities or women in a labor market, the better able they are to successfully challenge white men's monopoly of good jobs (Tienda & Lii 1987:145). Others, however, contend that there is a positive correlation between women's and minorities' share of jobs, their threat to white and male workers, and the severity of the latter's response (Blalock 1982:56). Studies at the occupational level support the threat rather than the power hypothesis (see, e.g., Frisbie & Niedert 1977:1028–29), but researchers have not shown a relationship at the establishment level, where such a response should occur.[4]

Large and growing establishments are able to accommodate heterogeneity without denying employment to dominant-group members or requiring them to work with groups they wish to avoid. Thus, both establishment size and establishment growth should be positively associated with the employment of minorities and women (for evidence at the job or occupational level, see Baron 1984:43, Baron et al 1991:Table 1, Reskin & Roos 1990). Of course, there are other reasons to expect establishment size to foster racial and gender heterogeneity: Organizational size is positively related to sophisticated personnel systems (Pfeffer 1977:557), formalization, and job differentiation, which, as indicated below, contribute to diversity in firms. The associations between establishment size and racial and gender heterogeneity are not always consistent with this expectation.[5] Organizational size was negatively associated with the percentage of female workers in California establishments in the 1960s and 1970s (Bielby & Baron 1986:787), perhaps because the association between size and slack resources allows organizations to indulge preferences for white or male workers (Cohn 1985:219, Tolbert & Oberfield 1991:311). However, more recent national data show the expected positive correlations for job

[4]Historical research recounts resistance by employees of establishments to the incursion of outsiders (Anderson 1982, Skrentny 1996), and the positive correlation between an establishment's level of unionization and white men's share of jobs (Szafran 1982:181) is consistent with exclusion by the dominant group.

[5]Heterogeneity, according to P Blau (1977:77–78), refers to the distribution of people among different groups such that the more equally sized the groups, the more heterogeneous the population.

shares for women (Carrington & Troske 1994:523, 1998a:456) and minorities (Moss & Tilly 1996, Holzer 1996:102; P Moss & C Tilly, unpublished data).[6]

The limited evidence regarding the effect of growth suggests that it expands employment for women. For example, the growth of sociology departments was positively associated with the number of women on their faculties (Kulis & Miller-Loessi 1992:103). The increasing heterogeneity of the labor pools from which establishments hire should also foster an association between growth and turnover on the one hand and an establishment's demographic composition on the other (Mittman 1992:30).[7] However, no research has examined this possibility.

The more attractive an organization—as reflected in its pay, benefits, promotion opportunities, and working conditions—the greater the incumbents' incentive to exclude outsiders. Consistent with this expectation, women are overrepresented at lower-paying plants, and men are overrepresented at better-paying plants (Carrington & Troske 1998a:460). More generally, whites and men are overrepresented in core firms, whereas women and especially minorities are concentrated in firms on the economic periphery (Howell & Reese 1986:93). Although an establishment's sex and race composition and the attractiveness of its characteristics should be reciprocally related (F Blau 1977: 77–80), two longitudinal studies suggest that employment conditions causally precede an establishment's sex and race composition. For example, establishments that upgraded skills and improved advancement opportunities became more male dominated (Baron 1984:44), and the change in average salaries between 1978 and 1983 was negatively associated with the proportion of women administrators colleges and universities employed in 1983 (Pfeffer & Davis-Blake 1987:19–20).

Labor Costs and Group Status

Race and sex differences in employment costs and prestige influence the employment of equally productive workers who differ in race or sex, although labor costs are relevant primarily to establishments that face pressures to contain expenses (Reskin 1991:183). However, establishments that can afford higher-priced white male labor are likely to purchase it because it tends to confer status on the employer. Consistent with this reasoning, the more labor intensive an establishment's activities, the more it should depend on female and minority workers. At the industry level, labor-intensive production technology is associated with the overrepresentation of women (Wallace & Chang 1990: 341). By the same reasoning, the more competitive an establishment's market

---

[6]The median small independent establishment is 99% white (Kalleberg et al 1996:55).

[7]Growth does not inevitably benefit underrepresented groups because white men can often monopolize new jobs in desirable work settings (Baron 1984:43).

or the lower its revenues, the greater its incentive to employ workers who customarily work for low pay. The results of three studies support this expectation. First, the higher a restaurant's prices, the more likely serving jobs will be offered to men rather than women (Neumark 1996:933). Second, women are overrepresented in industries dominated by small firms with competitive market structures and low profit margins (Wallace & Chang 1990:341). Third, women's greater representation in private rather than public universities may reflect the greater economic constraints faced by the former (Tolbert & Oberfield 1991:311–12). There is some evidence at the occupational level that employers' efforts to deskill jobs are accompanied by the employment of relatively more women (Baron & Bielby 1980:754), but we located no firm-level studies of the link between deskilling and an establishment's composition.

Antidiscrimination laws make discrimination against minorities and women potentially costly, but not all establishments are subject to these laws. Federal law banning sex discrimination in employment exempts firms with fewer than 15 workers, and enforcement efforts have often targeted large firms.[8] In addition, affirmative action regulations apply only to firms that do at least $50,000 worth of business with the federal government and have at least 50 employees (Reskin 1998). Thus, effects of establishment size may include the effects of vulnerability to equal employment opportunity and affirmative action regulations. In addition, comparisons of the composition of firms with and without federal contracts or of those that reportedly do and do not practice affirmative action indicate that the executive order requiring affirmative action—when enforced—prompted modest gains in the representation of African Americans and white women in firms required to practice affirmative action (Salancik 1979:390, Holzer 1996:85). Scrutiny by the California state regulatory agency substantially increased government agencies' employment of women and minorities (Baron 1984:51–52, Baron et al 1991:1394), and case studies of firms that have been targets of enforcement activities are consistent with equal employment opportunity and affirmative action regulations having increased the employment of women and minorities (N diTomaso, unpublished data).

Government employers are thought to be more receptive to women and minorities than are private-sector employers, for political reasons. Because the former are obligated to provide equal employment opportunity and because government employment practices are subject to public scrutiny, they should employ relatively more minorities than do private-sector employers. Available

---

[8]Title VII of the 1964 Civil Rights Act prohibits sex or race discrimination in establishments with at least 15 workers; an 1866 civil rights law bars race discrimination in employment contracts regardless of establishment size.

data indicate that this is the case for minorities but not women (BF Reskin, un-published data).

Market-Based Incentives

The clientele for an organization's services or products may create a sex- or race-specific demand for workers, especially in establishments in which employees interact with customers (Blum et al 1994:243, Tolbert & Oberfield 1991:305, Mittman 1992:17).[9] For example, the sex composition of university faculties varied directly with the sex composition of student bodies (Tidball 1986, Tolbert & Oberfield 1991:311), the share of a restaurant's customers who were men affected the restaurant's employment of male servers (Neumark 1996:935), and the proportion of blacks and women that federal agencies served correlated positively with each group's employment in the agencies (Borjas 1982: 292, 294). In a cross section of organizations, the proportion of black workers correlated positively with the proportion of customers who were black (Holzer 1996:102, Carrington & Troske 1998b:251).

Employment Practices

The hiring practices of establishments strongly affect their composition. Variation in the mechanisms employers use to recruit workers gives rise to variation in organizations' sex and race composition. Particularly important is whether recruitment procedures are formalized (Mittman 1992:16). Formalized practices or formal structures such as a personnel or human resources department reduce the use of sex and race as hiring criteria by limiting decision makers' discretion (Mayhew 1968, Baron & Bielby 1980:742, Szafran 1982: 175, Konrad & Linnehan 1995:805, Kalleberg et al 1996:135; P Moss & C Tilly, unpublished data). Recruitment through state employment agencies or community groups increased the representation of black men—and to a lesser degree Latinos (P Moss & C Tilly, unpublished data).

Recruitment through informal networks, in contrast, reproduces an establishment's composition because workers usually tell people who are similar to them about jobs (Kalleberg et al 1996:135). Thus, construction firms' recruitment of workers through informal ties blocked employment of African Americans (Waldinger & Bailey 1991:299). Firms were more likely to offer jobs to people who were referred by others than to those who were not referred, partly because personal ties provide information to applicants about the organization's hiring process (e.g., good times to apply for jobs) (Fernandez & Weinberg 1997:900). Methods of selection also affect an organization's composition. Subjective hiring procedures and vague criteria free decision makers

---

[9]Ethnic enclaves epitomize customer-employee matching by creating both a supply of and a demand for minority workers (Tienda & Lii 1987:144, Waldinger et al 1990:21).

to favor persons of their own race or sex (Kanter 1977, Baron 1984:55). Thus, firms that relied primarily on interviews to screen applicants employed fewer African Americans than those that did not (Moss & Tilly 1995:371), whereas the use of tests enhanced blacks' share of jobs, net of firm size, occupation, and neighborhood composition (Neckerman & Kirschenman 1991:443–45).[10]

Because an establishment's practices are influenced by the norms and environments that existed when it was founded and because hiring practices tend to become institutionalized, older establishments employ fewer women or minorities than do younger ones (Baron et al 1991:1394). As longitudinal research confirms, an establishment's demographic composition tends to reproduce itself through its hiring practices. Thus, educational administrators were typically the same sex and race as their predecessors, net of the composition of the recruitment pools (Konrad & Pfeffer 1991:153), and the proportion of savings and loan association employees who were female was positively related to the association's likelihood of hiring women (Cohen et al 1998).

THE CONSEQUENCES OF AN ORGANIZATION'S RACE AND SEX COMPOSITION

Social behavior occurs within organizations, and as Pfeffer (1991:792) observed, it is shaped not only by the attributes of individual actors but by their distribution within the organization. For this reason, demography is an important structural property of organizations. For example, in his classic article on organizational demography, Pfeffer (1983:303–4) wrote that "the relative proportions of [groups] condition the form and nature of social interaction and group processes" that in turn affect workers' "psychological well-being, attitudes, and even job performance."

The demography of organizations matters, of course, because it is within organizations that the micro- and macro-level processes that affect workers are played out (Baron & Bielby 1980:743). An establishment's sex and race composition can be particularly consequential because workplaces are likely to be more heterogeneous than are the other settings in which people interact.[11]

Although theorists agree on the importance of composition, they disagree on why or how the sex or race compositions of workplaces affect workers. The heart of their disagreement is over why numerical majorities respond nega-

---

[10]Although formal procedures such as written applications and the verification of educational and criminal records enhanced a firm's likelihood of employing black men, skills tests were more common in high-skilled jobs for which blacks were underrepresented among qualified candidates, and checks on education and criminal record were used to select low-skill workers who were disproportionally black (P Moss & C Tilly, unpublished data).

[11]Occupational segregation, because it involves sex- and race-specific occupational specialization, makes intergroup contact especially likely in establishments that include diverse occupations.

tively to minorities. Blalock (1956, 1957, 1967) argued that a minority's share of workers in a geographic area (or a labor market) affects majority-group members' behavior. He reasoned that the larger the minority group relative to the majority group, the more threatened the majority group will be, as more minorities mean more competition for the majority group (as well as a greater risk of status contamination through contact with someone from a low-status group and a greater chance of challenge to their customary practices) (see, e.g., Allmendinger & Hackman 1995:426). Although Blalock focused on race composition, his theory should hold for sex composition as well (see, e.g., Cassirer 1996).

Both Kanter (1977) and P Blau (1977) disagreed with Blalock on the effect of minorities' share. Kanter argued that the sex ratio in an organization affects men's perceptions of and reactions to women. Belonging to a numerical minority (under 15%) heightens a group's visibility, thereby subjecting it to stereotyping by the majority group. The majority's perceptual distortions can adversely affect the minority's performance. The greater the minority's representation, however, the more likely the majority is to perceive them realistically and to interact with them without focusing on group differences.

In 1977, P Blau (pp. 78–83) argued that the closer the sizes of the groups (i.e. the more heterogeneous an organization's composition), the less salient group membership is to the in-group and hence the less likely the in-group is to discriminate against the out-group (see also Taylor 1981). All else being equal, the greater the disparity between the sizes of the two groups, the less contact majority group members have with minorities, but the more contact minorities have with members of the majority. The preponderant group responds to this asymmetry, according to Blau, by discouraging contact with the numerical minority group. However, the smaller the disparity in the groups' sizes and, thus, the greater likelihood of interaction, the less likely members of the preponderant group are to avoid interacting with the minority. However, Blau (1994) later recognized that the salience of some statuses are so overarching that it overwhelms the structural effect of relative group size and he acknowledged that sex is such a status (p. 82).

Both Blau and Kanter asserted that the processes through which composition affects interaction and individual workers are invariant, regardless of whether the statistical majority group belongs to the socially dominant or subordinate sex or race. Each assumed that the more equal the groups' share of the workforce, the less salient group membership and the weaker its effects. For this reason, Blau focused on heterogeneity rather than on minority group relative size. In contrast, Blalock (1967) contended that the consequences of composition differ for socially subordinate and socially dominant numerical minority groups because only the socially dominant group enjoys the power to adversely affect groups that pose a competitive threat.

In this section, we review the research on the effects of an organization's sex and race composition on workers' relationships, their job satisfaction, how they are evaluated, their earnings, and their performance. We discuss these topics in the order implied by the causal process through which an organization's composition is thought to matter: the effect on workers, on intergroup relations, and on organizations themselves. Much of this research is based on work groups, not entire organizations. The dynamics reported in this research presumably apply to small establishments, the vast majority of business establishments,[12] but probably do not hold for large organizations.

Effects on Workers

INTERGROUP CONTACT AND ISOLATION   The relative sizes of groups employed in the same establishment affect the probability of minority-majority group interaction (P Blau 1977, Jacobs 1986). Research by South and his colleagues (1982:595, 1983:374–75) confirmed the importance of a work group's composition on intergroup contact: Each sex's share of the work group correlated positively with workers' contact with members of that sex. But the preference to associate with similar others exacerbates the effect of a group's relative size. Thus, the greater exposure that results from increased representation is not sufficient for positive contacts. Social psychologists point out that demographic similarity mediates the effect of contact, with people attracted to and identified with others who resemble them (Tajfel 1982:29, Byrne & Neuman 1992). Identification in turn hypothetically increases attraction and enhances communication, cohesion, and commitment to the collectivity. Consistent with this reasoning, women in the minority in their work groups felt more isolated than either women who were in the majority, or men, regardless of their share of group members (Konrad et al 1992:131), and women in mixed groups initiated less interaction and were addressed less frequently than women in all-female groups (Aries 1976:15, Carlock & Martin 1977:31).

INTERGROUP CONFLICT AND COHESION   Following Blalock's reasoning, Wharton & Baron (1991:369) hypothesized that sex-based conflict was less likely in predominantly male than in mixed-sex settings in which the presence of women constitutes a greater threat to men's prerogatives. If sex-balanced organizations reduce men's well-being, then hostility toward women should occur more often in such settings and cohesiveness should be lower (Ibarra 1992:423–24). We could locate no organizational-level multivariate research bearing on this point.

---

[12]In 1994, 87% of business establishments had fewer than 20 employees (US Bur. Census 1998:Table 847).

Work-group homogeneity hypothetically fosters interpersonal attraction and trust, which, in turn, maintain group cohesion. Research is consistent with this reasoning. For example, the percentage of women in 76 work groups in a public agency correlated negatively with the amount of social support they received (South et al 1983:376–77). Within major symphony orchestras, members' perception of the quality of their relationships displayed a negative bivariate association with the percentage of female members in the symphony; in minor orchestras, the association between members, although weak, was positive (Allmendinger & Hackman 1995:446). Among blue-collar work groups, gender but not racial heterogeneity led to more emotional conflict (Pelled 1996:241).

In contrast, the percentage of women in university departments was positively related to workers' perceptions of cohesion, with men in all-male departments expressing the least cohesion and men in predominantly female departments expressing the most (Wharton & Bird 1996:109). Perhaps the threat stemming from heterogeneity induces cohesion among members of the majority group. Finally, the proportion of women in a work group was positively associated with the support for advancement that men received from both male and female coworkers and negatively associated with the support that females receive from their male coworkers (South et al 1987:274–76). (Work-group sex composition was not associated with how much support women received from female coworkers.)

According to a meta-analysis of case studies of organizations, neither gender nor racial homogeneity nor the sex composition of the work group was associated with workers' solidarity (Hodson et al 1993:407, Hodson 1995: 149). Of course, the absence of associations does not rule out the possibility that race or sex heterogeneity exacerbates antagonism between workers from different races or sexes.

VISIBILITY, PERFORMANCE PRESSURE, AND STRESS   According to Kanter (1977:210–14) and Taylor (1981), workers who are minorities in their work setting are highly visible to members of the majority group, and this visibility hypothetically subjects them to performance pressure. The two studies that address this issue are consistent with that expectation. Racial tokenism, as measured by the proportion of blacks or women with whom African American leaders worked, was associated with experiencing performance pressure (Jackson et al 1995:550–51). Similarly, women in a law school with fewer female students reported more performance pressure than women in a school with more female students (Spangler et al 1978:164–65), and female students in academic departments with low proportions of women received lower grades than did their counterparts in departments with more female students, although males' grades were unaffected by their department's sex composition (Alexander & Thoits 1985:335–38). Exacerbating the stress associated with being in the minority is an organization's tendency to assign minorities to roles as representatives of their race or sex (Jackson et al 1995:550–51).

STEREOTYPING AND EVALUATION BIAS   Dominant groups hypothetically shore up the boundaries between themselves and minority groups by focusing on the differences between a minority group and themselves, while ignoring the differences among the minority group members—in other words, by stereotyping persons who belong to numerical minority groups in terms of group membership. Consistent with this expectation, women in male-dominated work groups experienced more sex stereotyping than did women in female-dominated groups (Konrad et al 1992:131). In one study, students working on Masters of Business Administration (MBA) degrees were more likely to attribute stereotypically feminine traits to women in an applicant pool when the women numbered fewer than three in eight than when there were at least three (Heilman 1980).

By ascribing to women and racial minorities undesirable characteristics and by blinding evaluators to evidence that would challenge their stereotypes, sex and race stereotyping negatively biases the evaluation of women and minorities (Heilman 1984, Gerber 1989, Foschi et al 1994). Skewed race and sex ratios affect these processes (Nieva & Gutek 1980, Tsui & O'Reilly 1989). According to a meta-analysis of social psychological research (Kraiger & Ford 1985:61), African Americans were evaluated least favorably in work settings in which their share was small. Research on sex composition shows the same pattern. MBA students participating in an experiment judged women to be less qualified when they were one quarter or less of the applicant pool than when they were at least three eighths of the pool (Heilman 1980). In addition, in an analysis of 486 jobs across several firms, the percentage of women in blue-collar and clerical jobs in a given firm was positively related to supervisors' ratings of women's performance, net of women's education and ability, but supervisors' evaluations of blacks were lower than those of whites, regardless of the race composition of the job (Sackett et al 1991:265). According to a study of the evaluation of small groups of promotion candidates at a utility company, group composition affected workers' evaluations on several dimensions (Schmitt & Hill 1977). The most consistent finding was that the greater white men's share of the group, the more positive were evaluators' assessments of individual white men. However, white men's numbers were negatively related to the evaluation of white women on six of the dimensions, although none of the correlations differed significantly from zero. The number of white women in a group was positively related to the evaluation of black women as forceful and negatively related to evaluators' assessment of their effectiveness at communicating in writing, whereas the more white men there were in a group, the less forceful evaluators viewed black women (Schmitt & Hill, 1977:263, Table 2).[13]

However, contrary to predictions by Blau and Kanter about the positive effects of intergroup contact, the amount of interaction male bank managers had with female managers was unrelated to their attitudes toward women managers (Bhatnagar & Swamy 1995:1295).

In sum, although the evidence is mixed, the greater a minority group's representation, the less distorted evaluations tend to be.

JOB SATISFACTION, ORGANIZATIONAL ATTACHMENT, AND TURNOVER   Theoretically, the negative reactions of dominant group members to minorities are commensurate with the minority group's representation. These negative reactions, which include reduced group cohesion, should erode the job satisfaction of both groups (Blalock 1967). Research on work groups offers mixed support for this prediction but suggests that the psychological impact of being a member of a gender minority may differ by sex (Tolbert et al 1998:21). According to Wharton & Bird (1996:110), men in predominantly male and mixed-sex work groups were more satisfied than men in all-male groups. In addition, both sexes in gender-balanced work groups were more satisfied than workers in homogeneous groups, with workers in male-dominated groups reporting the least satisfaction (Fields & Blum 1997:190). However, female managers reported lower job satisfaction when they worked in organizations with high proportions of men (Burke & McKeen 1996:1100), and women's representation was negatively related to job satisfaction in both sexes in symphony orchestras (Allmendinger & Hackman 1995:435) and university departments (Wharton et al 1999). One study hints that this inconsistency may stem from differences in the group to which female and male workers are oriented. The sex composition of the departments in a military supply depot increased women's satisfaction but did not affect men's satisfaction, but having more women at his hierarchical level lowered a man's overall satisfaction (Martin & Harkreader 1993: 329). The presence of women appears to increase men's satisfaction with one aspect of their jobs, however. Women's share of manufacturing jobs was positively related to both sexes' satisfaction with their earnings, presumably because more female establishments had lower earners in workers' reference group (Loscocco & Spitze 1991:14). Similarly, in a national survey of establishments, the racial heterogeneity of establishments was positively related to employees' perception regarding the extent of earnings inequality (Kalleberg & van Buren 1994:942–44), probably because of the lower pay of workers of color.

---

[13]There were too few black men for the researchers to reliably assess compositional effects on their evaluation.

In a study of 151 work units within three large organizations, Tsui et al (1992:569) found that the organizational attachment of men and whites dropped as the race and sex heterogeneity of their work groups increased. In contrast, and consistent with Blalock's reasoning, women's attachment increased and that of nonwhites was not affected.

To the extent that the presence of women and racial minorities threatens white men who respond in ways that distress women and minorities, the greater the proportion of women and minorities in customarily white or male workplaces, the higher turnover rates for all workers. Research partially supports this proposition. In three large organizations, sex heterogeneity was associated with men's, but not women's, intention to leave the organization (Tsui et al 1992:569), and in a Canadian sample, the proportion of men in an organization was positively related with the intention of managerial and professional women to quit (Burke & McKeen 1996:1100–101). However, consistent with the reasoning of Kanter and Blau, the presence of women in academic departments was unrelated to men's turnover and reduced women's turnover only in settings in which women were at least 35% of the employees (Tolbert et al 1995:570–71).

Effects on Organizations

PERFORMANCE   Theories offer contradictory predictions regarding the effect of composition on performance. If homogeneity fosters trust and cohesion and facilitates communication, it should enhance group performance. However, Kanter argued that as the minority-majority ratio approaches parity, the less performance pressure on numerical minority groups and the better their performance. Both these theories imply curvilinear relationships, but the former predicts a positive relationship between performance and the size of the disparity between the groups' sizes, whereas the latter predicts a negative correlation. In keeping with these contradictory predictions, two establishment-level studies reported contradictory findings. In firms with considerable market power, the proportion of women was positively related to profitability, which may signal performance (JK Hellerstein, D Neumark & KR Troske, unpublished data). But in symphony orchestras—organizations in which performance requires interdependence—the bivariate relationships between the percentage of women in an orchestra and each sex's perceptions of orchestral functioning were negative (Allmendinger & Hackman 1995:436). The higher emotional conflict among sex-heterogeneous work groups reduced their productivity (Pelled 1996:241).

HIRING PATTERNS   As noted above, demographic patterns tend to be self-perpetuating. First, the sex and race composition of a workplace influences an employer's conceptions of appropriate employees (Kanter 1977, Acker 1990,

Baron 1991, Perry et al 1994:796–98). Given homosocial reproduction, evaluations of potential employees by gatekeepers are likely to depend on the prospective workers' demographic similarity to "organizational elites" (Baron 1984:57). Second, the most common recruitment method—hiring through informal networks—perpetuates an establishment's sex and race composition (Braddock & McPartland 1987:8). Third, the social environment of predominantly white or predominantly male work settings may be sufficiently inhospitable as to exclude women or people of color (Bergmann & Darity 1981:49, Swerdlow 1989, Padavic 1991). Research confirms this expectation. In police agencies, women's application rates were more closely related to the proportion of women already employed in the job than to an agency's recruitment efforts (Martin 1991:499), and as noted, the greater women's share of employees in savings and loan associations, the more likely women were to be hired (Cohen et al 1998).

JOB SEGREGATION AND PROMOTION STRUCTURES   Given the possibility that whites and men resist the employment of outsiders, organizations that employ relatively more women or minorities may segregate them to insulate majorities from contact with equal-status minorities (Kulis & Miller-Loessi 1992:95).[14] However, Bielby & Baron (1984:51, 53; Baron & Bielby 1985:238–39, 247) found that an establishment's level of sex segregation was negatively associated with women's share of the workforce, net of occupational composition and other occupational characteristics. In fact, a longitudinal analysis of California state agencies indicated that as the job shares of women and, to a lesser degree, racial minorities increased, agencies became less sex segregated (Baron et al 1991:1388, 1395).

Heterogeneity can affect an organization's structure through its impact on the balance of power. To the extent that the majority's perception of threat is directly related to minorities' share of jobs and the majority can shape organizational practices to protect its self-interest, women's or minorities' share of jobs will be negatively related to their outcomes (pay, assignments, promotion, opportunities). Consistent with this reasoning, the percentage of minority workers across establishments was negatively related to the likelihood of promotion for black workers but not white workers (Baldi & McBrier 1997:489). On the other hand, if a minority group's size is positively related to its power, it should also be positively related to its opportunities and rewards. In keeping with this expectation, the proportion of women employed by savings and loan associations was positively related to the likelihood of the savings and loan

[14]According to DiPrete (1989:113–14), the designers of the civil service used job-title distinctions to segregate higher-status professional positions that employed mostly white men from lower-status clerical and manual jobs that employed men and women of color and white women.

promoting women (Cohen et al 1998). In addition, although the causal order of these relationships is unclear, several cross-sectional studies show a positive relationship between the percentage of female workers in an establishment and the percentage of female managers (Blum, et al 1994:260, Shenhav & Haberfeld 1992:131, Stover 1994:396; BF Reskin & DB McBrier, unpublished data), and one observed a positive bivariate correlation between percentage of blacks and blacks' share of managerial jobs in medium-to-large Detroit firms (Shenhav & Haberfeld 1992:131).

WAGES   The devaluation of activities that are associated with lower-status groups might lead the sex or race composition of establishments to affect the pay of workers. In occupations and jobs, the percentage of female workers is negatively associated with wages, net of appropriate controls (see Baron & Newman 1989:123, England 1992, Kilbourne et al 1994). However, devaluation should occur at the establishment level only if (a) most of the jobs in an establishment involve activities that are sex-typed and typical of just one sex (for example, a social welfare agency) or (b) a single entity (e.g., a civil service commission) sets pay for several establishments and hence can systematically vary pay for all workers in an establishment based on an establishment's race or sex composition.[15]

Five studies show establishment-level effects of demographic composition on one or both sexes or races; a sixth reported no association. Using data from industry wage surveys conducted between 1973 and 1983, Groshen (1991: 466–68) found that the greater women's share of workers in establishments, the less all workers earned. In Detroit firms, women's earnings were curvilinearly related to their share of jobs: In establishments with less than 12% female employees, the correlation was positive, but in establishments with more than 12% female employees it was negative (men's pay was unaffected) (Shenhav & Haberfeld 1992:137). Also, the earnings of manufacturing workers—especially women—were negatively related to women's share of plant work (Carrington & Troske 1998a:460–62).[16] A 1991 study of almost half a million workers employed in more than 28,000 establishments showed that, net of workers' sex and the sex composition of the industry, occupation, and job, the percentage of female employees in an establishment was negatively related to

[15]The process of differentially evaluating activities depending on their sex or race label must occur for the entity that sets pay. Devaluation occurs at the occupational level because some occupations are labeled as female work. There is almost no empirical evidence of race-based devaluation, presumably because whites so outnumber minorities that occupations are not labeled as minorities' work.

[16]Kalleberg & van Buren (1994:944) found that an organization's sex heterogeneity was positively related to earnings dispersion, but the percentage of workers that was female had no effect.

workers' earnings. Net of a variety of control variables, an establishment's sex composition explained between one ninth and one fifth of the pay gap between the sexes (K Bayard, JK Hellerstein, D Neumark & KR Troske, unpublished data). Similarly, the wages of black workers fell with blacks' share of an establishment's employment, whereas the wages of white workers rose with blacks' share of employment (Carrington & Troske 1998b:258). Finally, an establishment's sex composition did not significantly affect workers' earnings, net of the effect of the sex composition of their occupations and jobs (Huffman et al 1996:201). In sum, the majority of the research indicates that the representation of women and minorities in establishments is negatively related to their own earnings and sometimes to those of men. The inconsistent findings may reflect the fact that organizational practices can mitigate any tendency toward devaluation (Baron 1991:123).

BENEFITS   If white and male workers have more power than women and minorities or are more valued, the more white and male an establishment's workforce, the more fringe benefits the establishment should provide. Empirical research on two national samples of organizations provides mixed support for this expectation. The greater women's share of employment, the less likely employers were to offer personal benefits and bonuses, and the greater the proportion of employees who were not white, the less likely establishments were to offer many personal and family benefits (Knoke 1994:972–75). However, other analyses of these data showed a curvilinear relationship between women's share of full-time employment and benefits, with the proportion of females positively associated with both conventional and family benefits for establishments whose employees were at least 50% male, and negative for establishments whose employees were over half female (C Deitch & ML Huffman, unpublished data). Whether at least 10% of the establishment's employees were minority did not affect any of the benefits the researchers examined. According to research based on a second sample of establishments, the proportion of employees who were female was positively associated with organizations having work-family programs and—in unionized workplaces—with the likelihood that the organization provided parental leave (Osterman 1995:693). The proportion of employees who were female did not affect whether a sample of northern Indiana establishments provided childcare benefits (Glass & Fujimoto 1995:400), however.

CONCLUSIONS

We can think of the demographic composition of establishments as both social fact and social structure. As social fact, the race and sex composition of individual establishments is a significant feature of the environment in which employees interact. In the aggregate, an establishment's race and sex composition provides a rough gauge of the extent to which ascribed characteristics segregate the workforce. Moreover, variation in the race and sex composition of establishments that differ on wages, benefits, working conditions, and advancement opportunities provides the opportunity to investigate sex and race stratification in employment.

The writings of P Blau (1977) make the case for viewing demographic composition as social structure. Pfeffer (1991:790) concurred, arguing that an organization's demography constitutes a theoretical and empirical reality whose effects are distinct from the aggregated effects of the behaviors or attitudes of its members (Pfeffer 1983:303–4). Scholars can examine the interrelationship between demographic structures and other organizational structures, such as internal labor markets, reward systems, and the like, as well as the structural effect of composition on workers' experiences. Below we summarize what such research has revealed about the determinants and consequences of an organization's sex and race structures. We conclude by recommending a brief research agenda.

Determinants of an Organization's Sex and Race Composition

Research indicates that an establishment's composition is a function of the race and sex composition of the qualified labor supply and that employers affect this supply by the qualifications they impose. Employers' preferences for or aversions to prospective workers on the basis of their sex and race affect an establishment's composition, although these effects are conditional on whether firms are subject to government antidiscrimination and affirmative action regulations. Although, hypothetically, majority group workers' responses to the composition of the labor supply affect their opposition to the employment of racial minorities and women, no establishment-level research has tested this hypothesis. Several studies have confirmed that indicators of the attractiveness of an establishment as an employment setting are negatively related to the share of jobs women and racial minorities hold, although none has pinpointed the mechanisms underlying this relationship. In general, the more establishments pay, the less likely they are to employ racial minorities and women, and those that have formalized their employment practices are more likely to do so.

Consequences of an Organization's Sex and Race Composition

It is axiomatic in sociology that context affects attitudes and behaviors, and theorists concur that workplace composition is consequential for workers and work organization (Pfeffer 1983, 1991:790). For example, as Ridgeway & Smith-Lovin (1999) pointed out, situational factors "overdetermine" inequality in male-female interaction. Research confirms the importance of composition for workers and for organizational outcomes, such as performance, hiring and promotion practices, levels of job segregation, and wages and benefits. However, theoretical accounts of the effects of group composition on workers disagree over the underlying mechanisms and the direction of compositional effects. Specifically, they disagree over whether the relationship between outgroups' relative numbers and majority-group resistance is positive or negative, and whether the hypothesized response by the majority group is limited to social majorities or occurs as well among societal minorities (e.g. women) when they constitute a numerical majority in an establishment.

Research on the effects of an organization's sex and race composition on workers' intergroup contacts, cohesion, job satisfaction, and how they are evaluated does not resolve the disagreement. Much of the research on the likelihood of contact, liking, isolation, and stereotyping conforms to Blau's predictions, and research on evaluation bias and stereotyping is consistent with Kanter's theory of tokenism. In contrast, research on intergroup hostility and job satisfaction is generally consistent with Blalock's majority-threat theory. As noted below, however, many studies are preliminary, and there is rarely a set of consistent findings based on well-specified models from which to draw final conclusions.

Future Research

REPLICATION AND EXTENSION   Although the topic of an organization's sex and race composition is linked intellectually to that of occupational segregation, the latter constitutes a specialty area with a cohesive body of knowledge that displays considerable consensus on segregation's causes and consequences. In contrast, the research we have reviewed is not a cohesive research area. We drew eclectically on psychology, economics, and management as well as sociology and, within these disciplines, from several specialty areas. Although the empirical results reviewed above are generally consistent with some theory or with a priori conjecture, any general conclusions must be preliminary. Many findings are based on bivariate relationships and hence are starting points, at best, for more systematic study.

CONTINGENT RELATIONSHIPS   It seems likely that many of the observed determinants and effects of composition depend on unmeasured organizational characteristics such as firm size, sector (public or private), labor process, workers' interdependency, recruitment methods, and region, among others. For example, Baron & Bielby (1985:239) speculated that larger shifts in sex composition may be required to achieve desegregation in big firms relative to small ones. The results of laboratory experiments, although revealing as to processes, do not incorporate contextual factors that condition the social psychological outcomes in actual work settings. In other words, assessments of the determinants or consequences of an organization's race and sex composition must be based on properly specified models. With a few exceptions, the studies we reviewed either were not designed to examine the causes and consequences of an organization's demographic composition or their designs were inadequate for this purpose.

UNDERLYING CAUSAL MECHANISMS   Even for relationships that appear to be robust, the causal processes are uncertain. This is particularly true with respect to the finding that an establishment's proportion of female or minority workers is negatively related to workers' earnings. We know that it is within establishments that employment decisions are made and their consequences are played out; we have yet to determine the causal processes that lead structures to matter for workers and organizations.

LINEARITY OF EFFECTS OF COMPOSITION ON WORKERS   Blalock (1967) assumed that the relationship between a racial minority's share and the exclusionary responses of majority group members was negative and linear. In contrast, both Kanter and Blau hypothesized nonlinear relationships. Kanter suggested that when women's share of the work group exceeds a token level, they should encounter less stereotyping and more acceptance as individuals rather than as women, whereas Blau argued that the closer the groups' relative sizes, the less salient its minority status and the less severe the reactions by the majority status group.

Few researchers have tested for threshold effects of composition, and only a few have been observed in the hypothesized direction. These include negative effects of the proportion of women on salaries (Pfeffer & Davis-Blake 1987: 14–15); on orchestral functioning, the quality of relationships between players, and players' job involvement (Allmendinger & Hackman 1995:456–57); on female turnover (Tolbert et al 1995); and on sex stereotyping and the devaluation of female candidates (Heilman 1980). Research on the effects of organizational demography can uncover the reasons for the negative effects of the presence of women and racial minorities only when they test models that allow threshold effects and, thus, permit them to test competing theories

RACE COMPOSITION   Even a cursory reading of the reviewed research reveals that the research on race composition is much scantier than that on sex composition. Although medium-to-large organizations express strong concerns with workplace diversity—especially racial and ethnic diversity—little scholarship is available to guide organizations. The extant scholarship focuses either on gender composition or on race composition; we found almost no research that simultaneously takes gender and race into account to examine, for example, what establishment characteristics are associated with the employment of women of color. In addition, we located no establishment-level research that goes beyond black and white in conceptualizing race, although Hispanics' share of the labor force was 84% that of African Americans' in 1996 (US Bureau of the Census 1998:Table 621), and responses to Hispanic, Asian, and Native American women and men may differ from those to African American women and men.

As Bielby & Baron (1984) and Davis-Blake (1992) pointed out, an organization's demography is slow to change. However, as labor pools become more heterogeneous, so too will the American workplace. Workers will increasingly encounter members of other sexes, races, and ethnic groups at work. The research reviewed here indicates that increasing gender and racial heterogeneity of organizations is likely to alter intergroup relations among workers and may affect an establishment's performance.[17] One consequence is the attention that corporations are giving to concerns related to diversity (Kelly & Dobbin 1998). This concern with diversity provides both the opportunity and the need for systematic attention by researchers.

ACKNOWLEDGMENTS

We are grateful to Rachel Rosenfeld for her comments on a previous version of this chapter and to Pamela Tolbert for sharing with us a preprint of her forthcoming chapter.

[17]For example, whites employed in firms that practiced affirmative action were more likely than other whites to believe that blacks experience race discrimination and were more supportive of race-targeted interventions (Taylor 1995:1406).

> **Visit the *Annual Reviews* home page at**
> **http://www.AnnualReviews.org.**

Literature Cited

Acker JR. 1990. Hierarchies, jobs, bodies: a theory of gendered organizations. *Gend. Soc.* 4:139–58s

Alexander VD, Thoits PA. 1985. Token achievement: an examination of proportional representation and performance outcomes. *Soc. Forces* 64(2):332–40

Allmendinger J, Hackman JR. 1995. The more, the better? A four-nation study of the inclusion of women in symphony orchestras. *Soc. Forces* 74:423–60

Anderson KT. 1982. Last hired, first fired: black women workers during World War II. *J. Am. Hist.* 69:82–97

Aries E. 1976. Interaction patterns and themes of male, female and mixed groups. *Small Group Behav.* 7:7–18

Baldi S, McBrier DB. 1997. Do the determinants of promotion differ for blacks and whites? Evidence from the U.S. labor market. *Work Occup.* 24:478–97

Baron JN. 1984. Organizational perspectives

on stratification. *Annu. Rev. Sociol.* 10: 37–69

Baron JN. 1991. Organizational evidence of ascription in labor markets. In *New Approaches to Economic and Social Analyses of Discrimination*, ed. R Cornwall, P Wunnava, pp. 113–43. New York: Praeger

Baron JN, Bielby WT. 1980. Bringing the firm back in: stratification, segmentation, and the organization of work. *Am. Sociol. Rev.* 45:737–65

Baron JN, Bielby WT. 1985. Organizational barriers to gender equality: sex segregation of jobs and opportunities. In *Gender and the Life Course*, ed. A Rossi, pp. 233–51. New York: Aldine

Baron JN, Bielby WT. 1986. The proliferation of job titles in organizations. *Admin. Sci. Q.* 31:561–86

Baron JN, Mittman BS, Newman AE. 1991. Targets of opportunity: organizational and environmental determinants of gender integration within the California civil service, 1979–1985. *Am. J. Sociol.* 96: 1362–401

Baron JN, Newman AE. 1989. Pay the man: effects of demographic composition on prescribed wage rates in the California civil service. In *Pay Equity: Empirical Inquiries*, ed. RT Michael, H Hartmann, B O'Farrell, pp. 107–29. Washington, DC: Natl. Acad.

Bergmann BR, Darity W. 1981. Social relations, productivity, and employer discrimination. *Mon. Labor Rev.* 104(4):47–49

Bhatnagar D, Swamy R. 1995. Attitudes toward women as managers: Does interaction make a difference? *Hum. Relat.* 48(11):1285–307

Bielby WT, Baron JN. 1984. A woman's place is with other women: sex segregation within organizations. In *Sex Segregation in the Workplace*, ed. BF Reskin, pp. 27–55. Washington, DC: Natl. Acad

Bielby WT, Baron JN. 1986. Men and women at work: sex segregation and statistical discrimination. *Am. J. Sociol.* 91:759–99

Blalock HM. 1956. Economic discrimination and Negro increase. *Am. Sociol. Rev.* 21: 584–88

Blalock HM. 1957. Percent nonwhite and discrimination in the south. *Am. Sociol. Rev.* 22:677–82

Blalock HM. 1967. *Toward a Theory of Minority-Group Relations.* New York: Wiley

Blalock HM. 1982. *Race and Ethnic Relations.* Englewood Cliffs, NJ: Prentice Hall

Blau FD. 1977. *Equal Pay in the Office.* Lexington, MA: Lexington Books

Blau PM. 1977. *Inequality and Heterogeneity.* New York: Free Press

Blau PM. 1994. *Structural Contexts of Opportunity.* Chicago: Univ. Chicago Press

Blum TC, Fields DL, Goodman JS. 1994. Organizational-level determinants of women in management. *Acad. Manage. J.* 37:241–68

Borjas G. 1982. The politics of employment discrimination in the federal bureaucracy. *J. Law Econ.* 25:271–99

Braddock JH, McPartland JM. 1987. How minorities continue to be excluded from equal employment opportunity: research on labor markets and institutional barriers. *J. Soc. Issues* 43:5–39

Burke RJ, McKeen CA. 1996. Do women at the top make a difference? Gender proportions and the experiences of managerial and professional women. *Hum. Relat.* 49(8):1093–104

Byrne D, Neuman JH. 1992. The implications of attraction research for organizational issues. In *Issues, Theory, and Research in Industrial Psychology*, ed. K Kelley. New York: Elsevier

Carlock CJ, Martin PY. 1977. Sex composition and the intensive group experience. *Soc. Work* 22:27–32

Carrington WJ, Troske KR. 1994. Gender segregation in small firms. *J. Human Res.* 30: 503–33

Carrington WJ, Troske KR. 1998a. Sex segregation in U.S. manufacturing. *Ind. Labor Relat. Rev.* 51:445–64

Carrington WJ, Troske KR. 1998b. Interfirm segregation and the black/white wage gap. *J. Labor Econ.* 16:231–60

Cassirer NR. 1996. Race composition and earnings: effects by race, region, and gender. *Social Sci. Res.* 25:375–99

Cohen LE, Broschak JP, Haveman HA. 1998. And then there were more? The effects of organizational sex composition on hiring and promotion. *Am. Sociol. Rev.* 63: 711–27

Cohn S. 1985. *The Process of Occupational Sex-Typing: The Feminization of Clerical Labor in Great Britain.* Philadelphia, PA: Temple Univ. Press

Cotter DA, DeFiore JA, Hermsen JM, Kowalewski BM, Vanneman R. 1998. The macro-level effect of occupational integration. *Am. Sociol. Rev.* 62:714–34

Davis-Blake A. 1992. The consequences of organizational demography: beyond social integration effects. *Res. Sociol. Organ.* 10: 175–97

DiPrete TA. 1989. *The Bureaucratic Labor Market: The Case of the Federal Civil Service.* New York: Plenum

England P. 1992. *Comparable Worth: Theories and Evidence.* New York: de Gruyter

Farkas G, Vicknair K. 1996. Appropriate tests of racial wage discrimination require controls for cognitive skill. *Am. Sociol. Rev.* 61:557–60

Fernandez RM, Weinberg N. 1997. Sifting and sorting: personal contacts and hiring in a retail bank. *Am. Sociol. Rev.* 62:883–902

Fields DL, Blum TC. 1997. Employee satisfaction in work groups with different gender composition. *J. Organ. Behav.* 18(2): 181–96

Foschi M, Lai L, Sigerson K. 1994. Gender and double standards in the assessment of job applicants. *Soc. Psychol. Q.* 57(4): 326–39

Frisbie W, Niedert L. 1977. Inequality and the relative size of minority populations: a comparative analysis. *Am. J. Sociol.* 82: 1007–30

Gerber GL. 1989. The more positive evaluations of men than women on gender-stereotyped traits. *Psychol. Rep.* 65(1): 275–86

Glass J, Fujimoto T. 1995. Employer characteristics and provision of family responsive policies. *Work Occup.* 22:380–411

Groshen EL. 1991. The structure of the female male wage differential—is it who you are, what you do, or where you work? *J. Hum. Resour.* 26(3):457–72

Heilman ME. 1980. The impact of situational factors on personnel decisions concerning women: varying the sex composition of the applicant pool. *Organ. Behav. Hum. Decis. Process.* 26:386–95

Heilman ME. 1984. Information as deterrent against sex discrimination: the effects of applicant sex and information type on preliminary employment decisions. *Organ. Behav. Hum. Decis. Process.* 33(2): 174–86

Hodson R. 1995. Cohesion or conflict? Race, solidarity, and resistance in the workplace. *Res. Sociol. Work* 5:135–59

Hodson R, Welsh S, Rieble S, Jamison CS, Creighton S. 1993. Is worker solidarity undermined by autonomy and participation? Patterns from ethnographic literature. *Am. Sociol. Rev.* 58:398–416

Holzer HJ. 1996. *What Employers Want.* New York: Russell Sage Found.

Holzer HJ, Neumark D. 1999. Are affirmative action hires less qualified? Evidence from employer-employee data on new hires. *J. Labor Econ.* In press

Howell FM, Reese WA. 1986. Sex and mobility in the dual economy. *Work Occup.* 13: 77–96

Huffman ML, Velasco SC, Bielby WT. 1996. Where sex composition matters most: comparing the effects of job versus occupational sex composition on earnings. *Sociol. Focus* 29:189–207

Ibarra H. 1992. Homophily and differential returns: sex differences in network structure and access in an advertising firm. *Admin. Sci. Q.* 37:422–47

Jackson PB, Thoits PA, Taylor HF. 1995. Composition of the workplace and psychological well-being: the effects of tokenism on America's black elite. *Soc. Forces* 74: 543–57

Jacobs JA. 1986. Trends in workplace contact between men and women, 1971–1981. *Sociol. Soc. Res.* 70:202–5

Jacobs JA. 1989. Long-term trends in occupational segregation by sex. *Am. J. Sociol.* 95:160–73

Jones J, Rosenfeld RA. 1989. Women's occupations and local labor markets: 1950–1980. *Soc. Forces* 67:666–92

Kalleberg AL, Knoke D, Marsden PV, Spaeth JL. 1996. *Organizations in America: Analyzing Their Structures and Human Resources Practices.* Thousand Oaks, CA: Sage

Kalleberg AL, van Buren ME. 1994. The structure of organizational earnings inequality. *Am. Behav. Sci.* 37:930–47

Kanter RM. 1977. *Men and Women of the Corporation.* New York: Basic Books

Kelly E, Dobbin F. 1998. How affirmative action became diversity management: employer response to antidiscrimination law, 1961 to 1996. *Am. Behav. Sci.* 41(7): 960–84

Kennelly I. 1999. You've got that single-mother element: employers' images of African American women. *Gend. Soc.* 13:168

Kilbourne BS, England P, Beron K. 1994. Effects of individual, occupational, and industrial characteristics on earnings: intersections of race and gender. *Soc. Forces* 72:1149–76

Knoke D. 1994. *Cui bono?* Employee benefit packages. *Am. Behav. Sci.* 37(7):963–78

Konrad AM, Linnehan F. 1995. Formalized HRM structures: coordinating equal employment opportunity or concealing organizational practices? *Acad. Manage. J.* 38:787–820

Konrad AM, Pfeffer J. 1991. Understanding the hiring of women and minorities in educational institutions. *Sociol. Educ.* 64: 141–57

Konrad AM, Winter S, Gutek BA. 1992. Diversity in work group sex composition: implications for majority and minority workers. *Res. Sociol. Organ.* 10:115–40

Kraiger K, Ford JK. 1985. A meta-analysis of ratee race effects in performance ratings. *J. Appl. Psychol.* 70(1):56–65

Kulis S, Miller-Loessi KA. 1992. Organizations, labor markets, and gender integration in academic sociology. *Soc. Perspect.* 35:93–117

Loscocco KA, Spitze G. 1991. The organizational context of women's and men's pay satisfaction. *Soc. Sci. Q.* 72(1):3–19

Martin PY. 1985. Group sex composition in work organizations: a structural-normative model. *Res. Sociol. Organ.* 4:311–49

Martin PY, Harkreader S. 1993. Multiple gender contexts and employee rewards. *Work Occup.* 20:296–336

Martin SE. 1991. The effectiveness of affirmative action: the case of women in policing. *Justice Q.* 8:489–504

Mayhew L. 1968. Ascription in modern societies. *Sociol. Inq.* 38:105–20

Mittman BS. 1992. Theoretical and methodological issues in the study of organizational demography and demographic change. *Res. Sociol. Organ.* 10:3–53

Moss P, Tilly C. 1995. Skills and race in hiring: quantitative findings from face-to-face interviews. *East. Econ. J.* 21:357–74

Moss P, Tilly C. 1996. Soft skills and race: an investigation of black men's employment problems. *Work Occup.* 23:252–76

Neckerman KM, Kirschenman J. 1991. Hiring strategies, racial bias, and inner-city workers: an investigation of employers' hiring decisions. *Soc. Probl.* 38:433–47

Neumark D. 1996. Sex discrimination in the restaurant industry: an audit study. *Q. J. Econ.* 111:915–41

Nieva VF, Gutek BA. 1980. Sex effects on evaluation. *Acad. Manage. Rev.* 5:267–76

Osterman P. 1994. How common is workplace transformation and who adopts it? *Ind. Labor Relat. Rev.* 47(2):173–88

Osterman P. 1995. Work/family programs and the employment relationship. *Admin. Sci. Q.* 40:681–700

Padavic I. 1991. Attraction of male blue-collar jobs for black and white women: economic need, exposure, and attitudes. *Soc. Sci. Q.* 72:33–49

Pelled LH. 1996. Relational demography and perceptions of group conflict and performance: a field investigation. *Int. J. Confl. Manage.* 7(3):230–46

Perry EL, Davis-Blake A, Kulik CT. 1994. Explaining gender-based selection decisions: a synthesis of contextual and cognitive approaches. *Acad. Manage. Rev.* 19(4): 796–820

Pfeffer J. 1977. Toward an examination of stratification in organizations. *Admin. Sci. Q.* 22:553–67

Pfeffer J. 1983. Organizational demography. *Res. Organ. Behav.* 5:299–357

Pfeffer J. 1991. Organization theory and structural perspectives on management. *J. Manage.* 17:789–803

Pfeffer J, Davis-Blake A. 1987. The effect of the proportion of women on salaries: the case of college administrators. *Admin. Sci. Q.* 32:1–24

Reskin BF. 1991. Labor markets as queues: a structural approach to changing occupational sex composition. In *Macro-Micro Linkages in Sociology*, ed. J Huber, pp. 170–91. Newbury Park, CA: Sage

Reskin BF. 1993. Sex segregation in the workplace. *Annu. Rev. Sociol.* 19:241–70

Reskin BF. 1998. *The Realities of Affirmative Action in Employment.* Washington, DC: Am. Sociol. Assoc.

Reskin BF, Roos P. 1990. *Job Queues, Gender Queues: Explaining Women's Inroads into Male Occupations.* Philadelphia, PA: Temple Univ. Press

Ridgeway CL, Smith-Lovin L. 1999. The gender system in interaction. *Annu. Rev. Sociol.* 25:191-216

Sackett PR, DuBois CLZ, Noe AW. 1991. Tokenism in performance evaluation: the effects of work group representation on male-female and white-black differences in performance ratings. *J. Appl. Psychol.* 76:263–67

Salancik GR. 1979. Interorganizational dependence and responsiveness to affirmative action: the case of women and defense contractors. *Acad. Manage. J.* 22:375–94

Schmitt N, Hill T. 1977. Sex and race composition of assessment center groups as a determinant of peer and assessor ratings. *J. Appl. Psychol.* 62(3):261–64

Shenhav Y, Haberfeld Y. 1992. Organizational demography and inequality. *Soc. Forces* 71:123–43

Skrentny JD. 1996. *The Ironies of Affirmative Action.* Chicago: Univ. Chicago Press

South SJ, Bonjean CM, Markham WT, Corder J. 1982. Social structure and intergroup interaction: men and women of the federal bureaucracy. *Am. Sociol. Rev.* 47: 587–99

South SJ, Bonjean CM, Markham WT, Corder J. 1983. Female labor force participation and the organizational experiences of male workers. *Sociol. Q.* 24:367–80

South SJ, Bonjean CM, Markham WT, Corder J. 1987. Sex differences in support for organizational advancement. *Work Occup.* 14(2):261–85

Spangler E, Gordon MA, Pipkin RM. 1978. Token women: an empirical test of Kanter's hypothesis. *Am. J. Sociol.* 84:160–70

Stover DL. 1994. The horizontal distribution of female managers within organizations. *Work Occup.* 21:385–402

Swerdlow M. 1989. Men's accommodations to women entering a nontraditional occupation: a case of rapid transit operatives. *Gend. Soc.* 3:373–87

Szafran RF. 1982. What kinds of firms hire and promote women and blacks? A review of the literature. *Sociol. Q.* 23(Spring): 171–90

Tajfel H. 1982. Social psychology of intergroup relations. *Annu. Rev. Psychol.* 33: 1–39

Taylor MC. 1995. White backlash to workplace affirmative action: peril or myth? *Soc. Forces* 73:1385–414

Taylor SE. 1981. A categorization approach to stereotyping. In *Cognitive Processes in Stereotyping and Intergroup Behavior*, ed. D Hamilton, pp. 83–114. Hillsdale, NJ: Erlbaum

Tidball ME. 1986. Baccalaureate origins of recent national science doctorates. *J. Higher Educ.* 57(6):606–20

Tienda M, Lii D. 1987. Minority concentration and earnings inequality: blacks, Hispanics, and Asians compared. *Am. J. Sociol.* 93: 141–65

Tolbert PS, Graham ME, Andrews AO. 1998. Gender group composition and work group relations: theories, evidence, and issues. In *Handbook of Gender Organizations*, ed. G Powell. In press

Tolbert PS, Oberfield AA. 1991. Sources of organizational demography: faculty sex ratios in colleges and universities. *Sociol. Educ.* 64:305–15

Tolbert PS, Simons T, Andrews AO, Rhee J. 1995. The effects of gender composition in academic department on faculty turnover.

Ind. Labor Relat. Rev. 48:562–79

Tsui AS, Egan TD, O'Reilly CA. 1992. Being different: relational demography and organizational attachment. *Admin. Sci. Q.* 37:549–79

Tsui AS, O'Reilly C. 1989. Beyond simple demographic effects: the importance of relational demography in superior-subordinate dyads. *Acad. Manage. J.* 32: 402–23

US Bur. Census. 1998. *Statistical Abstract of the United States: 1997.* Washington, DC: US Dep. Commerce

Waldinger R, Aldrich H, Ward R. 1990. *Ethnic Entrepreneurs: Immigrant Business in Industrial Societies.* Newbury Park, CA: Sage

Waldinger R, Bailey T. 1991. The continuing significance of race: racial conflict and racial discrimination in construction. *Polit. Soc.* 19:291–323

Wallace M, Chang CF. 1990. Barriers to women's employment: economic segmentation in American manufacturing. *Res. Soc. Stratif. Mobil.* 9:337–61

Wharton AS, Baron JN. 1991. Satisfaction? The psychological impact of gender segregation on women at work. *Sociol. Q.* 32: 365–87

Wharton AS, Bird SR. 1996. Stand by your man: homosociality, work groups, and men's perceptions of difference. In *Masculinities in Organizations*, ed. C Cheng, pp. 97–114. Thousand Oaks, CA: Sage

Wharton AS, Rotolo T, Bird SR. 1999. Social context at work: a multilevel analysis of job satisfaction. *Sociol. Forum.* In press

Annu. Rev. Sociol. 1999. 25:363–94

RECENT DEVELOPMENTS AND CURRENT CONTROVERSIES IN THE SOCIOLOGY OF RELIGION

Darren E. Sherkat

Department of Sociology, Vanderbilt University, Nashville, Tennessee 37235;
e-mail: sherkade@ctrvax.vanderbilt.edu

Christopher G. Ellison

Department of Sociology, University of Texas-Austin, Austin, Texas 78712,
e-mail: cellison@mail.la.utexas.edu

KEY WORDS: rational choice, politics, family health, social control

ABSTRACT

The sociology of religion is experiencing a period of substantial organizational and intellectual growth. Recent theoretical and empirical papers on the sociology of religion appearing in top journals in sociology have generated both interest and controversy. We begin with a selective overview of research on religious beliefs and commitments. Second, we investigate the influence of religion on politics, the family, health and well-being, and on free space and social capital. Finally, we review rational choice theories in the sociology of religion and the controversies surrounding applications of these perspectives.

INTRODUCTION

The sociology of religion is experiencing a period of substantial organizational and intellectual progress. Social scientific organizations devoted to the study of religion have experienced unprecedented growth in meetings attendance and membership, and a sociology of religion section was recently added in the American Sociological Association. Recent theoretical and empirical papers

363

on the sociology of religion appearing in top journals have generated interest and controversy. Indeed, for the first time since the 1960s, scholars who typically specialize in other substantive areas are doing research on, or theorizing about, the sociology of religion. This development is a tremendous surprise to many sociologists, who accepted the expectations of secularization theories that promised declining importance of religion in social life, diminished strength for religious organizations, and waning religious commitment among individuals. However, by the late 1970s, events throughout the world revealed an undeniably strong influence of religion in the late twentieth century. For social scientists, the rise of fundamentalist religion in the United States and elsewhere (Marty & Appleby 1991), and the public debates about cults and new religious movements, were probably the most significant events that led to a reevaluation of the importance of religion. Theoretical and empirical connections between the sociology of religion and other areas of sociology—especially family, medical sociology, and social movements—also played a role in reviving interest in the sociology of religion.

Many contemporary controversies are rooted in debates between scholars wedded to secularization theories and those who explain religious behaviors and trajectories through a different lens. Secularization theory has a long history in the social sciences and played a considerable role in the development of the sociology of religion (Hadden 1987). Secularization is an ideological impulse strongly rooted in the Western Enlightenment, and one that resonates with the conventional wisdom of many Western elites (Hadden 1987, Lechner 1991, Stark & Bainbridge 1985). Secularization theorists generally agree that societal-level differentiation is a master process driving secularization (Dobbelaere 1985, Lechner 1991, Tschannen 1991, Chaves 1994). Yet, theorists are divided on the implications and scope of the perspective. Tschannen (1991) arrays seven secularization theorists according to their views on 12 separate dimensions (among these are differentiation, pluralization, rationalization, scientization, and unbelief). Dobbelaere (1985) argues that there are two discrete secularization paradigms with four distinct levels of analysis. Recent advocates reformulate secularization theories to focus on religious "authority" (Chaves 1994). The wide variety of secularization perspectives and interpretations, combined with a dearth of concrete operational hypotheses, led some critical commentators to argue that the perspective is not a theory at all (Hadden 1987). Whatever its status as a theory, many scholars still investigate religious phenomena from the vantage point of secularization, and debates about its relevance are far from over.

Critiques of secularization theory began to emerge as evolutionary functionalist theories lost favor in the 1970s. Sociologists objected to romantic notions of a unified collective consciousness and the imposition of Western European cultural and economic trajectories on the rest of the world. Historical sociologists and anthropologists noted that the premodern world was fraught with diverse religious beliefs and practices, and even unbelief (Douglas 1982). Other theorists argued that differentiation and disenchantment are often counterposed by dedifferentiation and reenchantment (Tiryakian 1992), and that the functional differentiation of religious institutions does not prevent religious influences on politics, the economy, culture, and other aspects of social life (Beyer 1994). The complexity of religious phenomena—and the profound importance of individual experiences for religious action—were difficult to comprehend from the lens of secularization theories. While many scholars work diligently to try to salvage this framework, even such luminary secularization theorists as Peter Berger have rejected it (*Christian Century*, Oct. 29, 1997). Alternative perspectives were lacking until the late 1970s, when Rodney Stark and William Sims Bainbridge began the work that would culminate in their influential theoretical opuses (1985, 1987), and when scholars examining social movements began to turn their attention to religious movements (Hall 1988a, Snow 1993, Rochford 1985, Zald 1982). Fresh theoretical perspectives, and a precipitous increase in methodological rigor, led many to proclaim the ascendance of a "new paradigm" rooted in rational choice theory and empirical analysis (Warner 1993).

We begin our review with a selective overview of research on religious beliefs and commitments, with a slant towards research on the United States. Next, we examine the influence of religion on: (*a*) politics, (*b*) the family, (*c*) health and well-being, and (*d*) free space and social capital. The remainder of the review presents rational choice theories of religion and the substantive and theoretical controversies surrounding their applications.

Religious Beliefs and Commitments in the Contemporary United States

Scholarly examinations of religious beliefs, participation, and affiliation have focused on three elements: (*a*) the distribution of beliefs and commitments, (*b*) trends in beliefs and attachments, and (*c*) predictors of religiosity. Religious beliefs are remarkably salient in the United States, and General Social Survey (GSS) data reveal that: (*a*) nearly 63% believe in God without doubts, while only 2.2% do not believe in God, (*b*) around a third of Americans believe that the Bible is the actual word of God, and more than 80% think it divinely inspired, (*c*) 77% believe in heaven, 63% in hell, and 58% in the devil. Trends in these beliefs are difficult to document because of changes in question wording and sampling procedures. However, analyses of Gallup data seem to indicate a slight drop in some measures of religious orthodoxy, particularly biblical inerrancy (Glenn 1987, Greeley 1989, Smith 1992), though early polls did not use comparable sampling or call-back procedures. In contrast, beliefs in

God and beliefs in an afterlife are remarkably stable (Greeley 1989, Harley & Firebaugh 1993).

Levels of religious participation and rates of membership in religious organizations remain high compared to other nations and other voluntary activities (Verweij et al 1997). GSS data indicate that 61% of Americans claim membership in a religious organization, 29% claim to attend church weekly or more often, and 45% report attending church at least monthly. There is considerable debate about the specific level of participation in the United States, focusing on the validity of self-reported church attendance in survey data. Some researchers claim that Americans overreport their church attendance, and that actual rates of attendance are about one half of what people claim in surveys—suggesting that around 22% of Americans attend religious services in a given week (Hadaway et al 1993). Still, even this conservative estimate of rates of religious participation is far higher than weekly rates of activity in other voluntary organizations. Critical assessments of rates of overreporting point to problems in determining the population of church affiliates, the nature of attendance reports, and anomalies created by low survey response rates; these studies suggest that overreporting is far less common (Hout & Greeley 1998, Woodberry 1998). Further, most investigations find no significant trend in religious participation, or a slight decrease accounted for by Catholic declines in the 1960s (Hout & Greeley 1987, Glenn 1987, Greeley 1989, but see Presser & Stinson 1998). Americans also donate substantial amounts of time and money to religious organizations, averaging $440 per year for households in the GSS (Hoge & Yang 1994). Indeed, contributions to the top 15 *reporting* denominations exceeded $18 billion in 1996, and 6 of the 10 largest denominations did not report contributions (Bedell 1997). Contributions, combined with expenditures on other religious activities and items (e.g. literature, music, clothing), make religion a huge industry in the United States (Moore 1994) and a large component of the nonprofit sector of the economy (Wuthnow 1991b).

One of the most interesting aspects of religiosity is that commitments are divided among competing groups. Sectarian differences and religious diversity are ubiquitous throughout the world; religious pluralism is often viewed, however, as a hallmark of religion in the United States (Tiryakian 1993). There are over 2100 religious groups in America, including a variety of cults or new religious movements (Melton 1996). Of these groups 133 report a confirmed membership of over 55 million, and 137 million adherents (Bradley et al 1992). GSS data (1989–1996) indicate that 25% of Americans identify themselves as Catholic, nearly 26% affiliate with Baptist or conservative Protestant bodies (e.g. Assembly of God, Churches of Christ, Church of God in Christ, Nazarene, Pentecostal), liberal and moderate Protestants (e.g. Episcopal, Presbyterian, Methodists, and Lutherans) account for 29%, more than 9% are nonreligious, 2.5% are Jewish, and almost 2% claim other non-Christian faiths. Religious identification varies considerably across racial and ethnic groups. Among African Americans: 54% claim Baptist affinities, and another 11% identify with conservative sects like the Church of God in Christ; 11% are Methodist, only 7% are Catholic, and less than 2% affiliate with non-Christian groups like the various Islamic groups (Ellison & Sherkat 1990). Ethnic diversity is having an impact on religious pluralism, and research has begun to investigate ethnic immigrant religions (Warner & Wittner 1998), though much more is warranted. It is also notable that religious affiliations are concentrated in particular regions of the country. Catholics are concentrated in the Northeast and Southwest, while Lutherans are plentiful in the upper Midwest. Baptists command the South, and Mormons are most common in the intermountain West (Bradley et al 1992). Approximately one third of Americans switch religious affiliations, and nearly a third of switchers make more than one switch (Roof 1989). Both survey data and denominational statistics indicate that conservative Protestant sects, Jehovah's Witnesses, Mormons, and nonreligion have seen marginal "growth" from religious switching or other sources, while moderate and liberal Protestant churches tend to be losing ground (Bedell 1997, Ellison & Sherkat 1990, Hadaway & Marler 1994, but see Smith 1992). Contrary to popular opinion, however, rates of religious switching are not increasing (Sullins 1993).

Research consistently finds religious beliefs and behaviors to be a function of: (*a*) family and denominational socialization, (*b*) gender, (*c*) social status, and (*d*) life course events and aging. Parents influence their children's religious beliefs and commitments both directly through the socialization of beliefs and commitments (Hoge et al 1994, Kelley & De Graaf 1997, Myers 1996, Sherkat 1998) and by channeling other social relationships (Cornwall 1989). Parents are more likely to transmit religiosity and affiliation when they have common religious commitments (Myers 1996, Sandomirsky & Wilson 1990, Sherkat 1991), and conservative Protestant and Catholic spouses are more likely to win children's loyalty when spouses are divided (Nelsen 1990). Conservative Protestant sects socialize their members to have more traditional religious beliefs, and to participate in religious activities more often. Consequently, members of conservative religious denominations are less likely to become irreligious, and they donate more time and money to religious organizations (Hoge & Yang 1994, Iannaccone et al 1995, Sherkat 1998, Sherkat & Wilson 1995).

Women participate more frequently in religious organizations, are less likely to become irreligious, and hold significantly more orthodox religious beliefs than men (De Vaus & McAllister 1987, Miller & Hoffman 1995, Sherkat 1998, Wilson & Sherkat 1994). Despite seemingly misogynist gender-role prescriptions and proscriptions (Peek et al 1991), religious organizations provide social settings and support that encourage women's participation and even allow for considerable leadership opportunities (Bartkowski 1997, McNamara 1984, Stark & Bainbridge 1985). Further, young women may be socialized into religious beliefs and commitments more vigorously and more successfully, and their structural location in the home may help solidify and perpetuate these commitments (De Vaus & McAllister 1987). Theorists have also speculated that higher risk aversion among women may lead them to be more religious (Miller & Hoffman 1995).

Social status has varying influences on religious beliefs and commitments. Higher levels of education have a negative impact on measures of traditional religious beliefs; however, education also spurs participation in religious organizations (Iannaccone 1997, Johnson 1997, Sherkat 1998). People with higher incomes donate more money to religious organizations, though their contributions as a percentage of income are generally found to be lower (Hoge & Yang 1994). Individuals with higher incomes tend to substitute contributions to religious organizations for attendance (Iannaccone 1997). Educational attainment increases the likelihood of relinquishing affiliation with religious organizations, and exceeding the educational attainment of peers in the denomination of origin prompts apostasy and religious switching (Sherkat 1991, Sherkat & Wilson 1995).

The close association between religious commitments, family formation, and childrearing evidences itself in a number of life course influences on religious behaviors. Generally, marriage and childrearing boost religious participation, while divorce and cohabitation reduce religious activity (Stolzenberg et al 1995, Thornton et al 1992, Myers 1996, Sherkat 1998). Importantly, the timing of life course events has been shown to mediate their influence on religious behaviors. When individuals marry and have children at "normatively appropriate" ages, they will benefit more from the social support provided to parents in religious organizations. Research shows that people who have children in their late 20s or early 30s increase their religious participation while those who rear their children earlier do not (Stolzenberg et al 1995). Religious intermarriage increases rates of religious switching (Lazerwitz 1995, Sherkat 1991, Sandomirsky & Wilson 1990), as spouses jointly negotiate religious commitments. Aging boosts religious participation, perhaps because of increased integration, desire for social support, or a heightened need for explanations of the meaning of life (Stark & Bainbridge 1987). Researchers are divided on whether cohort or period effects drive overall rates of religious participation (Chaves 1989), though persuasive analyses indicate that cohort and period effects are accounted for by life cycle factors (Firebaugh & Harley 1991, Hout & Greeley 1990).

Finally, scholars have investigated the importance of region and geographic mobility on religiosity. Regional concentrations of denominations have led to some characteristic patterns in the United States, generally described as a more "devoted" South and a relatively irreligious West (Shibley 1996, Smith et al 1998, Stark & Bainbridge 1985). Recent research demonstrates that migration to less committed regions diminishes religious devotion, while moving to more pious areas enhances religious participation and the importance of faith (Smith et al 1998). African Americans from the South, and especially the rural South, have high rates of religious participation and are unlikely to switch to nonreligion (Ellison & Sherkat 1995, Sherkat & Ellison 1991). Additionally, geographic mobility often disrupts social ties and leads to changes in religious affiliation, including conversion to new religious movements (Sherkat 1991, Stark & Bainbridge 1985).

THE INFLUENCE OF RELIGION ON SOCIAL LIFE

Renewed interest in the sociology of religion has been stimulated by attention given to the effects of religious beliefs, commitments, and institutions in other arenas of social life. Not only has religion stubbornly refused to disappear, it continues to hold sway over (a) political beliefs and commitments, (b) family relations, (c) health and well-being, and (d) free social space and social capital.

Religion, Social Movements, and Politics

The study of the connection between religion and politics was given new life by the "rise" of politicized Christianity (mostly conservative) in the 1970s, and revolutionary Islamic movements in the Middle East (Jelen 1998, Marty & Appleby 1991). Many scholars have long downplayed the significance of religion in world politics, yet longstanding political conflicts in Ireland, India, Sri Lanka, Palestine, Bosnia, and a host of other places have distinctively religious roots (Hadden 1987, Smith 1996a). Religious beliefs, commitments, and resources are an important part of building and maintaining ethnic identities, and they provide the ideological and actual resources brought to bear in ethnic conflicts ranging from the struggles over civil rights in the United States, to economic justice in Latin America, to Islamic and Zionist movements in the Middle East (Beyer 1994, Billings & Scott 1994, Casanova 1994, Moaddel 1996, Smith 1996a). For most of the 1970s and 1980s, scholars examining social movements neglected cultural influences on social movement activism. Yet, resource mobilization theorists pointed out the powerful importance of religion in the struggle for African American civil rights—providing organizational and symbolic resources, leadership, a premobilized constituency embedded in dense social networks, and an indigenous source of funding—and this helped call attention to the connection between religion and social movements (Morris 1984, Oberschall 1993, Zald 1982). Recent developments in social movement theory have emphasized the importance of cultural institutions for social movements (Johnston & Klandermans 1995, Morris & Mueller 1992). This cultural turn in the analysis of social movements has led to a re-examination of how religious ideologies and institutions might: (*a*) provide a groundwork for the framing of movement issues, (*b*) enhance the resonance of movement positions, (*c*) generate social legitimacy to enhance mobilization and stave off repression, and (*d*) lend narratives to social movements that help provide a rationale for action and a foundation for collective identities and group solidarity (Hunt et al 1994, Oberschall & Kim 1996, Smith 1996a). Among the recent findings from studies investigating the connection between religion and social movements are that "identity" and "constitutionalist" Christian ideologies and organizational resources are essential elements of right wing hate groups (Aho 1990, Barkun 1994), that activists from liberal Protestant and Catholic groups were instrumental in movements for legalizing abortion (Staggenborg 1991), that conservative Christianity provides considerable symbolic and actual resources for antiabortion groups like Operation Rescue (Blanchard 1994, Williams & Blackburn 1996), and that faithful Catholics and liberal Protestants were pivotal in movements opposing US policy in Central America (Smith 1996b).

In the United States, religious beliefs and commitments have a substantial impact on politicized beliefs about moral issues like pornography (Sherkat & Ellison 1997), abortion (Cook et al 1992), and homosexuality (Leege & Kellstedt 1993). The apparent gulf between "orthodox" religious adherents who base their commitments on the authority of sacred texts and "progressive" congregants who situate morals in modern social contexts led some to speculate that politicized moral issues are increasingly polarized between organized camps in a "culture war" (Hunter 1991). Yet, recent investigations fail to find trends in the polarization of a range of political and moral values within and across religious groups (Hoffman & Miller 1998, Davis & Robinson 1996, Di-Maggio et al 1996), and several inquiries cast serious doubt on the salience of orthodox versus progressive identities (Williams 1997). One investigation suggests that conservative Protestants were not increasingly mobilized in presidential elections, and that a shift toward the Democrats by liberal Protestants is the main trend in partisanship (Manza & Brooks 1997). Yet, Layman (1997) finds that members of conservative Protestant denominations have become more Republican since 1980, and that religious commitment increasingly predicts Republican voting. While rumors of war are exaggerated, contemporary research has demonstrated a continuing influence of religion on political beliefs and commitments in the contemporary United States, and a growing body of literature documents how religious beliefs and commitments inform political values and behaviors (Jelen 1998, Leege & Kellstedt 1993, Woodberry & Smith 1998).

Religion and Family Issues

The past decade has seen a modest resurgence of interest in the links between religion and family. An earlier generation of research tended to focus on Catholic-Protestant differences in family values and practices (Lenski 1961), yet many of these differences have disappeared because of upward mobility and assimilation of Catholic ethnic groups, considerable diversity among Protestant bodies, religious intermarriage, and changes in Catholicism since the 1960s (Alwin 1986, Ellison & Sherkat 1993a). Recent research on the religion-family connection has examined (*a*) adolescent sexuality, (*b*) marriage and fertility, (*c*) childrearing, and (*d*) gender roles.

Religious factors clearly influence adolescent sexual attitudes and reproductive behavior. Young women who attend services regularly, value religion in their lives, and maintain denominational ties are less likely than others to become sexually active prior to marriage, or to use contraceptives (Brewster et al 1998, Thornton & Camburn 1989, Forste & Heaton 1988, Goldscheider & Mosher 1991, Kahn et al 1990). While members of other denominations have liberalized their views about premarital sex, active conservative Protestants have not (Petersen & Donnenwerth 1997). Interestingly, among white adolescent women, the influence of conservative Protestant affiliation on the likelihood of remaining a virgin actually increased during the 1980s, perhaps due to the heightened activity of Christian advocacy groups such as True Love Waits (Brewster et al 1998).

Conservative Protestants marry earlier than members of other religious groups, including Catholics (Mosher et al 1992, Hammond et al 1993). Couples' church attendance and religious devotion are associated with greater marital happiness and adjustment, and lower risk of conflict (including domestic violence) and dissolution (Filsinger & Wilson 1984, Call & Heaton 1997, Ellison et al 1999a). Embeddedness within religious communities may validate couples' relationship commitments, encourage values of love and caring, and promote the subordination of egoistic desires (Scanzoni & Arnett 1987, Larson & Goltz 1989). In addition, same-faith marriages are happier and less likely to end in divorce than mixed-faith marriages (Glenn 1982, Heaton & Pratt 1990). The degree of theological distance separating partners is linked with marital dissatisfaction and conflict (including domestic violence) (Ortega et al 1988, Curtis & Ellison 1998, Ellison et al 1999a), and heterogamous marriages involving one fundamentalist or sectarian partner are at greatest risk of disharmony and dissolution (Lehrer & Chiswick 1993).

Religious heterogamy also depresses fertility rates among Catholics and Mormons (Lehrer 1996). Fertility is comparatively high among conservative Protestants, which may result from pronatalist theologies and high levels of religious commitment (Marcum 1986), or from early marriage and low socioeconomic status (Mosher et al 1992, Hammond et al 1993). Catholics had higher fertility rates than Protestants for much of the twentieth century (Westoff & Jones 1979), yet this pattern has shifted dramatically. Among non-Hispanic whites, the total fertility rate is lower for Catholics than for Protestants, primarily because Catholics tend to marry later and less frequently (Mosher et al 1992, Sander 1993). Mormons have the highest total fertility rate of any major religious grouping, while the religiously unaffiliated have the lowest fertility rates and the greatest propensity toward childlessness (Heaton et al 1994, Mosher et al 1992).

After decades of neglect, recent studies have shed new light on religious influences on children and parenting. For instance, one analysis links the religiosity of mothers and maternal grandmothers with more positive mother-child bonds, even into young adulthood (Pearce & Axinn 1998). Moreover, a growing body of literature has focused on the distinctive childrearing philosophies of conservative Protestants. In popular advice manuals for parents, fundamentalist and evangelical authors express a marked preference for well-defined, gendered parental roles, and hierarchical (rather than egalitarian) parent-child relations (Bartkowski & Ellison 1995). In addition, conservative Protestants are disproportionately likely to endorse and use corporal punishment (Ellison & Sherkat 1993b, Ellison et al 1996). Although critics worry that evangelicalism legitimates authoritarian and abusive childrearing practices (Greven 1990, Capps 1995), such concerns may be exaggerated. Religious childrearing manuals offer careful advice on how to administer mild-to-moderate corporal punishment (Ellison 1996). Further, conservative Protestant parents yell at their children less frequently, and express verbal and physical affection to their children more often than other parents (Wilcox 1998). Evangelical fathers, and those who are generally more religious, also spend more quality time with their children than other fathers do (Wilcox 1999). Perhaps for these reasons, one recent study finds no systematic negative consequences of corporal punishment for conservative Protestant children (Ellison et al 1999b).

Religious beliefs and commitments are central for establishing and reenforcing gender roles. Scholars have found that traditional religious beliefs, regular religious attendance, and conservative Protestant and Mormon ties buttress support for patriarchal gender roles (Hertel & Hughes 1987, Peek et al 1991). At the same time, there is considerably greater heterogeneity on gender attitudes among conservative Protestants than among others (Gay et al 1996). Although conservative Protestant women—especially those in homogamous unions, and those with young children—exhibit weaker labor force attachment than do other women (Lehrer 1995, Sherkat 1999); a growing number of conservative Protestant women work outside the home, prompting selective accommodation and ideological work among clergy and church officials (Iannaccone & Miles 1990, Demmitt 1992). In addition, while the gender segregation of household labor is somewhat more pronounced among homogamous evangelical couples than others, this difference is modest in magnitude (Ellison & Bartkowski 1997). Further, ethnographic studies find that decision-making in evangelical households involves extensive collaboration and negotiation between partners, with little evidence of male dominance (McNamara 1984, Bartkowski 1997). Moreover, women's roles in conservative religious groups suggest considerable complexity, even when doctrines and organizational cultures marginalize women. Several studies identify numerous means by which women find fulfillment and even empowerment in conservative variants of Protestantism and Judaism (Stacey & Gerard 1990, Davidman 1990, Pevey et al 1996, Griffith 1997).

Religion, Health, and Well-Being

In recent years, multidisciplinary research on the connection between religion, health, and well-being has flourished. Studies using longitudinal data, sophisticated analytic techniques, and exhaustive multivariate controls have reported substantial positive effects of religious involvement on various mental and physical health outcomes, including mortality (Hummer et al 1999, Idler & Kasl 1992, Musick 1996, Oxman et al 1995, Strawbridge et al 1997, Williams et al 1991). Extending Durkheimian themes of religion as an integrative and regulatory social force (Levin 1996, Ellison & Levin 1998), scholars have begun specifying the processes through which religion may influence health and well-being, including the following: (a) health behaviors and individual lifestyles, (b) social integration and support, (c) psychological resources, (d) coping behaviors and resources, and (f) various positive emotions and healthy beliefs, among other factors.

Religious involvement may promote mental and physical well-being by regulating personal behaviors in ways that decrease the risk of disease. In a well-documented example, religious attendance and affiliation with conservative or sectarian groups are inversely related to alcohol, tobacco, and substance use and abuse, which in turn are linked with chronic diseases (Koenig et al 1994, Troyer 1988). Moreover, most religious communities have teachings that discourage various types of deviant behavior (e.g., risky sexual practices, illegal conduct), provide guidance on family issues, and direct life-style choices in ways that may reduce exposure to various stressful events and conditions (Ellison 1994).

Religious congregations offer regular opportunities for social activity and interaction and so provide fertile terrain for the cultivation of friendships. Communities of coreligionists are valuable sources of informal social support and emotional assistance, providing instrumental aid to those in need as well as companionship and comfort to members experiencing stressful life events

(Taylor & Chatters 1988, Ellison & George 1994). Many congregations sponsor formal programs designed to aid persons in need (e.g., antipoverty, health information, family services) as well as pastoral counseling (Caldwell et al 1992, Kimble 1995). Religious groups foster a sense of community, leading members to feel loved, valued, and cared for; religious support may be particularly effective because of shared norms of altruism and reciprocity, and common beliefs about suffering and helping behavior (Ellison 1994, Wuthnow 1994).

Recent studies reveal that religious involvement may foster mental and physical health by enhancing of self-esteem and personal efficacy, especially among certain populations such as elders and African Americans (McIntosh & Spilka 1990, Ellison 1993 , Krause 1995). Individuals may enhance feelings of personal control or self-worth through cultivating a personal relationship with loving and caring "divine others" (gods), who can be engaged through prayer or meditation in a quest for solace and guidance (Pollner 1989, McIntosh & Spilka 1990, Ellison 1991). The nature of religious fellowship may contribute to favorable self-assessments by affirming and bolstering role identities and commitments or by fostering positive reflected appraisals (Ellison 1993).

It is increasingly evident that religious understandings and behaviors are common and effective coping strategies for many individuals dealing with a broad array of chronic and acute stressors, particularly bereavement and health problems (including physical disability) (Mattlin et al 1990, Idler 1995, Pargament et al 1990). A growing literature underscores the importance of religious cognitions in shaping the diverse ways in which individuals interpret and assign meaning to undesirable events and conditions, assess the degree of threat posed by such problems, and gauge their own capacity for dealing with them (Pargament 1997).

Investigators have also posited a wide range of additional mechanisms that may link religion with health, including positive emotions such as love, contentment, and forgiveness, as well as hope and optimism that often grow out of personal faith (Koenig et al 1997). Certain ritual or worship experiences—especially ecstatic or cathartic services—may confer mental and physical health benefits as well (Griffith et al 1984, Idler & Kasl 1997). At the same time, researchers in this burgeoning field are also beginning to explore aspects of religious communities—e.g., "toxic faith," maladaptive religious coping, congregational conflicts—that may tax the health and well-being of their members (Ellison & Levin 1998).

Free Social Space and Social Capital

A growing literature suggests that religious communities may serve as "free social space" for certain marginalized groups and may provide members with "social capital" that can be mobilized toward instrumental ends (Greeley1997, Warner 1993). Social capital can contribute to positive outcomes by (a) providing values and norms that channel behavior in certain directions and away from others, (b) promoting the circulation of information, and (c) encouraging both long-term investments of time and energy and exchange relations, within contexts governed by norms of reciprocity, trust, and mutual obligation (Coleman 1988, Portes 1998). Throughout US history, various groups have responded to conditions of cultural and/or structural marginality by creating new religious organizations, cultivating new modes of spiritual expression, and forming semi-autonomous enclaves within established religious institutions (Warner 1993). In the broadest terms, these "free spaces" have served some or all of the following functions: (a) affording spiritual fulfillment and psychological satisfaction, (b) providing opportunities for authentic religous expression, and sustaining ethnic and other group cultures and identities, (c) articulating and addressing group-specific needs that are ignored in other arenas, and (d) promoting awareness of common interests and fostering collective mobilization (Warner 1997). Among the numerous contemporary examples of this diverse phenomenon are organizations focused on the spiritual needs and social concerns of gays and lesbians, such as the Metropolitan Community Church, and various caucuses and fellowships within mainstream denominations (Warner 1995); diverse feminist spirituality groups, including an array of pagan and Wiccan groups (Griffin 1995); and religious groups established by various racial/ethnic minorities.

Perhaps the preeminent example of religion as "free space" is found in the vibrant African American church tradition. For generations, religious institutions have occupied positions of symbolic centrality within African American communities, serving as vital sources of collective self-help and community development, moral reform, social service delivery, community leadership, and political mobilization (Lincoln & Mamiya 1990, Morris 1984, Pattillo-McCoy 1998). Emerging research is illuminating the complex roles of various new immigrant congregations—e.g., in (re)creating and (re)vitalizing religious traditions and ethnic communities within major US cities (see Warner & Wittner 1998). Taken together, these studies are showing that immigrant congregations—representing diverse faith traditions—often afford social networks, information and skills, and other resources that facilitate the psychological adjustment and upward mobility of recent entrants (Bankston & Zhou 1996, Kwon et al 1997, Chong 1998, Warner & Wittner 1998, Yang 1998).

In addition, religion has long been thought to deter crime and deviance, for a wide range of reasons: (a) the internalization of religious norms and moral messages; (b) the fear of divine punishment (the so-called "hellfire" effect); (c) the threat of social sanctions for coreligionists; (d) the desire for approval from reference groups within religious communities; and (*e*) the lack of exposure to (or time for) deviant pursuits due to involvement in religious activities and networks, among other possible religious effects (Cochran et al 1988, Grasmick et al 1991, Evans et al 1995, Stark & Bainbridge 1997). However, studies in this area differ about how, and even whether, religion deters crime and delinquency. While some researchers have suggested that such a link may be spurious (Cochran et al 1994), others maintain that the effects of religion are contingent on the type or seriousness of the offense, or the distinctiveness of religious norms (vs. secular norms) pertaining to the offense (Tittle & Welch 1983). Proponents of the "moral communities" hypothesis argue that the power of religion to deter deviance is maximized in contexts (e.g., schools, congregations, communities) characterized by high overall levels of religiosity (Welch et al 1991, Stark 1996a) or religious homogeneity (Ellison et al 1997).

Recent studies have clarified religious differences in responses to crime and deviance. On average, conservative Protestants assign greater seriousness to most types of crimes than other persons (Curry 1996), and they endorse more retributive and punitive sanctions against offenders (Grasmick & McGill 1994). Provocative recent studies also suggest that prison religious programs and personal spirituality may reduce behavior problems among inmates and may lower the risk of recidivism in this population (Johnson et al 1997). Gaining a clearer understanding of the nature of the complex religion-crime connection should be an important priority for future research.

Interest in the constraining role of religion has been complemented in recent years by a renewed focus on the prosocial impact of faith communities, spurred partly by broader interests in communitarian themes. Although laboratory and field experiments generally report that religion has little bearing on spontaneous helping behaviors or individual altruism (Batson et al 1993), several studies show that survey respondents who report praying frequently are rated as "friendlier" and more cooperative by interviewers (Morgan 1983, Ellison 1992). Most religious communities promote voluntarism and charity, for a wide range of pragmatic and theological reasons. An emerging literature documents the prominent place of religious and religiously-sponsored organizations within the broad voluntary sector as well as how religious groups channel members into prosocial pursuits (Wuthnow 1991a,b). Individual-level studies consistently report that regular churchgoers devote more time than others to volunteer activities—in church-affiliated groups and throughout the broader community (Wilson & Janoski 1995).

Moreover, under the guidance of adult lay leaders and clergy, church-sponsored voluntary and charitable campaigns often mobilize young people for blood drives, supporting homeless shelters, programs aiding the poor and elderly, and the like—thus teaching vital lessons about civic commitment and caring for others (Donahue & Benson 1995, Greeley 1997, Wuthnow 1995). Religious socialization is often directed toward broader issues of character and purpose (Donahue & Benson 1995). Religious communities may encourage young people to focus on long-range goals, perseverance, and conformity to rules. They also may prompt adults to make long-term investments in the lives of youths. Indeed, religious institutions are among the few remaining social settings that bring young people together with caring, unrelated adult role models on a regular basis (Ellison & Muller 1996). Such religious influences can be especially important during adolescence and young adulthood, when parental influence often diminishes.

A large body of research from the 1960s through the early 1970s examined the influence of religious commitments on life chances, focusing on how Catholics may be socialized into values and communities opposed to educational attainment. However, waning Catholic-Protestant differences and a dearth of theory to explain remaining religious variations in educational attainment stifled this research agenda by the 1980s (Darnell & Sherkat 1997). Recent research has revived interest in the connection between religion and educational attainment by focusing on values that might promote or proscribe educational pursuits. One recent study based on a national sample of high school students found that those who participate regularly in religious activities tend to devote somewhat more time to school work, cut classes less often, and are more likely to graduate than their nonreligious counterparts (Ellison & Muller 1996). A growing body of research examines distinctive forms of social capital within Catholic school communities and documents their positive effects on a wide range of educational and social outcomes (Bryk et al 1993). In addition, mounting evidence indicates that religious involvement promotes educational attainment among urban African American and immigrant youths and may divert them from oppositional youth cultures (Bankston & Zhou 1996, Freeman 1986).

However, the norms and values of cultural minorities sometimes conflict with those promoted in public education, and aggrieved groups use free social spaces to defend against the assimilative influences of secular education. In earlier periods, Catholic schools developed for this purpose. At present, a key dimension of cultural conflict involves widespread fundamentalist and evangelical Protestant alienation from public schools, which are viewed as alien, hostile institutions steeped in "secular humanism" (Sikkink 1999). In response, some Conservative Protestants have pursued various alternative educational strategies, including home schooling and Christian academies. Although some studies have tended to emphasize the insularity and rigidity of fundamentalist schools (Peshkin 1986, Rose 1988), other accounts point to the selective incorporation of norms and strategies from mainstream education culture (Wagner 1990). For most Conservative Protestants, however, cultural alienation from the public schools clearly has not led to the abandonment of public education (Sikkink 1999). To the contrary, religious conservatives and Christian Right activists have vigorously contested local school board elections and have pressed debates over curricula and textbooks, censorship, and other policy issues at state and district levels around the country. However, conservative Christians have encouraged their children to avoid secular institutions of higher education. Biblical inerrantist parents and youths apparently heed the warnings of prominent activists, as evidenced by young fundamentalists' significantly lower rates of college attendance and avoidance of college preparatory curricula in high school and the negative effect that inerrantist parents have on young people's postsecondary educational attainment (Darnell & Sherkat 1997, Sherkat & Darnell 1999). Future research should continue to investigate the importance of distinctive cultural communities on the life circumstances and life chances of their members.

RATIONAL CHOICE THEORIES AND RELIGION

Just over a decade ago, Wuthnow (1988:500) cogently remarked that the sociology of religion "...has grown more rapidly in inductive empirical research and in subspecializations than it has in attempts to identify theoretically integrative concepts." Today, this statement is less true. The wealth of empirical findings about religious beliefs, commitments, and institutions and their consequences left the field open for new theoretical insights, and the trickle of theoretical perspicacity that began in the late 1970s turned into a flood by the early 1990s. The most notable and contested theoretical developments in the sociology of religion have come from rational choice perspectives (Young 1997). There are two schools of rational choice thought about religion. Supply-side theorists emphasize the importance of constraining and facilitating factors on the collective production of religious value—and assume that underlying preferences for religious goods remain stable. Demand-side theorists highlight shifting preferences and the influence of social constraints on individuals' choices. At the heart of all rational choice perspectives is the market analogy applied to religion, and the following axioms are common to studies in this genre: that religious markets involve exchanges for general supernatural compensators—promises of future rewards and supernatural explanations for life events and meaning (Stark & Bainbridge 1985, 1987). Like other commodities, religious goods are produced, chosen, and consumed. Supernatural compensators and explanations cannot be proven or disproved, so religious goods are risky. Social relationships are the most likely sources of information about religious wares and help reassure consumers of the value of religious goods. Uncertainty about the worth of compensators and explanations lowers their value and increases the likelihood that individuals will diversify religious investments (Iannaccone 1995a, Stark & Bainbridge 1987, Stark 1996b). Religious organizations are firms dedicated to the production of religious value. Congregations are franchises led by entrepreneurial salespeople (ministers), who create value for customers. Firms are limited in their range of product offerings, and only those lacking an organizational hierarchy (e.g. Baptists) or nourishing an institutional commitment to pluralism (e.g. Roman Catholics) can sustain much diversity (Finke & Stark 1992, Iannaccone 1991, Stark 1998).

Religious Human Capital

Iannaccone's (1990) religious human capital theory has been a source of both inspiration and controversy (Bruce 1993, Spickard 1998). According to this theory, religious participation builds individuals' stock of religious capital. Religious capital—in the form of knowledge and familiarity with doctrines, rituals, hymns, and the like—is then used to produce religious value in future religious collective actions. Familiar religious settings facilitate the effective use of religious capital and enhance religious production. Alien religious rituals, understandings, and communities hamstring the collective production of religious value because religious human capital cannot be utilized effectively. Just as experienced cooks are able to produce valuable meals with familiar ingredients, well-capitalized religious congregants are able to generate valuable religious experiences. As in all supply-side theories, preferences are viewed as stable, and only the capacity to produce religious value shifts. Further, the primary constraints on religious production are the levels of human capital possessed by individuals or collectivities. If they so desire, individuals are viewed as free to choose religious options they might desire, and any negative externalities of religious consumption are considered gratuitous costs (Iannaccone 1992, 1994).

Iannaccone (1990) uses this theory to explain a variety of religious phenomena. First, human capital stocks are seen to limit people's ability to switch religious affiliations, and if a switch is made, a similar denomination will be sought—one where previously acquired human capital can be used. Hence, Methodists would tend to switch to similar groups like the Presbyterians or the Baptists, rather than more unfamiliar traditions like the Catholic or Hindu. Young adults are more likely to switch affiliations because they are less invested in their religious commitments. Couples from different religious backgrounds are not as capable of collectively producing religious value; hence they will curtail religious participation. Women are argued to be more productive religious participants than men, owing to their relative specialization in religious tasks. The relative contribution of time and money to religious organizations has also been explained using this general framework (Iannaccone

1997). Stark (1996b) uses human capital theory to help explain the relative attractiveness of Christianity to Jews in the Roman Empire—since Christianity builds on a Jewish foundation, Jews did not have to develop entirely new religious capital stocks. Indeed, new religious movements that spring from familiar religious traditions are much more successful than those that construct entirely novel religious philosophies or that operate in alien environments (Stark & Bainbridge 1985, 1987).

Preferences and Religious Choices

While the human capital approach views prior religious activity as enhancing individuals' abilities to collectively produce religious value, demand-side perspectives argue that prior religious experiences influence people's desires for religious goods. It is important to note that this viewpoint has firm roots in economic theories of endogenously shifting preferences (cf Von Weizsaker 1971, Elster 1983). Usually, religious experiences enhance desires for familiar religious goods, and preferences are said to be adaptive (Sherkat 1997, 1998, Sherkat & Wilson 1995). Familiarity with religious compensators, explanations, and organizations makes those customary beliefs and commitments more valuable—rather than making persons better able to produce value with the religious articles. Preference shifts do not always support the status quo, since individuals might learn alternative preferences when novel information is introduced through social ties or changing life circumstances such as education, cross-cultural contact, geographic mobility, social movement participation, or social mobility. Further, religious seekers often have counteradaptive preferences, rejecting familiar religious goods in favor of novel compensators and explanations (Sherkat 1997).

Sherkat & Wilson (1995) demonstrate that distinctive religious beliefs in adolescence—particularly biblical inerrancy—are predictive of choosing to switch to conservative denominations versus liberal groups or no affiliation. This holds independent of prior levels of religious participation, which also enhances the likelihood of choosing conservative groups over liberal ones and decreases chances of apostasy. Together, these suggest that both human capital and preferences influence religious decision making. Religious socialization from parents and denominations indicates the development of preferences for particular religious goods, and these direct later participatory and affiliation choices (Sherkat 1998, Sherkat & Wilson 1995). The influence of status mobility on religious choices may arise in part from new preferences generated by changing life circumstances—harkening to Weber's notion of differential theodicies across status groups (Sherkat & Wilson 1995). Miller & Hoffman (1995) demonstrate how risk preferences are predictive of religious behavior, and they show that gender differences in risk preferences help explain gender differences in religiosity. Because religious beliefs and actions involve a risk that one might be wrong, and because there is little to lose by maintaining religious belief, risk averse individuals choose piety rather than chance the eternal consequences of error (Durkin & Greeley 1991, Miller & Hoffman 1995). Recent applications have also linked the dynamic nature of preferences and their guiding role in religious market behavior with structuration theories (Sewell 1992). Religious preferences are seen as schemata that guide religious choices, while religious participation involves interactions with religious resources. Interactions with religious resources usually sustain religious schemata but may result in learning new preferences (Sherkat 1997, 1998). The nexus of rational choice and structuration theories allows an integration of both institutional and individual elements of religious markets as well as a synthetic framework for the incorporation of the effects of family, workplace, education, politics, etc on religion—and of religion on these other realms of social life.

Social Influences on Individual's Religious Choices

Social influences on choices are an important topic of discussion in economic theory, and sociologists have paved the way for such analyses through models of normative constraints (Akerlof 1997, Bernheim 1995, Sen 1993). All choices are embedded within sets of social relations that influence decision-making, and religious choices are particularly prone to such inducements. When social influences drive religious choices, preferences for supernatural compensators and explanations have little bearing on the type or quantity of religious goods chosen. Social influences on choices come from three sources: (a) sympathy—when religious consumption is driven by the desire to make others feel good, (b) example setting—when the motivation for religious action is to show others how they should behave, and (c) rewards or punishments (Sherkat 1997). Sympathy provides an explanation for parental and spousal influences on religious choices—people often attend religious services or choose religious denominations to please their loved ones. Feelings of closeness to parents inhibit the likelihood of apostasy (Sherkat & Wilson 1995). Parents regularly make religious choices to set an example for children, and having children increases rates of religious participation and reduces the chance that an individual will become irreligious (Myers 1996, Stolzenberg et al 1995, Sherkat 1998).

Religious choices are often linked to secular rewards and punishments. Religious groups frequently serve as conduits for a variety of secular privileges (e.g. social support, access to mating markets, daycare, and economic activities), and social ties to coreligionists provide solidary incentives for participation in religious organizations. In contrast, connections to people outside of the religious group can impose costs that prevent recruitment and hinder commitment, especially when religious choices are considered deviant as with new religious movements (Stark & Bainbridge 1985, 1987). In communities where social ties are consolidated across family, work, friendship networks, neighborhoods, and other social arenas, individuals will be given considerable social rewards or suffer penalties for refusing participation in dominant religious institutions. These nonreligious sanctions limit religious voluntarism. Among African Americans, religious benefits are less predictive of religious participation in the South—especially the rural South—compared to the non-South. In the South, social opportunities for African Americans are limited, save for those provided by the near-monopoly Baptist and Methodists churches. Homogamy norms and residential and occupational segregation consolidate social ties and make some moderate level of religious participation necessary in order to enjoy social status and other social benefits (Ellison 1995, Ellison & Sherkat 1995, Sherkat & Cunningham 1998). A similar pattern is found among Mormons (Phillips 1998), where rates of participation and commitment are higher in the Mormon stronghold of the intermountain West.

Explaining the Church-Sect Cycle

Stark & Bainbridge's (1985, 1987) church-sect cycle provides an important theoretical model for understanding the trajectories of success and decline in religious organizations. Their model emphasizes both supply and demand elements. The definition and classification of religious organizations are pivotal for understanding this perspective. Religious groups vary in their degree of tension with broader society. Churches have little tension with worldly institutions, since they reject exclusive otherworldly explanations. Sects claim to have exclusive access to scarce supernatural compensators—and these claims also put them in a state of tension with the dominant society (Stark & Bainbridge 1985, 1987, Iannaccone 1988). Sects are attractive to less privileged groups because they renounce the importance of worldly gain and pleasure. Since the dispossessed always outnumber the upper classes—and may even recruit them through social ties—sectarian religious groups have broad appeal and grow rapidly when not subject to persecution (Finke & Stark 1992).

Religious organizations and their constituencies are not static, however. Successful sects spawn bureaucratic organizations to oversee movement resources and coordinate tasks vital to their soteriological mission. The professional staffs of these organizations are no longer directly beholden to the constituency of the movement, and these religious elites can begin to impress their own religious desires on the sect. Since religious elites are most likely to be upwardly mobile, they will seek more worldly religious goods. Upwardly mobile members of the sect will also prefer these more worldly religious goods, and contributions from elite members may further spur a shift in the religious goods produced by the sect. Seminaries and review boards allow religious elites to control the production of religious goods and to enforce product homogeneity by dictating seminary and ministerial appointments and by sanctioning deviants. The end result is a gradual replacement of otherworldly theologies and a salvation oriented mission with more worldly philosophies and a focus on secular concerns (Stark & Bainbridge 1985, 1987, Montgomery 1996, Finke & Stark 1992).

While sects tend to reduce their level of tension and become churches, many members prefer the otherworldly religion of the original sect. Some members will choose to exit the former sect, defecting to groups that maintain a high state of tension and offer exclusive supernatural compensators and explanations. Other congregants may voice opposition to changes, which can result in expulsion or schism, and the formation of a new sect. The Methodists are a classic American example. Beginning in the early nineteenth century as an otherworldly salvation-oriented sect, the Methodists gradually built seminaries, began paying full-time ministers, rejected principles of individual perfectionism, and replaced their soteriological focus with staid systematic theology. As they shifted their religious products, sectarian movements broke off and formed the Free Methodists, and various Holiness sects that sought to bring back the "old time religion" (Finke & Stark 1992). Sometimes those seeking otherworldly compensators find them in new religions—cults. Revivalist sects and/or novel cults fill the market niche for vividly otherworldly supernatural compensators and thereby limit secularization that might otherwise result as churchly movements gain ascendance.

Strictness and Strength

Beginning with Kanter's (1972) work on communal movements, scholars have recognized that groups that make stringent demands on members are more successful, and this success is rooted in the rational actions of members (Hall 1988b). Religious movements are no exception, and recently social scientists have formulated theories that explain the generative functions of strictness in religious movements. Drawing on Kelley's (1972) work on the growth and strength of strict religious groups, Iannaccone (1992, 1994) explains the advantages of strictness by appealing to increases in the collective production of religious value. Strict religious groups weed out unproductive members who free ride on the collective production efforts of more committed members. Iannaccone argues that because strict churches impose sacrifices and stigma on members, free riders shy away, and the more devoted membership generates higher per capita religious benefits. Committed members sacrifice some secular value; however, the faithful are repaid in bountiful religious goods produced in cooperation with equally engaged fellow congregants. The thesis fits nicely with historical research demonstrating the relative success of exclusive conservative religious groups (Finke & Stark 1992), higher levels of resource mobilization in conservative denominations (Iannaccone et al 1995), and variations in mobilization for Catholic religious orders (Finke 1997). Iannaccone's model also addresses cases where sacrifices or stigma are too high and when adjustments must be made to attain some necessary amount of secular utility (Iannaccone & Miles 1990). Less committed individuals have been shown to switch into less demanding liberal groups, while more active individuals choose strict groups (Sherkat & Wilson 1995)

The "strict church" thesis is both influential and controversial (Chaves 1995, Demerath 1995, Ellison 1995, Iannaccone 1995b, Marwell 1996, Spickard 1998), and criticism had been leveled on both theoretical and empirical grounds. Wallis (1991) points out that freeriding is limited by metapreferences that enhance the value of participation, and "in-process" benefits that can only be enjoyed by hearty participants. Marwell (1996) argues that sacrifice conflates strictness with resource mobilization and hence selects on the dependent variable of organizational strength. Tullock (1996) remarks that free riding is not important because religious goods are private goods like fire insurance. The joint maximization of religious and secular value may also be more feasible than Iannaccone asserts—one can be a devout conservative Protestant, Orthodox Jew, or Mormon and still enjoy all of the material aspects of secular life. This subverts Iannaccone's (1988) model by preventing joint production possibility frontiers from becoming concave.

Preferences for strictures may also be important determinants of religious participation (Sherkat 1997). Indeed, most members of strict religious organizations do not consider it a sacrifice to eschew ties with infidels, or refrain from drunkenness, homosexuality, and non-marital sex—and people may choose religious groups that affirm these preferences. Exclusive meaning systems that provide valued explanations may be the key benefit generated by "strict" groups (Stark & Bainbridge 1985, 1987), and these beliefs are unrelated to collective production, instead resembling private goods. Empirical critiques point out alternative interpretations for the growth and success of religious groups, and the imperfect relationship between strictness and growth. Perrin & Mauss (1993) find little in the way of sacrifices or stigma incurred by members of unquestionably strong and growing megachurches. Studies of church growth fail to provide reasonable confirmation that the range of "strict" churches is growing (Smith 1992, Lazerwitz 1995), and many argue that growth and strength are more likely a function of age structure, marketing techniques, geographic location, and birth rates (Roozen & Hadaway 1993).

Pluralism and Religiosity

The effect of religious pluralism on religiosity has been the subject of vigorous debates. Supply-side theorists argue that religious pluralism invigorates religious market activity, in contradiction to Durkheimian theorists who contend that a unified religion will enhance devotion and bolster religious institutions (Berger 1967). Drawing on Adam Smith, supply-side theorists contend that religious monopolies produce expensive, inferior religious goods (Finke & Stark 1988, 1992, Finke et al 1996, Iannaccone 1991). Diverse religious offerings are needed in a healthy religious market because religious preferences vary across status groups, ethnic origins, class positions, and life experiences (Stark & Bainbridge 1985, 1987). Pluralism is claimed to be the natural state of religious economies, and religious monopolies can only be maintained through state regulation. Separation of church and state ensures that religious institutions compete for the scarce, voluntarily sacrificed, resources of members, rather than being able to extract assets through taxes (Iannaccone 1991). Established churches taking advantage of state subsidies tend to guarantee lifetime employment for clergy (no matter how incompetent), provide parsonages for staff, maintain spectacular physical plants, and the like. Yet, part time ministers and volunteers may better serve local congregations because they share the life experiences of congregants. Competition makes institutions more efficient, and entrepreneurial salespeople vigorously market religious products—tailoring them to the desires of constituents, rather than following the preferences of religious elites (Finke & Stark 1992, Iannaccone 1991).

Considerable evidence from the United States and elsewhere shows the positive effects of pluralism, and negative effects of monopolies and state regulation (Chaves & Cann 1992, Christiano 1987, Finke & Stark 1988, Finke et al 1996, Hamberg & Pettersson 1994, Iannaccone 1991, Olds 1994, Stark & Iannaccone 1994). In the nineteenth century United States, religious pluralism bolstered membership and demand for clergy. In the presence of competition, Catholic churches are more effective in mobilizing high commitment members and are more innovative in their marketing of religious goods (Stark 1998, Stark & McCann 1993). Stark (1997) argues that exposure to the religious free market in the United States explains why first generation German immigrants are relatively irreligious, yet by the third generation they are like other Americans. Further, religious deregulation is linked to the preponderance of new religious movements in Europe (Stark 1993), as well as the flowering of religious groups in the former Soviet Union (Greeley 1994) and Latin America (Gill 1996). However, some scholars have found an inverse relationship between pluralism and church membership in US counties in the early twentieth century and later (Blau et al 1992, 1993, Breault 1989, Land et al 1991, Olson 1998). At issue in this debate are proper analytic methods and units of analysis. The positive effect of pluralism on membership rates requires a control for percent Catholic, and this is highly correlated with the pluralism index. Critics argue that colinearity problems create an artifactual positive effect of pluralism on membership, and that the positive effect of percent Catholic on adherence rates is inconsistent with the pluralism thesis. Supply siders claim that colinearity is not a significant problem, and that Catholicism maintains internal diversity and its positive effect is consistent with theory (Iannaccone 1991, Finke & Stark 1989, 1992). Second, advocates of the pluralism thesis persuasively argue that cities are the appropriate unit of analysis. Counties are too large and can mask local monopolies—particularly before the advent of automobiles (Finke et al 1996, Finke & Stark 1998). The timing of religious deregulation plays a role in explaining contrasting findings from the nineteenth and twentieth centuries; recently deregulated religious markets are more likely to respond to increased competition. Further, there are probably limits to the positive effects of diversity—beyond a few competing firms, there may be no additional positive effects of diversity on religious adherence.

CONCLUDING NOTE

The sociological rediscovery of religion comes at a time when other aspects of culture are also seeing renewed interest. The teleologies of Marxist and structural functionalist theories that drove cultural factors to the periphery of the discipline have become less salient in the diverse global setting of modern sociology. The theoretical infrastructure for studying religious markets has developed rapidly since the mid-1980s. What is clearly lacking are rigorous attempts to provide a theoretical and empirical link across levels of analysis. Future studies need to (*a*) disentangle the relative effects of preference shifts versus household productivity, (*b*) discern when religious value is collectively produced vs when it is a private good with intrinsic value, (*c*) specify the sources and magnitude of social influences on choices, (*d*) examine the influence of organizational processes on market dynamics (e.g. the effect of denominational conflict and organizational strength on individuals' choices and aggregate offerings), and, (*e*) model aggregate markets in a way that takes into account existing preference/human capital structures and organizational factors. Advances in multilevel modeling make such investigations possible; however, data gaps and operationalization problems limit what can be done at present. In a similar vein, investigations of religious beliefs and commitments and their influences have been hamstrung by a dearth of high quality, nationally representative panel data. Many data collection efforts neglect religious factors entirely, others only include coarse measures of religious identification and/or single items on religious participation at one point in time. These data gaps create serious problems for research in the sociology of religion, especially when research questions focus on racial and ethnic or religious subgroups with distinctive qualities.

Visit the *Annual Reviews home page* at
http://www.AnnualReviews.org.

Literature Cited

Aho JA. 1990. *The Politics of Righteousness: Idaho Christian Patriotism.* Seattle: Univ. Wash. Press

Akerlof GA. 1997. Social distance and social decisions. *Econometrica* 65:1005–27

Alwin DF. 1986. Religion and parental childrearing orientations: Evidence for a Catholic–Protestant convergence. *Am. J. Sociol.* 92:412–40

Bankston CL, Zhou M. 1996. The ethnic church, ethnic identification, and the social adjustment of Vietnamese adolescents. *Rev. Relig. Res.* 38:18–37

Barkun M. 1994. *Religion and the Racist Right.* Chapel Hill: Univ. N Carolina Press

Bartkowski JP. 1997. Debating patriarchy: discursive disputes over spousal authority among evangelical family commentators. *J. Sci. Stud. Relig.* 36:393–410

Bartkowski JP, Ellison CG. 1995. Divergent perspectives on childrearing in popular manuals: conservative Protestants vs. the mainstream experts. *Sociol. Relig.* 56: 21–34

Batson CD, Schoenrade PA, Ventis WL. 1993. *Religion and the Individual: A Social Psychological Perspective.* New York: Oxford Univ. Press

Bedell KB. 1997. *Yearbook of American and Canadian Churches.* Nashville, TN: Abingdon

Bernheim BD. 1995. A theory of conformity. *J. Polit. Econ.* 102:841–77

Berger PL. 1967. *The Sacred Canopy.* New York: Anchor

Beyer P. 1994. *Religion and Globalization.* London: Sage

Billings DB, Scott SL. 1994. Religion and political legitimation. *Annu. Rev. Sociol.* 20: 173–202

Blanchard D. 1994. *The Anti-Abortion Movement and the Rise of the Religious Right.* New York: Twayne

Blau JR, Land KC, Redding K. 1992. The expansion of religious affiliation: an explanation of the growth of church participation in the U. S., 1850-1930. *Soc. Sci. Res.* 21: 329–52

Blau JR, Redding K, Land KC. 1993. Ethnocultural cleavages and the growth of church membership in the United States. *Sociol. For.* 8: 609–37

Bradley MB, et al. 1992. Churches and church membership in the United States, 1990. Atlanta: Glenmary Res.

Breault KD. 1989. New evidence on religious pluralism, urbanism, and religious participation. *Am. Sociol. Rev.* 54: 1048–53

Brewster KL, Cooksey EC, Guilkey DK, Rindfuss RR. 1998. The changing impact of religion on the sexual and contraceptive behavior of adolescent women in the United States. *J. Marr. Fam.* 60:493–504

Bruce S. 1993. Religion and rational choice: a critique of economic explanations of religious behavior. *Sociol. Relig.* 54:193–205

Bryk AS, Lee VE, Holland PB. 1993. *Catholic Schools and the Common Good.* Cambridge, MA: Harvard Univ. Press

Caldwell CH, Green AD, Billingsley A. 1992. The black church as a family support system: instrumental and expressive functions. *Natl. J. Sociol.* 6:21–40

Call VR, Heaton TB. 1997. Religious influence on marital stability. *J. Sci. Stud. Relig.* 36:382–492

Capps DA. 1995. *The Child's Song: The Religious Abuse of Children.* Louisville, KY: Westminster/John Knox

Casanova J. 1994. *Public Religions in the Modern World.* Chicago, IL: Univ. Chicago Press

Chaves M. 1989. Secularization and religious revival: evidence from US church attendance rates,1972–1986. *J. Sci. Stud. Relig.* 28:464–77

Chaves M. 1994. Secularization as declining religious authority. *Soc. Forc.* 72:749–74

Chaves M. 1995. On the rational choice approach to religion *J. Sci. Stud. Relig.* 34: 98–104

Chaves M, Cann DE. 1992. Regulation, pluralism, and religious market structure. *Rational. Soc.* 4:272–90

Chong KH. 1998. What it means to be Christian: the role of religion in the construction of ethnic identity and boundary among second-generation Korean Americans. *Sociol. Relig.* 59:259–86

Christiano KJ. 1987. *Religious Diversity and Social Change: American Cities, 1890–1906.* Cambridge: Cambridge Univ. Press

Cochran JK, Beeghley L, Bock EW. 1988. Religiosity and alcohol behavior: an exploration of reference group theory. *Sociol. Forum* 3:256–76

Cochran JK, Wood PB, Arneklev, BJ. 1994. Is the religiosity-delinquency relationship spurious? A test of arousal and social control theories. *J. Res. Crime Delinq.* 31: 92–123

Coleman JS. 1988. Social capital in the creation of human capital. *Am. J. Sociol.* 94: S95–S120

Cook EA, Jelen TG, Wilcox C. 1992. *Between Two Absolutes: Public Opinion and the Politics of Abortion.* Boulder, CO: Westview

Cornwall M. 1989. The determinants of religious behavior: a theoretical model and empirical test. *Soc. Forc.* 68:572–92

Curry TR. 1996. Conservative Protestantism and the perceived wrongfulness of crimes. *Criminology* 34:453–64

Curtis KT, Ellison CG. 1998. *Religious heterogamy and spousal conflict among US married couples.* Paper presented at the Annu. Meet. Mid–South Sociol. Assoc., Lafayette, LA

Darnell A, Sherkat DE. 1997. The impact of Protestant fundamentalism on educational attainment. *Am. Sociol. Rev.* 62:306–16

Davidman L. 1990. *Tradition in a Rootless World: Women Turn to Orthodox Judaism.* Berkeley: Univ. Calif. Press

Davis NJ, Robinson RV. 1996. Are the rumors of war exaggerated? Religious orthodoxy and moral progressivism in America? *Am. J. Sociol.* 102:756–87

De Vaus D, McAllister I. 1987. Gender differences in religion: a test of the structural location theory. *Am. Sociol. Rev.* 52:172–81

Demerath NJ. 1995. Rational paradigms, a-rational religion, and the debate over secularization. *J. Sci. Stud. Relig.* 34:105–12

Demmitt KP. 1992. Loosening the ties that bind: the accomodation of dual-earner families in a conservative Protestant church. *Rev. Relig. Res.* 34:3–19

DiMaggio P, Evans J, Bryson B. 1996. Have Americans' social attitudes become more polarized? *Am. J. Sociol.* 102:690–755

Dobbelaere K. 1985. Secularization theories and sociological paradigms: a reformulation of the private-public dichotomy and the problem of social integration. *Sociol. Anal.* 46:377–87

Donahue MJ, Benson PL. 1995. Religion and the well-being of adolescents. *J. Soc. Issues* 51:145–60

Douglas M. 1982. The effects of modernization on religious change. *Daedalus* 111: 1–19

Durkin JT, Greeley AM. 1991. A model of religious choice under uncertainty: on re-

sponding rationally to the nonrational. *Ration. Soc.* 3:178–96

Ellison CG. 1991. Religious involvement and subjective well-being. *J. Health Soc. Behav.* 32:80–99

Ellison CG. 1992. Are religious people nice people? Evidence from the national survey of black Americans. *Soc. Forces* 71: 411–30

Ellison CG. 1993. Religious involvement and self-perception among black Americans. *Soc. Forces* 71:1027–55

Ellison CG. 1994. Religion, the life stress paradigm, and the study of depression. In *Religion in Aging and Health: Theoretical Foundations and Methodological Frontiers,* ed. JS Levin, pp. 78–121. Thousand Oaks, CA: Sage

Ellison CG. 1995. Rational choice explanations of individual religious behavior: notes on the problem of social embeddedness. *J. Sci. Stud. Relig.* 34:89–97

Ellison CG. 1996. Conservative Protestantism and the corporal punishment of children: clarifying the issues. *J. Sci. Stud. Relig.* 35:1–16

Ellison CG, Bartkowski JP. 1997. *Conservative Protestantism and the household division of labor.* Pap. presented Annu. Meet. Assoc. Sociol. Relig., Toronto

Ellison CG, Bartkowski JP, Anderson KL. 1999. Are there religious variations in domestic violence? *J. Fam. Issues.* 20:87–113

Ellison CG, Bartkowski JP, Segal ML. 1996. Conservative Protestantism and the parental use of corporal punishment. *Soc. Forc.* 74:1003–28

Ellison CG, Burr JA, McCall, PL. 1997. Religious homogeneity and metropolitan suicide rates. *Soc. Forc.* 76:273–99

Ellison CG, George, LK. 1994. Religious involvement, social ties, and social support in a Southeastern community. *J. Sci. Stud. Relig.* 33: 46–61

Ellison CG, Levin JS. 1998. The religion-health connection: evidence, theory, and future directions. *Health Educ. Behav.* 25: 700–20

Ellison CG, Muller, C. 1996. *Religious involvement, social capital, and adolescent outcomes: evidence from the NELS-88.* Pap. presented Annu. Meet. Soc. Sci. Stud. Relig., Nashville

Ellison CG, Musick MA, Holden GW. 1999. *The effects of corporal punishment on children: Are they less harmful for conservative Protestants?* Pap. presented *Soc. Sci. Stud. Relig.,* Boston

Ellison CG, Sherkat DE. 1990. Patterns of religious mobility among black Americans. *Sociol. Q.* 31:551–68

Ellison CG, Sherkat DE. 1993a. Obedience and autonomy: religion and parental values reconsidered. *J. Sci. Stud. Relig.* 32: 313–29

Ellison CG, Sherkat DE. 1993b. Conservative Protestantism and support for corporal punishment. *Am. Sociol. Rev.* 58: 131–44

Ellison CG, Sherkat DE. 1995. The semi-involuntary institution revisited: regional variations in church participation among black Americans. *Soc. Forc.* 73: 1415–37

Elster J. 1983. *Sour Grapes: Studies in the Subversion of Rationality.* Cambridge: Cambridge Univ. Press

Evans TD, Cullen FT, Dunaway RG, Burton VS. 1995. Religion and crime reexamined: the impact of religion, secular controls, and social ecology on adult criminality. *Criminology* 33:195–224

Filsinger EE, Wilson, MR. 1984. Religiosity, socioeconomic rewards, and family development: predictors of marital adjustment. *J. Marriage Fam.* 46:663–70

Finke R. 1997. An orderly return to tradition: explaining the recruitment of members into Catholic religious orders. *J. Sci. Stud. Relig.* 36:218–30

Finke R, Guest AM, Stark R. 1996. Mobilizing local religious markets: religious pluralism in the Empire State, 1855–1865. *Am. Sociol. Rev.* 61:203–18

Finke R, Stark R. 1988. Religious economies and sacred canopies: religious mobilization in American cities. *Am. Sociol. Rev.* 53:41–49

Finke R, Stark R. 1989. Evaluating the evidence: religious economies and sacred canopies. *Am. Sociol. Rev.* 54: 1054–56

Finke R, Stark R. 1992. *The Churching of America: Winners and Losers in Our Religious Economy.* New Brunswick, NJ: Rutgers Univ. Press

Finke R, Stark R. 1998. Reply: religious choice and competition. *Am. Soc. Rev.* 63: 761–66

Firebaugh G, Harley B. 1991. Trends in US church attendance: secularization and revival, or merely lifecycle effects. *J. Sci. Stud. Relig.* 30:487–500

Forste RT, Heaton TB. 1988. Initiation of sexual activity among female adolescents. *Youth Soc.* 19:250–68

Freeman RB. 1986. Who escapes? The relation of churchgoing and other background factors to the socioeconomic performance of black youths from inner-city tracts. In *The Black Youth Unemployment Crisis,* ed. RB Freeman, HJ Holzer. Chicago: Univ. Chicago Press

Gay DA, Ellison CG, Powers DA. 1996. In search of denominational subcultures: religious affiliation and 'pro-family' issues revisited. *Rev. Relig. Res.* 38:3–17

Glenn ND. 1987. Social trends in the United States: evidence from sample surveys. *Pub. Opin. Q.* 51:S109–S126

Glenn ND. 1982. Interreligious marriage in the US: patterns and recent trends. *J. Marriage Fam.* 44:555–66

Goldscheider C, Mosher WD. 1991. Patterns of contraceptive use in the United States: the importance of religious factors. *Stud. Fam. Plan.* 22:102–15

Grasmick HG, Bursik RJ, Cochran JK. 1991. 'Render unto Caesar what is Caesar's': religiosity and taxpayers' inclinations to cheat. *Sociol. Q.* 32:251–66

Grasmick HG, McGill AL. 1994. Religion, attribution style, and punitiveness toward juvenile offenders. *Criminology* 32: 23–45

Greeley A. 1989. *Religious Change in America.* Cambridge, MA: Harvard Univ. Press

Greeley A. 1994. A religious revival in Russia? *J. Sci. Stud. Relig.* 33:253–72

Greeley A. 1997. Coleman Revisited. *Am. Behav. Sci.* 40:587–94

Greven P. 1990. *Spare the Child: The Religious Roots of Punishment and the Psychological Impact of Physical Abuse.* New York: Knopf

Griffin W. 1995. The embodied goddess: feminist witchcraft and female divinity. *Sociol. Relig.* 56:35–48

Griffith EH, Young J, Smith D. 1984. An analysis of the therapeutic elements in a black church service. *Hosp. Commun. Psychiatry* 35:464–69

Griffith M. 1997. *God's Daughters: Evangelical Women and the Power of Submission.* Berkeley: Univ. Calif. Press

Hadaway CK, Marler PL. 1994. All in the family: religious mobility in America. *Rev. Relig. Res.* 35:97–116

Hadaway CK, Marler PL, Chaves M. 1993. What the polls don't show: a closer look at U.S. church attendance. *Am. Sociol. Rev.* 58:741–52

Hadden JK. 1987. Toward desacralizing secularization theory. *Soc. Forc.* 65: 587–611

Hall JR. 1988a. Collective welfare as resource mobilization in Peoples' Temple: a case study of a poor people's religious social movement. *Sociol. Anal.* 49:64s–77s.

Hall JR. 1988b. Social organization and pathways of commitment: types of communal groups, rational choice theory, and the Kanter thesis. *Am. Sociol. Rev.* 53:679–92

Hamberg EM, Pettersson T. 1994. The religious market: denominational competition and religious participation in contemporary Sweden. *J. Sci. Stud. Relig.* 33: 205–15

Hammond JA, Cole BS, Beck SH. 1993. Religious heritage and teenage marriage. *Rev. Relig. Res.* 35:117–33

Harley B, Firebaugh G. 1993. Americans' belief in an afterlife: trends over the past two decades. *J. Sci. Stud. Relig.* 32:269–78

Heaton TB, Goodman KL, Holman TB. 1994. In search of a peculiar people: Are Mormon families really different? In *Contemporary Mormonism: Social Science Perspectives*, ed. M Cornwall, TB Heaton, LA Young, pp. 87–117. Urbana: Univ. Ill. Press

Heaton TB, Jacobson CK, Fu XN. 1992. Religiosity of married couples and childlessness. *Rev. Relig. Res.* 33:244–55

Heaton TB, Pratt EL. 1990. The effects of religious homogamy on marital satisfaction and stability. *J. Fam. Issues* 11:191–207

Hertel BM, Hughes M. 1987. Religious affiliation, attendance, and support for pro family issues in the United States. *Soc. Forc.*, 65:858–82

Hoffman JP, Miller AS. 1998. Denominational influences on socially divisive issues: polarization or continuity? *J. Sci. Stud. Relig.* 37:528–46

Hoge DR, Yang F. 1994. Determinants of religious giving in American denominations: data from two nationwide surveys. *Rev. Relig. Res.* 36:123–49

Hoge DR, Johnson B, Luidens DA. 1994. *Vanishing Boundaries: the Religion of Mainline Protestant Baby Boomers.* Louisville, KY: John Knox

Hout M, Greeley A. 1987. The center doesn't hold: church attendance in the United States 1940–1984. *Am. Sociol. Rev.* 52: 325–45

Hout M, Greeley A. 1990. The cohort doesn't hold. *J. Sci. Stud. Relig.* 29:519–24

Hout M, Greeley A. 1998. What church officials' reports don't show: another look at church attendance data. *Am. Sociol. Rev.* 63: 113–19

Hummer RA, Rogers RG, Nam CB, Ellison CG. 1999. Religious involvement and US adult mortality. *Demography.* In press

Hunt SA, Benford RD, Snow DA. 1994. Identity fields: framing processes and the social construction of movement identities. In *New Social Movements: From Ideology to Identity*, ed. E Larana, H Johnston, JR. Gusfield, pp 185–208. Philadelphia, PA: Temple Univ. Press

Hunter JD. 1991. *Culture Wars.* New York: Basic Books

Iannaccone LR. 1988. A formal model of church and sect. *Am. J. Sociol.* 94:s241–68

Iannaccone LR. 1990. Religious practice: a human capital approach. *J. Sci. Stud. Relig.* 29:3:297–314

Iannaccone LR. 1991. The consequences of religious market structure: Adam Smith and the economics of religion. *Rationality Soc.* 3:2:156–77

Iannaccone LR. 1992. Sacrifice and stigma: reducing freeriding in cults, communes, and other collectivities. *J. Polit. Econ.* 100:2:271–91

Iannaccone LR. 1994. Why strict churches are strong. *Am. J. Sociol.* 99: 1180–1211

Iannaccone LR. 1995a. Risk, rationality, and religious portfolios. *Econ. Inq.* 33: 285–95

Iannaccone LR. 1995b. Second thoughts: a response to Chaves, Demerath, and Ellison. *J. Sci. Stud. Relig.* 34:113–20

Iannaccone LR. 1997. Skewness explained: a rational choice model of religious giving. *J. Sci. Stud. Relig.* 36:141–57

Iannaccone LR, Miles CA. 1990. Dealing with social change: the Mormon Church's response to change in women's roles. *Soc. Forc.* 68:1231–50

Iannaccone LR, Olson DV, Stark R. 1995. Religious resources and church growth. *Soc. Forc.* 74:705–31

Idler EL. 1995. Religion, health, and nonphysical senses of self. *Soc. Forc.* 74: 683–704

Idler EL, Kasl SV. 1992. Religion, disability, depression, and the timing of death. *Am. J. Sociol.* 97:1052–79

Idler EL, Kasl SV. 1997. Religion among disabled and nondisabled persons. II: Attendance at religious services as a predictor of the course of disability. *J. Gerontol.: Soc. Sci.* 52B:306–16

Jarvis GK, Northcott HC. 1987. Religion and differences in morbidity and mortality. *Soc. Sci. Med.* 25:813–24

Jelen TG. 1998. Research in religion and mass political behavior in the United States. *Am. Polit. Q.* 26:110–34

Johnson BR, Larson DB, Pitts TG. 1999. Religious programming, institutional adjustment, and Recidivism among former inmates in Prison Fellowship Programs. *Justice. Q.* 14:145–66

Johnson DC. 1997. Formal education vs. religious belief: soliciting new evidence with multinomial logit modeling. *J. Sci. Stud. Relig.* 36:231–46

Johnston H, Klandermans B. 1995. *Social Movements and Culture.* Minneapolis, MN: Univ. Minn. Press

Kahn JR, Rindfuss, RR, Guilkey, DK. 1990. Adolescent contraceptive method choices. *Demography* 27:323–35

Kanter RM. 1972. *Commitment and Community*. Cambridge, MA: Harvard Univ. Press

Kelley DM. 1972. *Why Conservative Churches are Growing*. New York. Harper

Kelley J, De Graaf ND. 1997. National context, parental socialization, and religious belief: results from 15 nations. *Am. Sociol. Rev.* 62:639–59

Kimble MA. 1995. Pastoral care. In *Aging, Spritualty, and Religion: A Handbook*, ed. MA Kimble, SH McFadden, JW Ellor, JJ Seeber, pp. 131–47. Minneapolis, MN: Fortress

Koenig HG, George LK, Meador, KG, Blazer DG, Ford SM. 1994. Religious practices and alcoholism in a southern adult population. *Hosp. Commun. Psychiatry* 45: 225–31

Koenig HG, Cohen HJ, George LK, Hays JC, Larson DB, Blazer DG. 1997. Attendance at religious services, interleukin-6, and other biological parameters of immune function in older adults. *Int. J. Psychiatry Med.* 27:233–50

Krause N. 1998. Stressors in highly valued roles, religious coping, and mortality. *Psychol. Aging.* 13:242–55

Kwon VH, Ebaugh HR, Hagan J. 1997. The structure and function of cell group ministry in a Korean church. *J. Sci. Stud. Relig.* 36:247–56

Land KC, Deane G, Blau JR. 1991. Religious pluralism and church membership: a spatial diffusion model. *Am. Sociol. Rev.* 56: 237–49

Larson LL, Goltz, JW. 1989. Religious participation and marital commitment. *Rev. Relig. Res.* 30:387–400

Layman GC. 1997. Religion and political behavior in the US: the impact of beliefs, affiliations, and commitment from 1980–1994. *Pub. Opin. Q.* 61:288–316

Lazerwitz B.1995. Denominational retention and switching among American Jews. *J. Sci. Stud. Relig.* 34:499–506

Lechner F. 1991. The case against secularization: a rebuttal. *Soc. Forc..* 69:1103–19

Leege DC, Kellstedt LA. 1993. *Rediscovering the Religious Factor in American Politics.* Armonk, NY: ME Sharpe

Lehrer EL. 1995. The effects of religion on the labor supply of married women. *Soc. Sci. Res.* 24:281–301

Lehrer EL. 1996. Religion as a determinant of marital fertility. *J. Pop. Econ.* 9:173–96

Lehrer EL, Chiswick CU. 1993. Religion as a determinant of marital stability. *Demography* 30:385–404

Lenski G. 1961. *The Religious Factor.* Garden City, NY: Doubleday

Levin JS. 1996. How religion influences mor-

bidity and health: reflections on natural history, salutogenesis and host resistance. *Soc. Sci. Med.* 43:849–64

Lincoln CE, Mamiya LH. 1990. *The Black Church in the African American Experience.* Durham, NC: Duke Univ. Press

Manza J, Brooks C. 1997. The religious factors in US presidential elections, 1960–1992. *Am. J. Sociol.* 103:38–81

Marcum JP. 1986. Explaining Protestant fertility: belief, commitment, and homogamy. *Sociol. Q.* 27:547–58

Marty ME, Appleby RS. 1991. *Fundamentalisms Observed.* Chicago: Univ. Chicago Press

Marwell G. 1996. We still don't know if strict churches are strong, much less why. *Am. J. Sociol.* 101:1097–108

Mattlin JA, Wethington E, Kessler RC. 1990. Situational determinants of coping and coping effectiveness. *J. Health Soc. Behav.* 31:103–22

McIntosh D, Spilka B. 1990. Religion and physical health: the role of personal faith and control beliefs. *Res. Soc. Sci. Stud. Relig.* 2:167–94

McNamara PH. 1984. Conservative Christian families and their moral world: some reflections for sociologists. *Sociol. Anal.* 46: 93–99

Melton JG. 1996. *Encyclopedia of American Religions.* Detroit, MI: Gale Res.

Miller AS, Hoffman JP. 1995. Risk and religion: an explanation of gender differences in religiosity. *J. Sci. Stud. Relig.* 34: 63–75

Moaddel M. 1996. The social bases and discursive context of the rise of Islamic fundamentalism: the cases of Iran and Syria. *Sociol. Inq.* 66:330–55

Montgomery JD. 1996. The dynamics of the religious economy: exit, voice, and denominational secularization. *Rational. Soc.* 8:81–110

Moore RL. 1994. *Selling God.* Oxford, UK: Oxford Univ. Press.

Morgan SP. 1983. A research note on religion and morality: Are religious people nice people? *Soc. Forc.* 61:683–92

Morris AD. 1984. *The Origins of the Civil Rights Movement.* New York: Free Press

Morris AD, Mueller CM. 1992. *Frontiers in Social Movement Theory.* New Haven, CT: Yale Univ. Press

Mosher WD, Williams LB, Johnson DP. 1992. Religion and fertility in the United States: new patterns. *Demography* 29:199–214

Musick MA. 1996. Religion and subjective health among Black and white elders. *J. Health Soc. Behav.* 37:221–37

Myers SM. 1996. An interactive model of religiosity inheritance: the importance of family context. *Am. Sociol. Rev.* 61:858–66

Nelsen HM. 1990. The religious identification of children of interfaith marriages. *Rev. Relig. Res.* 32:122–34

Oberschall A. 1993. *Social Movements.* New Brunswick, NJ: Transaction

Oberschall A, Kim H. 1996. Identity and action. *Mobilization* 1:63–86

Olds K. 1994. Privatizing the church: disestablishment in Connecticut and Massachusetts. *J. Polit. Econ.* 102:277–97

Olson DVA. 1998. Comment: religious pluralism in contemporary U.S. counties. *Am. Soc. Rev.* 63:759–61

Ortega ST, Whitt HP, Williams JA. 1988. Religious homogamy and marital happiness. *J. Fam. Issues* 9:224–39

Oxman TE, Freeman DH, Manheimer ED. 1995. Lack of social participation or religious strength and comfort as risk factors for death after cardiac surgery in the elderly. *Psychosom. Med.* 57:5–15

Pargament KI. 1997. *The Psychology of Religion and Coping.* New York: Guilford Press

Pargament KI, Ensing DS, Falgout K, Olsen H, Reilly B, Van Haitsma K, Warren R. 1990. God Help Me: (I): Religious coping efforts as predictors of the outcomes to significant negative life events. *Am. J. Commun. Psychol.* 18:793–824

Pattillo-McCoy M. 1998. Church culture as a strategy of action in the black community. *Am. Sociol. Rev.* 63:767–84

Pearce LD, Axinn WG. 1998. The impact of family religious life on the quality of mother-child relations. *Am. Sociol. Rev.* 63:810–28

Peek CW, Lowe GD, Williams LS. 1991. Gender and God's Word: another look at religious fundamentalism and sexism. *Soc. Forc.* 69:1205–21

Perrin RD, Mauss AL. 1993. Strictly speaking: Kelley's quandary and the Vineyard Christian Fellowship. *J. Sci. Stud. Relig.* 32: 125–35

Peshkin A 1986. God's choice: the total world of a fundamentalist school. Chicago: Univ. Chicago Press

Petersen LR, Donnenwerth GV. 1997. Secularization and the influence of religion on beliefs about premarital sex. *Soc. Forc.* 75:1071–89

Pevey C, Williams CL, Ellison CG. 1996. Male god imagery and female submission: lessons from a southern Baptist ladies' Bible class. *Qual. Sociol.* 19:173–93

Phillips R. 1998. Religious market share and Mormon Church activity. *Sociol. Relig.* 59:117–30

Pollner M. 1989. Divine relations, social rela-

tions, and well–being. *J. Health Soc. Behav.* 30:92–104

Portes A. 1998. Social capital: its origins and applications in modern sociology. *Annu. Rev. Sociol.* 22:1–24

Presser S, Stinson L. 1998. Data collection mode and social desirability bias in self-reported religious attendance. *Am. Sociol. Rev.* 63:137–145

Rochford EB. 1985. *Hare Krishna in America.* New Brunswick, NJ: Rutgers Univ. Press

Roof WC. 1989. Multiple religious switching. *J. Sci. Stud. Relig.* 28:530–35

Roozen DA, Hadaway CK. 1993. *Church and Denominational Growth.* Nashville: Abingdon

Rose SD. 1988. *Keeping Them Out of the Hands of Satan: Evangelical Schooling in America.* New York: Routledge, Chapman, Hall

Sander W. 1993. Catholicism and marriage in the United States. *Demography* 30:373–84

Sandomirsky S, Wilson J. 1990. Processes of disaffiliation: religious mobility among men and women. *Soc. Forc.* 68(4): 1211–29

Scanzoni J, Arnett, C. 1987. Enlarging the understanding of marital commitment via religious devoutness, gender role preferences, and locus of marital control. *J. Fam. Issues* 8:136–56

Sen A. 1993. Internal consistency of choice. *Econometrica* 61:495–521

Sewell WH. 1992. A theory of structure: duality, agency, and transformation. *Am. J. Sociol.* 98:1–29

Sherkat DE. 1991. Leaving the faith: testing theories of religious switching using survival models. *Soc. Science Res.* 20:171–87

Sherkat DE. 1997. Embedding religious choices: integrating preferences and social constraints into rational choice theories of religious behavior. In *Rational Choice Theory and Religion: Summary and Assessment,* ed. LA Young, pp. 65–86. New York: Routledge

Sherkat DE. 1998. Counterculture or continuity? Competing influences on baby boomers. Religious orientations and participation. *Soc. Forc.* 76:1087–1115

Sherkat DE. 1999. That they be keepers of the home: the effect of conservative religion on early and late transitions into housewifery. *Rev. Relig. Res.* In press

Sherkat DE, Cunninham SA. 1998. Extending the semi-involuntary institution regional differences and social constraints on private religious consumption among African Americans. *J. Sci. Stud. Relig.* 37:383–96

Sherkat DE. Darnell A. 1999. The effect of parents' fundamentalism on children's educational attainment: examining differences by gender and children's fundamentalism. *J. Sci. Stud. Relig.* 38:23–35

Sherkat DE, Ellison CG. 1997. The cognitive structure of a moral crusade: conservative Protestantism and opposition to pornography. *Soc. Forc.* 75:957–80

Sherkat DE, Ellison CG. 1991. The politics of black religious change: disaffiliation from black mainline denominations. *Soc. Forc.* 70:431–54

Sherkat DE, Wilson J. 1995. Preferences, constraints, and choices in religious markets: an examination of religious switching and apostasy. *Soc. Forc.* 73:993–1026

Shibley M. 1996. *Resurgent Evangelicalism in the US.* Columbia: Univ. South Carolina Press

Sikkink D 1999. The social sources of alienation from public schools. *Soc. Forc.* Forthcoming

Smith C. 1996a. *Disruptive Religion: The Force of Faith in Social Movement Activism.* New York: Routledge

Smith C. 1996b. *Resisting Reagan.* Chicago: Univ. Chicago Press.

Smith C, Sikkink D, Bailey J. 1998. Devotion in Dixie and beyond. *J. Sci. Stud. Relig.* 37:494–506

Smith TW. 1992. Are conservative churches growing? *Rev. Relig. Res.* 33:305–29

Snow DA. 1993. *Shakabuku: a study of the Nichiren Shoshu Buddhist movement in America.* New York: Garland

Spickard JV. 1998. Rethinking religious social action: What is rational about rational choice theory? *Sociol. Relig.* 59:99–115

Stacey J, Gerard SE. 1990. 'We are not doormats': the influence of feminism on contemporary evangelicals in the United States. In *Uncertain Terms: Negotiating Gender in American Culture,* ed. F Ginsberg, AL Tsing, pp. 98–117. Boston: Beacon

Staggenborg S. 1991. *The Pro-Choice Movement.* Oxford, UK: Oxford Univ. Press

Stark R. 1993. Europe's receptivity to new religious movements: round two. *J. Sci. Stud. Relig.* 32:389–97

Stark R. 1996a. Religion as context: hellfire and delinquency, one more time. *Sociol. Relig.* 57:163–73

Stark R. 1996b. *The Rise of Christianity.* Princeton, NJ: Princeton Univ. Press

Stark R. 1997. German and German American religiousness: approximating a crucial experiment. *J. Sci. Stud. Relig.* 36:182–93

Stark R. 1998. Catholic contexts: competition, commitment, and innovation. *Rev. Relig. Res.* 39:197–208

Stark R, Bainbridge WS. 1985. *The Future of Religion: Secularization, Revival, and Cult Formation.* Berkeley: Univ. Calif. Press

Stark R, Bainbridge WS. 1987. *A Theory of Religion.* Toronto: Lang

Stark R, Bainbridge WE. 1997. *Religion, Deviance, and Social Control.* New York: Routledge

Stark R, Iannaccone LR. 1994. A supply-side reinterpretation of the "secularization" of Europe. *J. Sci. Stud. Relig.* 33:230–52

Stark R, McCann JC. 1993. Market forces and Catholic commitment: exploring the new paradigm. *J. Sci. Stud. Relig.* 32:111–24

Strawbridge WJ, Cohen RD, Shema SJ, Kaplan GA. 1997. Frequent attendance at religious services and mortality over 28 years. *Am. J. Pub. Health* 87:957–61

Stolzenberg RM, Blair-Loy M, Waite LJ. 1995. Religious participation in early adulthood: age and family life cycle effects on church membership. *Am. Sociol. Rev.* 60:84–103

Sullins DP. 1993. Switching close to home: volatility or coherence in Protestant affiliation patterns? *Soc. Forc.* 72:399–419

Taylor RJ, Chatters LM. 1988. Church members as a source of informal social support. *Rev. Relig. Res.* 30:193–202

Thornton A, Axinn WG, Hill DH. 1992. Reciprocal effects of religiosity, cohabitation, and marriage. *Am. J. Sociol.* 98: 628–51.

Thornton A, Camburn D. 1989. Religious participation and adolescent sexual behavior and attitudes. *J. Marriage Fam.* 51:641–53

Tiryakian EA. 1993. American religious exceptionalism: a reconsideration. *Ann. Am. Acad. Polit. Soc. Sci.* 527:40–54

Tiryakian EA. 1992. Dialectics of modernity: reenchantment and dedifferentiation as counterprocesses. In *Social Change and Modernity,* ed. H Haferkamp, N Smelser, pp. 78–96. Berkeley: Univ. Calif. Press

Tittle CR, Welch MR. 1983. Religiosity and deviance: toward a contingency theory of constraining effects. *Soc. Forc.* 61:653–82

Troyer H. 1988. Review of cancer among four religious sects: evidence that lifestyles are distinctive sets of risk factors. *Soc. Sci. Med.* 26:1007–17

Tshannen O. 1991. The secularization paradigm: a systematization. *J. Sci. Stud. Relig.* 30:395–415

Tullock G. 1996. On group size and the free-rider hypothesis: another hypothesis. *Pub. Choice* 87:185

Verweij J, Ester P, Nauta R. 1997. Secularization as an economic and cultural phenomenon: a cross-national analysis. *J. Sci. Stud. Relig.* 36:309–24

Von Weizsaker CC. 1971. Notes on endogenous change of tastes. *J. Econ. Theory* 3: 345–72

Wagner MB. 1990. *God's Schools: Choice and Compromise in American Society.* New Brunswick, NJ: Rutgers Univ. Press

Wallis JL. 1991. Church ministry and the free rider problem: religious liberty and disestablishment. *Am. J. Econ. Sociol.* 50: 183–96

Warner RS. 1993. Work in progress toward a new paradigm for the sociological study of religion in the United States. *Am. J. Sociol.* 98:1044–93

Warner RS. 1995. The Metropolitan Community Churches and the gay agenda: the power of pentecostalism and essentialism. *Relig. Soc. Order.* 5:67–94

Warner RS. 1997. Religion, boundaries, and bridges. *Sociol. Relig.* 58:217–38

Warner RS, Wittner JG. 1998. *Gatherings in Diaspora: Religious Communities and the New Immigration.* Philadelphia, PA: Temple Univ. Press

Welch MR, Tittle CR, Petee T. 1991. Religion and deviance among adult Catholics: a test of the "moral communities" hypothesis. *J. Sci. Stud. Relig.* 30:159–72

Westoff CF, Jones, EF. 1979. The end of 'Catholic' fertility. *Demography* 16:209–17

Wilcox WB. 1998. Conservative Protestant childrearing: authoritarian or authoritative? *Am. Sociol. Rev.* 63:796–809

Wilcox WB. 1999. *Religion and paternal involvement: product of religious commitment or American convention?* Pap. presented at Ann. Meet. Am. Sociol. Assoc., Chicago

Williams DR, Larson DB, Buckler RE, Heckmann RC, Pyle CM. 1991. Religion and psychological distress in a community sample. *Soc. Sci. Med.* 32:1257–62

Williams RH. 1997. *Culture Wars in American Politics.* New York: Aldine De Gruyter

Williams RH, Blackburn J. 1996. Many are called but few obey: ideological commitment and activism in operation rescue. In *Disruptive Religion: The Force of Faith in Social Movement Activism,* ed. C Smith, pp. 167–88. New York: Routledge

Wilson J, Janoski T. 1995. The contribution of religion to volunteer work. *Sociol. Relig.* 56:137–52

Wilson J, Sherkat DE. 1994. Returning to the fold. *J. Sci. Stud. Relig.* 33:148–61

Woodberry RD. 1998. When surveys lie and people tell the truth: How surveys oversample church attenders. *Am. Sociol. Rev.* 63:119–22

Woodberry RD, Smith C. 1998. Fundamentalism et al. *Annu. Rev. Sociol.* 24:25–56

Wuthnow R. 1988. Sociology of religion. In *Handbook of Sociology,* ed. NJ Smelser, RS Burt, pp. 473–509

Wuthnow R. 1991a. *Acts of Compassion.* Princeton, NJ: Princeton Univ. Press

Wuthnow R. 1991b. *Between States and Markets.* Princeton, NJ: Princeton Univ. Press

Wuthnow R. 1994. *Sharing the Journey: Support Groups and America's New Quest for Community.* New York: Free Press

Wuthnow R. 1995. *Learning to Care: Elementary Kindness in an Age of Indifference.* New York: Oxford Univ. Press

Yang F. 1998. Chinese conversion to evangelical Christianity: the importance of social and cultural contexts. *Sociol. Relig.* 59:237–59

Young LA. 1997. *Rational Choice Theory and Religion: Summary and Assessment.* New York: Routledge

Zald MN. 1982. Theological crucibles: social movements in and of religion. *Rev. Relig. Res.* 23:317–36

Annu. Rev. Sociol. 1999. 25:395–418

CULTURAL CRIMINOLOGY

Jeff Ferrell

Department of Criminal Justice, Northern Arizona University, Flagstaff, Arizona, 86011-5005; e-mail: Jeff.Ferrell@nau.edu

KEY WORDS: crime, culture, media, subculture, meaning

ABSTRACT

As an emergent orientation in sociology, criminology, and criminal justice, cultural criminology explores the convergence of cultural and criminal processes in contemporary social life. Drawing on perspectives from cultural studies, postmodern theory, critical theory, and interactionist sociology, and on ethnographic methodologies and media/textual analysis, this orientation highlights issues of image, meaning, and representation in the interplay of crime and crime control. Specifically, cultural criminology investigates the stylized frameworks and experiential dynamics of illicit subcultures; the symbolic criminalization of popular culture forms; and the mediated construction of crime and crime control issues. In addition, emerging areas of inquiry within cultural criminology include the development of situated media and situated audiences for crime; the media and culture of policing; the links between crime, crime control, and cultural space; and the collectively embodied emotions that shape the meaning of crime.

INTRODUCTION

The concept of "cultural criminology" denotes both specific perspectives and broader orientations that have emerged in criminology, sociology, and criminal justice over the past few years. Most specifically, "cultural criminology" represents a perspective developed by Ferrell & Sanders (1995), and likewise employed by Redhead (1995) and others (Kane 1998a), that interweaves particular intellectual threads to explore the convergence of cultural and criminal processes in contemporary social life. More broadly, the notion of cultural criminology references the increasing analytic attention that many criminologists now give to popular culture constructions, and especially mass media

0360-0572/99/0815-0395$08.00

constructions, of crime and crime control. It in turn highlights the emergence of this general area of media and cultural inquiry as a relatively distinct domain within criminology, as evidenced, for example, by the number of recently published collections undertaking explorations of media, culture, and crime (Anderson & Howard 1998, Bailey & Hale 1998, Barak 1994a, Ferrell & Sanders 1995, Ferrell & Websdale 1999, Kidd-Hewitt & Osborne 1995, Potter & Kappeler 1998). Most broadly, the existence of a concept such as cultural criminology underscores the steady seepage in recent years of cultural and media analysis into the traditional domains of criminological inquiry, such that criminological conferences and journals increasingly provide room and legitimacy for such analysis under any number of conventional headings, from juvenile delinquency and corporate crime to policing and domestic violence.

Given this range, across tightly focused theoretical statements and particular case studies to wider analytic and substantive (re)orientations, this essay incorporates the work of the growing number of scholars who consciously identify their work as cultural criminology but also includes the work of those who more generally explore the various intersections of cultural and criminal dynamics. Further, while it considers existing works that might now be retroactively gathered under the heading of cultural criminology, it focuses on recent scholarship, and especially on work now developing in and around the fields of criminology and criminal justice. Thus, cultural criminology at this point can be seen to denote less a definitive paradigm than an emergent array of perspectives linked by sensitivities to image, meaning, and representation in the study of crime and crime control. Within this broad and fluid framework, a number of theoretical, methodological, and substantive orientations can be seen to provide a degree of commonality as well.

FOUNDATIONS OF CULTURAL CRIMINOLOGY

Historical and Theoretical Frameworks

At its most basic, cultural criminology attempts to integrate the fields of criminology and cultural studies or, put differently, to import the insights of cultural studies into contemporary criminology. Given this, much scholarship in cultural criminology takes as its foundation perspectives that emerged out of the British/Birmingham School of cultural studies, and the British "new criminology" (Taylor et al 1973), of the 1970s. The work of Hebdige (1979, 1988), Hall & Jefferson (1976), Clarke (1976), McRobbie (1980), Willis (1977, 1990), and others has attuned cultural criminologists to the subtle, situated dynamics of deviant and criminal subcultures, and to the importance of symbolism and style in shaping subcultural meaning and identity. Similarly, the work of Cohen (1972/1980), Cohen & Young (1973), Hall et al (1978), and others has influenced contemporary understandings of the mass media's role in constructing the reality of crime and deviance, and in generating new forms of social and legal control. At times, contemporary scholarship in cultural criminology simply assumes this intellectual foundation or utilizes it only partially. At other times, though, cultural criminology's lineage in British cultural studies and the British new criminology is made explicit (Cohen 1996, Redhead 1995:33–46). In the introduction to a recent volume on crime and the media, for example, Kidd-Hewitt (1995) outlines five key works that set the agenda for subsequent research into crime, representation, and social control: Young (1971), Cohen (1972/1980), Cohen & Young (1973), Chibnall (1977), and Hall et al (1978).

As a hybrid orientation, though, cultural criminology has been built from more than a simple integration of 1970s British cultural studies into contemporary American criminology. Certainly, cultural criminologists continue to draw on the insights of cultural studies as a developing field and on current cultural studies explorations of identity, sexuality, and social space (During 1993, Grossberg et al 1992). Moreover, with its focus on representation, image, and style, cultural criminology incorporates not only the insights of cultural studies, but the intellectual reorientation afforded by postmodernism. In place of the modernist duality of form and content, and the modernist hierarchy that proposes that form must be stripped away to get at the meaningful core of content, cultural criminology operates from the postmodern proposition that form is content, that style is substance, that meaning thus resides in presentation and re-presentation. From this view, the study of crime necessitates not simply the examination of individual criminals and criminal events, not even the straightforward examination of media "coverage" of criminals and criminal events, but rather a journey into the spectacle and carnival of crime, a walk down an infinite hall of mirrors where images created and consumed by criminals, criminal subcultures, control agents, media institutions, and audiences bounce endlessly one off the other. Increasingly, then, cultural criminologists explore the "networks...of connections, contact, contiguity, feedback and generalized interface" (Baudrillard 1985:127; see Pfohl 1993) out of which crime and crime control are constructed, the intertextual "media loops" (Manning 1998) through which these constructions circulate, and the discursive interconnections that emerge between media institutions, crime control agents, and criminal subcultures (Kane 1998b). As part of this exploration, they in turn investigate criminal and deviant subcultures as sites of criminalization, criminal activity, and legal control, but also as "subaltern counterpublic[s]," as "parallel discursive arena[s] where members...invent and circulate counterdiscourses" and "expand discursive space" (Fraser 1995:291).

Grounded as it is in the frameworks of cultural studies and postmodernism, cultural criminology is at the same time firmly rooted in sociological perspectives. Perhaps because of its emergence out of sociological criminology, though, cultural criminology has to this point drawn less on the sociology of culture than it has on various other sociological orientations more closely aligned, historically, with criminology. Central among these is the interactionist tradition in the sociology of deviance and criminology (Becker 1963, Pfuhl 1986). In examining the mediated networks and discursive connections noted above, cultural criminologists also trace the manifold interactions through which criminals, control agents, media producers, and others collectively construct the meaning of crime. In so doing, cultural criminologists attempt to elaborate on the "symbolic" in "symbolic interaction" by highlighting the popular prevalence of mediated crime imagery, the interpersonal negotiation of style within criminal and deviant subcultures, and the emergence of larger symbolic universes within which crime takes on political meaning. These understandings of crime and crime control as social and political constructions, and this endeavor to unravel the mediated processes through which these constructions occur, also build on more recent constructionist perspectives in sociology (Best 1995). Yet while cultural criminology certainly draws on constructionist sociology, it also contributes to constructionist orientations a sensitivity to mediated circuits of meaning other than those of the "mass" media, and it offers a spiraling postmodern sensibility that moves beyond dualisms of crime event and media coverage, factual truth and distortion, which at times frame constructionist analysis (Ferrell & Websdale 1999).

Finally, cultural criminology emerges in many ways out of critical traditions in sociology, criminology, and cultural studies, incorporating as it does a variety of critical perspectives on crime and crime control. Utilizing these perspectives, cultural criminologists attempt to unravel the politics of crime as played out through mediated anti-crime campaigns; through evocative cultural constructions of deviance, crime, and marginality; and through criminalized subcultures and their resistance to legal control. To the extent that it integrates interactionist, constructionist, and critical sociologies, cultural criminology thus undertakes to develop what Cohen (1988:68) has called "a structurally and politically informed version of labeling theory," or what Melossi (1985) has similarly described as a "grounded labeling theory"—that is, an analysis that accounts for the complex circuitry of mediated interaction through which the meaning of crime and deviance is constructed and enforced. Put more simply, cultural criminology heeds Becker's (1963:183, 199) classic injunction—that we "look at all the people involved in any episode of alleged deviance...all the parties to a situation, and their relationships"—and includes in this collective examination those cultural relationships, those webs of meaning and perception in which all parties are entangled.

In its mix of historical and theoretical foundations, cultural criminology can thus be seen to incorporate both more traditional sociological perspectives and more recently ascendant cultural studies and postmodern approaches. As such,

cultural criminology likewise embodies the creative tension in which sociology and cultural studies/postmodernism often exist (Becker & McCall 1990,
Denzin 1992, Pfohl 1992), a tension which at its best produces attentiveness to
structures of power and nuances of meaning, to fixed symbolic universes and
emergent codes of marginality, to the mediated expansion of legal control and
the stylized undermining of legal authority—and to the inevitable confounding
of these very categories in everyday criminality.

Methodological Frameworks

Cultural criminology's melange of intellectual and disciplinary influences also
surfaces in the methodologies that cultural criminologists employ. In exploring the interconnections of culture and crime, researchers utilize ethnographic
models rooted in sociology, criminology, cultural studies, and anthropology;
modifications of these models suggested by recent developments in feminist,
postmodern, and existentialist thought; and a range of methods geared toward
media and textual analysis. Further, as will be seen, researchers at times combine or overlay these methods in the course of particular projects. Nonetheless,
there remains within the broad framework of cultural criminology a significant
split between methodologies oriented toward ethnography and field work
practice, and those oriented toward media and textual analysis.

Ethnographic research in cultural criminology reflects the long-standing
attentiveness of cultural studies researchers to precise nuances of meaning
within particular cultural milieux. Willis (1977:3), for example, notes that his
use of ethnographic techniques was "dictated by the nature of my interest in
'the cultural.' These techniques are suited to record this level and have a sensitivity to meanings and values...." At the same time, ethnographic research in
cultural criminology reflects the sociological and criminological tradition of
deep inquiry into the situated dynamics of criminal and deviant subcultures
(Adler 1985, Becker 1963, Humphreys 1975); especially influential here are
Polsky's (1969) manifesto on the necessary politics and practice of field research among deviant and criminal populations, and Hagedorn's (1990) more
recent echoing of these themes. In addition, the practice of field research
within cultural criminology incorporates recent reconsiderations of field
method among sociologists, criminologists, and anthropologists (Burawoy et
al 1991, Ferrell & Hamm 1998, Van Maanen 1995a), and among feminists,
postmodernists, and existentialists (Fonow & Cook 1991, Clough 1992, Denzin 1997, Sanders 1995, Adler & Adler 1987) inside and outside these disciplines. Together, these works suggest that field research operates as an inherently personal and political endeavor, profoundly engaging researchers with
situations and subjects of study. These works thus call for reflexive reporting
on the research process, for an "ethnography of ethnography" (Van Maanen

1995b), which accounts for the researcher's own role in the construction of meaning.

An extreme version of this ethnographic perspective within cultural criminology, yet one rooted in sociological paradigms, is the notion of "criminological *verstehen*" (Ferrell & Hamm 1998). Drawing on Weber's (1978:4–5) formulation of *verstehen* in terms of "interpretive understanding" and "sympathetic participation," and on later refinements within qualitative methodology (Adler & Adler 1987), the concept of criminological *verstehen* denotes a field researcher's subjective appreciation and empathic understanding of crime's situated meanings, symbolism, and emotions, in part through the sorts of directly participatory research that can foster a methodology of attentiveness. From this view, the researcher's own experiences and emotions emerge as windows into criminal events and criminal subcultures, and into the collective experiences and understandings of those involved in them. While certainly fraught with personal and professional danger, and limited by issues of individual and collective identity, this approach seeks to move deep inside the cultures of crime and crime control by dismantling dualistic epistemic hierarchies that position the researcher over and apart from research subjects, abstract analysis over and beyond situated knowledge, and sanitary intellect over and outside human experience and emotion. The concept of criminological *verstehen* thus includes the researcher, and the researcher's own situated experiences, in the collective construction of crime's reality.

Alternatively, other bodies of research in cultural criminology are based not in researchers' deep participatory immersion in criminal worlds, but in their scholarly reading of the various mediated texts that circulate images of crime and crime control. The range of substantive scholarship that has recently emerged is itself remarkable, exploring as it does both historical and contemporary texts, and investigating local and national newspaper coverage of crime and crime control (Brownstein 1995, Websdale & Alvarez 1998, Perrone & Chesney-Lind 1997, Howe 1997); filmic depictions of criminals, criminal violence, and criminal justice (Newman 1998, Cheatwood 1998, Niesel 1998); television portrayals of crime and criminals (Tunnell 1998, Fishman & Cavender 1998); images of crime in popular music (Tunnell 1995); comic books, crime, and juvenile delinquency (Nyberg 1998, Williams 1998); crime depictions in cyberspace (Greek 1996); and the broader presence of crime and crime control imagery throughout popular culture texts (Barak 1995, Marx 1995, Surette 1998, Kidd-Hewitt & Osborne 1995, Kooistra 1989). Many of these studies utilize conventional content analysis techniques to measure the degree of crime coverage, the distribution of source material, or the relative presence of crime imagery. Others incorporate less formal, descriptive accounts of prominent media constructions (Barak 1996), or illustrative case-by-case comparisons among media texts. Still others, often influenced by feminist methodology and epistemology, develop imaginative readings, counter-readings, and "sociological deconstructions" (Pfohl & Gordon 1986, see Young 1996, Clough 1992) of crime texts and criminal justice formations.

While this divergence between ethnography and textual analysis does characterize much of the scholarship in cultural criminology, a number of scholars have in fact begun to produce works that usefully integrate these two methodological orientations. Chermak (1995, 1997, 1998), for example, has combined content analysis with ethnographic observation and interviewing to produce multilayered studies that explore not only the sources and symbolic characteristics of mediated crime accounts, but the organizational dynamics underlying them. Situating her work in "the overlapping fields of ethnography and cultural studies," Kane (1998b:8, 1998a) has engaged in extensive, cross-cultural field research in order to analyze and place herself within, "contrasting public discourses of public health and law" around AIDS and HIV. By integrating ethnographic research among neo-Nazi skinheads with detailed analysis of popular music's historical and thematic structures, Hamm (1993, 1995) has succeeded in explicating the broad symbolic underpinnings of the skinhead subculture and the specific place of musical idioms within it. Ferrell (1996) has likewise interwoven extended participant observation among urban graffiti writers with an analysis of media and criminal justice campaigns against them to reveal the ongoing, reflexive process by which each party to the conflict has reappropriated and reconstructed the meanings of the other.

These and other emerging works suggest that any sharp disjunction between ethnographic research and textual/media analysis in cultural criminology not only makes little sense methodologically, but to some degree actually undermines the very mandate of cultural criminology itself. At first glance, this methodological disjunction would seem to be justified by a parallel disjunction in subject matter, with ethnography best suited for exploring criminal subcultures and situations, and textual analysis best suited for investigating media constructions of crime and crime control. Yet, as contemporary research begins to show, these subjects are never as distinct as they first seem. The mass media and associated culture industries certainly produce an ongoing flood of crime images and crime texts; but media audiences, deviant and criminal subcultures, control agencies, and others subsequently appropriate these texts and images, and in part reconstruct their meaning as they utilize them in particular social situations. Similarly, the many subcultures concerned with crime and crime control—from gang members and graffiti writers to police associations and political interest groups—themselves produce complex circuits of communication, and within this circuitry all manner of images and symbols. These situated media in turn circulate within and between social worlds, generate competing symbolic references and public perceptions of crime, and regularly reappear as caricature within the realm of mass media entertainment and reporting on crime. Thus, as before, it is not criminal subcultures and situations that merit the attention of cultural criminologists, nor mediated constructions of crime, but rather the confounding and confluence of these categories in every-day life. And in this hall of mirrors, in this world of spiraling symbolism and fluid meaning, neither traditional ethnography nor textual analysis suffices— but instead some mix of method that can begin to situate the researcher inside the complex swirl of culture and crime.

In this sense ethnography and media/textual analysis, whether utilized indi-vidually or in combination, produce at their best interpretive case studies— case studies that expose the dynamic cultural situations out of which crime and crime control are constructed. In fact, Ferrell & Sanders (1995:304–8) argue that the subtlety and complexity of these dynamics are such that cultural crimi-nology is best served by an accumulation of in-depth case studies, rather than by more shallow survey research or more abstract statistical analysis. Yet while this reliance on case study method (Geis 1991, Ragin & Becker 1992) may enhance the analytic sophistication of cultural criminology, it may also function to marginalize it from the criminological and sociological main-stream. Feagin et al (1991:270), for example, contend that case study sociol-ogy has now been overtaken, and to some degree delegitimated, by a form of "mainstream journal-article sociology" which "accents quantitative-statistical data interpreted in a hypothetico-deductive positivistic framework."

The long sweep of scholarly history reminds us that, for cultural criminol-ogy as for other emergent perspectives, such marginalization may or may not develop, and may or may not endure. Should marginalization result from cul-tural criminology's reliance on case study method and interpretive analysis, though, it would dovetail doubly with the larger project of cultural criminol-ogy. First, this sort of methodological marginalization would perhaps suit an approach developed out of cultural studies, postmodernism, critical and femi-nist theory, and other perspectives long suspect within certain quarters of mainstream social science. Second, as will be seen, the contemporary practice of cultural criminology embodies not only theoretical and methodological frameworks exterior to the positivist mainstream, but an intellectual politics foreign to traditional notions of objectivity and detachment as well.

CONTEMPORARY AREAS OF INQUIRY

Framed by these theoretical and methodological orientations, cultural crimi-nological research and analysis have emerged in the past few years within a number of overlapping substantive areas. The first two of these can be charac-terized by an overly simple but perhaps informative dichotomy between "crime as culture" and "culture as crime." The third broad area incorporates the variety of ways in which media dynamics construct the reality of crime and crime control; the fourth explores the social politics of crime and culture and the intellectual politics of cultural criminology.

Crime as Culture

To speak of crime as culture is to acknowledge at a minimum that much of what we label criminal behavior is at the same time subcultural behavior, collectively organized around networks of symbol, ritual, and shared meaning. Put simply, it is to adopt the subculture as a basic unit of criminological analysis. While this general insight is hardly a new one, cultural criminology develops it in a number of directions. Bringing a postmodern sensibility to their understanding of deviant and criminal subcultures, cultural criminologists argue that such subcultures incorporate—indeed, are defined by—elaborate conventions of argot, appearance, aesthetics, and stylized presentation of self and thus operate as repositories of collective meaning and representation for their members. Within these subcultures as in other arenas of crime, form shapes content, image frames identity. Taken into a mediated world of increasingly dislocated communication and dispersed meaning, this insight further implies that deviant and criminal subcultures may now be exploding into universes of symbolic communication that in many ways transcend time and space. For computer hackers, graffiti writers, drug runners, and others, a mix of widespread spatial dislocation and precise normative organization implies subcultures defined less by face-to-face interaction than by shared, if second-hand, symbolic codes (Gelder & Thornton 1997:473–550).

Understandably, then, much research in this area of cultural criminology has focused on the dispersed dynamics of subcultural style. Following from Hebdige's (1979) classic exploration of "subculture: the meaning of style," cultural criminologists have investigated style as defining both the internal characteristics of deviant and criminal subcultures and external constructions of them. Miller (1995), for example, has documented the many ways in which gang symbolism and style exist as the medium of meaning for both street gang members and the probation officers who attempt to control them. Reading gang styles as emblematic of gang immersion and gang defiance, enforcing court orders prohibiting gang clothing, confiscating gang paraphernalia, and displaying their confiscated collections on their own office walls, the probation officers in Miller's study construct the meanings of gang style as surely as do the gang members themselves. Likewise, Ferrell (1996) has shown how contemporary hip hop graffiti exists essentially as a "crime of style" for graffiti writers, who operate and evaluate one another within complex stylistic and symbolic conventions, but also for media institutions and legal and political authorities who perceive graffiti as violating the "aesthetics of authority" essential to their ongoing control of urban environments. More broadly, Ferrell (in Ferrell & Sanders 1995:169–89) has explored style as the tissue connecting cultural and criminal practices and has examined the ways in which subcultural style shapes not only aesthetic communities, but official and unofficial reactions to subcultural identity. Finally, Lyng & Bracey (1995) have documented the multiply ironic process by which the style of the outlaw biker subculture came first to signify class-based cultural resistance, next to elicit the sorts of media reactions and legal controls that in fact amplified and confirmed its meaning, and finally to be appropriated and commodified in such a way as to void its political potential. Significantly, these and other studies (Cosgrove 1984) echo and confirm the integrative methodological framework outlined above by demonstrating that the importance of style resides not within the dynamics of criminal subcultures, nor in media and political constructions of its meaning, but in the contested interplay of the two.

If subcultures of crime and deviance are defined by their aesthetic and symbolic organization, cultural criminology has also begun to show that they are defined by intensities of collective experience and emotion as well. Building on Katz's (1988) wide-ranging exploration of the sensually seductive "foreground" of criminality, cultural criminologists like Lyng (1990, 1998) and Ferrell (1996) have utilized *verstehen*-oriented methodologies to document the experiences of "edgework" and "the adrenalin rush"—immediate, incandescent integrations of risk, danger, and skill—that shape participation and membership in deviant and criminal subcultures. Discovered across a range of illicit subcultures (Presdee 1994, O'Malley & Mugford 1994, Tunnell 1992: 45, Wright & Decker 1994:117), these intense and often ritualized moments of pleasure and excitement define the experience of subcultural membership and, by members' own accounts, seduce them into continued subcultural participation. Significantly for a sociology of these subcultural practices, research (Lyng & Snow 1986) shows that experiences of edgework and adrenalin exist as collectively constructed endeavors, encased in shared vocabularies of motive and meaning (Mills 1940, Cressey 1954). Thus, while these experiences certainly suggest a sociology of the body and the emotions, and further *verstehen*-oriented explorations of deviant and criminal subcultures as "affectually determined" (Weber 1978:9) domains, they also reveal the ways in which collective intensities of experience, like collective conventions of style, construct shared subcultural meaning.

Culture as Crime

The notion of "culture as crime" denotes the reconstruction of cultural enterprise as criminal endeavor—through, for example, the public labeling of popular culture products as criminogenic, or the criminalization of cultural producers through media or legal channels. In contemporary society, such reconstructions pervade popular culture and transcend traditional "high" and "low" cultural boundaries. Art photographers Robert Mapplethorpe and Jock

Sturges, for example, have faced highly orchestrated campaigns accusing them of producing obscene or pornographic images; in addition, an art center exhibiting Mapplethorpe's photographs was indicted on charges of "pandering obscenity," and Sturges's studio was raided by local police and the FBI (Dubin 1992). Punk and heavy metal bands, and associated record companies, distributors, and retail outlets, have encountered obscenity rulings, civil and criminal suits, high-profile police raids, and police interference with concerts. Performers, producers, distributors, and retailers of rap and "gangsta rap" music have likewise faced arrest and conviction on obscenity charges, legal confiscation of albums, highly publicized protests, boycotts, hearings organized by political figures and police officials, and ongoing media campaigns and legal proceedings accusing them of promoting—indeed, directly causing—crime and delinquency (Hamm & Ferrell 1994). More broadly, a variety of television programs, films, and cartoons have been targeted by public campaigns alleging that they incite delinquency, spin off "copy-cat" crimes, and otherwise serve as criminogenic social forces (Ferrell 1998, Nyberg 1998).

These many cases certainly fall within the purview of cultural criminology because the targets of criminalization—photographers, musicians, television writers, and their products—are "cultural" in nature, but equally so because their criminalization itself unfolds as a cultural process. When contemporary culture personas and performances are criminalized, they are primarily criminalized through the mass media, through their presentation and re-presentation as criminal in the realm of sound bites, shock images, news conferences, and newspaper headlines. This mediated spiral, in which media-produced popular culture forms and figures are in turn criminalized by means of the media, leads once again into a complex hall of mirrors. It generates not only images, but images of images—that is, attempts by lawyers, police officials, religious leaders, media workers, and others to craft criminalized images of those images previously crafted by artists, musicians, and film makers. Thus, the criminalization of popular culture is itself a popular, and cultural, enterprise, standing in opposition to popular culture less than participating in it, and helping to construct the very meanings and effects to which it allegedly responds. Given this, cultural criminologists have begun to widen the notion of "criminalization" to include more than the simple creation and application of criminal law. Increasingly, they investigate the larger process of "cultural criminalization" (Ferrell 1998:80–82), the mediated reconstruction of meaning and perception around issues of culture and crime. In some cases, this cultural criminalization stands as an end in itself, successfully dehumanizing or delegitimating those targeted, though no formal legal charges are brought against them. In other cases, cultural criminalization helps construct a perceptual context in which direct criminal charges can more easily follow. In either scenario, though, media dynamics drive and define the criminalization of popular culture.

The mediated context of criminalization is a political one as well. The contemporary criminalization of popular culture has emerged as part of larger "culture wars" (Bolton 1992) waged by political conservatives and cultural reactionaries. Controversies over the criminal or criminogenic characteristics of art photographers and rap musicians have resulted less from spontaneous public concern than from the sorts of well-funded and politically sophisticated campaigns that have similarly targeted the National Endowment for the Arts and its support of feminist/gay/lesbian performance artists and film festivals. In this light it is less than surprising that contemporary cultural criminalization is aimed time and again at marginal(ized) subcultures—radical punk musicians, politically militant black rap groups, lesbian and gay visual and performance artists—whose stylized celebration of and confrontation with their marginality threaten particular patterns of moral and legal control. Cultural criminalization in this sense exposes yet another set of linkages between subcultural styles and symbols and mediated constructions and reconstructions of these as criminal or criminogenic. In addition, as a process conducted largely in the public realm, cultural criminalization contributes to popular perceptions and panics, and thus to the further marginalization of those who are its focus. If successful, it constructs a degree of social discomfort that reflects off the face of popular culture and into the practice of everyday life.

Media Constructions of Crime and Crime Control

The mediated criminalization of popular culture exists, of course, as but one of many media processes that construct the meanings of crime and crime control. As noted in earlier discussions of textual methodologies, cultural criminology incorporates a wealth of research on mediated characterizations of crime and crime control, ranging across historical and contemporary texts and investigating images generated in newspaper reporting, popular film, television news and entertainment programming, popular music, comic books, and the cyberspaces of the Internet. Further, cultural criminologists have begun to explore the complex institutional interconnections between the criminal justice system and the mass media. Researchers like Chermak (1995, 1997, 1998) and Sanders & Lyon (1995) have documented not only the mass media's heavy reliance on criminal justice sources for imagery and information on crime, but more importantly, the reciprocal relationship that undergirds this reliance. Working within organizational imperatives of efficiency and routinization, media institutions regularly rely on data selectively provided by policing and court agencies. In so doing, they highlight for the public issues chosen by criminal justice institutions and framed by criminal justice imperatives, and they in turn contribute to the political agendas of the criminal justice system and to the generation of public support for these agendas. In a relatively nonconspiratorial but nonetheless powerful fashion, media and criminal justice organizations thus coordinate their day-to-day operations and cooperate in constructing circumscribed understandings of crime and crime control.

A large body of research in cultural criminology examines the nature of these understandings and the public dynamics of their production. Like cultural criminology generally, much of the research here (Adler & Adler 1994, Goode & Ben-Yehuda 1994, Hollywood 1997, Jenkins 1992, Sparks 1995, Thornton 1994) builds on the classic analytic models of cultural studies and interactionist sociology, as embodied in concepts such as moral entrepreneurship and moral enterprise in the creation of crime and deviance (Becker 1963), and the invention of folk devils as a means of generating moral panic (Cohen 1972/1980) around issues of crime and deviance. Exploring the epistemic frameworks surrounding everyday understandings of crime controversies, this research (Fishman 1978, Best 1995, Acland 1995, Reinarman 1994, Reinarman & Duskin 1992, Websdale 1996) problematizes and unpacks taken-for-granted assumptions regarding the prevalence of criminality and the particular characteristics of criminals, and the research traces these assumptions to the interrelated workings of interest groups, media institutions, and criminal justice organizations.

Emerging scholarship in cultural criminology also offers useful reconceptualizations and refinements of these analytic models. McRobbie & Thornton (1995), for example, argue that the essential concepts of "moral panic" and "folk devils" must be reconsidered in multi-mediated societies; with the proliferation of media channels and the saturation of media markets, moral panics have become both dangerous endeavors and marketable commodities, and folk devils now find themselves both stigmatized and lionized in mainstream media and alternative media alike. Similarly, Jenkins's (1999) recent work has begun to refine understandings of crime and justice issues as social and cultural constructions. Building on his earlier, meticulous deconstructions of drug panics, serial homicide scares, and other constructed crime controversies, Jenkins (1994a,b) argues that attention must be paid to the media and political dynamics underlying "unconstructed" crime as well. Jenkins explores the failure to frame activities such as anti-abortion violence as criminal terrorism, situates this failure within active media and political processes, and thus questions the meaning of that for which no criminal meaning is provided.

Through all of this, cultural criminologists further emphasize that in the process of constructing crime and crime control as social concerns and political controversies, the media also construct them as entertainment. Revisiting the classic cultural studies/new criminology notion of "policing the crisis" (Hall et al 1978), Sparks (1995; see 1992), for example, characterizes the production and perception of crime and policing imagery in television crime dramas as a process of "entertaining the crisis." Intertwined with mediated moral panic over crime and crime waves, amplified fear of street crime and stranger violence, and politically popular concern for the harm done to crime victims, then, is the pleasure found in consuming mediated crime imagery and crime drama. To the extent that the mass media constructs crime as entertainment, we are thus offered not only selective images and agendas, but the ironic mechanism for amusing ourselves to death (Postman 1986) by way of our own collective pain, misery, and fear. Given this, contemporary media scholarship in cultural criminology focuses as much on popular film, popular music, and television entertainment programming as on the mediated manufacture of news and information, and it investigates the collapsing boundaries between such categories. Recent work in this area targets especially the popularity of "reality" crime programs (Fishman & Cavender 1998). With their mix of street footage, theatrical staging, and patrol-car sermonizing, reality crime programs such as "C.O.P.S.," "L.A.P.D.,"and "True Stories of the Highway Patrol" generate conventional, though at times contradictory, images of crime and policing. Along with talk shows devoted largely to crime and deviance topics, they in turn spin off secondary merchandising schemes, legal suits over videotaped police chases and televised invasions of privacy, and criminal activities allegedly induced by the programs themselves. Such dynamics demonstrate the entangled reality of crime, crime news, and crime entertainment, and suggest that as mediated crime constructions come to be defined as real, "they are real in their consequences" (Thomas 1966:301).

The Politics of Culture, Crime, and Cultural Criminology

Clearly, a common thread connects the many domains into which cultural criminology inquires: the presence of power relations, and the emergence of social control, at the intersections of culture and crime. The stylistic practices and symbolic codes of illicit subcultures are made the object of legal surveillance and control or, alternatively, are appropriated, commodified, and sanitized within a vast machinery of consumption. Sophisticated media and criminal justice "culture wars" are launched against alternative forms of art, music, and entertainment, thereby criminalizing the personalities and performances involved, marginalizing them from idealized notions of decency and community and, at the extreme, silencing the political critiques they present. Ongoing media constructions of crime and crime control emerge out of an alliance of convenience between media institutions and criminal justice agencies, serve to promote and legitimate broader political agendas regarding crime control, and in turn function to both trivialize and dramatize the meaning of crime. Increasingly, then, it is television crime shows and big budget detective movies, nightly newscasts and morning newspaper headlines, recurrent campaigns against the real and imagined crimes of the disenfranchised that constitute

Foucault's (in Cohen 1979:339) "hundreds of tiny theatres of punishment"—theatres in which young people, ethnic minorities, lesbians and gays, and others play villains deserving of penalty and public outrage.

At the same time, cultural criminologists emphasize and explore the various forms that resistance to this complex web of social control may take. As Sparks (1992, 1995) and others argue, the audiences for media constructions of crime are diverse in both their composition and their readings of these constructions; they recontextualize, remake, and even reverse mass media meanings as they incorporate them into their daily lives and interactions. Varieties of resistance also emerge among those groups more specifically targeted within the practice of mediated control. Artists and musicians caught up in contemporary "culture wars" have refused governmental awards, resigned high-profile positions, won legal judgments, organized alternative media outlets and performances, and otherwise produced public counterattacks (Ferrell 1998). Within other marginalized subcultures, personal and group style certainly exists as stigmata, inviting outside surveillance and control, but at the same time is valued as a badge of honor and resistance made all the more meaningful by its enduring defiance of outside authority (Hebdige 1988). Likewise, as Lyng (1990, 1998) and Ferrell (1996) emphasize, those immersed in moments of illicit edgework and adrenalin construct resistance doubly. First, by combining in such moments high levels of risk with precise skills and practiced artistry, those involved invent an identity, a sense of crafted self, that resists the usual degradations of subordinate status and deskilled, alienated labor. Second, as these moments become more dangerous because targeted by campaigns of criminalization and enforcement, participants in them find an enhancement and amplification of the edgy excitement they provide, and in so doing transform political pressure into personal and collective pleasure. In investigating the intersections of culture and crime for power relations and emerging forms of social control, then, cultural criminologists carry on the tradition of cultural studies (Hall & Jefferson 1976) by examining the many forms of resistance that emerge there as well.

Moreover, cultural criminology itself operates as a sort of intellectual resistance, as a diverse counter-reading and counter-discourse on, and critical "intervention" (Pfohl & Gordon 1986:94) into, conventional constructions of crime. In deconstructing moments of mediated panic over crime, cultural criminologists work to expose the political processes behind seemingly spontaneous social concerns and to dismantle the recurring and often essentialist metaphors of disease, invasion, and decay on which crime panics are built (Brownstein 1995, 1996, Reinarman 1994, Reinarman & Duskin 1992, Murji 1999). Beyond this, Barak (1988, 1994a) argues for an activist "newsmaking criminology" in which criminologists integrate themselves into the ongoing mediated construction of crime, develop as part of their role in this process alternative images and understandings of crime issues, and in so doing produce what constitutive criminologists (Henry & Milovanovic 1991, Barak 1995) call a "replacement discourse" regarding crime and crime control. Much of cultural criminology's ethnographic work in subcultural domains functions similarly, as a critical move away from the "official definitions of reality" (Hagedorn 1990:244) produced by the media and the criminal justice system and reproduced by a "courthouse criminology" (see Polsky 1969) that relies on these sources. By attentively documenting the lived realities of groups whom conventional crime constructions have marginalized, and in turn documenting the situated politics of this marginalization process, cultural criminologists attempt to deconstruct the official demonization of various "outsiders" (Becker 1963)—from rural domestic violence victims (Websdale 1998) to urban graffiti writers (Ferrell 1996, Sanchez-Tranquilino 1995), gay hustlers (Pettiway 1996), and homeless heroin addicts (Bourgois et al 1997)—and to produce alternative understandings of them. Approaching this task from the other direction, Hamm (1993) and others likewise venture inside the worlds of particularly violent criminals to document dangerous nuances of meaning and style often invisible in official reporting on such groups. In its politics as in its theory and method, then, cultural criminology integrates subcultural ethnography with media and institutional analysis to produce an alternative image of crime.

TRAJECTORIES OF CULTURAL CRIMINOLOGY

In describing an emergent orientation like cultural criminology, it is perhaps appropriate to close with a brief consideration of its unfinished edges. The following short discussions are therefore meant to be neither systematic nor exhaustive; they simply suggest some of what is emerging, and what might productively emerge, as cultural criminology continues to develop.

Situated Media, Situated Audiences

The dynamic integration of subcultural crime constructions and media crime constructions has surfaced time and again in this essay as one of cultural criminology's essential insights. This insight further implies that the everyday notion of "media" must be expanded to include those media that take shape within and among the various subcultures of crime, deviance, and crime control. As noted in the above methodological discussions, various illicit subcultures certainly come into regular contact with the mass media, but in so doing appropriate and reinvent mass media channels, products, and meanings. Further, illicit subcultures regularly invent their own media of communication; as McRobbie & Thornton (1995:559) point out, even the interests of "folk devils" are increasingly "defended by their own niche and micro-media." Thus, alternative and marginalized youth subcultures self-produce a wealth of zines (alternative magazines) and websites; street gang members construct elaborate edifices of communication out of particular clothing styles, colors, and hand signs; and graffiti writers develop a continent-wide network of freight train graffiti that mirrors existing hobo train graffiti in its ability to link distant subcultural members within a shared symbolic community. As also suggested in above discussions, multiple, fluid audiences likewise witness efflorescences of crime and crime control in their everyday existence, consume a multitude of crime images packaged as news and entertainment, and in turn remake the meaning of these encounters within the symbolic interaction of their own lives. Investigating the linkages between "media" and crime, then, means investigating the many situations in which these linkages emerge, and moreover the situated place of media, audience, and meaning within criminal worlds (see Vaughan 1998). Ultimately, perhaps, this investigation suggests blurring the analytic boundary between producer and audience—recognizing, in other words, that a variety of groups both produce and consume contested images of crime—and moving ahead to explore the many microcircuits of meaning that collectively construct the reality of crime.

The Media and Culture of Policing

Increasingly, the production and consumption of mediated meaning frames not only the reality of crime, but of crime control as well. Contemporary policing can in fact hardly be understood apart from its interpenetration with media at all levels. As "reality" crime and policing television programs shape public perceptions of policing, serve as controversial tools of officer recruitment and suspect apprehension, and engender legal suits over their effects on street-level policing, citizens shoot video footage of police conduct and misconduct—some of which finds its way, full-circle, onto news and "reality" programs. Meanwhile, within the police subculture itself, surveillance cameras and on-board patrol car cameras capture the practices of police officers and citizens alike and, as Websdale (1999) documents, police crime files themselves take shape as "situated media substrates" which, like surveillance and patrol car footage, regularly become building blocks for subsequent mass media images of policing. The policing of a postmodern world emerges as a complex set of visual and semiotic practices, an expanding spiral of mediated social control (Manning 1998, 1999a,b).

From the view of cultural criminology, policing must in turn be understood as a set of practices situated, like criminal practices, within subcultural conventions of meaning, symbolism, and style. In this regard, Kraska & Kappeler (1995:85) integrate perspectives from police studies, feminist literature, and critical theory to explore the subcultural ideologies, situated dynamics, and broader "cultural and structural context" within which police deviance and police sexual violence against women develop. Perhaps most interesting here, in light of the reflexive methodologies discussed above, is Kraska's (1998) grounded investigation of police paramilitary units. Immersing himself and his emotions in a situation of police paramilitary violence, Kraska details the stylized subcultural status afforded by particular forms of weaponry and clothing, and he documents the deep-seated ideological and affective states that define the collective meaning of such situations. With crime control as with crime, subcultural and media dynamics construct experience and perception.

Crime and Cultural Space

Many of the everyday situations in which crime and policing are played out, and in fact many of the most visible contemporary controversies surrounding crime and policing issues, involve the contestation of cultural space. Incorporating perspectives from cultural studies, cultural geography, and postmodern geography (Merrifield & Swyngedouw 1997, Scott & Soja 1996, Davis 1992), the notion of cultural space references the process by which meaning is constructed and contested in public domains (Ferrell 1997). This process intertwines with a variety of crime and crime control situations. Homeless populations declare by their public presence the scandal of inequality, and they are in turn hounded and herded by a host of loitering, vagrancy, trespass, public lodging, and public nuisance statutes. "Gutter punks" invest downtown street corners with disheveled style, "skate punks" and skateboarders convert walkways and parking garages into playgrounds, Latino/a street "cruisers" create mobile subcultures out of dropped frames and polished chrome—and face in response aggressive enforcement of laws regarding trespass, curfew, public sleeping, and even car stereo volume. Street gangs carve out collective cultural space from shared styles and public rituals; criminal justice officials prohibit and confiscate stylized clothing, enforce prohibitions against public gatherings by "known" gang members, and orchestrate public gang "round-ups." Graffiti writers remake the visual landscapes and symbolic codes of public life, but they do so in the face of increasing criminal sanctions, high-tech surveillance systems, and nationally coordinated legal campaigns designed to remove them and their markings from public life.

As with the mediated campaigns of cultural criminalization discussed above, these conflicts over crime and cultural space regularly emerge around the marginalized subcultures of young people, ethnic minorities, and other groups, and thus they raise essential issues of identity and authenticity (Sanchez-Tranquilino 1995). Such conflicts in turn incorporate a complex criminalization of these subcultures as part of a systematic effort to erase their self-constructed public images, to substitute in their place symbols of homogeneity and consensus, and thereby to restore and expand the "aesthetics of authority" noted in above discussions. Ultimately, these disparate conflicts over crime and cultural space reveal the common thread of contested public meaning, and something of the work of control in the age of cultural reproduction.

Bodies, Emotions, and Cultural Criminology

Perhaps the most critical of situations, the most intimate of cultural spaces in which crime and crime control intersect are those in and around the physical and emotional self (Pfohl 1990). Throughout this essay such situations have been seen: the development of subcultural style as marker of identity and locus of criminalization; the fleeting experience of edgework and adrenalin rushes, heightened by risk of legal apprehension; the utilization of researchers' own experiences and emotions in the study of crime and policing. These situations suggest that other moments merit the attention of cultural criminology as well, from gang girls' construction of identity through hair, makeup, and discourse (Mendoza-Denton 1996) and phone fantasy workers' invocation of sexuality and emotion (Mattley 1998), to the contested media and body politics of AIDS (Kane 1998b, Watney 1987, Young 1996:175-206). Together, these and other situations in turn suggest a criminology of the skin (see Kushner 1994)—a criminology that can account for crime and crime control in terms of pleasure, fear, and excitement and that can confront the deformities of sexuality and power, control and resistance that emerge in these inside spaces. They also demand the ongoing refinement of the reflexive, *verstehen*-oriented methodologies and epistemologies described above—of ways of investigating and knowing that are at the same time embodied and affective (Scheper-Hughes 1994), closer to the intimate meaning of crime and yet never close enough.

CONCLUSIONS

As an emerging perspective within criminology, sociology, and criminal justice, cultural criminology draws from a wide range of intellectual orientations. Revisiting and perhaps reinventing existing paradigms in cultural studies, the "new" criminology, interactionist sociology, and critical theory; integrating insights from postmodern, feminist, and constructionist thought; and incorporating aspects of newsmaking, constitutive, and other evolving criminologies, cultural criminology seek less to synthesize or subsume these various perspectives than to engage them in a critical, multifaceted exploration of culture and crime. Linking these diverse intellectual dimensions, and their attendant methodologies of ethnography and media/textual analysis, is cultural criminology's overarching concern with the meaning of crime and crime control. Some three decades ago, Cohen (1988:68, 1971:19) wrote of "placing on the agenda" of a culturally informed criminology issues of "subjective meaning," and of deviance and crime as "meaningful action." Cultural criminology embraces and expands this agenda by exploring the complex construction, attribution, and appropriation of meaning that occurs within and between media and political formations, illicit subcultures, and audiences around matters of crime and crime control. In so doing, cultural criminology likewise highlights the inevitability of the image. Inside the stylized rhythms of a criminal subculture, reading a newspaper crime report or perusing a police file, caught between the panic and pleasure of crime, "there is no escape from the politics of representation" (Hall 1993:111).

ACKNOWLEDGMENTS

I thank Neil Websdale for his generous contributions to this essay; Phoebe Stambaugh and Brian Smith for assistance with source material; and two anonymous *Annual Review of Sociology* reviewers for their insightful comments.

> **Visit the *Annual Reviews* home page at
> http://www.AnnualReviews.org.**

Literature Cited

Acland CR. 1995. *Youth, Murder, Spectacle: The Cultural Politics of 'Youth in Crisis'.* Boulder, CO: Westview

Adler PA. 1985. *Wheeling and Dealing.* New York: Columbia Univ. Press

Adler PA, Adler P. 1987. *Membership Roles in Field Research.* Newbury Park, CA: Sage

Adler PA, Adler P, eds. 1994. *Constructions of Deviance: Social Power, Context, and Interaction.* Belmont, CA: Wadsworth

Anderson SE, Howard GJ, eds. 1998. *Interrogating Popular Culture: Deviance, Justice, and Social Order.* Guilderland, NY: Harrow & Heston

Bailey FY, Hale DC, eds. 1998. *Popular Culture, Crime, and Justice.* Belmont, CA: West/Wadsworth

Barak G. 1988. Newsmaking criminology: reflections on the media, intellectuals, and crime. *Justice Q.* 5:565–87

Barak G, ed. 1994a. *Media, Process, and the Social Construction of Crime: Studies in Newsmaking Criminology.* New York: Garland

Barak G, ed. 1994b. *Varieties of Criminology.* Westport, CT: Praeger

Barak G. 1995. Media, crime, and justice: a case for constitutive criminology. See Ferrell & Sanders 1995, pp. 142–66

Barak G, ed. 1996. *Representing O.J.: Murder, Criminal Justice, and Mass Culture.* Guilderland, NY: Harrow & Heston

Baudrillard J. 1985. The ecstasy of communication. In *Postmodern Culture*, ed. H Foster, pp. 126–34. London: Pluto

Becker HS. 1963. *Outsiders: Studies in the Sociology of Deviance.* New York: Free Press

Becker HS, McCall M, eds. 1990. *Symbolic Interaction and Cultural Studies.* Chicago: Univ. Chicago Press

Best J, ed. 1995. *Images of Issues: Typifying Contemporary Social Problems.* New York: Aldine de Gruyter. 2nd ed.

Bolton R, ed. 1992. *Culture Wars: Documents*

from the Recent Controversies in the Arts. New York: New Press

Bourgois P, Lettiere M, Quesada J. 1997. Social misery and the sanctions of substance abuse: confronting HIV risk among homeless heroin addicts in San Francisco. *Soc. Probl.* 44:155–73

Brownstein HH. 1995. The media and the construction of random drug violence. See Ferrell & Sanders 1995, pp. 45–65

Brownstein HH. 1996. *The Rise and Fall of a Violent Crime Wave: Crack Cocaine and the Social Construction of a Crime Problem.* Guilderland, NY: Harrow & Heston

Burawoy M, Burton A, Ferguson AA, Fox KJ, Gamson J, et al. 1991. *Ethnography Unbound: Power and Resistance in the Modern Metropolis.* Berkeley: Univ. Calif. Press

Cheatwood D. 1998. Prison movies: films about adult, male, civilian prisons: 1929–1995. See Bailey & Hale 1998, pp. 209–31

Chermak S. 1995. *Victims in the News: Crime and the American News Media.* Boulder, CO: Westview

Chermak S. 1997. The presentation of drugs in the news media: the news sources involved in the construction of social problems. *Justice Q.* 14:687–718

Chermak SM. 1998. Police, courts, and corrections in the media. See Bailey & Hale 1998, pp. 87–99

Chibnall S. 1977. *Law and Order News: An Analysis of Crime Reporting in the British Press.* London: Tavistock

Clarke J. 1976. Style. See Hall & Jefferson 1976, pp. 175–91

Clough P. 1992. *The End(s) of Ethnography: From Realism to Social Criticism.* Newbury Park, CA: Sage

Cohen S, ed. 1971. *Images of Deviance.* Harmondsworth, UK: Penguin

Cohen S. 1972/1980. *Folk Devils and Moral Panics.* London: Macgibbon & Kee

Cohen S. 1979. The punitive city: notes on the dispersal of social control. *Contemp. Crises* 3:339–63

Cohen S. 1988. *Against Criminology.* New Brunswick, NJ: Transaction

Cohen S. 1996. Review of *Cultural Criminology. Justice Q.* 13:737–40

Cohen S, Young J, eds. 1973. *The Manufacture of News: Deviance, Social Problems, and the Mass Media.* London: Constable

Cosgrove S. 1984. The zoot-suit and style warfare. *Radical Am.* 18:38–51

Cressey D. 1954. The differential association theory and compulsive crime. *J. Crim. Law Criminol.* 45:49–64

Davis M. 1992. *City of Quartz.* New York: Vintage

Denzin NK. 1992. *Symbolic Interaction and Cultural Studies: The Politics of Interpretation.* Cambridge, MA: Blackwell

Denzin NK. 1997. *Interpretive Ethnography.* Thousand Oaks, CA: Sage

Dubin S. 1992. *Arresting Images: Impolitic Art and Uncivil Actions.* London: Routledge

During S, ed. 1993. *The Cultural Studies Reader.* London: Routledge

Feagin JR, Orum AM, Sjoberg G, eds. 1991. *A Case for the Case Study.* Chapel Hill, NC: Univ. N. Carol. Press

Ferrell J. 1996. *Crimes of Style: Urban Graffiti and the Politics of Criminality.* Boston: Northeastern Univ. Press

Ferrell J. 1997. Youth, crime, and cultural space. *Soc. Justice* 24:21–38

Ferrell J. 1998. Criminalizing popular culture. See Bailey & Hale 1998, pp. 71–83

Ferrell J, Hamm MS, eds. 1998. *Ethnography at the Edge: Crime, Deviance, and Field Research.* Boston: Northeastern Univ. Press

Ferrell J, Sanders CR, eds. 1995. *Cultural Criminology.* Boston: Northeastern Univ. Press

Ferrell J, Websdale N, eds. 1999. *Making Trouble: Cultural Constructions of Crime, Deviance, and Control.* Hawthorne, NY: Aldine de Gruyter

Fishman M. 1978. Crime waves as ideology. *Soc. Probl.* 25:531–43

Fishman M, Cavender G, eds. 1998. *Entertaining Crime: Television Reality Programs.* Hawthorne, NY: Aldine de Gruyter

Fonow M, Cook J, eds. 1991. *Beyond Methodology: Feminist Scholarship as Lived Research.* Bloomington, IN: Indiana Univ. Press

Fraser N. 1995. Politics, culture, and the public sphere: toward a postmodern conception. In *Social Postmodernism: Beyond Identity Politics,* ed. L Nicholson, S Seidman, pp. 287–312. Cambridge, UK: Cambridge Univ. Press

Geis G. 1991. The case study method in sociological criminology. See Feagin et al 1991, pp. 200–23

Gelder K, Thornton S, eds. 1997. *The Subcultures Reader.* London: Routledge

Goode E, Ben-Yehuda N. 1994. *Moral Panics.* Cambridge, MA: Blackwell

Greek C. 1996. O.J. and the internet: the first cybertrial. See Barak 1996, pp. 64–77

Grossberg L, Nelson C, Treichler PA, eds. 1992. *Cultural Studies.* New York: Routledge

Hagedorn JM. 1990. Back in the field again: gang research in the nineties. In *Gangs in*

America, ed. CR Huff, pp. 240–59. Newbury Park, CA: Sage

Hall S. 1993. What is this 'black' in black popular culture? *Soc. Justice* 20:104–14

Hall S, Critcher C, Jefferson T, Clarke J, Roberts B. 1978. *Policing the Crisis: Mugging, the State, and Law and Order*. Houndmills, UK: MacMillan

Hall S, Jefferson T, eds. 1976. *Resistance Through Rituals: Youth Subcultures in Post-War Britain*. London: Hutchinson

Hamm MS. 1993. *American Skinheads: The Criminology and Control of Hate Crime*. Westport, CT: Praeger

Hamm MS. 1995. Hammer of the Gods revisited: neo-Nazi skinheads, domestic terrorism, and the rise of the new protest music. See Ferrell & Sanders 1995, pp. 190–212

Hamm MS, Ferrell J. 1994. Rap, cops, and crime: clarifying the 'cop killer' controversy. *ACJS Today* 13:1,3,29

Hebdige D. 1979. *Subculture: The Meaning of Style*. London: Methuen

Hebdige D. 1988. *Hiding in the Light*. London: Routledge

Henry S, Milovanovic D. 1991. Constitutive criminology: the maturation of critical theory. *Criminology* 29:293–315

Hollywood B. 1997. Dancing in the dark: ecstasy, the dance culture, and moral panic in post ceasefire Northern Ireland. *Crit. Criminol.* 8:62–77

Howe A. 1997. "The war against women": media representations of men?s violence against women in Australia. *Violence Against Women* 3:59–75

Humphreys L. 1975. *Tearoom Trade: Impersonal Sex in Public Places*. New York: Aldine de Gruyter. Enlarged ed.

Jenkins P. 1992. *Intimate Enemies: Moral Panics in Contemporary Great Britain*. Hawthorne, NY: Aldine de Gruyter

Jenkins P. 1994a. *Using Murder: The Social Construction of Serial Homicide*. Hawthorne, NY: Aldine de Gruyter

Jenkins P. 1994b. 'The Ice Age': the social construction of a drug panic. *Justice Q.* 11:7–31

Jenkins P. 1999. Fighting terrorism as if women mattered: anti-abortion violence as unconstructed terrorism. See Ferrell & Websdale 1999, pp. 319–46

Kane S. 1998a. Reversing the ethnographic gaze: experiments in cultural criminology. See Ferrell & Hamm 1998, pp. 132–45

Kane S. 1998b. *AIDS Alibis: Sex, Drugs and Crime in the Americas*. Philadelphia: Temple Univ. Press

Katz J. 1988. *Seductions of Crime: Moral and Sensual Attractions in Doing Evil*. NY: Basic Books

Kidd-Hewitt D. 1995. Crime and the media: a criminological perspective. See Kidd-Hewitt & Osborne 1995, pp. 1–24

Kidd-Hewitt D, Osborne R, eds. 1995. *Crime and the Media: The Post-Modern Spectacle*. London: Pluto

Kooistra P. 1989. *Criminals as Heroes: Structure, Power, and Identity*. Bowling Green: Bowling Green State Univ. Popular Press

Kraska PB. 1998. Enjoying militarism: political/personal dilemmas in studying U.S. police paramilitary units. See Ferrell & Hamm 1998, pp. 88–110

Kraska PB, Kappeler VE. 1995. To serve and pursue: exploring police sexual violence against women. *Justice Q.* 12:85–111

Kushner T. 1994. A socialism of the skin. *Nation* 259:9–14

Lyng S. 1990. Edgework: a social psychological analysis of voluntary risk taking. *Am. J. Sociol.* 95:851–86

Lyng S. 1998. Dangerous methods: risk taking and the research process. See Ferrell & Hamm 1998, pp. 221–51

Lyng S, Bracey ML. 1995. Squaring the one percent: biker style and the selling of cultural resistance. See Ferrell & Sanders 1995, pp. 235–76

Lyng S, Snow D. 1986. Vocabularies of motive and high-risk behavior: the case of skydiving. In *Advances in Group Processes*, ed. E Lawler, pp. 157–79. Greenwich, CT: JAI

Manning PK. 1998. Media loops. See Bailey & Hale 1998, pp. 25–39

Manning PK. 1999a. Semiotics and social justice. In *Social Justice/Criminal Justice*, ed. BA Arrigo, pp. 131–49. Belmont, CA: West/Wadsworth

Manning PK. 1999b. Reflections: the visual as a mode of social control. See Ferrell & Websdale 1999, pp. 255–75

Marx GT. 1995. Electric eye in the sky: some reflections on the new surveillance and popular culture. See Ferrell & Sanders 1995, pp. 106–41

Mattley C. 1998. (Dis)courtesy stigma: fieldwork among phone fantasy workers. See Ferrell & Hamm 1998, pp. 146–58

McRobbie A. 1980. Settling accounts with subcultures: a feminist critique. *Screen Ed.* 34:37–49

McRobbie A, Thornton SL. 1995. Rethinking 'moral panic' for multi-mediated social worlds. *Br. J. Sociol.* 46:559–574

Melossi D. 1985. Overcoming the crisis in critical criminology: toward a grounded labeling theory. *Criminology* 23:193–208

Mendoza-Denton N. 1996. 'Muy macha': gender and ideology in gang-girls' discourse about makeup. *Ethnos* 61:47–63

Merrifield A, Swyngedouw E, eds. 1997. *The Urbanization of Injustice*. Washington Square, NY: New York Univ. Press

Miller JA. 1995. Struggles over the symbolic: gang style and the meanings of social control. See Ferrell & Sanders 1995, pp. 213–34

Mills CW. 1940. Situated actions and vocabularies of motive. *Am. Sociol. Rev.* 5:904–13

Murji K. 1999. Wild life: constructions and representations of yardies. See Ferrell & Websdale 1999, pp. 179–201

Newman G. 1998. Popular culture and violence: decoding the violence of popular movies. See Bailey & Hale 1998, pp. 40–56

Niesel J. 1998. The horror of everyday life: taxidermy, aesthetics, and consumption in horror films. See Anderson & Howard 1998, pp. 16–31

Nyberg AK. 1998. Comic books and juvenile delinquency: a historical perspective. See Bailey & Hale 1998, pp. 61–70

O'Malley P, Mugford S. 1994. Crime, excitement, and modernity. See Barak 1994b, pp. 189–211

Perrone PA, Chesney-Lind M. 1997. Representations of gangs and delinquency: wild in the streets? *Soc. Justice* 24:96–116

Pettiway LE. 1996. *Honey, Honey, Miss Thang: Being Black, Gay, and on the Streets*. Philadelphia: Temple Univ. Press

Pfohl S. 1990. Welcome to the Parasite Cafe: postmodernity as a social problem. *Soc. Probl.* 37:421–42

Pfohl S. 1992. *Death at the Parasite Cafe: Social Science (Fictions) and the Postmodern*. New York: St. Martin's

Pfohl S. 1993. Twilight of the parasites: ultramodern captial and the new world order. *Soc. Probl.* 40:125–51

Pfohl S, Gordon A. 1986. Criminological displacements: a sociological deconstruction. *Soc. Probl.* 33:94–113

Pfuhl EH Jr. 1986. *The Deviance Process*. Belmont, CA: Wadsworth. 2nd ed.

Polsky N. 1969. *Hustlers, Beats, and Others*. Garden City, NY: Anchor

Postman N. 1986. *Amusing Ourselves to Death*. London: Heinemann

Potter GW, Kappeler VE, eds. 1998. *Constructing Crime: Perspectives on Making News and Social Problems*. Prospect Heights, IL: Waveland

Presdee M. 1994. Young people, culture, and the construction of crime: doing wrong versus doing crime. See Barak 1994b, pp. 179–87

Ragin CC, Becker HS. 1992. *What is a Case? Foundations of Social Inquiry*. New York: Cambridge Univ. Press

Redhead S. 1995. *Unpopular Cultures: The Birth of Law and Popular Culture*. Manchester, UK: Manchester Univ. Press

Reinarman C. 1994. The social construction of drug scares. See Adler & Adler 1994, pp. 92–104

Reinarman C, Duskin C. 1992. Dominant ideology and drugs in the media. *Intern. J. Drug Pol.* 3:6–15

Sanchez-Tranquilino M. 1995. Space, power, and youth culture: Mexican American graffiti and Chicano murals in East Los Angeles, 1972–1978. In *Looking High and Low: Art and Cultural Identity*, ed. BJ Bright, L Bakewell, pp. 55–88. Tucson, AZ: Univ. Ariz. Press

Sanders CR. 1995. Stranger than fiction: insights and pitfalls in post-modern ethnography. *Stud. Symb. Interact.* 17:89–104

Sanders CR, Lyon E. 1995. Repetitive retribution: media images and the cultural construction of criminal justice. See Ferrell & Sanders 1995, pp. 25–44

Scheper-Hughes, N. 1994. Embodied knowledge: thinking with the body in critical medical anthropology. In *Assessing Cultural Anthropology*, ed. R Borofsky, pp. 229–42. New York: McGraw-Hill

Scott A, Soja E, eds. 1996. *The City: Los Angeles and Urban Theory at the End of the Twentieth Century*. Berkeley: Univ. Calif. Press

Sparks R. 1992. *Television and the Drama of Crime: Moral Tales and the Place of Crime in Public Life*. Buckingham, UK: Open Univ. Press

Sparks R. 1995. Entertaining the crisis: television and moral enterprise. See Kidd-Hewitt &Osborne 1995, pp. 49–66

Surette R. 1998. *Media, Crime, and Criminal Justice: Images and Realities*. Belmont, CA: West/Wadsworth. 2nd ed.

Taylor I, Walton P, Young J. 1973. *The New Criminology: For a Social Theory of Deviance*. New York: Harper & Row

Thomas WI. 1966. The relation of research to the social process. In *W.I. Thomas on Social Organization and Social Personality*, ed. M Janowitz, pp. 289–305. Chicago: Univ. Chicago Press

Thornton S. 1994. Moral panic, the media, and British rave culture. In *Microphone Fiends: Youth Music and Youth Culture*, eds. A Ross, T Rose, pp. 176–92. New York: Routledge

Tunnell KD. 1992. *Choosing Crime: The Criminal Calculus of Property Offenders*. Chicago: Nelson-Hall

Tunnell KD. 1995. A cultural approach to crime and punishment, bluegrass style. See Ferrell & Sanders 1995, pp. 80–105

Tunnell KD. 1998. Reflections on crime, criminals, and control in newsmagazine television programs. See Bailey & Hale 1998, pp. 111–22

Van Maanen J, ed. 1995a. *Representation in Ethnography*. Thousand Oaks, CA: Sage

Van Maanen J. 1995b. An end to innocence: the ethnography of ethnography. See Van Maanen 1995a, pp. 1–35

Vaughn D. 1998. Rational choice, situated action, and the social control of organizations. *Law Soc. Rev.* 32:501–39

Watney S. 1987. *Policing Desire: Pornography, AIDS and the Media*. Minneapolis: Univ. Minn. Press

Weber M. 1978. *Economy and Society*. Berkeley: Univ. Calif. Press

Websdale N. 1996. Predators: the social construction of 'stranger-danger' in Washington State as a form of patriarchal ideology. *Women Crim. Justice* 7:43–68

Websdale N. 1998. *Rural Woman Battering and the Justice System: An Ethnography*. Thousand Oaks, CA: Sage

Websdale N. 1999. Police homicide files as situated media substrates. See Ferrell & Websdale 1999, pp. 277–300

Websdale N, Alvarez A. 1998. Forensic journalism as patriarchal ideology: the newspaper construction of homicide-suicide. See Bailey & Hale 1998, pp. 123–141

Williams J. 1998. Comics: a tool of subversion? See Anderson & Howard 1998, pp. 97–115

Willis P. 1977. *Learning to Labor: How Working Class Kids Get Working Class Jobs*. New York: Columbia Univ. Press

Willis P. 1990. *Common Culture: Symbolic Work at Play in the Everyday Cultures of the Young*. Milton Keynes, UK: Open Univ. Press

Wright R, Decker S. 1994. *Burglars on the Job*. Boston: Northeastern Univ. Press

Young A. 1996. *Imagining Crime: Textual Outlaws and Criminal Conversations*. London: Sage

Young J. 1971. The role of the police as amplifiers of deviancy, negotiators of reality and translators of fantasy. In *Images of Deviance*, ed. S Cohen, pp. 27–61. Harmondsworth, UK: Penguin

Annu. Rev. Sociol. 1999. 25:419–40

IS SOUTH AFRICA DIFFERENT?
Sociological Comparisons and Theoretical Contributions from the Land of Apartheid

Gay Seidman

Department of Sociology, University of Wisconsin, Madison, Wisconsin 53706;
e-mail: seidman@ssc.wisc.edu

KEY WORDS: race, development, democratization

ABSTRACT

For most of the past 50 years, South Africa served as the outlier in sociological discussions of racial inequality: From the late 1940s, when most of the world was moving away from strict racial classification and segregation, apartheid provided social scientists with their most extreme example of the dynamics of racial segregation and exclusion. Yet while apartheid South Africa was unique, social scientists have also used it in comparative studies to explore the underlying dynamics of racial capitalism: Insights from South Africa have offered sociologists new ways to think about migrant labor; the construction of ethnicity; racial exclusion and colonial relationships; relationships between business, white workers and capitalist states; and oppositional social movements. With the end of legal apartheid, South Africa is poised to move into a new position in the annals of social science. From being an outlier, it is increasingly used an an exemplar, in discussions of democratic transitions, development strategies and globalization, and postcolonial transformations. Still to come, perhaps, are comparative studies that draw on insights from other parts of the world to re-examine aspects of South African society that have been left relatively unexplored — ironically including issues around racial identities and changing patterns of race relations as South Africa constructs a new non-racial democracy.

0360-0572/99/0815-0419$08.00

INTRODUCTION

As everyone knows, South Africa is unique: For fifty years, it stood in the annals of social science as a monument to racial inequality. It appeared in most discussions as the place where white supremacy, authoritarian labor controls, and draconian security laws blocked normal patterns of gradual integration and modernization, where white privilege was entrenched and implacable. Since World War II, as the rest of the world tried to meet the challenges of civil rights movements and decolonization, apartheid symbolized resistance to the winds of change; South Africa consistently anchored the end point of the spectrum of racial orders, the place where racial inequality stood still (Massey & Denton 1993, Rex 1971, Marks 1998).

Given this almost axiomatic position, it would be surprising that South Africa's subtle transformation as a comparative case has gone unnoticed, were it not that other changes have been so much more dramatic. The thrilling release of political prisoners, the end of apartheid's strict racial segregation, the first democratic elections—all these have been far more visible than the re-invention of South Africa as a more-or-less ordinary society, which may serve as a basis for making larger claims about racial capitalism in an era of globalization, post-colonial state formation, social movements and democratization, migrant labor patterns, even race relations.

But this shift deserves a closer look. For some fifty years, South Africa has occupied a distinctive status: To social scientists, the country that produced apartheid appeared unique, a case that should be compared to others only in an attempt to explain its unusual trajectory—in contrast to the more ordinary social science assumption that most societies have at least a few common, or at least comparable features. To some extent, of course, this status was shaped by politics. Apartheid's opponents sought to isolate South Africa, distinguishing apartheid from other forms of racial capitalism. But South Africa's unique status also reflected a theoretical bias. More industrialized than any other part of Africa, yet more colonial than any other industrialized society, South Africa fit uneasily into ordinary social science categories; instead, it served as the case that demonstrated that racial divisions do not always disappear with industrialization. By the late twentieth century, of course, most analysts were willing to accept that racial inequalities had not disappeared in any society—industrialized or otherwise—yet South Africa's outlier status generally remained unquestioned.

Since South Africa's first democratic elections in 1994, however, comparisons have taken a very different tone: South Africa now seems to offer new insights into a larger set of cases, as social scientists bring South Africa firmly into the mainstream. Instead of treating South Africa as the last bastion of a dying order, or the place where social processes follow a unique logic, social scientists are increasingly treating South Africa as almost paradigmatic: as a site for exploring colonial ambiguities and post-colonial legacies, as a model for democratic transitions, or as a site for exploring development possibilities in the context of globalization. Just as South Africa itself has reinserted itself into international affairs on a new basis, social scientists are beginning to reinsert South Africa into broader debates, both as a way to explore new, hitherto-overlooked questions about South African society, and to use insights from South Africa to open new questions about broader social processes (Greenstein 1997).

South Africa's changing status in comparative studies alters the kinds of questions social scientists can ask about its society, and the lessons they can draw from it. In this essay, I first look at earlier comparative studies, where South Africa's unique status determined the logic of comparisons, as most studies sought to explain South African exceptionalism. Yet even at the height of apartheid, some comparativists used apartheid's extreme character to pursue broader theoretical questions about the relationship between race, class, and the state, exploring the character of racial capitalism, migrant labor systems, ethnicity, and social movements. In the present moment, South Africa often appears as something of an exemplar, suggesting new possible avenues for democratization and development. But finally, I suggest that perhaps the moment has come when South Africans may be able to look abroad, to reconsider South Africa's own most unusual feature, its strict racial hierarchy.

THE HIGHEST STAGE OF WHITE SUPREMACY

For decades, South Africa's unique status rested on the extreme character of apartheid: It represented a conscious system of social engineering, gradually constructed following the Nationalist Party's election victory in 1948, explicitly designed to maintain white supremacy. To an unparalleled degree, South Africa demonstrates the persistence of racial inequality despite industrialization—the case that disproved any lingering tendency among modernization theorists to treat racial oppression as atavistic or vestigal. At a time when decolonization movements were spreading and civil rights movements were challenging racial discrimination in the United States, South Africa was moving toward intensified segregation and toward complete disenfranchisement of its African majority—to the point that it denied its African inhabitants not only the right to vote, but even the right to call themselves South African.

The outlines of apartheid are well-known. Under a series of laws passed after the 1948 election—by a parliament that represented only the roughly twenty percent of the population classified as "white"—all South Africans were assigned at birth to a racial category (broadly: white, Asian, Colored, or African). Most legal and political rights were tied to racial status. Segregation was extreme: Interracial sex or marriage was prohibited, and public facilities—from schools and libraries to parks and restaurants—were strictly divided along racial lines. Inequality was built into the system: Even the curricula used for students of different races reflected the state's official vision of white supremacy. Residential areas were completely segregated by law: Under the Group Areas Act, blacks were moved to new townships far from the centers of town. Blacks could commute into work by day, but under apartheid, South Africa's cities were expected to be "white by night"—except, of course, for the nannies and waiters, janitors and domestic workers who continued to provide services to white citizens.

But apartheid went beyond exclusionary politics, urban segregation, or unequal public facilities. Long before the Nationalist Party took power in 1948, the British colonial government had passed the 1913 Land Act, creating native reserves which set aside 13% of South Africa's land area for the roughly 75% of the population classified as African. After 1948, these reserves became "homelands" for black South Africans: Blacks could work in white-designated areas, but they could never hope for citizenship in a larger South Africa. Instead, they were officially assigned to one of the African areas that were one day to be set adrift as "independent" countries. Blacks working in "white" South Africa were required to carry passes to show they had permission to live, work, or travel in white-designated areas, and faced prison terms if they were caught without passes. Apartheid's policy of "separate development" treated rural Africans as a temporary sojourners, who would leave their families behind while they came to work in white South Africa's mines, farms, and factories, but return to their "homelands" at the end of their working lives. This circulatory migrant labor system was apartheid's cornerstone: Black South Africans were denied citizenship in the land of their birth, but would continue to provide cheap labor to white-ruled South Africa.

For most of the apartheid era, comparisons between South Africa and other countries emphasized the unique characteristics of South African segregation. Apartheid was "the highest stage of white supremacy," a carefully constructed scaffolding designed to protect white domination of the black majority far into the future (Cell 1982). Not surprisingly, most comparisons sought to explain why South Africa was different, offering reasons for South Africa's peculiarly virulent form of racial control. Before the mid-twentieth century, South Africa had not seemed so different from other European colonies, where white domination was unquestioned, and where white settler control over native populations was ubiquitous (Cooper 1996); but when decolonization began to take off after World War II, South Africa seemed to take a divergent path. Why, when the "winds of change" were sweeping across Africa in the 1940s, did South Africa turn toward new racial restrictions, rather than moving toward integration? From a similar starting point—a relatively similar racial order, in which white minorities controlled black majorities through political exclusion, through strict segregation, and through racialized controls at the workplace—South Africa moved in a different direction.

South African exceptionalism was generally traced to dynamics in the white population, primarily in the relationship between mine-owners, white state officials, and white workers. Many studies attributed South Africa's odd trajectory to the character of the state. While some analysts argued that apartheid emerged out of the dynamics of Afrikaans nationalism and an unusually autonomous state bureaucracy (O'Meara 1983, Posel 1991), most comparative analysts link racial concerns more explicitly to economic ones: Whites were protecting racial privilege, but they were also reinforcing a system that provided cheap black labor to white-owned mines and farms (Evans 1997). White supremacy involved not only racial discrimination, but, just as importantly, a specifically racial class system, where racial identities marked class status. Conscious state policies recreated the racial character of South African capitalism: policies to uplift "poor whites" or to limit black farmers' opportunities consistently reinforced racial inequality (Bundy 1979, van Onselen 1982).

This perspective stimulated a series of detailed historical studies exploring the character of a state that permitted citizenship only to whites. The relationships between different factions of capital and the state, between white workers and the state, between white farmers and white industrialists, all helped explain the rigid character of South African minority rule. Careful historical studies helped explain how institutions that were common to many colonial situations—racial hierarchies, native reserves, vagrancy laws, and the like—developed into the apartheid system, as different segments of the white population promoted sectoral interests under the umbrella of white domination.

Some comparative studies viewed apartheid as the outcome of white workers' appeals to a racially-motivated state. Early in the twentieth century, as the mining industry emerged around Johannesburg, white workers sought to preserve a privileged position in the labor market by blocking black workers from semi-skilled positions. Enlisting the help of the state and white mineowners to prevent the displacement of white workers by lower-paid blacks, white workers organized around the infamous slogan, "Workers of the World, Unite! And Fight for a White South Africa" (Simons & Simons 1983). Researchers disagree on explanations for white workers' racialized vision, sometimes emphasizing the way a racially exclusionary state reinforced racially divided labor markets (Bonacich 1981, Fredrickson 1981), sometimes emphasizing the way upper-class white politicians could manipulate working class racial attitudes (Cell 1982). But clearly, through most of this century, white workers generally allied with their employers and white politicians, rather than seeking to build a class-based coalition with the Africans who were increasingly joining the wage labor force.

Rejecting the emphasis on white workers, some researchers focused instead on business elites and the state, emphasizing elite concerns about sustaining white supremacy (Posel 1991) or state and business concerns about maintaining control over a black workforce (Burawoy 1981, Davies 1979, Johnstone 1976). In a study comparing South Africa, the United States, Ireland, and Israel, Greenberg (1980) argued that South Africa's peculiarly racial capitalism had a sectoral basis. Agricultural and mining capital were far more interested in retaining racialized controls over workers than was manufacturing capital. Many of apartheid's peculiarities—especially the combination of a migrant labor system, the pass law system, and the job reservation system, which blocked black mobility into even semi-skilled jobs—were attributed to white farmers' and mineowners' concerns that manufacturers would pay higher wages, drawing black workers to cities and raising the cost of labor throughout South Africa. In the United States, southern manufacturers finally abandoned strict segregation and racially defined labor markets in order to stabilize an industrial workforce. South African manufacturers, in contrast, appeared unable to persuade other whites to abandon racial controls over workers and were forced to learn to live with the high turnover, skills shortages, and instability that came with strict apartheid.

Yet while some analysts suggested that these pressures would, over time, lead to conflicts between industrialists and state bureaucrats (Adam 1971, James 1987, Lipton 1986, Price 1991), Greenberg (1987) suggested these conflicts might be exaggerated. South African manufacturers often worked closely with government officials to bend the rules, reducing inefficiencies while retaining tight control over black workers.

Apartheid as Prism

Yet even while some social scientists sought to explain South African exceptionalism, there has always been another side. South Africa has also served as a prism—in part, perhaps, because the extreme character of apartheid lays bare the underlying dynamics of racial capitalism. South Africa's contribution to a broader sociology has, rather surprisingly, rested in large part in some of those areas where apartheid makes South African society unique: migration, ethnicity, and discussions of class formation and social movements.

Probably South Africa's most important contribution to a broader understanding of racial capitalism comes from a series of studies of Southern Africa's migrant labor system, beginning with research suggesting that African families' subsistence agriculture subsidized capital by supplementing the wages of migrant workers (Arrighi 1973, Levy 1982, Wolpe 1972). Burawoy (1977) was one of the first researchers to use South Africa as a prism into broader patterns of racial capitalism: he compared the role of the South African and Californian states in perpetuating and controlling circulatory migrant streams, arguing that in both cases migrant labor subsidized capital and states by pushing the costs of education, pensions, and other social services, along with the costs of feeding workers' families—across the border. Together, the South African studies contributed to a new approach to migration, emphasizing questions of labor supply, labor control, and the structural position occupied by migrants in the receiving area. By the mid-1980s, sociologists were drawing on insights derived from South Africa to examine migration in cases as far flung as the West Indies, Europe, and Mexico, looking at how states control the flow and circulation of migrants in terms of labor supplies and labor control, and at how migration flows are deeply intertwined with the racialization of labor streams (Miles 1993, Portes & Borocz 1989).

This structuralist view can, of course, be overstated. Even in South Africa, recent studies have offered a slightly less schematic view, emphasizing the active role that migrants themselves played in shaping the migrant process and exploring the gendered character of South Africa's migrant stream. Several recent studies have described the circulatory migratory pattern as an employer response to worker demands, instituted because workers sought to maintain a rural foothold as they moved into waged labor (Atkins 1993, Harries 1994, Crush et al 1991, Crush & James 1995, James 1992, Moodie & Ndatshe 1994). Similarly, studies by feminist sociologists have emphasized agency, stressing black South African women's responses to the constraints imposed by a gendered migrant process. Under apartheid, African men were hired to work for cash, while African women were expected to remain in rural areas, engaged in subsistence agriculture unless they found jobs as domestic workers in white households. Over the century, African women have regularly moved to urban areas, legally or illegally, undermining the strict household division envisaged by apartheid's planners, finding new opportunities in the interstices of the urban economy (Berger 1992, Bozzoli & Nkotsoe 1991, Cock 1989, Walker 1990, Ramphele 1993)

If South Africa's migratory labor system provided new insights into migrant labor patterns world-wide, so too did apartheid's attempt to reinforce tribalism among blacks. In much of Africa, colonial administrations assumed that ethnic (often called "tribal" or "customary") identities were fundamental to Africans' worldview, and "traditional" bonds are frequently used to explain political dynamics in post-colonial societies. In South Africa, however, ethnicity among Africans has been politicized from above: Apartheid planners explicitly sought to link ethnic identities for Africans to specific "homelands" in an attempt to legitimate "separate development." Rejecting this process, black South African politicians asserted a national South African identity for blacks, insisting that ethnic identities had been broken down through urbanization and delegitimated through white efforts to manipulate and separate blacks. South

Africa's township culture was a celebrated mix of elements long before globalization became a buzzword in cultural studies (Coplan 1995), and urban anti-apartheid activists often rejected ethnic labels as irrelevant (Greenstein 1995).

For social scientists, Southern Africa proved a fruitful site to explore the construction of ethnicity. Africa played a key role in international historiographic debates in the early 1980s, as European historians began to acknowledge the way nineteenth-century colonialists invented traditions around the world (Hobsbawm & Ranger 1983). Researchers in Southern Africa demonstrated how colonial administrators in the early twentieth century tended to codify as "customary" practices that had previously been flexible and contested—often, strengthening the power of chiefs over subjects, and husbands over wives (Berry 1993, Channock 1989, Klug 1995, Griffiths 1997). In a remarkable study, Wilmsen (1989) dramatically demonstrates the extent to which anthropologists, too, contributed to the reification of Southern African ethnic identities: The much-studied Kalahari "bushmen," often treated as the last isolated remnants of paleolithic culture, may in fact represent simply a desert underclass, pushed out of farming into hunting and gathering while their more successful cousins managed to find a foothold in the rapidly changing colonial economy along the edge of the desert.

As historians began to explore the way colonial states manipulated and redefined the ethnic categories that appeared so naturalized by the late twentieth century (Vail 1991), Southern Africa provided an important test case. But South Africa also demonstrated the way ethnic categories took on new meaning in the context of social change. As apartheid's framework channeled rural Africans through ethnically defined political institutions, these newly constructed identities—however artificial or invented—took on real importance in individuals' lives: Bantustan authorities became the source of work permits and drivers' licenses, as well as providers of education for rural black children (Mare 1992). Ethnically divided labor markets and circulatory migration reinforced links to rural settings; rural South African life became dependent on miners' remittances, but miners also interpreted their experiences at work through an ethnic lens (Guy & Thabane 1988, Moodie & Ndatshe 1994).

In a recent and important study of the post-colonial state in Africa, Mamdani (1996) argues that contemporary South Africa offers an archetypal illustration of the legacies of indirect rule: The bifurcated, racialized colonial state granted citizenship to whites in urban areas, but placed rural Africans under the control of strong rural chiefs, who used claims of ethnicity and tradition to legitimate domination. In struggles between rural-based migrant workers and township residents, he argues, we see dynamics common to most post-colonial societies in Africa: The legacies of ethnically defined colonial state institutions play out in urban settings. Contemporary politicians and ordinary citizens alike view ethnic allegiance as a reasonable basis for claims on the central state.

Again, however, just as recent research has challenged some of the most structurally determinist perspectives on migration, recent research on ethnicity in Southern Africa has shifted somewhat, moving beyond the strict instrumentalism embodied in a vision of ethnicity-as-invention, or even the subsequent notion that invented ethnic institutions channel political aspirations in the present. Recently, researchers have begun to examine the ambiguities of the colonial encounter, exploring the way African intellectuals, even traditional chiefs, used the cultural repertoire offered them by colonial society to contest power within African society as well as within the colonial environment (Landau 1995, Comoroffs 1997, van Onselen 1996). Traces of what Marks (1986) aptly termed the "ambiguities of dependence"—the reliance of African bantustan leaders on the support of a white-minority regime in Pretoria—can be seen throughout Southern African society, as Africans sought to use aspects of European literacy, religion, medicine, even architecture, for their own benefit. Indeed, contrasting the anti-colonial discourse of black South Africans with the Palestinian movement for self-determination, Greenstein (1995) suggests that black South Africans' aspirations were fundamentally shaped by colonial encounters, to such an extent that from the turn of the century, few black South Africans could envisage a future that did not include a white presence (see also Younis 1999). And finally, some researchers are beginning to explore the other side of this relationship, asking when and how white South Africans have drawn on and reinterpreted certain facets of indigenous African culture—including, recently, in settings such as a Zulu theme park, designed to attract tourists to a specific, commercialized interpretation of "traditional" culture (Hamilton 1998).

If South Africa illustrated the role of settler minorities in reshaping and reinventing "indigenous" culture, it has also provided a site for exploring oppositional social movements, where subaltern groups sought to create new cultures of resistance and challenge. Most studies of the anti-apartheid opposition have been quite historically specific. Not surprisingly, many have focused on the racial dynamic of apartheid, looking at how black activists mobilized a national resistance to white supremacy. Yet recognizing the complicated relationship between colonizer and colonized, the most historically nuanced of these studies have acknowledged a persistent tension between the street-corner appeal of calls of black supremacist rhetoric and the insistence by more respectable South African leaders that whites would be welcome in a future South Africa (Bradford 1987, Beinart & Bundy 1987, Callinicos 1987, Gerhardt 1978, Lodge 1983, Marx 1992, Peires 1989).

Several studies explore white involvement in the anti-apartheid resistance, acknowledging the contradictory situation in which sympathetic whites could provide important resources and support for black nationalism, but where issues of leadership, autonomy, and alliances are constantly framed in racialized terms (Simons & Simons 1983, Lazerson 1994). Conversely, several studies explored the way life in a militarized white society and white nationalism affected white South Africans, looking at the impact of racial tension on individuals' psyches, on definitions of masculinity and femininity, and on understandings of class identities (Crapanzano 1985, Cock & Nathan 1989).

Recently, a new dimension has been added to our understanding of the South African anti-apartheid movement, as analysts begin to explore the transnational side of black activism. This kind of transnational study may reflect a very immediate concern with globalization and transnationalism in the late twentieth century; but as historians Campbell (1995) and Fredrickson (1995) each demonstrate, interactions between black South African activists and African-American activists have been important throughout this century, providing intellectual and financial resources to movements on both sides of the ocean. Similarly, foreign funding has played a key role in the internal politics of the anti-apartheid movement, specifically in strengthening women's voices (Seidman 1999).

But while these studies raise interesting issues, they are more specific to the South African situation, perhaps, than studies that look at a range of other dynamics in the mobilization of the anti-apartheid resistance. Interestingly, the militant labor movement and most of the new urban groups that emerged to form a legal opposition in the 1970s and 1980s generally rejected racial identity as a basis for mobilization: Although they mobilized communities in racially segregated townships, activists generally used nonracial principles in defining social movement constituencies. Obviously, racial discrimination and exclusion have been key issues, from the point of view of social movement mobilization, but anti-apartheid groups have frequently framed their concerns in other terms, as students, workers, township residents, women.

In the 1980s, oppositional social movements in South Africa provided an important corrective to international social-movement theories that limited their vision to industrialized societies. Many of the South African studies explored the relationship between industrialization, urbanization, the changing character of the black community and its growing ability to challenge the apartheid state. Much research focused on the changing role of African workers in the economy and their ability to disrupt production as a consequence of industrialization. Before the 1970s, discussions of the labor process in South Africa tended to emphasize the apartheid state's control over workers. Rapid growth in the nonracial trade union movement, however, prompted sociologists to examine the character of labor militance. Rapid industrialization changed the experiences and racial composition of the industrial workforce over the century, increasing the capacity of African workers to assert demands at the workplace; changing patterns of production, with changing skill requirements, altered the ability of African workers to challenge employer and state control over their lives outside the factory (Freund 1988, Crankshaw 1994, Webster 1985).

South Africa's militant labor movement challenged many of the assumptions made in the literature about democratization and development, suggesting that unions can play a key role in democratic change (Lambert & Webster 1988). South Africa's racially segregated communities are unusual, but the links between union activism and community groups that were organized during the 1980s are not unique: A comparison with Brazil's democratization process suggests that despite an authoritarian pattern of industrialization, workers in both cases were able to use workplace organizations in support of community demands for political and economic change (Seidman 1994).

Despite the racial dimension of South African society, the concerns expressed by social movements within the anti-apartheid coalition echo the kinds of concerns expressed during democratization processes elsewhere: Poor communities insist that full citizenship must involve the provision of basic services such as health care, education, and infrastructure as well as the right to vote (Abel 1995, Escobar & Alvarez 1992, Marx 1992, Mayekiso 1996, Murray 1987, Murray 1994, Seidman 1994). Despite the repression that marked apartheid's last years, South Africa's urban movements provide an unusually visible site for exploring the character of oppositional social movements during democratization, and they offer new insights into the emergence of demands for a redefined, inclusionary citizenship in post-colonial settings.

Post-Apartheid, Post-Colonial

Since its first democratic elections in 1994, South Africa has moved into a new category: Instead of appearing as an outlier, it is now increasingly treated as an exemplar, a case that illustrates the post-colonial condition. Led by an unusually articulate and self-conscious group of reformers and blessed by an unusual degree of international legitimacy, South Africa in the 1990s appears to offer new ways to think about both the consolidation of democracy and strategies for development at the turn of the century. Conversely, South African social scientists are beginning to look beyond South Africa's borders for new insights into some of the most thorny issues of South African sociology— including, perhaps most ironically, issues of race and racial politics.

Perhaps the most obvious area where South African scholarship promises new insights lies in the general area of democratization. Early studies of the democratic transition in South Africa tended to draw heavily on Latin American examples, suggesting that anti-apartheid activists should steer a careful course between the *dictaduras* and *dictablandas* of the apartheid regime to avoid provoking a white backlash (Van Zyl Slabbert 1992, Adam & Moodley 1993). But South Africa's popular social movements gives discussions of the consolidation of democratization an unusual tone. Thus, for example, Adler & Webster (1996) suggested that in contrast to Latin America, where trade union leaders were advised to restrain their followers' demands during the democratization process to avoid pushing elites into the arms of authoritarian generals (Przeworski 1991, Valenzuela 1989), South African unionists can insist on demands for redistribution, because their claims may receive sympathetic attention from reformist policymakers. While scholars from Latin America, Eastern Europe, and the rest of Africa have increasingly recognized limits to the transition from authoritarianism (e.g., Jelin & Hershberg 1996), South African discussions continue to stress the possibility of rapid change in institutional framework and political culture.

Thus, for example, South Africa in the 1990s serves as an exemplar for how post-authoritarian regimes might deal with the legacies of human rights violations and repression. Most democratization processes have involved burying the past; authoritarian figures are frequently granted full amnesty and permitted complete integration into the new democratic order. South Africa, by contrast, took a firmer stance, offering amnesty only to those who fully disclose their participation in gross violations of human rights and threatening prosecution of those who did not cooperate. Although the Truth and Reconciliation Commission drew on examples from around the world, its planners sought to avoid some of the pitfalls of similar commissions—particularly, to avoid the powerlessness that prevented many such commissions from exploring the participation of still-powerful authoritarian figures in acts of repression and violence (Asmal et al 1997). Steering a careful course between forgetting the past and provoking further social conflict, the Truth and Reconciliation Commission has changed the debate about how to deal with the painful memories of the authoritarian past. Although the process is hardly complete, the South African TRC has already become a subject of much discussion among activists and social scientists around the world, as they begin to analyze what appears to have been a relatively successful innovation.

This kind of institutional innovation is not limited to the truth and reconciliation process. The thorough-going reform of the South African state provides other examples of similar innovation, as South African policy-makers build on examples from around the world, but add their own adaptations. Specific innovations—ranging from the successful integration of two previously-opposed armed forces, to the creation of a Gender Commission that will examine the implications for gender equity of every new law—have made South Africa's democratic transition unusually far-reaching. South Africa's experiences seem to stand apart from the "show elections" that have marked so many transitions; as a result, general discussions of democratization are likely to seem oddly incomplete if they overlook the South African experiences over the next decade.

Similarly, South Africa is likely to become an increasingly visible example in the literature on development, illustrating the possibilities and constraints inherent in a newly globalized world economy. Historically, South Africa's developmental trajectory has been rather anomalous: Although like most former colonies it depends on the export of a single primary commodity, that commodity—gold—long occupied a unique position in international markets. Further, South Africa was able to develop a relatively diversified industrial base during the period of strict apartheid. Despite one of the highest gini coefficients in the world, South Africa under apartheid experienced rapid spurts of economic growth—although South Africa's white minority regime could not shift its position within the hierarchy of the world system.

But in the 1990s, democratization coincided with another dramatic shift in South Africa's relationship to the rest of the world. Gold is no longer the backbone of the international financial system, and, as a result, South Africa is no longer the uniquely wealthy late-industrializer it once appeared to be. Changes in the international prices of gold have revealed that among the legacies of apartheid is classic underdevelopment. Since 1987, a steep drop in the world price for gold—largely the result of the collapse of the Bretton-Woods system of international exchange rates—makes gold just another commodity, and South Africa faces fluctuating international prices for a commodity that makes up about half the value of its exports. In the context of the democratic transition, the gold industry cannot rely on its historic response of simply further reducing wages for black workers (Martin 1983, James 1992). Instead, it has a new response: restructuring the industry to increase productivity and reduce the labor force in the mines (Freund 1993, Leger & Nichol 1991).

The impact on rural Southern Africa has been devastating: From independent Mozambique and Lesotho to former bantustan areas like the Transkei, households that previously depended on miners' remittances are now virtually without incomes. Repeated studies have shown the perverse effect of long-term circulatory migrancy in rural areas, as remittances from migrant workers have become essential for families to purchase the basic inputs needed for subsistence agriculture. Without remittances, hiring a plough or purchasing seeds becomes prohibitively expensive (Murray 1992, Moodie & Ndatsche 1994). Although mining is low-paid, dangerous work, the mines long provided jobs for blacks denied literacy and other skills; the industry's current downsizing closes off an option on which households across rural southern Africa had come to depend. Among apartheid's legacies is the collapse of the very industry that lay at the heart of the system. Ironically, one of the first demands made on South Africa's first democratically elected government by the militant black mineworkers union involved support for failing mines, as a way to sustain rural black communities that have become completely dependent on miners' remittances (Commission to Investigate the Development of a Comprehensive Labour Market Policy 1996).

As gold becomes more vulnerable to price fluctuations, South Africa looks like many other developing countries. Its strategists hope to diversify exports, moving away from dependence on a single commodity to find new market niches for manufactured and agricultural products. Somewhat paradoxically, South Africa's reintegration into the world economy may build on the fact that South Africa had developed a relatively successful manufacturing sector through import-substitution policies during the post-war era. One reason why the mining crisis has been ignored by many commentators is that South Africa appeared relatively successful in diversifying its economy. Had it not been for its racial inequalities, its record of manufacturing growth might well have been envied by other late industrializers around the world. Through high tarrif barriers and subsidies to local manufacturers and joint ventures—very much along the lines that would be called import-substitution industrialization in places like Mexico or India—a developmental South African state successfully promoted domestic industries and joint ventures, buying technology and supplying cheap inputs like electricity, steel, and petrochemicals (Clark 1994)

In the 1990s, however, those strategies appear less appealing; international pressures for open economies are changing the context of development, creating new constraints and possibilities for developing economies. South Africa's new government is finding itself forced to reconstruct its relationship to the outside world. The new pressures of economic integration and globalization have prompted a wholesale revision of South Africa's trade and export policies, as it seeks to position itself in competitive global markets. Instead of protecting domestic markets, the South African government now expects local producers to compete on a global scale; meanwhile, local producers are struggling to deal with a flood of new imports on local market shelves. Debates in Pretoria about economic policy and the impact of a global world economy on South African consumers and producers echo debates around the world at the turn of the century: How can any developing country attract new investment, restructure its industries to make them more productive, and find new international markets for their products, in ways that will both sustain economic growth over the long term and raise workers' wages (Baker et al 1993, Evans 1995, Guimaraes 1996)? For developing countries everywhere, the unfolding of South Africa's economic trajectory over the next ten years will reveal a great deal about the possibilities and constraints facing democratic developmentalist states in an era of globalization.

South Africa is not just another developing country, of course; it stands out from the rest, in its visibility and in the legitimacy of its current reform efforts. South Africa offers a remarkably visible and transparent example of restructuring. Since the 1994 elections, the wholesale reconstruction of state institutions have involved open and heated public debate. What should the new government do about inherited inequalities of wealth and power? Can representatives from labor unions, business, and the state reasonably hope to arrive at mutually acceptable policies in some kind of merger of corporatism and democracy (Patel 1994, Baskin 1996)? Given the persistence of racial divisions at work, can labor and management work together to replace the authoritarian labor practices of the past with the kind of cooperative arrangements often considered essential for higher productivity and industrial flexibility (Joffe et al 1993)? Especially since the highly mobilized anti-apartheid opposition spawned an energetic and vocal public sphere in post-apartheid South Africa, these debates are remarkably vivid, involving public discussion and commentary on state policies that might go unremarked elsewhere. In contrast to the rather opaque processes familiar from other developmental states, the design of development policy in a democratic South Africa is a highly visible process, offering the possibility of new insights into the dynamics of negotiations between states, business, and citizenry in the process of restructuring.

South Africa thus also holds out unusual promise, both to its citizens and to the rest of the developing world. Having defeated a system regarded as uniquely evil, the South African government retains extraordinary legitimacy, with internationally respected leadership and international acknowledgment that the inequities inherited from the apartheid era demand redress. In this context, South Africa's trajectory over the next few years will be of great interest. Its efforts to deal with the legacies of apartheid—with an authoritarian culture that remains riddled with racial hierarchies, with extreme inequalities of income and wealth, with rapidly growing squatter areas whose residents have been denied basic education or health care, and, of course, with the legacies of migrant labor and land dispossession—will resonate throughout the post-colonial world. Apartheid was indeed extreme, but many of its patterns are paralleled elsewhere; especially given the general good will and support accorded the new government, South African experiments may illustrate new strategies for addressing problems of growth or persistent inequalities in a globalized world.

Rethinking Race

Yet while South Africa may hold up a mirror, even a beacon, for the rest of the post-colonial world, it is also possible that South Africa's integration into global scholarly discourses could shed new light on South Africa. Ironically, that light may shine precisely on the area where South Africa has been considered most unique: The dynamics of race remain perhaps more unexplored in South Africa than anywhere else, and South African scholarship is only now beginning to problematize questions around the racial identities, racial politics, and racial formations that would appear so central to a divided society.

It is ironic that in a situation where racial differences have been so visible—and in a situation where complexities of racial identities and racial politics were played out in daily newspapers, as individuals confronted the tension between rigid legal racial categories and the more fluid reality of human lives—discussions about race have generally been left out of progressive scholarly work. For many social scientists, the omission reflected a conscious decision to avoid any link to the scientific racism so rampant in South African science. Although some of South Africa's most internationally renowned scholars demonstrated that racial categories cannot be physically defined (Tobias 1972), conservative white South African scientists were often deeply complicit in the reification of racial difference (Dubow 1995)—often to an absurd extreme, as when mining industry researchers experimented with different racial abilities to withstand heat, as if melanin somehow altered the fundamental functioning of the human body. And, of course, for many South African social scientists, racial identities hardly seemed problematic: Racial categories were so explicitly built into the legal and social framework that they seemed almost biological (van den Berghe 1978).

But even in South Africa, racial identities are fluid; racial politics are not set in stone, and racial dynamics merit more specific attention than they have often received. South African racial politics have not been static, but we have little sense of how and why they changed. Over time, we know that changing racial visions—among white nationalists, black consciousness activists, and nonracialists—were rooted in specific social movements, at specific conjunctures of South African history, but this area remains a fruitful site for further investigation (Greenstein 1993).

At the individual level, we have remarkably little sense of how South Africans experienced, responded to, or even challenged apartheid's rigid racial categories in their daily lives. Yet over the nearly fifty years that these categories carried legal implications, thousands of individuals were re-classified, either at their own behest or by official decree. Myriad complicated sagas of hidden relationships across "color lines," of corrupt officials and bribery, of "passing" and exposure—these issues underscore the social construction of race, both in terms of delineating categories and in terms of assigning social meaning to those categories. Yet few social scientists have thus far explored what this seamy underside of apartheid's neat schema meant for individuals, or how South Africans conceptualized or responded to the dilemmas posed by a messy reality. We know little that is not anecdotal or fictionalized about how people "passed" in more privileged racial categories, or, sometimes, rejected the possibility of "passing"; conversely, we have only a few faint glimpses of how people have managed to retain pride and culture in the face of white domination—or of the compromises made along the way. Similar questions can be asked of those classified "white": In the United States, some groups of immigrants found it easier to be included as "white" than did others (Roediger 1991), but we know little of those dynamics in South Africa. How did individuals deal with the contradictions created by classification: The situation of "poor whites," for example, or the "honorary white" status granted some people who might, in a less rigid system, have been called Japanese? Colonial racial categories must be dissected in relation to concerns over sexuality, class, and control (Stoler 1995), but these issues have scarcely been touched in South African historiography (see, however, McClintock 1995). Such questions cry out for serious inquiry—not, of course, the kind of fatuous generalization offered in work like Degler's 1971 study of Brazil's much-proclaimed but never substantiated "mulatto escape hatch," but a serious investigation of how individuals living under apartheid strategized, accommodated, and resisted the categorization that determined their life chances, and the racial domination that pervaded their lives.

At the more aggregate level, there is a crying need for more serious historical investigation of the construction of group political identities across apartheid's racial categories. As Omi & Winant (1986) have shown for the United States, racial identities are often malleable, as activists mobilize new constituencies to promote a racial political project in a specific setting. South Africa offers a remarkable setting to explore the tensions and obstacles to this process. Activists have long proclaimed unity among the "non-white" majority, especially since the Black Consciousness movement emerged in the 1970s, but in fact, these claims obscure real racial tensions within the "black" population. Incorporated on very different terms into South African society, people classified African, Indian, or Colored often express deep racial prejudice against other groups. Under apartheid, few anti-racist scholars were willing to even acknowledge such sentiments, fearing to reinforce divisions. But since the first democratic election, an explosion of new claims based largely on racial identities—claims to "real" indigeneity, to protected minority status, to restitution—has underscored the persistence of these divisions. Accepting the rhetoric of nonracialism, or the democratic fiction that all citizens are individuals with equal status, could create an explosive tinderbox for South Africa; conversely, understanding the underlying dynamics of how racialized group identities are constructed and maintained may be crucial to dealing with apartheid's divisive legacies.

These issues are not simply of historic interest. Without a better sense of the dynamics of race in South Africa—the lived dynamics, that is, not simply the legal categories described so often in discussions of apartheid—we have no way to conceptualize potential changes in the future. For now, we have no real sense of how racial patterns might change in the post-apartheid era, or how best reformers might seek to change them. In less than ten years, for example, a black elite has emerged in South Africa, staffing the top levels of the civil service and taking seats in corporate boardrooms; but we know little about the character of their interactions with white subordinates, or the extent to which racial hierarchies really change. How will white civil servants work with new black politicians? How will white South African mining managers respond to the new political context, as they restructure the mining process in the context of democratization and downsizing?

As yet, there are no studies of the impact of national affirmative action policies on racial hierarchies; we have only preliminary studies of persistent racial discrimination in hiring, training and promotion. Similarly, the remarkably complicated processes of South African school desegregation cry out for research: How do teachers raised under apartheid—and often deeply implicated in the racial thinking so prevalent in South African societies—deal with the problems of integration, when students come from wildly different backgrounds, different cultures, different languages? To what extent, and how, can universities challenge the racial hierarchies of skills and accreditation that have so long marked even the most liberal white institutions, when faculty remain committed to retaining "standards" developed under apartheid? These kinds of questions cry out for comparative studies. South Africa is hardly the first country to experience decolonization, or even to attempt redress for racial dispossession and discrimination in the context of consolidating a new democracy. Other experiences may well suggest new perspectives, new approaches to the challenges of confronting apartheid's multiple legacies.

But while comparisons are inevitable, they would be most useful if they employed a true comparative metric. South African scholars have moved away from the presumption that their society is unique, but they remain relatively eclectic in their approach to other cases. Throughout the democratic transition, academics and policy-makers have drawn selectively on examples from around the world, using comparisons to bolster an argument rather than to explore seriously the similarities and differences across cases. To help shed new light on South Africa, comparative studies will have to beware the danger of superficial comparisons that may obscure more than they illuminate.

Literature Cited

Abel R. 1995. *Politics by Other Means: Law in the Struggle against Apartheid, 1980–1994.* New York: Routledge

Adam H. 1971. *Modernizing Racial Domination: The Dynamics of South African Politics.* Berkeley: Univ. Calif. Press

Adam H, Moodley K. 1993. *Opening of the Apartheid Mind: Options for the New South Africa.* Berkeley: Univ. Calif. Press

Adler G, Webster E. 1996. Challenging transition theory: The labor movement, radical reform and transition to democracy in South Africa. *Polit. Soc.* 23(1):75–106

Arrighi G. 1973. Labour supplies in historical perspective: a study of the proletarianization of the African peasantry in Rhodesia. In *Essays in the Political Economy of Africa,* ed. G Arrighi, J Saul. New York: Monthly Rev.

Asmal K, Asmal L, Roberts R. 1997. *Reconciliation Through Truth: A Reckoning of Apartheid's Criminal Governance.* New York: St. Martin's Press

Atkins K. 1993. *The Moon is Dead! Give Us Our Money: The Cultural Origins of an African Work Ethic, Natal, South Africa, 1843–1900.* Portsmouth: Heinemann

Baker P, Alex Boraine A, Krafchick W, eds. 1993. *South Africa in the World Economy in the 1990s.* Cape Town: David Philip

Baskin J, ed. 1996. *Against the Current: Labour and Economic Policy in South Africa.* Johannesburg: Ravan

Beinart W, Bundy C. 1987. *Hidden Struggles in Rural South Africa: Politics and Popular Movements in the Transkei and Eastern Cape.* Johannesburg: Ravan

Berger I. 1992. *Threads of Solidarity: Women in South African Industry, 1900–1980.* Bloomington: Indiana Univ. Press

Berry S, 1993. *No Condition Is Permanent: The Social Dynamics of Agrarian Change in Sub-Saharan Africa.* Madison: Univ. Wisc. Press

Bonacich E. 1981. Capitalism and race relations in South Africa: a split-labor market analysis. *Polit. Power Soc. Theory* 2: 239–277

Bozzoli B, Nkotsoe M. 1991. *Women of Phokeng: Consciousness, Life Strategy, and Migrancy in South Africa, 1900–1993.* Johannesburg: Ravan

Bradford H. 1987. *A Taste of Freedom: The History of the ICU in South Africa.* New Haven: Yale Univ. Press

Bundy C. 1979. *The Rise and Fall of the South African Peasantry.* London: Heinemann

Burawoy M. 1977. The functions and reproduction of migrant labor: comparative material from Southern Africa and the United States. *Am. J. Sociol.* 81(5):1050–87

Burawoy M. 1981. The capitalist state in South Africa: Marxist and sociological perspectives on race and class. *Polit. Power Soc. Theory* 2:279–335

Callinicos L. 1987. The people's past: towards transforming the present. In *Class, Community and Conflict,* ed. B Bozzoli, pp. 44–64. Johannesburg: Ravan

Campbell J. 1995. *Songs of Zion: The African Methodist Episcopal Church in the United States and South Africa.* Oxford, UK: Oxford Univ. Press

Cell J. 1982. *The Highest Stage of White Supremacy: The Origins of Segregation in South Africa and the American South.* Cambridge, UK: Cambridge Univ. Press

Channock M. 1989. Neither customary nor legal: African customary law in an era of family law reform. *Int. J. Law Family* 3: 72–88

Clark NL. 1994. *Manufacturing Apartheid: State Corporations in South Africa.* New Haven: Yale Univ. Press

Cock J. 1989. *Maids and Madams: Domestic Workers Under Apartheid.* London: Women's Press

Cock J, Nathan L, eds. 1989. *Society at War: The Militarization of South Africa.* New York: St. Martin's Press

Commission to Investigate the Development of a Comprehensive Labour Policy, 1996. *Restructuring the South African Labour Market.* Pretoria: Government Printer

Commoroff J, Commoroff J. 1997. *Of Revelation and Revolution: The Dialectics of Modernity on a South African Frontier.* Vols 1 and 2. Chicago: Univ. Chicago Press

Cooper F. 1996. *Decolonization and African Society: The Labor Question in French and British Africa.* Cambridge, UK: Cambridge Univ. Press

Coplan D. 1995. *In the Time of Cannibals: The Word Music of South Africa's Basotho Migrants.* Chicago: Univ. Chicago Press

Crankshaw O. 1994. *Race, Class and the Changing Division of Labour Under Apartheid.* London: Routledge

Crapanzano V. 1985. *Waiting: The Whites of South Africa.* New York: Granada

Crush J, Jeeves A, Yudelman D. 1991. *South Africa's Labor Empire: A History of Black Migrancy to the Gold Mines.* Boulder, CO: Westview

Crush J, James W. eds.1995. *Crossing Boun-*

daries: Mine Migrancy in a Democratic South Africa. Cape Town: Inst. for Democracy in South Africa

Davies RH. 1979. Capital, State and White Labour in South Africa, 1900–1960: An Historical Materialist Analysis of Class Formation and Class Relations. Brighton, UK: Harvester

Degler C. 1971. Neither Black Nor White: Slavery and Race Relations in Brazil and the United States. New York: Macmillan

Dubow S. 1995. Scientific Racism in Modern South Africa. Cambridge, UK: Cambridge Univ. Press

Escobar A, Alvarez S, eds. 1992. The Making of Social Movements in Latin America. Boulder, CO: Westview

Evans I. 1997. Bureaucracy and Race: Native Administration in South Africa. Berkeley: Univ. Calif. Press

Evans P. 1995. Embedded Autonomy: States and Industrial Transformation. Princeton, NJ: Princeton Univ. Press

Fredrickson G. 1981. White Supremacy: A Comparative Study in American and South African History. Oxford, UK: Oxford Univ. Press

Frederickson G. 1995. Black Liberation: A Comparative History of Black Ideologies in the United States and South Africa. Oxford, UK: Oxford Univ. Press

Freund B. 1988. The African Worker. Cambridge, UK: Cambridge Univ. Press

Freund B. 1993. South African gold mining in transformation. In South Africa's Economic Crisis, ed. S Gelb. Cape Town: David Philip

Gerhardt G. 1978. Black Power in South Africa: The Evolution of an Ideology. Berkeley: Univ. Calif. Press

Greenberg SB. 1980. Race and State in Capitalist Development. New Haven: Yale Univ. Press

Greenberg SB. 1987. Legitimating the Illegitimate: State, Markets and Resistance in Suth Africa. Berkeley: Univ. Calif. Press

Greenstein R. 1995. Genealogies of Conflict: Class, Identity and State in Palestine/Israel and South Africa. Hanover: Wesleyan Univ. Press

Greenstein R. 1993. Racial formation: towards a comparative study of collective identities in South Africa and the United States. Soc. Dynamics 19(2):1–29

Greenstein R. ed. 1997. Comparative Perspectives on South Africa. London: Macmillan

Griffiths A. 1997. In the Shadow of Marriage: Gender and Justice in an African Community. Chicago: Univ. Chicago Press

Guimaraes SP. 1996. South Africa and Brazil: Risks and Opportunities in the Turmoil of Globalization. Rio de Janeiro: CNPq and IPRI

Guy J, Thabane M. 1988. Technology, ethnicity and ideology: Basotho miners and shaft-sinking on the South African Gold Mines. J. Southern African Stud. 14:2: 257–78

Hamilton C. 1998. Terrific Majesty: The Powers of Shaka Zulu and the Limits of Historical Invention. Cambridge, MA: Harvard Univ. Press

Harries P.1994. Work, Culture, and Identity: Migrant Laborers in Mozambique and South Africa, c. 1860–1910. Portsmouth, NH: Heinemann

Hobsbawn E, Ranger T, eds. 1983. The Invention of Tradition. Cambridge, UK: Cambridge Univ. Press

James WG, ed. 1987. The State of Apartheid. Boulder, CO: Lynne Reiners

James WG. 1992. Our Precious Metal: African Labour in South Africa's Gold Industry, 1970–1990. Bloomington: Indiana Univ. Press

Jelin E, Hershberg E, eds. 1996. Constructing Democracy: Human Rights, Citizenship and Society in Latin America. Boulder, CO: Westview

Joffe A, Kaplan D, Kaplinsky R, Lewis D. 1993. Meeting the global challenge: a framework for industrial revival in South Africa. In South Africa in the World Economy in the 1990s, ed. P. Baker, A. Borraine, W Krafchik. Cape Town: David Philip

Johnstone F. 1976. Class, Race and Gold: A Study of Class Relations and Racial Discrimination in South Africa. London: Routledge & Kegan Paul

Klug H. 1995. Defining the property rights of others: political power, indigenous tenure and the construction of customary land law. J. Legal Pluralism and Unofficial Law 35:119–48

Lambert R, Webster E. 1988. The reemergence of political unionism in contemporary South Africa? In Popular Struggles in South Africa, ed. W. Cobbett. New Jersey: Africa World Press

Landau P. 1995. The Realm of the Word: Language, Gender and Christianity in a Southern African Kingdom. Portsmouth, NH: Heinemann

Lazerson J. 1994. Against the Tide: Whites in the Struggle Against Apartheid. Boulder, CO: Westview

Leger JP, Nicol M. 1991. Gold Mining in South Africa: Priorities for Restructuring. Working Paper Number 1. Univ. Cape Town, Econ. Trends Res. Group, Dev. Policy Res. Unit

Levy N.1982. *The Foundations of the South African Cheap Labour System.* London: Routledge & Kegan Paul

Lipton M. 1986. *Capitalism and Apartheid: South Africa 1910–1986.* Cape Town: David Philip

Lodge T. 1983. *Black Politics in South Africa Since 1945.* Johannesburg: Ravan

Mamdani M. 1996. *Citizen and Subject: Contemporary Africa and the Legacy of Late Colonialism.* Princeton, NJ: Princeton Univ. Press.

Mare G. 1992. *Brothers Born of Warrior Blood: Politics and Ethnicity in South Africa.* Johannesburg: Ravan

Marks S. 1986. *The Ambiguities of Dependence: Class, Nationalism and the State in Twentieth Century Natal.* Baltimore, MD: Johns Hopkins Press

Martin W. 1983. Cycles, trends or transformations? Black labor migration to the South African gold mines. In *Labor in the Capitalist World-Economy,* ed. C Bergquist. Beverley Hills: Sage Press

Marx A. 1992. *Lessons of Struggle: South African Internal Opposition, 1960–1990.* Oxford, UK: Oxford Univ. Press

Massey D, Denton N. 1993. *American Apartheid: Segregation and the Making of the Underclass.* Cambridge, MA: Harvard Univ. Press

Mayekiso M. 1996. *Township Politics: Civic Struggles for a New South Africa,* ed. Patrick Bon. New York: Monthly Rev.

McClintock A. 1995. *Imperial Leather: Race, Gender and Sexuality in the Colonial Context.* New York: Routledge

Miles R.1993. *Racism after 'Race Relations'.* London: Routledge

Moodie TD, Ndatshe V. 1994. *Going for Gold: Men, Mines, and Migration.* Berkeley: Univ. Calif. Press

Murray C. 1992. *Black Mountain: Land, Class and Power in the Eastern Orange Free State, 1800s to 1980s.* Johannesburg: Univ. the Witwatersrand Press for the Int. African Inst., London.

Murray M. 1987. *South Africa: Time of Agony, Time of Destiny.* London: Verso

Murray M. 1994. *Revolution Deferred: The Painful Birth of Post-Apartheid South Africa.* London: Verso

O'Meara D. 1983. *Volkscapitalisme: Class, Capital and Ideology in the Development of Afrikaner Nationalism,* 1934–1948. Johannesburg: Ravan

Omi M, Winant H. 1986. *Racial Formation in the United States from the 1960s to the 1980s.* New York: Routledge & Kegan Paul

Patel E, ed. 1994. *Worker Rights: From Apart-*

heid to Democracy—What Role for Organized Labour? Johannesburg: Juta

Peires JB. 1989. *The Dead Will Arise: Nongqawuse and the Great Xhosa Cattle-killing Movement of 1856–7.* Bloomington: Indiana Univ. Press

Portes A, Borocz J. 1989. Contemporary immigration: theoretical perspectives on its determinants and modes of incorporation. *Int. Migration Rev.* 23 (3):606–28

Posel D. 1991. *The Making of Apartheid: Conflict and Compromise.* Oxford, UK: Clarendon

Price R. 1991. *The Apartheid State in Crisis.* New York: Oxford Univ. Press

Przeworski A. 1991. *Democracy and the Market.* Cambridge, UK: Cambridge Univ. Press

Ramphele M. 1993. *A Bed Called Home: Life in the Migrant Hostels of Cape Town.* Athens: Ohio Univ. Press

Rex J. 1971. The plural society: the South African case. *Race* 12:4

Roediger D. 1991. *The Wages of Whiteness: Race and the Making of the American Working Class.* London: Verso

Seidman G. 1994. *Manufacturing Militance: Workers' Movements in Brazil and South Africa, 1970–1985.* Berkeley: Univ. Calif. Press

Seidman, G. 1999. Gendered citizenship: South Africa's democratic transition and the construction of a gendered state. *Gender Soc.* Forthcoming

Simons J, Simons R. 1983. *Class and Color in South Africa.* London: Int. Defense and Aid. 2nd ed.

Stoler A. 1995. *Race and the Education of Desire: Foucault's History of Sexuality and the Colonial Order of Things.* Durham, NC: Duke Univ. Press

Tobias P. 1972. *The Meaning of Race.* Johannesburg: South African Inst. of Race. 2nd. ed. Relations

Vail L, ed. 1991. *The Creation of Tribalism in Southern Africa.* Berkeley: Univ. Calif. Press

Valenzuela JS. 1989. Labor movements in transitions to democracy. *Compar. Polit.* 2194:445–472

Van den Berghe P. 1978. Race and ethnicity: a sociobiological perspective. *Ethnic Racial Stud.* 1(4):402–11

Van Onselen C. 1982. *Studies in the Social and Economic History of the Witwatersrand, 1886–1914.* 2 vols. London: Longman

Van Onselen C. 1996. *The Seed Is Mine: The Life of Kas Maine, a South African Sharecropper 1894–1985.* Cape Town: David Philip

Van Zyl Slabbert F.1992. *The Quest for Democracy: South Africa in Transition*. London: Penguin

Walker C. 1990. Gender and the development of the migrant labor system, c. 1850–1930. In *Women and Gender in Southern Africa to 1945*, ed. C. Walker, 168–196. London: James Currey

Webster E. 1985. *Cast in a Racial Mould: Labor Process and Trade Unionism in the Foundries*. Johannesburg: Ravan

Wilmsen E. 1989. *Land Filled with Flies: A Political Economy of the Kalahari*. Chicago: Univ. Chicago Press

Wolpe H. 1972. Capitalism and cheap labour—power in South Africa: from segregation to apartheid. *Econ. Soc.* 111: 425–56

Younis M. 1999. *Liberation and Democratization: The South African and Palestinian Freedom Movments*. Minneapolis: Univ. Minnesota Press. Forthcoming

Annu. Rev. Sociol. 1999. 25:441–66

POLITICS AND INSTITUTIONALISM:
Explaining Durability and Change

Elisabeth S. Clemens and James M. Cook

Department of Sociology, University of Arizona, Tucson, Arizona 85721;
e-mail:clemens@u.arizona.edu, jcook@u.arizona.edu

KEY WORDS: institutional theory, politics, social change

ABSTRACT

From the complex literatures on "institutionalisms" in political science and sociology, various components of institutional change are identified: mutability, contradiction, multiplicity, containment and diffusion, learning and innovation, and mediation. This exercise results in a number of clear prescriptions for the analysis of politics and institutional change: disaggregate institutions into schemas and resources; decompose institutional durability into processes of reproduction, disruption, and response to disruption; and, above all, appreciate the multiplicity and heterogeneity of the institutions that make up the social world. Recent empirical work on identities, interests, alternatives, and political innovation illustrates how political scientists and sociologists have begun to document the consequences of institutional contradiction and multiplicity and to trace the workings of institutional containment, diffusion, and mediation.

INTRODUCTION

Institutions endure. As a reaction against methodological individualism, technological determinism, and behavioralist models that highlight the flux of individual action or choice (March & Olsen 1989), the resurgence of institutional analysis in recent years has forcefully reminded social scientists of the significance of this "relative permanence of a distinctly social sort" (Hughes 1936:180, Zucker 1988:25). Observing that organizations and nation-states resemble one another more than one would predict given their different circumstances (DiMaggio & Powell 1983, Meyer & Rowan 1977, Meyer et al 1977),

441

institutionalist analyses have developed compelling explanations for the relative absence of variation across cases or over time. Institutional arguments may also explain persistent differences, as when national industrial policies toward comparable technical issues consistently diverge (Dobbin 1994). In both instances, the core theoretical insight is the same: The patterning of social life is not produced solely by the aggregation of individual and organizational behavior but also by institutions that structure action.

This important contribution has generated new puzzles. One challenge follows from institutionalism's emphasis on enduring constraint. Institutions, it too often seems, "explain everything until they explain nothing" (Thelen & Steinmo 1992:15). Insofar as institutional arguments maintain that variation and change are minimized, those same arguments are ill-suited to the explanation of change (North 1981, Orren & Skowronek 1994, Powell 1991: 183–200). A second challenge is to determine the locus of change. Insofar as institutional change happens, where and when is it most probable and why?

These questions are particularly relevant for political sociologists. In organizational and economic sociology, "institution" is often taken to mean formal law and state organizations (e.g. Congress, the Department of Agriculture) or the models of organization they embody. Consequently, the resurgence of interest in institutional analysis signals an opportunity for a more expansive conversation among these subfields. Yet the capacity of these "institutions" to constrain political action and policy variation appears to marginalize the processes of conflict and innovation that are central to politics (Campbell 1998, DiMaggio 1988, Hicks 1995, Hirsch & Lounsbury 1997, Stryker 1999). This concern has been directed with greatest force toward that sociologically rooted "new institutionalism" which has become predominantly (although not necessarily) associated with the constitutive role of culturally legitimate models of organization and action (e.g. DiMaggio & Powell 1983, 1991, Meyer & Rowan 1977). For political sociologists, therefore, the renewed interest in institutions constitutes a faustian bargain. Wider attention to political entities such as the state or law comes at the price of obscuring political processes.

This dilemma, we argue, results from the tendency to equate institutions with stability or durability. For many political scientists and sociologists, the massively reinforced and embedded array of the state exemplifies the concept of institution. Given the image of the state as concrete, powerful, and constraining, change is most easily understood as the product of some sort of exogenous shock that disrupts an established order (Krasner 1984, Thelen & Steinmo 1992:15). If, on the other hand, institutions are understood as self-sustaining higher-order effects (Jepperson 1991; Zucker 1977; on institutional self-replication, Stinchcombe 1968:108–18; on the reproduction of structure, Sewell 1992:19), theories about the sources of stability and instability can be developed and tested.

Rather than focusing on the trait of durability, this second formulation raises questions about reliable reproduction, potential sources of change, and responses to disruption. This approach also requires a disaggregation of the capacity of institutions to constrain and constitute action. This change in focus is indicated by the substitution of "institutional" for "state-centered" in the theoretical language of political sociology (Orloff 1993:41); the distinction between state-centered and societal accounts of policy development has been blurred by the recognition that policies themselves may induce interests (Moe 1987:281–83, Pierson 1994:27–50). In their efforts to conceptualize the interrelationships between political actors and institutions, many scholars have turned to the dualistic terms of "structuration theory" (Archer 1988, Giddens 1984, Sewell 1992) to distinguish both the "virtual" aspects of institutions—the model, template, or schema—and the resources, interactions, and interpretive processes that make that pattern self-sustaining.

These theoretical reformulations have generated an increasingly rich appreciation of the conditions, mechanisms, and processes that account for durability and change in political institutions. Disaggregation of the monolithic entity of "the state" also facilitates exchanges with institutionalist arguments developed in organizational analysis, social psychology, and simulation studies of social dynamics. In the sections that follow, we first survey the complicated definitional terrain of "institutionalism" and then sketch the components of change that emerge from the recent literature in political science and sociology: mutability, contradiction, multiplicity, containment and diffusion, learning and innovation, and mediation.

This exercise results in a number of clear prescriptions for the analysis of institutional change: disaggregate institutions into schemas and resources; decompose institutional durability into processes of reproduction, disruption, and response to disruption; and, above all, appreciate the multiplicity and heterogeneity of the institutions that make up the social world (Friedland & Alford 1991; see also Clemens 1997:45–59, 1999; Orren & Skowronek 1994). Recent empirical work demonstrates how these institutional processes generate both durability and change, although mutability remains relatively unexplored. Under the banners of the "new institutionalisms," political scientists and sociologists have begun to document the consequences of institutional contradiction and multiplicity and to trace processes of containment, diffusion, innovation, and mediation.

WHAT IS AN INSTITUTION? AND WHY DO INSTITUTIONS ENDURE?

The enemy of my enemy is my friend. This basic political dynamic underlies much of the complexity of the current institutional turn across the social sciences. The common "enemy" was provided by the dominance of reductionist, behaviorist, methodologically individualist, and functionalist arguments in social science theory in the decades following World War II (March & Olsen 1989). Against this background, efforts to reassert the significance of "higher order" constraints or influences on action developed in numerous disciplines (for reviews, see DiMaggio & Powell 1991, Hall & Taylor 1996, Scott 1995, Thelen & Steinmo 1992). Faced with regularities where a purely individualistic, instrumental model of action would predict instability, rational choice theorists in political science directed attention to conventions, such as the committee system in Congress, that help to solve collective action problems (see Shepsle & Weingast 1987, Moe 1987 on the "positive theory of institutions"). A related "choice-within-constraint" framework has claimed the title of "the new institutionalism in sociology" (in contrast to the "new institutionalism in organizational analysis"); here the emphasis is on exploring the interrelationships among formal rules, informal norms, social networks, and purposive action (Brinton & Nee 1998).

Within political science and sociology, a part of the reaction against methodological individualism took the forms of neo-Marxist and neo-Weberian theories of the (relative) autonomy of the state (e.g. Nordlinger 1981, O'Connor 1973, Skocpol 1979, 1985), which in turn fueled a vibrant, interdisciplinary return to institutional and policy history (March & Olsen 1984, 1989, Skocpol 1992, Skowronek 1982). Confronted with the persistent divergence of national policy responses to similar political challenges, comparativists in political science, history, and sociology also called for renewed attention to the state and other institutions that structure political decision-making and conflict (Dobbin 1994, Hall 1986, Katzenstein 1985, Steinmo et al 1992). Intrigued by the unanticipated uniformity of firms in the modern economy and of nations within the world polity, sociologists argued for the power of taken-for-granted or legitimate models (rather than solely instrumental calculations) in shaping patterns of action and organization (DiMaggio & Powell 1983, Meyer & Rowan 1977). But although each of these literatures had a distinctive intellectual lineage, all concurred in claiming the label "institutional."

Faced with this abundance of theoretical claims, each empirically plausible, many commentators have enumerated the differences between old and new institutionalisms as well as among the multiplying "new institutionalisms" (DiMaggio & Powell 1991, Hall & Taylor 1996, Scott 1995, Stinchcombe 1997). Others bemoan the lack of familiarity among institutional approaches and called for disciplined eclecticism (Campbell 1998, Ethington & McDonagh 1995, Finnemore 1996, Hall & Taylor 1996, Koelble 1995). In this latter spirit, we privilege a basic definition over the familiar distinctions among institutions as constraining or constitutive, as operating through regulative, normative, or cognitive mechanisms: Institutions exert patterned higher-order effects on the actions, indeed the constitution, of individuals and organizations without requiring repeated collective mobilization or authoritative intervention to achieve these regularities (Jepperson 1991). Marriage, money, and the corporate form are institutions to the extent that these models of social relations and exchange are reliably reproduced through the actions of individuals and groups without requiring either repeated authoritative intervention or collective mobilization.

Such reliable higher-order effects have been attributed to distinct mechanisms, none mutually exclusive. First, institutions may negatively constrain action, define opportunity, and facilitate patterns of interaction. Here the imagery is architectural or maze-like, echoing Hobbes' claim that "the use of Lawes . . . is not to bind the People from all voluntary actions; but to direct and keep them in such a motion, as not to hurt themselves by their own impetuous desires, rashnesse, or indiscretion, as Hedges are set, not to stop Travellers, but to keep them in the way" ([1651] 1968:388). In this formulation, desires and interests are conceptually distinct from institutions (although institutions may also shape preferences; see Steinmo 1993, Wildavsky 1987). Political scientists have tended to adopt this sense of institution as external constraint, as a schema massively embedded in resources for social control rather than internalized by well-socialized actors (on the conceptual alternative of "institution as equilibrium," see Calvert 1995). Retaining a strong sense of the political actor as institutionally underdetermined (Hicks 1995:1226, Smith 1988: 90–96), these analyses conceptualize institutions as configurations of rules and resources either inherited from the past (Thelen & Steinmo 1992) or constructed to solve collective action or decision-making problems (Shepsle & Weingast 1987). Although differing in the prominence of instrumental action and explicit bargaining or design in their accounts of institutional origins, both variants conceptualize institutions as "humanly devised constraints that shape human interaction" (North 1990:3). Institutions endure to the extent that they are not disrupted by exogenous shocks such as war or so long as shifts in other opportunities do not lead individual actors and coalitions to defect from institutionalized arrangements.

Institutions may also provide positive models for how to do something. Approaches that predominate in sociology conceive of institutions as models, schemas, or scripts for behavior. Consequently, institutions endure because these models become "taken for granted" through repeated use and interaction (Berger & Luckmann 1967, DiMaggio & Powell 1991:19–22) or "legitimate" through the endorsement of some authoritative or powerful individual or organization (Meyer & Rowan 1977). Institutions are understood as models that provide substantive guides for practical action. Institutions are durable to the extent that these models are reinforced through socialization or interaction or legitimation while alternative scripts remain unimaginable. The distinctions between normative and cognitive variants are necessarily blurred insofar as the process of institutionalization, as understood by ethnomethodologists, "is one in which the moral becomes factual" (Zucker 1977:726). Although the cognitive or cultural emphasis in institutional analysis is often linked to the charge that institutionalism is apolitical, the processual question of how social arrangements and beliefs come to be taken for granted resonates with political theorists' articulation of a "third level of power": "the means through which power influences, shapes or determines conceptions of the necessities, possibilities, and strategies of challenge in situations of latent conflict" (Gaventa 1980:15, see also Lukes 1974).

Both theoretical models may account for the same empirical observations. If a mouse repeatedly takes the same path across a table, this regular pattern may be due to either to the presence of a maze that obstructs many possible changes in direction or to effective socialization through behavior modification. However, since the mouse may be well-socialized *and* in a maze, these "institutionalisms" are properly understood as complements, rather than as mutually exclusive explanations. Recognition of the multiple sources of regular patterns in social life has the further advantage of allowing one to conceptualize institutional durability as a continuous variable. Given a well-built maze and thoroughly conditioned mouse, one would not expect the mouse to deviate from the appointed path; given a less sturdy maze and a mouse bent on escape, the outcome is less certain.

The theoretical literature employs varied combinations of these two basic images of institutions: the first constraining and proscriptive, the second constitutive and prescriptive. One strategy has been to sort the social world into domains governed by noninstitutional "instrumental logics" or technical considerations and those governed by "logics of appropriateness" (March & Olsen 1989, Meyer et al 1983). This approach is undermined, however, by the increasing recognition of the socially constructed character of technical rationality (Espeland 1998, Porter 1995) as well as by attention to how actors perceive and interpret information (North 1995, Ikegami 1995:340). The once-stark lines between rational choice (the "positive theory of institutions") and historical or cultural institutional analyses have been eroded by the elaboration of a "choice-theoretic" or "choice-within-constraints" version of institutional theory, which adopts a culturally or contextually nuanced sense of "thick rationality" (Nee 1998:10–11). Network analysis has also diminished the distinction between these imageries. Networks may generate durable ties and practices through constitutive processes of social interaction or by shaping the opportunities and obstacles to exchange and cooperate (Nee & Ingram 1998, Powell 1991:190, Zucker 1988:29). From many directions, the development of institutional analysis has muted the conventional distinctions among institutionalisms.

Rather than highlighting the theoretical differences among these arguments, the tales of a mouse in a maze underscore the multiple dimensions of institutional durability. Given that regular patterns of social action may be produced by external constraints or internalized models, those regularities will be stronger to the extent that these multiple sources of regularity coincide and reinforce one another. In light of the potential for complex interactions among institutional processes (Stryker 1994, 1999), the following discussions are organized around the outcomes that combine to produce institutional durability and change: reproduction, disruption, and responses to disruption.

COMPONENTS OF INSTITUTIONAL CHANGE: REPRODUCTION AND DISRUPTION

Following the resurgence of interest in institutional theory, scholars soon faced the puzzle of explaining institutional change. Initial arguments stressed the alternation of stable institutions and dramatic change, a tempo captured in Krasner's (1984) appropriation of the evolutionary concept of "punctuated equilibrium." In this formulation, institutions are stable until disrupted by some force exogenous to the institutional system itself (see Sewell 1992:3, 16): war or global economic changes may disrupt national regimes, new laws may disrupt institutionalized economic arrangements (Fligstein 1990).

Recent work has greatly refined the causal imagery of some external force or legislative deus ex machina smacking into stable institutional arrangements and creating indeterminacy. Historical analyses demonstrate how choices among institutional arrangements may be "constitutive moments" or branching points that channel subsequent political and economic developments (Berk 1994, Rothstein 1992, 1998). At the same time, the concrete imagery of "state as [relatively autonomous] structure" is increasingly replaced by an understanding of institutions as constituted by a cultural component (variously labeled a model, schema, template, or rule) embedded in, or sustained by, or enacted through resources and/or social networks (see Archer 1988, Giddens 1984, Sewell 1992; for alternative formulations of "culture as a resource" see Pedriana & Stryker 1997:638–42). This distinction between schemas and resources provides a framework for thinking about sources of institutional change: within or among schemas; within or among resources; or between schemas and resources. The second of these has received little attention to date, but analyses of institutional change offer multiple variations on the first and last possibilities. Schemas may be more or less mutable; they may embody internal contradictions; or multiple schemas or institutional rules may be potentially relevant to a context for action. Within an existing system of institutional rules, resources and networks may contain variations or facilitate diffusion;

they may support learning or innovation, thereby incrementally altering schemas; or they may mediate the impact of exogenous shocks and environmental changes on institutions.

Schemas and Institutional Change

Cognitive, cultural, or normative variants of institutional theory typically emphasize the role of existing models·or scripts in shaping behavior, particularly but far from exclusively under conditions of uncertainty. But variation is rarely addressed in such arguments. Are there characteristics of models, or the conditions under which they are adopted, that produce more or less reliable reproduction of established templates? Focusing on the role of established schemas in maintaining institutional stability, this section addresses three possible sources of change: mutability, internal contradictions, and multiplicity.

MUTABILITY   Although much political analysis concerns the change from one sort of institutional order or regime to another, a more fundamental form of institutional change involves the loss of order or growth of social entropy (Zucker 1988). Reliable reproduction in the face of stochastic change is thus central to the concept of institution: "institutions are those social patterns that, when chronically reproduced, owe their survival to relatively self-activating social processes" (Jepperson 1991:145).

At the most basic level, some sets of rules or models of action may be more mutable than others. For example, Crawford & Ostrom (1995:583) begin with the concept of an *institutional statement*, "a shared linguistic constraint or opportunity that prescribes, permits, or advises actions or outcomes for actors (both individual and corporate)." Such statements about "shared strategies" of action specify to whom the statement applied; for what purposes; under what conditions; with what sanctions; and whether the statement must, must not, or may be followed. Clear implications for institutional mutability may be derived from the last of these components. If followed, an exclusively "must" set of institutional rules would maximize accurate reproduction; a set of "must not" rules would function as Hobbes' hedges, predicting only the boundaries of what is doable; and a thoroughly "may" set would minimize the institutional determination of social action promoting mutation and innovation.

Institutional statements that neither demand nor prohibit a particular behavior promote heterogeneity of action. Actors relate to institutional rules as a repertoire or tool kit (Clemens 1997, Minkoff 1994, Swidler 1986) of alternative models or schemas. The presence of alternatives lessens the institutional determination of action while also facilitating innovation through recombination. Haveman & Rao (1997:1620) demonstrate that in an environment of multiple competing institutional mandates, hybrid forms can emerge that combine various properties of competing models. Thus, the contrasts among "must," "must not," and "may" systems of statements illuminate one dimension of variation in the capacity of institutional arrangements to sustain reliable reproduction.

INTERNAL CONTRADICTIONS   Building on a biological analogy, mutability may be understood as stochastic. Social theory, however, frequently asserts that change is determined by the character of prior arrangements, specifically by their internal contradictions. Captured most forcefully in the concept of the dialectic, this insight highlights the instabilities inherent in certain systems of belief or practice. Often, these instabilities unfold developmentally, as when the faculty–graduate student relationship designed to produce new colleagues must be transformed from a supervisory into a collegial relationship; the success of the first institutional arrangement requires its own transformation. Analogous dynamics are invoked in analyses of political mobilization and formal institutions. Models or scripts for behavior may be appropriate in one situation, yet dysfunctional in the new conditions brought about by following the script. Mass membership movements that successfully disrupt existing institutions may be superseded by leadership movements that exploit the openings produced by that disruption (Schwartz 1976); presidential candidates who present themselves as loyal party members in order to secure the nomination then seek to use the autonomous powers of the presidency to succeed on the terms of that office (Skowronek 1993).

In accounts of macrohistorical change, the power of internal contradiction is most associated with Marxian dialectics. And, like capitalism, institutions may produce their own grave-diggers. Citizenship classifications used to administer empires or federations may construct "minorities" or "nationalities" that become the basis for challenges to the rule of the central state (Anderson 1983, Brubaker 1996). Policies that require workers to fund their own insurance through unions may strengthen those unions as the organizational base of a politicized working class (Rothstein 1992). To the extent that institutional arrangements embody contradictions or generate challengers, reliable reproduction will be less likely.

MULTIPLICITY   Institutional contradictions may be fully internal to a particular model for social action, but they may also be generated by tensions among multiple institutions (Sewell 1992:16–19). In the absence of alternatives—or due to the failure to perceive or conceive of them—institutional arrangements generate regularities in social action and may become "taken for granted." This ethnomethodological precept has clear parallels in political analyses. Revolution becomes possible once institutions, however fragile or robust, are no longer perceived as inevitable (Stinchcombe 1978:40; on "cognitive liberation," see McAdam 1982:48–51).

Yet what are the conditions under which what was once taken for granted comes to be perceived as less than inevitable? For Gramsci, hegemony was continually challenged by the contradiction between two theoretical consciousnesses: "one which is implicit in his activity and which in reality unites him with all his fellow-workers in the practical transformation of the real world; and one, superficially explicit or verbal, which he has inherited from the past and uncritically absorbed" (1971:333). The existence of multiple institutions (e.g. competing models of authority or exchange) can have similar consequences. Beginning with a description of role strain, Eckstein (1966: 234) emphasizes disjuncture as a source of instability and congruence as a source of stability: "a government will tend to be stable if its authority pattern is congruent with the other authority patterns of the society of which it is a party." The same insight informs the imagery of peripheries, margins, borderlands, and interstices in accounts of institutional change (Clemens 1997: 92–93, Mann 1986:15–19, Morrill 1999). Whether one assumes instrumental actors constrained by institutions or well-socialized actors who have internalized schemas, action becomes less predictable where multiple institutions compete or no institution is firmly established.

Resources, Schemas, and Change

Mutability, internal contradictions, and multiplicity do not automatically produce significant change. The consequences of variation in reliable reproduction for institutional change are powerfully conditioned by the extent to which those variations are contained, diffused, or mediated. Here, prospects for institutional change are powerfully shaped by the interaction of schemas with social networks and other resources in processes of diffusion, innovation, and mediation. As will be evident, these factors interact in diverse ways, suggesting the complex topography of institutional change.

CONTAINMENT AND DIFFUSION   Attention to networks provides one account for minimizing mutability. Zucker (1988:31) argues that the density of network ties enhances the reinforcement of existing institutions, rendering social systems more stable and coherent. Experimental and simulation studies sustain these claims, demonstrating that processes of social influence are more effective and durable when cognitive claims are embedded in quite minimal attributions of organizational hierarchy or legitimation (Zucker 1977) or in systems of social ties (Carley 1989, 1991).

In the absence of exogenous disturbances, therefore, institutional reproduction should be most reliable when (*a*) institutional statements are nondiscretionary and substantive ("must" statements); (*b*) social heterogeneity is minimized (Blau & Schwartz 1984, Carley 1991, Suitor & Keeton 1997), and (*c*) social ties are dense and rarely extend across significant social distances (Carley 1989, Feld 1981, Mark 1998). Conversely, institutional change will be highest when (*a*) models of action are understood to be discretionary, (*b*) social heterogeneity is high, and (*c*) social networks are fragmented and cross important social cleavages. In their study of political centralization in Renaissance Florence, Padgett & Ansell (1993) present a striking analysis of how the Medici harnessed disjunctures among elite networks and controlled their own followers by segregating ties based on marriage and economic relationships.

Dense network ties also establish the conditions for maintaining order and punishing defectors from institutional arrangements (North 1990:36–40). Grief et al (1995) demonstrate how the ability of merchant guilds to provide security for long distance trade against the predations of foreign rulers depended on the existence of densely connected merchant communities capable of punishing any individual who traded with an untrustworthy ruler. Adams (1996) argues that the Dutch East India company used its monopoly on trade with the metropole to control its agents in the colony; with the development of the British trading empire in India, would-be defectors or entrepreneurs had alternative opportunities to structure the terms of trade.

Network ties may also facilitate the diffusion of institutions (Strang & Meyer 1993, Strang & Soule 1998). Extensive literatures on the adoption of the model of the nation-state within the world polity (e.g. Meyer et al 1992, Strang 1990, Strang & Chang 1993), of policy adoption across subnational units (Soule & Zylan 1997), and of organizational responses to changes in law (e.g. Dobbin et al 1994, Edelman 1990, Sutton et al 1994, Tolbert & Zucker 1983) demonstrate how ties, connectedness, visibility, and proximity facilitate the adoption of new organizational forms or policies (for a review, see Schneiberg & Clemens 1999).

Insofar as networks may facilitate either containment or diffusion, the juxtaposition of these studies raises a basic question. Under what conditions do social networks have the homeostatic properties associated with feedback models and historicist explanations (Stinchcombe 1968:103–20)? And under what conditions do networks propagate initially small variations producing path-dependent trajectories of social change (North 1990:93–98)?

LEARNING AND INNOVATION   The content of institutions can change over time as a result of learning as well as of variation and diffusion. Within the constraints imposed by particular technological or economic configurations, actors can modify institutions to solve new problems, to facilitate network-based collective learning, or to achieve increasing efficiency (March 1991, Powell et al 1996, Thelen 1991). The path of learning, while conditioned by previous cognitive models (Heclo 1974), can also involve trial and error experimentation taking old rules in new directions (Levitt & March 1988). Zhou (1993) argues that insofar as organizational learning tends toward a greater fit with environmental demands over time, new organizations and those in chang-ing environments should display more learning-based change.

Diffusion processes may also spur innovation as actors seek to accommo-date newly adopted institutional rules to existing practices, resources, and competing schemas (Campbell 1988:382–83, Soysal 1994, Stryker 1999, Westney 1987). Such efforts entail the "transposition" of dispositions (Bour-dieu 1977) or schemas to new settings: "Knowledge of a rule or schema by definition means the ability to transpose or extend it creatively. If this is so, then *agency*, . . . the capacity to transpose and extend schemas to new contexts, is inherent in the knowledge of cultural schemas that characterizes all mini-mally competent members of society" (Sewell 1992:18). But such recombina-tions of schema and context may produce innovation. The greater the muta-bility or multiplicity of institutional arrangements, the more likely that such efforts to transpose models and embed them in different social networks or resources will disrupt reliable reproduction.

While experimentation may be an important part of institutional change, not all actors are equally likely to experiment. Groups marginal to the political system are more likely to tinker with institutions for two reasons. Denied the social benefits of current institutional configurations, marginal groups have fewer costs associated with deviating from those configurations (Leblebici et al 1991, Stearns & Allan 1996). Challengers may innovate with the aim of us-ing an alternative model of mobilization or policy to gain access to the polity (Clemens 1993, Hirsch 1986, Morrill 1999, Schneiberg 1998). Mutability and multiplicity enhance the stock of alternative schemas available to be trans-posed to new efforts; internal contradictions increase the probability that chal-lengers will exist to exploit these alternatives.

INSTITUTIONAL MEDITATION   In addition to contributing to an endogenous model of institutional change, contradiction and multiplicity usefully compli-cate the analysis of exogenous shock. To the extent that homogeneity and an absence of alternatives figure prominently in our understandings of institu-tional stability, decreases in heterogeneity will increase the relative impor-tance of exogenous shock as a source of change (Stryker 1999). In addition, exogenous changes may either intensify or dissipate contradictions within ex-isting institutions. Consider the dilemma of a newly elected president caught between a debt to the party organization for a successful campaign and a desire to demonstrate presidential greatness by striking out in new directions; in this dilemma, a crisis may actually delay the realization of the inevitable contradic-tion (Skowronek 1993:263). Events may also "disrupt the operative systems of ideas, beliefs, values, roles, and institutional practices of a given society" cre-ating a space in which political actors struggle to reestablish interpretive frames for multiple audiences (Ellingson 1995:103). Here again, heterogeneity enhances the fragility of organizing ideological templates: "The simultaneous existence of many collective action frames makes them more vulnerable to disconfirming evidence than scientific paradigms, because constituents have the option of turning to competing frames" (Babb 1996:1034).

Exogenous shocks or environmental changes may have effects by altering the salience of institutions or their relationship to domains of social life. The impact of swings in public opinion or the mobilization of new constituent groups is mediated by the openness of political systems to these changes (Amenta et al 1992, Amenta et al 1994, Amenta 1998). Using a resource dependency analysis, Sparrow (1996) compares multiple policy domains to demonstrate how ties of dependence either magnified or interrupted the momentum for institutional change stemming from military mobilization for World War II. Other comparisons across policy domains (Hooks 1990, 1993) or nations (Carruthers 1994, Orloff 1993, Weir & Skocpol 1985) address the relative autonomy of various agencies within national governments—their capacity to sustain innovative policy in the absence of exogenous shock or to persist in established routines in the midst of economic or geopolitical turmoil.

Once these potential sources of institutional disruption are identified, political sociologists appear to have made greater progress in explaining institutional change than is suggested by recent overviews of institutional theory (but see Scott 1995:66–77). Studies document how models of political organization become increasingly taken-for-granted and enmeshed in networks of dependence, expectation, and alliance. Analyses of policy innovation and change regularly invoke the same principles: innovation is generated by networks that crosscut important institutional boundaries; societal heterogeneity facilitates the mobilization of political challengers and constitutes loci of structural indeterminacy that may be exploited by political entrepreneurs. These basic theoretical claims infuse much recent research on the sources of institutional durability and transformation.

EXPLANATIONS OF DURABILITY AND CHANGE

Crosscutting the familiar distinctions among regulative, normative, and cognitive aspects of institutions, this survey of the components of institutional change redirects attention to heterogeneity and the processes by which heterogeneity disrupts reliable reproduction. Echoing the basic understanding of institutions as higher-order effects, scholars have addressed how the organization of rule constitutes both the identities and interests of actors. For the analysis of institutional change, the critical question is to what extent do these constituted identities and interests converge with or diverge from the schemas and distribution of resources that organize rule?

Institutional theory also suggests that more is at stake in politics than Lasswell's (1936) famous formulation of "who gets what, when, how?" The ultimate distribution of benefits is determined, at least in part, by a different sort of politics that centers on expanding or eliminating alternatives and opportunities for exit. Struggles over the available set of alternatives, in turn, shape the space for a distinctive style of politics in which entrepreneurs or challengers seek to "transpose" (Sewell 1992) schemas for collective action or policy responses from one social setting to another.

Political Institutions as Constitutive of Actors

Rejecting the naturalism of methodological individualism, one of the core insights of institutional theory is that institutions constitute actors (Meyer & Jepperson 1999). By extension, different kinds of institutional orders constitute different kinds of actors and different patterns of ties among them. This line of argument pushes beyond the claim that one's institutional position shapes preferences and interests to assert that core identities of political actors are shaped by broader institutional arrangements.

The seed of this process lies in the character of states as projects of social control. Control, in turn, requires knowledge or legibility of the world that is to be ruled. "Legibility," Scott (1998:2) argues, is "a central problem in statecraft." But purely textual imagery is misleading, he argues, because to make the world knowable is to transform the world. Categories are not simply imposed; the practices of rule seek to transform the world to fit the categories. The effort of state agents to document the distribution of income or wealth both changes individual behavior and leads to the cultural transformation of the meaning of activities—such as reproductive or caring labor—that are not defined as producing income (McCaffery 1997). The puzzle is whether these processes enhance or undermine the reproduction of the institutions of social governance.

Attention to how the constitution of identities generates challenges to the organization of rule is central to the study of nationalism and national identity. Relations of ruling constitute the identities of rulers and ruled alike. Anderson's analysis in *Imagined Communities* (1983) exemplifies both processes: intertwined administrative careers limited to the colonies generate a shared identity among creole elites; the imposition of colonial practices of rule on a particular territory elicits a territorially grounded national identity among the ruled. Both identities embodied developmental contradictions—colonial administrators doomed to be subordinate to the metropole, the colonized taught to celebrate the history of the metropole as an independent nation—that eventually fueled nationalist revolutions.

Deployed in worlds that are always already organized and meaningful, the constitutive powers of political institutions frequently have unintended consequences. Brubaker (1996) traces how the Soviet regime used the construct of nationality—as an attribute of both persons and places—to organize the administration of its ethnically heterogeneous territories. Although the Soviet Union itself was not organized as a nation state, this template for identity was displaced to regional and ethnic entities, made real through administrative practices such as the passport system, and thus eventually served as fuel for the thoroughly nationalist disintegration of the USSR. In the struggle to block construction of a dam on their reservation, the Yavapai of Arizona constructed "a portrait of themselves in categories that made sense to them" and that resisted the efforts of federal bureaucrats to subsume the unique and incommensurable character of their land within the cost-benefit framework of technocratic analysis. With the defeat of the dam, effective political activism was incorporated as an important component of their collective identity (Espeland 1998: 219–22). In a study of the property tax revolts that culminated in California's Proposition 13, Lo (1990) traces the disintegration of the legitimacy of state government built on the promise of delivering great public education, impressive highways, and safe neighborhoods. Having reconstituted the citizen as consumer, this politics of technocratic social provision helped to draw more migrants to the state, which drove up housing prices, which drove up taxes, which led those citizen-consumers to hobble their government with drastic restrictions on revenue collection while they continued to demand high-quality public services.

Given the destabilization so often associated with the constitution of national or citizen identities, under what conditions do institutionally constituted identities contribute to reliable reproduction? For Bourdieu (1994:3–4), the project of constructing the state entails not only the Weberian requirement of a monopoly over physical violence but also an incarnation of "itself simultaneously in objectivity, in the form of specific organizational structures and mechanisms and in subjectivity in the form of mental structures adapted to them." Ikegami (1995:5) elegantly demonstrates the intertwined processes of state-formation and the construction of cultural models of the self and institutional settings that enhanced "the trustworthiness of individuals who had otherwise strong centrifugal tendencies." Her analysis forcefully transcends the distinction between exogenous constraint and subjective constitution often used to organize discussions of the multiple "new institutionalisms": "The distinctive character of the state lies in its ability to create and sustain a number of institutions that variously affect people's lives. Although each institution by itself is not necessarily embedded in or intended to serve a particular purpose of moral or ideological regulation, taken together they form an institutional field that deeply affects individuals' decision-making. New institutional constraints resulting from state-making transform a society's wider cultural environment in critical and unforeseen ways" (Ikegami 1995:33).

Institutions as Constituting Interests

In addition to constituting identities, formal political institutions structure interests and incentives. One important mechanism for generating commitments of constituents to policies involves altering the costs and benefits of a particular line of action. In a study of tax expenditures in the United States, Howard (1997) provides particularly clear examples of this process. Introduced in the early years of the federal income tax, the home mortgage interest deduction came to profoundly shape individual investment decisions and the housing market once the income tax become a mass tax during World War II. The shift from owning to renting became more costly as house-sellers faced both the loss of the deduction and the tax on any appreciation in their home's value (on the behavioral consequences of income taxation for gender inequality and family organization, see McCaffery 1997). As importantly, the federally subsidized expansion of the residential real estate market gave rise to third parties—organized realtors, bankers, and developers—who have been far more active in protecting this tax expenditure than the individual taxpayers who are its explicit beneficiaries. A similar process is evident in health care where federal expenditures on hospital construction, Medicare, and Medicaid have stimulated the development of a thickly organized field of stakeholders (Laumann & Knoke 1987, Skocpol 1996; for social policy generally, see Pierson 1994).

The response of political regimes to societal demands also shapes the subsequent development of those organized interests. Skocpol (1992) explores the "policy feedback processes" by which nineteenth-century social spending reinforced the mobilization of constituencies such as Civil War veterans. Such beneficial feedback cycles may be established quite unintentionally. Swedish unionists failed to secure a state-run, compulsory system of unemployment insurance and settled for a voluntary system, managed by unions; ironically, this "Ghent" system created powerful incentives for workers to join unions and contributed to the emerging dominance of the Swedish Social Democratic Party (Rothstein 1992). Feedback cycles may also demobilize or depoliticize organized claimants. Whereas British workers in the nineteenth century became increasingly oriented to political action as more mobilization produced legislative results, their American counterparts repeatedly saw legislative victories annulled by the courts and, in time, abandoned political strategies in favor of business unionism (Hattam 1993).

Success in articulating, passing, and implementing policy often depends on embedding a proposed program in an array of supportive constituencies. Comparative studies of welfare state development point to the extent to which party systems mobilize cross-class constituencies (Amenta 1998, Orloff 1993, Skocpol 1992, Steinmo & Watts 1995). Debt can generate the same results as spending. Those who have extended credit to "kings, rulers, states and governments . . . have a financial interest in the ability of sovereigns to repay their debts and therefore they acquire a political interest in the survival of the sovereign regime. They become its allies" (Carruthers 1996:4). Opposition to indebtedness is thus also opposition to certain kinds of entangling alliances (Skowronek 1993:64). Instrumental rationality and constitutive identities reinforce one another: "Reproduction ensues when rules induce roles, which induce interests, which induce strategic exchanges, which lock in patterns of collective action that depend on the rules" (Padgett & Ansell 1993:1259–60).

At the level of taken-for-grantedness, effective politicians may enhance the obviousness of a particular policy by building deep analogies to already institutionalized models or widely held norms (Campbell 1998:394–98). National approaches to economic regulation, Dobbin (1994) argues, were modelled on basic templates of political governance. The proponents of Social Security consciously invoked the imagery of individual savings accounts (only recently secured by the Federal Deposit Insurance Corporation) to build a constituency for Old Age, Disability, and Survivors' Insurance; only as more citizens came to depend on what was initially a less prominent component of the 1935 legislation was this novel program transformed into the "third rail" of American politics (Amenta 1998, Zollars & Skocpol 1994). Once entrenched, Social Security could then provide an analogical foundation for Medicare and Medicaid during the 1960s (Skocpol 1996).

Such embedded analogies may also render some policy alternatives risky or unthinkable. Prior commitment to a color-blind model of civil rights presented an obstacle to African-American leaders interested in the possibilities of affirmative action; those policies were ultimately implemented under the rubric of "crisis management" in response to the urban riots of the 1960s (Skrentny 1996). In conjunction with the War on Poverty, employment policy became increasingly linked to racial politics and, therefore, unavailable for use as a tool of macroeconomic policy as in the 1930s (Weir 1992). This realignment of policies and imputed beneficiaries tainted an alternative that had once cemented the alliance of organized workers and the Democratic party.

These cases highlight the politics of effective institution-building. The institutional effects attributable to normative legitimacy or taken-for-grantedness (e.g. home ownership as the American dream or Medicare as an unquestioned, allegedly earned entitlement) are reinforced by the more explicitly political mobilization of a set of stakeholders and alignment of incentives. To the extent that rules of access or the configuration of agencies facilitate the influence of these stakeholders, the policy domain becomes increasingly institutionalized, shaping the terms on which new actors or new issues are encountered. With this "institutional thickening," the ability of political actors to achieve significant policy retrenchment or reconstruction is increasingly limited (Pierson 1994, Skowronek 1993).

Institutions as Eliminating Alternatives

The absence of alternatives and opportunities for exit enhances the prospects for reliable reproduction of any project of social control. If societies are conceptualized as "social cages" constructed from "multiple overlapping and intersecting sociospatial networks of power" (Mann 1986:1), such cages may be weakened by disruption of any network. If ideological power is weakened, alternatives become imaginable. New opportunities for economic exchange among actors at the periphery erode the capacity of central brokers to exercise control through their monopoly on trade (Adams 1996). This image of change informs macro-comparative studies of societal transformation, particularly those addressing the classic problem of "the rise of the west." Comparing China and Europe, Chirot (1985) attributes the dynamism of the latter in part to its more varied geography, political decentralization, and complex patterns of political conflict.

These arguments reinforce a theme found in many theoretical reflections on the politics of state-formation and institution-building. If alternative sets of prescriptions and proscriptions (or the perception of them) are suppressed, currently dominant institutional arrangements are more likely to persist. Formal political institutions have great capacities for eliminating alternatives. At a "constitutive moment" in an American political economy disordered by the Civil War and industrialization, debates over how to organize railroads were "at the center of a nearly half-century-long struggle to reimpose order on an inchoate world" (Berk 1994:13). Although regional railroads with practices foreshadowing modern "flexible specialization" were an already realized option a series of judicial decisions consolidated the model of the centralized, national railroad.

Institutional arrangements may also suppress alternatives by decoupling the components necessary to enact a particular policy. The distribution of surplus food is a possible response to poverty at home and abroad, but programs such as food stamps are lodged institutionally in the agricultural policy domain and are more responsive to the market conditions confronting American farmers than to the malnutrition of children (Laumann & Knoke 1987). The segregation of capacities for policy formation in think tanks and for policy implementation in state agencies undercuts the ability of the US political system to generate viable policy innovations (Weir 1992).

Finally, the interpretation of experience (Ellingson 1995) may eliminate alternatives from the repertoire available to political entrepreneurs. Voss (1996) compares the consequences of the defeat of broad-based, politically oriented labor movements in the late nineteenth century. In Britain, defeat was interpreted through a Marxist lens that predicted many failures on the road to socialism. The model retained its legitimacy and was resurrected a few decades later. In the United States, however, the collapse of the Knights of Labor discredited this model of mobilization just as the failure of the People's Party delegitimated the third party model among farmers (Clemens 1997:156–61).

The Politics of Institutional Change

The presence of multiple institutional orders or alternatives constitutes an opportunity for agency (Sewell 1992:19) in which political entrepreneurs seek to negotiate multiple sets of expectations or to embed their project more firmly in one of the possible institutional foundations (Friedland & Alford 1991, Pedriana & Stryker 1997, Skowronek 1993). Common to these arguments is a distinctive type of political action: "The essence of institutional entrepreneurship is to align skillfully an organizational form and the specific institution it embodies with the master rules of society" (Haveman & Rao 1997:1614, see also Swidler 1986).

Given this oblique style of politics, significant change may escape notice. When political entrepreneurs seek to transform the overarching institutions of political life, they face particularly high demands to embed calls for change within accepted models. Consequently "no institution is created de novo" (Riker 1995:121), and the most ambitious innovators may well cloak their efforts for change in appeals to restore tradition (Skowronek 1993, also Fligstein 1996, Fligstein & Mara-Drita 1996, Ikegami 1995:364, Pedriana & Stryker 1997:679, Skrentny 1996:154–58).

Alternatively, political challengers may mobilize by deploying familiar models of social organization in unfamiliar ways. At the turn of the century, a wide range of political challengers in the United States sought to circumvent the major political parties and to increase popular control over policy outcomes. Organized workers, who were relatively integrated into the party system, had the least success in sustaining alternative vehicles for mobilization; women, by contrast, were formally and culturally excluded from the fraternal world of electoral politics but showed the greatest innovation in refashioning models drawn from social clubs and business practices as the templates for novel forms of political engagement (Clemens 1997). Finally, challengers faced with the constraints of existing organizational schemas may simply invent new ones. Confronting a construction of scientific expertise premised on disinterestedness, activist scientists attempted to reconcile the contradiction between their professional identity and their political commitments by founding public interest science organizations (Moore 1996).

This style of political entrepreneurship presumes a degree of fragmentation or the availability of alternative models for mobilization and intervention. Analyzing changes in US policy on racial inequality, Skrentny (1996) argues that the organizational complexity of the federal government and the routines of different agencies generated alternative "solutions" to the grievances manifested in urban riots. The presence of alternatives created a space for political action and policy innovation. The opportunities for entrepreneurship are further complicated when there are multiple audiences for whom new political events or arrangements must be interpreted and legitimated (Ellingson 1995, Stryker 1999). As Padgett & Ansell argue, "robust action" is grounded in "multivocality–the fact that single actions can be interpreted coherently from multiple perspectives simultaneously" (1993:1263). Yet not every actor confronts the conditions of institutional multiplicity or possesses the skills to exploit them. In our efforts to appreciate human agency, we should beware of assuming "every actor a Cosimo de' Medici."

When institutions are challenged, what factors determine their resistance or capacity to restore the status quo ante? Research in comparative politics provides rich examples of how variations in institutional structure produce differences in the degree to which changes in the environment (e.g. shifts in public opinion or economic conditions) are translated into political outcomes. In the United States, the combination of federalism and the division of authority among the branches of the federal government presents obstacles to the establishment of new national policies and fragments constituencies; monarchical or parliamentary regimes may have a greater capacity to act autonomously from entanglements with organized interests or elected representatives (Dunlavy 1994, Steinmo 1993, Steinmo & Watts 1995).

The obverse of the autonomy or capacity of state agencies is the degree of access that societal actors enjoy with respect to political decision-making. Looking at the fate of a range of social policies proposed during the New Deal, Amenta (1998) documents how electoral arrangements sustained Southern Democrats in their opposition to reform and necessitated particularly widespread Democratic victories in the north to secure new progressive policies. This line of argument is refined further by comparative analysis of the articulation of societal and state actors with one another. Immergut (1992) attributes variations in national health care policy to the distinctive constellations of "veto points" built into different regimes. Kriesi (1996) uses the concept of opportunity structures to compare the relationship of social movements to national polities. These arguments underscore the variability of the robustness of institutional arrangements in the face of exogenous shock or endogenous challenge.

IN CONCLUSION

In the mid-1980s, the call went out to "bring the state back in" (Evans et al 1985) and to challenge the hegemony of behavioralism and methodological individualism in political science and sociology. The slogan itself only crystallized a turn toward institutional analysis in process across diverse fields within the social sciences. Initially, this resurgent interest in political institutions produced an image of the state as a concrete, massive, autonomous force within politics. Emphasizing durability and embeddedness, this imagery made it difficult to address the sources and mechanisms of institutional change.

More recently, however, a wide array of scholars have responded to this dilemma by reconsidering their imagery of the state and of political institutions more generally. Drawing on diverse theoretical resources, they have increasingly disaggregated "the state," recognizing both that societies are often structured by multiple institutions and that institutions themselves are complex embeddings of schemas into resources and networks. In the place of an all-or-nothing durability of the state, analyses of institutional change increasingly address the multiple processes of institutional reproduction, disruption, and responses to disruption.

Although many surveys emphasize the different theories of action (instrumental, normative, cognitive) that inform the various "new institutionalisms," when refracted through the sensibilities of a structuralist these literatures converge on a series of implications for the study of institutional change. For example, institutional multiplicity should undermine reliable reproduction, whether strategic actors are playing off competing alternatives, normative actors are torn between competing ideals, or actors are trying to make reconcile diverse cognitive schemas. Mutability, contradiction, learning, containment or diffusion, and mediation are additional conditions or processes that influence the likelihood and the trajectories of institutional change. Taken together, these literatures suggest that the analysis of institutional change rests on an appreciation of the heterogeneity of institutional arrangements and the resulting patterns of conflict or prospects for agency and innovation.

ACKNOWLEDGMENTS

For their valuable comments and criticism, we would like to thank Bruce Carruthers, Frank Dobbin, Ron Jepperson, Woody Powell, Marc Schneiberg, Robin Stryker, Marc Ventresca, and the members of the Social Organization Seminar at the University of Arizona.

> Visit the *Annual Reviews home page* at
> http://www.AnnualReviews.org.

Literature Cited

Adams J. 1996. Principals and agents, colonialists and company men: The decay of colonial control in the Dutch East Indies. *Am. Sociol. Rev.* 61:12–28

Amenta E. 1998. *Bold Relief: Institutional Politics and the Origins of Modern American Social Policy.* Princeton, NJ: Princeton Univ. Press

Amenta E, Carruthers BG, Zylan Y. 1992. A hero for the aged? The Townsend Movement, the political mediation model, and U.S. old-age policy, 1934–1950. *Am. J. Sociol.* 98: 308–39

Amenta E, Dunleavy K, Bernstein M. 1994. Stolen thunder? Huey Long's Share Our Wealth, political mediation, and the Second New Deal. *Am. Sociol. Rev.* 59: 678–702

Anderson B. 1983. *Imagined Communities: Reflections on the Origin and Spread of Nationalism.* New York: Verso

Archer MS. 1988. *Culture and Agency: The Place of Culture in Social Theory.* New York: Cambridge Univ. Press

Babb S. 1996. 'A True American System of Finance': frame resonance in the U.S. labor movement, 1866 to 1886. *Am. Sociol. Rev.* 61:1033–52

Berger PL, Luckmann T. 1967. *The Social Construction of Reality.* New York: Doubleday

Berk G. 1994. *Alternative Tracks: The Constitution of American Industrial Order, 1865–1917.* Baltimore, MD: Johns Hopkins Univ. Press

Blau PM, Schwartz JE. 1984. *Crosscutting Social Circles: Testing a Macrostructural Theory of Intergroup Relations.* Orlando, FL: Academic

Bourdieu P. 1977. *Outline of a Theory of Practice.* New York: Cambridge Univ. Press

Bourdieu P. 1994. Rethinking the state: genesis and structure of the bureaucratic field. *Sociol. Theory* 12(1):1–18

Brinton MC, Nee V, eds. 1998. *The New Institutionalism in Sociology.* New York: Russell Sage

Brubaker R. 1996. *Nationalism Reframed: Nationhood and the National Question in the New Europe.* New York: Cambridge Univ. Press

Calvert RL. 1995. Rational actors, equilibrium, and social institutions. See Knight & Sened 1995, pp. 57–93

Campbell JL. 1998. Institutional analysis and the role of ideas in political economy. *Theory Soc.* 27:377–409

Carley K. 1989. The value of cognitive foundations for dynamic social theory. *J. Math. Sociol.* 14:171–208

Carley K. 1991. A theory of group stability. *Am. Sociol. Rev.* 56:331–54

Carruthers BG. 1994. When is the state autonomous? Culture, organization theory, and the political sociology of the state. *Sociol. Theory* 12(1):19–44

Carruthers BG. 1996. *City of Capital: Politics and Markets in the English Financial Revolution.* Princeton, NJ: Princeton Univ. Press

Chirot D. 1985. The rise of the west. *Am. Sociol. Rev.* 50(2):181–94

Clemens ES. 1993. Organizational repertoires and institutional change: women's groups and the transformation of U.S. politics, 1890–1920. *Am. J. Sociol.* 98:755–98

Clemens ES. 1997. *The People's Lobby: Organizational Innovation and the Rise of Interest Group Politics in the United States, 1890–1925.* Chicago: Univ. Chicago Press

Clemens ES. 1999. Coherence and discontinuity: periodization and the problem of change. In *Social Time and Social Change,* ed. R Kalleberg, F Engelstad, pp. 62–83. Oslo: Norwegian Univ. Press

Crawford SES, Ostrom E. 1995. A grammar of institutions. *Am. Polit. Sci. Rev.* 89(3): 582–600

DiMaggio PJ. 1988. Interest and agency in institutional theory. In *Institutional Patterns and Organizations: Culture and Environment,* ed. LG Zucker, pp. 3–21. Cambridge, MA: Ballinger

DiMaggio PJ, Powell WW. 1983. The iron cage revisited: institutional isomorphism and collective rationality in organizational fields. *Am. Sociol. Rev.* 48:147–60

DiMaggio PJ, Powell WW. 1991. Introduction. See Powell & DiMaggio 1991, pp. 1–38

Dobbin F. 1994. *Forging Industrial Policy: The United States, Britain, and France in the Railway Age.* New York: Cambridge Univ. Press

Dobbin F, Sutton JR, Meyer JW, Scott WR. 1994. Equal opportunity law and the construction of internal labor markets. In *Institutional Environments and Organizations: Structural Complexity and Individualism,* ed. WR Scott, JW Meyer & Associates, pp. 272–300. Thousand Oaks, CA: Sage

Dunlavy CA. 1994. *Politics and Industrialization: Early Railroads in the United States and Prussia.* Princeton, NJ: Princeton Univ. Press

Eckstein H. 1966. *Division and Cohesion in Democracy: A Study of Norway.* Princeton, NJ: Princeton Univ. Press

Edelman LB. 1990. Legal environments and organizational governance: the expansion of due process in the American workplace. *Am. J. Sociol.* 95:1401–40

Ellingson S. 1995. Understanding the dialectic of discourse and collective action: public debate and rioting in antebellum Cincinnati. *Am. J. Sociol.* 101:100–44

Espeland WN. 1998. *The Struggle for Water: Politics, Rationality, and Identity in the American Southwest.* Chicago: Univ. Chicago Press

Ethington P, McDonagh E. 1995. The eclectic center of the new institutionalism. *Soc. Sci. Hist.* 19:469–77

Evans PB, Rueschemeyer D, Skocpol T, eds. 1985. *Bringing the State Back In.* New York: Cambridge Univ. Press

Feld S. 1981. The focused organization of social ties. *Am. J. Sociol.* 86:1015–35

Finnemore M. 1996. Norms, culture, and world politics: insights from sociology's institutionalism. *Int. Org.* 50:325–47

Fligstein N. 1990. *The Transformation of Corporate Control.* Cambridge, MA: Harvard Univ. Press

Fligstein N. 1996. Markets as politics: a political-cultural approach to market institutions. *Am. Sociol. Rev.* 61: 656–73

Fligstein N, Mara-Drita I. 1996. How to make a market: reflections on the attempt to create a single market in the European Union. *Am. J. Sociol.* 102:1-33

Friedland R, Alford RR. 1991. Bringing society back in: symbols, practices, and institutional contradictions. See Powell & DiMaggio 1991, pp. 232–63

Gaventa J. 1980. *Power and Powerlessness: Quiescence and Rebellion in an Appalachian Valley.* Urbana: Univ. Ill. Press

Giddens A. 1984. *The Constitution of Society: Outline of a Theory of Structuration.* Berkeley: Univ. Calif. Press

Gramsci A. 1971. *Selections from the Prison Notebooks.* New York: Int. Publ.

Grief A, Milgrom P, Weingast BR. 1995. Coordination, commitment and enforcement: the case of the merchant guild. See Knight & Sened 1995, pp. 27–56

Hall PA. 1986. *Governing the Economy: The Politics of State Intervention in Britain and France.* Cambridge, UK: Polity

Hall PA, Taylor RCR. 1996. Political science and the three new institutionalisms. *Polit. Stud.* 44(5):936–58

Hattam VC. 1993. *Labor Visions and State Power: The Origins of Business Unionism in the United States.* Princeton, NJ: Princeton Univ. Press

Haveman H, Rao H. 1997. Structuring a theory of moral sentiments: institutional and organizational coevolution in the early thrift industry. *Am. J. Sociol.* 102: 1606–51

Heclo H. 1974. *Modern Social Politics in Britain and Sweden: From Relief to Income Maintenance.* New Haven, CT: Yale Univ. Press

Hicks A. 1995. Is political sociology informed by political science? *Soc. Forces* 73(4): 1219–29

Hirsch PM. 1986. From ambushes to golden parachutes: corporate takeovers as an instance of cultural framing and institutional integration. *Am. J. Sociol.* 91: 800–37

Hirsch PM, Lounsbury M. 1997. Ending the family quarrel: toward a reconciliation of 'old' and 'new' institutionalisms. *Am. Behav. Sci.* 40:406–18

Hobbes T. (1651) 1968. *Leviathan,* ed. CB Macpherson. London: Penguin

Hooks G. 1990. From an autonomous to a captured state agency: the decline of the New Deal in agriculture. *Am. Sociol. Rev.* 55: 29–43

Hooks G. 1993. The weakness of strong theories: the U.S. state's dominance of the World War II investment process. *Am. Sociol. Rev.* 58:37–53

Howard C. 1997. *The Hidden Welfare State: Tax Expenditures and Social Policy in the United States.* Princeton, NJ: Princeton Univ. Press

Hughes EC. 1936. The ecological aspect of institutions. *Am. Sociol. Rev.* 1:180–89

Ikegami E. 1995. *The Taming of the Samurai: Honorific Individualism and the Making of Modern Japan.* Cambridge, MA: Harvard Univ. Press

Immergut EM. 1992. The rules of the game: the logic of health policy-making in France, Switzerland, and Sweden. See Steinmo et al 1992, pp. 57–89

Jepperson RL. 1991. Institutions, institutional effects, and institutionalism. In *The New Institutionalism in Organizational Sociology,* ed.WW Powell, PJ DiMaggio, pp. 143–63. Chicago: Univ. Chicago Press

Katzenstein PJ. 1985. *Small States in World Markets: Industrial Policy in Europe.* Ithaca, NY: Cornell Univ. Press

Knight J, Sened I, eds. 1995. *Explaining Social Institutions.* Ann Arbor: Univ. Mich. Press

Koelble TA. 1995. The new institutionalism in

political science and sociology. *Comp. Polit.* 27(2):231–43

Krasner SD. 1984. Approaches to the state: alternative conceptions and historical dynamics. *Comp. Polit.* 16(2):223–46

Kriesi H. 1996. The organizational structure of new social movements in a political context. See McAdam et al 1996, pp. 152–84

Lasswell HD. 1936. *Politics: Who Gets What When, How.* New York: McGraw-Hill

Laumann EO, Knoke D. 1987. *The Organizational State: Social Choice in National Policy Domains.* Madison: Univ. Wis. Press

Leblebici H, Salancik GR, Copay A, King T. 1991. Institutional change and the transformation of interorganizational fields: an organizational history of the U.S. radio broadcasting industry. *Admin. Sci. Q.* 36:333–63

Levitt B, March JG. 1988. Organizational learning. *Annu. Rev. Sociol.* 14:319–40

Lo CYH. 1990. *Small Property versus Big Government: Social Origins of the Property Tax Revolt.* Berkeley/Los Angeles: Univ. Calif. Press

Lukes S. 1974. *Power: A Radical View.* London: Macmillan

Mann M. 1986. *The Sources of Social Power, Volume I: A History of Power From the Beginning to A.D. 1760.* New York: Cambridge Univ. Press

March JG. 1991. Exploration and exploitation in organizational learning. *Org. Sci.* 2:71–87

March JG, Olsen JP. 1984. The new institutionalism: organizational factors in political life. *Am. Polit. Sci. Rev.* 78:734–49

March JG, Olsen JP. 1989. *Rediscovering Institutions: The Organizational Basis of Politics.* New York: Free Press

Mark NP. 1998. Beyond individual differences: social differentiation from First Principles. *Am. Sociol. Rev.* 63:309–30

McAdam D. 1982. *Political Process and the Development of Black Insurgency, 1930–1970.* Chicago: Univ. Chicago Press

McAdam D, McCarthy JD, Zald MN, eds. 1996. *Comparative Perspectives on Social Movements: Political Opportunities, Mobilizing Structures, and Cultural Framings.* New York: Cambridge Univ. Press

McCaffery EJ. 1997. *Taxing Women.* Chicago: Univ. Chicago Press

Meyer JW, Jepperson RL. The actor and the other: cultural rationalization and the ongoing evolution of modern agency. See Powell & Jones Forthcoming

Meyer JW, Ramirez FO, Rubinson R, Boli-Bennett J. 1977. The world educational revolution, 1950–1970. *Sociol. Educ.* 50: 242–58

Meyer JW, Ramirez FO, Soysal YN. 1992. World expansion of mass education, 1870–1980. *Sociol. Educ.* 65:128–49

Meyer JW, Rowan B. 1977. Institutionalized organizations: formal structure as myth and ceremony. *Am. J. Sociol.* 83:340–63

Meyer JW, Scott WR, Deal TE. 1983. Institutional and technical sources of organizational structure: explaining the structure of educational organizations. In *Organizational Environments: Ritual and Rationality,* JW Meyer, WR Scott, pp. 45–67. Beverly Hills, CA: Sage

Minkoff DC. 1994. From service provision to institutional advocacy: the shifting legitimacy of organizational forms. *Soc. Forces* 72:943–70

Moe TM. 1987. Interests, institutions, and positive theory: the politics of the NLRB. *Stud. Am. Polit. Dev.* 2:236–99

Moore K. 1996. Organizing integrity: American science and the creation of public interest science organizations. *Am. J. Sociol.* 101:1592–1627

Morrill C. Forthcoming. Institutional change and interstitial emergence: the growth of alternative dispute resolution in American law, 1965–1995. See Powell & Jones Forthcoming

Nee V. 1998. Sources of the new institutionalism. See Brinton & Nee 1998, pp. 1–15

Nee V, Ingram P. 1998. Embeddedness and beyond: institutions, exchange, and social structure. See Brinton & Nee 1998, pp. 19–45

Nordlinger EA. 1981. *On the Autonomy of the Democratic State.* Cambridge, MA: Harvard Univ. Press

North DC. 1981. *Structure and Change in Economic History.* New York: Norton

North DC. 1990. *Institutions, Institutional Change and Economic Performance.* New York: Cambridge Univ. Press

North DC. 1995. Five propositions about institutional change. See Knight & Sened 1995, pp. 15–26

O'Connor J. 1973. *The Fiscal Crisis of the State.* New York: St. Martin's

Orloff AS. 1993. *The Politics of Pensions: A Comparative Analysis of Britain, Canada, and the United States, 1880–1940.* Madison: Univ. Wis. Press

Orren K, Skowronek S. 1994. Beyond the iconography of order: notes for a 'new institutionalism.' In *The Dynamics of American Politics,* pp. 311–30. ed. LC Dodd, C Jillson. Boulder, CO: Westview

Padgett JF, Ansell C. 1993. Robust action and the rise of the Medici, 1400-1434. *Am. J. Sociol.* 98 (6):1259–319

Pedriana N, Stryker R. 1997. Political culture

wars 1960s style: Equal Employment Opportunity-Affirmative Action law and the Philadelphia Plan. *Am. J. Sociol.* 103: 633–91

Pierson P. 1994. *Dismantling the Welfare State: Reagan, Thatcher, and the Politics of Retrenchment.* New York: Cambridge Univ. Press

Porter TM. 1995. *Trust in Numbers: The Pursuit of Objectivity in Science and Public Life.* Princeton, NJ: Princeton Univ. Press

Powell WW. 1991. Expanding the scope of institutional analysis. See Powell & DiMaggio 1991, pp. 183–203

Powell WW, DiMaggio PJ, eds. 1991. *The New Institutionalism in Organizational Analysis.* Chicago: Univ. Chicago Press

Powell WW, Jones DL, eds. *Bending the Bars of the Iron Cage: Institutional Dynamics and Processes.* Chicago: Univ. Chicago Press. Forthcoming

Powell WW, Koput KW, Smith-Doerr L. 1996. Interorganizational collaboration and the locus of innovation: networks of learning in biotechnology. *Admin. Sci. Q.* 41:116–45

Riker W. 1995. The experience of creating institutions: the framing of the United States Constitution. See Knight & Sened 1995, pp. 121–44

Rothstein B. 1992. Labor market institutions and working-class strength. In *Structuring Politics,* see Steinmo et al 1992, pp. 33–56

Rothstein B. 1998. *Just Institutions Matter: The Moral and Political Logic of the Universal Welfare State.* New York: Cambridge Univ. Press

Schneiberg M. 1998. *From associations and states to markets and hierarchies: endogenous price shifts, models of rational order, and the process of institutional change.* Presented at the Am. Sociol. Assoc., San Francisco

Schneiberg M, Clemens ES. The typical tools for the job: research strategies in institutional analysis. See Powell & Jones Forthcoming

Schwartz M. 1976. *Radical Protest and Social Structure: The Southern Farmers' Alliance and Cotton Tenancy, 1880–1890.* New York: Academic

Scott JC. 1998. *Seeing Like a State: How Certain Schemes to Improve the Human Condition Have Failed.* New Haven: Yale Univ. Press

Scott W. 1995. *Institutions and Organizations.* Thousand Oaks, CA: Sage

Sewell WH Jr. 1992. A theory of structure: duality, agency, and transformation. *Am. J. Sociol.* 98:1–29

Shepsle KA, Weingast BR. 1987. The institutional foundations of committee power. *Am. Polit. Sci. Rev.* 81:85–104

Skocpol T. 1979. *States and Social Revolutions: A Comparative Analysis of France, Russia, and China.* New York: Cambridge Univ. Press

Skocpol T. 1985. Bringing the state back in: strategies of analysis in current research. In *Bringing the State Back In,* ed. PB Evans, D Rueschemeyer, T Skocpol, pp. 3–37. New York: Cambridge Univ. Press

Skocpol T. 1992. *Protecting Soldiers and Mothers: The Political Origins of Social Policy in the United States.* Cambridge, MA: Belknap/Harvard Univ. Press

Skocpol T. 1996. *Boomerang: Clinton's Health Security Effort and the Turn against Government in U.S. Politics.* New York: Norton

Skowronek S. 1982. *Building a New American State: The Expansion of National Administrative Capacities, 1877–1920.* New York: Cambridge Univ. Press

Skowronek S. 1993. *The Politics Presidents Make: Leadership from John Adams to George Bush.* Cambridge, MA: Belknap/Harvard Univ. Press

Skrentny JD. 1996. *The Ironies of Affirmative Action: Politics, Culture, and Justice in America.* Chicago: Univ. Chicago Press

Smith RM. 1988. Political jurisprudence, the 'new institutionalism,' and the future of public law. *Am. Polit. Sci. Rev.* 82(1): 89–108

Soule SA, Zylan Y. 1997. Runaway train? The diffusion of state-level reform in ADC/AFDC eligibility requirements, 1950–1967. *Am. J. Sociol.* 103:733–62

Soysal YN. 1994. *Limits of Citizenship: Migrants and Postnational Membership in Europe.* Chicago: Univ. Chicago Press

Sparrow BH. 1996. *From the Outside In: World War II and the American State.* Princeton, NJ: Princeton Univ. Press

Stearns LB, Allan KD. 1996. Institutional environments: the corporate merger wave of the 1980s. *Am. Sociol. Rev.* 61:599–718

Steinmo S. 1993. *Taxation and Democracy: Swedish, British and American Approaches to Financing the Modern State.* New Haven: Yale Univ. Press

Steinmo S, Thelen K, Longstreth F, eds. 1992. *Structuring Politics: Historical Institutionalism in Comparative Analysis.* New York: Cambridge Univ. Press

Steinmo S, Watts J. 1995. It's the institutions, stupid! Why comprehensive national health insurance always fails in America. *J. Health Polit. Policy Law* 20:329–72

Stinchcombe AL. 1968. *Constructing Social*

Theories. New York: Harcourt, Brace & World

Stinchcombe AL. 1978. *Theoretical Methods in Social History.* New York: Academic

Stinchcombe AL. 1997. On the virtues of the old institutionalism. *Annu. Rev. Sociol.* 23: 1–18

Strang D. 1990. From dependency to sovereignty: an event history analysis of decolonization 1870–1987. *Am. Sociol. Rev.* 55: 846–60

Strang D, Chang PMY. 1993. The International Labor Organization and the welfare state: institutional effects on national welfare spending, 1960–80. *Int. Org.* 47: 235–62

Strang D, Meyer J. 1993. Institutional conditions for diffusion. *Theory Soc.* 22: 487–511

Strang D, Soule SA. 1998. Diffusion in organizations and social movements: from hybrid corn to poison pills. *Annu. Rev. Sociol.* 24:265–90

Stryker R. 1994. Rules, resources, and legitimacy processes: some implications for social conflict, order, and change. *Am. J. Sociol.* 99(4):847–910

Stryker R. 1999. Legitimacy processes as institutional politics: implications for theory and research in the sociology of organizations. In *Research in the Sociology of Organizations: Organizational Politics,* ed. SB Bacharach, EJ Lawler. Greenwich, CT: JAI

Suitor J, Keeton S. 1997. Once a friend, always a friend? Effects of homophily on women's support networks across a decade. *Soc. Networks* 19:51–62

Sutton JR, Dobbin F, Meyer JW, Scott WR. 1994. The legalization of the workplace. *Am. J. Sociol.* 99:944–71

Swidler A. 1986. Culture in action: symbols and strategies. *Am. Sociol. Rev.* 51:273–86

Thelen K. 1991. *Union of Parts: Labor Politics in Postwar Germany.* Ithaca, NY: Cornell Univ. Press

Thelen K, Steinmo S. 1992. Historical institutionalism in comparative politics. See Steinmo et al 1992, pp. 1–32

Tolbert P, Zucker L. 1983. Institutional sources of change in the formal structure of organizations: the diffusion of civil service reform, 1880–1935. *Admin. Sci. Q.* 28:22–39

Voss K. 1996. The collapse of a social movement: the interplay of mobilizing structures, framing, and political opportunity in the Knights of Labor. see McAdam et al 1996, pp. 227–58

Weir M. 1992. *Politics and Jobs: The Boundaries of Employment Policy in the United States.* Princeton, NJ: Princeton Univ. Press

Weir M, Skocpol T. 1985. State structures and the possibilities for 'Keynesian' responses to the Great Depression in Sweden, Britain, and the United States. In *Bringing the State Back In,* ed. PB Evans, D Rueschemeyer, T Skocpol, pp. 107–63. New York: Cambridge Univ. Press

Westney DE. 1987. *Imitation and Innovation: The Transfer of Western Organizational Patterns to Meiji Japan.* Cambridge, MA: Harvard Univ. Press

Wildavsky A. 1987. Choosing preferences by constructing institutions: a cultural theory of preference formation. *Am. Polit. Sci. Rev.* 81:1–21

Zhou X. 1993. Occupational power, state capacities, and the diffusion of licensing in the American states, 1890 to 1950. *Am. Sociol. Rev.* 58:536–52

Zollars C, Skocpol T. 1994. Cultural mythmaking as a policy tool: the Social Security Board and the construction of a social citizenship of self-interest. *Res. Democr. Soc.* 2:381–408

Zucker LG. 1977. The role of institutionalization in cultural persistence. *Am. Sociol. Rev.* 42:726–43

Zucker LG. 1988. Where do institutional patterns come from? Organizations as actors in social systems. In *Institutional Patterns and Organization: Culture and Environment,* ed. LG Zucker, pp. 23–52. Cambridge, MA: Ballinger

Annu. Rev. Sociol. 1999. 25:467–87

SOCIAL NETWORKS AND STATUS ATTAINMENT

Nan Lin

Department of Sociology, Duke University, Box 90088, Durham, North Carolina 27708-0088; e-mail: nanlin@duke.edu

KEY WORDS: social resources, social capital, social networks, status attainment

ABSTRACT

This essay traces the development of the research enterprise, known as the social resources theory, which formulated and tested a number of propositions concerning the relationships between embedded resources in social networks and socioeconomic attainment. This enterprise, seen in the light of social capital, has accumulated a substantial body of research literature and supported the proposition that social capital, in terms of both access and mobilization of embedded resources, enhances the chances of attaining better statuses. Further, social capital is contingent on initial positions in the social hierarchies as well as on extensity of social ties. The essay concludes with a discussion of remaining critical issues and future research directions for this research enterprise.

INTRODUCTION

Status attainment can be understood as a process by which individuals mobilize and invest resources for returns in socioeconomic standings. Resources in this context are defined as valued goods in society, however consensually determined (Lin 1982, 1995), and values are normative judgments rendered on these goods which in most societies correspond with wealth, status, and power (Weber 1946). Socioeconomic standings refer to valued resources attached to occupied positions. These resources can be classified into two types: personal resources and social resources. Personal resources are possessed by the individual who can use and dispose them with freedom and without much concern

467

for compensation. Social resources are resources accessible through one's direct and indirect ties. The access to and use of these resources are temporary and borrowed. For example, a friend's occupational or authority position, or such positions of this friend's friends, may be ego's social resource. The friend may use his/her position or network to help ego to find a job. These resources are "borrowed" and useful to achieve ego's certain goal, but they remain the property of the friend or his/her friends.

The theoretical and empirical work for understanding and assessing the status attainment process can be traced to the seminal study reported by Blau & Duncan (1967). The major conclusion was that, even accounting for both the direct and indirect effects of ascribed status (parental status), achieved status (education and prior occupational status) remained the most important factor accounting for the ultimate attained status. The study thus set the theoretical baseline for further modifications and expansions. All subsequent theoretical revisions and expansions must be evaluated for their contribution to the explanation of status attainment beyond those accounted for by the Blau-Duncan paradigm (Kelley 1990, Smith 1990). Several lines of contributions since, including the addition of sociopsychological variables (Sewell & Hauser 1975), the recast of statuses into classes (Wright 1979, Goldthorpe 1980), the incorporation of "structural" entities and positions as both contributing and attained statuses (Baron & Bielby 1980, Kalleberg 1988), and the casting of comparative development or institutions as contingent conditions (Treiman 1970) have significantly amplified rather than altered the original Blau-Duncan conclusion concerning the relative merits of achieved versus ascribed *personal resources* in status attainment.

In the last three decades, a research tradition has focused on the effects on attained statuses of social resources. The principal proposition is that social resources exert an important and significant effect on attained statuses, beyond that accounted for by personal resources. Systematic investigations of this proposition have included efforts in: (*a*) developing theoretical explanations and hypotheses; (*b*) developing measurements for social resources; (*c*) conducting empirical studies verifying the hypotheses; and (*d*) assessing the relative importance of social resources as compared to personal resources in the process of status attainment. These investigations have been carried out in North America, Europe, and Asia, in multiple political economies, and have involved scholars of many nations and cultures. The accumulation and advances in theory and research have considerably expanded the intellectual horizon of sociological analysis in status attainment and, thus, in social stratification and social mobility. The purposes of this chapter are (*a*) to review the theoretical and empirical foundations of these lines of investigation, (*b*) summarize sampled studies and results, and (*c*) propose issues and directions for future research.

Before proceeding with the tasks outlined, I wish to identify the limitations of this review. It focuses on resources in the networks; as such, it does not review effects of properties of social networks per se (e.g., densities, centrality, bridging) unless they implicate accessed resources (what influence these characteristics may exert on the access and use of social resources). Second, the outcome of focus is the status attained rather than whether a job search is successful. The latter has a substantial literature of its own and is better summarized elsewhere (e.g., Granovetter 1995). This essay touches on aspects of job searches to the extent that they affect attained statuses. Finally, I am only reviewing the literature available in English. I am aware of an expanding literature in Europe, but unfortunately my language limitations do not allow for such coverage here.

FORMATIVE STUDIES AND THEORETICAL FOUNDATIONS

Contributions of social network analysis to status attainment can be traced to the seminal study conducted by Mark Granovetter (1974), who interviewed 282 professional and managerial men in Newton, Massachusetts. The data suggested that those who used interpersonal channels seemed to land more satisfactory and better (e.g., higher income) jobs. Inferring from this empirical research, substantiated with a review of job-search studies, Granovetter proposed (1973) a network theory for information flow. The hypothesis of "the strength of weak ties" was that weaker ties tend to form bridges that link individuals to other social circles for information not likely to be available in their own circles, and such information should be useful to the individuals.[1]

However, Granovetter never suggested that access to or help from weaker rather than stronger ties would result in better statuses of jobs thus obtained (1995:148). Clues about the linkage between strength of ties and attained statuses came indirectly from a small world study conducted in a tri-city metropolitan area in upstate New York (Lin et al 1978). The task of the participants in the study was to forward packets containing information about certain target persons to others they knew on first-name basis so that the packets might eventually reach the target persons. The study found that successful chains (those

---

[1]On the surface, this hypothesis might be seen as simply the inverse of the long-familiar hypothesis that stronger ties are formed among those who share similar characteristics and lifestyles; this is known as the homophily principle or the like-me hypothesis (Homans 1950, Lazarsfeld & Merton1954, Laumann 1966, Lin 1982). What the strength-of-weak-tie argument contributed, however, was a challenge to the taken-for-granted and attributed value given to strong ties or the homophily principle—strong ties, promoting group solidarity, are socially valuable. By shifting our attention to the weaker ties, Granovetter alerted us that weak ties, promoting access to different and new information, are socially valuable as well.

packets successfully forwarded to the targets) involved higher-status intermediaries until the last nodes (dipping down in the hierarchy toward the locations of the targets). Successful chains also implicated nodes that had more extensive social contacts (who claimed more social ties) and yet these tended to forward the packets to someone they had not seen recently (weaker ties). The small world study thus made two contributions. First, it suggested that access to hierarchical positions might be the critical factor in the process of status attainment. Thus, the possible linkage between strength of ties and status attainment might be indirect: The strength of weak ties might lie in their accessing social positions vertically higher in the social hierarchy, which had the advantage in facilitating the instrumental action. Second, the study implicated behavior rather than a paper-and-pencil exercise, as each step in the packet-forwarding process required actual actions from each participant. Thus, the study results lend behavioral validity to those found in previous status attainment paper-pencil studies.

Based on these studies, a theory of social resources has emerged (Lin 1982, 1990). The theory begins with an image of the macro-social structure consisting of positions ranked according to certain normatively valued resources such as wealth, status, and power. This structure has a pyramidal shape in terms of accessibility and control of such resources: The higher the position, the fewer the occupants; and the higher the position, the better the view it has of the structure (especially down below). The pyramidal structure suggests advantages for positions nearer to the top, both in terms of number of occupants (fewer) and accessibility to positions (more). Individuals within these structural constraints and opportunities take actions for expressive and instrumental purposes. For instrumental actions (attaining status in the social structure being one prime example), the better strategy would be for ego to reach toward contacts higher up in the hierarchy. These contacts would be better able to exert influence on positions (e.g., recruiter for a firm) whose actions may benefit ego's interest. This reaching-up process may be facilitated if ego uses weaker ties, since weaker ties are more likely to reach out vertically (presumably upward) rather than horizontally relative to ego's position in the hierarchy.

Three propositions were thus formulated: (*a*) the social resources proposition: that social resources (e.g., resources accessed in social networks) exert effect on the outcome of an instrumental action (e.g., attained status), (*b*) the strength of position proposition: that social resources, in turn, are affected by the original position of ego (as represented by parental resources or previous resources), and (*c*) the strength of ties proposition: that social resources are also affected by the use of weaker rather than stronger ties. A subsequent variation of the last proposition is the extensity of the proposition: that social resources are affected by extensity of direct and indirect ties (see *Issues and Future Directions*).

SOCIAL RESOURCES AND SOCIAL CAPITAL: A THEORETICAL CONVERGENCE

Parallel but independent of the development of the social resources theory, another general sociological theory emerged in the late 1970s and early 1980s (Bourdieu 1986, Coleman 1988)—the social capital theory. While social capital may refer to a variety of features in the social structure, according to different scholars (e.g., community norms—Coleman 1990; group solidarity—Hechter 1983, Portes & Senssenbrenner 1993; participation in voluntary and civil organizations—Putnam 1995), it has become clear (Lin 1995, Flap 1996, Tardos 1996, Burt 1997, Portes 1998) that social capital refers primarily to resources accessed in social networks. Further, the theory also focuses on the instrumental utility of such resources (capital as an investment or mobilization). The convergence of the social resources and social capital theories complements and strengthens the development of a social theory focusing on the instrumental utility of accessed and mobilized resources embedded in social networks. It places the significance of social resources in the broader theoretical discussion of social capital and sharpens the definition and operationalization of social capital as a research concept. The three propositions stated above remain valid in the framework of social capital (i.e., the social capital proposition, the strength of position proposition, and the strength of ties proposition). The following discussion reflects the merged notions of social capital and social resources. At the empirical and research levels, social resources are used, whereas at the general theoretical level, social capital is employed.

RESEARCH MODELS AND EVIDENCE

Research on the relationships between social resources and status attainment examines two processes, as illustrated in Figure 1. One process focuses on the access to social capital—resources accessed in ego's general social networks. In this process, human capital (education, experiences), initial positions (parental or prior job statuses), and ego's social ties (e.g., extensity of ties) are hypothesized to determine the extent of resources ego can access through such connections (network resources). Further, network resources, education, and initial positions are expected to affect attained statuses such as occupational status, authority positions, sectors, or earnings. We may identify this model as the accessed social capital model.

Another process focuses on the mobilization of social capital in the process of status attainment—the use of social contact and the resources provided by the contact in the job-search process. As can be seen in Figure 1, status of the contact used is seen as the mobilized social capital in the status attainment process. It is hypothesized that contact status, along with education and initial positions, will exert a significant and important effect on attained statuses of the job obtained. Contact status, in turn, is to be affected by education, network resources, and the tie strength between ego and the contact. Strength of ties may be measured either with a perceived strength (e.g., intimacy of relationship) or a role category (e.g., kin, friends, and acquaintances). We shall call this model the mobilized social capital model.

In both types of analyses, other factors may be added to the basic model, including age, gender, race/ethnicity, indications of job experience or tenure, the work sector, and the industry or organization, either as control variables or as opportunity/constraint factors. We turn now to a brief review of the literature, which proceeds first with the mobilized social capital model, as it received initial research attention, followed by the accessed social capital, and models incorporating both access and mobilization processes. A summary of the studies and findings appears in Table 1.

Mobilized Social Capital[2]

The initial empirical examination of the model was conducted by Lin and his associates (Lin et al 1981, Lin et al 1981). The study with data from a representative community sample in metropolitan Albany, New York, of more than 400 employed males confirmed that contact status exerted effects on attained status, beyond and after accounting for parental status and education effects. It also confirmed that contact status was affected positively by father's status and negatively by the strength of ties between ego and contact. The results provided the initial confirmation of all three propositions of the social capital theory. Ensel (1979) extended the investigation to both men and women in a study of employed adults in the state of New York. While confirming that contact status significantly affected attained status, he found that male seekers were much more likely to reach higher-status contacts than were females. Further, women were more likely to use female contacts in job searches while males overwhelmingly used male contacts. When women did use male contacts, their disadvantage in reaching higher-status contacts as compared to men was significantly reduced. The study was one of the first studies providing direct evidence that males, being positioned advantageously in the hierarchy, had better social capital. Secondly, female disadvantages in mobilizing male contacts,

---

[2]The fact that this estimation procedure only studies a subsample of labor-force participants who use personal contacts in job searches raised concern about the selectivity bias on the estimations. In surveys of community labor populations, anywhere from 20% to over 61% of the job-seekers indicate the use of personal contacts (for a summary, see Granovetter 1995:139–41). Yet, studies of selectivity bias have revealed no major differences in the characteristics of those who used personal contacts as compared to those who used formal channels or direct applications in job searches. Younger and less experienced workers do show a slightly greater tendency to use personal contacts. Thus, most studies have incorporated age and/or work experience as controls to account for possible bias.

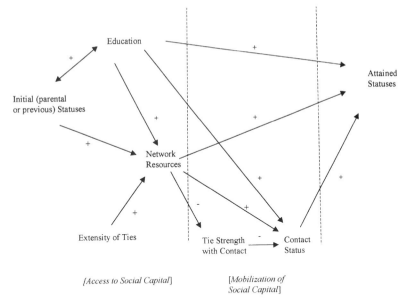

Figure 1   The social capital model of status *attainment*

and thereby accessing better social capital, accounted in part for their inferior status attainment. Further replication and extension of the model was conducted by Marsden & Hurlbert (1988) with an analysis of the transition to current jobs for 456 men in the 1970 Detroit Area Study. The study confirmed that contact status (occupational prestige and sector) exerted the strongest effect on attained prestige and sector, respectively. They also found that contact's prestige and being in the core sector were respectively related to prestige and sector of prior job, confirming the strength of position proposition. On the other hand, they did not confirm the strength of tie proposition; contact status was not associated with the strength of ties between ego and contact.

Extension of the model to other societies quickly followed. De Graaf & Flap (1988) lend further support to the social resources proposition in their analyses with a sample of 628 males in a 1980 West German survey and 466 males in a 1982 Dutch survey. They did not examine the strength of position or the strength-of-tie propositions for social resources. The Netherlands Family Survey of 1992 provided some data on male-female comparisons in the social capital effect. Moerbeek et al (1995) used father's occupation as the indicator of social capital when the father was mentioned as the social contact, and they found it exerted a positive and significant effect on the statuses of first and current/last jobs for both men and women. Wegener (1991) analyzed a 1987 data set from Germany of 604 men and women aged forty-two and thirty-two

Table 1   Summary of studies and findings

Study	Social resources effect (outcome var.)	Position effect	Tie effect
MOBILIZED SOCIAL CAPITAL MODEL			
Lin, Ensel & Vaughn (1981, USA)	yes	yes	yes
Marsden & Hurlbert (1988, USA)	yes	yes	no
Ensel (1979, USA)	yes	—	—
DeGraaf & Flap (1988, The Netherlands)	yes	—	—
Moerbeek, Utle & Flap (1996, The Netherlands)	yes	yes	—
Wegener (1991, West Germany)	yes	—	—
Requena (1991, Spain)	no	—	—
Barbieri (1996, Italy)	yes	yes	—
Hsung, Sun & She (1986, Taiwan)	yes	—	—
Hsung & Hwang (1992, Taiwan)	yes	yes	no
Bian & Ang (1997, Singapore)	yes	—	yes*
Volker & Flap (1996, East Germany)	yes	yes*	no
Bian (1997, China)	yes	—	no
ACCESSED SOCIAL CAPITAL MODEL			
Name Generator Methodology			
Campbell, Marsden & Hurlbert (1986, USA)	yes	—	—
Sprengers, Tazelaar & Flap (1988, The Netherlands	yes	yes	yes*
Barbierer (1996, Italy)	yes	yes	—
Boxman, DeGraaf & Flap (1991, The Netherlands)	yes	—	—
Boxman & Flap (1990, The Netherlands)	yes	—	—
Burt (1992, USA)	yes	—	—
Burt (1997, 1998, USA)	yes*	—	—
Position Generator Methodology			
Lin & Dumin (1986, USA)	yes	yes	yes*
Hsung & Hwang (1992, Taiwan)	yes	—	—
Volker & Flap (1997, East Germany)	yes	yes	yes
Angelusz & Tardos (1991, Hungary)	yes	no	—
Erickson (1995, 1996, Canada)	yes	—	yes*
Erickson (1998, Canada)	yes	—	—
Belliveau, O'Reilly & Wade (1996, USA)	yes	—	—
JOINT ACCESSED/MOBILIZED MODEL			
Boxman & Flap (Boxman 1992; H Flap, E Boxman, unpublished paper, The Netherlands)	yes	—	—
Flap & Boxman (1998, The Netherlands)	yes	—	—
Volker & Flap (1997, East Germany)	yes	—	—
Lai, Lin & Leung (1998, USA)	yes	yes	yes

—: not reported; *conditional confirmations; detail in text.

and found that contact status significantly affected the prestige of the job found, confirming the social resources proposition. However, the strength-of-ties proposition and the strength-of-position hypotheses were not examined. Barbieri (1996), reporting a study conducted of 500 newly hired persons in the administrative area of Milan, Italy, found that contact status significantly affected present job status, having already accounted for effects from father's status, education, and first and previous job statuses, confirming the social resources proposition. Further, he found that father's status indirectly affected contact status, through education, lending some support to the strength of tie proposition. His model did not include measures of the strength of tie between ego and contact and did not examine the strength of tie proposition. Requena's study in Spain (1991) provided the only disconfirming evidence for the social resources proposition, as it showed that greater social resources did not provide better jobs, even though these did affect the income attainment. He speculated that the lack of social resources effects was in part due to the rigid bureaucratization of Spain's employment policies and practices.

Systematic tests of the theory have been carried out in Asia as well. A series of studies were conducted by Hsung and others in Taiwan, which is also a capitalist state but in another region of the world. One study (Hsung & Sun 1988) surveyed the labor force in the manufacturing industry and another (Hsung & Hwang 1992) examined the labor force in a metropolitan area (Taichung). Both studies supported the social resources proposition: that contact status significantly affected the status of obtained first and current jobs, after accounting for father's education and occupational status, education, and, in the case of current job, prior job status. Hsung & Hwang (1992) also found modest support for the strength-of-position argument, while father's education and occupational status had only a modest effect on contact status for the first job and no significant effect on contact status for the current job. For strength of ties, a composite measure (closeness with contacts, frequency of visits, frequency of calls, and content of relation) indicated only a slightly negative relationship with contact status of the first job and no relationship with contact status of the current job. In addition, Bian & Ang (1997) conducted a study in 1994 of 512 men and women in Singapore that strongly confirmed the social resources proposition: Contact status significantly affected obtained status. Helper status was strongly related to occupational status of the current job, along with age, education, and prior job status. For all respondents, weaker ties reached higher-status contacts. However, the weakest ties (not intimate at all) did not have any effect on contact status, a finding similar to that in the 1988 Tianjin study to be described shortly. For those reaching helpers indirectly, the association between tie strength and contact status was a negative one. However, stronger ties between the intermediary and the helper were more likely to result in reaching a higher-status helper.

A major extension of the research paradigm has examined the propositions in different political economies, such as state socialism. In a 1988 study, conducted in Tianjin, China, including 1,008 men and women, Bian (1997) found that helpers' job status (measured by the hierarchical level of his/her work unit) was strongly associated with attained work unit status in the job change, along with education and prior job status. The overall effect of the tie strength between ego and the helper on the helper's status was insignificant. Further analyses showed that medium-strength ties reached helpers with better status, which was true for the tie strength between ego and the intermediaries as well as the intermediaries and the helpers. Moreover, in a retrospective panel study conducted by Volker & Flap (1996) in Leipzig and Dresden, two cities in the former GDR (German Democratic Republic), the occupational prestige of the contact person had strong and significant effects on both the first job and 1989 job prestige. Thus, the social resources proposition was confirmed. However, strength of ties (measured by intensity of relationship between ego and the contact) had no effect on contact statuses or the attained occupational status and income. Neither father's education nor occupational prestige affected contact status for the 1989 job search. However, education had a significant effect on contact status. Since the father's status had direct effects on education, these results confirmed the indirect effect of the strength of positions, mediated through education.

Accessed Social Capital

Two methods measure accessed social capital: name generators and position generators. The name generator is the more common method and has been used extensively in the network literature. The general technique is to pose one or more questions about ego's contacts in certain role relationships (e.g., neighborhood, work), content areas (e.g., work matters, household chores), or intimacy (e.g., confiding, most intimate, etc). Such questions generate a list of contacts ranging from three to five or as many as volunteered by ego. From these lists, relationships between ego and contacts and among contacts, as well as contacts' characteristics, were generated. Social capital measures are constructed to reflect the contacts' diversity and range in resources (education, occupation) as well as characteristics (gender, race, age). A number of problems are associated with the use of name generators to measure social capital, including variations in distributions being affected by the content or role and number of names. As a result, the data tend to reflect stronger ties, stronger role relations, or ties in close geographic limits (Campbell & Lee 1991).

Position generators, first proposed by Lin and associates (Lin & Dumin 1986), use a sample of structural positions salient in a society (occupations, authorities, work units, class, or sector) and ask respondents to indicate contacts (e.g., those known on first-name basis), if any, in each of the positions. Further, relationships between ego and contact for each position can be identified. Thus, instead of sampling content or role areas, the position generator samples hierarchical positions. It is content free and role/location-neutral. Instead of counting and measuring data from specific names (persons) generated, the position generator counts and measures access to structural positions. An example position-generator instrument is shown in Table 2. The name-generator methodology has been employed in research over a longer period of time, while the position-generator methodology has emerged in more recent studies. The following section reports on the studies and results for each methodology on accessed social capital and status attainment.

NAME GENERATORS STUDIES   Campbell et al (1986) examined the associations between network resources and socioeconomic statuses with name-generator data from the 1965–66 Detroit Area Study and found that the resource compositions of networks (mean and maximal education, mean and maximal prestige) were significantly associated with attained statuses such as occupational prestige and family income. In the Milan study, Barbieri (1996) also constructed three measures for social capital from name-generator data and found them to affect present job status, after accounting for parental statuses, experience, human capital (years of schooling), and first and previous job statuses. Further, social capital was affected by father's status, confirming the strength of position proposition (the study did not examine the strength-of-ties proposition).

Several studies have assessed the associations between accessed social capital and attained statuses among certain labor populations. Access to social capital by the unemployed was the focus of the study conducted by Sprengers et al (1988). Among a group of 242 Dutch men aged 40–55 who became unemployed in or before 1978, those with better social capital were more likely to

Table 2 Position generator for measuring accessed social capital: an example

Here is a list of jobs (*show card*). Would you please tell me if you happen to know someone (on a first-name basis) having each job?

Job	1. Do you know anyone having this job?	2. How long have you known this person (no. of years)?	3. What is your relationship with this person?	4. How close are you with this person?	5. His/her gender	6. His/her job
Job A						
Job B						
Job C						
etc.						

*If you know more than one person, think of the one person whom you have known the longest.

find jobs within a year after unemployment, especially those with access to so-cial capital through weak ties. Those with better social capital did not find a better occupational status or income when they found re-employment. How-ever, better social capital increased optimism about job opportunities, which in turn increased the intensity of the job search, leading to finding more and better jobs. Further, the more restricted the labor market was, the more intense those with greater social capital tended to be in job searches. After a year of unem-ployment, the ones with better social capital among strong ties (relatives) also tended to have a better chance to be re-hired in the next one to three years. The study also found that those with better education, former occupations, and higher incomes tended to have better social capital, confirming the strength of position hypothesis. Focusing on 1359 top managers of larger companies in the Netherlands, Boxman, De Graaf & Flap (1991) found that both education and social capital (measured with work contacts in other organizations and memberships in clubs and professional associations) had direct effects on in-come. The job-search activities of 365 persons in the Netherlands who finished vocational training were also studied by Boxman & Flap (1990) in 1989. Data were obtained from job seekers and employers as well as contacts used by the job seekers, and preliminary analyses showed that for income, the more impor-tant predictors were gender (in favor of men), social capital, career perspec-tive, and company-specific skills.

Early promotion and better bonuses were the outcomes assessed by Burt (1992) for managers in a large electronic components and computing equip-ment firm. Using the extent to which each ego was embedded in a constrained network (fewer contacts, more dense relations, and more contacts related to a single contact) as a measure of social capital, he found a negative association between structural constraints and early promotion. That is, there was the sug-gestion that access to diverse resources in one's networks enhanced the oppor-tunity to locate information and influence useful for promoting one's position in the firm. For men in senior positions in the investment banking division of a large American financial organization, similar negative association between constrained networks and bonuses was found (Burt 1997).

POSITION GENERATORS STUDIES   Lin & Dumin (1986) analyzed the data from the Albany study in which a list of 20 occupations was sampled from the US 1960 census listing of occupations, with all occupations ranked according to the job prestige scores. Then, at equal intervals on the job prestige scale scores, occupations were identified. From the group of occupations at the sampled interval, the most popular (frequency of occupants) occupation was selected. Each respondent was asked if he had any contact (person with whom on first-name basis) in each of the positions. If more than one contact was indi-cated, they were asked to focus on the most familiar one. For each accessed position, the respondent identified the contact's relationship (relative, friend, or acquaintance). From the data matrix, Lin & Dumin constructed two social resources access measures: the highest status accessible (the position accessed with the highest prestige score) and the range of statuses accessed (difference between the highest and lowest accessed statuses). Analyses showed that the two measures were positively and significantly related to current occupational status. Further analysis showed that respondents' original positions (father's occupational prestige score or white collar–blue collar and high-low occupational groupings) and these two measures were related positively and significantly, confirming the strength of position hypothesis. When they analyzed the relationships between the three types of ties (relatives, friends, acquaintances) and the access variables, they found that friends as well as acquaintances provided the best access to both the highest status position and the range of accessed statuses.

Hsung & Hwang (1992) also incorporated network resources in their Taichung study, as cited earlier. Adapting the position generator methodology with 20 occupations, they failed to find significant effects for the highest status accessed and for the difference between the lowest and highest occupational statuses accessed. However, they did find significant effects on the first job status of a measure of "the total amount of network resources" that was based on the sum status scores of all occupations accessed. This measure, however, did not have any effect on current job status.

Volker & Flap (1996), in their East Germany study, used the position generator methodology to ask respondents to identify, among 33 occupations, whether they knew anyone in any of the occupations, and if so, what their relationships were (relatives, friends, and acquaintances). For 1989 occupational status, the effect of the highest status accessed was positive and significant, while controlling for father's education and occupation, the respondent's own education and sex, and the prestige of their first job. This variable also had a positive and moderately significant ($p < .10$) effect on 1989 income, when 1989 occupational prestige was added to the equation along with all other independent variables for 1989 job prestige. This result confirmed the social resources proposition. Further, Volker & Flap found that both relatives and acquaintances accessed better occupations (upper-white, or higher prestige) than did friends. On the other hand, acquaintances did access a greater range (difference between the highest and lowest prestige jobs) of occupations than did either relatives or friends. Since the highest occupational prestige accessed turned out to be the best predictor for attained status, the effects of weak ties were not found (as relatives and acquaintances were almost equally likely to access high-prestige occupations). The father's occupational prestige was positively related to the highest occupation prestige accessed in general as well as for each group of occupations accessed through relatives, friends, and acquaintances. Thus, the strength of position proposition was confirmed. In pre-1989 Hungary (1987–1988), Angelusz & Tardos (1991) also used the position generator to identify "weakly tied" relations or resources. This variable was found to be significantly associated with wages, after accounting for the effects of sex, education, residence, and age.

In her study of 161 licensed guard and investigator firms in Toronto in 1991–1992, Erickson (1995, 1996) used Wright's (1979) class dimensions (control of property, control of organizations, and control of skill) to select 19 job positions. Data were gathered from 154 employers, 46 supervisors, 80 managers, and 112 owners. She found that social capital (diversity in accessing various positions) contributed to cultural capital, job autonomy, and authority, which in turn generated better job returns. For becoming an owner, network diversity made a more direct and significant contribution. In another study on social capital, Erickson (1998) differentiated two types of social capital: global and local. Local settings refer to geographic areas (neighborhoods), ethnic areas (ethnic communities and enclave economies), or organizations (schools, voluntary organizations, social movements, or firms). In a telephone survey with a sample of 352 participants in the Toronto LETS (Local Employment and Trading System), Erickson asked the respondents to identify contacts in a list of 30 occupations, both in and outside the LETS system. Analyses showed that global social capital was associated with global (age, gender—being female, education, and employment status) variables and local social capital with local activities (time in LETS, markets and swaps attended in LETS, social events, and steering committee meetings attended in LETS).

Joint Effects of Accessed and Mobilized Social Capital

Since there are two types of social capital in the process of status attainment, a logical step would be to examine accessed and mobilized social capital in a single study. The theoretical question posed is the extent to which accessed social capital facilitates and mobilizes social capital: that is, whether having more accessed social capital increases the likelihood of mobilizing better social capital. The structural opportunity and advantage implied in this hypothesis is apparent. However, it is also to be expected that the correspondence should not be overwhelming—not all persons accessed with rich social capital are expected to take advantage or be able to mobilize social capital for the purpose of obtaining better socioeconomic status. An element of action and choice should also be significant. Several studies have lent support to this hypothesis.

Flap & Boxman (H Flap, E Boxman, unpublished paper), for example, in their study of vocational training graduates showed that contact status (mobilized social capital) affected attained occupational status, whereas accessed social capital did not. The East Germany study (Volker & Flap 1996) is another study in which both accessed and mobilized social capital were measured. It was found that the highest occupation prestige accessed in the position-generator methodology was significantly and positively related to the status of the contact person used in the 1989 job search, but its direct effect on the 1989 job prestige, while positive, was only modest in significance (p < .10). The contact person's prestige had a much stronger effect. In fact, its direct effect on 1989 job prestige was stronger than education, once the first job prestige was also incorporated (and was the most significant predictor).

Lai et al (1998) also examined the joint effects of accessed and mobilized social capital on status attainment with the Albany data (Lin et al 1981). Incorporating both the network resources measures from the position generator (Lin & Dumin 1986) and the contact resources (contact status in the job search) in structural equation models, they showed that current job status was significantly and directly affected by education (achieved status) and contact status. Contact status was, in turn, affected by parental statuses (ascribed status), education, network resources, and weaker ties with the contact. Thus, it is clear that mobilized social capital directly influences status outcome, and mobilized social capital is affected by accessed social capital, along with ascribed and achieved statuses.

ISSUES AND RESEARCH DIRECTIONS

Research has provided consistent support to the proposition that social capital, in the form of social resources, makes a significant contribution to status attainment beyond personal resources. This association persists across societies (different nation-states and political economies), industrialization and development levels, populations in the labor market (recent graduates, new hires, job changers), different sectors in the economy (industries, organizations, positions in organizations), or status outcomes (occupation, authority, sector, promotion, bonuses). The association remains significant across differential conceptualization (accessed versus mobilized capital) and measurement (name generators versus position generators). Yet, there remain important issues to be conceptualized and studied in the future. In the following, a number of these are briefly identified and discussed.

Informal and Formal Channels of Job Search

It is clear by now that use of informal channels by itself offers no advantage over other channels, especially formal channels, in attained status. In fact, if anything, informal channels tend to be used by the disadvantaged: females, the less educated, and the less skilled. The statuses attained therefore tend to be lower. Yet, among those who use informal channels, social resources (statuses of the contacts) make a major difference. Several issues remain. First, is it really true that the advantaged do not need to use informal channels, as they possess greater human capital and can apply directly to high-status positions? The evidence is mixed. For some jobs that have specific job requirements (dealing with technology and hardware, for example), credentials regarding skills and training in the formal application may be sufficient to obtain the positions. However, for other critical jobs (high-level managers and human-interfaced positions), formal credentials often are insufficient to convey the social skills and resources so essential for occupants' performances. The necessary informal or shadow channels through which such information is conveyed, yet not detected in survey instruments, remain an important methodological challenge. Secondly, for the disadvantaged, social capital is restricted (the strength of position argument). Within this restricted range of resources, there is little information as to whether the disadvantaged are also less likely to mobilize the optimal resources available to them, thus creating double jeopardy. Knowledge about the choice behaviors of the advantaged and the disadvantaged will be helpful in sorting through the structural constraints and choice constraints.

Strength or Extensity of Ties?

While the social resources proposition and the strength-of-position propositions have been consistently confirmed (see Table 1), much ambiguity has resulted regarding the strength-of-ties proposition. Strength of ties in and of itself should not be expected to exert a direct effect on status outcomes (Granovetter 1995), and much research evidence points to the absence of a direct association (e.g., Bridges & Willemez 1986, Marsden & Hurlbert 1988, Forse 1997). The modified proposition that weaker ties might access better social resources also lacks consistent empirical support (see Table 1). Yet, social capital is theorized to contain both structural effects and agency effects; further specifications of network or the choices within structural constraints may eventually turn out to be meaningful. Several lines of investigation have provided some leads. For example, it has been argued that the effect of strength of ties on social resources accessed or mobilized may be contingent on the original status. Some studies have pointed to the ceiling effect of the tie strength: At or near the top level of the hierarchy, it is the strong ties that tend to yield successful job attainment (Lin et al 1981, Erickson 1995, 1996). Also, the weakest ties are clearly not useful (Bian 1997, Bian & Ang 1997), since ties with no strength offer no incentive for exchanges. On the other hand, the strongest ties, by the same token, may be useful despite the restricted range of resources accessed. They, by definition, represent commitment, trust, and obligation and, therefore, the motivation to help. Willingness and effort to search other ties by these strong ties may be critical under institutional uncertainties or constraints (e.g., under state socialism, Bian 1997, Rus 1995; or tight market situations, Sprengers et al 1988). Organizational constraints and opportunities may also condition the relative utility of weaker or stronger ties (Lin 1990).

An alternative route of theorizing the network effects on social capital shifts the focus from the strength of ties to extensity of ties. There is persistent evidence that extensity or size of network ties are significantly related to richness or diversity in social resources (e.g., Lin & Dumin 1986, Angelusz & Tardos 1991, Burt 1997). Having both strong and weak ties enhances extensity of networks, and extensive ties afford better opportunities for individuals to locate the resources useful for instrumental actions. Thus, we may propose an *extensity-of-ties proposition*: the more extensive the networks, the better social resources to be accessed and mobilized.

Further Development of the Position Generator

In order to ascertain the causal sequence, the time framework of the contacts needs to be specified. For example, the generator may wish to indicate that "when you were looking for the first (or current) job, did you know of anyone who had this kind of work?" Also, it is important to sample the positions from a meaningful hierarchy in a given society. In addition to occupational status or prestige, work units, sectors, authority, or autonomy may confer important statuses in certain societies. Catering to the significance of meaningful statuses/classes in a given society is thus an important consideration in identifying the positions in the generators (Erickson 1995).

Inequality of Social Capital

Differential access to social capital deserves much greater research attention. It is conceivable that social groups (gender, race) have different access to social capital because of their advantaged or disadvantaged structural positions and social networks. Thus, for example, inequality of social capital offers less opportunities for females and minority members to mobilize better social resources to attain and promote careers. For the disadvantaged to gain a better status, strategic behaviors require accessing resources beyond the usual social circles [for example, females use male ties (Ensel 1979) to find sponsors in the firm (Burt 1998) and join clubs dominated by males (Beggs & Hurlbert 1997); or for blacks to find ties outside their own neighborhood or with those employed (Green et al 1995); or for Mexican-origin high schoolers to find ties of nonMexican origin or to establish ties with institutional agents such as teachers and counselors (Stanton-Salazar & Dornbusch 1995, Stanton-Salazar 1997]. Systematic data will enhance our understanding of the inequalities in social capital as an explanatory framework for inequality in social stratification and mobility and behavior choices to overcome such inequalities.

Recruitment and Social Capital

The relationships between social capital and status attainment apply to both supply and demand sides of the labor market. So far, research literature has primarily concentrated on the supply side—the status attainment process from job-seekers' perspective. The demand side of the model—the recruitment process from the organization's perspective—has only begun to emerge (Boxman & Flap 1990, Boxman et al 1991, Burt 1997, Erickson 1995, 1996, Fernandez & Weinberg 1996). There are reasons to believe that social capital is important for firms in selective recruitments, as firms must operate in an environment where social skills and networks play critical roles in transactions and exchanges. This is especially true of certain types of positions. Thus, we may anticipate that certain positions require more social capital than other positions in a firm. First, top-level executives are expected to possess rich social capital, as they need to deal and manage people both within and outside the firm. In fact, we may postulate that at the highest level of management, social capital far outweighs human capital for occupants. Thus, it can be hypothesized that firms such as IBM and Microsoft may be more likely to recruit experienced managers with social skills than with computer expertise for their CEOs, and that top universities need presidents who have the social skills to negotiate with faculty, students, parents, and alumni and to raise funds rather than to produce distinguished scholarship. Secondly, we should expect positions that deal with persons (e.g., nurses) rather than machines or technologies (e.g., programmers) to be filled with occupants with better social capital. Third, positions at the edge of the firm are more likely to be filled by those with better social capital than others (e.g., salesperson, public relations, or managers at remote sites) (Burt 1997). Firms with more needs for such positions, therefore, should be expected to use informal sources in recruitments more extensively. Such hypotheses will help empirical specifications and testing.

Social Capital versus Human Capital

The relationship between social capital and human capital is theoretically important. Some scholars (Bourdieu 1986, Coleman 1990) have proposed that social capital helps produce human capital. Well-connected parents and social ties can indeed enhance the opportunities for individuals to obtain better education, training, and skill and knowledge credentials. On the other hand, it is clear that human capital induces social capital. Better educated and better trained individuals tend to move in social circles and clubs rich in resources. The harder question is: Given both, which is more important in enhancing status attainment? Several studies cited in this chapter suggest that social capital may be as important or even more important than human capital (education, and work experience) in status attainment (Lin et al 1981, Marsden & Hurlbert

1988), while others show the opposite (DeGraaf & Flap 1988, Hsung & Sun 1988, Hsung & Hwang 1992). Industrialization probably is not the explanation, as the former group includes studies conducted in the United States, and the latter the Netherlands and Taiwan. More likely, it suggests an association between specific educational institutions and methods of job allocations and searches. As Krymkowski (1991) showed in a comparative analysis of data from the United States, West Germany, and Poland in the 1970s, both West Germany and Poland showed greater associations between social origins and education and between education and occupational allocations than did the United States. Yet, there is no clear evidence that the educational system in Taiwan resembles the West German and Dutch systems more than the US system. The contrasting results from these countries thus remain to be explained.

Still more intriguing is possible interactions between human capital and social capital. Boxman et al (1991) found that human capital had its greatest effect on income when social capital was low and that human capital had its least effect on income when social capital was high. Further, in the study of Dutch managers, Flap & Boxman (1998) found that for top managers, social capital helped to earn more income at any level of human capital, but the returns of human capital decreased at higher levels of social capital. If these patterns can be confirmed, they would suggest that human capital supplements social capital in status attainment. That is, when social capital is high, attained status will be high, regardless of the level of human capital; and when social capital is low, human capital exerts a strong effect on attainment. Or, given certain minimal levels of human and social capital, social capital is the more important factor in accounting for status attainment.

> **Visit the *Annual Reviews home page* at
> http://www.AnnualReviews.org.**

Literature Cited

Angelusz R, Tardos R. 1991. The strength and weakness of weak ties. In *Values, Networks and Cultural Reproduction in Hungary*, ed. P Somlai, pp. 7–23. Budapest: Coordinating Council of Prog.

Barbieri P. 1996. *Household, social capital and labour market attainment.* ECSR Workshop. Max Planck Inst. Hum. Dev. Educ., Berlin, August 26–27

Baron JN, Bielby WT980. Bringing the frm back in: stratification, segmentation, and the organization of work. *Am. Sociol. Rev.* 45:737–65

Beggs JJ, Hurlbert JS. 1997. The social context of men's and women's job search ties: voluntary organization memberships, social resources, and job search sutcomes. *Sociol. Perspect.* 40(4):601–22, 24

Bian Y. 1997. Bringing strong ties back in: indirect connection, bridges, and job search in China. *Am. Sociol. Rev.* 62(3):36–385, 3

Bian Y, Ang S. 1997. Guanxi networks and job mobility in China and Singapore. *Soc. Forc.* 75:981–1006

Blau PM, Duncan OD. 1967. *The American Occupational Structure*. New York: Wiley

Bourdieu P. 1983/1986. The forms of capital. In *Handbook of Theory and Research for the Sociology of Education*, ed. JG Richardson, pp. 241–58. Westport, CT: Greenwood

Boxman EAW, De Graaf PM, Flap HD. 1991. The impact of social and human capital on the income attainment of Dutch managers. *Soc. Networks* 13:51–73

Boxman EAW, Flap HD. 1992. Social capital and occupational chances. Int. Sociol. Assoc. XII World Congr. Sociol.. Madrid, July.

Bridges WP, Villemez WJ. 1986. Informal hiring and income in the labor market. *Am. Sociol. Rev.* 51:574–82

Burt RS. 1992. *Structural Holes: The Social Structure of Competition.* Cambridge, MA: Harvard Univ. Press

Burt RS. 1997. The contingent value of social capital. *Admin. Sci. Q.* 42:339–65

Burt RS. 1998. The gender of social capital. *Ration. Soc.* 10(1):5–46, 1

Campbell KE, Lee BA. 1991. Name generators in surveys of personal networks. *Soc. Networks* 13:203–21

Campbell KE, Marsden PV, Hurlbert JS. 1986. Social resources and socioeconomic status. *Soc. Networks* 8(1), 1

Coleman JS. 1988. Social capital in the creation of human capital. *Am. J. Sociol.* 94: S95–S121

Coleman JS. 1990. *Foundations of Social Theory.* Cambridge, MA: Harvard Univ. Press

De Graaf ND, Flap HD. 1988. With a little help from my friends. *Soc. Forc.* 67(2): 452–72, 2

Ensel WM. 1979. Sex, social ties, and status attainment. Albany, NY: State Univ. New York at Albany Press

Erickson BH. 1995. *Networks, success, and class structure: a total view.* Sunbelt Social Networks Conf. Charleston, SC, February

Erickson BH. 1996. Culture, class and connections. *Am. J. Sociol.* 102(1):217–51, 1

Erickson BH. 1998. Social capital and its profits, local and global. The Sunbelt XVIII and 5th Eur. Int. Conf. on Soc. Networks. Sitges, Spain, May 27–31

Fernandez RM, Weinberg N. 1996. Getting a job: networks and hiring in a retail bank. Stanford Univ., March

Forse M. 1997. Capital social et emploi. *L'Annee Sociol.* 47(1):143–81, 1

Goldthorpe JH. 1980. *Social Mobility and Class Structure in Modern Britain.* New York: Oxford Univ. Press

Granovetter M. 1973. The strength of weak ties. *Am. J. Sociol.* 78:1360–80

Granovetter M. 1974. *Getting a Job.* Cambridge, MA: Harvard Univ. Press

Granovetter M. 1995. *Getting a Job.* Chicago: Univ. Chicago Press. Rev. ed.

Green GP, Tigges LM, Browne I. 1995. Social resources, job search, and poverty in Atlanta. *Res. in Commun. Sociol.* 5:161–82

Hechter M. 1983. A theory of group solidarity. In *The Microfoundations of Macrosociology,* ed. M Hechter, pp. 16–57. Philadelphia: Temple Univ. Press

Homans GC. 1950. *The Human Group.* New York: Harcourt, Brace

Hsung R-M, Hwang Y-J. 1992. Job mobility in Taiwan: job search methods and contacts status. XII Int. Sunbelt Soc. Network Conf. San Diego, February

Hsung R-M, Sun C-S. 1988. *Social Resources and Social Mobility: Manufacturing Employees.* Taiwan: Natl. Sci. Council

Kalleberg A. 1988. Comparative perspectives on work structures and inequality. *Annu. Rev. Sociol.* 14:203–25

Kelley J. 1990. The failure of a paradigm: loglinear models of social mobility. in *John H. Goldthorpe: Consens and Controversy,* ed. J Clark, C Modgil, S Modgil, pp. 319–346; 349–57. London: Falmer

Krymkowski DH. 1991. The process of status attainment Among men in Poland, the U. S., and West Germany. *Am. Sociol. Rev.* 56:46–59

Lai GW, Lin N, Leung S. 1998. Network resources, contact resources, and status attainment. *Soc. Networks* 20(2):159–78, 2

Laumann EO. 1966. *Prestige and Association in an Urban Community.* Indianapolis: Bobbs- errill

Lazarsfeld PF, Merton RK. 1954. Friendship as social process: a substantive and methodological analysis. In *The Varied Sociology of Paul F. Lazarsfeld,* ed. PL Kendall, pp. 298–348. New York: Columbia Univ. Press

Lin N. 1982. Social resources and instrumental action. In *Social Structure and Network Analysis,* ed. PV Marsden, N Lin, pp. 131–45. Beverly Hills, CA: Sage

Lin N. 1990. Social resources and social mobility: a structural theory of status attainment. In *Social Mobility and Social Structure,* ed. RL Breiger, pp. 247–171. New York: Cambridge Univ. Press

Lin N. 1995. Les Ressources Sociales: Une Theorie Du Capital Social. *Rev. Francaise de Sociol.* XXXVI(4):685–704, 4

Lin N, Dayton P, Greenwald P. 1978. Analyzing the instrumental use of relations in the context of social structure. *Sociol. Methods Res.* 7:149–66

Lin N, Dumin M. 1986. Access to occupations

through social ties. *Soc. Networks* 8: 365–85

Lin N, Ensel WM, Vaughn JC. 1981. Social resources and strength of ties: structural factors in occupational status attainment. *Am. Sociol. Rev.* 46(4):393–405, 4

Lin N, Vaughn JC, Ensel W. 1981. Social resources and occupational status attainment. *Soc. Forc.* 59:1163–81

Marsden PV. Hurlbert JS. 1988. Social resources and mobility outcomes: a replication and extension. *Soc. Forc.* 66(4): 1038–59, 4

Moerbeek H, Ultee W, Flap H. 1995. That's what friends are for: ascribed and achieved social capital in the occupational career. The Eur. Soc. Network Conf. London

Portes A. 1998. Social capital: its origins and applications in modern sociology. *Annu. Rev. Sociol.* 22:1–24

Portes A, Sensenbrenner J. 1993. Embeddedness and immigration: notes on the social determinants of economic action. *Am. J. Sociol.* 98(6):1320–50, 6

Putnam RD. 1995a. Bowling alone, revisited. *Responsive Commun.*, Spring, 18–33

Requena F. 1991. Social resources and occupational status attainment in Spain: a cross-national comparison with the United States and the Netherlands. *Int. J. Compar. Sociol.* XXXII(3–4):233–42, 3–4

Rus A. 1995. *Access and Mobilization—Dual Character of Social Capital: Managerial Networks and Privatization in Eastern Europe.* New York: Columbia Univ.

Sewell WH, Hauser RM. 1975. *Education, Occupation & Earnings: Achievement in the Early Career.* New York: Academic Press

Smith MR. 1990. What is new in new structuralist analyses of earnings? *Am. Sociol. Rev.* 55:827–41

Sprengers M, Tazelaar F, Flap HD. 1988. Social resources, situational constraints, and reemployment. *Netherlands J. Sociol.* 24: 98–116

Stanton-Salazar RD. 1997. A social capital framework for understanding the socialization of racial Minority children and youths. *Harvard Educ. Rev.* 67(1):1–40, 1

Stanton-Salazar RD, Dornbusch SM. 1995. Social capital and the reproduction of inequality: information networks among Mexican-origin high school students. *Sociol. Educ.* 68:116–35

Tardos R. 1996. Some remarks on the interpretation and possible uses of the social capital concept with special regard to the Hungarian case. *Bull. Method. Sociol.* 53: 52–62, 53

Treiman DJ. 1970. Industrialization and social stratification. In *Social Stratification: Research and Theory for the 1970s*, ed. EO Laumann, pp. 207–34. Indianapolis: Bobbs–Merrill

Volker B, Flap H. 1996. *Getting Ahead in the GDR: Human Capital and Social Capital in the Status Attainment Process Under Communism.* Universiteit Utrecht, the Netherlands

Weber M. 1946. *Max Weber: Essays in Sociology (Translated by H. H. Gerth and C. Wright Mills).* New York: Oxford Univ. Press

Wegener B. 1991. Job mobility and social ties: social resources, prior job and status attainment. *Am. Sociol. Rev.* 56:1–12

Wright EO. 1979. *Class Structure and Income Determination.* New York: Academic Press

Annu. Rev. Sociol. 1999. 25:489–516

SOCIOECONOMIC POSITION AND HEALTH: The Independent Contribution of Community Socioeconomic Context[1]

Stephanie A. Robert

School of Social Work, University of Wisconsin-Madison, Madison, Wisconsin
53706; e-mail: sarobert@facstaff.wisc.edu

KEY WORDS: social class, socioeconomic status, neighborhood, mortality, income inequality

ABSTRACT

Is living in a relatively poor community bad for your health; is living in a relatively affluent community good for your health; or is it only your own socioeconomic position that matters to your health no matter where you live? This article (*a*) presents a conceptual model suggesting the basic pathways that may link community socioeconomic context to individual health, (*b*) reviews recent research that has examined whether the socioeconomic context of communities impacts the health of individual residents, over and above their own socioeconomic position, (*c*) discusses conceptual and methodological challenges of current research, and (*d*) suggests new directions for future research such as the importance of more closely examining how age, race, gender, and individual socioeconomic position may moderate the impact of community socioeconomic context on individual health and mortality.

[1]Portions of this article are adapted from Robert 1996, Robert 1998, Robert & House in press a, Robert & House in press b.

0360-0572/99/0815-0489$08.00

INTRODUCTION

This review introduces readers to a topic that has been receiving a phenomenal increase in attention in recent years. This area of inquiry investigates how the socioeconomic context of communities (e.g., median income, percentage of adults with twelve or more years of education, inequality in income distribution) affects the health of individual residents, regardless of their individual socioeconomic position. For example, why is it that people living in high poverty communities tend to have worse health than people living in low poverty communities? Is it simply because people living in poor communities tend to be poor themselves, or is there something else about living in poor communities that is bad for the health of all residents, no matter whether they are rich or poor themselves?

Ecological or aggregate-level studies have consistently shown that the socioeconomic context of communities is associated with the morbidity and mortality rates of communities (Crombie et al 1989, Guest et al 1998). For example, a recent study by Guest and colleagues (1998) showed that community socioeconomic factors (levels of unemployment and education) were strongly associated with both infant mortality and working-age mortality in Chicago communities. Moreover, other research indicates that inequality in income distribution in a nation, state, region, or community is associated with higher morbidity and mortality rates, over and above the impact of the average socioeconomic level (Ben-Shlomo et al 1996, Kaplan et al 1996, Kennedy et al 1996, Lynch et al 1998, Wilkinson 1992, 1996). For example, Kaplan and colleagues (1996) showed that greater inequality in income distribution within US states is associated with higher state mortality rates and other poor health outcomes measured at the state level, after controlling for state median income. Still other research, finding individual-level socioeconomic data unavailable, has used aggregate community socioeconomic variables as proxies for individual-level socioeconomic position and has found these aggregate measures of socioeconomic position to be associated with individual health and mortality (Krieger 1992, Figueroa & Breen 1995).

Although these studies provide important information about the distribution of disease in society, such research is unable to conclude whether the association between community socioeconomic context and aggregate or individual measures of health either, one, simply reflects the relationship between individual socioeconomic position and individual health of residents, or two, reflects the fact that community socioeconomic context affects characteristics of the community environment that can affect the health of all residents.

The distinction between these two explanations is crucial in terms of its public health and policy implications. If the association between community socioeconomic context and health simply reflects the sum of relationships at the individual level, we might choose to improve health by targeting individuals with lower socioeconomic position rather than targeting communities with lower socioeconomic profiles. Yet we might also decide that focusing interventions in communities with lower socioeconomic profiles is an efficient way of reaching a high number individuals with low socioeconomic position. However, if the socioeconomic context of communities contributes something unique to the health of its residents, beyond the residents' own socioeconomic position, then community interventions are not optional, but rather are necessary to improve overall individual and population health.

In order to determine whether community socioeconomic context has independent effects on the health of residents, research needs to use data and methods that include information about both the socioeconomic position of individuals and the socioeconomic context of their communities. This review focuses on such research. I first describe a basic conceptual model that summarizes the proposed relationship between community socioeconomic context and individual health as it has been examined in recent research. I then review current empirical evidence for the independent effects of community socioeconomic context on individual health. Finally, I discuss some of the methodological and conceptual challenges to research in this area and suggest directions for future research.

I am limiting the scope of this review by focusing on *socioeconomic* context of communities, including any factors broadly representing community economic status (e.g., income level, income inequality, poverty level), material standards (e.g., percentage of households with access to a vehicle, average home value), educational status (e.g., percent of community with a given level of education), occupational status (e.g., unemployment, percentage of workers in a given occupational class), or some combination thereof. I am further limiting the scope of the review by focusing on physical aspects of health (e.g., mortality, self-rated health, specific chronic or acute conditions, functional limitations, birth outcomes), rather than considering broader conceptions of health that include emotional, psychological, or social health and well-being (though see Aneshensel & Sucoff 1996). I use the term socioeconomic position to refer to the broad range of socioeconomic circumstances in which individuals are hierarchically stratified (e.g., education, income, occupation, level of assets).

BASIC CONCEPTUAL MODEL

We know that one's own socioeconomic position strongly determines one's health, but what is it that one's community socioeconomic context can contribute? Why might living in a lower socioeconomic community be bad for one's health per se, or why would living in a higher socioeconomic community be protective of one's health? No comprehensive theories describe the complex mechanisms through which community context may affect individual health, but a number of theories and frameworks suggest multiple potential pathways through which these effects may occur. Figure 1 demonstrates a basic conceptual model that emphasizes some of the major pathways linking community socioeconomic context to individual health. The thick lines represent main effects, the thin lines represent interaction effects, and the dotted lines represent relationships that have gone relatively unexplored to date, but that may have crucial implications for our understanding of whether and/or how community socioeconomic context affects individual health.

In Figure 1, the sequence of boxes along the bottom reflects the way that most research has investigated socioeconomic inequalities in health. This pathway suggests that the socioeconomic position of individuals is a function of age, race, and gender, and in turn affects a broad array of individual biological, psychological, behavioral, and social characteristics, conditions, and experiences, which then affect health (Williams 1990, House et al 1994, Lynch et al 1996). Because of the consistently strong relationship between individual socioeconomic position and health, along with the fact that one's own socioeconomic position may affect the type of community in which one chooses to or is able to live, it might be that any association between community socioeconomic context and individual health is simply spurious.

However, as reflected in the conceptual model, it may be that community socioeconomic context plays an important role in affecting health. The model

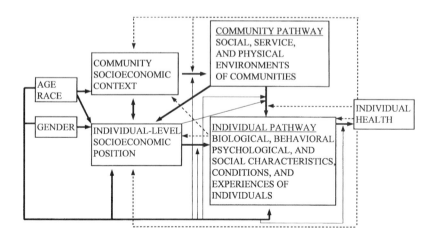

Figure 1 Conceptual model: relationship between community socioeconomic context and individual health. Thick lines represent main effects, thin lines represent interaction effects, and dotted lines represent understudied reciprocal effects.

suggests that community socioeconomic context affects health through two major pathways: (*a*) by shaping the socioeconomic position of individuals, and (*b*) by directly affecting the social, service, and physical environments of communities shared by residents, which then affect the individual characteristics, conditions, and experiences of individuals that more directly impact health.

The first pathway suggests that the opportunities and constraints presented in communities with different socioeconomic contexts can shape the educational attainment, job prospects, and income level of individuals (Foster & McLanahan 1996, Garner & Raudenbush 1991, Jencks & Mayer 1990, Wilson 1987), which then more directly affect health. The second pathway is less intuitive, and as I discuss later, not well investigated. I describe in more detail some of the specific aspects of the social, service, and physical environments that may ultimately link community socioeconomic context to individual health independent of pathways through individual socioeconomic position.

Explanations for Independent Effects of Community Socioeconomic Context on Individual Health

SOCIAL ENVIRONMENT OF COMMUNITIES   Although not necessarily focusing on health outcomes, a number of sociological theories and frameworks—in particular, urban ecological theory, social disorganization theory, social capital theory, and Wilson's (1987) theory of concentration and social isolation effects in inner cities—suggest how the social environment of communities, particularly how the impact of high poverty communities, can affect individual development and outcomes over and above individual socioeconomic position.

Both early and more contemporary urban ecology and social disorganization theories describe how the socioeconomic characteristics of communities are associated with the degree of residential mobility, ethnic heterogeneity, social organization, and social cohesion in communities that are responsible for problem behavior such as crime and delinquency (e.g., Kornhauser 1978, Sampson & Groves 1989, Sampson & Morenoff 1997, Shaw & McKay 1931) and that may be important to health outcomes as well.

For example, communities or regions with low socioeconomic levels or high inequality in income distribution often have high levels of actual or perceived crime (Hsieh & Pugh 1993), which can directly and indirectly affect the health of all residents (Macintyre et al 1993, Sooman & Macintyre 1995). Actual crime can directly affect health through bodily harm, while fear of crime can indirectly affect health by increasing stress, promoting social isolation, preventing the health-promoting practice of walking for exercise, and preventing access to services for those fearful of traveling freely in the community. Older adults living in deteriorating hotels in the Tenderloin district of San Francisco listed crime as the most important *health* problem for older adults in their area (Minkler 1992).

Recent theories on social capital (Coleman 1988, Putnam 1993) stress the importance of social relationships, social organization, norms of reciprocity, and civic participation in promoting social good in society. This idea has recently been extended to suggest that income inequality within communities, regions, states, and countries leads to lower levels of social cohesion and trust among residents, as well as feelings of relative deprivation, which in turn, can affect health (Kawachi et al 1997, Kawachi & Kennedy 1997, Wilkinson 1996).

Wilson (1987) suggests ways that concentration effects and social isolation in inner cities could impact a number of outcomes for inner city residents, and although he does not specifically focus on the health outcomes of these processes, his ideas suggest a number of mechanisms through which concentration effects and social isolation in inner cities might affect health. For example, his ideas are consistent with contagion or epidemic models that suggest that people's behavior is influenced by the norms or values of those around them (Crane 1991, Jencks & Mayer 1990). Therefore, living in communities with low socioeconomic profiles may negatively affect a person's health-promoting attitudes and behaviors by exposing a person to neighbors who are less likely to practice health-promoting behaviors than would neighbors with higher socioeconomic position. In fact, some evidence indicates that living in communities with lower socioeconomic levels is associated with a greater likelihood of smoking (Kleinschmidt et al 1995, Diez-Roux et al 1997, Reijneveld 1998), higher systolic blood pressure (Diez-Roux et al 1997), and higher serum cholesterol (Diez-Roux et al 1997), even after controlling for individual socioeconomic factors.

SERVICE ENVIRONMENT OF COMMUNITIES   The socioeconomic context of communities may affect access to adequate or high quality services for all residents. Municipal services such as policing, fire, and sanitation may be less adequate in lower socioeconomic communities, impacting the health and safety of all residents (Wallace & Wallace 1990). People in lower socioeconomic communities often have to travel outside of their communities to have access to more affordable and higher quality food (Troutt 1993). The existence of, quality of, and access to medical and social services (such as congregate meals, senior centers, mental health services, and family services) may also differ by socioeconomic characteristics of communities. Necessary or high quality medical and social services may not even exist in a community, even if some residents are able to pay for them, or access to those services may be hampered by barriers such as inadequate or unsafe transportation systems.

Moreover, income inequality at the community, region, state, or country levels may be associated with mortality rates over and above the impact of average income levels because areas that tolerate greater income inequality may also be those less likely to provide generous human, social, and health resources that ultimately affect the health of all residents (Davey Smith 1996, Kaplan et al 1996, Lynch et al 1998).

PHYSICAL ENVIRONMENT OF COMMUNITIES   Lower socioeconomic communities may have worse pollution that affects the health of all residents. The quality of air and water and the location of toxic waste dumps and incinerators may all differ by the socioeconomic characteristics of communities (General Accounting Office 1983, Bullard 1990). Communities with lower socioeconomic levels may offer less healthy housing, work places, and recreational options, with greater potential exposure to toxins such as lead paint, asbestos, and pest infestation (Troutt 1993).

SUMMARY   In sum, the socioeconomic context of communities may affect characteristics of the social, service, and physical environments of communities to which all community residents are exposed, regardless of their own socioeconomic position. These patterned community exposures in turn affect the individuals' biological, psychological, behavioral, and social characteristics, conditions, and experiences that are more proximate determinants of individual health. This model shows that although community socioeconomic context and individual socioeconomic position may each affect the other, they also may have separate pathways linking them to health.

Interactions Between Community Socioeconomic Characteristics and Age, Race, and Gender

As depicted in the conceptual model, age, race, and gender affect health through multiple pathways. Most of these pathways are relatively well known, such as the indirect effects of age, race, and gender on health through their impact on individual socioeconomic position. Less commonly conceived of are the potential roles that age, race, and gender may play in moderating the impact of community socioeconomic context on individual health, as depicted by two of the thin arrows in Figure 1. Research on individual socioeconomic position and health shows that there are age, race, and gender differences in this relationship (Robert & House in press a). Most notably, individual socioeconomic position is more strongly associated with health in middle age and early old age, whereas it is weakly associated with health and mortality in young adulthood and at later old ages (House et al 1990, 1994). Perhaps age, race, and gender moderate the relationship between *community* socioeconomic context and health as well.

Figure 1 suggests that age, race, and gender may moderate the effects of community socioeconomic context on individual health in two ways. First, these factors may affect a person's degree of exposure to the social, service, and physical environments of communities. For example, because of differences in work force participation, children, older adults, and women may on average spend more time actively interacting with and effectively being "exposed to" their community environments, compared to working age adult men. Moreover, older adults may have more "exposure" to their community environments due to longer length of residence and to less involvement in labor force activity outside their residential community.

Second, age, race, and gender may affect the impact of the community social, service, and physical environments on the individual pathways that are more closely linked to health. A number of gerontological theories suggest that the community context is more important to older adults than to younger adults (i.e., Lawton 1970, 1977, Lawton & Simon 1968) and that this may have repercussions for their health (Robert 1996). Community context may also be particularly important to the health of women who care for small children at home.

For example, the health of older adults and of women at home with children may be particularly affected if they live in communities with unsupportive social and service environments. Whereas weak social ties in the community and poor medical and social services may mean less to people who have few service needs and who are able to seek social support elsewhere, lack of emotional, informational, and functional social support in the community may be particularly damaging to the health of community members who must rely more heavily on community service and social support resources.

Interactions Between Community Socioeconomic Characteristics and Individual-Level Socioeconomic Position

The ultimate impact of the social, service, and physical environments of one's community on health may be somewhat moderated by one's own socioeconomic position, as indicated by one of the thin arrows in Figure 1. Even if the community socioeconomic context may affect the health of all or most residents, the nature of those effects may be somewhat different depending on individual socioeconomic position.

For example, a "double jeopardy" hypothesis might suggest that living in communities with lower socioeconomic levels may be particularly detrimental to the health of individuals who have lower socioeconomic position themselves. Alternately, a "relative deprivation" hypothesis might suggest that individuals with lower socioeconomic position may be worse off living in communities with higher socioeconomic levels than in communities with lower socioeconomic levels because they might experience health effects of structural relative deprivation when competing with neighbors with higher socioeconomic position for scarce resources, and/or psychosocial relative deprivation when comparing oneself to neighbors with higher socioeconomic position. Such theories provide contradictory but intriguing and testable hypotheses about the interactions between individual and community socioeconomic context in affecting individual health.

Summary

The conceptual model shows that community socioeconomic context may affect individual health both through its impact on the socioeconomic position of individual residents and through a pathway that is independent of the socioeconomic position of individual residents. Characteristics of the social, service, and physical environments of communities vary by the socioeconomic context of communities, and may affect the health of all residents regardless of their own socioeconomic position. Age, race, gender, and individual-level socioeconomic position may each modify the relationship between community socioeconomic context and individual health. The dotted arrows in the model represent some of the complex relationships that need to be considered when investigating the effects of community socioeconomic context on individual health. These pathways will be discussed later.

INDEPENDENT EFFECTS OF COMMUNITY SOCIOECONOMIC CONTEXT ON INDIVIDUAL HEALTH: THE EVIDENCE

Recent research has focused on testing the piece of the conceptual model that suggests that community socioeconomic context has effects on individual health over and above the effects of individual socioeconomic position. Such research has taken existing individual-level data from surveys (with information about individual socioeconomic position, individual health, and/or mortality) and then attached community socioeconomic variables (e.g., percentage of community residents in poverty, mean family income) that derive from census summary statistics about the census areas that each respondent lives in (e.g., in the United States: census tracts, block groups, enumeration districts, zip codes). Such research can generally be divided into research on the health effects of the socioeconomic level of communities and the inequality in income distribution of communities.

Socioeconomic Level of Communities

With few exceptions (Ecob 1996, Sloggett & Joshi 1994, Reijneveld 1998), studies have generally found that community socioeconomic level is associated with individual health (Diez-Roux et al 1997, Hochstim et al 1968, Jones & Duncan 1995, Kaplan et al in press, Krieger 1992, O'Campo et al 1997, Reijneveld 1998, Robert 1998, Sloggett & Joshi 1998) and mortality (Anderson et al 1997, Haan et al 1987, LeClere et al 1997, Davey Smith et al 1998, Waitzman & Smith 1998a), over and above the impact of individual socioeconomic position.

Some of the seminal work in this area by Haan and colleagues (1987) showed that, in a population of adults age 35 and older living in Oakland, California in 1965, the effects of residence in a poverty area on nine-year mortality persisted after controlling for age, race, sex, and for separate measures of socioeconomic position and other health risk factors. A recent study by Waitzman & Smith (1998a) confirmed these effects of poverty residence on mortality risk in a study of adults living in urban areas in the United States who were part of the National Health and Nutrition Examination Survey in 1971 through 1974 and who were followed through 1987. The association between poverty residence and mortality persisted for those aged 25–54 (rate ratio = 1.78, CI = 1.33, 2.38 for all-cause mortality) but not for those aged 55–74, after adjusting for age, race, sex, marital status, household income, formal education, poverty status, baseline health, and multiple behavioral and biological risk factors.

Other recent studies have examined the independent effects of community socioeconomic context on mortality in national samples of the United States, using various measures of community socioeconomic context other than residence in a poverty area. Anderson and colleagues (1997) linked the National Longitudinal Mortality Study to 1980 census tract data to assess the multilevel effects of income on all-cause mortality among black and white adults in the United States from 1979 to 1991. Their results indicated that median income of census tracts had statistically significant independent effects on mortality for those age 25 to 64 of both sexes and races after controlling for family income. There were no similar effects for those ages 65 or older. LeClere and colleagues (LeClere et al 1997, 1998) similarly linked the 1986 to 1990 National Health Interview Survey with the National Death Index and with census tract level data from the 1990 census. In one study (LeClere et al 1997) they found that community median income had an independent effect on all-cause mortality for men, but not for women, after controlling for individual-level education, income-to-needs ratio, age, race, and marital status. In a later study, LeClere and colleagues (1998) found that median family income, percentage of households receiving public assistance, percentage of people at or below 75% of the poverty level, percentage of adult unemployment, and percentage of black residents, each predicted women's heart disease mortality after controlling for individual-level education, income, employment status, age, ethnicity, body mass index, pre-existing conditions, and marital status. These effects were stronger in women under age 65 compared to those ages 65 and older.

Studies have similarly found that community socioeconomic context is associated with various measures of health other than just mortality, net of individual socioeconomic position (Diez-Roux et al 1997, Hochstim et al 1968, Jones & Duncan 1995, Kaplan et al in press, Krieger 1992, O'Campo et al 1997, Reijneveld 1998, Robert 1998, Sloggett & Joshi 1998). Among a national sample of adults in the United States in 1986, Robert (1998) found that percentage of families earning $30,000 or more and percentage adult unemployment in respondents' census tracts each had an independent association with number of chronic conditions, over and above the effects of respondents' individual- or family-level education, income, and assets, and their age, race, and sex. Similarly, percentage of households receiving public assistance had independent associations with self-rated health, after controlling for the same individual- and family-level variables. An economic disadvantage index composed of three community socioeconomic factors had independent associations with both self-rated health and number of chronic conditions, though the index did not perform much better than the strongest single community socioeconomic variable.

Sloggett & Joshi (1998) found that living in more socioeconomically deprived wards in England was associated with poor health, net of individual and family socioeconomic circumstances (employment status, occupational class, housing tenure, car access), and that level of community deprivation was a better predictor of poor health (e.g. long-term limiting illness, giving birth to a baby of low birthweight) than it was of mortality. Jones & Duncan (1995) also investigated the independent effects of a ward-level deprivation index on three health measures among a sample of adults in England. They found associations between ward-level deprivation scores and respiratory functioning, self-rated health, and heart symptoms, over and above individual socioeconomic characteristics, including social class, employment status, housing tenure, and income, as well as demographic and health behavior measures. They concluded that the linear nature of the relationship between the ward deprivation index and the three health measures supports the idea that there is a gradient effect of community socioeconomic context on health rather than solely a threshold or deprivation effect.

Along with Jones & Duncan (1995), others (LeClere et al 1997, Robert 1998) found that the effects of community socioeconomic context on health and mortality are not simply due to effects of living in severely deprived communities. For example, LeClere and colleagues (1997) found that the association between community median income and male all-cause mortality was reflected by more of a gradient relationship than a deprivation relationship, with those living in communities with the highest median income quartile less likely to die than even those in the second highest income quartile communities.

Therefore, it is not just conditions in extremely deprived neighborhoods that account for community socioeconomic effects on health, but rather community conditions distinguishing higher socioeconomic communities from each other as well. In fact, Sloggett & Joshi (1998) found that adjusting for individual socioeconomic factors virtually eliminated the health impact of living in the most deprived wards in England, whereas some health protective effects of living in the least deprived communities remained.

Although some of the studies reviewed here had limited individual-level socioeconomic controls (e.g., Anderson et al 1997, Davey Smith et al 1998, Haan et al 1987) that might lead to an overestimation of the independent community socioeconomic effects, other studies found persisting community socioeconomic effects even after controlling for several measure of individual socioeconomic variables (e.g., Diez-Roux 1997, LeClere et al 1997, Robert 1998). Nevertheless, even in the studies noting independent community socioeconomic effects on health and mortality, the independent community effects were relatively small in magnitude and were certainly smaller than the independent effects of the individual socioeconomic variables, as most of the researchers were careful to point out.

In fact, several studies found that the association between community socioeconomic context and individual health and mortality was no longer statistically significant after controlling for individual socioeconomic variables. For example, an earlier study by Sloggett & Joshi (1994) found that level of deprivation of social wards in England no longer predicted nine-year mortality for people ages 16 to 65 after controlling for a number of individual socioeconomic indicators (work status, occupational class, and housing tenure). And although Robert (1998) found some independent associations between community socioeconomic measures and both number of chronic conditions and self-rated health, she found no such associations when looking at functional limitations as the outcome. Similarly, although Reijneveld (1998) found that community socioeconomic characteristics had some independent effects on long-term physical limitations after controlling for individual socioeconomic factors among residents of Amsterdam, The Netherlands, the individual socioeconomic factors accounted for all of the association between community socioeconomic factors and both self-rated health and physical complaints. Ecob (1996) found that an area deprivation index was no longer associated with self-rated health, limiting long-standing illness, and standardized respiratory function, after controlling for individual socioeconomic factors. Interestingly, both Reijneveld (1998) and Ecob (1996) found stronger independent associations between community socioeconomic context and health risk factors (e.g., smoking, waist-hip ratio) than between community socioeconomic context and measures of health outcomes.

SUMMARY   In sum, research has generally found that there are independent effects of community socioeconomic level on individual health and mortality risk, net of individual socioeconomic position. However, the studies found that individual socioeconomic position greatly mediated the relationship between community socioeconomic level and individual health and mortality, with individual socioeconomic position explaining all of the association between community socioeconomic level and individual health and mortality in some studies. Moreover, even those studies finding independent effects of community socioeconomic level on health and mortality found these effects to be small in magnitude, particularly relative to the independent effects of individual socioeconomic position. Where independent community effects were detected, they were seen not only in the most socioeconomically deprived communities, but also when comparing communities with high socioeconomic levels to those with socioeconomic levels just below them.

Inequality in Income Distribution of Communities

Beyond finding effects of the income level of communities on health, research has found that inequality in income distribution at the societal level is associated with life expectancy in more developed countries, after average income levels are controlled for (Rodgers 1979, van Doorslaer et al 1997, Wilkinson 1992, 1996), and that inequality in income distribution at regional and state levels within the United States and England is associated with mortality rates after controlling for average socioeconomic levels (Ben-Shlomo et al 1996, Kaplan et al 1996, Kennedy et al 1996, Lynch et al 1998). However, recent debate (Robert & House in press b, Lynch & Kaplan 1997) has centered around two issues. One is whether these ecological relationships reflect a causal relationship whereby inequality in income distribution affects or reflects the social cohesion and social capital of a society, region, or state (Kawachi et al 1997), or the willingness of its residents to invest in education, health care, housing, or other forms of human and social capital (Davey Smith 1996, Kaplan 1996), which then more directly affect individual and population health. The other is whether these ecological relationships simply or largely reflect the curvilinear relationship between income and mortality at the individual level (Fiscella & Franks 1997, Gravelle 1998).

Only recently have studies begun testing the second explanation that the association between inequality in income distribution and individual mortality is entirely or primarily driven by individual socioeconomic position. Fiscella & Franks (1997) found that community income inequality (at approximately the county level) relates to individual-level mortality in the United States, just as it does to aggregate life expectancy. However, they found that once family income is controlled, the relationship between community income inequality and individual mortality becomes minimal and nonsignificant. Because Fiscella & Franks derived their aggregate inequality measures from data on their survey respondents, rather than from an independent (e.g., census) source, their aggregate inequality variables may or may not represent the true aggregate inequality values within these communities. As a result, their findings have been criticized as overly conservative at best and as uninterpretable at worst (Soobader & LeClere, in press, Waitzman & Smith 1998b, Lynch & Kaplan 1997). More recent studies have demonstrated that the effects of socioeconomic inequality at the level of states, counties, or metropolitan areas on morbidity and mortality are substantially but not entirely mediated by individual or household income (Soobader & LeClere, in press, Waitzman & Smith 1998b, Kennedy et al 1998, Daly et al 1998).

Waitzman & Smith (1998b) matched death certificate information to the 1986–1994 National Health Interview Surveys for respondents ages 30 and older living in 33 of the largest metropolitan statistical areas (MSAs) in the United States (representing 40% of the population). They calculated the degree of concentrated poverty and concentrated affluence within each of the 33 MSAs and measured the association between spatial concentration of poverty and affluence and individual mortality risk in these urban areas. The individual risk of mortality was heightened by living in an MSA with greater spatial concentration of poverty for people ages 30–64 after controlling for family income, age, sex, and race. However, this effect was no longer statistically significant once level of poverty in the MSA was included in these models. There were no consistent or strong effects of concentrated affluence on mortality for those ages 30–64. However, there were associations between both concentrated poverty and concentrated affluence on the risk of mortality for those ages 65 and older after controlling for family income, age, sex, race, and even after further controls for median income and proportion poor in the MSA.

Soobader & LeClere (in press) tested whether income inequality at the county level has effects on individual self-perceived health, after controlling for individual socioeconomic position and county socioeconomic levels. They combined 1990 census information at the census tract and county levels with individual-level data on white males ages 25–64 in the 1989–1991 National Health Interview Survey. They found that income inequality at the county level exerts an independent effect on self-perceived health, over and above county median income, percentage in poverty in the county, and individual socioeconomic factors.

Moreover, Soobader & LeClere also tested the hypothesis that inequality in income distribution may have stronger effects on individual health when measured at larger levels of aggregation (counties, states, regions) rather than at smaller levels of aggregation (census tracts, communities). Wilkinson (1992, 1996) was the first to suggest that both socioeconomic levels and socio-economic inequalities within communities, regions, states, and countries may be important to health, but that they each may operate more strongly at different geographic levels. Specifically, Wilkinson suggested that in smaller geographic areas such as communities (census tracts or block groups), socioeconomic level may be particularly important to the health of residents. However, in larger geographic areas such as states or nations, socioeconomic inequality may operate to further determine inequalities in health and mortality. Soobader & LeClere (in press) tested Wilkinson's hypothesis by comparing the effects of income inequality on self-perceived health at both the census tract and county levels in the United States. As reported above, they found independent effects of income inequality at the county level on individual self-perceived health. However, at the census tract level, median income, percentage in poverty, and individual socioeconomic factors are associated with self-perceived health with no additional effects of income inequality on self-perceived health. This study is the first to provide evidence in support of Wilkinson's hypothesis that both socioeconomic levels and socioeconomic inequalities may be important to health, but that they each may operate more strongly at different geographic levels.

Other recent research provides some evidence that state-level income inequality is associated with individual risk of death (Daly et al 1998) and individual health status (Kennedy et al 1998) after controlling for individual socioeconomic position. However, because neither study controls for state socioeconomic *level* (such as state poverty level or state median income), it is unclear whether the effects persist in the presence of state income level.

SUMMARY   In comparison to the larger number of studies reviewed earlier investigating the independent impact of community socioeconomic <u>level</u> on individual health and mortality, there are few studies on which to base conclusions about the impact of community socioeconomic <u>inequality</u> on individual health and mortality, over and above individual socioeconomic position and average community socioeconomic level. The few studies investigating this question have provided mixed results.

Subgroup Variation in Effects of Community Socioeconomic Context

Perhaps even more interesting or more important than testing whether there are independent effects of community socioeconomic context on individual health is testing whether there are subgroup variations in these community effects.

This section reviews evidence regarding whether and how independent effects of community socioeconomic context on individual health vary by age, race, gender, and individual socioeconomic position.

AGE   The research reviewed earlier generally found smaller or nonexistent associations between community socioeconomic level and mortality for older adults compared to younger and middle-aged adults, after controlling for individual socioeconomic position (Anderson et al 1997, Haan et al 1987, Waitzman & Smith 1998a, b). In contrast, Robert (1996) found that some community socioeconomic characteristics were better predictors of adult health at middle and older ages compared to younger ages, and that community socioeconomic characteristics were sometimes better predictors of health than individual socioeconomic measures at these middle and older ages.

Moreover, the research by Waitzman & Smith (1998b), described above, found that although community socioeconomic level (median income and proportion poor in MSAs) was not predictive of mortality among those ages 65 and older, after controlling for family income, the spatial distribution of both poverty and affluence was associated with mortality risk after controlling for age, sex, race, family income, and for socioeconomic level of MSAs among those ages 65 and older. Living in MSAs with high concentrations of poverty was associated with a higher risk of mortality, and living in MSAs with high concentrations of affluence was associated with a lower risk of mortality, among people ages 65 and older. There were no similar effects for adults ages 30–64. In contrast, Daly and colleagues (1998) found that state income inequality was associated with individual mortality risk only among nonelderly individuals.

GENDER   As discussed earlier, community socioeconomic characteristics may be particularly salient to the lives and health of women compared to men, particularly for women who do not work outside the home. In support of this hypothesis, Diez-Roux and colleagues (1997) found that for white women, living in more disadvantaged communities was associated with increased coronary heart disease odds, even after controlling for individual socioeconomic measures, with much weaker effects for white men. Similarly, Sloggett & Joshi (1998) found that women in England who classify themselves as housewives have particularly poor health if they live in socioeconomically deprived wards. In contrast, LeClere et al (1997) found that community socioeconomic indicators were better predictors of mortality for men than for women (after controlling for measures of individual-level socioeconomic position), and Anderson et al (1997) found no gender differences in the association between community median income and all-cause mortality (after controlling for family income).

RACE   Research on the effects of communities on child and adolescent development and outcomes generally find less powerful community effects among black people than among white people (Brooks-Gunn et al 1997). For example, there is some evidence that living in communities with high socioeconomic levels only enhances the educational attainment of black males if the neighbors are themselves black (Duncan et al 1997). Are there race differences in the impact of community socioeconomic context on health and mortality as well?

Diez-Roux and colleagues (1997) found that for African-American men living in poor neighborhoods in Jackson, Mississippi, in the late 1980s, coronary heart disease prevalence actually decreased as neighborhood characteristics worsened. The reverse was true for black women and for white men and women for whom living in poor neighborhoods was generally associated with greater risk of coronary heart disease. However, other research finds no race differences in the effects of community socioeconomic context on health and mortality (Anderson et al 1997, Kaplan et al, in press; Collins et al 1997).

In addition to examining whether race moderates the effects of community socioeconomic context on health, future research should further examine how race differences in health may be mediated by community socioeconomic context. For example, we know that black people are more likely to live in lower socioeconomic communities than white people with the same individual socioeconomic position (Jargowsky 1997). These race differences in residential context might help explain race differences in health. Many research studies find that although individual socioeconomic position greatly mediates the association between race and health, some race effects on health remain (Williams & Collins 1995). Do race differences in community socioeconomic context help further explain race differences in health?

Some studies found evidence that race differences in health and mortality that persisted after controlling for individual socioeconomic position were eliminated after further considering community socioeconomic context (Robert 1998, Haan et al 1987, LeClere et al 1998). Although generally consistent with theories about the role of residence in explaining racial disadvantage (Jargowsky 1997, Massey & Denton 1993, Wilson 1987), such ideas have gone relatively untested, particularly as they relate to health outcomes.

INDIVIDUAL-LEVEL SOCIOECONOMIC POSITION   Some of the most confusing evidence regarding community socioeconomic effects on health has to do with how community socioeconomic context interacts with individual socioeconomic position to affect health. As discussed earlier, investigating these multilevel interactions allows one to test a number of hypotheses, including a double jeopardy hypothesis and a relative deprivation hypothesis. Some research finds no statistically significant interactions between community socioeconomic context and individual socioeconomic position when predicting health (e.g. Diez-Roux et al 1997) and mortality (Sloggett & Joshi 1998). Yet others do find significant multilevel interactions with conflicting evidence for double jeopardy and relative deprivation hypotheses.

Supporting a double jeopardy hypothesis, Waitzman & Smith (1998b) found that the impact of concentrated poverty and proportion of poor within MSAs on individual mortality risk for those ages 30–64 was strongest for individuals with household incomes of less than $15,000, but that effects were also seen for those with low to middle incomes as well ($15,000–$49,999). There seemed to be no effects of concentrated affluence or poverty on individuals with high family income ($50,000+). In contrast, Sloggett & Joshi (1998) found that living in deprived wards in England was not particularly detrimental to the health of low income people compared to high income people. Both low and high income people have poor health in deprived wards, but the health of low income people is not markedly better in less deprived areas while the health of high income people is, resulting in greater socioeconomic disparities in health in less deprived wards. Similarly, Kaplan and colleagues (in press) found that the association between poverty area residence and incidence of disability was driven by effects among those with adequate levels of income. For those with inadequate or marginal incomes, poverty area residence had virtually no effects on disability incidence, whereas disability incidence was strongly associated with poverty area residence among those with adequate levels of income.

Providing some support for a relative deprivation hypothesis, Yen & Kaplan (in press) found that people in the Alameda county study with low income had the highest mortality risk in census tracts with the highest socioeconomic profile. Yet Collins et al (1997) found that both black and white babies were less likely to have very low birthweight if they were born in communities that had a higher socioeconomic level than the socioeconomic level of their parents (though a very small proportion of black babies were born in this beneficial situation compared to the proportion of white babies).

These and other studies (Jones & Duncan 1995, O'Campo et al 1997) provide evidence that there are some interactions between community socioeconomic context and individual socioeconomic position that affect health, though conclusions about the specific form and meaning of these relationships are unclear.

Explanations for Independent Effects of Community Socioeconomic Context on Health: The Evidence

Although I presented earlier many potential explanations for the independent effects of community socioeconomic context on individual health, over and above individual socioeconomic context, it is unclear what actually explains this relationship. Only a few studies have examined specific mediating factors, and these have focused on known individual behavioral and biological health risk factors.

For example, Diez-Roux and colleagues (1997) found that the independent effects of community socioeconomic context on increased odds of coronary heart disease in women persisted after controlling for individual socioeconomic position, and these effects persisted even after controlling further for a number of coronary heart disease risk factors considered simultaneously including cholesterol levels, smoking behavior, blood pressure, body mass index, diabetes, leisure index, sport index, work index, and serum fibrinogen.

Waitzman & Smith (1998a) showed that the impact of poverty-area residence on all-cause mortality was only somewhat reduced after controlling simultaneously for marital status, household income as a percentage of the poverty line, formal education, alcohol consumption, body mass index, smoking, exercise frequency, baseline health status, hypertension, and cholesterol level. The relative risk of mortality for poverty-area residence was 2.01 after controlling for age, sex, and race, and this was only reduced to 1.78 after controlling further for all the individual socioeconomic position and health risk factors just listed. Other studies similarly show that adjusting for a few individual health risk factors does not eliminate the independent effects of community socioeconomic context on individual health (Haan et al 1987, Jones & Duncan 1995, LeClere et al 1998).

In contrast, Davey Smith and colleagues (1998) found that, in their sample of adults in England, independent effects of community socioeconomic deprivation on all-cause and cardiovascular disease mortality that remained after controlling for occupational class were virtually eliminated by controlling simultaneously for individual health risk factors including diastolic blood pressure, cholesterol, body mass index, smoking, angina, ischemia, and bronchitis.

It may be premature to continue examining explanations for the independent effects of community socioeconomic context on individual health until some of the more thorny methodological and conceptual issues of current studies are addressed (see later discussion). However, these few studies suggest that the independent effects of community socioeconomic context on individual health and mortality are not entirely due to a few well-known individual health risk factors.

METHODOLOGICAL AND CONCEPTUAL CHALLENGES

There are methodological and conceptual limitations to the current body of research that will need to be addressed in future research before grand conclusions can be made about the true nature of and explanations for the relationship between community socioeconomic context and individual health.

Reverse Causation

Does community socioeconomic context affect individual health, or does health affect the type of community that a person remains in or moves into (see Figure 1)? Although some of the studies reviewed here are cross-sectional and unable to distinguish the directionality of causation (e.g. Reijneveld 1998, Robert 1998, Sloggett & Joshi 1998), the studies focusing on mortality outcomes while controlling for baseline health suggest that community socioeconomic context has effects on individual health (e.g. Waitzman & Smith 1998a, LeClere et al 1998, Davey Smith et al 1998, Haan et al 1987). However, future research should more fully consider the dynamics of individual health, individual socioeconomic position, and community socioeconomic context over time.

Selection Bias

The association between community socioeconomic context and individual health may be overestimated if unmeasured factors affect both the type of neighborhood one lives in and one's health. Robert (1998) found that including measures of parental socioeconomic position did not affect the relationship between community socioeconomic context and individual health, and research on the effects of community context on child development found no evidence of selection bias after testing whether a number of typically unmeasured family factors changed estimated community effects (Duncan et al 1997). In order to eliminate the possibility of selection bias, future research should more carefully consider whether there are some unmeasured factors, such as personality traits, that affect both one's health and where one lives.

Measuring Community

The effects of community socioeconomic level on health may be underestimated in these studies because of crude measures of community boundaries. All of the studies described above relied on convenient census boundaries to delineate communities. Clearly, census areas do not necessarily correspond with the self-defined communities of individual respondents. Although physical and service environments of communities may be more appropriately characterized at larger census levels, the social patterns of individuals often do not correspond with such boundaries. Some individuals may have meaningful social networks and interactions that are bounded within a very small neighborhood area, while the social patterns of others may transcend large geographical boundaries. Although much more difficult to do, future research should include information about self-defined communities or at least purposefully delineate community boundaries to more closely match the theoretical constructs being tested, in order to get a more accurate picture of the relationship between community socioeconomic context and individual health.

Measuring Community Socioeconomic Context

Some studies have measured community socioeconomic context using one or more indicators considered separately or simultaneously (e.g. LeClere et al 1997), whereas other studies have constructed indices of community socioeconomic context by combining a number of separate indicators into one index or community classification scheme (e.g. Jones & Duncan 1995), and some studies have used separate indicators and indices (e.g. Robert 1998). The advantage of using a number of indicators is that we can more directly observe which characteristics of communities are most strongly associated with individual health, though we understand less about how the community socioeconomic variables work together to provide a unique community socioeconomic context. The advantage of using a community socioeconomic index is that it may more fully describe the overall nature of the community socioeconomic context, although it may obscure our understanding of whether specific aspects of the community context may be particularly important to health. Future research should continue to examine both the separate, simultaneous, and combined effects of a variety of community variables.

Future research also needs to investigate more closely the shape of the relationship between community socioeconomic context and individual health. For example, the research described earlier indicated that there are health effects of not only extreme community socioeconomic deprivation, but also of high levels of affluence, and gradations in between as well. Further research is needed to examine whether and under what circumstances a gradient relationship exists between community socioeconomic context and health, and whether and under what circumstances there is a tipping or threshold relationship.

In addition, future research needs to more thoroughly address how socioeconomic characteristics of communities interact with other characteristics of communities to impact health. For example, LeClere and colleagues highlight the additional importance of percentage of female headed families in predicting heart disease mortality among women (1998), and of community racial concentration in predicting overall mortality (1997). Beyond the role of racial concentration, the role of racial residential segregation in affecting the health of individuals (Collins & Williams 1999) needs to be explored further since racial residential segregation and community socioeconomic context are interrelated in complex ways and may similarly work together and separately to affect individual health.

The effects of community socioeconomic context on health may have been underestimated in these studies because of failure to consider the impact of length of residence in communities. People living in a community for a long time are more "exposed" to their community than people who recently moved there. Those "exposed" for longer may be more likely to have their health affected by their community's characteristics. Future research should explore the impact of length of community residence, rather than just community residence, on the relationship between community socioeconomic context and individual health. Moreover, if we knew people's residential histories, we could examine the potential health impact of their community socioeconomic context as it varied over their life course rather than considering only their current community context.

Just as individuals may change residences over time, communities may change over time as well. Stability and change in communities are related to the level of social organization of communities (Sampson 1991), which in turn may affect health. Future research should examine what impact stability and change in communities might have on the health of residents.

Measuring Individual Socioeconomic Position

The independent effects of community socioeconomic context on health may be overestimated in these studies if they are simply capturing an unmeasured dimension of individual- or family-level socioeconomic position (Hauser 1970, 1974, Krieger et al 1997). For example, community socioeconomic context may better reflect a person's permanent or lifetime income than do measures of current family income and assets. However, the combination of multiple measures of socioeconomic position in some of the studies reviewed here makes it unlikely that most of the community effects are due to poor measurement of individual socioeconomic position.

Statistical Methods

Sociologists and others have long understood that there are statistical challenges involved in analyzing data at multiple levels (i.e. socioeconomic data at both the individual and community levels), such as the serial correlation that occurs when individuals within the same communities have common community variables (Blalock 1984, Boyd & Iversen 1979, DiPrete & Forristal 1994, Diez-Roux 1998, Von Korff et al 1992). Although special statistical techniques, such as hierarchical linear modeling (e.g. HLM, Bryk & Raudenbush 1992), have been designed for use with multilevel or contextual studies, few studies have actually employed such methods to study the impact of community socioeconomic context on individual health (exceptions include Diez-Roux et al 1997, Ecob 1996, Reijneveld 1998), raising questions about whether the significance of community effects has been overestimated in many studies (e.g., Davey Smith et al 1998, Haan et al 1987, Hochstim et al 1968, LeClere et al 1997, LeClere et al 1998, Sloggett & Joshi 1994, 1998, Waitzman & Smith 1998a). Some studies using data with sample designs less conducive to hierarchical linear modeling techniques (e.g. Anderson et al 1997, Robert 1998) have used software (e.g. SUDAAN, Shah et al 1992) to specifically address serial correlation problems. Although differences in study sample designs greatly affect which statistical technique is most appropriate (Robert 1998, Duncan et al 1997, Lynch & Kaplan 1997), future research should more explicitly test and compare the results of different statistical methods for use with multilevel models.

Moderating Effects of Age, Race, Gender, and Socioeconomic Position

As discussed earlier, research has not adequately addressed questions about how age, race, gender, and individual socioeconomic position moderate the effects of community socioeconomic context on individual health. When testing whether there are moderating effects, researchers will need to specify: (*a*) whether community socioeconomic context matters only to the health and mortality of people in some subgroups while not to others, or (*b*) whether community socioeconomic context matters to the health of all individuals, while also being particularly important to some subgroups. These differences may seem subtle, but they suggest different types of mediating mechanisms and intervention strategies.

Explaining the Relationship Between Community Socioeconomic Context and Individual Health

It is important to emphasize at this point that research has focused on examining the independent effects of community socioeconomic context on individual health after controlling for individual socioeconomic position without exploring evidence for the indirect effects of community socioeconomic context on health *through* individual socioeconomic position. Therefore, although the independent effects of community socioeconomic context may be relatively small in magnitude, the overall importance of community socioeconomic context to individual health may be more substantial to the degree that community socioeconomic context shapes the socioeconomic position of residents. Although sociologists and others have had interest in the effects of community context on individual socioeconomic position (Brooks-Gunn et al 1997, Foster & McLanahan 1996, Garner & Raudenbush 1991), many of these studies suffer from the same methodological limitations discussed here (Duncan et al 1997), and they have not specifically tested for the ultimate health outcomes of these relationships. Future research should consider the full effects of community socioeconomic context on individual health both through and independent of individual socioeconomic position.

As for investigating the specific mediating factors that link community socioeconomic context to health, it seems premature to test for the relative explanatory weight of different factors when we still need better specification of the basic relationship between community socioeconomic context and individual health. However, it is not too early to develop more comprehensive and theoretically driven models specifying the potential mechanisms that may connect community socioeconomic context to health and describing the conditions under which they might act and interact to affect health. Because much of the research on community socioeconomic context and health has been more epidemiological than sociological to date, it has lacked infusion of sociological theory despite the many sociological theories that may have direct relevance, such as some of the seminal social disorganization, stratification, and social ecology theories (Shaw & McKay 1931, Kornhauser 1978, Blau 1977) as well as more recent theories regarding inner city poverty, social disorganization, and residential segregation (Wilson 1987, Jencks & Peterson 1991, Sampson & Morenoff 1997, Massey & Denton 1993).

FINAL THOUGHTS

Although the studies reviewed here demonstrate that the independent effects of community socioeconomic context on individual health are relatively small in magnitude, I and others (e.g. Duncan et al 1997) believe that most of the methodological and conceptual limitations of current research suggest that studies to date have generally underestimated community effects. The independent community effects *controlling* for individual-level socioeconomic position have been underestimated due to methodological flaws, and the indirect community effects *through* individual socioeconomic position have been understudied to date.

In order to move research in this area forward, future sociological research should particularly: (*a*) address many of the methodological limitations discussed above, (*b*) examine more thoroughly how age, race, gender, and individual socioeconomic position moderate the effects of community socioeconomic context on individual health, (*c*) integrate existing sociological theories and extend them to more formally propose testable relationships between community socioeconomic context and individual health, (*d*) examine the indirect effects of community socioeconomic context on individual health through individual socioeconomic position, and (*e*) investigate what role racial residential segregation plays in creating or explaining community socioeconomic effects on health. Although we are ultimately interested in what it is about living in communities of lower or higher socioeconomic contexts that may be detrimental to or protective of health, it is currently premature to test formally and accurately the relative weight of different explanations for community effects using current methods before we address some of the basic methodological and theoretical issues just discussed. Moreover, the knowledge gained through the use of increasingly sophisticated quantitative methods, as discussed here, could be well supplemented by qualitative approaches to examining people's health in the context of their community environments.

ACKNOWLEDGMENTS

I would like to thank Jim House, Felicia LeClere, and John Lynch for their comments on an earlier version of this manuscript. Support for this work came from the Robert Wood Johnson Foundation Scholars in Health Policy Research Program.

> **Visit the *Annual Reviews* home page at http://www.AnnualReviews.org.**

Literature Cited

Anderson RT, Sorlie P, Backlund E, Johnson N, Kaplan GA. 1997. Mortality effects of community socioeconomic status. *Epidemiology* 8(1):42–7

Aneshensel CS, Sucoff CA. 1996. The neighborhood context of adolescent mental health. *J. Health Soc. Behav.* 37:293–310

Ben-Shlomo Y, White IR, Marmot M. 1996. Does the variation in the socioeconomic characteristics of an area affect mortality? *Br. Med. J.* 312:1013–4

Blalock HM. 1984. Contextual-effects models: theoretical and methodological issues. *Annu. Rev. Sociol.* 10:353–72

Blau P. 1977. *Inequality and Heterogeneity*. New York: Free Press

Boyd JHJ, Iversen GR. 1979. *Contextual Analysis: Concepts and Statistical Techniques*. Belmont, CA: Wadsworth

Brooks-Gunn J, Duncan GJ, Aber JL, eds. 1997. *Neighborhood Poverty: Context and Consequences for Children*, Vol. 1. New York: Russell Sage Found.

Bryk AS, Raudenbush SW. 1992. *Hierarchical Linear Models*. London: Sage

Bullard RD. 1990. *Dumping in Dixie: Race, Class, and Environmental Quality*. Boulder, CO: Westview

Coleman JS. 1988. Social capital in the creation of human capital. *Am. J. Sociol.* 94(Suppl.):S95–S120

Collins JW, Herman AA, David RJ. 1997. Very-low-birthweight infants and income incongruity among African American and white parents in Chicago. *Am. J. Public Health* 87(3):415–17

Collins C, Williams DR. 1999. Segregation and mortality: the deadly effects of racism? *Sociol. Forum.* In press

Crane J. 1991. The epidemic theory of ghettos and neighborhood effects on dropping out and teenage childbearing. *Am. J. Sociol.* 96:1236–59

Crombie IK, Kenicer MB, Smith WCS, Tunstall-Pedoe HD. 1989. Unemployment, socioenvironmental factors, and coronary heart disease in Scotland. *Br. Heart J.* 61:172–77

Daly MC, Duncan GJH, Kaplan GA, Lynch JW. 1998. Macro-to-micro links in the relations between income inequality and mortality. *Milbank Q.* 76(3):315–39

Davey Smith G. 1996. Income inequality and mortality: Why are they related? *Br. Med. J.* 313:987–88

Davey Smith G, Hart C, Watt G, Hole D, Hawthorne V. 1998. Individual social class, area-based deprivation, cardiovascular disease risk factors, and mortality: the Renfrew and Paisley study. *J. Epidemiol. Commun. Health* 52:399–405

Diez-Roux AV. 1998. Bringing context back into epidemiology: variables and fallacies in multilevel analysis. *Am. J. Public Health* 88(2):216–22

Diez-Roux AV, Nieto FJ, Muntaner C, Tyroler HA, Comstock GW, et al. 1997. Neighborhood environments and coronary heart disease: a multilevel analysis. *Am. J. Epidemiol.* 146(1):48–63

DiPrete TA, Forristal JD. 1994. Multilevel models: methods and substance. *Annu. Rev. Sociol.* 20:331–57

Duncan GJ, Connell JP, Klebanov PK. 1997. Conceptual and methodological issues in estimating causal effects of neighborhoods and family conditions on individual development. In *Neighborhood Poverty: Context and Consequences for Children*, ed. J Brooks-Gunn, GJ Duncan, JL Aber, pp. 219–50. New York: Russell Sage Found.

Ecob R. 1996. A multilevel modelling approach to examining the effects of area of residence on health and functioning. *J. Roy. Statist. Soc. A* 159(1):61–75

Figueroa JB, Breen N. 1995. Significance of underclass residence on the stage of breast or cervical cancer diagnosis. *AEA Pap. Proc.* 85(2):112–16

Fiscella K, Franks P. 1997. Poverty or income inequality as a predictor of mortality: longitudinal cohort study. *Br. Med. J.* 314:1724–27

Foster EM, McLanahan S. 1996. An illustration of the use of instrumental variables: Do neighborhood conditions affect a young person's chance of finishing high school? *Psychol. Meth.* 1(3):249–60

Garner CL, Raudenbush SW. 1991. Neighborhood effects on educational attainment: a multilevel analysis. *Sociol. Educ.* 64:251–62

Gravelle H. 1998. How much of the relation between population mortality and unequal distribution of income is a statistical artefact? *Br. Med. J.* 316:382–85

Guest AM, Almgren G, Hussey JM. 1998. The ecology of race and socioeconomic distress: infant and working-age mortality in Chicago. *Demography* 35(1):23–34

Haan M, Kaplan GA, Camacho T. 1987. Poverty and health: prospective evidence from the Alameda county study. *Am. J. Epidemiol.* 125(6):989–98

Hauser RM. 1970. Context and consex: a cautionary tale. *Am. J. Sociol.* 75:645–64

Hauser RM. 1974. Contextual analysis revisited. *Sociol. Meth. Res.* 2(3):365–75

Hochstim JR, Athanasopoulos DA, Larkins JH. 1968. Poverty area under the microscope. *Am. J. Public Health* 58:1815–27

House JS, Kessler RC, Herzog AR, Mero RP, Kinney AM, Breslow MJ. 1990. Age, socioeconomic status, and health. *Milbank Q.* 68(3):383–411

House JS, Lepkowski JM, Kinney AM, Mero RP, Kessler RC, Herzog AR. 1994. The social stratification of aging and health. *J. Health Soc. Behav.* 35:213–34

Hsieh CC, Pugh MD. 1993. Poverty, income inequality, and violent crime: a meta-analysis of recent aggregate data studies. *Crim. Justice Rev.* 18:182–202

Jargowsky PA. 1997. *Poverty and Place: Ghettos, Barrios, and the American City*. New York: Russell Sage Found.

Jencks C, Mayer SE. 1990. The social consequences of growing up in a poor neighborhood. In *Inner-City Poverty in the United States*, ed. LE Lynn Jr, MGH McGeary, pp. 111–86. Washington, DC: Natl. Acad. Press

Jencks C, Peterson PE. 1991. *The Urban Underclass*. Washington, DC: Brookings Inst.

Jones K, Duncan C. 1995. Individuals and their ecologies: analysing the geography of chronic illness within a multilevel modelling framework. *Health & Place* 1(1):27–40

Kaplan GA, Pamuk ER, Lynch JW, Cohen RD, Balfour JL. 1996. Inequality in income and mortality in the United States: analysis of mortality and potential pathways. *Br. Med. J.* 312:999–1003

Kaplan GA, Shema SJ, Balfour JL, Yen IH. 1999. Poverty area residence and incidence of disability. *Am. J. Public Health.* In press

Kawachi I, Kennedy BP. 1997. Health and social cohesion: Why care about income inequality? *Br. Med. J.* 314:1037–40

Kawachi I, Kennedy BP, Lochner K, Prothrow-Stith D. 1997. Social capital, income inequality, and mortality. *Am. J. Public Health* 87(9):1491–98

Kennedy, BP, Kawachi I, Glass R, Prothrow-Stith D. 1998. Income distribution, socioeconomic status and self-rated health in the United States. *Br. Med. J.* 317:917–21

Kennedy BP, Kawachi I, Prothrow-Stith D. 1996. Income distribution and mortality: cross sectional ecological study of the Robin Hood index in the United States. *Br. Med. J.* 312:1004–7

Kleinschmidt I, Hills M, Elliott P. 1995. Smoking behaviour can be predicted by neighbourhood deprivation measures. *J. Epidimiol. Commun. Health* 49(2):S72–S7

Kornhauser R. 1978. *Social Sources of Delinquency*. Chicago: Univ. Chicago Press

Krieger N. 1992. Overcoming the absence of socioeconomic data in medical records: validation and application of a census-based methodology. *Am. J. Public Health* 82(5):703–10

Krieger N, Williams DR, Moss NE. 1997. Measuring social class in US public health research: Concepts, methodologies, and guidelines. *Annu. Rev. Public Health* 18: 341–78

Lawton MP. 1970. Ecology and aging. In *The Spatial Behavior of Older People*, ed. LA Pastalan, DH Carson. Ann Arbor: Univ. Mich. and Wayne State Univ. Inst. of Gerontology

Lawton MP. 1977. The impact of the environment on aging and behavior. In *Handbook of the Psychology of Aging*, ed. JE Birren, KW Schaie, pp. 276–301. New York: Van-Nostrand Reinhold

Lawton MP, Simon B. 1968. The ecology of social relationships in housing for the elderly. *Gerontologist* 8(2):108–15

LeClere FB, Rogers RG, Peters KD. 1997. Ethnicity and mortality in the United States: individual and community correlates. *Soc. Forc.* 76(1):169–98

LeClere FB, Rogers RG, Peters K. 1998. Neighborhood social context and racial differences in women's heart disease mortality. *J. Health Soc. Behav.* 39:91–107

Lynch JW, Kaplan GA. 1997. Understanding how inequality in the distribution of income affects health. *J. Health Psychol.* 2(3):297–314

Lynch JW, Kaplan GA, Cohen RD, Tuomilehto J, Salonen JT. 1996. Do cardiovascular risk factors explain the relation between socioeconomic status, risk of all-cause mortality, cardiovascular mortality, and acute myocardial infarction. *Am. J. Epidemiol.* 144(10):934–42

Lynch JW, Kaplan GA, Pamuk ER, Cohen RD, Heck KE, et al. 1998. Income inequality and mortality in metropolitan areas of the United States. *Am. J. Public Health* 88(7):1074–80

Macintyre S, Maciver S, Sooman A. 1993. Area, class and health: Should we be focusing on places or people? *J. Soc. Policy* 22(2):213–34

Massey DS, Denton NA. 1993. *American Apartheid: Segregation and the Making of the Underclass*. Cambridge, MA: Harvard Univ. Press

Minkler M. 1992. Community organizing among the elderly poor in the United States: a case study. *Int. J. Health Serv.* 22(2):303–16

O'Campo P, Xue X, Wang M-C, Caughy MOB. 1997. Neighborhood risk factors for low birthweight in Baltimore: a multilevel analysis. *Am. J. Public Health* 87(7): 1113–8

Putnam R. 1993. The prosperous community: social capital and public life. *Am. Prospect* 25(March/April):26–28

Reijneveld SA. 1998. The impact of individual and area characteristics on urban socioeconomic differences in health and smoking. *Int. J. Epidemiol.* 27:33–40

Robert SA. 1996. *The effects of individual-, family-, and community-level socioeconomic status on health over the life course.* PhD thesis. Univ. Michigan, Ann Arbor

Robert SA. 1998. Community-level socioeconomic status effects on adult health. *J. Health Soc. Behav.* 39:18–37

Robert SA, House JS. 1999a. Socioeconomic inequalities in health: An enduring sociological problem. In *Handbook of Medical Sociology*, eds. CE Bird, P Conrad, AM Fremont. In press

Robert SA, House JS. 1999b. Socioeconomic inequalities in health: integrating individual-, community-, and societal-level theory and research. In *Handbook of Social Studies in Health and Medicine*, eds. G Albrecht, S Scrimshaw, R Fitzpatrick. In press

Rodgers GB. 1979. Income and inequality as determinants of mortality: an international cross-section analysis. *Popul. Stud.* 33: 343–51

Sampson RJ. 1991. Linking the micro- and macrolevel dimensions of community social organization. *Soc. Forc.* 70(1):43–64

Sampson RJ, Groves WB. 1989. Community structure and crime: Testing social disorganization theory. *Am. J. Sociol.* 9(4): 774–802

Sampson RJ, Morenoff JD. 1997. Ecological perspectives on the neighborhood context of urban poverty: past and present. In *Neighborhood Poverty: Policy Implications in Studying Neighborhoods*, ed. J Brooks-Gunn, GJ Duncan, JL Aber, pp. 1–22. New York: Russell Sage

Shah BV, Barnwell BG, Hunt PN, LaVange LM. 1992. *SUDAAN User's Manual Release 6.0.* Research Triangle Park, NC: Res. Triangle Inst.

Shaw C, McKay H. 1931. Report of the causes of crime. In *Social Factors in Juvenile Delinquency*. Washington, DC: US Gov. Print. Off.

Sloggett A, Joshi H. 1994. Higher mortality in deprived areas: community or personal disadvantage? *Br. Med. J.* 309:1470–74

Sloggett A, Joshi H. 1998. Deprivation indicators as predictors of life events 1981–1992 based on the UK ONS longitudinal study. *J. Epidemiol. Comm. Health* 52(4): 228–33

Soobader M, LeClere FB. 1999. Aggregation and the measurement of income inequality effects on morbidity. *Soc. Sci. Med.* In press

Sooman A, Macintyre S. 1995. Health and perceptions of the local environment in socially contrasting neibhourhoods in Glasgow. *Health & Place* 1(1):15–26

Troutt DD. 1993. *The Thin Red Line: How the Poor Still Pay More.* San Francisco, CA: Consumers Union of US, Inc., West Coast Regional Off.

US General Accounting Office. 1983. *Siting of hazardous waste landfills and their correlation with racial and economic status of surrounding communities.* Washington, DC: U.S. General Accounting Off.

van Doorslaer E, Wagstaff A, Bleichrodt H, Calonge S, Gerdtham U–G, et al. 1997. Income-related inequalities in health: some international comparisons. *J. Health Econ.* 16:93–112

Von Korff M, Koepsell T, Curry S, Diehr P. 1992. Multi-level analysis in epidemiologic research on health behaviors and outcomes. *Am. J. Epidemiol.* 135(10):1077–82

Waitzman NJ, Smith KR. 1998a. Phantom of the area: Poverty-area residence and mortality in the United States. *Am. J. Public Health* 88(6):973–76

Waitzman NJ, Smith KR. 1998b. Separate but lethal: the effects of economic segregation on mortality in metropolitan America. *Milbank Q.* 76(3):341–73

Wallace R, Wallace D. 1990. Origins of public health collapse in New York City: the dynamics of planned shrinkage, contagious urban decay and social disintegration. *Bull. N. Y. Acad. Med.* 66(5):391–434

Wilkinson RG. 1992. Income distribution and life expectancy. *Br. Med. J.* 301:165–68

Wilkinson RG. 1996. *Unhealthy Societies: The Afflictions of Inequality.* New York: Routledge

Williams DR. 1990. Socioeconomic differentials in health: a review and redirection. *Soc. Psychol. Q.* 53(2):81–99

Williams DR, Collins C. 1995. US socioeconomic and racial differences in health: patterns and explanations. *Annu. Rev. Sociol.* 21:349–86

Wilson WJ. 1987. *The Truly Disadvantaged: The Inner City, the Underclass, and Public Policy.* Chicago: Univ. Chicago Press

Yen IH, Kaplan GA. 1999. Neighborhood social environment and risk of death: multilevel evidence from the Alameda County Study. *Am. J. Epidemiol.* In press

Annu. Rev. Sociol. 1999. 25:517–39

A RETROSPECTIVE ON THE CIVIL RIGHTS MOVEMENT: Political and Intellectual Landmarks

Aldon D. Morris

Department of Sociology, Northwestern University, Evanston, Illinois 60201-1330;
e-mail: amorris@casbah.acns.nwu.edu

KEY WORDS: segregation, race, M. L. King, change, tactics, social movement theory

ABSTRACT

This review provides an analysis of the political and intellectual contributions made by the modern civil rights movement. It argues that the civil rights movement was able to overthrow the Southern Jim Crow regime because of its successful use of mass nonviolent direct action. Because of its effectiveness and visibility, it served as a model that has been utilized by other movements both domestically and internationally. Prior to the civil rights movement social movement scholars formulated collective behavior and related theories to explain social movement phenomena. These theories argued that movements were spontaneous, non-rational, and unstructured. Resource mobilization and political process theories reconceptualized movements stressing their organized, rational, institutional and political features. The civil rights movement played a key role in generating this paradigmatic shift because of its rich empirical base that led scholars to rethink social movement phenomena.

INTRODUCTION

What would America be like if we could turn back the clock to 1950? One thing is certain, the pre-civil rights movement era would stand in stark contrast to the America that currently exists just two years before the new millennium. In terms of race relations, the contrast is so sharp that we are justified to speak of a pre- and post- civil rights movement period. The civil rights movement is clearly one of the pivotal developments of the twentieth century. The task of

517

0360-0572/99/0815-0517$08.00

this chapter is to elucidate the factors that made this movement such an important force in America and abroad. The chapter also concerns itself with how the civil rights movement has affected the theoretical developments in the field of social movements. The first concern is to discuss why the civil rights movement was necessary in the first place.

The Jim Crow regime was a major characteristic of American society in 1950 and had been so for over seven decades. Following slavery it became the new form of white domination, which insured that Blacks would remain oppressed well into the twentieth century. Racial segregation was the linchpin of Jim Crow, for it was an arrangement that set Blacks off from the rest of humanity and labeled them as an inferior race (see Morris 1984:2). Elsewhere I characterized Jim Crow as a tripartite system of domination (Morris 1984) because it was designed to control Blacks politically and socially, and to exploit them economically. In the South, Blacks were controlled politically because their disenfranchisement barred them from participating in the political process. As a result, their constitutional rights were violated because they could not serve as judges nor participate as jurors.

Economically Blacks were kept at the bottom of the economic order because they lacked even minimal control over the economy. Throughout the first half of the twentieth century, most rural Blacks worked as sharecroppers and hired hands where they were the victims of exploitation because of the unequal economic arrangements they were forced to enter. As Blacks migrated to Southern and Northern cities they found that their economic status did not change radically; in these settings they were forced onto the lowest rungs of the unskilled wage sectors. Therefore, "in 1950 social inequality in the work place meant that nonwhite families earned nationally 54% of the median income of white families" (Morris 1984:1).

The social oppression Blacks experienced prior to the civil rights movement was devastating. The Jim Crow system went to great lengths to impress on Blacks that they were a subordinate population by forcing them to live in a separate inferior society. Moreover, the fact that Blacks had to use separate toilets, attend separate schools, sit at the back of buses and trains, address whites with respect while being addressed disrespectfully, be sworn in on different bibles in the court room, purchase clothes without first trying them on, pass by "white only" lunch counter seats after purchasing food, and travel without sleep because hotels would not accommodate them—all these—resulted in serious psychological damage.

The role that violence and terror played against Blacks during the Jim Crow period has been documented. John Hope Franklin (1967) detailed the violence that white supremacist groups, including the Ku Klux Klan and the Knights of the White Camellia, heaped upon African Americans. He wrote that such groups "used intimidation, force, ostracism in business and society, bribery at the polls, arson, and even murder to accomplish their deeds" (Franklin 1967: 327). The lynch rope was one of the most vicious and effective means of terror used against Blacks. In a painstaking analysis of lynching in one Southern state, Charles Payne (1994) wrote that "between the end of Reconstruction and the modern civil rights era, Mississippi lynched 539 Blacks, more than any other state. Between 1930 and 1950—during the two decades immediately preceding the modern phase of the civil rights movement—the state had at least 33 lynchings" (1947:7).

As late as the 1950s the Jim Crow regime remained firmly intact, effectively oppressing the Southern Black population. Earlier in the century W.E.B. DuBois had predicted that the problem of the twentieth century was the problem of the color line (DuBois 1903). By the 1950s racial realities suggested that the color line was not likely to undergo substantial change during the twentieth century. As late as the 1940s, the majority of white Americans still held racist views that squarely supported white supremacy. Larry Bobo summarized the evidence:

> The available survey data suggest that anti-Black attitudes associated with Jim Crow racism were once widely accepted. The Jim Crow social order called for a society based on deliberate segregation by race. It gave positive sanction to anti-Black discrimination in economics, education, and politics...All of this was expressly premised on the notion that Blacks were the innate intellectual, cultural and temperamental inferiors to whites (Bobo 1997:35).

In their heyday, systems of domination often appear unshakable. By 1950 the Jim Crow regime appeared to rest on a solid foundation of white supremacy capable of enduring indefinitely.

Beneath the placid appearance of permanent dominance there may exist substantial resistance. For the Black population such resistance had gathered steam long before 1950. It is often the case that students of protest overlook resistance until it becomes highly visible and threatens dominant interests. The inability to grasp such "subterranean" forces is more pronounced when the oppressed population is perceived as inferior and incapable of generating the agency required to transform domination. As I discuss later, this certainly was the case for African Americans. We now have nuance studies documenting the continuity of Black protest and Black insurgent ideologies. Vincent Harding's (1983) study, *There Is A River*, details the numerous protests that African Americans initiated throughout the slave period and the radical visions associated with these struggles. George Fredrickson's (1995) *Black Liberation*, does a masterful job documenting how African Americans developed radical ideologies from the nineteenth century to the present that have guided their struggles and played significant roles in liberation ideologies on the continent of Africa. These studies make clear that African Americans have long possessed a protest tradition that is continually refashioned and interjected into new rounds of struggles.

Early years in the twentieth century African Americans launched protests directly attacking racial inequality. Between 1900 and 1906 Southern Blacks developed boycott movements against Jim Crow streetcars in most major cities of the South (Meier & Rudwick 1976:267–89). By the turn of the twentieth century Black women had organized local and national clubs through which they relentlessly fought both for the overthrow of Jim Crow and for women's rights (Collier-Thomas 1984:35–53). The National Association for the Advancement of Colored People (NAACP) was founded in 1909–1910. This was an important development because the NAACP was the first national protest organization organized specifically to attack the Jim Crow regime and racial inequality. It immediately began attacking the legal basis of racial subordination during the Jim Crow era (McNeil 1983, Tushnet 1987). The NAACP would win major legal cases against racial segregation throughout the first half of the twentieth century especially with regards to segregated schools.

Major developments occurred in the 1920s that challenged entrenched ideas of white supremacy and Black inferiority. The Garvey movement, organized in 1920, rapidly became the largest mass movement Black America had ever produced. Its main message was that Black people, Black culture, Black history and Africa were noble and that Black people had created great civilizations that rivaled Western civilization on every front. Garvey preached that Blacks should return to Africa. This praising of things Black flew directly in the face of white hegemonic beliefs. Large numbers of African Americans were receptive to this message. Otherwise the Garvey movement could never have developed into a major mass movement.

The Harlem Renaissance of the 1920s was a major literary movement that carried a similar message. This movement produced what has come to be characterized as protest literature. It aimed at creating a "New Negro" who was proud of her Black heritage and prepared to fight for Black liberation. This protest theme was clearly represented in lines of Claude McKay's poem, "If We Must Die" where he declared, "Oh, Kinsmen! We must meet the common foe/ Though far outnumbered, let us show us brave/ And for their thousand blows deal one deathblow!" (McKay 1963:31).

During this period Black protests accompanied the proliferating Black protest literature. Jaynes & Williams found that "between 1929 and 1941, Northern Blacks organized a series of 'don't buy where you can't work' campaigns in which white owned ghetto businesses were boycotted unless they agreed to hire Blacks" (Jaynes & Williams 1989). But it was a movement organized just a decade prior to the explosion of the modern civil rights movement that was the clearest harbinger of things to come. In the early 1940s A Philip Randolph organized the March on Washington Movement (MOWM). Randolph had become convinced that a mass nonviolent movement of African Americans was the central force needed to overthrow racial inequality. Throughout 1941, Randolph, Black leaders, and organizers across America worked to build a Black nonviolent direct action movement (Garfinkel 1969). It was named the March on Washington Movement because Randolph decided to target racial discrimination in the defense industries by marching on Washington and the White House by the thousands. Such a mass march, he reasoned, would embarrass the nation and President Roosevelt who were in the midst of fighting racism abroad during World War II. On the eve of the March Randolph and Black leaders throughout the nation had organized thousands of Blacks who were prepared to march on Washington. The March never occurred because Roosevelt suspected that it was a real possibility that thousands of Blacks would march on his White House. On June 25, 1941 he issued an Executive Order that banned racial discrimination in the nation's defense industries. Thus, the very threat of protest by a massive Black nonviolent direct action movement bore fruit in the early 1940s.

Two sharply contrasting developments occurred in the early 1950s that severely threatened the Jim Crow system. They were the 1954 Supreme Court ruling in the Brown vs. Board of Education case and the lynching of Emmett Till in 1955. In the Brown case the NAACP won a major Supreme Court ruling that declared racially segregated schools unconstitutional (Kluger 1975). This ruling literally swept away the legal grounds on which Jim Crow stood. African Americans were filled with hope by the ruling, believing that finally it was realistic for them to believe that legal racial segregation was on its deathbed. Morehouse College President, Benjamin Mays, captured the Black reaction when he stated "we all underestimated the impact of the 1954 decision…people literally got out and danced in the streets…The Negro was jubilant" (Mays Interview 1978). The Southern white power structure had a completely different reaction. They rebuked the Supreme Court for its decision, vowing never to integrate the schools nor to dismantle the Jim Crow regime. The Brown ruling caused sharp battle lines to be drawn between the white South and African Americans.

In August of 1955, Emmett Till, a fourteen year old Black male from Chicago, was lynched in Money, Mississippi for whistling at a white woman (Whitefield 1988). The crime was extremely brutal, and it was a reminder to the Black community that whites would utilize all means, including murder, to uphold Jim Crow. An all-white jury exonerated Till's murderers of the crime. The black response to Till's lynching differed from the usual pattern. Till's mother and the Black press generated national publicity pertaining to the gross injustice of the lynching. Because of the widespread attention this lynching received, the brutality and raw racism of the Jim Crow regime were placed on a national stage where it was debated and denounced.

The generation of young Blacks who would lead the student wing of the modern civil rights movement was coming of age precisely at the time of Till's lynching. This murder played an important role in radicalizing them. They were shocked at the brutality of the crime and outraged when the murderers were allowed to go free by the white judicial system. Many of them began embracing ideas of activism because they themselves felt vulnerable. They were well aware that the white community and many adults within the black community refused to fight for justice. Thus, the Till lynching pushed them toward political activism (see Moody 1968, Ladner 1979, Whitfield 1988). The hope generated by the Brown Ruling and the outrage caused by Till's lynching, helped set the stage for the emergence of the modern civil rights movement.

Structural Prerequisites Of The Civil Rights Movement

Oppressed groups are not always in a position to generate change through social protest. Favorable social conditions play an important role in creating the circumstances conducive to protest. Social movement scholars (McAdam 1982, Tarrow 1994) have asserted that social protest is more likely to occur if there exists a favorable political opportunity structure. Such a structure had developed prior to the rise of the modern civil rights movement. As McAdam has argued (1982), by the time the civil rights movement began to unfold, Blacks had amassed a new level of political power because of the Northern Black vote. That vote could be used to push a Black agenda, especially given its emerging importance in presidential elections.

The politics of the Cold War was an additional factor making Black protest a viable option. The United States and the Soviet Union were locked in an intense battle to win over newly independent Third World countries, especially those in Africa. The issue of American racism was an impediment to an American foreign policy bent on persuading African nations to align themselves with America. Racism and democracy were opposing ideologies, and Black leaders were aware that America's treatment of Blacks could be a stumbling block in America's quest to become the major superpower. Wide-scale Black protest, therefore, stood a good chance of exposing the contradiction between racism and democracy.

The coming of age of modern communication technologies in the 1950s and early 1960s was another development that could be exploited by a Black protest movement. The widespread use of television was a case in point. As early as 1958, over 83% of American households owned television sets (Sterling & Kittross 1978). These technologies were capable of providing a window through which millions could watch Black protest and become familiar with the issues it raised. Likewise, by the early 1960s communications satellites were launched into orbit. This development made it possible for Black protest to be viewed globally, thus enhancing its ability to affect the international arena.

A development internal to the Black community also increased the probability that widespread protest could be launched and sustained. This was the great migration that occurred during the period of the two World Wars and that continued throughout the 1950s. During this period large numbers of Blacks moved to cities in both the South and the North. This migration led to institution building especially within the Black Church and community organizations. These were the kinds of institutions through which protest could be organized and supported. The urban setting also provided the Black community with dense social networks through which social protest could be organized rapidly. In short, by the 1950s the Northern Black vote, the politics of the Cold War, the rise of modern communication technologies, and Black mass migration constituted favorable social conditions conducive to the rise of a massive Black movement.

The existence of favorable conditions does not guarantee that collective action will materialize. Agency is required for such action to occur. People must develop an oppositional consciousness that provides them with a critique of the status quo and reasons to believe that acting collectively will lead to change. They must develop the willingness to make sacrifices that may endanger their physical well being or cause them to lose jobs. They must be willing to devote time to collective action that may cause them to neglect or curtail other important but routine activities. Creativity is crucial to social movements because they require new ways of doing things and they thrive on innovations. People who participate in movements have to place themselves in learning situations where they can be taught to act creatively. Structural prerequisites may be conducive to collective action, but without human agency such conditions will not even be recognized, let alone exploited.

THE MODERN CIVIL RIGHTS MOVEMENT

The impact of the civil rights movement on race relations and the nation's social fabric has been monumental. This pivotal movement has had significant influence on social movements in a wide array of countries. The intent here is not to provide a detailed account of the modern civil rights movement. Such accounts are available in the vast literature that has emerged over the last twenty years (e.g. Carson 1981, Sitkoff 1981, McAdam 1982, Blumberg 1984, Morris 1984, Garrow 1986, Bloom 1987, Fairclough 1987, Branch 1988, Lawson 1991, Robnett 1997). The purpose here is to present an analysis of why this movement by a relatively powerless group was able to overthrow the formal Jim Crow system and how it became a model for other protest movements here and abroad. My analysis draws heavily from the previously mentioned literature.

The most distinctive aspect of the modern civil rights movement was its demonstration that an oppressed, relatively powerless group, can generate social change through the widespread use of social protest. For nearly two decades, this movement perfected the art of social protest. The far ranging and complex social protest it generated did *not* emerge immediately. Rather it evolved through time making use of trial and error.

By the mid 1950s Southern Black leaders had not yet fully grasped the idea that the fate of Jim Crow rested in the hands of the Black masses. Even though protest against racial inequality occurred throughout the first half of the century, it tended to be localized and limited in scope. With the exception of the Garvey Movement and A Philip Randolph's March On Washington Movement (MOWM), the mass base of the prior protests was too restricted to threaten the Jim Crow order. Both the Garvey and MOWM movements had limited goals and were relatively short lived. By 1950 the legal method was the dominant weapon of Black protest, and it required skilled lawyers rather than mass action. The legal method depended on the actions of elites external to the Black community whereby Blacks had to hope that white judges and Supreme Court justices would issue favorable rulings in response to well-reasoned and well-argued court cases.

The 1955 Montgomery, Alabama, year-long mass-based bus boycott and the unfolding decade of Black protest changed all this. These developments thrust the power capable of overthrowing Jim Crow into the hands of the Black community. Outside elites, including the courts, the Federal Government, and sympathetic whites, would still have roles to play. However, massive Black protest dictated that those roles would be in response to Black collective action rather than as catalysts for change in the racial order. A decisive shift in the power equation between whites and Blacks grew out of the struggle to desegregate Alabama buses.

The Montgomery bus boycott revealed that large numbers of Blacks—indeed an entire community—could be mobilized to protest racial segregation. The Montgomery boycott demonstrated that protest could be sustained indefinitely: the boycott endured for over a year. The boycott revealed the central role that would be played by social organization and a Black culture rooted in a protest tradition, if protests were to be successful. The Black Church, which had a mass base and served as the main repository of Black culture, proved to be capable of generating, sustaining, and culturally energizing large volumes of protest. Its music and form of worship connected the masses to its protest tradition stemming back to the days of slavery.

Out of Montgomery came the Montgomery Improvement Association (MIA), the first highly visible social movement organization (SMO) of direct action protests. It was both church based and structurally linked to the major community organization of the Black community. A young Black minister, Martin Luther King, Jr., who came to personify the role of charismatic leader, was chosen to lead the movement. Finally, it was the boycott method itself that shifted power to the Black masses, for it required that large numbers of individuals engage in collective action. The requirement that the boycott adopt nonviolent direct action was crucial, for it robbed the white power structure of its ability to openly crush the movement violently without serious repercussions. The mass media, especially television, radio, and the Black press, as well as communication channels internal to the Black community, proved capable of disseminating this new development across the nation. A ruling by the Supreme Court, that declared bus segregation in Alabama unconstitutional, sealed the victory for the movement. It was clear, however, that the ruling was in response to Black protest and that Jim Crow could be defeated if the lessons of the Montgomery movement could be applied in movements across the South which targeted all aspects of racial segregation.

For more than a decade, such movements did occur across the South. Numerous local communities throughout the South, supported by the national Black community and sympathetic whites, perfected the use of mass-based nonviolent direct action. The disruptive tactics included boycotts, sit-ins, freedom rides, mass marches, mass jailings, and legal challenges. The 1960 student sit-ins at segregated lunch counters were especially important because within a month these protests had become a mass movement, which spread throughout the South and mobilized an important mass base. That base initially consisted largely of Black college students but also came to include high school and elementary students. The sit-in tactic was innovative because other tactics spun off of it, including "wade ins" at segregated pools, "kneel-ins" and "pray-ins" at segregated churches, and "phone-ins" at segregated businesses.

The sit-in movement was also critical because it led to the formation of the Student Nonviolent Coordination Committee (SNCC), which became a social movement organization of students through which local communities were organized and mobilized into social protest (Morris 1984). This organization increased the formal organizational base of the movement, which already included the Southern Christian Leadership Conference (SCLC), the Congress of Racial Equality (CORE), the NAACP, and numerous local movement organizations. The sit-in movement and SNCC constituted the framework through which large numbers of white college students came to participate in the civil rights movement.

It was during the early to mid 1960s that the modern civil rights movement became the organized force that would topple Jim Crow. In this period highly public demonstrations occurred throughout the South and came to be increasingly strengthened by Northern demonstrations that were organized in support. These protests created a crisis because they disrupted social order and created an atmosphere that was not conducive to business and commerce in the South (Bloom 1987). They often caused white officials to use violence in their efforts to defeat the movement. By this time Martin Luther King Jr. had become a national and international charismatic figure. As James Lawson put it, "Any time King went to a movement, immediately the focus of the nation was on that community...He had the eyes of the world on where he went. And in the Black community, it never had that kind of person...It gave the Black community an advantage [that] it has never had" (Lawson 1978).

The intensity and visibility of demonstrations caused the Kennedy Administration and the Congress to seek measures that would end demonstrations and restore social order (Morris 1984, Schlesinger 1965). The demonstrations and the repressive measures used against them generated a foreign policy nightmare because they were covered by foreign media in Europe, the Soviet Union and Africa (see Fairclough 1987, Garrow 1986). As a result of national turmoil and international attention, the Jim Crow order was rendered vulnerable.

The Birmingham, Alabama, confrontation in 1963 and the Selma, Alabama, confrontation in 1965 generated the leverage that led to the overthrow of the formal Jim Crow order. In both instances, the movement was able to generate huge protest demonstrations utilizing an array of disruptive tactics that caused social order to collapse. The authorities in each locale responded with brutal violence that was captured by national and international media. The Birmingham movement sought to dismantle segregation in Birmingham and to generate national legislation that would invalidate racial segregation writ large. Because the Birmingham confrontation was so visible and effective it engendered additional protests throughout the South. Within ten weeks following the Birmingham confrontation, "758 demonstrations occurred in 186 cites across the South and at least 14,733 persons were arrested" (Sale 1973:83).

The goal of the 1965 Selma movement was to generate the necessary pressure that would lead to national legislation that would enfranchise Southern Blacks. The Selma confrontation commanded the same level of attention as the confrontation in Birmingham. Over 2,600 demonstrators were jailed, and on March 21 thousands of people from across the nation initiated a highly visible march from Selma to Montgomery. During the confrontations two Northern whites and a local Black demonstrator were murdered by Alabama lawmen. As in Birmingham, the Selma confrontations outraged the nation and drew widespread international attention. Once again the movement had maneuvered the Federal government into a corner where it had to play a role in resolving a crisis.

Because of the Birmingham movement and its aftermath, the Federal government issued national legislation outlawing all forms of racial segregation and discrimination. Thus, on June 2, 1964 President Johnson signed into law the 1964 Civil Rights Act. Similarly, to resolve the crisis created by Selma, the Congress passed national legislation that enfranchised Southern Blacks. Johnson signed the 1965 Voting Rights Bill into law on August 6, 1965. The 1964 Civil Rights Act and the 1965 Voting Rights Bill brought the formal regime of Jim Crow to a close.

By overthrowing Jim Crow in a matter of ten years, the civil rights movement had taught the nation and the world an important lesson: a mass-based grass roots social movement that is sufficiently organized, sustained, and disruptive is capable of generating fundamental social change. James Lawson captured it best when he concluded, "Many people, when they are suffering and they see their people suffering, they want direct participation... So you put into the hands of all kinds of ordinary people a positive alternative to powerlessness and frustration. That's one of the great things about direct action" (Lawson 1978). Structural opportunities helped facilitate the rise of the modern civil rights movement, but it was the human agency of the Black community and its supporters that crushed Jim Crow.

NATIONAL AND INTERNATIONAL SIGNIFICANCE OF THE CIVIL RIGHTS MOVEMENT

Scholars of social movements have increasingly come to recognize the pivotal role that the civil rights movement has played in generating movements in America and abroad. A consensus is emerging that the civil rights movement was the catalyst behind the wave of social movements that crystallized in the United States beginning in the middle of the 1960s and continuing to the present (see Evans 1980, Freeman 1983, Morris 1984, 1993, Adam 1987, McAdam 1988, Snow & Benford 1992, Tarrow 1994, Groch 1998). This body of literature has shown that movements as diverse as the student movement, the women's movement, the farm workers' movement, the Native American movement, the gay and lesbian movement, the environmental movement, and the disability rights movement all drew important lessons and inspiration from the civil rights movement. It was the civil rights movement that provided the model and impetus for social movements that exploded on the American scene.

A myriad of factors were responsible for the civil rights movement's ability to influence such a wide variety of American social movements. The ideas that human oppression is not inevitable and that collective action can generate change were the most important lessons the civil rights movement provided other groups. As Angela Davis (1983) has pointed out, the Black freedom struggle in America has taught other groups about the nature of human oppression and important lessons about their own subjugation. This was certainly the case with the civil rights movement, and this message was amplified by the great visibility accorded the movement by mass media, especially television.

The legal achievements of the civil rights movement were crucial to its capacity to trigger other movements. The 1964 Civil Rights Act was paramount in this regard for it prohibited a wide array of discriminations based on race, color, religion, national origin, and sex (Whalen & Whalen 1985). The modern women's movement was first to take advantage of this aspect of the Civil Rights Act because women in Congress had to struggle to get the word "sex" included in the legislation precisely because its opponents recognized that the incorporation of sex would have far ranging implications for the place of women in society. The general point is that this legislation, and others generated by the civil rights movement, created the legal framework through which other groups gained the constitutional right to demand changes for their own population and they were to do so in the context of their movements for change.

A repertoire of collective action, as Tilly (1978) has pointed out, is crucial to the generation of protest. It was the civil rights movement that developed the repertoire utilized by numerous American social movements. This movement sparked the widespread use of the economic boycott, sit-ins, mass marches and numerous tactics that other movements appropriated. It also developed a cultural repertoire including freedom songs, mass meetings, and freedom schools that would also be utilized by a variety of movements. New movements could hit the ground running because the Black movement had already created the repertoires capable of fueling collective action.

The civil rights movement also revealed the central role that social movement organizations played in mobilizing and sustaining collective action. Organizations like SCLC, NAACP, CORE and SNCC were very visible in the civil rights movement and were the settings in which a variety of activists including women and students were drawn into civil rights activism. These social movement organizations provided the contexts that served as the training ground for activists who would return to their own populations to organize social movements.

Social movement theory has not developed a viable framework for understanding why at certain moments in history oppressed groups are able to develop the moral courage and make the extraordinary sacrifices that collective action requires. But the fact that African Americans were willing to be beaten, jailed, and killed for their activism while exuding unprecedented levels of dignity surely played an important role in encouraging other groups to confront authorities in their quest for change. As we glance backward, it becomes exceedingly clear that it was the civil rights movement that fertilized the ground in which numerous American social movements took root and flowered into widespread collective action.

The American civil rights movement has had an impact beyond the shores of America. Many of the same reasons the civil rights movement influenced American social movements, appear to also be the source of its influence on international movements. The major exception is that the civil rights movement did not serve as the training ground for many of the activists who initiated movements outside the United States. What is clear, however, is that numerous international movements were influenced by the US civil rights movement.

A similarity that movements share across the world is that they usually must confront authorities who have superior power. The major challenge for such movements is that they must develop a collective action strategy that will generate leverage enabling them to engage in power struggles with powerful opponents. The strategy of nonviolent direct action was first developed by Gandhi in South Africa and then used by Gandhi in the mass movement that overthrew British colonialism in India. Ghandi's use of nonviolence was important to the civil rights movement because some key leaders of the civil rights movement—James Farmer, Bayard Rustin, James Lawson and Glenn Smiley—had studied Gandhi's movement and became convinced that nonviolence could be used by African Americans. Additionally, Gandhi became a hero and a source of inspiration for Martin Luther King Jr. It was the American civil rights movement that perfected and modernized nonviolent direct action. Because of this achievement, the civil rights movement was the major vehicle through which nonviolent direct action was spread to other movements internationally. Nonviolent direct action has enabled oppressed groups as diverse as Black South Africans, Arabs of the Middle East, and pro-democracy demonstrators in China to engage in collective action. Leaders of these movements have acknowledged the valuable lessons they have learned from the civil rights movement (see Morris 1993). As Tarrow (1994) has pointed out, nonviolent direct action is a potent tool of collective action because it generates disruption and uncertainty that authorities must address. Tarrow captured how nonviolent direct action has spread domestically and internationally following the civil rights movement when he wrote:

> Although it began as a tool of nationalist agitation in the Third World, nonviolent direct action spread to a variety of movements in the 1960s and 1970s. It was used in the Prague Spring, in the student movements of 1968, by the European and American Peace and environmental movements, by opponents of the Marcos regime in the Philippines and of military rule in Thailand and Burma (Tarrow 1994:109).

As McAdam (1995) has argued, it is possible that the lessons of the civil rights movement crossed national boundaries through complex diffusion processes. Although McAdam leaves the mechanisms of diffusion unspecified, interviews by the author with leaders of the movements in South Africa,

China, and the West Bank provide insights. Mubarak Awad, one of the central leaders of the Intifadah Movement on the West Bank, conveyed that they absorbed the lessons of America's nonviolent direct action civil rights movement by acquiring films on the Black movement and Martin Luther King, and showing them on Jordanian television so that the lessons of that movement could be widely disseminated and applied (1990). Shen Tong, one of China's 1989 pro-democracy leaders revealed that "my first encounter with the concept of nonviolence was in high school when I read about Martin Luther King Jr. and Mahatma Gandhi" (1990). Patrick Lekota, a leader of the United Democratic Front in South Africa, explained that many of the leaders of the National African Congress gained their knowledge of the Black movement when they studied in the United States and that literature concerning the civil rights movement was widely spread in South Africa where "it was highly studied material" (1990). Similarly, in the early days of the Solidarity movement in Poland, Bayard Rustin, a major tactician of the civil rights movement, was summoned to Poland to give a series of colloquia and speeches on how nonviolent direct action worked in the civil rights movement. Summarizing the responses, Rustin stated, "I am struck by the complete attentiveness of the predominantly young audience, which sits patiently, awaiting the translation of my words" (Rustin, undated report). Additionally, leaders of these movements indicated that King, the charismatic leader who won the Nobel Peace Prize, was another important factor that fixed international attention upon the civil rights movement.

Because the civil rights movement developed a powerful tactical, ideological, and cultural repertoire of collective action available to a worldwide audience through mass media and an extensive literature, it has served as a model of collective action nationally and internationally. Awareness of the civil rights movement is so widespread globally that oppressed people in distant lands seek out knowledge of its lessons so they can employ it in their own struggles. Diffusion processes are important in this regard, but they merely complement the active pursuit of information pertaining to the civil rights movement by those wishing to engage in collective action here and abroad. The national anthem of the civil rights movement, "We Shall Overcome," continues to energize and strengthen the resolve of social movements worldwide.

THE CIVIL RIGHTS MOVEMENT AND THE STUDY OF SOCIAL MOVEMENTS

In a recent book (1993), the sociologist James McKee explored the question as to why no sociological scholar anticipated the civil rights movement and Black protest that rocked the nation throughout the 1960s and early 1970s. After an extensive examination of the literature, he argued that this failure could not be attributed to the lack of theory or empirical data because the sociology of race relations had a wealth of both. Rather, he maintained that it was the assumptions underlying these theories that prevented sociologists from anticipating the civil rights movement. He argued that prior to the movement, sociologists viewed Southern rural Blacks as a culturally inferior, backward people. He concluded that "there was a logical extension of this image of the American Black: a people so culturally inferior would lack the capability to advance their own interests by rational action...Blacks were portrayed as a people unable on their own to affect changes in race relations..." (1993:8). In short, the study of race relations lacked an analysis of Black agency.

Collective behavior and related theories of social movements, which dominated the field prior to the 1970s, were similar in that they lacked a theory of Black agency. The problem was even more pronounced for theories of social movements prior to the civil rights movement, for those theories operated with a vague, weak version of agency to explain phenomena that are agency driven. Those theories conceptualized social movements as spontaneous, largely unstructured, and discontinuous with institutional and organizational behavior (Morris & Herring 1987). Movement participants were viewed as reacting to various forms of strain and doing so in a non-rational manner. In these frameworks, human agency was conceptualized as a reactive agency, created by uprooted individuals seeking to reestablish a modicum of personal and social stability. External uncontrollable factors were in the driver seat, directing the agency encompassed in collective action.

Resource mobilization and political process models of social movements reconceptualized social movement phenomena as well as the human agency that drives them. The civil rights movement and the movements it helped spur, were pivotal in the reconstruction of social movement theory. The civil rights movement provided a rich empirical base for the reexamination of social movements because the structures and dynamics of that movement could not be reconciled with existing social movement theories. Central themes of current social movement theory— the role of migration and urbanization, mobilizing structures including social networks, institutions and social movements organizations, tactical repertoires and innovations, dissemination of collective action, culture and belief systems, leadership, the gendering phenomenon and movement outcomes—have been elaborated in the context of the civil rights movement because those structures and processes were germane to that movement.

Theories prior to the civil rights movement had argued that migration and urbanization were vital to collective action because they produced the social strain and ruptured belief systems that drove people into collective action to reconstitute the social order. Scholars of the civil rights movement (Obserchall

1973, McAdam 1982, Morris 1984) have produced convincing evidence to the contrary. Black migration and urbanization facilitated the civil rights movement because it led to the institutional building and the proliferation of dense social networks across localities and across neighborhoods in cities through which the movement was mobilized and sustained. This finding helped solidify the proposition that migration and urbanization may facilitate social movements because of their capacity to produce and harden the social organization critical to the production of collective action.

The social organization underlying collective action encompasses a movement's mobilizing structures. These structures include formal and informal organizations, communication networks, local movement centers, social movement organizations and leadership structures. Morris (1984) and McAdam (1982) developed detailed analyses of the crucial role that Black churches, colleges and informal social networks played in the mobilization and development of the civil rights movement. Morris (1984) demonstrated that the civil rights movement was comprised of local movements and that it was local mobilizing structures that produced the power inherent in the civil rights movement. To capture this phenomenon, he developed the concept of "local movement center" and defined it as the social organization within local communities of a subordinate group, which mobilizes, organizes, and coordinates collective action aimed at attaining the common ends of that subordinate group. Without those mobilizing structures, it is doubtful that the movement would have been able to consolidate the resources required to confront and prevail over white racists and powerful state structures. These findings helped to discredit arguments maintaining that movements were spontaneous and discontinuous with pre-existing social structures.

The civil rights movement afforded scholars the opportunity to examine the fundamental role played by social movement organizations (SMOs) in the creation and coordination of collective action. That movement was loaded with SMOs operating at the local and national levels. By examining these SMOs, scholars (Morris 1984, Barkan 1986, Haines 1984) have assisted in the development of an interorganizational analysis of social movement organizations. Morris analyzed how each of the major SMOs of the civil rights movement shaped collective action by carving out its own spheres of organizational activity and producing the leaders, organizers, and tactics that provided the movement with its power and dynamism. At the interorganizational level, these organizations engaged in competition, cooperation, and conflict. What has been learned from this interorganizational standpoint, is that when SMOs compete and cooperate they can produce greater volumes of collective action by sharing knowledge, and resources and by triggering tactical innovations. SMOs can be destructive to social movements when they engage in intense conflict and generate warring factions. This appears to have been the case in

Albany, Georgia in 1962 when the movement failed to reach its goals because of the conflict between SCLC and SNCC (see Morris 1984:239–250). By examining the civil rights movement, Haines (1984) demonstrated how interorganizational relations between SMOs can affect the outcomes of a movement because the agenda of radical organizations can cause authorities, because of their fear of radical alternatives, to concede to the demands of moderate SMOs. Research prior to the civil rights movement tended to conceive SMOs as by-products of social movements and thus as not germane to their causation and outcomes. The visibility of SMOs in the civil rights movement and their obvious centrality, have helped scholars to reconceptualize the role of SMOs and give them the theoretical attention they merit.

The civil rights movement has served as a rich empirical base for the analysis of social movement tactics. The widespread use and development of nonviolent direct action tactics is one of the crowning achievements of the civil rights movement. The labor movement and other grassroots movements of the 1930s adopted versions of some of the tactics—the sit-down strike, freedom songs, labor schools, community-based organizing— that would be used by the civil rights movement. Nevertheless, it was the civil rights movement that expanded these tactics and employed them in contexts where they would have enormous impact world-wide. Indeed, the importance of the tools of nonviolent direct action and especially the sit-in, which the civil rights movement utilized and made famous around the globe, led Tarrow to declare that these tactics were "perhaps the major contributions of our century to the repertoire of collective action" (Tarrow 1994:108). Several formulations by scholars examining the tactical repertoire of the civil rights movement have been developed. In an analysis of the 1960 sit-ins, Morris (1981) demonstrated that this tactic spread rapidly because of the mobilizing structures already in place by 1960, and because the tactics of nonviolent direct action fitted into the ideological and organizational framework of the Black church, which preached against violence and extolled the virtues of redemptive suffering.

In an analysis of tactical innovations within the civil rights movement, McAdam (1983) examined how tactical innovations increased the collection action of that movement and affected its outcomes. He argued that once authorities learn to neutralize a tactic, movement leaders had to devise a new tactic or risk a decline in collection action and the defeat of the movement. A study by Morris (1993) confirmed the important role of tactical innovation but took issue with McAdam as to how the process worked in the civil rights movement. He found that the tactical innovation process of the civil rights movement consisted of activists developing and adding new tactics to existing ones and employing them dynamically. The use of multiple tactics increased the possibility of generating a crisis, which served as the leverage to achieve movement demands. A great deal more theoretical work on movement tactics is needed and the civil rights movement will continue to provide a rich terrain for such theorizing.

The development of cycles of protest is intimately related to the development of tactical and cultural repertoires. Tarrow (1994:154) has defined a cycle of protest as "a phase of heightened conflict and contention across the social system." During such phases, collective action diffuses rapidly from more mobilized to less mobilized sectors and it generates "sequences of intensified interactions between challengers and authorities" (p. 154). A cycle of protest occurred in the United States following the civil rights movement when numerous movements—antiwar, women, farm workers, Native Americans, gay and lesbians, etc.—sprang into action. This cycle was not limited to national boundaries; it was also replicated in Europe during the same period. A major theoretical task is to explain the cycles of protest (McAdam 1995). The civil rights movement has figured prominently in such theorizing because it was the initiator movement that set this cycle in motion. Tarrow (1994) and McAdam (1995) have utilized the case of the civil rights movement to argue that such cycles are likely to occur when there exists an initial movement that has been successful in developing a repertoire of tactical, organizational and ideological lessons that can be transplanted to other movements under conditions favorable to social protest. Because the civil rights movement provided such a clear example of a protest cycle initiator, it continues to inform scholars about the processes by which a "family of movements" burst on the social scene.

CULTURE AND CIVIL RIGHTS MOVEMENT

Social movement scholars are increasingly coming to recognize that cultural factors weigh heavily in collective action (see Morris & McClurg Mueller 1992). In order for people to be attracted to and participate in collective action, they must come to define a situation as intolerable and changeable through collective action. To do so they develop injustice frames (Gamson 1992) and undergo cognitive liberation (McAdam 1982). Black cultural beliefs and practices were pronounced in the civil rights movement, and they affected strategic choices in that movement and figured significantly in the cycles of protest that it helped trigger. Morris (1984) analyzed how Black music, prayers, and religious doctrines were refashioned to critique Black oppression and to promote solidarity and to function as a tool of mobilization for the civil rights movement.

David Snow and his colleagues (1986, 1992) have produced the most compelling formulation as to why belief systems are germane to collective action. Parts of their analysis rest squarely on dynamics of the civil rights movement. Snow and his colleagues (1986) argued that framing processes constitute one of the major avenues through which collective action is generated, disseminated, and sustained. For them, frame alignment is the key process because it refers to "the linkage of individual and SMO interpretive orientations, such that some set of individual interests, values and beliefs and SMO activities, goals and ideology are congruent and complementary" (1986:484). Thus, SMO leaders are able to recruit and mobilize movement participants through creative ideological work whereby frames are bridged, amplified and extended. Snow & Benford's (1992) concept of an innovative master frame is explicitly derived from an analysis of the civil rights movement. Master frames are generic frames of meaning and one of their variable features is their capacity to generate "diagnostic attribution, which involved the identification of a problem and the attribution of blame or causality" (Snow & Benford 1992: 138). When an innovative master frame becomes elaborated it "allows for numerous aggrieved groups to tap it and elaborate their grievances in terms of its basic problem-solving schema" (p. 140). Snow & Benford argued that the civil rights movement developed an elaborate civil rights master frame. That master frame was so significant because its "punctuation and accentuation of the idea of equal rights and opportunities amplified a fundamental American value that resonated with diverse elements of Americans society and thus lent itself to extensive elaboration" (p. 148). Because of its master frame, they argued that the civil rights movement was able to play a pivotal role in generating cycles of protest. More theorizing is needed on the central role that culture plays in social movements, and the civil rights movement will continue to be a key reservoir for such work because much of what it has to teach scholars about culture and collective action remains untapped.

GENDER AND CIVIL RIGHTS MOVEMENT

Rosa Parks is known as the mother of the civil rights movement because her refusal to give a white man her seat on a segregated bus sparked the Montgomery, Alabama bus boycott. Parks' resistance and civil rights activity were not unlike those of countless Black women such as Ella Baker, Septima Clark, Fannie Lou Hammer, and Diane Nash (see Crawford et al 1990, Barnett 1993, Payne 1994, Robnett 1997). Black women played crucial roles in the civil rights but they did so in the context of a society and a movement characterized by high levels of patriarchy. Morris (1984) detailed the roles that Black women played in the origins of the civil rights movement, and he discussed how their contributions were restricted by male sexism within the movement.

Recent studies (Barnett 1993, Payne 1995, Robnett 1997) examining the role of women in the civil rights movement have sought to understand how the movement itself was gendered and how this reality affected movement dynamics. Payne and Barnett analyzed how Black women played pivotal organizing roles, often behind the scene, that enabled the movement to perform the multi-faceted, mobilization and organizational tasks crucial for wide-scale collective action. These studies, however, make it clear that these women performed these duties not because of natural inclinations to work behind the scene. They did so because they were dedicated to the goals of the movement and because male-dominated hierarchies limited the types of contributions they could make.

Robnett's study (1997) has produced some important insights on how gendering affected the civil rights movement. She found that despite the sexism, the contributions of many Black women encompassed a great deal more than backstage organizing. Black women constituted the bridge leaders of the civil rights movement. Bridge leadership is "an intermediate layer of leadership, whose tasks include bridging potential constituents and adherents, as well as potential formal leaders, to the movement" (Robnett 1997:191). Because these women were excluded from formal leadership positions because of their gender, they could act in more radical ways than men, given their allegiances to the grassroots and their freedom from state constraints. Given the structural location of this leadership it had more latitude to do the movement's emotional work which increased its mobilization capacity and generated greater strategic effectiveness. The majority of bridge leaders in the civil rights movement were Black women because that "was the primary level of leadership available to women" (Robnett 1997:191). Scholars such as Robnett have just begun to unpack the gendering dynamic of movements. The civil rights movement provides a rich empirical case for the continuance of this work because it was a movement in which women and men converged in their activity for the sake of liberating a people.

LEADERSHIP AND CIVIL RIGHTS MOVEMENT

Two theoretical issues thrust up by the civil rights movement have not received much attention. We do not have a theory that explains the relationship between preexisting protest traditions and the rise and trajectory of new social movements. Black leaders from previous movements played important roles in the civil rights movement. The expertise of leaders such as Ella Baker, A Philip Randolph, Bayard Rustin, and Septima Clark supplied the movement with vision and technical knowledge pertaining to collective action. By the time of the modern civil rights movement, the NAACP had developed a sophisticated legal strategy to attack racial segregation. This strategy became one of the central features of the nonviolent direct action movement. A preexisting Black culture containing a variety of oppositional themes supplied the modern movement with much of its cultural content and anchored it to the cultural traditions of the Black community. There can be little doubt that this preexisting protest tradition help to solidify this movement and affected its trajectory from the outset. A theoretical formulation of preexisting protest traditions is needed for a comprehensive understanding of movement emergence and outcomes.

Current social movement theory has made little progress in the analysis of social movement leadership. Movement scholars have too readily assumed that movement leadership is a matter of common sense not requiring theoretical analysis (see McAdam et al 1988:716). The civil rights movement reveals, however, that movement leadership is a complex phenomenon that remains relatively unexplored theoretically. Morris (1984) found that charismatic leadership played a key role in the civil rights movement but functioned differently from the way it was characterized in Weber's classic formulation, given that it was rooted in preexisting institutions and organizational structures. Robnett's (1997) finding concerning bridge leadership reveals the complex composition that leadership structures can assume in movements and the way such structures are shaped by durable practices in the larger society. Additional theorizing is needed to uncover the processes by which individuals are chosen to become movement leaders and how factors internal to the movement constrain the strategic options available to them. The social class of leaders appears to be important in determining leadership style and the degree to which they can be successful in mobilizing movement participants across social classes. Thus, as the civil movement reveals, movement leadership is a complex variable phenomenon that should receive attention from social movement scholars.

LOOKING BACKWARD TO MOVE FORWARD

By looking back we can appreciate the tremendous contributions the civil rights movement has made to social change and to the reconceptualization of an intellectual discipline. Because of that movement and those it triggered, social movement scholars have had to formulate new ideas and rethink why and how social movements continue to reshape the social landscape. As Gamson put it:

> If there hadn't been a civil rights movement there might not have been an anti-war movement, if there hadn't been these movements there might not have been an environmental movement. Without these movements there wouldn't have been people coming into the field who were receptive to a new orientation (Morris & Herring 1987:184).

The civil rights movement helped trigger a paradigmatic shift in the field of social movements and collective action. It did not do so alone, for other historic and contemporary movements worldwide have provided empirical puzzles that have assisted in the reconceptualization of the field. But the intellectual work based on the civil rights movement has been substantial and transformational. This movement has provided scholars with empirical and theoretical puzzles that should continue to push the field forward until new path—breaking social movements arise and shake up the field once again.

I close by returning to McKee's issue regarding Black agency. The civil rights movement revealed that that agency resides in Black social networks, institutions, organizations, cultures, and leaders, and in the creativity of a people who have had to engage in a chain of struggles to survive relentless oppression and to maintain their dignity. What is more, that movement helped other groups to locate their own agency, who then harnessed it in activities that have generated important changes in America and the world.

ACKNOWLEDGMENTS

I would like to thank professors Jeff Manza, Arthur Stinchcombe, and Mayer Zald for their insightful comments on an earlier version of this chapter. I also thank Kiana Morris for her assistance in the preparation of the manuscript.

> **Visit the *Annual Reviews home page* at**
> **http://www.AnnualReviews.org.**

Literature Cited

Adam B. 1987. *The Rise of a Gay and Lesbian Movement.* Boston: Twayne

Awad M. 1990. Interview, Feb. 9, Boston, Mass

Barkan S. 1986. Interorganizational Conflict in the Southern Civil Rights Movement. *Sociol. In.* 56:190–209

Barnett B. 1993. Invisible black women leaders in the civil rights movement: the triple constraints of gender, race and class. *Signs* 7(2):162–82

Bloom JM. 1987. *Class, Race and the Civil Rights Movement.* Bloomington: Indiana Univ. Press

Blumberg RL. 1984. *Civil Rights: The 1960s Freedom Struggle.* Boston: Twayne

Bobo L. 1997. The color line, the Dilemma, and the dream: race relations in America at the close of the twentieth century. In *Civil Rights and Social Wrongs: Black-White Relations Since World War II,* ed. J Higham, pp. 31–55. University Park, Penn: Penn. State Univ. Press

Branch T. 1988. *Parting the Waters: America in the King Years.* New York: Simon & Schuster

Carson C. 1981. *In Struggle: SNCC and the Black Awakening of the 1960s.* Cambridge: Harvard Univ. Press

Collier-Thomas B. 1984. *Black Women Organized for Social Change 1800–1920.* Washington DC: Bethune Mus. Arch.

Crawford V, Rouse J, Woods B. 1990. *Women in the Civil Rights Movement.* Brooklyn, NY: Carlson

Davis A. 1981. *Women, Race and Class.* New York: Random House

DuBois WEB. 1903. *The Souls of Black Folk.* Greenwich, CT: Fawcett

Evans S. 1980. *Personal Politics.* New York: Vintage Books

Fairclough A. 1987. *To Redeem the Soul of America: The Southern Christian Leadership Conference and Martin Luther King, Jr.* Athens: The Univ. Georgia Press

Franklin JH. 1967. *From Slavery to Freedom: A History of American Negroes.* New York: Knopf

Fredrickson GM. 1995. *Black Liberation.* New York: Oxford Univ. Press

Freeman J, ed. 1983. *Social Movements of the Sixties and Seventies.* New York: Longman

Gamson W. 1992. The social psychology of collective action. See Morris & McClurg Mueller 1992, pp. 53–76

Garfinkel H. 1969. *When Negroes March: The March on Washington Movement in the*

Organizational Politics for FEPC. New York: Atheneum

Garrow D. 1986. *Bearing the Cross: Martin Luther King, Jr., and the Southern Christian Leadership Conference.* New York: Morrow & Co

Groch S. 1998. *Pathways to protest: the making of oppositional consciousness by people with disabilities.* PhD thesis. Northwestern Univ., Evanston.

Haines H. 1984. Black radicalization and the funding of civil rights: 1957–1970. *Soc. Prob.* 32:31–43

Harding V. 1983. *There Is a River: The Black Struggle for Freedom in America..* New York: Vantage Books

Jaynes G, Williams R Jr, eds. 1989. *A Common Destiny: Blacks and American Society.* Washington, DC : Natl. Acad. Press

Kluger R. 1975. *Simple Justice.* New York: Knopf

Ladner J. 1979. The South: Old-New Land. *New York Times,* May 17, 1973, p. 23

Lawson J. 1978. Interview, October 2. Los Angeles, Calif

Lawson S. 1991. *Running for Freedom.* Philadelphia: Temple Univ. Press

Lekota P. 1990. Interview. February 9, Boston, Mass

Mays BE. 1978. Interview. September 20. Atlanta, Ga

McAdam D. 1982. *Political Process and the Development of Black Insurgency.* Chicago: Univ. Chicago Press

McAdam D. 1983. Tactical innovation and the pace of insurgency. *Am.. Sociol. Rev.* 48: 735–54.

McAdam D. 1988. *Freedom Summer.* New York: Oxford Univ. Press.

McAdam D. 1995. "Initiator" and "Spin-off" movements: diffusion processes in protest cycles. In *Repertoires and Cycles of Collective Action,* ed. M Traugott, pp. 217–39. Durham, NC: Duke Univ. Press

McAdam D, McCarthy J, Zald M. 1988. Social movements. In *Handbook of Sociology,* ed. NJ Smelser, p. 695–737. Newbury Park, CA: Sage.

McKay C. 1963. If we must die. In *American Negro Poetry,* ed. A Bontemps, p. 31. New York: Hill & Wang

McKee JB. 1993. *Sociology and the Race Problem.* Urbana: Univ. Ill. Press

McNeil G. 1983. *Groundwork: Charles Hamilton Houston and the Struggle for Civil Rights.* Philadelphia: Univ. Penn. Press

Meier A, Rudwick E. 1976. *Along the Color Line: Explorations in the Black Experience.* Urbana: Univ. Ill. Press

Moody A. 1968. *The Coming of Age in Mississippi.* New York: Dial Press

Morris A. 1981. Black southern student sit-in movement: an analysis of internal organization. *Am. Sociol. Rev.* 46:744–67

Morris A. 1984. *The Origins of the Civil Rights Movement: Black Communities Organizing for Change.* New York: Free Press

Morris A. 1993. Birmingham confrontation reconsidered: an analysis of the dynamics and tactics of mobilization. *Am. Sociol. Rev.* 58:621–36

Morris A, Herring C. 1987. Theory and research in social movements: a critical review. *Annu. Rev. Polit. Sci.* 2:137–98

Morris A, McClurg Mueller C, eds. 1992. *Frontiers in Social Movement Theory.* New Haven, CT: Yale Univ. Press

Oberschall A. 1973. *Social Conflict and Social Movements.* Englewood Cliffs, NJ: Prentice-Hall

Payne C. 1994. *I've Got the Light of Freedom.* Berkeley: Univ. Calif. Press

Robnett B. 1997. *How Long? How Long?* New York: Oxford Univ. Press

Rustin B. No date. *Report on Poland.* New York: A. Philip Randolph Inst.

Sale K. 1973. *SDS.* New York: Vintage Books

Schlesinger AM Jr. 1965. *A Thousand Days.* Boston: Houghton Mifflin.

Sitkoff H. 1981. *The Struggle for Black Equality, 1945–1980.* New York: Hill & Wang

Snow D, Benford R. 1992. Master frames and cycles of protest. See Morris & McClurg Mueller 1992, pp. 133–55

Snow D, Rochford E Jr, Worden S, Benford R. 1986. Frame alignment processes, micromobilization, and movement participation. *Am. Soc. Rev.* 51:464–81

Sterling C, Kittross J. 1978. *Stay Tuned: A Concise History of American Broadcasting.* Belmont: Wadsworth

Tarrow S. 1994. *Power in Movement: Social Movements, Collective Action and Politics.* Cambridge Univ. Press

Tilly C. 1978. *From Mobilization to Revolution.* Reading, Mass: Addison-Wesley

Tong S. 1990. *Shen Tong's King Center Address.* Atlanta, GA: Martin Luther King Cent. Soc. Change

Tushnet M. 1987. *The NAACP's Legal Strategy against Segregated Education, 1925–1950.* Chapel Hill: Univ. NC Press

Whalen C, Whalen B. 1985. *The Longest Debate: A Legislative History of the 1964 Civil Rights Act.* Cabin John, MD.: Seven Lakes Press

Whitfield S. 1988. *A Death In the Delta: The Story of Emmett Till.* New York: Free Press

Annu. Rev. Sociol. 1999. 25:541–74

ARTISTIC LABOR MARKETS AND CAREERS

Pierre-Michel Menger
Centre de sociologie des arts, Ecole des Hautes Etudes en Sciences Sociales, Centre National de la Recherche Scientifique, 75006 Paris, France; e-mail: menger@ehess.fr

KEY WORDS: uncertainty, occupational choice, multiple job, oversupply

ABSTRACT

Artistic labor markets are puzzling ones. Employment as well as unemployment are increasing simultaneously. Uncertainty acts not only as a substantive condition of innovation and self-achievement, but also as a lure. Learning by doing plays such a decisive role that in many artworlds initial training is an imperfect filtering device. The attractiveness of artistic occupations is high but has to be balanced against the risk of failure and of an unsuccessful professionalization that turns ideally non-routine jobs into ordinary or ephemeral undertakings. Earnings distributions are extremely skewed. Risk has to be managed, mainly through flexibility and cost reducing means at the organizational level and through multiple job holding at the individual level. Job rationing and an excess supply of artists seem to be structural traits associated with the emergence and the expansion of a free market organization of the arts.

Reviewing research done not only by sociologists, but also by economists, historians and geographers, our chapter focuses on four main issues: the status of employment and career patterns, the rationales of occupational choice, occupational risk diversification, and the oversupply of artists.

INTRODUCTION

Artistic labor markets are puzzling and challenging ones for social scientists. As this review essay will show, theoretical work and empirical studies, stemming from various perspectives, may be brought together in order to solve some of these puzzles. The way these markets expand may help to understand what is a stake. Evidence of sustained growth in artistic employment over the

541

last 20 years is amply documented by several surveys and Census sources, and trends are quite similar in most advanced countries. In the United States, over the period 1970–1990, the number of artists grew at a rate of 127%—much more rapidly than the civilian labor force, and the rate of increase has continued to be high. The total number of women artists increased faster, and all artistic occupations, with the exception of musicians, have seen a steady shift toward a higher proportion of women. By contrast, ethnic composition of the artistic workforce remains considerably disequilibrated, the nonclassical music sphere being this time one of the relatively few exceptions.

The pattern of change, of course, varies across the different artistic occupations, but the trend is almost everywhere the same. The overall picture of artistic labor markets and of their growth is, however, a quite paradoxical one: Employment but also underemployment and unemployment have been increasing steadily and simultaneously over the period. Obviously, fluctuations in supply and demand of artistic labor do not provide a satisfying explanation of what appears to be highly unbalanced growth. Several historical studies on artistic professions have repeatedly insisted on an "oversupply of artists" phenomenon, which they have associated with changes in the organizational apparatus of the art worlds or with technological innovations, or, more radically, with the emergence and expansion of a free market organization for the arts. But in each case, ad hoc arguments may overshadow structural disequilibria: The present development of labor markets for the arts, by highlighting an apparently irresistible trend toward flexibility, helps to explain the underlying processes of such a course of development, namely the built-in pervasive uncertainty of artistic undertakings and careers and the ways for individuals, as well as for organizations, to handle uncertain prospects and to manage the correlated individual and business risks.

One may speculate as to why artistic employment growth has been so rapid. As for demand factors, increases in real disposable per capita income have shifted demand curves for the arts and resulted in an increasing fraction of national income and employment being devoted to the arts. In Europe in particular, the steady growth of federal and local government subsidies, mainly in the 1970s and the 1980s, has accounted for much of the employment gain, perhaps more than for the overall change in consumer demand for artistic products and performances, due to the large expansion of the nonprofit sector of services for artistic training and for conservation and display of cultural heritage. Public spending under nonarts headings (e.g. local economic development, urban regeneration) as well as support for the cultural industries has also stimulated opportunities for cultural employment.

Here, it should be noted that the definition of art and culture has obviously been broadened as cultural policies have developed. A more relativistic view of culture has become increasingly legitimate as public support has taken into consideration the local community level and its whole apparatus (amateur activities, associations, so called sociocultural activities) by setting up links between art, culture, leisure, schooling, and social work. At the same time, one may note an opposing trend in cultural policies: the development of a discourse about culture as a real economic sector. A new form of "cultural accountancy" has in fact emerged that seeks to quantify the economic output of public spending on culture. Of course, the wider the definition of culture, the more culture can claim to play an economic role, and the stronger the economic rationale of public support may appear to be, at least at first sight.

In terms of the increased demand for selective occupations, several industrial sectors that draw heavily on the skills of artists and other creative occupations underwent rapid expansion during the 1980s. The most sriking change within the cultural industries was the rapid growth of the audiovisual and broadcasting sector, and along with it, of the advertising industry as well as that of the new media industries (video, corporate video) and of the computer game industry. No less striking is that employment in these growing sectors is mainly on a short-term contract or freelance basis, which magnifies the shift toward numerical flexibility observed elsewhere in the economy (Smith 1997). One should mention also the expansion of the crafts and of the design sector, which increasingly contribute to the rise in the numbers of artists in the Census data (Feist 1998).

These changes not only rely on demand factors but also raise definitional issues concerning what the artistic occupations are, where the boundaries of the artistic sector lie, and whether one should rather adopt a more expansive approach, both in terms of cultural occupations, so as to include arts-related occupations, and in terms of the cultural sector. Recent research on British Census data (O'Brien & Feist 1995, Pratt 1997) builds on an occupational as well as on a sectoral breakdown; the redefined categorizations cross both classifications. As a result, cultural work appears to spread across a number of professional occupations and industrial activities. Thus, in Great Britain, among the individuals involved in the cultural sector, 25% work in the cultural industries with cultural occupations, 40% have cultural occupations outside the cultural industries, and 35% work in the cultural industries without cultural occupations.

More generally, the set of methodological decisions and disputes that goes with any study of artistic labor markets is by no means negligible, since they reflect conflicting and evolving views of art and artistic occupations and may considerably bear on the scientific understanding of them.

The list of the limitations and discrepancies of Census data as well as of non-Census data opens almost every research report on artistic occupations: To mention only a few major issues, such a list may identify as problems the definition of who is a professional artist and how his or her occupation is determined; the delimitation of each specific artistic field, and the inclusion or exclusion of peripheral specialties within a field in a way that may be inconsistent over time or vary from one survey to the other; the variations in job classifications and the periodic addition of new occupations to the artists' subset in the Census classification; the lack of any serious treatment of multiple job holding, which is pervasive in the arts, whatever the combination of jobs and occupations inside or outside the sphere of arts may be.

Regarding the tricky issue of the comparative strengths and limitations of survey vs Census data, one need only mention the primary source of most variations: the definition of the artist. The Census uses a parsimonious classification rule, which narrowly interprets the "chief job activity or business last week" in terms of the kind of industry or employer concerned, the occupational content and the type of organizational sector. Surveys, by contrast, generally use one or several criteria, drawn from a list of at least eight (Frey & Pommerehne 1989) and are susceptible to categorizing various activities as art in accordance with the particular interests of the researcher (Becker 1982). The most controversial of these criteria is, of course, that of subjective self-definition as an artist: Although it seems to work in all ways except as a market test, it encapsulates a temporal dimension of occupational commitment, since artists may at times or repeatedly cycle between several jobs or experience occupational and sectoral mobility and yet continue to think of themselves as artists.

As stated by Adler (quoted in Jeffri & Greenblatt 1996), "a study of artists in a society in which occupational membership is (fortunately) not defined or restricted by a guild, an academy or a state system of licensing can neither comfortably ignore problems of occupational definition nor resolve them." Indeed, although some of the most remarkable studies by sociologists, economists, and art historians on art labor markets and careers have been historical ones (White & White 1965, Montias 1982, Warnke 1989, Ehrlich 1985), the definition of the artist as well as the orderly course of an artistic career appear today to be dependent variables in the process of how highly competitive and contestable labor and product markets, interacting or not with state and public intervention, operate and evolve.

The terms of such theoretical and methodological issues are by no means new in sociology since labels, taxonomies, and classification systems are core issues in interactionist and constructivist theories. One should note that sociologists deal with such matters more cautiously than do economists: While the former run the risk of questioning endlessly the significance of any quantitative measurement, the latter run that of taking for granted that Census data (almost the only source they use) will lead to strong results by virtue of sophisticated econometric computation, once they have acknowledged the obvious limitations from which the data suffer.

Despite all these discrepancies, a review of a number of recent studies on art labor markets will bring to light findings that seem hardly disputable and whose summary will allow us to highlight the key issues for a comprehensive approach to artistic labor markets.

Artists as an occupational group are on average younger than the general work force, are better educated, tend to be more concentrated in a few metropolitan areas, show higher rates of self-employment, higher rates of unemployment and of several forms of constrained underemployment (nonvoluntary part-time work, intermittent work, fewer hours of work), and are more often multiple job holders. They earn less than workers in their reference occupational category, that of professional, technical, and kindred workers, whose members have comparable human capital characteristics (education, training, and age) and have larger income inequality and variability. These traits are even more striking in the 1990s, according to the most recent reports using Census and BLS data, which enable general comparisons over time (in France the equivalent sources are Census and Enquêtes Emploi of INSEE).

One may suspect that, according to such a bundle of characteristics, an increase in the number of artists as reported in the Census data may be far from corresponding to a similar increase in the level of activity, since the former trend may have different and contradictory meanings: If there is more work but an ever more rapidly growing number of individuals, a fiercer competition takes place that implies higher inequalities in the access to employment, more variability in the level and schedule of activity, and, on the whole, work rationing for those who share the labor pie and cycle more often from work to unemployment or from arts work to arts-related or non-arts work.

Extensive job and sectoral mobility as well as multiple job holding considerably affect the use of conventional work and unemployment indicators. Unemployment rates may be mismeasured for several related reasons: Individuals with artistic occupations may switch temporarily to work mainly in nonartistic occupations when unable to make a living in their primary vocational field, without stopping to produce art works. They would therefore not be classified as unemployed in their artistic occupation if they are primarily engaged in nonartistic work during the Census week. Accordingly, plotting change over time raises several difficulties. International comparisons are of course even more problematic.

A closer examination of descriptive statistics would provide us with considerable details about each of these traits, and it would in particular allow for the kind of fine-tuned differentiation between the several categories of artists that we find in the comprehensive NEA report on *Artists in the Work Force* (1996), in the Australian report by Throsby & Thompson (1994), in the British one by O'Brien & Feist (1995), or in French official annual reports based on Census and Labor Survey data (*Observatoire de l'emploi culturel* 1998a & 1998b).

Yet, our main aim here is rather to review explanatory models of work organization and labor supply in the arts and to focus on four main issues: the status of employment and career patterns, the rationales of occupational choice, occupational risk diversification, and the oversupply of artists. Our approach is deliberately multidisciplinary, since a number of studies have been done in sociology, economics, history, and geography that may be usefully brought together and confronted.

EMPLOYMENT STATUS AND CAREERS

Generally speaking, although current trends show an increased blurring of the following distinction, employment strategies in general labor markets contrast, on the one hand, firms that emphasize low turnover and high productivity, bear costs of screening, trying out, and training, and use optimal reward schemes based on long-term contracts and tenured jobs, with, on the other, organizations that operate with casual workers and short-term contractual ties. How does this distinction apply to the arts? Wherever stable employment through long-term contracts exists for artists and craftworkers, it is to be found almost exclusively in large organizations operating on a pluri-annual basis—permanent organizations like symphony orchestras, opera houses, conservatories, or architecture firms—although these large organizations do increasingly hire personnel on a short-term basis. Temporary organizations or small cultural organizations use mainly or exclusively short-term contracts. Finally, creative artists operating as independent freelancing workers may themselves be seen as small firms building subcontractual relations with artistic organizations. On the whole, short-term contractual or subcontractual relationships prevail in artistic labor markets.

Normally, contingent employment possesses the characteristics that define "secondary" labor markets, where workers are mainly low-trained and low-paid and productivity differences between individuals are small. Yet most employed artists work under this form of employment and craft workers in the cultural sector are increasingly hired on such a basis. A paradoxical picture emerges, in which rather highly skilled and quite differentiated workers maintain weak employer attachments. Moreover, people (as well as organizations) may combine the different contractual forms: For example, musicians in orchestras can also be hired as freelancers for some studio recording jobs and hold a teaching position in a conservatory, so that the employment status distinction becomes blurred at the individual level. In fact, many opportunities can be found within a whole range of contractual arrangements: An artist's success often goes along with increasingly strategic choices and, by contrast, less successful careers mean entrapment in constraining contractual formulas.

Among the salaried artists working on a long-term basis, musicians and their careers meet a rather well-patterned job system that has often been studied (Westby 1960, Faulkner 1973, Allmendinger et al 1994). Bureaucratic careers can be found in permanent orchestras with positions ranging on a well-defined scale of status: A majority of the orchestral players interviewed by Faulkner (1973) become anchored in their organization, experience no or little mobility, and, unless they feel entrapped, adjust and become committed to their role in a stable work setting. But Kanter's (1989) distinction between three main career structures—bureaucratic, professional, and entrepreneurial—applies only partly because of organizational and sectoral mobility. Indeed, advancement on the job ladder is limited since top ranks are filled up mainly through external recruiting, so that the mechanics of vacancy chains operate rather poorly. Individual career opportunities and their main elements—responsibilities, challenges, training, influence, earnings—develop through mobility within a stratified set of organizations ranked on a hierarchy of prestige, musical excellence, calibre of musicianship, working conditions, and operating budgets, either toward similar or higher positions in higher ranking orchestras or toward higher status positions in lower ranked orchestras.

Such moves are few in a professional lifetime: As described by Westby, each musician behaves like his own employment agency, compiles an inventory of probable and possible jobs, gets information about the approximate ages, professional histories, and abilities of the current holders of the most desirable jobs, so as to be prepared for an opportunity that may appear only once in a lifetime. The curvilinear profile of such career mobility means that the artist has to move early to reach the peak of this organizational set, and that chances of mobility diminish rather quickly after the age of 30 or 35, at least with respect to the top level tier of prestigious organizations. Publishing houses (Powell 1985) and architecture firms (Blau 1984, Champy 1998) are additional examples of permanent organizations that combine constraining hierarchies of jobs and career development through lateral mobility.

However, an increasing proportion of salaried cultural workers now work under a short-term contractual basis. The steady increase in the number of artists across all art sectors during the 1970s, 1980s, and 1990s appears to be driven by two forces: the rise of contigent work and the rapid increase of independent, self-managed work, with increasing numbers of artists now to be found in the sectors where self-employed practitioners work, such as creative writing, visual arts, and the crafts. This overall trend is reported in recent American (Alper et al 1996), British (O'Brien & Feist 1995), Australian (Throsby & Thompson 1994), and French surveys (*Observatoire de l'emploi culturel* 1998a,b).

Contingent work, insofar as it usually corresponds to the secondary labor market where workers are highly mobile and poorly skilled and jobs are very routine, seems at first sight somewhat paradoxical in the arts. Yet, employment and work organization in the arts are indeed characterized by highly skilled, highly mobile, and well-paid workers moving from one employer to the next while accumulating experience through on-the-job training and highly diversified jobs. This is especially true of the performing arts, which appear to have been quite avant-garde in designing and experiencing the process of increasingly flexible labor markets (on Hollywood, see Storper 1989; for a somewhat idealized view of the Hollywood flexibility model, see Kanter 1995; and see Smith 1997, for the trend toward flexibility in the general labor markets).

Why does this paradoxical type of casual labor occur and develop so rapidly in the arts? Let's consider the organizational characteristics of artistic production. Casual employment structure and the corresponding search for flexibility are a core feature of artistic work, due to the "high rate of change over time of the content of activities," according to Stinchcombe's (1968) phrasing in his pioneering work on the craft administration of production and structures of activities. This occurs for at least four reasons. First, artistic products are often designed as prototypes and their market value depends on their originality and on a more or less pronounced differentiation or, as Caves (2000) argues, on a mixture of vertical and horizontal differentiation. According to these two contrasting properties, artworks are conceived as unique, which makes each artist into a monopolist, and are relatively substituable, which results in a monopolistic competition once differentiation is conceived along a continuum, as an 'infinite-variety' property in Caves' formulation. Secondly, the combination of activities needed to produce a movie, play, or opera involves a large number of different artistic occupations and crafts, and each participant shifts to a new project just hours, days, or weeks after the initial one, with new requirements and challenges. Thirdly, tastes (especially in the most speculative art markets such as popular music, *hyped* contemporary painting, blockbuster novels, mass audience-designed movies and serials) undergo unpredictable shifts. Finally, uncertainty can be seen as a built-in characteristic of the creative process. On the supply side, it makes artistic work highly attractive, since predictable outcomes would lead to routine work (Menger 1989). On the demand side, consumer versatility and taste for novelty give social and economic value to newness and originality to the extent that these are unpredictable. Uncertainty must be considered as the true condition of the breakthrough innovation that opens up to its author a new (temporary) monopoly, and, simultaneously, uncertainty is also the threat contained in the destructive aspect of every true innovation.

Flexibility can be attained through three main social requirements: a system of performance contracts, a system for transmitting information about the performance capacities of people, and a minimization of overhead costs (Stinchcombe 1968). The performing arts meet these requirements: for each project—film, opera, or theater performance, musical show, etc—new teams are formed and then dispersed. Networks help to build the stable relationships that are needed to lower transaction costs. They facilitate hiring procedures through patronage and trustworthy ties among peers, and they convey reliable information about skills and talents quite rapidly, since formal screening and hiring processes would often be inefficient and too costly in a casual work scheme.

The distinction between short contractual arrangements (at firm level) and employment processes (at industry level) is blurred by the multisided activities of each worker as well as by the dense formal or informal relations between employers. Indeed, artistic production is based on three components: (*a*) a nexus of ties between firms involved in the different parts of the production process and between the many employers who draw from the artistic labor pool, (*b*) an original way of processing information through this network in order to minimize the costs and length of the sorting and hiring operations, and (*c*) conventional industry-wide negotiations and arrangements regarding wage and fringe benefit schemes. An effective way to overcome the complexities of the disintegration of the production process is to rely on spatial concentration. Especially dense transactional relationships between production units have geographically sensitive cost structures. The greater the costs per transaction, the greater the probability that firms will agglomerate in order to benefit from external economies of scale (Storper & Walker 1989, Scott 1997, Quingley 1998).

Artistic activities show a very high level of spatial concentration in a few locations or even in one dominant city in each country. It is also remarkable that even in the presence of the active decentralization of cultural public policy, the concentration of artists and art professionals does not decline. The Parisian case is striking: during the 1980s, the population of artists and professionals involved in cultural production expanded rather rapidly in France (+ 55% between 1982 and 1991), but the share of artists living and working in Paris and Ile-de-France also increased (from a 45.8% to a 54.1% rate; see Menger 1993).

In their extensive study on the vertical disintegration and flexible specialization trend in the Hollywood film industry and its effects on the labor market, Christopherson & Storper (1989) show that through subcontracting, financing, and distribution of independent producers, utilization of less costly production methods, and expansion of auxillary markets, the demand for short-term contract workers increased. They go on to explain how changes in labor supply occurred as well. Using pension data sources, they demonstrate that the aggregate quantity of work available (i.e. the total hours of work), even if increasing, increases far less rapidly than the pool of individuals employed intermittently, generating a growing competition and resulting in a decreasing average participation in production.

In the case of casual work, the risk of unemployment is pervasive, and insurance devices through long-term contractual relationships are, by definition, missing. The typical worker will view the risk of unemployment as something that must be compensated for by a higher hourly wage. Compensation for uncertain labor prospects is in fact observed in the performing arts since intermittent artists and workers earn much higher hourly wages than do those employed on a long-term basis. The wage premium is the price that employers must pay in order to draw on a reserve army of underemployed individuals whose availability has to be secured. A loss of flexibility in employment decisions would be more costly for firms. Yet this compensating differential scheme operates only imperfectly, since hourly wages are not higher for greatly underemployed workers than for their more successful colleagues.

Compensating wage differentials therefore play their role mainly at the industry level. Individual differences in hiring probabilities are, by contrast, not subject to compensation: here is another kind of risk. This is simply to say that casual work in the performing arts stems from the freelance status of employment. In such a context, accumulation of hiring records acts as a reputation signal in a self-reinforcing process: hiring calls for more hiring. As the intermittent working system expands, at any given time the number of job candidates more and more exceeds the supply of full-time jobs. New forms of employment instability and new forms of labor market segmentation appear, since the quantity of work allocated varies considerably across the workforce. As job allocation takes place on an individual basis and involves on-the-job accumulation of skills and reputation, experienced and network-building artists and workers are frequently hired; by contrast, younger or less skilled individuals, loosely connected with the most active entrepreneurs, form a peripheral population facing discontinuous employment and longer spells without work. Thus, differences in annual earnings of workers may reflect differences in hours worked more than in wage rates (Christopherson & Storper 1989, Rannou & Vari 1996, Debeauvais et al 1997).

In a vertical disintegration of production and highly flexible work scheme, firms minimize their risks by using contractual relationships that transmit the market uncertainty down the hierarchy of control to subcontractors and ultimately to individual workers. Contingent workers thus become more and more like independent workers, cycling between employers and between work and unemployment spells. In that sense, freelance artists may be better thought of as operators of small businesses. Although asymmetrical, the relationship between the employer and the freelancer is that of a matching process where both sides build a career interdependently, as carefully demonstrated by Faulkner in his study of the Hollywood job system (1983, Faulkner & Anderson 1987). Artists as well as entrepreneurs accumulate a history of results, and their performance ratings translate into reputations and into distinct industry identities.

Careers are two-sided affairs, with entrepreneurs making distinctions among qualified artists, and artists (directors, screenwriters, composers, etc) making distinctions among film productions. In a market of projects, careers advance incrementally through recurrent and nonrecurrent matches. Artists learn how to spread their occupational risks by forming career portfolios, i.e. by mixing one-shot ties, which are the normal feature of a loosely coupled hiring system, and recurrent "bread and butter" accounts with a few producers. Faulkner shows that such a spreading of accounts allows the artist to hedge his or her bets, to get information about a wider environment, and to accumulate credits in a human capital investment program, through a variety of work, stylistic diversification, and adaptation to changing teams.

As cumulative productivity profiles greatly differ, distinct matching proclivities segment the labor market, and matchings are neatly stratified in equivalent classes of market agents. Yet given the high variance in activities, and the volatility of the cultural industries, career advancement and attainment are never secured.

Neither a stage process nor a simple interactional process (Abbott 1990), such career trajectories combine traits from professional as well as from entrepreneurial careers, as defined by Kanter. Artists rely on skills as well as on opportunities to take on evermore challenging assignments that bring them greater knowledge and more rewards; they have an external market value based on reputation; they exhibit less loyalty to particular organizations than to their professional community; and they may manage their working life much as property owners do when spreading their risks. To that extent, they may be compared to small firms and their labor market to a network of small units trading along matching processes from one project to another. The analogy with small firms may be taken one step further when multiple job holding and role versatility are brought into the picture, as shown below. The large number of small artistic organizations and their high rate of turnover may be explained that way, since composers (Burke 1997), choreographers (Sussman 1984), and stage directors (Menger 1997) can easily set up companies or fringe firms by relying on a portfolio of resources and multiple roles.

According to Weick's notion of self-designing organizations (Weick 1979, Weick & Berlinger 1989), careers in such a labor system are subjectively patterned because they are committed to impermanence, to cumulative learning and exploration, rather than tied to external career markers. Regarding the dynamics of personal growth and achievement, one striking feature of careers in the arts is their temporal aspect. To consider only each end of a working life in the arts: Precocity often plays a significant role, not only as a mythical feature of the "self-generating genius" topos described by Kris & Kurz (1987), but also as a symptom of the ambiguity of the transition from training to work, since many creative artists and performers produce serious work and get credits before their formal training is complete (Menger 1997). Conversely, late starters are particularly prevalent among writers (Throsby & Thompson 1994), and the increasing occupational flexibility of careers also leads to late entry for a second career, whether this corresponds to a deferred vocational choice or to reconversion following redundancy, as is the case in the crafts sector surveyed by Knott (1994). Of course, self-employment status typically allows for such switches.

The span of a career varies greatly with the type of art (e.g. dance vs creative writing), with the subsector of each art world (classical dance vs contemporary dance), with the nature of the occupation in it (performing vs creative work), and with the organizational and market features of each world. Sharply contrasting examples can be cited: A conductor's career may extend until near the end of his life with almost no time for retirement, but classical dancers have career schedules constrained by severe physical requirements. In the high arts sphere, reputation may be a factor of exceptional longevity, and that from a twofold point of view: The sense of achievement is enhanced, well beyond the average working-life term (Anzieu 1981), and the reputation as capital may be converted into an artistic and economic rent, since the famous artist faces a rather inelastic demand for his praised work (Moulin 1987). By contrast, skyrocketing success in the mass market arts and entertainment industries is subject to sudden shifts in market demand toward new competitors and is characterized by highly volatile reputations.

Self-employment is today the most frequent work status in the arts. Proportions vary with national contexts and occupations, but trends are similar: Self-employment increasingly acts as a driving force in the expansion of artistic labor markets. The careers of self-employed artists display most of the attributes of the entrepreneurial career form: the capacity to create valued output through the production of works for sale, the motivation for deep commitment and high productivity associated with their occupational independence—control over their own work, a strong sense of personal achievement through the production of tangible outputs, the ability to set their own pace, but also a high degree of risk-taking, as shown by the highly skewed distribution and high variability of earnings, as well as the low amount of time allocated on average to their primary creative activity (Alper et al 1996). Thus, as stressed by Freidson (1986a), self-employment may bring with it only an illusory independence and autonomy: The freelancers who fail to move into the inner circles of successful colleagues get locked in a precarious situation.

In theory, because most creative artists are self-employed, it would seem meaningless to equate fewer working hours with unemployment spells or underemployment levels. Their income, which reflects whether their works are in demand (that is, whether they are sold and at what price), does not derive from a quantity of working time at a given wage rate (Frey & Pommerehne 1989).

Creative artists and craftspeople decide whether or not to continue to work in their chosen field according to their income and to the stream of their expected earnings. If their income is low, because of low demand for their work, a simple increase in production, through more work, may have no effect, and an excess supply of the works for sale at lower prices may not easily trigger an equilibration process because the price acts as a signal of quality and a decrease in the price of works of a contemporary artist will promptly be interpreted negatively. Oversupply of the works they produce cannot be defined at any given price. That's why so many creative artists, since they can make their own work opportunities, may, despite working hard and being fully committed, suffer from low or very low income levels, and develop a sense of null or even negative correlation between effort and earnings, an effect reported in many studies (e.g. Jeffri 1991, Moulin 1992).

THE RATIONALES OF OCCUPATIONAL CHOICE

In most advanced countries, Census data provide quite similar pictures about artists' earnings. Mean annual earnings appear to be less than those in occupational groups that require similar levels of professional training and qualification. Filer (1986), in a quite provocative paper, has refuted the "myth of the starving artist" by estimating the income penalty to be less than 10% in the artistic occupations and by estimating on 1970 and 1980 Census data that artists have a higher probability of remaining in their occupation five years later than do workers in all nonartistic occupations. But his study does not distinguish between arts and nonarts sources of income nor, within income derived from art, between that from creative activity and that from arts-related work. Moreover, the income penalty estimated by Filer varies greatly among the different artistic groups (e.g. −69% for dancers, + 58% for actors and directors).

In short, as summarized by Wassall & Alper (1992) and by Throsby (1994) in their review of a number of recent studies, artists actually appear to suffer from significant income penalties, to have more variable income both across time for an individual artist and across artists at a given point in time, and to get lower returns from their educational investments than is the case in other comparable occupations. Although data based on similar sources and similar methodological design may be difficult to obtain for a careful comparison of each category of artists' incomes over time, the distributional evidence remains the same. The skewed distribution of artists' income is strongly biased toward the lower end of the range: Artistic careers are and remain risky.

Despite the evidences of low returns from vocational creative work and of the high degree of income inequality, artists are not deterred from entering such an occupation in growing numbers, nor is there as much withdrawal from artistic careers as would be expected. Are artists irresistibly committed to a labor of love, or are they true risk-lovers, or perhaps "rational fools" to use a notion developed by Sen?

The "labor of love" argument (Freidson 1990) insists that occupational commitment and achievement in the arts cannot be matched to the monetary considerations of a market economy of exchange; they should better be conceived as skilled and sustained activities that entail a social value that artists carry out by making a living in host occupations such as teaching. Artists' notion of their "calling," analyzed by Kris & Kurz (1987) as a historically recurring feature of artistic biographical narrative, calls to mind the "inner drive" reported by Jeffri & Throsby (1994) as the foremost criterion of professionalism according to US visual artists. The ideology inherited from the "art for art's sake" era may even reverse the meaning of success and failure, so that only recognition by the peer group matters, at least in high art worlds (Bourdieu 1992). One way to deal with this ideological dimension is to turn it into an inherent cultural trait—a kind of occupational characteristic that goes along with artistic life or, to be more precise, that blurs the boundaries between occupation and private life, and between their respective rationales. However, once this trait is regarded as belonging to the initial socialization process of the artist via a very early manifestation of ability and taste for the arts, such an explanation turns out to be highly deterministic and ultimately tautological. Artists are presumed to commit to their art and to link to their community of fellow artists, whatever degree of success in the market they may meet. Inescapable commitment results in a highly inelastic labor supply function

The second argument is that of occupational choice under uncertainty. Artists may be risk-lovers (whatever origin one may assign to this preference), or they may be induced to take risks by a probabilistic miscalculation. Occupations where enormous rewards are concentrated in the hands of a small number of practitioners, whereas the majority of entrants may do poorly, entail a high degree of uncertainty. Entry into these fields has, to a large extent, the aspect of a lottery where players overestimate their chances, as has been emphasized by A Marshall (1947). The analogy with a lottery is actually ambiguous: While it is helpful to think of the skewed distribution of incomes as a matrix of payoffs, it is also misleading because it suggests that success is purely random and has nothing to do with individual abilities and characteristics.

A third, less deterministic view may be offered that substantiates an occupational choice dimension without overshadowing the characteristics either of work or of workers. Rewards in artistic jobs are of two sorts: Aside from monetary rewards, there are the so-called nonmonetary rewards or "psychic income" flows, which have in fact been regarded for a long time as an essential dimension of work. Analytically speaking, every job can be regarded as a bundle of characteristics, resulting in several possible combinations.

Wage differentials compensate for more or less attractive work and equalize among workers the total monetary and nonmonetary advantages or disadvantages.

This economic theory of equalizing differences (Rosen 1986), which goes back to Adam Smith, seeks to explain the diversity of characteristics of work and workers in such a way as to give central consideration to individual preferences and choice, provided that there is perfect information on both sides of the market. Artistic work can be considered as highly attractive along a set of measurable dimensions of job satisfaction that include the variety of the work, a high level of personal autonomy in using one's own initiative, the opportunities to use a wide range of abilities and to feel self-actualized at work, an idiosyncratic way of life, a strong sense of community, a low level of routine, and a high degree of social recognition for the successful artists. All these benefits have a so-called shadow price, which may be compensated for by a lower income than would be expected from less amenable jobs. It should be noted that in strong contrast to the ideological argument, especially to its deterministic aspect, people discover what a nonroutine job really is only by experiencing it.

The benefits derived from nonmonetary income are, however, not of a uniform magnitude: An analysis in terms of equalizing differences requires that we adjust the total amount of these benefits according to the job, the level of professional achievement, and the conditions that prevail for those in the profession who, still waiting for success, are forced to take on secondary jobs. Comparisons between artists salaried by an organization and independent artists (Fohrbeck & Wiesand 1975, Taylor 1987) reveal, for example, that the latter obtain higher levels of nonmonetary satisfaction but have lower average incomes than do salaried artists, due to higher levels of job-insecurity, higher rates of unemployment, and greater variance in individual incomes around the mean. Some of the studies that have been done on the activities of certain categories of salaried artists even go so far as to reject, to a great extent, the presence of any compensating "psychic income": The emblematic case of orchestra musicians illustrates the countermythology of the artist subjected to the constraints of an organization, resigned to a humdrum and narrowly specialized labor, very distant from what long years of apprenticeship oriented toward individual accomplishment in a soloist career had led him or her to expect (Arian 1971).

It should be also stressed, as does Spilerman (1977), that the salience of particular job facets might vary with a worker's age. Artists offer many examples of a "career-line vulnerability to aging." As they get older, freelancers like actors appear to be increasingly sensitive to job insecurity and to the steady strain of searching for jobs, gathering information about new projects, and maneuvering repeatedly to remain visible in a highly competitive labor market (Laplante 1990, Menger 1997). Orchestral musicians (Faulkner 1973) and dancers (Federico 1983) experience well-patterned sequences of job change over their life cycle: the upward mobility chances of the former decrease quite abruptly after about age 35, which induces them to adjust their occupational commitment, and the latter have to plan their reconversion at about the same age. Of course, shifts in career patterns may be provoked by changes in market conditions or by aesthetic innovations. Modern dancers start and end their careers later than classical dancers. Painters today can expect official recognition and financial success much sooner than their predecessors could: As Moulin (1992) and Galenson (1999) show from different perspectives, changes both in the nature of modern painting and in the market for contemporary art may shift demand towards the works of the early period of an artist's career. Very young artists can therefore expect high immediate reputation, but the market also turns out to be more volatile and reputations vanish sooner.

The economic argument is attractive for its elegant parsimony. The artists who remain in artistic occupations despite low earnings and highly uncertain earnings prospects gain something else that has to be taken into account in order to preserve the rational occupational choice frame: The additional income flow that one would expect to draw from another occupation, according to one's skills and qualifications, has been exchanged in return for psychic goods. However, such an argument holds only in a conceived world of activity in which there is no room for anything else but exchange and arbitration based on a series of minute and well-informed calculations.

Moreover, the compensating differentials argument formulates its notion of the compensating wage premium with respect only to the differences in average income levels across occupations, once standardized for a number of individual income-related characteristics (mainly education, experience, age, sex, ethnicity, location of residence, and of work). However, from a distributional perspective, artistic occupations show a high variance in income. Poverty rates among US artists are higher than those for all other professional and technical workers (Alper et al 1996). Again, the inequalities and uncertainties reflected in this large dispersion of rewards may be conceived as double-sided. Factors behind this skewedness include, first of all, differences in talent, insofar as these differences are rewarded by the organizations that hire the artists and are perceived and valued by the surrogate and final consumers. Stinchcombe (1986 [1963]) distinguishes between talent as a complementary factor of production and talent as a nearly additive factor. The former is found in firms, activities, and positions (e.g. scientific research, "winner take all" systems, soloist performances in violin concertos) where output value may benefit more than proportionately from differences in individual levels of ability; accordingly, earnings inequalities are high. By contrast, the distribution of rewards is less skewed and seniority a more important factor where individual performance has a less dramatic impact on the value of the total production, as in a symphony orchestra. Moreover, in the first case, due to the differential skews of the distributions of talent and income, small differences in talent can become magnified in wide earnings differences, as Rosen (1981) shows in his superstar model. On the demand side, lesser quality is a poor substitute for greater quality, so that preferences are strongly biased toward the latter; on the supply side, due to joint consumption technology (that of mass production and the distribution of art and entertainment through records, books, TV, radio etc), the marginal costs of production do not rise in proportion to the size of a seller's market, but profits do. The appealing and paradoxical result of such a model is disputable, since the basic assumption that small differences in talent may lead to huge return differentials requires a measurement of talent and quality other than income (Hamlen 1991, 1994); however, it is consistent with the distribution of incomes observed in the industries relying on scale economy of joint consumption (see Laplante 1990, and Menger 1997, for differences in actors' earnings distribution in theater vs TV and cinema). In a sense, this model may help to underscore the impact of evaluative biases, too. The process of valuation of art and artists is indeed subject to considerable inflexibilities, asymmetries, and imperfections.

To speak of reputation instead of talent, provided that reputation is conceived as a social process, as Becker (1982) or White (1993) do, highlights the fact that the appraisal of art and artists varies with the organizational traits of each art world, since it reflects the cooperative and competitive activities of the various members. Several dimensions of appraisal exist, of which the spot market value of the outcome is only one. Deferred financial success occurs especially in art markets where the appraisal is initially undertaken by a narrow community of experts and learned consumers, and where a capital of recognition may be accumulated that is eventually converted into an increasing share of demand, which may provide the most famous artists with a slowly increasing flow of earnings (Bourdieu 1992). Thus, at each point in time, the distribution of earnings ranks artists whose cumulative career experiences differ widely; in that respect, income differentials may serve as a proxy for talent measurement if talent is equated not only with a flow of marketable abilities but also with a stock of recognizable characteristics, investments, and achievements. In an imperfectly competitive market, as the markets for artistic services and products are, considerable informational problems arise concerning how consumers can know and appraise the many characteristics of a large amount of highly differentiated goods. As Becker (1982) points out, the condition of perfect information among tastemakers and consumers holds quite exceptionally. Employers have search and information costs, as do consumers. Both may minimize their search costs by using price or the artist's visibility as an index of quality: Rather than being a causal factor, talent becomes a dependent variable, socially determined by the behavior of employers on one side of the market and consumers on the other side (Towse 1993). This is why talent may be conceived as embodying not only artistic abilities and technical skills, but also behavioral and relational ones. For example, Peterson & White (1989), studying the local world of studio musicians in Nashville, and Faulkner (1983), in his study on composers in the Hollywood film industry, show that those performers who succeed in a highly competitive market master several kinds of skills in order to secure a monopolistic control over the hiring system.

To consider talent as an initial endowment that is unequally distributed, and that only needs a proper occasion to be set in motion and to express itself, misses another fundamental feature, that of uncertainty in its twofold manifestation: that of uncertainty regarding the chances of individual success in a course of action and that of strategic uncertainty, which relates individual expectations to the behavior of other artists, as well as to the gatekeepers' and consumers' evaluations and preferences in a competitive market.

According to an expressivist model of praxis that can be traced back at least to Hegelian philosophy (Habermas 1988) and that plays a major role in Marx's theory of labor (Elster 1985), self-actualization through creative work entails a basic distinction between labor as a routine and alienating activity and work as a nonroutine pursuit. This distinction plays a major role in Arendt's (1959) theory of work as a nonutilitarian kind of lasting human achievement, as well as in Freidson's (1986b) view that artistic professions present a challenge to conventional conceptions about vocation and labor. Stinchcombe's (1968) analysis of uncertainty as a variance-related concept demonstrates how people have recourse to superstitious beliefs (luck, divination, supernatural coercion) or to their more sophisticated equivalents (genius, creativity) in dealing with highly uncertain activities: Talent for dealing with uncertainty turns out to challenge any measurement of its characteristics. Hirschman's (1986) classification of different kinds of work in terms of the varying predictability of their intended outcome brings to light the noninstrumental nature of the artist's striving effort. In the uncertain course of creative action, the strenuous overcoming of obstacles takes place through alternations of tension and the anticipated savoring of the future result. Therefore self-actualization through work, which makes artistic activity so attractive, occurs only if the outcome is unpredictable. The possibilities of personal invention are wide open, and at the same time, the artist is never sure that she will express herself in her work as she expected to.

The two kinds of incentives in occupational choice that have been mentioned up to this point can be related as follows: Nonroutine work, the most celebrated examples of which are artistic, scientific, and entrepreneurial work, provides psychic and social gratification proportional to the degree of uncertainty of success. The more the work is nonroutine, the less one can be certain about the immediate or long-term chances of individual achievement. It should, however, not be overlooked that artistic work also entails routine aspects, both in relative terms—the various artistic occupations and the various individual achievements in each of them may also, of course, be ranked according to how routine or nonroutine the work is—and in absolute terms—no artist could every time reconstruct afresh his own frame of activity, and no collective work could be achieved if conventions didn't exist as stabilizing forces (Becker 1982). The fact remains that the nonroutine dimension of artistic creative work is the most demanding, the most rewarding, and the most acclaimed one, and that which gives it such a great social value.

This also means that performance in nonroutine activities hardly depends on skills that could be easily objectified, transmitted, and certified in the training system. Indeed, the impact of schooling on earnings is typically smaller for artists than it is either for all workers or for managers, professionals, and technical workers (Filer 1990). Insofar as nonroutine activity refers to a wide range of changing and challenging work situations, it therefore implies that abilities may be revealed and skills acquired only progressively, in the course of action, through a process of learning-by-doing, which is highly informative and which cannot be perfectly anticipated ab initio. Even if one were to assume that innate abilities command success much more than formal training, talent could express itself only by coping with work situations that reveal the multiple characteristics of what artistic achievement really is. It should be added that if talent could be detected more rapidly, then quit rates in artistic professions would be much higher.

A dynamic occupational choice model may help to explain how workers accumulate skills through experience and learning-by-doing. As nonroutine work implies a steady human capital investment, it takes place in a matching process where jobs are "tied packages of work and learning" (Rosen 1986) and are ranked along their varying learning potentials, as shown in Faulkner's (1983) research on the work of freelance composers in Hollywood. The attractiveness of artistic jobs can therefore partly derive from their high learning potential, at least as long as the work is nonroutine enough.

Marx's rather solipsistic conception of self-actualization virtually precludes the possibility of failure, both because everyone is endowed with the same abilities and because competition as a source of alienation must be avoided. Yet the risk of failure is a built-in characteristic of artistic undertakings. Moreover, failure or success does not merely depend on the creators' own appraisal of their work, unless their art world forms a community of producers who have no interest in others' production nor in anyone's consumption (Elster 1985). Individuation through creative work, which greatly accounts for the admiration of artists, requires that others have an interest in one's work, and, consequently, that some competitive comparison occurs. This points to the

strategic side of uncertainty, that is, to uncertainty about the choices and behaviors of other agents, as in games of incomplete information. Firstly, competition cannot be separated from the individualistic search for systematic originality and innovation that has been characterizing the production of art since
the nineteenth century, so that artists, like all other social actors, do not behave
other than interdependently and competitively. Secondly, uncertainty as it
stems from the nonroutine and noninstrumental aspect of work brings to light
another characteristic: Competition is highly indeterminate, since work experiences have more or less to be constantly renewed in order to be attractive and
fertile. Uncertainty plays a major role not only during the early part of a career
but throughout the whole span of the professional lifetime. One can never be
sure whether one's next film or record will be a hit or will at least be held in
high esteem by peers; the only certainty in work is that it will always have to
cope with discontinuities and a high rate of change in content.

In a rational behavior model, expected risky occupational outcomes should
be experienced in a way quite similar to that predicted by the theory of option
pricing in finance. An optimal sequential decision scheme orders occupational
alternatives with respect to risk; it is rational to choose the job with the greater
risk first and to switch to a less risky alternative if the outcome turns out to be
unfavorable.

This approach gains much greater realism and explanatory power when informational considerations are brought in, as in the job matching approach of
occupational choice (Miller 1984) that fits rather well with the results of surveys on the careers of freelancers (Menger 1997). A job applicant only learns
gradually how well he is suited for a particular artistic occupation and to what
extent he can expect to meet success in it. It is a trial and error process: One becomes more and more informed about the various facets of the occupation and
about one's own abilities through doing the job. One tries to find the occupation or the job for which one is best suited. Many artistic occupations provide
this kind of information only through the learning-by-doing process, either because formal training is not strictly required to enter the professional community and to succeed (in some artistic occupations like that of writer, formal
training plays a more minor role, although there does exist in the US a huge industry in creative writing classes), or because formal training doesn't act as an
efficient means for selecting talents and screening abilities. This is probably
why so many artists think of themselves as self-taught, even in occupations
where formal training plays a true role (Moulin 1992). For example, most actors, while rather satisfied with the technical aspects of their training, are nonetheless critical of the lack of preparation. More information about one's abilities and chances of successful professionalization is mainly acquired in the
course of practicing (Jackson et al 1994, Menger 1997). Yet the learning and
information acquisition process is costly. Jobs where one can benefit more

from learning by doing are on average less well-paid initially than jobs where applicants can be selected on the basis of university degrees or through other immediate skill certifications.

High variance in the earnings distribution, according to this model, means therefore that, on the one hand, young and inexperienced artistic workers accept low rewards in exchange for information about the job and about themselves, which allows many of them, after a while, to estimate more precisely their chances and thus to opt to leave the occupation, or at least, to give up the project of making a comfortable living in the arts.

On the other hand, a small number of artists will successfully benefit from the learning process. In other words, scarcity of talent always remains a key factor that explains the super incomes (be these monetary or nonmonetary) of a few highly rated artists, but no one is able, ex ante, to make an accurate estimation of the value of his or her talents and skills, and to assess the chances she or he has to get them priced and recognized.

However, the application of this job matching model to artistic occupations raises two issues. Firstly, it may be asked how much information one needs before being able to assess the quality of one's job match, considering that occupational practice acquires so many different and changing forms, takes place in so many environments, and in relation to many diverse employers and patrons. In addition, this high variability in practice probably influences the artist's behavior regarding risk-taking. In some respects, each work experience in the performing arts, such as theater or movie production, is unique and new, each team of artists and technicians is different. One can get the feeling that there is no end to the learning process and to the assessment of one's talent and that no situation is really crucial when one has to decide how far to go ahead in such a career. This could explain why many artists maintain for so long the hope that they will eventually become famous, even after death. Romantic writers and poets invented a well-known psychological and ideological device for fighting against short-term disenchantment: the "loser is eventually the winner" game (Sartre 1971, Bénichou 1985). Secondly, once multiple job holding is taken into account, risk diversification considerations may advocate for an enlarged definition of occupational choice, where several related jobs provide switching opportunities that, instead of building irreversible sequences of choices, may result in a cycling pattern of allocation of occupational time between various kindred activities.

In this case, an interesting way to test the assumption that, against the standard economic view, workers may derive satisfaction from the process of work itself and not just from the income it earns, is to study whether artists turn down better-paid jobs in order to pursue their vocational work. In estimating labor supply functions for Australian artists with arts and nonarts wage rates as explanatory variables, Throsby (1992) shows that artists supply the nonarts labor market only up to the point where an adequate return was received to support their primary artistic work.

OCCUPATIONAL RISK DIVERSIFICATION

Both sociological and economic studies of artistic occupations show how artists can be induced to face the constraints of a rationed labor market and how they learn to manage risky careers by resorting to the insurance devices that are at hand. Pioneering empirical research (Baumol & Bowen 1966) has found that artists may improve their economic situation in three main ways, which are not incompatible and may be combined: Artists can be supported by private sources (working spouse, family, or friends) or by public sources (subsidies, grants and commissions from the state, sponsorship from foundations or corporations, and other transfer income from social and unemployment insurance); they can work in cooperative-like associations by pooling and sharing their income and by designing a sort of mutual insurance scheme; and finally, they can hold multiple jobs.

Most studies, both in sociology and in economics, have focused on this last means, since apart from being widespread and becoming more so, it brings into light a puzzling feature of the artistic labor market: that of the diversification of risk through one's own human capital and labor, which seems a much more unusual phenomenon than risk management through financial assets and income from various sources. In fact, it brings artists close to entrepreneurs since, like property owners who can spread their risk by putting bits of their property into a large number of concerns, multiple job holders put bits of their efforts into different jobs (Drèze 1987).

Multiple job holding shows a general upward trend, and artistic workers rank among the highest in the percentage of all workers who have secondary jobs; in addition, artistic occupations rank at the top in the percentage of all jobs held as secondary jobs. If one adds the numbers of primary and secondary job holders in a given occupation, so as to estimate the total number of practitioners in that occupation, almost every artistic occupation appears among the 25 occupations employing the largest proportions of their workers through a secondary job (Amirault 1997). Wassall & Alper (1992) review a number of surveys that document the extent of multiple job holding among artists, including their own 1981 survey of 3000 New England artists, which found that only 24% of artists did not hold a nonartistic job.

As shown by Throsby (1992, 1994, 1996) in his studies on artists' income and labor supply, not only must economic studies recognize the arts/nonarts earnings distinction as providing a more complete picture of artists' income sources, but they must also recognize that simple dichotomy in itself does not go far enough. In order to capture the full range of relationships between labour supply and earnings experienced by artists, a three-way division of working time and earnings is essential (Throsby 1996, Menger 1997, Paradeise 1998): that between (*a*) the creative activity itself, which corresponds to the primary creative labor and the tasks associated to the preparation of the artistic product (thinking, dreaming, searching for materials, rehearsing, practicing); (*b*) arts-related work, which includes the various activities within the particular art world that do not contribute directly to producing the artistic product, but still rely on the skills and qualifications possessed by the professional artist; common examples of such work would be teaching activities and management tasks in artistic organizations; (*c*) nonarts work, which may differ considerably both among individuals, among the arts, and over the individual life-cycle in an artistic career. For example, recent US Census and survey data report that while a majority of authors (as primary occupation) hold secondary jobs in other professional occupations and especially in educational fields, actors' and singers' secondary jobs are mainly in sales, clerical, or service jobs—jobs with a history of low pay and poor benefits (Alper et al 1996; see also Kingston & Cole 1986).

The range of various resources and jobs may be compared to a portfolio of financial assets (Faulkner 1983, Menger 1989). This way of handling uncertainty has already been evoked above in the case of the freelancer, who may insure himself against downswings on the employers' side as well as strengthen his position by building a career portfolio that is mixed with tightly and loosely coupled work associations. With sectoral diversification of hirings, artists may also be financially better off and have greater career continuity in a highly fragmented labor market.

Holding other jobs outside one's vocational field of activity corresponds to a better known scheme of occupational risk diversification, though the hackneyed examples of artists forced to hold jobs totally unrelated to their art are partially misleading. In facing the constraints of job rationing in their artistic field or those of an unsuccessful position in the art market, artists manage the risks of their main commitment to their art through job diversification, but the composition of their portfolio also evolves as their personal position in the art world at different stages of their career solidifies or gets weaker. The sources of income and multiple job earnings are much more dispersed at the beginning of an artist's professional life and come under greater control when the artist's reputation grows and when his or her ability to select among different opportunities allows him or her to reach a more careful balance between constraints and fulfilling commitments. Instead of thinking statically in the terms of the old dilemma—freedom or alienation—the portfolio model of occupational risk management offers new insights for the dynamic study of how artists cope with uncertainty throughout their career and allow the maintainance of the centrality of choice for the course of that career.

However, in focusing on the combination of insecure and secure sources of income, the "diversification of risk" approach fails to deal with the characteristics of the different kinds of work that may be associated with the creative one. It is assumed that a secondary job doesn't provide the artist with anything else except income. Indeed another, complementary, dimension of multiple job holding is overshadowed, which concerns above all the relationship between creative work and related artistic work, and which is described in the "role versatility" scheme (Nash 1970[1955]). In certain art worlds, like that of "serious" music, high technical skill requirements act as a selective barrier to entry as well as an integrating device among the professionals employed in the various occupational roles (composer, performer, conductor, publisher, and so forth), whose differentiation has increased with the professionalization process. Through role versatility, the composer may reduce the financial risk in his creative activity but also extend his control over the distribution process of his music, facilitate his interaction and communication with the other roles, and increase his prestige among his peers. Roles simultaneously or successively played are thought of in terms of positions in various spheres, as in Abbott & Hrycak's (1990) work on eighteenth century German composers, or as in Baker & Faulkner's study (1991) that examines the shifting combinatorial patterns in Hollywood filmmaking and sees roles as resources to enact positions in evolving organizational settings.

More generally, sociologists of art are good at exploring how organizational or aesthetic innovations induce role combinations and hybridizations and transform both the content of cooperative activities and the extent of control over new market resources—see Moulin 1992, on the case of the entrepreneurial artists who work as performers and producers of services in the contemporary visual art markets; Christopherson 1996, on the emergence of entrepreneurial filmmakers whose managerial skills blur the lines between management and labor; Kealy 1979, on the emergence of the hybrid 'artist mixer' in rock music; Hesmondhalgh 1996, on the entrepreneurial strategies of sound mixers and DJ's in the dance music record sector.

Wherever practice needs a specific training, the center of the artistic role constellation is traditionally the teaching role, the most frequent 'pool' profession (Abbott 1988) or 'host occupation' (Freidson 1986b) for creative artists. This teaching position in the arts has been compared by Baumol as well as by Freidson to the role of teaching in academic life, which hosts and supports research activities; this might explain why creative artists so often consider themselves researchers. The paradox of artists whose educational profile as a group is close to that of managerial and professional occupational categories but has far less impact on their earnings can also be solved. Throsby (1996) shows that relationships between arts income and art training may be strong for arts-related activities such as teaching whereas income from primary creative practice is more influenced by on-the-job experience. Human capital and role versatility considerations militate for arts-related rather than nonarts jobs and portfolio choice considerations for stable salaried supplementary jobs: teaching fits best. White (1993) suggests that the artist as teacher combines two opposing forms of career, one (teacher) that represents the image of the traditional career, since it entails seniority and some ordered sense of cumulation from training, and another (the artist as genius) that is built on originality and conveys a sense of destructive creation. That paradoxical role combination is especially striking in avant-garde music (Menger 1983) and visual arts (Moulin 1992).

Methods for dealing with risk may be classified in terms of individual, co-operative and collective action (Peacock & Weir 1975). In a sense, multiple job holding and role versatility blur the frontier between individual and collective action: Artists, as suggested above, may better be conceived as small firms, drawing resources and building careers from changing combinations of roles, income sources, work settings, and employment statuses. Similarly, artists may share the occupational risk by pooling their resources together as in the case of groups of visual artists (Simpson 1981, Crane 1987), who provide each of their members with mutual support, or of the main symphony orchestras in London, which operate on a self-managed organizational basis, with musicians being shareholders of their own company and cumulating that position with freelance hirings elsewhere (Peacock 1970). Most of the small organizations in the live performing arts (dance companies, chamber orchestras, baroque and contemporary music ensembles), work on this co-operative basis, which recurrently brings together workers who are themselves already mini-firms.

Sociological studies on the collective action of unions in the arts are fewer than those devoted to state and public support for the arts. One common feature of the unions' intervention concerns the income transfers and redistributions that may allow workers to adapt to more flexible and more disequilibrated artistic labor markets. Apart from traditional direct (grants, awards, salaries, income guarantees) and indirect (purchases of works, tax and social security facilities) forms of public support to artists, which are mostly prevalent in European countries (Mitchell 1992) and mainly intended for self-employed creative artists, collective action regarding the artistic labor markets deals with the funding of nonprofit organizations such as performance companies that employ artists as well as with the impact of increasing flexibility. Paul & Kleingartner (1994) show that in the US film and TV industries, the actors', writers' and directors' unions, unlike craft unions, have expanded in spite of the introduction of highly flexible production. A three-tier compensation structure allows artists both to be covered on an egalitarian basis (through minimum pay rates), to allow those whose market value exceeds union scale to negotiate additional compensation, and to get additional payments (residuals) for the reuse of the films and TV programs to which they have contributed. This last device can hardly be underestimated. Residual compensation, whose total amount now matches total initial compensation, softens the impact of work intermittency by generating a passive income stream. As film and audiovisual markets expand and flexibility increases, residuals as the focus of labor relations in that sector symbolize the shifts that result from the collective bargaining process. The French unemployment insurance system put in place for artists and craft workers in the performing arts plays a similar role of compensating these intermittent workers for their recurrent unemployment spells (Menger & Gurgand 1996).

THE OVERSUPPLY OF ARTISTS

The oversupply of artists has been underscored nearly as often as sociologists, economists, and historians have dealt with artistic labor markets. One could hardly find a piece of research where an excess supply of artists is not documented. Disequilibrium seems to be a sort of permanent critical situation. In the first half of the nineteenth century, the glut of novelists and poets in Paris, as analyzed by the late Cesar Graña (1964), led to Parisian bohemianism and accounted for the success of the "art for art's sake" ideology, which acted as a compensating device for the subordination of the artist to the impersonal market forces. In several other European countries, literary proletariats were similarly spawned by the mid-century publishing boom.

   The Impressionists' revolution took place in a Parisian art world whose institutional apparatus—the Academic system—was collapsing, as the pressure from the greatly expanded number of professional painters on a framework conceived to handle a few hundred men increased and as the functional gaps in the system widened. White & White (1965) show how control was lost over the flow of recruits through art schools, the flow of paintings produced, and the careers of the painters: A free market took over to launch innovative artists and movements, on a more flexible and also much riskier basis of open competition involving dealers, critics, painters, and buyers. Supply was no more to be regulated, so that oversupply was known to become a permanent feature of that market. In Berlin and Münich, at the turn of the century, the art market, as depicted by Lenman (1989), was similarly overcrowded with painters competing for recognition and success. Periodic panics about the glut and the high rate of unemployment didn't deter students from entering art schools in growing numbers. In his minute study of the music profession in Britain, Ehrlich (1985) reports substantial evidence of a glut at the turn of the nineteenth century, at the end of a 60-year period during which musicians had become one of the fastest growing professional groups; he shows how musicians, aside from lamenting over the damnable flood, tried to react to the pressures of relentless competition and its consequences (very low fees and depressed incomes, underdealing practices,...) by establishing professional associations and trade unions, despite increasing segmentation among the workforce.

In each of these cases, a similar array of factors is invoked: a rising level of demand (enhanced by factors such as urbanization, increasing educational level, growing incomes, more leisure time, public support), changes in the commercialization of art, which bring market principles of organization and bargaining into harmony with the stream of artistic innovations, and technological innovations affecting the transmission and the distribution of art. Unlike short-term fluctuations that may be provoked by fads and fashions, long-run shifts causing an increase in private and/or public demand trigger an expansion in training facilities, and more artists appear. But, as Ehrlich shows in the case of musicians, inflexibilities may dramatically hinder the equilibration process if demand turns down, as in the case of the briefly flourishing demand for musicians in cinemas that collapsed with the coming of talkies. Existing practitioners are trapped in a disintegrating market while new aspirants continue to flood in. The training system may play an unintended role in the self-congesting spiral of oversupply, since teaching positions and kindred activities in nonprofit art organizations shelter artists from occupational risks.

Innovations in artistic production, as a result of the interaction between new techniques, aesthetic shifts, and market transformations, have often been studied in respect to their impact on labor supply. Some of these innovations tend to lower or to modify the usual skill requirements and/or the quantity of input factors in the production process, resulting in an increase of the artists' productivity, a growing competition among them, and a declining control over entry and professional practice through the traditional devices of the professionalization system. Among numerous possible examples, we may cite the new methods of production of paintings in seventeenth-century Holland (Montias 1996), the deskilling process at stake in many avant-garde innovations in visual arts (Moulin 1992), and the pop music revolution (Peacock & Weir 1975) and the success of dance music (Hesmondhalgh 1996), which can be partly explained as the result of the widespread availability of production technology, of the transformation of the record industry, of shifts in authorship, and of the segmentation of market demand. Technical innovations, like motion pictures, radio, television, records, and other recent changes, increase the extent of scale economies in artistic and entertainment activities (Rosen 1981). As the market supply of works and services grows, the scope of each performer's audience gets larger, and more numerous artists are induced to enter the labor market, though some occupational trades and niches of specialization may disappear. Even if there is a resultant greater concentration of the distribution of rewards among the most talented, who can operate on an international scale, the lure of enormous rewards and large social recognition may favor an occupational gambling behavior, as success seems like a lottery game in a more speculative market of talents.

In itself, the population of small-sized cultural organizations has been described as a contributing factor to innovativeness, but effects on artistic employment have not been underlined as much. Indeed, the population of employers and small organizations in the cultural sector is surprisingly numerous; in the cultural industry, although oligopolistic market control by major companies remains a striking feature, mainly through the control of distribution and finance (Aksoy & Robins 1992 and Storper's reply 1993), a vertical disintegration scheme at the production level can hardly be overstressed, resulting in an increasing number of independent film producers (Christopherson & Storper 1989, Storper 1989), record companies (Burke 1997), and publishing houses (Boin & Bouvaist 1989). In the performing arts, the expansion of the nonprofit sector and the increase in public support have favored the multiplication of dance companies (Sussmann 1984) and theater groups (Menger 1997). Even if demographic trends concerning the rise and fall of organizations differ across the various arts scenes (for an extreme example, see the case of dance music; Hesmondhalgh 1998), on the whole, the expansion of the craft-administered production sector, with its growing product differentiation, acts as an inflationary labor supply factor since it draws on an increasing number of aspiring young artists. Lower costs pose fewer barriers to entry, but a substantial share of the risks are transferred to the artists who face a fiercer competition and more uncertain career prospects.

Here one should think not only in terms of artists' oversupply at an aggregate level, as a result of growing interfirm competition in more contestable markets, but also of an intraorganizational process designed to deal with an uncertain and turbulent market environment. Organizational flexibility in the arts plays a major causal role in structural oversupply. Employers in project-based organizations seek to draw from a large pool of artists and personnel in order to build efficient and well-matched teams, because they may gain from the variety of talents and skills at hand, and to reduce overheads. Similarly, for record companies or book publishers, as highlighted in Hirsch's pioneering paper (Hirsch 1972) and Coser et al (1982), overproduction of new items, along with allocation of numerous personnel to boundary-spanning roles and cooptation of mass-media gatekeepers, is a rational organizational response to an environment of low capital investments and demand uncertainty, especially in the most speculative and entrepreneurial segments of the market. Because of a strategy of differential promotion of the numerous items released, the corporate sponsoring is only focused on a small proportion of them.

More generally, however, the notion of oversupply has to be questioned (Killingsworth 1983), since it refers to a disequilibrium in only one of the labor markets that artists supply, that of their principal vocational work. As stated above, when multiple job holders cycle between rationed and less- or unconstrained job markets, or when individual, cooperative, and collective devices of compensation for and insurance against risk are at hand, notions of underemployment or oversupply may be hard to apply, provided that work under such a steady "management of risk" scheme is more attractive than occupational alternatives outside the arts sphere.

The oversupply issue may then be split into two more precise questions: How constrained and rationed is the vocational job market? And how does the market of arts-related jobs evolve?

Regarding the first issue, it appears that under a highly flexible working scheme, the competitive nature of the artistic labor markets is enhanced so as to increase the variability of individual situations. Indeed, estimating one's chances of success may be increasingly difficult since long-term career prospects disappear behind a daily strain of getting credits; and variance in reputations is accordingly higher too. Thus, the explanation of oversupply by the 'risk-taking behavior' scheme seems to be especially appealing: where information about the quality of the individual occupational match is delivered only through on-the-job experiences which are more and more fragmented, and aspirants are not screened at the entry. Oversupply consequently stems from the sorting mechanism on which the competitive labor market relies: The resulting segmentation of the artistic work force means that at each point in time there seem to be shortages of talented workers and an excess supply of less talented ones (Towse 1996).

As to the second issue, part of the arts-related contingent jobs or stable positions are offered by publicly supported institutions. Employers of course are better off if they do not incur the major part of the costs of securing pools of employable artists. One unintended consequence may be a highly unbalanced growth in artistic employment. Through short-term contractual ties, employers take no responsibility for most of the elements that constitute a career, so the social and human costs of the structural excess supply of workers fall on public cultural policy as well as on personal means of risk management. Moreover, market organizations sort out talents without any relativistic scruple, in contrast to public support policies.

CONCLUSION

The contemporary artistic scene is more contestable. On the one hand, the valuation process is subject to more volatility, leaving more room for speculative bets and for joint action by several categories of actors to promote artistic movements, innovations, and fashions. On the other hand, a paradoxical alliance has emerged that unites the obsessive conservation of cultural heritage (the result of a long-term selection process) with the promotion and support of the New. Because they are consecrated and offered for public admiration in museums, concert programs, books, and audiovisual or computerized archives, an ever-increasing number of pieces of art and culture act as permanent reminders; one cannot forget that this selection has emerged from an even greater stock of works whose significance and value needed time to be correctly appraised and sorted out. This legitimates a transfer of the title and merit of past artists and creators onto their contemporary heirs, be these known or unknown at this time.

Uncertainty here plays a major and highly ambiguous role. On the one hand, as discussed above, uncertainty means that art is a risky business. On the other, uncertainty, as it surrounds any decision to support new artistic creation, also provides a true rationale for the public support of artists.

According to DiMaggio (1986), uncertainty is at the core of the evaluation of any work, and this uncertainty principle bears on collective choices, from both an intra- and an intergenerational equity point of view. Uncertainty, as it disappears over time, turns into an extremely skewed distribution of fame and success, in the long term.

Thus, it can be claimed that it is in the interests of society at large to nurture an oversupply of artists so as to have the best possible choice of talented artists. Indeed, as pointed out by Nisbett & Ross (1980), people sometimes may require overly optimistic or overly pessimistic subjective probabilities to goad them into effective action or to prevent them from taking dangerous actions. The social benefits of individually erroneous subjective probabilities may be great even when the individual pays a high price for the error.

Cultural policies as regarding patterns of public support for artistic labor markets may be at odds with the way firms and entrepreneurs take advantage of the attractiveness of artistic occupations and of individual erroneous expectations. Increasing flexibility, which can be associated with higher rates of artistic innovation or, at least, with increasing differentiation in production, transfers more and more of the occupational risk down onto artists. Artists may only partly manage it through individual strategies of diversification. Public policies are burdened with another part of the costs of insurance against individual risk (that of low income and low reputation) as well as social risk—that of having innovations underrated and of experiencing a suboptimal cultural development.

Actually we never know exactly of which kind is the uncertainty that, in the short term, has to be managed through insurance devices: Is it exogenous or endogenous? Should a lack of jobs and an unsuccessful career be attributed to insufficient ability? Or is it due to insufficient demand for the kind of ability with which the artist is endowed? Moreover, ability and talent themselves may be ambiguous: "Talent" should be considered not only as an exogenous factor of market success but also as an endogenous factor shaped by competition through innovation. The more competition raises the rate of innovation or, at least, of differentiation between prototype-like works, in exploiting and stimulating consumer demand for novelty, the more the sorting mechanism will be based on shifting specifications of marketable talent.

Only some of the occupational risks in the arts are insurable. One tends to forget this when the enormous variance in artists' reputations and incomes is ascribed to an endemic crisis of cultural underconsumption because, presumably, demand is on the whole too weak, or, to take another symptom of the same social dysfunction, because consumer preferences are shaped by market forces and by the inequalities on which class societies are based and so become fixed on a desperately limited number of works and artists.

Indeed, this argument neglects the role of an essential factor in the professionalization of artists and in the remuneration of talent by the market: competition and its endorsements, through which those qualities that are temporarily the most prized also become the rarest. Full employment in the artistic labor market would require, on the one hand, a regulation on entry into the profession, and, on the other, either sufficient homogeneity on the supply-side or a high enough degree of insensitivity to differences in quality on the demand-side, such that the substitutability of artists and goods in the various sectors of production ensures against disequilibrium in the market. But, then, on what is that other requirement, that of the free expression of individual creativity, to be based? On artistic individualism; the product of a movement of progressive autonomization and professionalization of the sphere of artistic activities, according to the Weberian analysis, and the force behind competition among artists. To isolate the nonmonetary dimensions of artistic work and imagine that the practice of artistic activity could be at once fully satisfying and risk-free is to ignore the two interconnected principles of the evolution of artistic life. It was professionalization by the market as the organizational form of artistic practices that made possible the triumph of creative individualism; but professionalization also maximizes the role of risk in the choice and exercise of professions in which those who feel called upon to create are infinitely more numerous than those who can succeed.

ACKNOWLEDGMENTS

I would like to thank Geoffrey Turnovsky for his help in preparation of the manuscript and an anonymous reviewer for insightful comments and helpful suggestions.

Visit the *Annual Reviews home page* at
http://www.AnnualReviews.org.

Literature Cited

Abbott A. 1988. *The System of Professions.* Chicago: Univ. Chicago Press

Abbott A. 1990. Conceptions of time and events in social science methods. *Hist. Meth.* 23(4):140–50

Abbott A, Hrycak A. 1990. Measuring resemblance in sequence data: an optimal matching analysis of musicians' careers. *Am. J. Sociol.* 1:144–85

Aksoy A, Robins K. 1992. Hollywood for the 21st century: global competition for critical mass in image markets. *Cambridge J. Econ.* 16:1–22

Allmendinger J, Hackman R, Lehman E. 1994. *Life and Work in Symphony Orchestras.* Harvard Bus. Sch., Rep. N°7

Alper N, Wassall G, Jeffri J, Greenblatt R, Kay A, et al. 1996. *Artists in the Work Force: Employment and Earnings 1970–1990,* Natl. Endowment for the Arts, Santa Anna, CA: Seven Locks Press

Amirault T. 1997. Characteristics of multiple jobholders. *Monthly Labor Rev.* March: 9–15

Anzieu D. 1981. *Le corps de l'oeuvre.* Paris: Gallimard

Arendt H. 1959. *The Human Condition.* Garden City, NJ: Doubleday Anchor Press

Arian E. 1971. *Bach, Beethoven and Bureaucracy.* AL: Univ. Alabama Press

Baker WE, Faulkner RR. 1991. Role as resource in the Hollywood film industry. *Am. J. Sociol.* 2:279–309

Baumol WJ, Bowen WG. 1966. *Performing Arts: the Economic Dilemma.* New York: Twentieth Century Fund

Becker HS. 1982. *Art Worlds.* Berkeley: Univ. Calif. Press

Bénichou P. 1985. *Le sacre de l'écrivain.* Paris: Corti

Blau JR. 1984. *Architects and Firms.* Cambridge, MA: MIT Press

Boin JG, Bouvaist JM. 1989. *Du printemps des éditeurs à l'âge de raison.* Paris: La Documentation Française

Bourdieu P. 1992. *Les règles de l'art.* Paris: Seuil

Burke AE. 1997. Small firm start-up by composers in the recording industry. *Small Bus. Econ.* 9:463–71

Caves RE. 2000. *Getting Our Act Together: The Economic Organization of Creative Industries.* Harvard: Harvard Univ. Press. Forthcoming

Champy F. 1998. *Les architectes et la commande publique.* Paris: PUF

Christopherson S. 1996. Flexibility and adaptation in industrial relations: the exceptional case of the US media entertainment industries. In *Under the Stars,* ed. L Gray, R Seeber, pp. 86–112. Ithaca: Cornell Univ. Press

Christopherson S, Storper M. 1989. The effects of flexible specialization on industrial politics and the labour market: the motion picture industry. *Indust. Labour Relat. Rev.* 42:331–47

Coser LA, Kadushin C, Powell WW. 1982. *Books. The Culture and Commerce of Publishing.* New York: Basic Books

Crane D. 1987. *The Transformation of the Avant-Garde.* Chicago: Univ. of Chicago Press

Debeauvais R, Menger P-M, Rannou J, Vari S, Laplante B. 1997. *Le spectacle vivant,* Paris, La Documentation Française, Collection Contrats d'Etudes Prospectives

DiMaggio P. 1986. Can culture survive the marketplace? In *Nonprofit Enterprise in the Arts. Studies in Mission and Constraint,* ed. P DiMaggio, pp. 65–92. New York: Oxford Univ. Press

Drèze J. 1987 [1979]. Human capital and risk-bearing. In *Essays on Economic Decisions under Uncertainty.* Cambridge, MA: Cambridge Univ. Press

Ehrlich C. 1985. *The Music Profession in Britain since the Eighteenth Century.* Oxford: Clarendon

Elster J. 1985. *Making Sense of Marx.* Cambridge, UK: Cambridge Univ. Press

Faulkner R. 1973. Career concerns and mobility motivations of orchestra musicians. *Sociol. Q.* 14:334–49

Faulkner R. 1983. *Music on Demand.* New Brunswick: Transaction Books

Faulkner R, Anderson A. 1987. Short-term projects and emergent careers: evidence from Hollywood. *Am. J. Sociol.* 92: 879–909

Federico R. 1983. The decision to end a performing career in ballet. In *Performers and Performances,* ed. J Kamerman, R Martorella, pp. 57–69. New York: Praeger

Feist A. 1998. Great Britain. In *New Frontiers for Employment in Europe,* ed. C Bodo, R Fisher. Rome: Circle Publ. N°9

Filer RK. 1986. The "Starving artist"—Myth or reality? Earnings of artists in the United States. *J. Polit. Econ.* 96:56–75

Filer RK. 1990. Arts and academe: the effects of education on earnings of artists. *J. Cult. Econ.* 2:15–38

Fohrbeck K, Wiesand A. 1975. *Der Künstler-Report.* München: Hanser Verlag

Frey B., Pommerehne W. 1989. *Muses and Markets*. Oxford: Basil Blackwell

Freidson E. 1986a. *Professional Powers*. Chicago: Univ. Chicago Press

Freidson E. 1986b. L'analyse sociologique des professions artistiques. *Rev. française de sociol.* 27:431–43

Freidson E. 1990. Labors of love: a prospectus. In *The Nature of Work: Sociological Perspectives*, ed. K Erikson, SP Vallas, pp. 149–61. New Haven: Yale Univ. Press

Galenson DW. 1999. The careers of modern artists: evidence from auctions of contemporary art. *Working paper*. Univ. Chicago and NBER

Graña C. 1964. *Bohemian versus Bourgeois*. New York: Basic Books

Habermas J. 1988. *Le discours philosophique de la modernité*, tr. fr. Paris: Gallimard.

Hamlen W Jr. 1991. Superstardom in popular music: empirical evidence. *Rev. Econ. Stat.* 4:729–33

Hamlen W Jr. 1994. Variety and superstardom in popular music. *Econ. Inq.* 3:395–406

Hesmondhalgh D. 1996. Flexibility, post-Fordism and the music industry. *Media, Cult. Soc.* 18:469–88

Hesmondhalgh D. 1998. The British dance music industry. *Br. J. Sociol.* 2:234–51

Hirsch P. 1972. Processing fads and fashions. *Am. J. Sociol..* 77:639–59

Hirschman AO. 1986. *Rival Views of Market Society*. New York: Viking

Jackson C, Honey S, Hillage J, Stock J. 1994. *Careers and Training in Dance and Drama*. Brighton: Inst. Manpower Stud.

Jeffri J. 1991. *The Artists Training and Career Project: Painters*. New York: Columbia Univ.

Jeffri J, Throsby D. 1994. Professionalism and the visual artist. *European J. Cultur. Policy.* 1:99–108

Kanter RM. 1989. Careers and the wealth of nations: a macro-perspective on the structure and implications of career forms. In *Handbook of Career Theory*, ed. M Arthur, D Hall, B Lawrence, pp. 506–21. Cambridge, MA: Cambridge Univ. Press

Kanter RM. 1995. *World Class: Thriving Locally in the Global Economy*. New York: Simon & Schuster

Kealy E. 1979. The case of sound mixers and popular music. *Sociol. Work Occup.* 1:3–29

Killingsworth M. 1983. *Labor Supply*. Cambridge, UK: Cambridge Univ. Press

Kingston P, Cole J. 1986. *The Wages of Writing*. New York: Columbia Univ. Press

Knott J. 1994. *Crafts in the 1990s*. London: The Crafts Council

Kris E, Kurz O. 1987. *L'image de l'artiste*, tr.fr. Marseille, Ed. Rivages.

Laplante B. 1990. *La vocation de l'acteur*. Montréal: Univ. Montreal, unpublished PhD.

Lenman R. 1989. Painters, patronage and the art market in Germany 1850–1914, *Past Present* 123:109–40

Marshall A. 1947. *Principles of Economics*. New York: MacMillan. 8th ed.

Menger PM. 1983. *Le Paradoxe du musicien*. Paris: Flammarion

Menger PM. 1989. Rationalité et incertitude de la vie d'artiste. *L'Année Sociol.* 39: 111–51

Menger PM. 1993. L'hégémonie parisienne. Economie et politique de la gravitation artistique. *Annales ESC* 6:1565–1600

Menger PM. 1997. *La profession de comédien*. Paris: La Documentation Française

Menger PM, Gurgand M. 1996. Work and compensated unemployment in the performing arts: exogenous and endogenous uncertainty in artistic labour markets. In *Economics of the Arts*, V Ginsburgh, PM Menger, pp. 347–81. Amsterdam: North Holland

Miller R. 1984. Job matching and occupational choice. *J. Polit. Econ.* 92/1086–120

Mitchel R. 1992. Artists policies. In *European Symposium on the Status of the Artist,* ed. A Irjala, pp. 238–67 Helsinki: Unesco

Montias JM. 1982. *Artists and Artisans in Delft*. Princeton, NJ: Princeton Univ. Press

Montias JM. 1996. *Le marché de l'art aux Pays-Bas (15e - 17e siècles)*. Paris: Flammarion

Moulin R. 1987. *The French Art Market, A Sociological View*. New Brunswick, NJ: Rutgers Univ. Press

Moulin R. 1992. *L'artiste, l'institution et le marché*. Paris: Flammarion

Nash D. 1970[1955]. The American composer's career. In *The Sociology of Art and Literature*, ed. M Albrecht, J Barnett, M Griff, pp. 256–65. London: Duckworth

Nisbett R, Ross L. 1980. *Human Inference*. Englewood Cliffs: Prentice-Hall

O'Brien J, Feist A. 1995. *Employment in the Arts and Cultural Industries: An Analysis of the 1991 Census*. London: Arts Council England

Observatoire de l'emploi culturel. 1998a. *L'emploi dans le secteur de la culture en 1997*, note n°12. Paris: Ministère de la Culture

Observatoire de l'emploi culturel. 1998b. *L'emploi dans les professions culturelles en 1997*, note n°13. Paris: Ministère de la Culture

Paradeise C. 1997. *Les comédiens*. Paris: PUF

Paul A. Kleingartner A. 1994. Flexible production and the transformation of industrial relations in the motion picture and television industry. *Industrial Labor Relations Rev.* 4:662–78

Peacock A. 1970. *A Report on Orchestral Resources.* London: Arts Council of Great Britain

Peacock A, Weir R. 1975. *The Composer in the Market Place.* London: Faber

Peterson RA, White HG. 1989. The simplex located in art worlds. In *Art and Society*, ed. AW Foster, JR Blau, pp. 243–59. New York: SUNY Press

Powell WW. 1985. *Getting into Print.* Chicago: Univ. Chicago Press

Pratt AC. 1997.The cultural industries production system: a case study of employment change in Britain, 1984-1991. *Environ. Planning A*, 29:1953–74

Quingley J. 1998. Urban diversity and economic growth. *J. Econ. Perspect.* 2: 127–38

Rannou J, Vari S. 1996. *Les itinéraires d'emploi des ouvriers, techniciens et cadres intermittents de l'audiovisuel et des spectacles*, Paris: La Documentation Française

Rosen S. 1981. The economics of superstars. *Am. Econ. Rev.* 75: 845–58

Rosen S. 1986. The theory of equalizing differences. In *Handbook of Labour Economics*, ed. O Ashenfelter, R Layard, pp. 641–92. Amsterdam: North-Holland

Sartre JP. 1971. *L'idiot de la famille.* Paris: Gallimard

Scott AJ. 1997. The cultural economy of cities. *Int. J. Urban Regional Res.* 2:323–39

Simpson C. 1981. *SoHo: The Artist in the City.* Chicago: Univ. Chicago Press

Smith. V. 1997. New forms of work organization. *Annu. Rev. Sociol.* 23:315-39

Spilerman S. 1977. Careers, labor market structure, and socioeconomic achievement. *Am. J. Sociol.* 3:551–93

Stinchcombe A. 1968. *Constructing Social Theories.* Chicago: Univ. Chicago Press

Stinchcombe A. 1986. *Stratification and Organization.* Cambridge, UK: Cambridge Univ. Press

Storper M. 1989. The transition to flexible specialisation in the film industry. *Cambridge J. Econ.* 13:273–305

Storper M. 1993. Flexible specialisation in Hollywood: a response to Aksoy and Robins. *Cambridge J. Econ.* 17:479–84

Storper M., Walker R. 1989. *The Capitalist Imperative. Territory, Technology and Industrial Growth.* Oxford et New York: Basil Blackwell.

Sussmann L. 1984. Anatomy of the dance company boom. *Dance Research J.* 2: 23–28

Taylor B. 1987. Artists in the marketplace: a framework for analysis. In *Artists and Cultural Consumers*, ed. D Shaw, W Hendon, CR Waits, pp. 77–84. Akron: Assoc. for Cult. Econ.

Throsby D. 1992. Artists as workers. In *Cultural Economics*, ed. R Towse, A Khakee, pp. 201–8. Berlin: Springer Verlag

Throsby D. 1994. The production and consumption of the arts. *J. Econ. Lit.* XXXII: 1–29

Throsby D. 1996. Disaggregated earnings functions for artists . In *Economics of the Arts*, ed. V Ginsburgh, PM Menger, pp. 331–46. Amsterdam: North Holland

Throsby D, Thompson B. 1994. *But What Do You Do for a Living?* Redfern: Australia Council for the Arts

Towse R. 1993. *Singers in the Marketplace. The Economics of the Singing Profession.* Oxford, UK: Clarendon Press

Towse R. 1996. *The Economics of Artists' Labour Markets*, London: The Arts Council of England.

Warnke M. 1989. *L'artiste et la cour.* tr.fr. Paris: Ed. MSH

Wassall GH, Alper NO. 1992. Toward a unified theory of the determinants of the earnings of artists. In *Cultural Economics*, R Towse, A Khakee, pp. 187–99. Heidelberg: Springer Verlag

Weick K. 1979. *The Social Psychology of Organizing.* New York: Random House

Weick K, Berlinger L. 1989. Career improvisations in self-designing organizations. In *Handbook of Career Theory*, ed. M Arthur, D Hall, B Lawrence, pp. 313–28. Cambridge, UK: Cambridge Univ. Press

White HC, White CA. 1965. *Canvases and Careers.* New York: Wiley

White HC. 1993. *Careers and Creativity.* Boulder, CO: Westview

Westby D. 1960. The career experience of the symphony musician. *Soc. Forc.* March: 224–30

Annu. Rev. Sociol. 1999. 25:575–96

PERSPECTIVES ON TECHNOLOGY AND WORK ORGANIZATION

Jeffrey K. Liker

Industrial and Operations Engineering, University of Michigan, Ann Arbor, Michigan 48109-2117; e-mail: liker@umich.edu

Carol J. Haddad

Department of Interdisciplinary Technology, Eastern Michigan University, Ypsilanti, Michigan; e-mail: idt_haddad@online.emich.edu

Jennifer Karlin

Industrial and Operations Engineering, University of Michigan, Ann Arbor, Michigan 48109-2117; e-mail: jennifer.karlin@swe.org

KEY WORDS: technology impacts, technology implementation

ABSTRACT

This chapter summarizes and synthesizes some major perspectives on the relationship between technology and the nature of work. Given the complexity of technology and its impacts, the chapter elucidates different perspectives on this topic rather than summaries of detailed findings in a particular area of technology. The central thesis of the chapter is a follows: Technology's impact on work is contingent on a broad set of factors, including the reasons for its introduction, management philosophy, the labor-management contract, the degree of a shared agreement about technology and work organization, and the process of technology development and implementation. How this is viewed varies with different theoretical paradigms. Looking through a variety of paradigms provides a richer view of the phenomenon, though integrating these perspectives remains problematic. Historically, technology was treated as a deterministic causal force with predictable impacts. More recently there is a recognition of the complexity of technology and its relationship to work which is both bi-directional and dependent on a number of contingent factors. One set of factors integral to the "impact" of technology is the dynamics of the change process and in fact the change process and "out-

comes" are inextricably linked. We conclude that the social reality of technology implementation is highly complex. Very different technologies are
brought into very different social settings for very different reasons, often
with completely opposite effects and thus complex theories that recognize
the emergent and socially constructed nature of technology are needed.

INTRODUCTION

Among students of work organization, it is hard to imagine a topic that has
generated as much interest, and as much ambivalence, as the impact of advanced technology. The interest comes from the fact that technology is ubiquitous. Computers have invaded our workplace, our homes, our televisions, our
cars, our coffee makers, and our watches. In many ways they make our lives
easier, and those of us who adapt wonder how we ever lived without them. In
other ways technology complicates our lives, and simple tasks become complex. Think of the tinkering automobile owners who used to fix their own car-
buretor and tune-up their car; now they find when the engine won't start that
the problem is in a computer chip they cannot take apart and fix. Think of the
times we have struggled to get that paper out to a journal only to find the computer file won't open or the printer will not print. "My dog ate my paper" has
been replaced as a student excuse with "I lost my computer file."

While these anecdotes are merely quaint, the implications of technology for
work and the worker can be quite serious. On the one hand, the manager of
computer-integrated manufacturing may find that s\he has a fascinating, challenging job with numerous career alternatives. Similarly, the electrician in a
manufacturing plant sent to learn to repair programmable automation may find
a whole new world opens up of interesting work and job opportunities. On the
other hand, the skilled machinist may find the door slammed shut on his or her
career when programmable controllers can operate the lathe that used to be
adjusted manually.

We began work on this chapter expecting to summarize the state of knowledge on the "social impacts of technology." In reviewing our own experiences,
conducting research on this topic, and reviewing the recent literature, we
discovered a number of things:

There are many types of technology—Programmable controllers in factories running physical operations, transfer presses that automate an entire
stamping line, Computer-Aided-Design systems that automate pieces of draft-
ing work, word processors in offices, automatic tellers in banks, and on and on.
Surely these all are very different technologies with very different implications.

There are many social contexts for technology adoption—Bringing automation into an adversarial union-management environment where manage-

ment is seeking to downsize is fundamentally different from bringing that same technology into a rapidly growing company with a highly cooperative management-labor climate. Adding technology as a tool for a professional decision-maker is fundamentally different than automating clerical work where a claims adjuster becomes a clerk pushing buttons. Thus, the type of job you are starting with matters, as does the labor-management climate, and other contextual features.

There are many approaches to selecting and implementing technology— Technology selected with a high degree of participation, for example, by those people who will use the technology, is likely to be perceived in a fundamentally different way by the receiver than technology bought and implemented without any consultation. Trying a pilot in an area and then mutually evaluating the technology by a team is fundamentally different from shutting the plant down for a complete technological renovation and reopening the doors with people now in new jobs.

There are many different perspectives on the technology and on who wins and loses. A recent survey of the field (on which we drew heavily for this chapter) identified over 20 different research paradigms on the impact of technology (Lewis 1998). These paradigms see the problem, what constitutes useful data on the problem, and how to analyze that data in fundamentally different ways. Moreover, they have different value implications for whether the technology is good, bad, or indifferent.

Given the complexity of technology and its impacts, we decided to focus on different perspectives on this topic rather than on summaries of detailed findings in a particular area of technology. The central thesis of the chapter is as follows: Technology's impact on work is contingent on a broad set of factors, including the reasons for its introduction, management philosophy, the labor-management contract, the degree of a shared agreement about technology and work organization, and the process of technology development and implementation. How this is viewed varies with different theoretical paradigms. Looking through a variety of paradigms provides a richer view of the phenomenon, though integrating these perspectives remains problematic.

The purpose of this chapter is to summarize and synthesize some major perspectives on the relationship between technology and the nature of work. Historically, technology was treated as a deterministic causal force with predictable impacts. More recently, there is a recognition of the complexity of technology and its relationship to work that is both bi-directional and dependent on a number of contingent factors. One set of factors integral to the "impact" of technology is the dynamics of the change process, and in fact the change process and "outcomes" are probably inextricably linked.

To create some structure to our discussion, we introduce in the next section a "contingency model of technology and organization." Following that, we take a different slice and discuss the impact of technology through the lenses of a variety of different perspectives or paradigms. We conclude with a discussion of what this means for research in this area.

CONTINGENCY MODEL OF TECHNOLOGY AND ORGANIZATION

We have argued that the "impacts" of technology depend on a variety of factors (see also Liker et al 1993). Figure 1 presents a model that defines sets of variables that the impact of technology is contingent upon. This model is similar to an open-systems model that shows interactions between all sets of variables (Nadler & Tushman 1997). In fact the model can be shown as the effects of organizational context contingent upon the nature of technology. Our specific model in Figure 1 focuses on the impacts of technology because that is the focus of this chapter, not because we believe it has any absolute degree of supremacy in the model. In the next section we argue that the relative importance of each of the factors in Figure 1 and the definitions of these factors all vary across different sociological paradigms. In this section we simply provide a generic description of each.

Technology can be characterized in many different ways, from narrow notions of hardware only to broad concepts that include almost anything. We

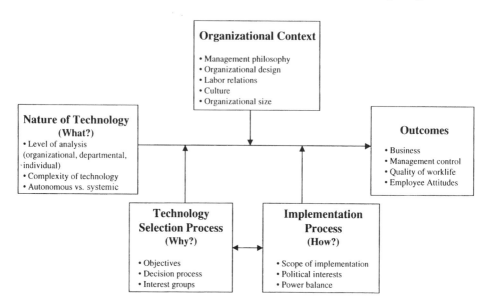

Figure 1

start with the definition by Tornatzky & Fleischer (1990:11) of technology as: "knowledge-derived tools, artifacts, and devices by which people extend and interact with their environment." While this definition is quite broad and includes "social technologies" like self-directed work teams and quality circles, for this paper we are focusing more narrowly on process technologies and their associated hardware and software.

There are many different ways to distinguish different types of technologies, for example, distinguishing computer-integrated technologies from stand alone automation. We can also look at technologies at varying levels of analysis. Woodward's (1965) classic study focused on technology at the organizational level. For example, the classification of technology as large batch refers to the core technology of a factory. She found that associated with making large batches of product were a set of organizational characteristics. It is quite common within the same factory to see multiple technologies even at the level of Woodward's generic description, for example, a batch operation (e.g., injection molded plastics) feeding a sequential, assembly operation. To capture these differences we need to move down to the department level.

Perrow's (1967) well-known classification of the complexity of technology at the department level identifies the degree of uncertainty associated with core departmental tasks. Tasks high in uncertainty tend to be associated with more loosely structured "organic" organizational forms, compared to routine, programmable tasks that can be managed by more mechanistic bureaucracies. But core tasks at the department level obscure the fact that different individuals may use different technologies, for example, the drafter using a drawing board may sit alongside one using a CAD terminal (Liker & Fleischer 1989).

Other types of classifications look at technologies as innovations when they are first brought into an organization. Rogers' (1983) well-known typology of innovations helps predict the extent of diffusion of the technology (e.g., relative advantage compared to alternatives, compatibility with existing values, trialability of the technology, etc). Another useful distinction is between autonomous and systemic technologies (Wolfe 1994, Brannen et al 1999). Autonomous technologies can be implemented as relatively independent units with relatively small impacts outside of the local area in which they are implemented. For example, if one robot is implemented in a corner of a large factory to do a specialty paint operation, it is apt to get relatively little attention except of course from the individuals who used to do the painting or those who now service the robot. On the other hand, a computer-integrated manufacturing system has a very broad scope and broad systemic impacts on almost all aspects of the business and all people in the factory. Of course, even this simple distinction is difficult to apply to an actual technology because any technology, no matter how seemingly isolated in its impact, will have broad systemic impacts on people and social organization.

The nature of the particular technology implemented obviously has a bearing on its impacts. But according to Figure 1, a set of organizational variables also play critical roles in shaping the impact, even of the same technology. For example, Shaiken (1985) observes cases in which programmable automation raises skill levels when NC programming is assigned to machinists and others, whereas skill levels are reduced when NC programming is assigned to specialist programmers. He argues this is the result of management discretion in designing jobs. These organizational variables can be characterized in many ways. We distinguish the organizational context, a static concept, from the processes of selecting the technology and the implementation process. By including the technology selection process, we are arguing that the motivations for bringing in the technology, and the process by which key decisions are made, shape both how the technology is implemented and the consequences of bringing in the technology. We show these context and process variables as moderators of the influence of technology. In sum, according to the model in Figure 1, outcomes of technology depend on characteristics of the technology itself that interact with the organizational context and process of selection and implementation.

MULTIPLE PARADIGMS ON TECHNOLOGY IMPACTS

While most, if not all, of the contemporary literature assumes the underlying structure of the contingency model in Figure 1, accounts of the same phenomenon vary dramatically across studies and researchers because of different paradigmatic views. One researcher will emphasize the nature of the technology chosen with a nod toward the implementation process. The next sees those issues as being equal in importance to culture and other pieces of the organization context. In order to make sense of the many paradigms, we constructed a 2x2 table, which categorizes the views along two axes (see Figure 2). We should state up front that the two dimensions in this table are more accurately viewed as continuous, with the cells being regions along the continuum.

The vertical axis distinguishes static views of technology impacts from dynamic views that consider a more complex interplay of technology and organization over time. On the static end of the scale, technology's impact is viewed as a billiard ball (Brannen et al 1999) in which the ball has a predictable impact on other balls on the table, though this impact may be complex to model mathematically. If context is considered in these paradigms, it is a static view of context that does not change over time or interact with the technology in complex ways. In static views the particular implementation process is largely inconsequential, and the outcomes are solely dependent on the choice of technology, existing organizational context, or both. The more dynamic paradigms

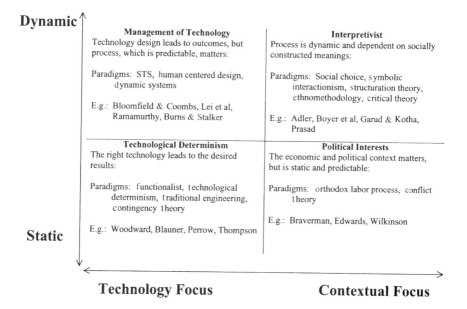

Dynamic

Management of Technology Technology design leads to outcomes, but process, which is predictable, matters: Paradigms: STS, human centered design, dynamic systems E.g.: Bloomfield & Coombs, Lei et al, Ramamurthy, Burns & Stalker	**Interpretivist** Process is dynamic and dependent on socially constructed meanings: Paradigms: Social choice, symbolic interactionism, structuration theory, ethnomethodology, critical theory E.g.: Adler, Boyer et al, Garud & Kotha, Prasad
Technological Determinism The right technology leads to the desired results: Paradigms: functionalist, technological determinism, traditional engineering, contingency theory E.g.: Woodward, Blauner, Perrow, Thompson	**Political Interests** The economic and political context matters, but is static and predictable: Paradigms: orthodox labor process, conflict theory E.g.: Braverman, Edwards, Wilkinson

Static

Technology Focus   **Contextual Focus**

Figure 2

look at the implementation of technology as a complex process that unfolds over time, and they highlight the social process of transformation.

The horizontal axis contrasts paradigms that focus primarily on the technology and its characteristics as having causal efficacy from those that focus primarily on the social context. A paradigm concerned with the social context rates the organizational context of the firm as equal to, or more important than, the technology itself. When these axes are combined, we have the four views depicted in Figure 2: technological determinism, management of technology, political interests, and interpretivist. We have sorted paradigms into these four categories, recognizing that some fit more neatly than others.

The functionalist, technological determinist, and traditional engineering paradigms focus largely on characteristics of the technology. Both static and acontextual, these perspectives assume that the right choice of technology will lead to desired outcomes regardless of the organizational context. Those who subscribe to the technological determinism paradigm view technology as the causal variable to which all other factors are subservient. In a societal sense, as Pacey (1983) notes, technological determinists "present technical advance as a process of steady development dragging human society along in its train" (p. 24). Both Woodward (1958) and Blauner (1964) saw a progression of technology, with more complex forms leading to a more humane, organic organization compared to the traditional assembly line. Some underlying propositions that apply to an industrial technology determinist view are: (*a*) Technology is the solution to the problems organizations face, particularly with respect to competitiveness; (*b*) organizations must adapt to accommodate the technology, after it is installed; (*c*) technology type determines the best organizational design (Woodward 1958, 1965); and (*d*) advanced technology tends to drive organizational change in a democratic direction toward reduced management control (Zuboff 1988, Walton & Susman 1987). In short, technology is not only a deterministic variable, but a static one as well.

As is usually the case with simplistic 2x2 tables, some paradigms do not fit neatly into one cell or another. For example, we include in the technology determinism cell the work of some contingency theorists as illustrated by some of the early work of Perrow (1967) and of Thompson (1967), even though their models consider organizational context to a degree. Their models are not unlike Woodward's argument that the best organizational form is contingent on some characteristic of the core technology. If you know the technology, you know the "right" organizational form. In Perrow's (1967) model, the key technology characteristic is the degree of uncertainty, which then determines how mechanistic versus organic the organization must be to be effective. In Thompson's (1967) model, the nature of interdependence inherent in the tasks and technology determines the degree of organizational interdependence needed for effectiveness. A more accurate representation of these theories would show them on the horizontal dimension somewhere in the middle between technology focus and contextual focus, though still toward the static end of the vertical dimension.

Management of technology, the group of paradigms that are process focused but that still concentrate to a large degree on characteristics of the technology, include sociotechnical systems (STS), human centered design, and dynamic systems (Majchrzak 1988, Liker & Majchrzak 1994). This framework assumes that the right technology design, in combination with the right implementation process, leads to the desired outcomes, provided the predictable process is followed with care. According to Bloomfield & Coombs (1992), the "deliberate interventions in the culture and therefore the understandings and practices of an organization" are the process by which the proper technology is embedded in the firm.

A management-of-technology (MOT) view conceives of technology in relation to the process of change. Technology management has become a cross-disciplinary academic field of inquiry, built from the foundations of strategic management theory, systems theory, organizational behavior, sociology, economics, finance, political science, and industrial relations (Badawy & Badawy 1993). Noori (1990) has described MOT as the link between engineering and management. The management of technological change embraces two tenets:

one, an integrative systems approach to change; and two, strategic planning of the technology. The systems perspective can itself be viewed through different lenses. Gaynor (1996) discusses the need to manage the system and the pieces, and to integrate "the 'pieces' into an acceptable 'whole' by focusing attention on the interdependence of the pieces " (p. 15). Sociotechnical theorists, on the other hand, believe that the way to attain systems integration is to systematically analyze the social/organizational and technological subsystems and re-design work processes as needed (Taylor & Asadorian 1986, Davis & Taylor 1979, Pasmore & Sherwood 1978). The strategic planning view most common in the MOT literature is premised on a belief that technology adoption and implementation proceed in linear, sequential fashion delineated by stages and guided by planning and strategy (D Preece 1995). A management-by-objectives approach is applicable to this paradigm of technological change (Sankar 1991:357). Again we should note that all these perspectives grouped together under MOT are not uniform. For example, arguably sociotechnical systems perspectives are in the middle between the technology focus and the contextual focus, and they try to achieve a balanced view of the two.

A third category of paradigms presented in the lower right-hand quadrant of Figure 2 is one in which the political context is considered, but in a static way. These paradigms assume people act and react according to static, predictable roles, which are generally determined by their places in the organizational hierarchy and relative power differentials. It should be noted that while their roles may be static and predictable, the outcomes are not. One example of this paradigm is labor process theory. Influenced by the writings of Karl Marx, labor process theorists believe that management introduces new workplace technology to exert control over the labor process and wrest it away from craft and production workers. Attempted management control takes many forms: the separation of work/task planning from execution (Braverman 1974), the replacement of labor—especially skilled craft labor—with machines (Marx 1906) or the use of machines to permit lesser-skilled workers to perform craft work (Yellowitz 1977), deskilling of work (Noble 1979, Wood 1982), monitoring of employee performance (Shaiken 1985), and reduction of union influence and power (Bennett 1977). At the heart of this struggle is capitalist competition, which pushes firms to seek newer, cheaper, and more predictable production methods (Edwards 1979). However, workers do not simply succumb to management attempts to control work, and they are sometimes victorious in disrupting production (Montgomery 1979).

The final view, where a dynamic process and context connect, is called interpretivist. The dynamic process and dependency on the social context of the firm in the interpretivist perspective are represented in paradigms such as social choice, structuration theory, and critical theory. Adler (1992:7) describes this as the "third generation" and what has become the dominant view of academic thought on the impact of implementing new technologies in a firm, one which "progressively veered away from the big generalizations." Dean et al (1992) call new technology a "Rorschach test for organizational leadership," where the social context of the firm is the framework through which the manager sees the choice and outcomes of technology.

The interpretivist perspective has its roots in symbolic interactionism and concepts of the social construction of reality. Barley (1986, 1988) has attempted to reconcile interactionist perspectives on technology, which suggest highly particularistic impacts of technology, with structural perspectives, which assume systematic effects, through the use of Gidden's (1979) concept of structuration. Barley (1986) argues that technology presents "an occasion for structuring." Structure in this sense is viewed as an emergent process rather than a static configuration. Technology is viewed as having a reality that can bring about patterned social interaction. Barley (1986) studied the introduction of CT scanner technologies in hospitals and found they had the effect of empowering technicians whose roles became more central to the interpretation of the data, making judgments formerly left to "professionals." But this occurred to differing degrees in the two hospitals he studied. He argues that specific features of the technology brought about new patterns of role interaction, albeit to different degrees in different contexts.

A different slant on this perspective is taken by feminist scholars who view technology as socially constructed around traditional gender roles (Wacjman 1991, Morgall 1993). The way technology is viewed and applied is shaped by the dominant male role in society. Weick emphasizes the subjective interpretations of technology and the high degree of uncertainty associated with technology through the concept of "equivoque," an experience "that admits of several possible or plausible interpretations and therefore can be esoteric, subject to misunderstandings, uncertain, complex, and recondite" (1990:2).

MULTIPLE PARADIGMS AND TECHNOLOGY IMPACTS

Management Philosophy

In Table 1, we apply these four theoretical paradigms to our model of technology and organization. Technological determinists assume that the best way of managing depends on characteristics of the technology. Long-linked, sequential technologies are best managed using Theory X (McGregor 1957) and Tayloristic approaches (Taylor 1947). Since there is little need for reciprocal interdependence on an assembly line, workers can work independently motivated by a system of rewards and punishment, with a top down planning system that is very effective (Woodward 1958, Thompson 1967). On the other hand, more complex technologies, like continuous process technologies that are more

Table 1 Paradigmatic views of technology impacts model

	Technological Determinism: • Technology is a causal variable • Organizations must adapt to technology	Management of Technology: • Organizations are open-systems • Technology and organization can be planned and integrated	Political Interests: • Static, predictable interests influence outcomes • Power differentials lead to conflict in capitalist enterprises	Interpretivist: • Technology is socially constructed • Technology implementation as an emergent process
Organizational Context:				
Philosophy	Contingency perspective; technology determines management approach	Strategic focus; socio-technical systems orientation	Marxist, conflict perspective	Open dialogue about emergent meanings
Culture	Traditional engineering	Planning and participation	Highly political; authoritarian	Emergent and dynamic learning organization
Org Design	Contingent on complexity of technology	Organic; matrix; flexible; open system; cross-functional	Bureaucratic; hierarchical; highly stratified; rigid roles; subdivision of labor	Organizing process
Labor Relations	Traditional and non-participative	Least antagonistic and most participatory	Highly adversarial	Negotiated order
Nature of Technology	Deterministic; measureable	Must fit with strategy	Control systems; labor displacing and deskilling	Socially constructed
Technology Selection Process	Technology is a given; organizational impacts studied	Technology selection should occur only after other steps in planning process have been followed; technology choice depends on strategic goals of organization	Dependent upon relative bargaining power of labor vs. management	Process of negotiating interpretations and meanings
Technology Implementation Process	Technology is put in place, and organization must adapt	There is a predictable process for implementing tech; steps must be followed sequentially; need user involvement	Management will attempt to control all decisions	Emergent; socially constructed
Outcomes	Outcomes are predictable and measureable but technology may not perform as expected because of engineering bias in design	If tech mgmt steps have been followed, outcomes can be quantitatively measured	Technology unlikely to perform as expected because of employee resistance and lack of employee consultation	Outcomes open to interpretation; emergent and variable over time

automated, break down in unpredictable ways and require more horizontal communication and empowered, skilled workers (Woodward 1958, Perrow 1967).

Marxist theory provides a philosophical foundation for most of the political interests paradigms. In these models capitalist enterprises are in a natural state of conflict (Edwards 1979), creating a perpetual tension of differing organizational goals and perspectives between labor and management.

The philosophical foundations of the management of technology paradigm are quite different. As discussed, there is an emphasis on managerial strategy guiding practice (Chandler 1962), but in this case applied to the adoption and implementation of new technology. A second philosophical basis for this MOT paradigm is sociotechnical systems (STS) theory, which emphasizes the interaction of system elements. Most applications of STS incorporate worker participation in planning and implementation of decisions (Walton 1985). Similarly, human-centered design assumes that certain predictable characteristics of technologies fit human cognitive and work styles, but that the particular configuration of appropriate features is best defined with the participation of users of the technology (Kidd 1988, 1992).

The interpretivist perspective leads largely to descriptive and analytic research that provides a rich picture of the process of technological change. It is less prescriptive but does lead to the philosophy of encouraging open dialogue and negotiation about new technologies, their possibilities, and their impacts. Prasad (1993) suggests that to avoid "mismanaged meanings" it is important to openly discuss users' interpretations. Simonsen (1997) prescribes methods for developing more contextualized designs. Garud & Kotha (1994) use the brain as a metaphor to generate insights into how firms might design flexible production systems. The brain is a self-organizing system capable of responding rapidly to a broad range of external stimuli. Using this metaphor they suggest a prescriptive model of collaborative technology design in which flexibility can be enhanced by employing practices that promote distributed processes occurring in a parallel manner. De Sanctis & Poole (1994) view "adaptive structuration" theory as a particularly powerful approach to understanding how new technologies focused on supporting collaborative group work can influence group structure and dynamics.

ORGANIZATIONAL CULTURE (IMPLIED BY PARADIGMS)

The philosophical orientations of top management clearly affect an organization's predominant culture. Zammuto & O'Connor (1992) find that firms have a wide range of success in implementing advanced manufacturing technologies and argue that organizational culture is one of the critical factors distinguishing different degrees of success.

Organizations managed using a technological determinist paradigm would tend to place great value on traditional engineering thinking. It is rooted in the belief, extending back to Andrew Ure and Charles Babbage, that application of mechanical principles to factory systems can enhance productive capacity and lower the cost of goods (Mitcham 1994). One engineering enthusiast blames "anti-technologists" for dampening the enthusiasm of engineers (Florman 1976).

The organizational culture in modern capitalist organizations suggested by a political interests perspective is one of highly authoritarian management and resisting workers, with continuing conflict between these groups. Formal power resides at the top of the organizational hierarchy, but those below earn informal and even formal power on the basis of knowledge, skill, and/or union bargaining strength. Labor-management communication and trust are low. Morale is low as well, except when front-line employees are able to exercise power through the means described above. Advanced technologies place greater power in the hands of managers and simply fuel the hierarchical and authoritarian culture.

The culture of an organization implied by a technology management perspective is very different, and in fact there is a great deal of variance within this paradigm. Great value is placed on planning for change to minimize unpredictability, and on involving cross-disciplinary teams in the process—teams that may also span hierarchical boundaries. Advanced technology is assumed to contribute to greater openness and sharing of information from this perspective (Noori 1990, Lei et al 1996, Walton & Susman 1987).

The interpretivist perspective is all about culture, but culture as an emergent phenomenon that is much more dynamic and fragile than structural perspectives would suggest (Prasad 1993). Thus, an interpretivist perspective does not presuppose a particular organizational culture associated with the implementation of new technology, but rather, tries to use overt symbols and deeper underlying assumptions to decode the culture of a particular organization.

LABOR RELATIONS

The final aspect of organization context we consider is labor relations. From a technological-determinist perspective, a traditional labor-management relationship is generally assumed. If one were to consider a unionized environment from this perspective, collective bargaining would focus on limited subjects, which do not include decisions about technology type or design, and with traditional lines of demarcation. From a political interests' perspective, labor relations play a central role as labor and management struggle to control technology (Wilkinson 1983). An organization from a technology management perspective is viewed as having the potential of participatory labor-management cooperation in the selection and design of technology guided by a common vision and set of interests. Walton & McKersie (1991) describe how a relationship characterized by mutual commitment/cooperation can be used to effectively manage technological change. Haddad (1994; and Haddad, in press) gives examples of worker and union involvement even at the technology design stage. Yet Cohen-Rosenthal (1997) chides sociotechnical theorists and practitioners for ignoring unions in their analyses and for making naive assumptions about political interests.

An interactionist perspective can account for varied labor relations outcomes of technology, depending on specific contextual features. Barley (1988) uses the concept of "roles" and views roles as an emergent, contextual feature of organization. He notes that the traditional role relationships between radiologists, physicians specializing in diagnosing X-rays, and radiological technicians were segregated and hierarchical. CT scanners altered the tasks and roles of radiologists and technologists. In one hospital the emergent roles significantly reduced status distances and correspondingly reduced conflict between radiologists and technologists, while this effect was much smaller in the second hospital, which operated in a different context. Pichault (1995) investigated four case studies of the introduction of computer-based information systems (in a chain store, bank, teaching hospital, and a news agency) and found very different influences on the distribution of power. Management style differences seemed to account to a large degree for these different patterns.

NATURE OF TECHNOLOGY

Each paradigm also has a different perspective on the nature of technology itself. A technological determinist organization most likely considers technology as self-regulating with a minimum of human intervention. Using Bright's (1966) typology, this would be machinery that "anticipates action required and adjusts to provide it." (II:210). The presumption is of course that workers add variability to the production process, and therefore that it is better to rely solely upon the technology. Butera & Thurman (1984), however, point out that even under conditions of full automation, significant operator involvement is needed because of frequent disturbances. A political interests organization would view the technology in terms of its potential for controlling and eliminating labor, with the added objective of deskilling the remaining jobs. Political interest theorists search for feedback systems, which they presume employers will use in seeking to monitor and control employee performance.

A firm adhering to the technology management perspective would see different types of technology as fitting with different strategic business objectives that can be identified a priori (Cleland & Bursic 1992, Preece 1995). In fact, technological change may come after organizational innovation (Haddad 1996), which is opposite the direction assumed under technological determinism. When the sociotechnical systems philosophy is factored in, additional criteria are likely to be considered, namely the potential of particular technology design features to support ease of use, organizational learning, human resource policies, and organizational structure and behavior. These include issues of the types of implementation approaches that best fit with the technology, such as training—how much and what type will be needed (Flynn 1988, Majchrzak 1988), the compensation and reward system, and the likelihood of middle management resistance (Noori 1990).

The interactionist perspective takes into account differences in meaning of the technology through design and implementation. The nature of technology is socially constructed. Turkle (1984:13) distinguishes between the "instrumental computer" and the "subjective computer." She observes how computers evoke a great deal of emotion and hold very different meanings for different people. In his study of the computerization of administrative services in an HMO, Prasad (1993) found a number of different and distinct conceptions of the computer. Some associated it with increased professionalism, making the hospital a more "professional place to work." Others used anthropomorphic imagery to talk about it, identifying its superhuman characteristics as if it were a living thing. By probing deeper Prasad (1993) was able to uncover some of the underlying reasons for these different images. For example, the "professionalism" perspective was linked in some employees' minds with an underlying anxiety that this relatively "small" hospital was not a professional place to work; for them the computer was a symbol of a more modern, sophisticated facility. Let us contrast this with a small, family-oriented factory in the Midwest where programmable automation was brought in, threatening to eliminate the jobs of some employees and enhance the positions of others (Liker et al 1987). There were sharp differences in the meaning of the technology in these two groups of employees, which corresponded directly with their position in the social structure. Threatened employees spoke passionately about the technology in terms of feelings of loss, while those whose jobs were enhanced spoke more dispassionately about what the technology would mean for their new challenging roles and the competitiveness of the firm. One does not see the threatened feelings of a portion of the shopfloor workers among the hospital "professionals." Similarly, even expert systems were not perceived as threatening to accountants who knew that only an inconsequential portion of their jobs could be automated by the expert systems and who had a choice of whether or not to use them (Liker & Sindi 1997).

TECHNOLOGY SELECTION AND IMPLEMENTATION

The views of technology selection and implementation processes also vary across the four paradigms. The technological determinism framework has generally started with the assumption that firms have already adopted the technology. It is taken as a given. But one would assume that the technology is selected by the managers, generally with the advice of the engineering unit, based on rational, technical criteria. The implications for organizational design can then be worked out afterward. Though this perspective recognizes one has to change the organization to fit the technology, it is a matter of design, almost like an architect designing a physical structure. As for the implementation process, new technology precedes organizational or human resource changes, and the organization is left to adapt. There is no conception of managing a change process.

From a political interests perspective, management will attempt to exert control over technology selection and implementation decisions by centralizing decision-making—in the hands of upper-management during the selection process, and with middle managers and technologists during the implementation process (Zammuto & O'Connor 1992). However, Thomas (1994) among others recognizes that upper-management control cannot be assumed, for "choices of technology could be influenced as much by efforts to alter structure and power relations as they could by efforts to reinforce or reproduce existing relations" (p. 229).

In a firm following the prescriptive tenets of technology management, the selection and implementation processes are planned according to a rational, predictable logic, and a great deal of research and thought have gone into how to make these decisions and how to plan the change process to increase the probability of successful outcomes. During the selection phase, data about technology needs are systematically collected and analyzed (Bancroft 1992), and choices are made about which technology types best meet the strategic needs of the organization. Cost-benefit analyses are also performed as part of the planning and justification process (Gerwin & Kolodny 1992, Gaynor 1990, Noori 1990), and these procedures, too, influence technology choice. As part of the implementation process, plans are developed to prepare the site for the technology, provide user support, manage training and operations, and maintain the new technology to reduce the chances of system failure (Bancroft 1992, Majchrzak & Gasser 1992). Ramamurthy (1995), based on survey data, finds evidence that manufacturing firms using a high-quality planning system, measured in terms of scope/comprehensiveness and adaptability, achieved higher performance from their advanced manufacturing systems, and managers were more satisfied with the outcomes than companies without a strong planning system.

As a different variant of the management of technology, STS proponents advocate technology selection and design as a participative process (Taylor & Asadorian 1986, Davis & Taylor 1979, Pasmore & Sherwood 1978). STS starts with an open-systems model and emphasizes interaction with the environment and that organizations are living, dynamic systems. Yet the classical tools of STS born out of the Tavistock Institute are primarily static, mapping variances in the technical system and relating them to static descriptions of roles and functions (Pasmore & Sherwood 1978). A broad cross-section of participants are brought through a visioning exercise to develop a vision of the future social and technical systems and how they can work together and then identify a detailed implementation plan. There is some recognition of the dynamic, unpredictable nature of the social and technical change, but the assumption is that the change can be managed much more smoothly by a cross-functional team systematically planning and executing according to plan.

The human-centered design perspective, rooted in human factors engineering, is even more focused on rational prediction and control of user reactions to the technology (Liker & Majchrzak 1994). At one extreme, Majchrzak & Gasser (1992) have attempted to develop an expert system that takes as inputs characteristics of the organizational structure, people, and culture and advises the user on the optimal design of the "human infrastructure" for technology and how to implement the technology. It is assumed that technology is a fixed thing to be used by an organism whose reactions can be predicted and controlled. (More recent versions of this technology allow for user interaction with the system as technology implementation progresses.)

While the interpretivist perspective does not focus on prediction and control, it has the potential of greatly enhancing our understanding of how technology decisions are really made and how the human side of technological change can be intelligently managed through the change process. It is recognized that there is no one reason for technology selection, and the social construction of the technology and the organization it will lead to are negotiated processes among many actors. The entire "enacted" process of selection and implementation is viewed as unfolding without clear dividing lines between a selection phase and an implementation phase. By understanding some of the general metaphors people use to understand the technology, how these meanings vary across individuals and groups in the organization, and analyzing the process as it unfolds, there would seem to be an opportunity for jointly developing the people and the technology toward desirable ends. The brain metaphor (Garud & Kotha 1994) discussed earlier provides what many interactionists might consider an effective design paradigm. This metaphor assumes a self-organizing, emergent process of design and implementation.

CONCLUSIONS

As we began the arduous task of synthesizing a voluminous literature on technology and work organization, we noticed its diversity and the contradictory claims and observations. Thus, to "review" the literature it seemed more useful to organize the diversity of views than try to identify common findings and yet "unanswered" questions. In identifying a range of perspectives on the implications of technology for work organization, we have not tried to develop our own prescriptions or to synthesize these disparate paradigms. We in fact do not believe they can be synthesized. As described by Morgan (1997), these paradigms are different metaphors that provide different windows on the same phenomenon. Morgan has emphasized repeatedly that multiple metaphors can be used to enhance our understanding of social reality so long as we recognize that they are metaphors and do not mistake the metaphor for the realities.

In the case of technology the social reality is quite complex. Very different technologies are brought into very different social settings for very different reasons, often with completely opposing effects. Statistical studies have attempted to generalize predictable effects of the technology and found statistically significant correlates (Dean et al 1992, Dean & Snell 1991, Hull & Collins 1987). But for each study finding that the computer centralizes power, another will find that computer technology decentralizes and democratizes the workplace. For example, Dean et al (1992) use a survey of 185 firms to see if the use of advanced manufacturing technology is associated with centralization of power, as Marxist theories would suggest, or decentralization, as the "idealist" perspective would suggest. They find mixed evidence, partly supporting both perspectives. Are such observations useful? One gets the picture of a dog endlessly chasing its tail, always out of reach. Bloomfield & Coombs (1992) argue that the question of whether technology centralizes or decentralizes power is the wrong question. The right question, they argue, is: What are the *symbolic* dimensions of the development of information systems, and how do these vary by professional discipline? This is certainly an interesting question, but is it sufficient to understand differences in meanings assigned to technology?

Figure 2 sorted paradigms into four quadrants. Admittedly, this is an oversimplification. Not all paradigms fit perfectly. For example, contingency theory could fit into the determinist or frozen roles' quadrant. Lewis (1998) identified over 20 paradigms and mapped them in a more complex way with many on the boundaries between quadrants. But the question is: Does this represent progress?

Lewis (1998) argues that by deconstructing views on technology impacts and then reconstructing them into a conceptual framework we make progress. The point is not to synthesize the paradigms but to "employ their distinctions, maintaining mutual co-existence within a multidimensional understanding" (p. 27). If one believes the model we presented in Figure 1, it seems clear that there are some benefits, and weaknesses, to each of the quadrants. All but the interpretivist perspective oversimplify reality, either by ignoring context or by taking a static perspective, or both. The interpretivist perspective accounts for process and context in a richer way, and as Adler (1992:8) poignantly observes: "The dominant image of the future of work in this research is that of a kaleidoscope of complex patterns, constantly shifting and forming no overall tendency." But with no ability to generalize we are left with highly particularistic accounts of the implementation of technology under a myriad of circumstances.

Adler (1992) provides some hope that a fourth generation of research, superceding the interactionist aversion to generalization, can take into account process and context in a dynamic way, yet leave room for the role of systematic social patterns. Adler (1992) argues this work moves beyond both class conflict and local variability. He argues this new generation allows for a "soft" technological determinism, "one that neither underestimates the causal roles of variables nor telescopes the time frame required for technological constraints to manifest themselves" (p. 9). Adler's edited volume does indeed present a richer and more complex collection of research than many of the simplistic views summarized in this chapter. Nonetheless, one does not get the sense of a synthesis or an agreement on general trends in the impacts of technology. Nor is there a consensus on the critical contextual factors that condition its impacts, nor of general trends in social processes likely to unfold.

Thus, we are left with many differing, competing perspectives painting different portaits of the impacts of technology. Perhaps diversity is a good thing, as Lewis (1998) argues. Perhaps the intellectual debate is all we can hope for. In the meantime, the speed of technological change is quickening and its complexity grows. It is rare that technological change is "autonomous" with localized effects; more likely, technology influences complex social networks and acts sometimes as an integrative force and other times as a disintegrative force that separates people. If complex phenomena call for complex theories, we will need even more complex theories to account for the impact of technological change.

ACKNOWLEDGMENTS

The authors gratefully acknowledge support given by the Air Force Office of Scientific Research through the Japan Technology Management Program at the University of Michigan, as well as support provided by a Spring-Summer Faculty Research Award granted by Eastern Michigan University.

Visit the *Annual Reviews home page* at
http://www.AnnualReviews.org.

Literature Cited

Adler PS. 1992. Introduction. In *Technology and the Future of Work*, ed. PS Adler, pp. 3–14. New York: Oxford Univ. Press

Badawy MK, Badawy AM. 1993. Directions for scholarly research in management of technology—editorial commentary. *J. Engin. Technol. Mgmt.* 10:1–5

Barley SR. 1986. Technology as an occasion for structuring: evidence from observations of CT scanners and the social order of radiology departments. *Admin. Sci. Q.* 31: 78–108

Barley SR. 1988. On technology, time, and social order: technically induced change in the temporal organization of radiological work. In *Making Time Ethnographies of High Technology Organizations*, ed. FA Dubinskas, pp. 123–69. Philadelphia: Temple Univ. Press

Bancroft NH. 1992. *New Partnerships for Managing Technological Change*. New York: Wiley

Bennett JW. 1977. *Iron workers in Woods Run and Johnstown: the union era, 1865–1895*. PhD diss., Univ. Pittsburgh, Penn.

Blauner, R. 1964. *Alienation and Freedom: The Factory Worker and His Industry*. Chicago: Univ. Chicago Press

Bloomfield BP, Coombs R. 1992. Information technology, control and power: the centralization and decentralization debate revisited. *J. Mgmt. Stud.* 29:459–84

Brannen MY, Liker JK, Fruin M. 1999. Recontextualization and factory-to-factory transfer from Japan to the U.S.: the case of NSK. In *Remade in America: Transplanting and transforming Japanese Production Systems*, ed. JK Liker, M Fruin, P Adler, pp. 117–52. New York: Oxford Univ. Press

Bright JR. 1966. The relationship of increasing automation to skill requirements. In *The Employment Impact of Technological Change*, Appendix, Vol. II, pp. 203–21. Washington, DC: Natl. Commiss. on Technol., Automation and Econ. Prog.

Burns T, Stalker GM. 1961 *The Management. of Innovation*. London: Tavistock

Butera F, Thurman JE. 1984. *Automation and Work Design. A Study Prepared by the International Labour Office*. Amsterdam: North-Holland

Chandler AD. 1962. *Strategy and Structure: Chapters in the History of the Industrial Enterprise*. Cambridge, MA: MIT Press

Cleland DI, Bursic KM. 1992. *Strategic Technology Management*. New York: AMA-COM

Cohen-Rosenthal, E. 1997. Sociotechnical systems and unions: nicety or necessity. *Hum. Relat.* 505:585–604

Davis LE, Taylor JC, eds. 1979. *The Design of Jobs*. Santa Monica, CA: Goodyear. 2nd ed.

Dean JW, Snell SA. 1991 Integrated manufacuring and job design: moderating effects of organizational inertia. *Acad. Mgmt. J.* 34(4):776–804

Dean JW, Yoon SJ, Susman GI. 1992. Advanced manufacturing technology and organizational structure: empowerment or subordination? *Organ. Sci.* 3:203–29

De Sanctis G, Poole MS. 1994. Capturing the complexity in advanced technology use: adaptive structurization theory. *Organ. Sci.* 5:121–47

Edwards R. 1979. *Contested Terrain: The Transformation of the Workplace in the Twentieth Century*. New York: Basic

Florman SC. 1976. *The Existential Pleasures of Engineering*. New York: St. Martin's

Flynn PM. 1988. *Facilitating Technological Change: The Human Resource Challenge*. Cambridge, MA: Ballinger

Garud R, Kotha S. 1994. Using the brain as a metaphor to model flexible production systems. *Acad. Mgmt. Rev.* 19:671–98

Gaynor GH. 1996. *Handbook of Technology Management*. New York: McGraw-Hill

Gaynor G. 1990. *Achieving the Competitive Edge Through Integrated Technology Management*. New York: McGraw-Hill

Gerwin D, Kolodny H. 1992. *Management. of Advanced Manufacturing Technology: Strategy, Organization and Innovation*. New York: Wiley

Giddens A. 1979. *Central Problems in Social Theory*. Berkeley, CA: Univ. Calif. Press

Haddad CJ. 1994. Concurrent engineering and the role of labor in product development. *Control Engin.Practice* 24:689–96

Haddad CJ. 1996. Operationalizing the concept of concurrent engineering: a case study from the U.S. auto industry. *IEEE Transact. Engin. Mgmt.* 432:124–32

Haddad CJ. 1999. Involving manufacturing employees in the early stages of product development: a case study from the U.S. automobile industry. In *New Product and Process Development Networks,* ed. U Juergens. Berlin: Springer. In press

Hull FM, Collins PD. 1987 High-technology batch production systems: Woodward's missing type. *Acad. Mgmt. J.* 30:786–97

Kidd PT. 1988. The social shaping of technology: the case of a CNC lathe. *Behav. Infor. Technol.* 7:192–204

Kidd PT. 1992 Interdisciplinary design of skill-based computer-aided technologies: interfacing in depth. *Int. J. Hum. Factors Manufact.* 2(3):209–28

LaPorte T, Consolini PM. 1991. January. Working in practice but not in theory: theoretical challenges of high-reliability organizations. *J. Public Admin. Res. Theory.* pp. 19–47. Cited in Pool R 1997. *Beyond Engineering: How Society Shapes Technology*

Lei D, Hitt MA, Goldhar JD. 1996. Advanced manufacturing technology: organizational design and strategic flexibility. *Organ. Stud.* 17:501–23

Lewis M. 1998. *Advanced manufacturing technology: a multiparadigm deconstruction and reconstruction of the literature.* Best Pap. Proc. Acad. Mgmt. Conf., San Diego, CA

Liker JK, Fleischer M. 1989. Implementing computer-aided design: the transition of non-users. *IEEE Transact. Engin. Mgmt.* 36(3):180–90

Liker JK, Majchrzak A, Choi T. 1993, Social impacts of advanced manufacturing technology: a review of recent studies and contingency formulation. *J. Engin. Technol. Mgmt.* 10:222–64

Liker JK, Majchrzak A. 1994. Designing the human infrastructure for technology. In *Organization and Manag. of Advanced Manufacturing*, ed. W Karwowski, G Salvendy, pp. 121–64. New York: Wiley

Liker JK, Sindi A. 1997. User acceptance of expert systems: a test of the theory of reasoned action. *J. Engin. Technol. Mgmt.* 14: 147–73

Liker JK, Roitman D, Roskies E. 1987 Changing everything all at once: work life and technological change. *Sloan Mgmt. Rev.* 28(4):29–48

Majchrzak A. 1988. *The Human Side of Factory Automation: Managerial and Human Resource Strategies for Making Automation Succeed.* San Francisco: Jossey-Bass

Majchrzak A, Gasser L. 1992. On using artificial intelligence to integrate the design of organizational and process change in U.S. manufacturing. *AI Soc.* 5:321–38

Marx K. 1906. *Capital.* Vol. I. Chicago: Kerr. Cited in Braverman, *op.cit.*, p. 186

McGregor D. 1957. The human side of enterprise. *Mgmt. Rev.* 46:22-28, 88-92. Cited in *Work, Organization and Power: Introduction to Industrial Sociology,* R Ford 1988, p. 89. Boston: Allyn & Bacon

Mintzberg H. 1979. *The Structuring of Organizations.* Englewood Cliffs, NJ: Prentice Hall

Mitcham C. 1994. *Thinking Through Technology: The Path Between Engineering and Philosophy.* Chicago: Univ. Chicago Press

Montgomery D. 1979. *Workers' Control in America: Studies in the History of Work, Technology and Labor Struggles.* Cambridge, UK: Cambridge Univ. Press

Morgall JM. 1993. *Technology Assessment: A Feminist Perspective.* Philadelphia: Temple Univ. Press

Morgan G. 1997. *Images of Organization.* Beverly Hills, CA: Sage

Nadler DA, Tushman ML. 1997. A congruence model for organization problem solving. In *Managing Strategic Innovation and Change,* ML Tushman, P Anderson, pp. 159–71. New York: Oxford Univ. Press

Noble DF. 1979. Social choice in machine design: the case of automatically controlled machine tools. In *Case Studies in the Labor Process,* A Zimbalist, pp. 18–47. New York: Monthly Rev.

Noori H. 1990. *Managing the Dynamics of New Technology: Issues in Manufacturing Manag.* Englewood Cliffs, NJ: Prentice-Hall

Pacey A. 1983. *The Culture of Technology.* Cambridge, MA: MIT Press. 6th ed.

Pasmore WA, Sherwood JJ, eds. 1978. *Sociotechnical Systems.* La Jolla, CA: Univ. Assoc.

Perrow C. 1967. A framework for the comparative analysis of organizations. *Am. Sociol. Rev.* 32:194–208

Pichault F. 1995. The managment of politics in technically related organizational change. *Organ. Stud.* 16(3):449–76

Prasad P. 1993. Symbolic processes in the implementation of technological change: a symbolic interactionist study of work computerization, *Acad. Mgmt. J.* 36:1400–29

Preece D. 1995. *Organizations and Technical Change: Strategy, Objectives and Involvement.* London: Routledge

Ramamurthy K. 1995. The influence of planning on implementation of advanced manufacturing technologies. *IEEE Transact. Eng. Mgmt.* 42:62–75

Rogers EM. 1983. *Diffusion of Innovation.* New York: Free Press. 3rd ed.

Sankar Y. 1991. *Management of Technological Change.* New York: Wiley

Shaiken H. 1985. *Work Transformed: Automation and Labor in the Computer Age.* New York: Holt, Rinehart & Winston

Simonsen J. 1997. Using ethnography in contextual design. *Commun. ACM* 40:82–88

Taylor FW. 1947. *Scientific Management.* New York: Harper & Row

Taylor JC, Asadorian RA. 1986. The implementation of excellence: STS Management. *Indust. Mgmt.* 274:5–15

Thomas RJ. 1994. *What Machines Can't Do: Politics and Technology in the Industrial Workplace*. Berkeley: Univ. Calif. Press

Thompson JD. 1967. *Organizations in Action.* New York: McGraw Hill

Tornatzky LG, Fleischer M. 1990. *The Processes of Technological Innovation,* Lexington, MA: Lexington Books

Turkle S. 1984. *The Second Self: Computers and the Human Spirit,* New York: Simon & Schuster

Wacjman J. 1991. *Feminism Confronts Technology*. University Park, PA: Penn. State Univ. Press

Walton RE. 1985. From control to commitment in the workplace. *Harvard Bus. Rev.* 27:77–84

Walton RE, McKersie RB. 1991. Managing new technology and labor relations: an opportunity for mutual influence. In *The Challenge of New Technology to Labor-Management Relations,* DC Mowery, BE Henderson, pp. 33–43. US Dep. Labor, Bur. Labor-Mgmt. Relat. and Coop. Prog., BLMT 135. Washington, DC: US Gov. Print. Off.

Walton RE, Susman GI. 1987. People policies for the new machines. *Harvard Bus. Rev.* March-April, 2:98–106

Weick K. 1990. Technology as equivogue: sensemaking and new technologies. In *Technology and Organizations.* ed. PS Goodman, LS Sproul, et al. San Francisco: Jossey-Bass

Wilkinson B. 1983. *The Shopfloor Politics of New Technology.* London: Heinemann Educ.

Wolfe RA. 1994, Organizational innovation: review, critique, and suggested research methods. *J. Mgmt. Stud.* 31L3)405–31

Wood S, ed. 1982. *The Degradation of Work? Skill, Deskilling and the Labour Process.* London: Hutchinson

Woodward J. 1958. *Management and Technology.* London: HMSO

Woodward, J. 1965. *Industrial Organization: Theory and Practice*. Oxford, UK: Oxford Univ. Press

Yellowitz I. 1977. Skilled workers and mechanization: the lasters in the 1890s. *Labor Hist.* 182:197–213

Zammuto RF, O'Connor EJ. 1992. Gaining advanced manufacturing technologies' benefits. *Acad. Mgmt. Rev. 174:*701

Zuboff S. 1988. *In the Age of the Smart Machine: The Future of Work and Power.* New York: Basic Books

Annu. Rev. Sociol. 1999. 25:597–622

ORGANIZATIONAL INNOVATION AND ORGANIZATIONAL CHANGE

J. T. Hage

Center for Innovation, University of Maryland, College Park, Maryland 20742;
e-mail: hage@socy.umd.edu, or J.t.hage@nias.nl

KEY WORDS: innovation, complex, organic, strategy, change

ABSTRACT

Three ideas—a complex division of labor, an organic structure, and a high-risk strategy—provoke consistent findings relative to organizational innovation. Of these three ideas, the complexity of the division of labor is most important because it taps the organizational learning, problem-solving, and creativity capacities of the organization. The importance of a complex division of labor has been underappreciated because of the various ways in which it has been measured, which in turn reflect the macroinstitutional arrangements of the educational system within a society. These ideas can be extended to the study of interorganizational relationships and the theories of organizational change. Integrating these theories would provide a general organizational theory of evolution within the context of knowledge societies.

ORGANIZATIONAL INNOVATION AND CHANGE

Although many lament the absence of cumulative findings in sociology, the study of organizational innovation is one instance where consistent findings have accumulated across more than thirty years of research. This was demonstrated in two recent reviews (Damanpour 1991, Zammuto & O'Connor 1992) published in the management literature. This present review has as one of its objectives to acquaint sociologists with the generalizations that have emerged and, as another objective, to extend beyond these previous reviews in three

0360-0572/99/0815-0597$08.00

distinctive ways: (*a*) by emphasizing the importance of the complexity of the division of labor; (*b*) by suggesting needed arenas of new research; and (*c*) by integrating organizational innovation with the more general topic of organizational change. This will broaden systemically the solid body of research already accumulated.

Innovation research, although previously not central to the concerns of many sociologists, now offers an opportunity to address a large number of important practical and theoretical issues. Here are a few examples. Practically, since a country's economic development depends largely on the continued launching of new products, governments have become concerned about innovation. Indeed, the new products and new services provide new employment opportunities and positive balances of trade, thus protecting the nation's standard of living. But innovation in products, services, technologies, and administrative practices is also relevant to other institutional sectors besides the economy; the study of organizational innovation, for instance, articulates with the study of significant breakthroughs in science, the development of superior military equipment, the creation of interdisciplinary programs in higher education (Blau 1973), the reform of welfare, etc. In other words, for anyone interested in some of the most basic problems of society, the subject of organizational innovation is relevant.

Theoretically, research on organizational innovation opens new perspectives on a number of interesting issues that have surfaced recently, including the issues of societal evolution and institutional change, the dynamics of knowledge societies (Bell 1973, Hage & Powers 1992), and the integration of macro and micro levels of analysis. Beyond sociology, organizational innovation can make important contributions to several important arenas of new research in economics. The most obvious one is research on national systems of innovation (Lundvall 1992, Nelson 1993), but it is equally relevant to endogenous theories of economic growth (Romer 1986, 1990, Solow 1992) more generally.

The first section of this review examines the general pattern of findings and emphasizes the importance of three critical variables: (*a*) the organic structure, (*b*) the organizational strategy; and (*c*) the complexity of the division of labor. In this section, we discuss the definition of innovation. The second section focuses on the new areas of potential research on organizational innovation. Here the emphasis is put on considering inputs and feedbacks as well as extending innovation studies to interorganizational relationships and the institutional level of analysis. Throughout this discussion, continued reference is made to linkages with several topics in the economics literature. The third section then shifts to the relationship between organizational innovation and the more general literature on organizational change. Four distinctive perspectives of change are considered and integrated.

AN OVERVIEW OF ORGANIZATIONAL INNOVATION RESEARCH

The Theoretical Relevance of Innovation Research in the Study of Organizations

Despite the attractiveness of the idea of creative and flexible organizations, the topic of organizational innovation has never been central in either organizational or management theory and research (see such textbooks as Hall 1991, Scott 1992, or any of the management textbooks in organizational theory such as Daft 1989 and Mintzberg 1979). Yet, innovations reflect a critical way in which organizations respond to either technological or market challenges (Brenner 1987, Gomes--Casseres 1994, 1996, Smith et al 1992, Hage 1988). In particular, technological advance is increasingly the basis of competition between nations (Kitson & Michie 1998, Porter 1990). As Zammuto & O'Connor (1992) demonstrate, most systems of flexible manufacturing adopted in the United States have had little impact on flexibility and only half have improved productivity, raising serious questions as to why, and about the long-term prospects for the United States (Jaikumar 1986).

Businesses have come to realize the importance of innovation for survival in a world of global competition. A recent report from the British Department of Trade and Industry (Sullivan 1998) indicates that the major companies, irrespective of country—France, Germany, Italy, Japan, Sweden, United Kingdom, and the United States—spend between 4% and 5% of sales on research in the automobile and the commercial aircraft industries, from 5% to 8% in the three sectors of semi-conductors and computers, electrical products, and chemical products and 10% to 15%% in the health products, pharmaceuticals, and software sectors. In the past year, the research and development (R&D) spending in the top 300 companies world-wide increased 12.8%, with the largest increases in some 100 American companies. While this may be an exceptional increase, it continues the long-term trend since 1975 (Hage & Powers 1992:32) of annual growth of 4% to 5% above inflation per annum in private expenditure, at least in the American firms.

The Definition of Organization Innovation and Styles of Research

Organizational innovation has been consistently defined as the adoption of an idea or behavior that is new to the organization (Damanpour 1988, 1991, Daft & Becker 1978, Hage 1980, Hage & Aiken 1970, Zaltman, Duncan & Holbek 1973, Oerlemans et al 1998, Wood 1998, Zummato & O'Connor 1992). The innovation can either be a new product, a new service, a new technology, or a new administrative practice. The research usually focuses on *rates* of innovation and not on single innovations except in the instance of diffusion studies (e.g. Collins et al 1987, Ettlie et al 1984, Walton 1987) where the speed of adoption is an issue. The importance of studies of innovation rates rather than a case study of a single innovation must be stressed. In the metaanalysis of Damanpour (1991), he found that the greater the number of innovations considered in the research study, the more consistent the findings. *This is an important conclusion, namely, that the focus on rates of a phenomenon will produce more consistent results than the analysis of a single event.* Here lies one of the major methodological reasons why organizational sociologists have not always been able to observe an accumulation of findings.

Although the definition has remained consistent, the particular kinds of innovation examined have shifted across time as well as have the kinds of problems that have interested people. In the 1960s and 1970s the emphasis was on incremental change in public sector organizations (Allen & Cohen 1969, Daft & Becker 1978, Hage & Aiken 1967, Kaluzny et al 1972, Moch 1976), while in the 1980s and 1990s it has been on radical change in private sector organizations (Collins et al 1987, Cohn & Turyn 1980, Ettlie et al 1984, Gerwin 1988, Jaikumar 1986, Teece 1987, Walton 1987). Examples of the latter include flexible manufacturing (Collins et al 1987, Gerwin 1988, Teece 1987), retortable pouches (Ettlie et al 1984), robotics, automated handling of materials, or computer numerically controlled machines (Jaikumar 1986), and even ship automation (Walton 1987) and shoe production (Cohn & Turyn 1980). Furthermore, the measures for "radical" altered from subjective ones (Kaluzny et al 1972) to more objective ones (Cohn & Turyn 1980, Collins et al 1987, Ettlie et al 1984, Walton 1987).

As this shift in focus occurred, the nature of the problem being investigated also changed. Rather than simply count the number of adoptions within a particular time period, the analytical focus became differential implementation of radical innovations, most typically advanced manufacturing technologies (see Zammuto & O'Connor 1992).

What kinds of innovation have not been studied? This is always the more difficult but necessary question in any review. Essentially there are two kinds of organizational innovations that have not received much attention. The first lacuna is the examination of radical innovations in the components of assembled products such as cars, commercial airplanes, and trains. By and large the organizational innovation literature has focused on simple products or services rather than the assembled variety. But some of the most interesting radical innovations are occurring in the components of assembled products. To take cars as one example, there have been air bags, anti-lock disk brakes, geographical positioning systems, fuel efficient engines, etc. The second lacuna is radical innovations in what are called large-scale technical systems (Mayntz & Hughes 1988) such as electrical, railroad, and telephone systems. Some radical innovations in these areas include nuclear energy, high-speed trains, and coaxial cables. And this is to say nothing about the emergence of new radical large scale technical systems such as satellite television and internet. We need a shift in focus to assembled products and large-scale technical systems because of their importance in the post-industrial economy.

Consistency of Findings

In the two management reviews (Damanpour 1991, Zammuto & O'Connor 1992), two important themes about the determinants of innovation have emerged, namely, the importance of an organic structure (Burns & Stalker 1961) and pro-change values or high-risk strategies. The organic structure has long been a feature of various reviews (see Burns & Stalker 1961, Hage 1965, Aiken & Hage 1971, Zaltman et al 1973) as has the pro-change strategy (Hage & Dewar 1973, Hage 1980). What has been missed is the central role of the complexity of the division of labor (Hage 1965). Before considering this latter idea, however, the general ideas of the two management reviews need to be summarized.

THE DAMANPOUR (1991) REVIEW   This review contains a metaanalysis involving 23 studies in which four major contingencies—type of organization, type of innovation, stage of adoption, and scope of innovation—were controlled in the analysis of the impact of structure and strategy on innovation rates. In general, these contingencies did not eliminate most of the general findings although in certain instances they affected the size of the parameters.

For structural variables that in some way refer to the division of labor, Damanpour examined the impact of specialization (or number of occupations), departmentalization or functional differentiation (or number of departments), professionalism (education and/or involvement in professional activities), and a new one, the technical knowledge resources involved in the job. The first three had significant relationships with innovation. In the moderator analysis, however, it was specialization that had the most robust association across the four moderator variables. Technological knowledge resources represent a specific kind of human capital or expertise (Becker 1964, Schultz 1961). Again, there was a positive relationship with innovation, but only a few of the control variables could be considered because of the small number of studies involving this variable.

However, this positive relationship is consistent with a number of other findings in the literature on organizational innovation that are not generally known in the organizational literature. In several British and German plant comparisons (Daly et al 1985, Steedman & Wagner 1987, 1989), the researchers found that when managers did not have technical training relevant to their manufacturing they were slow to adopt new technologies.

The two other structural variables Damanpour (1991) examined in one way or another referred to characteristics of the organic organization—centralization and formalization. Centralization had a robust and negative relationship with innovation, whereas formalization had a weak and inconsistent one given various controls. The major strategy variable was managerial attitudes toward change, which in general had a positive relationship with innovation, though less robust than did centralization and specialization.

There is, however, an important qualification to be made about Damanpour's metaanalysis. Although the author has taken several dimensions of an organic structure (Burns & Stalker 1961), perhaps the most fundamental characteristics of this structure have not been examined in studies of innovation. Here are three examples: the idea of shifting leadership, the different mechanisms for facilitating communication, and the importance of technical progress as a goal.

THE ZAMMUTO AND O'CONNOR(1992) REVIEW   This review focuses specifically on the problems of the adoption of flexible manufacturing, including those for Britain (Bessant 1985, Ingersoll Engineers 1984, Primrose 1988), Japan (Jaikumar 1986), Australia (Fleck 1984), and the United States (Jaikumar 1986, Voss 1988), and thus it deals directly with the issue of unemployment and national standards of living. However, this study poses a new problem, namely, differential implementation. Few American firms achieved flexibility, and only one half had improvements in productivity. Given the work of Piore & Sabel (1984), who have argued that flexible specialized manufacturing represents what they call "the second industrial divide," and that of Pine (1993) on mass customization, these findings are disquieting.

The thesis of the Zammuto & O'Connor review is that it is an organic organization and a pro-change or high-risk strategy that provide the best chance for a successful implementation of flexible manufacturing so that both productivity and flexibility are achieved. Unlike the Damanpour (1991) review, this review is qualitative, but it has the advantage of including a number of engineering studies that are not part of the previous review.

Within the review, the authors mention the importance of the complexity of the job (Zammuto & O' Connor 1992:708), another new characteristic of the division of labor. Their argument that more complex jobs at the operative level facilitated organizational learning is similar to the one made for professionalism in the literature cited above. The importance of complex jobs in facilitating the adoption of new technologies is again demonstrated in a number of matched plant comparisons not cited in Zammuto & O'Connor's (1992) review (Prais et al 1989, Prais & Steedman 1989, Steedman & Wagner 1987, 1989; Steedman et al 1991). For instance, the German foremen typically performed the activities associated with several distinct positions found in British plants, including responsibility for quality control and production scheduling, activities regularly assigned to managers or engineers in American plants. More complex jobs at the bottom of the hierarchy were associated in the German plants with much greater flexibility in the work force and the ability of the German manufacturers to provide customization of their products. The German workers repaired their own machines, took responsibility for their maintenance, and exploited more effectively the range of capabilities in the machines, thus explaining how gains in both productivity and flexibility could be obtained from advanced manufacturing technologies. Admittedly, it is difficult to separate the unique effects of the German superior technical training from the complexity of the job because these two are related in the German instance.

A recent study (Collins et al 1988) on differential implementation of flexible manufacturing across a number of industries in the United States was not included in either of these two reviews, although it further substantiates the idea that flexible manufacturing systems were more likely to be adopted when there was complexity in the division of labor. This study used the diversity of occupational specialties as the measure of complexity and controlled for the prior level of automation, which almost none of the previous research studies reviewed did. The expected finding was the higher the level, the *less* the movement toward greater automation. *But the unexpected finding was that at higher levels of automation, complexity had a multiplier effect on further adoption of flexible manufacturing,* i.e. an interaction effect. Again, in quantitative terms this substantiates the qualitative comparisons of plants in Europe.

Zammuto & O'Connor (1992:717) also expanded the idea of decentralization by discussing the importance of participation of the workers during the implementation process, but they did not explain why this was successful. This provides another insight as to why the organic structure—decentralization, horizontal communication, and shifting leadership—facilitates the process of implementation. This allows for mobilizing the skills and knowledge that the employees have. In particular, Jaikumar's (1986) comparison of Japan and the United States across a number of industries and Walton's (1987) study of the adoption of innovations in the shipping industries of Britain, Germany, Japan, Norway, the Netherlands, and the United States both provide considerable evidence for this assertion. The continual gains in productivity—incremental process innovation—associated with quality work circles are also proof of this assertion (Lazonick 1998).

One of the weaknesses in the various studies of strategy relative to innovation is shifting definitions of the content of the strategy. In particular what has not been addressed is the degree of radicalness in the strategy itself. This is important because of Tushman & Andersen's work (1986), which indicates that dominant firms are more likely to adopt nonradical strategies, while new and weak firms are more likely to adopt radical ones.

Another issue not discussed in the Zammuto & O'Connor (1992) review but relevant to their analysis are the advantages for motivation of a high-risk strategy that is visionary. Resistance to radical changes, and especially when they involve the potential loss of jobs, as for example with automation, is a constant theme. But a high-risk strategy that contains a new vision about protecting employment is quite different. Beyond this, strategies that involve making the world better in some way have a considerable motivational impact on the employees as they are struggling with the implementation of the radical innovation (Hage & Aiken 1970). Economists have stressed the importance of incentives and especially the entrepreneurial rewards obtained from radical innovations (Baldwin & Scott 1987, Cayselle 1998) but have ignored the motivation of the employees or workers who may not directly benefit economically. In particular, the idea of public goods, that is gains for society, as a motivating factor is not part of their framework. Interestingly, items in the Hage & Dewar (1973) operationalization of change values stressed the gains for society rather than self-interest, whether for the organization or its members. The famous Kidder (1979) account of the development of a computer provides a dramatic illustration of how important making society better in some way is for the motivation of many people. In future research we need to more directly access whether or not the successful introduction of radical products or the implementation of radical process innovations involved some vision of a better society.

THE MISSING VARIABLE: THE COMPLEX DIVISION OF LABOR   Although both reviews discussed various aspects of the division of labor in organizations as an important feature that facilitated innovation, they did not directly reference the complexity of the division of labor as the most critical variable for stimulating innovation. Four of the potential six indicators were in the Damanpour (1991) review: specialization, departmentalization, professionalization, and technical knowledge resources, and one of them, the complexity of the job, was in the Zammuto & O'Connor (1992) review. Neither considered the importance of the presence of a research department, which would appear to be the most obvious prior condition for innovation and which appeared in the Cohen & Levinthal (1990) discussion of absorbtive capacity and was relevant to the literature on organizational learning. The true significance of the complexity of the division of labor can only be appreciated when one adds across these various dimensions.

Why is the complexity of the division of labor so critical for organizational innovation? The original argument made by Hage (1965) was that the complexity of the division of labor would lead to much greater adaptiveness or flexibility relative to changes in the environment (for some evidence for this assertion, see Smith et al 1992). However, this occurred via several different chains of reasoning: (*a*) the complexity reduced the amount of centralization and formalization, that is the bureaucracy; and (*b*) shifted the ends of the organization away from efficiency toward higher morale. These were further amplified in Hage & Aiken (1970) when they suggested that occupants of a diverse number of college-level trained occupations monitor the environment and learn about new ideas either as problems or as solutions. Given a diverse number of specialties, more aspects of the task environment are being monitored, generating a cross-fertilization of ideas. Coalitions of professionals form in differentiated units such as departments and struggle for scarce resources. Consistent with this idea but not separately analyzed is the finding about the relationship between the existence of a department and the number of new techniques associated with that occupational specialty (Moch & Morse 1977) or the presence of a research department (see Allen 1977), in part the idea of functional differentiation. In current work this is referred to as absorptive capacity (Cohen & Levinthal 1990). Damanpour (1991) reviews a number of these reasons under various indicators of complexity.

Given the current emphasis on the organic structure and pro-change strategies, why is the complexity of the division of labor more important? Neither concept—that is, neither the organic structure nor the pro-change or high-risk strategy—refer to the intellectual or problem-solving capacities or learning capacities (Cohen & Levinthal 1990) of the organization, to say nothing about the creative capacities. Diversity of knowledge is critical for creative, complex, and rapid problem solving (Smith et al 1992, Schoenberger 1994), which is increasingly required in the global market place (Hage & Powers 1992). Organic structures help mobilize this knowledge and strategies provide goals and motivation, but ultimately one has to have the knowledge base represented by complexity and its various indicators.

Given the considerable importance currently being attached to the management of knowledge and the learning organization in both the management and industrial economics literatures (Foss 1999, Nooteboom 1999), the concept of the degree of complexity needs to be stressed. Except for the advantages of a research department in improving the absorptive capacity (Cohen & Levinthal 1990), the other dimensions of complexity have not been considered in discussions of the learning organization. Nonaka & Takeuchi (1995) in their discussion of the knowledge organization have primarily stressed mechanisms of integration rather than the various measures of complexity. Perhaps most critically, most of this literature (Foss 1999) is not predictive because it does not ask, Why do some organizations learn more? Some have begun to suggest that the learning organization is the innovative organization (Nooteboom 1999), but again this begs the question as to what explains the higher rates of innovation and we are lead back to complexity.

THE VARIABLE TO BE IGNORED: ORGANIZATIONAL SIZE   Ever since the thesis of Schumpeter (Baldwin & Scott 1987) about the advantages of large size and/or market power (concentration), a number of studies in economics have tried to demonstrate whether or not he was correct. Most reviews have found that the picture is quite mixed (see reviews of Baldwin & Scott 1987, Cayselle 1998, Cohen & Levin 1989). The reason for this is that the economists have not divided their industrial sectors or sample of large firms into those with high complexity such as chemicals, computers, commerical airplanes, electrical products, drugs, etc and those with low complexity such as rubber tires, steel, processed foods, cement, cigarettes, etc. When this is done there is much more order in the data. In the former instance, even with relatively high levels of concentration, firms spend a great deal on research and product development while in the latter case they do not (Hage 1980). The same assertion can be made about small firms (see Nooteboom 1994). Many do not spend much money on research and development but those that do spend a great deal. Again, the difference is the degree of complexity (see Hage 1980 for the explicit organizational typology generated by large versus small size and low versus high complexity).

Furthermore, another problem with the variable of organizational size is the issue of how does one measure innovation in firms of varying size. As I observed in the beginning the usual research design for innovation research in sociology is a single industrial sector where there is a modal size. But in comparing across sectors, which is of more interest to industrial economists, the problem becomes whether or not the rate of innovation should be standardized on the size of the organization. An additional problem is the weighting issue. Across sectors, the amount of money required for a radical product innovation is vastly different. Compare 70 million dollars for a radical new drug with one billion for a new model car that might have only incremental improvements in its various components.

NEW ARENAS OF RESEARCH FOR ORGANIZATIONAL INNOVATION

Several ways exist for specifying new arenas of research. If one takes a systems perspective, it becomes easier to observe several limitations in the literature (Hage 1980). In general, little attention has been paid to the problem of inputs as a necessary control. Only recently have feedbacks become part of the literature. They are a necessary next step, especially for those interested in building some theory about evolution and in particular the characteristics of knowledge societies. Finally, there are several logical extensions of this literature, specifically to the study of networks and to the macroinstitutional level of analysis.

Controlling for Inputs

THE INPUT OF RESEARCH EXPENDITURES   *One of the major limitations of the large number of studies on organizational innovation is that there has not been any attempt to control for the amount of investment in research and development before testing whether the structure of the organization has a multiplier effect on the amount of innovation produced.* There is one exception (Hull 1988), and one not involved in either of the two management reviews. This study demonstrates that controlling for the investment in either research dollars or researchers, and controlling for size, the organic model provides a multiplier effect on the number of patents produced, while the opposite—the use of centralization and formalization—reduces their number. The sample includes a wide variety of research departments in major American companies, including most of the major pharmaceuticals. Unfortunately, this study is a rare exception to the typical ones in organizational sociology. Most organizational research has ignored the inputs of human capital and more critically the amount of money spent on research. Thus, one could always question whether or not innovation was a consequence of these inputs. By combining the economists' input-output modeling, in this instance the inputs of the number of researchers and the amount invested in research, and testing the impact of organizational characteristics such as complexity and the organic model to predict the amount of innovation, admittedly here only measured by patents (which has its own problems), one has both a much more convincing and a more powerful argument relative to the importance of structural variables in general and the complexity of the division of labor in particular.

Please observe that the multiplier is being provided not by technological progress but instead by the nature of the intervening organization. Likewise, the complexity of the organizational structure when it is integrated in an organic structure creates the innovation in products, services, and technologies by the same kind of logic. The basic thesis of a structural paradigm is that it augments what is invested, and it is this idea that should be tested. Following the logic of the economists, one would like to partition the amount of technological progress produced by innovation among the three components that have been suggested in this review. In other words how much is technological progress produced by the complexity of the division of labor, by an organic structure, or by a high-risk strategy? With answers to these questions, governments could more wisely select policies to facilitate one or another of these structural or strategic attributes.

The failure to study the impact of research departments and their organization on rates of innovation is all the more regrettable because, as was suggested at the beginning of this review, most of the major corporations in the world now allocate money for research expenditures, at minimum product development. Similarly, nations recognize that their economic vitality is dependent upon the effectiveness of their research programs. Therefore, the study of how to organize research becomes a strategic arena for organizational sociologists if they want to make a contribution to the study of economic progress.

Paradoxically, very few studies of industrial research departments and their characteristics exist in the literature, the Hull (1988) study being a major exception. In contrast, the sociology of science has studied public sector research departments and been concerned with the local knowledge problem (Knorr 1981, Latour & Woolgar 1979), rather than with how the organization of the research team or department affects the ability to make major discoveries. Complexity is also relevant to studies of organizational learning for the same reason; the complexity of the division of labor overcomes the single-loop reasoning problem of managers (Argyris & Schoen 1978).

THE INPUT OF PRIOR INNOVATION   A similar limitation of the research to date is that just as these studies generally do not control for the amount of inputs invested in producing organizational innovation, there is also little analysis of the prior history of innovation, what some might term the culture of the organization and others the prior strategy (presumably these ideas are in various ways related). Again, there is one major study (see Hage & Dewar 1973), which controlled for both the prior history of innovation, the attitudes of the power elite toward social change, and organizational structure, and it found that all three perspectives or paradigms—and with only three variables, one for each—explained some 70% of the variation in a three-year prediction study. Although Damanpour (1991) includes this study in his meta-analysis, the variable prior innovation is not, precisely because it is missing from most research studies. Future research on organizational innovation should control for the prior history of innovation as a critical explanation of the future behavior of the organization, even though it is not a particularly exciting idea that organizations repeat their behavior across time!

Another important reason for studying prior innovation is the problem of the product life-cycle. Abernathy & Utterbach (1978, Utterbach 1994) argue that, when a new industrial sector is created, the first phase involves a high rate of product innovation, the second phase a high rate of process innovation, and the third phase a relatively low rate of both. Except for Utterbach's work, no long-term historical studies of the evolution of industrial sectors across time have been conducted. There is a need for further work in this area.

THE INPUT OF A PERFORMANCE GAP   Any review of a topic should be quite explicit about issues that were once important and have not necessarily been pursued. In the context of innovation research, probably the most critical omission is the process approach. In the early work (Hage & Aiken 1970, Zaltman et al 1973), considerable attention was devoted to the problem of naming the stages in the process of change and sometimes to identifying the various problems associated with each stage (in particular, see Hage 1980). Much of this work has proved to be a dead end, perhaps in part because there have been few process studies.

However, one critical idea from this early work has remained and is worth emphasizing; that is the notion of a performance gap (Zaltman et al 1973) as the triggering mechanism for the introduction of innovation and particularly of radical change, including the transformation of the organizational form from one steady state such as mechanical to another such as mixed mechanical-organic. The Minnesota studies (Van de Ven Angle & Poole 1989), which are probably the single most important collective effort focusing on innovation today, have a large quantity of data demonstrating the role of crises in moving organizations to adopt radical innovations. Furthermore, this finding has also been substantiated in developing countries (Hage & Finsterbusch 1987).

The concept of a performance gap is especially interesting because it connects back to the ambiguities of the meaning of a high-risk strategy. The potential connection is clear: If individuals set very high standards, or high goals, they will perceive a large performance gap, which will lead them to adopt a high-risk strategy in order to close it.

Examining Feedbacks

Most of the literature on organizational innovation has concentrated on the causes of innovation but has not considered the feedbacks. Yet, we witness the beginning of some interesting work in this area, although it has not been connected closely to the study of innovation. A wide variety of potential feedbacks could be considered. Only three can be touched upon in this review: (a) the complexity of the division of labor and thus the organization; (b) the nature of competition; and (c) the survival of specific firms. Together they provide an evolutionary perspective, especially in knowledge societies.

ON THE COMPLEXITY OF THE DIVISION OF LABOR   One crucial kind of feedback is the impact of innovation on the complexity of the division of labor. What little evidence exists suggest that, rather than deskilling, there has been a shift to upgrade the skills and training of the labor forces in which innovation occurs. Dewar & Hage (1978) found that across a six-year period innovation did lead to the hiring of new occupations in the rehabilitation sector. A more dramatic illustration, in a study (Collins 1997) of a number of manufacturing plants, is the consequence of adding flexible manufacturing. This study found that both radical process and radical product innovation resulted in a considerable change in the composition of the labor force. Although the employee numbers remained about the same, the proportion of technical, professional, and managerial personnel increased. In other words, one critical feedback was the reduction in the number of unskilled and semi-skilled employees and their replacement with those who were more educated. Pianta (1998:82) found parallel results in a study of the impact of innovation on employment in Italian service sectors. More generally his research shows a decline in employment across many industrial sectors associated with improvements with productivity in Europe, the USA, and Japan, the implication being that this is because of radical new process technologies.

ON THE KIND OF COMPETITION   Another important kind of feedback is on the nature of competition. Tushman & Andersen (1986) have made a distinction between technologies that enhance capacities and those that destroy capabilities—where destroy means primarily the elimination of a number of firms—a needed refinement when assessing radical technologies and their impact. The successful organizations are likely to do the former, while new organizations are likely to introduce radical process innovations that destroy capabilities. The authors also demonstrate that the number of organizations declines when these radical process innovations are introduced. The beauty of their work is that it calls attention to the problem of discontinuities, a perspective that I believe is particular relevant for understanding postindustrial society (Bell 1973, Hage & Powers 1992) or knowledge societies.

ON SURVIVAL   Still a different way of posing the same question is to ask about the survival of particular companies. Given the argument in the introduction that firms must innovate to survive, one might ask two questions concerning this. Is it the case that plants and therefore firms that emphasize innovation are more likely to survive? And do those that survive have a complex division of labor and an organic structure as well as flexible manufacturing (characteristics suggested above as needed for success in competition for innovation)? In Hage et al (1993), 97 plants, including most of the major industrial sectors in the economy, were studied across 15 years, that is from 1973 to 1987. About 40% of the plants had closed during this period, indicating that many American businesses were unable to adjust to global competition.

An event history analysis demonstrated that the plants that survived longer were significantly more likely to have a diverse set of professional and scientific personnel (the number of managers did not make a difference) or a complex division of labor, to have invested more in flexible manufacturing, to be decentralized, to have fewer rules and procedures or be less bureaucratic, and to be located in industries that were research intensive. Controlling for industrial growth or market concentration ratio had no effect on these findings; in other words they were not a function of either product life cycle or monopoly control. Perhaps the most interesting finding was that the amount of money spent on research *by the entire industry* also led to a higher survival rate net of other factors. This documents the importance of both spill-over effects, a hot topic in economics (Romer 1986, Solow 1992) and the importance of the research department for absorptive capacity (Cohen & Levinthal 1990). But it is making an additional point, namely the collective benefits of individual firm investments in research. This suggests a win-win game.

New Areas for Research

INTERORGANIZATIONAL RELATIONSHIPS   All of the above research has focused on comparisons of organizations. Little research has occurred on whether or not the same ideas can be applied to joint ventures and interorganizational networks. Given the size of this expanding literature on joint ventures and interorganizational networks (for reviews see Alter & Hage 1993, Beamish & Killing 1997, Gomes-Casseres 1996, Jarillo 1993, Nohria & Eccles 1992, Powell 1990), it is surprising that few studies have been conducted on how successful these interorganization arrangements are for increasing innovation. Admittedly not all such arrangements are designed to maximize innovation, though most of them do involve at minimum the desire for access to new skills and areas of expertise, that is, concern for expanding the complexity of the division of labor (Badaracco 1991, Killing 1988). But in addition many joint ventures have set innovation as one of their objectives (Alter & Hage 1993, Contractor & Lorange 1988, Häkansson 1990, Hladik 1988, Laage-Hellman 1989).

Furthermore, more complex forms than joint ventures, such as consortia (Aldrich & Sasaki 1995) and strategic alliances (Gomes-Casseres 1996) are designed to generate innovations for an entire industry or to impose a new global standard. So far there has been only one study of the innovative effectiveness (for SEMATECH, Browning et al 1995) in a consortium. Yet, these new organizational forms represent ways of increasing the national competitiveness of the nation, and they deserve greater attention.

Kitson & Michie (1998) in a study of small businesses in the United Kingdom found that both fast growth firms and innovative firms were more likely to collaborate. The most typical reasons provided were gaining expertise of one kind or another. Both innovators and collaborators were more likely to have growth in profit margins than the non-innovative and non-collaborative firms. Unfortunately the fruits of collaboration relative to innovation were not directly measured, at least as reported in this study.

Another study (Oerlemans et al 1998), although not directly focused on joint ventures as such, was able to demonstrate that inter-organizational network variables contributed to the amount of innovation in a quite diverse sample of about 600 small firms in the Netherlands. The variables considered included interactions with trade organizations, national centers of applied research, consultants, important buyers and/or suppliers, chambers of commerce, and regional innovation centers. This study is important because it destroys the notion of the organization creating innovations on its own and has a much broader view of what they call the organization set than just joint ventures or collaborators along the supply chain.

These new forms can be easily incorporated within the basic framework of an organic structure, strategy of high risk, and a complex division of labor for stimulating innovation. Both Killing (1988) and Alter & Hage (1993) provide examples of how these concepts can be applied. However, neither of these studies actually examined comparatively the rates of innovation.

In research on the impact of the complexity of the division of labor, the organic nature of the interorganizational network, and the high-risk strategy, special attention should be paid to whether more radical innovations are developed in shorter periods of time. Actually, an argument made in the literature is that interorganizational networks appear to have these advantages (Gomes-Casseres 1996, Schoenberger 1994, Smith et al 1992, Stalk & Hout 1990), but this remains to be tested.

INTEGRATING THE MESO AND THE MACRO LEVELS OF ANALYSIS   One major objective of this review is to begin to link the macro institutional levels in society (Maurice et al 1986, Whitley 1992) with the meso analysis of organizational innovation by stipulating that the way in which knowledge is channelled affects the relative importance of specific indicators (for one model, see Walton 1987). The six indicators of complexity—specialization, departmentalization, professionalization, the technical knowledge involved in the training or education, the complexity of the job, and the presence or absence of a research department—reflect the alternative ways in which knowledge is "packaged." Thus, in the United States specialization and professionalism among managers and professionals are important, whereas in Europe the level of technical training and the scope of the job are more likely to be critical. This idea has been suggested in the "societal effects" approach to organizational analysis (Maurice 1978, 1995, Maurice Sellier & Silvestre 1986, Maurice et al 1980, Sorge 1996), which has emphasized the impact of education and values on the way in which the division of labor is structured in firms.

The same logic can be used to examine how research is institutionally arranged, which is the point of another important and relevant literature in economics (Nelson 1993, Lundvall 1992). Both the United States and Germany had pioneering companies that had industrial research laboratories. The close connection between research and education in both countries facilitated the early development of industrial laboratories (Mowry & Rosenberg 1993), a pattern largely absent in Japan. In contrast, the separation of research and higher education in France has slowed down certain forms of innovations.

The previous two perspectives stress the importance of the institutional embeddedness of the organization and how that shapes its internal characteristics. Another perspective, and one consistent with the previous arguments about examining the feedbacks of radical innovations, provides quite a different view. Two issues can be briefly considered: employment and institutional change.

The feedback of radical innovations on employment is quite mixed, as Pianta (1998) observes. On the one hand, radical process innovations reduce employment, as we have already observed. On the other hand, radical product innovations increase employment. Furthermore, these results are complicated by the relative speed of the introduction of the new products and processes. Countries which are the first to introduce even radical process innovations do not necessarily suffer losses in employment (Lazonick 1998). Some countries invest too late and reap few advantages from innovation (Valéry 1999). The reasons why are to be found in the nature of their institutional environment, which then relates back to the literature on the national systems of innovation (Lundvall 1992, Nelson 1993). This process is leading to specialization by nation in the areas in which they have comparative advantage (Porter 1990) but it is being driven by the innovation process and the relative speed with which it occurs.

Perhaps the most interesting and unexplored, at least in sociology, impact of radical innovations is their consequences for institutional change. The emergence of inter-organizational joint ventures and research consortia is perhaps the most dramatic illustration but it is not the only one. Consider the development of computer and softwear companies and how this has led to the creation of computer science departments, the resulting explosion in their enrollments, and the proliferation of new avenues of research. Furthermore, the computer and its software represents not only a whole new industrial sector in which there are many small firms but a considerable range of service companies—repair and maintenance, retailing, and training. One of the reasons as to why advanced industrial economies are really service economies is because of the proliferation of services relative to all of the various radical new products and processes being introduced. Any theory of organizational evolution should consider this feedback process on the institutional environment as part of its explanatory framework.

Finally, another promising direction for future research is to integrate organizational innovation with economic theories of growth, especially the new literature on endogenous patterns of economic growth (Romer 1986, Solow 1992). At several points, I have suggested how the theory of organizational innovation provides new insights into economic growth. Complexity as a measure of the diversity of human capital (Becker 1964, Schultz 1961) is a much more accurate way of estimating the effects of education on economic growth (Hage & Garnier 1993). The Hull (1988) study indicates how the way in which research is organized partially explains the multiplier effect associated with technical progress. This suggests that the input-output form of thinking involved in Cobb-Douglass equations should include variables for complexity and the organic structure as a way of developing a more accurate explanation for economic growth. Finally, once one builds in feedbacks, especially the major parameters used in economic growth theory, a more complex socioeconomic theory of economic growth becomes possible (for one attempt to do so, see Hage 1998).

AN OVERVIEW OF ORGANIZATIONAL CHANGE

The third objective of this review is to unite the general organizational literature on change with the studies of organizational innovation. This is less obvious than it might appear because the major perspectives—structural contingency theory, political theory, organizational ecology theory, and meso institutional theory—generally have not focused on the problem of organizational innovation per se. Nevertheless, they can be related by recognizing that in various ways their focus on environmental change can force or influence the choice of organizational form, whether mechanical or organic (Burns & Stalker 1961), which in turn can be linked to the relative emphasis on innovation.

This connection between the choice of form and the theory of organizational change can be made because each paradigm or perspective (Astley & Van de Ven 1983, Hage 1980)—structural contingency (Blau 1973, Blau & Schoenherr 1971, Hage 1980, Lawrence & Lorsch 1967, Perrow 1967); political (Hickson et al 1971, Hinings et al 1974, Pfeffer 1981, Pfeffer & Salancik 1974); organizational ecology (Baum 1996, Carroll 1987, Hannan & Freeman 1989, Hannan & Carroll 1992, Singh et al 1986) and meso institutional theory (DiMaggio & Powell 1983, Meyer & Rowan 1977, Powell & DiMaggio 1991, Scott 1987, Zucker 1987)— rests on a more or less explicit view of the environment. Given changes in the environment one or another form becomes favored for selection. In other words, does environmental change lead to changes in the nature of organizational form and especially the movement toward (or away from) an organic form with an emphasis on organizational innovation? As these connections are made, implicitly a number of new areas of research on innovation are suggested.

Structural Contingency Theory

The original insight of Burns & Stalker (1961) was that a stable demand led to the mechanical organization, whereas a changing demand created the need for an organic organization with its emphasis on innovation and flexibility. Hence the name structural contingency. Though not recognized for it, Lawrence & Lorsch (1967) were the ones who provided an evolutionary theory of increasing knowledge and its impact on these choices, suggesting that movement toward the organic form took place as departments of product development, applied research, and then basic research were being added to the structure of the organization. Building upon their work and that of Bell (1973) and others, Hage & Powers (1992) argue that more and more economic and political sectors must now emphasize either the organic model or interorganizational networks (Jarillo 1993, Nohria & Eccles 1992, Contractor & Lorange, 1988). The study of Hage et al (1993) provides empirical evidence for this set of ideas. These same ideas about evolution and knowledge societies can also be applied and tested with more complex forms such as interorganizational networks (Alter & Hage 1993, Contractor & Lorange 1988, Powell 1990) as discussed above. However, as yet, the contingencies that explain why one particular form of interorganizational network is better for which kind of innovation and in which institutional or societal context have not been developed.

In the previous section, it was suggested that it was worthwhile to examine the feedback effects on the complexity of the division of labor. As this increases, at some point the Lawrence & Lorsch (1967) solutions for integration break down. Firms (and government agencies) must split into either separate firms or "deconstruct" into profit centers, two processes occurring very frequently now (Hage & Powers 1992). How competencies, and more importantly their integration, impact on the boundaries of the organization (Foss 1999) lies at the heart of an evolutionary theory of the firm. Again, part of the answer to this problem lies in the institutional "packing" of knowledge that has already been discussed.

Political Theory

Political theory emerged in opposition to structural contingency theory and its implicit assumption that managers will also adjust to meet environment demands in ways that are appropriate for them. The central premise is that those departments or occupations (Hickson et al 1971, Hinings et al 1974) that handle the major contingency facing the organizations will become the dominant coalition. Pfeffer (1981) has indicated a number of ways in which the dominant coalition, once in power, can remain even if the basic contingencies for the organization change, thus offering an explanation for why some firms do not respond to environment change.

However, leaving aside which occurs first—changes in the major contingency or changes in the dominant coalition—shifts in the latter usually mean changes in strategy either toward or away from innovation. Therefore, the political model can be easily integrated with the findings on the importance of a high risk-strategy, usually a distinctive prerogative of this dominant coalition.

Another version is resource dependency theory (Pfeffer & Salancik 1974, 1978), which argues that the dominant coalition is beholden to those who control the purse strings of the organization. If they want innovation, it will occur. Again, changes in resource dependency generally have not been studied for their impact on innovation, though this has become a current concern with the shifting of welfare financing to state governments. Will this produce more reform, as has been argued?

Organizational Ecology Theory

An excellent review of the studies that have been done on organizational change within this perspective is to be found in Baum (1996). Baum's central insight is that the bulk of the organizational ecology approach has emphasized the selection of organizational form (for examples, see Hannan & Freeman 1984, 1989, Hannan & Carroll 1992, Singh et al 1986). The study of Hage et al (1993) provides a good example of how the mechanical form is being eliminated in the United States because of its inability to be flexible and its lack of innovation, while the organic form is being selected. In addition, there is now a renewed appreciation in this literature for trying to specificity the circumstances when adaptation occurs and when selection occurs. As yet, however, little attention has been paid to either the organic structure, the complexity of the division of labor, or innovation rates. In other words, in the debate about inertia versus adaptiveness (Hannan & Freeman 1984, Baum 1996), organizational ecologists have not considered whether a generic form such as a complex division of labor combined with an organic structure is adaptive.

But regardless of the relative absence of research on this topic, at the population level (Carroll 1987, Hannan & Freeman 1989, Baum 1996) adaptiveness can occur via the creation of a new specific form that allows for the population of organizations to adapt to new competitive circumstances such as globalization. Illustrations are research institutes in bio-medical research at the turn of the century, mini-mills in the steel industry, half-way homes in the rehabilitation service sector, the Italian network during the 1970s in textiles, luggage, and machine tools (Lazonick 1998, Piore & Sabel 1984), the commodity chain à la Nike in shoes, etc. These kinds of adaptation are especially interesting because they reflect radical innovations in the nature of the organization, a topic that has not been researched in the organizational literature on innovation. Furthermore, there is some indication in the literature that quite radical product and process innovations frequently have to have a new form. Again, we have another topic deserving of attention, not the least because of its implications for organizational evolution.

Although one would normally assume that organizational ecology would be primarily interested in the evolution of organizational forms across time, there has been surprisingly little research on this, with Aldrich & Mueller (1982) as a major exception. In their work the latter have focused on the evolution of the multidivisional form.

Institutional Theory

In the iron cage theory DiMaggio & Powell (1983) indicate the different ways in which organizational forms are adopted within a country. More recently, they (Powell & DiMaggio 1991) have stressed the importance of professional associations, foundations, and socialization agents as sources of change in organizational form. Again, none of this literature has been related to organic structure and the problem of rates of innovation. In a very different perspective, Ramirez & Boli (1987) demonstrated the role of military and societal failure as a motivation for adopting a similar form of primary school. Here lie the beginnings of a basic theory about institutional failure and change. Currently, a number of European countries are lamenting their lack of small high tech companies and are looking for institutional mechanisms to stimulate their growth.

The ideas about selection and adaptation can easily be combined with the political theory and with the structural contingency theory. Political theory would explain why some organizations do not adapt and thus are rejected. It can also explain how under certain circumstances, such as the emergence of a new elite, a new and more adaptive form might be created. Structural contingency theory offers insights as to which forms are most appropiate for what kinds of environments and the dynamics of competition. Structural contingency theory also makes clear how failures in evolution can occur when not all parts of the structure are compatible. Finally, institutional theory can explain how diffusion occurs within countries and even across them. It provides a different set of explanations for why countries may not respond to competitive pressures.

CONCLUSIONS

Across the last quarter century three basic ideas united much of the research (see list of studies in Hage 1980, Damanpour 1991, and Zammuto & O'Connor 1992). A complex division of labor, an organic structure, and a high-risk strategy together account for the varying rates of innovation across the organizations that have been studied. However, in this research there has been a tendency to neglect the inputs of research expenditures, feedback, and macro-institutional levels of analysis.

This literature can easily be extended in a number of directions. I have stressed three possibilities: the application of these ideas to the study of organizational relations, the integration with intitutional analysis, and the study of organizational change. Throughout the discussion two critical concepts can integrate a number of the ideas for future research that have been discussed—organizational evolution and feedbacks. There has been too much emphasis on the causes of organizational innovation and not enough attention to the consequences. We need to think "backwards!" If this were to be done, the different perspectives would then be integrated into a general theory of organizations.

ACKNOWLEDGMENTS

The author wishes to thank Madeleine Hage, who converted my drafts into something both readable and enjoyable. I also wish to thank Marius Meeus, a colleague at the Institute for Advanced Studies, for his calling to my attention a number of new pieces of literature in his critique of the previous draft of this paper. Finally, I also want to thank the Netherlands Institute for Advanced Studies for the fellowship that has been giving me time to think about these matters.

> **Visit the *Annual Reviews home page* at**
> **http://www.AnnualReviews.org.**

Literature Cited

Abernathy JM, Utterback WJ. 1978. Patterns of industrial innovation. *Tech. Rev.* (June): 40–47

Aiken M, Hage J. 1971 The organic organization and innovation. *Sociology* 5:63–82

Aldrich H, Mueller S. 1982. The evolution of organizational forms: technology, coordination and control. *Res. Org. Behav.* 4: 33–87

Aldrich H, Sasaki T. 1995. R and D consortia in the United States and Japan. *Res. Policy.* 24:301–16

Allen T. 1977. *Managing the Flow of Technology.* Cambridge, MA: MIT Press

Allen T, Cohen S. 1969. Information flows in R, D labs. *Admin. Sci. Q.* 20:12–19

Alter C, Hage J. 1993. *Organizations Working Together.* Newbury Park, CA: Sage

Argyris C, Schoen D. 1978. *Organizational Learning.* Reading, MA: Addison-Wesley

Astley G, Van de Ven A. 1983. Central perspectives and debates in organizational theory. *Admin. Sci. Q.* 28:245–73

Badaracco JL. 1991. *The Knowledge Link:* *How Firms Compete Through Strategic Alliances.* Boston: Harvard Bus. School

Baldwin WL, Scott JT. 1987. *Market Structure and Technological Change.* Chur, Switzerland: Harwood Academic

Baum J. 1996. Organizational ecology. In *The Handook of Organization Studies,* ed. S Clegg, C Hardy, W Nord. London: Sage

Beamish P, Killings JP. 1997. *Cooperative Strategies: North American Perspectives.* San Francisco, CA: New Lexington

Becker G. 1964. *Human Capital.* New York: Natl. Bur. Econ. Res.

Bell D. 1973. *Post–Industrial Society.* New York: Free Press

Bessant J. 1985. The integration barrier: problems in the implementation of advanced manufacturing technology. *Robotica* 3: 97–103

Blau P. 1973. *The Organization of Academic Work.* New York: Wiley-Intersci.

Blau P, Schoenherr R. 1971. *The Structure of Organizations.* New York: Basic Books

Brenner R. 1987. *Rivalry: In Business, Sci-*

ence, Among Nations. Cambridge: Cambridge Univ. Press

Browning L, Beyer J, Shetler J. 1995. Building cooperation in a competitive Industry: SEMATEC and the semiconductor industry. *Acad. Mgmt. J.* 38:113–51

Burns T, Stalker GM. 1961. *The Management of Innovation.* London: Tavistock

Carroll GR. 1987. *Publish and Perish: The Organizational Ecology of Newspaper Industries.* Greenwich, CT: JAI Press

Cohen WM, Levin RC. 1989. Empirical studies of innovation and market structure. In *Handbook of Industrial Organization, Vol. II,* ed. R Schmalensee, RD Willig, pp. 1060–98. Amsterdam: Elsevier

Cohen W, Levinthal D. 1990. Absorptive capacity: a new perspective on learning and innovation. *Admin. Sci. Q.* 35:128–52

Cohn S, Turyn R. 1980. The structure of the firm and the adoption of process innovations. *IEEE Trans. Eng. Mgmt.* 27: 98–102

Collins, P. 1997. *Loosening the Gordian knot: innovation, occupational inertia and change.* Revision of a paper in Best Paper Proc., Acad. Mgmt. for 1992

Collins P, Hage J, Hull F. 1988. Organizational and technological predictors of change in automaticity. *Acad. Mgmt. J.* 31:512–43

Contractor F, Lorange P. 1988. *Cooperative Strategies in International Business.* Lexington, MA: Lexington

Daft R. 1989. *Organizational Theory and Design.* St. Paul, MI: West

Daft R, Becker S. 1978. *Innovation in Organizations: Innovation Adoption in School Organizations.* New York: Elsevier

Daly A, Hitchens DM, Wagner K. 1985. Productivity, machinery and skills in a sample of British and German manufacturing plants. *Natl. Inst. Econ. Rev.* February: 48–61

Damanpour F. 1988. Innovation type, radicalness and the adoption process. *Commun. Res.* 15:545–67

Damanpour F. 1991. Organizational innovation: a meta-analysis of effects of determinants and moderators. *Acad. Mgmt. J.* 34: 555–90

Dewar R, Hage J. 1978. Size, technology, complexity, and structural differentiation: toward a theoretical synthesis. *Adm. Sci. Q.* 20:453–60

DiMaggio PJ, Powell WW. 1983. Institutional isomorphism: the iron case. *Am. Sociol. Rev.* 48:147–60

Donaldson L. 1996. The normal science of structural contingency theory. In *The Handbook of Organizational Studies,* ed. S

Clegg, C Hardy, W Herd, pp. 55–76. London: Sage

Duchesneau T, Cohn S, Dutton J. 1979. *A study of innovation in manufacturing: determinants, processes and methodological issues.* Vols 1, 2. Unpubl. rep. to NSF, Soc.Sci. Res. Inst., Univ. Maine

Foss NJ. 1999. Research in the strategic theory of the firm: "isolationism" and "integrationism." *J. Mgmt. Stud.* 36(4). Forthcoming

Ettlie JE, Bridges WP, O'Keefe RD. 1984. Organizational strategy and structural differences for radical versus incremental innovation. *Mgmt. Sci.* 30:682–95

Fleck J. 1984. The employment effects of robots. In *Proc. 1st Int. Conf. on Human Factors in Manufacturing,* ed. T Lupton, pp. 269–77. Kempston, UK: IFS Publ. and North-Holland

Gerwin D. 1988. A theory of radical innovation process for computer aided manufacturing technology. *IEEE Trans. Engin. Mgmt.* 35:90–100

Gomes-Casseres B. 1994. Group vs. group: how alliance networks compete. *Harvard Bus. Rev.* 92:62–66, and sequel

Gomes-Casseres B. 1996. *The Alliance Revolution: The New Shape of Business Rivalry.* Cambridge, MA: Harvard Univ. Press

Hage J. 1965. An axiomatic theory of organizations *Admin. Sci. Q.* 8:289

Hage J. 1980. *Theories of Organizations: Form, Process, and Transformation.* New York: Wiley

Hage J. 1988. *The Futures of Organizations.* Lexington, MA: DC Heath

Hage J. 1998. *An Endogenous Theory of Economic Growth Via Innovation: Organizational and Institutional Determinants, Feedbacks, and Disequilibriums.* Presented at Annu. Meet. Soc. For Advancement of Socio-Economics, Vienna 1998

Hage J, Aiken M. 1967. Social change and oganizational properties: a comparative analysis. *Am. J. Sociol.* 72:503–19

Hage J, Aiken M. 1970. *Social Change in Complex Organizations.* Englewood Cliffs, NJ: Prentice-Hall

Hage J, Dewar R. 1973. Elite values vs. organizational structure in predicting innovation. *Admin. Sci. Q.* 18:279–90

Hage J, Finsterbusch K. 1987. *Organizational Change as a Development Strategy: Models and Tactics for Improving Third World Organizations.* Boulder, CO: Lynee Rienner

Hage J, Garnier M. 1993. *The Technical Training Advantages: A Review of Voca-*

tional and Technical Education and Their Effects for Individuals, Plants, and Economic Growth in Britain, France, Germany and the United States. Rep. for Dep. Educ., Washington, DC

Hage J, Collins P, Hull F, Teachman J. 1993. The impact of knowledge on the survival of American manufacturing plants. *Soc. Forc.* 72:223–46

Hage J, Powers C. 1992. *Post-Industrial Lives.* Newbury Park, CA: Sage

Häkansson H. 1990. Technology collaboration in industrial networks. *Eur. Mgmt. J.* 8:371–79

Hall R. 1991. *Organizations: Structure and Process.* Englewood Cliffs, NJ: Prentice-Hall. 5th ed.

Hannan M, Freeman J. 1984. Structural inertia and organizational change. *Am. Sociol. Rev.* 49:149–64

Hannan M, Freeman J. 1989. *Organizational Ecology.* Cambridge, MA: Harvard Univ. Press

Hannan MT, Carroll G. 1992. *Dynamics of Organizational Populations: Density, Legitimation and Competition.* New York: Oxford Univ. Press

Hickson DJ, Hinings CR, Lee CA, Schneck RE, Pennings JM. 1971. A strategic contingencies theory of intraorganizational power. *Admin. Sci. Q.* 16:216–29

Hinings CR, Hickson DJ, Pennings JM, Scneck RE. 1974. Structural conditions of intraorganizational power. *Admin. Sci. Q.* 19:22–44

Hladik K. 1988. R, D and international joint ventures. In *Cooperative Strategies in International Business,* ed. F Contractor, P Lorange, pp. 187–204. Lexington, MA: Lexington

Hull F. 1988. Inventions from R & D: organizational designs for efficient research peformance. *Sociology* 22:393–15

Ingersoll Engineers. 1984. *The FMS Reports.* Kempston, UK: IFS Publ.

Jaikumar R. 1986. Postindustrial manufacturing. *Harvard Bus. Rev.* 64:69–76

Jarillo JC. 1993. *Strategic Networks: Creating the Borderless Organization.* Oxford, UK: Butterworth-Heine Mgmt.

Kaluzny A, Veney J, Gentry J. 1972. Innovation of health services: a comparative study of hospitals and health departments. *Health, Society* 52:51–82

Kidder T. 1979. *The Soul of the New Machine.* New York: Avon

Killing JP. 1988. Understanding alliances: the role of task and organizational complexity. In *Cooperative Strategies in International Business,* ed. F Contractor, P Lorange, pp. 55–67. Lexington, MA: Lexington

Kitson M, Michie J. 1998. Markets, competition and innovation. See Michie & Smith 1998, pp. 101–18

Knorr K. 1981. *The Manufacture of Knowledge: An Essay in the Constructivist and Contextual Nature of Science.* Oxford, UK: Pergamon

Laage-Hellman J. 1989. *Technological development in industrial networks.* PhD thesis. Univ. Uppsala, Uppsala, Sweden

Latour B, Woolgar S. 1979. *Laboratory Life: The Construction of Scientific Facts.* Princeton, NJ: Princeton Univ. Press

Lawrence P, Lorsch J. 1967 *Organizations and Environments.* Boston, MA: Harvard Bus. School

Lazonick W. 1998. Organizational learning and international competition. See Michie & Smith 1998, pp. 204–38

Lundvall BA. 1992. *National Systems of Innovation: Towards a Theory of Innovation and Interactive Learning.* London: Pinter

Maurice M. 1978. Study of "the societal effect": universality and specificity in organization research. In *Organizations Alike and Unlike,* ed. C Lammers, DJ Hickson, pp. 42–60. London: Routledge & Kegan Paul

Maurice M. 1995. The social foundations of technical innovation: engineers and the division of labour in France and Japan. In *The New Division of Labour,* ed. W Littek, T Charles, pp. 317–47. Berlin: de Gruyter

Maurice M, Sellier F, Silvestre JJ. 1986. *The Social Foundations of Industrial Power.* Cambridge, MA: MIT Press

Maurice M, Sorge A, Warner M. 1980. Societal differences in organizing manufacturing units: a comparison of France, West Germany and Great Britain. *Organ. Stud.* 1:59–86

Mayntz R, Hughes TP. 1988 *The Development of Large Technical Systems.* Frankfurt am Main: Campus Verlag

Meyer J, Rowan B. 1977. Institutionalized organization: formal structure as myth and ritual. *Am. J. Sociol.* 83:440–63

Michie J, Smith JG, eds. 1998. *Globalization, Growth and Governance: Creating an Innovative Economy.* Oxford: Oxford Univ. Press

Mintzberg H. 1979. *Structuring of Organizations.* Englewood Cliffs, NJ: Prentice-Hall

Moch M. 1976. Structure and organizational resource allocation. *Admin. Sci. Q.* 21: 661–74

Moch M, Morse E. 1977. Size, centralization and organizational adoption of innovations. *Am. Sociol. Rev.* 42: 716–25

Mowry D, Rosenberg N. 1993. The U.S. national innovation system. In *National Ino-*

vation Systems, ed. R Nelson, pp. 29–75. New York: Oxford Univ. Press

Nelson R. 1993. National Systems of Innovation. New York: Oxford Univ. Press

Nohria N, Eccles R. 1992. Networks and Organizations. Cambridge, MA: Harvard Bus. School

Nonaka I, Takeuchi H. 1995. Knowledge Creating Company. Oxford: Oxford Univ. Press

Nooteboom B. 1994. Innovation and diffusion in small firms: theory and evidence. Small Bus. Econ. 6: 327–47

Nooteboom B. 1999. Innovation, learning and industrial organization. Cambridge J. Econ. 23: Forthcoming

Oerlemans L, Meeus M, Boekema W. 1998. Do networks matter for innovation? The usefulness of the economic network approach in analyzing innovation. Tijdschr. Econ. So. Geogr. 89(3):298–309

Palumbo D. 1969. Power and role specificity in organizational theory. Public Admin. Rev. 29:237–48

Perrow C. 1967. A framework for the comparative analysis of organizations. Am. Sociol. Rev. 32 (April):194–209

Pfeffer J. 1981. Power in Organizations. Boston, MA: Pitman

Pfeffer J, Salacik G. 1974. Organizational decision making as a political process: the case of a university budget. Admin. Sci. Q. 19:135–51

Pfeffer J, Salancik G. 1978. The External Control of Organizations. New York: Harper & Row

Pianta M. 1998. New technology and jobs. See Michie & Smith, pp. 71–100

Pine BJ. 1993. Mass Customization: The New Frontier in Business Competition. Boston, MA: Harvard Bus. School

Piore MJ, Sabel CF. 1984. The Second Industrial Divide: Possibilities for Prosperity. New York: Basic

Powell WW. 1990. Neither market nor hierarchy: network forms of organizations. In Research in Organizational Behavior, ed. LL Cummings, B Staw, pp. 295–36. Greenwich, CT: JAI

Powell WW, DiMaggio P. 1991. The New Institutionalism in Organizational Analysis. Chicago: Univ. Chicago Press

Porter M. 1990. The Comparative Advantage of Nations. New York: Free Press

Prais SJ, Jarvis V, Wagner K. 1989. Productivity and vocational skills in Britain and Germany: Hotels. Natl. Inst. Econ. Rev. November

Prais SJ, Steedman H. 1986. Vocational training in France and Britain in the building trades. Natl. Inst. Econ. Rev. :116

Primrose, P. 1988. The effect of AMT investment on costing systems. J. Cost Mgmt. Manufacturing Indust. 2 (2):27–30

Ramirez F, Boli J. 1987. The political construction of mass schooling, European origins and worldwide institutionalization. Soc. Educ. 60:2–178

Romer P. 1986. Increasing returns and long-run growth. J. Polit. Econ. 94:1002–37

Romer P. 1990. Endogenous technological change. J. Polit. Econ. 98:71–102

Schoenberger E. 1994. Competition, time, and space in industrial change. In Commodity Chains and Global Capitalism, ed. G Gereffi, M Korzeniewicz, pp. 51–60. Westport, CT: Praeger

Schultz T. 1961. Investment in human capital. Am. Econ. Rev. 51:1–16

Scott WR. 1987. The adolescence of institutional theory. Admin. Sci. Q. 32:493–511

Scott HR. 1992. Organizations: Rational, Natural and Open Systems. Englewood Cliffs, NJ: Prentice-Hall. 3rd ed.

Singh JV, House R, Tucker D. 1986. Organizational change and organizational mortality. Admin. Sci. Q. 31:587–11

Smith K, Grimm C, Gannon M. 1992. Dynamics of Competitive Strategy. Newbury Park, CA: Sage

Solow RM. 1992. Siena Lectures on Endogenous Growth Theory. Siena: Univ. Siena

Sorge A. 1996. Societal effects in cross-national organizational studies: conceptualizing diversity in actors and systems. In The Changing European Firm: Limits to Convergence, ed. R Whitley, PH Kristensen, pp. 67–86. London, Routledge

Stalk G, Hout T. 1990. Competing Against Time: How Time-Based Competition Is Reshaping Global Markets. New York: Free Press

Steedman H, Mason G, Wagner K. 1991. Intermediate skills in the workplace: deployment, standards and supply in Britain, France and Germany. Natl. Inst. Econ. Rev. May:60–77

Steedman H, Wagner K. 1987. A second look at productivity, machinery and skills in Britain and Germany. Natl. Inst. Econ. Rev. November:84–95

Steedman H, Wagner K. 1989. Productivity, machinery and skills: clothing manufacture in Britain and Germany. Natl. Inst. Econ. Rev. pp. 40–57

Sullivan A. 1998. Research outlays: the real bottom line: expenditures color a company's outlook. Int. Herald Tribune July 4–5th, pp 15–17

Teece D. 1987. The Competitive Challenge: Strategies for Industrial Innovation and Renewal. Cambridge, MA: Ballinger

Tushman M, Andersen P. 1986. Technological discontinuities and organizational environments *Admin. Sci. Q.* 31:439–65

Utterback J. 1994. *Mastering the Dynamics of Innovation: How Companies Can Seize Opportunities in the Face of Technological Change.* Boston, MA: Harvard Bus. School

Utterback JM, Abernathy WJ. 1975. A dynamic model of process and product innovation. *Omega* 3:639–56

Valéry N. 1999. Survey on innovation in industry. *Economist* Feb. 20:1–28

van Cayseele PJG. 1998. Market structure and innovation: a survey of the last twenty years. *Economist* 146, 3:391–417

Van de Ven A, Angle H, Pool M. 1989. *Research on the Management of Innovation: The Minnesota Studies.* New York: Harper & Row

Voss CA. 1988. Success and failure in advanced manufacturing technology. *Int. J. Tech. Mgmt.* 3:285–97

Walton R. 1987. *Innovating To Compete: Lessons for Diffusing and Managing Change in the Workplace.* San Franciso, CA: Jossey-Bass

Whitley R. 1992. *Business Systems of East Asia.* London: Sage

Whitley R. 1993. *European Business Systems: Firms and Markets in their National Contexts.* London: Sage

Womack J, Jones D, Roos D. 1990. *The Machine that Changed the World.* New York: Rawson Assoc.

Wood E. 1998. Determinants of innovation in SME's. See Michie & Smith, pp. 119–45

Zaltman G, Duncan R, Holbek J. 1973. *Innovations and Organizations.* New York: Wiley

Zammuto R, O'Connor E. 1992. Gaining advanced manufacturing technologies benefits: the role of organizational design and culture. *Acad. Mgmt. Rev.* 17: 701–28

Zucker LG. 1987. Institutional theories of organization. *Am. Sociol. Rev.* 95:445–46

Annu. Rev. Sociol. 1999. 25:623–57

INEQUALITY IN EARNINGS AT THE CLOSE OF THE TWENTIETH CENTURY

Martina Morris

Departments of Sociology and Statistics, Pennsylvania State University, University Park, Pennsylvania 16802; e-mail morris@pop.psu.edu

Bruce Western

Department of Sociology, Princeton University, Princeton, New Jersey 08540; e-mail: western@princeton.edu

KEY WORDS: stratification, economic restructuring, labor force, income, social change

ABSTRACT

Median income in the United States has fallen and the distribution of income has grown markedly more unequal over the past three decades, reversing a general pattern of earnings growth and equalization dating back to 1929. Median trends were not the same for all groups—women's earnings generally increased—but the growth in earnings inequality has been experienced by all groups. Even white men employed full-time, year-round—traditionally the most privileged and secure group—could not escape wage stagnation and polarization. These patterns suggest research questions that go beyond conventional sociological interest in racial and gender wage gaps, refocusing attention on more general changes in labor market dynamics. The debates over the origins of the rise in US inequality cover a wide range of issues that can be roughly grouped into four categories: the changing demographics of the labor force, the impact of economic restructuring, the role of political context and institutions, and the dynamics of globalization. We review the empirical literature here, and challenge the field of sociology to reconstruct its research agenda on stratification and inequality.

INTRODUCTION

Median income in the United States has stagnated and the distribution of income grown markedly more unequal over the past three decades, reversing a

0360-0572/99/0815-0623$08.00

general pattern marked by earnings growth and equalization dating back to 1929. The journals in economics have been full of descriptions, analyses, and debates about this new trend, as has the popular press. It has been front page news on and off for at least the last decade. Earnings trends played a major role in the last two presidential campaigns, generating the ironic spectacle of Republican candidates raising the issue of income and jobs as one of their primary campaign themes. There have been ironies in the academic response as well. For example, if you had been reading only the flagship journals in sociology, you probably would not know about these trends. Sociologists have been strangely and remarkably silent on this issue. While stratification and inequality are among the few undisputed core areas in the field of sociology, sociological research in this area has continued to focus on trends in the earnings "gaps"— gender and race—or on poverty alone, leaving the broader trends— stagnation in earnings levels and growing polarization in earnings distributions—to the economists. Sociologists, in other words, have continued to focus on the question of how people are allocated to positions in the earnings distribution, rather than on the structure of those positions. If the structure had been stable, the narrow focus on allocation might be justifiable. But the last three decades have been a period of economic restructuring at many levels, and the impact on earnings distributions both within and between groups has been profound.

The purpose of this paper is to review the broad changes in earnings inequality, and the animated debates about the causes and consequences of these changes. We will restrict our focus to the trends in hourly wages and annual earnings and not address trends in family income, as the latter is affected by changes in family structure that would take us beyond the scope of this review. The debate over the origins of the new trends covers a wide range of issues that can be roughly grouped into four categories: the changing demographics of the labor force, the impact of economic restructuring, the role of political context and institutions, and the dynamics of "globalization." Most of the literature cited here comes from labor economics because that is where most of the research is conducted and published. We believe that sociological theory has a rich framework for integrating and understanding the broad changes now under way, and we offer this review as a challenge to the field; to critically evaluate the evidence and provide a sociologically informed response.

BASIC TRENDS IN EARNINGS IN THE TWENTIETH CENTURY

Income tax data suggest that earnings inequality had two peaks in this century. The first occurred just prior to World War I, and the second on the eve of the great depression (Williamson & Lindert 1980).[1] From the 1930s to the 1950s, a general secular decline in earnings inequality occurred, first documented by Kuznets (1953). A similar trend was documented for wealth by Lampman (1962). This leveling trend inspired Kuznets' classic argument on the "inverted U" curve linking economic development to inequality: The early stage of modern economic growth is fueled by capital accumulation and generates a corresponding rise in inequality, but this trend is temporary, and as a capitalist economy enters maturity inequality eventually declines (Kuznets 1955). Debate over the necessity of inequality for early growth remains a heated topic in development economics (Adelman & Morris 1973, Chenery 1974, Chenery et al 1986), and the causal link is disputed for the United States (Williamson & Lindert 1980).

The postwar years of prosperity were marked by a steady rise in median earnings and relative stability in earnings inequality. The benefits of economic growth were large and widely distributed. The annual income of the median worker more than doubled from 1950 to 1970, and those at the bottom of the earnings scale made even greater progress during this period (Danziger & Gottschalk 1995). It was, as many have pointed out in chastened hindsight, a rising tide that lifted all boats.

These trends made a dramatic reversal in the early 1970s. In 1973[2], median earnings began to stagnate and then decline, and during the 1980s earnings inequality rose dramatically. By the early 1990s, a significant number of workers were earning less than their counterparts in the 1960s, and the trends toward wage stagnation and polarization have continued through 1996 (Bernstein & Mishel 1997).

The trends since 1973 in hourly wages can be seen in Figure 1[3]. The data are taken from the Current Population Survey (CPS) outgoing rotation groups[4]. Each line represents the dollar value of the decile cutoff for deciles 1, 3, 5, 7,

[1]Data on the distribution of earnings are sketchy prior to the imposition of a federal income tax, first levied on the wealthy in 1913 and eventually extended to the general population in 1929. Readers interested in earlier years can consult Williamson & Lindert's (1980) book on the history of wealth and income inequality, and the references mentioned there.

[2]This year is often cited as marking a secular decline in the growth of wages, productivity, and total output (Levy & Murnane 1992, Kutscher 1993, Western & Healy 1999).

[3]There are at least four different measures of economic well-being that can be examined here: hourly wages, annual earnings, household total earnings, and wealth. All show the same basic pattern, with pronounced rises in inequality. We show hourly wages here because they do not confound labor supply components like hours worked and income pooling, with labor pricing. Wages are thus a better representative of the job structure.

[4]The 4-8-4 rotation system used in the CPS results in one fourth of the sample being retired each month. The retired sample is called "the outgoing rotation group" (ORG) (see Bureau of the Census 1978). The cumulative ORG sample over the course of a year is about three times larger than the sample for the March CPS series on employment and earnings. See Bernstein (1997) for a discussion of the differences among alternative Census data sets.

and 9, divided by the dollar value for this decile in 1973 (decile 1 is the lowest decile in the distribution and decile 9 is the highest). Values above 1 imply that the workers at this decile made real wage gains in that year relative to 1973, while values below 1 indicate a decline in the real wage value for that decile. The line for decile 1, for example, represents the relative wage earned by the worker at the tenth percentile of the wage distribution from 1973 to 1976. If we follow it across the graph, we can see that workers in this decile saw their real wages rise slightly from the mid 1970s to the beginning of the 1980s, fall precipitously during the 1980s, and continue to decline at a lower rate during the 1990s. By 1996, real wages for these workers had fallen about 13% in real terms. The wage of the median worker (5th decile) stagnated through most of the 1970s and 1980s, and then fell sharply in the 1990s, losing a total of about 10% over the two decades. Even at the 7th decile, wages declined, albeit more modestly. The only workers who did not experience a drop in their real wages were those at the top (9th decile): This group saw their wages rise by about 10%, mostly during the 1980s. Thus, the story of this period is not that the rich got richer and the poor got poorer, but that virtually everyone lost ground, and those at the bottom lost the most.

The trend for all workers, however, masks a striking difference in the fortunes of men and women during this period. The sex-specific decile graphs can be seen in Figure 2. Among men, there were no winners. Those at the top of the distribution managed to hold on to the value of their real wage from 1973 to

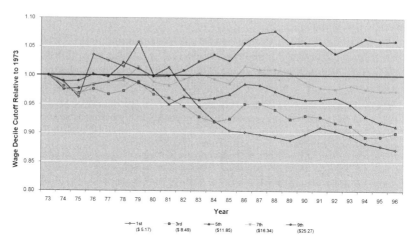

Figure 1   The lines trace the real value of wages at each decile relative to its value in 1973. The deciles are determined by the earnings distribution within sex. Data are for all workers, from the CPS, Outgoing Rotation Groups, and are available at: http://epinet.org/datazone/data/ orghourlyxoffs_all.xls. For more information see (Bernstein & Mishel 1997).

1996, but everyone else experienced losses. At the bottom decile, wages dropped by 20% in real terms. For women, by contrast, there were no losers, and those at or above the median all experienced some gains. The wage gains for the median woman worker were quite modest, about 5%. But the wage gains for women in the top decile were nearly 30%. When comparing the patterns for women and men, it is important to keep in mind that the trends here are constructed within group—relative to their own position in 1973. Thus the gains that women made at the top still only put their ninetieth percentile somewhere around the eightieth percentile of the men's distribution in 1996, and the median woman is still earning about as much as a thirty-fifth percentile man. It would be a mistake to say that women have gained parity with men (Bernhardt et al 1995), but they did make both relative and absolute gains over the past two decades (Blau & Kahn 1994, Blau 1998). About the only thing that men and women shared over this period was the growth in within-group inequality.

The next question for most sociologists is how the trends in earnings break down by race. The stylized facts are that the decline in the race gap in income that had begun in the 1960s came to a halt in the early 1970s (Juhn et al 1991) and reversed by the mid 1970s, leaving blacks in the early 1990s at about the levels they had been in the late 1970s. Here, as well, the growth in within group

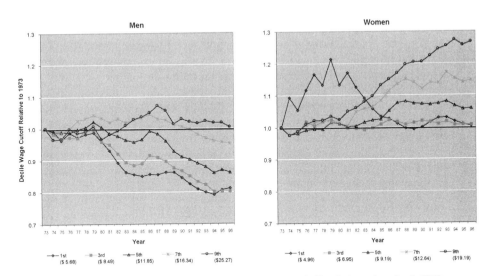

Figure 2   The lines trace the real value of wages at each decile relative to its value in 1973. Data are from the CPS, Outgoing Rotation Groups, and are available at: http://epinet.org/datazone/data/orghourlyxoffs_men.xls and _women.xls. For more information see Bernstein & Mishel (1997).

inequality was the one common thread: Polarization in the earnings of black men and women grew in the 1980s decade (Morris et al 1994).

These, then, are the basic trends. There are numerous reviews, descriptive and synthetic, to be found in the microeconomics literature (Burtless 1990, Bound & Johnson 1991, Katz & Murphy 1992, Levy & Murnane 1992, Danziger & Gottschalk 1993, Danziger & Gottschalk 1995). The key finding, however, is that earnings inequality has been growing among virtually all groups. Even among white men employed full-time, year-round, the group that has traditionally enjoyed the highest wages, most generous benefits, and greatest protection from cyclical downturns, the trends of wage stagnation and polarization have been marked. This leads to a set of research questions that breaks out of the usual "wage-gap" framework and begins to address the general issue of changes in labor market dynamics.

CHANGES IN SUPPLY: DEMOGRAPHIC SHIFTS IN THE LABOR FORCE

From 1950 to 1980 the labor force expanded by more than 44 million workers, a 70% increase. More than half of that expansion occurred during the 1970s (Kutscher 1993). The timing of the increase coincides with three dramatic changes in the composition of labor supply: the entry of the baby boom generation to the labor force, the growth of women's labor force participation, and the increase of legal and illegal immigration. Each of these factors could have had a large impact on the earnings distribution, and each has been the focus of a substantial literature that seeks to clarify the magnitude of this impact. The findings suggest that each of these factors has played a role, but not a key role, in growing inequality. The changing distribution of educational attainment has also attracted much attention, and here the findings have been interpreted as yielding greater evidence of some kind of causal role. A closer look at each literature, however, suggests that the issues are far from resolved. In particular, the debate about the role of education, what it represents, and what it explains, is at the leading edge of the supply side paradigm, and at the boundary of explanations that focus instead on shifts in demand.

Age: The Baby Baby Boom Enters the Labor Market

The baby boom generation is defined as the cohort born between 1946 and 1964. This cohort turned 18 from 1964 to 1980, years which roughly mark their transition into the labor force. The share of the labor force comprising young workers (20–34 years old) grew by over 40% during this period (Freeman 1980). Neoclassical economics would predict that this increase in the supply of workers with little experience would depress the relative wages of new workers (the classic work is Easterlin 1980) and, by extension, widen the overall wage distribution by lowering the wages in the bottom tail. There was, in fact, some evidence that the experience premium rose during the early years of the baby boom entry, and cross-national comparisons suggested that large cohort size did reduce the relative wages of younger workers by a small amount (for a review of this literature, see Bloom et al 1987).

But a number of studies suggest that the baby boom effect was not driving the growth in earnings inequality. First, the timing was off. Peak entry years for the baby boom cohort were during the 1960s and early 1970s, well before wages in the lower tail of the distribution collapsed (see Easterlin 1987:18). Second, empirical studies repeatedly documented that the growth in inequality was greater within age groups than between them (Dooley & Gottschalk 1982). And third, a recent study of the "baby bust" cohort, which should presumably benefit by the reverse logic, has shown that wages for this cohort while they are 25–34 years old are both absolutely lower than the boom cohort at the same age (by as much as 20% in some industries), and lower relative to older members of the labor force (Schrammel 1998). So the baby boom is now generally regarded as having played a minor role, at best, in the growth of earnings inequality.

Sex: Women Enter the Labor Market

Another profound change in the composition of the labor force was the steady rise in women's labor force participation. From 1950 to 1994, the fraction of women working for pay increased from 34% to 59%. Among prime-aged women (25–54), the increase was even stronger: 37% to 75%. As a result, women's share of the labor force rose from 30% to 46% (Spain & Bianchi 1996). As with the baby boom, this rapid influx of workers with low levels of experience and traditionally lower wages seemed a likely candidate for explaining the increase in overall earnings inequality. And as with the baby boom, this explanation fell short.

First, as is clearly visible in Figure 2, earnings data showed that the wage gap between the sexes was declining (Blau & Kahn 1994, Bernhardt et al 1995). This was an unexpected trend under the circumstances. One might expect that the general pattern of wage stagnation and decline should have been exacerbated for women by their rapidly increasing supply, but instead women in most segments of the earnings distribution saw real increases in their wages during this period. Compared to their male counterparts, women at the bottom of the distribution in particular held their ground. The net result was that while 50% of women's earnings were in the bottom decile of the men's distribution at the start of the 1970s, only 28% remained there by the end of the 1980s (Bernhardt et al 1995). The growing supply of women workers clearly did not depress their wages.

Second, inequality was growing rapidly within sex. The 90:10 earnings ratio for men grew from 3.6 to 4.4 from 1980 to 1996, and the ratio for women grew from 2.9 to 4.0 (based on data from Figure 2). While the decline in the gender wage gap was widely seen as heralding a new era of progress for women, the sharp polarization in earnings among women, as among men, made it clear that the benefits of this new era were going to be distributed more unequally than before. There was good reason to expect inequality to grow among women, as their levels of work experience and tenure rose strongly during this period, increasing the differentiation in human capital among them. While their stocks of work experience, and the returns to this experience rose during the 1980s (Spain & Bianchi 1996, Blau 1998), these and other human capital factors were found to explain 30–50% of the growing inequality in women's earnings (O'Neill & Polachek 1993, Wellington 1993). To the extent that both men's and women's earnings distributions reflected the same residual polarizing trend, rising earnings inequality could not be explained by the changing sex composition of the labor force.

If women were "perfect substitutes" for men in the labor market, one might read the evidence as consistent with the hypothesis that women's labor force entry placed them in direct competition with low-wage men, depressing the earnings for these men, but generally raising the earnings for women. This interpretation is complicated by occupational segregation. Occupational segregation by sex fell during the period from 1970 to 1990, but the rate of decline slowed in the second decade. Using the index of dissimilarity, the fraction of men or women who would have needed to change jobs to end segregation was 68% in 1970, 59% in 1980, and 53% in 1990 (Spain & Bianchi 1996, Table 4.6). This indicates the persistence of largely separate labor markets for men and women. Empirical studies find little evidence that increases in the female labor supply reduced the wages of men in the lower tail of the earnings distribution (Juhn & Kim 1999, but see also Topel 1994).

In sum, trends in women's labor force participation were clearly an important phenomenon during this period, but their impact on overall earnings inequality was probably modest at best. The way in which earnings inequality rose among both sexes suggests that other factors were at work.

Immigration: A New Wave of Unskilled Workers

A third demographic shift in the labor force was the change in ethnic composition. This shift was not as large as the age and sex changes described above, but there was a rapid influx of Asians and Latin Americans in the three decades following the 1965 amendments to the Immigration and Nationality Act. While 4.8% of the US population was foreign born in 1970, 15 million immigrants were added over the next 25 years, and by 1996 immigrants accounted for 9.3% of the population. Most immigrants are concentrated in just six states—California, New York, Texas, Florida, New Jersey, and Illinois— with over a fifth originating from Mexico (Jasso & Rosenzweig 1990, Borjas 1997).

Empirically, immigrants have less schooling on average than US natives. In addition, the educational attainment of foreign-born workers rose slowly, increasing the skills gap with native workers. By 1990, the proportion of high school dropouts among immigrants was about twice as high as among natives (Borjas 1994; for heterogeneity among nativity groups see Portes & Rumbaut 1996:58–66). If immigrants are substitutes for native workers, an increase in the number of immigrants would push wages down for less educated native workers.

Patterns of immigration and educational attainment motivated two main approaches to studying earnings inequality: spatial studies of earnings across localities, and aggregate analysis linking immigration rates to earnings for different education groups. Spatial studies capitalize on the concentration of immigrants in relatively few localities. Using 1970, 1980, and 1990 Census data, studies of cities find that the proportion of immigrants in local labor markets and the size of immigrant inflows have little effect on native earnings and changes in earnings (Altonji & Card 1991, LaLonde & Topel 1991) despite small effects on employment (Card 1997). Critics argue that city wage levels and trends are dominated by common variation unrelated to local immigration. Results are thus sensitive to time points chosen for analysis (Borjas 1996, Borjas 1997). In addition, outflows of natives in response to immigration may bias estimated effects on local wage structures (Borjas 1997). Aggregate analysis can address both these problems.

Borjas et al (1992, 1997) studied aggregate effects by analyzing the influence of immigration on the supply of workers with different levels of education. The wage effects of immigration can then be calculated with unobserved coefficients (or elasticities) that express the change in wages for a given change in the labor supply. Disaggregating labor supply effects by educational level provides estimates of the impact of immigration on earnings inequality by skill level. Since immigrants increase the supply of dropouts compared to high schools graduates, immigration is estimated to account for a large part— around 45%—of the rise in the dropout-high school wage differential between 1980 and 1995. The influence of immigration on high school and college graduates is negligible. Critics of this approach argue that the aggregate estimates depend on the choice of wage elasticity, and substantial uncertainty accompanies this quantity (Borjas et al 1992:240, Katz & Murphy 1992:69), leading to a wide range of estimates (e.g. Borjas 1997:56).

How much does immigration affect inequality? The answer so far depends strongly on research design. Spatial studies yield small estimates that are sensitive to the choice of survey year. Aggregate studies report large effects that are, nevertheless, highly uncertain.

Education: Declining Position of High School–Educated Workers

Another change in labor force composition that has attracted much attention is the distribution of education. This story has a couple of ironic twists. Figure 3 shows the change in educational attainment for men over time. While the popular perception is probably that college completion has risen slowly but steadily in the postwar period, this is not true for men. Completion of a college degree peaked in the 1970s, then declined slightly during most of the 1980s and early 1990s. Most regard the 1970s peak in college enrollment as an anomaly, attributing the high levels to Vietnam War draft evasion.[5] Whatever the reason, the number of college-educated workers grew relatively faster than non–college-educated in all age and sex groups throughout the 1970s. This was particularly true for young workers, where the number of college-educated workers grew by 85% for men and 150% for women from 1971 to 1979, compared to 13% and 66% rates of growth among the respective high-school–educated groups (this and other figures in this paragraph from Levy & Murnane 1992). As supply grew, the wage gap between college and high school–educated workers narrowed. For men, the college earnings premium fell from 22% to 13%, 50% to 35%, and 55% to 36% among the 10-year age groups bracketed by 25, 35, 45, and 54 years old, respectively. The comparable figures for women were declines from 41% to 23%, 47% to 30%, and 50% to 35%. This was a fairly dramatic shift, and one that attracted much popular and academic attention. A number of classic books were published on this issue, including *The Overeducated American* (Freeman 1976), and *Education and Jobs: The Great Training Robbery* (Berg 1970). America was seen to be producing too many educated workers, for jobs that had been increasingly "deskilled" with the introduction of modern technology (Braverman 1974).[6]

By the next decade, this decline in the earnings premium was reversed. Technological change was again claimed to be the driving force—this time by raising the demand for a high skill workforce. It was a remarkable about face.

A growing wage gap between high school and college–educated workers began to be documented in numerous studies by the mid 1980s (Dooley & Gottschalk 1985, Blackburn et al 1990, Murphy & Welch 1993). While most age-sex groups recouped during the 1980s the college premium losses that they had experienced during the 1970s, for the younger workers, the new gains

---

[5]Some economists focus instead on the post-peak decline and attribute this to the preceding fall in the education-related earnings premium. The assumption is that people would observe that the returns to a college degree were falling and would therefore choose not to go to college. The fact that women's attainment shows a consistent rise suggests this argument is wrong.

[6]This issue also led to the notion of "underemployment" and the development of the "Labor Force Utilization Framework" for measuring it (Clogg 1979).

sometimes exceeded the earlier losses (Levy & Murnane 1992, Table 5, Part 2). In contrast to the other compositional changes in the labor force, the "rising education premium" appeared to be one of the few features in earnings trends that clearly contributed to the growth in overall wage inequality.

Despite the (economist's) language used here, it should be kept in mind that the "rise" in the college premium was almost entirely driven by the *collapse* in the earnings of high-school graduates and dropouts. Both wages and to a lesser extent hours worked declined for this group. From 1979 to 1994 the real weekly earnings of college graduates rose by 5%, while the earnings of high-school graduates fell by 20% (Gottschalk 1997). This is what caused the doubling of the college premium.

Initially, the falling wages of the high-school educated were attributed to macroeconomic factors: a decline in demand for less-skilled workers arising from the trends in trade and immigration (Murphy & Welch 1988, Murphy & Welch 1992). As discussed elsewhere in this paper, evidence for these conjectures was mixed, leading to some influential reversals of opinion (Murphy & Welch 1993).

An alternative hypothesis regarding the rise in the education premium then gained some consensus: a rise in the rate of "skill-biased technological change." For some labor economists, the puzzle that needs to be explained is not the fall in wages among the high-school educated, but rather a rising col-

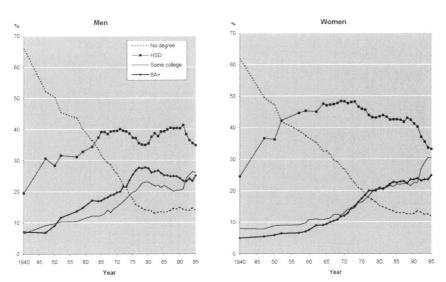

Figure 3   Each line represents the share of the 25–34-year-old population with the indicated educational attainment. Data are from the Census and CPS, and are available at: http://www.census.gov/population/socdemo/education/ table17.txt.

lege premium during a period of rising supply. The lower rates of college attendance in the late 1970s did not result in a decline in the share of college-educated workers, just a slower rate of growth. Measured in terms of "aggregate labor input"[7], the college-educated share of labor grew by 17.8% in the 1963–1971 period, by 24.1% the 1971–1979 period, and then by 15.6% in the 1979–1987 period (Murphy & Welch 1992, Table II). Simple economic logic implies that the demand for these "skilled" workers must therefore have risen more than the supply. The explanation for this increased demand is hypothesized to be a diffusion of technology in the workplace that requires higher levels of skills than in the past (Johnston & Packer 1987, Davis & Haltiwanger 1991, Bound 1992).

The evidence for a general increase in the demand for skills is weak, in large part because both skill and demand are notoriously difficult to measure. Educational attainment is often used as a proxy for skill, and the educational credentials of the workforce clearly rose during this period. But this is a measure of supply, and does not necessarily signify a shift in demand or job skill requirements. Educational attainment is, as well, a problematic proxy for individual skill. Howell and Wolff use the skill measures from the *Dictionary of Occupational Titles* as an alternative measure for skill demand (1991). While they do find an upgrading of cognitive and interactive skills and a declining demand for motor skills within industries, they also find that the wage effects are muted by the growth of moderate skill jobs in low-wage service industries. Another common proxy for skill demand is the share of non-production workers in an industry. This is the measure used by the most widely cited paper claiming that increased demand for skills is driving the growth in wage inequality. In this study by Berman et al (1994), the rising share of non-production workers in the manufacturing industry is found to be associated with the growth in wage dispersion in this sector. Using production work to proxy for lack of skills is at least as problematic as using educational attainment. Even if the proxy were acceptable, however, the timing of the changes in occupational composition does not match the timing of the wage changes. The share of non-production workers rises continuously from 1948 through 1982, and then begins a slight decline. Just as the growth in wage inequality begins, the demand for "skill" appears to fall.

The evidence for the more specific hypothesis of a technology-driven increase in demand for skills is equally weak. In a somewhat humorous exchange, one of the few papers to try to measure the extent of technological change in the workplace and its connection to wage differentials—"How computers have changed the wage structure" (Krueger 1993)—was answered with

---

[7]This is essentially the average number of hours worked for this group weighted by a time constant average wage. For details, see (Katz & Murphy 1992:39–40).

a paper entitled "The returns to computer use revisited: Have pencils changed the wage structure too?" (Pischke & DiNardo 1997). Krueger's study, using CPS data, found that computer use at work was associated with a 17% increase in wages in 1984, and a 19% increase in 1988. In the subsequent paper, Pischke & DiNardo, using a more detailed German work survey, find that pencils, calculators, and telephones have a similar effect. Entered simultaneously, each remains significant, though all of them, including computers, increase wages by only 5%. Another variable, "working while sitting," had similar wage impacts. Clearly, computer use, pencils, and sitting while working are potential proxies for a host of other factors that may be associated with wage differentials, the prime candidate of which is white-collar office work. Additional contributions to this literature can be found in Berman et al (1998) and Autor et al (1998).

The role of office workers in the growing education premium has been examined in a recent paper by Rose & Carneval (1997). Tracking the wage changes for the detailed three-digit occupational codes in the CPS from 1979 to 1995, they note that earnings for professionals in technical/scientific fields stagnated during this period, even in occupations closely tied to technological innovation. Among computer systems analysts with bachelor's degrees, for example, earnings rose by only 3% over the 16 years. Engineers, the largest occupation among science-related professionals, actually experienced earnings declines of about 1.5%. During this same period, earnings increased by 34% for all occupations in the category of "office work"[8], an increase that was driven by the nonscience, nontechnical business professionals and managers. Explaining this disparity in earnings growth as a function of skill-biased technological change would be difficult.

The current popularity of this technology thesis is therefore somewhat curious. Productivity has stagnated over the period that technological change is supposed to have led to a skill-intensive workplace (Kozicki 1997)[9], which requires us to believe that the change in technology was strong enough to reverse a half century of wage leveling, but still too weak to increase productivity (Mishel et al 1997). Perhaps, as Howell et al suggest, it is the "natural attraction of a simple story" that accounts for the tenacity of the technology thesis (1998). But the rapidity with which this story was embraced, and the vehemence with which it is defended suggest that something other than science makes this thesis attractive.

[8]Office workers are defined as managers, supervisors, fire sector employees, business professionals, employees of public administration and nonprofits, and support staff.

[9]The rate of growth in productivity has declined from an average about 2.8% per year in the 1948–1972 period to about 1.2% per year since 1973 (Bureau of Labor Statistics website data). The trend is often attributed to the shift in the industrial mix toward the service sector and to the rise in energy prices (Kozicki 1997).

In summary, changes in the wage premium associated with a college degree are more strongly implicated in the growth in wage inequality than either the baby boom or women's labor force entry. While inequality grew rapidly within age and sex groups, it grew more rapidly between education groups than within them. This leaves the question of causality open, however. The observed trends in the education premium are equally consistent with a microeconomic argument that emphasizes the role of skill-biased technological changes in raising the relative demand for highly educated workers, and with a macroeconomic argument that emphasizes the role of trade and immigration in lowering the relative demand for less educated workers. The evidence for the microeconomic argument is weak, and a number of the most recent studies have mounted compelling critiques of this argument at both the theoretical and empirical levels (cf Howell et al 1988 for a critical review of this literature). The macroeconomic argument is ultimately a story of economic restructuring and political resources, and this is what we turn to next.

CHANGES IN DEMAND: ECONOMIC RESTRUCTURING

While the demographics of the labor force changed substantially during the postwar boom years, changes of similar magnitude were also occurring in the structure of the labor market. The restructuring took two forms: continuing decline in manufacturing employment leading to the emergence of a "service economy" (Fuchs 1968), and a rise in market-mediated employment relations—outsourcing, subcontracting, and temporary, contingent, and part-time work contracts. In the popular press it is these factors, more than the demographic trends, that are linked to the perception of changing economic fortunes. A poll would probably show that most people associate the "baby-boom problem" with the looming social security crisis, and women's (paid) work with the changes in family structure. By contrast, the decline of the "rust belt" and the prospect of being "downsized" would probably strike a chord that resonates with many people who feel that their economic security, and their children's economic future, are increasingly at risk.

Deindustrialization

The trend toward growing employment in the service sector and shrinking employment in the manufacturing sector is a remarkably long and stable one. Figure 4 shows the relative employment shares of the goods-producing and service-producing sectors from 1950 to 1997 (Bureau of Labor Statistics 1998). By the end of this period, the share of employment in the manufacturing industry proper (the largest industry in the goods-producing sector) had declined to 15%, making it smaller than the retail trade industry, while the size of the serv-

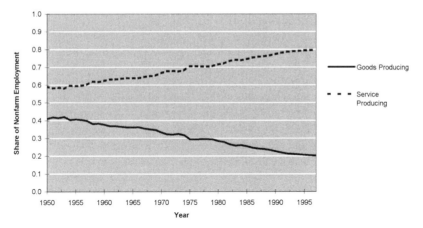

Figure 4   The lines represent the share of total nonfarm employment in the goods and service producing sectors from 1950 to 1997. Data are from the Bureau of Labor Statistics, series EES00000001, and are available at http://www.bls.gov/top20.html.

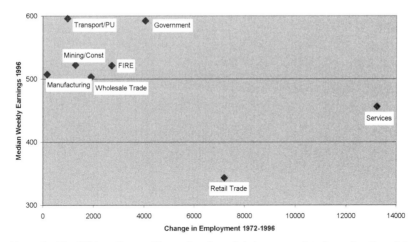

Figure 5   The 1996 median weekly earnings in each industry are plotted as a function of the growth in employment in that industry from 1972–1996. Data are from the Bureau of Labor Statistics, as reported in (Meisenheimer 1998).

ice industry proper had risen to 29%. This does not imply that the United States now produces fewer goods, as a concomitant trend has been a steep rise in productivity in the manufacturing sector (Kozicki 1997). The net result is that national manufacturing output has remained essentially stable. Kutscher & Personick (1986) record a small decline from 36.8% to 34.5% in manufacturing's share of gross duplicated output from 1959 to 1984, while Mishel (1989) reports a slight increase from 21.6% to 22%, using the Gross Domestic Product from 1948 to 1987. While manufacturing output may be stable, the population of jobs—and wages—has clearly changed.

Deindustrialization is associated for many with the substitution of bad jobs for good ones. Service sector jobs have traditionally paid less, offered fewer benefits, and more part-time employment. The gap in annual earnings between expanding industries (primarily in the service sector) and contracting industries (primarily in the goods-producing sector) reached $10,000 in the 1980s—a postwar high (Costrell 1988). The correlation between earnings and employment growth at the industry level from 1972 to 1996 can be seen in Figure 5 (taken from Meisenheimer II 1998). The inverse relation is striking: Higher wage industries are all growing much more slowly than the two lowest wage industries. (The X-axis here measures the change in number of persons employed, rather than the per cent or share change). The two fastest growing industries, services and retail trade, are also distinguished by lower rates of heath and pension benefits, and higher rates of part-time work, as can be seen in Table 1 (adapted from Meisenheimer 1998).

Table 1   Selected characteristics of jobs by industry[a]

	Services	Retail	Other	% lower (or higher) service	retail
Wages[b]					
Median wage	456	343	542.3	−16	−37
1st decile wages	217	191	251.8	−14	−24
9th decile wage	1050	774	1134.9	−7	−32
90:10 ratio	4.8	4.1	4.5	7	−10
Benefits[c]					
Health benefits	49.0	38.4	71.5	−31	−46
Pension benefits	35.2	25.7	56.8	−38	−55
Sick leave	55.1	35.3	61.3	−10	−42
Disability	31.4	22.3	48.2	−35	−54
Job Security					
Involuntary PT	5.0	9.4	2.4	108	292
Contingent work	7.4	3	4.7	59	−36

[a]Data taken from (Meisenheimer 1998)
[b]1996 March CPS, full time workers only
[c]1993 April CPS

With 80% of all jobs in the "service producing" sector, however, this sector is also fairly diverse. As a result the dispersion of wages in this sector is higher than in the goods producing sector. Low end service industries, like retail trade, provide wages that are 30% below average while high end services, like those found in the finance, insurance, and real estate sectors, offer wages that are about 8% higher on average. Within the service industry proper, the 90:10 earnings ratio is 7% higher than in other industries.

A rising share of employment in the service sector would thus be expected to generate trends consistent with the observed stagnation in wages and growing inequality. The stagnation effects have generally been supported by empirical studies (Costrell 1988) and reinforced by studies of the wage penalties experienced by displaced workers (see also the references cited in Bluestone & Harrison 1982, Ch. 3; Farber 1993), but the inequality effects of deindustrialization have not been consistently supported. Initial findings ranged from no significant effect (Raffalovich 1990), to effects that account for about 20% of the change in earnings dispersion (Tilly et al 1986). One source of the mixed findings is the use of different measures, sample restrictions, and time periods. In general, however, changes in the industrial mix have met the same analytic fate as compositional shifts in supply: Inequality was found to be growing within the sectors, not simply between them (Lawrence 1984, Grubb & Wilson 1989, Blackburn 1990). Perhaps in response to these inconsistent findings, the literature on deindustrialization increasingly shifted to regional studies (Carlino 1989, Rodwin & Sazanami 1989, Rodwin & Sazanami 1991, Grant & Wallace 1994). A recent study finds large effects of deindustrialization on growth in earnings inequality at the state level (Bernard & Jensen 1998).

Deindustrialization's contribution to current wage trends thus seems to be an unresolved question. The "good jobs-bad jobs" debate has increasingly taken a different path. In contrast to the idea that some industries provide good jobs with stable employment and high wages, while other industries provide bad jobs with low wages and no mobility, the demand-side research literature now recognizes that these employment strategies are being used together, not only within industries, but even within firms.

Employment Relations

The postwar years of earnings growth and equalization emerged during a unique period in American industrial history. The period was marked by the development of a system of employment relations often referred to as the "internal labor market" (Doeringer & Piore 1971). The key characteristic of an internal labor market is a formal hierarchy of jobs within firms that are filled primarily by internal promotion rather than through external recruitment. The resulting system serves to buffer employment relations—including decisions about wages, job mobility, and training—from the volatility of external market pressures. This substitution of organizational control for market mechanisms is a topic that has generated many of the classic works on the boundary between sociology and economics [Williamson 1975, Chandler 1977, Kerr 1977, Dunlop 1993 (1958)]. The origins of the system are sometimes traced to firms themselves, acting to "rationalize" the uncertainties of employment and productivity (Doeringer & Piore 1971) and to reduce transaction costs associated with the agency problem (Williamson 1975, Burawoy 1979). Others emphasize the role of unions in seeking better working conditions for their members (Jacoby 1985). A further impetus for change was the Federal Government, which enacted key employment legislation to meet the need for national economic planning and stable production during the two world wars (Baron et al 1986). In any case, the system was never wholeheartedly embraced by US managers (Jacoby 1990).

In stylized form, the internal labor market was characterized by the lifetime job. Workers started at one company, stayed with it, and were guaranteed job security and yearly raises. In return, employers obtained control over labor supply and a committed workforce, or at least a negotiated truce with labor. For jobs higher in the skill hierarchy, the system also provided customized training, since workers learned on the job and therefore brought firm-specific knowledge and tested skills to each new position (Piore & Sabel 1984, Kochan et al 1986).

The terms of this trade-off deteriorated for American employers in the mid-1970s. Cost reduction became an important basis of competition, and internal labor markets were a natural target. Cost reduction requires flexibility in who is hired, for how long, for how much, and for which tasks. To get this flexibility, some firms have adopted high-performance work systems that can benefit their employees as well as productivity (Piore & Sabel 1984, Pfeffer 1994). Other employers, however, are now more willing to rely instead on the external labor market, as the high-performance systems require significant initial investments in technology and training. With the changes in corporate financing and governance in the wake of banking deregulation, the "shareholder revolution" has skewed the incentives toward short- term growth in dividends, rather than long-term reinvestment of profits (for a review, see Applebaum & Berg 1996). The wave of "downsizing" that took place during the late 1980s and 1990s heralded this change. For the first time, employment losses finally reached deep into the white collar occupations (Cappelli 1992), though some question the extent of the change (Gordon 1996). There are many good reviews of this literature (Appelbaum 1987, Pfeffer & Baron 1988, Colclough & Tolbert 1992, Harrison 1994, Osterman 1994, Cappelli 1995).

In one of the first systematic studies of the growth in "market-mediated" employment relations, Belous (1989) documented a dramatic rise in the number of contingent workers during the 1980s. While the total labor force grew by 14% during this period, the number of agency temporary workers grew by 175%, part-time employment grew by 21%, employment in the business service sector—the primary provider of subcontracted human services—grew by 70%, and self-employment grew by 19%. Overall, the contingent workforce grew from about 25–28% of the workforce to 30–37% of the workforce during the decade (depending on the definition). Belous used standard employment categories from the Bureau of Labor Statistics to define contingent workers in his study, not all of which are mutually exclusive. This has led to some criticism that he overestimates the size of the contingent workforce.

A number of studies since Belous have wrestled with the definition of "contingent worker" in the attempt to develop better measures.[10] This has resulted in a wide range of estimates for the size of the contingent workforce. The most conservative definitions suggest that contingent workers comprised at most 5% of the workforce by 1995 (Polivka 1996a,b; see also Abraham 1990), while a survey of employers suggests a figure of 17% (EQW 1995). At the same time, nearly 80% of firms reported making use of flexible staffing arrangements, excluding the use of part-time workers, which is even more widespread (Mishel & Bernstein 1995:229, Houseman 1997). While agencies specializing in office temporary workers accounted for two thirds of the total temporary employment in 1972, this had fallen to 55% in 1982 (Abraham 1990). Increasingly, firms are turning to temporary workers to staff other specialized, nonclerical positions.

The growth in market-mediated employment has revived speculation regarding the emergence of a core/periphery structure in the labor market—this time within rather than between firms (or industries) (Belous 1989). To meet the dual needs of a stable and reliable workforce in positions that are central to organizational performance, and the flexibility to deal with rapid change induced by global competition, large firms may simply adopt a dual strategy: retaining the key elements of the internal labor market for a (now much reduced) set of core employees, and using flexible staffing arrangements for all other functions. Cappelli (1995) reviews the European literature on this topic and concludes that the evidence for it is weak.

Workplace studies do shed some light, however, on the technology debate. In contrast to the notion that new computer-based technologies have a universal upskilling effect on jobs, these studies suggest that the effect is more polarizing. On the one hand, changes in telephone technology make it possible to centralize customer service operations in large, low-wage call centers that re-

---

[10]This debate parallels in many ways the debates over measuring the size of the workforce employed in internal labor markets [e.g., Smith (1988) and Oi (1983)].

semble a modern-day assembly line. On the other hand, changes in computer networking have transformed the typical bank branch worker from a recording clerk into a sales-oriented investment analyst. Thus, technology may have played a role in growing inequality, but not in a skill-biased way (Capelli 1993, Hunter & Lafkas 1998).

Much of the work on changes in the nature of employment relations is based on case studies rather than national surveys. The natural unit of analysis is the firm, rather than the worker, which makes many of the more widely used surveys inappropriate for linking changes in firm structure to changes in employment outcomes. To the extent that firm-level changes are driving the overall trends in earnings, however, this is a key area for future research. It is also one that sits squarely on the traditional boundary between sociology and economics.

INSTITUTIONAL FACTORS: THE POLITICS OF THE WAGE-EFFORT BARGAIN

Supply and demand are powerful forces, but they operate in a larger political context. Political decisions determine the extent and types of regulatory constraints placed on market forces, as well as the redistributive measures adopted "post fisc." While market explanations dominate research on rising inequality, institutional conditions have received some consideration. The focus, however, has been narrow, restricted largely to the two major wage-setting institutions: the minimum wage and unions. There is also evidence for the effect of monetary policy on labor market outcomes. Much of this work focuses on the link between inflation rates and unemployment, rather than earnings inequality (but cf Galbraith 1998). Inflation and unemployment, however, are not neutral with respect to their distributional consequences (see e.g. Campagna 1974:362–65). Central banks are the main institution through which monetary policy is made and implemented, making them an important, and perhaps underappreciated, player in the distribution of earnings. We will not attempt to review the literature on these issues here. A good comparative historical survey of monetary institutions is provided by Eichengreen (1996); recent papers by Hall & Franzese (1998) and Iversen (1998) study how central banks and labor market institutions jointly influence unemployment.

The Minimum Wage

The federal minimum wage was frozen at \$3.35/hour from 1980 to 1990. As a result, the real dollar value fell by about 30% over the decade, the largest and longest continuous decline in the postwar period (cf Figure 1.2 of Card & Krueger 1995). Establishing the impact of the minimum wage on earnings is complicated because less than 10% of the working population is typically directly affected by changes in the minimum wage.[11]

Even if only the direct effects are considered, however, the 1990 increase is estimated to have reduced the previous decade's growth in wage inequality by about 30%, with no negative effects on employment (Card & Krueger 1995:297). Blackburn et al (1990) estimate that about 17% of the growth in the gap between the wages of college graduates and high-school dropouts may have been driven by the freeze in the minimum wage.

Minimum wages also have an indirect ratcheting effect on the overall wage structure—as wages above the minimum are changed to retain the relative ranking of occupational positions within hierarchies. While Card & Krueger find that this effect is only evident among wages in the first decile, the declines in this decile play a large role in the recent growth in inequality. A recent paper, using distributional methods, finds that the rise and fall of the minimum wage over the 1970s and 1980s explain about 25% of the changes in wage dispersion for men and over 30% for women (DiNardo et al 1996).

The typical minimum wage earner is often portrayed as a teenager working for spending money. It turns out that this portrayal is not accurate. More than 70% of those affected by the minimum wage hikes in 1990 and 1991 were adults, predominantly women and minorities. Over 35% were the sole wage-earner in their family, which is only slightly lower than the 41% figure for all workers. On average, minimum wage earners provided 45% of the family's annual earnings, compared to 65% for all workers (all figures from Ch. 9 in Card & Krueger 1995).

The decade-long freeze in the minimum wage coincided with the dramatic decline in the real earnings among those at the bottom of the distribution, both in terms of timing and in terms of magnitude. The evidence is fairly consistent in supporting a causal role.

Unions

A large research literature shows the equalizing effect of labor unions on the earnings distribution, so the decline in unionization also provides a plausible account of the rise in earnings inequality.[12] In 1970, unions represented about 27% of all wage and salary earners in the United States; by 1993 only 15% of

[11]Those affected include both those earning the current minimum, and those earning more than the current minimum but less than the future minimum.

[12]While neoclassical theory claims that unions raise inequality between organized and unorganized workers (Friedman 1962), there is strong evidence that the reverse is true. Unions compress earnings within firms, standardize wage rates across firms, and raise the pay of low-wage workers (Freeman & Medoff. 1984, ch. 5). These equalizing effects overshadow inequality due to the union wage premium. In addition, the effects of unionization spill into the economy as a whole, as nonunion firms bring wages into line with collective agreements to defuse demands for union representation (Leicht 1989).

workers were unionized (Visser 1996). Although union organization fell steadily from a highpoint of 35% in the mid-1950s, the decline accelerated through the 1980s. Union representation fell most sharply among men, in the private sector, and in manufacturing industries (OECD 1991). Because unions tend to raise the average wage and compress the distribution of wages, the basic trends in observed wages are consistent with those predicted by a fall in unionization rates: stagnation or decline in median wages coupled with increased wage dispersion.

Empirical studies have used several methods to estimate the effect of falling unionization on the increase in wage dispersion. The most common method uses aggregate differences between union and non-union wage distributions to derive the effects of compositional shifts in workforce coverage. Using a simple reweighting, Freeman (1993) calculates that a 10% decline in union density would explain roughly half of the observed growth in earnings variance among blue-collar workers from 1978 to 1988. More sophisticated compositional adjustments control for a wide range of covariates (and in one case, unobserved heterogeneity) and produce estimates that range from about 10% (for 1981–1988; Dinardo & Lemieux 1996) to 20% (for 1973–1993; Card 1998). These estimates are smaller in part because the analyses are based on earnings dispersion for all male workers. An alternative approach is to use longitudinal data on job displacement to estimate the wage loss (or gain) associated with moving from a unionized to a non-unionized position. The estimates here suggest that when a job change is accompanied by the loss of union status, the wage penalty is on the order of 20% after controlling for other covariates (for US workers, Freeman 1993; for Canadian workers, Kuhn & Sweetman, 1998). Because unionized workers typically have more to lose from displacement, Kuhn & Sweetman estimate that about 75% of the total wage losses were experienced by the 13% of workers who lost union coverage when they changed jobs. The dispersion in both post-transition wages and wage losses is also higher for transitions into non-unionized jobs. Using these methods, Freeman estimates that overall declining union density accounts for about 21% of the rise in wage inequality.

A final method employs the international variation in union density to estimate its effect on wage dispersion. Using simple correlations between union density and several different estimates of country-specific variance in log earnings across industrialized nations during the 1980s, the bivariate R^2 ranges from 35% to 64% (Freeman, 1993). The bivariate correlation between the change in earnings inequality from 1978 to 1987 and the 1979 union density is -0.61. While these figures are simple descriptive correlations, they are consistent with the evidence from other methods.

Few studies examine the impact of unionization trends on women, in large part because women are less likely to hold a unionized job. Studies that do, however, find that the changes in unionization among women have had little effect on their wage dispersion. (Asher & DeFina 1997, DiNardo et al 1996, Card 1998)

Overall, these findings suggest that the decline in union density may account for about 20% of the overall rise in male wage inequality, and as much as 50% of the rise for male blue-collar workers. As with other potential explanatory factors, however, there is also evidence of increasing earnings inequality among union members (Freeman 1993, Dinardo & Lemieux 1996, although cf Bratsberg & Ragan 1997).

GLOBALIZATION

By highlighting the role of the nation state, globalization would appear to hold strong interest for sociological approaches to inequality. Dependency theorists have studied how globalization impoverishes countries at the periphery of the world economy, however, and inequality in the core countries has received little attention. As with most work on current trends on US inequality, research on the link between globalization and the labor market is dominated by economists.

In economics, globalization describes transnational flows of people, goods and services, and capital. Immigration to the United States, trade with developing countries, foreign investment, and outsourcing are all thought to lower demand for low-wage US workers. As a result, wages fall at the bottom of the earnings distribution and inequality rises. In contrast to dependency theory, recent economic studies examine how economic ties between North and South, and East and West undermine the prosperity of workers in wealthy countries.

Trade

The consequences of trade for inequality are often considered alongside the effects of immigration (Abowd & Freeman 1991, Borjas et al 1992, Borjas & Ramey 1993, Borjas 1997). Like immigration, imports from less developed countries (LDCs) embody relatively large amounts of less-skilled labor. Increasing consumption of LDC imports thus increases the implicit supply of less-skilled labor, forcing down the wages of local less-skilled workers. While this factor content approach is common in labor economics, some trade economists instead emphasize the role of prices. In a price analysis, LDC imports force down the price of local import-competing goods, which in turn reduces the pay of less-skilled workers in import-competing industries (Cline 1997:35–46 summarizes the theory). The empirical intuition remains the same: Imports from low-wage countries reduce the wages of less-skilled workers in the United States.

Trends in trade superficially support the effects of globalization. From 1960 to 1990, US manufacturing imports increased more than threefold as a proportion of gross domestic product (GDP), and by around fivefold as a proportion of manufacturing GDP. These gross trends conceal the growing role of LDC producers. Between 1978 and 1990, manufacturing imports as a proportion of GDP increased by 35%, while LDC imports increased by 75%. In this period, the share of imports from developing countries had grown 7 percentage points to account for 36% of all imports (Sachs & Shatz 1994:10). By 1998, the four largest LDC exporters to the United States—Taiwan, Mexico, Korea, and China—earned more than $200 billion from US sales.

Despite these trends, evidence for trade effects is mixed. Research falls into two main categories: A majority of studies find neutral or small effects while a few report large trade effects (review essays include Deardorf & Hakura 1994, Burtless 1995, Cline 1997). The leading proponents of large trade effects are Leamer (1993, 1994) and Wood (1994, 1995). Leamer (1994) uses data from 3- and 4-digit industries in 13 OECD countries to forecast the impact of NAFTA on the wages of low-skill US workers. Imports to OECD countries are concentrated in industries with low-skill workers, placing downward pressure on their wages. With this association between trade and wages, Leamer estimates that NAFTA will produce an annual earnings loss of around $1900 per low-skill worker, but a $6000 gain for each skilled worker. These forecasts more than account for the total increase in the US skilled/low-skill wage differential in the 1980s (Cline 1997:115). Wood's (1994) analysis also holds trade responsible for rising inequality. He begins by estimating how much native labor would have been used to produce LDC imports. These factor contents are then adjusted to allow that LDC imports may have already driven domestic producers out of the market. Further adjustments are made for trade in services and trade-induced technical change. With these adjustments, LDC trade is estimated to have reduced the demand for unskilled labor in OECD countries by more than 20% in 1990 (Wood 1995, 66). Although the adjustments driving this estimate are controversially large and informed mostly by theory rather than data, they underline the difficulty of drawing causal inferences about the influence of trade on the labor market [see Burtless 1995 for a critical review of Wood 1994; cf also Wood's general response to critics (1995:68–72)].

Typical estimates of trade effects are much smaller than those produced by Leamer or Wood. Krugman is particularly prominent in rejecting an important role for trade in raising inequality (see also Lawrence & Slaughter 1993, Krugman & Lawrence 1994, Krugman 1995). In his account, trade cannot be important because it contributes minimally to US output and its effects are concentrated in manufacturing industries that make up a small share of total employment. A back-of-the-envelope calculation suggests that trade reduced wages by $3.5 billion, against a total national income of $5.5 trillion (Krugman & Lawrence 1994). Although an extensive literature finds larger—but still modest—trade effects, few economists hold trade principally responsible for the rise in earnings inequality (key recent papers include Berman et al 1994, Sachs & Shatz 1994, Borjas 1997).

Despite this broad consensus, sharper measurement of production and worker characteristics casts some doubt on these results. For instance, Bernard & Jensen (1995) analyze data from 50,000 manufacturing establishments rather than the usual sample of 3-digit industries and estimate a large positive effect of exports on wages. Leamer (1994) finds that a common proxy for skill—the distinction between production and nonproduction workers—is unrelated to skill levels when detailed occupational codes are reviewed. These studies underline the preliminary character of existing research and suggest that future developments may involve greater disaggregation of skill and industry data.

Capial Flows

In contrast to research on trade and immigration, only a few studies have examined the link between capital flows and earnings inequality. Although public imagination was briefly captured by Ross Perot's "giant sucking sound" in the 1992 presidential campaign, academic research has been constrained by the limited relevance of available data. In theory, the effects of capital flows on inequality appear clear. As the movement of capital is liberalized, neighboring countries with low-wage labor will draw off investment, causing a fall in low-wage labor demand at home.

Capital flows can be divided into two broad categories, both of which affect the local wage structure. First, foreign direct investment captures spending on new plants and equipment overseas by US multinationals. Second, outsourcing describes the delegation of production to external suppliers. Foreign direct investment is unlikely to be the source of increasing US earnings inequality, as recent trends run in the wrong direction and the size of investment is small. Throughout most of the postwar period, the United States was the largest direct investor, accounting for nearly half of all OECD direct investment in the ten years from 1971. However, through the 1980s when earnings inequality rose substantially, both Japan and the United Kingdom surpassed US direct investment. Comparing the 1980s to the 1970s, the ratio of outward to inward investment shrunk by about 85% (Baldwin 1995). The overall magnitude of foreign direct investment is also very small compared to total investment. Net direct investment flows from 1980 to 1990 was only 0.73 of a percentage point of total gross fixed capital formation (Baldwin 1995:35). Most of these capital flows are among the wealthy OECD countries. Krugman (1994) estimates that in 1993—a peak year for emerging market investment—capital flows from advanced countries to LDCs equaled $100 billion out of $3.5 trillion in total investment. These figures suggest a net earnings loss in advanced countries of about 0.15% due to capital exports.

Feenstra & Hanson (1996) suggest that the impact of outsourcing may be larger than these direct investment effects. They argue that previous research underestimates the level of outsourcing because the usual definition—imports of materials by US firms—is too restrictive [cf Berman et al (1994) and Lawrence (1994)]. A broader definition includes all goods used in the production of, or sold under the brand name of, a US firm. With this definition, outsourcing grows at an increasing rate from the 1970s to the 1980s. A regression analysis of nonproduction workers' share of the wage bill in 450 4-digit industries shows the significant effect of outsourcing. Indeed, about a third of the annual change in this wage share is explained by outsourcing in the period 1979–1987. The use of industry data and reliance on nonproduction work as a measure of skill opens Feenstra & Hanson's work (1996) to criticisms leveled at the research on trade effects. Still, the study is distinguished by its attempt at precise measurement of outsourcing.

To summarize, the effects of capital flows have received relatively little attention, partly because they account for only a very small part of total investment. While outsourcing may capture some part of the total effect of trade and initial results are suggestive, aggregation of industry and skill categories has so far prevented a strong empirical test.

DISCUSSION

Capital is a social relation of production. Marx (1891:207)

The earnings distribution has undergone a set of rapid and dramatic changes over the past 25 years. Stagnation in real wages and a sustained rise in inequality fueled a collapse in the earnings of those at the bottom of the distribution. The effects at the median were not the same for all groups—most women made gains during the period—but the growing polarization in earnings was evident in all groups. Demographic shifts in the composition of the labor market, including the baby boom, the rise in women's labor market participation, and the growth in immigration were all plausible candidates for explaining the observed changes in the earnings structure. Empirical studies, however, have repeatedly documented at best a modest impact of these supply side factors. Education effects have been more consistently supported, but not explained. The penalty for not having a college degree has risen dramatically. While some have taken this as evidence of a technology-driven shift in demand for higher skilled workers, workplace studies suggest that the impact of technological change may be polarizing rather than simple upskilling. Demand was clearly restructured during this period, however, through both deindustrialization and the return to market-mediated employment relations. The empirical findings regarding the impact of this economic restructuring on inequality are mixed, but the complexity of the measurement issues here plays a greater role in obscuring the view. National labor market institutions, in particular unions and the minimum wage, have also had an impact. While institutions are among the most contested explanatory factors for labor economists, they enjoy some of the most consistent support in the evidence. All of these dynamics, finally, are subject to the pressures of "globalization," as the flows of capital, goods, and people across national boundaries modify the effective supply of and demand for specific kinds of labor, the resulting strength of traditional labor organizations, and the role of the monetary system in national politics.

So why has sociology ignored these trends? The issues could hardly be more central to our field, so it cannot be a matter of disciplinary irrelevance. There are perhaps several pieces to the answer. Sometime during the early 1970s, we ceded the study of earnings to the economists, retreating, perhaps, from the wave of neoclassical econometric formalism that overtook the study of wage determination. This left us with the more comprehensive but opaque measures like SES and occupational prestige. Even had we wanted to, it would have been impossible to develop a theory of SES or prestige determination that could have paralleled the theory of wage determination in neoclassical economics. The primary descriptive findings of stratification and mobility research, in any case, seemed to be that the American economic system was remarkably meritocratic, with achievement, rather than ascription, the dominant pattern. Problematic forms of inequality were then more narrowly located in persistent poverty and research was focused accordingly.

Economic sociology, on the other hand, continued to contribute an important critique of neoclassical models in the early 1970s by articulating the embeddedness of supply and demand factors in institutional contexts. A good selection of this work can be found in the edited volume *Sociological Perspectives on Labor Markets* (Berg 1981). The concept of a dual or segmented labor market played an important role in this literature, and eventually dovetailed with the study of systematic race and gender gaps in economic outcomes. While the segmented labor market literature foundered on the problem of defining the sectors, race and gender gap research flourished. Consistent with the institutional or structural imperative, sociologists who followed along this line specialized in the study of occupational segregation, often framing the research in terms of a challenge to the "human capital" paradigm in economics, or the mainstream stratification research tradition in sociology. In the process, however, important but difficult structural questions—what are the positions in the labor market and how are they constructed?—were replaced by relatively simpler allocation questions—who gets which positions?

The study of race and gender then itself evolved from the use of attribute categories as variables in an equation to a more fundamental set of questions regarding the social construction of the categories themselves. So 25 years later, we find ourselves fighting disciplinary boundary battles with literature and the humanities, rather than economics. Perhaps it is not surprising that we missed the boat.

The story is not over, however. Debates over the causes and consequences of the changes in earnings are still largely unresolved. From a sociological perspective, it is no accident that the economic approach has provided few concrete answers. Many of the unresolved issues concern the role of nonmarket forces in shaping and filtering the impact of supply and demand. The integration of different spheres of social organization has always been a more natural task for sociology. This suggests several directions for a sociological research agenda on inequality that span the macro to micro continuum.

From a macrosociological perspective, the rise in US earnings inequality raises basic questions about large-scale social change. Three issues stand out. The first concerns the relationship between inequality and development in advanced capitalist societies. A central question for macrosociology would be whether the current rise in inequality marks a qualitative break from the Kuznets style leveling of the past century, or just a temporary hiccup. A second key issue concerns the salience of the nation-state in shaping the impact of globalizing market forces. While the volume of international trade, capital, and migration flows have increased significantly, their effects may be tempered by the strength of national political actors. The cost of an increase in the supply of low-wage labor, for example, could be paid either by shareholders in the form of lower profits, by workers in unemployment or lower wages, or by consumers in the form of higher prices. Unmediated market forces are a political outcome, not an inevitability. A third issue for macrosociology is to consider the impact of globalizing the economy without globalizing the polity. The result is much like having a country with a stock market, but no government. Under what conditions would such a system evolve, and could it persist? In sum, placing current inequality trends in a broad macrosociological context can shed light on the historical relevance of those trends and speak to more general questions about large-scale social change in an increasingly more connected world.

At the level of middle-range institutional explanation, sociology has a traditional dialogue with economics that is relevant to current trends. Empirical labor markets provide only weak approximations to the competitive models of economic theory. There is a rich institutional context to inequality that extends well beyond the immediate wage-setting forces of the minimum wage and collective bargaining. Systems of education and training, labor exchanges, social welfare, and the penal system all figure prominently as institutional sources of inequality in sociological research (e.g. Bourdieu & Passeron 1979, Esping-Andersen 1990, Janoski 1990, Sampson & Laub 1993). This partial list of institutional influences suggests a distinctively sociological perspective, where earnings inequality is shaped by structures of power and inequality that originate outside the marketplace. Trends in US incarceration are especially suggestive in this context. A common argument in economics claims that recent trends in global markets confront labor market policy makers with a choice between unemployment and low wages (Blank 1998; but cf. the critical review by Howell et al 1998). European welfare and industrial relations institutions represent one side of this tradeoff, with labor market rigidities that maintain high wages at the cost of high unemployment. The unregulated US labor market represents the other side of the tradeoff, with low unemployment at the cost of low wages at the bottom. This economic folklore is challenged, however, if the incarcerated populations are included in the calculations. The American penal system has grown rapidly since the 1970s largely due to mandatory drug sentencing policies, and by 1995 about 5% of the adult male population was under some kind of correctional supervision (Bureau of Justice Statistics 1997). Including the incarcerated population as unemployed raises the U.S. male unemployment rate by about 2 points but has virtually no effect on the unemployment rate in European countries, largely erasing the U.S.-European difference in joblessness (Western & Beckett 1999; Buchele & Christiansen 1998). With the penal system defined as a labor market institution, low unemployment in the United States can be seen to result, in part, from a large and coercive state intervention in the marketplace. Institutions are thus as fundamental to the operation of the ostensibly unregulated US labor market as they are to the centralized industrial relations regimes of Western Europe.

More traditional sociological interests in firms and networks are also important here. Sociologists "bringing the firm back in" (Baron & Bielby 1980) to the analysis of economic mobility and inequality could readily extend this approach to the restructuring of corporate governance, finance, and employment relations over the past two decades. As multinational firms increasingly direct the visible hand, what implications does this have for our traditional understanding of organizational structure on labor market outcomes? Sociologists also know about networks, and networks serve as an informal nonmarket mechanism for linking people to jobs, filtering information, and segmenting the effective impact of supply and demand. For example, social networks feature prominently in immigration (Massey 1987, Portes & Rumbaut 1996). In contrast to economic assumptions regarding the substitutability of immigrant labor, research on immigrant networks suggests that ethnic enclaves provide a relatively self-contained economic structure, resulting in little competition between immigrants and natives and small labor-displacing effects of immigration (Waldinger et al 1990, Sassen 1995).

Finally, at the microlevel, two populations are affected by these broad trends: persons and jobs. Sociology and demography bring a distinctive perspective here as well. The study of economic mobility remains the key to a sociological perspective on the fine-grained dynamics of inequality. Mobility links labor market structure to individual life history, providing insight into the processes that generate economic differentiation, and evidence of meritocratic or ascriptive regimes. To a large extent, empirical sociological research has been dominated by the study of *inter*generational mobility (but see DiPrete 1993, DiPrete 1997), but *intra*generational mobility was a critical concept in much of the original theoretical work on dual labor markets. At root, what distinguished the dual segments was the absence or presence of internal labor markets, and this concept was inherently tied to the mobility process. The analysis of cross-sectional wage-gaps in the past two decades has lost sight of this focus. As the link between firm restructuring and wage inequality begins to be made, it is natural that we return to individuals' work histories in order to analyze whether wage growth has deteriorated, whether the rate of job changing has increased, and how the sequence unfolds over the life course (Bernhardt et al 1998, 1999). Economic restructuring is also changing the population of jobs. A demographic approach to these population changes could help to formalize the analysis of the birth, death, and migration of jobs (Keyfitz 1985:199–200; Davis et al 1996).

Sociology has an important role to play in understanding the recent trends in economic inequality. It is not just a question of earnings, but of fundamental changes in politics, markets, and life chances. The integrated analysis of social institutions and social change is at the heart of our disciplinary theory, but at the margins of our contemporary empirical work in the United States. If we cannot resolve this problem, we risk ceding our core areas of intellectual inquiry to other fields.

ACKNOWLEDGMENTS

The authors would like to thank Nan Astone, Annette Bernhardt, Michael Burawoy, Glen Cain, Paula England, Thomas Espenshade, Robert Hauser, Douglas Massey, and Erik Olin Wright for thoughtful comments and pointed critical remarks that have helped to shape this paper.

> **Visit the *Annual Reviews* home page at**
> **http://www.AnnualReviews.org.**

Literature Cited

Abowd J, Freeman RB, eds.. 1991. *Immigration, Trade and the Labor Market.* Chicago: Univ. Chicago Press

Abraham K. 1990. Restructuring the employment relationship: the growth of market-mediated work arrangements. In *New Developments in the Labor Market,* pp. 85–118. Cambridge, MA: MIT Press

Adelman I, Morris C. 1973. *Economic Growth and Social Equity in Developing Countries.* Stanford, CA: Stanford Univ. Press

Altonji JG, Card D. 1991. The effects of immigration on the labor market outcomes of less-skilled natives. In *Immigration, Trade, and the Labor Market,* ed. JM Abowd, RB Freeman. Chicago: Univ. Chicago Press

Appelbaum E. 1987. Restructuring work: temporary, part-time, and at-home employment. In *Computer Chips and Paper Clips: Technology and Women's Employment,* ed. Heidi Hartmann, pp. 268–310. Washington, DC: Natl. Acad.

Applebaum E, Berg P. 1996. Financial market constraints and business strategy in the USA. In *Creating Industrial Capacity: Towards Full Employment,* ed. J Michie, JG Smith. Oxford, UK: Oxford Univ. Press

Asher MA, DeFina R. 1997. The impact of changing union density on earnings inequality: evidence from the private and public sectors. *J. Labor Res.* 18:425–38

Autor DH, Katz LF, Krueger AB. 1998. Computing inequality: Have computers changed the labor market? *Q. J. Econ.* 113:1169–213

Baldwin RE. 1995. *The effect of trade and foreign direct investment on employment and relative wages. Working paper 5037,* Natl. Bur. Econ. Res. Cambridge, MA

Baron JN, Bielby WT. 1980. Bringing the firms back in: stratification, segmentation, and the organization of work. *Am. Sociol. Rev.* 45:737–65

Baron JN, Dobbins FR, Jennings PD. 1986. War and peace: the evolution of modern personnel administration in US industry. *Am. J. Sociol.* 92:350–83

Belous RS. 1989. *The Contingent Economy.* Washington, DC: Natl. Plan. Assoc.

Berg IE. 1970. *Education and Jobs: The Great Training Robbery.* New York: Praeger

Berg IE. 1981. *Sociological Perspectives on Labor Markets.* New York: Academic

Berman E, Bound J, Griliches Z. 1994. Changes in the demand for skilled labor within U.S. manufacturing: evidence from the Annual Survey of Manufactures. *Q. J. Econ.* 109:367–97

Berman E, Machin S, Bound J. 1998. Implications of skill-biased technological change: international evidence. *Q. J. Econ.* 113:1245–79

Bernard AB, Jensen JB. 1995. Exporters, jobs, and wages in US manufacturing 1976–1987. *Brookings Econ. Micro.* 67:1–19

Bernard AB, Jensen JB. 1998. *Understanding increasing and decreasing wage inequality. Working Paper 6571,* Natl. Bur. Econ. Res., Cambridge, MA

Bernhardt A, Morris M, Handcock M. 1995. Women's gains or men's losses? A closer look at the shrinking gender gap in earnings. *Am. J. Sociol.* 101:302–28

Bernhardt A, Morris M, Handcock M, Scott M. 1999. *Inequality and mobility: trends in wage growth for young adults. Work. Pap.* 99–03, Popul. Res. Ins., Penn. State Univ.

Bernhardt A, Morris M, Handcock M, Scott M. 1999. Trends in job instability and wages for young adult men. *J. Lab. Econ.* Forthcoming

Bernstein J, Mishel L. 1997. Has wage inequality stopped growing? *Mon. Labor Rev.* :3–16

Blackburn M. 1990. What can explain the increase in earnings inequality among males? *Ind. Rel.* 29:441–56

Blackburn ML, Bloom DE, Freeman RB. 1990. The declining economic position of less skilled American men. In *A Future of Lousy Jobs?,* ed. Gary Burtless, pp. 31–76. Washington, DC: Brookings Inst.

Blank RM. 1998. *Is There a Trade-Off Between Unemployment and Inequality? No Easy Answers: Labor Market Problems in the United States versus Europe. Public Policy Brief 33,* Levy Economics Institute

Blau FD. 1998. Trends in the well-being of American women, 1970–1995. *J. Econ. Lit.* 36:112

Blau FD, Kahn LM. 1994. Rising wage inequality and the U.S. gender gap. *Am. Econ. Rev.* 84:23–8

Bloom DE, Freeman RB, Korenman SD. 1987. The labor-market consequences of generational crowding. *Eur. J. Pop.* 3:131–76

Bluestone B, Harrison B. 1982. *The Deindustrialization of America: Plant Closings, Community Abandonment, and the Dismantling of Basic Industry.* New York: Basic Books

Borjas GJ. 1994. The economics of immigration. *J. Econ. Lit.* 32:1667–717

Borjas GJ. 1996. Searching for the effect of immigration on the labor market. *Am. Econ. Rev. Papers and Proceedings* 86: 246

Borjas GJ. 1997. How much do immigration and trade affect labor market outcomes? *Brookings Econ. Micro.* :1

Borjas GJ, Freeman RB, Katz LF. 1992. On the labor market effects of immigration and trade. In *Immigration and the Work Force: Economic Consequences for the United States and Source Areas*, ed. GJ Borjas, RB Freeman. Chicago: Univ. Chicago Press

Borjas GJ, Ramey V. 1993. *Foreign competition, market power and wage inequality: theory and evidence. Working paper 4556*, Natl. Bur. Econ. Res., Cambridge, MA

Bound J. 1992. Changes in the structure of wages in the 1980's : an evaluation of alternative explanations. *Am. Econ. Rev.* 82: 371–92

Bourdieu P, Passeron J–C. 1979. *The Inheritors.* Chicago, IL: Univ. Chicago Press

Bratsberg B, Ragan JF. 1997. Have unions impeded growing wage inequality among young workers. *J. Lab. Res.* 18:593–612

Braverman H. 1974. *Labor and Monopoly Capital, the Degradation of Work in the Twentieth Century.* New York: Monthly Rev. Press

Buchele R, Christensen J. 1998. Do employment and income security cause unemployment? A comparative study of the US and the E-4. *Camb. J. Econ.* 22: 117–36

Burawoy M. 1979. *Manufacturing Consent, Changes in the Labor Process under Monopoly Capitalism.* Chicago: Univ. Chicago Press

Bureau of Justice Statistics. 1997. *Correctional Populations in the United States, 1995.* Washington DC: Department of Justice.

Bureau of Labor Statistics. 1998. "http://www.bls.gov."

Bureau of the Census. 1978. *The Current Population Survey: Design and Methodology. Tech. Pap. 40.* Washington, DC: US Dep. Commerce .

Burtless G. 1990. Earnings inequality over the business and demographic cycles. In *A Future of Lousy Jobs?*, ed. Gary Burtless, pp. 77–122. Washington, DC: Brookings Inst.

Burtless G. 1995. International trade and the rise in earnings inequality. *J. Econ. Lit.* 333:800–16

Campagna AS. 1974. *Macroeconomics: Theory and Policy.* Boston: Houghton Mifflin.

Cappelli P. 1992. Examining managerial displacement. *Acad. Manag. J.* 35:203–17

Cappelli P. 1995. Rethinking employment. *Br. J. Indust. Relat.* 33:563

Card D. 1992. *The Effect of Unions on the Distribution of Wages: Redistiribution or Relabelling. Work. Pap. 4195.* Natl. Bur. Econ. Res., Cambridge, MA

Card D. 1997. *Immigrant Inflows, Native Outflows and the Local Labor Market Impacts of Higher Immigration. Work. Pap. 5927.* Natl. Bur. Econ. Res., Cambridge, MA

Card D. 1998. *Falling union membership and rising wage inequality: What's the connection?* Work. Pap. W6520, Nat. Bur. Econ. Res., New York

Card D, Krueger AB. 1995. *Myth and Measurement: The New Economics of the Minimum Wage.* Princeton, NJ: Princeton Univ. Press

Carlino GA. 1989. What can output measures tell us about deindustrialization in the nation and its regions? *Bus. Rev.* Jan/Feb:15–27

Chandler AD. 1977. *The Visible Hand: The Managerial Revolution in American Business.* Cambridge, MA: Harvard Univ. Press

Chenery HB. 1974. *Redistribution With Growth.* London: Oxford Univ. Press

Chenery HB, Robinson S, Syrquin M. 1986. *Industrialization and Growth, a Comparative Study.* New York: Oxford Univ. Press

Cline WR. 1997. *Trade and Income Distribution.* Washington DC: Inst. for Int. Econ.

Clogg CC. 1979. *Measuring Underemployment, Demographic Indicators for the United States.* New York: Academic Press

Colclough G, Tolbert CM. 1992. *Work in the Fast Lane: Flexibility, Divisions of Labor, and Inequality in High-Tech Industries.* New York: State Univ. NY Press

Costrell RM. 1988. *The Effects of Industry Employment Shifts on Wage Growth, 1947–1987.* U.S. Congress, Joint Econ. Com.. Washington, DC: USGPO

Danziger S, Gottschalk P, eds. 1993. *Uneven Tides: Rising Inequality in America.* New York: Russell Sage Found.

Danziger S, Gottschalk P. 1995. *America Unequal.* Cambridge, Mass.: Harvard Univ. Press

Davis SJ, Haltiwanger J. 1991. Wage dispersion between and within U.S. manufacturing plants: 1963–86. *Brookings Econ. Micro.* :115–200

Davis SJ, Haltiwanger JC, Schuh S. 1996. *Job Creation and Destruction.* Cambridge, MA: MIT Press

Deardorf AV, Hakura DS. 1994. Trade and wages—What are the questions? In *Trade and Wages: Leveling Wages Down?*, ed. J Bhagwati, MK Kosters, pp. 76–107. Washington, DC: AEI Press

DiNardo J, Fortin N, Lemieux T. 1996. Labor market institutions and the distribution of wages, 1973–1992: a semiparametric approach. *Econometrica* 64:1001–44

Dinardo J, Lemieux T. 1996. Diverging male wage inequality in the United States and Canada, 1981–1988: Do institutions explain the difference. *Ind. Labor Relat. Rev.* 50:629–51

DiPrete TA. 1993. Industrial restructuring and the mobility response of American workers in the 1980s. 58(1):74

DiPrete TA. 1997. Collectivist versus individualist mobility regimes? Structural change and job mobility in four countries. *Am. J. Sociol.* 103:318

Doeringer PB, Piore MJ. 1971. The theory of internal labor markets. In *Internal Labor Markets and Manpower Analysis,* Part 1, pp. 13–92. Lexington, MA: Heath

Dooley M, Gottschalk P. 1982. Does a younger male labor force mean growing earnings inequality? *Monthly Labor Rev.* 105:42–5

Dooley M, Gottschalk P. 1985. The increasing proportion of men with low earnings in the United States. *Demography* 22:25–34

Dunlop JT. 1993 [1958]. *Industrial Relations Systems.* Boston: Harvard Bus. School Press

Easterlin R. 1980. *Birth and Fortune.* New York: Basic Books

Eichengreen B. 1996. *Globalizing Capital: A History of the International Monetary System.* Princeton, NJ: Princeton Univ. Press

EQW. 1995. *The EQW National Employer Survey: First Findings.* Philadelphia: Natl. Ctr. on Educ. Quality of the Workforce

Esping–Andersen G. 1990. *Three Worlds of Welfare Capitalism.* Princeton, NJ: Princeton Univ. Press

Farber HS. 1993. The incidence and costs of job loss: 1982–91. *Brookings Econ. Micro.* 1:73–132

Feenstra RC, Hanson GH. 1996. *Globalization, Outsourcing, and Wage Inequality. Work. Pap. 5424,* Natl. Bur. Econ. Res., Cambridge, MA

Freeman RB. 1976. *The Overeducated American.* New York: Academic Press

Freeman RB. 1980. The effect of demographic factors on age-earnings profiles. *J. Hum. Res.* 14:289–318

Freeman RB. 1993. How much has deunionization contributed to the rise in male earnings inequality. In *Uneven Tides: Rising Inequality in America,* ed. S Danziger,

P Gottschalk, pp. 133–63. New York: Russell Sage Found.

Freeman RB, Medoff JL. 1984. *What Do Unions Do?* New York: Basic Books

Friedman M. 1962. *Capitalism and Freedom.* Chicago: Univ. Chicago Press

Fuchs V. 1968. *The Service Economy.* New York: Columbia Univ. Press

Galbraith JK. 1998. Inequality and unemployment. *Res. Econ. Inequality* 8:121–54

Gordon DM. 1996. *Fat and Mean : The Corporate Squeeze of Working Americans and the Myth of Managerial "Downsizing".* New York: Martin Kessler

Gottschalk P. 1997. Inequality, income growth, and mobility: the basic facts. *J. Econ. Persp.* 11:21–40

Grant DS, Wallace M. 1994. The political economy of manufacturing growth and decline across the American states, 1970–1985. *Soc. Forc.* 73:33

Grubb W, Wilson R. 1989. Sources of increasing inequality in wages and salaries, 1960–1990. *Monthly Labor Rev.* 112:3–13

Hall PA, Franzese RJ. 1998. Mixed signals: central bank independence, coordinated wage bargaining, and European Monetary Union. *Int. Organ.* 52:505–35

Harrison B. 1994. *Lean and Mean, The Changing Landscape of Corporate Power in the Age of Flexibility.* New York: Basic Books

Houseman SN. 1997. Flexible staffing arrangements in the U.S. *Worklife Rep.* 10:6

Howell DR, Duncan M, Harrison B. 1998. *Low wages in the US and high unemployment in Europe: A critical assessment of the conventional wisdom. Work. Pap. Ser. I, number 5,* New School for Social Research, Cent. for Econ. Policy Anal.

Howell DR, Wolff EN. 1991. Trends in the growth and distribution of skills in the U.S. workplace, 1960-1985. *Indust. Lab. Rel. Rev.* 44:486–502

Hunter LW, Lafkas JJ. 1998. Firm evidence of the information age? Information technology, work practices, and wages. *Proc. Indust. Relat. Res. Assoc.* Wharton Financial Inst. Ctr.

Iversen T. 1998. Wage bargaining, central bank independence, and the real effects of money. *Int. Organ.* 52:469–504

Jacoby SM. 1985. *Employing Bureaucracy: Managers, Unions and the Transformation of Work in American Industry, 1900–1945.* New York: Columbia Univ. Press

Jacoby SM. 1990. Norms and cycles: the dynamics of nonunion industrial relations in the United States, 1897–1987. In *New Developments in the Labor Market,* ed. KG

Abraham, RB McKersie, pp. 19–56. Cambridge, MA: MIT Press

Janoski T. 1990. *The Political Economy of Unemployment: Active Labor Market Policy in West Germany and the United States.* Berkeley: Univ. Calif. Press

Jasso G, Rosenzweig MR. 1990. *The New Chosen People. New York: Immigrants in the United States.* New York: Russell Sage Found.

Johnston WB, Packer AE. 1987. *Workforce 2000, Work and Workers for the Twenty-First Century.* Indianapolis, Ind: Hudson Inst.

Juhn C, Kim D. 1999. The effects of rising female labor supply on male wages. *J. Lab. Econ.* 17:23–48

Juhn C, Murphy KM, Pierce B. 1991. Accounting for the slowdown in black-white wage convergence. In *Workers and Their Wages*, ed. M Kosters, pp. 107–43. Washington, DC: Am. Enterprise Inst.

Katz LF, Murphy KM. 1992. Changes in relative wages, 1963–1987: supply and demand factors. *Q. J. Econ.* 107:35–78

Kerr C. 1977. *Labor Markets and Wage Determination: The Balkanization of Labor Markets and Other Essays.* Berkeley: Univ. Calif. Press

Keyfitz N. 1985. *Applied Mathematical Demography.* Berlin: Springer Verlag

Kochan TA, Katz HC, McKersie RB. 1986. *The Transformation of American Industrial Relations.* New York: Basic Books

Kozicki S. 1997. The productivity growth slowdown : diverging trends in the manufacturing and service sectors. *Econ. Rev.* 82:31–46

Krueger AB. 1993. How computers have changed the wage structure: evidence from Microdata, 1984–1989. *Q. J. Econ.* CVIII: 33

Krugman P. 1994. Does third world growth hurt first world prosperity? *Harvard Bus. Rev.* July/August:113–21

Krugman P. 1995. *Growing World Trade: Causes and Consequences (with discussion). Brookings Papers on Econ. Activity.* :327–77

Krugman P, Lawrence RZ. 1994. Trade, jobs, and wages. *Sci. Am.* 270:44–9

Kuhn P, Sweetman A. 1998. Wage loss following displacement: the role of union coverage. *Indust. Lab. Rel. Rev.* 51: 384–99

Kutscher RE. 1986. Deindustrialization and the shift to services. *Monthly Labor Rev.* 109:3–13

Kutscher RE. 1993. Historical trends, 1950–92, and current uncertainties. *Monthly Labor Rev.* 116:3–10

Kutscher RE, Personick VA. 1986. Deindustrialization and the shift to services. *Mon. Lab. Rev.* 109:3–13

Kuznets S. 1953. *Shares of Upper Income Groups in Income and Savings.* New York: Natl. Bur. of Econ. Res.

Kuznets S. 1955. Economic growth and income inequality (Presidential address). *Am. Econ. Rev.* 45:1–28

LaLonde RJ, Topel RH. 1991. Labor market adjustments to increased immigration. In *Immigration, Trade, and the Labor Market*, ed. JM Abowd, RB Freeman, pp. 167–200. Chicago: Univ. Chicago Press

Lampman RJ. 1962. *The Share of Top Wealth–holders in National Wealth, 1922–1956.* Princeton, NJ: Princeton Univ. Press

Lawrence R. 1984. Sectoral shifts and the size of the middle class. *Brookings Rev.* Fall: 3–11

Lawrence RZ. 1994. *Trade Multinationals and Labor. Work. Pap. 4836*, Natl. Bur. Econ. Res. Cambridge, MA

Lawrence RZ, Slaughter M. 1993. International trade and American wages in the 1980's: great sucking sound or small hiccup? *Brookings Econ. Micro.* 2:161–226

Leamer EE. 1993. Wage effects of a US–Mexican free trade agreement. In *The Mexico–I.S. Free Trade Agreement*, ed. PM Garber, pp. 57–125. Cambridge, MA: MIT Press

Leamer EE. 1994. *Trade, Wages and Revolving Door Ideas. Work. Pap. 4716.* Natl. Bur. Econ. Res. Cambridge, MA

Leicht K. 1989. On the estimation of union threat effects. *Am. Sociol. Rev.* 54:1035–45

Levy F, Murnane R. 1992. U.S. earnings levels and earnings inequality: a review of recent trends and proposed explanations. *J. Econ. Lit.* 30:1333–81

Marx K. 1891. Wage labour and capital. In *The Marx–Engels Reader*, ed. RC Tucker, pp. 203–17. New York: Norton

Massey DM. 1987. The social process of international migration. *Science* 237: 733–38

Meisenheimer II JR. 1998. The services industry in the 'good' versus 'bad' job debate. *Monthly Labor Rev.* :22–47

Mishel L. 1989. The late great debate on deindustrialization. *Challenge* 32:35–43

Mishel L, Bernstein J. 1995. *The State of Working America 1994–1995.* Washington, DC: Econ. Policy Inst.

Mishel L, Bernstein J, Schmitt J. 1997. *Did Technology Have Any Effect on the Growth of Wage Inequality in the 1980s and 1990s?* Washington, DC: Econ. Policy Inst.

Morris M, Bernhardt A, Handcock M. 1994.

Economic inequality: new methods for new trends. *Am. Sociol. Rev.* 59:205–19

Murphy KM, Welch F. 1988. *Wage differentials in the 1980s: The role of international trade.* Mont Pelerin Soc. Gen. Mtg.

Murphy KM, Welch F. 1992. The structure of wages. *Q. J. Econ.* 107:215–326

Murphy KM, Welch F. 1993. Industrial change and the rising importance of skill. In *Uneven Tides: Rising Inequality in America*, ed. S Danziger, P Gottschalk, pp. 101–32. New York: Russell Sage Found.

OECD. 1991. Employment Outlook. Paris: OECD

Oi WY. 1983. The fixed employment costs of specialized labor. In *The Measurement of Labor Costs*, ed. J Triplett. Chicago: Univ. Chicago Press

O'Neill J, Polachek S. 1993. Why the gender gap in wages narrowed in the 1980s. *J. Lab. Econ.* 11:205–28

Osterman P. 1994. Internal labor markets: theory and change. In *Labor Economics and Industrial Relations*, ed. C Kerr, P Staudohar. Cambridge, MA: Harvard Univ. Press

Pfeffer J. 1994. *Competitive Advantage Through People.* Cambridge, MA: Harvard Univ. Press

Pfeffer J, Baron J. 1988. Taking the workers back out: recent trends in the structuring of employment. *Res. Org. Behav.* 10: 257–303

Piore MJ, Sabel CF. 1984. *The Second Industrial Divide.* New York: Basic Books

Pischke J–S, DiNardo JE. 1997. The returns to computer use revisited: have pencils changed the wage structure too? *Q. J. Econ.* 112:291

Polivka AE. 1996a. Contingent and alternative work arrangements, defined. *Monthly Labor Rev.* 119:3–9

Polivka AE. 1996b. A profile of contingent workers. *Monthly Labor Rev.* 119:10–21

Portes A, Rumbaut RG. 1996. *Immigrant America: A Portrait.* Berkeley: Univ. Calif. Press

Raffalovich LE. 1990. Segmentation theory, economic performance, and earnings inequality. *Res. Soc. Stratif. Mobility* 9:251

Rodwin L, Sazanami H (eds.). 1989. *Deindustrialization and Regional Economic Transformation: The Experience of the United States.* London: HarperCollins Academic

Rodwin L, Sazanami H, eds. 1991. *Industrial Change and Regional Economic Transformation: The Experience of Western Europe.* London: HarperCollins Academic

Rose S, Carneval A. 1997. *The New Office Economy.* Princeton, NJ: Educ. Test. Serv.

Sachs JD, Shatz HJ. 1994. Trade and jobs in US manufacturing (with discussion). *Brookings Econ. Micro.* 1:1–84

Sampson RJ, Laub JH. 1993. *Crime in the Making: Pathways and Turning Points Through Life.* Cambridge, MA: Harvard Univ. Press

Sassen S. 1995. Immigration and local labor markets. In *Economic Sociology of Immigration: Essays on Networks, Ethnicity, and Entrepreneurship*, ed. A Portes, pp. 87–127. New York: Russell Sage Found.

Schrammel K. 1998. Comparing the labor market success of young adults from two generations. *Monthly Labor Rev.* :3–48

Smith RS 1988. Comparable worth: limited coverage and the exacerbation of inequality. *Indust. Lab. Relat. Rev.* 41:227–39

Spain D, Bianchi SM. 1996. *Balancing Act: Motherhood, Marriage, and Employment Among American Women.* New York: Russell Sage Found.

Tilly C, Bluestone B, Harrison B. 1986. What is making American wages more unequal? *Proc. Indust. Rel. Res. Assoc.* pp. 338–48

Topel RH. 1994. Regional labor markets and the determinants of wage inequality. *Am. Econ. Rev.* 84:17--22

Visser J. 1996. *Unionisation Trends Revisited.* Res. Pap. 1996/2. Ctr. for Eur. Soc. Indust. Relat. Amsterdam

Waldinger R, Aldrich H, Robin W, eds. 1990. *Ethnic Entrepreneurs: Immigrant Business in Industrial Societies.* Newbury Park, CA: Sage

Wellington AJ. 1993. Changes in the male/female wage gap, 1976–85. *J. Hum. Res.* 28:83–141

Western B, Beckett K. 1999. How unregulated is the U.S. labor market? The penal system as a labor market institution. *Am. J. Soc.* 104: In press

Western B, Healy K. 1999. Explaining the OECD wage slowdown: recession or labor decline? *Eur. Soc. Rev.* Forthcoming

Williamson JG, Lindert PH. 1980. *American Inequality: A Macroeconomic History.* New York: Academic Press

Williamson OE. 1975. *Markets and Hierarchies.* New York: Free Press

Wood A. 1994. *North-South Trade, Employment, and Inequality: Changing Fortunes in a Skill-Driven World.* New York: Oxford Univ. Press

Wood A. 1995. How trade hurt unskilled workers. *J. Econ. Persp.* 9:57

Annu. Rev. Sociol. 1999. 25:659–707

THE ESTIMATION OF CAUSAL EFFECTS FROM OBSERVATIONAL DATA

Christopher Winship and Stephen L. Morgan

Harvard University, Department of Sociology, William James Hall, 33 Kirkland Street, Cambridge, Massachusetts 02138; e-mail: winship@wjh.harvard.edu; smorgan@wjh.harvard.edu

KEY WORDS: causal inference, causal analysis, counterfactual, treatment effect, selection bias

---

ABSTRACT

When experimental designs are infeasible, researchers must resort to the use of observational data from surveys, censuses, and administrative records. Because assignment to the independent variables of observational data is usually nonrandom, the challenge of estimating causal effects with observational data can be formidable. In this chapter, we review the large literature produced primarily by statisticians and econometricians in the past two decades on the estimation of causal effects from observational data. We first review the now widely accepted counterfactual framework for the modeling of causal effects. After examining estimators, both old and new, that can be used to estimate causal effects from cross-sectional data, we present estimators that exploit the additional information furnished by longitudinal data. Because of the size and technical nature of the literature, we cannot offer a fully detailed and comprehensive presentation. Instead, we present only the main features of methods that are accessible and potentially of use to quantitatively oriented sociologists.

INTRODUCTION

Most quantitative empirical analyses are motivated by the desire to estimate the causal effect of an independent variable on a dependent variable. Although the randomized experiment is the most powerful design for this task, in most social science research done outside of psychology, experimental designs are infeasible. Social experiments are often too expensive and may require the

659

0360-0572/9/0815-0659$08.00

unethical coercion of subjects. Subjects may be unwilling to follow the experimental protocol, and the treatment of interest may not be directly manipulable. For example, without considerable power and a total absence of conscience, a researcher could not randomly assign individuals to different levels of educational attainment in order to assess the effect of education on earnings. For these reasons, sociologists, economists, and political scientists must rely on what is now known as observational data—data that have been generated by something other than a randomized experiment—typically surveys, censuses, or administrative records.

The problems of using observational data to make causal inferences are considerable (Lieberson 1985, LaLonde 1986). In the past two decades, however, statisticians (e.g. Rubin, Rosenbaum) and econometricians (e.g. Heckman, Manski) have made considerable progress in clarifying the issues involved when observational data are used to estimate causal effects. In some cases, this hard-won clarity has permitted the development of new and more powerful methods of analysis. This line of research is distinct from the work of sociologists and others who in the 1970s and 1980s developed path analysis and its generalization, covariance structure analysis. Despite their differences, both areas of research are often labeled causal analysis.

Statisticians and econometricians have adopted a shared conceptual framework that can be used to evaluate the appropriateness of different estimators in specific circumstances. This framework, to be described below, also clarifies the properties of estimators that are needed to obtain consistent estimates of causal effects in particular applications.

Our chapter provides an overview of the work that has been done by statisticians and econometricians on causal analysis. We hope it will provide the reader with a basic appreciation of the conceptual advances that have been made and some of the methods that are now available for estimating causal effects. Because the literature is massive and often technical, we do not attempt to be comprehensive. Rather, we present material that we believe is most accessible and useful to practicing researchers.

As is typical of the literature we are reviewing, we use the language of experiments in describing these methods. This usage is an indication of the advances that have been made; we now have a conceptual framework that allows us to use the traditional experimental language and perspective to discuss and analyze observational data. Throughout this chapter, we write of individuals who are subject to treatment, and we describe individuals as having been assigned to either a treatment or a control group. The reader, however, should not assume that the thinking and methods we review apply only to the limited set of situations in which it is strictly proper to talk about treatment and control groups. In almost any situation where a researcher attempts to estimate a causal effect, the analysis can be described, at least in terms of a thought experiment, as an experiment.

The chapter consists of three major sections. The first presents the conceptual framework and problems associated with using observational data to estimate causal effects. It presents the counterfactual account of causality and its associated definition of a causal effect. We also discuss the basic problems that arise when using observational data to estimate a causal effect, and we show that there are two distinct sources of possible bias: Outcomes for the treatment and control groups may differ even in the absence of treatment; and the potential effect of the treatment may differ for the treatment and control groups. We then present a general framework for analyzing how assignment to the treatment group is related to the estimation of a causal effect.

The second section examines cross-sectional methods for estimating causal effects. It discusses the bounds that data place on the permissible range of a causal effect; it also discusses the use of control variables to eliminate potential differences between the treatment and control groups that are related to the outcome. We review standard regression and matching approaches and discuss methods that condition on the likelihood of being assigned to the treatment. These latter methods include the regression discontinuity design, propensity score techniques, and dummy endogenous variable models. This section also discusses the use of instrumental variables to estimate causal effects, presenting their development as a method to identify parameters in simultaneous equation models and reviewing current research on what instrumental variables identify in the presence of different types of treatment-effect heterogeneity.

The third section discusses methods for estimating causal effects from longitudinal data. We present the interrupted time-series design, then use a relatively general model specification for the structure of unobservables to compare change-score analysis, differential linear growth rate models, and the analysis of covariance. The key lesson here is that no one method is appropriate for all cases. This section also discusses how to use data to help determine which method is appropriate in a particular application.

The paper concludes with a discussion of the general importance of the methods reviewed for improving the quality of quantitative empirical research in sociology. We have more powerful methods available, but more important, we have a framework for examining the plausibility of assumptions behind different methods and thus a way of analyzing the quality and limitations of particular empirical estimates.

BASIC CONCEPTUAL FRAMEWORK

In the past two decades, statisticians and econometricians have adopted a common conceptual framework for thinking about the estimation of causal effects—the counterfactual account of causality. The usefulness of the counterfactual framework is threefold. It provides an explicit framework for understanding (*a*) the limitations of observational data, (*b*) how the treatment assignment process may be related to the outcome of interest, and (*c*) the type of information that is provided by the data in the absence of any assumptions.

The Counterfactual Account Of Causality

Discussions of causality in the social sciences often degenerate into fruitless philosophical digressions (e.g., see McKim & Turner 1997, Singer & Marini 1987). In contrast, the development of the counterfactual definition of causality has yielded practical value. With its origins in the early work on experimental designs by Fisher (1935), Neyman (1923, 1935), Cochran & Cox (1950), Kempthorne (1952), and Cox (1958a,b), the counterfactual framework has been formalized and extended to nonexperimental designs in a series of papers by Rubin (1974, 1977, 1978, 1980, 1981, 1986, 1990; see also Pratt & Schlaifer 1984). However, it also has roots in the economics literature (Roy 1951, Quandt 1972). The counterfactual account has provided a conceptual and notational framework for analyzing problems of causality that is now dominant in both statistics and econometrics. Holland (1986), Pratt & Schlaifer (1988), and Sobel (1995, 1996) provide detailed exegeses of this work.

Let Y be an interval level measure of an outcome of interest, either continuous or discrete or a mixture of the two. Examples are earnings, mathematics aptitude, educational attainment, employment status, and age at death. Assume that individuals can be exposed to only one of two alternative states but that each individual could a priori be exposed to either state. Each state is characterized by a distinct set of conditions, exposure to which potentially affects the outcome of interest Y. We refer to the two states as treatment and control.[1]

Assume that one group of individuals is assigned to be observed in the treatment state and that a second group of individuals is assigned to be observed in the control state. The key assumption of the counterfactual framework is that individuals assigned to these treatment and control groups have potential outcomes in both states: the one in which they are observed and the one in which they are not observed. In other words, each individual in the treatment group has an observable outcome in the treatment state and an unobservable counterfactual outcome in the control state. Likewise, each individual in the control group has an observable outcome in the control state and an unobservable counterfactual outcome in the treatment state. Thus, the framework asserts that individuals have potential outcomes in all states, even though they can actually only be observed in one state.

---

[1] Any two states to which individuals could be assigned or could choose to enter can be considered treatment and control. The potential outcome framework also can be generalized to any number of alternative sets of treatment conditions.

Formalizing this conceptualization, the potential outcomes of each individual unit of analysis are defined as the true values of Y that would result from exposure to the alternative sets of conditions that characterize the two states named treatment and control. More formally, let Y_i^t and Y_i^c equal the potential outcomes for each individual i that would result from exposure to the treatment and control conditions. We assume that both potential outcomes exist in theory for every individual, although at most only one potential outcome can be observed for each individual.

The causal effect of the treatment on the outcome for each individual i is defined as the difference between the two potential outcomes in the treatment and control states:

$$\delta_i = Y_i^t - Y_i^c. \tag{1.}$$

Because both Y_i^t and Y_i^c exist in theory, we can define this individual-level causal effect. However, as detailed below, because we cannot observe both Y_i^t and Y_i^c for any single individual, we cannot observe or thus directly calculate any individual-level causal effects.

First note that this definition of a causal effect, while intuitively appealing, makes several assumptions.[2] The most crucial assumption among these is that a change in treatment status of any individual does not affect the potential outcomes of other individuals. Known as the stable unit treatment value assumption (SUTVA) (see Rubin 1980, 1986, 1990), this assumption is most commonly violated when there is interference across treatments (i.e. when there are interactions between treatments). The classical example is the analysis of treatment effects in agricultural research—rain that surreptitiously carries fertilizer from a treated plot to an adjacent untreated plot. Aside from simple interference, the SUTVA may also be violated in other situations, especially when "macro effects" of the treatment alter potential outcomes (see Garfinkel et al. 1992, Heckman et al. 1998). Consider the case where a large job training program is offered in a metropolitan area with a competitive labor market. As the supply of graduates from the program increases, the wage that employers will be willing to pay graduates of the program will decrease. When such complex effects are present, the powerful simplicity of the counterfactual framework vanishes.

Why can we not observe and calculate individual-level causal effects? In order to observe values of Y, we must assign individuals to be observed in one of the two states. To formalize this observation rule, define T_i as a dummy variable equal to 1 if an individual is assigned to the treatment group and equal

---

[2]One important assumption that we do not discuss is that the treatment must be manipulable. For example, as Holland (1986) argued, it makes no sense to talk about the causal effect of gender or any other nonmanipulable individual trait alone. One must explicitly model the manipulable mechanism that generates an apparent causal effect of a nonmanipulable attribute.

to 0 if an individual is assigned to the control group. The observed Y_i are equal to $Y_i = Y_i^t$ when $T_i = 1$ and $Y_i = Y_i^c$ when $T_i = 0$. As these definitions reveal, causal inference can be seen as a problem of missing data. The observed Y_i do not contain enough information to identify individual-level causal effects because individuals cannot be observed under both the treatment and the control conditions simultaneously.[3]

The main value of this counterfactual framework is that causal inference can be summarized by a single question: Given that the δ_i cannot be calculated for any individual and therefore that Y_i^t and Y_i^c can be observed only on mutually exclusive subsets of the population, what can be inferred about the distribution of the δ_i from an analysis of Y_i and T_i?

Average Effects And The Standard Estimator

Most of the literature has focused on the estimation of the average causal effect for a population. Let $\overline{Y}^t$ be the average value of Y_i^t for all individuals if they are exposed to the treatment, and let $\overline{Y}^c$ be the average value of Y_i^c for all individuals if they are exposed to the control. More formally, $\overline{Y}^t$ is the expected value of Y_i^t in the population, and $\overline{Y}^c$ is the expected value of Y_i^c in the population. The average treatment effect in the population is

$$\overline{\delta} = \overline{Y}^t - \overline{Y}^c \qquad\qquad\qquad 2.$$

or, again more formally, the expected value of the difference between $\overline{Y}^t$ and $\overline{Y}^c$ in the population.[4]

Because Y_i^t and Y_i^c are unobservable (or missing) on mutually exclusive subsets of the population, $\overline{Y}^t$ and $\overline{Y}^c$ cannot both be calculated. However, $\overline{Y}^t$ and $\overline{Y}^c$ can potentially be estimated, although not very well or without considerable difficulty except in special circumstances. Most methods discussed in this paper attempt to construct from observational data consistent estimates of $\overline{Y}^t$ and $\overline{Y}^c$ in order to obtain a consistent estimate of $\overline{\delta}$.

For example, consider the most common estimator, which we call the standard estimator for the average treatment effect. Let $\overline{Y}_{i \in T}^t$ be the expected value of Y_i^t for all individuals in the population who would be assigned to the treatment group for observation, and let $\overline{Y}_{i \in C}^c$ be the expected value of Y_i^c for all

---

[3]When one has longitudinal data, an effective strategy may be to use a person as his own control. This strategy only works if age does not otherwise affect the outcome and there are no exogenous period-specific effects. If change with age or period effects is possible, some type of adjustment is needed. We discuss methods that do this in the section on longitudinal analysis.

[4]In many presentations of the counterfactual framework, formal $E[.]$ notation is used. The average treatment effect of Equation 2 is written as $E[\delta] = E[Y^t - Y^c]$. The standard estimator in Equation 3 is considered an attempt to estimate $E[Y^t \mid T = 1] - E[Y^c \mid T = 0]$.

individuals in the population who would be assigned to the control group for observation. Both of these quantities can be calculated and thus effectively estimated by their sample analogs, the mean of Y_i for those actually assigned to the treatment group and the mean of Y_i for those actually assigned to the control group. The standard estimator for the average treatment effect is the difference between these two estimated means:

$$\hat{\delta} = \hat{\overline{Y}}^t_{i \in T} - \hat{\overline{Y}}^c_{i \in C},$$ 3.

where the hats on all three terms signify that they are the sample analog estimators (sample means) of the expectations defined above.

Note the two differences between Equations 2 and 3. Equation 2 is defined for the population, whereas Equation 3 represents an estimator that can be applied to a sample drawn from the population. All individuals in the population contribute to the three terms in Equation 2. However, each sampled individual can be used only once to estimate either $\overline{Y}^t_{i \in T}$ or $\overline{Y}^c_{i \in C}$. As a result, the way in which individuals are assigned (or assign themselves) to the treatment and control groups determines how effectively the standard estimator $\hat{\delta}$ estimates the true average treatment effect δ. As we demonstrate, many estimators are extensions of this standard estimator that seek to eliminate the bias resulting from inherent differences between the treatment and control groups.

To understand when the standard estimator consistently estimates the true average treatment effect for the population, let $\overline{Y}^t_{i \in C}$ and $\overline{Y}^c_{i \in T}$ be defined analogously to $\overline{Y}^t_{i \in T}$ and $\overline{Y}^c_{i \in C}$ above, and let π equal the proportion of the population that would be assigned to the treatment group. Decompose the average treatment effect in the population into a weighted average of the average treatment effect for those in the treatment group and the average treatment effect for those in the control group and then decompose the resulting terms into differences in average potential outcomes:

$$\begin{aligned}
\overline{\delta} &= \pi \overline{\delta}_{i \in T} + (1 - \pi)\overline{\delta}_{i \in C} \\
&= \pi \left(\overline{Y}^t_{i \in T} - \overline{Y}^c_{i \in T} \right) + (1 - \pi)\left(\overline{Y}^t_{i \in C} - \overline{Y}^c_{i \in C} \right) \\
&= \left[\pi \overline{Y}^t_{i \in T} + (1 - \pi)\overline{Y}^t_{i \in C} \right] - \left[\pi \overline{Y}^c_{i \in T} + (1 - \pi)\overline{Y}^c_{i \in C} \right] \\
&= \overline{Y}^t - \overline{Y}^c.
\end{aligned}$$ 4.

The quantities $\overline{Y}^t_{i \in C}$ and $\overline{Y}^c_{i \in T}$ that appear explicitly in the second and third lines of Equation 4 cannot be directly calculated because they are based on unobservable values of Y. If we assume that $\overline{Y}^t_{i \in T} = \overline{Y}^t_{i \in C}$ and $\overline{Y}^c_{i \in C} = \overline{Y}^c_{i \in T}$, then through substitution starting in the third line of (4):

$$\bar{\delta} = \left[\pi \overline{Y}^t_{i\in T} + (1 - \pi)\overline{Y}^t_{i\in C}\right] - \left[\pi \overline{Y}^c_{i\in T} + (1 - \pi)\overline{Y}^c_{i\in C}\right]$$
$$= \left[\pi \overline{Y}^t_{i\in T} + (1 - \pi)\overline{Y}^t_{i\in T}\right] - \left[\pi \overline{Y}^c_{i\in C} + (1 - \pi)\overline{Y}^c_{i\in C}\right] \qquad 5.$$
$$= \overline{Y}^t_{i\in T} - \overline{Y}^c_{i\in C}.$$

Thus, a sufficient condition for the standard estimator to consistently estimate the true average treatment effect in the population is that $\overline{Y}^t_{i\in T} = \overline{Y}^t_{i\in C}$ and $\overline{Y}^c_{i\in C} = \overline{Y}^c_{i\in T}$. In this situation, the average outcome under the treatment and the average outcome under the control do not differ between the treatment and control groups. In order to satisfy these equality conditions, a sufficient condition is that treatment assignment T_i be uncorrelated with the potential outcome distributions of Y^t_i and Y^c_i. The principal way to achieve this uncorrelatedness is through random assignment to the treatment.

By definition, observational data are data that have not been generated by an explicit randomization scheme. In most cases, treatment assignment will be correlated with the potential outcome variables. As a result, the standard estimator will usually yield inconsistent estimates of the true average treatment effect in the population when applied to observational data.

An important caveat is that the average treatment effect $\bar{\delta}$ is not always the quantity of theoretical interest. Heckman (1992, 1996, 1997) and Heckman et al. (1997b) have argued that in a variety of policy contexts, it is the average treatment effect for the treated that is of substantive interest. The essence of their argument is that in deciding whether a policy is beneficial, our interest is not whether on average the program is beneficial for all individuals but whether it is beneficial for those individuals who are either assigned or who would assign themselves to the treatment.

For example, if we are interested in determining whether a particular vocational education program in a high school is beneficial, it makes little sense to ask whether its effect is positive for all high school students. For college-bound students, the effects of the program may be negative. Even for non–college-bound students, the program may have positive effects only for some students. To the degree that students can estimate their likely benefit of enrolling in the program before actually doing so, we would expect that those students for whom the expected benefits are positive will be more likely to enroll in the program. The appropriate policy question is whether the program effects for this group of "self-selecting" students are positive and sufficiently large to justify the program costs. The policy–relevant piece of information in need of estimation is the size of the treatment effect for the treated. The average treatment effect for all students in the school is of little or no policy relevance.

As discussed below, it is also the case that in many contexts the average treatment effect is not identified separately from the average treatment effect for the treated. In most circumstances, there is simply no information available on how those in the control group would have reacted if they had instead received the treatment. This is the basis for an important insight into the potential biases of the standard estimator.

Define the baseline difference between the treatment and control groups as $(\overline{Y}^c_{i \in T} - \overline{Y}^c_{i \in C})$. This quantity can be thought of as the difference in outcomes between the treatment and control groups in the absence of treatment. With a little algebra, it can be shown that Standard estimator = True average treatment effect + (Difference in baseline Y) + $(1 - \pi)$ (Difference in the average treatment effect for the treatment and control groups), or in mathematical notation:

$$\overline{Y}^t_{i \in T} - \overline{Y}^c_{i \in C} = \overline{\delta} + \left(\overline{Y}^c_{i \in T} - \overline{Y}^c_{i \in C}\right) + (1 - \pi)(\overline{\delta}_{i \in T} - \overline{\delta}_{i \in C}). \qquad 6.$$

Equation 6 shows the two possible sources of bias in the standard estimator. The baseline difference, $(\overline{Y}^c_{i \in T} - \overline{Y}^c_{i \in C})$, is equal to the difference between the treatment and control groups in the absence of treatment. The second source of bias $(\overline{\delta}_{i \in T} - \overline{\delta}_{i \in C})$, the difference in the treatment effect for those in the treatment and control groups, is often not considered, even though it is likely to be present when there are recognized incentives for individuals (or their agents) to select into the treatment group. Instead, many researchers (or, more accurately, the methods that they use) simply assume that the treatment effect is constant in the population, even when common sense dictates that the assumption is clearly implausible (Heckman 1997, Heckman et al. 1997b, Heckman & Robb 1985, 1986, 1988; JJ Heckman, unpublished paper).

To clarify this decomposition, consider a substantive example—the effect of education on an individual's mental ability. Assume that the treatment is college attendance. After administering a test to a group of young adults, we find that individuals who have attended college score higher than individuals who have not attended college. There are three possible reasons that we might observe this finding. First, attending college might make individuals smarter on average. This effect is the average treatment effect, represented by $\overline{\delta}$ in Equation 6. Second, individuals who attend college might have been smarter in the first place. This source of bias is the baseline difference represented by $(\overline{Y}^c_{i \in T} - \overline{Y}^c_{i \in C})$ in Equation 6. Third, the mental ability of those who attend college may increase more than would the mental ability of those who did not attend college had they in fact attended college. This source of bias is the differential effect of treatment, represented by $(\overline{\delta}_{i \in T} - \overline{\delta}_{i \in C})$ in Equation 6.

To further clarify this last term in the decomposition, assume that those who have attended college and those who have not attended college had the same (average) initial mental ability. Assume further that only those who then attended college would have benefitted from doing so. If the treatment and control groups are of equal size, the standard estimator would overestimate the true average treatment effect by a factor of two. In this example, and in many other situations, the standard estimator yields a consistent estimate of the average treatment effect for the treated, not the average treatment effect for the entire population.

Equation 6 specifies the two sources of bias that need to be eliminated from estimates of causal effects from observational data. The remainder of the paper examines how this goal can be accomplished. Most of the discussion focuses on the elimination of the baseline difference $(\overline{Y}^c_{i \in T} - \overline{Y}^c_{i \in C})$. Fewer techniques are available to adjust for the differential treatment effects component of the bias $(\overline{\delta}_{i \in T} - \overline{\delta}_{i \in C})$.

Treatment Assignment Model

To proceed further, we need to develop a basic model for the assignment mechanism that generates the treatment and control groups. Our presentation of the assignment model follows Heckman & Robb (1985, 1986, 1988). Above, we specified that each individual has two potential outcomes, Y^t_i and Y^c_i, corresponding to potential exposure to the treatment and control. We noted that, in general, for any one individual only one of these two potential outcomes can be observed.

To develop an assignment model, we first write the potential outcomes Y^t_i and Y^c_i as deviations from their means:

$$Y^c_i = \overline{Y}^c + u^c_i,$$

$$Y^t_i = \overline{Y}^t + u^t_i.$$

Combining these two expressions with the observation rule given by the definition of the treatment assignment dummy variable T_i, the equation for any Y_i is

$$Y_i = \overline{Y}^c + T_i(\overline{Y}^t - \overline{Y}^c) + u^c_i + T_i(u^t_i - u^c_i)$$
$$= \overline{Y}^c + T_i\overline{\delta} + u_i,$$

7.

where $u_i = u^c_i + T_i(u^t_i - u^c_i)$. Equation 7 is known as the structural equation. This equation provides another way of thinking about the problem of consistently estimating the treatment effect. For the standard estimator—which is equivalent to the coefficient on T_i when Equation 7 is estimated by ordinary least squares (OLS)—to be a consistent estimate of the true average treatment effect, T_i and u_i must be uncorrelated.

Consider a supplemental equation, known as the assignment or selection equation, that determines T_i and is written in what is known as an index structure.

Let T_i^* be a latent continuous variable:

$$T_i^* = Z_i a + v_i, \qquad\qquad 8.$$

where $T_i = 1$ if $T_i^* \geq 0$ and $T_i = 0$ if $T_i^* < 0$, and where Z_i is a row vector of values on various exogenous observed variables that affect the assignment process, a is a vector of parameters that typically needs to be estimated, and v_i is an error term that captures unobserved factors that affect assignment.

Equations 7 and 8 are general. Additional covariates X_i can be included in Equation 7, as shown below in Equation 10, and X_i and Z_i may have variables in common. Both Z_i and v_i may be functions of an individual's potential outcome after exposure to the treatment (Y_i^t), an individual's potential outcome after exposure to the control (Y_i^c), or any function of the two potential outcomes, such as their difference $(Y_i^t - Y_i^c)$.

We can distinguish between two different ways that T_i and the error term in Equation 7, u_i, can be correlated (Heckman & Robb 1986, 1988; Heckman & Hotz 1989). When Z_i and u_i are correlated, but u_i and v_i are uncorrelated, we have "selection on the observables." In this case, some observed set of factors in Z_i is related to Y_i^c and/or Y_i^t. This form of selection results in data that are sometimes characterized as having ignorable treatment assignment— the probability of being assigned to the treatment condition is only a function of the observed variables (Rosenbaum & Rubin 1983, Rosenbaum 1984a,b). The second case is where u_i is correlated with v_i, resulting in "selection on the unobservables." Known as nonignorable treatment assignment, in this case the probability of assignment is a function of unobserved variables (and possibly observed variables as well). In the following sections, we examine methods that attempt to deal with both types of selection bias. Not surprisingly, remedies for bias from selection on the observables are easier to implement than are remedies for selection on the unobservables.

CROSS-SECTIONAL METHODS

Bounds For Treatment Effects

In a series of articles that have culminated in a book, Manski has investigated the bounds that are consistent with the data when weak assumptions alone are maintained (Manski 1995; see also Robins 1989). In this section, we point to the fact that in some circumstances the data, without any auxiliary assumptions, provide some information on the size of the treatment effect. Our discussion follows Manski (1994, 1995).

To see that the data can potentially bound a treatment effect, consider a case with a dichotomous zero-one outcome. The average treatment effect, $\bar{\delta}$, cannot exceed 1. The maximum treatment effect occurs when $\bar{Y}_{i \in T}^t = \bar{Y}_{i \in C}^t = 1$

Table 1 Hypothetical example illustrating the calculation of bounds on treatment effects

	Mean Outcome	
Groups	Y_i^c	Y_i^t
Observed mean outcomes[a]		
Control	$\overline{Y}_{i\in C}^c = 0.3$	$\overline{Y}_{i\in C}^t = ?$
Treatment	$\overline{Y}_{i\in T}^c = ?$	$\overline{Y}_{i\in T}^t = 0.7$
Largest possible treatment effect[b]		
Control	$\overline{Y}_{i\in C}^c = 0.3$	$\overline{Y}_{i\in C}^t = 1$
Treatment	$\overline{Y}_{i\in T}^c = 0$	$\overline{Y}_{i\in T}^t = 0.7$
Small possible treatment effect[c]		
Control	$\overline{Y}_{i\in C}^c = 0.3$	$\overline{Y}_{i\in C}^t = 0$
Treatment	$\overline{Y}_{i\in T}^c = 1$	$\overline{Y}_{i\in T}^t = 0.7$

[a]Standard estimator of treatment effect is 0.4.
[b]Implied upper bound of average treatment effect is 0.7.
[c]Implied lower bound of average treatment effect is -0.3.

and $\overline{Y}_{i\in T}^c = \overline{Y}_{i\in C}^c = 0$. Similarly, the average treatment effect cannot be less than -1. The minimum treatment effect occurs when $\overline{Y}_{i\in T}^t = \overline{Y}_{i\in C}^t = 0$ and $\overline{Y}_{i\in T}^c = \overline{Y}_{i\in C}^c = 1$. Thus, $\overline{\delta}$ is contained in an interval of length 2; more specifically, $\overline{\delta} \in [-1, 1]$.

Now assume that $\overline{Y}_{i\in T}^t = 0.7$ and $\overline{Y}_{i\in C}^c = 0.3$, as is shown in the hypothetical example in Table 1. Both quantities could be estimated from the data, and we do not consider the problem of sampling error. The standard estimator for the treatment effect in this case is $\overline{Y}_{i\in T}^t - \overline{Y}_{i\in C}^c = 0.4$. The largest possible treatment effect (Table 1) indicates the values of $\overline{Y}_{i\in C}^t$ and $\overline{Y}_{i\in T}^c$ that would produce the largest estimate of $\overline{\delta}$, 0.7. The smallest possible treatment effect (Table 1) indicates the values that would produce the smallest estimate of $\overline{\delta}$, -0.3. Thus, the constraints implied by the data guarantee that $\overline{\delta} \in [-0.3, 0.7]$, an interval of length 1, which is half the length of the maximum interval calculated before values for $\overline{Y}_{i\in T}^t$ and $\overline{Y}_{i\in C}^c$ were obtained from the data. Manski calls this interval the no-assumptions bound. Although this bound is still wide, it has substantially reduced our uncertainly about the range of $\overline{\delta}$. Manski (1995) shows that with a zero-one outcome variable, the no-assumptions bound will always be of length 1.

In general (see Manski 1994), the treatment effect will only be bounded when the outcome variable itself is bounded or when one is analyzing a function of the distribution of the dependent variable that is bounded. Because $\overline{Y}_{i\in C}^t$ and $\overline{Y}_{i\in T}^c$ are both unobserved, in the absence of any restriction they can take on any value from minus infinity to plus infinity. Thus, in the absence of any known restriction on $\overline{Y}^t_{i\in C}$ and $\overline{Y}^c_{i\in T}$, $\overline{\delta}$ can take on any value from minus infinity to plus infinity.

The goal of Manski's research is to analyze how additional assumptions narrow the bound for the estimated treatment effect while recognizing that the more assumptions an analysis entails, the less credible it is. He argues that researchers should first attempt to learn as much as possible about a treatment effect maintaining the weakest possible assumptions. Manski shows that weak and often plausible assumptions can substantially narrow the no-assumptions bound. For example, in many situations it may be reasonable to assume that the treatment effect cannot be negative (or alternatively positive) for any individual. Manski (1997) labels this assumption the monotone treatment response assumption. Under this assumption, the lower bound for the treatment effect is 0. Thus, for the example presented in Table 1, the bound for the treatment effect would be [0, 0.7].

Another possible assumption is that those who actually receive the treatment have higher average outcomes under potential exposure to both the treatment and control (i.e. $\overline{Y}^t_{i\in T} \geq \overline{Y}^t_{i\in C}$ and $\overline{Y}^c_{i\in T} \geq \overline{Y}^c_{i\in C}$). Manski & Pepper (1998) present this monotone treatment selection assumption with the example of the effect of education on wages. This case is equivalent to assuming that individuals with higher educational attainments would on average receive higher wages than would individuals with lower educational attainments, even if counterfactually the two groups had the same levels of educational attainment. For the example presented in Table 1, the monotone treatment selection assumption implies that the standard estimator would be an upper bound for the average treatment effect. Therefore, if we invoke the monotone treatment response and selection assumptions together, the bound on the treatment effect is [0, 0.4], which is considerably more narrow than the no-assumptions bound. Applications of Manski's approach can be found in Manski & Nagin (1998) and in Manski et al. (1992). We discuss Manski's work further below.

Regression Methods

The basic strategy behind regression analysis and related methods is to find a set of control variables that can be included in the regression equation in order to remove the correlation between the treatment variable and the error term. In order to understand the relationship between regression and other cross-sectional methods, it is worth formalizing this idea. Assume that we are interested in estimating Equation 8 above and that we believe the treatment indicator, T_i, is correlated with the error term, u_i, because treatment assignment is not random. We could attempt to deal with this problem by controlling for various observed Xs, estimating a regression equation of the form

$$Y_i = b_0 + T_i\bar{\delta} + X_i b + w_i.$$ 9.

Estimating Equation 9 by OLS is equivalent to following the double residual regression procedure (Malinvaud 1970, Goldberger 1991): (*a*) Regress Y_i on X_i and calculate $Y_i^* = Y_i - \hat{Y}_i$; (*b*) regress T_i on X_i and calculate $T_i^* = T_i - \hat{T}_i$; and (*c*) estimate $Y_i^* = T_i^*\bar{\delta} + w_i^*$, where $w_i^* = w_i - X_i b$. This three step procedure will yield the same estimate of $\bar{\delta}$ as OLS on Equation 9. Thus, OLS regression is equivalent to estimating the relationship between residualized versions of Y_i and T_i from which their common dependence on other variables has been subtracted out.

A number of techniques, all falling under what Heckman & Robb (1985) label control function estimators, can be understood as variants of this strategy. We discuss only a few such methods where a control function (i.e. some function of one or more variables) is entered into a regression equation in an attempt to eliminate the correlation between the treatment indicator variable and the error term. As is discussed below, instrumental variable techniques are based on a strategy that is the mirror image of the control function approach.

ANALYSIS OF COVARIANCE AND MATCHING   The analysis of covariance is probably the most common technique used to adjust for possible differences between treatment and control groups. Although it was originally developed to adjust for chance differences in observed Xs across treatment and control groups in randomized designs, it is now routinely used to attempt to control for differences between treatment and control groups in observational studies. Technically, the analysis of covariance is just a specific application of regression analysis. We consider a model somewhat more general than the standard model.

If we had a large data set and believed that either Y_i^c or δ_i varied as a function of the Xs, then one approach would be to stratify the sample on the Xs and carry out the analysis separately within each stratum. We could then estimate separate average treatment effects, $\bar{\delta}_x$, for each stratum. If a single treatment effect estimate was desired, we could then average these estimated effects across the strata, weighting each estimated treatment effect by the relative size of its stratum.

An analogous set of analyses could be mounted in a regression framework. Let the potential outcomes Y_i^t and Y_i^c depend on some set of variables X_i:

$$Y_i^c = b_0^c + X_i b + e_i^c$$ 10a.

and

$$Y_i^t = b_0^t + X_i(b + c) + e_i^t.$$ 10b.

The observed data can be written as a combination of these two equations:

$$Y_i = b_0^c + T_i(b_0^t - b_0^c) + X_i b + T_i(X_i c) + e_i. \qquad\qquad 11.$$

For individuals for whom $X_i = 0$, the treatment effect in Equation 11 is equal to $(b_0^t - b_0^c)$. The $X_i b$ term represents how the baseline level of Y_i, the Y_i^c, varies with the observed X_i. The hope is that by including the $X_i b$ term, we eliminate the baseline difference between the treatment and control groups, $(\overline{Y}_{i\in T}^c - \overline{Y}_{i\in C}^c)$.

The $X_i c$ term represents how the treatment effect, δ_i, varies with X_i. This term is not typically included in a standard analysis of covariance model. The hope is that by including the $X_i c$ term, we eliminate the difference in the treatment effects between the treatment and control groups, $(\overline{\delta}_{i\in T} - \overline{\delta}_{i\in C})$. This may often be an unrealistic assumption, because it implies that the researcher can forecast an individual's treatment effect just as accurately as the individual himself can. If individuals have pertinent information that is unavailable to the researcher (i.e. information that is not contained in the Xs), then it is likely that there will be differences in the treatment effects between the treatment and control groups that are not captured by observed Xs (Heckman 1989, 1992, 1996, 1997). Note that the treatment effect in Equation 11 is equal to $(b_0^t - b_0^c) + X_i c$. Obviously, this is not the treatment effect for the entire population but rather for individuals with characteristics X_i.

One problem with the regression approach is that it imposes a linearity constraint. Nonlinear terms can be added, but it is often difficult to know how the nonlinearity should be approximated. As White (1981) has shown, polynomial and related expansions may inadequately model nonlinearity and lead to biased estimates.

An alternative technique that avoids this problem is matching. Common in biomedical research but not in social scientific research, matching is closely related to the stratification procedure described above. Smith (1997) provides an excellent introduction for social scientists. Matching has several advantages. First, it makes no assumption about the functional form of the dependence between the outcome of interest and the other Xs. Second, matching ensures that only those portions of the distribution of the Xs in the observed data that contain individuals in both the treatment and control groups enter the estimation of the treatment effect.[5] Third, because fewer parameters are estimated than

---

[5]In two important empirical papers, Heckman et al (1997, 1998a) show that the bias due to selection on the unobservables, although significant and large relative to the size of the treatment effect, is small relative to the bias that results from having different ranges of Xs for the treatment and control groups and different distributions of the Xs across their common range. Matching solves both of the latter problems, although the average effect is not for the total population but only for that portion of the population where the treatment and control groups have common X values.

in a regression model, matching is more efficient. Efficiency can be important with small samples. A major problem with the traditional matching approach is that unless an enormous sample of data is available and there are more than a few Xs, it may be difficult to find both treatment and control cases that match. [See below for the ingenious solution to this problem developed by Rosenbaum & Rubin (1983)].

REGRESSION DISCONTINUITY DESIGN   A key limitation of the analysis of co-variance and related designs is that they do not directly conceptualize how the Xs are related to the likelihood of being assigned to the treatment group. Rather, the approach is to model the determinants of Y_i, thereby including Xs that are believed to affect the outcome and that may also be associated with assignment to the treatment group. By including many determinants of Y_i, one hopes to eliminate all differences between the treatment and control groups that are related to the outcome but that are not due to the treatment itself.

The philosophy behind regression discontinuity designs and propensity score methods is quite different from the strategy behind analysis of covariance. The strategy is to attempt to control for observed variables, Z_i, that affect whether an individual is assigned to the treatment group or the control group. By controlling for Zs that affect the treatment assignment, one hopes to eliminate any correlation between T_i and u_i in Equation 7.

The regression discontinuity design (Cook & Campbell 1979, Judd & Kenny 1981, Marcantonio & Cook 1994) is the simplest way of relating an observed variable, Z_i, to the assignment to a treatment group. The basic strategy is to find a Z_i that is related to the assignment of treatment in a sharply discontinuous way, as in Figure 1. The jump on the vertical axis at the point of treatment on the horizontal axis is the estimate of the main treatment effect. In Figure 1, the treatment effect is even more complex. The treatment also affects the slope of the relationship between Z and Y. Thus, the size of the treatment effect varies with Z.

The strength of the regression discontinuity design is determined by the accuracy of the estimate of the conditional relationship between Y and Z in the absence of treatment over the range of Z that receives the treatment. If the relationship between Z and Y is nonlinear, this can be highly problematic. Figure 2 provides an example. As can be seen from Figure 2, if we poorly estimate the values of Y that would be observed in the absence of treatment, we poorly estimate the effect of the treatment. The problem here is directly related to matching. One of the strengths of matching is that it ensures that we have both control and treatment cases over the range of Z that is relevant to the analysis. In the regression discontinuity design, the opposite is the case. There are no values of Z that contain both treatment and control cases. The power of the design hinges solely on the ability to extrapolate accurately.

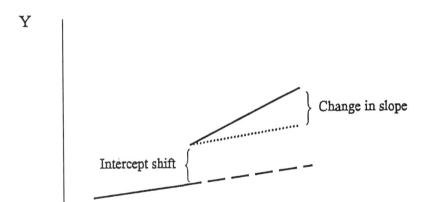

Figure 1   The regression discontinuity design. Note: If $Z \geq k$, the individual receives the treatment. If $Z < k$, the individual does not receive the treatment. (Solid line) Observed outcome; (dashed line) the assumed outcome in the absence of treatment.

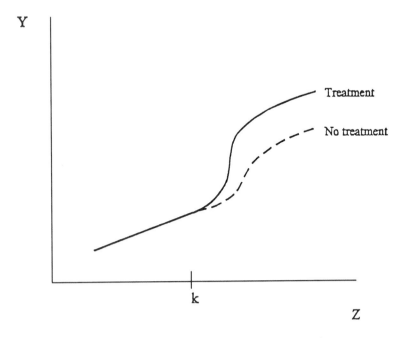

Figure 2   The regression discontinuity design with unrecognized nonlinearity.

PROPENSITY SCORES   The essence of the regression discontinuity design is the direct tie between the treatment assignment and an observed variable Z. The propensity score method (Rosenbaum & Rubin 1983, 1984, 1985; Rosenbaum 1984a,b, 1995; Rubin 1991; Rubin & Thomas 1996) provides a much more general approach that is nonetheless based on the same strategy as the regression discontinuity design. The propensity score for an individual is simply the probability that an individual, with a set of observed characteristics Z_i, is assigned to the treatment group instead of the control group, or

$$P(Z_i) = \text{Prob}(T = 1 \mid Z_i).$$ 12.

If treatment assignment is purely a function of the observed Zs (or in the language used above, selection is only on the observables), then conditional on the Zs, assignment is random with respect to the outcomes.[6] The importance of this result is that the analysis can then safely proceed after either matching or stratifying on the propensity score, $P(Z_i)$. In general, the propensity score will not be known but can be estimated using standard methods such as a logit or probit model.

Rosenbaum & Rubin (1983) show that there is nothing to be gained by matching (or stratifying) in a more refined way on the variables in Z than on just the propensity scores alone that are a function of the variables in Z. The propensity score contains all the information that is needed to create a balanced design—a design where the treatment and control groups do not differ with respect to Z in any way that is also related to treatment assignment T_i. This fact is of enormous importance because it means that matching can be done on a single dimension. As a result, even when there are many variables in Z that determine treatment assignment, matching is still feasible. Stratification on the propensity score is typically feasible only with large data sets.

A variety of matching schemes are possible. Nearest available matching on the estimated propensity score is the most common and one of the simplest (see Rosenbaum & Rubin 1985). First, the propensity scores for all individuals are estimated with a standard logit or probit model. Individuals in the treatment are then listed in random order.[7] The first treatment case is selected, and its propensity score is noted, and then matched to the control case with the closest propensity score. Both cases are then removed from their respective lists,

---

[6]See Rosenbaum & Rubin (1983) for a proof. Heckman et al (1997, 1998b) point out that this proof involves the true propensity score and that in most applications the propensity score needs to be estimated. It is unclear whether this is consequential.

[7]In most empirical applications of matching techniques, the treatment group is considerably smaller than the control group. This need not be the case in all applications, and if the reverse is true, the nearest available matching scheme described here runs in the opposite direction. Treatment cases would be matched to the smaller subset of control cases.

the second treatment case is matched to the remaining control case with the closest propensity score, and so on, until all treatment cases have received a matched control case. Other matching techniques that use propensity scores are implemented by (*a*) using different methods and different sets of Zs to estimate propensity scores, (*b*) matching on some important Zs first and then on propensity scores second, (*c*) defining the closeness of propensity scores and Zs in different ways, and/or (*d*) matching multiple control cases to each treatment case (see Rosenbaum 1995, Rubin & Thomas 1996, Smith 1997).

In principle, the propensity score can also be entered as a control variable in a regression model in a fashion similar to the inclusion of X_i in Equation 9 or 11. Rubin & Rosenbaum have advocated matching because it implicitly deals with the problem of nonlinearity and uses fewer degrees of freedom, making it more efficient. To better understand the propensity-score method, it is useful, however, to consider the approach within a regression framework.

Consider Equations 7 and 8 again. The assumption behind these two equations is that Z_i directly affects treatment assignment but does not directly affect either Y_i^t or Y_i^c. Z_i, however, is potentially correlated with u_i, which may include both observed and unobserved components. In some cases, the Z_i may overlap with observed components of u_i. However, we do not think of either the Z_i or the propensity score $P(Z_i)$ as being determinants of the outcome. Thus, Z_i does not belong in the structural Equation 7. Z_i determines assignment, not the outcome.

What are we doing if we enter the propensity score, or some nonlinear transformation of it, into Equation like 9 or 10, as if it were an X? Heckman & Robb (1986, 1988) have pointed out that Rosenbaum and Rubin's propensity-score method is one example of a control function. As discussed above, the goal when a control variable, in this case the propensity score, is entered into Equation 7 as a regressor is to make the treatment assignment variable uncorrelated with the new error term. Above, we noted that conditional on the propensity score, assignment to the treatment group is random by construction. This means that by entering the propensity score, or some nonlinear transformation of it, into regression Equation 9, for example, we are "subtracting out" of Y_i and T_i that component of their correlation that is due to the assignment process.

To understand what we are doing further, consider Figure 3 where we are interested in estimating the effect of T_i on Y_i, but we are concerned that T_i and u_i might be correlated. There are two reasons they might be correlated. First, u_i and T_i might be correlated because the Z_i or equivalently the propensity score, $P(Z_i)$, and T_i are correlated. This is selection on the observables. Second, there is a possibility that T_i and u_i are correlated because u_i and v_i are correlated. This is selection on the unobservables. The propensity-score method, however, assumes that all the selection is on the observables. Thus there is no

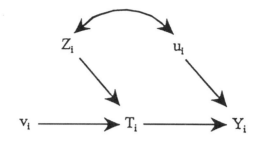

Figure 3   The propensity score strategy for the estimation of a treatment effect when selection is nonrandom.

arrow connecting u_i and v_i in Figure 3. This is a very strong assumption. It implies that there are no common omitted variables that determine both treatment assignment and the outcome. Estimation of the propensity-score model amounts to estimating the effect of T_i on Y_i where both variables have been residualized with respect to $P(Z_i)$. As Figure 3 indicates, conditional on Z_i, or equivalently the propensity score $P(Z_i)$, T_i and u_i are assumed to be uncorrelated. As a result, estimation by OLS using residualized Y_i and T_i consistently estimates the treatment effect.

SELECTION MODELS   Heckman's early work in the late 1970s on selection bias, particularly his lambda method, has received some attention in sociology. Since that time, considerable new research has appeared, primarily in the econometrics literature. Winship & Mare (1992) provide a review of much of this literature. Heckman's closely related work on dummy endogenous variables, pursued at the same time as his well-known selection-bias research, has received less attention (Heckman 1978). Although his terminology is different, his work also addresses the estimation of treatment effects when assignment is nonrandom.

The selection and nonrandom assignment problems are intimately connected. In essence, the nonrandom assignment problem is two selection problems in one. If the focus is only on Y_i^c, we have a selection problem because Y_i^c is only observed for individuals who are exposed to the control. Similarly, we have a selection problem if we focus solely on Y_i^t because it is only observed for individuals who are exposed to the treatment. In both cases, we are concerned that individuals have selected (or been selected) on the dependent variable and thus that treatment exposure is a function of Y_i^t, Y_i^c, or some function of the two. When this occurs, standard regression techniques yield an inconsistent estimate of the treatment effect.

Although completed prior to most of Rubin's and Rosenbaum's work on propensity scores, Heckman's work on the dummy endogenous variable problem can be understood as a generalization of the propensity-score approach. It is also another example of a control function estimator.[8] As with Rosenbaum's and Rubin's propensity score method, Heckman focuses on the selection Equation 9. Heckman, however, is interested in the conditional mean of T_i^*, the latent continuous variable, rather than the probability that $T_i = 1$. Specifically, using the linearity of Equation 8, he is interested in

$$E[T_i^* \mid Z_i a, T_i] = Z_i a + E[v_i \mid Z_i a, T_i].$$ 13.

Note that the expected value here of T_i^* is a function of both $Z_i a$ and T_i. This allows Heckman to take account of selection that may be a function of both the observables Z_i and the unobservables v_i. As shown in Figure 3, we now assume that u_i and v_i may be correlated. This correlation would occur if respondents know more about their potential outcomes under the treatment and control than the researcher and use their private information when "selecting" themselves into the treatment or control group.

If v_i is only correlated with observed components of u_i (i.e. the Xs in our notation), then the selection problem is easily solved. We can adjust for nonrandom assignment by simply controlling for these Xs when estimating Equation 8, as in the analysis of covariance and its extensions that are discussed above. However, if v_i is correlated with unobserved components of u_i, a more complicated solution is required.

If we could observe v_i, we could enter it into Equation 7 or 11 as a control variable, adopting a strategy similar in spirit to Rosenbaum's and Rubin's propensity score method. In so doing, we would control for a function of the assignment process in order to create residualized Y_i and T_i so that the residualized T_i would no longer be correlated with the new error term. The brilliance of Heckman's research was his recognition that although one could not observe v_i directly, one could calculate its expected value from Equation 13 and that this expected value of v_i could be used as a control variable (function) to consistently estimate Equation 7.

In order to calculate the expected value of v_i in Equation 13, one needs to make an assumption about the distribution of v_i. Typically, the distribution is assumed to be normal. If $f(.)$ is the normal density function and $F(.)$ is the corresponding cumulative distribution function, then

$$E[v_i \mid Z_i a, T_i] = \frac{f(Z_i a)}{[1 - F(Z_i a)]} \quad \text{when} \quad T_i = 1$$ 14a.

---

[8] The general selection model considered by Heckman (1979) can also be estimated by maximum likelihood or nonlinear least squares, although this involves stronger distributional assumptions than does the lambda method discussed here (see Winship & Mare 1992 for a brief discussion).

and

$$E[v_i \mid Z_i a, T_i] = \frac{-f(Z_i a)}{F(Z_i a)} \quad \text{when} \quad T_i = 0. \qquad \text{14b.}$$

Equation 14a simply gives the formula for lambda in a standard sample selection problem. In the treatment context, one would calculate a lambda for those in the treatment condition ($T_i = 1$) using Equation 14a and a lambda for those in the control equation using Equation 14b. These lambdas would then be entered into Equation 7 or, similarly, Equation 11 as controls, analogous to the inclusion of two more Xs. Thus, the procedure here is identical to Heckman's lambda method for correcting for selection bias, except that two distinct lambdas, one for the treatment and one for the control group, are utilized.

As Heckman and many others have come to recognize, estimates from his method can be sensitive to assumptions about the distribution of v_i. This issue is discussed in Winship & Mare (1992). Typically, if one is estimating, for example, Equation 11, there should be Zs in the selection equation that are not also Xs. Recently, Heckman and his colleagues (1998a) have suggested that one might, in the spirit of Rubin's and Rosenbaum's propensity score method, match on lambda. This strategy is similar to methods proposed by Powell (1987) and Honore & Powell (1994) for dealing with sample selection.

Instrumental Variables

When an independent variable in a regression model is endogenous (i.e. correlated with the error term), the traditional approach in econometrics is to use instrumental variables. In our context, if there is some variable (or set of variables) that affects assignment but does not affect the outcome, then this variable (or set of variables) can be used as an instrument to deal with the possibility that assignment to treatment is nonrandom. The power of the instrumental variable approach is derived solely from the assumption that the instrument only affects the outcome indirectly through the independent variables in the model. In general, this assumption cannot be tested.

Instrumental variable techniques were first developed by economists to estimate simultaneous equation models with jointly determined supply and demand equations from a set of competitive markets (Hood & Koopmans 1953). For any one market, only one point is observed—the competitive equilibrium price and quantity at the intersection of the supply and demand curves. In order to estimate the demand curve, a variable is needed that shifts the supply curve. One can then observe different points of intersection between the demand curve and the shifted supply curve. Similarly, in order to estimate the supply curve, a second variable is needed that shifts the demand curve so that one can observe

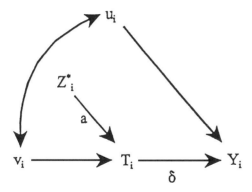

Figure 4 The instrumental variable strategy for the estimation of a treatment effect when selection is nonrandom.

different points of intersection between the supply curve and the shifted demand curve. Variables that fulfill these functions are instrumental variables for quantity supplied and quantity demanded, respectively.

TRADITIONAL INSTRUMENTAL VARIABLES In the counterfactual causality framework outlined above, an instrument is a variable that affects assignment but does not directly affect either Y_i^t or Y_i^c. Consider the simple path model in Figure 4, analogous to Figure 3, for the observed Y_i. In order to simplify the discussion, assume that u_i only contains unobserved determinants of Y_i (i.e. there are no Xs). Equivalently, assume that the effects of any Xs have already been conditioned out. In Figure 4, the potential instrument Z_i^* is assumed to be uncorrelated with u_i. Contrast this with Figure 3, where Z_i or more accurately the propensity score, $P(Z_i)$, is assumed to be (strongly) correlated with u_i. In Figure 3, the strength of the correlation between Z_i and u_i is sufficiently strong so that u_i and v_i, and thus u_i and T_i, are assumed to be uncorrelated. Figures 3 and 4 show that Z_i and Z_i^* relate to u_i in totally opposite ways.

Ignoring scale factors, or similarly assuming that all variables have been standardized, we can see that in Figure 4 the covariance between Z_i^* and Y_i is δa if the covariance between Z_i^* and T_i is a and δ is the direct effect of T_i on Y_i (i.e. the effect of T_i on Y_i not including its indirect effect through u_i). Thus, we can estimate the treatment effect as $\hat{\delta} = \mathrm{Cov}(Y_i, Z_i^*)/\mathrm{Cov}(T_i, Z_i^*)$.

One way of understanding instrumental variables is in terms of an exclusion restriction—the instrumental variable only affects the outcome indirectly through the treatment variable. In the previous section, we discussed the use of control functions—residualizing Y_i and T_i with respect to some X_i and Z_i (or set of Xs and Zs) such that the residualized T_i is no longer correlated with the resulting error term. Instrumental variable techniques attempt to achieve the same goal of creating a new T_i that is uncorrelated with the resulting error term but do so in the opposite way. Instead of constructing residualized variables, instrumental variables construct predicted Y_i and T_i where the predicted T_i is uncorrelated with the resulting error term. Analogous to steps (a) through (c) above, instrumental variable estimates can be obtained by the following two-stage procedure: (a) Regress Y_i on Z_i^* and calculate $\hat{Y}_i$; (b) regress T_i on Z_i^* and calculate $\hat{T}_i$; and (c) estimate $\hat{Y}_i = \hat{T}_i \bar{\delta} + w_i$. This three-step procedure illustrates another way of thinking about instrumental variables. We express both our dependent variable Y_i and independent variable T_i as functions of a third variable Z_i^* that is uncorrelated with the error term. Because Z_i^* is uncorrelated with the error term, the new predicted T_i, $\hat{T}_i$, is uncorrelated with the error term. We can then regress the new predicted Y_i, $\hat{Y}_i$, on $\hat{T}_i$ to obtain a consistent estimate of the treatment effect.

A comparison of alternative strategies based on instrumental variables and control functions is instructive. When using a propensity score, or more generally a control function strategy, we look for control variables, as in Figure 3, that are highly correlated with the error term in the structural equation so that after conditioning on these variables, the treatment indicator variable is no longer correlated with any portion of the error term that remains. When using an instrumental variables strategy, we look for a variable or set of variables, as in Figure 4, that is uncorrelated with the error term. If we can then express the outcome and treatment variables as functions of this variable or set of variables, we can calculate the treatment effect with a simple regression using the new variables that have been predicted from the instrument(s).

A third way of thinking about instrumental variables is as naturally occurring randomization (Angrist et al. 1996, Heckman 1996). This perspective is easiest to appreciate when the instrument is binary, because the standard instrumental variable estimator takes the simple form

$$\hat{\beta}_{IV} = \frac{(\bar{Y}_i \mid Z_i^* = 1) - (\bar{Y}_i \mid Z_i^* = 0)}{(\bar{T}_i \mid Z_i^* = 1) - (\bar{T}_i \mid Z_i^* = 0)}. \qquad 15.$$

known in econometrics as the Wald estimator. The numerator is the standard estimator for the treatment effect of Z_i^* on Y_i, and the denominator is the standard estimator for the treatment effect of Z_i^* on T_i. If Z_i^* is randomly assigned, as in the case of a natural experiment, then both estimates are consistent. Because we assume that Z_i^* only affects Y_i through T_i, the ratio of these two effects consistently estimates the effect of T_i on Y_i.

WEAKNESSES OF CONVENTIONAL IV TECHNIQUES   Instrumental variable (IV) techniques have three main weaknesses (see Heckman 1997 for a detailed discussion). First, assumptions that exclusion restrictions are valid are generally untestable and sometimes unbelievable. Second, the standard errors of IV estimates can be large if the instrument is weak or the sample size is not large. Third, IVs only consistently estimate the true average treatment effect when the treatment effect is constant for all individuals, an assumption that is often unreasonable. We discuss each of these problems in turn.

Even within economics, the assumed validity of an exclusion restriction is often controversial. Consider one of the most celebrated example of IVs— the draft lottery number as an instrument for veteran status in estimating the effect of military service on earnings (Angrist 1990). The case for excluding lottery number from the earnings equation that is the primary interest of the study is the randomization of the draft lottery (numbers assigned by day of birth). However, differential mortality patterns may lead to sample selection that spoils the randomization (Moffitt 1996). In addition, employers may behave differently with respect to individuals with different lottery numbers, investing more heavily in individuals who are less likely to be drafted. As a result, lottery number may be a direct, though probably weak, determinant of future earnings (Heckman 1995, 1997).

IV point estimates of treatment effects are often accompanied by wide confidence intervals.[9] The variance of the IV estimator for a bivariate regression with a single instrument is

$$\text{Var}(\hat{\beta}_{\text{IV}}) = \frac{\sigma_e^2 \, \text{Var}(Z_i^*)}{n \, \text{Cov}(T_i, Z_i^*)^2},$$ 16.

where n is the sample size and σ_e^2 is the variance of the error term. The standard error of an IV estimate is inversely proportional to both the covariance between T_i and Z_i^* and the sample size. To obtain precise estimates, either the sample size must be unusually large and/or T_i and Z_i^* must be strongly correlated. The latter case has led researchers to describe the perfect instrument as an apparent contradiction. A valid instrument must be uncorrelated with the error term but highly correlated with the treatment variable T_i. However, because T_i is correlated with the error term, motivating the use of instrumental variables in the first place, any variable that is highly correlated with T_i is likely also to be correlated with the error term, even though this is not necessarily so.

Angrist & Krueger (1991, 1992) have capitalized on the large size of census datasets, using quarter of birth as an instrument for education when estimating

---

[9]IV estimates always have larger variance than OLS estimates. Thus, even if it is known that OLS estimates are biased, they may be preferred to apparently unbiased IV estimates if the mean-squared error of OLS estimates is smaller.

the effect of education on earnings. Because of education laws regarding minimum ages for school entry and later voluntary dropping out, individuals born just before and just after specific cutoff dates (e.g. January 1) are likely to differ in their levels of educational attainment. Angrist & Krueger (1991, 1992) find that quarter of birth is indeed (weakly) correlated with educational attainment and assume that it has no direct effect on earnings. Because of the large size of the census samples they utilize, they are able to obtain precise IV estimates of the effect of education on earnings. Their work, however, has received considerable criticism (Bound et al. 1995; also see Winship 1998). All these critics point out that the covariance of earnings with quarter of birth and the covariance of educational attainment with quarter of birth are both weak. In this case, the instrumental variable estimator is essentially the ratio of two very small numbers, the covariance between quarter of birth and education and the covariance between quarter of birth and earnings. As a result, the IV estimate may potentially be unstable. Even if the direct effect of quarter of birth on earnings is small, it will make a substantial contribution to the covariance between these two variables. As a result, large biases in the IV estimate will occur. Bound et al (1995) discuss a variety of reasons that quarter of birth might have a small but non-zero direct effect on earnings. If this direct effect is non-zero, as they argue, then Angrist's and Krueger's IV estimates are likely to be substantially biased.

As already noted, the instrumental variable estimator only estimates the average treatment effect when the treatment effect is constant. What does it estimate when the treatment effect is heterogenous? Recent work by Imbens & Angrist (1994), Angrist & Imbens (1995), Angrist et al (1996), and Imbens & Rubin (1997) investigates this issue by extending the potential outcome framework discussed at the beginning of this paper. This extension is accomplished by assuming that treatment assignment is a function of an exogenous instrument Z_i^*.

For simplicity, assume that both the treatment and the instrument are binary, and that the instrument Z_i^* is a randomly assigned incentive to enroll in the treatment program (e.g. a cash subsidy). When both the treatment and incentive are binary, individuals eligible to receive the treatment can be categorized into four mutually exclusive groups. Individuals who would only enroll in the program if offered the incentive and thus who would not enroll in the program if not offered the incentive are labeled compliers [i.e. individuals for whom $T_i(Z_i^* = 0) = 0$ and $T_i(Z_i^* = 1) = 1$]. Likewise, individuals who would only enroll in the program if not offered the incentive are called defiers [i.e. individuals for whom $T_i(Z_i^* = 0) = 1$ and $T_i(Z_i^* = 1) = 0$]. Individuals who would always enroll in the program, regardless of the incentive, are called always-takers [i.e. individuals for whom $T_i(Z_i^* = 0) = T_i(Z_i^* = 1) = 1$]. Finally, individuals who would never enroll in the program, regardless of the incentive, are called never-takers [i.e. individuals for whom $T_i(Z_i^* = 0) = T_i(Z_i^* = 1) = 0$].

Based on the potential treatment assignment function, Imbens & Angrist (1994) define a monotonicity condition. In the binary-treatment-binary-instrument case, their condition requires that either $T_i(Z_i^* = 1) \geq T_i(Z_i^* = 0)$ or $T_i(Z_i^* = 1) \leq T_i(Z_i^* = 0)$ for all i. In words, the instrument must affect the treatment assignment of all individuals in the same direction and thus in a monotone fashion. For all individuals, an increase (decrease) in their Z_i^* must either leave their treatment condition the same or, among individuals who change, change them in the same way. There may be either defiers or compliers but not both among those eligible to receive the treatment. Conventional IV methods make no assumptions about the coexistence of compliers and defiers.[10]

When an exclusion restriction is satisfied and when the treatment assignment process satisfies the monotonicity condition, the conventional IV estimate is an estimate of what is known as the local average treatment effect (LATE), the average treatment effect for either compliers alone or for defiers alone, depending on which group exists in the population.[11] LATE is the average effect for the subset of the population whose treatment assignment is affected by the instrument. The individual-level treatment effects of always-takers and never-takers are excluded in the calculation of LATE. When the monotonicity condition is not satisfied and treatment effect heterogeneity seems likely, the conventional IV estimator yields a parameter estimate that has no clear interpretation.

LATE has three problems: (a) It is defined by the instrument, and thus different instruments define different average treatment effects for the same group of individuals eligible to receive the treatment; (b) it is an average treatment effect for a subset of individuals that is inherently unobservable no matter what the instrument; (c) it is hard to interpret when the instrument measures something other than an incentive to which individuals can consciously respond by complying or defying.

BOUNDS WITH INSTRUMENTAL VARIABLES   If IV techniques generally do not provide an estimate of the average treatment effect when there is treatment effect heterogeneity, then can IVs tell us anything at all about the average treatment effect? In a recent paper, Manski & Pepper (1998) investigate this question in some depth showing what can be learned when standard and when weaker IV assumptions are maintained.

---

[10]Note that when an instrument is valid, there must be at least some compliers or some defiers, otherwise the sample would be composed of only always-takers and never-takers. In this case, Z_i^* would not be a valid instrument because it would be uncorrelated with treatment assignment.

[11]The exclusion restriction that defines LATE is stronger than the conventional exclusion restriction that the instrument be mean-independent of the error term. Instead, Imbens & Angrist (1994) require that the instrument be fully independent of the error term. Imbens & Rubin (1997) argue that the strong independence restriction is more realistic because it continues to hold under transformations of the outcome variable. An assumption about the distribution of the outcome is thereby avoided.

Manski & Pepper (1998) define the traditional IV assumption in terms of mean independence. Specifically, in our notation, for arbitrary values s and s'

$$E\left[Y_i^t \mid X, Z_i^* = s\right] = E\left[Y_i^t \mid X, Z_i^* = s'\right] \qquad 17a.$$

and

$$E\left[Y_i^c \mid X, Z_i^* = s\right] = E\left[Y_i^c \mid X, Z_i^* = s'\right]. \qquad 17b.$$

In words, Equations 17a and 17b require that the mean values of the outcomes in each subpopulation defined by values of Z_i^* be equivalent to those in the population as a whole. The implication of this assumption is that the bounds assumption analysis, discussed earlier, and the monotone treatment response assumption alone also apply within each subpopulation defined by Z_i^*. As a result, the bound on the treatment effect can be defined as the intersection of the bounds across subpopulations defined by Z_i^* (see Manski 1994,1995; Manski & Pepper 1998). The common bound can only be narrowed with the aid of an IV if the bounds differ across subpopulations. Because the monotone treatment selection assumption, discussed briefly above, is an assumption about how treatment is assigned, it may or may not make sense to assume that it holds within subpopulations defined by the instrument.

As we and many others have noted, the standard IV assumption is a strong condition. Manski & Pepper consider a weaker assumption, the monotone IV assumption (MIV). It states that for $s \geq s'$,

$$E\left[Y_i^t \mid X, Z_i^* = s\right] \geq E\left[Y_i^t \mid X, Z_i^* = s'\right] \qquad 18a.$$

and

$$E\left[Y_i^c \mid X, Z_i^* = s\right] \geq E\left[Y_i^c \mid X, Z_i^* = s'\right]. \qquad 18b.$$

Thus, in Equations 18a and 18b, the mean values of both potential outcomes are weakly increasing functions in Z_i^*.

It is easier to demonstrate how the MIV condition bounds the mean of each outcome than it is to demonstrate directly how the MIV condition bounds the average treatment effect that is a function of these means. Without loss of generality, consider the mean of Y_i^t in the population. Under the standard IV assumption, the upper bound for this mean will be equal to the smallest upper bound across the different subpopulations defined by the instrument. Under the MIV assumption, the upper bound of the conditional mean within the subpopulation defined by a particular value, s', of the instrument will be equal to the smallest upper bound for all subpopulations defined by values of the instrument greater than or equal to s'. The upper bound for the overall mean of Y_i^t will simply be the weighted average of the subpopulation upper bounds where the weights are equal to the proportions of the sample in the various subpopulations defined by Z_i^*. The determination of the analysis for the lower bound of Y_i^t is analogous, as are the determination of the bounds on Y_i^c.

Manski & Pepper (1998) use the assumptions of monotone treatment response, monotone treatment selection, and MIV to determine the bounds on the effect of education on the logged wages of respondents to the National Longitudinal Survey of Youth. When they invoke monotone treatment response and selection assumptions, they find that the bound for the effect of a twelfth year of schooling is [0, 0.199], that the bound for the effect of a fifteenth year of schooling is [0, 0.255], and that the bound for the effect of a sixteenth year of schooling is [0, 0.256]. When they use the Armed Forces Qualifying Test as a monotone instrumental variable while still maintaining the monotone treatment response and selection assumptions, they obtain narrower bounds respectively of [0, 0.126], [0, 0.162], and [0, 0.167]. Although these bounds are somewhat broader than one might wish, they are consistent with the range of estimates typically found in the literature.

LONGITUDINAL METHODS

The use of longitudinal data to estimate treatment effects has a long history. Longitudinal data are useful because they allow individuals to serve as their own controls. The treatment effect for an individual can then be estimated as the change in the pretest and the posttest measurements of their outcome. Of course, any such estimator implicitly assumes that the outcome would have remained unchanged in the absence of treatment. As this is often an unrealistic assumption, we need to be able to estimate for those individuals in the treatment group how their outcomes would have evolved in the absence of treatment.

There are two possible sources of information for constructing this counterfactual trajectory. First, if there are multiple pretest observations, it may be possible to extrapolate from these observations and estimate what the outcome would have been in the absence of treatment, assuming that the future is similar to the past. Second, if there is a control group, then the evolution of its outcome may be used to model what the outcome would have been in the absence of treatment, assuming that the treatment and control groups are similar in key respects.

In the past two decades, many new techniques have been developed to utilize longitudinal data to estimate causal effects. Five important insights have emerged from this research: (*a*) in many circumstances, aggregate cohort-level data contain sufficient information to consistently estimate a causal effect (Heckman & Robb 1985, 1986, 1988); (*b*) whenever possible, the data should be used to test the appropriateness of alternative models; (*c*) multiple measurements of the outcome before and after the treatment are essential both for estimating sophisticated models and for testing the appropriateness of alternative specifications; (*d*) understanding the underlying behavior that generates assignment to the treatment and control groups is critical to the proper modeling of suspected unobservable effects; and (*e*) it is only possible to estimate the average treatment effect for the treated in most longitudinal models because the average treatment effect for the entire population is typically unidentified.

Heckman & Robb (1985, 1986, 1988) provide an extensive, although challenging, review of alternative methods for estimating causal effects using longitudinal (as well as cross-sectional) data. Space does not permit us to provide a similar review here. Moreover, we are confident that many readers would find a full exposition of the technical details of these models more overwhelming than illuminating. Our aim in this section, rather, is to provide an overview of commonly used methods, both old and new, and an assessment of their utility. In so doing, we hope to provide insight into the types of information that are available in longitudinal data to aid in the estimation of a causal effect. We discuss five basic models: interrupted time series models, fixed effect models, differential linear growth rate models, analysis of covariance models, and covariance stationary models.

Interrupted Time Series Design

Perhaps the simplest data structure for estimating causal effects, the interrupted time series (ITS) design uses standard time series methods on multiple observations over time for a single unit in order to estimate a causal effect of a variable. The core of the method involves the specification and estimation of the error structure (i.e. the nature of the interdependence of the period-specific error terms over time). A variety of textbooks provide comprehensive treatments of time series methods (e.g. Harvey 1990, Hamilton 1994, Judge et al 1985). We do not review them here.

The logic of the ITS design parallels that of the regression discontinuity design discussed earlier. In an ITS analysis, time plays the role of Z, and there are now multiple measures over time for a single unit of analysis. The unit might be a country, city, cohort of individuals, or a single person. It is assumed that the treatment is introduced at a specific time and has an immediate impact. The goal is then to estimate how the dependent variable would evolve over time in both the presence and absence of a treatment effect.

We now change notation slightly. Let Y_t be the outcome at time t. For an ITS analysis we do not need an "i" subscript because we are only analyzing data for a single unit of analysis. We continue to denote treatment by the dummy variable T.

We can formally represent the ITS model as

$$Y_t = b_{0_t} + T_t b_{1_t} + e_t. \qquad 19.$$

Note that both the intercept, b_{0_t}, and the treatment effect, b_{1_t}, potentially vary over time. This model is not identified without imposing further structure on how these two parameters are related to time. Return to Figure 1, which presents the basic intuition behind both the regression discontinuity design and the ITS design. For the ITS model, this figure assumes that Y_t, under both treatment and control conditions, grows linearly with time. This implies that for all t, the differences $b_{0_{t+1}} - b_{0_t}$ and $b_{1_{t+1}} - b_{1_t}$ are constants. The dashed line shows the predicted evolution for Y_t in the absence of the treatment. As shown in Figure 1, in this particular example, the treatment has caused a shift in Y_t and a change in the slope.

Equation 19 could be augmented by the inclusion of covariates, X_t. A frequent problem with time series analyses (unlike most cross-sectional analyses) is that the number of parameters in the model may be large relative to the number of observations. As a result, the amount of information available to estimate the parameters may be small. This problem can be especially acute when there is strong dependence among the period-specific error terms, e_t.

The ITS design has the same potential problems as the regression discontinuity design. An ITS analysis assumes that the future is sufficiently like the past that the past can be used to estimate how Y_t would have evolved in the absence of treatment. As with the regression discontinuity design, Figure 2 illustrates the bias in the estimate of the treatment effect that can result when this assumption does not hold.

At the beginning of this section, we noted that the availability of aggregated cohort-level data alone is sometimes sufficient for estimating a treatment effect. This conclusion can be presented in the framework of an ITS model where we assume that Y_t measures the average value for a cohort of individuals on some dependent variable (e.g. wages). Equation 19 is consistent with a specification in which all individuals receive the treatment. In this case, b_{1_t} represents the contemporaneous increase in wages caused by the treatment (e.g. training), and variation in b_1 over time represents the changes in wage growth caused by the treatment. What if only some known portion of the cohort, π, received training? As shown by Heckman & Robb (1985, 1986, 1988), we can still consistently estimate the average treatment effect for those who received training. In the situation where b_{1_t} does not vary with time, the average treatment effect for the treated equals (b_{1_t}/π).

The time series literature provides a host of sophisticated ways of modeling data. The core material in this literature is typically covered in a one- or even two-semester advanced graduate-level econometrics course. Time and space limitations prevent us from providing even a brief overview of these models. The time series literature also contains alternative conceptions of causality to those considered here. The key ideas are those of Granger causality and cointegration (see Harris 1995 and Hendry 1995 for definitions and further discussion; see Holland 1986 and Sobel 1995 for connections with the counterfactual framework). Robins (1986, 1987, 1997) provides a full analysis of the estimation of causal effects when a treatment may be applied repeatedly and at multiple times.

General Model Specification

The methods that we want to consider in the remainder of this section all assume that we have individual-level data with pretest and posttest values on the outcome for both treatment and control groups. The goal is to use the control group (as well as possible multiple pretest measures on the treatment group) to forecast what the values of the dependent variable would have been for the treatment group in the absence of treatment. This goal can only be accomplished if we know or can effectively estimate what the relationship would have been in the absence of treatment between the pretest and posttest values of the treatment and control groups.

Consider the simplest but by far the most common situation, where we have a single pretest and posttest value for the two groups. As Judd & Kenny (1981) demonstrated, even in a linear world there are at least three possibilities. These are shown in Figures 5a, b, and c. In all three figures, the observed values are identical. The estimate of the treatment effect, however, differs substantially, depending on what we assume would have happened to the treatment group if they had not been exposed to the treatment.

As is discussed below, Figures 5a, b, and c characterize three traditional models for estimating a causal effect with pretest and posttest data. To understand the assumptions behind each of these models, we first build a general model of which the three models are special cases. Consider the following model:

$$Y_{it} = b_{0_t} + T_{it}b_1 + \qquad \text{(Basic structural parameters)}$$

$$X_{it}b_{2_t} + T_{it}X_{it}b_3 + \quad \text{(Observed heterogeneity)} \qquad 20.$$

$$\lambda_{it} + T_{it}\alpha_i + e_{it} \qquad \text{(Unobserved heterogeneity)},$$

where $e_{it} = \rho e_{it-1} + v_{it}$. The first term is b_{0_t}, the intercept that varies with t in order to capture the general effects of time; b_1 is the treatment effect that we assume is time invariant. This assumption is not essential. Because we want to allow for the possibility that the treatment effect may vary across individuals, we assume that b_1 is the average treatment effect for the population of interest or the group for whom $X_{it} = 0$.

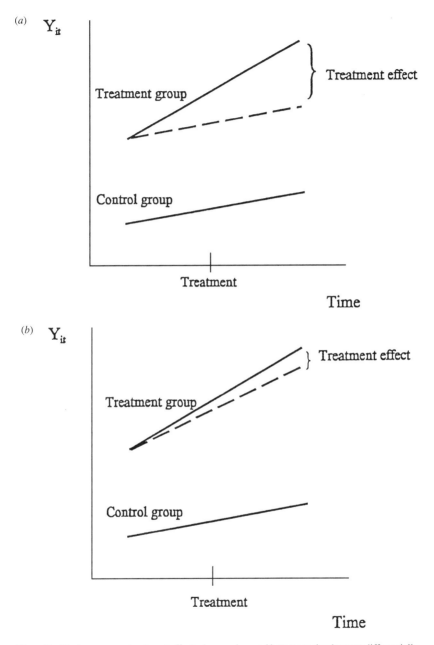

Figure 5   The true average treatment effect when unobserved heterogeneity does not differentially affect the rate of growth for both groups.

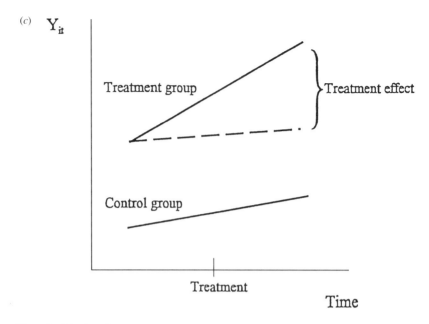

Figure 5   (Continued)

X_{it} consists of the values of fixed, current, past, and future values of exogenous control variables that are relevant at time t. The two terms in the second line of Equation 20, which are interactions of the two terms of the first line with X_{it}, represent observed heterogeneity. The coefficients in b_{2_t} represent (possibly time-varying) shifts in the intercept that are a function of X_{it}. The coefficients in b_3 represent interactions between X_{it} and the treatment effect. We assume that these interactions are time invariant, but this assumption is not essential.

The next three terms constitute the different components of the error term for Equation 20. The first two terms are measures of unobserved individual heterogeneity that are analogous to the two terms for observed individual heterogeneity in the second line. The first term, λ_{it}, represents an individual specific intercept that we allow to vary with time. Thus, the components of λ_{it} capture both constant (or fixed) differences between individuals as well as the possibility that Y_{it} may grow at different rates across individuals i in ways that are not captured in the Xs.

The second term, $T_{it}\alpha_i$, measures the degree to which the treatment differentially impacts each individual i. As with the previous treatment effect terms, we assume that this treatment effect is time invariant. In general, we would expect that individuals who are most likely to benefit from the treatment (i.e.

individuals who have high α_is) would self-select into the treatment. Unfortunately, longitudinal data typically do not provide a way to control for these differences. In most cases, it is only possible to estimate the average treatment effect for the treated, not the average treatment effect for the population as a whole.

The final component of Equation 20, e_{it}, represents an individual-and-period-specific component of the error term. We want to allow for interdependence among the e_{it} over time to capture what is known in the time series literature as transitory effects. We assume an autoregressive structure of order one (AR1), that is $e_{it} = \rho e_{it-1}$ where ρ is the correlation between e_{it} and e_{it-1}. More complicated dependence in the form of an autoregressive moving-average structure could be assumed. These are reviewed in the standard time series textbooks cited above.

Finally, v_{it} is a pure time-specific error that is uncorrelated with anything else. To simplify the exposition, we assume that v_{it} has constant variance across individuals. In the time series literature, v_{it} is often referred to as the innovation in the process. Because it is purely random, it cannot be forecast. Typically, it is assumed to be a priori unknown to both the individual and the analyst.

How does Equation 20 relate to Figures 5a–c? Assume for the moment (and for most of our discussion of longitudinal methods below) that all of the heterogeneity is represented by the unobservables. Standard techniques can be used to eliminate differences that are a function of observed Xs. When estimating the treatment effect, we would like the treatment and control groups to be identical, at least conditional on X.[12] Our concern is that the two groups may also differ in terms of the unobservable components found in Equation 20 because assignment to the treatment group may be a function of unobservable characteristics. The question then is whether there are techniques that can eliminate potential differences between the treatment and control groups that are a function of the unobservable components in Equation 20. After eliminating differences due to X, can we "control out" the effects of the unobservables that are potentially related to treatment assignment?

In Figure 5a, in the absence of a treatment, the parallel lines for the two groups indicate that the differences between Y_{it} for individuals in the treatment and control groups (on average) remain constant over time. This case is consistent with a model in which unobserved differences between the treatment and control group are a function solely of a λ_i that is time invariant or fixed, as would occur if we had omitted an X that was constant over time and correlated with the treatment variable. For example, if we were estimating the effects of additional schooling on wages, there might be unmeasured and thus unobserved components of family background that need to be controlled.

---

[12]In the linear models used in our exposition, it is only necessary that the expected values of the components on the right-hand side of Equation 20 be identical for the treatment and control groups.

Figure 5b illustrates a situation in which, in the absence of treatment, the growth rate for Y_{it} differs for individuals in the treatment and the control groups. Assume that the λ_{it} change linearly with time such that $\lambda_{it} - \lambda_{it-1} = \tau_i$, where τ_i is a constant for each individual i for all t. In Figure 5b the rate of increase (in the absence of the treatment) in λ_{it}, τ_i, is higher for those in the treatment group than for those in the control group. As an example, more intelligent individuals may be more likely to continue in school, but whether they are in school or not (that is, whether they receive the treatment or not), they may still learn faster than individuals with less intelligence.

Figure 5c might result in two different ways. First, as in Figure 5b, the rate of increase in λ_{it}, τ_i, may differ between the treatment and control group. Here, however, the rate of increase is greater for those in the control group than for those in the treatment groups. For example, an increase in the incidence rate of disease might be greater in a control group if willingness to take other unobservable preventive measures (unrelated to the treatment regime itself) is greater on average for those in the treatment group.

A second circumstance when Equation 20 is consistent with Figure 5c is when ρ in Equation 20 is positive. In this case, if assignment to the treatment group instead of the control group is a function of e_{it}, then assignment is a function of transitory components of the unobservables. If assignment is only a function of transitory components, then over-time differences between the two groups would shrink to zero in the absence of treatment.

A number of empirical examples exist where assignment to the treatment group is a function of transitory components of the unobservables. The classic case, which reverses the labeling of the treatment and control groups in Figure 5c, is where individuals who are experiencing low wages in the near term are more likely to enroll in a job-training program because they experience lower opportunity costs (Ashenfelter 1978, Ashenfelter & Card 1985). Regression toward the mean in this case produces an apparent training effect because the wages of individuals who received training would have increased on average (regressed toward the mean) even in the absence of training. This case differs from the one presented in Figure 5c in that the treatment program is compensatory—individuals with the lower wages are in the treatment group.

Several approaches are available to consistently estimate the treatment effect, b_1, in Equation 20. The most obvious, but often difficult method, would be to use panel data to fully estimate a complicated model specification such as Equation 20. If the model is properly specified, then the treatment effect b_1 can be consistently estimated. In general, it will only be possible to estimate models of this type of complexity if one has multiple pretest and post test measures of Y_{it}. The technical issues involved in estimating models of this type vary across different model specifications.

Alternative Methods

Over the years, a number of simple methods for estimating treatment effects have been proposed. These include charge score analysis, the analysis of covariance, and their generalizations. We now consider these models and the conditions under which they give consistent estimates of the treatment effect, b_1. An extensive literature has argued the relative merits of these different approaches (see Judd & Kenny 1981; Holland & Rubin 1983; Allison 1990).

The appropriateness of a model depends on whether it provides a consistent estimate of the treatment effect in a particular context. This depends on whether the model's assumptions are congruent with the underlying process that generates the data. The appropriateness of a model for a specific situation can only be determined through theoretical and empirical analysis. No one statistical model is a panacea.

The problem of whether a model is consistent with an underlying process that generates Y_{it} is potentially complicated. As we discuss below, if one is to have confidence in one's results, it is essential to test the appropriateness of one's model specification. But what constitutes a proper model specification? As discussed above, one approach to consistently estimating the treatment effect in a longitudinal model is to attempt to specify and estimate a full model specification for Y_{it}. To accomplish this, it may be necessary to have multiple pre- and posttest observations on Y_{it}.

Our above discussion of Rubin's and Rosenbaum's propensity score, however, suggests that estimation of the full model for Y_{it} may not be necessary to correct for the effects of assignment. We demonstrated that if we could condition on the probability of assignment (or at least on those factors that determine assignment), the treatment effect could be consistently estimated even in the presence of omitted variables.

Does this mean that we can get away with not estimating the full model for Y_{it}? As Heckman has argued repeatedly over the years, in many situations this is not likely to be possible. If individual choice is involved in the assignment process, it is likely that individuals will choose to be in the treatment and control group based on the consequences of treatment for their future Y_{it}. In this case, individuals (at least crudely) use the previous history of their Y_{it}, plus the total history of Y_{it} for others, both pre- and posttreatment, to project the future values of their Y_{it} under both the treatment and control. If so, the assignment process will be a function of the parameters of the model that the individual uses to predict future Y_{it}.

The question then is what model is the individual using to predict their future Y_{it}? If it is simpler than the full model, then it may well be possible to condition on only those components of the model that determine assignment and consistently estimate the treatment effect. In many situations, it is unclear why an individual would not use something like the full model to predict future Y_{it}. Thus, we may be stuck with having to try to specify and estimate the full model that generates Y_{it}. Of course, the greatest concern is that the individual may be using a prediction model that is more complicated or more accurate than the one used by the analyst. This might be due to the fact that the analyst has used too simple a model and/or that the individual has access to information that the analyst has no way of incorporating into her model—either directly through observed Xs or indirectly through a particular specification of the structure of the unobservables. In this situation, it may simply be impossible to consistently estimate the treatment effect.

CHANGE SCORE OR FIXED EFFECTS MODELS   Change score or fixed-effect models are a common and simple method for estimating causal effects when pretest and posttest data are available for separate treatment and control groups. The basic model can be formalized in two ways. The standard change-score model is

$$(Y_{it} - Y_{it-1}) = c_0 + T_i c_1 + (X_{it-1} - X_{it-1})c_2 + u_{it}, \qquad 21.$$

where $T_i = 1$ if the individual received the treatment (and $T_i = 0$ otherwise), $c_0 = b_{0_t} - b_{0_{t-1}}, c_1 = b_1, c_2 = b_2$, and $u_{it} = e_{it} - e_{it-1}$. This model can also be formalized as a fixed effect model making its relation to Equation 20 more transparent:

$$Y_{it} = b_{0_t} + T_{it}b_1 + X_{it}b_2 + \lambda_i + e_{it}, \qquad 22.$$

where λ_i is a time invariant or fixed individual specific effect and the e_{it} for individual i and across time are assumed to be uncorrelated. The fixed-effect formulation allows for the possibility that multiple pretest and posttest outcomes may be observed on each individual. The model implies that there are permanent fixed differences between individuals in their Y_{it}. As a result, as the process evolves from time $t - 1$ to time t there will be regression toward the mean in Y_{it}, but the regression will be toward the individual specific mean of Y_{it} not the overall population mean of Y_{it}.

Because the λ_i terms represent all fixed, time-invariant differences between individuals, the effects of constant Xs are absorbed into λ_i. This is most apparent in Equation 21, where we see that only the effects of Xs that change over time are estimated. The fixed-effect model is equivalent to a standard regression model where a separate dummy variable has been included for each individual, which is then estimated by OLS. Alternatively, Equation 21 can be estimated by OLS. Heckman & Robb (1985, 1986, 1988) show that if we know the identity of individuals who will receive the treatment, then the fixed-effect model can be estimated from cohorts based on repeated cross sections.

As can be seen from Equation 22, the fixed-effect model is a constrained version of the general model in Equation 20 because it assumes there is no transitory component to the error term ($\rho = 0$) and the effect of the X_{it} are invariant with respect to time ($b_{2_t} = b_2$). The first constraint implies that any unobserved differences between the treatment and control groups must be constant over time, as shown in Figure 5a. As with all the longitudinal models we consider, the fixed-effects model also assumes that the effect of the treatment is constant across individuals ($b_3 = \alpha_i = 0$). If this is not the case, then the treatment effect estimate is a consistent estimate only of the average treatment effect for the treated, not the average treatment effect for the entire population.

The fixed-effect model will only provide consistent estimates of the treatment effect if Equation 22 correctly models the time series structure of Y_{it} or if the fixed effects, λ_i, are the only unobservables that determine assignment to the treatment group. Framed in terms of Heckman's concern above about the consequences of assignment due to individual choice, the fixed-effect model will provide consistent estimates of the treatment effect only if assignment is a function of the fixed effects in Equation 20. However, it only makes sense for an individual to make choices this way if in fact Equation 22, the pure fixed-effects specification, is the correct model for Y_{it}.

DIFFERENTIAL RATE OF GROWTH MODELS   In many situations it may be the case that not only are there fixed unobserved individual differences, λ_i, but that there are differences across individuals in the rate of change in Y_{it}. We allow for this possibility by permitting λ_{it} to vary with time. The simplest case is where we assume that the λ_{it} grow linearly but at different rates across individuals (i.e. $\lambda_{it} - \lambda_{it-1} = \tau_i$, a constant growth rate for individual i across all t). Figures 5b and c are illustrative of this type of process. For example, consistent with Figure 5b, we might believe that some individuals learn faster than others, or that because of previous education and training some individuals' wages would grow faster than others.

The differential growth rate model can be estimated as a standard regression model using OLS by including a dummy variable for each individual entered in the equation by themselves and also interacted with time. Alternatively, the model can be estimated by applying OLS to the double difference of both the right- and left-hand sides of Equation 20. If λ_{it} grows quadratically or as a function of even a higher-order polynomial in time, this can be dealt with by differencing further.[13] The differential growth rate model will consistently

[13] In these models, the variance of the outcome or equivalently of the error term may grow without bound. As a result, these models do not have a typical autoregressive moving-average structure. We know of no methods for estimating the differential growth rate model when it includes a transitory auto-regressive component.

estimate the treatment effect only if it accurately models the process generating Y_{it} or assignment is only a function of an individual's fixed effect and individual growth parameter (Heckman & Robb 1985, 1986, 1988).

ANALYSIS OF COVARIANCE MODELS   The most common model used to estimate causal effects when both pretest and posttest data are available is the analysis-of-covariance model. In its simplest form, the model is

$$Y_{it} = b_0 + Y_{it-1}\gamma + T_{it}b_1 + u_{it}, \qquad\qquad 23.$$

where b_1 is an estimate of the treatment effect and Equation 23 is estimated by OLS.[14] The coefficient γ is equal to the pooled within-treatment group regression of Y_{it} on Y_{it-1}. If u_{it} has constant variance (which is generally assumed and which we also assume), then in the absence of treatment, γ is equal to the correlation between Y_{it} and Y_{it-1}, (that is, the intracluster correlation with each individual considered a separate cluster). As a result, when u_{it} has constant variance, γ must be less than or equal to one. It measures the degree to which each individual's Y_{it} regresses between times $t - 1$ and t toward the overall mean of Y_{it}. This regression toward the mean differs from that in the fixed effects model where the individual Y_{it} regress toward individual specific means.

To simplify the exposition, consider the properties of the analysis-of-covariance model in the absence of treatment for all individuals. If we generalize to allow for multiple time periods, then the analysis-of-covariance model is equivalent to an autoregressive model of degree 1:

$$Y_{it} = b_{0_t} + e_{it}, \qquad\qquad 24.$$

where $e_{it} = \rho e_{it-1} + v_{it}$. Here ρ is the correlation between temporally adjacent e_{it}, and v_{it} is pure random error that is assumed to be independent of everything. b_{0_t} is a time-varying intercept that follows the generating equation $b_{0_{t+1}} - b_{0_t} = \rho(b_{0_t} - b_{0_{t-1}})$. This model is a constrained version of Equation 20. It makes the strong assumption that all differences in Y_{it} across individuals are transitory. There are no fixed or permanent differences or differences across individuals in the growth rates of their Y_{it}. Thus, Equation 24 implies that between Y_{it-1} and Y_{it} there will be regression toward the mean of a very strong form. Y_{it} across all individuals regress toward the same grand mean.

---

[14] As written, econometricians would typically interpret Equation 23 as indicating that i is determined in part by its lagged value Y_{it-1}. Under this interpretation, Equation 23 should be estimated using instrumental variables, because under almost any reasonable assumption about the error structure, Y_{it-1} will be correlated with u_{it}, invalidating OLS. Heckman & Robb (1985, 1986, 1988) point out that equations with lagged Y_{it}s can be dealt with by putting them in reduced form. This strategy then yields equations similar in form to Equation 20 which can be dealt with by the techniques discussed here and in their papers.

If Y_{it} is in fact generated by Equation 24, then $\rho = \gamma$. In most situations, however, we would expect that Y_{it} would have both fixed and transitory components. A simple specification that captures this idea is

$$Y_{it} = b_{0_i} + \lambda_i + e_{it}, \qquad 25.$$

where $e_{it} = \rho e_{it-1} + v_{it}$ and where ρ and v_{it} are as in Equation 24. In this case, $\gamma = [\text{var}(\lambda_i) + \rho\text{var}(e_{it})]/[\text{var}(\lambda_i) + \text{var}(e_{it})]$ which is necessarily greater than or equal to the correlation ρ. If there is no transitory component, $\text{var}(e_{it}) = 0$, and γ is still less than one because regression toward the mean is due to the pure random component, v_{it}. If there is no permanent component, then $\gamma = \rho$.

The key to understanding the analysis-of-covariance model is to rewrite Equation 23 as

$$(Y_{it} - Y_{it-1}\gamma) = b_0 + T_{it}b_1 + u_{it}. \qquad 26.$$

Equation 26 shows that γ is a measure of the degree to which Y_{it} should be adjusted by its previous pretreatment value, Y_{it-1}. Specifically, γ measures the degree to which the pretest difference in the treatment and control group Y_{it-1} should be used to correct the post-treatment difference in Y_{it} in estimating the treatment effect:

$$\text{Treatment effect} = b_1 = \left(\overline{Y}^t_{it} - \overline{Y}^c_{it}\right) - \gamma\left(\overline{Y}^t_{it-1} - \overline{Y}^c_{it-1}\right). \qquad 27.$$

If $\gamma = 0$, then no adjustment is needed. The treatment effect is simply equal to the average difference between the treatment and control group in Y_{it}. This would be appropriate only if the Y_{it} were a function of the pure random component of the unobservables, v_{it}.

If $\gamma = 1$, then the Y_{it} are fully adjusted. The treatment effect is then equal to the difference in Y_{it} between the treatment and control groups net of their initial difference. In the latter case, the analysis of covariance model is equivalent to the change-score/fixed-effect model discussed above. This would be appropriate if there is no transitory component in Equation 26.

Assume that Equation 25—which models Y_{it} as a function of fixed, transitory, and random effects—holds and that we estimate γ from the data. In this case $1 > \hat{\gamma} > \rho$. $\hat{\gamma} = 1$ only if there is no transitory component or random component, that is, v_{it} in Equation 25. $\hat{\gamma} = \rho$ only if there is no fixed effect term in Equation 25.[15]

---

[15] If there is measurement error in Y_{it}s, the measurement error will bias downward the estimate of γ, resulting in an underadjustment for pretreatment differences between the treatment and control groups. This underadjustment will bias the estimate of the treatment effect.

Consider the assignment of individuals to the treatment and control groups. If assignment is a function of the fixed effects λ_i, then no adjustment is needed to the pretreatment difference in Y_{it}. Using the estimated γ in Equation 27 will overstate the treatment effect because the correct adjustment factor is $\gamma = 1$. The analysis-of-covariance model will only give a consistent estimate of the treatment effect in this situation if the estimated $\gamma = 1$. This will occur, however, only when there is no transitory term, e_{it}, or random component, v_{it} in Equation 25. In this case, the prediction of Y_{it} from previous values is trivial because Y_{it} is a constant.

If assignment were a function of only the transitory component, e_{it}, and Y_{it} depends on a fixed component, using the estimated γ would result in an understatement of the treatment effect because the correct adjustment factor is $\gamma = \rho$, which is necessarily less than the estimated γ. In general, the estimated γ will be the correct adjustment factor only if selection is on Y_{it-1}. In this case, in the absence of treatment, the expected shrinkage in the difference in the pretreatment means of Y_{it} for the treatment and control groups and their posttreatment difference is proportional to γ.

But under what circumstances would it make sense for assignment to be based only on Y_{it-1}? As Heckman has argued, if Y_{it} were generated according to, for instance, Equation 25 or the even more complicated Equation 20, it would be reasonable to assume that an individual would want to use values of Y_{it} prior to Y_{it-1} to predict Y_{it}. In essence, one could imagine an individual (at least crudely) estimating their individual specific fixed effect and growth rate so that they could accurately predict what their Y_{it} would be in the absence of treatment. Assuming that is known, values of Y_{it} prior to Y_{it-1} could be ignored only in the situation where Y_{it} had a simple AR1 structure, i.e. where Y_{it} is generated by Equation 24. This leads us to a strong and negative conclusion about the applicability of the analysis-of-covariance model. An analysis of covariance generally will only properly adjust for the pretreatment difference in outcomes between the treatment and control group if treatment assignment is solely a function of the pretreatment outcome, Y_{it-1}. In general, an individual would only choose his assignment based on Y_{it-1} if prior values of Y_{it} or other relevant information were not available or if Y_{it} followed an AR1 specification, as in Equation 24. The latter condition is an extremely strong assumption because it implies that all unobserved differences between individuals are only transitory.

COVARIANCE STATIONARY MODELS   The change-score and analysis-of-covariance models (or, similarly, their specifications respectively as a pure fixed-effect model and a pure transitory-effect model) represent extreme model specifications. These two extremes make strong assumptions about how, in the absence of treatment, the difference between the pretreatment mean Y_{it} for the treatment and control groups will change during the posttreatment period. In the change-score model, the assumption is that there will be no change. For the analysis-of-covariance model, the assumption is that there will be shrinkage of a specific amount. In particular, the shrinkage will be equivalent to the amount of regression toward the mean observed at the individual level. Thus, although ρ is estimated from the data, the analysis-of-covariance model simply assumes that this is the correct shrinkage factor.

In most instances, we would like to use a method that allows for both fixed and transitory effects in the generation of Y_{it} or at least in the assignment process. Equivalently, we would like to estimate how much adjustment is appropriate when estimating the treatment effect using pretreatment differences between the treatment and control groups. The change score and analysis-of-covariance models simply assume alternative levels of adjustment.

Heckman & Robb (1985) show that it is possible to estimate a model that combines an individual fixed effect along with a transitory AR1 component. In fact, all that needs to be assumed is that the process is covariance stationary.[16] This model is consistent with most autoregressive moving-average specifications, including the change-score/fixed effect and analysis-of-covariance models. Assume that you have at least three equally spaced (in time) measures of Y_{it}, at least two of which occur prior to treatment. Label these times respectively $t - 2$, $t - 1$, and t, with only t occurring after the treatment. Assuming there are no relevant Xs for the moment, it is easy to show through multiplication and two substitutions that the covariance between Y_{it} and Y_{it-1} is equal to

$$\text{Cov}(Y_{it}, Y_{it-1}) = \text{Cov}(Y_{it-1}, T_i)b_1 + \text{Cov}(Y_{it}, Y_{it-2}), \qquad 28.$$

where T_i is as before a dummy variable treatment indicator and b_1 is the treatment effect. All three of these covariances can be estimated from the data, allowing us to solve out for b_1. If additional time periods are available, the assumption of stationary covariance can be tested. An overall test of the model can be obtained by comparing alternative estimates of the treatment effect using different time-period triplets.

Testing Alternative Models

The point of the above discussion is that traditional methods such as change-score analysis and the analysis of covariance are flawed because they make strong assumptions that are rarely examined and almost never tested. Without

---

[16] A process is covariance stationary if it has a finite mean and finite variance and the covariance between any two Y over time is only a function of the time elapsed between them.

confidence that their assumptions are valid, resulting estimates of a causal effect have no guaranteed validity.

When only a single pretest measure and a single posttest measure are available, the appropriateness of alternative models cannot be tested. At best one can only make arguments for one specification as opposed to another on theoretical grounds. Hopefully, by embedding these models in Equation 20, we have made it clear to the reader what the nature of these arguments would have to be. With multiple waves of data, however, it becomes possible to determine whether a particular specification is appropriate for the data being analyzed.

One approach would be to use both pre- and posttest data to determine the structure of the unobservables in the data. This is a standard topic in the analysis of panel data. An extensive collection of relevant papers is provided in Maddala (1993). We note that it can often be difficult to determine which among the possible specifications is appropriate because different specifications can produce similar patterns in the data. Also, standard time series methods typically will not work because they assume that the error term consisting of different unobserved components is uncorrelated with any of the observed right-hand-side variables. In this paper, we are interested in situations where the treatment variable may be correlated with unobserved components.

Fortunately, less-sophisticated and more easily applied methods can be used. In order to consistently estimate the treatment effect, it is not necessary that we correctly specify the full structure of the unobservables. Rather, we must only control for those aspects of the unobservables that differ between the treatment and control groups. Heckman & Hotz (1989) discuss an imaginative way of testing this condition that is also simple. One should take all the pretest observations and then analyze them as if they consisted of both pretest and posttest data, testing whether a treatment effect is significant on the pretest observations alone. Because no treatment has yet occurred, no treatment effect should be observed. If a pretreatment effect is found, this is strong evidence that one's model is misspecified. Whatever procedure has been used to control for unobserved differences between the treatment and control group has failed because the significant pretreatment effect indicates that there are still differences between the two groups that have not been accounted for. The posttest data can be used in a similar way. In this case, no treatment effect should be found if the model has been correctly specified, because no additional treatment has occurred. It may, however, be necessary to account for the possibility that the treatment effect dissipates over time. A third possible test is to enter past and future values of the outcome as regressors. If the model is appropriately specified, they should have no effect on the current outcome (Heckman & Hotz 1989).

CONCLUSION

We have tapped only a fraction of the methods and literature that has appeared over the past couple of decades relevant to estimating causal effects. Our intention has been to focus on methods that are relatively accessible and likely to be useful to quantitatively oriented researchers. We hope the reader is impressed by how far the research literature has gone beyond standard regression models.

The appropriateness of alternative models for the estimation of a causal effect depends both on the structure of the data that are available and on the nature of the substantive problem. Given the large number of options, it is critical that researchers, to the degree that it is possible, test for the appropriateness of a chosen specification. Otherwise, a variety of methods should be implemented to determine how robust the treatment effect estimate is to alternative methods.

Besides providing the reader with an introduction to a variety of methods that can be used to estimate causal effects, we hope that we have also presented a conceptual scheme that will be useful to all researchers in trying to think through their own particular analysis problems. In particular, we have shown how a counterfactual interpretation of causality leads to a precise definition of what is meant by a causal effect. Furthermore, this definition points to two important sources of bias in the estimation of treatment effects: (*a*) initial differences between the treatment and control groups in the absence of treatment, and (*b*) the difference between the two groups in the potential effect of the treatment. The latter component is particularly important in situations where there is likely to be selection into the treatment group based on the projected effects of the treatment.

The estimation of causal effects continues to be one of the most active areas of research in both statistics and econometrics. Perhaps one of the most important new developments is the investigation of the quality of estimates that are produced by the different techniques we have discussed. Rubin and Rosenbaum are actively involved in applying matching methods based on the propensity score to different problems. Heckman and his coworkers have been examining matching as well as other methods. It is important to note that they have been extending the methods discussed here to semi-parametric and nonparametric approaches. Their findings (Heckman et al 1997a,b, 1998a,b), using the Job Training Partnership Act data, suggest that at least in some circumstances, the assumption of specific functional forms can be an important source of bias.

ACKNOWLEDGMENT

We thank Gary King, Peter Marsden, William Morgan, Herb Smith, Michael Sobel, Peng He, and Aage Sørensen for helpful comments. The research was supported in part by the National Science Foundation through grant no. SBR

9411875 awarded to Winship and a graduate research fellowship awarded to Morgan.

Literature Cited

Allison PD. 1990. Change scores as dependent variables in regression analysis. In *Sociological Methodology 1990*, ed. CC Clogg, 20:93–114. Washington, DC: Am. Sociol. Assoc.

Angrist JD. 1990. Lifetime earnings and the Vietnam era draft lottery: evidence from Social Security administrative records. *Am. Econ. Rev.* 80:313–36

Angrist JD, Imbens GW. 1995. Two-stage least squares estimation of average causal effects in models with variable treatment intensity. *J. Am. Stat. Assoc.* 90:431–42

Angrist JD, Imbens GW, Rubin DB. 1996. Identification of causal effects using instrumental variables. *J. Am. Stat. Assoc.* 91:444–72

Angrist JD, Krueger AB. 1991. Does compulsory school attendance affect schooling and earnings? *Q. J. Econ.* 106:979–1014

Angrist JD, Krueger AB. 1992. The effect of age at school entry on educational attainment: an application of instrumental variables with moments from two samples. *J. Am. Stat. Assoc.* 87:328–36

Ashenfelter O. 1978. Estimating the effect of training programs on earnings. *Rev. Econ. Stat.* 60:47–57

Ashenfelter O, Card D. 1985. Using the longitudinal structure of earnings to estimate the effect of training programs. *Rev. Econ. Stat.* 67:648–60

Bound J, Jaeger DA, Baker RM. 1995. Problems with instrumental variables estimation when the correlation between the instruments and the endogenous explanatory variable is weak. *J. Am. Stat. Assoc.* 90:443–50

Cochran WG, Cox GM. 1950. *Experimental Design*. New York: Wiley. 2nd ed.

Cook TD, Campbell DT. 1979. *Quasi-Experimental: Design and Analysis Issues for Field Settings*. Boston, MA: Houghton Mifflin

Cox DR. 1958a. *Planning of Experiments*. New York: Wiley

Cox DR. 1958b. The interpretation of the effects of non-additivity in the Latin square. *Biometrika* 45:69–73

Fisher RA. 1935. *The Design of Experiments*. Edinburgh: Oliver & Boyd

Garfinkel I, Manski CF, Michalopoulos C. 1992. Micro experiments and macro effects. See Manski & Garfinkel 1992, pp. 253–73

Goldberger AS. 1991. *A Course in Econometrics*. Cambridge, MA: Harvard Univ. Press

Hamilton JD. 1994. *Time Series Analysis*. Princeton, NJ: Princeton Univ. Press

Harris RID. 1995. *Using Cointegration Analysis in Econometric Modelling*. New York: Prentice Hall

Harvey A. 1990. *The Econometric Analysis of Time Series*. Cambridge, MA: MIT Press. 2nd ed.

Heckman JJ. 1978. Dummy endogenous variables in a simultaneous equation system. *Econometrica* 46:931–61

Heckman JJ. 1979. Selection bias as a specification error. *Econometrica* 47:153–61

Heckman JJ. 1989. Causal inference and nonrandom samples. *J. Educ. Stat.* 14:159–68

Heckman JJ. 1992. Randomization and social policy evaluation. See Manski & Garfinkel 1992, pp. 201–30

Heckman JJ. 1995. *Instrumental Variables: A Cautionary Tale*. Cambridge, MA: Natl. Bur. Econ. Res.

Heckman JJ. 1996. Randomization as an instrumental variable. *Rev. Econ. Stat.* 77:336–41

Heckman JJ. 1997. Instrumental variables: a study of implicit behavioral assumptions used in making program evaluations. *J. Hum. Resour.* 32:441–62

Heckman JJ, Hotz VJ. 1989. Choosing among alternative nonexperimental methods for estimating the impact of social programs: the case of manpower training. *J. Am. Stat. Assoc.* 84:862–80

Heckman JJ, Ichimura H, Smith J, Todd P. 1998a. Characterizing selection bias using experimental data. *Econometrica* 6:1017–99

Heckman JJ, Ichimura H, Todd P. 1997a. Matching as an econometric evaluation estimator: evidence from evaluating a job training programme. *Rev. Econ. Stud.* 64:605–54

Heckman JJ, Ichimura H, Todd P. 1998b. Matching as an econometric evaluation estimator. *Rev. Econ. Stud.* 65:261–94

Heckman JJ, Lochner L, Taber C. 1998c. General-equilibrium treatment effects: a study of tuition policy. *Am. Econ. Rev.* 88(2):381–92

Heckman JJ, Robb R. 1985. Alternative methods for evaluating the impact of interventions. In *Longitudinal Analysis of Labor Market Data*, ed. JJ Heckman, B Singer, pp. 156–245. Cambridge, UK: Cambridge Univ. Press

Heckman JJ, Robb R. 1986. Alternative methods for solving the problem of selection bias in evaluating the impact of treatments on outcomes. In *Drawing Inferences from Self-Selected Samples*, ed. H Wainer, pp. 63–113. New York: Springer-Verlag

Heckman JJ, Robb R. 1988. The value of longitudinal data for solving the problem of selection bias in evaluating the impact of treatment on outcomes. In *Panel Surveys*, ed. G Duncan, G Kalton, pp. 512–38. New York: Wiley

Heckman JJ, Smith J, Clements N. 1997b. Making the most out of programme evaluations and social experiments: accounting for heterogeneity in programme impacts. *Rev. Econ. Stud.* 64:487–535

Hendry F. 1995. *Dynamic Econometrics*. New York: Oxford Univ. Press

Holland PW. 1986. Statistics and causal inference. *J. Am. Stat. Assoc.* 81:945–70

Holland PW, Rubin DB. 1983. On Lord's Paradox. In *Principles of Modern Psychological Measurement: A Festschrift for Frederic M. Lord*, Ed. H Wainer, S Messick, pp. 3–25. Hillsdale, NJ: Erlbaum

Honore BE, Powell JL. 1994. Pairwise difference estimators of censored and truncated regression models. *J. Econom.* 64:231–78

Hood WC, Koopmans TC, eds. 1953. *Studies in Econometric Method*. New York: Wiley

Imbens GW, Angrist JD. 1994. Identification and estimation of local average treatment effects. *Econometrica* 62:467–75

Imbens GW, Rubin DB. 1997. Estimating outcome distributions for compliers in instrumental variables models. *Rev. Econ. Stud.* 64:555–74

Judd CM, Kenny DA. 1981. *Estimating the Effects of Social Interventions*. New York: Cambridge Univ. Press

Judge G, Hill C, Griffiths W, Lee T. 1985. *The Theory and Practice of Econometrics*. New York: Wiley

Kempthorne O. 1952. *Design and Analysis of Experiments*. New York: Wiley

LaLonde RJ. 1986. Evaluating the econometric evaluations of training programs with experimental data. *Am. Econ. Rev.* 76:604–20

Lieberson S. 1985. *Making It Count: The Improvement of Social Research and Theory*. Berkeley: Univ. Calif. Press

Maddala GS. 1993. *The Econometrics of Panel Data*, Vols. 1, 2. Hants, UK: Elgar

Malinvaud EB. 1970. *Statistical Methods of Econometrics*. Amsterdam: North-Holland

Manski CF. 1994. The selection problem. In *Advances in Econometrics*, Vol. I, ed. C Sims, pp. 147–70. Cambridge, UK: Cambridge Univ. Press

Manski CF. 1995. *Identification Problems in the Social Sciences*. Cambridge, MA: Harvard Univ. Press

Manski CF. 1997. Monotone treatment response. *Econometrica* 65:1311–34

Manski CF, Garfinkel I, eds. 1992. *Evaluating Welfare and Training Programs*. Cambridge, MA: Harvard Univ. Press

Manski CF, Nagin DS. 1998. Bounding disagreements about treatment effects: A case study of sentencing and recidivism. *Sociol. Methodol.* 28:99–137

Manski CF, Pepper JV. 1998. *Monotone instrumental variables: with an application to the returns to schooling*. Presented at Winter Meet. Am. Sociol. Assoc., Chicago

Manski CF, Sandefur GD, McLanahan S, Powers D. 1992. Alternative estimates of the effect of family structure during adolescence on high school graduation. *J. Am. Stat. Assoc.* 87:25–37

Marcantonio RJ, Cook TD. 1994. Convincing quasi-experiments: the interrupted time series and regression-discontinuity designs. In *Handbook of Practical Program Evaluation*, ed. JS Wholey, HP Hatry, KE Newcomer, pp. 133–54. San Francisco: Jossey-Bass

McKim VR, Turner SP. 1997. *Causality in Crisis: Statistical Methods and the Search for Causal Knowledge in the Social Sciences*. South Bend, IN: Univ. Notre Dame Press

Moffitt RA. 1996. Comment on "Identification of causal effects using instrumental variables" by Angrist, Imbens, and Rubin. *J. Am. Stat. Assoc.* 91:462–65

Neyman JS. 1923. On the application of probability theory to agricultural experiments. Essay on principles. Transl. DM Dabrowska, TP Speed, 1990, in *Stat. Sci.* 5:465–80 (From Polish)

Neyman J. 1935. Statistical problems in agricultural experimentation. *J. R. Stat. Soc.* 2:107–80

Powell JL. 1987. *Semiparametric estimation of bivariate latent variables models. Working pap. no. 8704.* Madison, WI: Univ. WI, Soc. Syst. Res. Inst.

Pratt JW, Schlaifer R. 1984. On the nature and discovery of structure. *J. Am. Stat. Assoc.* 79:9–33

Pratt JW, Schlaifer R. 1988. On the interpretation and observation of laws. *J. Econom.* 39:23–52

Quandt R. 1972. A new approach to estimating switching regression. *J. Am. Stat. Assoc.* 67:306–10

Robins JM. 1986. A new approach to causal

inference in mortality studies with a sustained exposure period-application to control of the healthy worker survivor effect. *Math. Model* 7:1393–512

Robins JM. 1987. Addendum to 'A new approach to causal inference in mortality studies with sustained exposure period-application to control of the healthy worker survivor effect.' *Comp. Math. Appl.* 14:923–45

Robins JM. 1989. The analysis of randomized and nonrandomized AIDS treatment trials using a new approach to causal inference in longitudinal studies. In *Health Service Research Methodology: A Focus on AIDS*, ed. L Sechrest, H Freeman, A Mulley, pp. 113–59. Washington, DC: US Public Health Serv.

Robins JM. 1997. Causal inference from complex longitudinal data. In *Latent Variable Modeling and Applications to Causality. Lecture Notes in Statistics* Ed. M Berkane. 120:69–117. New York: Springer-Verlag

Rosenbaum PR. 1984a. The consequences of adjustment for a concomitant variable that has been affected by the treatment. *J. R. Stat. Soc.* 147:656–66

Rosenbaum PR. 1984b. From association to causation in observational studies: the role of tests of strongly ignorable treatment assignment. *J. Am. Stat. Assoc.* 79:41–48

Rosenbaum PR. 1995. *Observational Studies*. New York: Springer-Verlag

Rosenbaum PR, Rubin DB. 1983. The central role of the propensity score in observational studies for causal effects. *Biometrika* 76:41–55

Rosenbaum PR, Rubin DB. 1984. Reducing bias in observational studies using subclassification on the propensity score. *J. Am. Stat. Assoc.* 79:516–24

Rosenbaum PR, Rubin DB. 1985. Constructing a control group using multivariate matched sampling methods that incorporate the propensity score. *Am. Stat.* 39:33–38

Roy AD. 1951. Some thoughts on the distribution of earnings. *Oxford Econ. Pap.* 3:135–46

Rubin DB. 1974. Estimating causal effects of treatments in randomized and nonrandomized studies. *J. Educ. Psychol.* 66:688–701

Rubin DB. 1977. Assignment to treatment group on the basis of a covariate. *J. Educ. Stat.* 2:1–26

Rubin DB. 1978. Bayesian inference for causal effects: the role of randomization. *Ann. Stat.* 6:34–58

Rubin DB. 1980. Discussion of "Randomization analysis of experimental data in the Fisher randomization test" by Basu. *J. Am. Stat. Assoc.* 75:591–93

Rubin DB. 1981. Estimation in parallel randomized experiments. *J. Educ. Stat.* 6:377–400

Rubin DB. 1986. Which ifs have causal answers? Discussion of "Statistics and causal inference" by Holland. *J. Am. Stat. Assoc.* 83:396

Rubin DB. 1990. Formal modes of statistical inference for causal effects. *J. Stat. Plan. Inference* 25:279–92

Rubin DB. 1991. Practical implications of modes of statistical inference for causal effects and the critical role of the assignment mechanism. *Biometrics* 47:1213–34

Rubin DB, Thomas N. 1996. Matching using estimated propensity scores: relating theory to practice. *Biometrics* 52:249–64

Singer B, Marini MM. 1987. Advancing social research: an essay based on Stanley Lieberson's *Making It Count*. In *Sociological Methodology 1987*, ed. CC Clogg, pp. 373–91. Washington, DC: Am. Sociol. Assoc.

Smith HL. 1997. Matching with multiple controls to estimate treatment effects in observational studies. *Sociol. Methodol.* 27:325–53

Sobel ME. 1995. Causal inference in the social and behavioral sciences. In *Handbook of Statistical Modeling for the Social and Behavioral Sciences*, ed. G Arminger, CC Clogg, ME Sobel, pp. 1–38. New York: Plenum

Sobel ME. 1996. An introduction to causal inference. *Sociol. Methods Res.* 24:353–79

White H. 1981. Consequences and detection of misspecified nonlinear regression models. *J. Am. Stat. Assoc.* 76:419–33

Winship C. 1998. *Multicollinearity and model misspecification: a Bayesian analysis*. Presented at Winter Meet. Am. Sociol. Assoc., Chicago

Winship C, Mare RD. 1992. Models for sample selection bias. *Annu. Rev. Sociol.* 18:327–50

SUBJECT INDEX

CUMULATIVE INDEXES

CONTRIBUTING AUTHORS, VOLUMES 1–25

Hernandez DJ, 12:159–80
Hickson DJ, 13:165–92
Hill GD, 8:161–86
Hindelang MJ, 7:107–28
Hirschman C, 9:397–423;
20:203–33
Hogan DP, 12:109–30
Holden KC, 17:51–78
Hollander P, 8:319–51
Holz JR, 5:193–217
Homans GC, 12:xiii–xxx
Horwitz AV, 10:95–119
House JS, 14:293–318
Hout M, 21:137–62
Hoynes W, 18:373–93

I

Ihinger-Tallman M, 14:25–48

J

Jacobs JA, 22:153–85
Janson C-G, 6:433–56
Jaret C, 9:499–525
Jenkins JC, 9:527–53;
18:161–85
John D, 22:299–322
Johnson MP, 2:161–207
Jones RA, 9:447–69
Juster SM, 13:193–216

K

Kalleberg AL, 5:351–79;
14:203–25
Kalmijn M, 24:395–421
Kalton G, 12:401–29
Kanazawa S, 23:191–214
Kandel DB, 6:235–85
Kang DL, 25:121–44
Kanter RM, 2:269–98;
7:321–49
Kariya T, 16:263–99
Karlin J, 25:575–96
Kasarda JD, 11:305–28;
17:467–501
Katz AH, 7:129–55
Keating KM, 14:149–72
Kennedy MD, 22:437–58
Kerckhoff AC, 21:323–47
Kertzer DI, 9:125–49;
17:155–79
Kiecolt KJ, 14:381–403
Kimeldorf H, 18:495–517
Kluegel JR, 7:29–56
Kmec JA, 25:335–61

Knoke D, 12:1–21
Kohli M, 10:215–37
Kollock P, 14:467–90;
24:183–214
Kolosi T, 14:405–19
Komarovsky M, 17:1–25
Korteweg AC, 25:47–71
Kourvetaris GA, 8:289–317
Kozloff MA, 4:317–43
Krecker ML, 16:241–62
Kreps GA, 10:309–30
Kuklick H, 9:287–310
Kurz K, 13:417–42

L

Lachmann R, 15:47–72
LaFree G, 19:113–37;
25:145–68
Laitin DD, 24:423–52
Lammers CJ, 4:485–510
Land KC, 9:1–26
Landis KR, 14:293–318
Laslett B, 15:381–404
Laub JH, 18:63–84
Laumann EO, 4:455–84
Lawler EJ, 25:217–44
Lehrer E, 12:181–204
Leicht KT, 23:215–31
Leifer EM, 12:233–53
Lenski G, 20:1–24
Lever H, 7:249–62
Levine S, 4:317–43
Levitt B, 14:319–40
Levitt PR, 6:213–34
Lewis GF, 2:35–53
Lichter DT, 23:121–45
Lie J, 23:341–60
Light J, 4:145–70
Liker JK, 25:575–96
Lin N, 25:467–88
Lincoln JR, 13:289–312
Lipman-Blumen J, 1:297–337
Lipset SM, 22:1–27
Liska AE, 13:67–88;
23:39–61
Lo CYH, 8:107–34
Long JS, 21:45–71
Longshore D, 11:75–91
Lubeck PM, 18:519–40
Lumsden CJ, 16:161–95
Luschen G, 6:315–47
Lye DN, 22:79–102

M

Machalek R, 10:167–90
Machlis GE, 14:149–72

Macke AS, 4:57–90
Macy MW, 20:407–36;
21:73–91
Maddox GL, 5:113–35
Maier T, 16:263–99
Maines DR, 3:235–59
Manza J, 21:137–62
March JG, 14:319–40
Mare RD, 18:327–50
Marini MM, 15:343–80
Markovsky B, 20:407–36
Marks C, 17:445–66
Marsden PV, 4:455–84;
16:435–63
Martindale D, 2:121–43
Marx GT, 1:363–428
Massey DS, 7:57–85
Matras J, 6:401–31
Matthews R, 22:401–35
Mauss AL, 10:437–60
Mayer KU, 15:187–209;
23:233–61
Maynard DW, 17:385–418
McBride K, 13:289–312
McBrier DB, 25:335–61
McCall GJ, 10:263–82
McEwen CA, 6:143–85
McFalls JA Jr, 16:491–519
McLanahan S, 13:237–57
McMahon AM, 10:121–40
McNicoll G, 18:85–108
McPhail C, 9:579–600
McQuail D, 11:93–111
Mechanic D, 1:43–65;
16:301–27; 22:239–70
Meier RF, 8:35–55
Menaghan EG, 17:419–44
Menger P-M, 25:541–74
Merton RK, 13:1–28
Meyer JW, 1:223–46;
6:369–99; 10:461–82
Michalowicz J, 10:417–35
Miller J, 8:237–62
Mirowsky J, 12:23–45
Mizruchi MS, 22:271–98
Model S, 14:363–80
Modell J, 17:205–224
Moen P, 18:233–51
Mohr JW, 24:345–70
Morgan DL, 22:129–52
Morgan SL, 25:659–706
Morgan SP, 22:351–75
Morris AD, 25:517–39
Morris M, 25:623–57
Morse EV, 1:339–61
Mortimer JT, 4:421–54
Moseley KP, 4:259–90
Moskos CC Jr, 2:55–77
Mukerji C, 12:47–66
Müller W, 13:417–42

CHAPTER TITLES, VOLUMES 1–25

SOCIAL PROCESSES

DEMOGRAPHY